Creo Parametric 12.0

A Power Guide for Beginners and Intermediate Users

CADArtifex

A premium provider of learning products and solutions

www.cadartifex.com

Creo Parametric 12.0: A Power Guide for Beginners and Intermediate Users

Author: Sandeep Dogra
Email: info@cadartifex.com

Published by
CADArtifex
www.cadartifex.com

ISBN: 978-9394074248

NOTICE TO THE READER

The publisher and the author make no representations or warranties with respect to the accuracy or completeness of the contents of this work/text and specifically disclaim all warranties, including without limitation warranties of fitness for a particular purpose. The Publisher does not guarantee any of the products described in the text or perform any independent analysis in connection with any of the product information contained in the text. No warranty may be created or extended by sales or promotional materials. This work is sold with the understanding that the publisher is not engaged in rendering legal, accounting, or other professional services. Neither the publisher nor the author shall be liable for damages arising herefrom. Further, readers should be aware that Internet Websites listed in this work may have changed or disappeared between when this work was written and when it is read.

Examination Copies

Textbooks received as examination copies in any form such as paperback and eBook are for review only and may not be made available for the use of the student. These files may not be transferred to any other party. Resale of examination copies is prohibited.

Electronic Files

The electronic file/eBook in any form of this textbook is licensed to the original user only and may not be transferred to any other party.

Disclaimer

The author has made sincere efforts to ensure the accuracy of the material described herein, however the author makes no warranty, expressed or implied, with respect to the quality, correctness, accuracy, or freedom from error of this document or the products it describes.

Dedication

First and foremost, I would like to thank my parents for being a great support throughout my career and while writing this book.

Heartfelt gratitude goes to my wife and my sisters for their patience and support in fulfilling this challenge.

I would also like to acknowledge and commend the dedication of the team at CADArtifex. Their meticulous efforts in editing and refining the content of this textbook have been instrumental in ensuring its quality and accuracy to the highest standards.

Contents at a Glance

Table of Contents

Part 3. Working with Assemblies

Part 4. Creating Drawings

Preface

Creo Parametric, developed by PTC Inc. (Parametric Technology Corporation), one of the biggest technology providers of engineering, offers a complete range of 3D software tools that let you create, simulate, publish, and manage your design data. By providing advanced solid modeling techniques and field-proven technology, PTC enables its customers to stay one step ahead of increasing competition with its strategic vision. PTC helps companies to quickly adopt changes that are being created at the convergence of the physical and digital worlds through IoT, 3D printing, digital twins, and augmented reality.

Creo Parametric delivers a rich set of integrated tools that are powerful and intuitive to use. It is a feature-based, parametric solid-modeling mechanical design and automation software that allows you to convert 2D sketches into solid models by using simple yet highly effective modeling tools. Creo Parametric provides a wide range of tools that allow you to create real-world components and assemblies. These real-world components and assemblies can then be converted into 2D engineering drawings for production, additive manufacturing, IoT, and model-based definition (MBD). Additionally, you can validate your designs by simulating their real-world conditions and assessing their environmental impact.

Creo Parametric 12.0: A Power Guide for Beginners and Intermediate Users is a comprehensive textbook designed for both instructor-led courses and self-paced learning. It is ideal for engineers, designers, and students who want to master parametric 3D mechanical design using Creo Parametric.

With **12 detailed chapters spanning 736 pages**, this book covers all major functionalities of Creo Parametric, including **Sketch, Part, Assembly, and Drawing modes**. The content is structured to help new users get started quickly while also offering valuable insights for intermediate learners and instructors.

This textbook emphasizes not only how to use Creo tools but also how to apply **design concepts** effectively. Every chapter features **step-by-step tutorials** for hands-on practice, along with **test drives** at the end to reinforce learning and improve design skills.

Who Should Read This Book

This book is written with a wide range of Creo Parametric users in mind, varying from beginners to advanced users as well as Creo Parametric instructors. The easy-to-follow chapters of this book allow you to easily understand different design techniques, Creo Parametric tools, and design principles.

What Is Covered in This Textbook

Creo Parametric 12.0: A Power Guide for Beginners and Intermediate Users textbook is designed to help you understand everything you need to know to start using Creo Parametric with clear step-by-step tutorials. This textbook covers the following topics:

Chapter 1, "***Introduction to Creo Parametric,***" introduces the Creo Parametric interface, different Creo Parametric modes, and various components of the startup user interface. It also explains how to set the working directory, erase objects of the current session, save an object, open an object, delete older versions of a design, change the background color, customize the Ribbon and Quick Access Toolbar, and close a file.

Chapter 2, "***Drawing Sketches and Applying Dimensions,***" discusses how to invoke the Sketching environment, specify units, define grids and snap settings, draw sketches, create datum geometries, work with construction mode, apply constraints, work with weak dimensions, apply dimensions, and edit dimensions.

Chapter 3, "***Editing and Modifying Sketches,***" introduces various editing tools for editing and modifying sketch entities. It also explains how to insert a pre-defined shape of geometry, a sketch, or a drawing file in the Sketching environment.

Chapter 4, "***Creating Base Feature of a Solid Model,***" discusses how to create 3D solid and thin extrude features as well as revolve base features of a model. It also explains how to navigate a model, manipulate the view orientation of the model to the predefined standard views, and change the display style of a model.

Chapter 5, "***Creating Datum Geometries,***" introduces three default planes: Front, Top, and Right. As these may not be enough for creating models having multiple features, therefore, the chapter discusses how to create additional datum planes. Additionally, this chapter also explains creating a datum axis, datum coordinate system, and datum point.

Chapter 6, "***Advanced Modeling - I,***" introduces advanced options for creating extruded and revolved features. The chapter discusses how to create cut features, project the edges of existing features onto the current sketching plane, edit an existing feature and the sketch of a feature, and measure different geometrical parameters such as length, angle, area, and volume. It also explains assigning appearances, and material, and calculating the mass properties of a model.

Chapter 7, "***Advanced Modeling - II,***" discusses how to create sweep features, helical sweep features, volume helical sweep features, blend features, swept blend features, and rotational blend features.

Chapter 8, "***Patterning and Mirroring,***" introduces various patterning and mirroring tools. After completing this chapter, you can create different types of patterns such as dimension patterns, direction patterns, axis patterns, fill patterns, table patterns, reference patterns, curve patterns, variable patterns, and geometry patterns. Also, you can mirror a feature or features about a mirroring plane as well as copy and paste a feature.

Chapter 9, "***Advanced Modeling - III,***" discusses how to create simple holes using a predefined rectangle profile, a standard hole profile (countersink, counterbore, or tip angle), and a sketched profile. It explains how to create industry-standard holes such as tapped, tapered, drilled, and clearance as per the standard specifications. This chapter also explains creating cosmetic threads, various types of rounds, chamfers, profile ribs, trajectory ribs, and shell features.

Chapter 10, "***Working with Assemblies - I,***" discusses how to create assemblies by using the bottom-up assembly approach and how to apply predefined constraint sets such as Pin, Slider, Cylinder, and

Planar. It explains how to apply user-defined constraints such as Distance, Angle Offset, Parallel, and Coincident to assemble the components of an assembly. This chapter also describes on moving and rotating individual components of an assembly as well as editing constraints.

*Chapter 11, "**Working with Assemblies - II**,"* discusses how to create assemblies by using the top-down assembly approach. It explains how to edit a component of an assembly within the Assembly environment or by opening the component in the Part modeling environment. It introduces the editing of existing constraints, displaying constraints and features of components in the Model Tree of the Assembly mode, and patterning and mirroring assembly components. The chapter discusses the creation of assembly features, suppressing or resuming the components of an assembly, inserting multiple copies of a component in an assembly, checking interference between components, creating an exploded view of an assembly, switching between exploded and unexploded views of an assembly, and creating the Bill of Material (BOM).

*Chapter 12, "**Working with Drawings**,"* discusses how to create 2D drawings from parts and assemblies. It introduces various drawing views such as general views, projection views, section views, auxiliary views, and detailed views of a component or an assembly, along with the concept of angle of projection. This chapter also explains defining the angle of projection, creating a new drawing template or format, applying reference and driving dimensions, modifying drawing properties, editing the hatching and text style of a view, and adding notes, bill of material (BOM), and balloons.

Icons/Terms used in this Textbook

The following icons and terms are used in this textbook:

Note

Note: Notes highlight information requiring special attention.

Tip

Tip: Tips provide additional advice, which increases the efficiency of the users.

Flyout

A Flyout is a list in which a set of tools are grouped, see Figure 1.

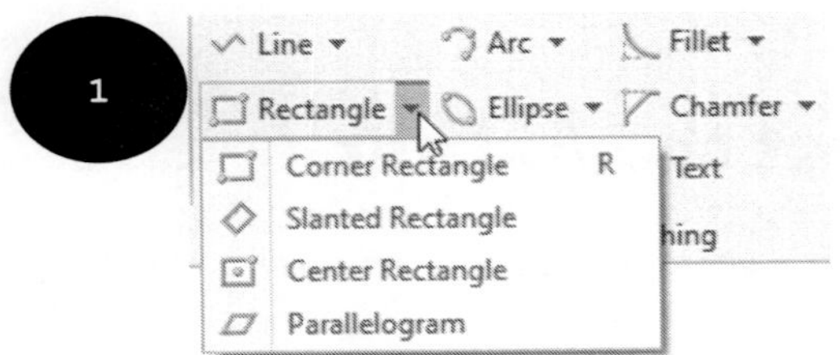

Drop-down List

A drop-down list is a list in which a set of options are grouped, see Figure 2.

Field
A Field allows you to enter a new value or modify an existing value, see Figure 2.

Check box
A Check box allows you to turn on or off the usage of a particular option, see Figure 2.

Button
A Button allows you to turn on or off the function of a particular option, see Figure 2.

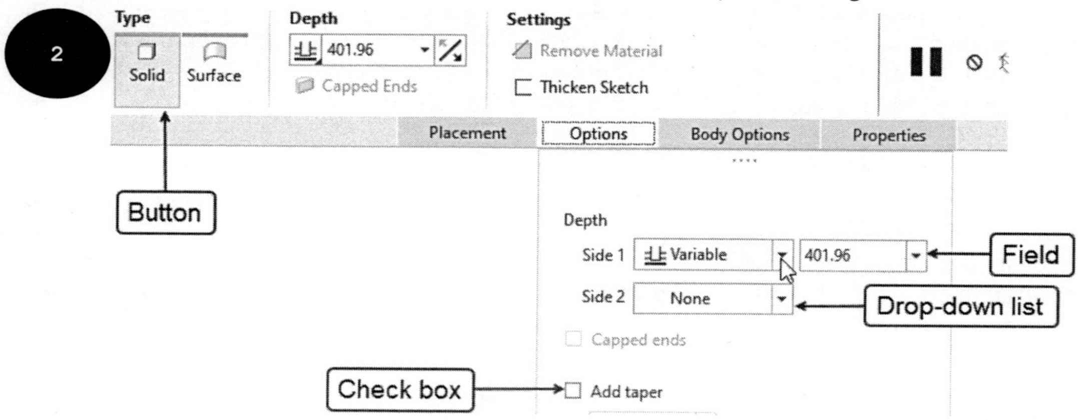

How to Download Online Resources
Students and faculty members can **download all parts/models** used in the illustrations, Tutorials and Hands-on Test Drives (exercises) of the textbook. In addition, faculty can also download PowerPoint Presentations (PPTs) of each chapter of the textbook.

To download the free online teaching and learning resources of the textbook, log on to our website (*cadartifex.com/login*). If you are a new user, you need to first register (*cadartifex.com/register*) for downloading the online resources of the textbook.

Interactive Support for Your Learning
In the book, you'll find **QR codes** next to key tutorial steps for certain tutorials. Scan these codes to access video demonstrations, designed to help you through any challenging parts of the process.

How to Contact the Author
We value your feedback and suggestions. Please email us at *info@cadartifex.com*. You can also log on to our website *www.cadartifex.com* to provide your feedback about the textbook as well as download the free learning resources.

We thank you for purchasing **Creo Parametric 12.0: A Power Guide for Beginners and Intermediate Users** textbook. We hope that the information and concepts introduced in this textbook help you accomplish your professional goals.

CHAPTER

1

Introduction to Creo Parametric

In this chapter, the following topics will be discussed:

- Installing Creo Parametric
- Getting Started with Creo Parametric
- Starting a New File
- Identifying Creo Parametric Files
- Setting the Working Directory
- Erasing Objects of the Current Session
- Saving an Object
- Saving a Copy of an Object
- Opening an Object
- Deleting Older Versions of a Design
- Changing Background Color
- Customizing the Ribbon
- Customizing the Quick Access Toolbar
- Closing a File

Welcome to the world of Computer Aided Design (CAD) with Creo Parametric. It is a product of PTC Inc. (Parametric Technology Corporation), one of the biggest technology providers in engineering, offering a complete range of 3D software tools that let you create, simulate, publish, and manage your design data. By providing advanced solid modeling techniques and field-proven technology, PTC enables its customers to stay one step ahead in the ever-increasing competition with its strategic vision. PTC helps companies quickly adapt to changes resulting from the convergence of the physical and digital worlds through IoT, 3D printing, digital twins, and augmented reality.

Creo Parametric delivers a rich set of integrated tools that are powerful and intuitive to use. It is a feature-based, parametric solid-modeling mechanical design and automation software that allows you to convert 2D sketches into solid models by using simple yet highly effective modeling tools. Creo Parametric provides a wide range of tools that allow you to create real-world components and assemblies. These real-world components and assemblies can then be converted into 2D engineering drawings for production, additive manufacturing, IoT, and model-based definition (MBD). Additionally, you can validate your designs by simulating their real-world conditions and assessing their environmental impact.

Installing Creo Parametric

If you do not have Creo Parametric installed on your system, you first need to get it installed. However, before you start installing Creo Parametric, you need to evaluate the system requirements and ensure that it is capable of running Creo Parametric adequately. Below are the system requirements for installing Creo Parametric.

1. Operating Systems: Windows 10 64-bit Editions, Windows 11, Windows Server 2022 & 2025
2. RAM: Minimum 8 GB or higher (Recommended 16GB or higher)
3. Graphics Card: 3D capable graphics cards that at least support OpenGL 4.0.

For more information about the system requirements for Creo, visit the PTC website at *ptc.com/support/-/media/support/refdocs/Creo_Parametric/12/creo12_hardware_notes.pdf?sc_lang=en*

Once the system requirements have been fulfilled, install Creo Parametric software by using the downloaded Creo Parametric setup files.

Getting Started with Creo Parametric

Once Creo Parametric is installed on your system, double-click on the **Creo Parametric** icon on the desktop of your system. The system prepares for start-up by loading all the required files of Creo. Once all the required files have been loaded, the startup user interface of Creo Parametric appears along with the **Resource Center** window, see Figure 1.1. The **Resource Center** window is used for accessing online Creo resources, PTC Communities, PTC Events, and so on. If you do not want this window to be displayed next time you launch Creo Parametric, then simply select the **Do not show window again** check box located at the bottom of the **Resource Center** window. Next, close the **Resource Center** window. The startup user interface of Creo Parametric appears as shown in Figure 1.2.

1.1

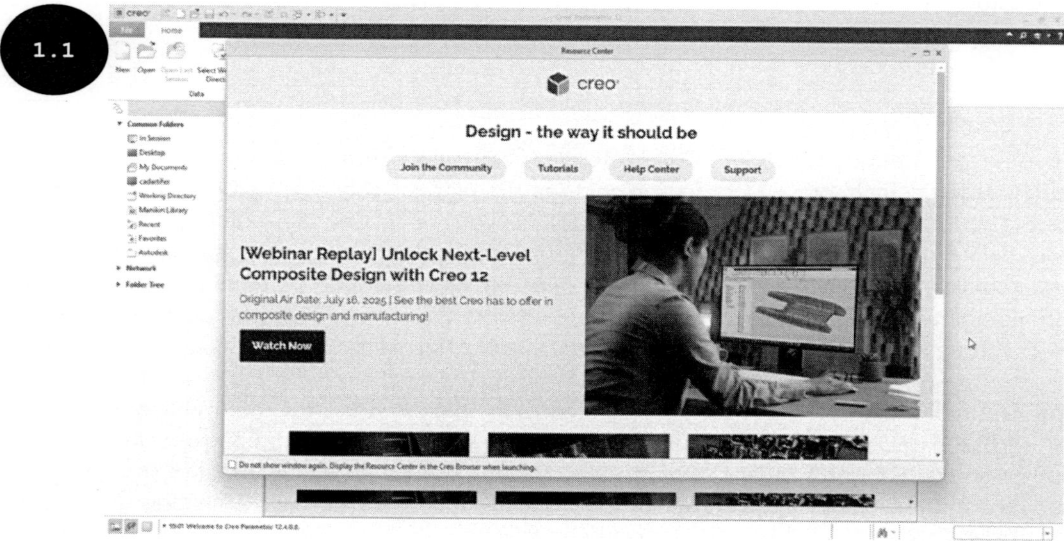

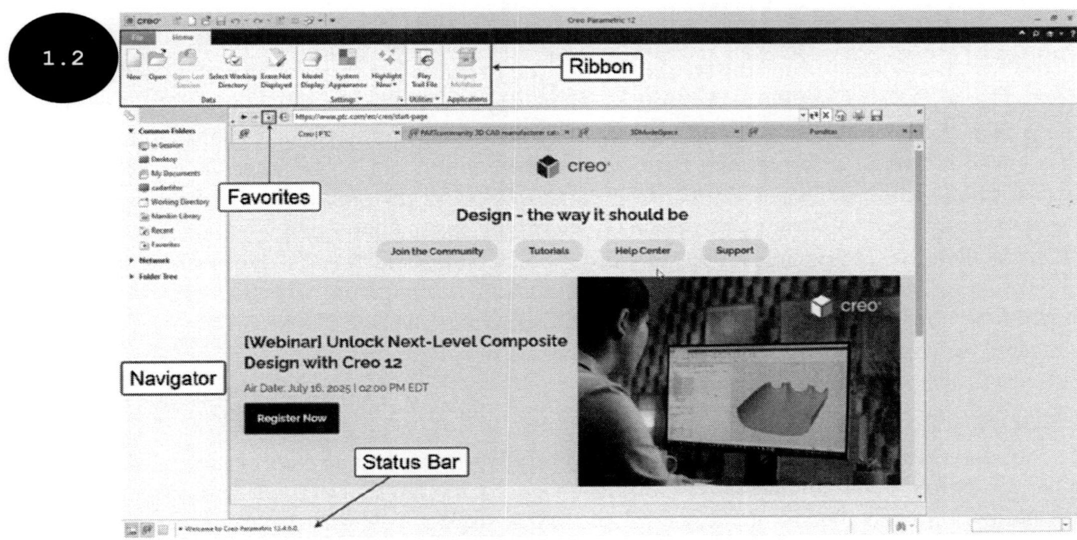

Tip: If the display of the **Resource Center** window is turned off, then you can turn on its display by clicking on **File > Help > Online Resources** in the **File** menu and then clearing the **Do not show window again** check box at the bottom of the **Resource Center** window that appears.

It is evident from the startup user interface of Creo Parametric that it is very user-friendly. Some of the components of the startup user interface of Creo Parametric are discussed below.

Navigator

The **Navigator** is available on the left side of the screen and consists of three tabs: **Model Tree**, **Folder Browser**, and **Favorites**, see Figure 1.3. The **Model Tree** tab is available when a model is opened in Creo Parametric and displays the **Model Tree** which keeps a record of all operations or features used for creating the model. You will learn more about the **Model Tree** later in this chapter. The **Folder Browser** tab displays a list of folders available on your local computer. It allows you to quickly access any folder of your system. The **Favorites** tab allows you to access files that are saved in the **Personal Favorites** folder. Note that you can turn on or off the display of **Navigator** by clicking on the **Show Navigator** button available at the lower left side of the **Status Bar**.

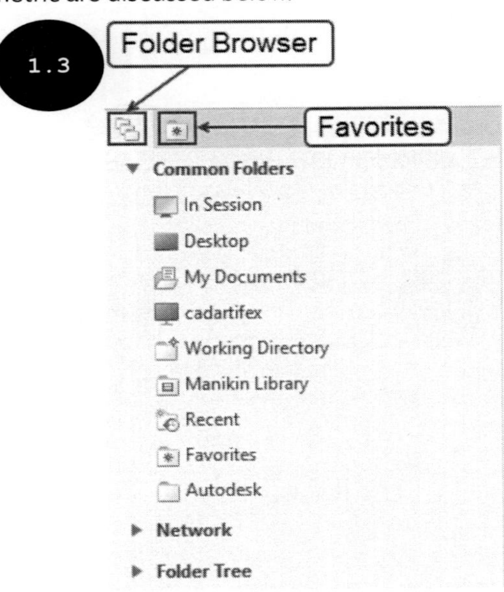

Note: If the **Favorites** tab is not displayed in the **Navigator** as shown in Figure 1.3, then click on **Favorites** in the **Browser** window to add it in the **Navigator**, refer to Figure 1.2.

Browser

In Creo Parametric, when you start a new session, the **Browser** appears on the screen with Four tabs, refer to Figure 1.2. The **Creo PTC** tab offers users the opportunity to join the community of creo users, access help topics, video tutorials, and support. The **PART community 3D CAD manufacturer catalogs** tab is linked to the PTC community page (*ptc.partcommunity.com/*). This page allows you to access the PTC online community portal that offers certified 2D and 3D models from global manufacturers. The **3D ModelSpace** tab is linked to the PTC 3D model space library page (*3dmodelspace.com/ptc*). This page allows you to download 3D standard models. The **Punditas AI Advisor** tab is linked to the Punditas AI Advisor landing page (*home.punditas.com/Advisor/landing*). This page provides real-time guidance on how to use a feature and work with Creo. You can switch between the tabs and browse to any URL or web page similar to other web browsers.

Ribbon

The **Ribbon** is available at the top of the screen and is composed of a series of tabs in which a set of similar tools are grouped in different groups, see Figure 1.4. Note that in the startup user interface of Creo Parametric, only the **Home** tab is available in the **Ribbon**. You will learn more about the **Ribbon** later in this chapter. By using the tools in the **Data** group of the **Home** tab, you can start a new file, open an existing file, open the last session, specify a working directory, and erase objects that are not displayed in the current session of Creo Parametric. These functions are discussed next.

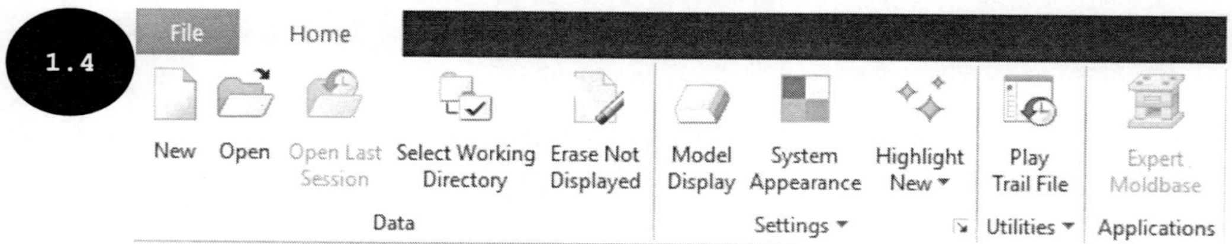

Starting a New File

In Creo Parametric, you can start a new file by using the **New** tool of the **Data** group in the **Home** tab, refer to Figure 1.4. You can also access the **New** tool in the **File** menu and the **Quick Access Toolbar**, see Figures 1.5 and 1.6.

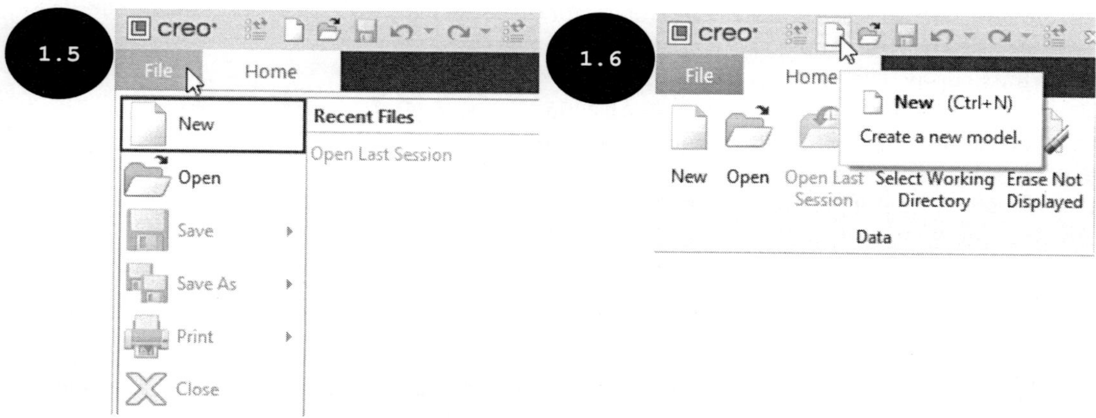

To start a new file, click on the **New** tool or press CTRL + N. The **New** dialog box appears, see Figure 1.7. In this dialog box, you can select the type and sub-type of the file to be started. By default, the **Part** radio button is selected in the **Type** area and the **Solid** radio button in the **Sub-type** area of the dialog box. As a result, on clicking the **OK** button in the dialog box, the Part mode will be invoked for creating a 3D solid part. The methods for invoking the Part mode, Assembly mode, and Drawing mode by using the **New** dialog box are discussed next.

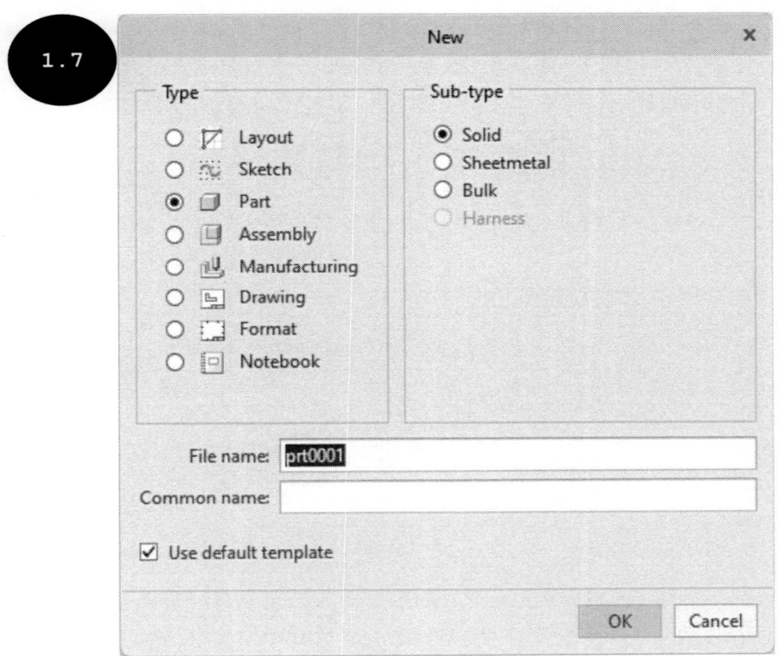

Invoking the Part Mode

To invoke the Part mode for creating a 3D solid part, ensure that the **Part** radio button is selected in the **Type** area and the **Solid** radio button in the **Sub-type** area of the **New** dialog box. Next, specify the name of the part in the **File name** field of the dialog box. By default, the **Use default template** check box is selected in the dialog box. As a result, the default Creo template (**inlbs_part_solid_abs**) with the predefined unit system (length in inches, mass in lbm, and time in seconds) is used for creating the part. To select a template other than the default one, clear the **Use default template** check box in the dialog box and then click on the **OK** button. The **New File Options** dialog box appears, see Figure 1.8.

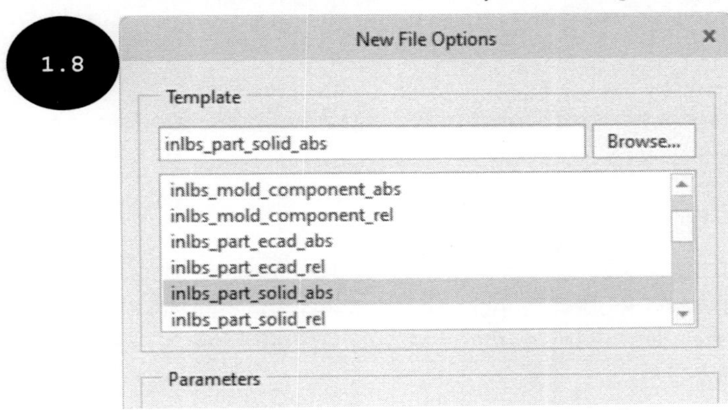

In the **New File Options** dialog box, select the required template and then click on the **OK** button in the dialog box. The Part mode is invoked, and the startup user interface of the Part mode appears, as shown in Figure 1.9.

1.9

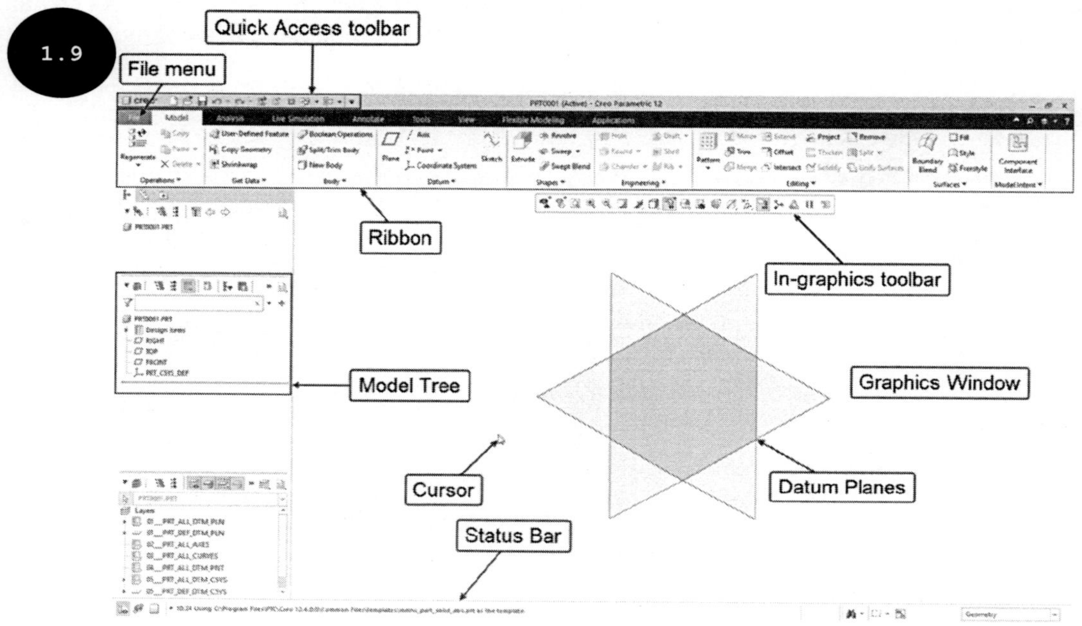

Note: In Figure 1.9, the background color of the graphics area is changed to white for clarity of the image. You will learn about changing the background color later in this chapter.

It is evident from the startup user interface of the Part mode that Creo Parametric is very user-friendly. Some of the components of the startup user interface are discussed next.

Ribbon

The **Ribbon** is available at the top of the graphics window and is composed of a series of tabs such as **Home, Analysis,** and **Annotate** in which a set of similar tools are grouped together in different groups, see Figure 1.10. Note that the availability of tabs, groups, and tools in the **Ribbon** depends upon the currently invoked mode of Creo Parametric.

1.10

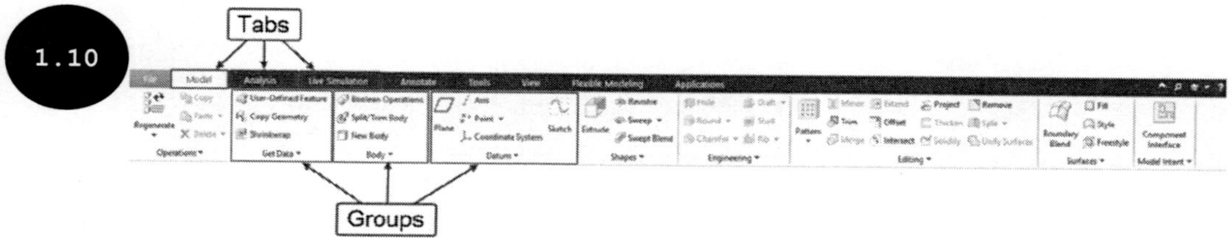

You can also minimize the **Ribbon** to increase the size of the graphics window. To do so, right-click anywhere in the **Ribbon** and then select the **Minimize the Ribbon** check box in the shortcut menu that appears, see Figure 1.11.

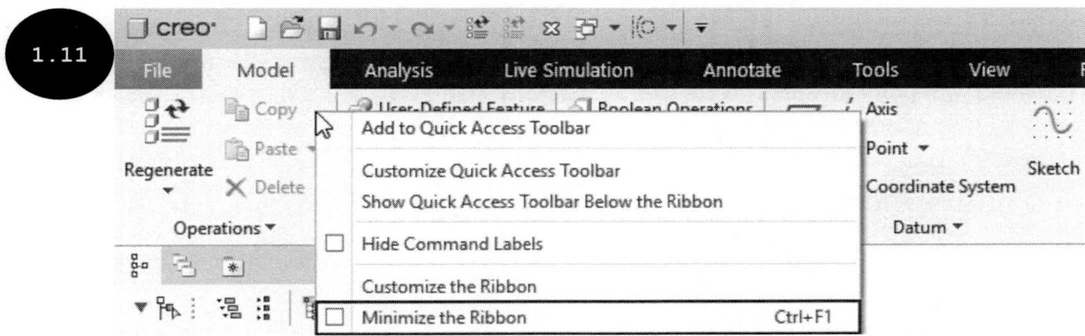

Quick Access Toolbar

The **Quick Access Toolbar** is provided with frequently used tools such as **New**, **Open**, **Save**, **Save As**, **Undo**, **Redo**, and **Regenerate**, see Figure 1.12. It is available at the top of the **Ribbon**.

File Menu

You can invoke the **File** menu by clicking on the **File** button available at the top left corner of the **Ribbon**, see Figure 1.13. It contains tools for starting a new file, opening an existing file, saving a file, closing a file, managing a file, preparing a model for distribution, managing the current session of Creo Parametric, and setting Creo Parametric options and configurations. You can also access the recently opened files by using the **File** menu.

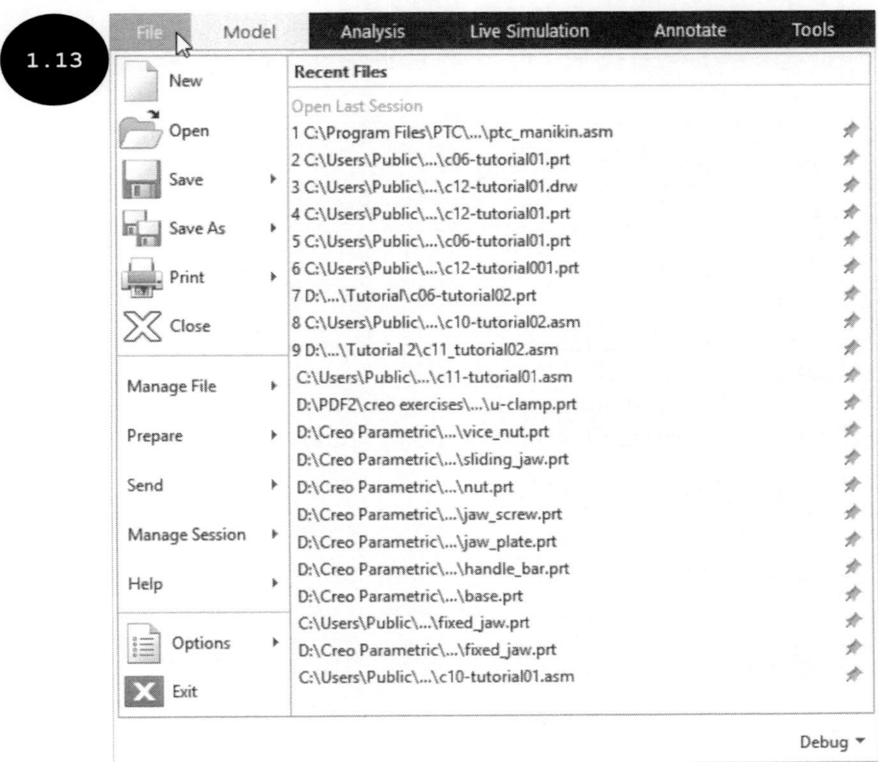

In-graphics Toolbar

The **In-graphics** toolbar is available at the top middle section of the graphics window, see Figure 1.14. It is provided with different sets of tools that are used for manipulating the view and display of a model available in the graphics window.

Model Tree

The **Model Tree** appears on the left side of the graphics window and keeps a record of all operations or features used for creating a model, see Figure 1.15. Note that the first created feature appears at the top and the next created features appear one after the other in an order in the **Model Tree**. Note that in the **Model Tree**, three default datum planes and a coordinate system appear by default.

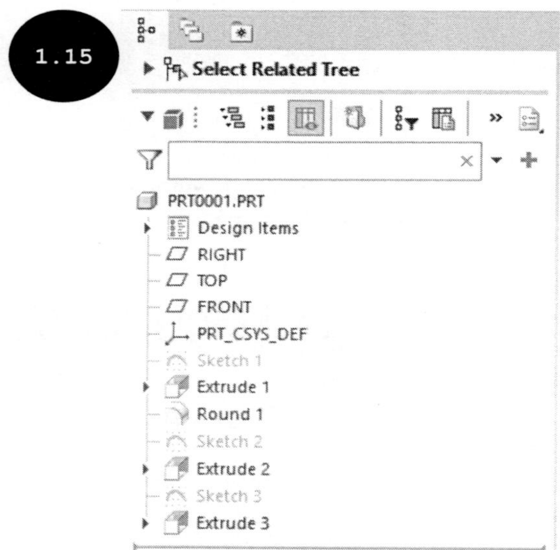

Status Bar

The **Status Bar** is available at the bottom of the graphics window and provides information about the action to be taken based on the currently active tool. It also contains tools to toggle the display of full-screen mode, **Navigator**, and **Browser**, see Figure 1.16. You can also filter the selection mode by selecting the required option in the **Filter** and **Selection** drop-down lists of the **Status Bar**, respectively.

Invoking the Assembly Mode

The Assembly mode is used for creating assemblies. To invoke the assembly mode for creating an assembly, click on the **New** tool in the **Quick Access Toolbar** or press the CTRL + N keys. The **New** dialog box appears. In this dialog box, select the **Assembly** radio button in the **Type** area and the **Design** radio button in the **Sub-type** area. Next, specify the name of the assembly in the **Name** field of the dialog box. By default, the **Use default template** check box is selected in the dialog box. As a result, the default Creo template with the predefined unit system is used for creating the assembly. To select a template other than the default one, clear the **Use default template** check box in the dialog box and then click on the **OK** button. The **New File Options** dialog box appears. In this dialog box, select the required template and then click on the **OK** button. The Assembly mode is invoked, and the startup user interface of the Assembly mode appears, as shown in Figure 1.17.

1.17

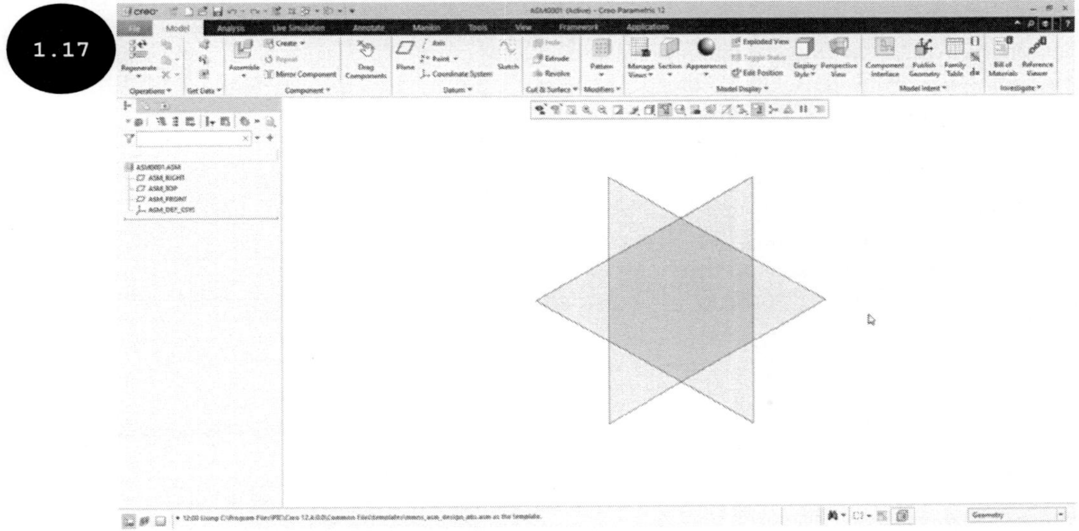

After invoking the Assembly mode, you can create an assembly by assembling two or more components. Figure 1.18 shows an assembly. You will learn more about creating assemblies in later chapters.

1.18

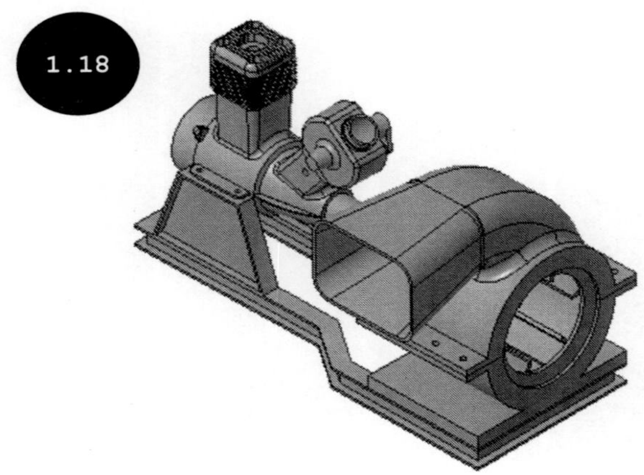

Invoking the Drawing Mode

The Drawing mode is used for creating 2D drawings of a component or an assembly. To invoke the Drawing mode, click on the **New** tool in the **Quick Access Toolbar** or press the CTRL + N keys. The **New** dialog box appears. In this dialog box, select the **Drawing** radio button in the **Type** area and then enter a name for the drawing file in the **Name** field of the dialog box. Next, clear the **Use default template** check box in the dialog box to select the required drawing template and then click on the **OK** button. The **New Drawing** dialog box appears, see Figure 1.19. The options in the **New Drawing** dialog box are used for defining a drawing template to create drawing views. You can define a default template, a format, or an empty template by selecting the required radio button in the **Specify template** area of the dialog box. After specifying the required drawing template, click on the **OK** button in the dialog box. The Drawing mode is invoked, and the startup user interface of the Drawing mode appears, as shown in Figure 1.20.

1.19

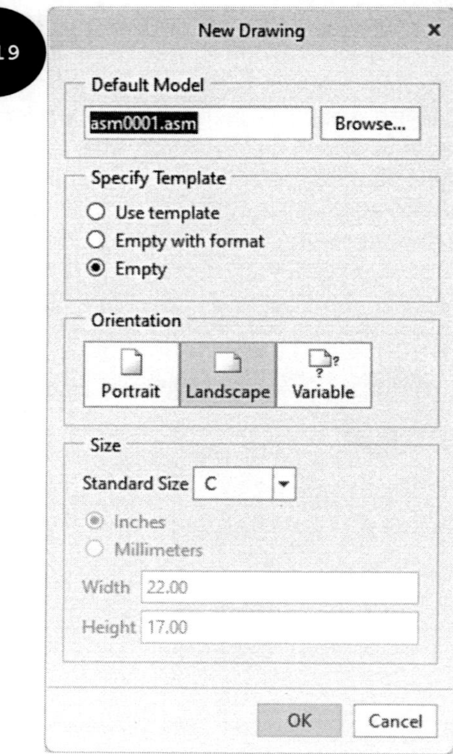

1.20

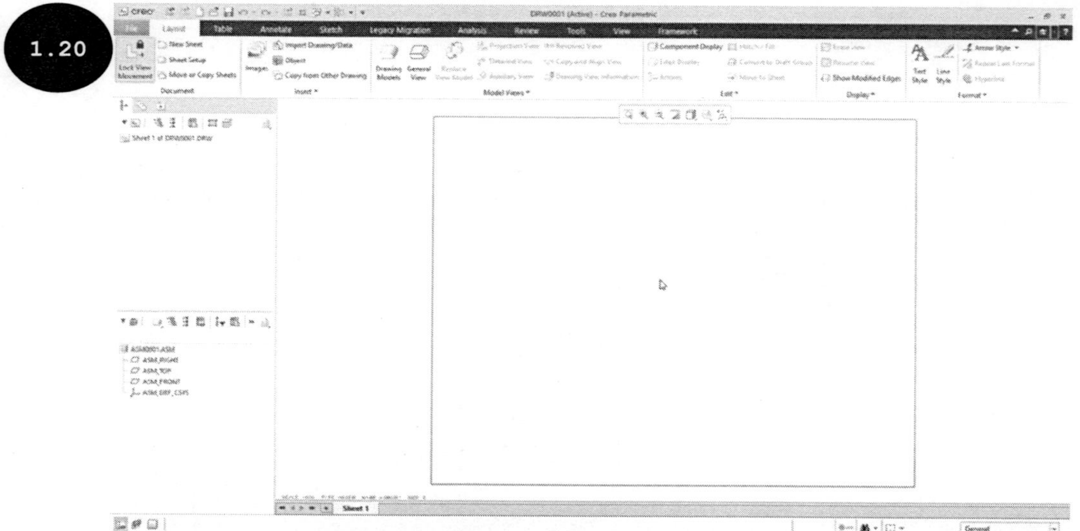

After invoking the Drawing mode, you can generate various drawing views of a component or an assembly. You will learn about generating various drawing views, applying dimensions, creating BOM, and so on, in later chapters. Figure 1.21 shows a drawing with dimensions for your reference only.

1.21

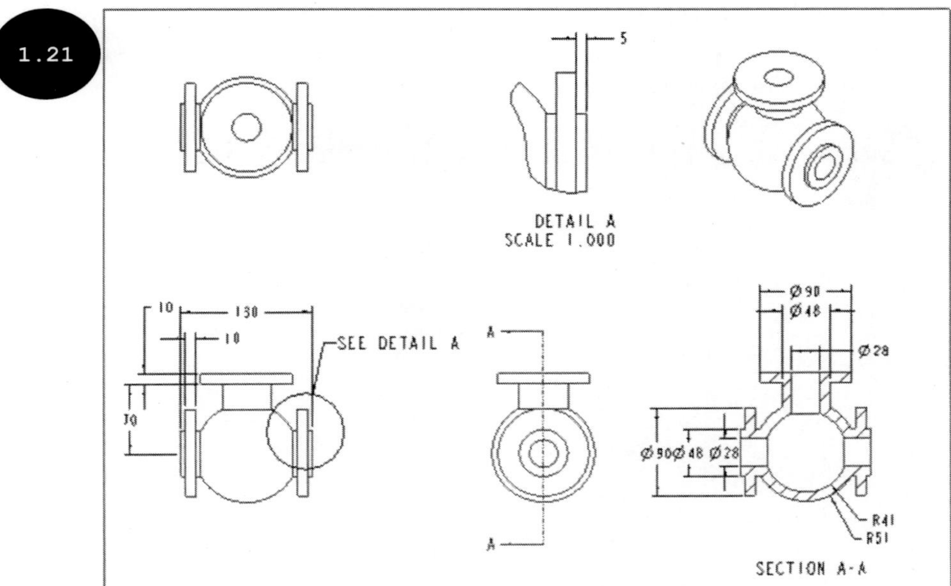

Identifying Creo Parametric Files

The files or models created in different modes (Sketch, Part, Assembly, and Drawing) of Creo Parametric have different file extensions, see the table given below:

Mode	File Extension / Format
Sketch mode	.sec
Part mode	.prt
Assembly mode	.asm
Drawing mode	.drw

Tip: You can invoke the Sketch mode for creating a sketch by selecting the **Sketch** radio button in the **Type** area of the **New** dialog box. Besides, you can also invoke the sketch mode within the Part mode of Creo Parametric. You will learn about creating sketches in later chapters.

Setting the Working Directory

After starting Creo Parametric, it is important to first set up a working directory for saving the files of the current session of Creo Parametric. You can set any folder created in a local drive of your system as the working directory. However, it is recommended to set a working directory such that all the files of a project are saved in a common folder making it easier to manage and avoid missing components of an assembly or a drawing file.

To set a working directory, click on **File > Manage Session > Select Working Directory** in the **File** menu, see Figure 1.22. The **Select Working Directory** window appears. In this window, browse to the required location of a local drive of your system and then select the desired folder as the working directory. Next, click on the **OK** button in the dialog box. The selected folder becomes the working directory for saving all the files of the current session of Creo Parametric.

1.22

Alternatively, to set the working directory, click on the **Working Directory** folder of the **Folder Browser** tab in the **Navigator** that appears on the left side of the screen when you start a new session of Creo Parametric, see Figure 1.23. A list of folders appears in the **Browser**. Next, browse to the required location and then select the desired folder. The selected folder becomes the working directory of the current session of Creo Parametric.

1.23

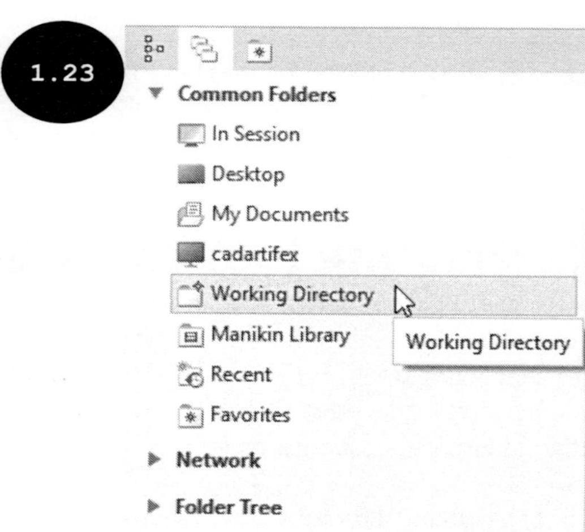

You can also click on the **Select Working Directory** tool in the **Data** group of the **Home** tab that appears in the **Ribbon** when you start a new session of Creo Parametric to set the working directory, see Figure 1.24.

1.24

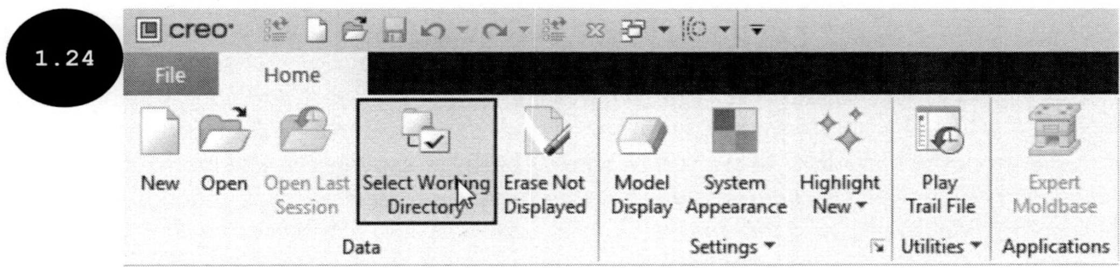

Erasing Objects of the Current Session

All the files that you create or open in the current session of Creo Parametric are saved in the temporary memory even after the file has been closed. As a result, Creo Parametric does not allow you to specify a name for a file that was previously used in the session. Also, when you open an assembly, the previously created or opened components in the session will be opened, if the names of the components being opened match with them.

To overcome this issue, it is recommended to remove all the files from the temporary memory that are not currently displayed in the current session of Creo Parametric. To do so, click on the **File > Manage Session > Erase Not Displayed** in the **File** menu. The **Erase Not Displayed** dialog box appears with a list of all the objects that are not displayed in the current session, see Figure 1.25. Next, click on the **OK** button in the dialog box. All the objects are removed from the temporary memory.

1.25

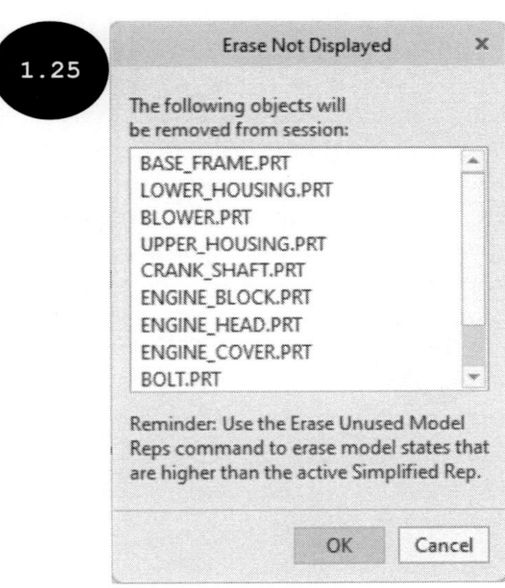

You can also remove or erase the object that is being displayed in the current session of Creo Parametric. To do so, click on **File > Manage Session > Erase Current** in the **File** menu. The **Erase Confirm** dialog box appears, see Figure 1.26. Click on the **Yes** button in this dialog box to confirm the action of erasing the current object from the session.

1.26

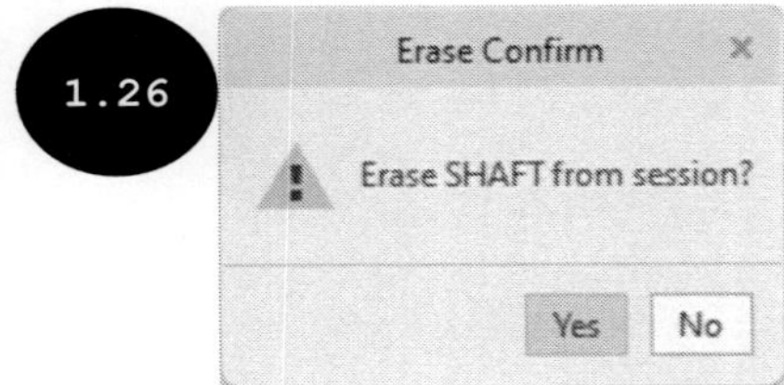

Saving an Object

To save an object, click on the **Save** tool in the **Quick Access Toolbar** or press the CTRL + S key. The **Save Object** dialog box appears such that it gets browsed to the folder which is defined as the working directory. Also, the name of the object appears in the **Model Name** field of the dialog box. Next, click on the **OK** button in the dialog box. The object is saved in the specified working directory.

In Creo Parametric, every time you save an object by using the **Save** tool, a new version of the object is saved in the working directory because Creo Parametric keeps track of each version of your design and saves all versions as backup files. However, when you open an object, the latest version of the file gets opened in Creo Parametric. After completing the design, you can delete all the older versions of your design from the hard disk of your computer except the latest version. The methods for opening an object and deleting all the older versions of a design are discussed later in this chapter.

Saving a Copy of an Object

In Creo Parametric, you can save a copy of an object in the same or different working directory. To do so, ensure that the object is opened in the current session of Creo Parametric. Next, click on **File > Save As > Save a Copy** in the **File** menu. The **Save a Copy** dialog box appears. In this dialog box, browse to the location where the copy of the object is to be saved and then specify a new name for the copy of the object in the **File Name** field of the dialog box. Next, click on the **OK** button. A copy of the object is saved in the native Creo Parametric file format in the specified location.

You can also save or export an object to other file formats such as Inventor file, CATIA file, NX file, SolidWorks file, IGES file, STEP file, Neutral file, PDF file, etc. To do so, click on the **File > Save As > Save a Copy** in the **File** menu. The **Save a Copy** dialog box appears. In the **Type** drop-down list of the dialog box, select the required file format in which you want to export the object, see Figure 1.27. You can scroll down in the **Type** drop-down list to access more options. After selecting the file format, browse to the required location and then specify a new name for the object in the **File Name** field of the dialog box. Next, click on the **OK** button. A copy of the object is saved in the selected file format.

1.27

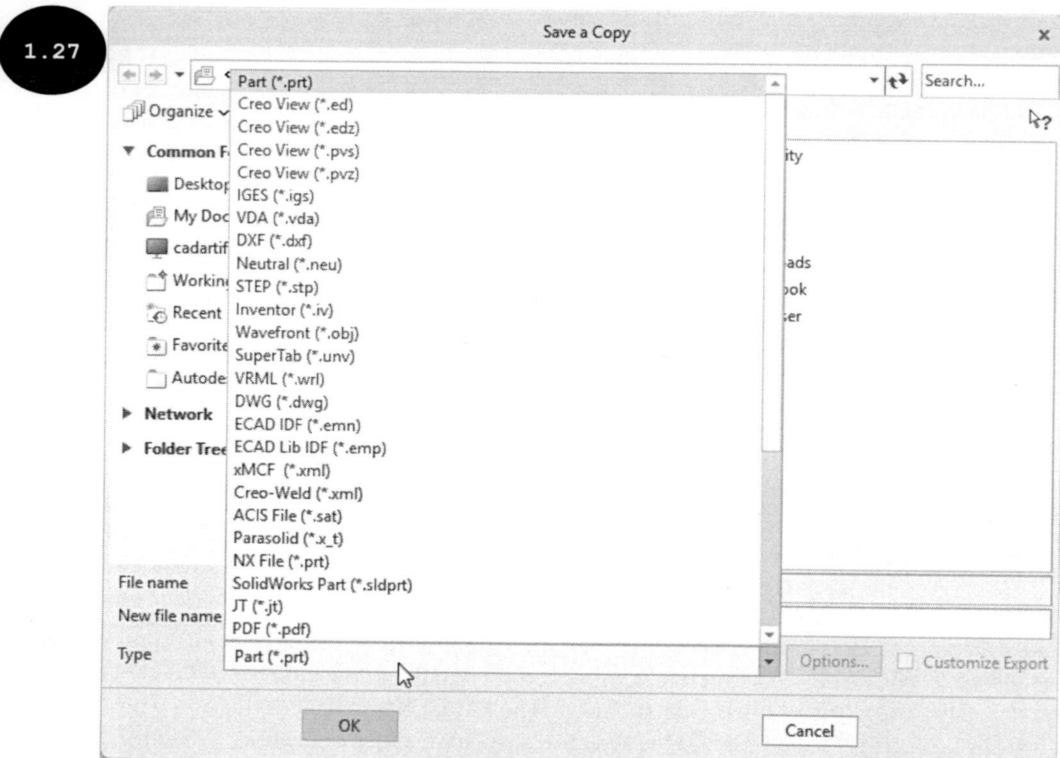

Opening an Object

To open an object in Creo Parametric, click on the **Open** tool in the **Quick Access Toolbar** or press the CTRL + O key. The **File Open** dialog box appears. In this dialog box, the **Creo Files (.prt, .asm, .drw, .frm, .mfg, .lay, .sec, .dgm, .int, .g, .tmu, .tmz, .apr, .cem)** option is selected in the **Type** drop-down list, by default. As a result, the objects that are saved in the native Creo Parametric file format appear in the dialog box. Next, select the object to be opened and then click on the **Open** button in the dialog box. The selected object is opened in the current session of Creo Parametric.

Note: In Creo Parametric, when you open an object, the latest version of the file gets opened. To open an older version of a design, invoke the **File Open** dialog box by clicking on the **Open** tool. Next, browse to the location where the object to be opened is saved. By default, only the latest version of the object appears in the **File Open** dialog box. To display all versions of the design, invoke the **Tools** flyout in the **File Open** dialog box and then select the **All Versions** check box, see Figure 1.28. All the versions of the design appear in the dialog box. Next, select the required version and then click on the **Open** button in the dialog box. The selected version of the design gets opened in Creo Parametric.

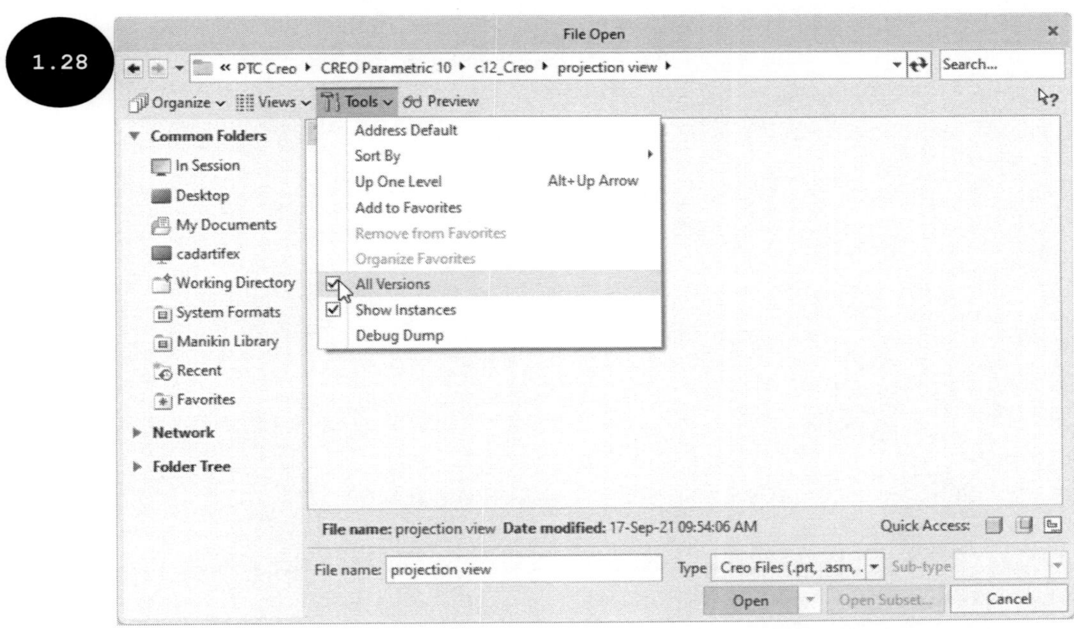

In Creo Parametric, you can also open or import objects created in other CAD applications such as Inventor, CATIA, NX, SolidWorks, etc. To do so, invoke the **File Open** dialog box and then select the required file format in the **Type** drop-down list of the dialog box. Next, select the object to be opened and then click on the **Open** button in the dialog box. Similarly, you can also open files that are saved in universal CAD formats such as IGES, STEP, and Parasolid by selecting the respective file format in the **Type** drop-down list of the **File Open** dialog box.

Deleting Older Versions of a Design

As discussed earlier, every time you save an object by using the **Save** tool, a new version of the object is saved in the working directory. To delete all the older versions of a design from the hard disk of your computer except the latest version, click on **File > Manage File > Delete Old Versions** in the **File** menu, see Figure 1.29. The **Delete Old Versions** dialog box appears, see Figure 1.30. In this dialog box, click on the **Yes** button to confirm the action of deleting all the older versions of the design from the hard disk of your computer.

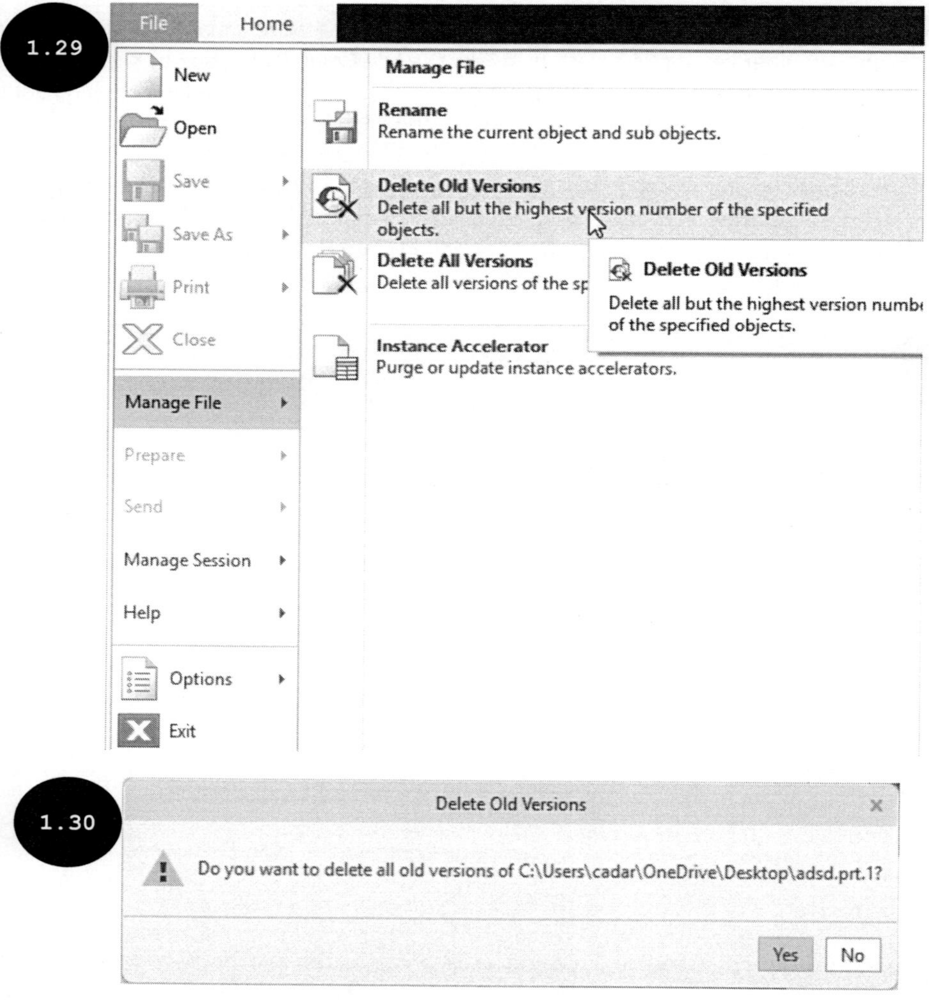

Note: In Creo Parametric, you can also delete all the versions of a design including its latest version. However, be careful before deleting all versions of a design as it may result in loss of data. To delete all versions of a desin, click on **File > Manage File > Delete All Version** in the **File** menu. The **Delete All Confirm** dialog box appears. In this dialog box, click on the **Yes** button to delete all versions of the design including its latest version.

Changing Background Color

To change the background color of the graphics window of Creo Parametric, click on **File > Options** in the **File** menu. The **Creo Parametric Options** dialog box appears. In this dialog box, click on the **System Appearance** option in the left panel of the dialog box. The options for defining the system appearances or colors appear on the right panel of the dialog box. Next, expand the **Graphics** node in the right panel of the dialog box by clicking on the arrow available on its left, see Figure 1.31. In the expanded **Graphics** node, invoke the **Background Color** palette by clicking on the **Color** button on the left of the **Background** option, see Figure 1.31. Next, select the required color from the palette or click on the **More Colors** option to invoke the **Color Editor** dialog box for defining the background color. The options in the **Color Editor** dialog box are used for defining the settings for the required color. To define a white color for the background, enter **255**, **255**, and **255** in the **R**, **G**, and **B** fields in the **Color Editor** dialog box. After defining the required color for the background, click on the **OK** button in the **Color Editor** dialog box. Next, click on the **OK** button in the **Creo Parametric Options** dialog box. The background color of the graphics window is changed, as per specification.

1.31

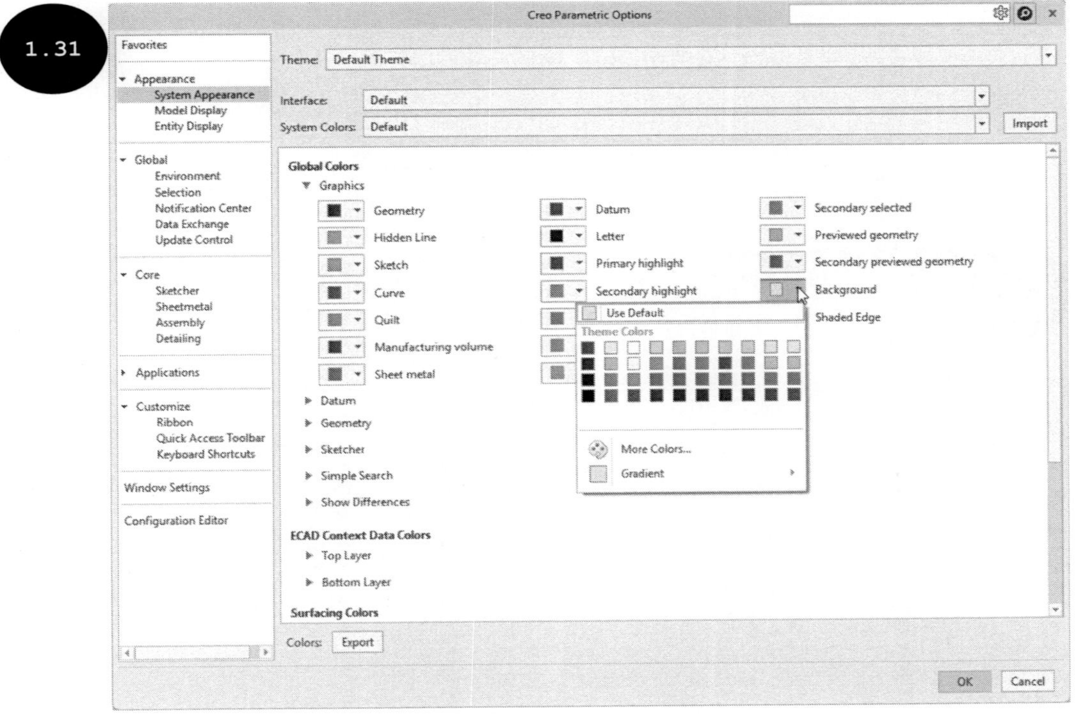

Tip: You can similarly also change the appearance or color of the other entities of Creo Parametric such as curve, sketch, datum, selected entity, previewed geometry, and so on, by using the respective color palette of the dialog box.

Customizing the Ribbon

In addition to the default set of tools in the **Ribbon**, you can customize the **Ribbon** to add more tools, as required. To customize the **Ribbon**, right-click anywhere on the **Ribbon** to display a shortcut menu, see Figure 1.32. Next, click on the **Customize the Ribbon** option in the shortcut menu that appears. The **Creo Parametric Options** dialog box appears with the **Ribbon** option selected in the **Customize** section on the left panel of the dialog box, see Figure 1.33. Also, a list of current tabs of the **Ribbon** with an available set of groups in each tab appears in the **Current Command** list on the right panel of the dialog box. Now, to add a tool in the **Ribbon**, drag and drop the tool from the **All Command** list at the right panel of the dialog box to the required location in the **Ribbon** or in the **Current Command** list of the dialog box.

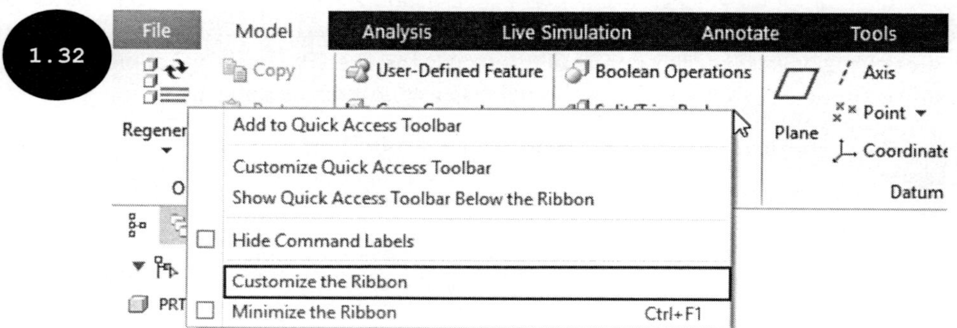

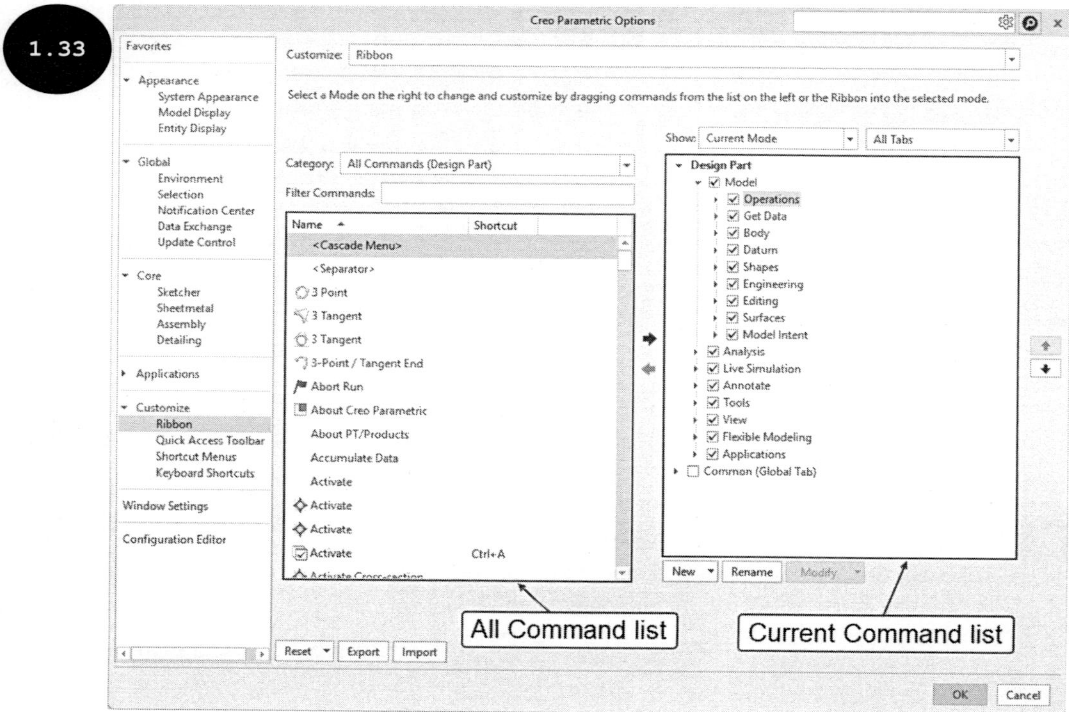

You can also add a new tab in the **Ribbon**. To do so, right-click on the **Current Command** list in the dialog box and then select the **Add New Tab** option in the shortcut menu that appears. Similarly, to add a group in a tab, select the tab and then right-click to display a shortcut menu. Next, click on the **Add New Group** option in the shortcut menu. A new group gets added in the selected tab. You can add multiple groups in a tab and then add required tools in each group by dragging and dropping the tools from the **All Command** list to the **Current Command** list of the dialog box.

Customizing the Quick Access Toolbar

Similar to customizing the **Ribbon**, you can customize the **Quick Access Toolbar** to add more frequently used tools. To do so, right-click anywhere on the **Quick Access Toolbar** to display a shortcut menu, see Figure 1.34. Next, click on the **Customize Quick Access Toolbar** option in the shortcut menu. The **Creo Parametric Options** dialog box appears with the **Quick Access Toolbar** option selected in the **Customize** section on the left panel of the dialog box. Now, you can drag and drop tools from the **All Command** list in the right panel of the dialog box to the required location in the **Quick Access Toolbar** or the **Current Command** list of the dialog box.

1.34

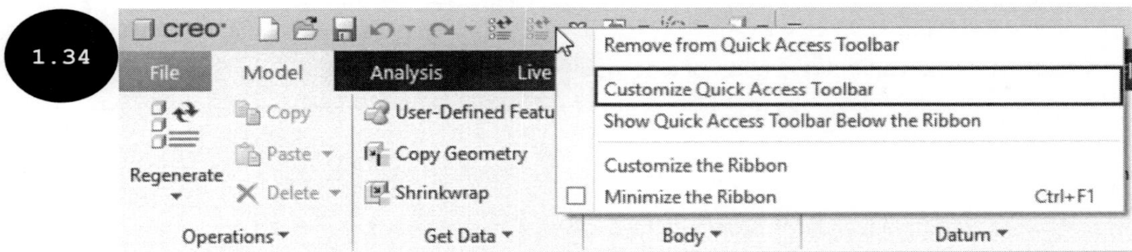

Closing a File

After completing a design and saving it in the working directory, you can close the design file. To do so, click on **File > Close** in the **File** menu. The currently displayed design file gets closed.

Summary

In this chapter, you have learned about system requirements for installing Creo Parametric, invoking different modes (Part, Assembly, and Drawing) of Creo Parametric, setting the working directory, identifying Creo Parametric files, erasing objects of the current session, saving an object, saving a copy of an object, opening an object, deleting older versions of a design, changing background color, customizing the **Ribbon**, customizing the **Quick Access Toolbar**, and closing a file.

Questions

Complete and verify the following sentences:

- The **Navigator** consist of three tabs: _________, _________, and _________ .
- The _________ is composed of a series of tabs in which a set of similar tools are grouped.

- The _________ keeps a record of all operations or features used for creating a model.
- The _________ tool in the Status Bar is used for toggling the display of full-screen mode.
- The _________ tool is used for removing all files from the temporary memory that are not currently displayed in the current session of Creo Parametric.
- The _________ tool is used for deleting all the older versions of a design from the hard disk of your computer except the latest version.
- You cannot minimize the **Ribbon** to increase the size of the graphics window. (True/False)
- In Creo Parametric, every time you save an object, a new version of the object is saved in the working directory. (True/False)
- In Creo Parametric, when you open an object, the latest version of the file gets opened, by default. (True/False)
- You cannot open an older version of a design. (True/False)

CHAPTER

2

Drawing Sketches and Applying Dimensions

In this chapter, the following topics will be discussed:

- Invoking the Part Mode
- Specifying Units
- Invoking the Sketching Environment
- Working with Selection of Planes
- Specifying Grids and Snap Settings
- Drawing Sketch Entities
- Creating Datum Geometries
- Working with Construction Mode
- Applying Constraints
- Working with Weak Dimensions
- Applying Dimensions
- Editing Dimensions

Creo Parametric is a feature-based, parametric, solid modeling mechanical design and automation software. Before you start creating solid 3D components in Creo Parametric, you need to understand it. To design a component in this software, you need to create all its features one by one, see Figures 2.1 and 2.2. Note that the features are divided into two main categories: sketch-based features and placed features. A feature created using a sketch is known as a sketch-based feature, whereas a feature created by specifying placement on an existing feature without using a sketch is known as a placed feature. Of the two categories, the sketch-based feature is the first feature to design any real-world component. It is therefore important, to first learn to draw a sketch.

Figure 2.1 shows a component consisting of an extrude feature and chamfer. Out of these two features, the extrude feature is created using a sketch, therefore, this is known as a sketch-based feature. On the other hand, since no sketch is used in creating the chamfer, this feature is known as a placed feature. Figure 2.2 depicts the process for creating this model.

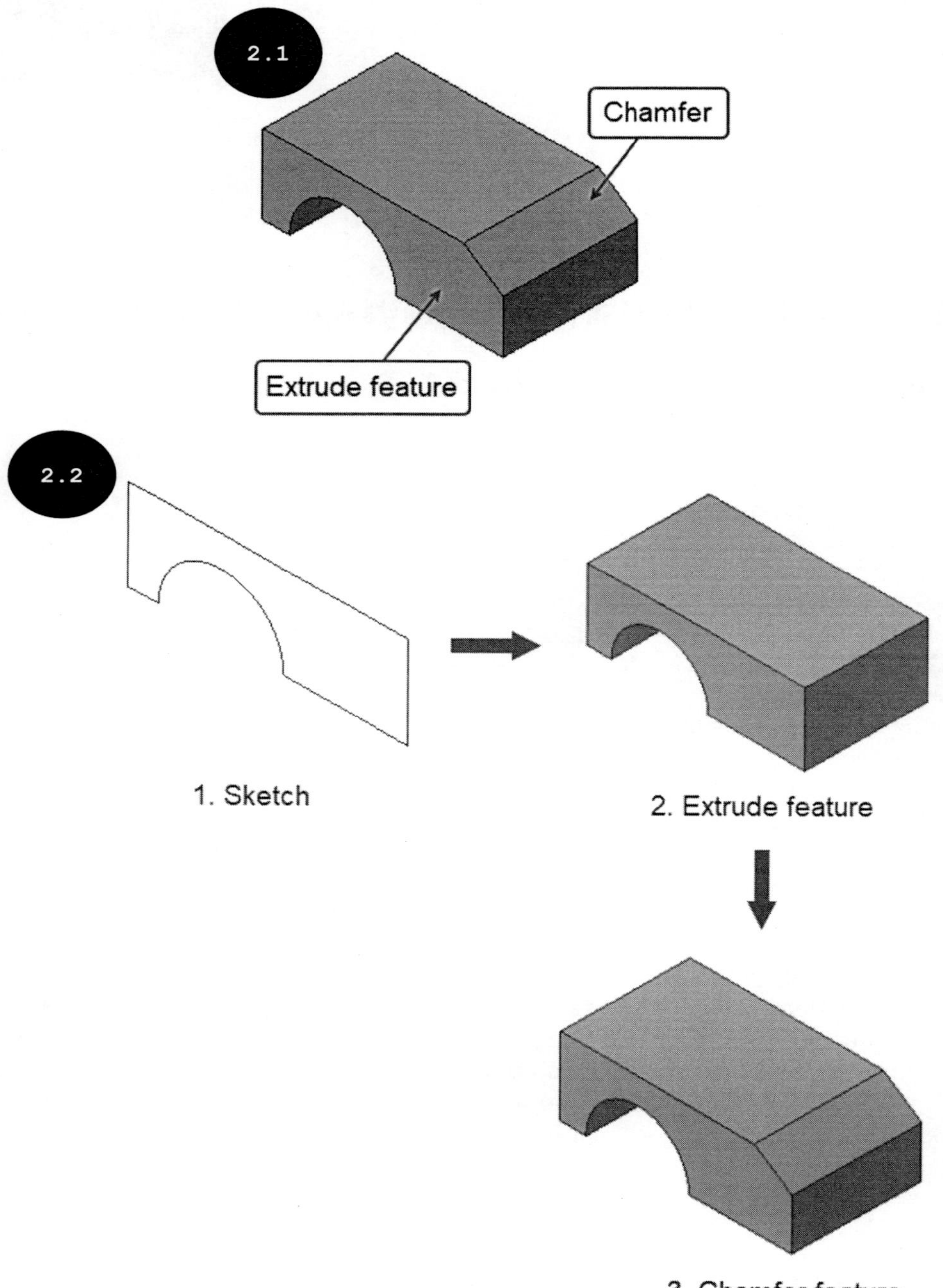

As the first feature of any component is sketch-based, you need to first learn how to create sketches in the Sketching environment. In Creo Parametric, the Sketching environment can be invoked within the Sketch mode as well as the Part mode.

Invoking the Part Mode

Start Creo Parametric by double-clicking on the **Creo Parametric 12.4.0.0** icon on your desktop. After loading the required files, the startup user interface of Creo Parametric appears along with the **Resource Center** window, see Figure 2.3. The **Resource Center** window is used for accessing online Creo resources, PTC Communities, PTC Events, and so on. This window appears every time you start Creo Parametric. If you do not want this window to be displayed the next time you start Creo Parametric, select the **Do not show window again** check box at the bottom of the **Resource Center** window. Next, close the **Resource Center** window. The startup user interface of Creo Parametric appears, see Figure 2.4.

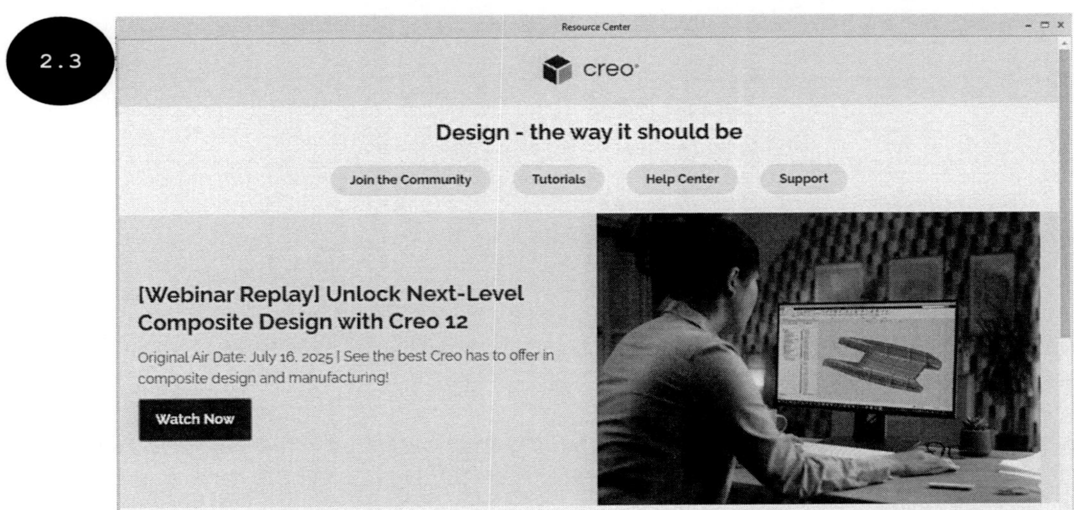

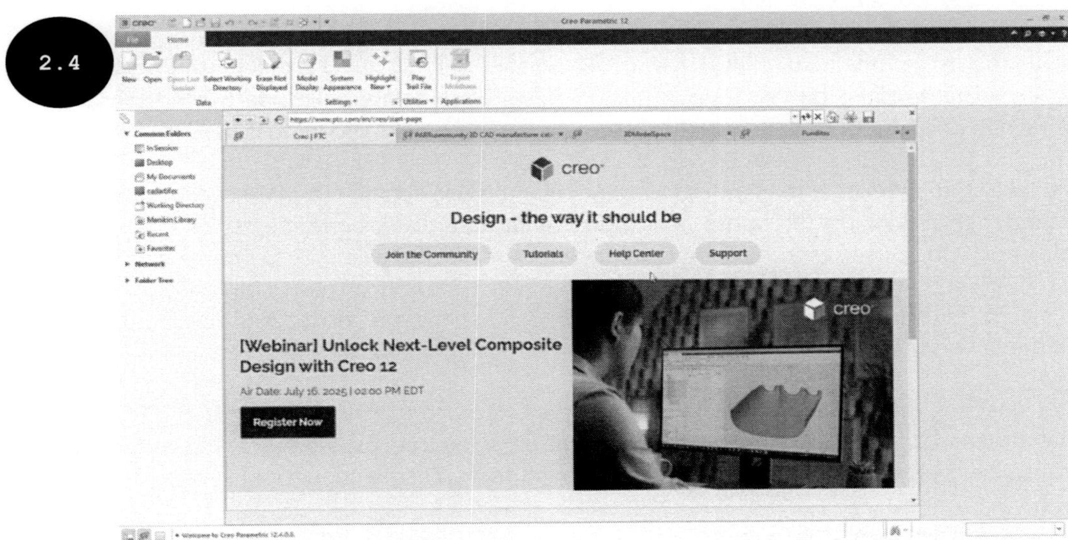

Once the startup user interface of Creo Parametric has been invoked, click on the **New** tool in the **Data** group of the **Home** tab in the **Ribbon**. The **New** dialog box appears, see Figure 2.5.

2.5

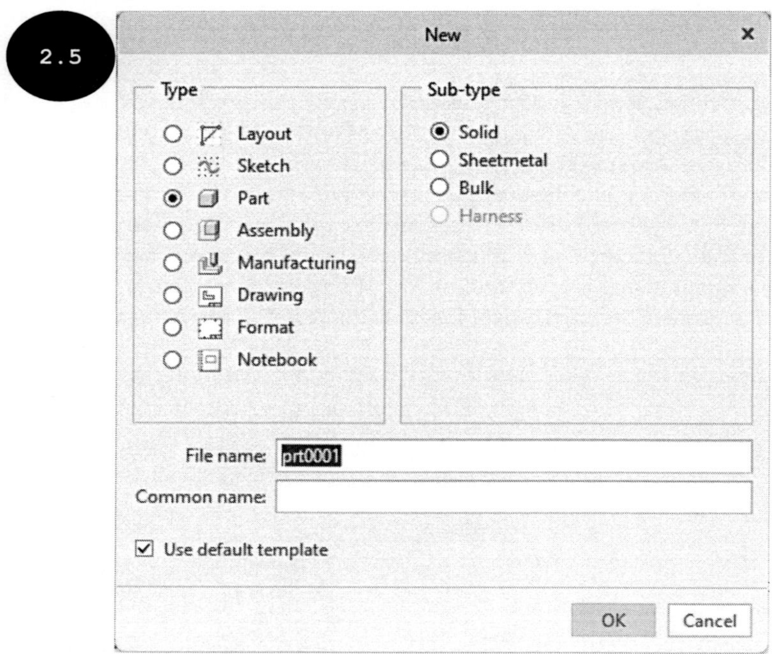

In the **New** dialog box, the **Sketch** radio button is used for invoking the Sketch mode, and the **Part** radio button is used for invoking the Part mode.

To invoke the Part mode, ensure that the **Part** radio button is selected in the **Type** area and the **Solid** radio button is selected in the **Sub-type** area, see Figure 2.5. Next, enter the name of the part file in the **File name** field of the dialog box.

Besides, you also need to define a template for the part file. A template contains some properties of the file such as a predefined unit system and file type. By default, the **Use default template** check box is selected in the dialog box. As a result, the default Creo template (**inlbs_part_solid_abs**) with the predefined unit system (length in inches, mass in lbm, and time in seconds) is used for the part file.

To select a template other than the default one, clear the **Use default template** check box in the dialog box and then click on the **OK** button. The **New File Options** dialog box appears, see Figure 2.6. In this dialog box, you can select the required template for the file. For example, to open a part file with the Metric unit system with absolute accuracy, you can select the **mmns_part_solid_abs** template in the dialog box. In this template, the length is measured in millimeters, the mass is measured in Newton, and the time is measured in seconds.

After selecting the required template, click on the **OK** button in the dialog box. The Part modeling environment of the Part mode is invoked and three default datum planes; Front, Top, and Right, which are mutually perpendicular to each other, appear in the graphics window, see Figure 2.7.

Similarly, you can invoke the Sketch mode using the **Sketch** radio button of the **New** dialog box.

2.6

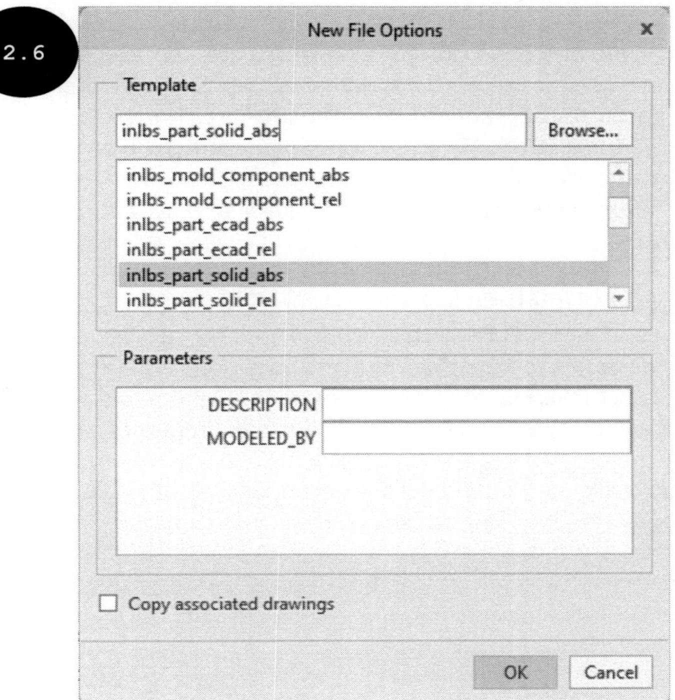

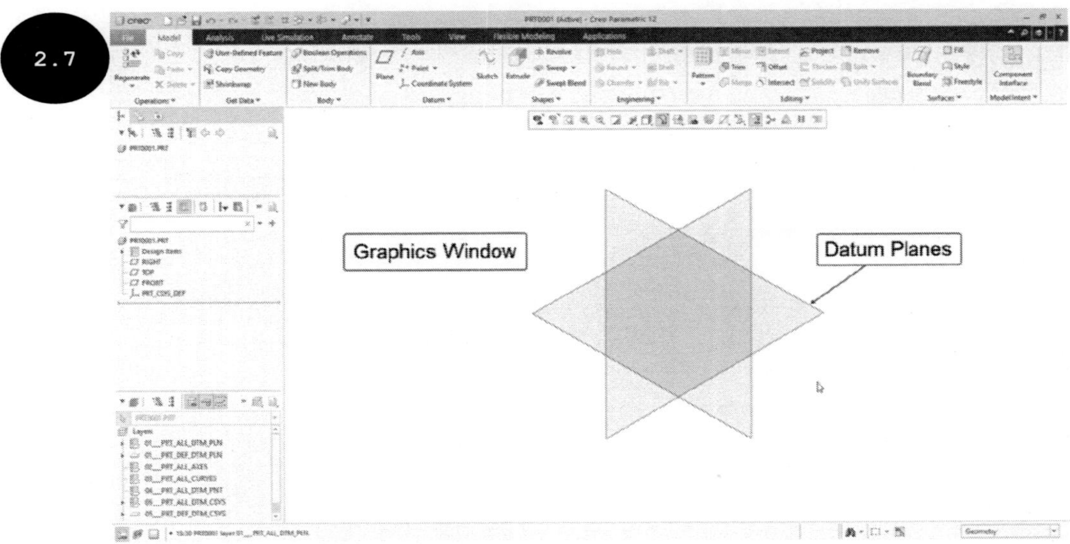

Tip: When you invoke a Part file, the unit system associated with the selected template is defined as the default unit system for that Part file. However, you can modify the default unit settings at any point of your design for any particular file. You will learn more about specifying units later in this chapter.

Note: In Creo Parametric, two different suffixes; _abs and _rel are used for templates. The templates with _abs refer to absolute accuracy and _rel refer to relative accuracy. The absolute accuracy of a model defines the smallest allowable length of the model that Creo Parametric can display or interpret without any error. The default absolute accuracy value is 0.00039 inches or .01 millimeters. As a result, Creo Parametric can accurately display the edges of the model with a length greater than or equal to 0.00039 inches or 0.01 millimeters, respectively.

To edit or change the default absolute accuracy of the model, click on **File** > **Prepare** > **Model Properties**. The **Model Properties** window appears, see Figure 2.8. In this window, click on the **change** option to the right of the **Accuracy** option, see Figure 2.8. The **Accuracy** dialog box appears. In this dialog box, you can specify the required accuracy value and then click on the **Regenerate** button. Next, exit the **Model Properties** window.

The relative accuracy of a model defines the ratio of the smallest length of the model to the overall part size (bounding box). The default relative accuracy value is 0.0012. As a result, if the part size of the model is 10 inches, then Creo Parametric can accurately display the edges of the model with a length greater than or equal to 0.012 inches (relative accuracy = smallest length of the model / part size).

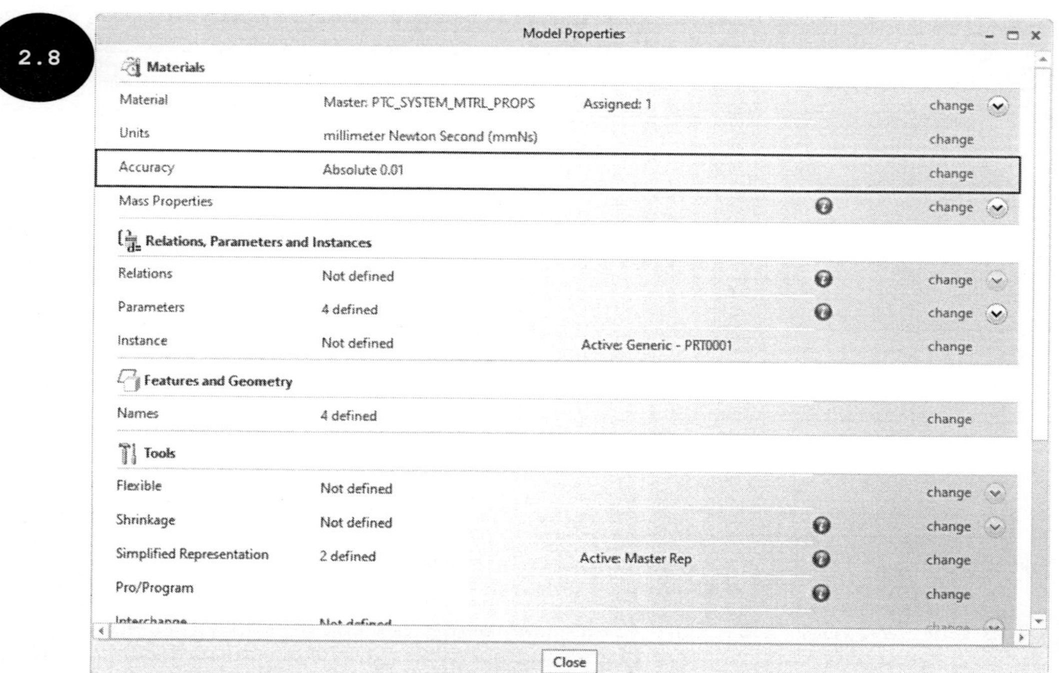

2.8

Specifying Units

As discussed earlier, when you invoke a part file, the unit system associated with the selected template is defined as the default unit system for that part file. However, you can modify the default unit settings at any point of your design for any particular file. To do so, click on the **File** button in the upper left corner of the screen. The **File** menu appears, see Figure 2.9. In this menu, click on **Prepare > Model Properties**. The **Model Properties** window appears, see Figure 2.10. Next, click on the **change** option on the right of the **Units** option in the window, see Figure 2.10. The **Units Manager** dialog box appears, see Figure 2.11.

2.9

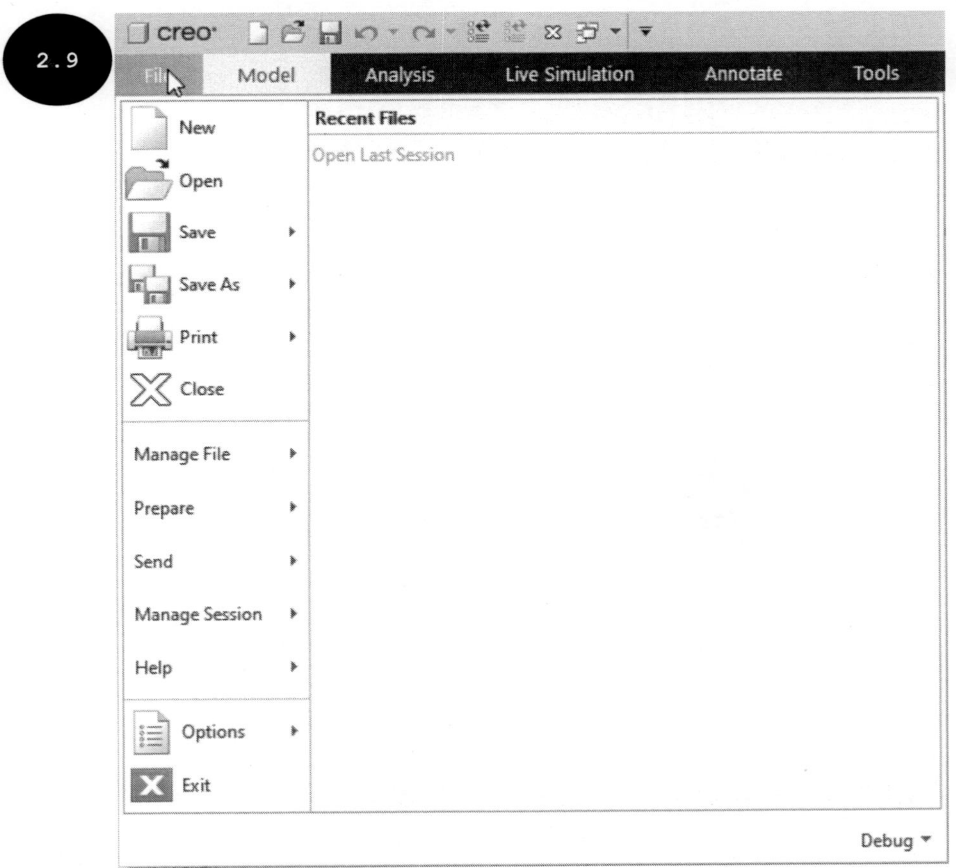

In the **Systems of Units** tab of this dialog box, a list of predefined unit systems appears. You can select any of these as the unit system of the current file. For example, to set the metric unit system for the currently opened file, select the **millimeter Kilogram Sec (mmKs)** unit system. Note that in this unit system, the length is measured in millimeters, mass is calculated in kilograms, and time is represented in seconds. After selecting the desired unit system, click on the **Set** button in the dialog box. The **Changing Model Units** window appears, which asks to confirm whether you want to convert the current dimensions as per the new unit system or interpret dimensions only. Select the required radio button [**Convert dimensions (for example, 1" becomes 25.4mm)** or **Interpret dimensions (for example, 1" becomes 1mm)**] in the **Changing Model Units** window and then click on the **OK** button. The selected unit system becomes the unit system for the current file.

2.10

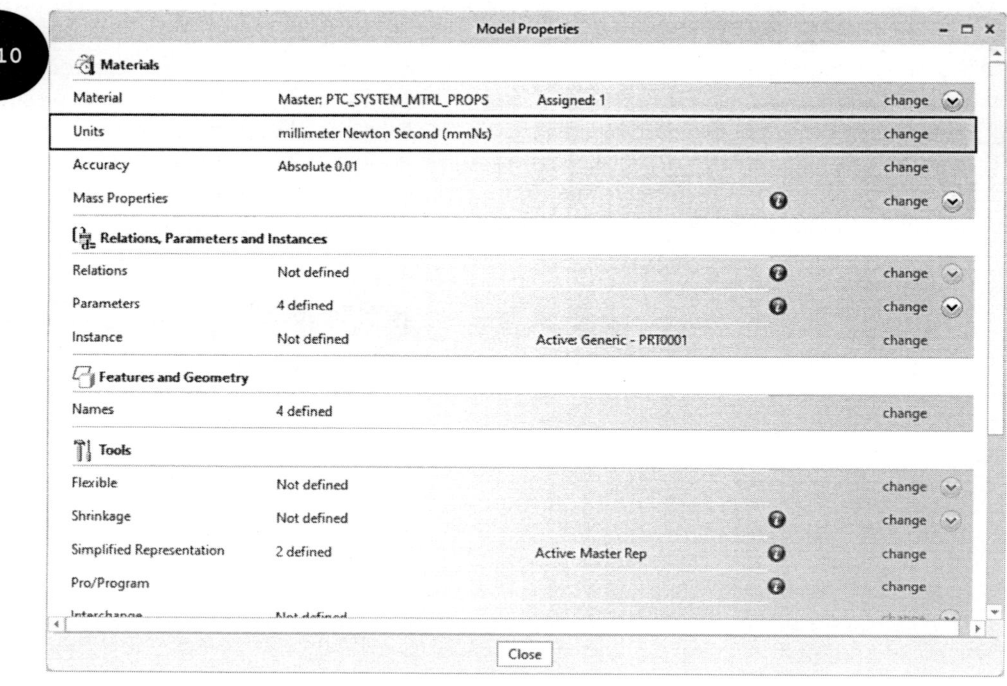

2.11

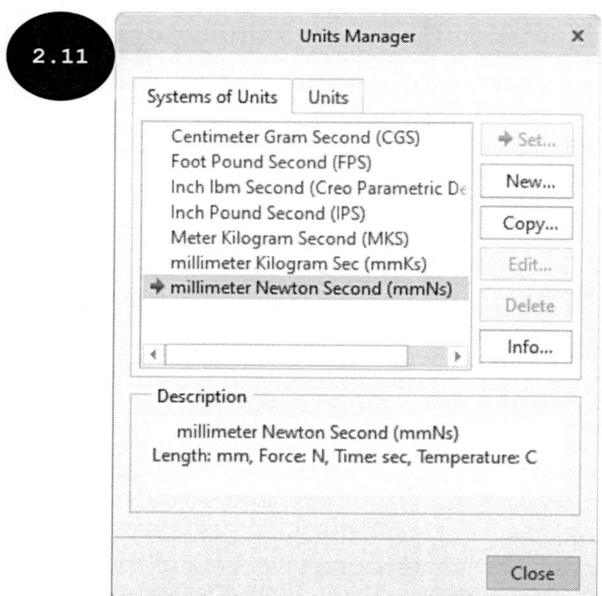

You can also create a new unit system for the currently opened file as per your requirement by using the **Units Manager** dialog box. To do so, click on the **New** button in the **Units Manager** dialog box. The **System of Units Definition** dialog box appears, see Figure 2.12. In this dialog box, specify the name of the unit system in the **Name** field and then select the type of unit system in the **Type** area of the dialog box. Next, select the desired unit of measurement in the respective drop-down lists of the **Units** area in the dialog box and then click on the **OK** button. The unit system is created and added to the list of unit systems in the **Units Manager** dialog box. Now, you can make the newly created unit system as the unit system of the current file. After selecting the desired unit system for the current file, click on the **Close** button in the **Units Manager** dialog box.

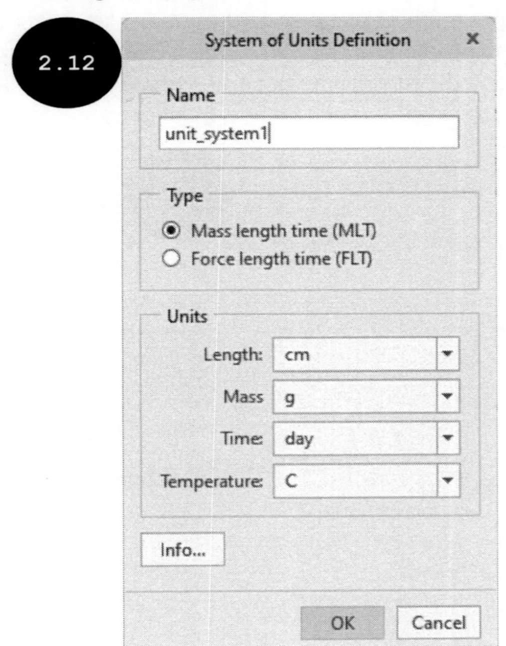

Invoking the Sketching Environment

After the Part mode is invoked, you need to invoke the Sketching environment to create the sketch of the first feature of a model. To invoke the Sketching environment, click on the **Sketch** tool in the **Datum** group of the **Model** tab, see Figure 2.13. The **Sketch** dialog box appears, see Figure 2.14. Also, you are prompted to select a plane or a surface to define the sketching plane. You can select any of the default datum planes as the sketching plane for creating a sketch.

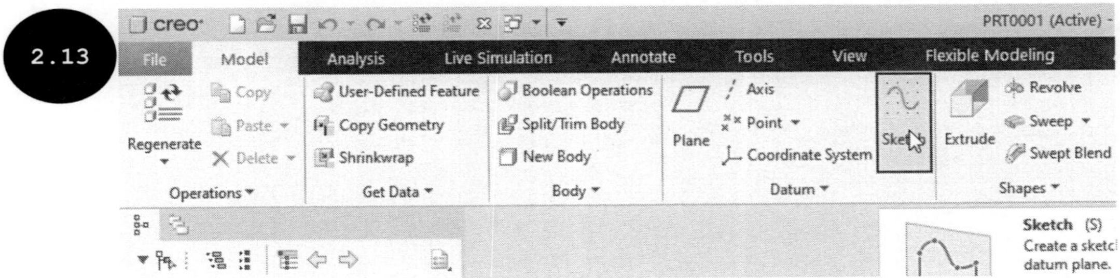

To select a plane, move the cursor over the plane to be selected and then click the left mouse button when it gets highlighted in the graphics window. The name of the selected plane appears in the **Plane**

field in the **Placement** tab of the dialog box, see Figure 2.15. Also, a reference plane and its orientation are selected by default in the **Reference** field and **Orientation** drop-down list of the dialog box, respectively, see Figure 2.15. In this figure, the Right plane is selected as the reference plane, and its orientation is defined as **Right** in the **Orientation** drop-down list. This means that the Right plane will be oriented toward the right side in the Sketching environment to make the sketching plane appear normal to the screen. You can define a reference plane and its orientation other than the default selection, as per requirement. After selecting a sketching plane and a reference plane, click on the **Sketch** button in the dialog box. The Sketching environment of the Part mode is invoked with the display of the **Sketch** tab in the **Ribbon**. Also, the selected datum plane becomes the sketching plane for creating the sketch, see Figure 2.16.

Note: In this textbook, the background color of the graphics window has been set to white for clarity. The method for changing the background color of the graphics window has been discussed in Chapter 1.

Now, you can start creating the sketch on the sketching plane by using different sketching tools in the **Sketch** tab of the **Ribbon**. Before you start creating the sketch, it is recommended to change the orientation of the sketching plane normal to the viewing direction, so that you can create the sketch easily, if it is not oriented normal to the viewing direction, by default. To do so, click on the **Sketch View** tool in the **In-graphics** toolbar, see Figure 2.17. The sketching plane becomes normal to the viewing direction.

2.17

Note: You can also invoke the Sketching environment of the Sketch mode for creating the sketch. To do so, click on the **New** tool in the **Quick Access Toolbar**. The **New** dialog box appears. In this dialog box, click on the **Sketch** radio button and then enter a name for the sketch in the **File name** field of the dialog box. Next, click on the **OK** button. The Sketching environment of the Sketch mode is invoked.

Working with Selection of Planes

As discussed earlier, to invoke the Sketching environment of the Part mode, you need to select a datum plane as the sketching plane for creating a sketch. Note that the selection of a correct datum plane is very important to define the right orientation of the model. Figure 2.18 shows the isometric view of a model having a length of 200 mm, width of 100 mm, and height of 40 mm. To create a model with the same orientation and dimensions, select the Top plane as the sketching plane and then draw a rectangular sketch having dimensions 200 mm X 100 mm. However, if you select the Front plane as the sketching plane for creating this model, you need to draw a rectangular sketch of 200 mm X 40 mm. Likewise, if you select the Right plane as the sketching plane, you need to draw a rectangular sketch of 100 mm X 40 mm.

2.18

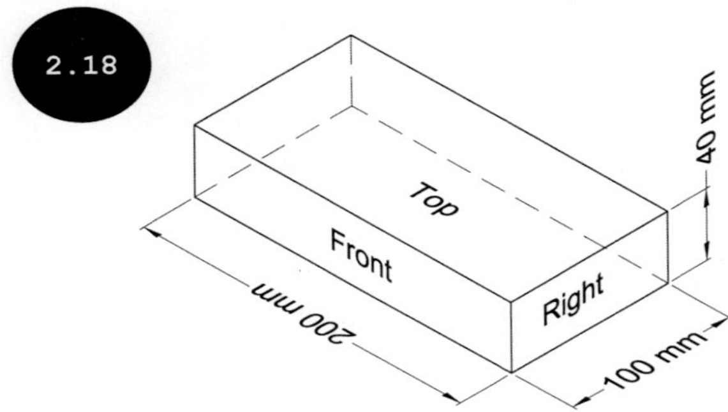

Once the Sketching environment has been invoked, you can start drawing the sketch using different sketching tools of the **Sketching** group in the **Sketch** tab of the **Ribbon**. However, before you start drawing the sketch, it is important to understand grids and snap settings.

Specifying Grids and Snap Settings

Grids help you specify points in the drawing area for creating sketch entities and act as reference lines. By default, the display of grids is turned off in the drawing area. You can turn on the display of grids in the drawing area and specify snap settings such that the movement of the cursor is restricted at specified intervals.

To turn on the display of grids, click on the **Sketcher Display Filters** tool in the **In-graphics** toolbar. The **Sketcher Display Filters** flyout appears, see Figure 2.19. In this flyout, click on the **Grid Display** tool. The grid appears in the drawing area with default settings, see Figure 2.20.

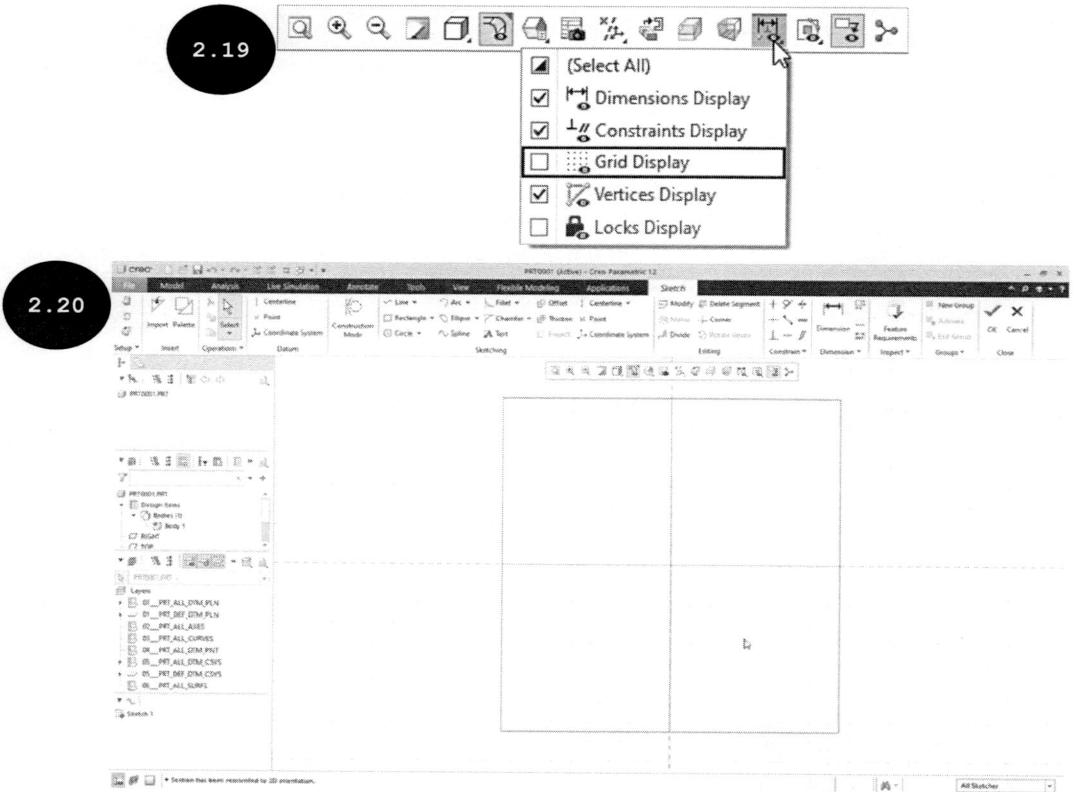

To control the grid settings, click on the down arrow in the **Setup** group of the **Sketch** tab. The **Setup** flyout appears, see Figure 2.21. In this flyout, click on the **Grid** tool. The **Grid Settings** dialog box appears, see Figure 2.22.

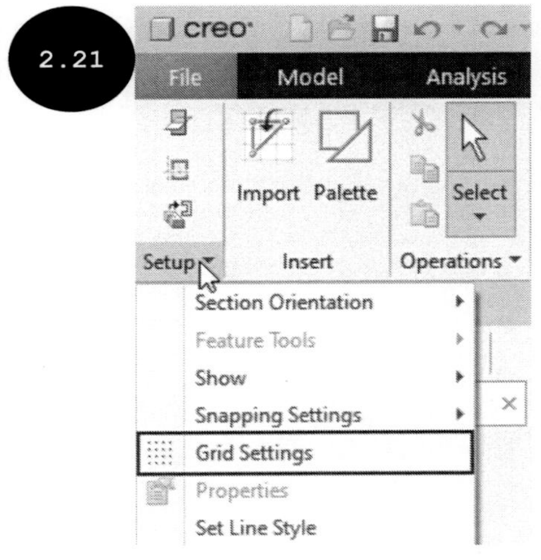

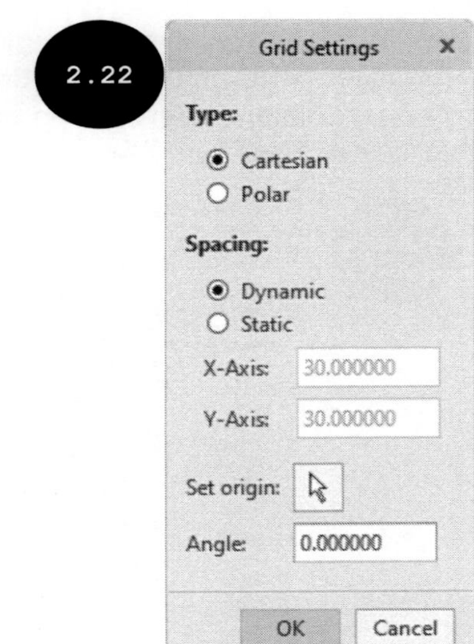

Creo Parametric supports the Cartesian and Polar grid types. By default, the Cartesian grid type appears in the drawing area. You can select the required grid type radio button (**Cartesian** or **Polar**) in the **Type** area of the **Grid Settings** dialog box. Next, select the method (**Dynamic** or **Static**) for defining the spacing between the grid lines.

By default, the **Dynamic** radio button is selected in the **Spacing** area of the dialog box, see Figure 2.22. As a result, the spacing between the grid lines is adjusted automatically based on the user's zoom in or zoom out operations. On selecting the **Static** radio button, you can define the X and Y grid spacing in the respective fields of the **Spacing** area.

Note that the availability of fields in the **Spacing** area for defining the grid spacing depends on the type of grid selected (**Cartesian** or **Polar**). You can also define the angle of the grid lines by using the **Angle** field of the dialog box. Besides, you can also reset the grid origin by using the **Set origin** button of the dialog box. To do so, click on the **Set origin** button and then click on a point in the drawing area. After specifying the grid settings, click on the **OK** button to apply the changes and exit the dialog box.

After defining the grid settings, you can turn on the Snap mode for snapping the cursor on the grid lines while creating drawing entities. To do so, click on the **File** button in the upper left corner of the screen. The **File** menu appears. In this menu, click on the **Options** tool. The **Creo Parametric Options** dialog box appears, see Figure 2.23. In this dialog box, click on the **Sketcher** option to display the options for defining the sketcher settings on the right panel of the dialog box. Next, scroll down the dialog box and select the **Snap to grid** check box in the **Sketcher grid** area of the dialog box, see Figure 2.23.

You can also control the grid settings by using the options available in this area of the dialog box. Next, click on the **OK** button in the dialog box. The **Creo Parametric Options** dialog box appears, which informs that the changes made in the settings will be applied to the current session only and confirms whether you want to save settings to a configuration file. Click on the **No** button to make the changes only in the current session and to exit the dialog box. If you click on the **Yes** button, you can save the settings to a configuration file to apply the same settings to other sessions of Creo Parametric as well.

Alternatively, to turn on the Snap mode in the current session of Creo Parametric, click on the down arrow in the **Setup** group of the **Sketch** tab. The **Setup** flyout appears, see Figure 2.24. In this flyout, click on the **Snapping Settings** tool and then select the **Snap to grid** check box in the cascading menu that appears, see Figure 2.24.

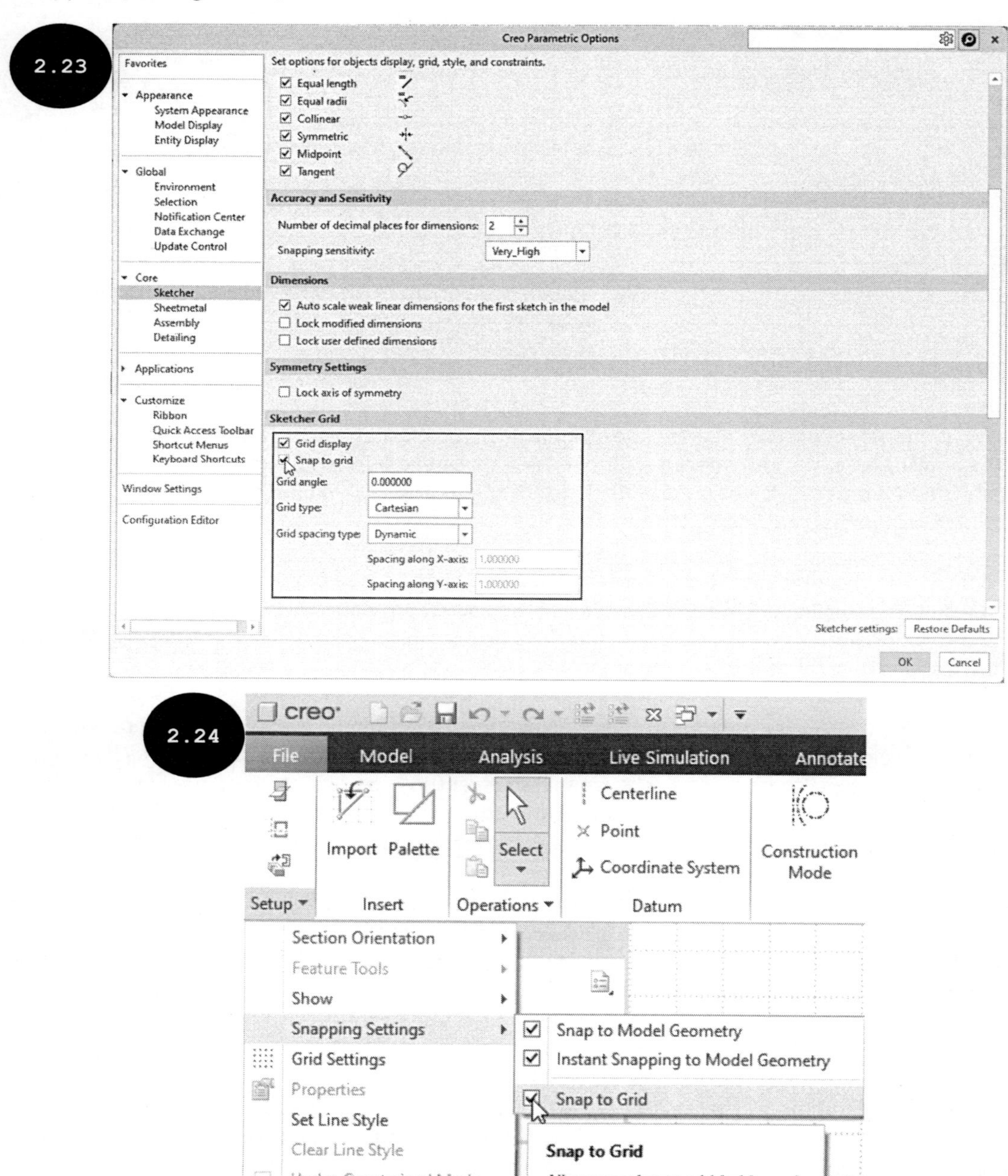

Drawing Sketch Entities

In the Sketching environment, you can draw a sketch of a feature using the tools available in the **Sketching** group of the **Sketch** tab in the **Ribbon**, see Figure 2.25. Methods for creating different types of sketch entities are discussed next.

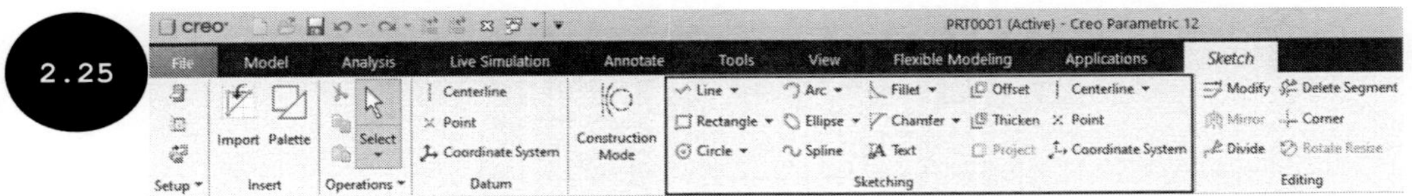

Drawing a Line

A line is defined as the shortest distance between two points. In Creo Parametric, you can create a line by using the **Line Chain, Line Tangent Line** and **Line Mid-point** tools available in the **Line** flyout of the **Sketching** group, see Figure 2.26. This flyout can be invoked by clicking on the arrow next to an active line tool in the **Sketching** group, see Figure 2.26.

The **Line Chain** tool is used for creating a line or a continuous chain of lines. The **Line Tangent** tool is used for creating a tangent line between two existing entities. The **Line Mid-point** tool is used for creating a line by specifying its midpoint and an endpoint. The method for drawing lines using these tools is discussed next.

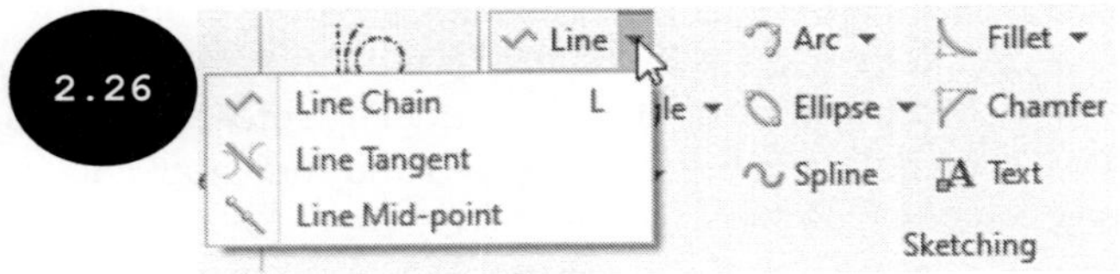

Drawing a Line or Chain of Lines

The method for drawing a line or a continuous chain of lines using the **Line Chain** tool is discussed below:

1. Click on the **Line Chain** tool in the **Line** flyout of the **Sketching** group, see Figure 2.27. The **Line Chain** tool gets activated. Alternatively, you can press the **L** key to activate this tool.

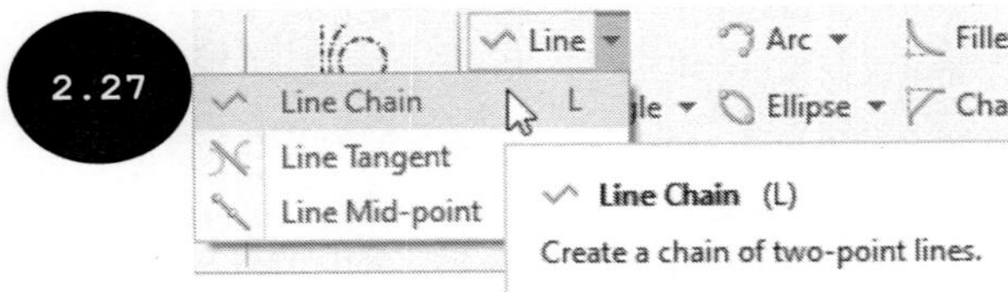

2. Click to specify the start point of the line in the drawing area.

3. Move the line cursor away from the start point. A rubber band line appears with one of its ends fixed at the start point and the other end attached to the cursor, see Figure 2.28.

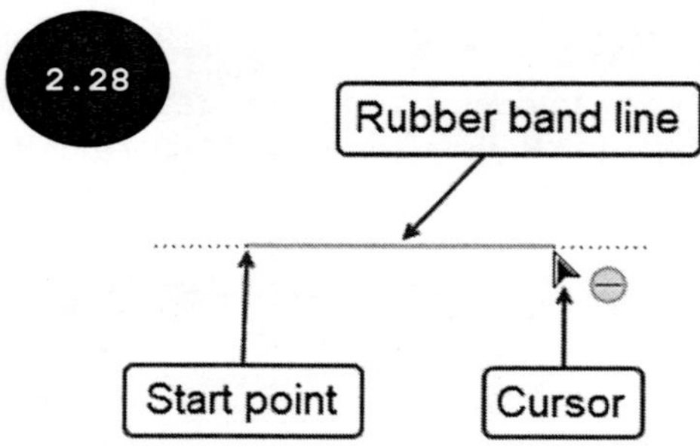

Note: If you move the cursor horizontally or vertically after specifying the start point of the line, a symbol of horizontal ⊖ or vertical ⦶ constraint appears near the cursor. The symbol of constraint indicates that if you left click to specify the endpoint of the line, the corresponding constraint will be applied. You will learn more about constraints later in this chapter.

4. Left-click anywhere in the drawing area to specify the endpoint of the line. A line between the specified points is drawn. Also, notice that the rubber band line is still displayed with one of its ends fixed to the last specified point and the other end attached to the cursor. This indicates that a chain of continuous lines can be drawn by clicking the left mouse button in the drawing area.

Tip: As Creo Parametric is a parametric, 3D solid modeling software, you can first draw a sketch by specifying arbitrary points in the drawing area and then apply dimensions. You will learn about dimensioning sketch entities later in this chapter.

5. Once all the line entities have been drawn, press the middle mouse button to terminate the creation of a continuous chain of lines. Next, press the middle mouse button again to exit the **Line Chain** tool. The line entities are drawn, and the weak dimensions appear in the drawing area, see Figure 2.29. In Creo Parametric, weak dimensions are applied automatically to the sketch entities, see Figure 2.29. You will learn more about weak dimensions later in this chapter. Also, the open ends of the sketch appear with red-colored square boxes.

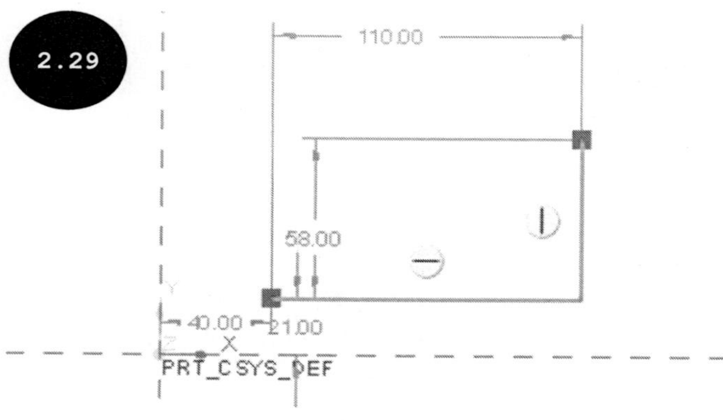

Note: In Figure 2.29, the display of datum planes is turned off for clarity of image. To turn on or off the display of datum planes, click on the **Datum Display Filters** tool in the **In-graphics** toolbar. A flyout appears, see Figure 2.30. In this flyout, click on the **Plane Display** tool.

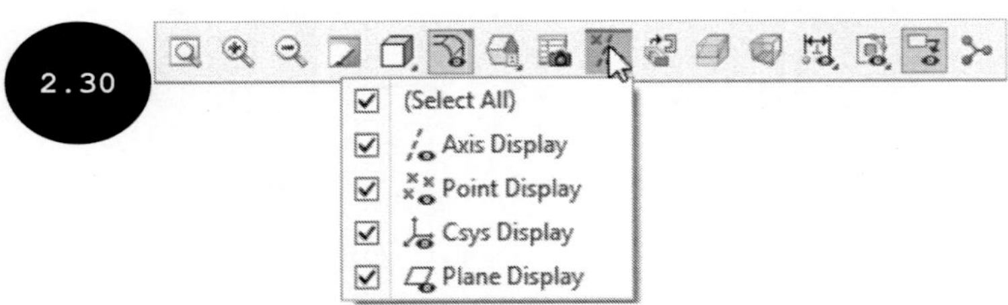

Drawing a Tangent Line

The method for drawing a tangent line between two existing entities (arc and circle entities) using the **Line Tangent** tool is discussed below:

1. Click on the arrow next to the active line tool in the **Sketching** group of the **Sketch** tab. The **Line** flyout appears, see Figure 2.31.

2. Click on the **Line Tangent** tool in the **Line** flyout, see Figure 2.31. The **Line Tangent** tool gets activated.

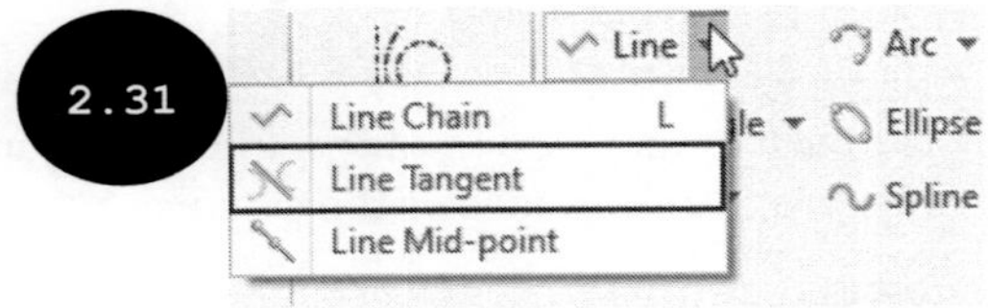

Note: To create a tangent line using the **Line Tangent** tool, ensure that at least two entities (arcs, circles, or an arc and a circle) are drawn in the Sketching environment. You will learn about drawing arc and circle entities later in this chapter.

3. Click to specify the first entity (an arc or a circle) in the drawing area as the first tangent entity, see Figure 2.32. Next, move the cursor away from the specified point. A rubber band tangent line appears with one end fixed at the specified point and the other end attached to the cursor.

4. Click to specify the second entity (an arc or a circle) when the cursor snaps on it, see Figure 2.32. A tangent line is drawn between the selected entities. Next, press the middle mouse button to exit the **Line Tangent** tool.

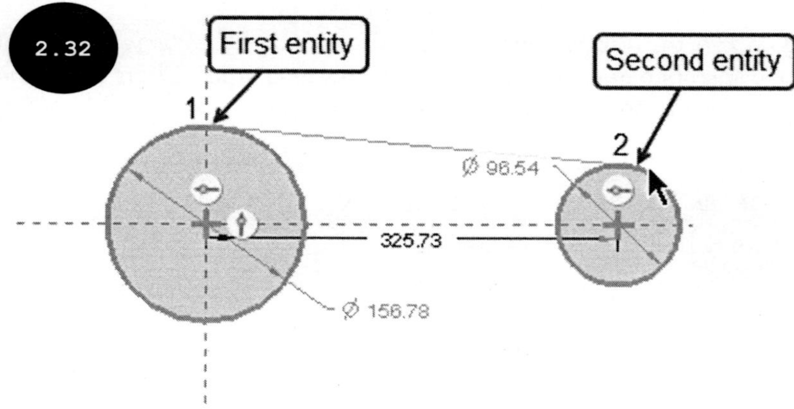

Drawing a Mid-point Line

The method for drawing a mid-point line using the **Line Mid-point** tool is discussed below:

1. Invoke the **Line** flyout and then click on the **Line Mid-point** tool, see Figure 2.33. The **Line Midpoint** tool gets activated.

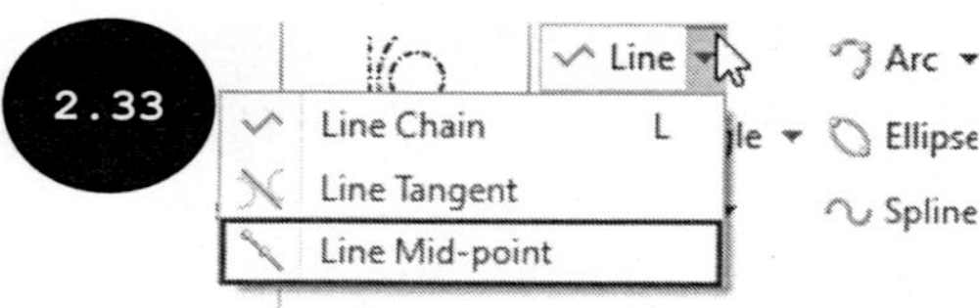

2. Click in the drawing area to specify the midpoint of the line, see Figure 2.34. A rubber band line appears with the midpoint fixed and an end follows the cursor.

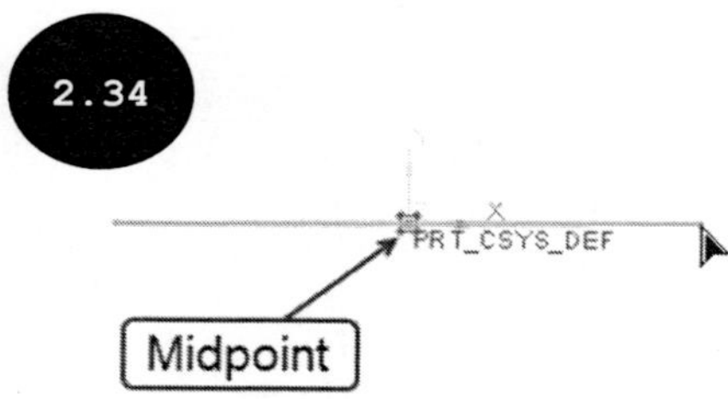

3. Move the cursor to the required location and click to define the endpoint. A line symmetric about the specified midpoint is drawn and the tool remains actived. Press the middle mouse button to exit the **Line Mid-point** tool.

Drawing a Rectangle

In Creo Parametric, you can draw a rectangle by different methods using the tools in the **Rectangle** flyout of the **Sketching** group in the **Sketch** tab, see Figure 2.35. To invoke the **Rectangle** flyout, click on the arrow next to the active rectangle tool in the **Sketching** group, see Figure 2.35. The methods for drawing rectangles using these tools are discussed next.

2.35

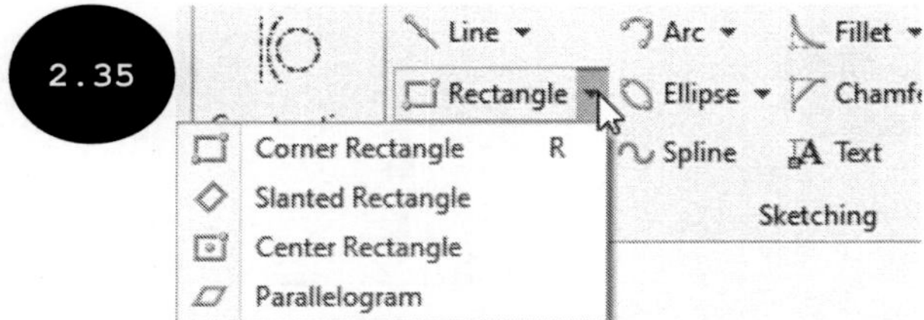

Drawing a Rectangle using the Corner Rectangle Tool

The **Corner Rectangle** tool is used for drawing a rectangle by specifying two diagonally opposite corners. The first specified corner defines the position of the rectangle, and the second corner defines the length and width of the rectangle, see Figure 2.36. The method for drawing a rectangle using the **Corner Rectangle** tool is discussed below:

2.36

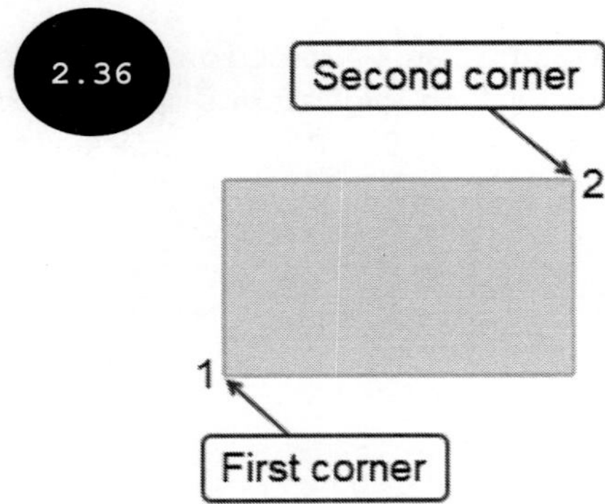

1. Invoke the **Rectangle** flyout, refer to Figure 2.35.

2. Click on the **Corner Rectangle** tool in the **Rectangle** flyout. The **Corner Rectangle** tool gets activated. Alternatively, you can press the **R** key to activate this tool.

3. Click anywhere to specify the first corner of the rectangle in the drawing area.

4. Move the cursor away from the first specified corner and then click to specify the diagonally opposite corner of the rectangle. After specifying the second corner of the rectangle in the drawing area, a rectangle is drawn, and the **Corner Rectangle** tool is still active. You can continue creating rectangles by specifying two diagonally opposite corners.

5. Press the middle mouse button to exit the tool. Figure 2.37 shows a rectangle created by specifying its two diagonally opposite corners. In Creo Parametric, weak dimensions are applied automatically to the sketch entities, see Figure 2.37. You will learn about weak dimensions later in this chapter.

2.37

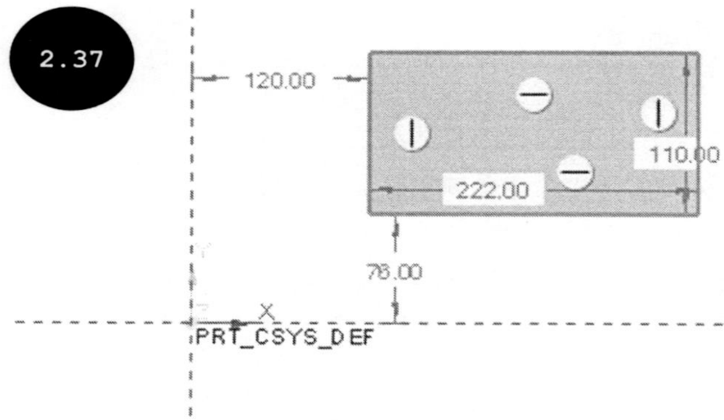

Note: In Figure 2.37, the display of datum planes is turned off for clarity of image. To turn on or off the display of datum planes, click on the **Datum Display Filters** tool in the **In-graphics** toolbar. A flyout appears, see Figure 2.38. In this flyout, click on the **Plane Display** tool.

2.38

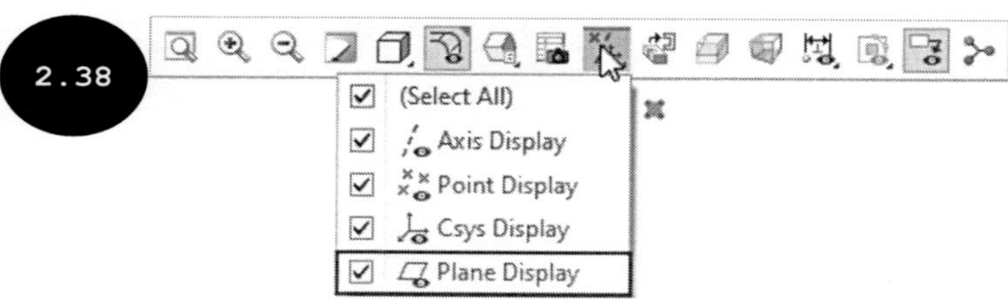

Drawing a Rectangle using the Slanted Rectangle Tool

The **Slanted Rectangle** tool is used for drawing a slanted rectangle by specifying 3 points. The first two points define the width and orientation of the rectangle, and the third point defines the length of the rectangle, see Figure 2.39. The method for drawing a slanted rectangle using the **Slanted Rectangle** tool is discussed below:

2.39

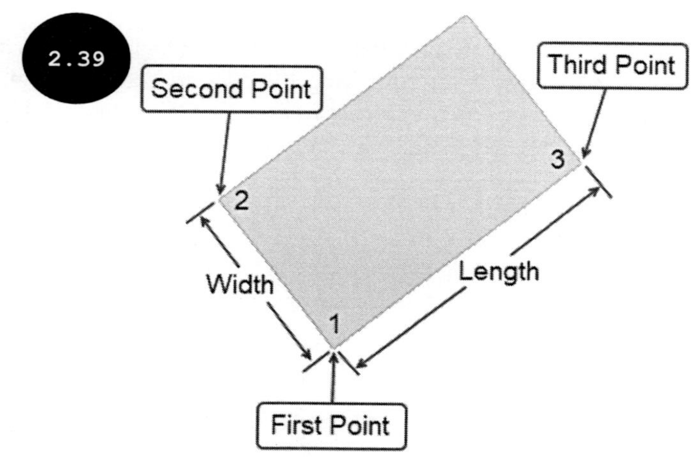

Note: In this chapter, some of the figures are numbered for your reference only, see Figure 2.39. These numbers represent the sequence of points specified in the drawing area for creating an entity by clicking the left mouse button.

1. Invoke the **Rectangle** flyout by clicking on the arrow next to the active rectangle tool in the **Sketching** group of the **Sketch** tab in the **Ribbon**.

2. Click on the **Slanted Rectangle** tool in the **Rectangle** flyout. The **Slanted Rectangle** tool gets activated.

3. Click anywhere to specify the first point of the rectangle in the drawing. The first point defines the first corner of the rectangle.

4. Move the cursor away from the first specified point in the drawing area. A rubber band line attached to the cursor appears.

5. Click to specify the second point of the rectangle in the drawing area. Note that the first and second points define the width and orientation of the rectangle, refer to Figure 2.39.

6. Move the cursor away from the second specified point in the drawing area. A preview of the rectangle appears with one end attached to the cursor, see Figure 2.40.

7. Click to specify the third point, which defines the length of the rectangle. A rectangle is drawn, and the **Slanted Rectangle** tool is still active.

8. Press the middle mouse button to exit the tool. Figure 2.41 shows a slanted rectangle created by specifying 3 points in the drawing area.

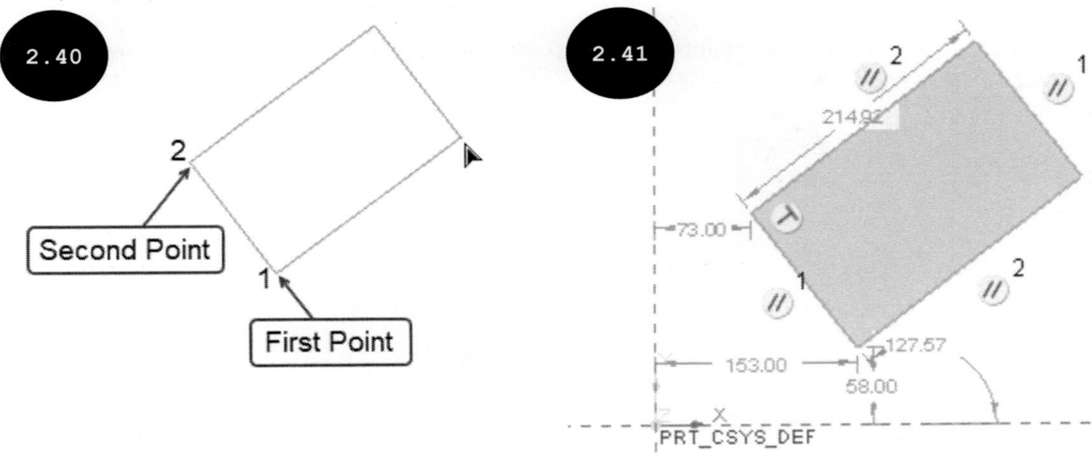

Note: In Creo Parametric, weak dimensions are applied automatically to the sketch entities. You will learn about weak dimensions later in this chapter.

Drawing a Rectangle using the Center Rectangle Tool

The **Center Rectangle** tool is used for drawing a rectangle by specifying a center point and a corner point, see Figure 2.42. The method for drawing a rectangle by using this tool is discussed below:

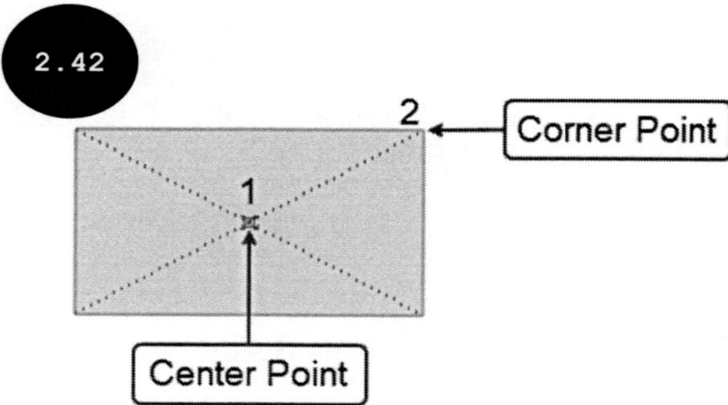

1. Invoke the **Rectangle** flyout in the **Sketching** group of the **Sketch** tab and then click on the **Center Rectangle** tool, see Figure 2.43. The **Center Rectangle** tool gets activated.

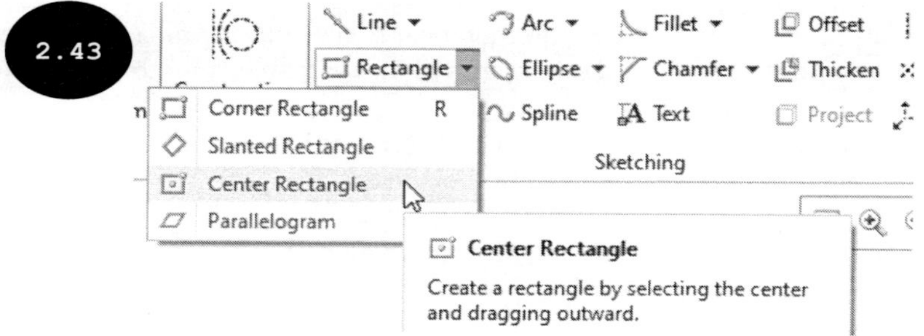

2. Click anywhere to specify the center point of the rectangle in the drawing area.

3. Move the cursor away from the specified point in the drawing area. A preview of the rectangle appears such that its center point is fixed at the specified point and a corner is attached to the cursor, see Figure 2.44.

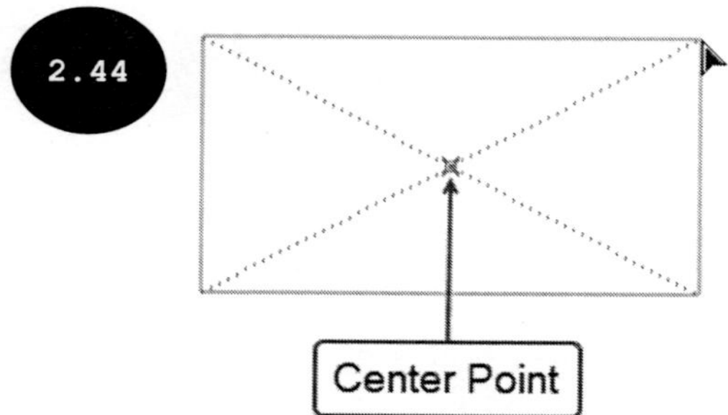

4. Click to specify the corner point of the rectangle in the drawing area. A rectangle is drawn.

5. Press the middle mouse button to exit the tool. Figure 2.45 shows a rectangle drawn by specifying its center point and a corner point in the drawing area.

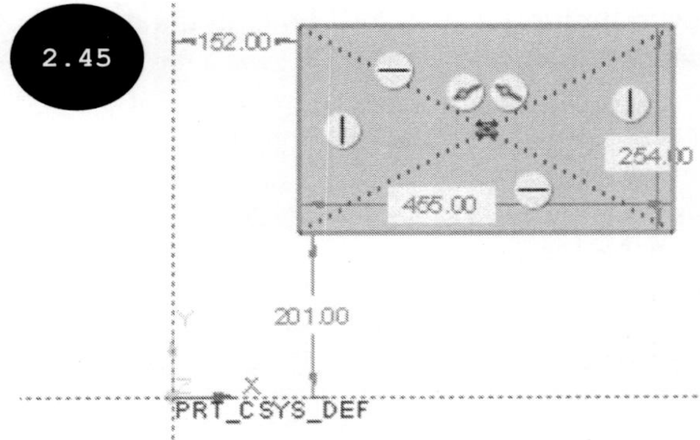

Drawing a Parallelogram

The **Parallelogram** tool is used for drawing a parallelogram, whose sides are not perpendicular to each other. You can draw a parallelogram by specifying three corners. The first two corners define the width and orientation of the parallelogram, and the third corner defines the length and the angle between the parallelogram sides, see Figure 2.46. The method for drawing a parallelogram by using the **Parallelogram** tool is discussed below:

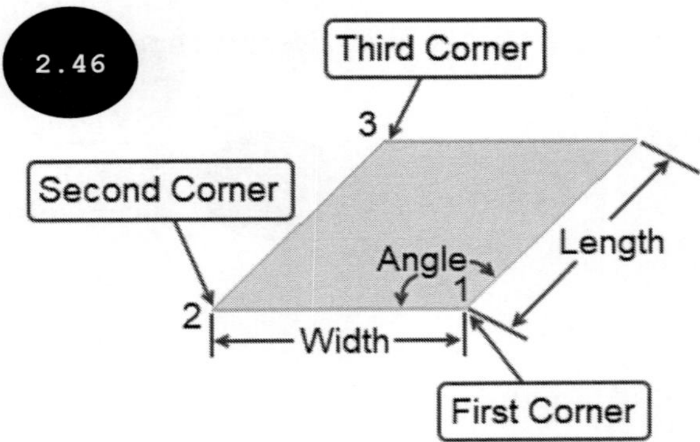

1. Invoke the **Rectangle** flyout and then click on the **Parallelogram** tool, see Figure 2.47. The **Parallelogram** tool gets activated.

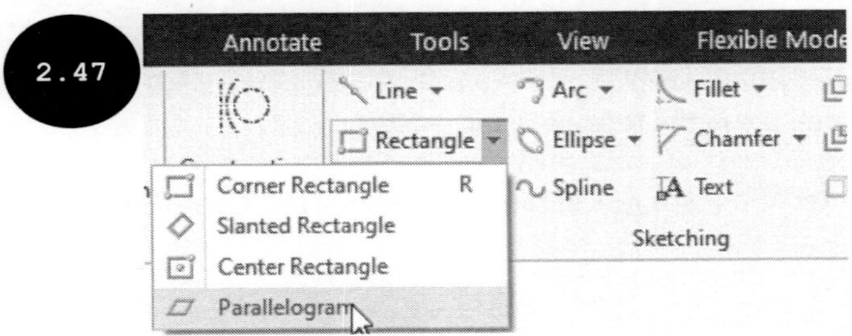

2. Click to specify the first corner of the parallelogram, refer to Figure 2.46.

3. Move the cursor away from the first specified corner in the drawing area. A rubber band line attached to the cursor appears.

4. Click to specify the second corner of the parallelogram in the drawing area, refer to Figure 2.46.

5. Move the cursor away from the second specified corner in the drawing area. A preview of the parallelogram appears in the drawing area.

6. Click to specify the third corner of the parallelogram. A parallelogram is drawn, and the **Parallelogram** tool is still active. Next, press the middle mouse button to exit the tool.

Drawing a Circle

In Creo Parametric, you can draw a circle by different methods using the tools in the **Circle** flyout of the **Sketching** group in the **Sketch** tab, see Figure 2.48. To invoke the **Circle** flyout, click on the arrow next to the active circle tool in the **Sketching** group, see Figure 2.48. The methods for drawing circles by using these tools are discussed next.

Drawing a Circle using the Center and Point Tool

The **Center and Point** tool is used for drawing a circle by specifying the center point and a point on the circumference of the circle, see Figure 2.49. The method for drawing a circle using this tool is discussed below:

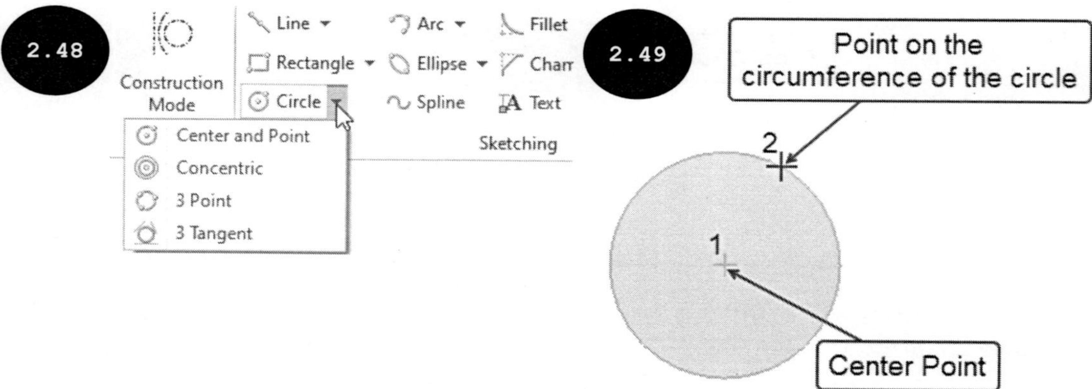

1. Invoke the **Circle** flyout by clicking on the arrow next to the active circle tool in the **Sketching** group of the **Sketch** tab in the **Ribbon**, refer to Figure 2.48.

2. Click on the **Center and Point** tool in the **Circle** flyout. The **Center and Point** tool gets activated.

3. Click to specify the center point of the circle in the drawing area. A preview of the circle attached to the cursor appears.

4. Click to specify a point on the circumference of the circle in the drawing area. A circle is drawn and the **Center and Point** tool is still active.

5. Press the middle mouse button to exit the tool. Figure 2.50 shows a circle created by specifying its center point and a point on the circumference of the circle in the drawing area.

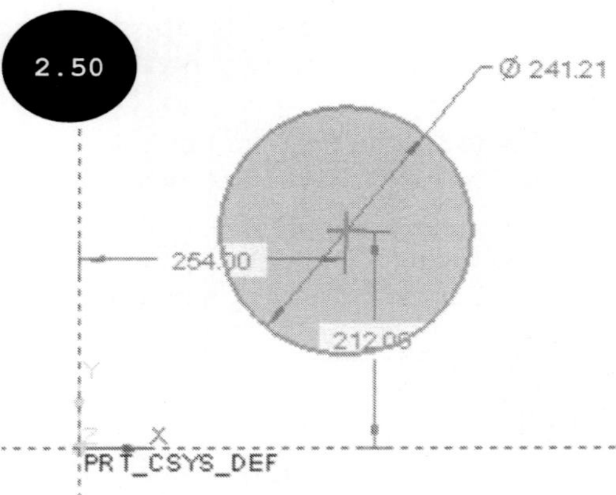

Drawing a Circle using the 3 Point Tool

The **3 Point** tool is used for drawing a circle by specifying three points on the circumference of the circle, see Figure 2.51. The method for drawing a circle by using this tool is discussed below:

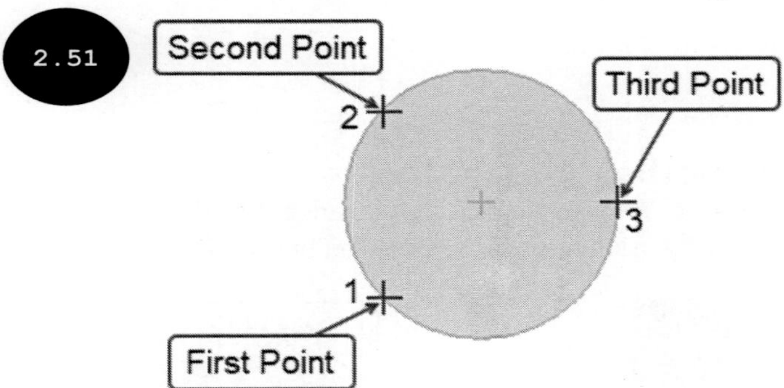

1. Invoke the **Circle** flyout in the **Sketching** group of the **Sketch** tab and then click on the **3 Point** tool, see Figure 2.52. The **3 Point** tool gets activated.

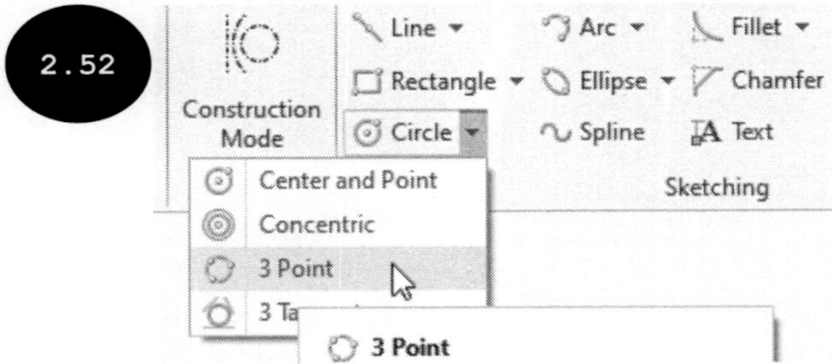

2. Click to specify the first point on the circumference of the circle in the drawing area.

3. Move the cursor away from the first specified point and then click to specify the second point on the circumference of the circle.

4. Move the cursor away from the second specified point. A preview of the circle appears such that it passes through the two specified points, see Figure 2.53.

5. Click to specify the third point on the circumference of the circle. A circle is drawn by defining three points on its circumference and the **3 Point** tool is still active.

6. Press the middle mouse button to exit the tool. Figure 2.54 shows a circle created by defining three points on the circumference of the circle.

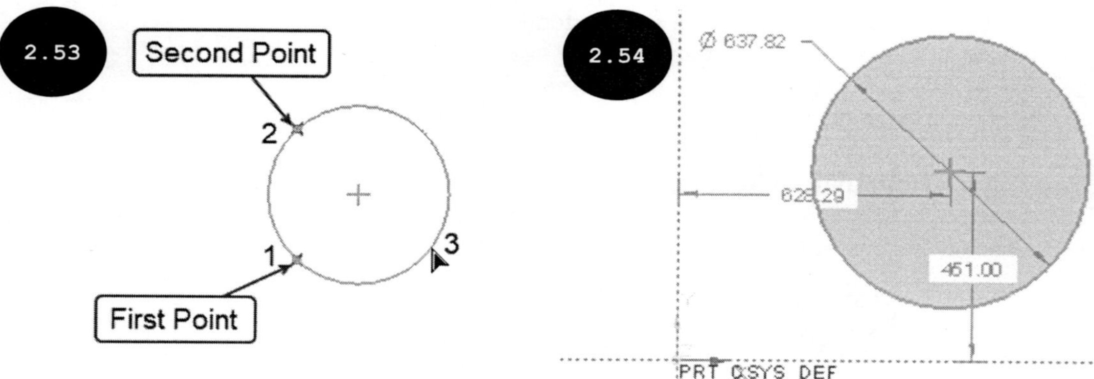

Drawing a Circle using the 3 Tangent Tool

The **3 Tangent** tool is used for drawing a circle that is tangent to three entities, see Figure 2.55. The method for drawing a circle by using this tool is discussed below:

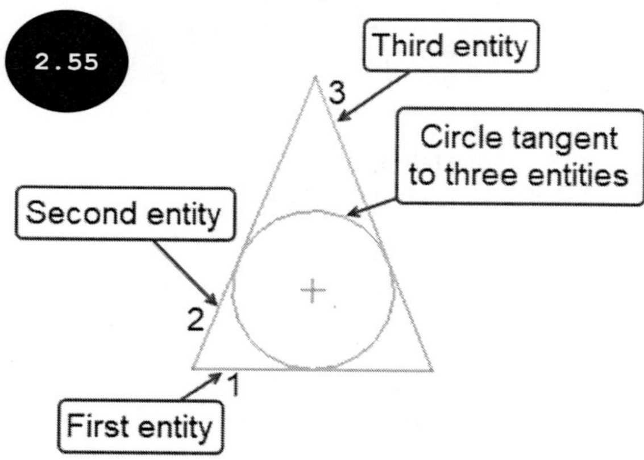

1. Invoke the **Circle** flyout in the **Sketching** group of the **Sketch** tab and then click on the **3 Tangent** tool. The **3 Tangent** tool gets activated.

2. Click to specify the first tangent entity in the drawing area and then move the cursor away from the specified entity. A rubber band line with one end attached to the cursor appears.

3. Click to specify the second tangent entity in the drawing area. A preview of the circle appears such that it is tangent to the specified entities.

4. Click to specify the third tangent entity in the drawing area. A circle is drawn such that it is tangent to the three specified entities. Next, press the middle mouse button to exit the tool.

Drawing a Circle using the Concentric Tool

The **Concentric** tool is used for drawing a circle that is concentric to an existing arc or a circular entity/edge. The method for drawing a circle by using this tool is discussed below:

1. Invoke the **Circle** flyout in the **Sketching** group and then click on the **Concentric** tool. The **Concentric** tool gets activated.

2. Move the cursor toward an existing arc or a circle entity of the sketch (see Figure 2.56), and then click on it when it gets highlighted in the drawing area. You can also select a circular or a semi-circular edge of the existing feature to draw a concentric circle.

3. Move the cursor to a distance in the drawing area. The preview of a circle that is concentric to the selected entity (arc or circle) appears in the drawing area.

4. Click to specify a point in the drawing area that defines the radius of the circle. A circle that is concentric to the selected entity is drawn in the drawing area. Also, the preview of another concentric circle appears attached to the cursor. You can create multiple circles that are concentric to the selected entity (arc or circle), one after the other, by specifying points in the drawing area.

5. Press the middle mouse button twice to exit the **Concentric** tool. Figure 2.57 shows a circle created concentric to an arc of the sketch.

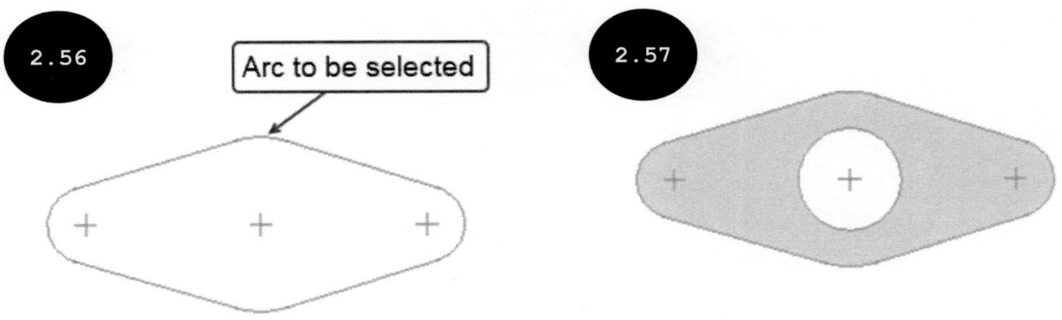

Note: In Figures 2.56 and 2.57, the display of dimensions and constraints is turned off in the drawing area for clarity of images. To turn on or off the display of dimensions and constraints, click on the **Sketcher Display Filters** tool in the **In-graphics** toolbar. A flyout appears, see Figure 2.58. In this flyout, click on the **Dimensions Display** and **Constraints Display** tools, respectively.

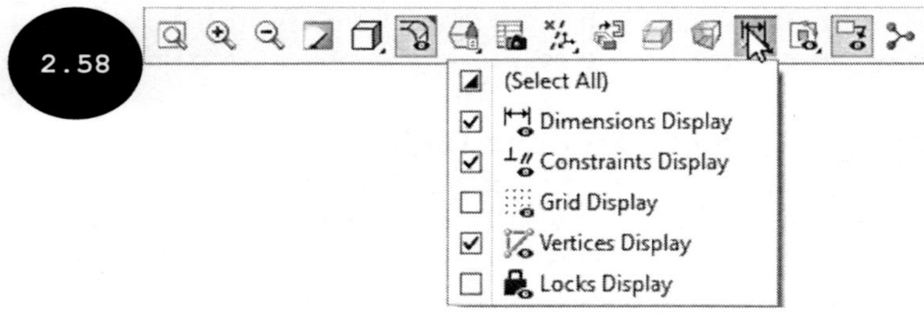

Drawing an Arc

In Creo Parametric, you can draw an arc by different methods using the tools available in the **Arc** flyout of the **Sketching** group, see Figure 2.59. To invoke the **Arc** flyout, click on the arrow next to the active arc tool in the **Sketching** group, see Figure 2.59. The methods for drawing arcs using these tools are discussed next.

Drawing an Arc using the 3-Point / Tangent End Tool

The **3-Point / Tangent End** tool is used for drawing an arc by defining 3 points on the arc length, see Figure 2.60. The first two points define the start and endpoints of the arc, and the third point defines the arc length. The method for drawing an arc by using this tool is discussed below:

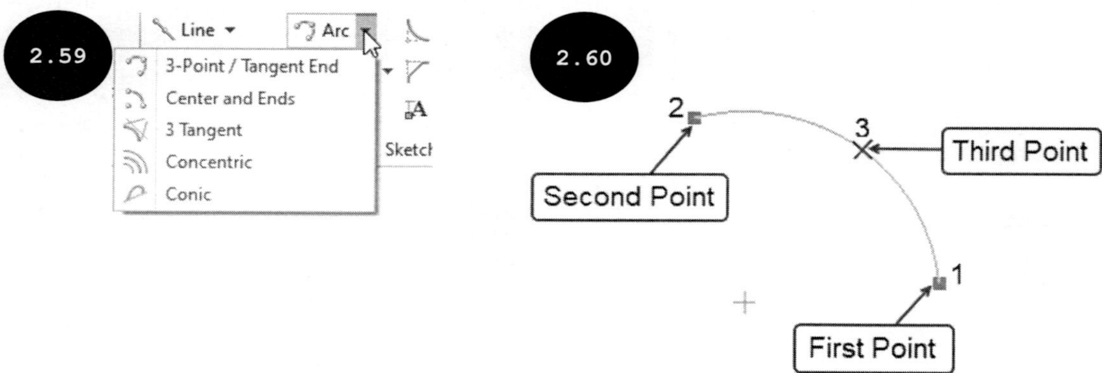

1. Invoke the **Arc** flyout by clicking on the arrow next to the active arc tool in the **Sketching** group (refer to Figure 2.59), and then click on the **3-Point / Tangent End** tool.

2. Click to specify the start point (first point) of the arc in the drawing area.

3. Move the cursor away from the specified start point and then click to specify the endpoint (second point) of the arc in the drawing area.

4. Move the cursor away from the specified endpoint. A preview of the arc appears in the drawing area. Next, click to specify a point (third point) on the arc length. An arc is drawn and the **3-Point / Tangent End** tool is still active.

5. Press the middle mouse button to exit the tool. Figure 2.61 shows an arc created by defining 3 points in the drawing area.

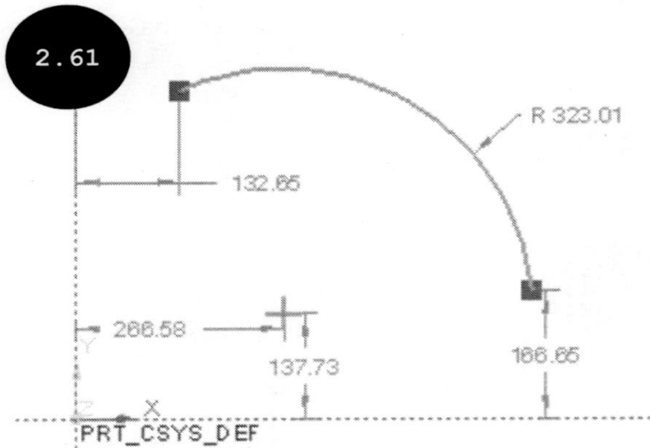

Drawing an Arc using the Center and Ends Tool

The **Center and Ends** tool is used for drawing an arc by defining the center point, start point, and endpoint, see Figure 2.62. The method for drawing an arc by using this tool is discussed below:

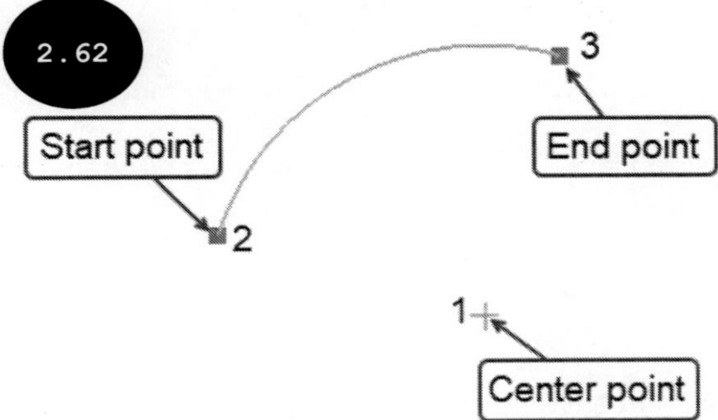

1. Invoke the **Arc** flyout in the **Sketching** group of the **Sketch** tab and then click on the **Center and Ends** tool, see Figure 2.63.

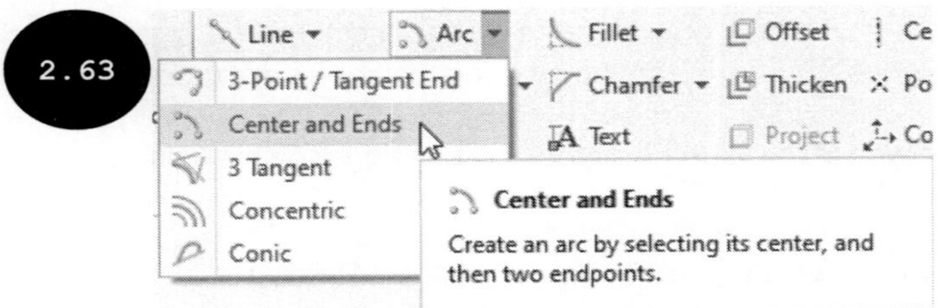

2. Click to specify the center point of the arc in the drawing area.
3. Move the cursor away from the specified center point. A construction circle attached to the cursor appears in the drawing area.
4. Click in the drawing area to define the start point of the arc.
5. Move the cursor clockwise or anti-clockwise. A preview of the arc appears in the drawing area.

6. Click to specify the endpoint of the arc in the drawing area. An arc is drawn. Next, press the middle mouse button to exit the tool.

Drawing an Arc using the 3 Tangent Tool

The **3 Tangent** tool is used for drawing an arc that is tangent to three entities, see Figure 2.64. The method for drawing an arc by using this tool is discussed below:

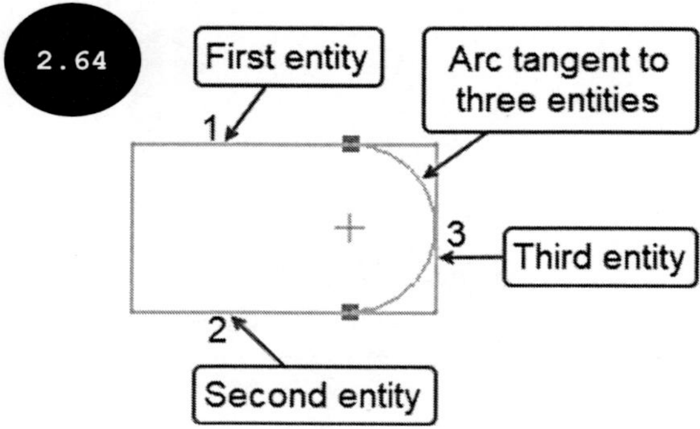

1. Invoke the **Arc** flyout in the **Sketching** group and then click on the **3 Tangent** tool.

2. Click to specify the first tangent entity in the drawing area and then move the cursor away from the specified entity. A rubber band line with one end attached to the cursor appears.

3. Click to specify the second tangent entity in the drawing area. A preview of the arc appears such that it is tangent to the specified entities.

4. Click to specify the third tangent entity in the drawing area. An arc is drawn such that it is tangent to the three specified entities. Next, press the middle mouse button to exit the tool.

Drawing an Arc using the Concentric Tool

The **Concentric** tool is used for drawing an arc that is concentric to an existing arc or a circular entity/edge. The method for drawing an arc by using this tool is discussed below:

1. Invoke the **Arc** flyout in the **Sketching** group and then click on the **Concentric** tool. The **Concentric** tool gets activated.

2. Move the cursor toward an existing arc or a circle entity of the sketch (see Figure 2.65), and then click on it when it gets highlighted in the drawing area. You can also select a circular or a semi-circular edge of the existing feature.

3. Move the cursor to a distance in the drawing area. The preview of a construction circle that is concentric to the selected entity (arc or circle) appears in the drawing area.

4. Click to specify the start point of the arc in the drawing area.

5. Move the cursor clockwise or anti-clockwise. A preview of the arc appears in the drawing area, which is concentric to the selected entity.

6. Click to specify the endpoint of the arc in the drawing area. The concentric arc is drawn. Also, a preview of another concentric circle appears attached to the cursor. You can create multiple arcs that are concentric to the selected entity one after the other by specifying the start and endpoints in the drawing area.

7. Press the middle mouse button twice to exit the **Concentric** tool. Figure 2.66 shows an arc created concentric to the arc of the sketch.

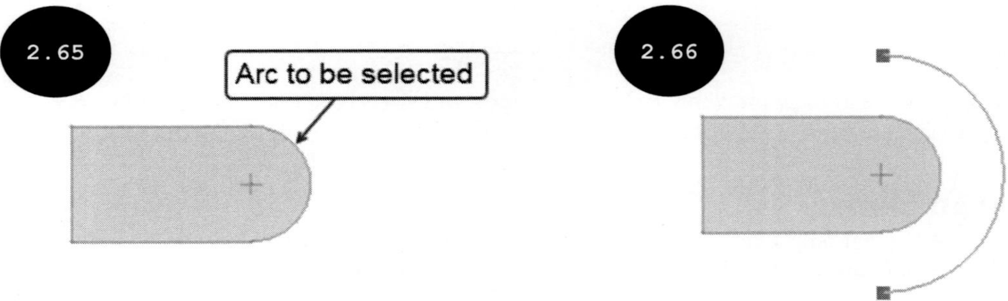

Drawing an Arc using the Conic Tool

The **Conic** tool is used for drawing a conic arc by specifying two endpoints and an apex point, see Figure 2.67. The method for drawing a conic arc by using this tool is discussed below:

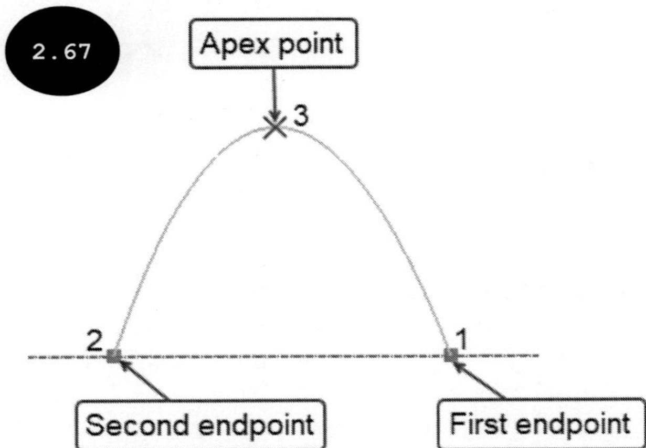

1. Invoke the **Arc** flyout in the **Sketching** group and then click on the **Conic** tool, see Figure 2.68. The **Conic** tool gets activated.

2. Click to specify the first endpoint in the drawing area.

3. Move the cursor away from the first specified endpoint in the drawing area and then click to specify the second endpoint in the drawing area at the desired location.

4. Move the cursor away from the second specified endpoint. A preview of the conic arc appears with its apex attached to the cursor, see Figure 2.69. Also, a construction line appears passing through the specified endpoints in the drawing area.

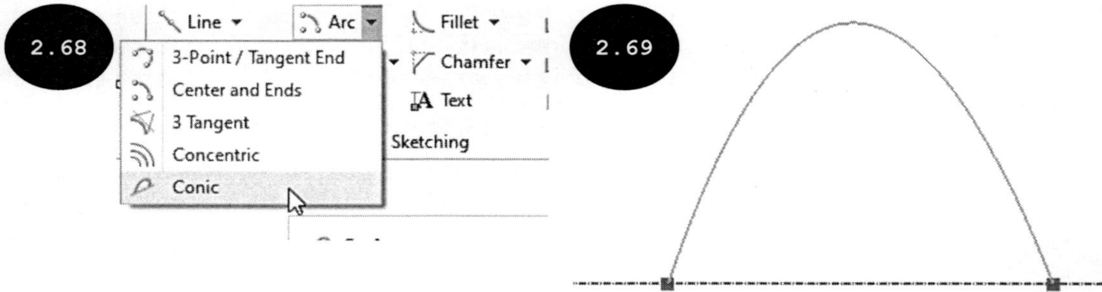

5. Click to specify the apex point when the desired shape and size of the conic arc is achieved in the drawing area. A conic arc is drawn. Next, press the middle mouse button to exit the tool.

Drawing an Ellipse

An ellipse is drawn by defining its major axis and minor axis, see Figure 2.70. You can draw an ellipse by using the **Axis Ends Ellipse** and **Center and Axis Ellipse** tools in the **Ellipse** flyout, see Figure 2.71. To invoke the **Ellipse** flyout, click on the arrow next to the active ellipse tool in the **Sketching** group of the **Sketch** tab in the **Ribbon**. The methods for drawing an ellipse by using these tools are discussed next.

Drawing an Ellipse using the Axis Ends Ellipse Tool

The **Axis Ends Ellipse** tool is used for drawing an ellipse by defining the endpoints of the major axis and minor axis. The method for drawing an ellipse by using this tool is discussed below:

1. Invoke the **Ellipse** flyout by clicking on the arrow next to the active ellipse tool in the **Sketching** group (refer to Figure 2.71), and then click on the **Axis Ends Ellipse** tool.

2. Click to specify the first endpoint of the major axis of the ellipse in the drawing area, see Figure 2.72.

3. Move the cursor away from the first specified endpoint in the drawing area. A construction line appears with one end attached to the cursor.

4. Click to specify the second endpoint of the major axis in the drawing area, see Figure 2.72. Next, move the cursor to a distance. A preview of the ellipse appears, see Figure 2.72.

5. Click to specify a point in the drawing area to define the minor axis of the ellipse. An ellipse is drawn. Next, press the middle mouse button to exit the tool.

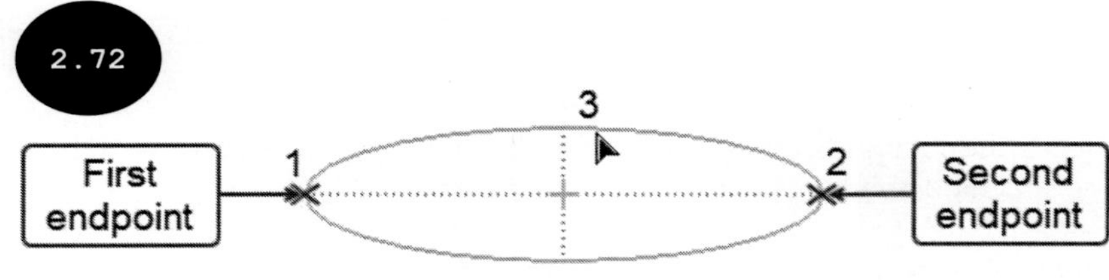

Drawing an Ellipse using the Center and Axis Ellipse Tool

The **Center and Axis Ellipse** tool is used for drawing an ellipse by defining the center point and endpoints of the major axis and minor axis. The method for drawing an ellipse by using this tool is discussed below:

1. Invoke the **Ellipse** flyout in the **Sketching** group and then click on the **Center and Axis Ellipse** tool.

2. Click to specify the center point of the ellipse in the drawing area.

3. Move the cursor away from the specified center point in the drawing area, see Figure 2.73. A preview of the ellipse axis appears.

4. Click to specify the endpoint of the major axis of the ellipse. A preview of the ellipse appears in the drawing area, see Figure 2.73.

5. Click to specify a point in the drawing area to define the minor axis of the ellipse. An ellipse is drawn. Next, press the middle mouse button to exit the tool.

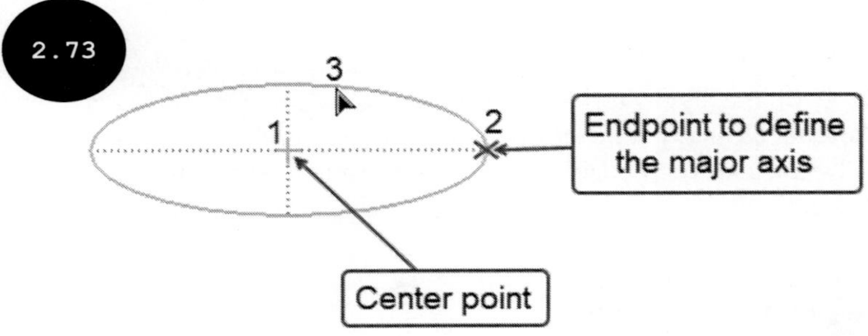

Drawing a Spline

A spline is defined as a curve having a high degree of smoothness and is used for creating free-form features. You can draw a spline by specifying two or more control points in the drawing area. The method for drawing a spline is discussed below:

1. Click on the **Spline** tool in the **Sketching** group of the **Sketch** tab in the **Ribbon**, see Figure 2.74. The **Spline** tool gets activated.

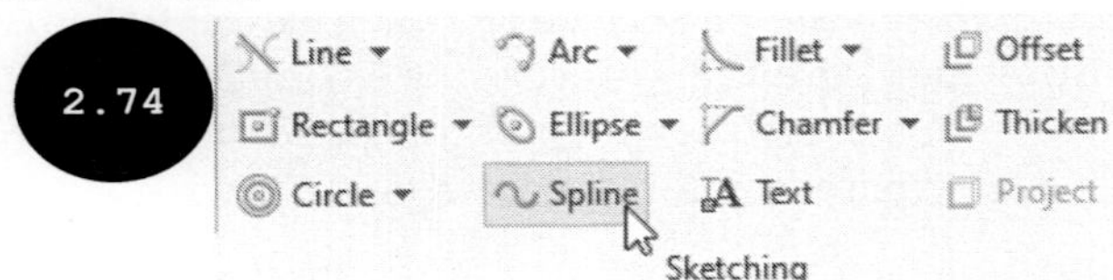

2. Click to specify the first point of the spline in the drawing area. A rubber band curve appears with one end attached to the cursor.

3. Click to specify the second point of the spline in the drawing area. A preview of the spline passing through the specified points appears in the drawing area, see Figure 2.75.

4. Click to specify the third point of the spline in the drawing area. A preview of the spline passing through the specified points appears.

5. Similarly, you can specify multiple points of the spline one by one. After specifying all the points of the spline, press the middle mouse button twice to terminate the creation of the spline and exit the tool. Figure 2.76 shows a spline created by specifying five points. Note that the first and last points of the spline are known as endpoints and the points in between the endpoints through which the spline passes are known as interpolation points, see Figure 2.76.

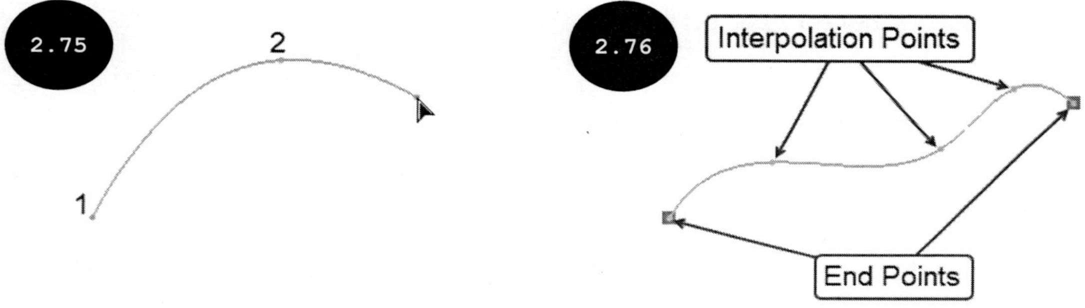

Note: In Figure 2.76, the display of dimensions and constraints is turned off in the drawing area for clarity of images. To turn on or off the display of dimensions and constraints, click on the **Sketcher Display Filters** tool in the **In-graphics** toolbar. A flyout appears, see Figure 2.77. In this flyout, click on the **Dimensions Display** and **Constraints Display** tools, respectively.

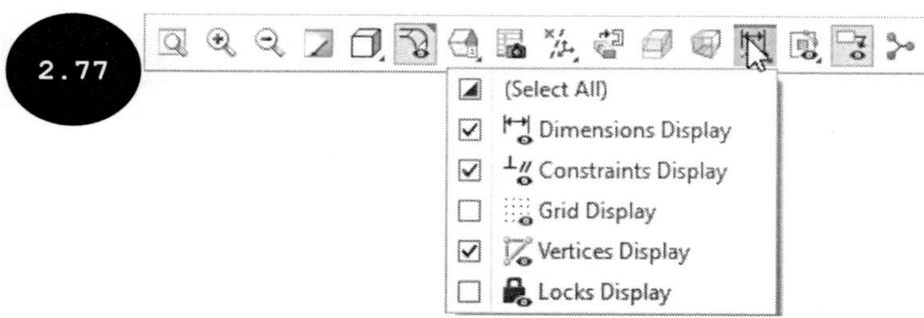

Drawing a Construction Centerline

Construction centerlines are defined as reference or construction lines, which are drawn to aid sketching. In Creo Parametric, you can draw a construction centerline using the **Centerline** and **Centerline Tangent** tools of the **Centerline** flyout, see Figure 2.78. To invoke the **Centerline** flyout, click on the arrow next to an active centerline tool in the **Sketching** group of the **Sketch** tab. The methods for drawing a construction centerline by using these tools are discussed next.

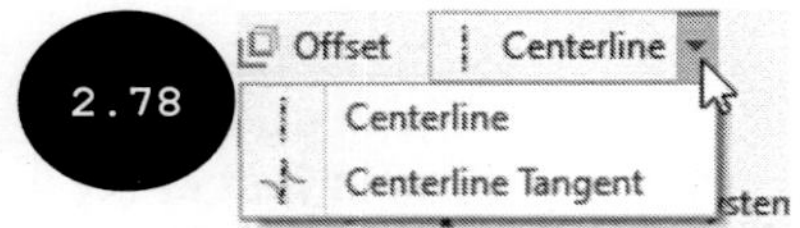

Drawing a Construction Centerline using the Centerline Tool

The **Centerline** tool is used for drawing a construction centerline by specifying two points in the drawing area. The method for drawing a construction centerline by using this tool is discussed below:

1. Click on the **Centerline** tool in the **Sketching** group of the **Sketch** tab in the **Ribbon**. The **Centerline** tool gets activated.

2. Click to specify the first point in the drawing area. A preview of a centerline passing through the specified point appears in the drawing area.

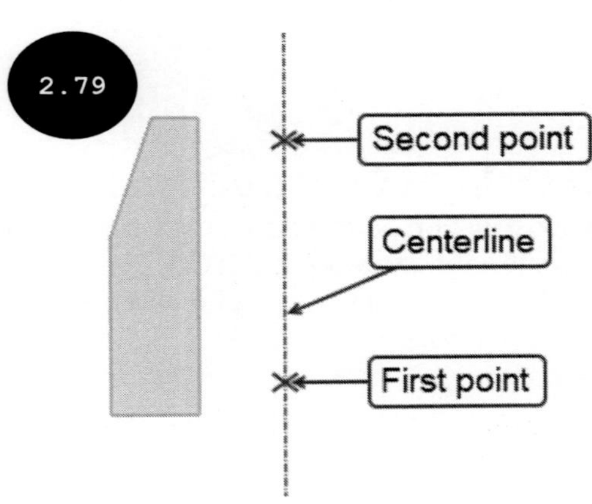

3. Click to specify the second point in the drawing area. A construction centerline of infinite length passing through the specified points is drawn in the drawing area, see Figure 2.79.

4. Similarly, you can draw multiple construction centerlines by specifying two points in the drawing area. Once the construction centerline has been drawn, press the middle mouse button to exit the **Centerline** tool.

Drawing a Construction Centerline using the Centerline Tangent Tool

The **Centerline Tangent** tool is used for drawing a construction centerline that is tangent to two entities (arc or circle). The method for drawing a construction centerline by using this tool is discussed below:

1. Invoke the **Centerline** flyout in the **Sketching** group and then click on the **Centerline Tangent** tool, see Figure 2.80. The **Centerline Tangent** tool gets activated.

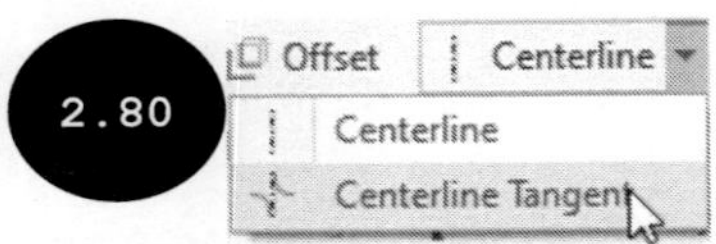

2. Click to specify a point on the first tangent entity in the drawing area and then move the cursor away from the specified point. A rubber band line with one end attached to the cursor appears.

3. Click to specify a point on the second tangent entity in the drawing area. A construction centerline passing through two specified points and tangent to the entities is drawn, see Figure 2.81. Next, press the middle mouse button to exit the **Centerline Tangent** tool.

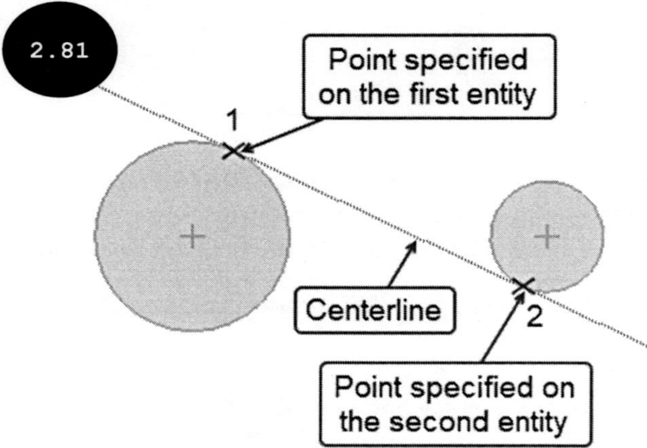

Creating a Construction Point

A construction point acts as a reference entity within the Sketching environment for creating other drawing entities of a sketch. In Creo Parametric, you can create a construction point by using the **Point** tool in the **Sketching** group of the **Sketch** tab. The method for creating a construction point by using this tool is discussed below:

1. Click on the **Point** tool in the **Sketching** group, see Figure 2.82. The **Point** tool gets activated.

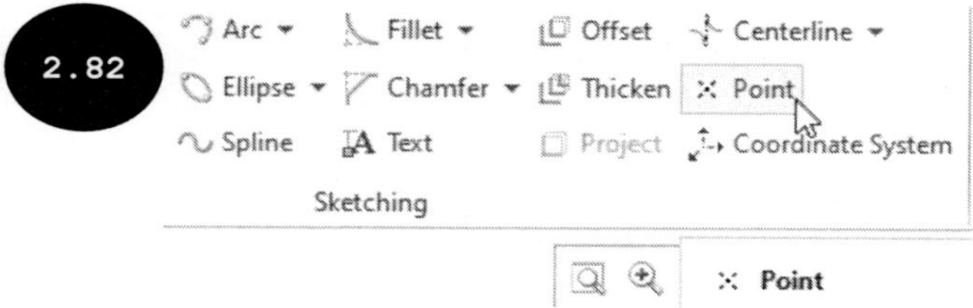

2. Click to specify the location of the point in the drawing area. A construction point is created, and the **Point** tool is still active. You can create multiple construction points one by one by clicking the left mouse button in the drawing area.

3. After creating the construction points, press the middle mouse button to exit the **Point** tool.

Creating a Construction Coordinate System

A construction coordinate system acts as a reference object within the Sketching environment for dimensioning sketch entities. You can create a construction coordinate system by using the **Coordinate System** tool in the **Sketching** group of the **Sketch** tab. The method for creating a construction coordinate system by using this tool is discussed below:

1. Click on the **Coordinate System** tool in the **Sketching** group of the **Sketch** tab, see Figure 2.83. The **Coordinate System** tool gets activated, and a coordinate system gets attached to the cursor.

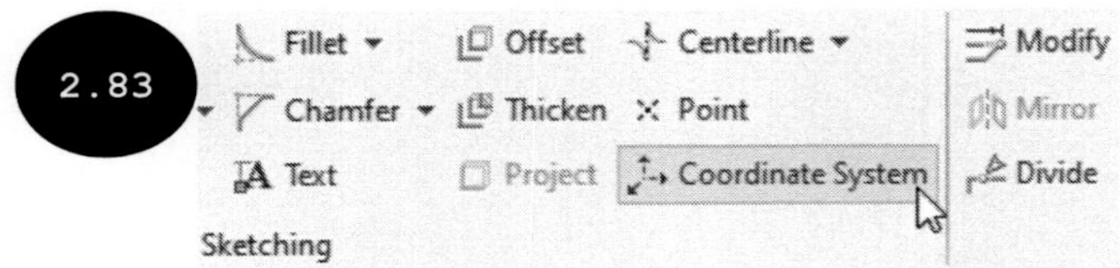

2. Click to specify a placement point for the coordinate system in the drawing area. A construction coordinate system is created, and the **Coordinate System** tool is still active. You can create multiple construction coordinate systems one by one by specifying the placement points in the drawing area.

3. Once the construction coordinate system has been created, press the middle mouse button to exit the tool.

Creating Datum Geometries

In addition to creating construction entities such as centerline, point, and coordinate system, you can create datum geometries (centerline, point, and coordinate system) with the only difference that the datum geometries can also be used outside the Sketching environment as reference geometries. The tools for creating datum geometries are available in the **Datum** group of the **Sketch** tab, see Figure 2.84. The methods for creating datum geometries are the same as discussed earlier while creating construction entities.

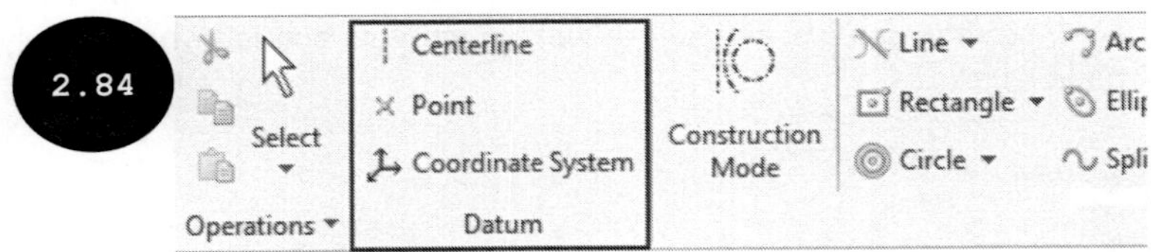

Working with Construction Mode

In Creo Parametric, you can switch modes for creating new entities from solid sketch entities to construction entities using the **Construction Mode** tool, see Figure 2.85.

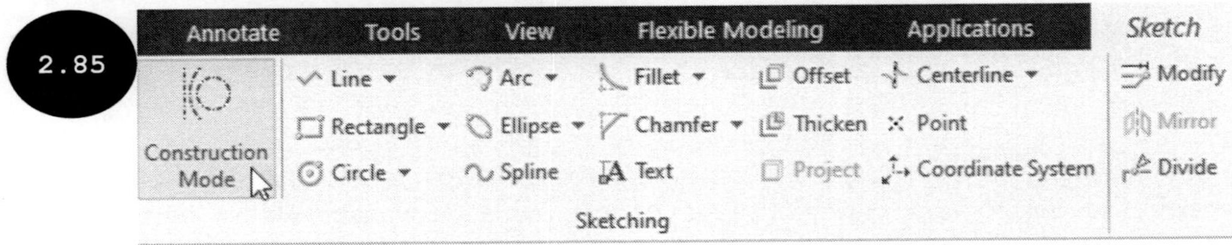

By default, the **Construction Mode** tool is not activated. As a result, you can create solid sketch entities by using the sketching tools available in the **Sketching** group of the **Sketch** tab. On activating the **Construction Mode** tool by clicking on it, the sketch entities created in the drawing area by using the sketching tool will act as construction entities and can only be used as reference entities. Figure 2.86 shows a circle created by using the **Center and Point** tool after activating the **Construction Mode** tool in the **Sketch** tab of the **Ribbon**.

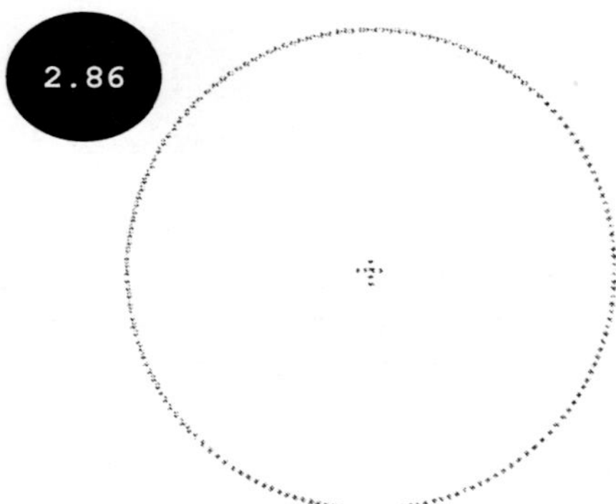

Applying Constraints

After creating a sketch using the sketching tools, you need to apply the required constraints and dimensions so that the sketch becomes fully defined and the entities of the sketch can no longer change shape, size, and position on being dragged. In Creo Parametric, some of the constraints such as horizontal, vertical, and coincident are applied automatically while drawing sketch entities. For example, after specifying the start point of a line entity, if you move the cursor horizontally toward left or right, a symbol of horizontal constraint appears near the cursor, see Figure 2.87. This indicates that if you specify the endpoint of the line, a horizontal constraint will be applied to the line entity. Likewise, on moving the cursor vertically upward or downward after specifying the start point of a line entity, a symbol of vertical constraint appears, see Figure 2.87 which gets applied immediately on specifying the endpoint of the line.

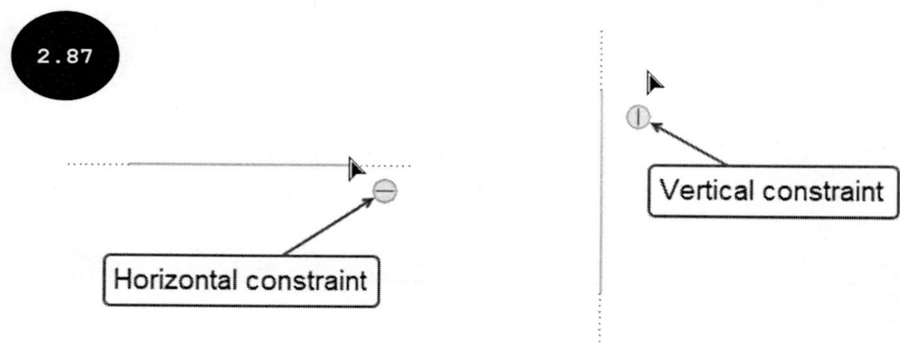

In addition to the automatically applied constraints, you can also apply constraints manually. In Creo Parametric, the tools for applying various types of constraints are available in the **Constrain** group of the **Sketch** tab in the **Ribbon**, see Figure 2.88. Various types of constraints are discussed next.

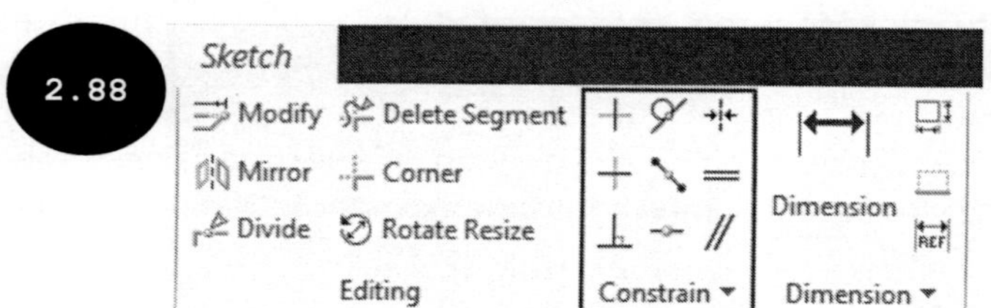

Applying Horizontal Constraint

Horizontal constraint is used for changing the orientation of an entity to horizontal and then forcing it to remain so. This constraint can be applied to a line, centerline, or between two points/vertices. To apply a horizontal constraint, click on the **Horizontal** tool in the **Constrain** group of the **Sketch** tab, and then click on an entity or two points one by one. The selected entity or points become horizontal. After applying the constraint, press the ESC key to exit the tool.

Applying Vertical Constraint

Vertical constraint is used for changing the orientation of an entity to vertical and then forcing it to remain so. This constraint can be applied to a line, centerline, or between two points/vertices. To apply this constraint, click on the **Vertical** tool in the **Constrain** group and then click on an entity or two points one by one. The selected entity or points become vertical. After applying the constraint, press the ESC key to exit the tool.

Applying Perpendicular Constraint

Perpendicular constraint is used for making two line entities perpendicular to each other and then forcing them to remain perpendicular. To apply this constraint, click on the **Perpendicular** tool in the **Constrain** group and then click on two line entities one by one. The selected line entities become perpendicular to each other. After applying the constraint, press the ESC key to exit the tool.

Applying Tangent Constraint

Tangent constraint is used for making two entities such as a circle and a line, tangent to each other. You can also make two circles, two arcs, two ellipses, and a combination of these entities tangent to each other. To apply this constraint, click on the **Tangent** tool of the **Constrain** group and then click on two entities one by one. The selected entities become tangent to each other. After applying the constraint, press the ESC key to exit the tool.

Applying Coincident Constraint

Coincident constraint is used for making two points/vertices coincide and then forcing them to remain so. You can also align two entities (lines, circles, arcs, or ellipses) with each other or a point with a line/arc/circle/ellipse by applying the coincident constraint. To apply this constraint, click on the **Coincident** tool and then click on two points or entities one by one. The selected points or entities coincide with each other. After applying the constraint, press the ESC key to exit the tool.

Applying Mid-point Constraint

Mid-point constraint is used for making a point coincident at the middle of a line or an arc entity. To apply this constraint, click on the **Mid-point** tool. Next, click on a point and then click on a line or an arc. The selected point becomes coincident at the middle of the selected line/arc. After applying the constraint, press the ESC key to exit the tool.

Applying Symmetric Constraint

Symmetric constraint is used for making two points/vertices symmetric about a centerline. To apply this constraint, click on the **Symmetric** tool and then click on two points/vertices one by one. Next, click on a centerline. The selected points become symmetric about the centerline. After applying the constraint, press the ESC key to exit the tool.

Applying Equal Constraint

Equal constraint is used for making two or more than two arcs/circles/lines/ellipses equal to each other. Note that on applying the equal constraint, the length of line entities and radii of the arc/circle/ellipse entities become equal to each other. You can also make the curvature of a spline and a line/arc equal to each other by using the equal constraint. To apply this constraint, click on the **Equal** tool in the **Constrain** group and then select two or more entities one by one. The selected entities become equal to each other. After applying the constraint, press the ESC key to exit the tool.

Applying Parallel Constraint

Parallel constraint is used for making two or more line entities parallel to each other and then forcing them to remain parallel. To apply the parallel constraint, click on the **Parallel** tool in the **Constrain** group, and then click on two or more line entities one by one. The selected entities become parallel to each other. After applying the constraint, press the ESC key to exit the tool.

Tip: You can turn on or off the display of constraints in the drawing area. To do so, click on the **Sketcher Display Filters** tool in the **In-graphics** toolbar. A flyout appears. In this flyout, click on the **Constraints Display** tool to change the display option.

Working with Weak Dimensions

In Creo Parametric, when you create a sketch in the Sketching environment, the weak dimensions are applied automatically to the entities of the sketch. These weak dimensions are for your reference only and do not restrict the entities to change their shape, size, or position. They appear in light blue color in the Sketching environment. Figure 2.89 shows a sketch with weak dimensions. It is recommended to convert the weak dimensions into strong dimensions before you exit the Sketching environment. The methods for converting a weak dimension into a strong dimension are discussed below:

2.89

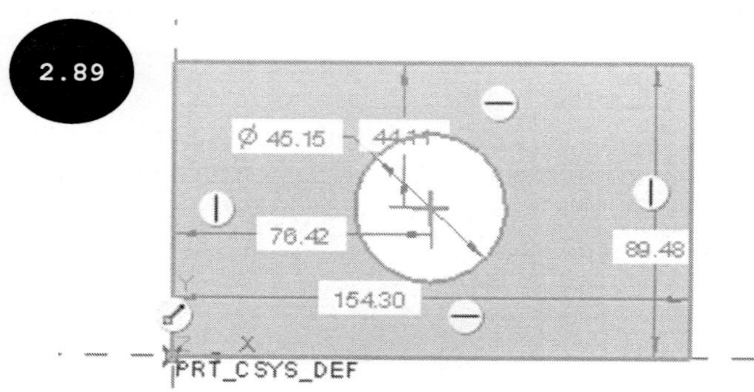

- Edit a weak dimension to convert it into a strong dimension by double-clicking on it or by using the **Modify** tool of the **Editing** group in the **Sketch** tab. You will learn more about the **Modify** tool later in this chapter.

- Apply a new strong dimension to the sketch entity by using the **Dimension** tool of the **Dimension** group. Note that on applying a strong dimension to an entity, the weak dimension of the entity gets removed automatically. You will learn about applying dimensions later in this chapter.

- Click on a weak dimension in the drawing area. A Mini toolbar appears, see Figure 2.90. In this Mini toolbar, click on the **Strong** tool. The dimension value appears in an edit field. You can enter a new dimension value in this edit field. Next, press the middle mouse button. The selected dimension becomes a strong dimension.

2.90

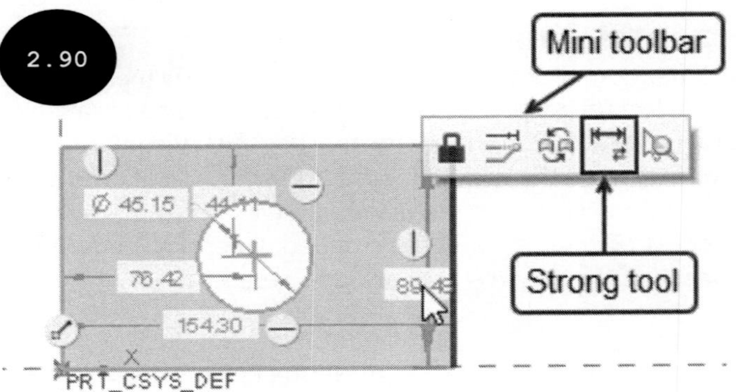

Note: If you do not want weak dimensions to be displayed automatically on the sketch entities, click on **File > Options**. The **Creo Parametric Options** dialog box appears. In this dialog box, click on the **Sketcher** option on the left panel, see Figure 2.91. The options to control the sketcher settings appear on the right panel of the dialog box. Next, clear the **Show weak dimensions** check box in the **Object display settings** area of the dialog box, see Figure 2.91. Next, click on the **OK** button in the dialog box. The **Creo Parametric Options** window appears. Click on the **No** button in this dialog box to make the change only in the current session. If you want this change to be applied to the other sessions of Creo Parametric as well, then click on the **Yes** button to save the settings to the configuration file.

2.91

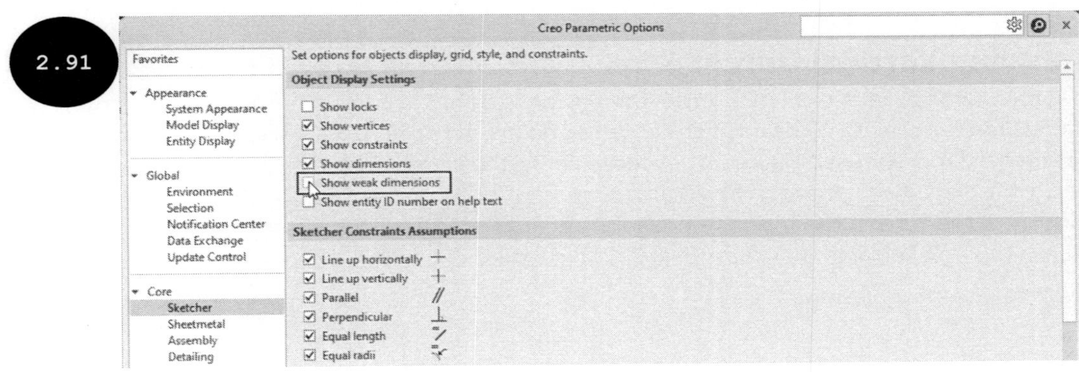

Applying Dimensions

Once a sketch has been drawn and the required constraints have been applied, you need to apply dimensions by using the **Dimension** tool. The dimensions applied by using this tool are known as strong dimensions. As Creo Parametric is a parametric software, the parameters of sketch entities such as length and angle are controlled or driven by strong dimensions. On modifying the value of a strong dimension, the respective sketch entity also gets modified accordingly.

The **Dimension** tool is used for applying dimensions depending upon the type of sketch entity or entities selected. For example, on selecting an arc, the radius dimension is applied and on selecting a line, the linear dimension is applied. The methods for applying various types of dimensions by using the **Dimension** tool are discussed next.

Applying Horizontal Dimensions

To apply a horizontal dimension, click on the **Dimension** tool in the **Dimension** group of the **Sketch** tab in the **Ribbon** and then select the required sketch entity or entities. You can select a horizontal sketch entity, two points, or two vertical sketch entities for applying the horizontal dimension, see Figure 2.92. After selecting the entities, press the middle mouse button to specify the placement point for the horizontal dimension in the drawing area. An edit field appears with a display of the current dimension value of the selected entity or entities. Enter the required dimension value in this edit field and then press ENTER. The horizontal dimension is applied, see Figure 2.92.

Tip: After selecting two points, you need to move the cursor vertically upward or downward to specify the placement point of the horizontal dimension by pressing the middle mouse button.

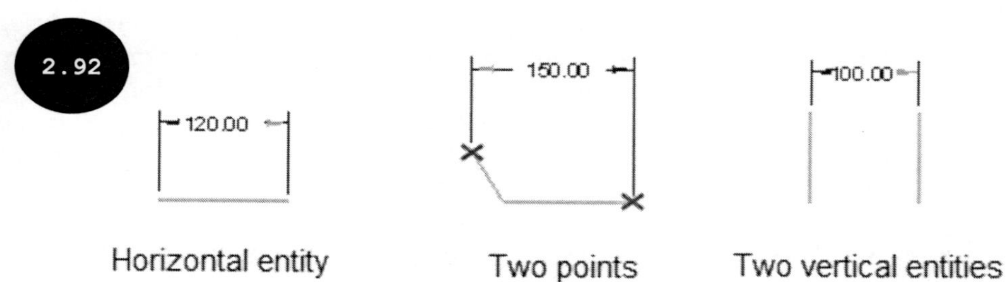

Applying Vertical Dimensions

To apply a vertical dimension, click on the **Dimension** tool and then select the required sketch entity or entities. You can select a vertical sketch entity, two points, or two horizontal sketch entities for applying the vertical dimension, see Figure 2.93. After selecting the entities, press the middle mouse button to specify the placement point for the vertical dimension in the drawing area. An edit field appears with a display of the current dimension value of the selected entity/entities. Enter the required dimension value in this edit field and then press ENTER. The vertical dimension is applied, see Figure 2.93.

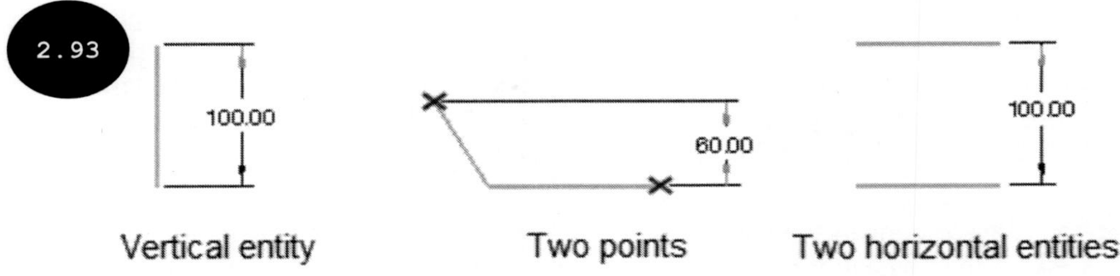

Tip: After selecting two points, you need to move the cursor horizontally toward right or left to specify the placement point of the vertical dimension by pressing the middle mouse button.

Applying Aligned Dimensions

To apply an aligned dimension, click on the **Dimension** tool and then select the required sketch entity or entities. You can select an aligned sketch entity or two points for applying the aligned dimension, see Figure 2.94. The aligned dimension is generally used for measuring the aligned length of an inclined line. Note that after selecting one or more entities for applying the aligned dimension, you need to specify the placement point parallel to the selected entity/entities by pressing the middle mouse button.

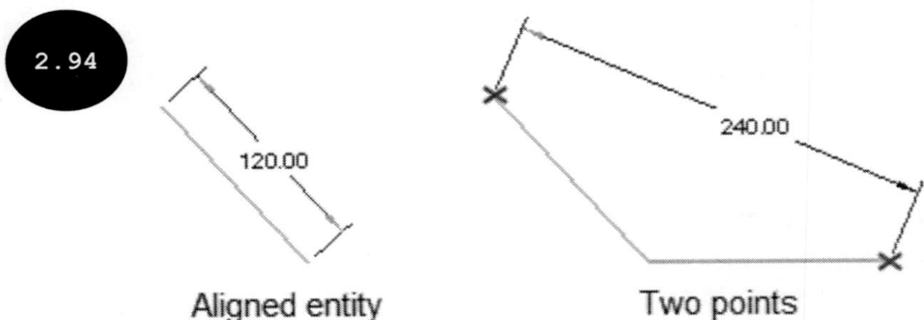

Applying Angular Dimensions

You can apply angular dimensions between two non-parallel line entities or an arc. To apply an angular dimension between two non-parallel line entities, click on the **Dimension** tool and then click on two non-parallel line entities in the drawing area one by one. Next, move the cursor to a location where you want to place the dimension and then press the middle mouse button to specify the placement point. An edit field appears with the current angle value. Enter the required angular value in this edit field and then press ENTER. The angular dimension is applied between the two selected line entities. Note that the angular dimension applied between the selected entities depends upon the location of the placement point specified, see Figure 2.95.

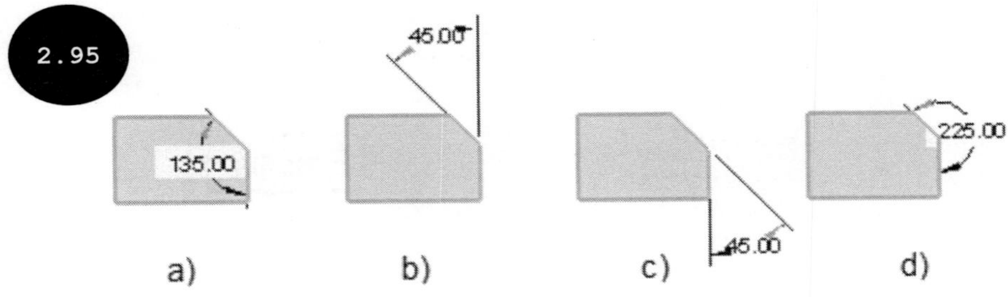

To apply an angular dimension to an arc by specifying three points, activate the **Dimension** tool and then select the start, center, and endpoints of the arc in the drawing area one by one, see Figure 2.96. Next, move the cursor to a location where you want to place the angular dimension, and then press the middle mouse button to specify the placement point. An edit field appears. Enter the required angular value in this edit field and then press ENTER. The angular dimension is applied to the arc, see Figure 2.96.

Tip: You can also convert the angular dimension of an arc to the arc length dimension. To do so, click on the angular dimension of the arc in the drawing area. A Mini toolbar appears, see Figure 2.97. In this Mini toolbar, click on the **Length** tool.

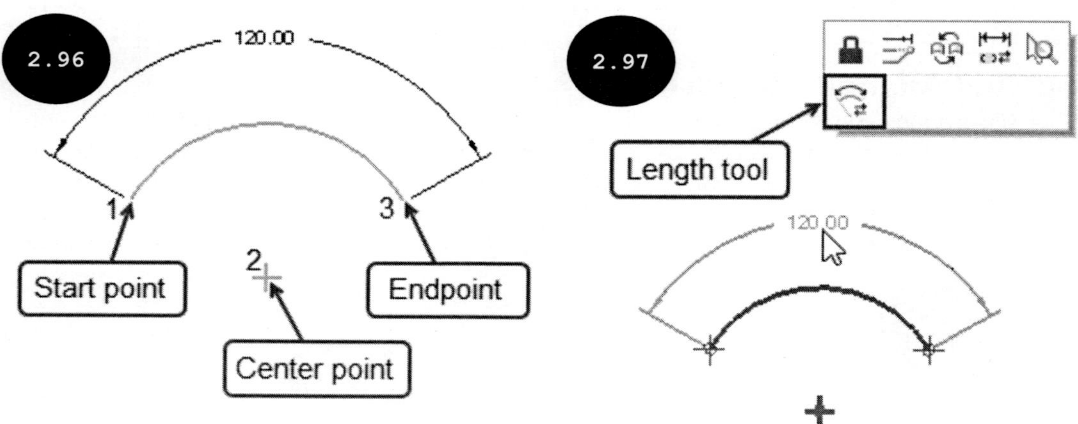

Applying Arc Length Dimensions

Similar to applying angular dimension to an arc, you can apply arc length dimension to an arc. To do so, click on the **Dimension** tool to activate it. Next, click on the start point and the endpoint of the arc one by one and then select a point on the arc, see Figure 2.98. Next, press the middle mouse button at the desired location to specify the placement point for the arc length dimension. An edit field appears with the display of the current arc length value. Enter the required arc length value in this edit field and then press ENTER. The arc length dimension is applied, see Figure 2.98.

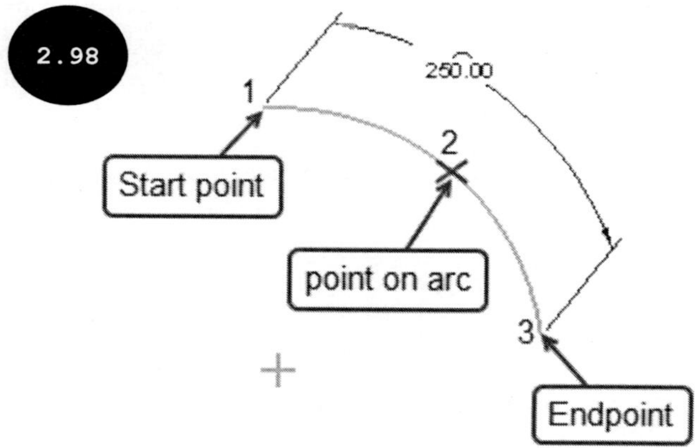

Tip: You can also convert the arc length dimension of an arc to the angular dimension. To do so, click on the arc length dimension of the arc in the drawing area. A Mini toolbar appears. In this Mini toolbar, click on the **Angle** tool.

Applying Radius Dimensions

A radius dimension can be applied to an arc or a circle. To apply a radius dimension, click on the **Dimension** tool and then click on an arc or a circle in the drawing area. Next, press the middle mouse button at the desired location to specify the placement point for the radius dimension. An edit field appears with the display of the current radius value. Enter the required radius value in this edit field and then press ENTER. The radius dimension is applied, see Figure 2.99.

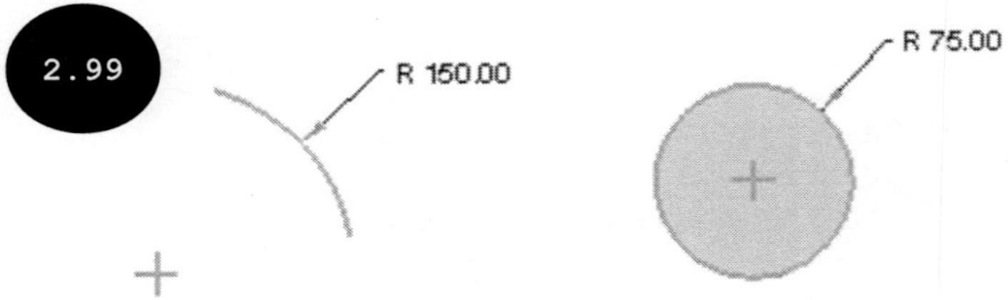

Applying Diameter Dimensions

Similar to applying a radius dimension, you can apply a diameter dimension to an arc or a circle. To do so, click on the **Dimension** tool and then double-click on an arc or a circle in the drawing area. Next, press the middle mouse button at the desired location to specify the placement point for the diameter dimension. An edit field appears with a display of the current diameter value. Enter the required diameter value in this edit field and then press ENTER. The diameter dimension is applied, see Figure 2.100.

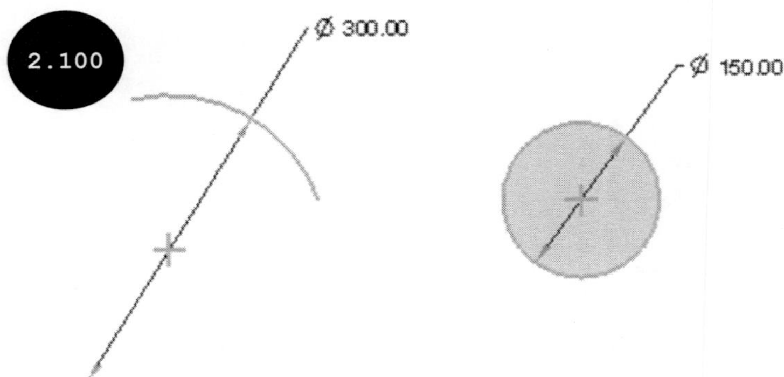

Applying Linear Diameter Dimensions

Linear diameter dimensions can be applied to a sketch of a revolved feature, see Figure 2.101. To apply a linear diameter dimension, click on the **Dimension** tool and then click on a linear sketch entity of the sketch. Next, click on a centerline as the revolving axis of the sketch and then click on the previously selected linear sketch entity again. Next, press the middle mouse button at the desired location to specify the placement point for the linear diameter dimension. An edit field appears. Enter the required linear diameter value in this edit field and then press ENTER. The linear diameter dimension is applied, see Figure 2.101. In this figure, three linear diameter dimensions are applied.

2.101

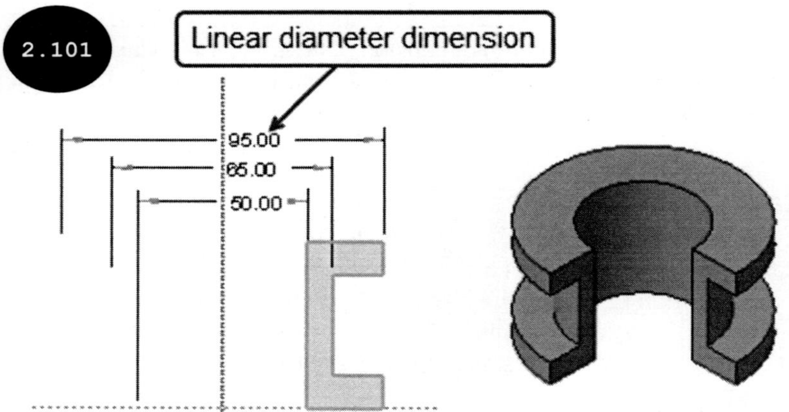

Note: By default, on dragging the sketch entities, the modified dimensions or the user-defined dimensions (strong dimensions) associated with the entities will also get modified, accordingly. To lock the modified dimensions or the user-defined dimensions, click on **File > Options**. The **Creo Parametric Options** dialog box appears. In this dialog box, click on the **Sketcher** option and then select the **Lock user defined dimensions** or **Lock modified dimensions** check box in the **Dimensions** area, see Figure 2.102. Next, click on the **OK** button. The **Creo Parametric Options** window appears. Now, you can save the changes in the configuration file so that the changes will be applied to the other sessions of Creo Parametric as well by clicking on the **Yes** button. If you want the changes to be applied only in the current session, click on the **No** button in the **Creo Parametric Options** window.

2.102

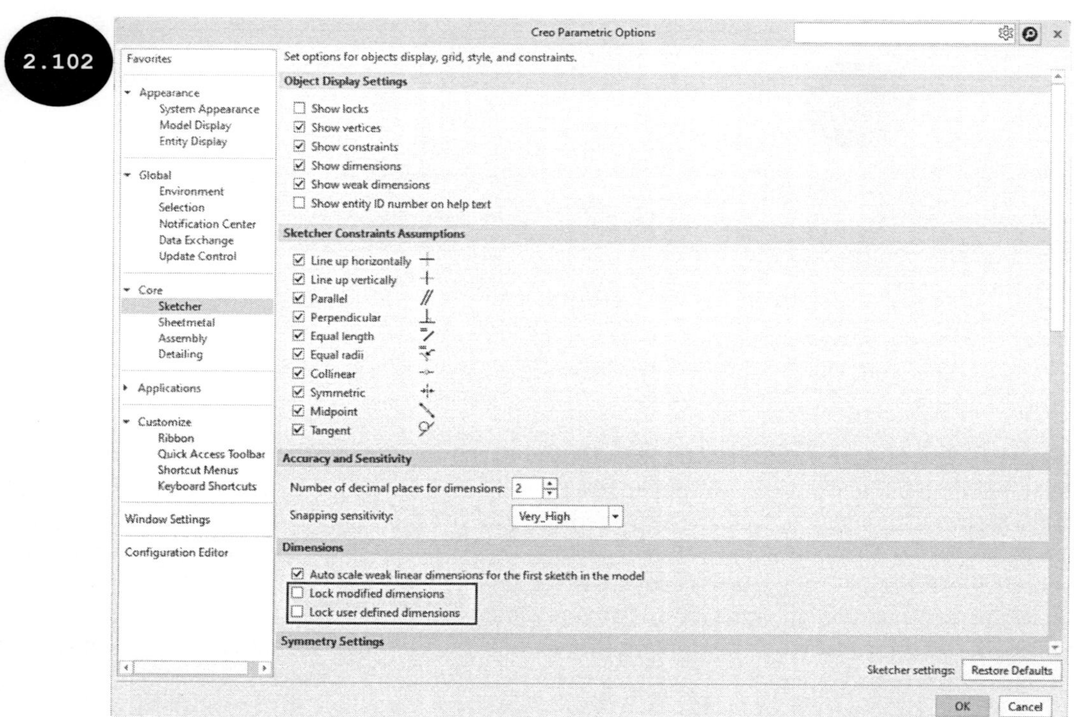

Applying Baseline and Ordinate Dimensions

Ordinate dimensions are measured from a baseline dimension. The baseline dimension is defined as the starting point from where all other dimensions are measured, see Figure 2.103. To apply ordinate dimensions, you first need to apply a baseline dimension to an entity that acts as a base or origin entity, see Figure 2.103. Generally, the ordinate dimensions are used for the components created by using CNC machines to avoid differences in dimension values due to the maximum and minimum tolerance limits.

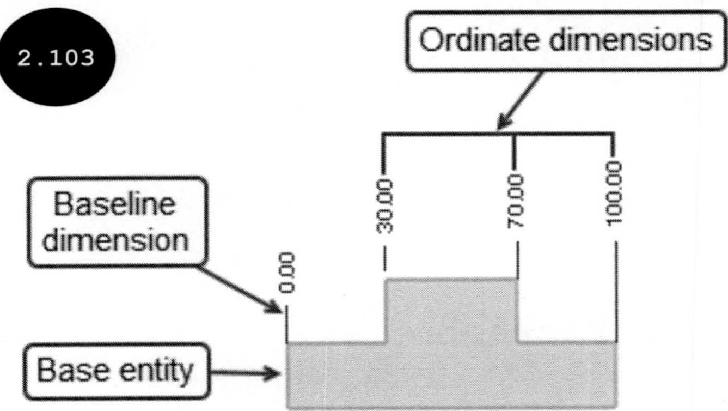

You can apply a horizontal or a vertical baseline dimension by using the **Baseline** tool of the **Dimension** group in the **Sketch** tab, see Figure 2.104. To apply a vertical baseline dimension, click on the **Baseline** tool in the **Dimension** group and then click on a vertical entity as the base entity. Next, press the middle mouse button to specify the placement point of the baseline dimension. The vertical baseline dimension is applied with a 0.00 dimension value, see Figure 2.105. Next, press the ESC key to exit the **Baseline** tool.

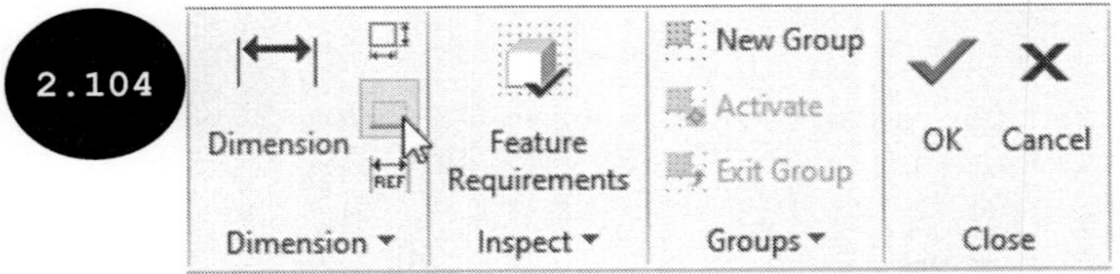

After applying the vertical baseline dimension, you can apply vertical ordinate dimensions by using the **Dimension** tool. To do so, click on the **Dimension** tool and then click on the vertical baseline dimension. Next, click on a vertical entity to be measured from the selected baseline dimension and then press the middle mouse button. The ordinate dimension is applied to the selected entity which is measured from the selected baseline dimension. Similarly, you can apply ordinate dimensions to other vertical entities of the sketch, see Figure 2.105. Next, press the ESC key to exit the tool.

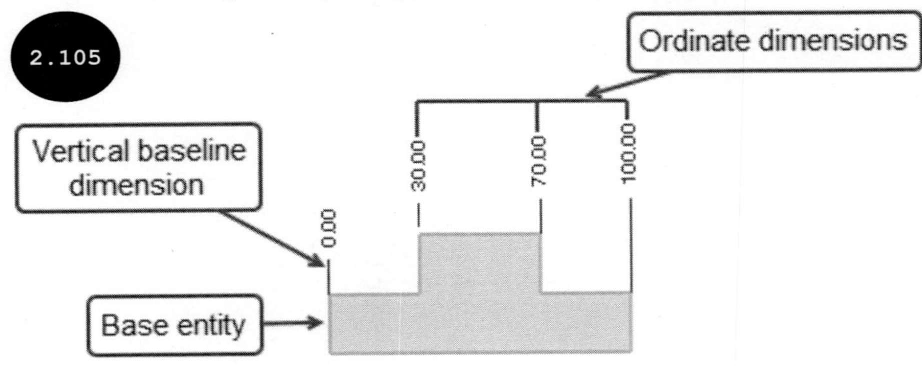

Similar to applying the vertical baseline dimension to a vertical entity, you can apply a horizontal baseline dimension to a horizontal entity by using the **Baseline** tool and then horizontal ordinate dimensions by using the **Dimension** tool, see Figure 2.106.

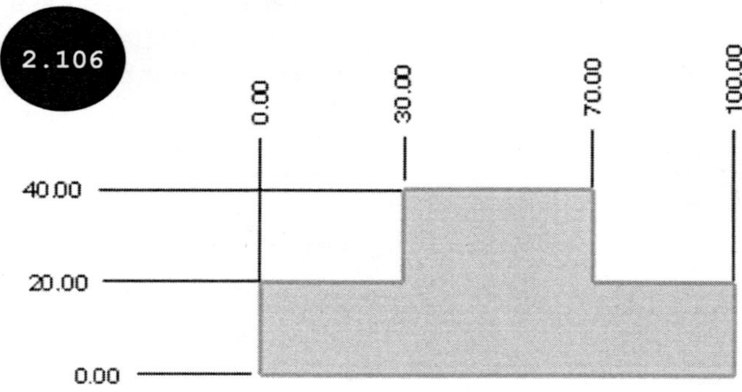

Applying Reference Dimensions

In Creo Parametric, you can also apply reference dimensions to sketch entities. The reference dimensions are for reference only and do not control the shape, size, and position of the entities. To apply a reference dimension, click on the **Reference** tool in the **Dimension** group of the **Sketch** tab, see Figure 2.107. Next, select one or more entities in the drawing area. The reference dimension is applied. Figure 2.108 shows a reference dimension applied to a horizontal entity.

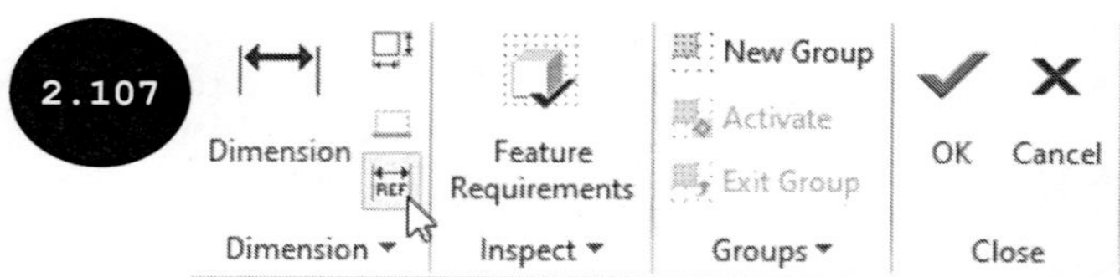

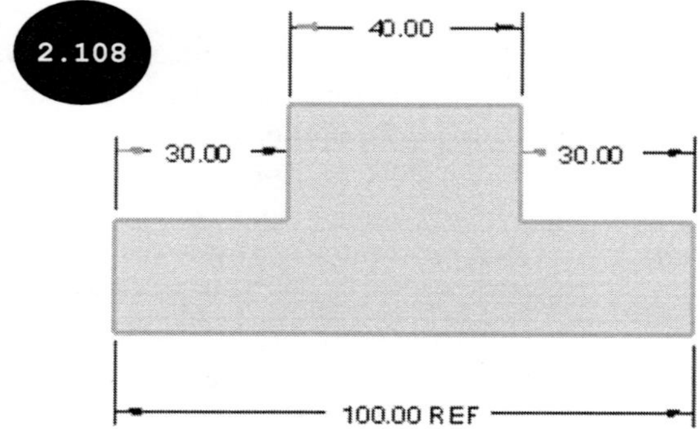

Editing Dimensions

In Creo Parametric, you can edit strong dimensions as well as weak dimensions by using the **Modify** tool of the **Editing** group in the **Sketch** tab (see Figure 2.109), or by double-clicking on the dimensions. Both the methods for editing dimensions are discussed next.

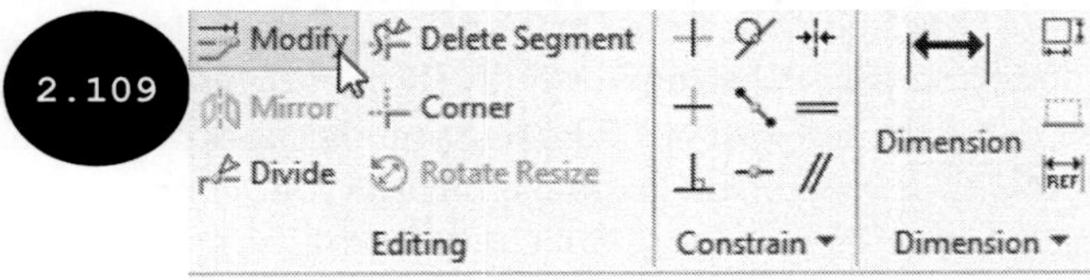

Note: On editing a weak dimension, the edited dimension automatically gets converted into a strong dimension.

Editing Dimensions using the Modify Tool

To edit dimensions by using the **Modify** tool, select the dimensions to be edited. You can select a dimension by clicking on it in the drawing area. To select multiple dimensions, press the CTRL key and then click on the dimensions one by one in the drawing area. You can also select multiple dimensions by defining a window around the dimensions to be edited. Note that the selected dimensions appear in green color in the drawing area. After selecting one or more dimensions, click on the **Modify** tool in the **Editing** group of the **Sketch** tab, see Figure 2.110. The **Modify Dimensions** dialog box appears and all the selected dimensions are listed in it, see Figure 2.111. Note that in this dialog box, the current values of the selected dimensions are visible in the respective edit fields. You can edit these values one by one by entering the desired dimension values in their respective edit fields. Alternatively, you can increase or decrease the dimension values by dragging the thumbwheel that is available on the right of each edit field in the dialog box to the right or left, respectively.

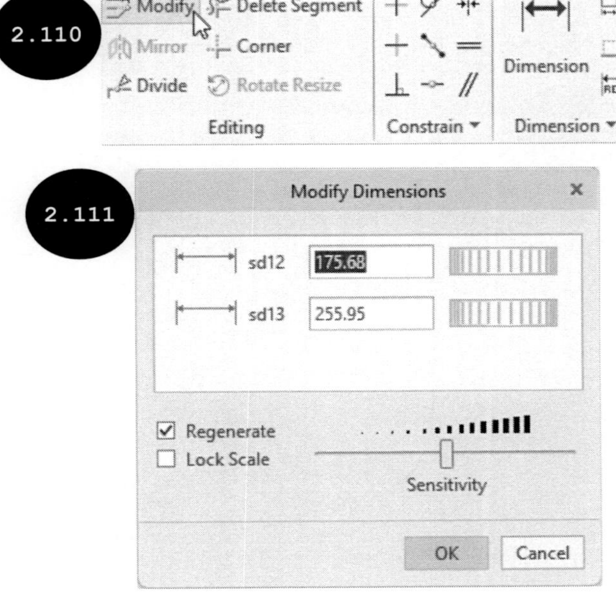

Tip: While editing a dimension value by clicking on an edit field in the **Modify Dimensions** dialog box, the respective dimension gets highlighted in the drawing area for your reference.

By default, the **Regenerate** check box is selected in the **Modify Dimensions** dialog box, see Figure 2.111. Due to this, on modifying a dimension value in the **Modify Dimensions** dialog box, the same modification is reflected in the sketch, dynamically. However, if the **Regenerate** check box is cleared, the modifications made in the dimension values will not reflect in the sketch until you click on the **OK** button in the dialog box to accept the changes and exit the dialog box. If you are modifying more than one dimension value, it is recommended to clear the **Regenerate** check box before making any modification.

By selecting the **Lock Scale** check box of the **Modify Dimensions** dialog box, you can lock the scale of the dimension values. On doing so, when you modify a dimension value, all the remaining dimension values of the selected dimensions get modified automatically by the same scale.

After modifying the dimension values of the selected dimensions in the dialog box, click on the **OK** button.

Editing Dimensions by Double-Clicking

In addition to editing dimensions by using the **Modify** tool, you can edit a dimension by double-clicking on it. To do so, double-click on a dimension value in the drawing area. An edit field appears with the current dimension value. Enter a new dimension value in this edit field and then press ENTER. The dimension value gets modified and updated in the drawing area. Similarly, the other dimensions can be modified.

Tutorial 1

Draw the sketch shown in Figure 2.112. All dimensions are in mm.

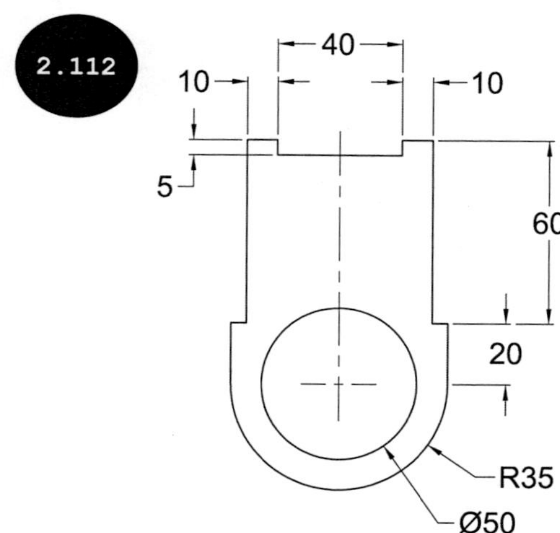

Section 1: Starting Creo Parametric

1. Start Creo Parametric by double-clicking on the Creo Parametric icon on your desktop.

Section 2: Setting the Working Directory

After starting Creo Parametric, you need to set a working directory to save files of the current session of Creo Parametric. You can set any folder created in a local drive of your system as the working directory. However, it is recommended to create a folder with the name "*Creo Parametric*" in a local drive of your system and then create another folder inside it with the name "*Chapter 2*" to set it as the working directory.

1. Click on **File** > **Manage Session** > **Select Working Directory**, see Figure 2.113. The **Select Working Directory** window appears.

2.113

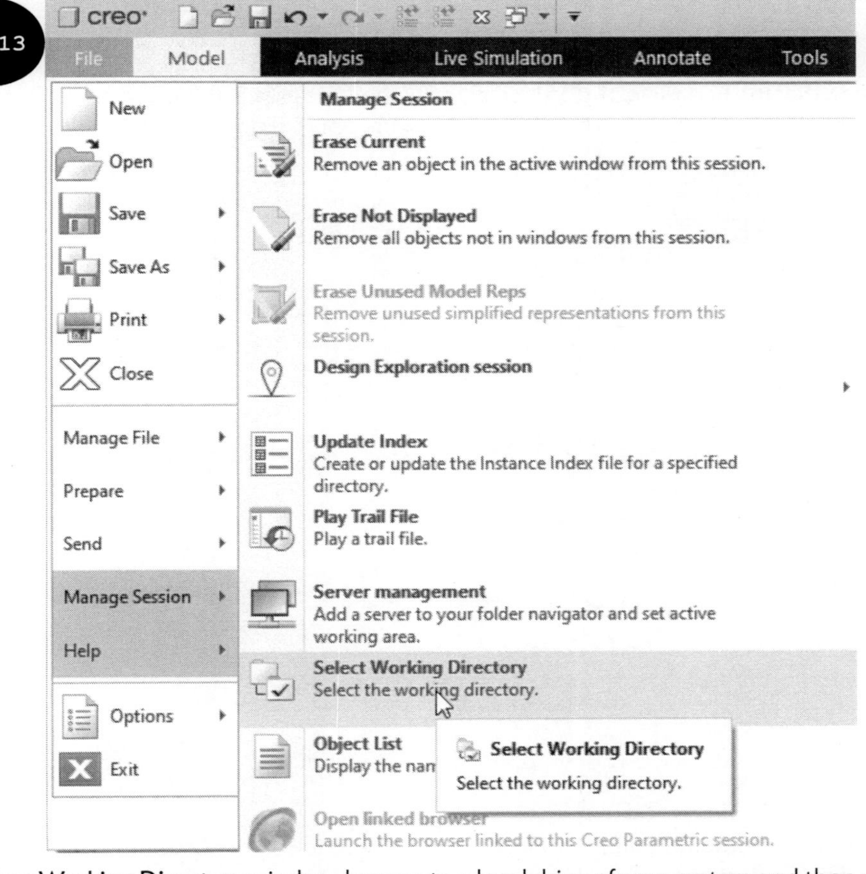

2. In the **Select Working Directory** window, browse to a local drive of your system and then create a folder with the name *Creo Parametric*. You can create a folder by right-clicking in the empty area of the **Select Working Directory** window and then clicking on the **New Folder** tool in the shortcut menu that appears. Alternatively, click on the arrow next to the **Organize** tool in the window and then click on the **New Folder** tool.

3. Create another folder with the name *Chapter 2* in the *Creo Parametric* folder.

Note: You can also create these folders in a local drive of your system before invoking the **Select Working Directory** window.

4. Click on the **OK** button to set the working directory to <<*Creo Parametric**Chapter 2*\.

Section 3: Invoking the Sketching Environment

In Creo Parametric, you can invoke the Sketching environment of the Sketch mode and the Part mode. In this section, you will invoke the Sketching environment of the Part mode for creating the sketch.

1. Click on the **New** tool in the **Data** group of the **Home** tab. The **New** dialog box appears, see Figure 2.114.

2. Ensure that the **Part** radio button is selected in the **Type** area and the **Solid** radio button is selected in the **Sub-type** area of the dialog box (see Figure 2.114), to invoke the Part mode.

3. Clear the **Use default template** check box and then click on the **OK** button in the dialog box. The **New File Options** dialog box appears, see Figure 2.115.

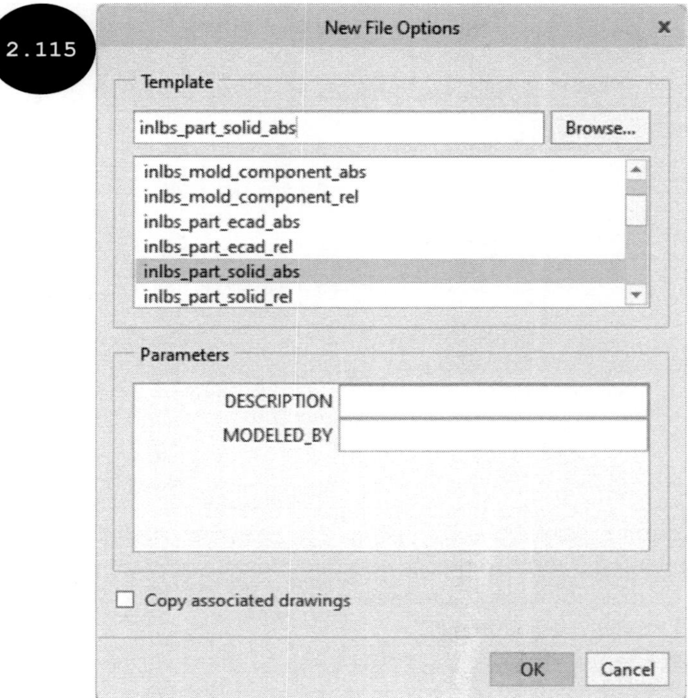

4. In the **New File Options** dialog box, select the **mmns_part_solid_abs** template and then click on the **OK** button. The Part mode is invoked with the **mmns_part_solid_abs** template. In this template, length is measured in millimeters, mass is measured in Newton, and time is measured in seconds.

   Now, you can invoke the Sketching environment for creating the sketch.

5. Click on the **Sketch** tool in the **Datum** group of the **Model** tab, see Figure 2.116. The **Sketch** dialog box appears and you are prompted to select a plane or a surface to define the sketching plane.

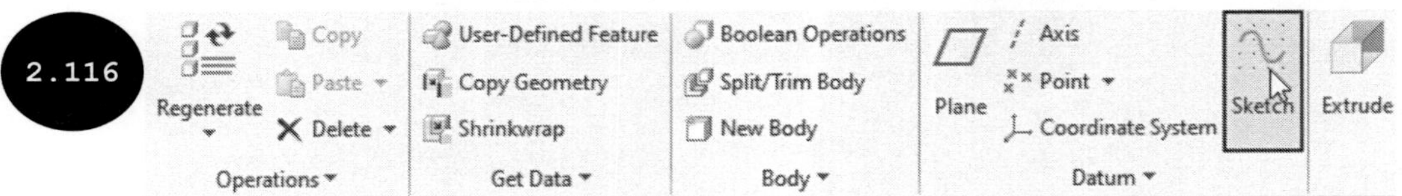

6. Move the cursor over the Front plane in the graphics window and then click the left mouse button when it gets highlighted in the graphics window. The Front plane gets selected as the sketching plane and its name appears in the **Plane** field of the **Sketch** dialog box, see Figure 2.117. Also, a reference plane and its orientation are selected automatically in the **Reference** field and **Orientation** drop-down list of the dialog box, respectively, see Figure 2.117.

2.117

7. Click on the **Sketch** button in the dialog box. The Sketching environment is invoked. Also, the Front plane is oriented normal to the viewing direction. If the Front plane is not oriented normal to the viewing direction by default, then you need to do it by clicking on the **Sketch View** tool in the **In-graphics** toolbar, see Figure 2.118.

2.118

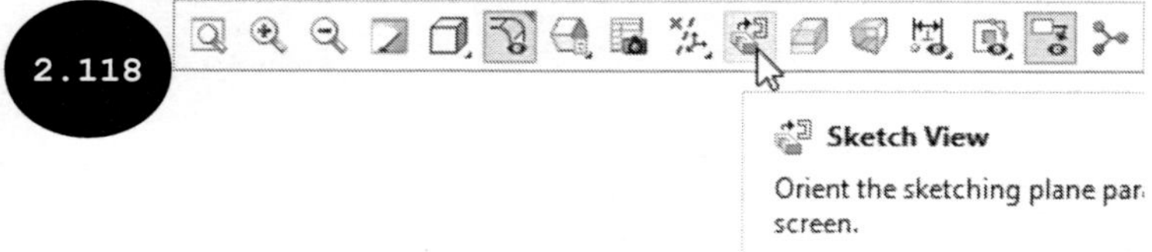

Section 4: Drawing the Sketch

Once the Sketching environment is invoked, you need to start drawing the sketch.

1. Click on the arrow next to the **Circle** tool in the **Sketching** group. A flyout appears, see Figure 2.119. Next, click on the **Center and Point** tool in the flyout.

2.119

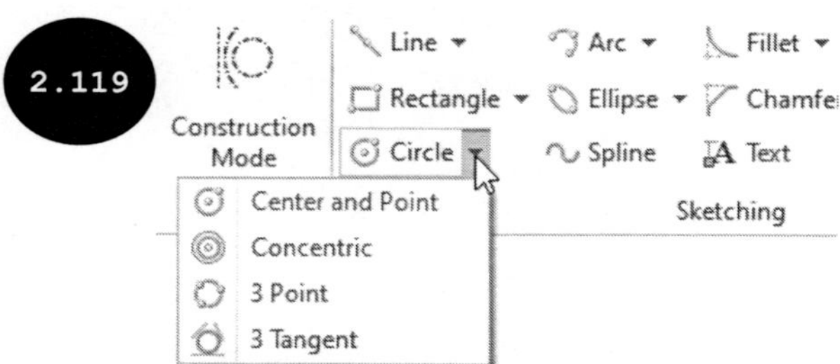

2. Move the cursor to the origin and then click to specify the center point of the circle, when the cursor snaps to the origin.

3. Move the cursor away from the origin and then click to specify a point arbitrarily in the drawing area. A circle is drawn and the **Center and Point** tool is still active. Next, press the middle mouse button to exit the tool. A weak diameter dimension is applied automatically to the circle, see Figure 2.120.

Note: As the circle is drawn by specifying a point arbitrarily in the drawing area, you will find a variation in the weak diameter dimension value in this case.

Now, you need to draw an arc concentric to the previously drawn circle.

4. Click on the arrow next to the **Arc** tool in the **Sketching** group. A flyout appears, see Figure 2.121. Next, click on the **Concentric** tool in the flyout.

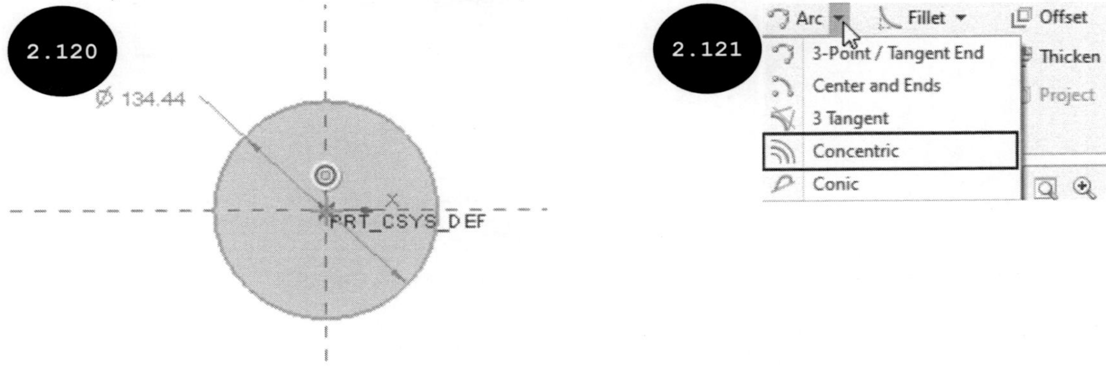

5. Click on the previously drawn circle in the drawing area. The preview of a construction circle that is concentric to the selected circle appears in the drawing area.

6. Move the cursor horizontally toward the right and then click to specify the start point of the arc, outside the circle, when the cursor snaps to the horizontal reference line, see Figure 2.122.

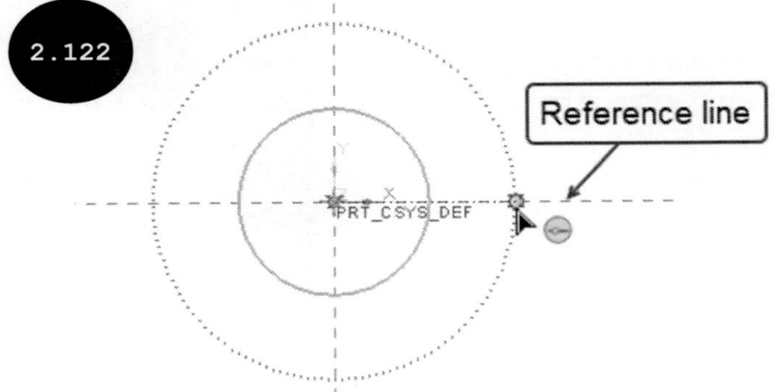

7. Move the cursor clockwise and then click to specify the endpoint of the arc when the cursor snaps to the horizontal reference line on the other side, see Figure 2.123. An arc concentric to the circle is drawn and the **Concentric** tool is still active. Press the middle mouse button to exit the tool.

Now, you need to draw the line entities of the sketch.

8. Click on the arrow next to the Line tool in the **Sketching** group. A flyout appears, see Figure 2.124. Next, click on the **Line Chain** tool. The **Line Chain** tool gets activated. Alternatively, press the **L** key to activate this tool.

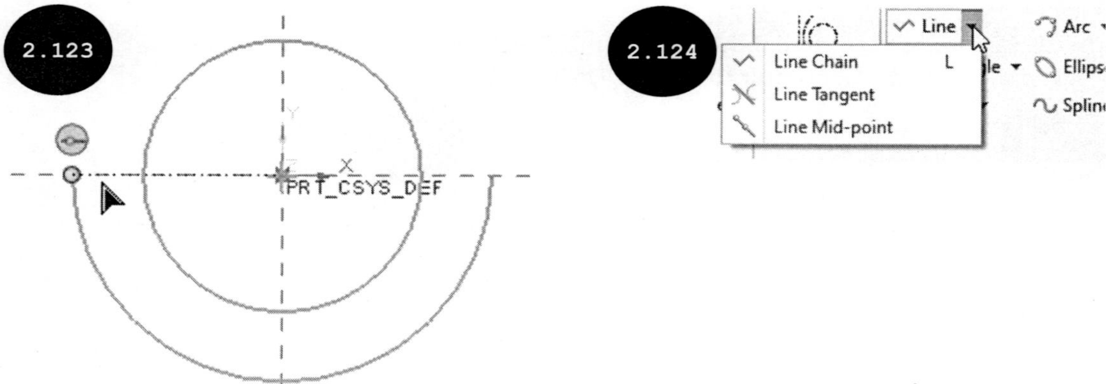

9. Move the cursor to the start point of the previously drawn arc in the drawing area and then click to specify the start point of the line when the cursor snaps to it.

10. Move the cursor vertically upward to a distance and then click to specify the endpoint of the line when the symbol of vertical constraint appears near the cursor, see Figure 2.125. A line is drawn, and a rubber band line with one end fixed at the last specified point and the other end attached to the cursor appears in the drawing area.

11. Move the cursor horizontally toward the left to a distance, and then click to specify the endpoint of the line when the symbol of horizontal constraint appears near the cursor, see Figure 2.126. A line is drawn and a rubber band line appears attached to the cursor in the drawing area.

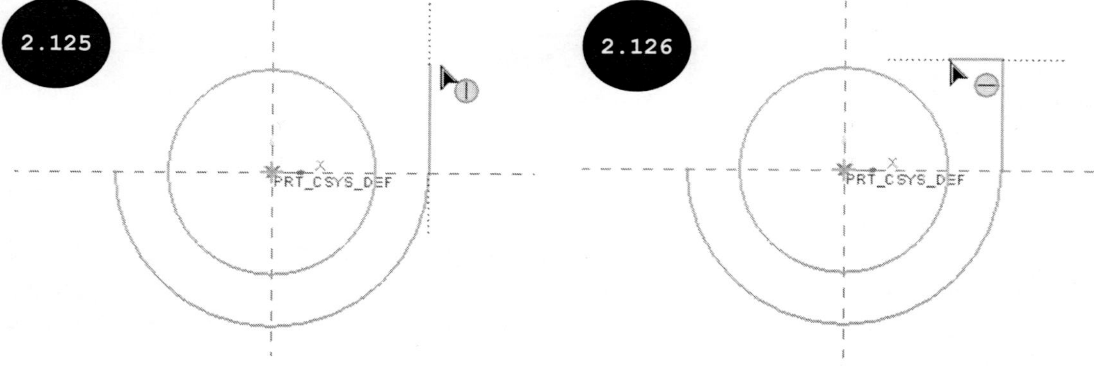

12. Similarly, draw the remaining line entities of the sketch by specifying points arbitrarily in the drawing area, see Figure 2.127.

2.127

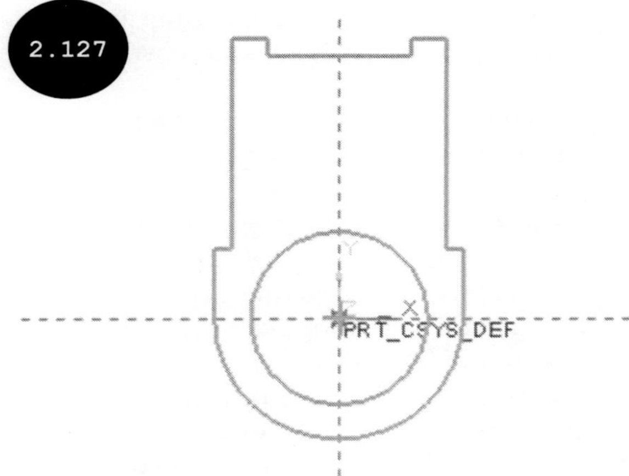

13. After drawing all the line entities of the sketch, press the middle mouse button twice to terminate the creation of a continuous chain of lines and exit the tool.

Section 5: Applying Constraints

Now, you need to apply the required constraints to the entities of the sketch.

1. Click on the **Equal** constraint tool in the **Constrain** group, see Figure 2.128. The **Equal** constraint tool gets activated.

2. Click on the vertical line entities (L1 and L11) one by one (refer to Figure 2.129), and then press the middle mouse button. Equal constraint is applied between the selected entities and the **Equal** constraint tool is still active.

2.128

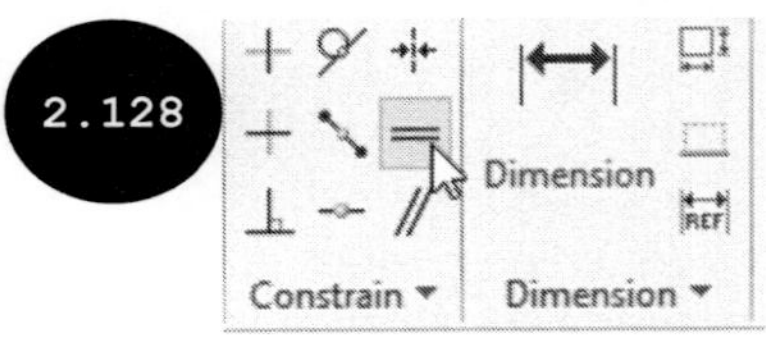

2.129

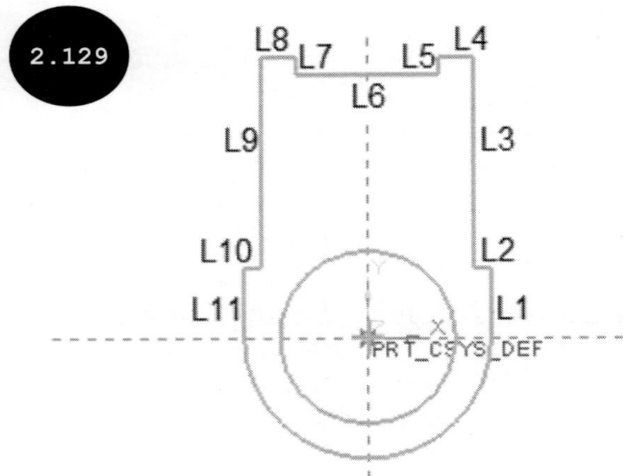

3. Click on the horizontal line entities (L2 and L10) one by one (refer to Figure 2.129), and then press the middle mouse button. Equal constraint is applied and the **Equal** constraint tool is still active.

4. Click on the vertical line entities, L3 and L9 (refer to Figure 2.129), and then press the middle mouse button. Equal constraint is applied and the **Equal** constraint tool is still active.

5. Click on the horizontal line entities L4 and L8 (refer to Figure 2.129), and then press the middle mouse button. Equal constraint is applied and the **Equal** constraint tool is still active.

6. After applying equal constraints between the lines, press the ESC key to exit the tool.

Note: When you apply a constraint or a dimension manually, sometimes the **Resolve Sketch** dialog box appears, see Figure 2.130. This dialog box appears, if the application of constraint or dimension conflicts with any of the existing constraints or dimensions (strong dimensions) and prompts you to delete the conflicted constraints or dimensions to resolve the sketch. In the **Resolve Sketch** dialog box, a list of all the conflicted constraints or dimensions appear. You can also undo the currently applied constraint or dimension by clicking on the **Undo** button of the dialog box. To delete a conflicted constraint or dimension, select it in the dialog box. The selected constraint or dimension gets highlighted in the drawing area. Next, click on the **Delete** button in the dialog box. You may need to delete one or more constraints or dimensions to resolve the sketch.

2.130

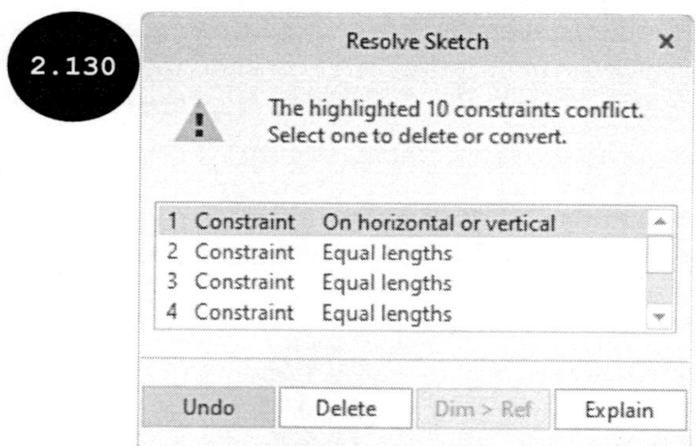

7. Ensure that the horizontal constraint is applied to all the horizontal line entities and vertical constraint is applied to all the vertical line entities. These constraints are applied automatically while drawing the entities. However, if not applied automatically, you can apply the horizontal and vertical constraints by using the **Horizontal** and **Vertical** tools of the **Constrain** group.

Section 6: Applying Strong Dimensions

Now, you need to apply strong dimensions to the sketch. You can apply strong dimensions by using the **Dimension** tool. Alternatively, you can modify the weak dimensions to convert them into strong dimensions. In this section, you will modify the weak dimensions of the sketch.

1. Select all the weak dimensions of the sketch by drawing a window around the dimensions, see Figure 2.131. You can draw a window by dragging the cursor. The selected dimensions are highlighted in green.

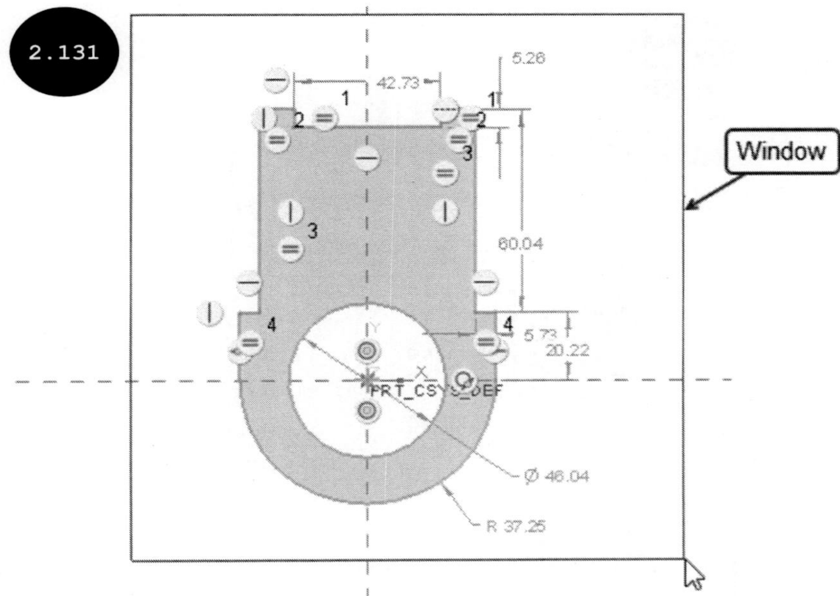

2. Click on the **Modify** tool in the **Editing** group, see Figure 2.132. The **Modify Dimensions** dialog box appears, see Figure 2.133. In this dialog box, a list of all the selected dimensions appears.

3. Clear the **Regenerate** check box in the **Modify Dimensions** dialog box so that the modifications made in the dimension values will not reflect in the sketch until you exit the dialog box.

4. Change the values of all the dimensions one by one by entering new values in the respective edit fields of the **Modify Dimensions** dialog box. You can refer to Figure 2.112 for new dimension values. Note that when you click on an edit field in this dialog box to enter the new value, the respective dimension gets highlighted in the drawing area for your reference.

5. After entering new values for all the dimensions, click on the **OK** button. All the dimensions get updated with new dimension values and are converted into strong dimensions in the drawing area. Next, click anywhere in the drawing area to exit the selection of dimensions in the drawing area. Figure 2.134 shows the final sketch after modifying all the dimensions.

2.134

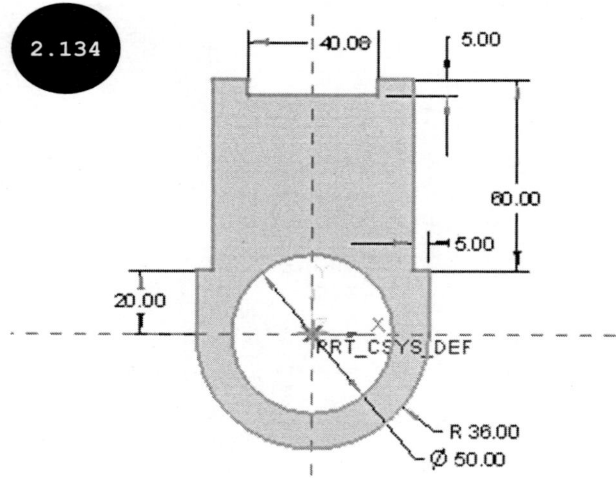

Note: After modifying the dimensions, you need to arrange them properly by dragging them to a new location in the drawing area, see Figure 2.134.

Section 7: Saving the Sketch

Now, you need to save the sketch.

1. Click on the **Save** tool in the **Quick Access Toolbar**. The **Save Object** dialog box appears with default name of the sketch.

2. Click on the **OK** button. The sketch is saved with the default name in the specified working directory. Note that the sketches created in the Sketching environment of Creo Parametric are saved with *.SEC* file extension.

Tutorial 2

Draw the sketch shown in Figure 2.135. All dimensions are in mm.

2.135

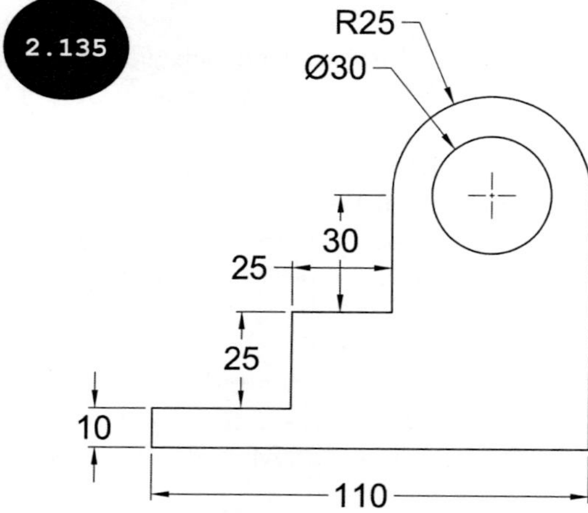

Section 1: Starting Creo Parametric

1. Start Creo Parametric by double-clicking on the Creo Parametric icon on your desktop, if not started already.

Section 2: Setting the Working Directory

After starting Creo Parametric, you need to set a working directory to save files of the current session of Creo Parametric. It is recommended to create a folder with the name "*Creo Parametric*" in a local drive of your system and then create another folder inside it with the name "*Chapter 2*" to set it as the working directory. You need to create these folders, if not created in Tutorial 1 of this chapter.

1. Click on **File > Manage Session > Select Working Directory**. The **Select Working Directory** window appears. In this window, browse to the *Chapter 2* folder of the *Creo Parametric* folder in the local drive of your system. You need to create these folders, if not created, in Tutorial 1 of this chapter.

2. Click on the **OK** button. The working directory is set to <<*Creo Parametric**Chapter 2*\.

Section 3: Invoking the Sketching Environment

In Creo Parametric, you can invoke the Sketching environment of the Sketch mode and the Part mode. In this section, you will invoke the Sketching environment of the Sketch mode for creating the sketch.

1. Click on the **New** tool in the **Data** group of the **Home** tab. The **New** dialog box appears, see Figure 2.136.

2. Select the **Sketch** radio button in the **Type** area of the dialog box, see Figure 2.136.

2.136

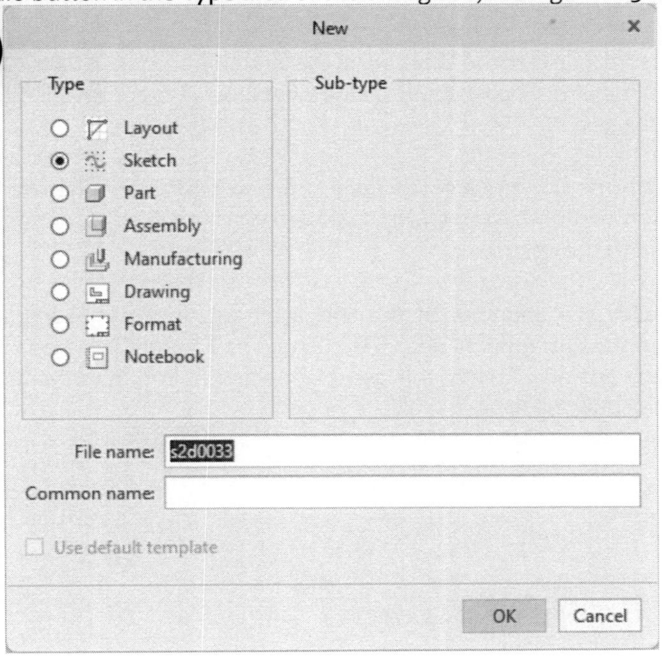

3. Enter **Tutorial02** as the name of the sketch in the **File name** field of the dialog box and then click on the **OK** button. The Sketching environment of the Sketch mode is invoked, see Figure 2.137. Now, you can directly start creating the sketch by using the sketching tools.

2.137

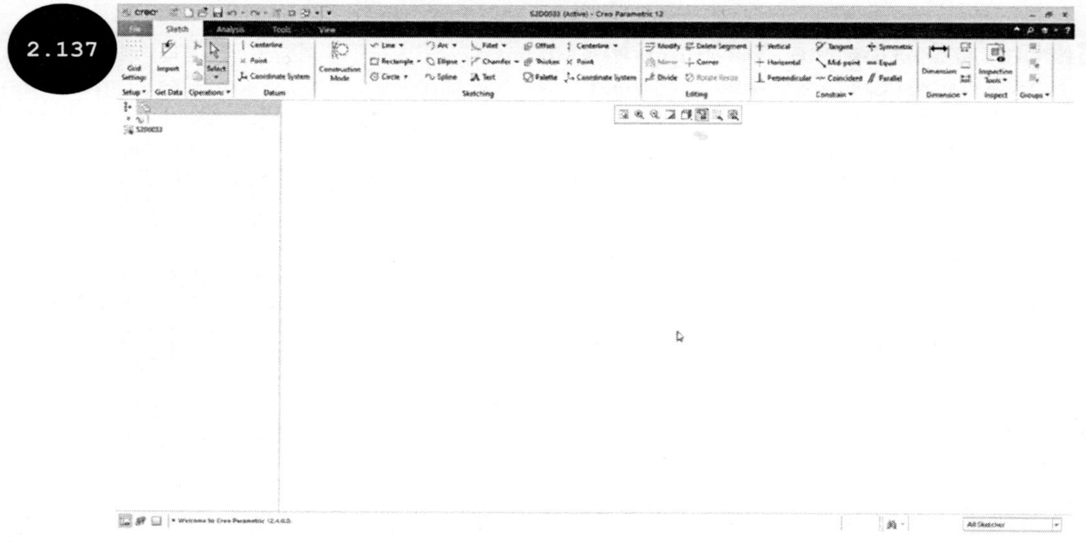

Note: In this textbook, the background color of the drawing area has been set to white for clarity of image. The method for changing the background color is discussed in Chapter 1.

Section 4: Drawing the Sketch

Once the Sketching environment is invoked, you need to start drawing the sketch.

1. Click on the arrow next to the **Line** tool in the **Sketching** group. A flyout appears (see Figure 2.138), then click on the **Line Chain** tool. The **Line Chain** tool gets activated. Alternatively, press the L key to activate this tool.

2. Click to specify the start point of the line in the drawing area and then move the cursor horizontally toward the left. A rubber band line appears with one end fixed at the specified point and the other end attached to the cursor.

3. Click to specify the endpoint of the line, arbitrarily in the drawing area when the symbol of horizontal constraint appears near the cursor, see Figure 2.139. The line is drawn and a rubber band line with one end fixed at the last specified point and the other end attached to the cursor appears in the drawing area.

4. Move the cursor vertically upward to a distance and then click to specify the endpoint of the line when the symbol of vertical constraint appears near the cursor, see Figure 2.140. The line is drawn and a rubber band line appears attached to the cursor in the drawing area.

5. Move the cursor horizontally toward the right and then click to specify the endpoint of the line when the symbol of horizontal constraint appears near the cursor, see Figure 2.141.

6. Similarly, draw the three remaining line entities (L4, L5, and L6) of the sketch by specifying arbitrary points in the drawing area, refer to Figure 2.142.

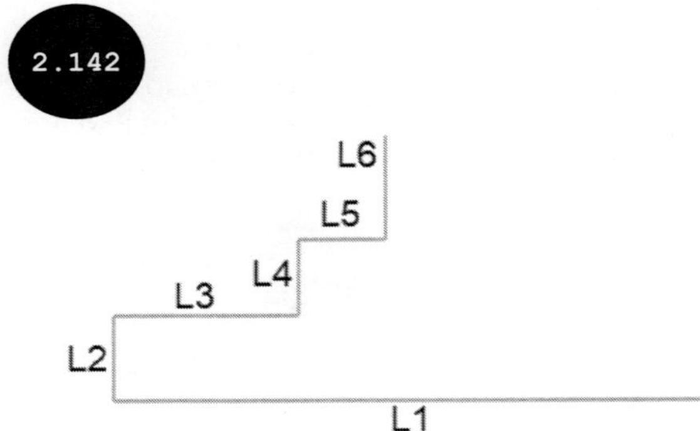

7. Press the middle mouse button to terminate the creation of a continuous chain of lines. Note that the **Line Chain** tool is still active.

8. Move the cursor to the start point of the first drawn line in the drawing area and then click to specify the start point of the line when the cursor snaps to it.

9. Move the cursor vertically upward and then click to specify the endpoint of the line when the symbol of vertical and horizontal constraints appear near the cursor, see Figure 2.143.

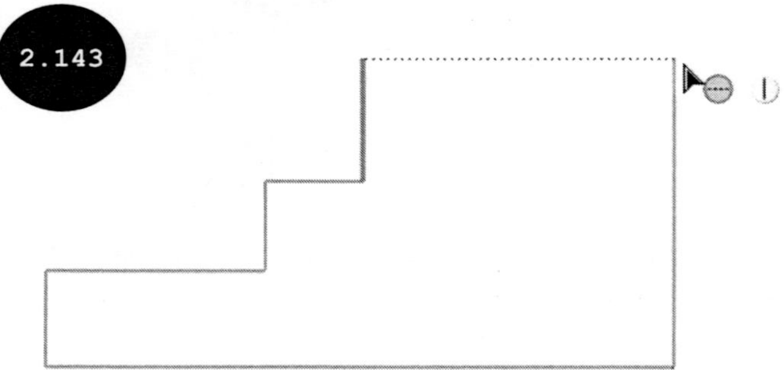

10. Press the middle mouse button twice to exit the tool.

Now, you need to draw an arc.

11. Click on the arrow next to the Arc tool in the **Sketching** group. The **Arc** flyout appears, see Figure 2.144. Next, click on the **3-Point / Tangent End** tool in the flyout.

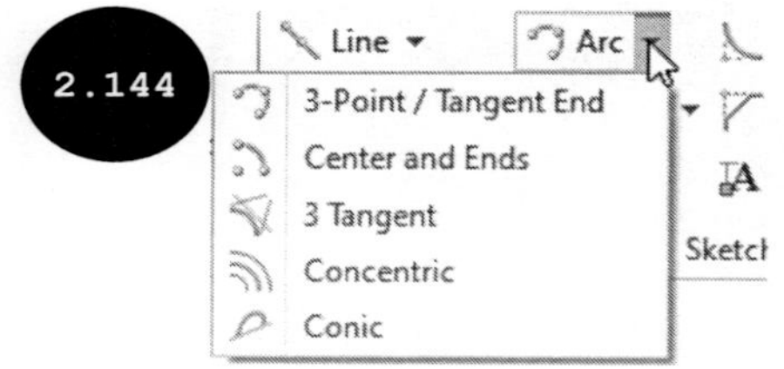

12. Move the cursor to the endpoint of the previously drawn line and then click to specify the start point of the arc when the cursor snaps to it, see Figure 2.145.

13. Move the cursor vertically upward to a distance and then move it anti-clockwise. The preview of an arc tangent to the line appears in the drawing area.

14. Click to specify the endpoint of the arc when the cursor snaps to the endpoint of the vertical line (L6), see Figure 2.146. The arc is drawn and the **3-Point / Tangent End** tool is still active. Press the middle mouse button to exit the tool.

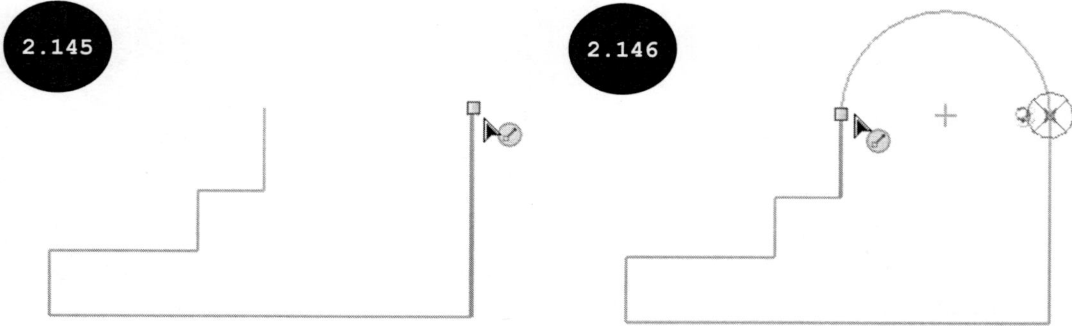

Now, you need to draw a circle.

15. Click on the arrow next to the Circle tool in the **Sketching** group. The **Circle** flyout appears, see Figure 2.147. Next, click on the **Concentric** tool in the flyout.

16. Click on the previously drawn arc of the sketch. The preview of a circle concentric to the selected arc appears attached to the cursor.

17. Click to specify a point inside the arc. A circle concentric to the arc is drawn and the preview of another concentric circle appears attached to the cursor.

18. Press the middle mouse button twice to exit the tool. Figure 2.148 shows the sketch after creating all its entities.

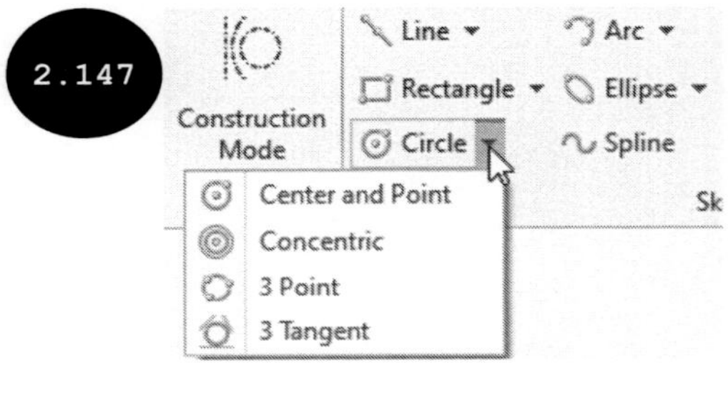

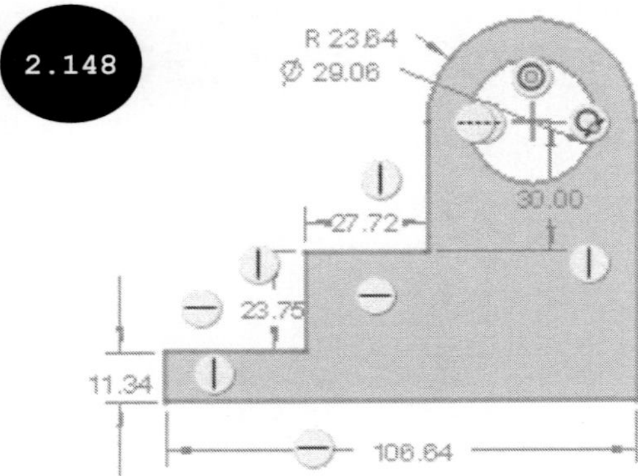

Section 5: Applying Constraints

1. Ensure that the horizontal constraint is applied to all the horizontal line entities and the vertical constraint is applied to all the vertical line entities. These constraints are applied automatically while drawing the entities. However, if not applied automatically, you can apply them manually by using the **Horizontal** and **Vertical** tools of the **Constrain** group, respectively.

Section 6: Applying Strong Dimensions

Now, you need to apply strong dimensions to the sketch. You can apply strong dimensions by using the **Dimension** tool. You can also modify the weak dimensions of the sketch to convert them into strong dimensions. In this section, you will modify the weak dimensions of the sketch.

1. Select all the weak dimensions of the sketch by drawing a window around the dimensions. You can draw a window by dragging the cursor.

2. Click on the **Modify** tool, see Figure 2.149. The **Modify Dimensions** dialog box appears with a list of all the selected dimensions.

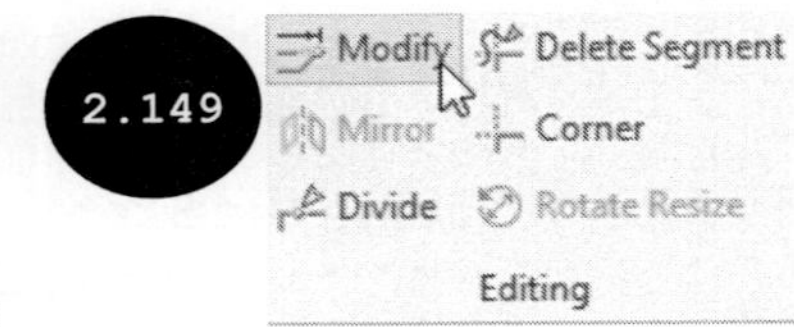

3. Clear the **Regenerate** check box in the **Modify Dimensions** dialog box so that the modifications made in the dimension values will not reflect in the sketch until you exit the dialog box.

4. Change the values of all the dimensions one by one by entering the new value in the respective edit fields of the **Modify Dimensions** dialog box. You can refer to Figure 2.135 for dimension values. Note that when you click on an edit field in this dialog box for entering the new value, the respective dimension gets highlighted in the drawing area.

5. After entering new dimension values for all the dimensions, click on the **OK** button. All the dimensions get updated with new dimension values and are converted into strong dimensions in the drawing area. Next, click anywhere in the drawing area. Figure 2.150 shows the final sketch after modifying all the dimensions.

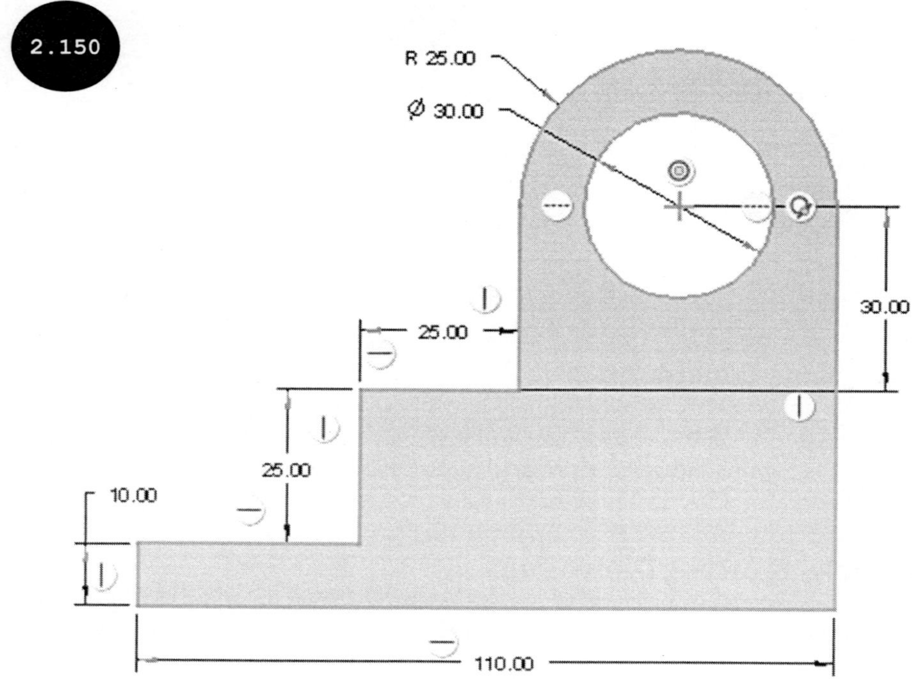

Note: After modifying the dimensions, you need to arrange them properly by dragging them to a new location in the drawing area, see Figure 2.150.

Section 7: Saving the Sketch

Now, you need to save the sketch.

1. Click on the **Save** tool in the **Quick Access Toolbar**. The **Save Object** dialog box appears.

2. Click on the **OK** button. The sketch is saved in the specified working directory. Note that the sketches created in the Sketching environment of Creo Parametric are saved with *.SEC* file extension.

Hands-on Test Drive 1

Draw the sketch shown in Figure 2.151. All dimensions are in mm.

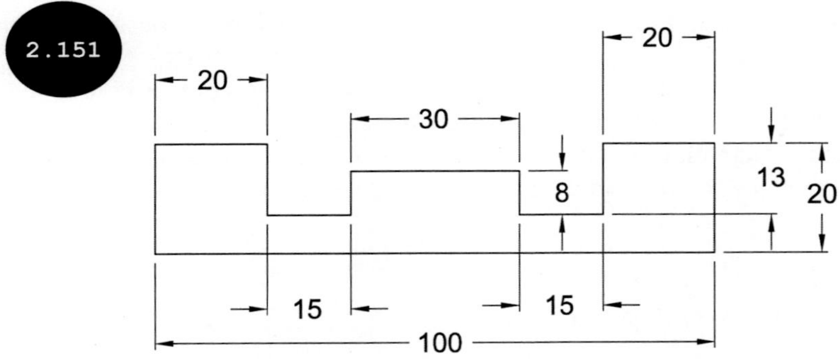

Hands-on Test Drive 2

Draw the sketch shown in Figure 2.152. All dimensions are in mm.

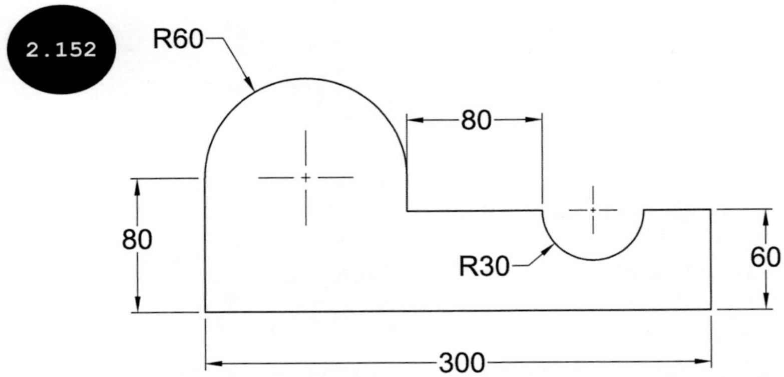

Hands-on Test Drive 3

Draw the sketch shown in Figure 2.153. All dimensions are in mm.

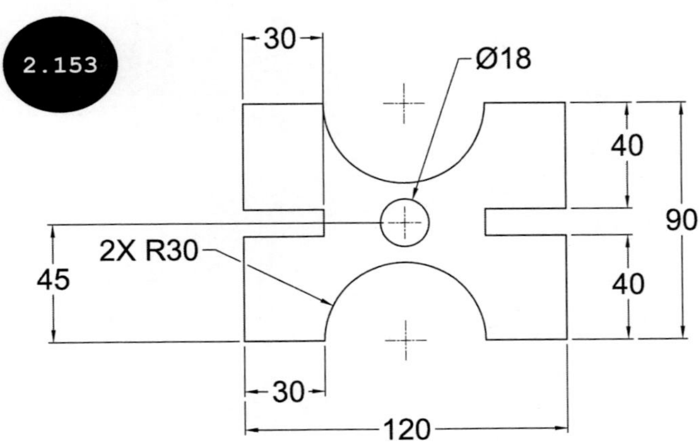

Summary

In this chapter, we have thoroughly discussed the methods for accessing the Sketching environment within both Part mode and Sketch mode. Additionally, we have covered the procedures for specifying units, grids, and snap settings, providing a foundational understanding of these crucial elements.

Furthermore, we have explored various methods for drawing sketches by using sketching tools such as **Line Chain**, **Line Tangent**, **Corner Rectangle**, **Slanted Rectangle**, **Parallelogram**, and **Spline**. Additionally, we have discussed the creation of datum geometries, the use of construction mode, application of constraints, the use of weak dimensions, application of dimensions, and the editing of dimensions.

Questions

Complete and verify the following sentences:

- Features are divided into two main categories: _________ and _________.
- The _________ feature of any real-world component is a sketch-based feature.
- To draw an ellipse, you need to define its _________ axis and _________ axis.
- The ______ tool is used for drawing an arc that is concentric to an existing arc or a circular entity/edge.
- The ______ tool is used for switching between the mode of creating new entities from the solid sketch entities and the construction entities.
- Datum geometries can also be used outside the Sketching environment as reference geometries (True/False).
- You cannot lock the modified dimensions or the user-defined dimensions (True/False).

CHAPTER

3

Editing and Modifying Sketches

In this chapter, the following topics will be discussed:

- Trimming Sketch Entities
- Creating Corners by Trimming/Extending Entities
- Dividing Entities
- Moving, Rotating, and Scaling Entities
- Mirroring Entities
- Offsetting Entities
- Offsetting Entities Bi-directionally
- Creating a Sketch Fillet
- Creating a Sketch Chamfer
- Inserting Text in Sketching Environment
- Inserting Pre-defined Shapes of Geometries
- Inserting a Sketch or a Drawing File

Editing and modifying a sketch plays an important role in giving the sketch its desired shape. In Creo Parametric, various editing operations such as trimming unwanted sketch entities, creating corners by trimming or extending entities, mirroring, dividing entities, moving, scaling, and rotating sketch entities can be performed by using the editing/modifying tools in the Sketching environment. In this chapter, you will learn about the editing tools. You will also learn about creating fillets, chamfers, offset, and inserting text in the Sketching environment.

Trimming Sketch Entities

You can trim unwanted sketch entities by using the **Delete Segment** tool in the **Editing** group of the **Sketch** tab, see Figure 3.1.

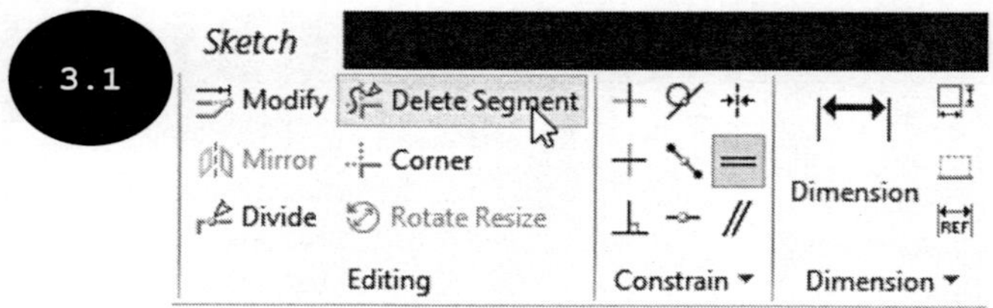

To trim sketch entities, click on the **Delete Segment** tool in the **Editing** group. The **Delete Segment** tool gets activated and you are prompted to select or drag the cursor over the entities to be trimmed. Move the cursor over the entity to be trimmed, and then click on it when the entity is highlighted in a different color, see Figure 3.2. The selected entity is trimmed from its nearest intersection, see Figure 3.3. Similarly, you can trim multiple entities one by one by clicking on them.

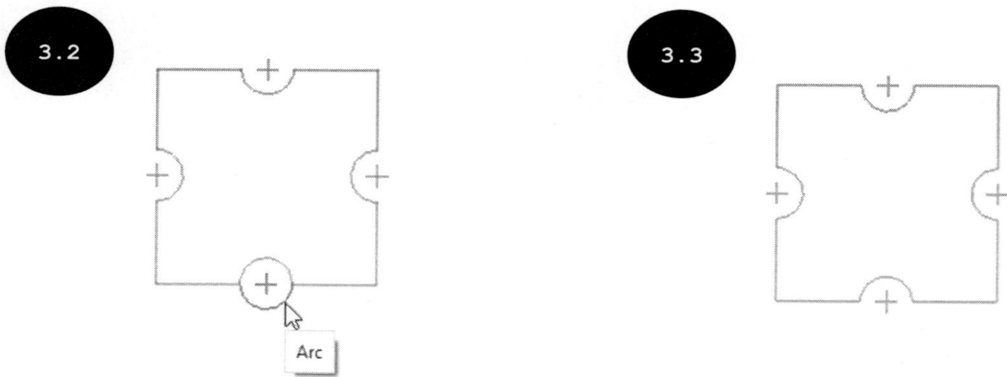

Alternatively, you can also trim the entities by dragging the cursor over the entities to be trimmed. When you drag the cursor by pressing and holding the left mouse button after activating the **Delete Segment** tool, a tracing line following the cursor appears, see Figure 3.4. Also, the portion of the sketch entities coming across the tracing line gets highlighted in green color. Next, release the left mouse button. The entities get trimmed from their nearest intersection, see Figure 3.5.

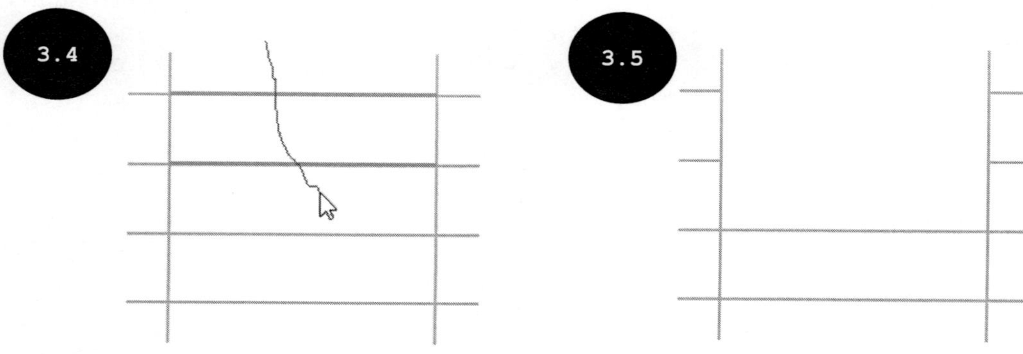

Creating Corners by Trimming/Extending Entities

You can create a corner between two entities by trimming or extending them using the **Corner** tool of the **Editing** group in the **Sketch** tab. To do so, click on the **Corner** tool in the **Editing** group, see Figure 3.6. The **Corner** tool gets activated and you are prompted to select two entities. Next, click on two sketch entities one by one. A corner is created between the selected entities either by trimming or extending the entities, see Figures 3.7 and 3.8. In Figure 3.7, the corner is created by extending the selected entities, whereas in Figure 3.8, the corner is created by trimming the selected entities.

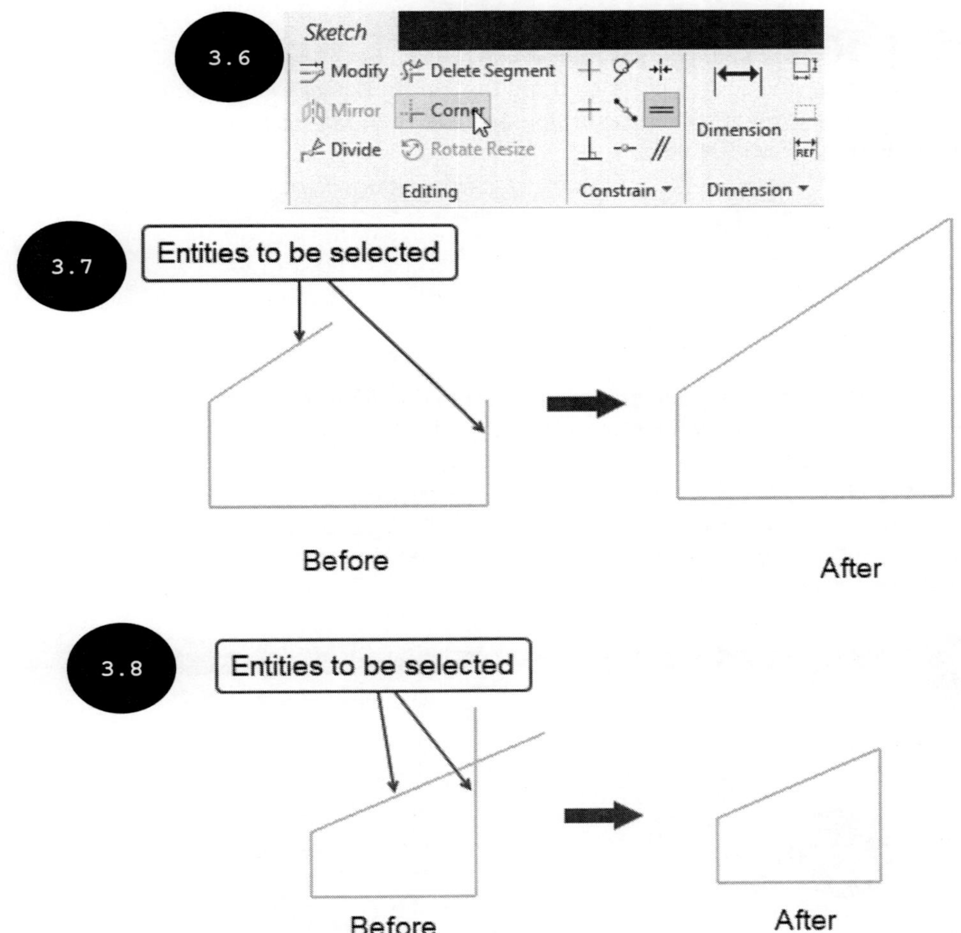

Dividing Entities

You can divide an entity into multiple segments by using the **Divide** tool of the **Editing** group in the **Sketch** tab. To do so, click on the **Divide** tool in the **Editing** group, see Figure 3.9. The **Divide** tool gets activated. Next, move the cursor over the entity to be divided and then click to specify a point on it at the location where you want to divide the entity, see Figure 3.10. The entity gets divided into two segments at the location where the point has been specified. Note that two segments of an entity act as two different entities. After dividing the entity, press the middle mouse button to exit the **Divide** tool.

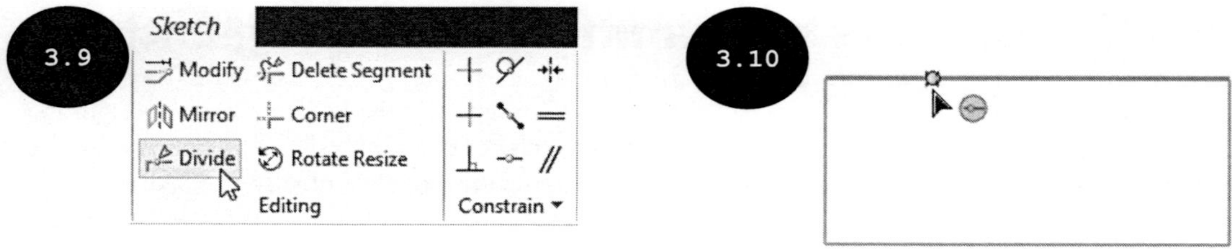

Moving, Rotating, and Scaling Entities

You can move, rotate, and scale entities by using the **Rotate Resize** tool of the **Editing** group in the **Sketch** tab, see Figure 3.11. Note that this tool gets enabled in the **Editing** group only after selecting one or more entities in the drawing area.

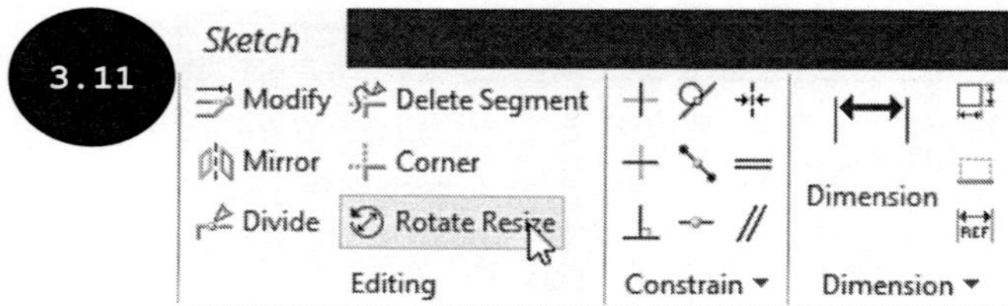

To move, rotate, or scale, select one or more entities in the drawing area by clicking the left mouse button. You can select multiple entities by pressing the CTRL key. Alternatively, you can select multiple entities by dragging the cursor around the entities to be selected. After selecting one or more entities, click on the **Rotate Resize** tool of the **Editing** group, see Figure 3.11. The **Rotate Resize** tab appears in the **Ribbon**, see Figure 3.12. Also, a rectangular box with the Move, Rotate, and Scale handles appears around the selected entity/entities in the drawing area, see Figure 3.13. In this figure, all the entities of the rectangle are selected.

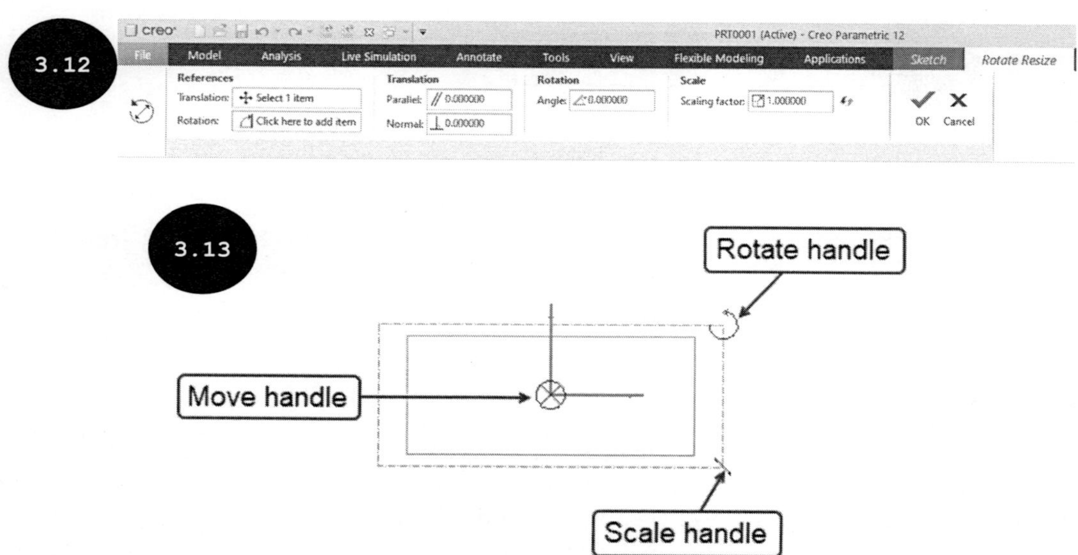

To move the selected entities, press and hold the left mouse button on the Move handle and then drag the cursor to the new location. Next, release the left mouse button. The selected entities are moved to the new location. Alternatively, enter the horizontal and vertical distance in the **Parallel** and **Normal** fields of the **Rotate Resize** tab in the **Ribbon**, respectively, to move the selected entities.

To rotate the selected entities, press and hold the left mouse button on the Rotate handle and then drag the cursor, clockwise or anti-clockwise. Next, release the left mouse button at the required angle of rotation. Alternatively, enter the rotational angle in the **Angle** field of the **Rotate Resize** tab. By default, entities rotate around an imaginary center point of the selected entities. However, you can define a center point for rotating the entities by using the **Enter reference to rotate entity** field of the **Rotate Resize** tab.

Similarly, you can scale selected entities to increase or decrease their size by using the Scale handle or the **Scaling factor** field of the **Rotate Resize** tab.

After editing the selected entities, press the middle mouse button or click on the green tick mark in the **Rotate Resize** tab of the **Ribbon** to exit the tool.

Mirroring Entities

In Creo Parametric, you can mirror sketch entities about a mirroring line by using the **Mirror** tool of the **Editing** group. You can select a line, a centerline, a construction line, a straight curve, a linear edge, or a linear projected geometry as the mirroring line. To do so, select one or more entities to be mirrored in the drawing area by clicking the left mouse button. You can select multiple entities by clicking the left mouse button after pressing the CTRL key or by dragging the cursor around the entities to be selected. After selecting the entities to be mirrored, click on the **Mirror** tool of the **Editing** group, see Figure 3.14. The **Mirror** tool gets activated. Next, select a straight sketch entity, an edge, or a curve in the drawing area as the mirroring line, see Figure 3.15. The selected entities get mirrored about the selected mirroring line, see Figure 3.16. Next, click anywhere in the drawing area to exit the current selection set.

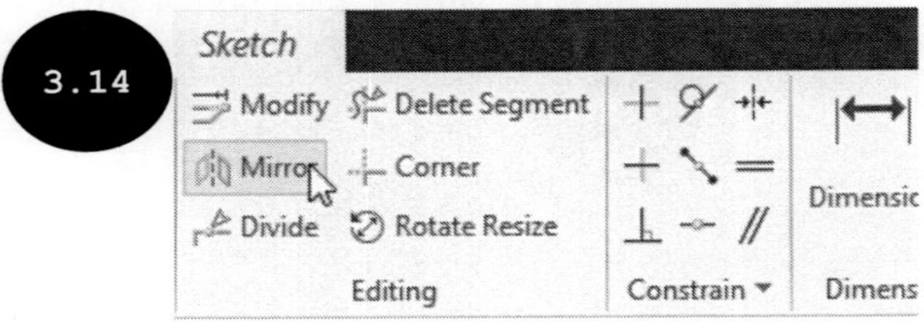

Note: The **Mirror** tool gets enabled in the **Editing** group only after selecting one or more entities in the drawing area.

Offsetting Entities

You can offset sketch entities or edges of an existing feature at a specified offset distance by using the **Offset** tool of the **Sketching** group, see Figure 3.17. By using the **Offset** tool, you can offset a single entity, a chain of entities, or a loop of entities. The different methods for offsetting entities are discussed next.

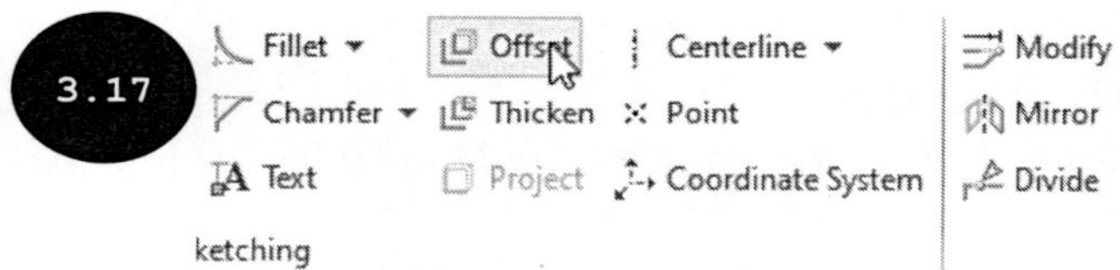

Offsetting a Single Entity

To offset a single entity (a sketch entity or an edge), click on the **Offset** tool of the **Sketching** group, see Figure 3.17. The **Type** window appears, see Figure 3.18. In this window, the **Single** radio button is selected, by default. As a result, you are prompted to select a sketch entity or an edge. Click on an entity or an edge. The **Offset Input** field appears at the top center of the drawing area, see Figure 3.19. Also, an arrow appears in the drawing area pointing toward the direction of offset, see Figure 3.20.

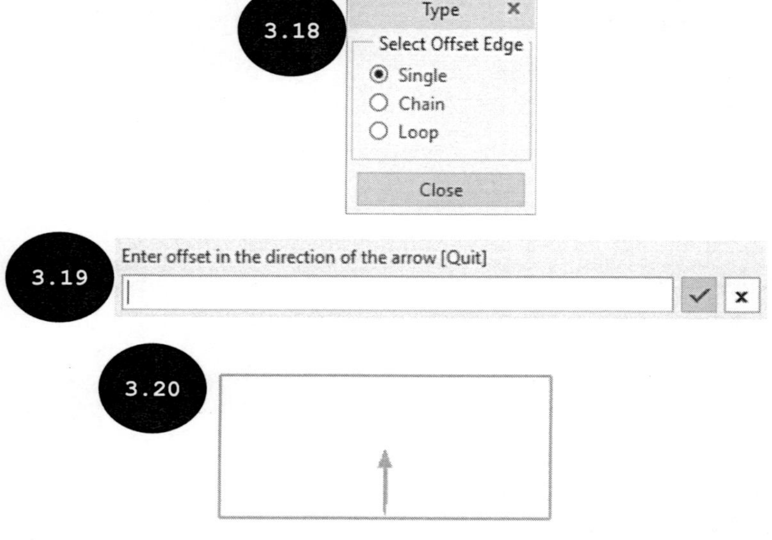

Enter the offset distance value in the **Offset Input** field, which appears at the top center of the drawing area. Note that to offset the selected entity in the direction of the arrow that appears in the drawing area, you need to enter a positive value, whereas to offset in the opposite direction of the arrow, you need to enter a negative value in the **Offset Input** field. After entering the offset distance value, click on the green tick-mark button in the **Offset Input** field or press the middle mouse button. The selected entity gets offset at the specified offset distance in the drawing area.

Offsetting a Chain of Entities

To offset a chain of continuous entities (sketch entities or edges), click on the **Offset** tool of the **Sketching** group. The **Type** window appears, refer to Figure 3.18. In this window, click on the **Chain** radio button. You are prompted to specify a chain of entities by selecting two entities or two edges. Select two entities one by one by clicking the left mouse button to define a chain of entities. The **Menu Manager** window appears in the drawing area, see Figure 3.21. Also, a chain of entities, which is formed by the selected entities is selected and highlighted in green color in the drawing area. Note that the **Menu Manager** dialog box appears only if the entities of a closed sketch are selected. Click on the **Accept** option in the **CHOOSE** menu of the **Menu Manager** window to accept the selected chain of entities. You can also click on the **Next** option in the **CHOOSE** menu to cycle through the alternative chain of entities formed by the selected entities. As soon as you click on the **Accept** option in the **CHOOSE** menu, the **Offset Input** field and an arrow appear in the drawing area, see Figure 3.22. Next, enter the offset distance value in the **Offset Input** field and then press the middle mouse button. The selected chain of entities gets offset at the specified offset distance in the drawing area. Note that to offset the selected chain of entities in the direction of the arrow that appears in the drawing area, you need to enter a positive value, whereas to offset in the opposite direction of the arrow, you need to enter a negative value in the **Offset Input** field. Figure 3.22 shows two sketch entities selected and Figure 3.23 shows the sketch after offsetting the chain of entities.

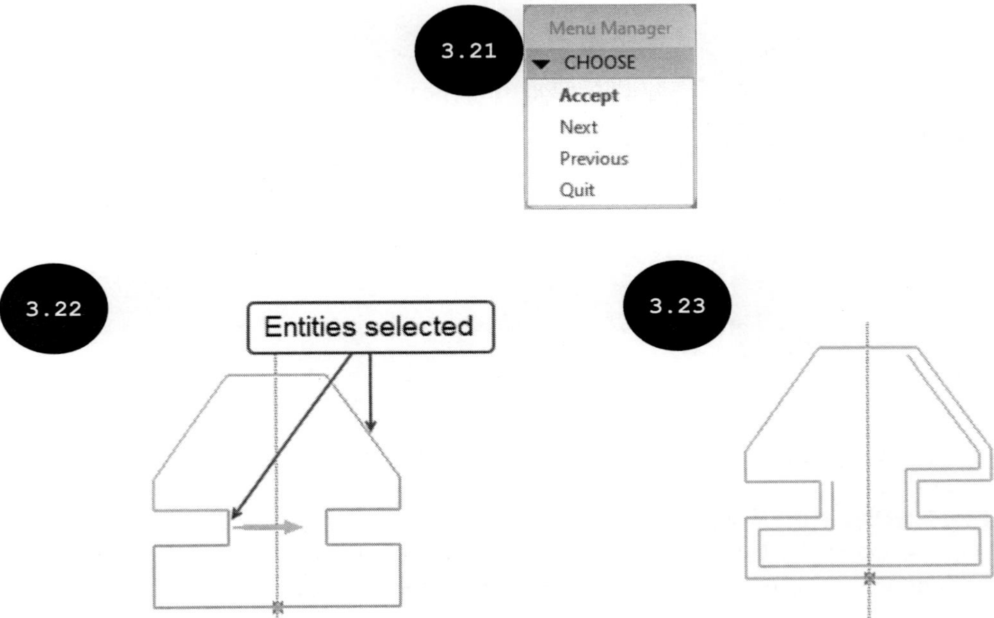

Offsetting a Loop

You can also offset an open or closed loop by using the **Offset** tool. To do so, click on the **Offset** tool and then select the **Loop** radio button in the **Type** window that appears. Next, select an entity to define the loop. The loop of entities, which are end-to-end connected to the selected entity are selected and highlighted in green color in the drawing area. Enter the offset distance value in the **Offset Input** field that appears at the top center of the drawing area. Next, press the middle mouse button. The selected loop gets offset at the specified offset distance in the drawing area.

Offsetting Entities Bi-directionally

In Creo Parametric, you can also offset entities (single, chain, or loop) bi-directionally (both sides of the parent entity/entities) by using the **Thicken** tool of the **Sketching** group, see Figure 3.24. In this figure, an open loop is offset on both sides, symmetrically.

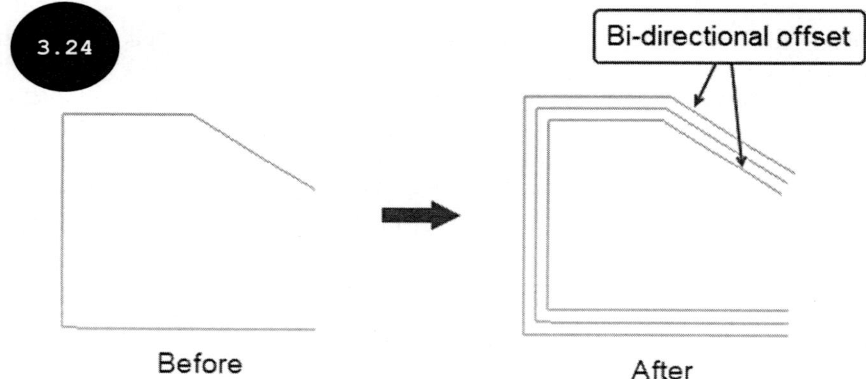

To offset entities bi-directionally, click on the **Thicken** tool of the **Sketching** group, see Figure 3.25. The **Type** window appears, see Figure 3.26. The options in the **Type** window are discussed next.

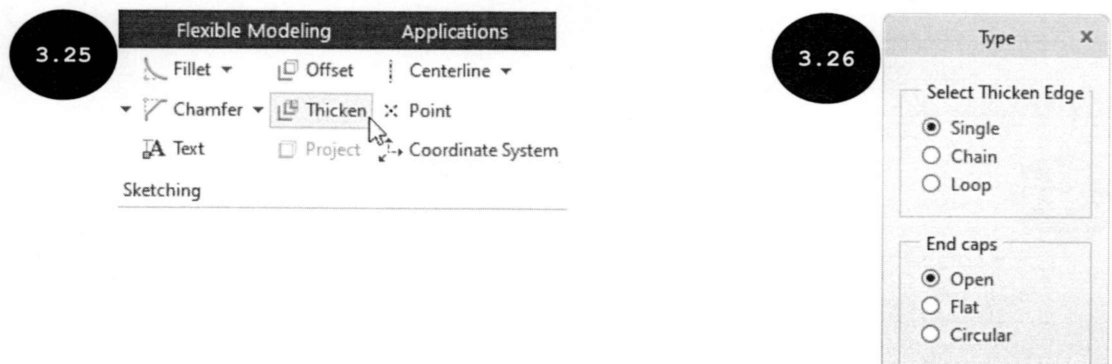

Select Thicken Edge Area

The options in the **Select Thicken Edge** area of the **Type** window are the same as discussed earlier. By using these options, you can either select a single entity, a chain of entities, or a loop to be offset.

End caps Area

The options in the **End caps** area of the **Type** window are used for capping the open ends of offset **entities** with lines or arcs, see Figures 3.27 and 3.28.

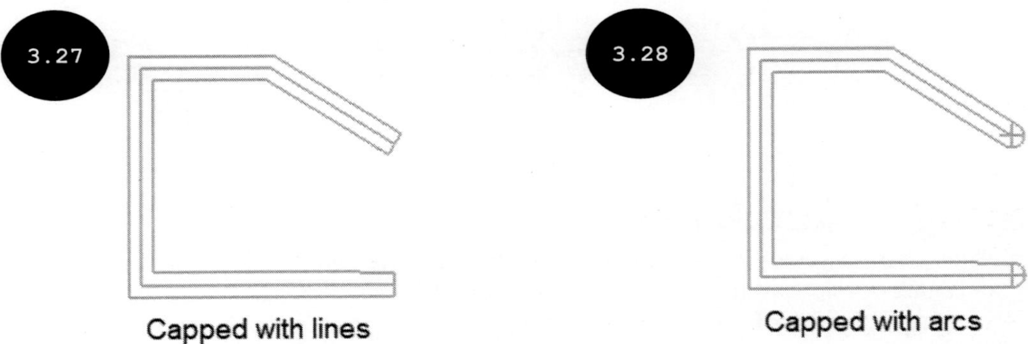

Capped with lines

Capped with arcs

By default, the **Open** radio button is selected in the **End caps** area. As a result, the open ends of the offset entities will not be capped and will remain open in the drawing area, see Figure 3.29. The **Flat** radio button is used for capping the open ends with lines, (whereas the **Circular** radio button is used for capping the open ends with arcs, refer to Figure 3.28.

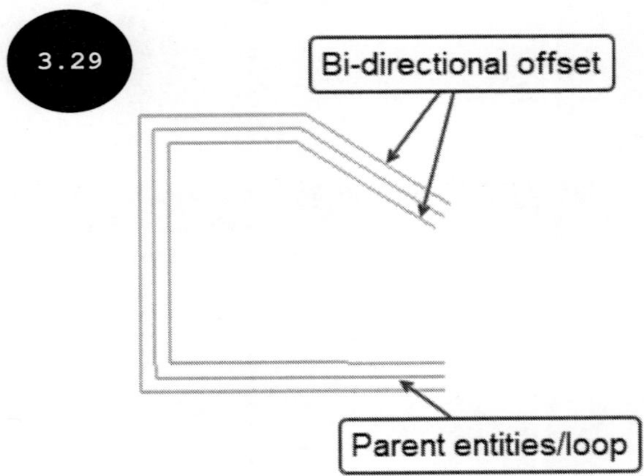

After selecting the required radio button in the **Select Thicken Edge** area and the **End caps** area of the **Type** window, click on an entity in the drawing area. Note that to offset a chain of entities, you need to select two entities to define the chain. As soon as you select an entity, the **Thickness Input** field appears at the top center of the drawing area. Enter the total thickness/offset distance value in this field (refer to Figure 3.30), and then press the middle mouse button. The **Offset Input** field appears. Enter the offset distance value in the direction of the arrow that appears in the drawing area, refer to Figure 3.30. Next, press the middle mouse button twice. The bi-directional offset entities are created at the specified offset distance.

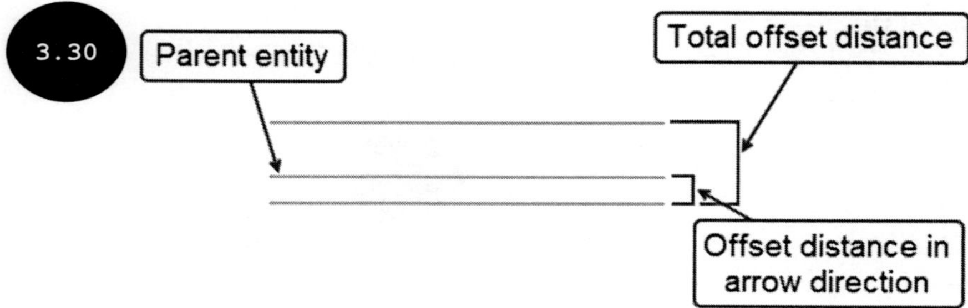

Creating a Sketch Fillet

A sketch fillet is used for removing the corner at the intersection of two sketch entities by creating a tangent circular arc or elliptical arc, see Figure 3.31. In Creo Parametric, you can create fillets by using the tools available in the **Fillet** flyout of the **Sketching** group, see Figure 3.32. The different tools for creating fillets are discussed next.

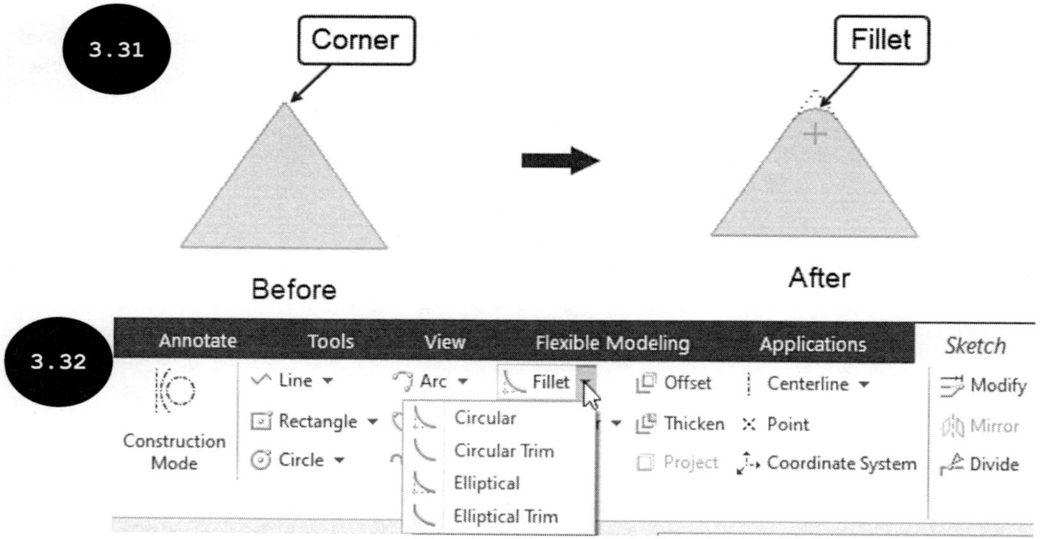

Circular Tool

The **Circular** tool is used for removing a corner at the intersection of two sketch entities by creating a tangent circular arc of constant radius with construction lines meeting at the intersection point, see Figure 3.33.

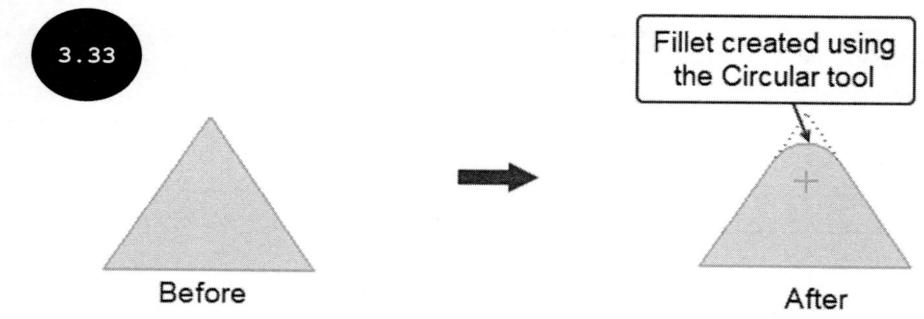

Note that you can also create a circular fillet between two non-parallel line entities that do not form a corner by using this tool, see Figure 3.34. The method for creating a fillet by using the **Circular** tool is discussed next.

1. Invoke the **Fillet** flyout and then click on the **Circular** tool, see Figure 3.35. You are prompted to select two entities.

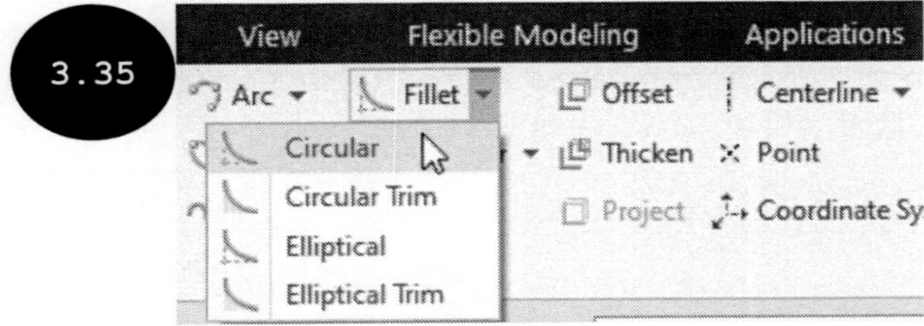

2. Select two entities in the drawing area one by one. As soon as you select entities, a circular fillet of default radius value gets applied between the selected entities, refer to Figure 3.36. Note that the **Circular** tool is still active.

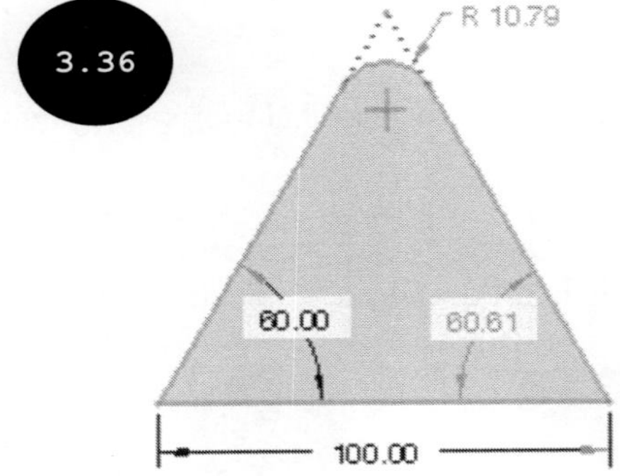

3. Similarly, you can click on other sets of entities one by one in the drawing area to create fillets.

4. After creating all the fillets, press the middle mouse button to exit the tool. Now, you can specify the fillet radius value as required by modifying the weak dimension.

Circular Trim Tool

Similar to creating a circular fillet by using the **Circular** tool, you can create a circular fillet by using the **Circular Trim** tool with the only difference that in the **Circular Trim** tool, the intersection point between the selected entities gets trimmed and is not represented by construction lines, see Figure 3.37.

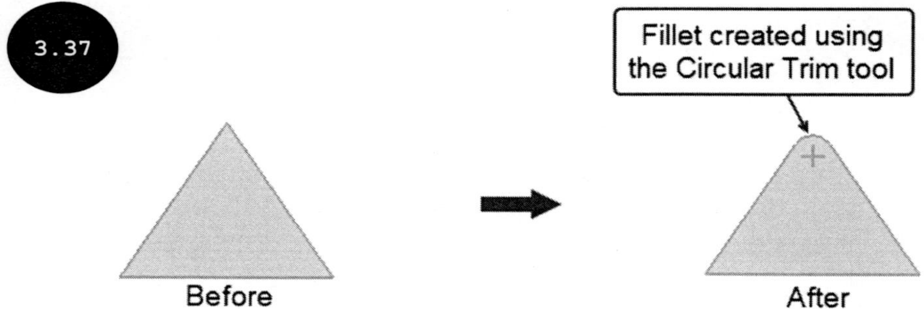

Elliptical Tool

The **Elliptical** tool is used for removing a corner at the intersection of two sketch entities by creating an elliptical arc with construction lines meeting at the intersection point, see Figure 3.38. The method for creating a fillet by using the **Elliptical** tool is discussed next.

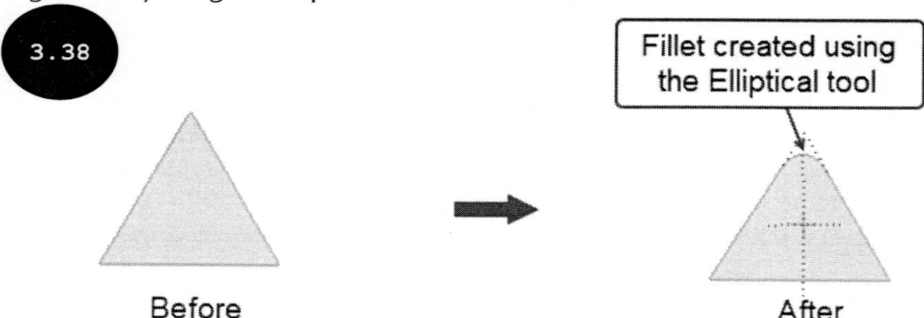

1. Invoke the **Fillet** flyout and then click on the **Elliptical** tool, see Figure 3.39. You are prompted to select two entities.

2. Select two entities in the drawing area one by one. As soon as you select entities, an elliptical fillet with default parameters gets applied between the selected entities, see Figure 3.40. Also, the **Elliptical** tool is still active.

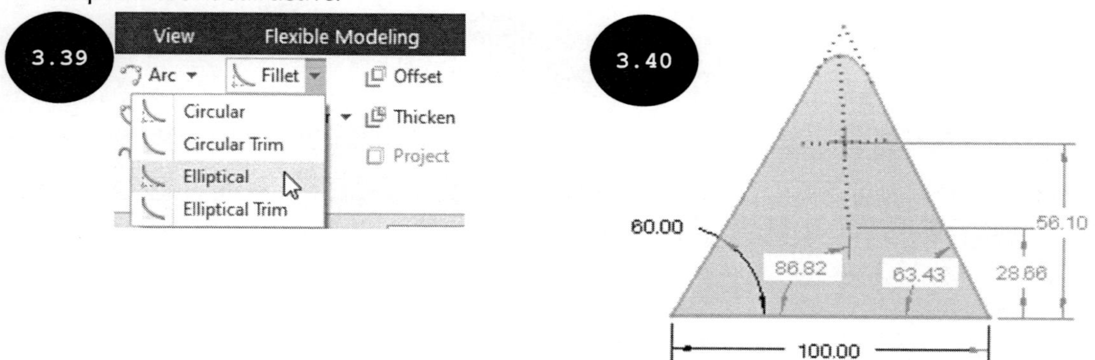

3. Similarly, you can click on a different set of entities one by one in the drawing area to create fillets.

4. After creating all the fillets, press the middle mouse button to exit the tool. Now, you can modify the weak dimensions (major and minor axes dimensions) of the elliptical fillets, as required.

Elliptical Trim Tool

Similar to creating an elliptical fillet by using the **Elliptical** tool, you can create an elliptical fillet by using the **Elliptical Trim** tool with the only difference that in the **Elliptical Trim** tool, the intersection point between the selected entities gets trimmed and is not represented by construction lines, see Figure 3.41.

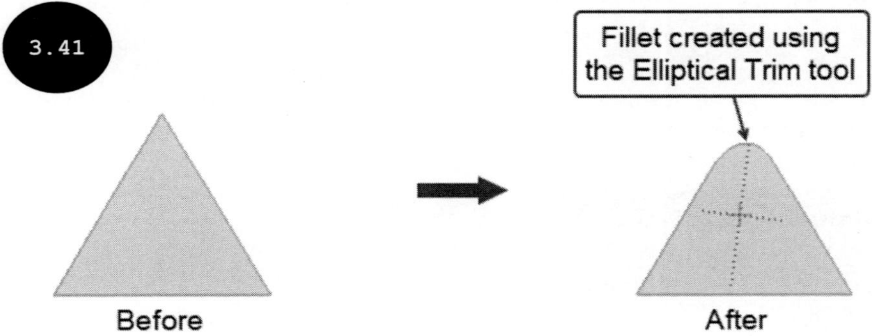

Creating a Sketch Chamfer

A chamfer is a beveled corner created at the intersection of any two non-parallel line entities, see Figure 3.42. In Creo Parametric, you can create a chamfer by using the **Chamfer** and **Chamfer Trim** tools. Both these tools are available in the **Chamfer** flyout of the **Sketching** group (see Figure 3.43) and are discussed next.

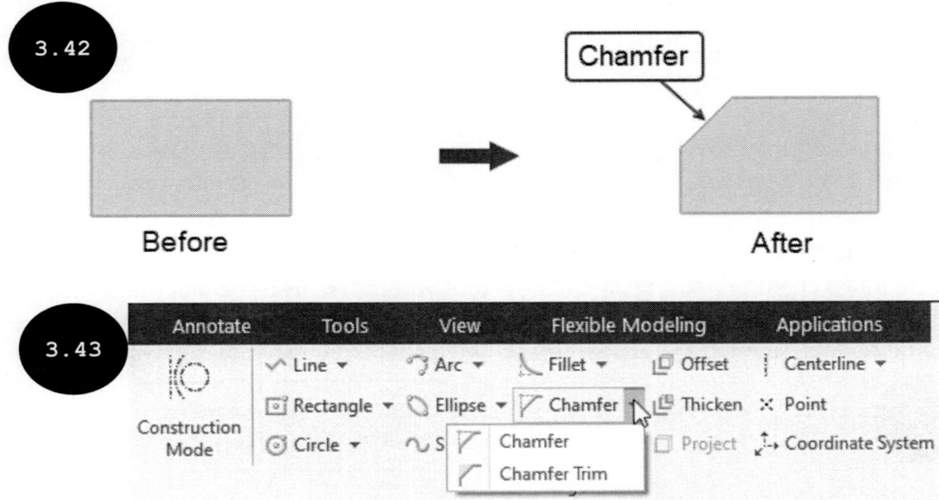

Chamfer Tool

The **Chamfer** tool is used for creating a beveled corner at the intersection of any two non-parallel line entities with construction lines meeting at the intersection point, see Figure 3.44. The method for creating a chamfer by using the **Chamfer** tool is discussed next.

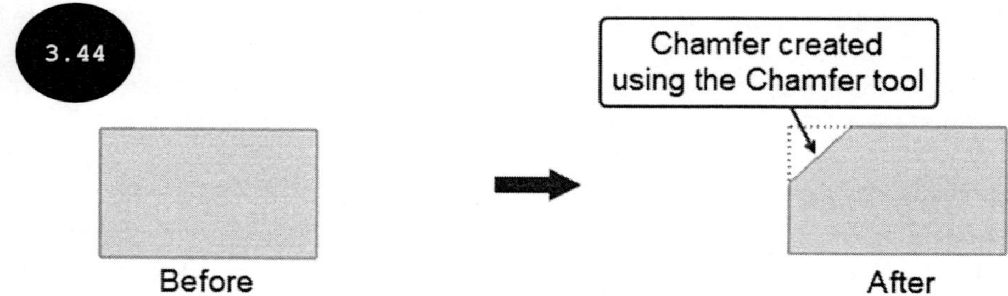

1. Invoke the **Chamfer** flyout in the **Sketching** group and then click on the **Chamfer** tool, see Figure 3.45. You are prompted to select two entities.

2. Select two entities in the drawing area one by one. As soon as you select the entities, a chamfer with default parameters gets created between the selected entities, see Figure 3.46. Also, the **Chamfer** tool is still active.

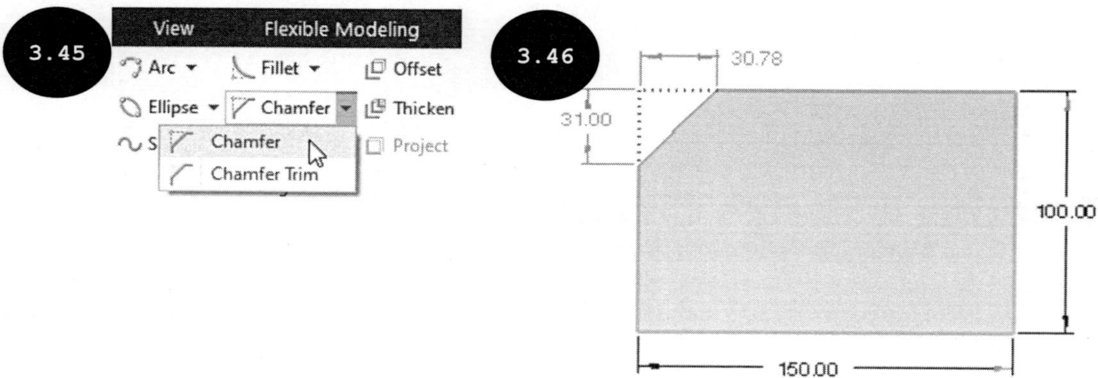

3. You can click on other sets of entities one by one in the drawing area to create chamfers in a similar manner.

4. After creating all the chamfers, press the middle mouse button to exit the tool. Now, you can specify the chamfer parameters by modifying the weak dimension, as required.

Chamfer Trim Tool

Similar to creating a chamfer by using the **Chamfer** tool, you can create a chamfer by using the **Chamfer Trim** tool with the only difference that in the **Chamfer Trim** tool, the intersection point between the selected entities gets trimmed and is not represented by construction lines, see Figure 3.47.

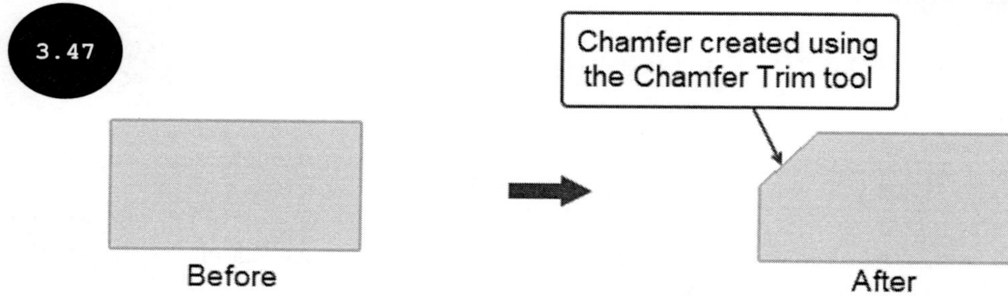

Inserting Text in Sketching Environment

In Creo Parametric, you can add text in the Sketching environment by using the **Text** tool of the **Sketching** group, see Figure 3.48.

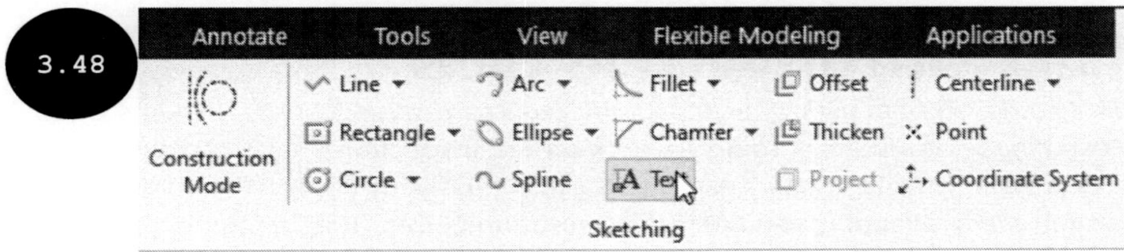

On clicking the **Text** tool, you are prompted to specify the start point of a line in the drawing area to determine the position of the text. Click in the drawing area where you want to place the text. A rubber band line gets attached to the cursor with one end fixed at the specified point, and you are prompted to specify the second point of the line to determine the text height and orientation. Click in the drawing area to specify the second point of the line such that the length of the line defines the text height and the angle defines the text orientation. As soon as you specify the second point, the **Text** dialog box appears, see Figure 3.49. You can type single-line text upto 79 characters in the **Enter text** field of the dialog box. You can also specify other parameters such as text font, text alignment, aspect ratio, slant angle, and spacing using the respective options of the dialog box.

In Creo Parametric, you can also insert symbols by clicking on the button available adjacent to the **Enter text** field, see Figure 3.49. On doing so, the **Text Symbol** dialog box appears, see Figure 3.50. In the **Text Symbol** dialog box, click on the required symbol to be inserted. The selected symbol gets inserted in the **Enter text** field of the **Text** dialog box as well as in the drawing area. After inserting the required symbols, click on the **Close** button in the **Text Symbol** dialog box to exit the dialog box.

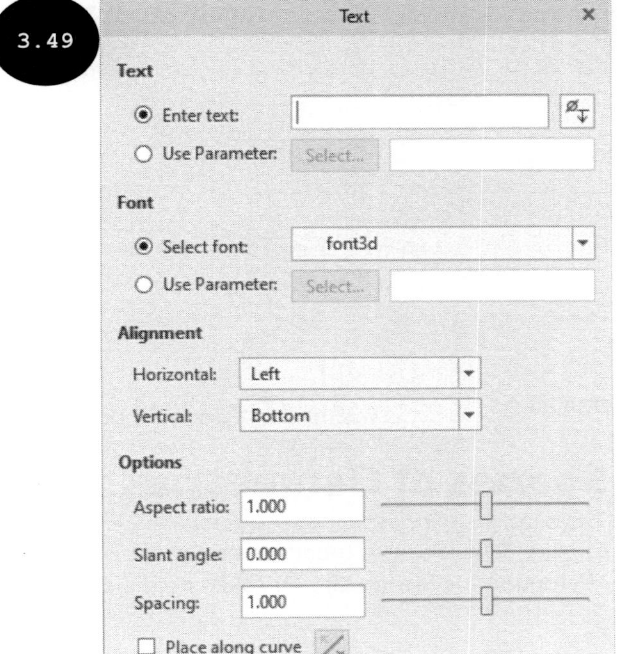

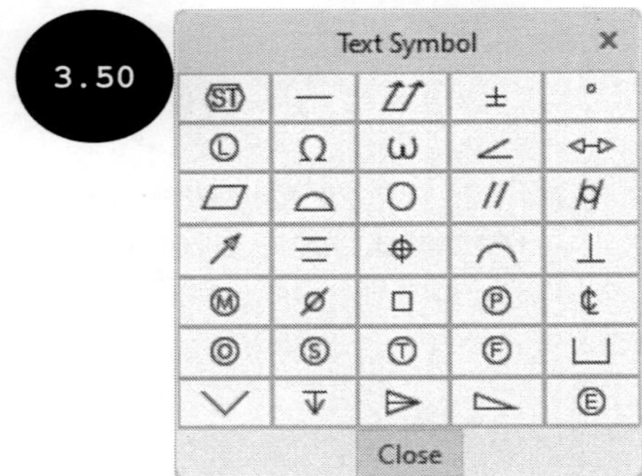

Note: Figure 3.49 shows the **Text** dialog box invoked in the Sketching environment of the Part mode.

Working with Inspection Tools

In Creo Parametric, you can highlight overlapping geometry, intersections, junctions, open ends, and shaded closed loops of a sketch. To do so, click on the **Inspection Tools Display Filters** tool in the **In-Graphics** toolbar. A flyout appears, see Figure 3.51. In this flyout, click on the respective check boxes for highlighting the overlapping geometries, intersection points, junction points, open ends, and/or shaded closed loops of the sketch, refer to Figure 3.52.

3.51

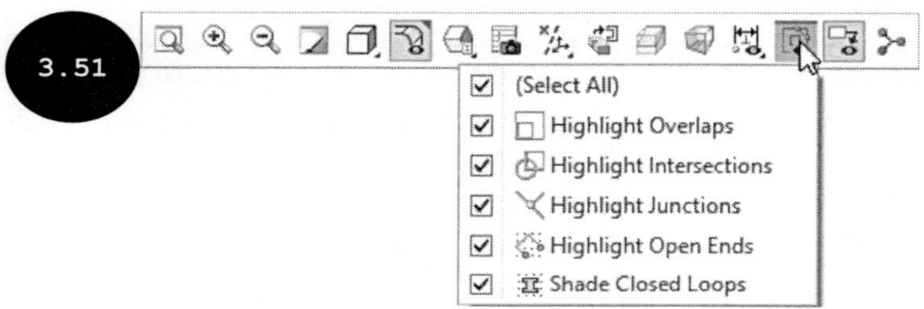

Figure 3.52 (a) shows highlighted overlap geometries, where an arc and a circle overlap each other. Figure 3.52 (b) shows highlighted intersection points, where a circle and a rectangle intersect each other. Figure 3.52 (c) shows highlighted junction points, where a circle, a rectangle, and a line meet each other. Figure 3.52 (d) shows highlighted open ends and Figure 3.52 (e) shows a highlighted shaded closed loop.

3.52

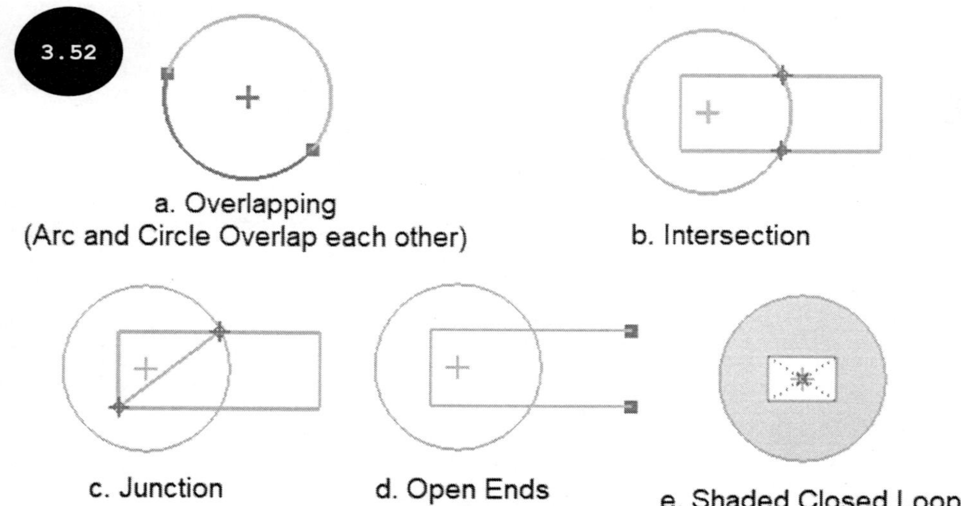

Inserting Pre-defined Shapes of Geometries

In Creo Parametric, you can insert pre-defined shapes of geometries such as polygons, stars, and profiles into the current Sketching environment by using the **Palette** tool of the **Insert** group, see Figure 3.53. To do so, click on the **Palette** tool in the **Insert** group of the **Sketch** tab. The **Sketcher Palette** dialog box appears, see Figure 3.54.

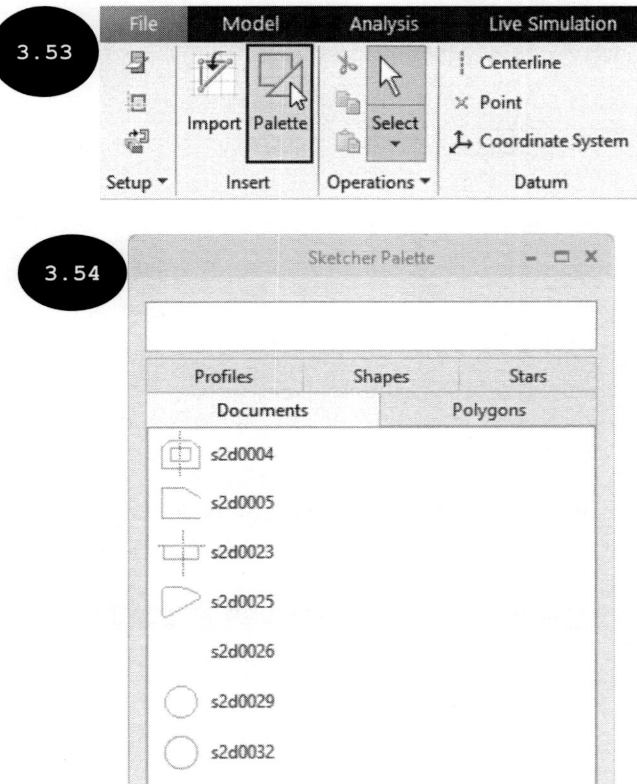

The **Sketcher Palette** dialog box contains four tabs: **Profiles, Shapes, Stars, Documents and Polygons**. These tabs contain different shapes of geometries. For example, the **Polygons** tab contains different polygon shapes of geometries and the **Stars** tab contains different star shapes of geometries. You can click on the required tab in this dialog box to display the respective shapes available in it.

Tip: In addition to the default pre-defined shapes of geometries, you can customize the **Sketcher Palette** dialog box to add user-defined shapes of geometries. To do so, create user-defined shapes of sketches in the Sketching environment and then save them in the current working directory one by one. Next, invoke the **Sketcher Palette** dialog box by clicking on the **Palette** tool in the **Insert** group of the **Sketch** tab. Notice that all the sketches that are saved in the current working directory appear in a separate tab of the **Sketcher Palette** dialog box. Note that the name of the tab is same as the name of the specified working directory folder.

Alternatively, you can also use existing sketches as user-defined shapes. To do so, go to the location *C:\Program Files\PTC\Creo 12.4.0.0\Common Files\text\sketcher_palette* of your system (see Figure 3.55), and then create a new folder with a name, as required in this location. Next, copy and paste the existing sketches to be used as user-defined shapes in the newly created folder. After doing so, when you invoke the **Sketcher Palette** dialog box in the **Sketching** environment of Creo Parametric, a new tab with the user-defined shapes appears in it. Note that the name of the new tab in the **Sketcher Palette** dialog box is the name of the folder created in the *C:\Program Files\PTC\Creo 12\Common Files\text\sketcher_palette* location.

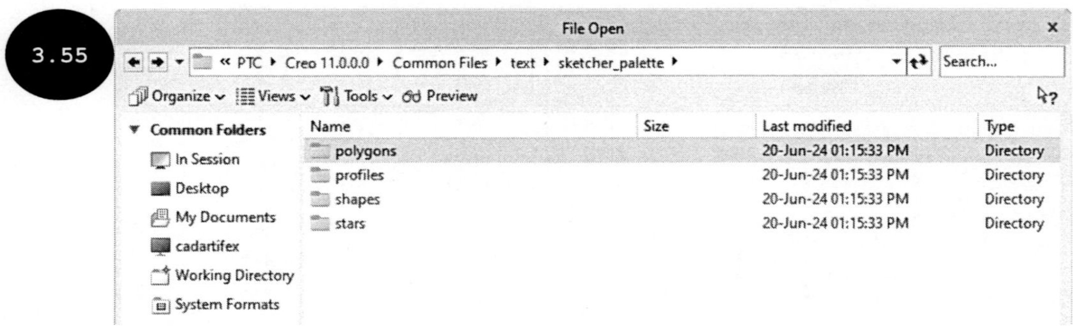

To insert a pre-defined shape of geometry into the current Sketching environment, drag and drop it into the Sketching environment from the **Sketcher Palette** dialog box. As soon as you drag and drop a pre-defined shape of geometry, the **Import Section** tab appears in the **Ribbon**, see Figure 3.56. Also, the move, rotate, and scale handles appear with the inserted shape in the Sketching environment, see Figure 3.57. You can move, rotate, and scale the inserted pre-defined shape by using these handles or by using the options available in the **Import Section** tab of the **Ribbon**. Next, press the middle mouse button to place the inserted pre-defined shape in the Sketching environment.

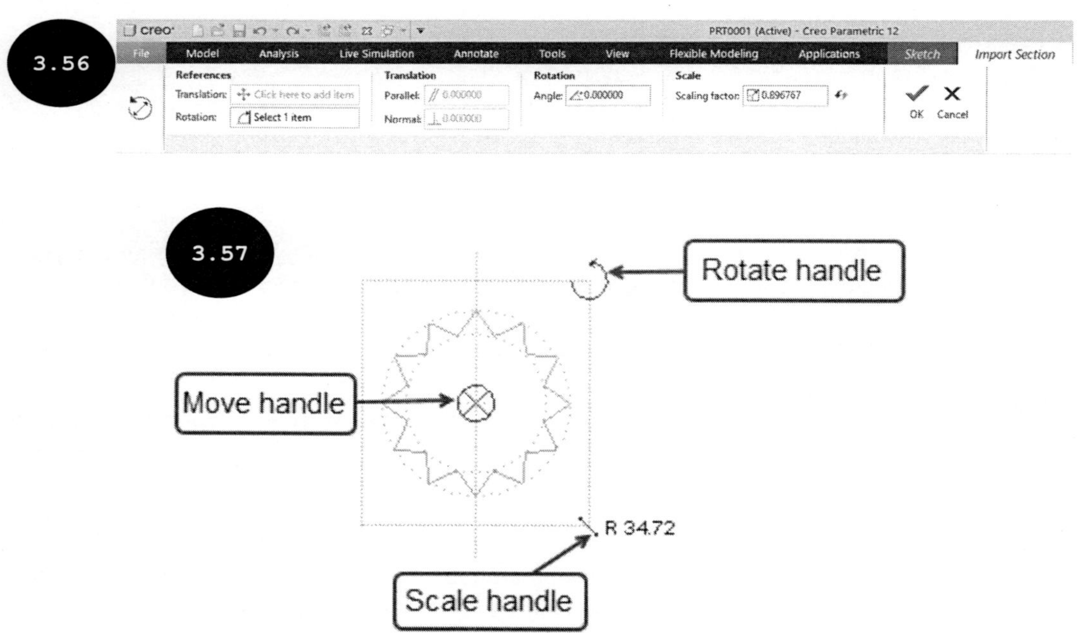

Alternatively, to insert a pre-defined shape of geometry into the Sketching environment, double-click on a pre-defined shape in the **Sketcher Palette** dialog box and then click in the drawing area. The selected pre-defined shape of geometry appears in the drawing area with the move, rotate, and scale handles. You can use these handles to move, rotate, and scale the geometry. Next, press the middle mouse button to place the geometry in the Sketching environment.

Inserting a Sketch or a Drawing File

In addition to inserting pre-defined shapes of geometries such as polygons, stars, and profiles, you can also insert an existing sketch (*.sec*) or a drawing (*.drw*) file into the current Sketching environment. To do so, click on the **Import** tool in the **Insert** group of the **Sketch** tab, see Figure 3.58. The **Open** dialog box appears, see Figure 3.59.

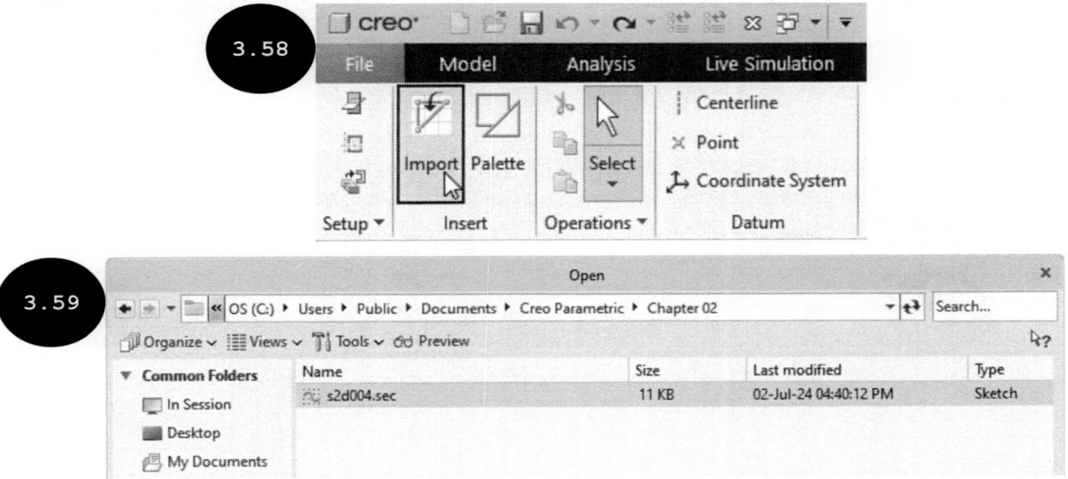

Browse to the location where the required file to be opened is saved and then select the required file type [*Drawing (*.drw), Sketch (*.sec), IGES (.igs, .iges), DXF (*.dxf), DWG (*.dwg), or Adobe Illustrator (*.ai)*] from the **Type** drop-down list of the dialog box. For example, to open a sketch, which is created in Creo Parametric, you need to select the **Sketch (*.sec)** file type in the **Type** drop-down list. Similarly, to open an AutoCAD drawing, you need to select the **DWG (*.dwg)** file type in the **Type** drop-down list. Next, select the file to be opened in the dialog box and then click on the **Open** button. Next, click on the drawing area to specify the placement point for the selected file. The selected file appears in the drawing area with move, rotate, and scale handles. These handles can be used to perform the desired functions. Also, the **Import Section** tab appears in the **Ribbon**. Next, press the middle mouse button to confirm the placement of the file in the Sketching environment.

Tutorial 1

Draw the sketch shown in Figure 3.60. All dimensions are in mm.

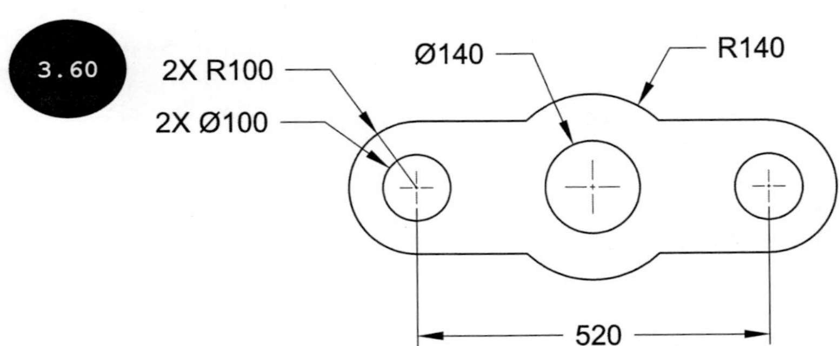

Section 1: Starting Creo Parametric

1. Start Creo Parametric by double-clicking on the Creo Parametric icon on your desktop.

Section 2: Setting the Working Directory

After starting Creo Parametric, you need to set up a working directory to save the files of the current session of Creo Parametric. You can set any folder created in a local drive of your system as the working directory. However, it is recommended to create a folder with the name "*Chapter 3*" inside the "*Creo Parametric*" folder in the local drive of your system. If the "*Creo Parametric*" folder is not already created in the earlier chapter then you need to create this folder.

1. Click on **File > Manage Session > Select Working Directory**, see Figure 3.61. The **Select Working Directory** window appears. In this window, browse to the *Creo Parametric > Chapter 3* location of your system. You need to create these folders, if not already created earlier.

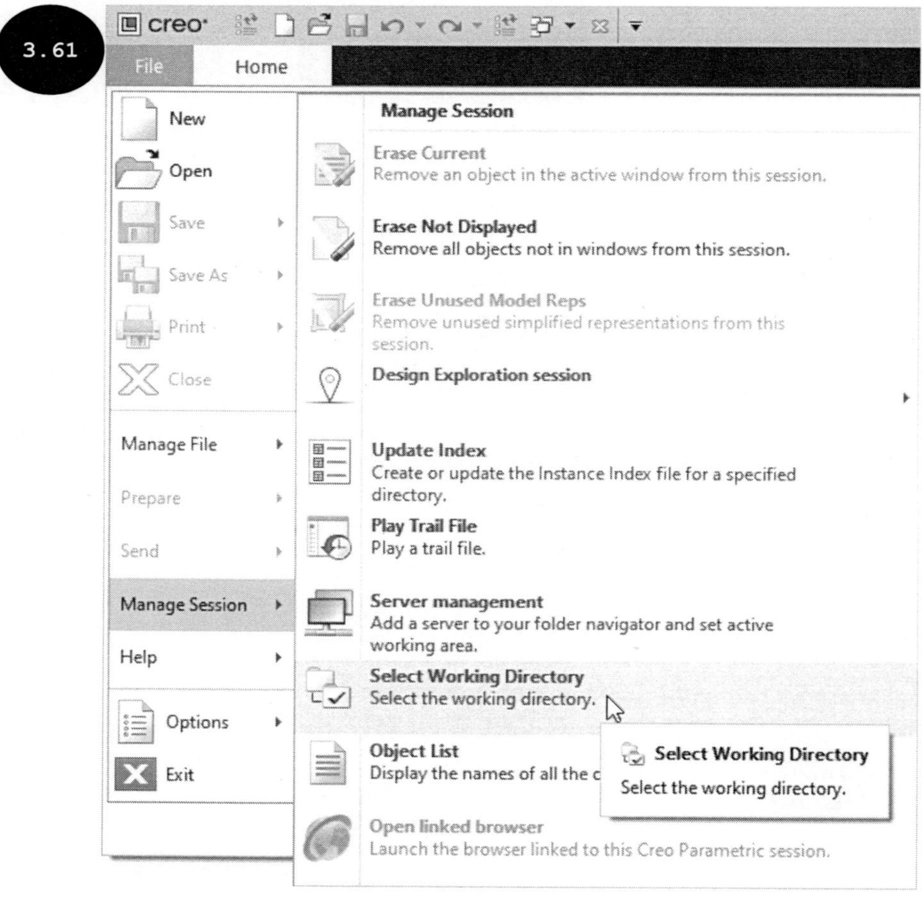

2. Click on the **OK** button to set the working directory to <<*Creo Parametric\Chapter 3*\.

Section 3: Invoking the Sketching Environment

Now, you need to invoke the Sketching environment of the Sketch mode for creating the sketch.

1. Click on the **New** tool in the **Data** group of the **Home** tab. The **New** dialog box appears, see Figure 3.62.

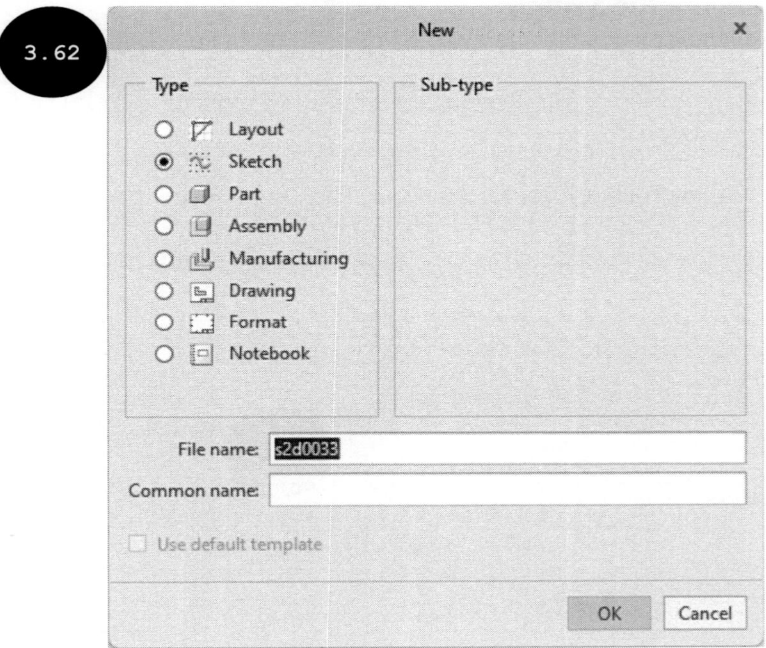

2. Select the **Sketch** radio button in the **Type** area of the dialog box and then enter **Tutorial01** in the **File name** field as the name of the sketch.

3. Click on the **OK** button in the dialog box. The Sketching environment of the Sketch mode is invoked and the initial screen of the Sketching environment appears as shown in Figure 3.63.

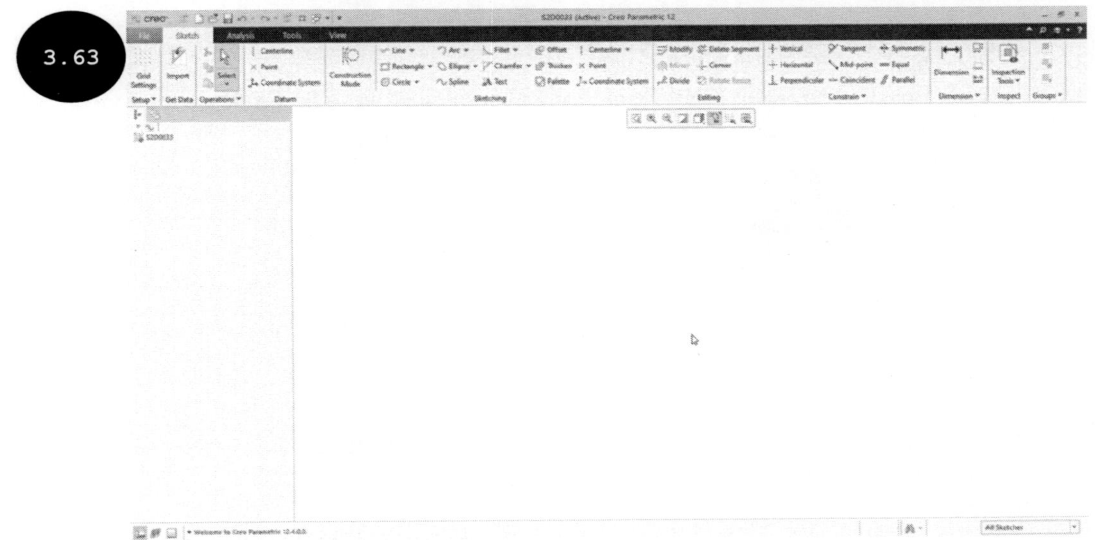

Note: In this textbook, the background color of the drawing area has been set to white for clarity of images. The method for changing the background color is discussed in Chapter 1.

Section 4: Drawing the Sketch

Once the Sketching environment is invoked, you need to start drawing the sketch.

1. Click on the arrow next to the Rectangle tool in the **Sketching** group. The **Rectangle** flyout appears, see Figure 3.64.

2. Click on the **Center Rectangle** tool in the flyout. The **Center Rectangle** tool gets activated.

3. Click anywhere in the drawing area to specify the center point of the rectangle.

4. Move the cursor away from the specified center point and then click to specify a corner of the rectangle in the drawing area, see Figure 3.65. The rectangle is drawn and the **Center Rectangle** tool is still active.

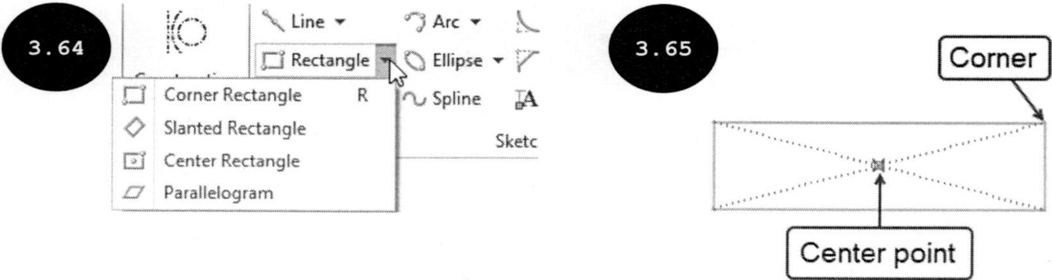

5. Press the middle mouse button to exit the tool. Weak dimensions are applied automatically to the rectangle.

   Now, you need to create circles in the sketch.

6. Click on the arrow next to the **Circle** tool in the **Sketching** group. The **Circle** flyout appears, see Figure 3.66. In this flyout, click on the **Center and Point** tool.

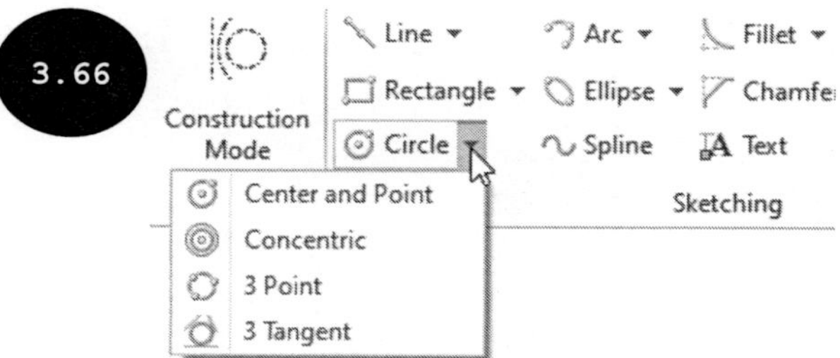

7. Move the cursor to the center point of the rectangle and then click to specify the center point of the circle when the cursor snaps to it, see Figure 3.67.

8. Move the cursor away from the specified center point and then click to specify a point outside the rectangle in the drawing area, see Figure 3.68. The circle is drawn and the **Center and Point** tool is still active. After creating the circle, do not exit the tool.

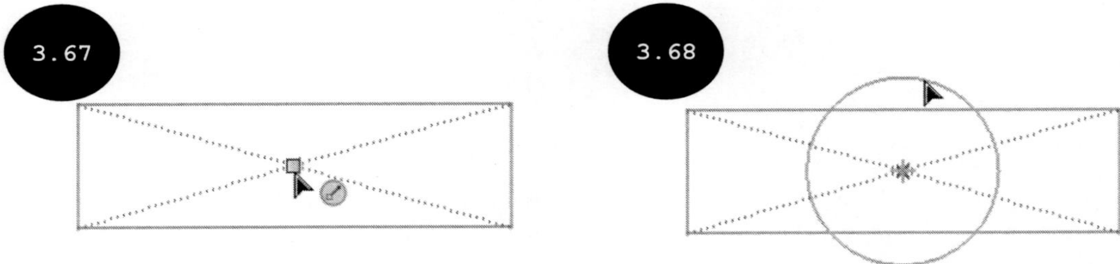

9. Create three more circles as per the method described above, see Figure 3.69. In this figure, the circles are numbered for your reference only.

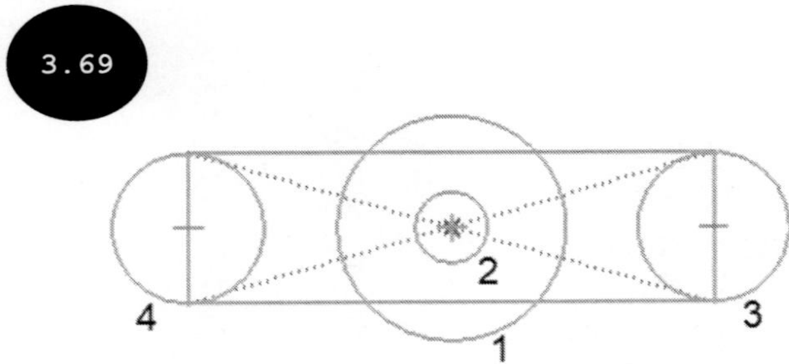

10. After creating the circles, press the middle mouse button to exit the **Center and Point** tool. Weak dimensions are applied automatically to the sketch.

Section 5: Trimming Sketch Entities

Now, you need to trim the unwanted entities of the sketch.

1. Click on the **Delete Segment** tool in the **Editing** group, see Figure 3.70. You are prompted to select entities to be trimmed.

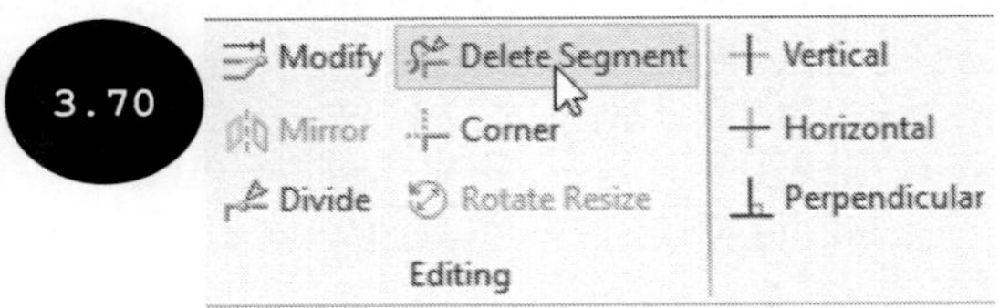

2. Move the cursor over the portion of the lower horizontal line of the rectangle which lies inside the circle, see Figure 3.71.

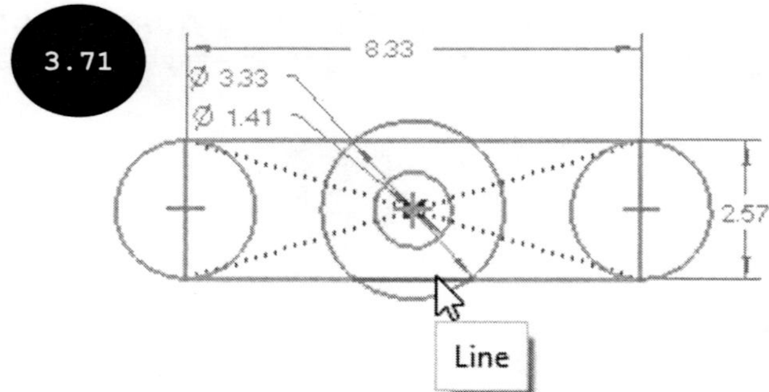

3. Click the left mouse button when the entity is highlighted in the drawing area, see Figure 3.71. The selected portion of the entity is trimmed, see Figure 3.72.

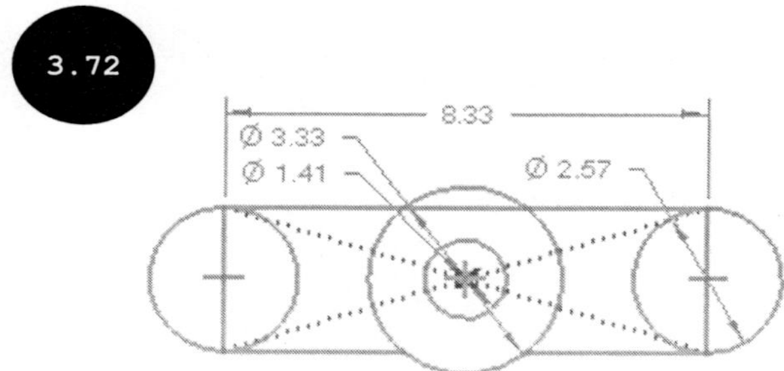

4. Similarly, click on the other unwanted entities of the sketch one by one to trim them. Figure 3.73 shows the sketch after trimming all the unwanted entities. Note that you may need to zoom into the sketch while trimming the unwanted entities by scrolling up or down the middle mouse button.

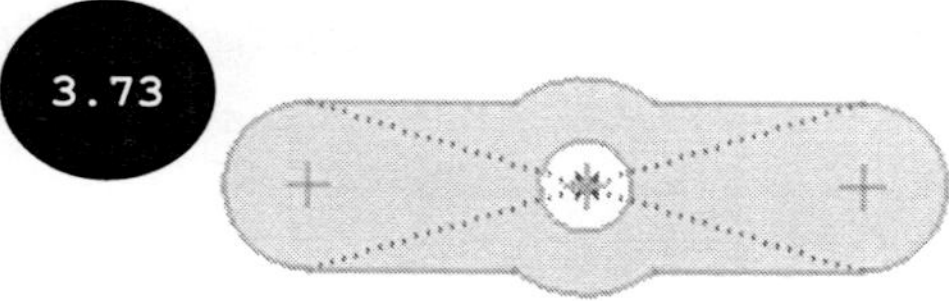

Note: In Figure 3.73, the display of weak dimensions and constraints are turned off for clarity of image. To turn off the weak dimensions, click on **File > Options** to invoke the **Creo Parametric Options** dialog box. Next, click on the **Sketcher** option on the left panel of the dialog box and then clear the **Show weak dimensions** check box in the **Object display settings** area of the dialog box. Next, click on the **OK** button. The **Creo Parametric Options** window appears. In this window, click on the **No** button to restrict the change only to the current session of Creo Parametric.

To turn off the display of constraints, click on the **Sketcher Display Filters** tool in the **In-graphics** toolbar. A flyout appears, see Figure 3.74. In this flyout, clear the **Constraints Display** check box. The **Dimensions Display** check box of this flyout is used for turning on or off the display of dimensions in the drawing area.

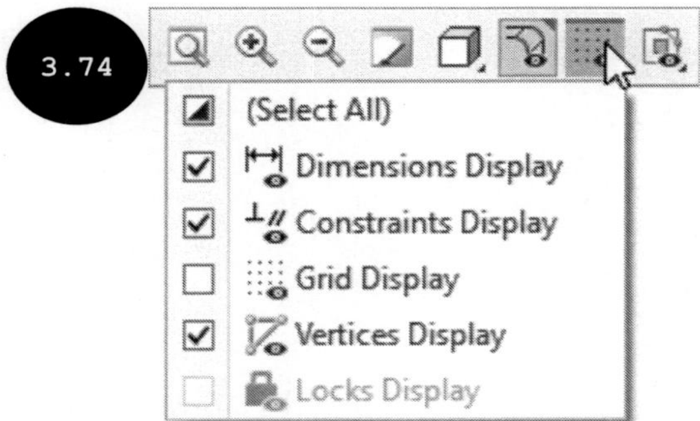

Section 6: Deleting Reference Entities

Now, you need to delete the reference entities of the sketch.

1. Press the CTRL key and then click on the reference entities of the sketch one by one, see Figure 3.75. Next, press the DELETE key. Figure 3.76 shows the sketch after deleting the reference entities of the sketch.

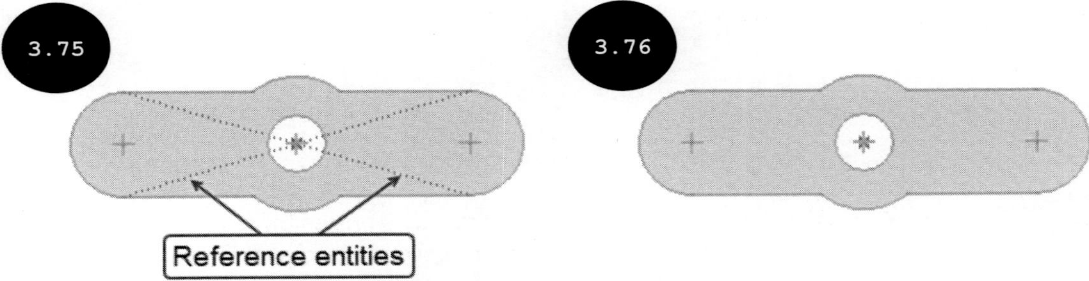

Section 7: Creating Remaining Circles

Now, you need to create the remaining circles of the sketch.

1. Invoke the **Circle** flyout (see Figure 3.77), and then click on the **Concentric** tool.

2. Move the cursor toward the right arc of the sketch and then click on it when it gets highlighted, see Figure 3.78. The preview of a circle concentric to the selected arc appears attached to the cursor.

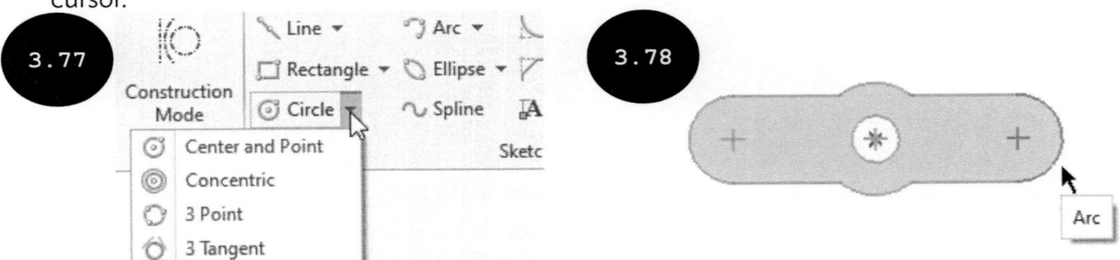

3. Click to specify a point inside the arc. A circle concentric to the arc is drawn, see Figure 3.79. Also, the preview of another concentric circle appears attached to the cursor. Next, press the middle mouse button to terminate the creation of a concentric circle. Note that the **Concentric** tool is still active.

3.79

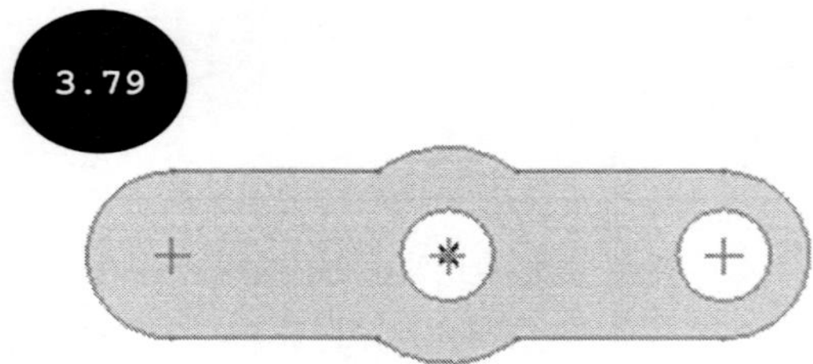

4. Similarly, draw another circle that is concentric to the left arc of the sketch, see Figure 3.80. Next, press the middle mouse button twice to exit the tool.

3.80

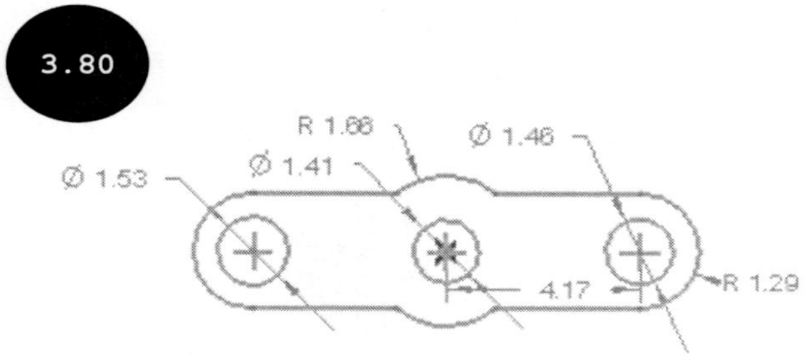

Note: In Figure 3.80, the shaded display style of the sketch is turned off for clarity of image. To turn on or off the shaded display style of the sketch, click on the **Shade Closed Loops** tool in the **Inspect** group of the **Sketch** tab, see Figure 3.81. Also, the display of constraints is turned off in the figure. The method to turn on or off the display of constraints has been discussed earlier.

3.81

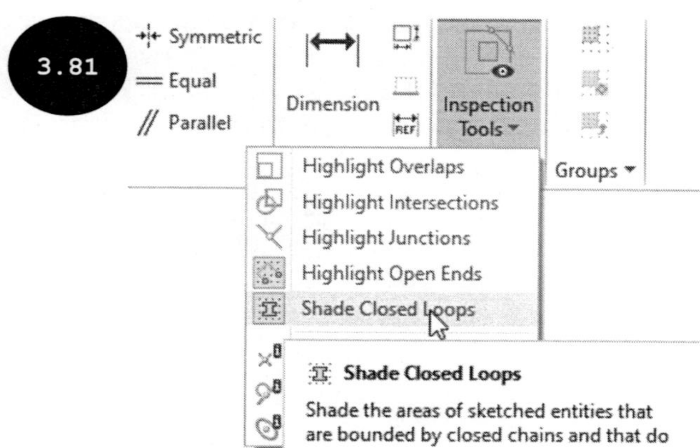

Section 8: Applying Constraints

1. Ensure that an equal constraint is applied between the left and right circles of the sketch. You can apply an equal constraint by using the **Equal** tool of the **Constrain** group.

Section 9: Applying Dimensions

Now, you need to apply dimensions to the sketch. You can apply dimensions by using the **Dimension** tool. You can also modify the weak dimensions of the sketch to convert them into strong dimensions. In this section, you will modify the weak dimensions of the sketch.

1. Select all the weak dimensions of the sketch by drawing a window around the dimensions. You can draw a window by dragging the cursor.

2. Click on the **Modify** tool in the **Editing** group, see Figure 3.82. The **Modify Dimensions** dialog box appears with a list of all the selected dimensions.

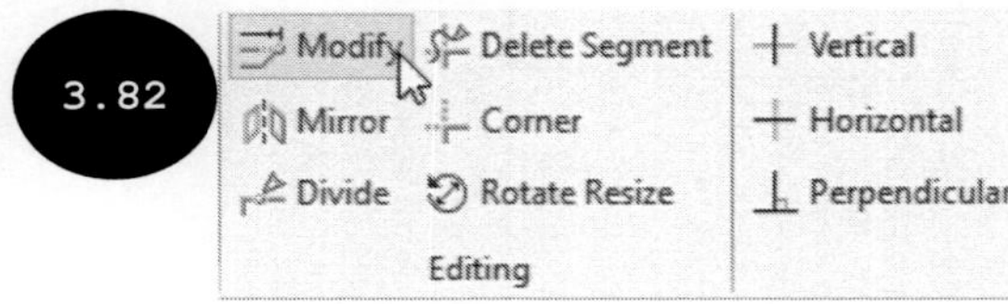

3. Clear the **Regenerate** check box in the **Modify Dimensions** dialog box so that the modifications made in the dimension values are not reflected in the sketch until you exit the dialog box.

4. Change the values of all the dimensions one by one by entering the new value in the respective edit fields of the **Modify Dimensions** dialog box. You can refer to Figure 3.60 for dimension values. Note that when you click on an edit field in this dialog box to enter a new value, the respective dimension gets highlighted in the drawing area.

5. After entering new dimension values for all the dimensions, click on the **OK** button. All the dimensions get updated with new dimension values and are converted to strong dimensions in the drawing area. Next, click anywhere in the drawing area. Figure 3.83 shows the final sketch after modifying all the dimensions.

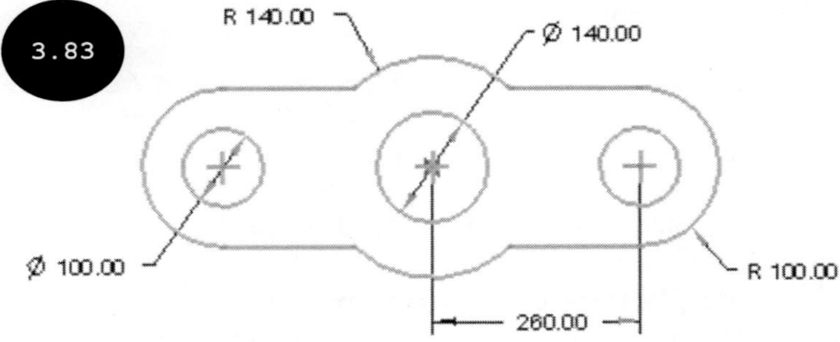

Section 10: Saving the Sketch

Now, you need to save the sketch.

1. Click on the **Save** tool in the **Quick Access Toolbar**. The **Save Object** dialog box appears.

2. Click on the **OK** button. The sketch is saved in the specified working directory. Note that the sketches created in the Sketching environment of Creo Parametric are saved with *.SEC* file extension.

Tutorial 2

Draw a sketch of the revolved feature shown in Figure 3.84. The 3D model shown in the figure is for your reference only. You will learn about creating 3D models in later chapters. All dimensions are in mm.

3.84

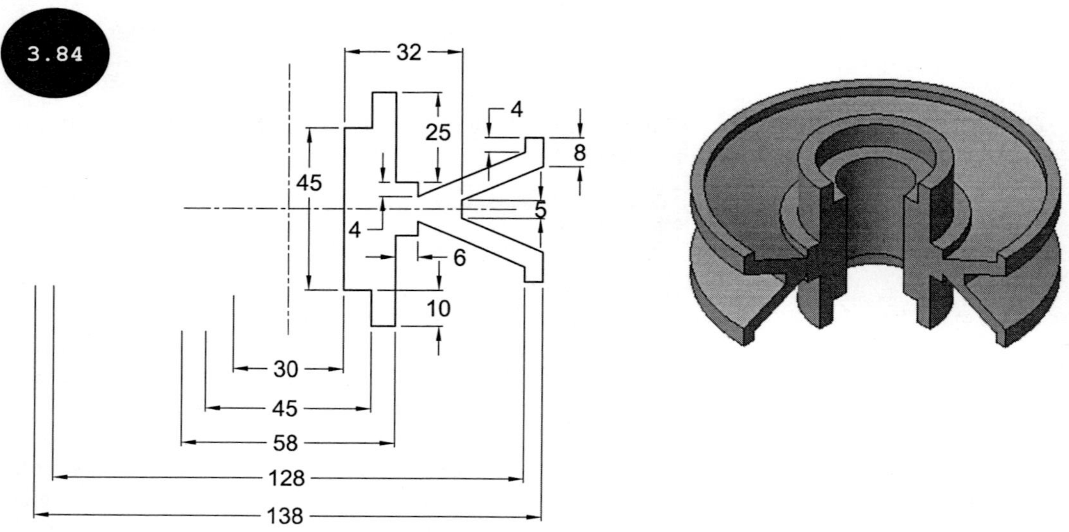

Section 1: Starting Creo Parametric

1. Start Creo Parametric by double-clicking on the Creo Parametric icon on your desktop.

Section 2: Setting the Working Directory

After starting Creo Parametric, you need to set up a working directory to save the files of the current session of Creo Parametric.

1. Click on **File > Manage Session > Select Working Directory**. The **Select Working Directory** window appears. In this window, browse to the *Creo Parametric > Chapter 3* location of your system. You need to create these folders, if not already created earlier.

2. Click on the **OK** button to set the working directory to <<*Creo Parametric**Chapter 3*\\.

Section 3: Invoking the Sketching Environment

Now, you need to invoke the Sketching environment of the Sketch mode for creating the sketch.

1. Click on the **New** tool in the **Data** group of the **Home** tab. The **New** dialog box appears.

2. Select the **Sketch** radio button in the **Type** area of the **New** dialog box to invoke the Sketching environment of the Sketch mode, see Figure 3.85.

3. Enter **Tutorial02** in the **File name** field of the dialog box as the name of the sketch, see Figure 3.85.

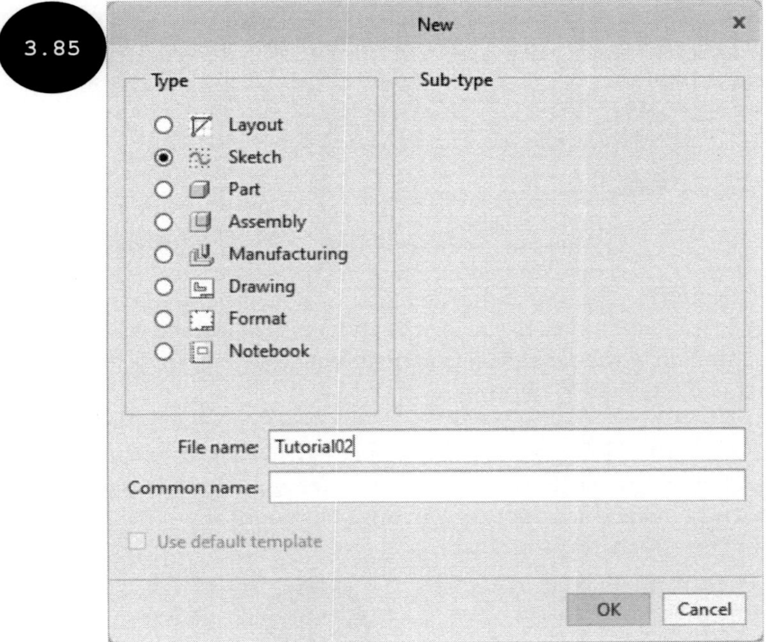

3.85

4. Click on the **OK** button in the dialog box. The Sketching environment of the Sketch mode is invoked and the initial screen of the Sketching environment appears.

Section 4: Drawing the Upper Half of the Sketch

Once the Sketching environment is invoked, you need to start drawing the sketch. In this section, you need to draw the upper half of the sketch.

1. Click on the **Centerline** tool in the **Sketching** group of the **Sketch** tab, see Figure 3.86. The **Centerline** tool gets activated.

2. Draw a vertical and a horizontal centerline in the drawing area one by one, see Figure 3.87. Next, press the middle mouse button to exit the **Centerline** tool.

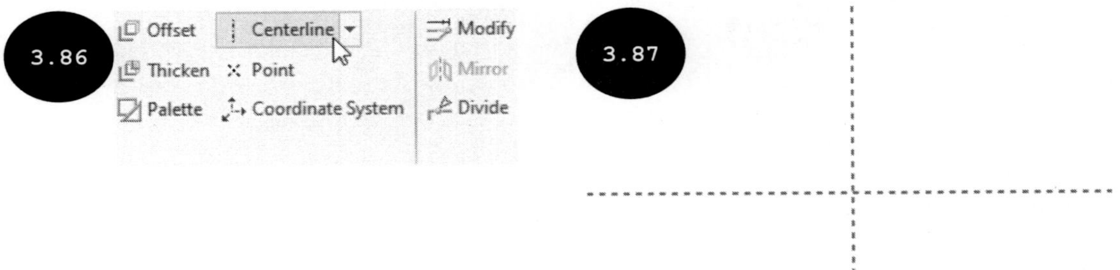

3.86

3.87

3. Click on the arrow next to the **Line** tool in the **Sketching** group. The **Line** flyout appears, see Figure 3.88. Next, click on the **Line Chain** tool in the flyout to activate it. Alternatively, press the **L** key to activate this tool.

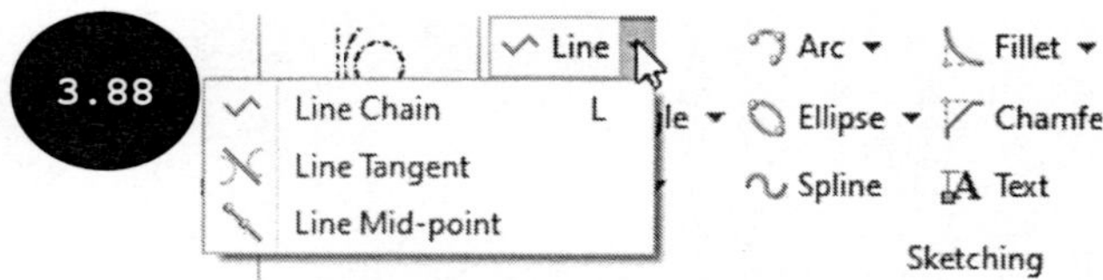

4. Move the cursor over the horizontal centerline at a distance from the vertical centerline (see Figure 3.89), and then click to specify the start point of the line when the cursor snaps to the horizontal centerline. A rubber band line appears with one of its ends fixed at the specified point and the other end attached to the cursor.

5. Move the cursor vertically upward to a distance and then click to specify the endpoint of the line when the symbol of vertical constraint appears near the cursor, see Figure 3.90. A vertical line is drawn. Also, a rubber band line appears with one of its ends fixed at the previously specified point and the other end attached to the cursor.

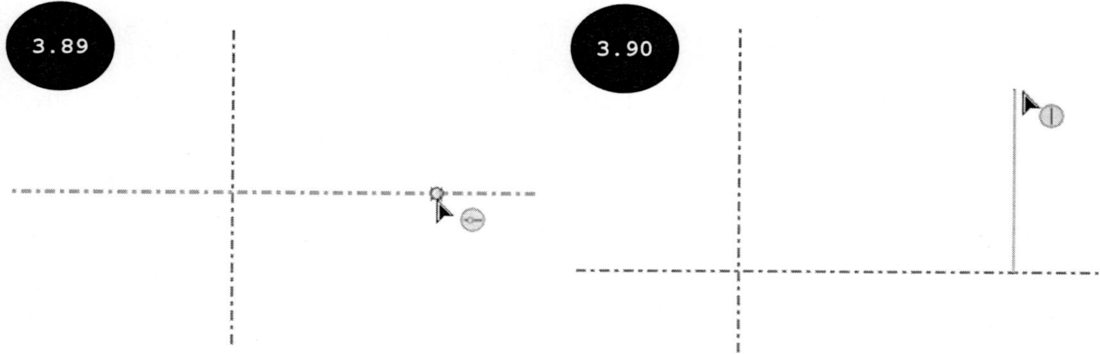

6. Move the cursor horizontally right to a distance and then click to specify the endpoint of the line when the symbol of horizontal constraint appears near the cursor, see Figure 3.91.

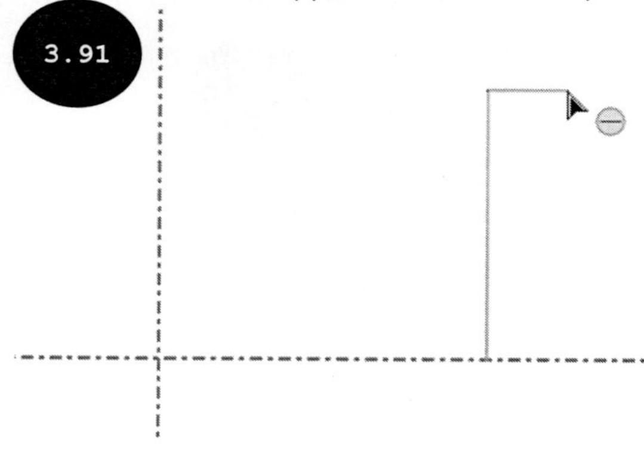

7. Similarly, create the other line entities of the upper half of the sketch by specifying the endpoints of the lines. Figure 3.92 shows the upper half of the sketch after creating all its entities. Next, press the middle mouse button to exit the **Line Chain** tool.

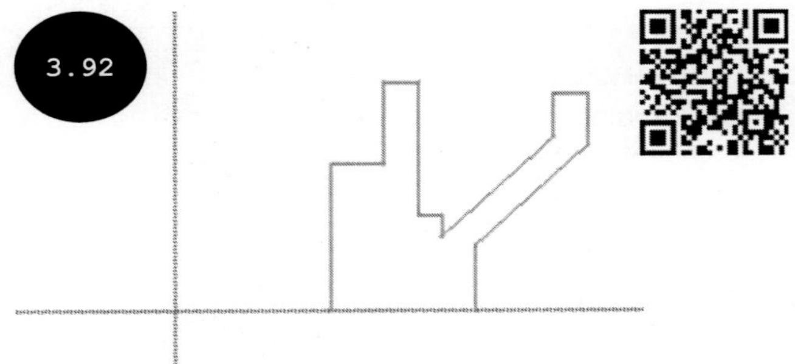

Note: While drawing the sketch, ensure that equal constraints are not automatically applied between the entities of the sketch.

Section 5: Mirroring Sketch Entities

After creating the upper half of the sketch, you need to mirror it to create the lower half.

1. Select all the entities of the sketch by drawing a window around them. You can draw a window around the entities to be selected by dragging the cursor.

2. Click on the **Mirror** tool in the **Editing** group. You are prompted to select a straight sketch entity.

3. Click on the horizontal centerline as the mirroring line. The lower half of the sketch is created, see Figure 3.93. In this figure, the display of constraints is turned off for clarity of image.

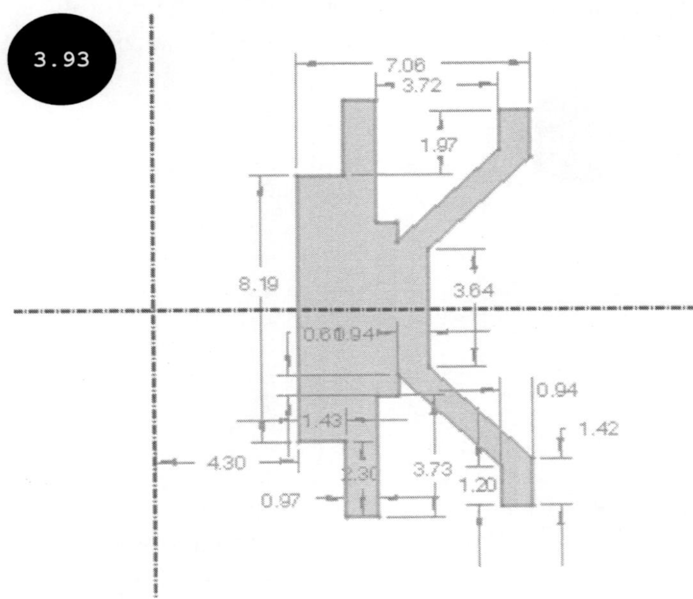

Note: As the sketch entities are drawn by specifying arbitrary points in the drawing area, you will find differences in the weak dimension values in this case.

Section 6: Applying Dimensions

Now, you need to apply dimensions to the sketch. You need to first apply linear diameter dimensions to the sketch and then modify the dimension values.

1. Click on the **Dimension** tool in the **Dimension** group of the **Sketch** tab.

2. Click to select the leftmost vertical line of the sketch, see Figure 3.94. Next, click on the vertical centerline and then click on the previously selected vertical line again. Next, press the middle mouse button in the drawing area. An edit field appears with a display of the current linear diameter dimension value. Do not modify the current dimension value at this moment.

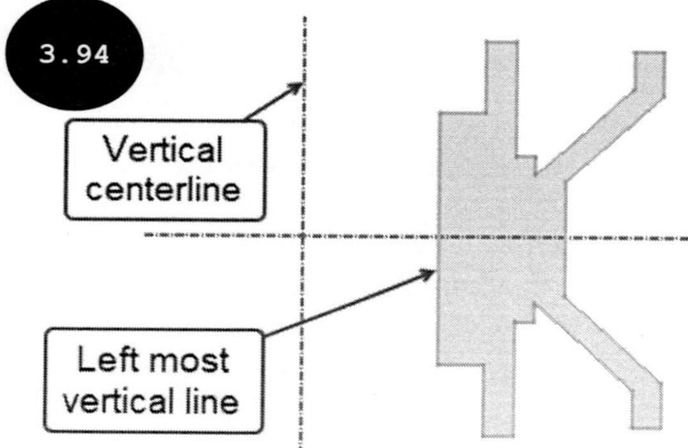

3. Press the ENTER key to accept the current dimension value. The linear diameter dimension is applied with the current dimension value, see Figure 3.95. Note that the value of the applied linear diameter dimension will be different in your case. You will modify the dimension values later in this tutorial.

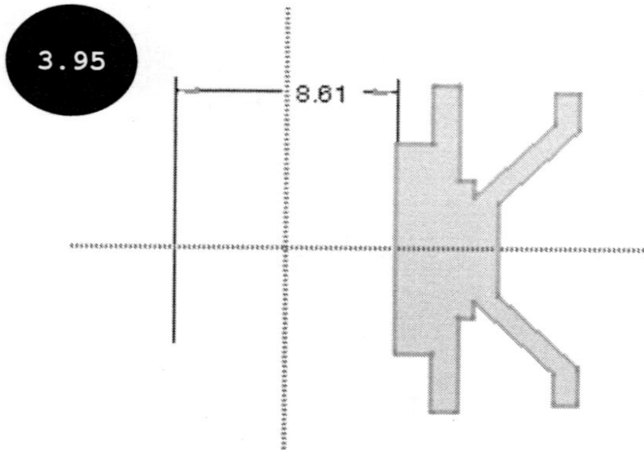

Note: In Figures 3.94 and 3.95, the constraints and weak dimensions are turned off. The method to turn on or off the constraints and weak dimensions has already been discussed earlier.

4. Apply the remaining linear diameter dimensions with their current dimension values in a similar manner, see Figure 3.96. In this figure, the display of weak dimensions is turned off. Also, the values of the applied dimensions will be different in your case. After applying the linear diameter dimensions, press the ESC key to exit the **Dimension** tool.

3.96

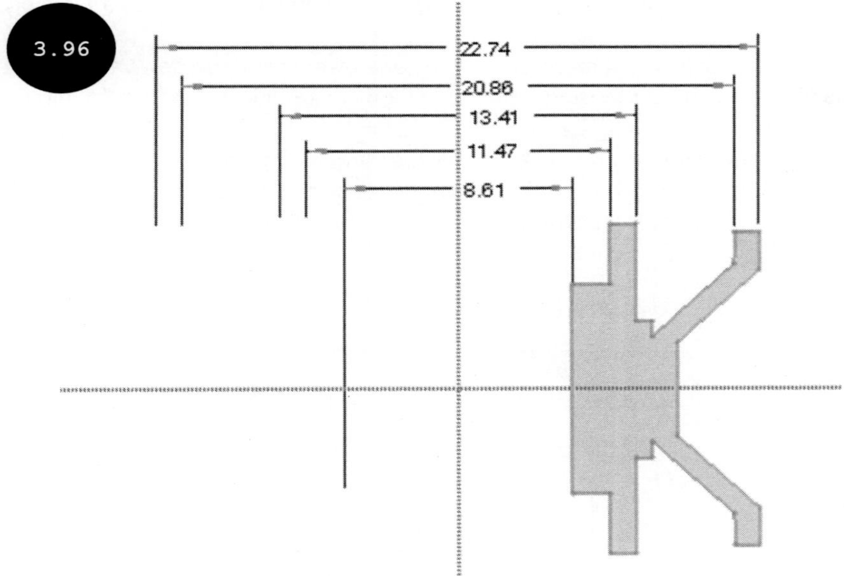

Note: While applying the linear diameter dimensions, if the **Resolve Sketch** dialog box appears, you need to delete the equal constraint to resolve the sketch, see Figure 3.97.

3.97

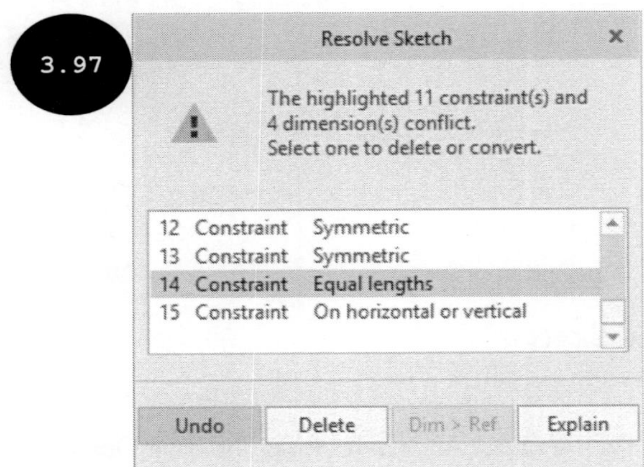

Section 7: Modifying Dimensions

Now, you need to modify the linear diameter dimensions and the weak dimensions.

1. Select all the dimensions of the sketch including the weak dimensions by drawing a window around them. You can draw a window to select dimensions by dragging the cursor.

2. After selecting all the dimensions, click on the **Modify** tool in the **Editing** group. The **Modify Dimensions** dialog box appears.

3. Clear the **Regenerate** check box in the **Modify Dimensions** dialog box so that the modifications made in the dimension values are not reflected in the sketch until you exit the dialog box.

4. Change the values of all the dimensions one by one by entering the new values in the respective edit fields of the **Modify Dimensions** dialog box. You can refer to Figure 3.84 for dimension values.

5. After entering new dimension values for all the dimensions, click on the **OK** button. All the dimensions get updated with new dimension values and are converted to strong dimensions in the drawing area. Next, click anywhere in the drawing area. Figure 3.98 shows the final sketch after modification of all the dimensions.

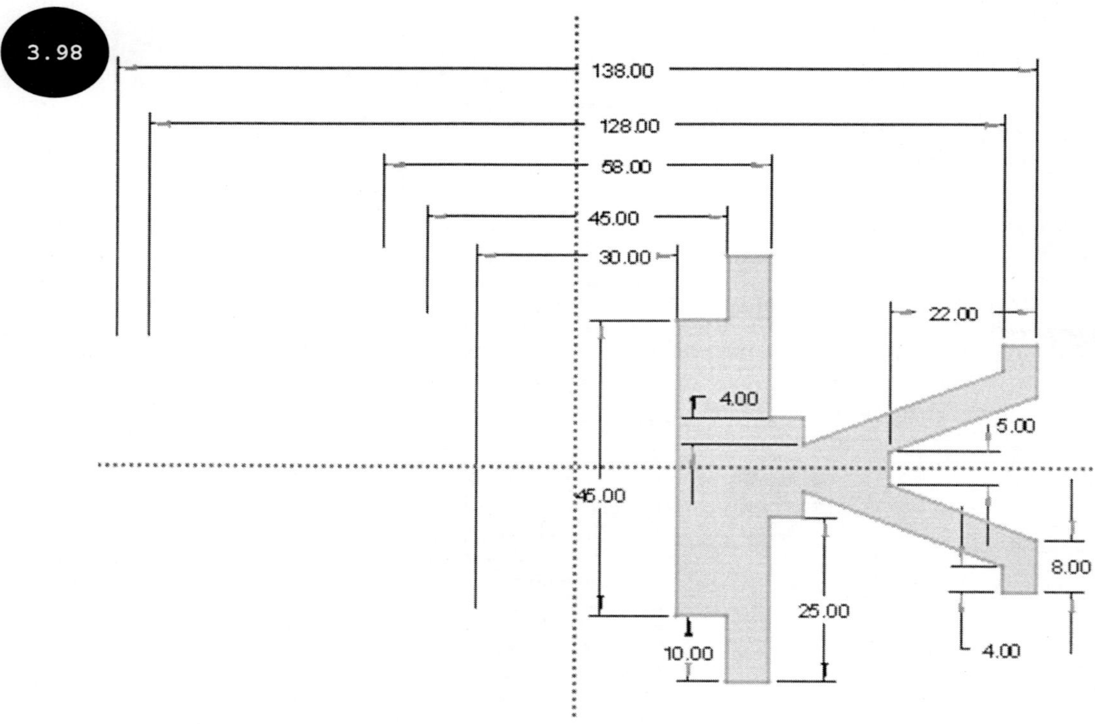

Section 8: Saving the Sketch

Now, you need to save the sketch.

1. Click on the **Save** tool in the **Quick Access Toolbar**. The **Save Object** dialog box appears.

2. Click on the **OK** button. The sketch is saved in the specified working directory.

Hands-on Test Drive 1

Draw the sketch shown in Figure 3.99. All dimensions are in mm.

3.99

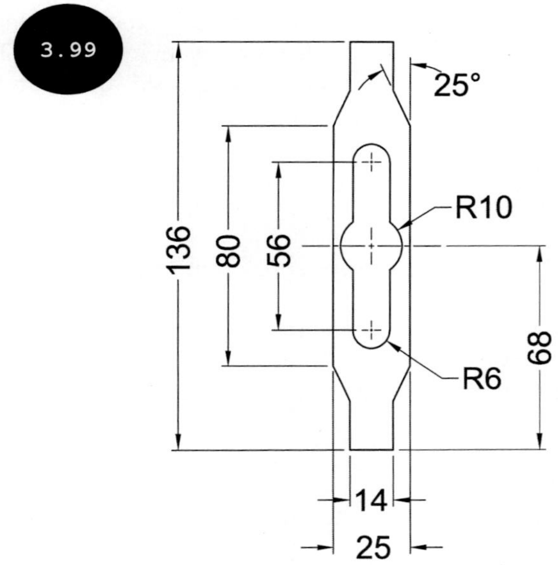

Hands-on Test Drive 2

Draw the sketch shown in Figure 3.100. All dimensions are in mm.

3.100

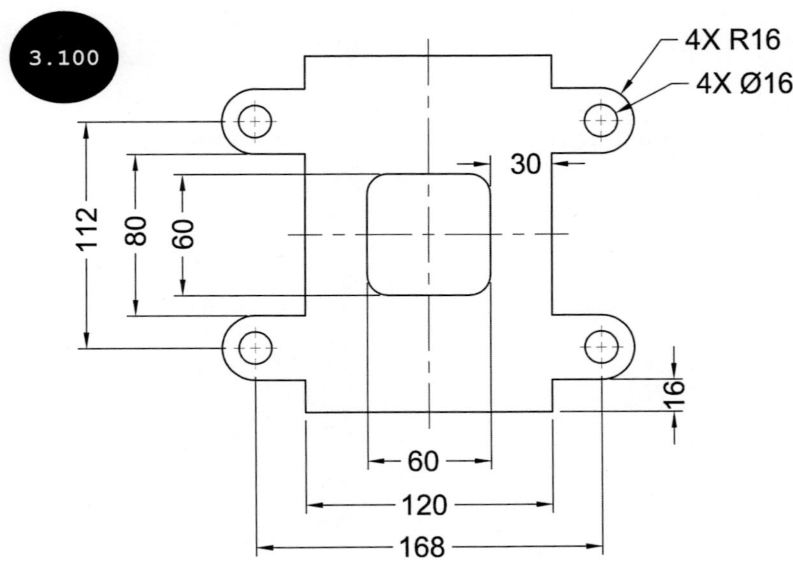

Summary

In this chapter, you have learned about editing and modifying sketch entities by using various editing tools such as **Delete Segment**, **Corner**, **Divide**, **Rotate Resize**, **Mirror**, **Offset**, **Fillet**, and **Chamfer**. You have also learned how to insert pre-defined shapes of geometries in the Sketching environment by using the **Palette** tool, how to insert text in the Sketching environment by using the **Text** tool, and how to insert a sketch or a drawing file in the Sketching environment by using the **Import** tool.

Questions

Complete and verify the following sentences:

- The _________ tool is used for trimming the unwanted entities of a sketch.
- The _________ tool is used for creating a corner between two entities of a sketch.
- You can divide an entity into multiple segments by using the _______ tool.
- You can move, rotate, and scale entities by using the _______ tool.
- You can offset sketch entities or edges of an existing feature at a specified offset distance by using the _______ tool.
- The _______ tool is used for offsetting entities (single, chain, or loop) bi-directionally.
- The _______ tool is used for inserting pre-defined shapes of geometries such as polygons, stars, and profiles into the current Sketching environment.
- You can customize the **Sketcher Palette** dialog box to add user-defined shapes of geometries. (True/False)
- You cannot insert an existing sketch (.sec) or a drawing (.drw) file into the current Sketching environment. (True/False)

CHAPTER
4

Creating Base Feature of a Solid Model

In this chapter, the following topics will be discussed:

- Creating an Extrude Feature
- Creating a Revolve Feature
- Navigating a 3D Model in Graphics Window
- Manipulating View Orientation of a Model
- Changing the Display Style of a Model

Once a sketch has been created and fully defined by applying proper constraints and dimensions, you can convert the sketch into a solid feature by using the feature modeling tools. All the feature modeling tools are available in the **Model** tab of the **Ribbon** in the Part mode, see Figure 4.1.

4.1

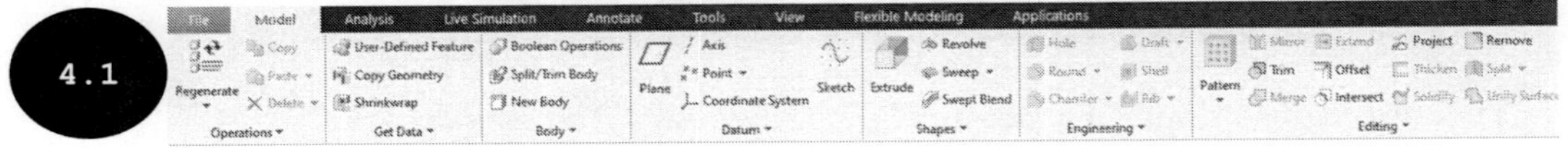

Note that the tools in the **Engineering** and **Editing** groups of the **Model** tab are not enabled, initially. These tools are enabled after creating the base feature of a model. The base feature of a model is also known as the first feature or the parent feature of a model. In Creo Parametric, you can create the base feature by using the **Extrude**, **Revolve**, **Sweep**, **Helical Sweep**, or **Swept Blend** tools available in the **Shapes** group of the **Model** tab. You will learn about creating features using the **Sweep**, **Helical Sweep**, and **Swept Blend** tools in the later chapters. In this chapter, you will learn about creating a base feature by using the **Extrude** and **Revolve** tools.

Creating an Extrude Feature

An extrude feature is created by adding or removing material normal to the sketching plane. In Creo Parametric, you can create an extrude feature by using the **Extrude** tool. Note that the sketch of the extruded feature defines its geometry. Figure 4.2 shows different extruded features created by adding material in the respective sketches.

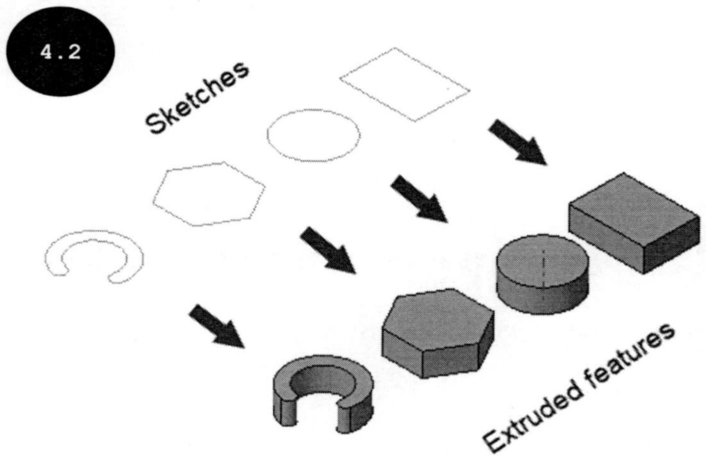

After creating a sketch by using the sketching tools in the Sketching environment of the Part mode, click on the **OK** button (green tick-mark) in the **Close** group of the **Sketch** tab, see Figure 4.3. The Part modeling environment is invoked and the sketch created in the Sketching environment appears in the graphics window. Note that the method for invoking the Sketching environment within the Part mode has been discussed in Chapter 2.

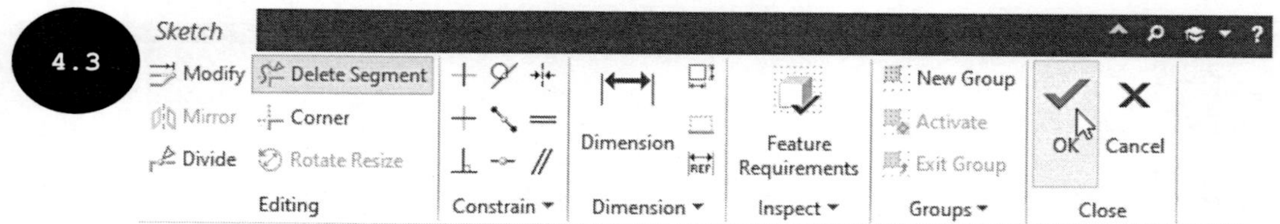

In the Part modeling environment, click on the **Extrude** tool in the **Shapes** group of the **Model** tab. The **Extrude** tab appears in the **Ribbon**, see Figure 4.4. Also, you are prompted to select either a sketch to be extruded or a sketching plane to create the sketch. Select the sketch to be extruded in the graphics window. A preview of the extrude feature appears, see Figures 4.5 and 4.6.

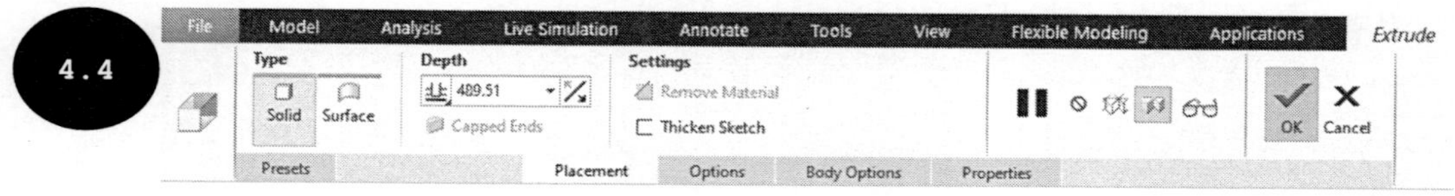

Figure 4.5 shows a rectangular sketch created on the Top Plane in the Sketching environment of the Part mode and Figure 4.6 shows a preview of the resultant extrude feature.

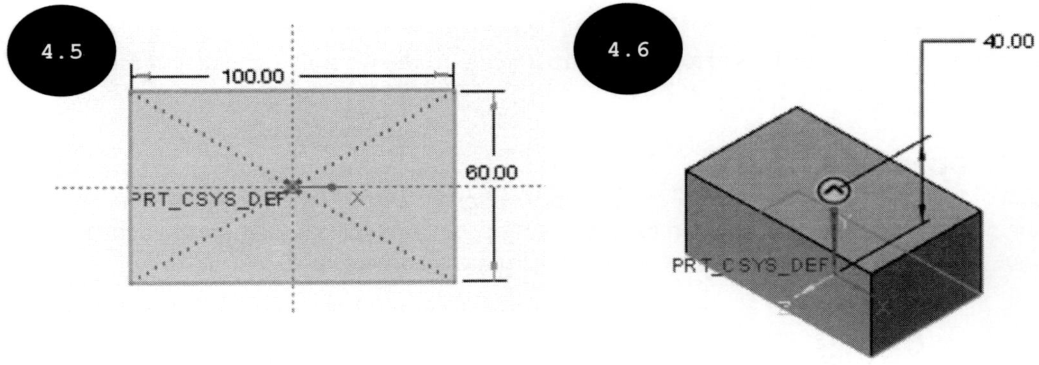

Note: You can select the sketch to be extruded before or after invoking the **Extrude** tool. If the sketch is selected before invoking the **Extrude** tool, then the sketch gets selected automatically and the preview of the extrude feature appears in the graphics window.

The options in the **Extrude** tab of the **Ribbon** are discussed below.

Placement Tab

By default, the **Placement** tab is activated and the **Placement** panel appears within the **Extrude** tab, see Figure 4.7. As a result, you can directly select a sketch to be extruded or a sketching plane for creating the sketch. In this panel, the **Sketch** field is used for selecting a sketch to be extruded, while the **Define** button is used for invoking the **Sketch** dialog box to define the sketching plane for creating the sketch. Note that as soon as you select a sketch, its name appears in the **Sketch** field of the **Placement** panel. Also, the **Define** button changes to the **Unlink** button. The **Unlink** button is used to break the link/association between the selected sketch and the feature and creates a copy of the sketch as an internal sketch of the feature.

Extrude as solid

The **Extrude as solid** button of the **Extrude** tab is used for creating a solid extrude feature by adding material to the sketch. By default, this button is activated. As a result, a preview of the solid extrude feature appears in the graphics area after selecting the sketch.

Extrude as surface

The **Extrude as surface** button is used for creating a surface extrude feature. Note that a surface feature has zero thickness and no mass properties.

Side 1 Drop-down list

The **Side 1** drop-down list is used for selecting a depth option for extruding the feature on side 1 of the sketching plane, see Figure 4.8. You can invoke this drop-down list by clicking on the active depth option, see Figure 4.8. The options in this drop-down list are discussed next.

4.8

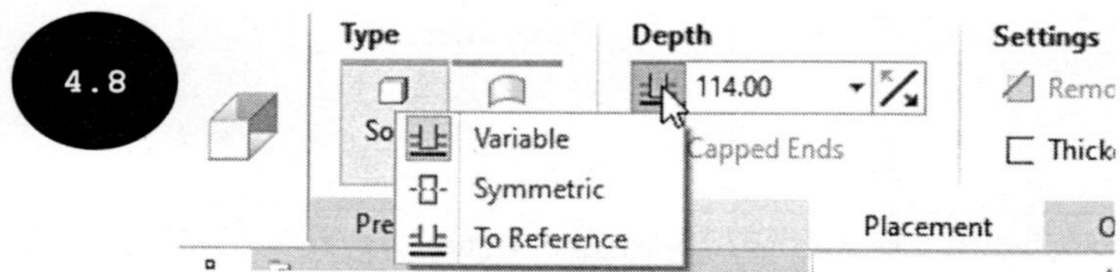

Note: You can also define the depth options for extruding the feature on side 1 and side 2 of the sketching plane by using the options in the **Options** tab of the **Extrude** tab. The **Options** tab is discussed later in this section.

Variable

The **Variable** option of the **Side 1** drop-down list is used for specifying the depth of the extrude feature by entering the depth value in the **Value** field of the **Extrude** tab, see Figure 4.9. You can also drag the handle available in the preview of the extrude feature to define the depth of the extrusion in the graphics window.

4.9

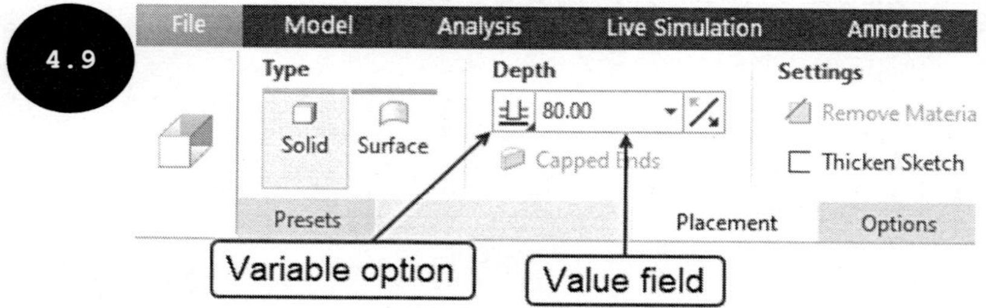

Symmetric

The **Symmetric** option of the **Side 1** drop-down list is used for extruding the feature symmetrically about the sketching plane, see Figure 4.10. After selecting this option, you can enter the depth value of extrusion in the **Value** field. Note that the depth value specified in the **Value** field is divided equally and creates a symmetrical extrusion on both sides of the sketching plane. For example, if the specified depth value is 36 mm then the resultant feature is created by adding 18 mm of material on each side (side 1 and side 2) of the sketching plane.

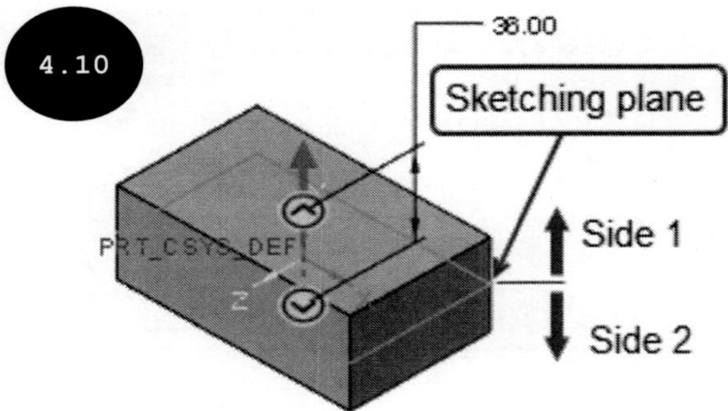

Note: The **To Reference** option of the **Side 1** drop-down list is discussed in later chapters while creating the second feature of the model. Also, the other options such as **To Next**, **Through All**, and **Through Until** are available in the drop-down list while creating the second feature of the model and are discussed in later chapters.

Flip Direction

The **Flip Direction** button of the **Extrude** tab is used for flipping the direction of the extrusion depth to the other side of the sketching plane.

Remove Material

The **Remove Material** button is used for creating a cut feature by removing material from the existing solid feature. Note that this button is not enabled while creating the base/first feature of a model.

Thicken Sketch

The **Thicken Sketch** button is used for creating a thin solid feature of specified wall thickness, see Figure 4.11. When you click on the **Thicken Sketch** button, a preview of the thin feature with the default wall thickness appears in the graphics window. Also, the **Value** field and the **Flip Direction** button appear next to the **Thicken Sketch** button in the **Extrude** tab, see Figure 4.12. The **Value** field is used for specifying the thickness value and the **Flip Direction** button is used for flipping the direction of thickness to one side, the other side, or both sides of the sketch.

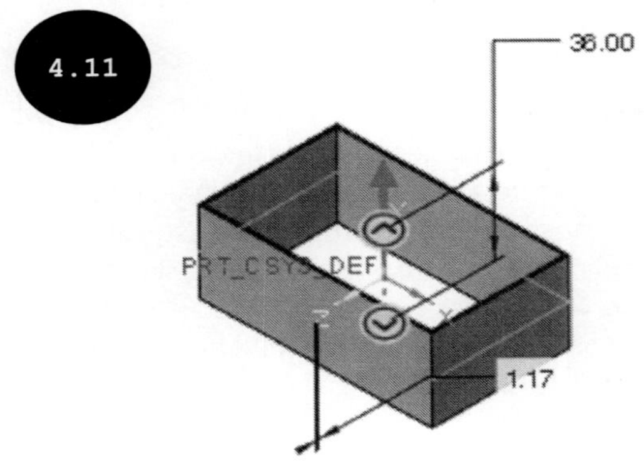

4.12

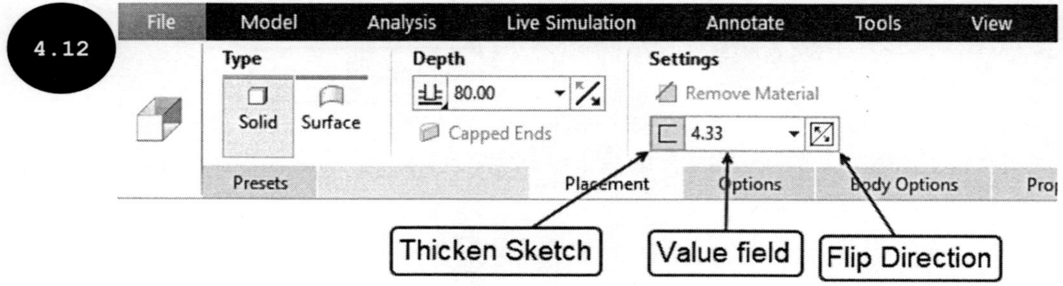

Capped Ends

The **Capped Ends** button is activated while creating a surface extrude feature and is used for closing the open ends of the surface feature.

Options Tab

The **Options** tab is used for defining the depth options for extruding a feature on side 1 as well as on side 2 of the sketching plane. Click on the **Options** tab in the **Extrude** tab. The **Options** panel appears, see Figure 4.13.

4.13

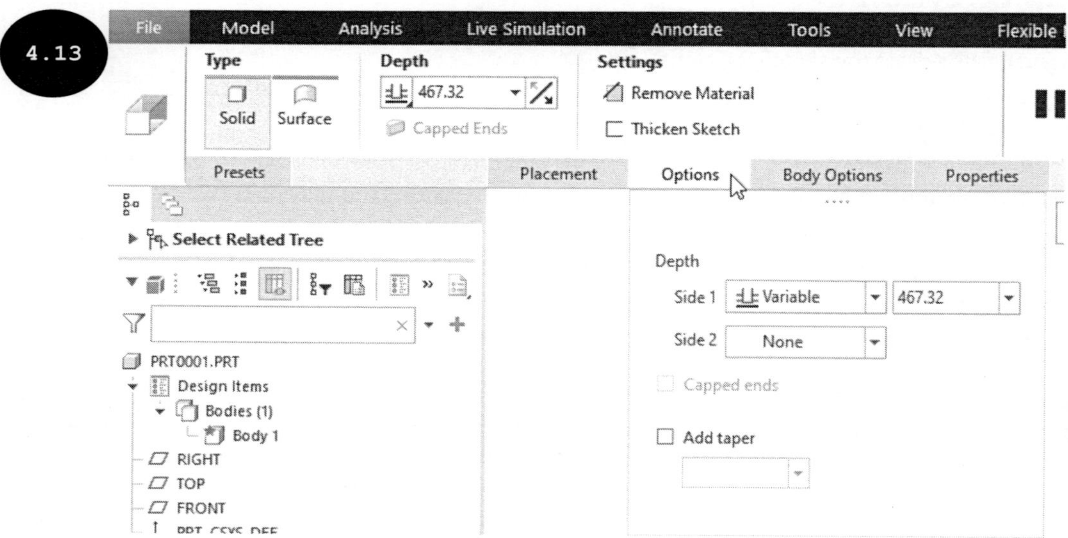

In the **Options** panel, the **Side 1** drop-down list is used for defining the depth option for the feature on side 1 of the sketching plane, as discussed earlier, whereas the **Side 2** drop-down list is used for defining the depth option for the feature on side 2 of the sketching plane. Note that the options in the **Side 2** drop-down list are the same as those the **Side 1** drop-down list, with the only difference being that these options are used for extruding the feature on side 2 of the sketching plane. Figure 4.14 shows the preview of a feature, extruded on both sides (side 1 and side 2) of the sketching plane with different extrusion depths. Note that the **Side 2** drop-down list will not be enabled, if the **Symmetric** option is selected in the **Side 1** drop-down list.

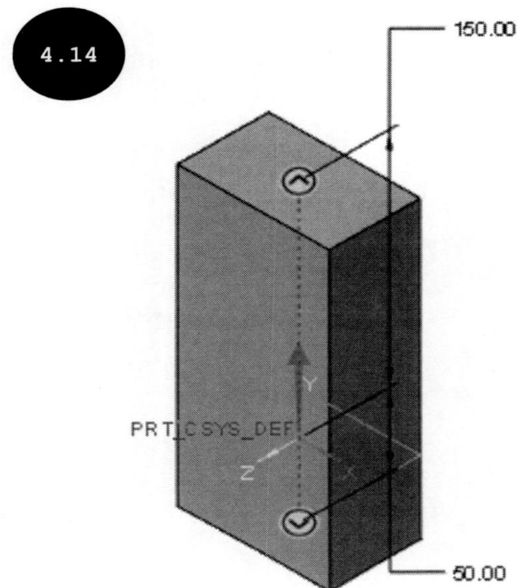

The **Capped ends** check box of the **Options** panel is used for closing a surface feature by adding caps on both its open ends. Note that this check box is enabled only when you create a surface feature by using a closed sketch. You can create a surface feature by using the **Extrude as surface** button of the **Extrude** tab, as discussed earlier. On selecting the **Capped ends** check box, the open ends of the surface feature are capped and a hollow surface feature is created.

The **Add taper** check box of the **Options** panel is used for tapering the extrude feature, see Figure 4.15. By default, the **Add taper** check box is cleared. As a result, the extrude feature is created without any tapering in it. To add tapering in an extrude feature, select the **Add taper** check box in the **Options** panel. A preview of the feature with a default draft angle appears in the graphics area. Also, the **Draft Value** field is enabled below this check box. You can enter the draft angle value in this field in a range between -89.9 degrees to 89.9 degrees. You can flip the direction of the draft by specifying a negative or positive draft angle value, see Figures 4.15 and 4.16.

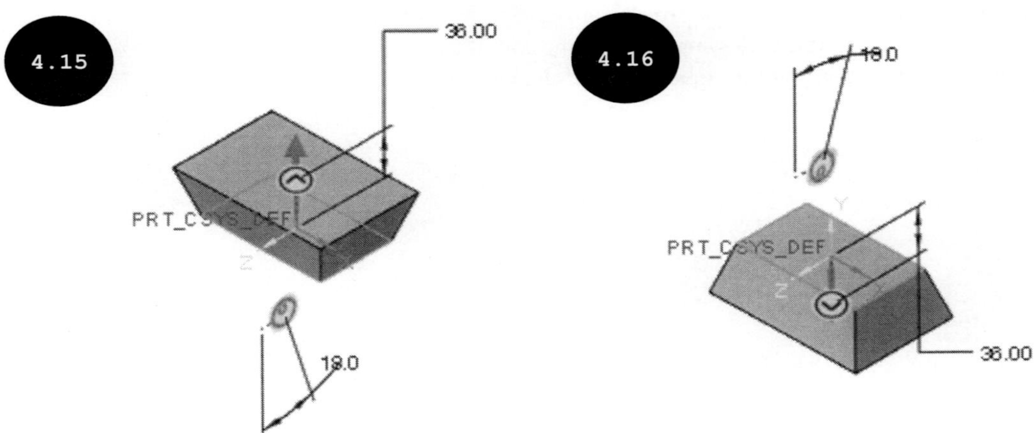

Body Options Tab

The **Body Options** tab is used for merging the feature being created with the existing body or for creating a new separate body. To do so, click on the **Body Options** tab. The **Body Options** panel appears, see Figure 4.17. In this panel, the **Create new body** check box is cleared, by default. As a result, the feature being created merges with the existing part body (Body 1). However, if you select this check box, the feature being created does not merge with the existing body and creates a new separate body (Body 2).

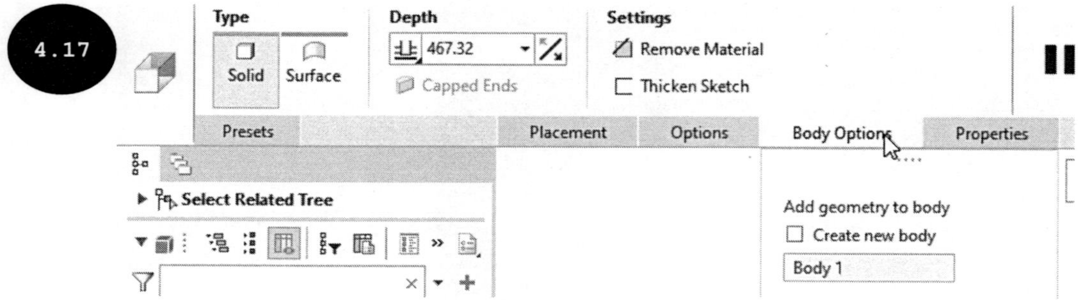

Properties Tab

The **Properties** tab of the **Extrude** tab is used for displaying detailed information about the feature. Click on the **Properties** tab. The **Properties** panel appears, see Figure 4.18.

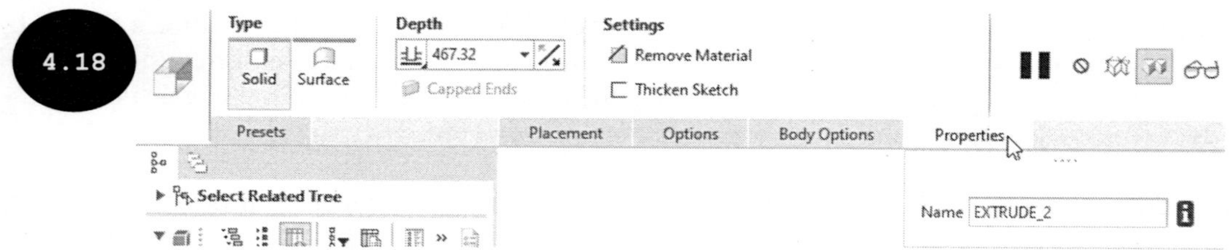

The **Name** field of the **Properties** panel is used for specifying a name for the feature. By default, the name of the extrude feature is specified as EXTRUDE_1, EXTRUDE_2, ... or EXTRUDE_n. You can enter a name for the feature as per your requirement in this field.

The **Information** button in the **Properties** panel is used for displaying detailed information such as name, material, extrusion direction, depth, dimension values, and so on about the feature in a browser window, see Figure 4.19. After reviewing the information of the feature, you can close this window by clicking on the cross sign in the top right corner of the window, see Figure 4.19.

4.19

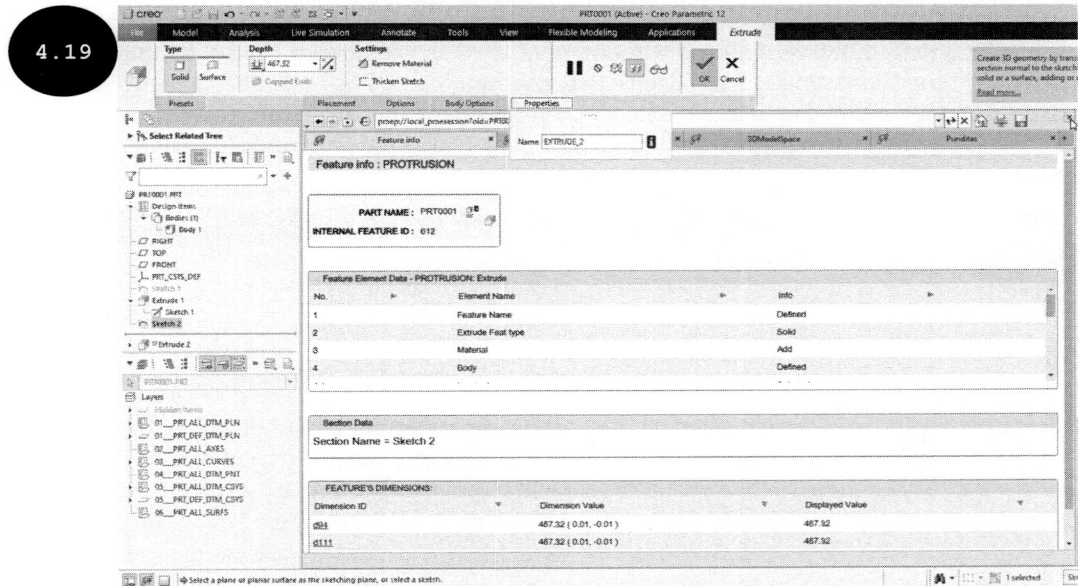

After specifying the required parameters for extruding the sketch, click on the green tick-mark button in the **Extrude** tab to accept the defined parameters and create the extrude feature.

Creating a Revolve Feature

A revolve feature is a feature created such that the material is added by revolving a sketch around an axis of revolution. Note that the sketch to be revolved should be on either side of the axis of revolution/centerline. You can create a revolved feature by using the **Revolve** tool of the **Shapes** group in the **Model** tab. Figure 4.20 shows sketches and the resultant revolved features created by revolving the sketch around the respective centerline of the sketch.

4.20

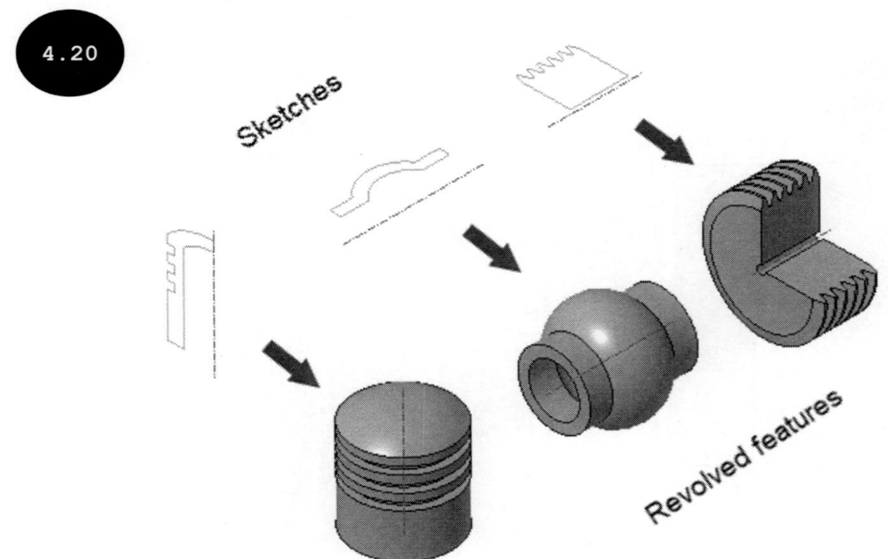

After drawing the sketch of a revolve feature along with a centerline as the axis of revolution by using the sketching tools in the Sketching environment of the Part mode, click on the **OK** button (green tick-mark) in the **Close** group of the **Sketch** tab, see Figure 4.21. The Part modeling environment is invoked and the sketch created in the Sketching environment appears in the graphics window. Note that the method for invoking the Sketching environment within the Part mode has been discussed in Chapter 2.

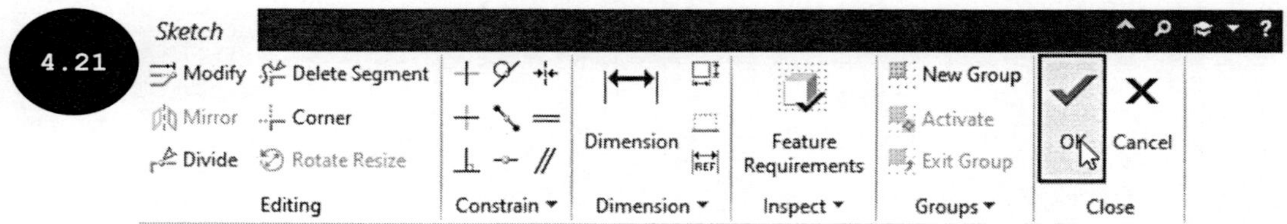

In the Part modeling environment, click on the **Revolve** tool in the **Shapes** group of the **Model** tab. The **Revolve** tab appears in the **Ribbon**, see Figure 4.22. You are also prompted to either select a sketch to be revolved or a sketching plane to create the sketch. Select the sketch to be revolved in the graphics window. A preview of the revolve feature appears in the graphics window, see Figures 4.23 and 4.24.

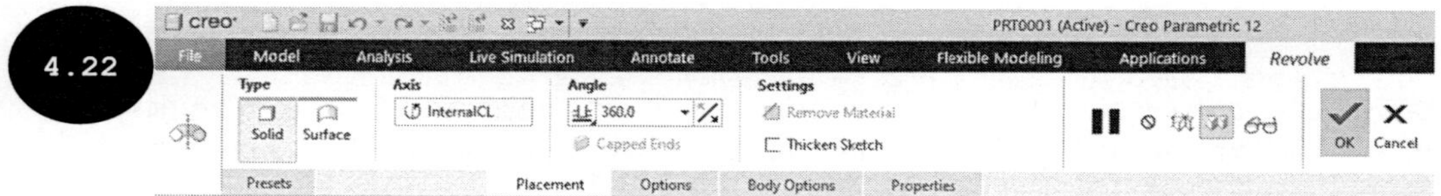

Figure 4.23 shows a sketch with a centerline created on the Front Plane in the Sketching environment and Figure 4.24 shows a preview of the resultant revolve feature.

Note: You can select the sketch to be revolved before or after invoking the **Revolve** tool. If the sketch having a centerline is selected before invoking the **Revolve** tool, then the preview of the revolve feature appears automatically in the graphics window.

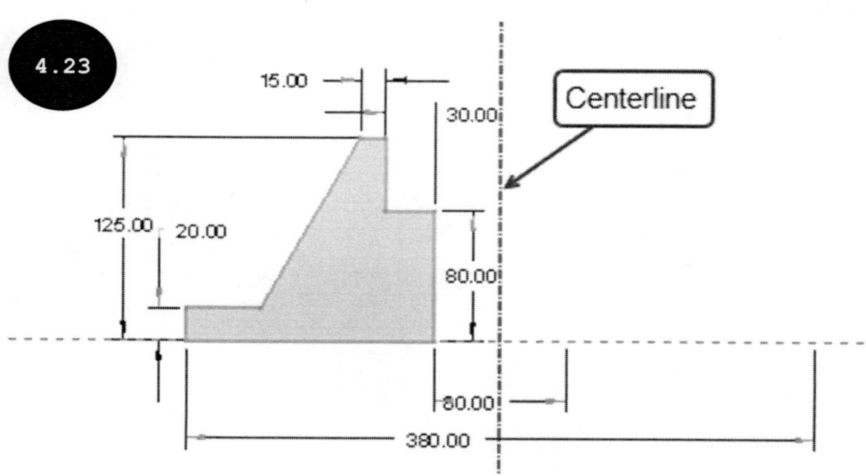

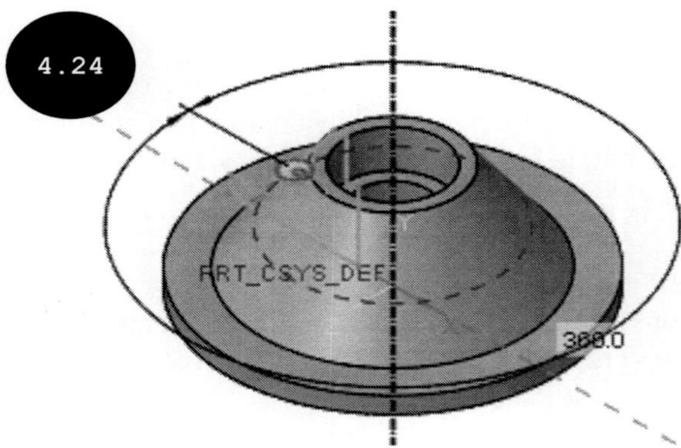

The options in the **Revolve** tab of the **Ribbon** are discussed below:

Placement Tab

By default, the **Placement** tab is activated and the **Placement** panel appears in the **Revolve** tab, see Figure 4.25. As a result, you can directly select a sketch to be revolved or a sketching plane for creating the sketch. In this panel, the **Sketch** field is used for selecting a sketch to be revolved, whereas the **Define** button is used for invoking the **Sketch** dialog box to define the sketching plane for creating the sketch of the revolve feature. Note that as soon as you select a sketch, its name appears in the **Sketch** field of the **Placement** panel. Also, the **Define** button changes to the **Unlink** button. The **Unlink** button is used for breaking the link or association between the selected sketch and the feature, and creates a copy of the sketch as an internal sketch.

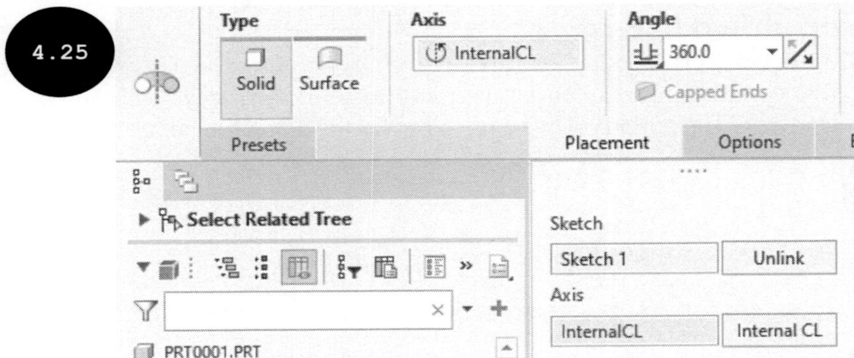

The **Axis** field of the **Placement** tab is used for selecting the axis of revolution of the revolved feature. You can select a linear sketch entity, a centerline, an axis, or a linear edge as the axis of revolution. The **Internal CL** button of the **Placement** tab is used for selecting the internal centerline of the sketch as the axis of revolution. Note that the **Axis** field gets enabled as soon as you select a sketch to be revolved. The **Internal CL** button gets enabled only when the selected sketch has an internal centerline drawn.

Note: If a centerline is drawn in the sketch to be revolved, then on selecting the sketch, its centerline will automatically be selected as the axis of revolution and a preview of the resultant revolve feature appears in the graphics window. However, if the sketch does not have any centerline, then on selecting the sketch, a preview of the revolve feature does not appear and you need to select the axis of revolution.

Revolve as solid

The **Revolve as solid** button of the **Revolve** tab is used for creating a solid revolve feature by revolving the sketch around the axis of revolution/centerline. By default, this button is activated. As a result, a preview of the solid revolve feature appears in the graphics window as soon as you select a sketch having an internal centerline.

Revolve as surface

The **Revolve as surface** button is used for creating a surface revolve feature. Note that a surface feature has zero thickness and no mass properties. Figure 4.26 shows the preview of a solid revolve feature and Figure 4.27 shows the preview of a surface revolve feature.

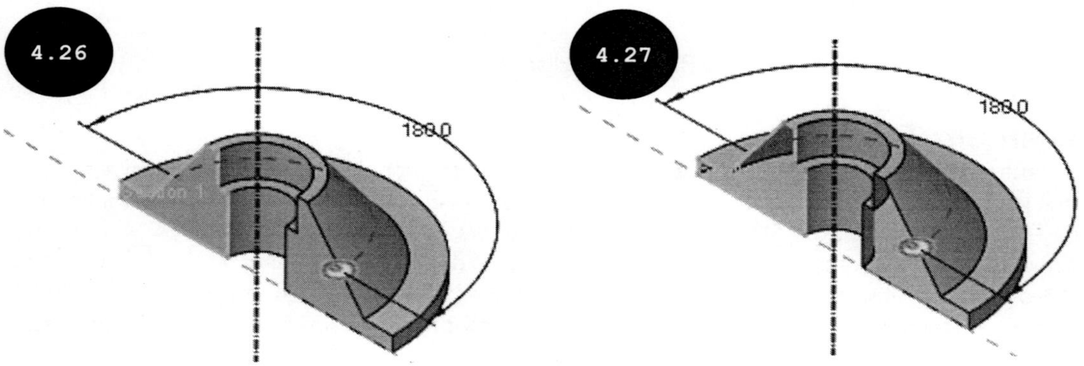

Side 1 Drop-down list

The **Side 1** drop-down list is used for selecting an angle option for revolving the feature on side 1 of the sketching plane, see Figure 4.28. You can invoke this drop-down list by clicking on the active angle option, see Figure 4.28. The options in this drop-down list are discussed next.

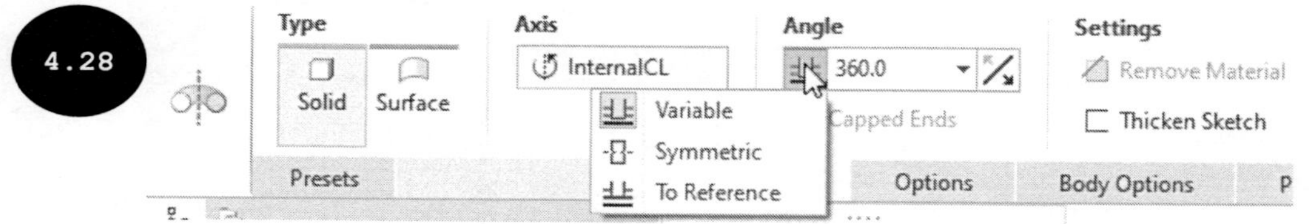

Note: You can also define the angle options for revolving the feature on side 1 and side 2 of the sketching plane by using the options in the **Options** tab. The **Options** tab is discussed later in this section.

Variable

The **Variable** option of the **Side 1** drop-down list is used for specifying the angle of the revolve feature by entering the angle value in the **Angle** field of the **Revolve** tab, see Figure 4.29. You can also drag the handle available in the preview of the revolve feature to define the angle of revolution in the graphics window.

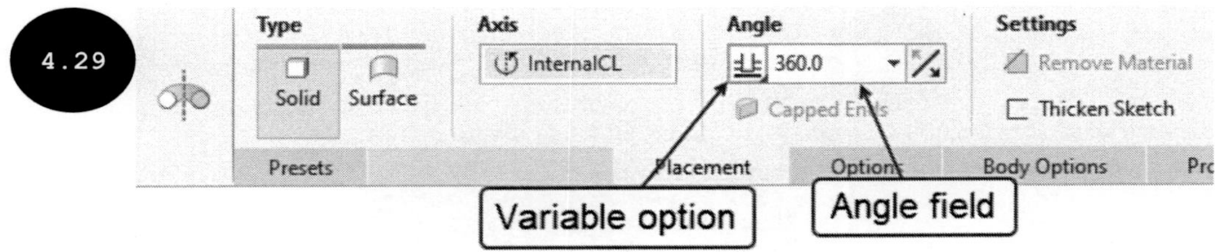

Symmetric

The **Symmetric** option of the **Side 1** drop-down list is used for revolving the feature symmetrically about the sketching plane, see Figure 4.30. After selecting this option, you can enter the angle value of revolution in the **Angle** field. Note that the specified angle value is divided equally on both sides of the sketching plane and creates a symmetrical revolve feature.

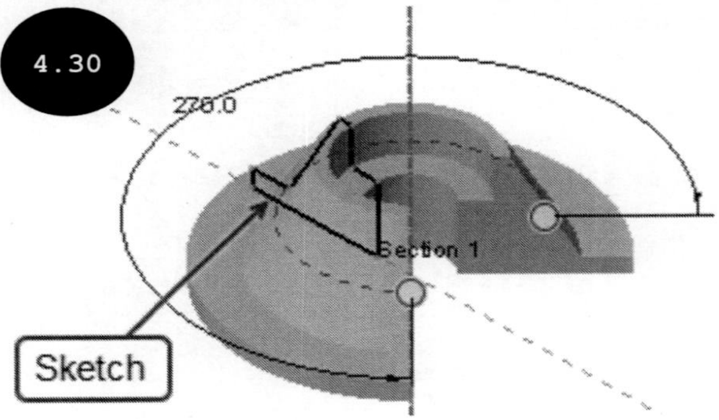

Note: The **To Reference** option of the **Side 1** drop-down list is discussed in later chapters while creating the second feature of the model.

Flip Direction

The **Flip Direction** button of the **Revolve** tab is used for flipping the direction of the revolve angle to the other side of the sketching plane.

Remove Material

The **Remove Material** button is used for creating a cut revolve feature by removing material from the existing solid feature. Note that this button is not enabled while creating the base/first feature of the model.

Thicken Sketch

The **Thicken Sketch** button is used for creating a thin revolve feature of specified wall thickness, see Figure 4.31. When you click on the **Thicken Sketch** button, a preview of the thin revolve feature with the default wall thickness appears in the graphics window. Also, the **Value** field and the **Flip Direction** button appear next to the **Thicken Sketch** button in the **Revolve** tab, see Figure 4.32. The **Value** field is used for specifying the thickness value and the **Flip Direction** button is used for flipping the direction of thickness to either side or both sides of the sketch.

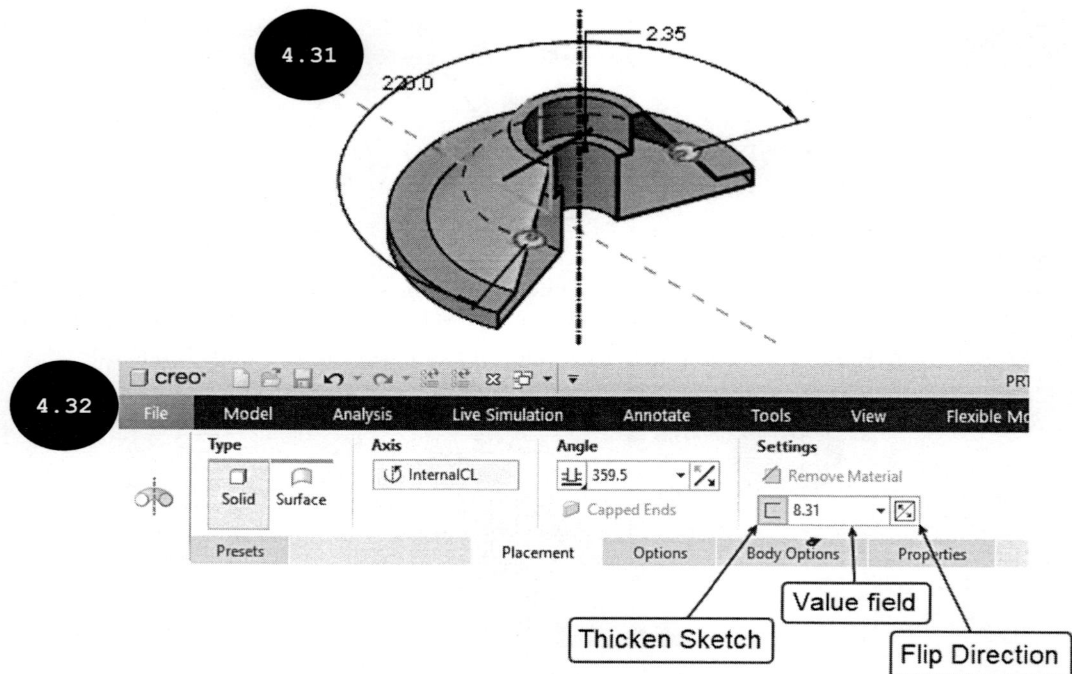

Capped Ends

The **Capped Ends** button is activated while creating a surface revolve feature and is used for closing the open ends of the surface feature.

Options Tab

The **Options** tab is used for defining the angle options for revolving the feature to side 1 as well as to side 2 of the sketching plane around the axis of revolution. Click on the **Options** tab in the **Revolve** tab. The **Options** panel appears, see Figure 4.33.

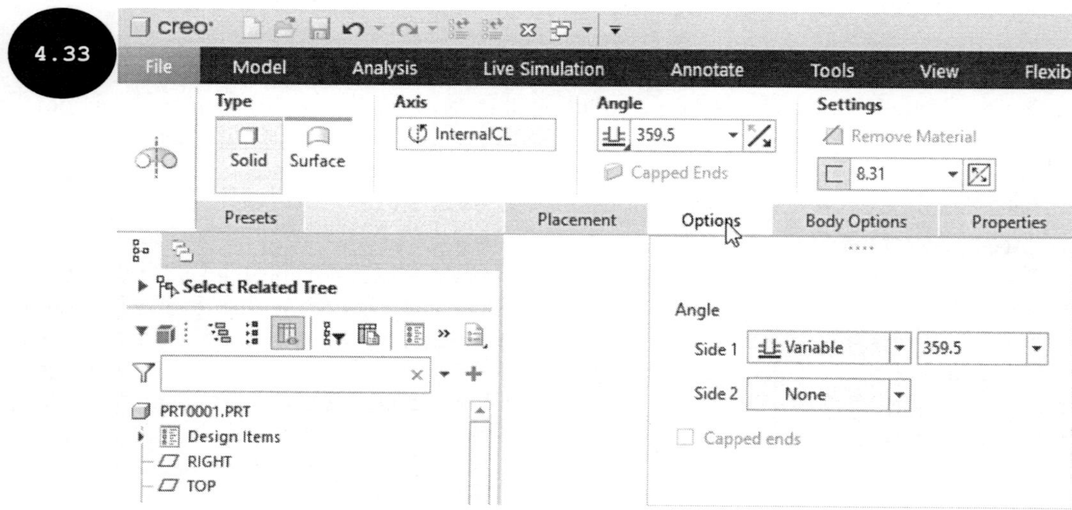

In the **Options** panel, the **Side 1** drop-down list is used for defining the angle option for the revolve feature on side 1 of the sketching plane, as discussed earlier, whereas the **Side 2** drop-down list is used for defining the angle option for the revolve feature on side 2 of the sketching plane.

Note that the options in the **Side 2** drop-down list are the same as those the **Side 1** drop-down list, with the only difference that these options are used to revolve the feature on side 2 of the sketching plane. Figure 4.34 shows the preview of a feature, revolved around both sides (side 1 and side 2) of the sketching plane with different angle values. Note that the **Side 2** drop-down list will not be enabled, if the **Symmetric** option is selected in the **Side 1** drop-down list.

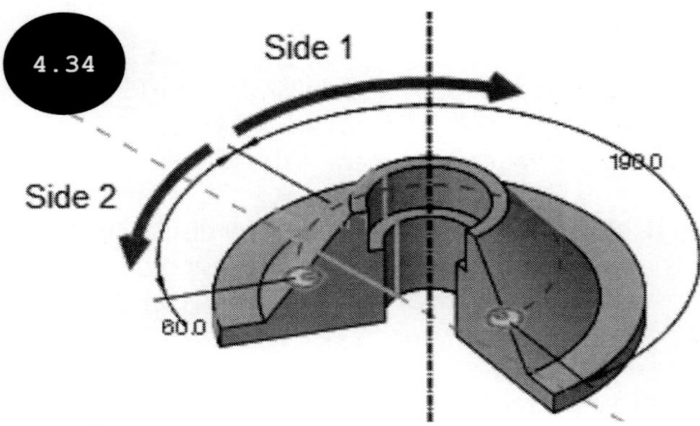

The **Capped ends** check box of the **Options** panel is used for closing a surface feature by adding caps on both its open ends. Note that this check box is enabled only when you create a surface feature by using a closed sketch. You can create a revolve surface feature by using the **Revolve as surface** button of the **Revolve** tab, as discussed earlier. On selecting the **Capped ends** check box, the open ends of the surface feature are capped and a hollow revolve surface feature is created.

Body Options Tab

The **Body Options** tab is used for merging the feature being created with the existing body or for creating a new separate body. To do so, click on the **Body Options** tab. The **Body Options** panel appears, see Figure 4.35. In this panel, the **Create new body** check box is cleared, by default. As a result, the feature being created merges with the existing part body (Body 1). However, if you select this check box, the feature being created does not merge with the existing body and creates a new separate body (Body 2).

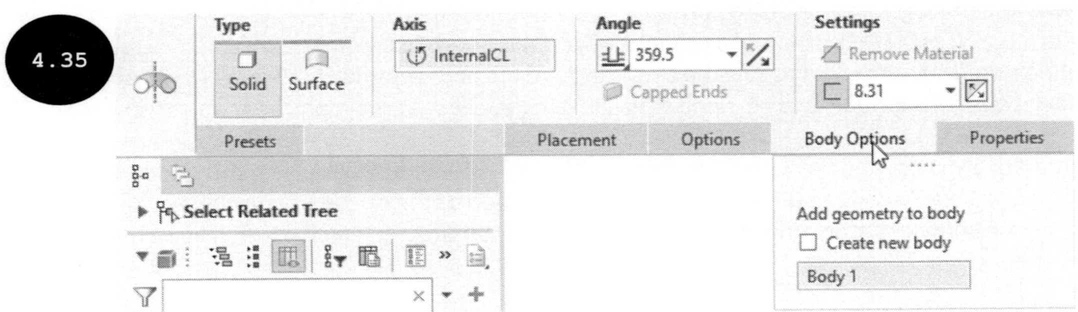

Properties Tab

The **Properties** tab of the **Extrude** tab is used for displaying detailed information about the feature. Click on the **Properties** tab. The **Properties** panel appears, see Figure 4.36.

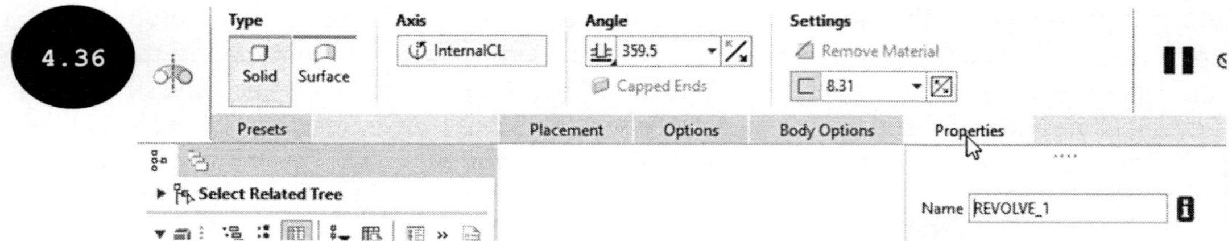

The **Name** field of the **Properties** panel is used for specifying a name for the revolve feature. By default, the name of the revolve feature is specified as REVOLVE_1, REVOLVE_2, ... or REVOLVE_n. You can enter a name for the feature as per your requirement in this field.

The **Information** button of the **Properties** panel is used for displaying detailed information such as name, material, revolving axis, direction, angle, sketch dimensions, etc. of the feature in a browser window. After reviewing the information about the feature, you can close this window by clicking on the cross sign in the top right corner of the window.

After specifying the required parameters for revolving the sketch, click on the green tick-mark button in the **Revolve** tab to accept the defined parameters and create the revolve feature.

Navigating a 3D Model in Graphics Window

In Creo Parametric, you can navigate a model by using the mouse buttons or the navigating tools. You can access the navigating tools in the **In-graphics** toolbar, see Figure 4.37. You can also access the navigating tools in the **Orientation** group of the **View** tab in the **Ribbon**. Different navigating tools are discussed below.

Zoom In

The **Zoom In** tool is used for enlarging a particular portion or area of a model by defining a boundary box. To enlarge a particular portion of a model, click on the **Zoom In** tool in the **In-graphics** toolbar. Next, define a boundary box by dragging the cursor around the portion/area of the model to be zoomed. The area inside the boundary box gets enlarged. Next, right-click in the graphics window to exit the tool.

Alternatively, press and hold the CTRL key and then click the middle mouse button once. Next, move the cursor to define the boundary box around the portion of the model to be enlarged, and then click the middle mouse button. The area inside the boundary box gets enlarged. Next, release the CTRL key.

Zoom Out

The **Zoom Out** tool is used for reducing the view of a model. To do so, click on the **Zoom Out** tool in the **In-graphics** toolbar. The current view of the model gets reduced. You can continue reducing the model view by clicking on the **Zoom Out** tool.

Alternatively, you can zoom in or zoom out the model view by using the mouse buttons. The methods are discussed below:

- Scroll the wheel of the mouse up or down to zoom into or zoom out of the model view.
- Press and hold the CTRL key and the middle mouse button. Next, drag the cursor upward or downward in the graphics window. On dragging the cursor upward, the model view gets reduced, whereas on dragging the cursor downward, the model view gets enlarged.

Note: In the process of zooming into or zooming out of the model view, the scale of the model remains the same. Only the viewing distance gets modified in order to enlarge or reduce the view of the model.

Refit

The **Refit** tool is used for fitting a model completely inside the graphics window. To do so, click on the **Refit** tool in **In-graphics** toolbar.

Zoom to Selected

The **Zoom to Selected** tool is used for enlarging the selected object or geometry completely in the graphics window. To do so, click on the object/geometry to be enlarged. The Mini toolbar appears in the graphics window, see Figure 4.38. In this toolbar, click on the **Zoom to Selected** tool. The selected geometry gets enlarged and fits in the graphics window. Alternatively, you can also click on the **Zoom to Selected** tool in the **Orientation** group of the **View** tab in the **Ribbon**, see Figure 4.39.

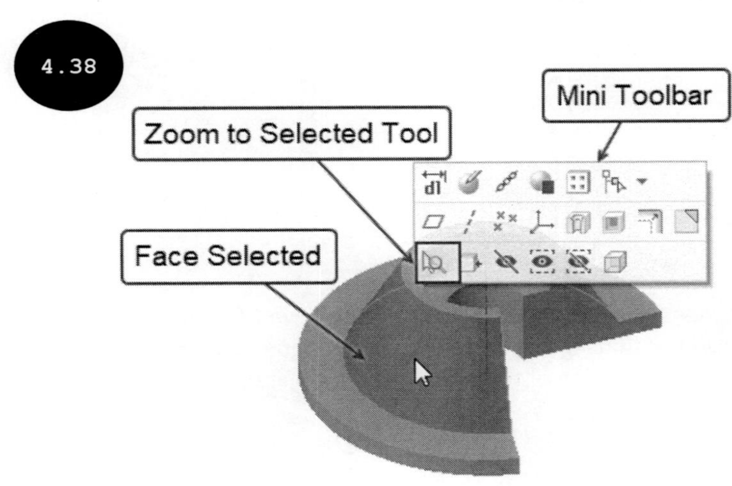

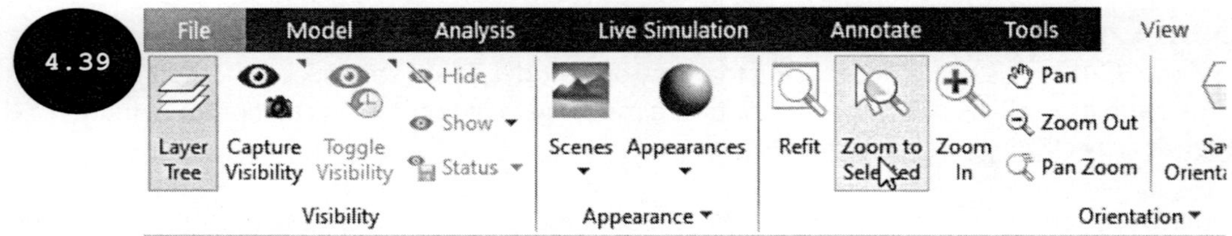

Pan

The **Pan** tool is used for panning/moving the model in the graphics window. To move the model, click on the **Pan** tool in the **Orientation** group of the **View** tab in the **Ribbon**, refer to Figure 4.39. Next, drag the cursor after pressing and holding the left mouse button. To exit the **Pan** tool, press the middle mouse button.

Alternatively, you can also pan the model by using the mouse buttons. To do so, press and hold the **SHIFT** key and the middle mouse button. Next, drag the cursor in the graphics window.

Rotate

To rotate a model in the graphics window, press and hold the middle mouse button and then drag the cursor.

Manipulating View Orientation of a Model

The manipulation of the view orientation of a 3D model is very important in order to review a model from different views and angles. In Creo Parametric, you can manipulate the orientation of a 3D model to predefined standard orientations such as front, top, right, left, and bottom by using the tools in the **Saved Orientations** flyout, see Figure 4.40. You can invoke this flyout by clicking on the **Saved Orientations** tool in the **In-graphics** toolbar or the **Orientation** group of the **View** tab in the **Ribbon**.

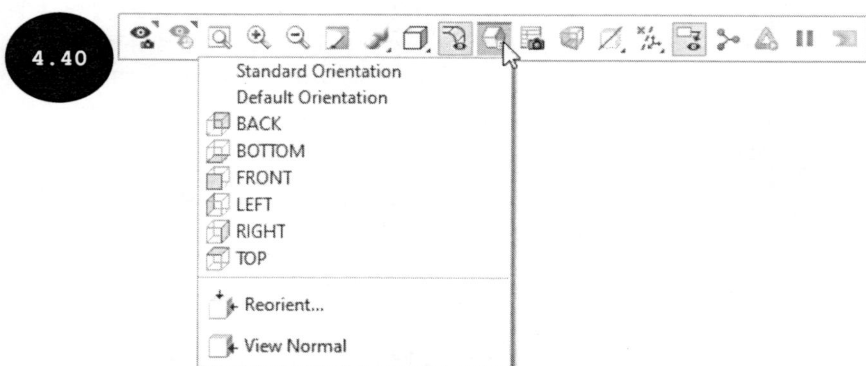

To manipulate the orientation of a model, click on the **Saved Orientations** tool in the **In-graphics** toolbar. The **Saved Orientations** flyout appears, refer to Figure 4.40. By using the tools of this flyout, you can manipulate the orientation of the model. The tools are discussed next.

BACK, BOTTOM, FRONT, LEFT, RIGHT, and TOP Tools

The BACK, BOTTOM, FRONT, LEFT, RIGHT, and TOP tools of the **Saved Orientations** flyout are used for displaying the predefined standard views such as back, bottom, front, left, right, and top of the model in the graphics window.

Standard Orientation/Default Orientation Tool

The **Standard Orientation/Default Orientation** tool of the **Saved Orientations** flyout is used for changing the orientation of the model to standard or default specified orientation.

By default, the standard orientation is set to Isometric. As a result, on clicking the **Standard Orientation/Default Orientation** tool, the orientation of the model changes to Isometric in the graphics window. You can set the standard/default orientation of the model to Isometric, Trimetric, or User-defined. To do so, click on **File > Options**. The **Creo Parametric Options** dialog box appears, see Figure 4.41. In this dialog box, click on the **Model Display** option and then select the required orientation; Isometric, Trimetric, or User-defined in the **Default model orientation** drop-down list as the default orientation of the model, see Figure 4.41. Next, click on the **OK** button. The **Creo Parametric Options** window appears. Click on the **Yes** button to save the settings in the configuration file so that the same settings reflect in the other sessions of Creo Parametric as well. If you want these settings to be reflected only in the current session of Creo Parametric, then click on the **No** button in this window.

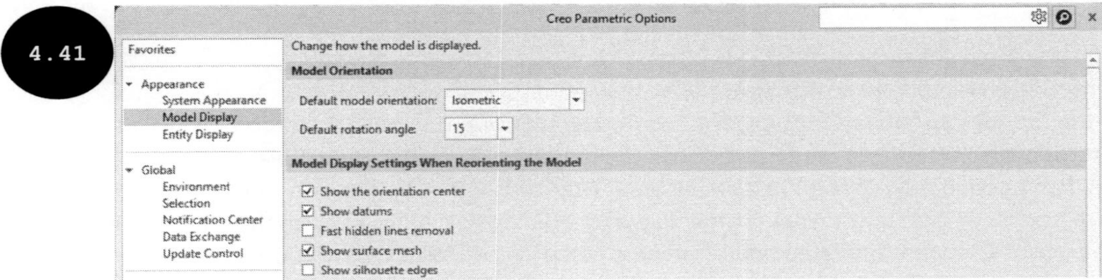

Reorient Tool

The **Reorient** tool is used for creating a custom or user defined orientation of the model. To do so, click on the **Reorient** tool in the **Saved Orientations** flyout, see Figure 4.42. The **View** dialog box appears, see Figure 4.43.

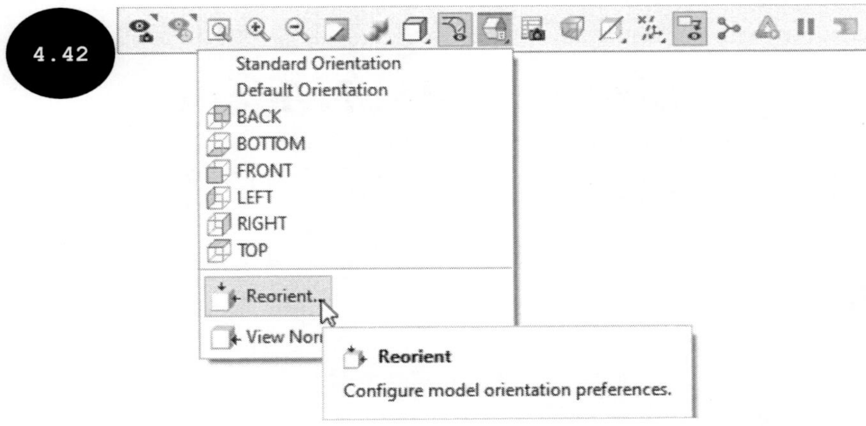

4.43

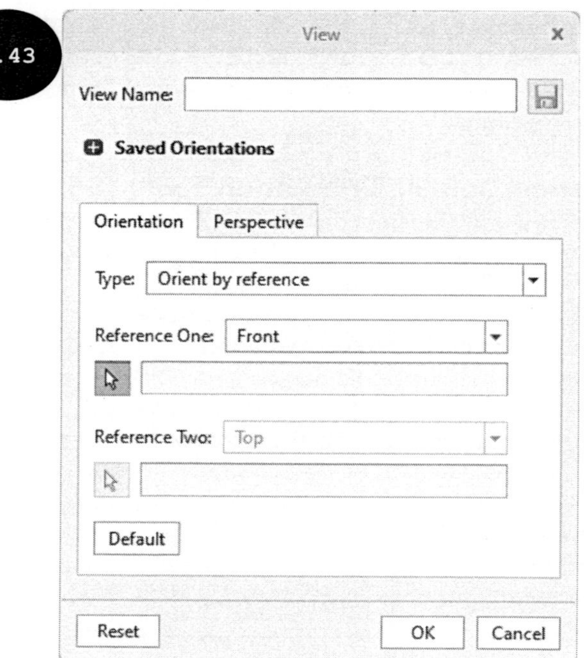

In the **View Name** field of the **View** dialog box, enter the name of the view. Next, set the orientation of the model, as required in the graphics window by using the navigating tools, as discussed earlier. Alternatively, you can set the orientation of the model by using the options available in the **Orientation** and **Perspective** tabs of the **View** dialog box. After setting the orientation of the model, click on the **Save** button next to the **View Name** field of the dialog box. Next, click on the **OK** button to exit the dialog box. The view is created and its name is listed in the **Saved Orientations** flyout. You can display the model as per the custom view created at any point in time by clicking on its name in the **Saved Orientations** flyout. Similarly, you can create multiple custom views for a model.

View Normal Tool

The **View Normal** tool is used for displaying the selected face/edge of a 3D model normal to the viewing direction.

Changing the Display Style of a Model

You can change the display style of a 3D model to shading with reflections, shading with edges, shading, no hidden, hidden line, or wireframe. The tools used for changing the display style of the model are available in the **Display Style** flyout of the **In-graphics** toolbar (see Figure 4.44) and are discussed next.

4.44

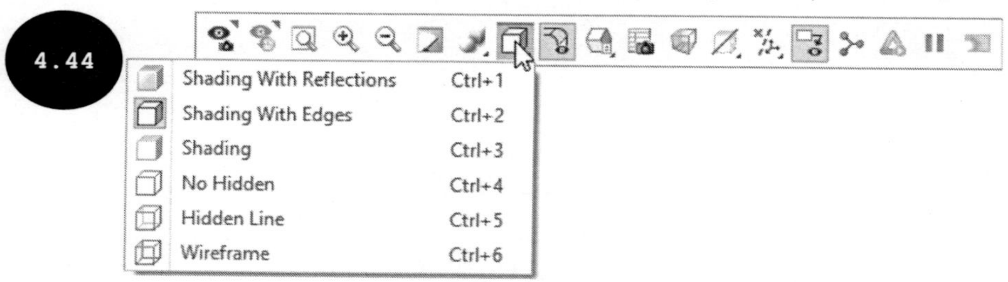

Shading With Reflections

The **Shading With Reflections** tool is used for displaying a model in shaded mode with reflections, see Figure 4.45.

Shading With Edges

The **Shading With Edges** tool is used for displaying a model in shaded mode with black edges, see Figure 4.46.

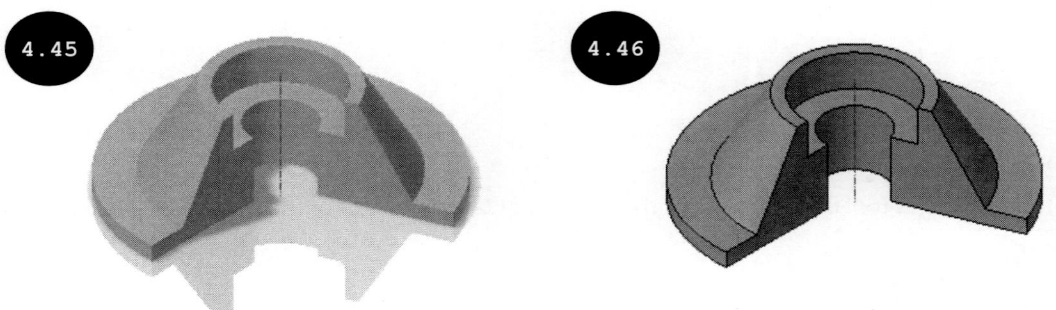

Shading

The **Shading** tool is used for displaying a model in shaded mode with no black edges, see Figure 4.47. This tool is activated by default. As a result, the model is displayed in shaded mode with no black edges in the graphics window, by default.

No Hidden

The **No Hidden** tool is used for displaying a model such that the hidden lines of the model are not visible in the display of the model, see Figure 4.48.

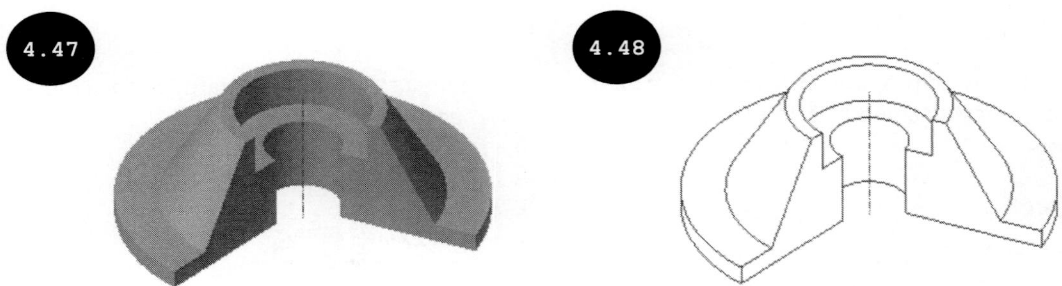

Hidden Line

The **Hidden Line** tool is used for displaying a model such that the visibility of the hidden lines of the model is turned on and appears in a faded display, see Figure 4.49.

Wireframe

The **Wireframe** tool is used for displaying a model such that the visibility of the front and hidden edges of the model appears in wireframe display style, see Figure 4.50.

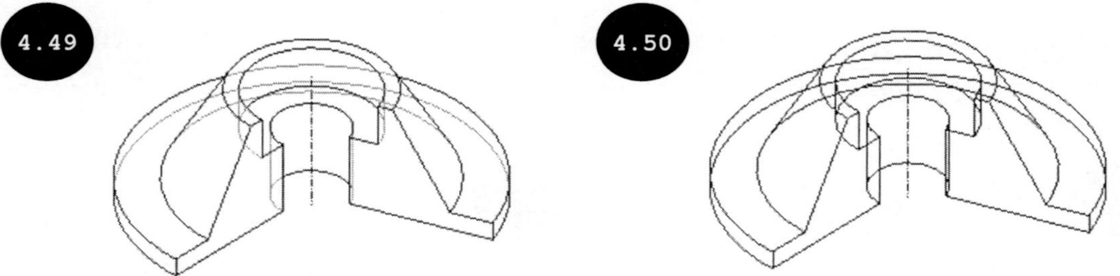

Tangent Edges

The **Tangent Edges** tool is used to toggle the visibility of tangent edges of the model, see Figure 4.51.

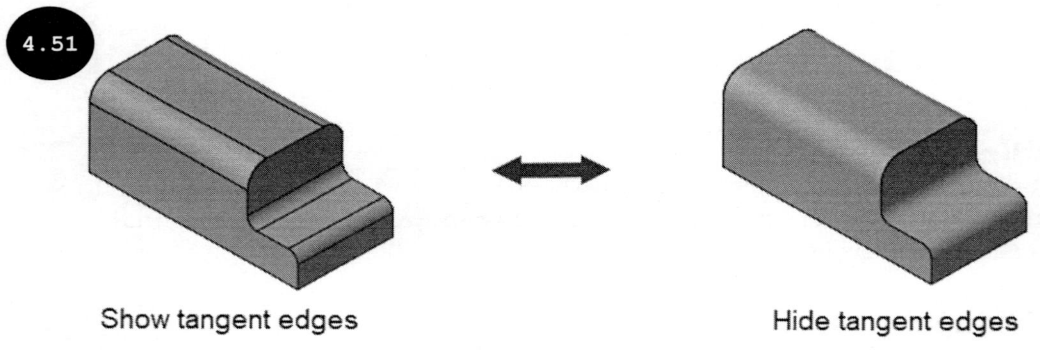

Tutorial 1

Import the sketch created in Tutorial 1 of Chapter 3 (see Figure 4.52) and then create the solid model by extruding it to a depth of 40 mm, see Figure 4.53. All dimensions are in mm.

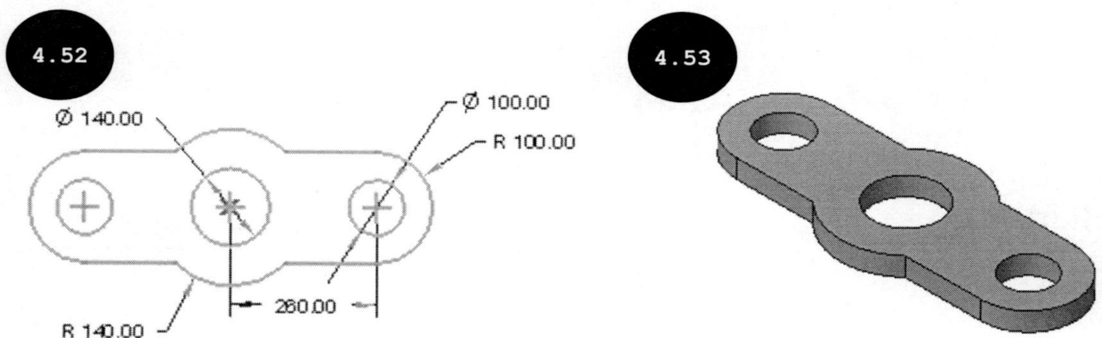

Section 1: Starting Creo Parametric

1. Start Creo Parametric by double-clicking on the Creo Parametric icon on your desktop.

Section 2: Setting the Working Directory

After starting Creo Parametric, you need to set a working directory to save the files of the current session of Creo Parametric. It is recommended to create a folder with the name "*Chapter 4*" inside the "*Creo Parametric*" folder in the local drive of your system. If the "*Creo Parametric*" folder is not already created then you need to create this folder.

1. Click on **File** > **Manage Session** > **Select Working Directory**, see Figure 4.54. The **Select Working Directory** window appears. In this window, browse to the *Creo Parametric* > *Chapter 4* location of your system. You need to create these folders, if not created earlier.

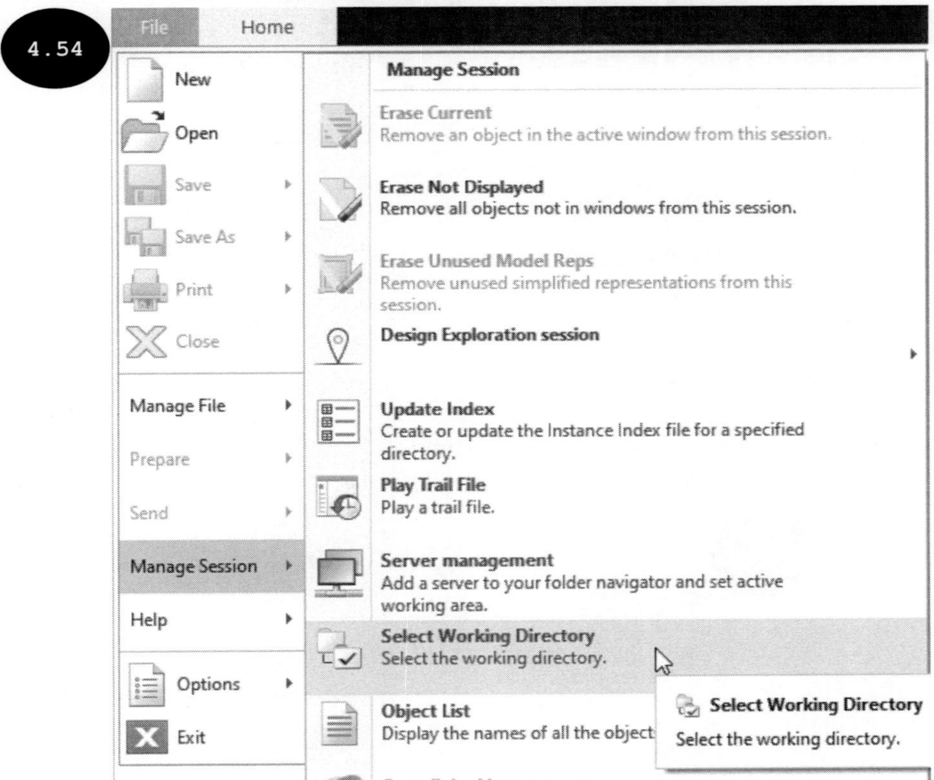

2. Click on the **OK** button to set the working directory to <<*Creo Parametric**Chapter 4*\.

Section 3: Invoking the Sketching Environment

Now, you will invoke the Sketching environment of the Part mode for importing the sketch created in Tutorial 1 of Chapter 3.

1. Click on the **New** tool in the **Data** group of the **Home** tab. The **New** dialog box appears, see Figure 4.55. Alternatively, press the CTRL + N keys to invoke the **New** dialog box.

2. Ensure that the **Part** radio button is selected in the **Type** area and **Solid** radio button is selected in the **Sub-type** area of the dialog box, see Figure 4.55.

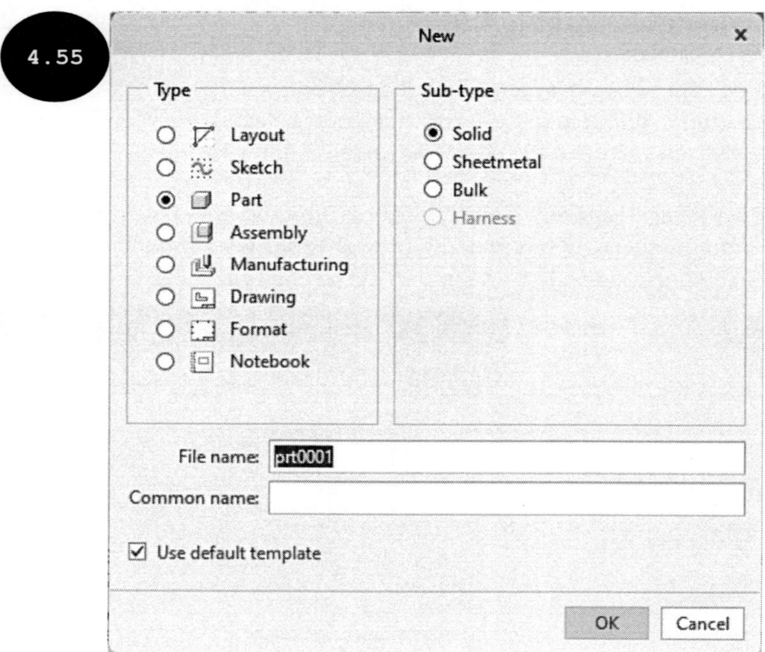

3. Enter **C04-Tutorial01** in the **File name** field of the dialog box.

4. Clear the **Use default template** check box and then click on the **OK** button in the dialog box. The **New File Options** dialog box appears, see Figure 4.56.

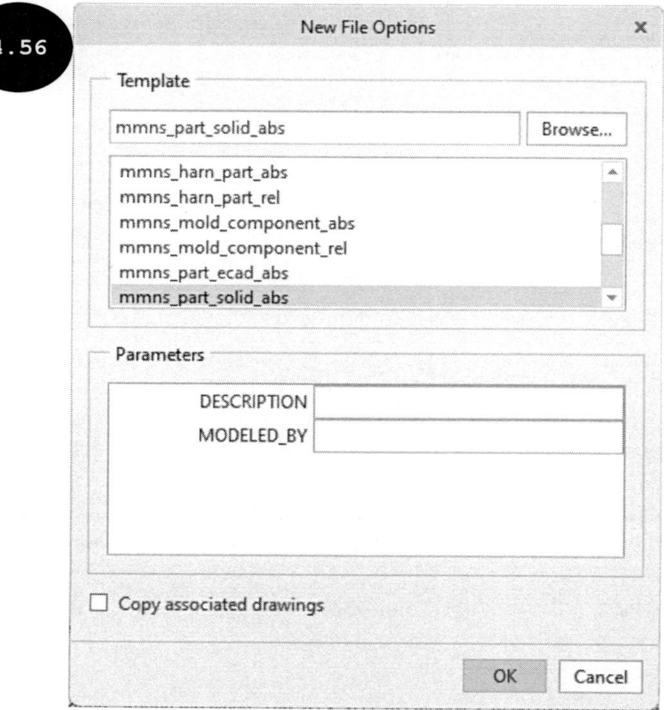

5. In the **New File Options** dialog box, select the **mmns_part_solid_abs** template and then click on the **OK** button. The Part mode is invoked with the **mmns_part_solid_abs** template. In this template, the length is measured in millimeters, mass is measured in Newton, and time is measured in seconds.

   Now, you need to invoke the Sketching environment within the Part mode.

6. Click on the **Sketch** tool in the **Datum** group of the **Model** tab, see Figure 4.57. The **Sketch** dialog box appears and you are prompted to select a plane or a surface to define the sketching plane.

4.57

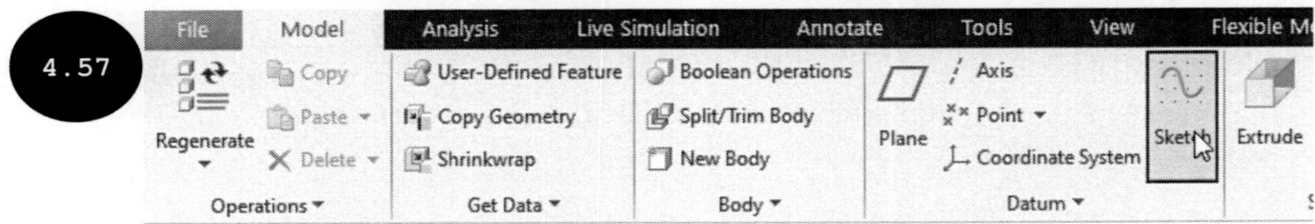

7. Move the cursor over the Top plane in the graphics window and then click the left mouse button when it gets highlighted in the graphics window. The Top plane gets selected as the sketching plane and its name appears in the **Plane** field of the **Sketch** dialog box, see Figure 4.58. Also, a reference plane and its orientation are selected automatically in the **Reference** field and **Orientation** drop-down list of the dialog box, respectively, see Figure 4.58.

4.58

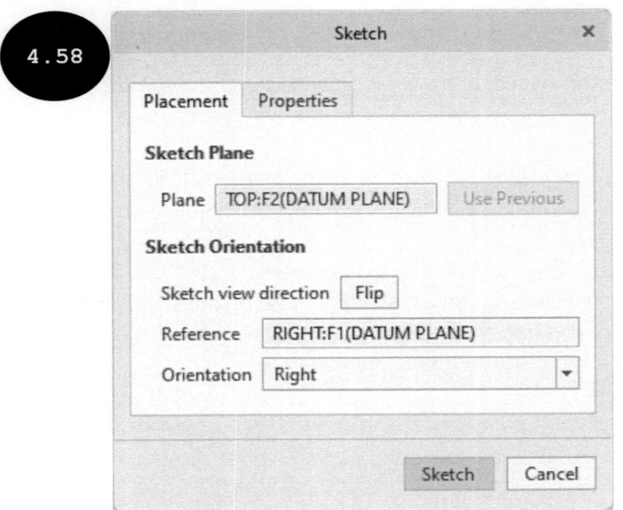

8. Click on the **Sketch** button in the dialog box. The Sketching environment is invoked. Also, the Top plane is oriented normal to the viewing direction. If the Top plane is not oriented normal to the viewing direction by default, then you need to do it by clicking on the **Sketch View** tool in the **In-graphics** toolbar, see Figure 4.59.

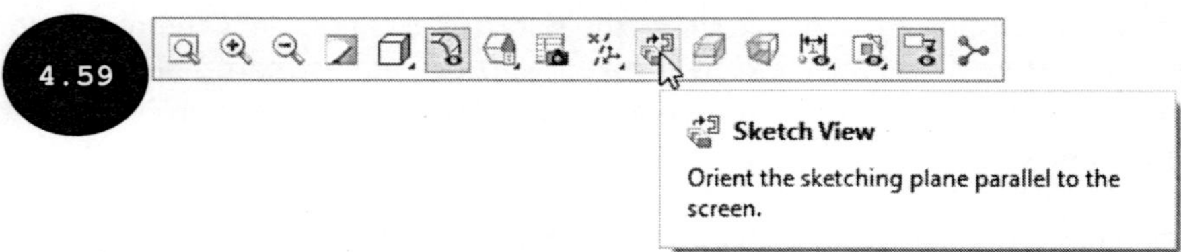

Section 4: Importing the Sketch

After invoking the Sketching environment of the Part mode, you need to import the sketch created in Tutorial 1 of Chapter 3.

Note: If you have not already created the sketch of Tutorial 1 in Chapter 3 then you first need to create it by using the sketching tools of the Sketching environment.

1. Click on the **Import** tool in the **Insert** group of the **Sketch** tab, see Figure 4.60. The **Open** dialog box appears.

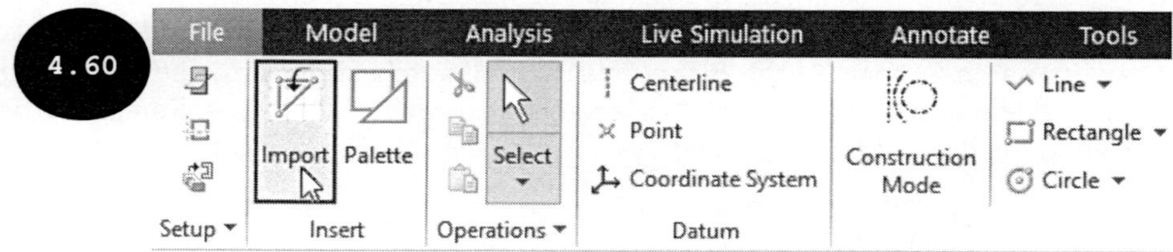

2. Ensure that the **Sketch (*.sec)** file type is selected in the **Type** drop-down list of the **Open** dialog box.

3. Browse to the *Chapter 3* folder in the *Creo Parametric* folder and then select the **Tutorial01** file (*.sec* file) created in Tutorial 1 of Chapter 3. Next, click on the **Open** button in the dialog box.

4. Click in the drawing area to specify a placement point for the selected file. The sketch of Tutorial 1 created in Chapter 3 appears in the drawing area with move, rotate, and scale handles, see Figure 4.61. Also, the **Import Section** tab appears in the **Ribbon**, see Figure 4.62.

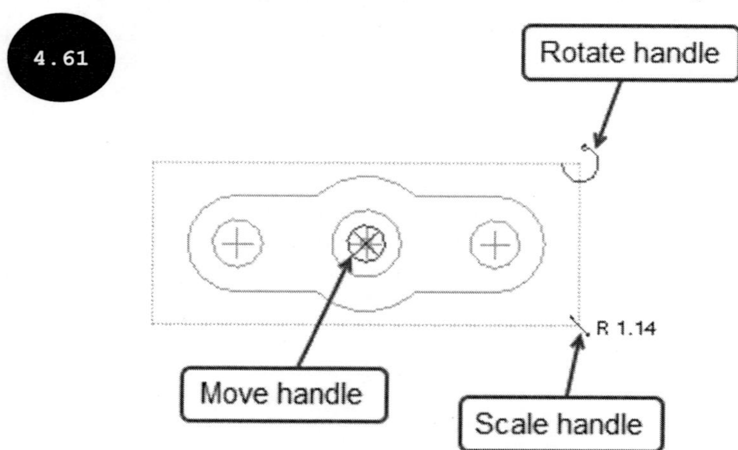

5. Enter **1** in the **Scaling factor** field of the **Import Section** tab in the **Ribbon**, see Figure 4.62 to import the sketch with its actual dimension values.

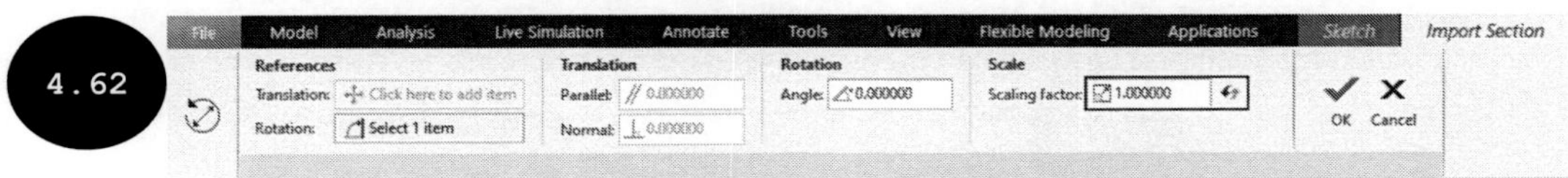

6. Drag the move handle of the sketch towards the origin by pressing and holding the left mouse button. Next, release the left mouse button when the cursor snaps to the origin and the symbol of coincident constraint appears, see Figure 4.63.

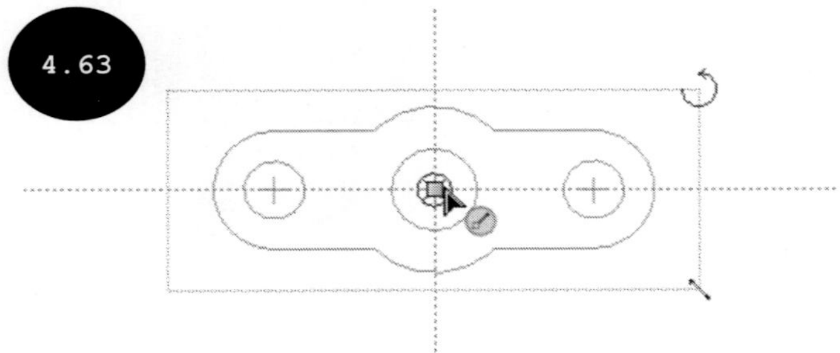

Note: In this figure, the display of datum planes and coordinate system is turned off for clarity of the image.

7. Click on the green tick-mark button in the **Import Section** tab of the **Ribbon**. The sketch of Tutorial 1, created in Chapter 3 is imported into the Sketching environment.

   Now, you need to exit the Sketching environment to create a 3D solid model by extruding the sketch.

8. Click on the **OK** button (green tick-mark) in the **Close** group of the **Ribbon** to exit the Sketching environment. The Part modeling environment is invoked and the sketch appears in green color, indicating that the sketch is selected in the graphics window.

Section 5: Extruding the Sketch

Now, in the Part modeling environment, you can extrude the sketch to create a 3D model.

1. Click on the **Extrude** tool in the **Shapes** group of the **Model** tab. A preview of the extrude feature appears in the graphics window with default parameters. Also, the **Extrude** tab appears in the **Ribbon**.

Note: If a sketch is not selected before invoking the **Extrude** tool then the preview of the feature will not appear and you will be prompted to select the sketch to be extruded. Select the sketch in the graphics window. A preview of the extrude feature appears in the graphics window.

2. Change the current orientation of the model to the standard orientation, see Figure 4.64. To change the orientation, click on the **Saved Orientations** tool in the **In-graphics** toolbar, see Figure 4.65. The **Saved Orientations** flyout appears. In this flyout, click on the **Standard Orientation** tool.

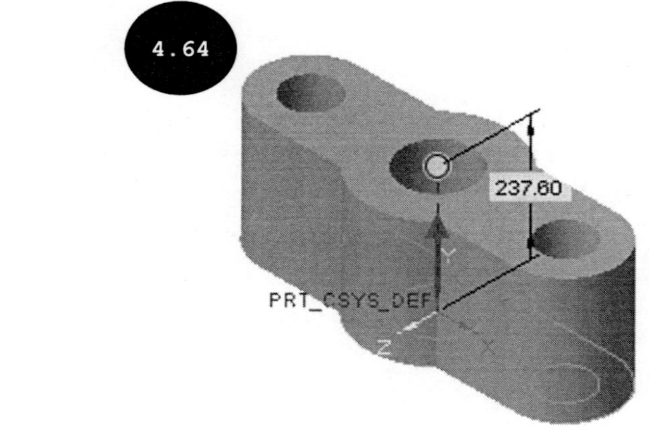

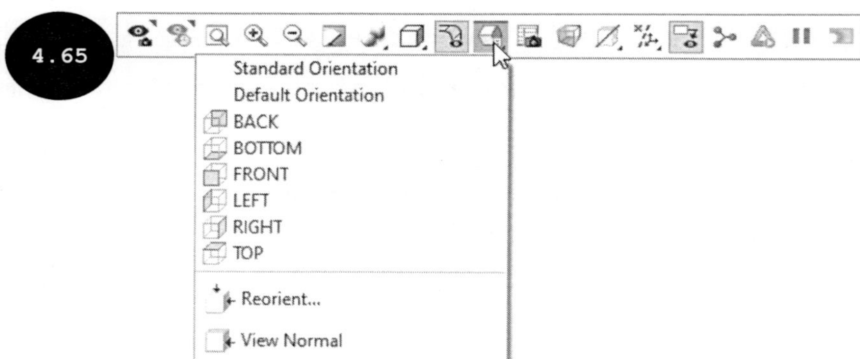

3. Ensure that the **Variable** option is selected in the **Side 1** drop-down list of the **Extrude** tab, see Figure 4.66.

4. Enter 40 as the depth of extrusion in the **Value** field of the **Extrude** tab, see Figure 4.66.

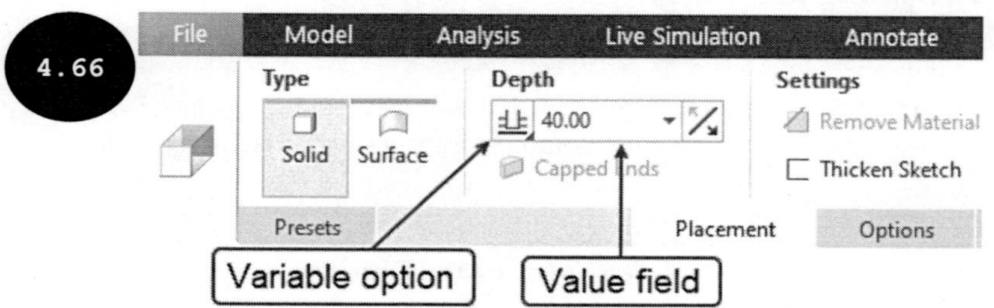

5. Click on the green tick-mark button in the **Extrude** tab. The extrude feature is created, see Figure 4.67. In this figure, the standard/default orientation of the model is set to Isometric.

4.67

Section 6: Saving the Model

Now, you need to save the model.

1. Click on the **Save** tool in the **Quick Access Toolbar**. The **Save Object** dialog box appears. Next, click on the **Working Directory** option in the left panel of the dialog box.

2. Click on the OK button in the dialog box. The model is saved in the specified working directory (<<*Creo Parametric**Chapter 4*\).

Tutorial 2

Create the revolve model as shown in Figure 4.68. All dimensions are in mm.

4.68

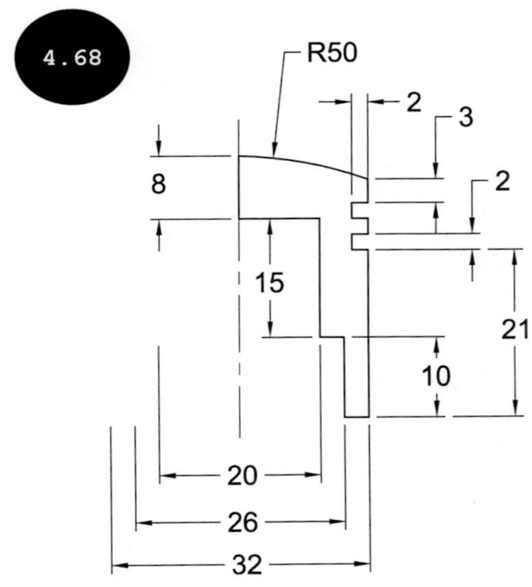

Section 1: Starting Creo Parametric

1. Start Creo Parametric, if not started already.

Section 2: Setting the Working Directory

After starting Creo Parametric, you need to set a working directory to save the files of the current session of Creo Parametric.

1. Click on **File > Manage Session > Select Working Directory**. The **Select Working Directory** window appears. In this window, browse to the *Creo Parametric > Chapter 4* location of your system. You need to create these folders, if not created earlier.

2. Click on the **OK** button to set the working directory to <<*Creo Parametric\Chapter 4*\\.

Section 3: Invoking the Sketching Environment

Now, you will invoke the Sketching environment of the Part mode for creating the sketch of the revolve feature.

1. Click on the **New** tool in the **Data** group of the **Home** tab. The **New** dialog box appears, see Figure 4.69. Alternatively, press the CTRL + N to invoke the **New** dialog box.

2. Ensure that the **Part** radio button is selected in the **Type** area and the **Solid** radio button is selected in the **Sub-type** area of the dialog box, see Figure 4.69.

4.69

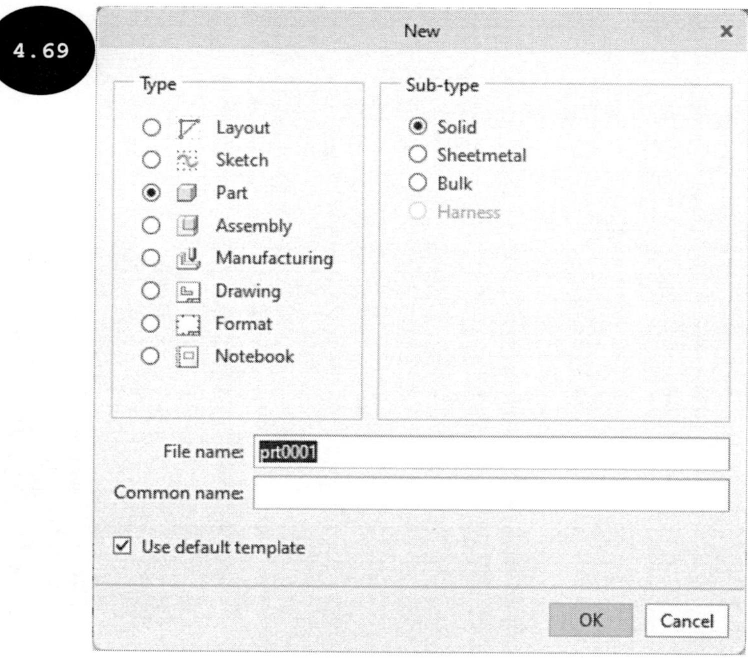

3. Enter **C04-Tutorial02** in the **File name** field of the dialog box.

4. Clear the **Use default template** check box and then click on the **OK** button in the dialog box. The **New File Options** dialog box appears, see Figure 4.70.

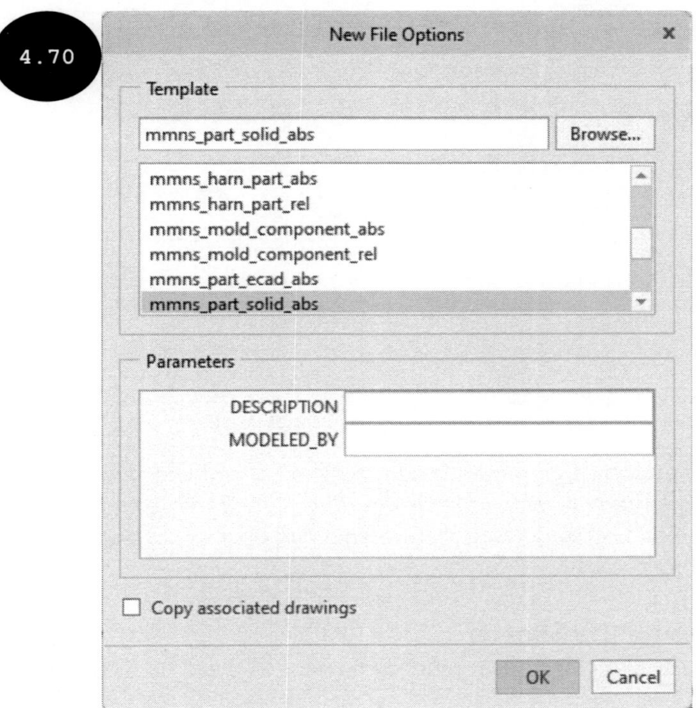

5. Select the **mmns_part_solid_abs** template in the **New File Options** dialog box and then click on the **OK** button. The Part mode is invoked with the **mmns_part_solid_abs** template. In this template, the length is measured in millimeters, mass is measured in Newton, and time is measured in seconds.

   Now, you need to invoke the Sketching environment of the Part mode.

6. Click on the **Sketch** tool in the **Datum** group of the **Model** tab, see Figure 4.71. The **Sketch** dialog box appears and you are prompted to select a plane or a surface to define the sketching plane.

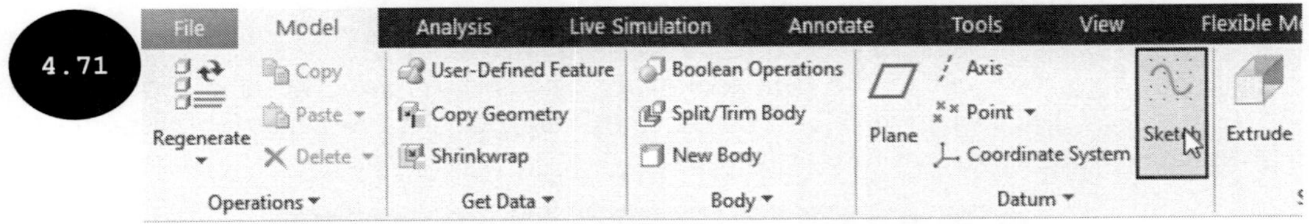

7. Move the cursor over the Front plane in the graphics window and then click the left mouse button when it gets highlighted. The Front plane gets selected as the sketching plane and its name appears in the **Plane** field of the **Sketch** dialog box, see Figure 4.72. Also, a reference plane and its orientation are selected automatically in the **Reference** field and **Orientation** drop-down list of the dialog box, respectively, see Figure 4.72.

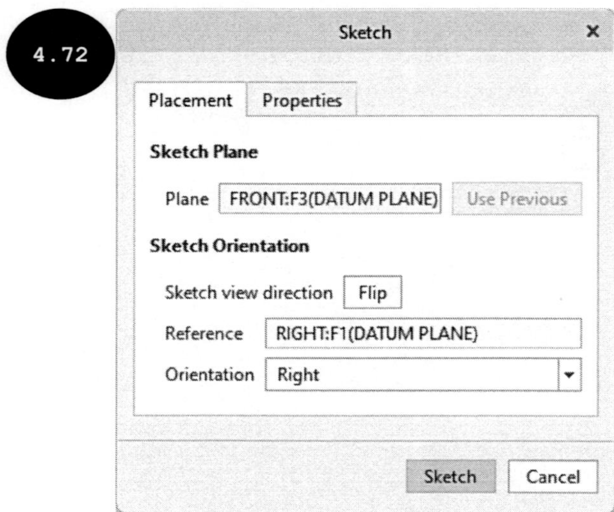

8. Click on the **Sketch** button in the dialog box. The Sketching environment is invoked. Also, the Front plane is oriented normal to the viewing direction. If the Front plane is not oriented normal to the viewing direction by default, then you need to do it by clicking on the **Sketch View** tool in the **In-graphics** toolbar.

Section 4: Drawing the Sketch

After invoking the Sketching environment, you need to draw the sketch of the feature.

1. Click on the **Centerline** tool in the **Sketching** group of the **Sketch** tab, see Figure 4.73. The **Centerline** tool gets activated.

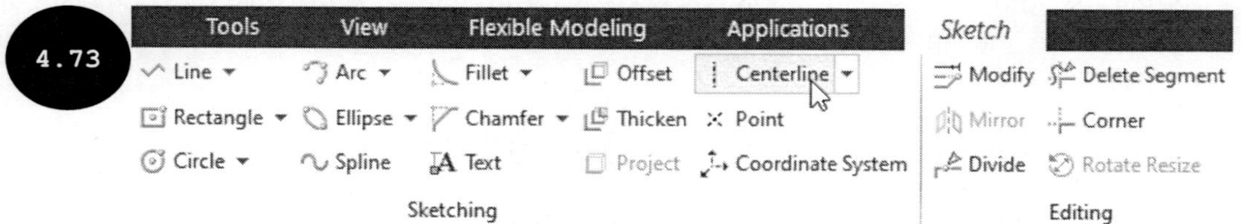

2. Draw a vertical centerline that passes through the origin in the drawing area. Next, press the middle mouse button to exit the **Centerline** tool.

3. Click on the arrow next to the Line tool in the **Sketching** group. The **Line** flyout appears (see Figure 4.74), following which, click on the **Line Chain** tool. The **Line Chain** tool gets activated. Alternatively, press the **L** key to activate this tool.

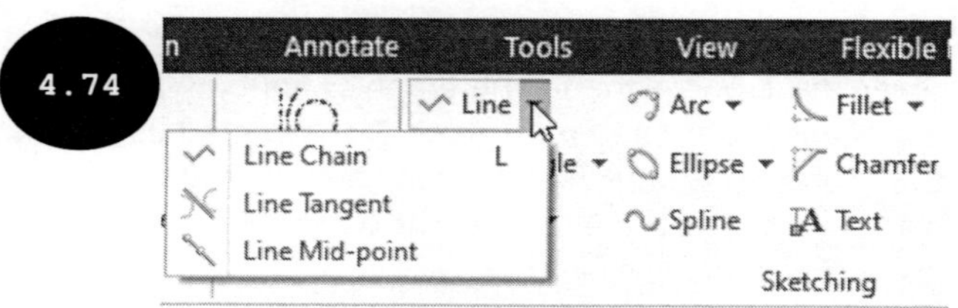

4. Move the cursor over the horizontal reference line at a distance from the vertical centerline, see Figure 4.75. Next, click to specify the start point of the line when the cursor snaps to the horizontal reference line. A rubber band line appears with its one end fixed at the specified start point and the other end attached to the cursor.

5. Move the cursor vertically upward and then click to specify the end point of the line, arbitrarily in the drawing area, when the symbol of vertical constraint appears near the cursor, see Figure 4.76. The line is drawn and a rubber band line with its one end fixed at the last specified point and the other end attached to the cursor appears in the drawing area.

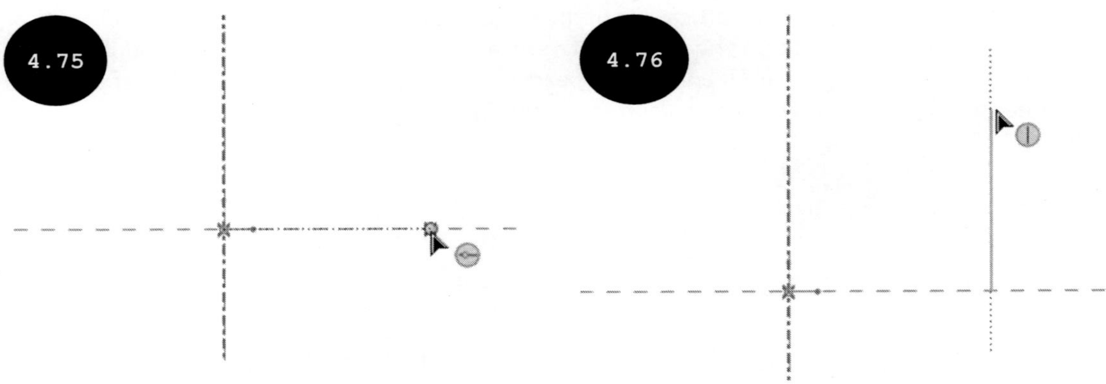

Note: In the figures, the display of datum planes and coordinate system is turned off for clarity of the image.

6. Similarly, draw the remaining entities of the sketch, see Figure 4.77. You can draw this sketch by using the **Line Chain** and **3-Point / Tangent End** tools of the **Sketching** group. The **3-Point / Tangent End** tool is used for drawing the arc of the sketch by specifying three points in the drawing area.

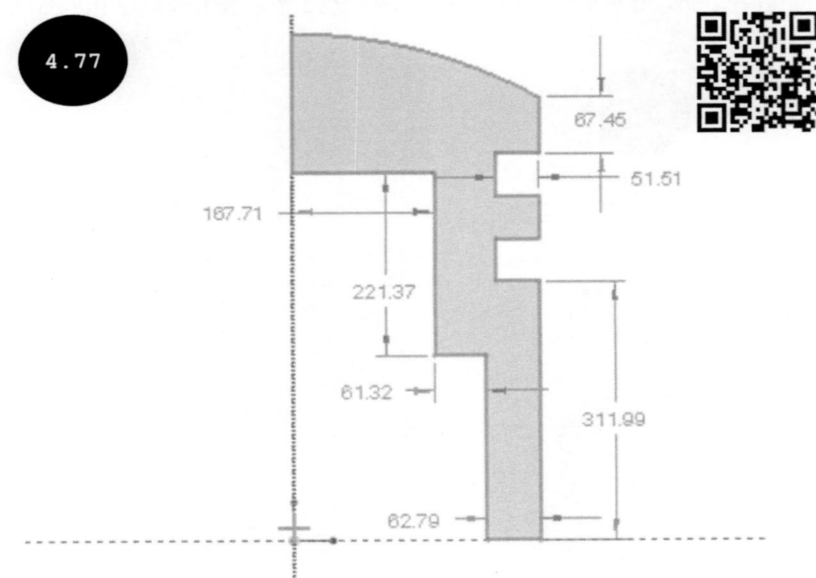

7. After drawing the sketch of the feature, press the middle mouse button to exit the currently active tool.

Section 5: Applying Dimensions

Now, you need to apply dimensions to the sketch. Since it is a sketch of the revolve feature, you need to first apply the linear diameter dimensions and then modify its dimension values.

1. Click on the **Dimension** tool in the **Dimension** group of the **Sketch** tab.

2. Click to select the right most vertical line of the sketch, see Figure 4.78. Next, click on the vertical centerline and then click on the right most vertical line again. Next, press the middle mouse button in the drawing area. An edit field appears with the display of the current linear diameter dimension value. Do not modify the current dimension value at this moment.

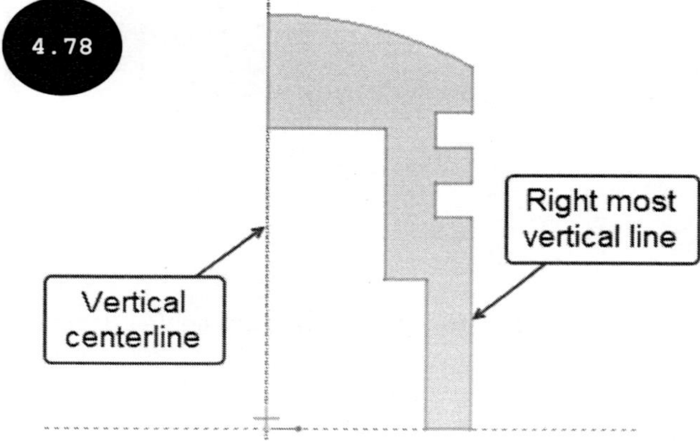

3. Press the ENTER key to accept the current dimension value. The linear diameter dimension is applied with the current dimension value, see Figure 4.79. Note that the value of the applied linear diameter dimension will be different in your case. You will modify the dimension values later in this tutorial.

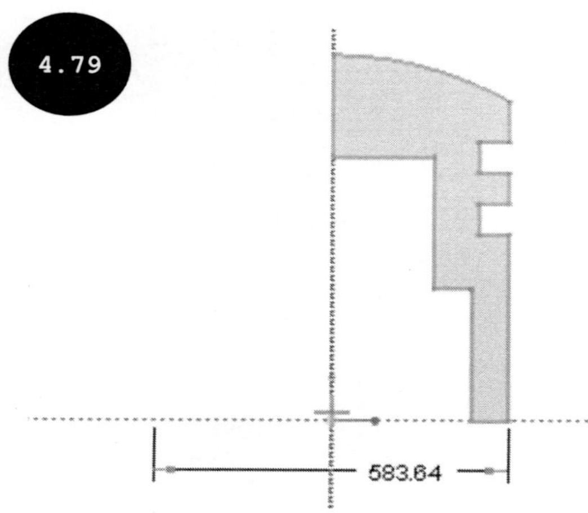

Note: In Figures 4.78 and 4.79, the constraints and weak dimensions are turned off. The method to turn on or off the constraints and weak dimensions has been discussed in earlier chapters.

4. Apply the remaining linear diameter dimensions with their current dimension values in a similar manner, see Figure 4.80. Note that the values of the applied dimensions and weak dimensions shown in this figure will be different in your case. After applying the linear diameter dimensions, press the ESC key to exit the **Dimension** tool.

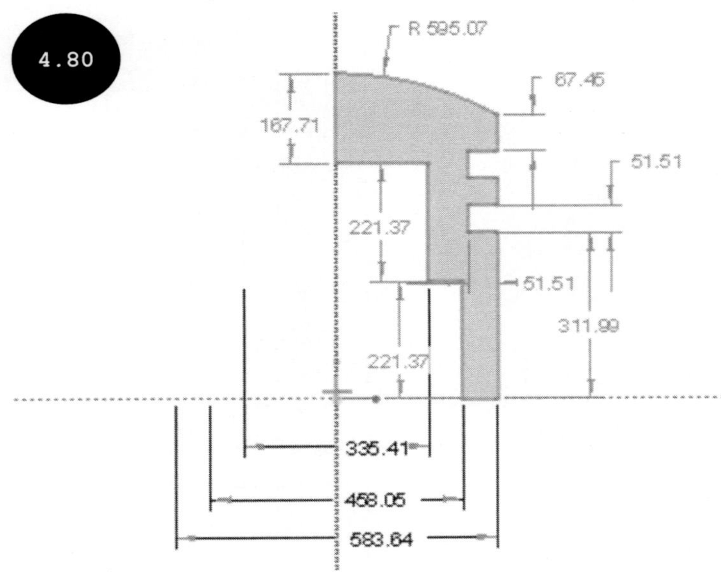

Section 6: Modifying Dimensions

Now, you need to modify the linear diameter dimensions and the weak dimensions of the sketch.

1. Select all the dimensions of the sketch including the weak dimensions by drawing a window around them. You can draw window to select dimensions by dragging the cursor.

2. After selecting all the dimensions, click on the **Modify** tool in the **Editing** group. The **Modify Dimensions** dialog box appears.

3. Clear the **Regenerate** check box in the **Modify Dimensions** dialog box so that the modifications made in the dimension values do not reflect in the sketch until you exit the dialog box.

4. Change the values of all the dimensions one by one by entering new values in the respective edit fields of the **Modify Dimensions** dialog box. You can refer to Figure 4.68 for dimension values.

5. After entering new dimension values for all the dimensions, click on the **OK** button. All the dimensions get updated with new dimension values and are converted to strong dimensions in the drawing area. Next, click anywhere in the drawing area. Figure 4.81 shows the sketch after modifying all the dimensions.

4.81

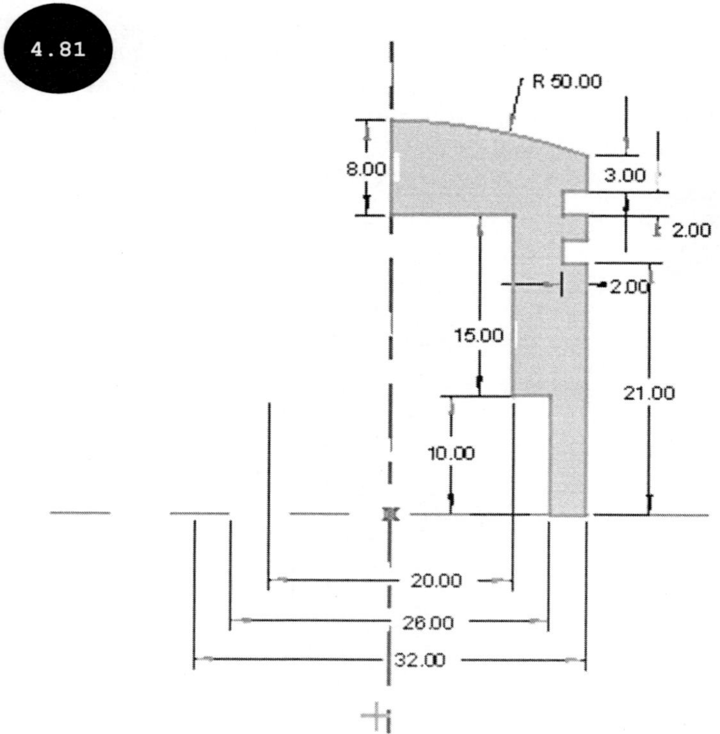

Now, you need to exit the Sketching environment to create a 3D solid model by revolving the sketch.

6. Click on the **OK** button (green tick-mark) in the **Close** group of the **Ribbon** to exit the Sketching environment. The Part modeling environment is invoked and the sketch appears in green color, indicating that the sketch is selected in the graphics window.

Section 7: Revolving the Sketch

Now, in the Part modeling environment, you can revolve the sketch to create a 3D model.

1. Click on the **Revolve** tool in the **Shapes** group of the **Model** tab. A preview of the revolve feature appears in the graphics window by revolving the sketch around its vertical centerline. Also, the **Revolve** tab appears in the **Ribbon**.

Note: If a sketch is not already selected before invoking the **Revolve** tool then the preview of the feature will not appear and you will be prompted to select a sketch to be revolved. Select the sketch in the graphics window. A preview of the revolve feature appears in the graphics window.

2. Change the current orientation of the model to the standard orientation, see Figure 4.82. To change the orientation, click on the **Saved Orientations** tool in the **In-graphics** toolbar, see Figure 4.83. The **Saved Orientations** flyout appears. In this flyout, click on the **Standard Orientation** tool.

4.82

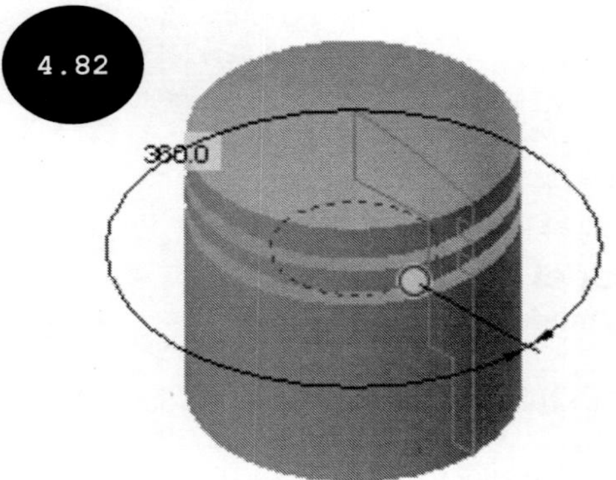

4.83

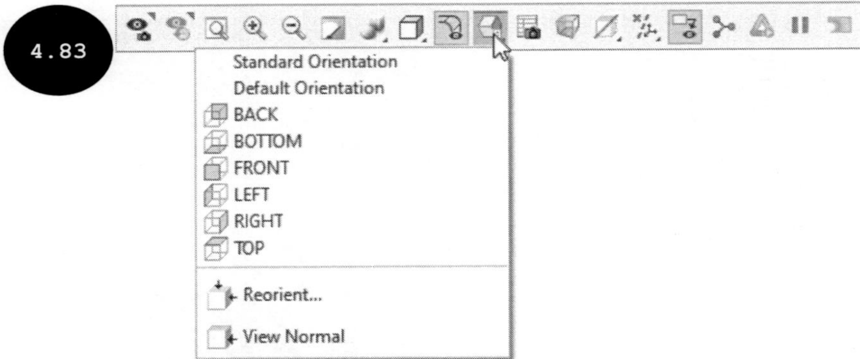

3. Ensure that the **Variable** option is selected in the **Side 1** drop-down list and the angle value is set to 360-degrees in the **Angle** field of the **Revolve** tab, see Figure 4.84.

4.84

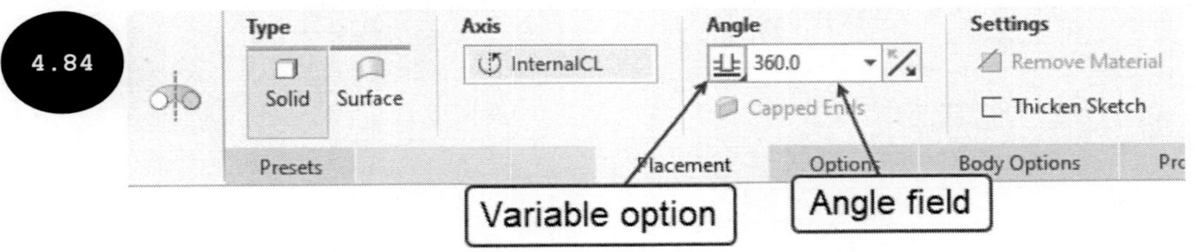

4. Click on the green tick-mark button in the **Revolve** tab. The revolve feature is created, see Figure 4.85. In this figure, the standard/default orientation of the model is set to Isometric.

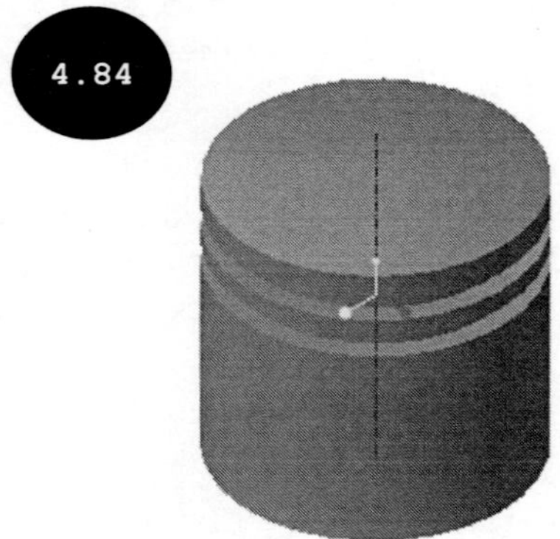

Section 8: Saving the Model

Now, you need to save the model.

1. Click on the **Save** tool in the **Quick Access Toolbar**. The **Save Object** dialog box appears.

2. Click on the **OK** button in the dialog box. The model is saved in the specified working directory (<<*Creo Parametric**Chapter 4*\).

Hands-on Test Drive 1

Create the model shown in Figure 4.86. The extruded depth of the model is 60 mm. All dimensions are in mm.

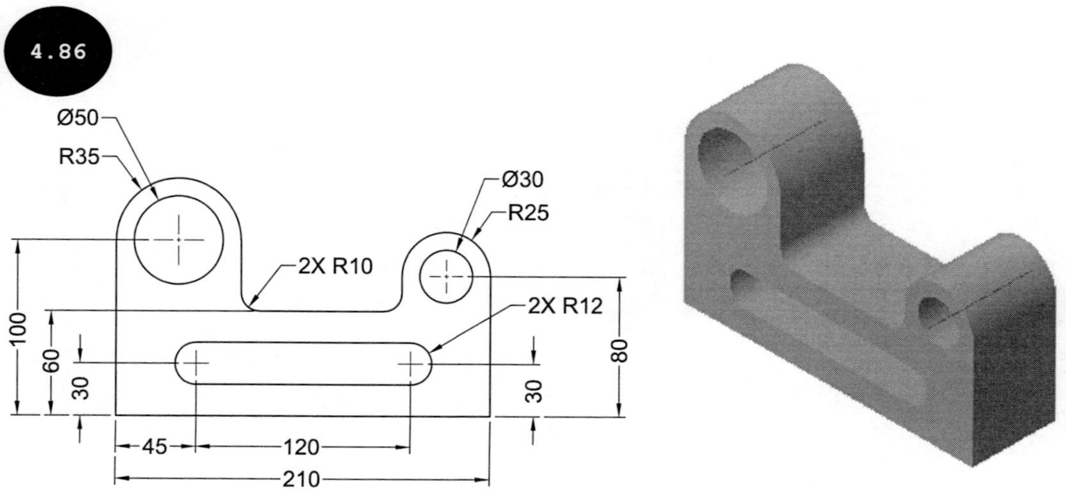

Hands-on Test Drive 2

Create the model shown in Figure 4.87. All dimensions are in mm.

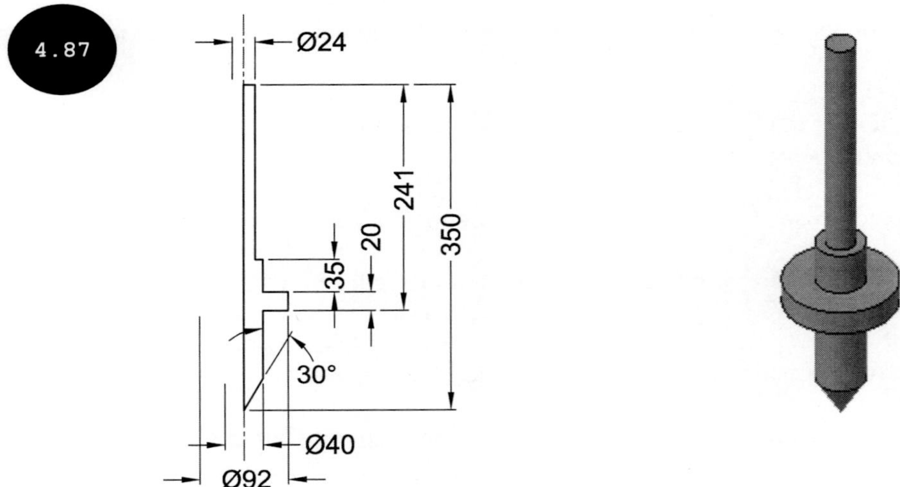

Summary

In this chapter, you have learned about creating extrude and revolve base features by using the **Extrude** and **Revolve** tools. The chapter discussed how to navigate a model by using the mouse buttons and navigation tools such as **Zoom In**, **Zoom Out**, **Refit**, **Zoom to Selected**, and **Pan**. It also discussed how to manipulate the view orientation of the model to predefined standard views such as front, top, right, and custom views. Besides, the chapter also explained changing the display style of the model.

Questions

Complete and verify the following sentences:

- The _________ tool is used for creating a feature by adding material normal to the sketching plane.
- The _________ tool is used for creating a feature by revolving the sketch around a centerline as the axis of revolution.
- The _________ tool is used for fitting a model completely inside the graphics area.
- The _________ check box of the **Options** panel in the **Extrude** tab is used for tapering the extrude feature.

- The ______ button of the **Properties** panel in the **Extrude** tab is used for displaying detailed information of the feature such as name, material, extrusion direction, depth, dimension values, and so on, in a browser window.
- The ______ option is used for extruding/revolving a feature symmetrically about the sketching plane.
- The ______ tool of the **Saved Orientations** flyout is used for changing the orientation of the model to standard orientation.
- The ______ tool is used for creating a custom or user defined orientation of the model.
- The ______ tool is used for displaying the selected face/edge of a 3D model normal to the viewing direction.
- By default, the standard orientation is set to Trimetric. (True/False)
- In Creo Parametric, you cannot navigate a model by using the mouse buttons. (True/False)
- While creating a revolved feature, if the sketch to be revolved has a centerline, then the drawn centerline is automatically selected as the axis of revolution. (True/False)

CHAPTER

5

Creating Datum Geometries

In this chapter, the following topics will be discussed:

- Creating Datum Planes
- Creating a Datum Axis
- Creating a Datum Coordinate System
- Creating a Datum Point

In Creo Parametric, three default datum planes; Front, Top, and Right are available, by default. You can use these datum planes to create the base feature of a model by extruding or revolving the sketch, as discussed in earlier chapters. However, to create a real-world model having multiple features, you may need additional datum planes. In other words, the three default datum planes may not be enough to create all features of a real-world model and you may need to create additional datum planes. Creo Parametric allows you to create additional datum planes for creating real-world models, as required. You can create additional datum planes by using the **Plane** tool, which is available in the **Datum** group of the **Model** tab, see Figure 5.1.

5.1

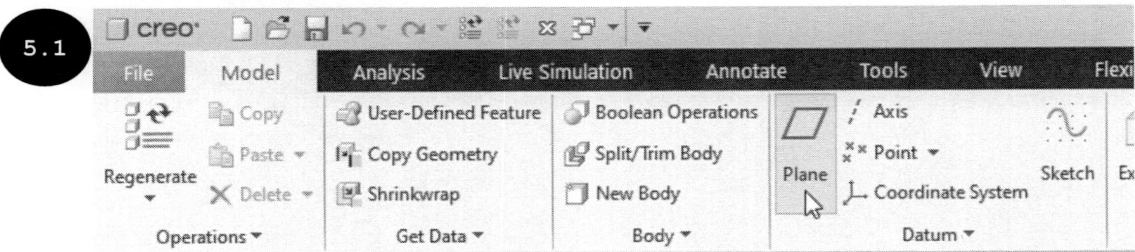

Figure 5.2 shows a model, which is created by creating all its features one by one. This model has four features. Its first feature is an extruded feature created on the right plane. The second feature is a user-defined datum plane created at an angle. The third feature is an extruded feature created on the user-defined datum plane. The fourth feature is a cut feature created on the top planar face of the third feature.

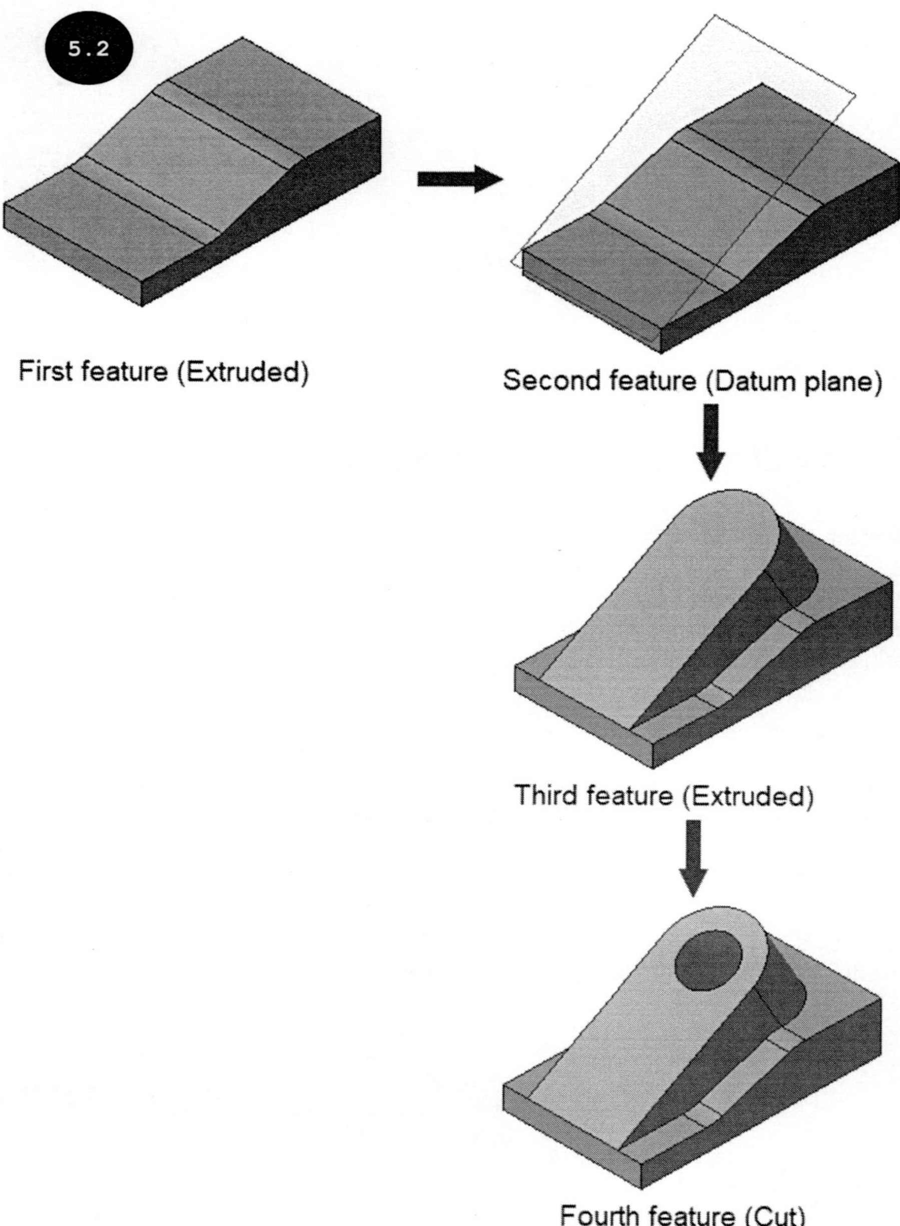

Note: It is clear from the above figure that additional datum planes may be required for creating a real world 3D model.

Creating Datum Planes

In Creo Parametric, you can create datum planes at an offset distance from an existing plane or planar face, parallel to an existing plane or planar face, at an angle to an existing plane or planar face, or normal to a curve by using the **Plane** tool.

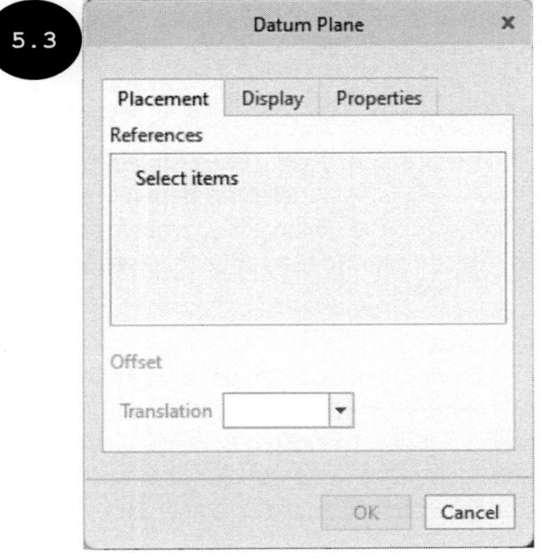

5.3

To create a datum plane, click on the **Plane** tool in the **Datum** group of the **Model** tab. The **Datum Plane** dialog box appears, see Figure 5.3. The options in this dialog box are used for creating different types of datum planes and are discussed next.

Placement

The **References** area of the **Placement** tab in the dialog box is used for selecting references for creating a datum plane. You can select a maximum of three references for creating a datum plane. Note that the selection of a reference depends upon the type of datum plane to be created. For example, to create a plane at an offset distance from the planar face of a model, you need to select the planar face of the model as a reference. As soon as you select a reference, its name appears in the **References** area and the most suitable constraint is selected in the **Constraint** drop-down list that appears next to the selected reference in the dialog box, see Figure 5.4. Note that on selecting a planar face or a plane as the first reference, the **Offset** constraint is selected in the **Constraint** drop-down list, by default, which allows you to create a datum plane at an offset distance from the selected reference. To select a required constraint in the **Constraint** drop-down list, click on the arrow next to the selected constraint. The **Constraint** drop-down list appears (see Figure 5.5), from which you can select the required constraint. The availability of constraints in this drop-down list depends upon the type of reference selected. The different constraints available in the **Constraint** drop-down list are discussed next.

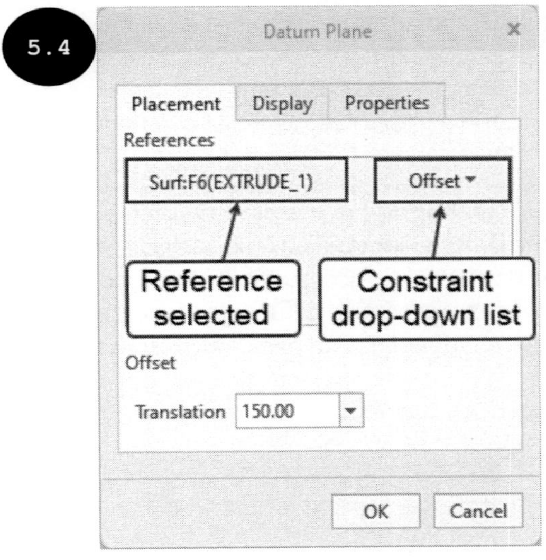

5.4

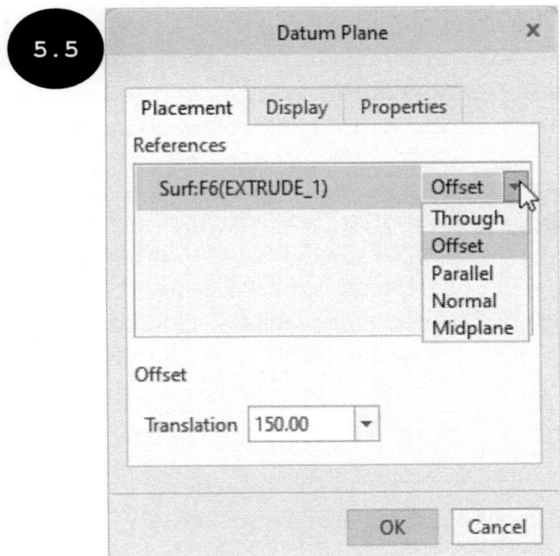

5.5

Offset

The **Offset** constraint is used for creating a datum plane at an offset distance from the selected reference. On selecting the **Offset** constraint in the **Constraint** drop-down list, the **Translation** field gets enabled in the **Offset** area of the dialog box. The **Translation** field allows you to enter an offset distance for creating the datum plane. Note that the **Offset** constraint is available in the **Constraint** drop-down list when the selected reference is a plane or a planar face of a model.

Parallel

The **Parallel** constraint is used for creating a datum plane parallel to the selected reference (a planar face or a plane). On selecting the **Parallel** constraint, the parallel constraint is applied between the selected reference and the plane. Note that for creating a plane parallel to a planar face or a plane, you also need to select a second reference. You will learn more about creating parallel planes later in this chapter.

Normal

The **Normal** constraint is used for creating a datum plane normal to a selected reference (a planar face or a plane). On selecting the **Normal** constraint, the normal constraint is applied between the selected reference and the plane. Note that for creating a plane normal/perpendicular to a planar face or a plane, you also need to select a second reference. You will learn more about creating a plane normal to a selected reference (a planar face or a plane) later in this chapter.

Midplane

The **Midplane** constraint is used for creating a datum plane in the middle of two planar faces. To do so, you need to select two planar faces as the first and second references. You will learn more about creating a datum plane in the middle of two planar faces later in this chapter.

Note: You can select more than one reference for creating a datum plane by pressing the CTRL key.

Through

The **Through** constraint is used for creating a datum plane that passes through three points or vertices. To do so, you need to select three points/vertices as the first, second, and third references. You can also create a datum plane passing through an edge and at an angle, parallel, or normal to a planar face. To do so, you need to select an edge as the first reference and a planar face as the second reference.

Note: In Creo Parametric, you need to focus more on creating datum planes rather than selecting options in the **Constraint** drop-down list of the **Datum Plane** dialog box, because when you select a reference geometry for creating a datum plane, the most suitable option/constraint gets automatically selected. Also, the preview of the respective datum plane appears in the graphics area. The methods for creating different types of datum planes are discussed later in this chapter.

Display

The options in the **Display** tab of the **Datum Plane** dialog box are used for controlling the display of datum planes, see Figure 5.6. The options in the **Display** tab are discussed next.

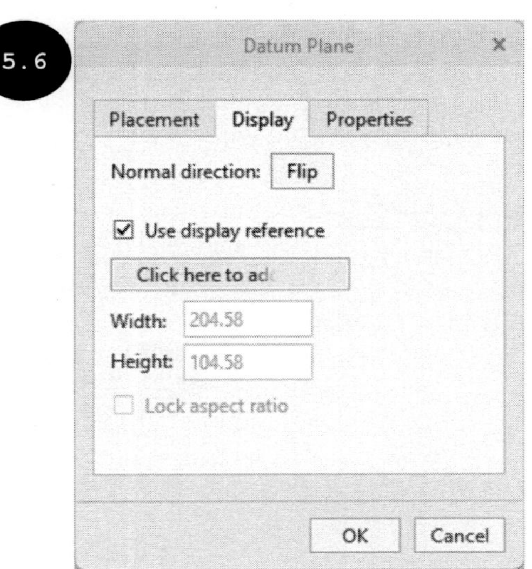

Flip

The **Flip** button in the **Display** tab is used for flipping/changing the normal direction of the datum plane. The arrow appearing in the graphics area points toward the normal direction of the plane. The normal direction of a plane defines the front side of the datum plane. Note that each datum plane has two sides, front and back. The boundary of the front side of a datum plane appears in brown, whereas the boundary of the back side appears in gray.

Use display reference

The **Use display reference** check box allows you to control the size of the datum plane by selecting a reference geometry. To do so, select the **Use display reference** check box in the dialog box. Next, you need to select a geometry as a reference for defining the size of the datum plane. On clearing the **Use display reference** check box, you can control the size of the datum plane by entering its width and height in the **Width** and **Height** fields in the dialog box, respectively, see Figure 5.7.

Note: You can also drag the handles that appear at each corner of the datum plane in the graphics area to adjust its size, dynamically, see Figure 5.8.

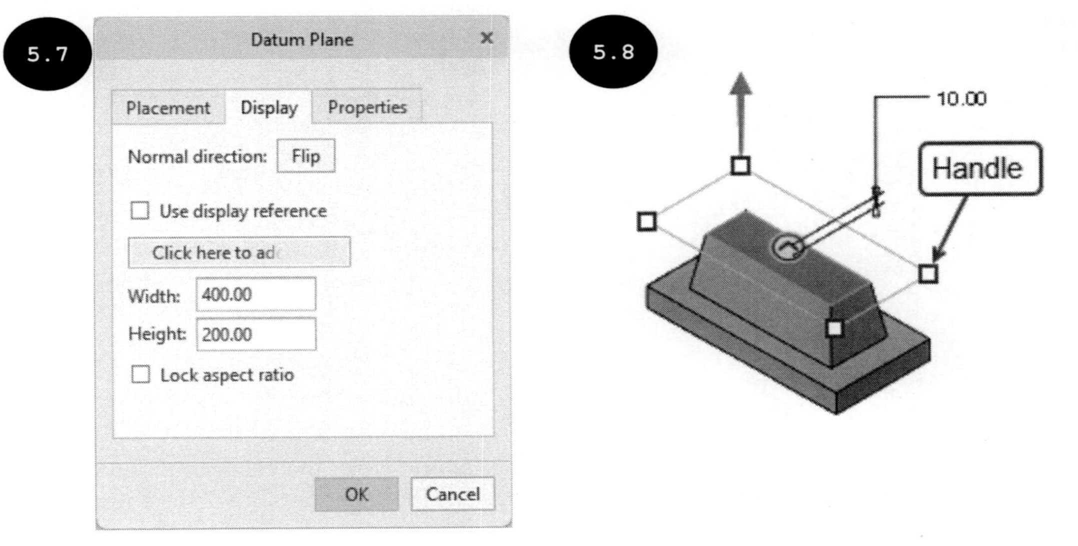

Lock aspect ratio

The **Lock aspect ratio** check box is used for maintaining the proportion between the width and height of the datum plane. Note that this check box is available when the **Use display reference** check box is cleared in the dialog box.

Properties

The **Name** field of the **Properties** tab of the dialog box is used for specifying a name for the datum plane, see Figure 5.9. By default, the name of a datum plane is assigned as DTM1, DTM2, DTM3, ..., or DTMn in a sequential order.

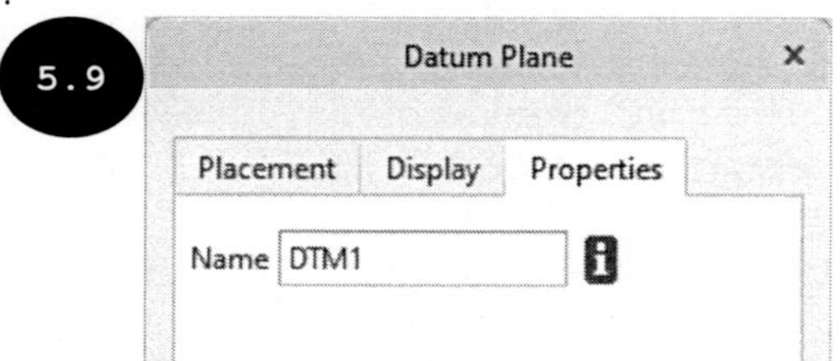

After selecting the required references for creating a datum plane and specifying other properties in the **Datum Plane** dialog box, click on the **OK** button. The method for creating different types of datum planes is discussed next.

Creating a Plane at an Offset Distance

1. Click on the **Plane** tool in the **Datum** group of the **Model** tab. The **Datum Plane** dialog box appears.

2. Select a planar face or a plane in the graphics area as the first reference. A preview of the offset plane appears in the graphics area, see Figure 5.10. Also, the name of the selected reference appears in the **References** area of the dialog box, and the **Offset** constraint is selected in the **Constraint** drop-down list, by default, see Figure 5.11.

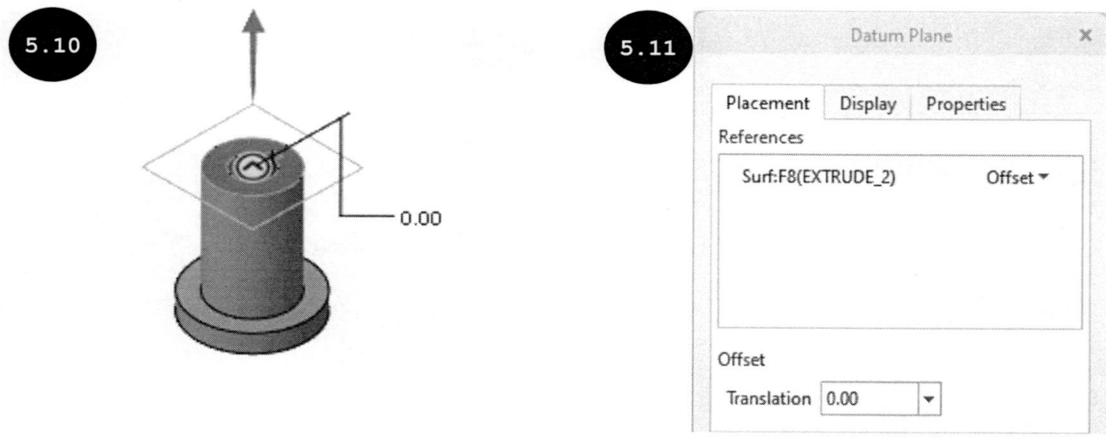

3. Enter the required offset distance value in the **Translation** field of the dialog box. You can also drag the handle that appears in the graphics area to adjust the offset distance of the datum plane, dynamically, see Figure 5.12.

Note: To reverse the direction of the datum plane, you need to either enter a negative offset distance value or drag the handle to the other side of the selected planar face.

4. Click on the **OK** button in the dialog box. A datum plane is created at the specified offset distance from the selected reference, see Figure 5.13.

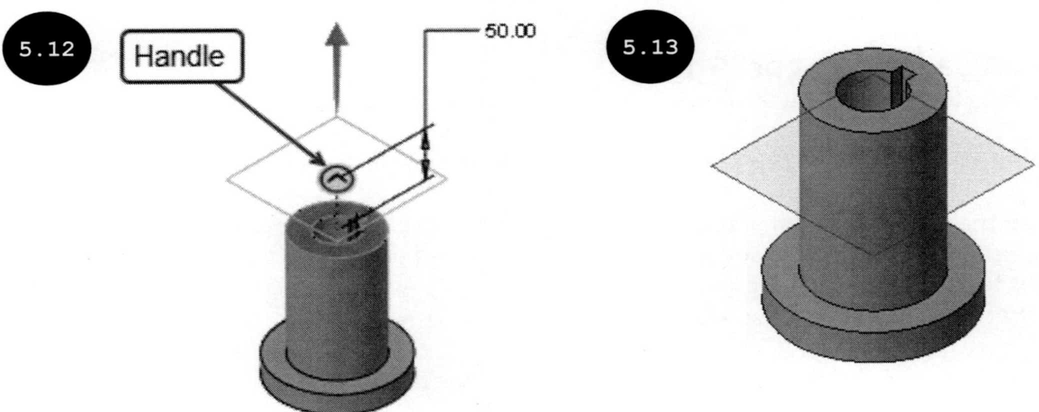

Creating a Parallel Plane

1. Click on the **Plane** tool in the **Datum** group. The **Datum Plane** dialog box appears.

2. Select a planar face or a plane in the graphics area as the first reference, see Figure 5.14.

Note: When you select a planar face or a plane as the first reference, the preview of an offset plane appears in the graphics area. Also, the name of the selected reference appears in the **References** area of the dialog box and the **Offset** constraint is selected in the **Constraint** drop-down list, by default.

3. Press the CTRL key and then select a point, a vertex, or a linear edge in the graphics area as the second reference. A preview of the datum plane parallel to the selected face and passing through the selected vertex/point appears in the graphics area, see Figure 5.14. In this figure, a vertex is selected as the second reference.

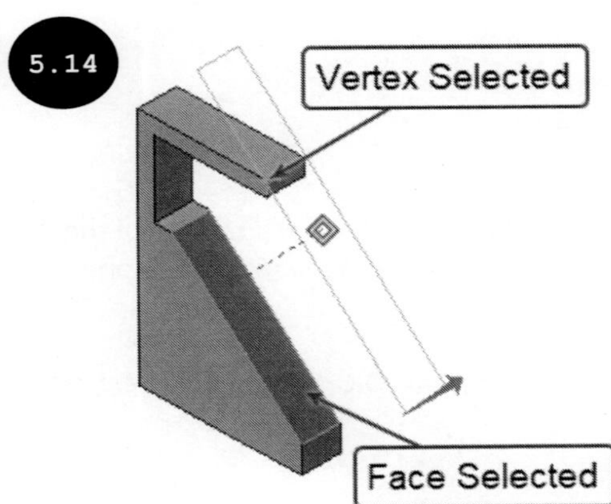

Note: On selecting a linear edge as the second reference, you need to select the **Parallel** constraint from the **Constraint** drop-down list that appears in front of the planar face reference in the **Reference** area of the dialog box.

4. Click on the **OK** button in the dialog box. A datum plane is created parallel to the selected planar face and passes through the selected vertex or edge.

Creating a Plane at an Angle

1. Click on the **Plane** tool in the **Datum** group. The **Datum Plane** dialog box appears.

2. Select a planar face or a plane in the graphics area as the first reference, see Figure 5.15.

3. Press the CTRL key and then select a linear edge, an axis, or a sketch line as the second reference. A preview of the datum plane at an angle to the selected planar face and passing through the selected edge appears in the graphics area, see Figure 5.15. Also, the **Rotation** field appears in the **Offset** area of the dialog box, see Figure 5.16.

4. Enter the required angle value in the **Rotation** field of the dialog box.

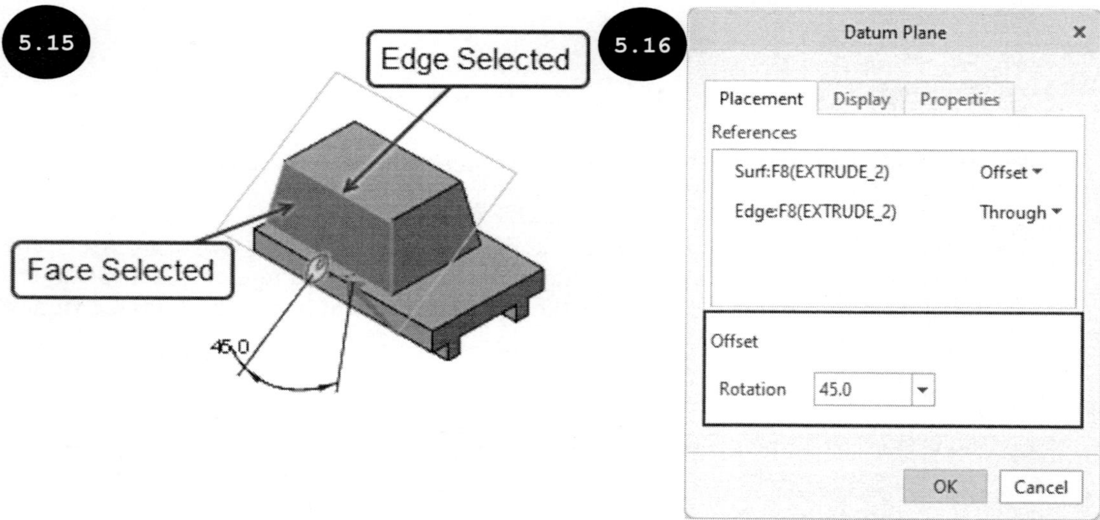

Note: To reverse the direction of the datum plane, you need to either enter a negative angle value or drag the handle that appears in the graphics area.

5. Click on the **OK** button in the dialog box. A datum plane is created at the specified angle.

Creating a Plane Passing through Three Points/Vertices

1. Click on the **Plane** tool in the **Datum** group. The **Datum Plane** dialog box appears.
2. Select a point or a vertex in the graphics area as the first reference.
3. Select the second point or vertex as the second reference by pressing the CTRL key.
4. Select the third point or vertex as the third reference by pressing the CTRL key. A preview of the datum plane passing through three points/vertices appears, see Figure 5.17.
5. Click on the **OK** button in the dialog box. The desired datum plane is created.

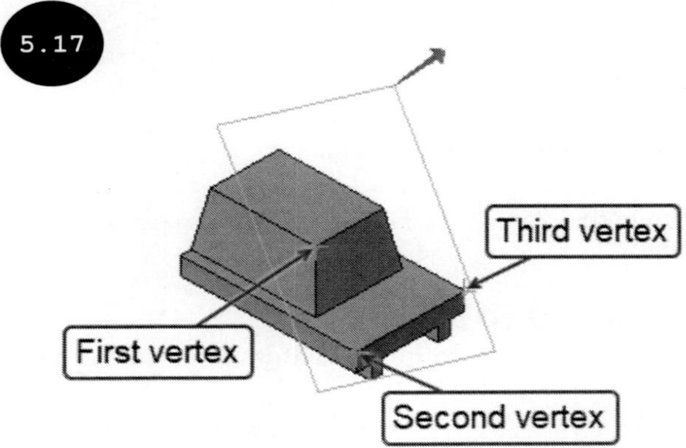

Creating a Plane at the Middle of Two Faces/Planes

1. Click on the **Plane** tool in the **Datum** group. The **Datum Plane** dialog box appears.
2. Select a planar face of the model as the first reference, see Figure 5.18.
3. Press the CTRL key and then select the second planar face of the model as the second reference, see Figure 5.18. A preview of the plane passing through the middle of the two selected faces appears in the graphics area, see Figure 5.18.

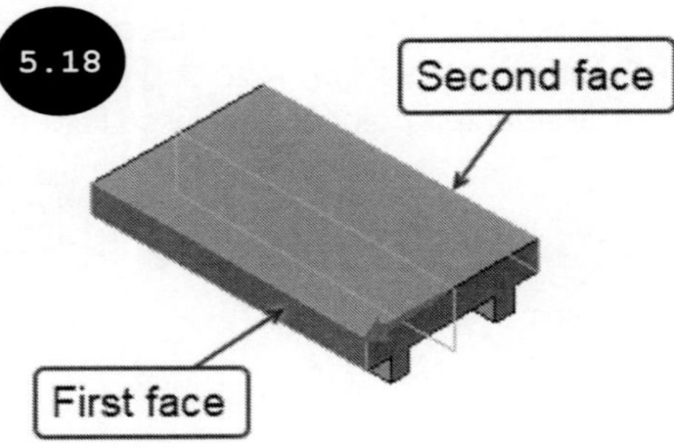

Note: Both the selected references must be parallel to each other for creating a datum plane in between. If you select two non-parallel references (planar faces or planes), then a plane bisecting the angle at the intersection of selected references will be created.

4. Click on the **OK** button in the dialog box. A datum plane is created between the two selected faces.

Creating a Plane Normal to a Planar Face/Plane

1. Click on the **Plane** tool in the **Datum** group. The **Datum Plane** dialog box appears.

2. Select a planar face or a plane in the graphics area as the first reference, see Figure 5.19.

3. Select the **Normal** constraint from the **Constraint** drop-down list that appears in front of the selected reference in the **References** area of the dialog box.

4. Press the CTRL key and then select a linear edge in the graphics area as the second reference. A preview of the datum plane normal to the selected face and passing through the selected edge appears in the graphics area, see Figure 5.19.

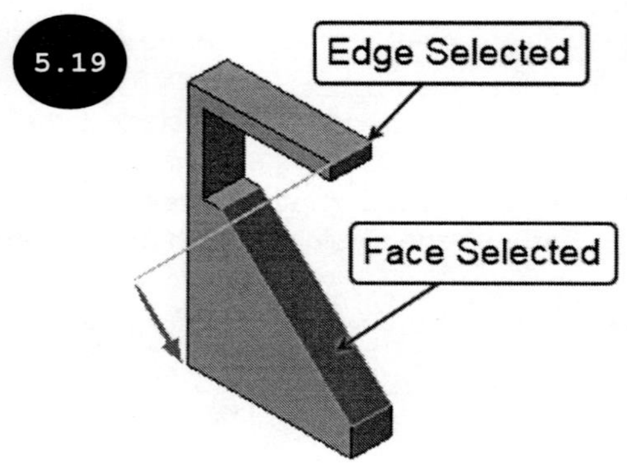

5. Click on the **OK** button in the dialog box. The desired datum plane is created.

Creating a Plane Normal to a Curve

1. Click on the **Plane** tool in the **Datum** group. The **Datum Plane** dialog box appears.

2. Select a curve in the graphics area as the first reference, see Figure 5.20.

3. Select the **Normal** constraint from the **Constraint** drop-down list that appears in front of the selected reference in the **References** area of the dialog box.

4. Press the CTRL key and then select an endpoint of the curve in the graphics area as the second reference, see Figure 5.20. A preview of the datum plane normal to the curve and passing through the selected point appears, see Figure 5.20.

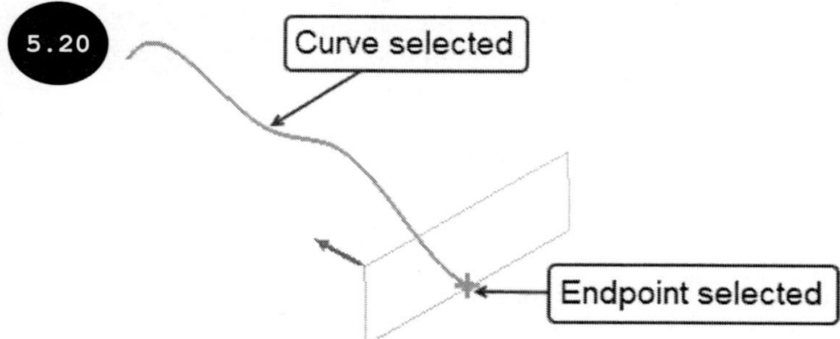

5. Click on the **OK** button in the dialog box. The desired datum plane is created.

Creating a Plane Tangent to a Cylindrical Face

1. Click on the **Plane** tool in the **Datum** group. The **Datum Plane** dialog box appears.

2. Select a cylindrical face of the model as the first reference, see Figure 5.21.

3. Select the **Tangent** constraint from the **Constraint** drop-down list that appears in front of the selected reference in the **References** area of the dialog box.

4. Press the CTRL key and then select a planar face or a plane as the second reference, see Figure 5.21. A preview of the plane tangent to the cylindrical face and normal to the planar face appears, see Figure 5.21.

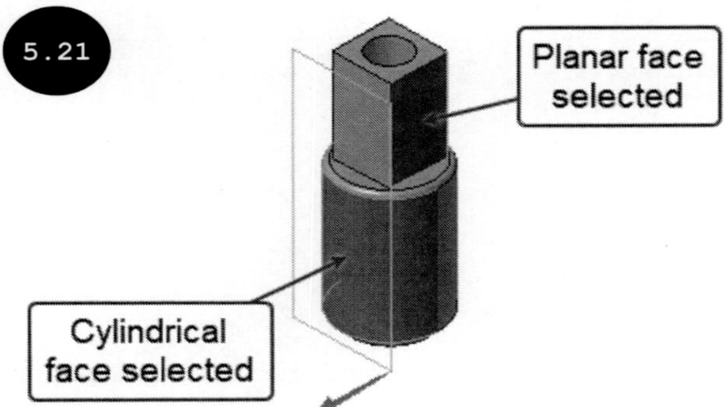

Note: When you specify the second reference (a planar face), the **Normal** constraint gets selected, automatically in the **Constraint** drop-down list that appears in front of it in the dialog box. As a result, the preview of the datum plane appears as tangent to the cylindrical face and normal to the selected planar face. If you select the **Parallel** constraint in the **Constraint** drop-down list, the preview of the tangent plane gets modified and appears as tangent to the cylindrical face and parallel to the selected planar face.

5. Click on the **OK** button. A datum plane tangent to the selected cylindrical face and normal or parallel to the planar face is created.

Creating a Datum Axis

Similar to creating a datum plane, you can create a datum axis. Datum axis is used as the axis of revolution for creating features such as revolved features and circular patterns. To create a datum axis, click on the **Axis** tool in the **Datum** group of the **Model** tab, see Figure 5.22. The **Datum Axis** dialog box appears, see Figure 5.23. The methods for creating different types of datum axes are discussed next.

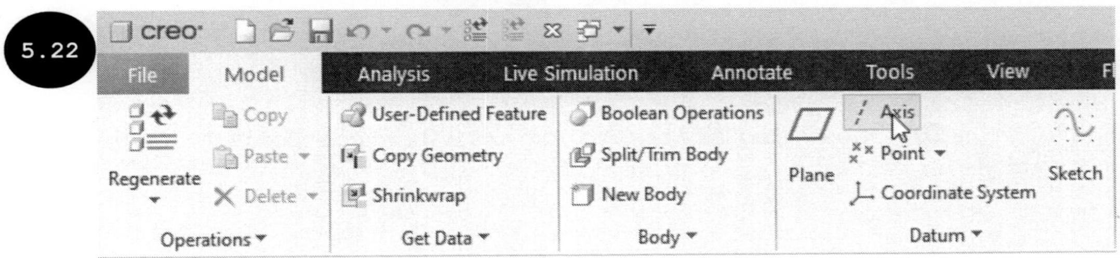

Creating a Datum Axis along a Linear Entity

1. Click on the **Axis** tool in the **Datum** group. The **Datum Axis** dialog box appears, see Figure 5.23.

2. Select a linear entity (an edge or a line) as the first reference in the graphics area. The preview of a datum axis appears along the selected entity, see Figure 5.24. Also, the **Through** constraint is selected in the **Constraint** drop-down list that appears in front of the selected reference in the **References** area of the dialog box, by default.

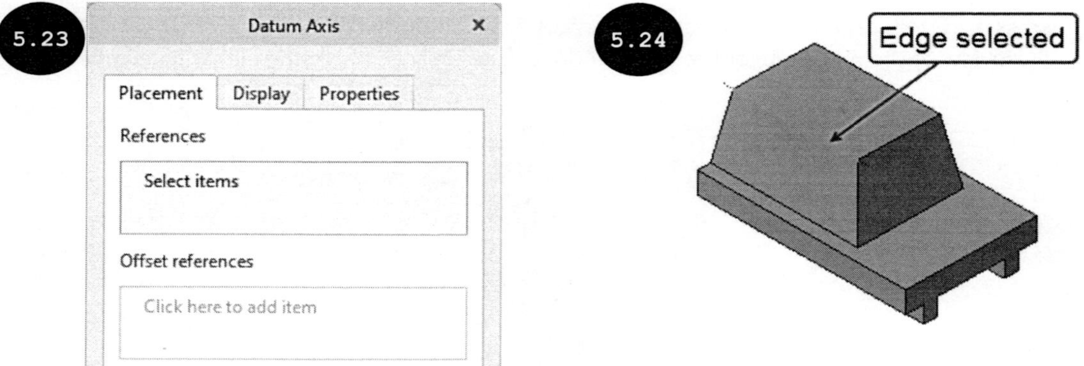

3. Click on the **OK** button in the dialog box. A datum axis is created along the selected linear entity.

Creating a Datum Axis at the Intersection of Two Planar Faces

1. Click on the **Axis** tool in the **Datum** group. The **Datum Axis** dialog box appears.

2. Select a planar face or a plane as the first reference in the graphics area, see Figure 5.25.

3. Press the CTRL key and then select the second planar face as the second reference in the graphics area, see Figure 5.25. A preview of the datum axis at the intersection of the selected references appears in the graphics area. Note that the planes or faces selected as references need to be non-parallel to each other.

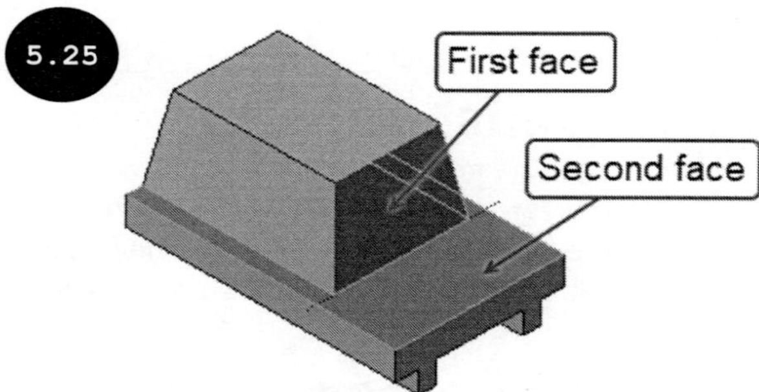

4. Click on the **OK** button in the dialog box. A datum axis at the intersection of the two planar faces is created.

Creating a Datum Axis Normal to a Planar Face

1. Click on the **Axis** tool in the **Datum** group. The **Datum Axis** dialog box appears.

2. Select a planar face or a plane as the first reference in the graphics area, see Figure 5.26. A preview of the datum axis normal to the selected face appears in the graphics area along with a placement handle and two offset handles, see Figure 5.26.

3. Click on the **Offset references** area in the **Placement** tab of the dialog box and then select two references (planes, planar faces, or linear edges) in the graphics area, see Figure 5.27. Alternatively, you can drag the offset handles to the references.

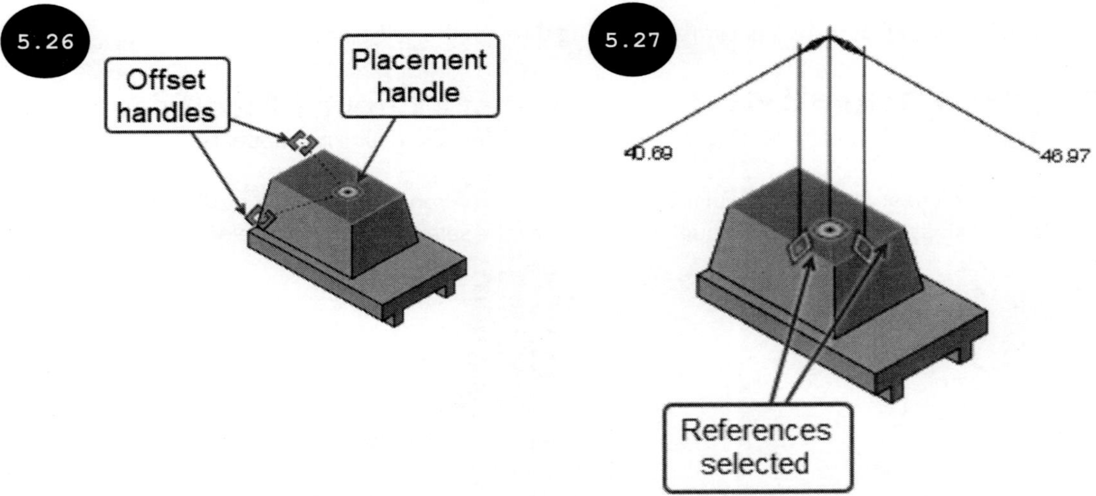

4. Edit the offset distance values by double-clicking on the dimensions that appear in the graphics area or next to the references in the dialog box to define the placement of the datum axis on the selected face, as required.

5. Click on the **OK** button. A datum axis normal to the selected face is created.

Creating a Datum Axis Passing Through Two Points/Vertices

1. Click on the **Axis** tool in the **Datum** group. The **Datum Axis** dialog box appears.

2. Select a vertex or a point in the graphics area as the first reference, see Figure 5.28.

3. Press the CTRL key and then select the second vertex as the second reference, see Figure 5.28. A preview of the datum axis passing through the selected vertices appears.

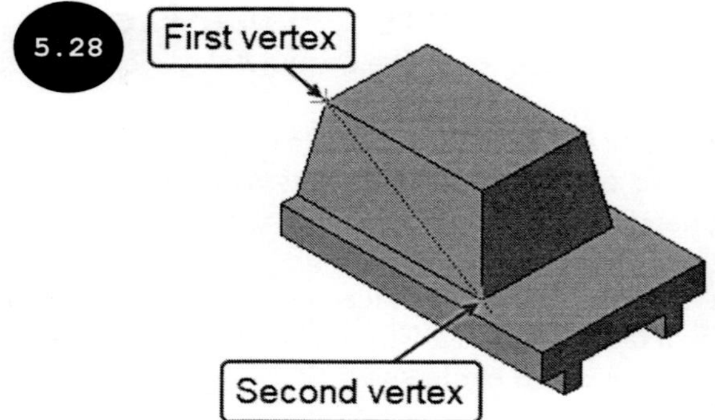

4. Click on the **OK** button. A datum axis passing through the selected vertices is created.

Creating a Datum Axis at the Center of a Circular Face/Edge

1. Click on the **Axis** tool in the **Datum** group. The **Datum Axis** dialog box appears.

2. Select a circular face or a circular edge as the first reference, see Figure 5.29. A preview of the datum axis appears passing through the center of the selected circular face or edge.

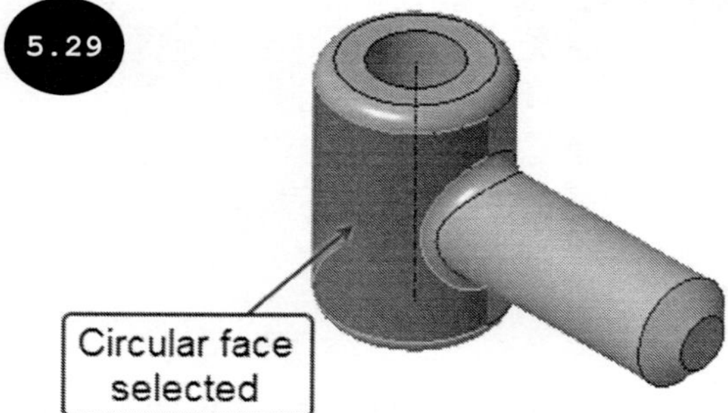

3. Click on the **OK** button. A datum axis at the center of the circular face is created.

Creating a Datum Axis Tangent to a Circular Edge

1. Click on the **Axis** tool in the **Datum** group. The **Datum Axis** dialog box appears.

2. Select a circular edge as the first reference, see Figure 5.30. A preview of the datum axis passing through the center of the selected circular edge appears.

3. Press the CTRL key and then select a vertex of the selected edge as the second reference, see Figure 5.30. A preview of the datum axis appears tangent to the circular edge and passes through the vertex.

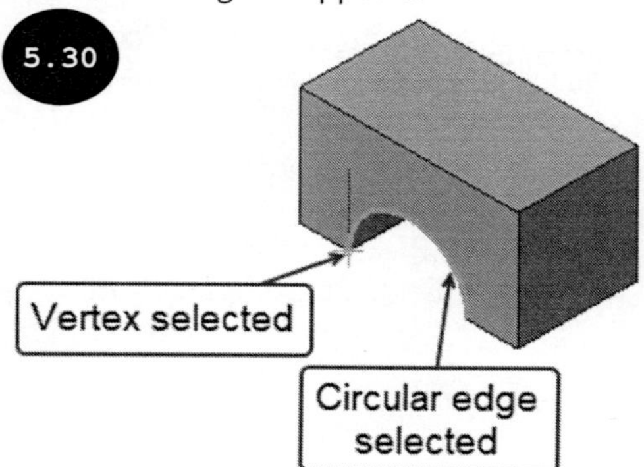

4. Click on the **OK** button. A datum axis tangent to the circular edge is created.

Creating a Datum Axis Normal to a Face and Passing through a Vertex

1. Click on the **Axis** tool in the **Datum** group. The **Datum Axis** dialog box appears.

2. Select a planar face or a plane as the first reference, see Figure 5.31.

3. Press the CTRL key and then select a vertex or a point as the second reference, see Figure 5.31. A preview of the datum axis normal to the face and passing through the vertex appears.

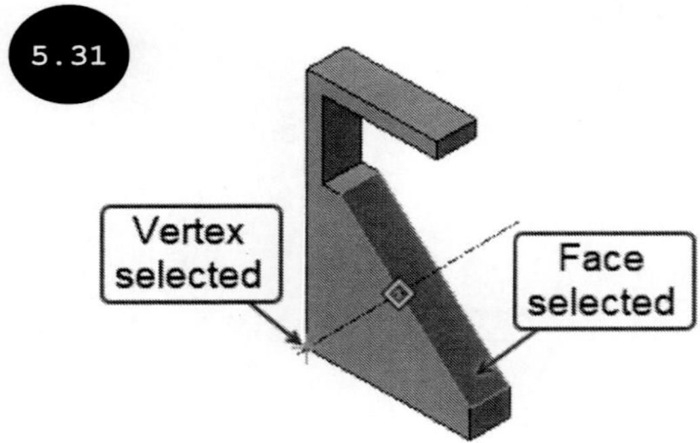

4. Click on the **OK** button. A datum axis normal to a face and passing through a vertex is created.

Creating a Datum Coordinate System

In addition to creating a datum plane and axis, you can also create datum coordinate systems by using the **Coordinate System** tool in the **Datum** group of the **Model** tab, see Figure 5.32. A coordinate system is mainly used for machining or analyzing a model by positioning the origin of the model relative to its features. You can also use a datum coordinate system for applying constraints, calculating mass properties, measurements, and so on. The methods for creating different types of coordinate systems are discussed next.

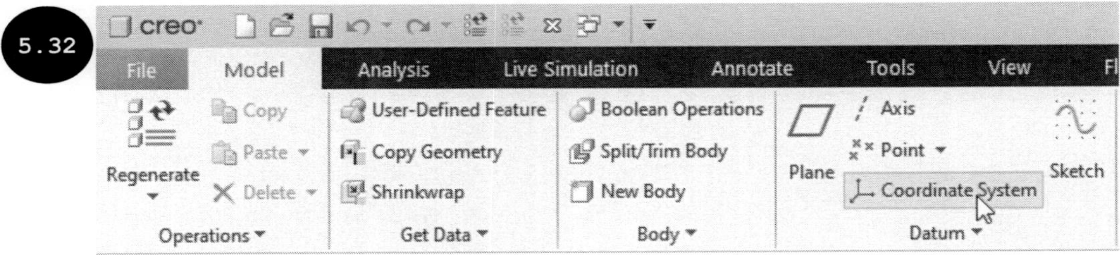

Creating a Coordinate System on a Face

1. Click on the **Coordinate System** tool in the **Datum** group. The **Coordinate System** dialog box appears.

2. Select a face (planar or circular) of the model as the first reference. A preview of the coordinate system appears on the selected face along with a placement handle that is filled with yellow color and two offset handles that are filled with red color, see Figure 5.33. In this figure, a planar face is selected for creating a coordinate system. Note that on selecting a face, the **Coordinate System** dialog box gets modified with additional options, see Figure 5.34.

5.33

5.34

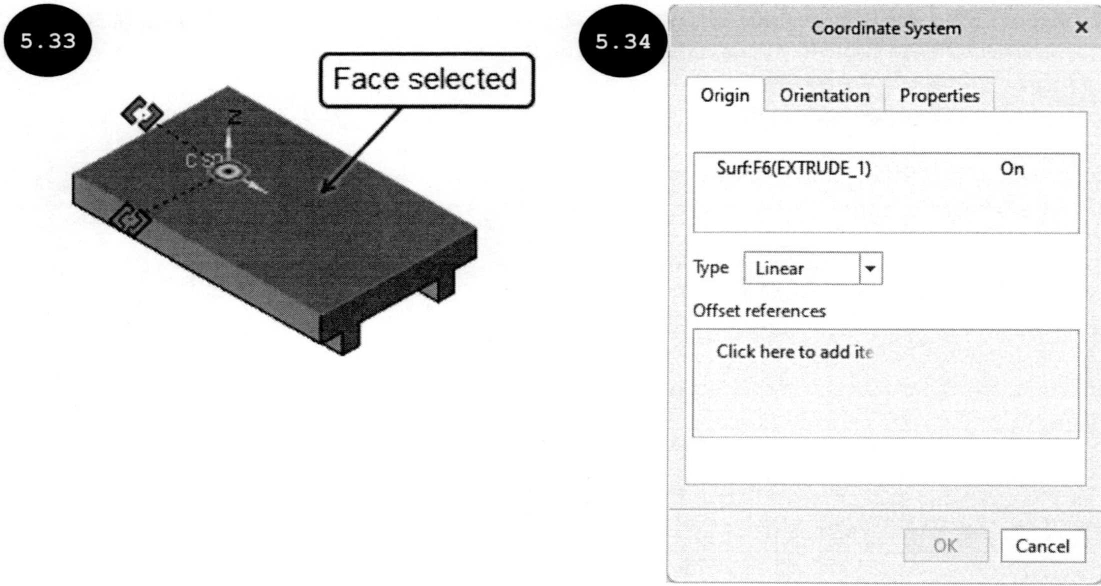

3. Select the required option in the **Type** drop-down list of the dialog box. The options in this drop-down list are discussed next.

Linear: When you select a planar face for creating the coordinate system, the **Linear** option is selected in the **Type** drop-down list, by default. This option allows you to specify two references (planes, planar faces, or linear edges) to define linear dimensions for the placement of a coordinate system, see Figure 5.35.

5.35

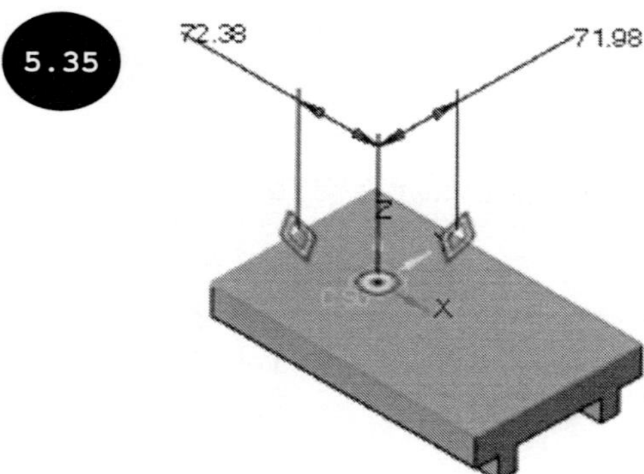

Radial: The **Radial** option allows you to specify two references to define a linear dimension and an angular dimension for the placement of a coordinate system, see Figure 5.36. Note that if a planar face is selected for creating the coordinate system, then you need to select a planar face as the first reference to define the angular dimension and a linear edge as the second reference to define the linear dimension for the placement of the coordinate system, see Figure 5.36. However, if a circular face is selected for creating the coordinate system, then you need to select two planar faces as the first and second references to define the angular and linear dimensions for the placement of the coordinate system, see Figure 5.37.

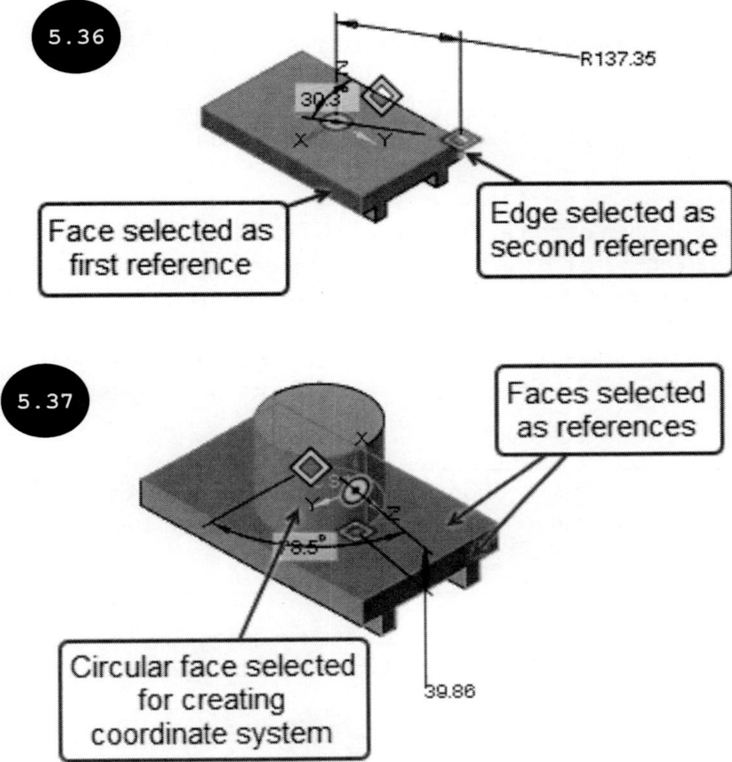

Diameter: The **Diameter** option allows you to specify two references to define an angular dimension and a diameter dimension for the placement of a coordinate system, see Figure 5.38. You need to select a planar face as the first reference to define the angular dimension and a linear edge as the second reference to define the diameter dimension. Note that this option is available only when a planar face is selected for creating the coordinate system.

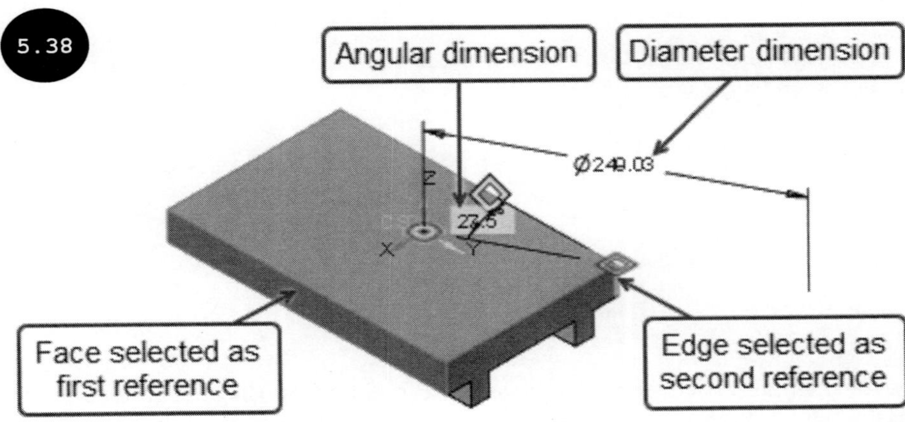

4. After selecting the required option (**Linear**, **Radial**, or **Diameter**) in the **Type** drop-down list, click on the **Offset references** area of the dialog box to select references.

5. Select two references by pressing the CTRL key to define the placement of the coordinate system. Note that the selection of references depends upon the option selected in the **Type** drop-down list of the dialog box.

6. Select the **Offset** or **Align** option in the drop-down list that appears in front of each reference in the **Offset references** area of the dialog box, see Figure 5.39. Note that these options appear only when the **Linear** option is selected in the **Type** drop-down list of the **Origin** tab in the dialog box. By default, the **Offset** option is selected. As a result, the dimensions appear in the graphics area to control the placement of the coordinate system with respect to the selected references. On selecting the **Align** option, the origin of the coordinate system gets aligned to the selected references.

Note: After selecting the **Offset** option, you can edit the dimension values that appear in the graphics area or next to the references in the dialog box as per requirement, by double-clicking on them.

7. Click on the **Orientation** tab in the **Coordinate System** dialog box. The options to change the orientation of the coordinate system appear in the dialog box, see Figure 5.40.

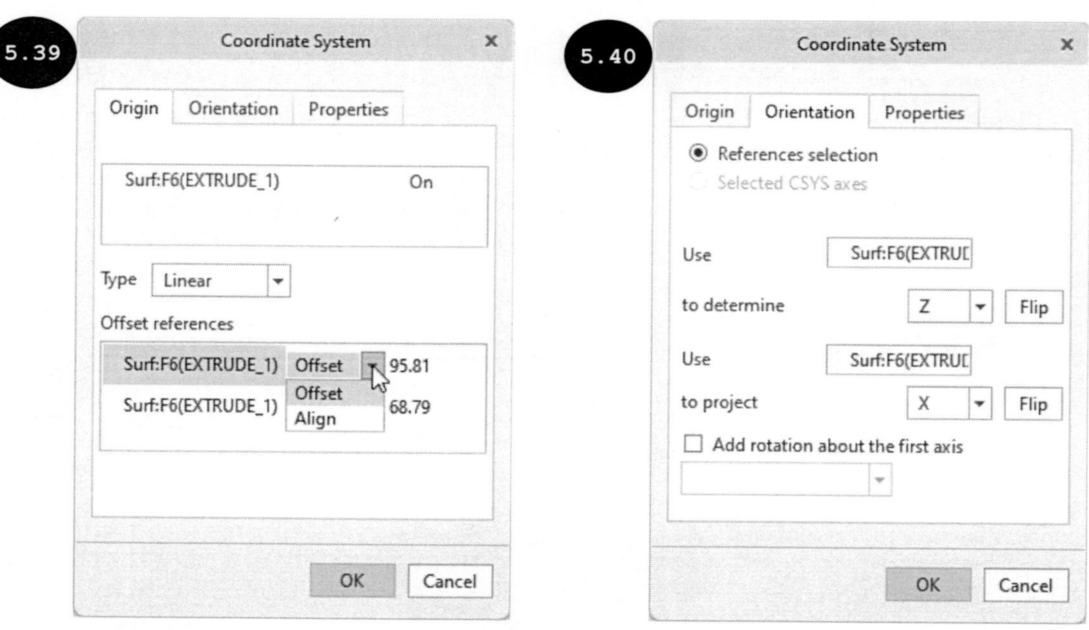

8. Change the orientation of the coordinate system as required, by using the options available in the **Orientation** tab of the dialog box. On selecting the **Add rotation about the first axis** check box, you can enter the rotational angle for the coordinate system in the field that appears below the check box.

9. Click on the **Properties** tab in the dialog box. The options to specify a name and to control the display of the coordinate system appear in the dialog box.

10. Specify a new name for the coordinate system or accept the default specified name in the **Name** field of the **Properties** tab. By default, the **Display coordinate system name** check box is selected in the **Properties** tab of the dialog box. As a result, the name of the coordinate system specified in the **Name** field appears in the graphics area. On selecting the **Display zoom-dependent** check box, you can control the size of the coordinate system by specifying the axis length of the coordinate system in the **Axis length** field of the dialog box. Note that the **Axis length** field is activated if the **Display zoom-dependent** check box is selected.

11. After specifying all parameters for creating the coordinate system, click on the **OK** button in the dialog box. The coordinate system is created.

Creating a Coordinate System Using an Existing Coordinate System

You can also create a coordinate system by using an existing coordinate system as a reference, the method for which is discussed below:

1. Click on the **Coordinate System** tool in the **Datum** group. The **Coordinate System** dialog box appears.

2. Select an existing coordinate system in the graphics area as a reference for creating the coordinate system. The **Coordinate System** dialog box gets modified with additional options, see Figure 5.41. Also, a preview of the coordinate system appears in the graphics area with default parameters.

5.41

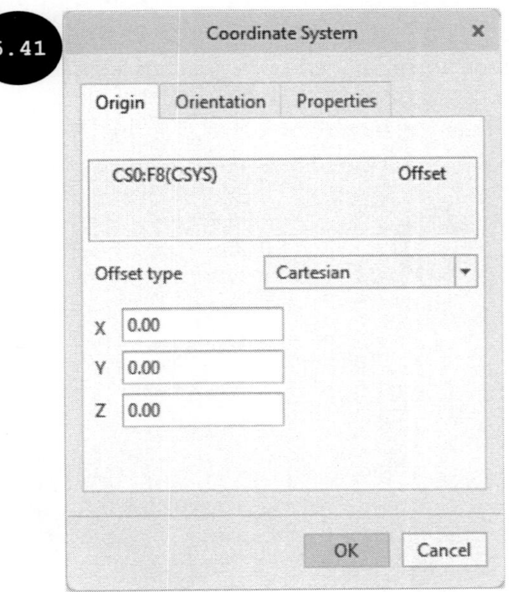

3. Select the required option (**Cartesian**, **Cylindrical**, **Spherical**, or **From File**) in the **Offset type** drop-down list of the dialog box. The options are discussed next.

Cartesian: By default, the **Cartesian** option is selected in the **Offset type** drop-down list. As a result, the **X**, **Y**, and **Z** fields appear in the dialog box. In these fields, you can specify the X, Y, and Z coordinates, respectively, for creating the new coordinate system with respect to the selected coordinate system.

Cylindrical: On selecting the **Cylindrical** option in the **Offset type** drop-down list, the **R**, **θ**, and **Z** fields appear in the dialog box. In these fields, you can enter the required translational (radial distance, angle, and axial distance) values for creating the new coordinate system.

Spherical: On selecting the **Spherical** option in the **Offset type** drop-down list, the **r**, **ϕ**, and **θ** fields appear in the dialog box. In these fields, you can enter the required translational values (radial distance and angle values) for creating the new coordinate system.

From File: On selecting the **From File** option in the **Offset type** drop-down list, the **Open** dialog box appears. In this dialog box, select a transformation file (*.trf*), which contains data for defining the location of the new coordinate system.

4. Enter the required translational values for creating the new coordinate system in the respective fields that appear in the dialog box.

5. Click on the **OK** button in the dialog box. The desired coordinate system is created.

Creating a Coordinate System at the Intersection of two Edges

1. Click on the **Coordinate System** tool in the **Datum** group. The **Coordinate System** dialog box appears.

2. Select a linear edge as the first reference in the graphics area, see Figure 5.42.

3. Press the CTRL key and then select the second edge as the second reference in the graphics area, see Figure 5.42. A preview of the coordinate system appears at the intersection of the selected edges.

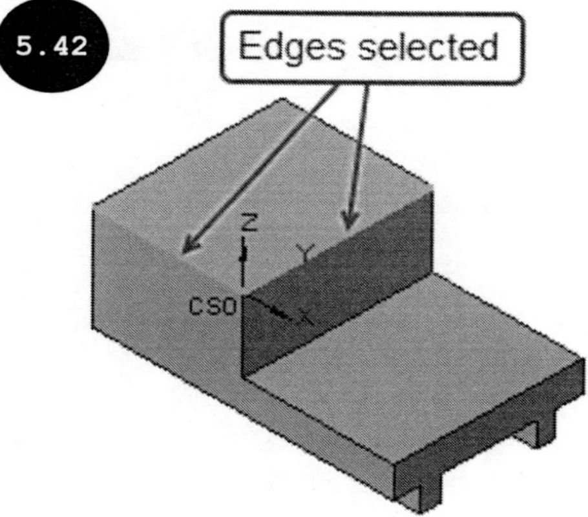

Tip: You can also control/flip the axes of the coordinate system by using the options available in the **Orientation** tab of the dialog box.

4. Click on the **OK** button in the dialog box. The desired coordinate system is created at the intersection of the two selected edges.

Creating a Coordinate System at the Intersection of Three Faces

1. Click on the **Coordinate System** tool in the **Datum** group. The **Coordinate System** dialog box appears.

2. Select three planar faces of the model one after the other by pressing the CTRL key as the first, second, and third references, see Figure 5.43. A preview of the coordinate system appears at the intersection of the selected faces.

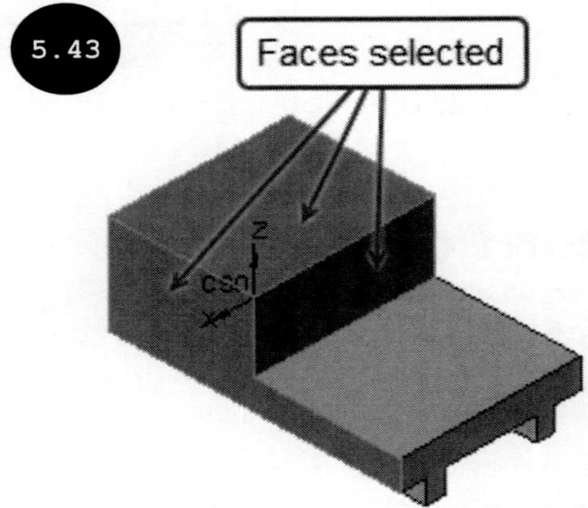

Tip: You can also control/flip the axes of the coordinate system by using the options available in the **Orientation** tab of the dialog box.

3. Click on the **OK** button in the dialog box. The desired coordinate system is created at the intersection of the three selected faces.

Creating a Coordinate System at the Center of a Circular Edge

1. Click on the **Coordinate System** tool. The **Coordinate System** dialog box appears.

2. Select a circular edge of the model as the first reference. A preview of the coordinate system appears at the center of the selected circular edge, see Figure 5.44.

3. Click on the **Orientation** tab in the **Coordinate System** dialog box and then click on the second **Use** field of the dialog box to select the second reference for creating the coordinate system.

4. Select a planar face of the model as the second reference in the graphics area, see Figure 5.45. Next, select the required option in the **to project** drop-down list of the dialog box to control the orientation of the **Coordinate System.**

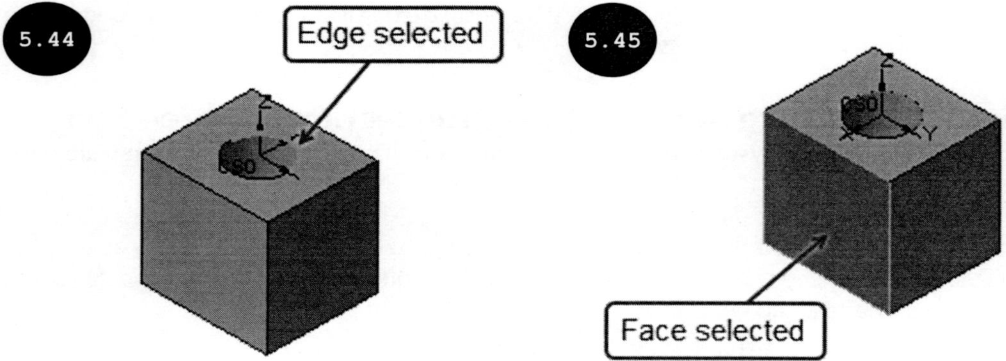

5. Click on the **OK** button. The desired coordinate system is created at the center of the selected circular edge.

Creating a Datum Point

A datum point can be created anywhere in a 3D model or space and is used as a datum for measuring distance, creating planes, and so on. You can create a datum point by using the **Point**, **Offset Coordinate System**, and **Field** tools. These tools are available in the **Point** flyout of the **Datum** group in the **Model** tab, see Figure 5.46. The methods for creating a datum point are discussed next.

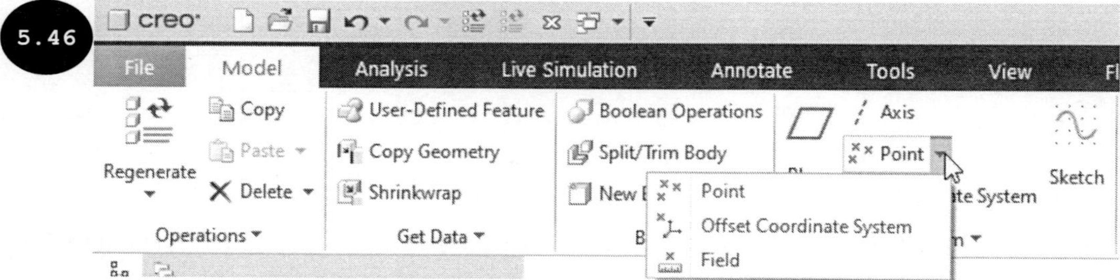

Creating a Datum Point Using the Point Tool

The **Point** tool is used for creating single or multiple points on a face, offset to a face, at the intersection of three faces or two edges, on a vertex, or on an edge. The methods for creating points by using the **Point** tool are discussed next.

Creating a Datum Point on a Face

1. Click on the **Point** tool in the **Datum** group. The **Datum Point** dialog box appears.

2. Select a face (planar or curved) as a reference. A preview of the datum point appears along with a placement handle and two offset handles on the selected face, see Figure 5.47. Also, the **Datum Point** dialog box gets modified with additional options, see Figure 5.48.

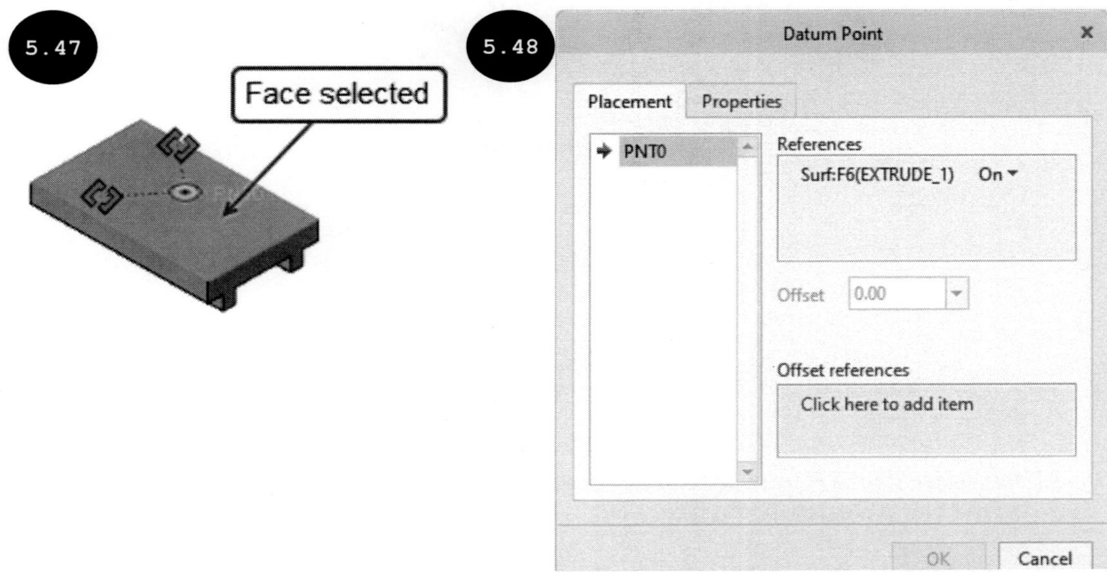

3. Ensure that the **On** option is selected in the **Constraint** drop-down list that appears in front of the selected reference in the **References** area of the dialog box.

Tip: The **On** option is used for creating a datum point on the face that is selected as the reference for creating the datum point.

4. Click on the **Offset references** area of the dialog box and then select two references by pressing the CTRL key to define the placement of the datum point on the selected face, see Figure 5.49. You can select planar faces or linear edges as the references. Alternatively, you can drag the offset handles that appear in the graphics area to the required references.

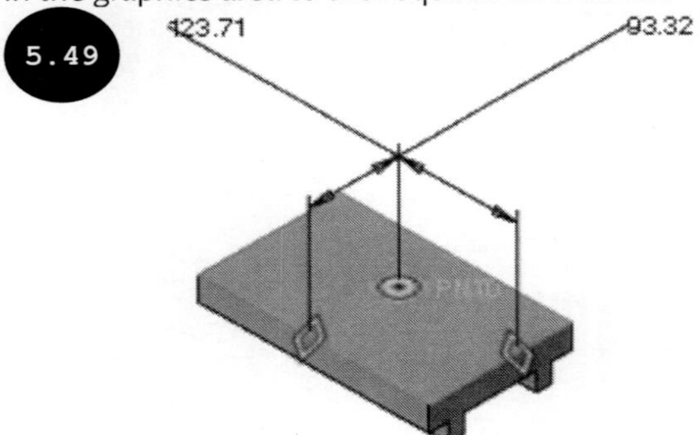

5. Edit the offset distance values by double-clicking on the dimensions that appear in the graphics area or next to the references in the dialog box to define the placement of the datum point on the selected face, as required.

Note: After specifying all references that are required for creating a datum point, the **New Point** option appears in the dialog box, see Figure 5.50. This option allows you to create the next datum point. You can create multiple datum points one after the other by using the **New Point** option of the **Datum Point** dialog box.

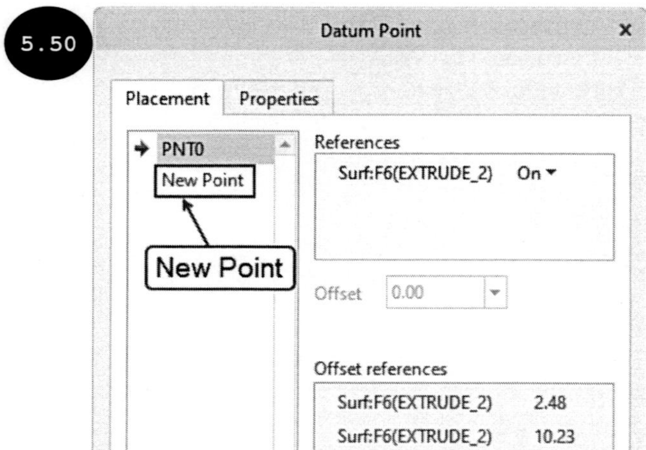

6. After specifying all references for creating a datum point, click on the **OK** button in the dialog box. A datum point is created on the face.

Creating a Datum Point Offset to a Face

1. Click on the **Point** tool in the **Datum** group. The **Datum Point** dialog box appears.

2. Select a face (planar or curved) as a reference. A preview of the datum point appears along with a placement handle and two offset handles on the selected face, see Figure 5.51. Also, the **Datum Point** dialog box gets modified with additional options.

3. Invoke the **Constraint** drop-down list by clicking on the **On** option that appears in front of the selected reference in the **References** area of the dialog box, see Figure 5.52.

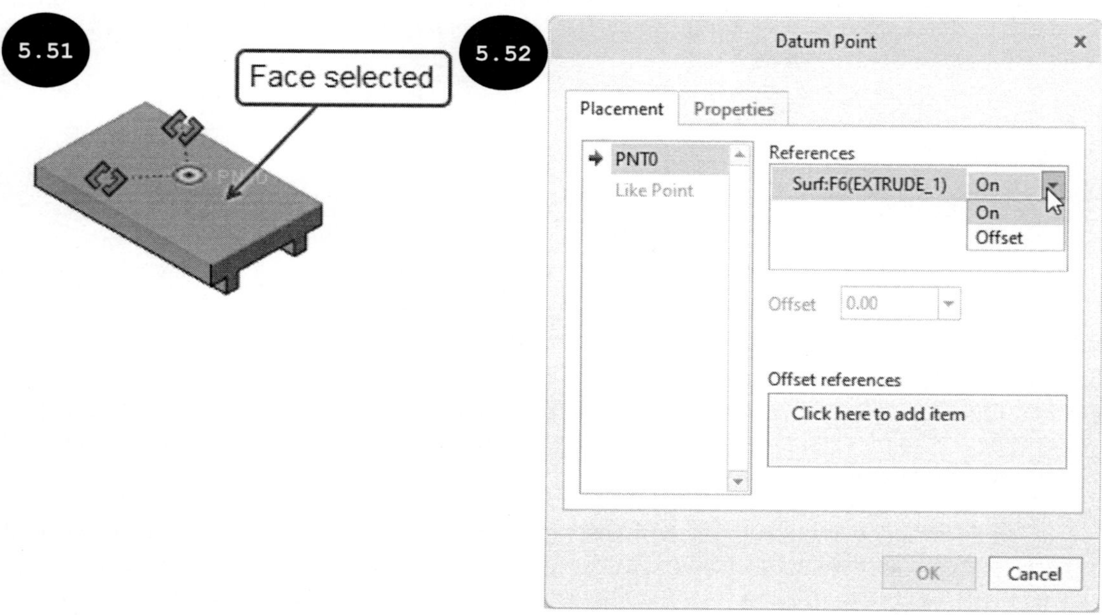

4. Select the **Offset** option in the **Constraint** drop-down list. The **Offset** field is enabled in the dialog box.

5. Enter the required offset distance in the **Offset** field of the dialog box. A preview of the datum point appears at the specified offset distance from the selected face, see Figure 5.53.

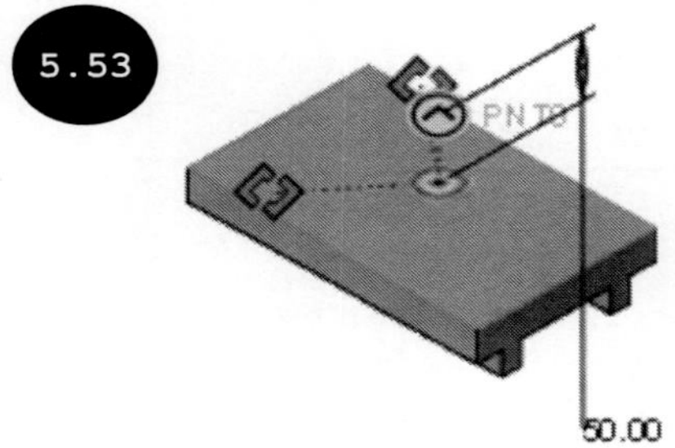

6. Click on the **Offset references** area of the dialog box and then select two references by pressing the CTRL key to define the placement of the datum point, see Figure 5.54. You can select planar faces or linear edges as the references. Alternatively, you can drag the offset handles that appear in the graphics area to the required references.

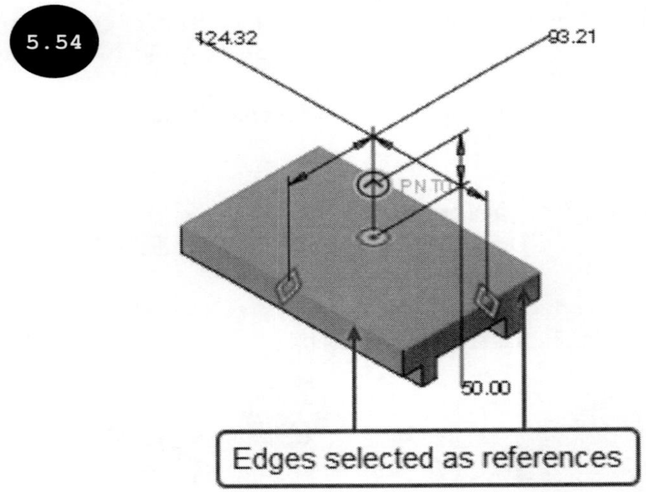

7. Edit the offset dimensions that appear in the graphics area or in the **Offset references** area of the dialog box, as required. To do so, double-click on the dimension to be edited and then enter the new dimension value. Next, press ENTER.

Note: After specifying all references that are required for creating a datum point, the **New Point** option appears in the dialog box, see Figure 5.55. This option allows you to create the next datum point. You can create multiple datum points one after the other by using the **New Point** option of the **Datum Point** dialog box.

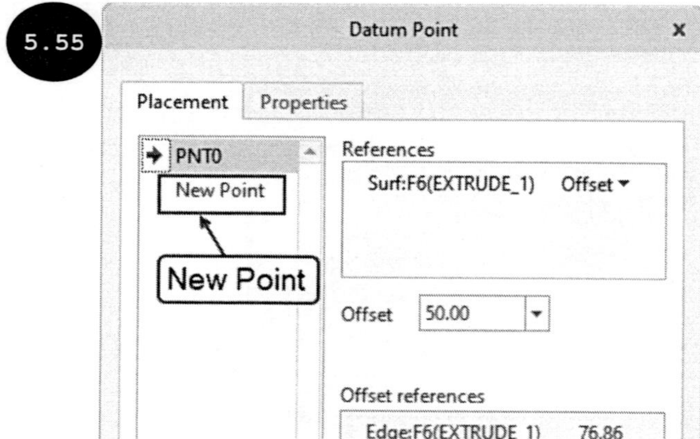

8. After specifying all references for creating a datum point, click on the **OK** button in the dialog box. A datum point at a specified offset distance from the selected face is created.

Creating a Datum Point at the Intersection of Three Faces or Two Edges

1. Click on the **Point** tool in the **Datum** group. The **Datum Point** dialog box appears.

2. Select three planar faces or two linear edges one after the other by pressing the CTRL key. A preview of the datum point at the intersection of selected faces or edges appears in the graphics area, see Figure 5.56. In this figure, three planar faces are selected.

3. Click on the **OK** button in the dialog box. A datum point is created at the intersection of three faces or two edges.

Creating a Datum Point on a Vertex

1. Click on the **Point** tool in the **Datum** group. The **Datum Point** dialog box appears.

2. Select a vertex of the model in the graphics area. A preview of the datum point appears on the selected vertex in the graphics area, see Figure 5.57.

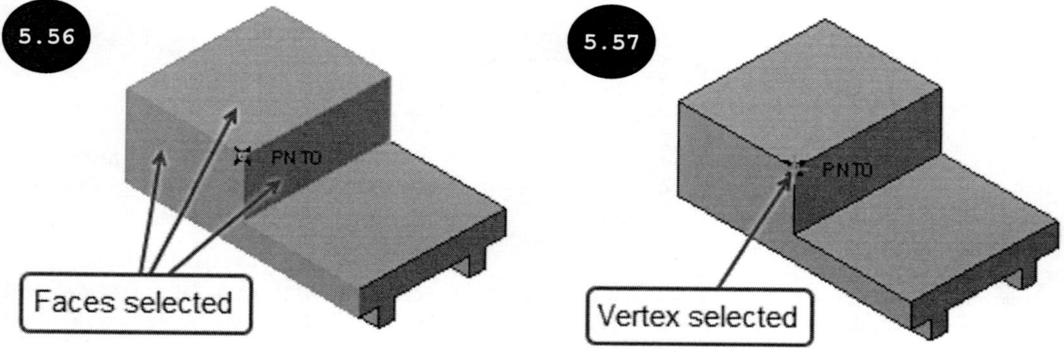

3. Click on the **OK** button in the dialog box. A datum point is created on the selected vertex.

Creating a Datum Point on an Edge

1. Click on the **Point** tool in the **Datum** group. The **Datum Point** dialog box appears.

2. Select an edge of the model as a reference. A preview of the datum point appears on the selected edge of the model in the graphics area, see Figure 5.58.

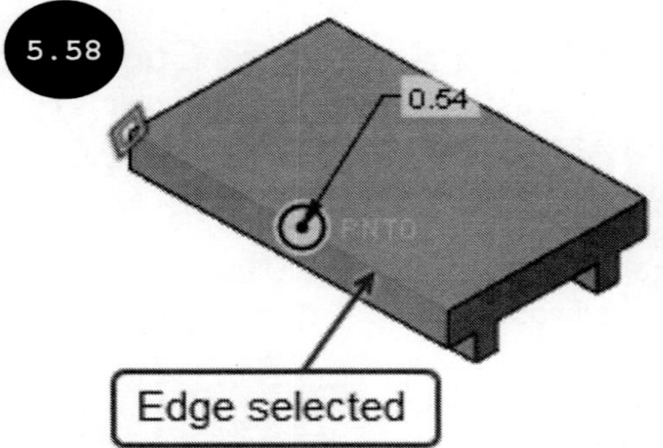

3. Select the **Ratio** or **Real** option in the **Offset** drop-down list of the dialog box to define the location of the datum point on the selected edge, see Figure 5.59.

   Ratio: The **Ratio** option allows you to define the location of the datum point on the selected edge in terms of a ratio (0 to 1). Note that 0 defines the start point of the edge and 1 defines the endpoint of the edge. You can enter any value from 0 to 1.

   Real: The **Real** option allows you to define the location of the datum point on the selected edge by specifying the actual distance value, which measures from the start point of the edge. You can choose an endpoint of the selected edge as the start point by clicking on the **Next End** button that is available next to the **End of curve** radio button in the dialog box.

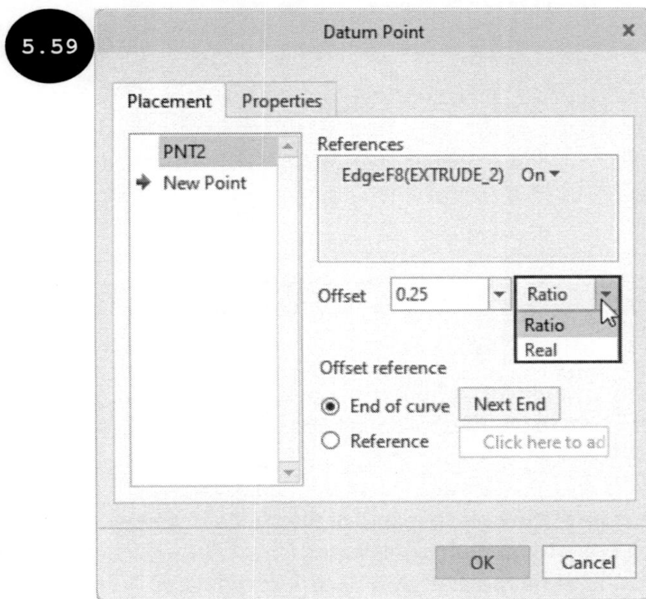

4. Enter a ratio or distance in the **Offset** field of the dialog box depending upon the option selected in the **Offset** drop-down list of the dialog box.

5. Click on the **OK** button in the dialog box. A datum point is created on the selected edge of the model.

Creating a Datum Point Using the Offset Coordinate System Tool

The **Offset Coordinate System** tool is used for creating datum points by specifying coordinates (X, Y, and Z) with respect to an existing coordinate system. The method for creating points by using the **Offset Coordinate System** tool is discussed below:

1. Click on the arrow next to the **Point** tool in the **Datum** group and then click on the **Offset Coordinate System** tool in the flyout that appears, see Figure 5.60. The **Datum Point** dialog box appears, see Figure 5.61.

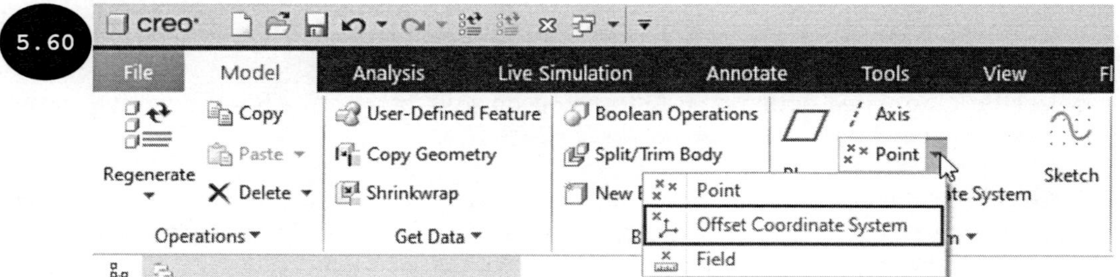

2. Select an existing coordinate system as a reference in the graphics area. The name of the selected coordinate system appears in the **Reference** field of the dialog box, see Figure 5.61.

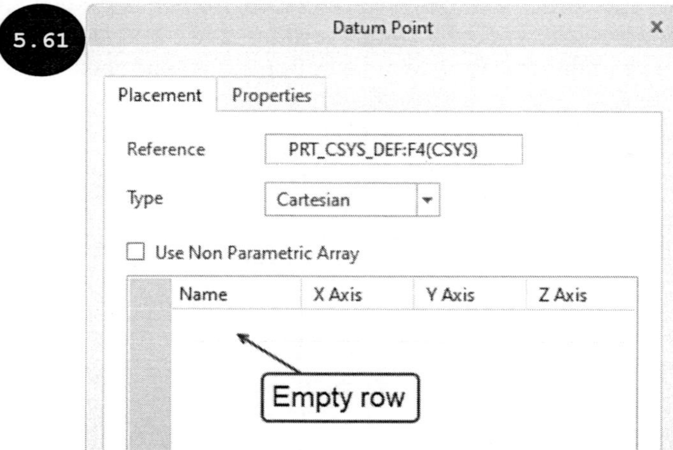

3. Select the **Cartesian**, **Cylindrical**, or **Spherical** option in the **Type** drop-down list of the dialog box as the coordinate system to be used for specifying the X, Y, and Z coordinates for creating datum points.

4. Click on the empty row at the bottom panel of the dialog box, refer to Figure 5.61. The first row is added in the dialog box with default coordinates (0, 0, 0), see Figure 5.62. Also, a preview of the datum point appears in the graphics area at default coordinates. Note that every row added in the dialog box represents a datum point.

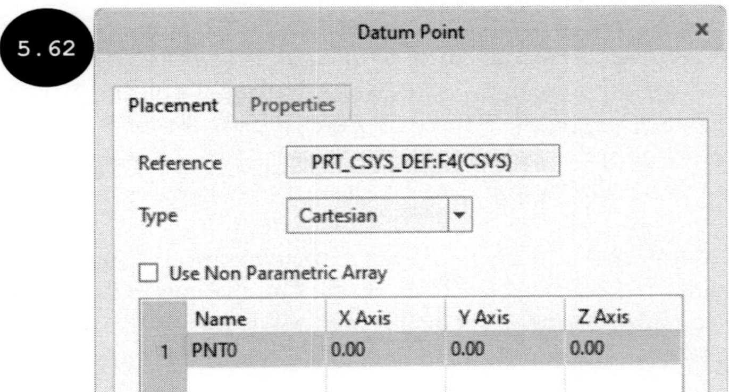

5. Click on the field corresponding to the first row and **X Axis** column in the dialog box. An edit field appears. In this edit field, enter the X coordinate of the datum point with respect to the coordinate system that is selected as the reference. Similarly, enter the Y and Z coordinates of the datum point. A preview of the datum point appears in the graphics area.

   After specifying the coordinates of the first datum point, you can create a second datum point.

6. Click on the empty row that appears below the first row in the dialog box. The second row is added in the dialog box with default coordinates (0, 0, 0), see Figure 5.63. Also, a preview of the second datum point appears in the graphics area.

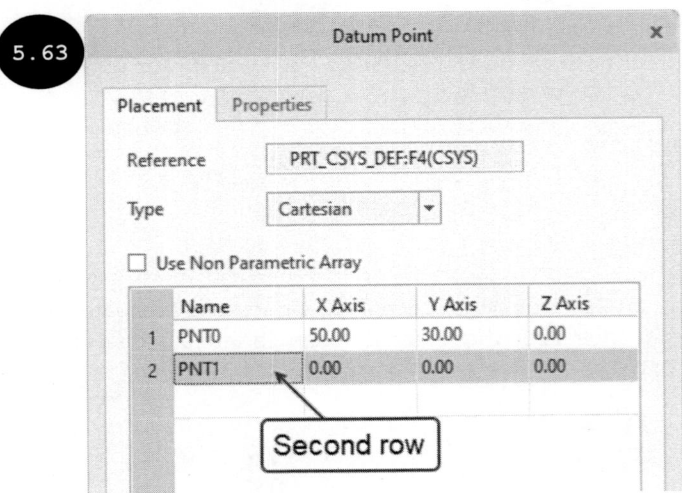

7. Specify the X, Y, and Z coordinates for the second point in the second row of the dialog box. A preview of the second datum point appears in the graphics area at the coordinates specified in the dialog box.

8. Similarly, you can create multiple datum points by adding multiple rows in the dialog box. Every row added in the dialog box represents a datum point.

Note: You can also save coordinates of all datum points specified in the dialog box as *.pts* file in your local drive for future use. To do so, click on the **Save** button in the dialog box. The **Save a Copy** dialog box appears. In this dialog box, browse the location where you want to save the file and then specify a name for the file in the **New file name** field of the dialog box. Next, click on the **OK** button. The file is saved as *.pts* file.

You can also import the *.pts* or *.ibl* file containing information about coordinates of the datum points in the dialog box. To do so, click on the **Import** button in the dialog box. The **Open** dialog box appears. Next, select the *.pts* or *.ibl* file and then click on **Open** button in the dialog box. The coordinate points of the selected file are entered in the dialog box.

9. Click on the **OK** button in the dialog box. The desired datum points are created.

Creating a Datum Point Using the Field Tool

The **Field** tool is used for creating a datum point on a selected reference. The method for creating points by using the **Field** tool is discussed below:

1. Click on the arrow next to the **Point** tool in the **Datum** group and then click on the **Field** tool in the flyout that appears, see Figure 5.64. The **Datum Point** dialog box appears, see Figure 5.65.

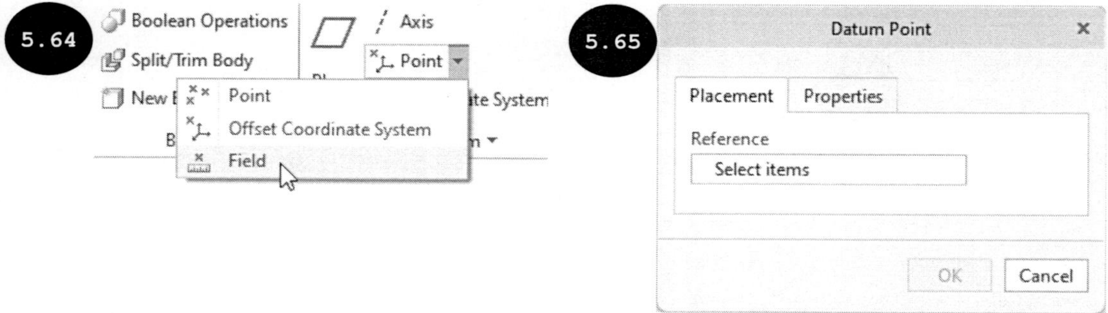

2. Click on a face or an edge (planar or curved) as a reference to create a datum point. A preview of the datum point appears on the selected reference with a placement handle, see Figure 5.66. Also, the name of the selected reference appears in the **Reference** field of the dialog box.

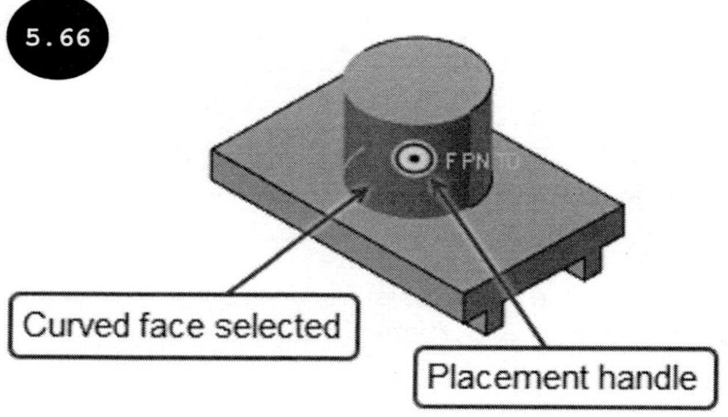

3. Drag the placement handle of the datum point to define its location on the selected reference, as required.

4. Click on the **OK** button in the dialog box. A datum point is created.

Tutorial 1

Create the multi-feature model shown in Figure 5.67. You need to create the model by creating all its features one by one. All dimensions are in mm.

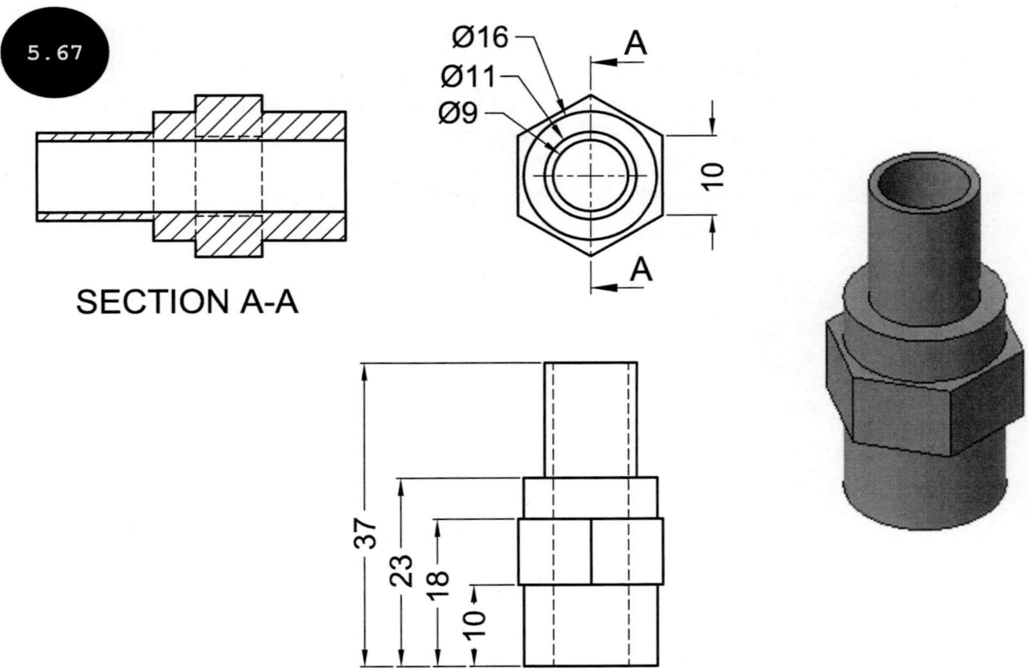

Section 1: Starting Creo Parametric

1. Start Creo Parametric by double-clicking on the Creo Parametric icon on your desktop.

Section 2: Setting the Working Directory

Now, you need to set the working directory to save the files of the current session of Creo Parametric. It is recommended to create a folder with the name "*Chapter 5*" inside the "*Creo Parametric*" folder in the local drive of your system. If the "*Creo Parametric*" folder is not already created then you need to create this folder.

1. Click on the **Select Working Directory** tool in the **Data** group of the **Home** tab, see Figure 5.68. The **Select Working Directory** window appears. In this window, browse to *Creo Parametric > Chapter 5*. You need to create these folders, if not created earlier.

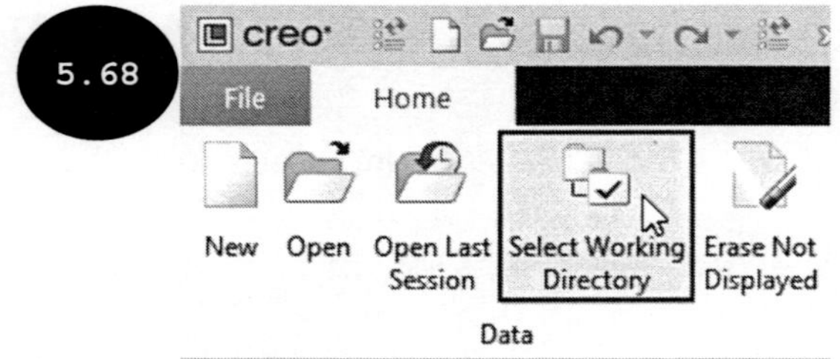

2. Click on the **OK** button in the dialog box. The working directory is set to <<*Creo Parametric\ Chapter 5*.

Section 3: Invoking the Part Mode

1. Click on the **New** tool in the **Data** group of the **Home** tab. The **New** dialog box appears, see Figure 5.69. Alternatively, press the CTRL + N to invoke the **New** dialog box.

2. Ensure that the **Part** radio button is selected in the **Type** area and the **Solid** radio button is selected in the **Sub-type** area of the dialog box, see Figure 5.69.

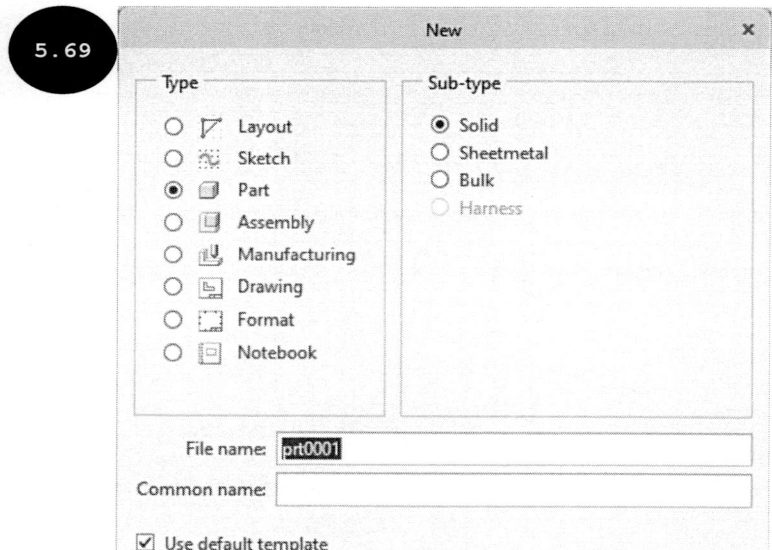

3. Enter **C05-Tutorial01** in the **File name** field of the dialog box as the name of the model.

4. Clear the **Use default template** check box and then click on the **OK** button in the dialog box. The **New File Options** dialog box appears, see Figure 5.70.

5. Select the **mmns_part_solid_abs** template in the **New File Options** dialog box and then click on the **OK** button. The Part mode is invoked with the **mmns_part_solid_abs** template. In this template, the length is measured in millimeters, mass is measured in Newton, and time is measured in seconds.

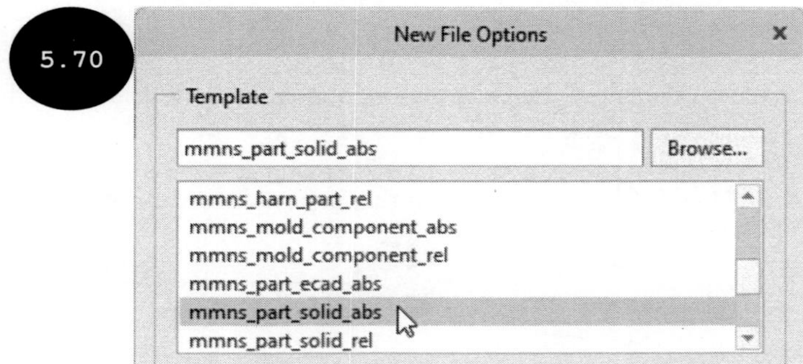

Section 4: Creating the Base/First Feature

1. Click on the **Sketch** tool in the **Datum** group, see Figure 5.71. The **Sketch** dialog box appears, see Figure 5.72.

2. Move the cursor over the Top plane in the graphics area and then click the left mouse button when it gets highlighted. The Top plane gets selected as the sketching plane and its name appears in the **Plane** field of the **Sketch** dialog box, see Figure 5.72. Also, a reference plane and its orientation are selected automatically in the **Reference** field and **Orientation** drop-down list of the dialog box, respectively, see Figure 5.72.

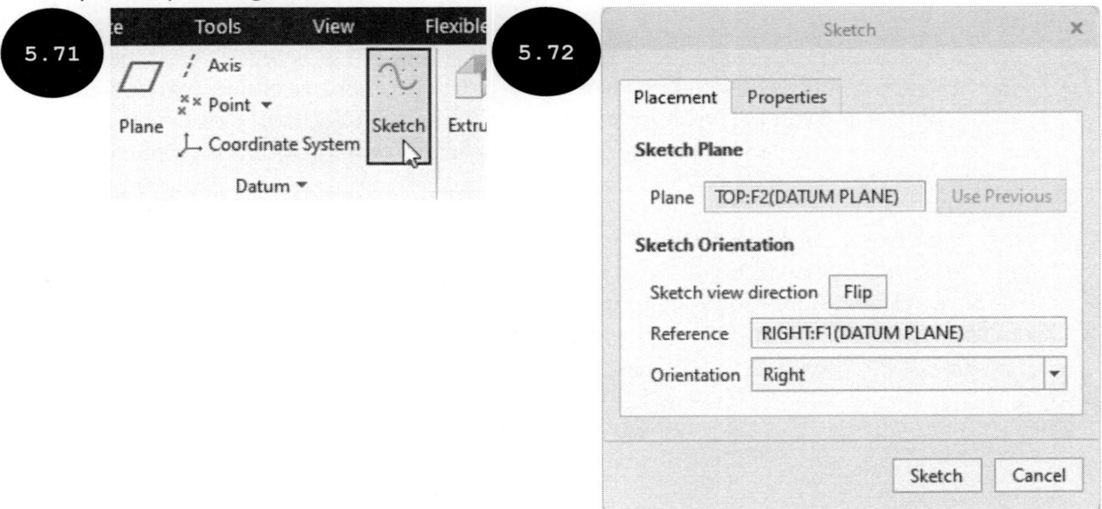

3. Click on the **Sketch** button in the dialog box. The Sketching environment is invoked. Also, the Top plane is oriented normal to the viewing direction.

Note: To orient the sketching plane normal to the viewing direction automatically every time on invoking the Sketching environment, you need to ensure that the **Make the sketching plane parallel to the screen** check box is selected in the **Creo Parametric Options** dialog box. To invoke this dialog box, click on the **File > Options**. Next, click on the **Sketcher** option in the left panel of the dialog box and then select the **Make the sketching plane parallel to the screen** check box on the right panel of the dialog box.

Now, you can draw the sketch of the base feature.

4. Draw two circles as the sketch of the base feature and apply dimensions, see Figure 5.73. Ensure that the center points of the circles are at the origin.

5. Click on the **OK** tool in the **Close** group to exit the Sketching environment, see Figure 5.74.

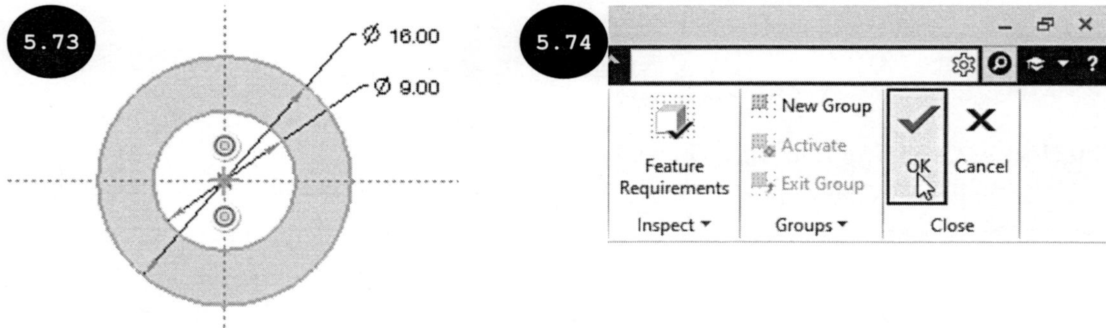

6. Click on the **Extrude** tool in the **Shapes** group of the **Model** tab. A preview of the extrude feature appears in the graphics window with default parameters. Also, the **Extrude** tab appears in the Ribbon.

Note: If a sketch is not selected before invoking the **Extrude** tool then a preview of the feature will not appear and you will be prompted to select the sketch to be extruded. Select the sketch in the graphics window. A preview of the extrude feature appears in the graphics window.

7. Change the current orientation of the model to the standard orientation, see Figure 5.75. In the figure, the standard orientation of the model is set to Isometric. To change the orientation, click on the **Saved Orientations** tool in the **In-graphics** toolbar, see Figure 5.76. The **Saved Orientations** flyout appears. In this flyout, click on the **Standard Orientation** tool.

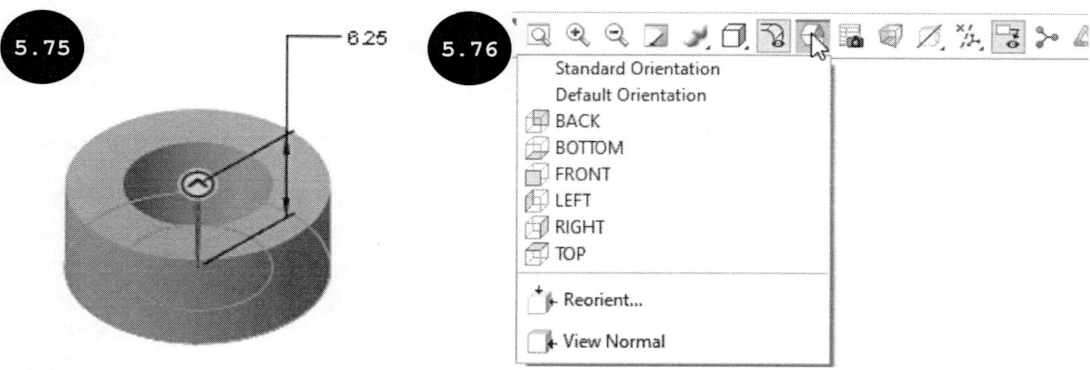

Note: By default, the standard orientation of the model is set to Isometric. However, you can change the standard/default orientation of the model to Isometric, Trimetric, or User-defined. The method for changing the standard orientation of the model has been discussed in Chapter 4.

8. Ensure that the **Variable** option is selected in the **Side 1** drop-down list, see Figure 5.77.

9. Enter **10** as the depth of extrusion in the **Value** field of the **Extrude** tab, see Figure 5.77.

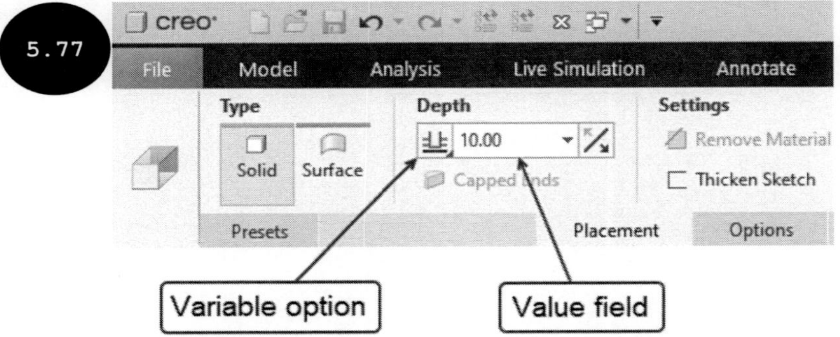

10. Click on the green tick-mark button in the **Extrude** tab. An extrude feature is created, see Figure 5.78. In this figure, the standard/default orientation of the model is set to Isometric. Also, the display of datum planes is turned off.

Section 5: Creating the Second Feature

1. Click on the **Sketch** tool in the **Datum** group. The **Sketch** dialog box appears.

2. Click on the top planar face of the base/first feature, see Figure 5.79. The top planar face of the base feature is selected as the sketching plane and its name appears in the **Plane** field of the **Sketch** dialog box. Also, a reference plane and its orientation are selected automatically in the **Reference** field and **Orientation** drop-down list of the dialog box, respectively.

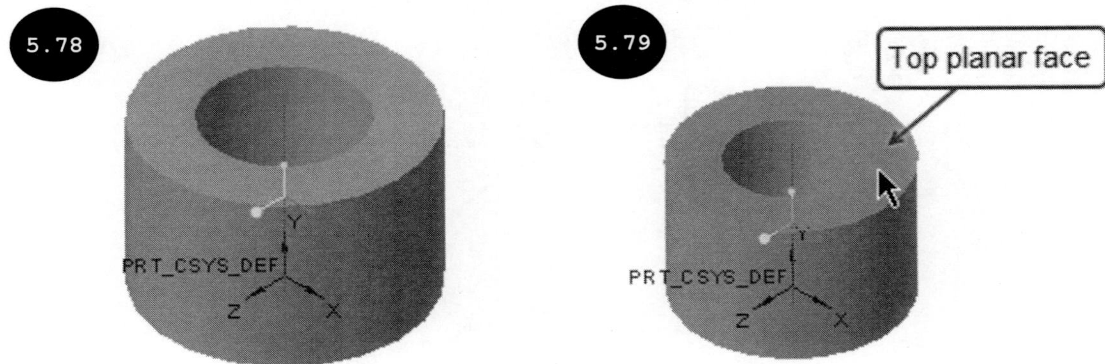

3. Click on the **Sketch** button in the dialog box. The Sketching environment is invoked. Also, the top planar face gets oriented normal to the viewing direction.

Now, you can draw the sketch of the second feature.

4. Click on the **Palette** tool in the **Insert** group, see Figure 5.80. The **Sketcher Palette** dialog box appears, see Figure 5.81.

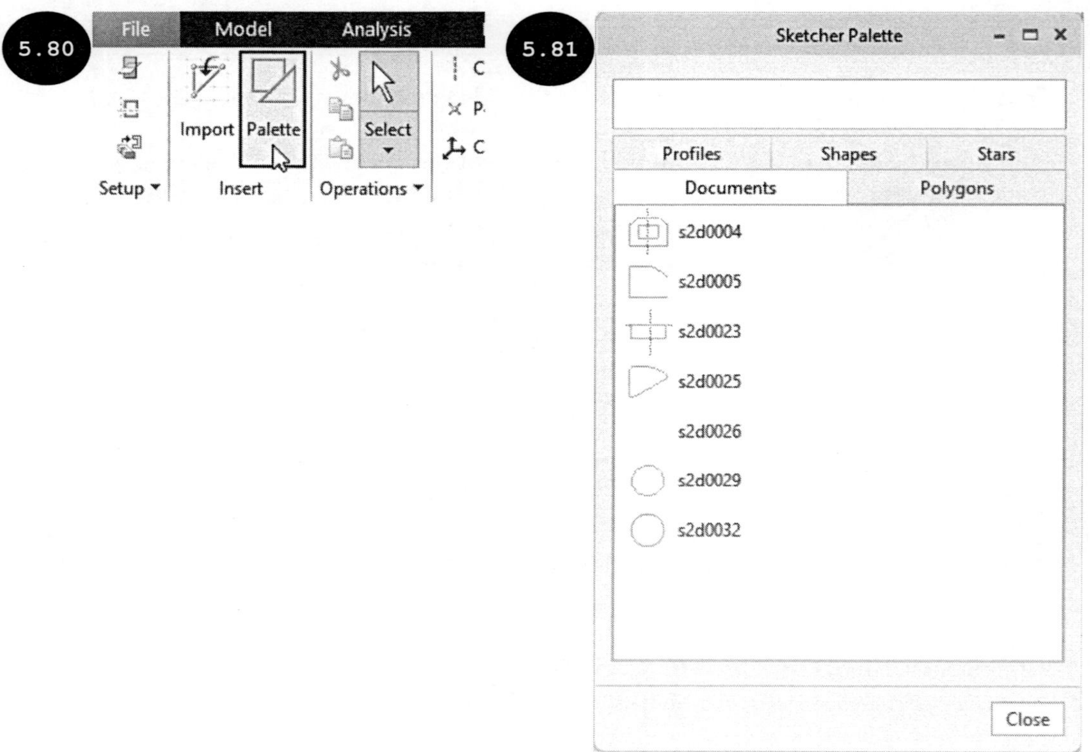

5. Click on the **Polygons** tab in the **Sketcher Palette** dialog box, then drag and drop the **6-Sided Hexagon** shape anywhere in the graphics area, see Figure 5.82. Note that as soon as you drag and drop the pre-defined shape in the graphics area, the **Import Section** tab appears in the **Ribbon**.

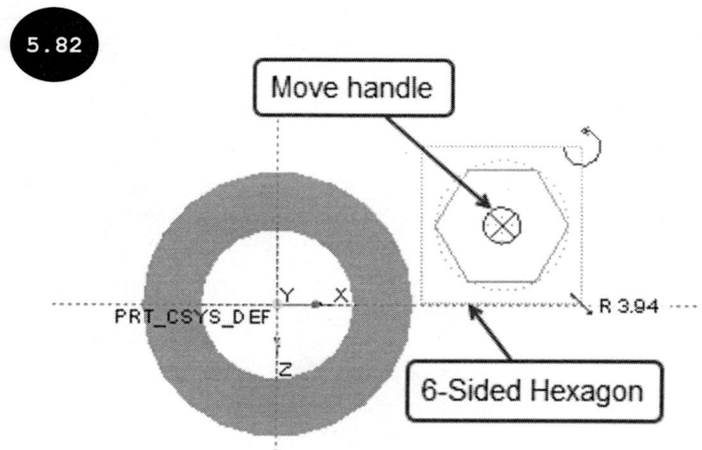

6. Place the center of the 6-sided hexagon shape on the origin. To do so, drag the move handle of the 6-sided hexagon shape toward the origin and then drop it when the cursor snaps to the origin and both the axes passing through the origin get highlighted, refer to Figure 5.83.

5.83

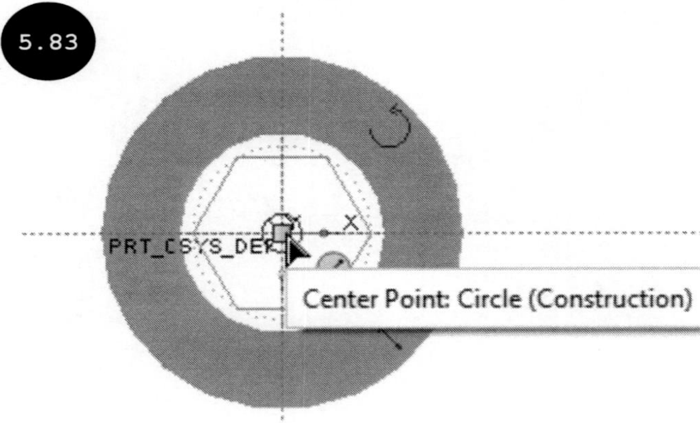

7. Enter **90** degrees in the **Angle** field of the **Import Section** tab that appears in the **Ribbon**, see Figure 5.84. The pre-defined shape gets rotated at the specified angle, see Figure 5.85.

5.84

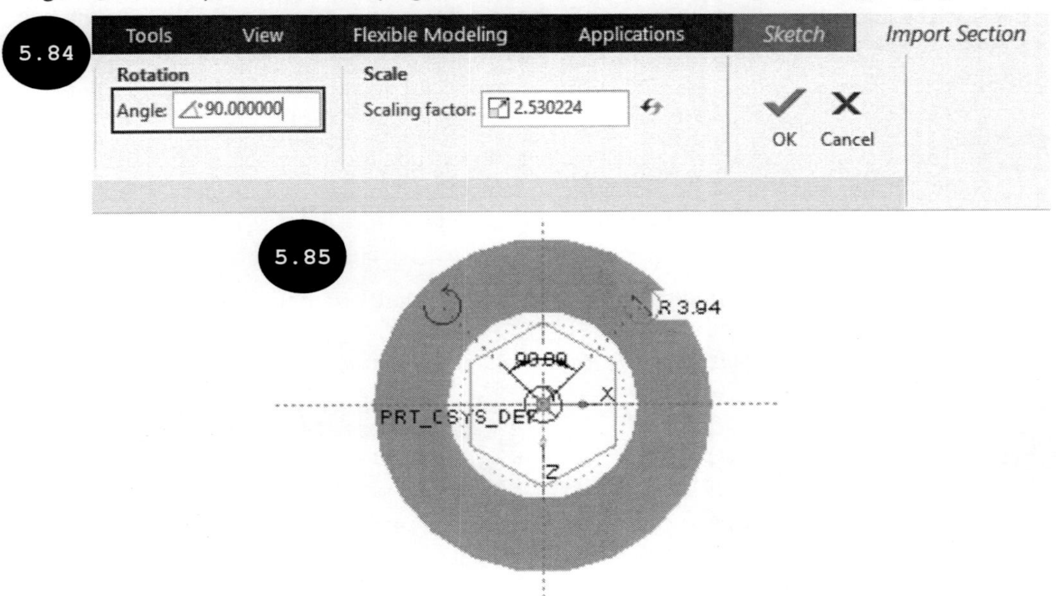

5.85

8. Click on the green tick-mark button in the **Import Section** tab of the **Ribbon**. The 6-sided hexagon is inserted in the Sketching environment. Next, close the **Sketcher Palette** dialog box.

9. Edit the length of the 6-sided hexagon to 10 mm, see Figure 5.86.

Note: On applying a dimension, if the center of the hexagon changes its position from the origin to anywhere in the graphics area, then you need to apply a coincident constraint between the origin and the center point of the hexagon.

10. Draw a circle of diameter 9 mm, see Figure 5.87. Note that the center point of the circle is at the origin.

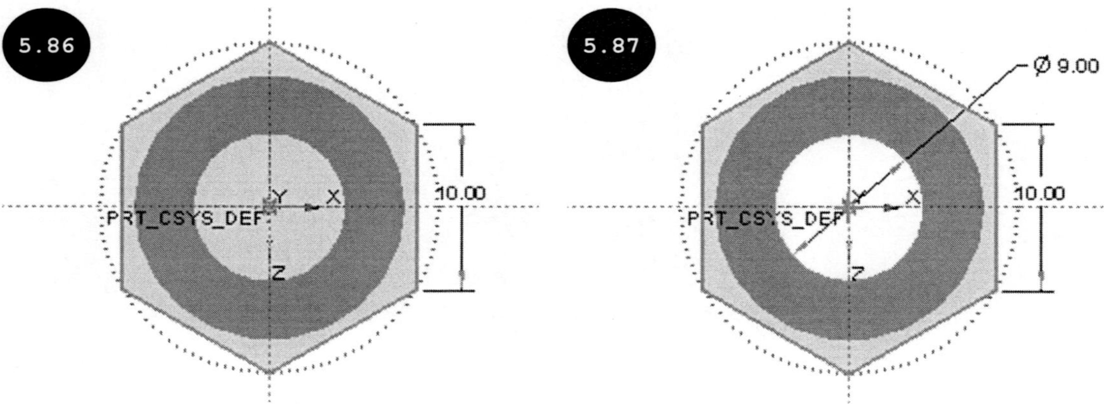

11. Click on the **OK** tool in the **Close** group of the **Sketch** tab in the **Ribbon** to exit the Sketching environment.

12. Click on the **Extrude** tool in the **Shapes** group of the **Model** tab. A preview of the extrude feature appears in the graphics window with default parameters. Also, the **Extrude** tab appears in the **Ribbon**.

Note: If a sketch is not selected before invoking the **Extrude** tool then a preview of the feature will not appear and you will be prompted to select the sketch to be extruded. Select the sketch in the graphics window. A preview of the extrude feature appears in the graphics window.

13. Change the current orientation of the model to the standard orientation, see Figure 5.88.

14. Enter **8** as the depth of extrusion in the **Value** field of the **Extrude** tab, see Figure 5.89.

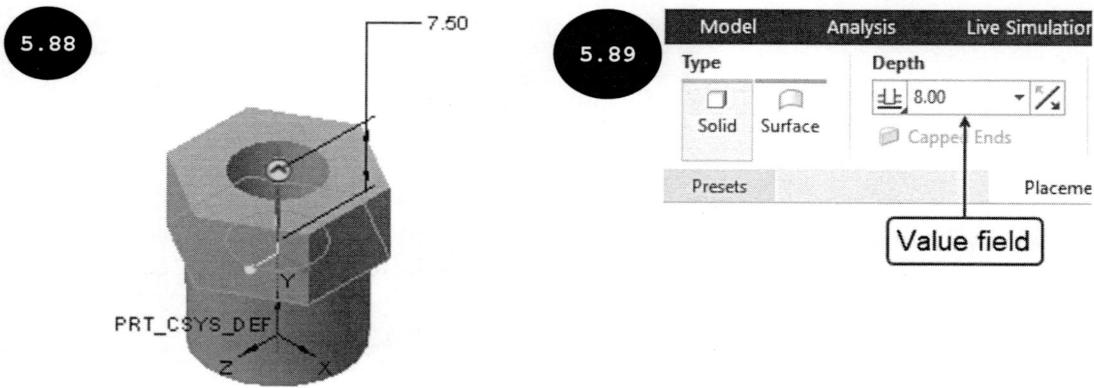

15. Click on the green tick-mark button in the **Extrude** tab. The extrude feature is created, see Figure 5.90.

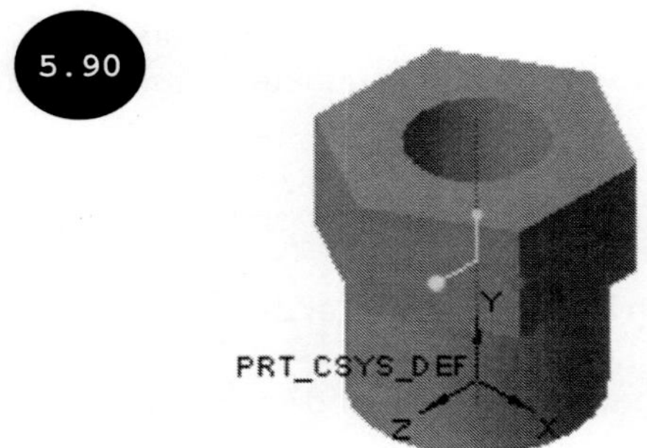

Section 6: Creating the Third Feature

1. Click on the **Sketch** tool in the **Datum** group. The **Sketch** dialog box appears.

2. Click on the top planar face of the second feature, see Figure 5.91. The top planar face of the second feature is selected as the sketching plane and its name appears in the **Plane** field of the **Sketch** dialog box. Also, a reference plane and its orientation are selected automatically in the **Reference** field and **Orientation** drop-down list of the dialog box, respectively.

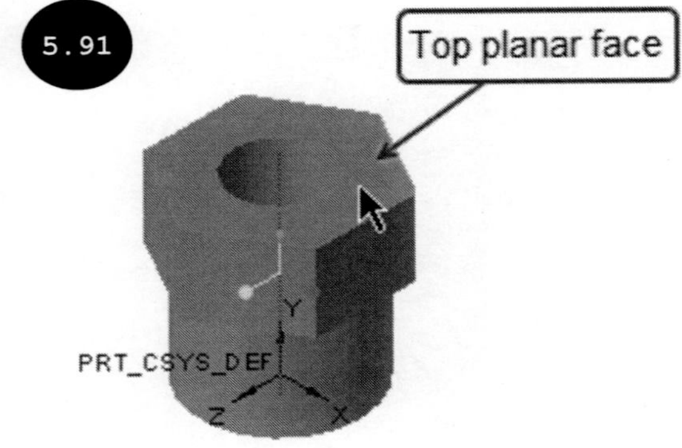

3. Click on the **Sketch** button in the dialog box. The Sketching environment is invoked. Also, the top planar face gets oriented normal to the viewing direction.

   Now, you can draw the sketch of the third feature.

4. Create the sketch of the third feature by creating two circles of diameter 9 mm and 16 mm by using the **Center and Point** tool, see Figure 5.92. Note that you need to edit the weak dimensions to convert them into strong dimensions.

5. Click on the **OK** tool in the **Close** group of the **Sketch** tab in the **Ribbon** to exit the Sketching environment, see Figure 5.93.

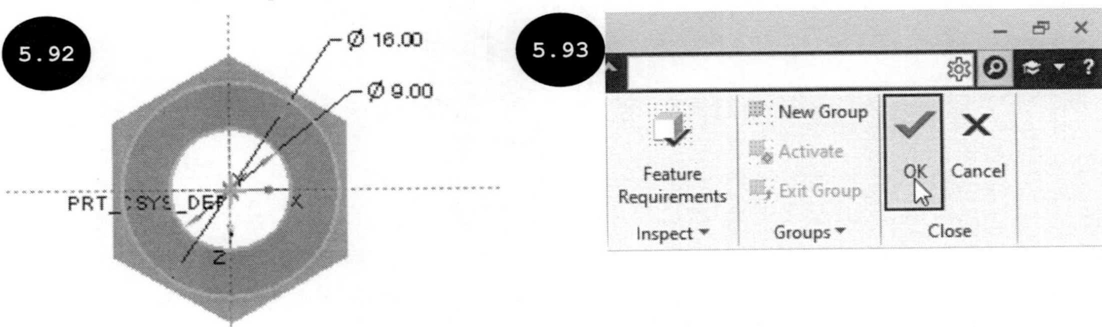

6. Click on the **Extrude** tool in the **Shapes** group of the **Model** tab. A preview of the extrude feature appears in the graphics window with default parameters. Also, the **Extrude** tab appears in the **Ribbon**.

7. Change the current orientation of the model to the standard orientation, see Figure 5.94.

8. Enter **5** as the depth of extrusion in the **Value** field of the **Extrude** tab.

9. Click on the green tick-mark button in the **Extrude** tab. The extrude feature is created, see Figure 5.95.

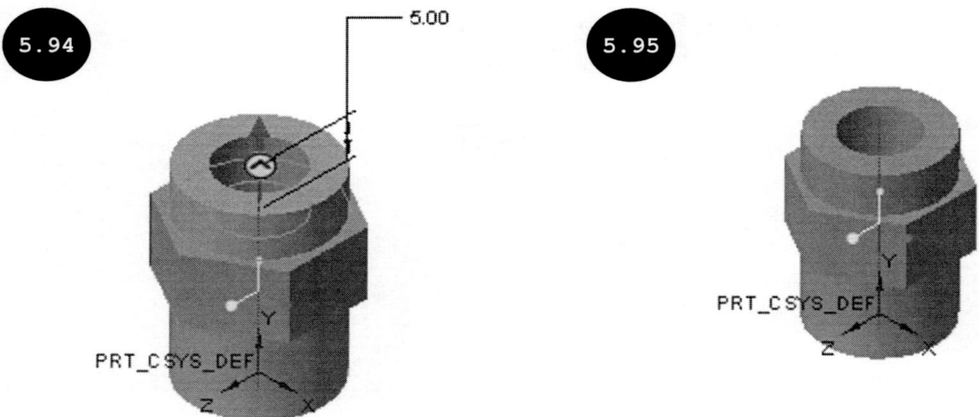

Section 7: Creating the Fourth Feature

1. Click on the **Sketch** tool in the **Datum** group. The **Sketch** dialog box appears.

2. Click on the top planar face of the third feature as the sketching plane, see Figure 5.96.

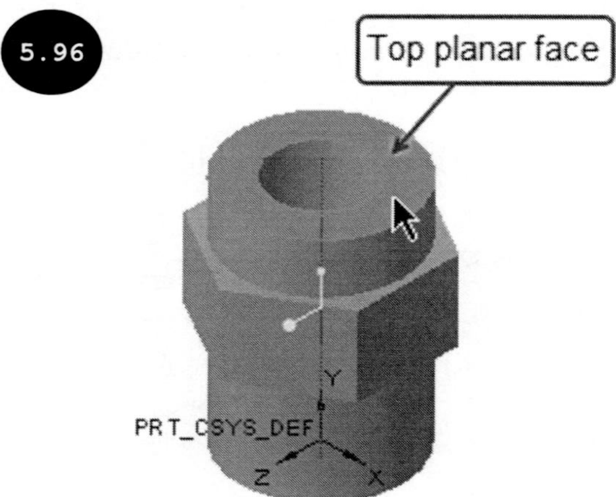

3. Click on the **Sketch** button in the dialog box. The Sketching environment is invoked. Also, the top planar face gets oriented normal to the viewing direction.

4. Create the sketch of the fourth feature by creating two circles of diameter 9 mm and 11 mm, see Figure 5.97.

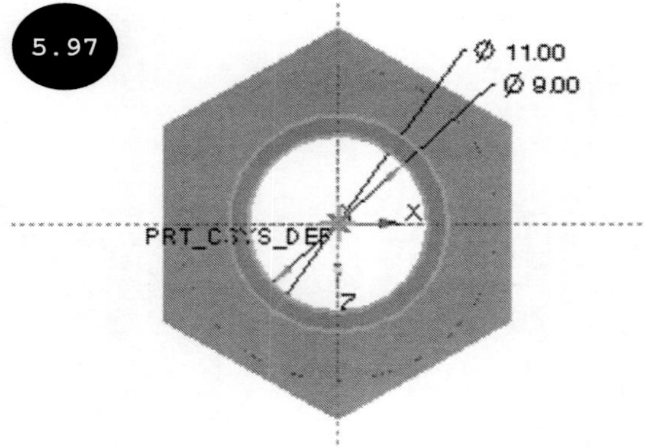

5. Exit the Sketching environment by clicking on the **OK** tool in the **Close** group of the **Ribbon**.

6. Click on the **Extrude** tool in the **Shapes** group of the **Model** tab. A preview of the extrude feature appears with default parameters. Also, the **Extrude** tab appears in the **Ribbon**.

7. Change the current orientation of the model to the standard orientation, see Figure 5.98.

8. Enter **14** as the depth of extrusion in the **Value** field of the **Extrude** tab.

9. Click on the green tick-mark button in the **Extrude** tab. The extrude feature is created, see Figure 5.99.

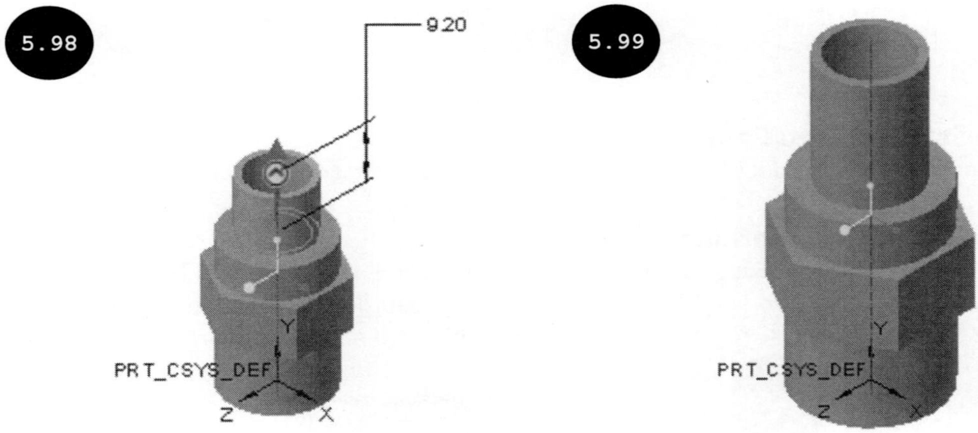

Section 8: Saving the Model

1. Click on the **Save** tool in the **Quick Access Toolbar**. The **Save Object** dialog box appears.

2. Click on the **OK** button in the dialog box. The model is saved with the name **C05-Tutorial01** in the specified working directory (<<*Creo Parametric**Chapter 5*\\).

Tutorial 2

Create the multi-feature model shown in Figure 5.100. All dimensions are in mm.

5.100

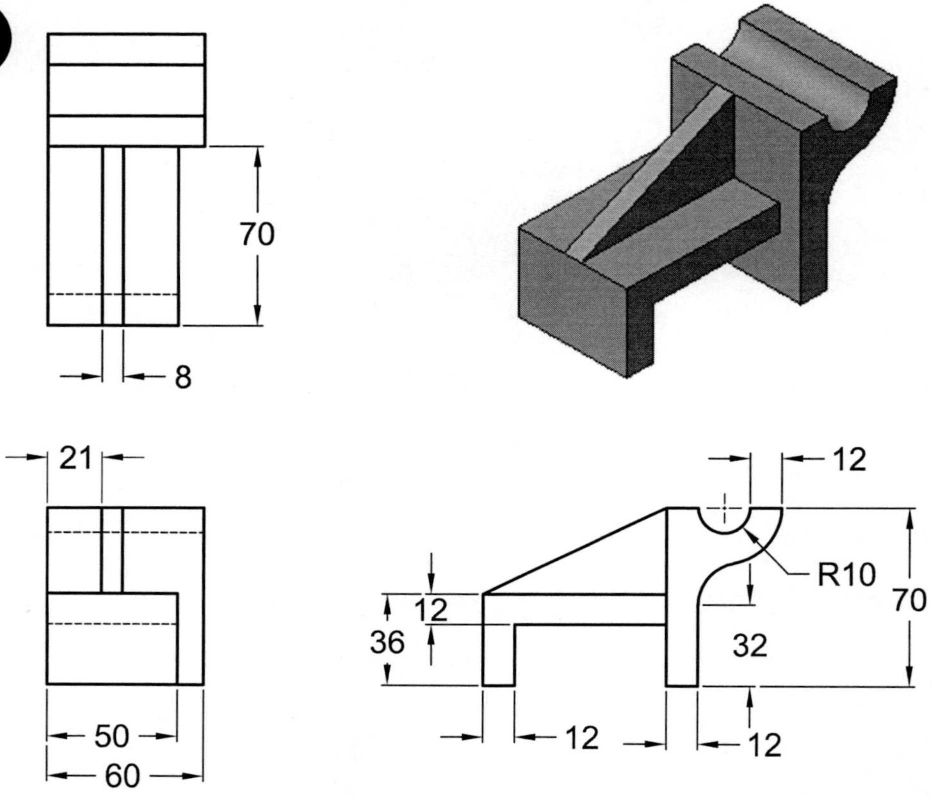

Section 1: Starting Creo Parametric

1. Start Creo Parametric by double-clicking on the Creo Parametric icon on your desktop.

Section 2: Setting the Working Directory

1. Click on the **Select Working Directory** tool in the **Data** group of the **Home** tab, see Figure 5.101. The **Select Working Directory** dialog box appears. In this dialog box, browse to the *Creo Parametric > Chapter 5*. You need to create these folders, if not created earlier.

5.101

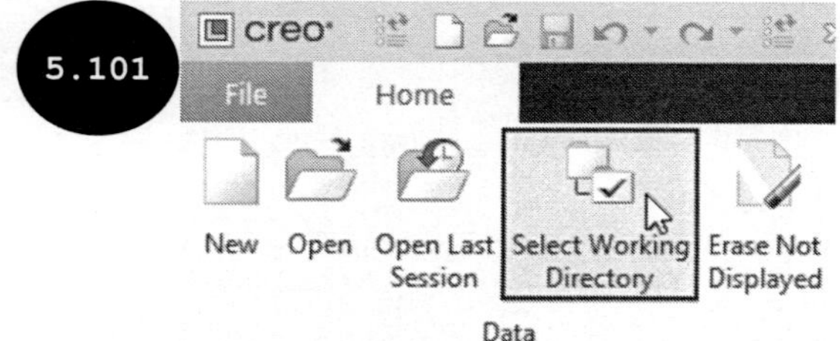

2. Click on the **OK** button in the dialog box. The working directory is set to <<*Creo Parametric\ Chapter 5*\.

Section 3: Invoking the Part Mode

1. Click on the **New** tool in the **Data** group of the **Home** tab. The **New** dialog box appears, see Figure 5.102. Alternatively, press CTRL + N to invoke the **New** dialog box.

2. Ensure that the **Part** radio button is selected in the **Type** area and the **Solid** radio button is selected in the **Sub-type** area of the dialog box, see Figure 5.102.

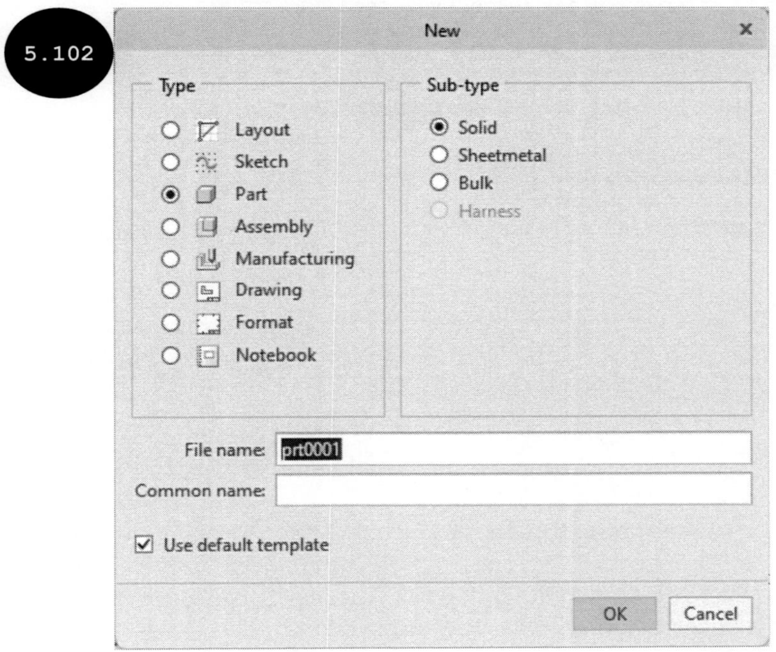

3. Enter **C05-Tutorial02** in the **File name** field of the dialog box as the name of the model.

4. Clear the **Use default template** check box and then click on the **OK** button in the dialog box. The **New File Options** dialog box appears, see Figure 5.103.

5. Select the **mmns_part_solid_abs** template in the **New File Options** dialog box and then click on the **OK** button. The Part mode is invoked with the **mmns_part_solid_abs** template. In this template, the length is measured in millimeters, mass is measured in Newton, and time is measured in seconds.

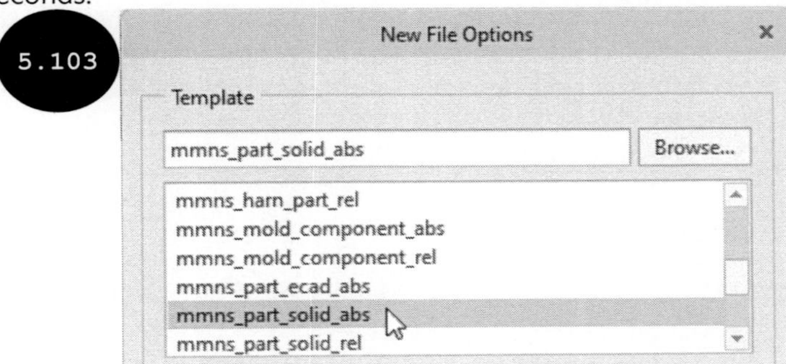

Section 4: Creating the Base/First Feature

1. Click on the **Sketch** tool in the **Datum** group, see Figure 5.104. The **Sketch** dialog box appears.

2. Click on the Right plane in the graphics area. The Right plane is selected as the sketching plane and its name appears in the **Plane** field of the **Sketch** dialog box, see Figure 5.105. Also, a reference plane and its orientation are selected automatically in the **Reference** field and **Orientation** drop-down list of the dialog box, respectively, see Figure 5.105.

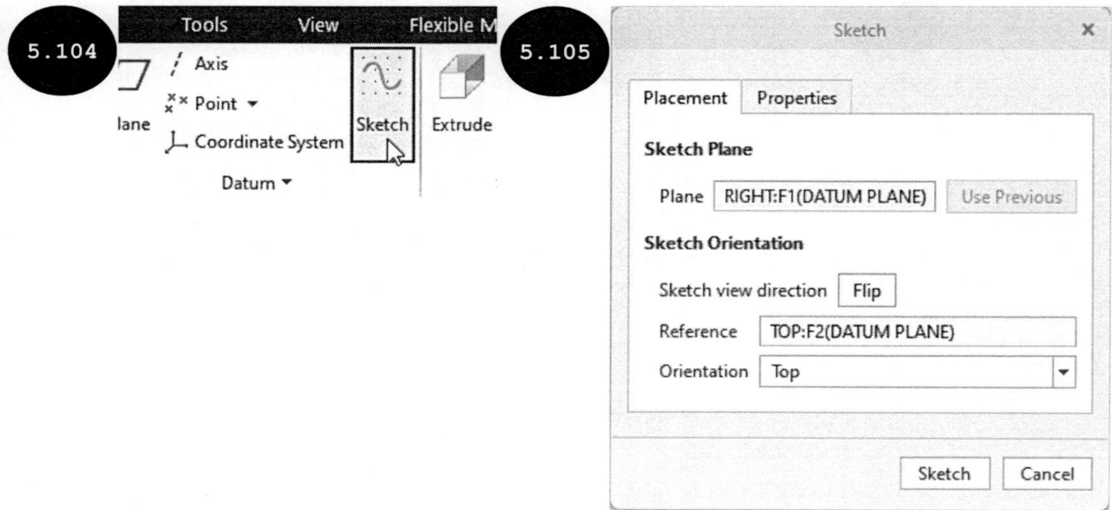

3. Click on the **Sketch** button in the dialog box. The Sketching environment is invoked. Also, the Right plane is oriented normal to the viewing direction.

   Now, you can draw the sketch of the base feature.

4. Create the sketch of the base feature and then apply the required relations and dimensions to the sketch, see Figure 5.106.

Tip: To make the sketch of the base feature fully defined, you need to apply the tangent constraint between line 2 and arc 3; arc 3 and arc 4 of the sketch, refer to Figure 5.107. Also, apply coincident constraint between the center points of arc 4 and arc 6, refer to Figure 5.107. Also, you need to apply equal constraint between line 5 and line 7. The sketch shown in the Figure 5.107 has been numbered for your reference only. The horizontal and vertical constraints are applied automatically while drawing the horizontal and vertical line entities of the sketch, respectively.

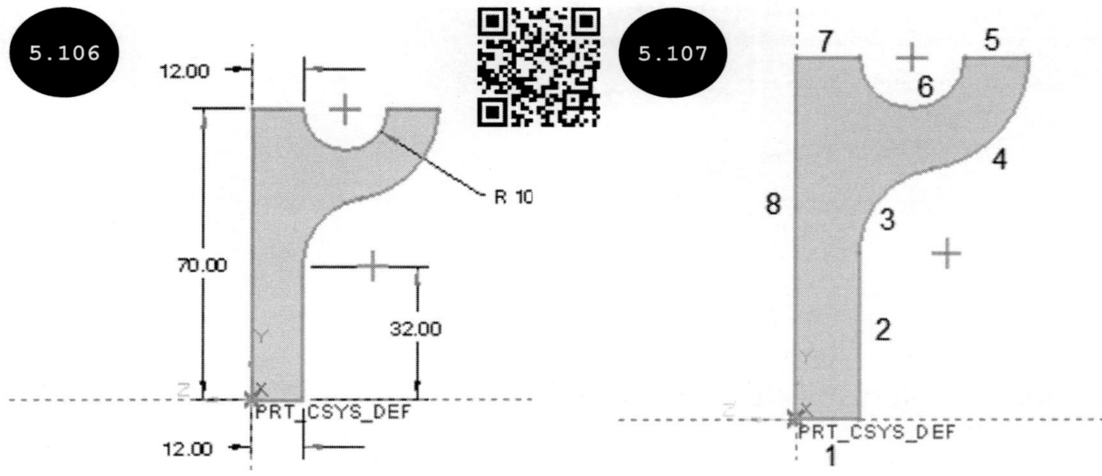

5. Click on the **OK** tool in the **Close** group to exit the Sketching environment, see Figure 5.108.

6. Click on the **Extrude** tool in the **Shapes** group of the **Model** tab. A preview of the extrude feature appears with default parameters. Also, the **Extrude** tab appears in the **Ribbon**.

7. Change the current orientation of the model to the standard orientation, see Figure 5.109.

8. Select the **Symmetric** option of the **Side 1** drop-down list of the **Extrude** tab to add the material symmetrically on both sides of the sketching plane, see Figure 5.110.

9. Enter **60** as the depth of extrusion in the **Value** field of the **Extrude** tab and then press ENTER. The preview of the extrude feature gets modified.

10. Click on the green tick-mark button in the **Extrude** tab. The extrude feature is created, see Figure 5.111.

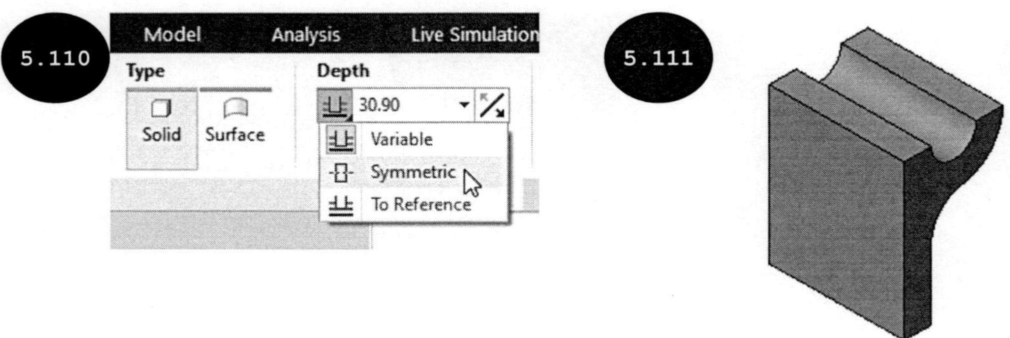

Section 5: Creating the Second Feature

To create the second feature of the model, you first need to create a datum plane at an offset distance of 10 mm from the right planar face of the base feature.

1. Click on the **Plane** tool in the **Datum** group, see Figure 5.112. The **Datum Plane** dialog box appears.

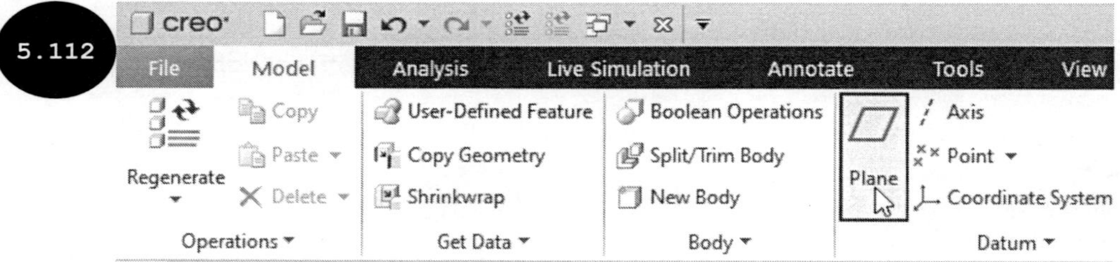

2. Select the right planar face of the base feature as the first reference. The preview of an offset datum plane appears, see Figure 5.113. Also, the **Offset** constraint is selected in the **Constraint** drop-down list in the **References** area of the dialog box, by default.

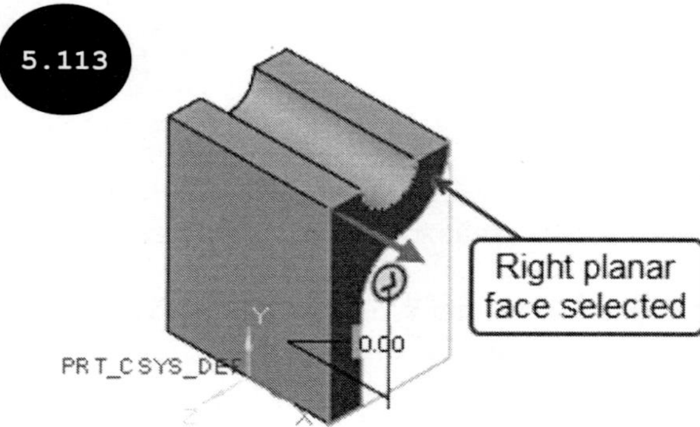

3. Enter -10 in the **Translation** field of the **Offset** area in the dialog box. Note that the negative value entered in the **Translation** field is used for reversing the direction of plane creation.

4. Click on the **OK** button in the dialog box. The offset datum plane is created, see Figure 5.114.

Note: In Figure 5.114, all other datum planes are turned off for clarity. To do so, click on the datum plane to be turned off and then click on the **Hide** tool in the Mini toolbar that appears in the graphics area, see Figure 5.115.

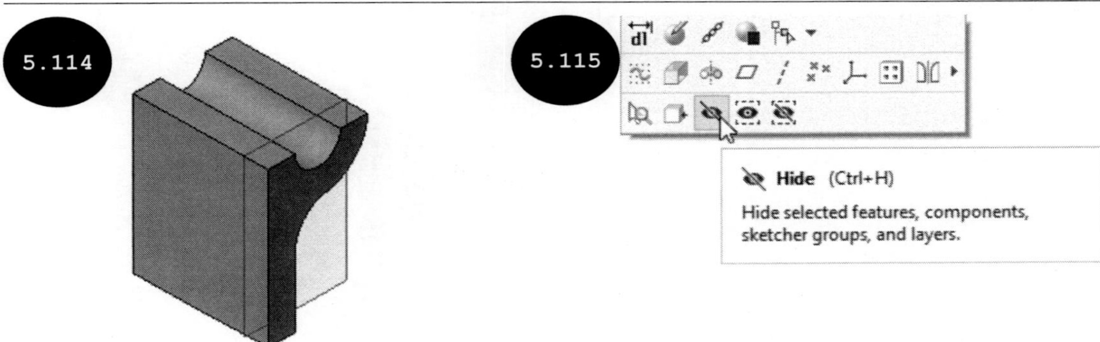

After creating the datum plane, create the second feature of the model.

5. Click on the **Sketch** tool in the **Datum** group of the **Model** tab in the **Ribbon**. The **Sketch** dialog box appears.

6. Select the newly created datum plane as the sketching plane and then click on the **Sketch** button in the dialog box. The Sketching environment is invoked and the selected datum plane is oriented normal to the viewing direction.

7. Create the sketch of the second feature and then apply the required dimensions to the sketch, see Figure 5.116.

8. Click on the **OK** tool in the **Close** group to exit the Sketching environment, see Figure 5.117.

9. Click on the **Extrude** tool in the **Shapes** group. A preview of the extrude feature appears with default parameters. Also, the **Extrude** tab appears in the **Ribbon**.

10. Change the current orientation of the model to the standard orientation.

11. Click on the **Flip Direction** button in the **Extrude** tab to reverse the direction of extrusion, see Figure 5.118. The preview of the extrude feature appears similar to the one shown in Figure 5.119.

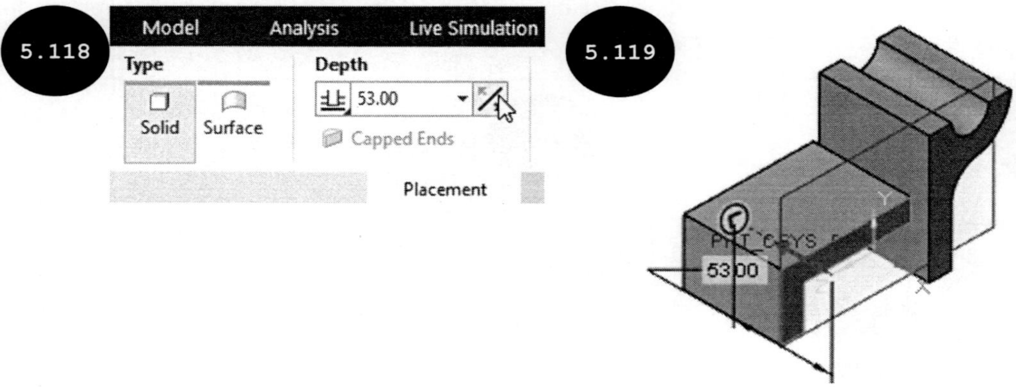

12. Enter **50** as the depth of extrusion in the **Value** field of the **Extrude** tab and then press ENTER. The preview of the extrude feature gets modified.

13. Click on the green tick-mark button in the **Extrude** tab. The extrude feature is created, see Figure 5.120.

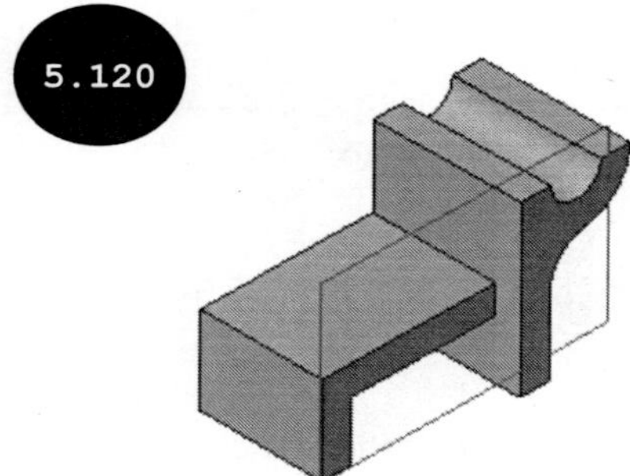

Section 6: Creating the Third Feature

To create the third feature of the model, you need to create a datum plane such that it passes through the middle of the second feature.

1. Click on the **Plane** tool in the **Datum** group. The **Datum Plane** dialog box appears.

2. Select the right planar face of the second feature as the first reference. The preview of an offset datum plane appears in the graphics area, see Figure 5.121.

3. Rotate the model such that the left planar face of the second feature can be viewed in the graphics area, see Figure 5.122. You can rotate the model by dragging the cursor after pressing and holding the middle mouse button.

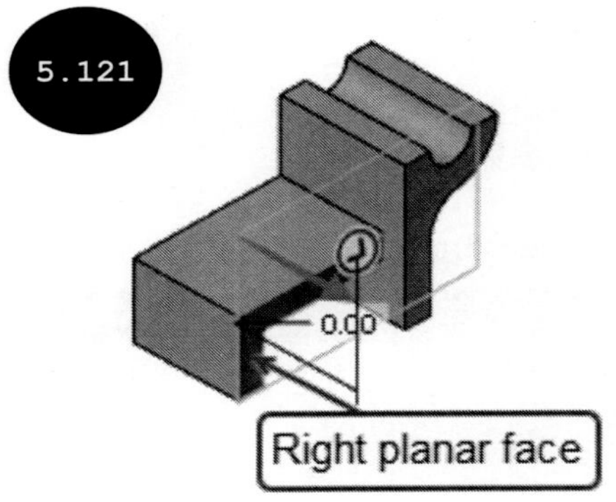

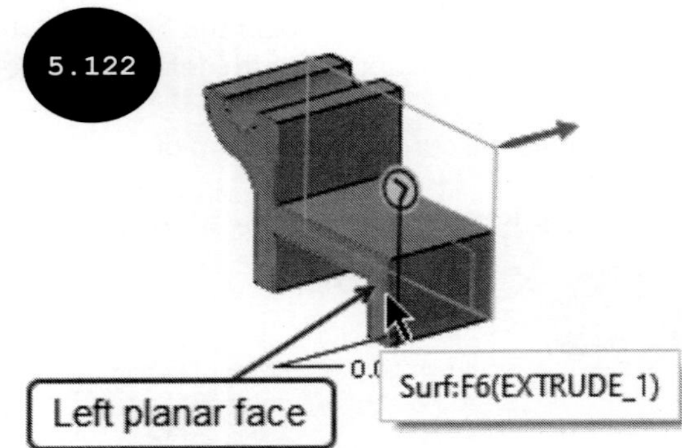

4. Press and hold the CTRL key and then select the left planar face of the second feature as the second reference. The preview of a datum plane in the middle of the two selected planar faces appears in the graphics area, see Figure 5.123. Note that in this figure, all other datum planes are turned off for clarity of the image.

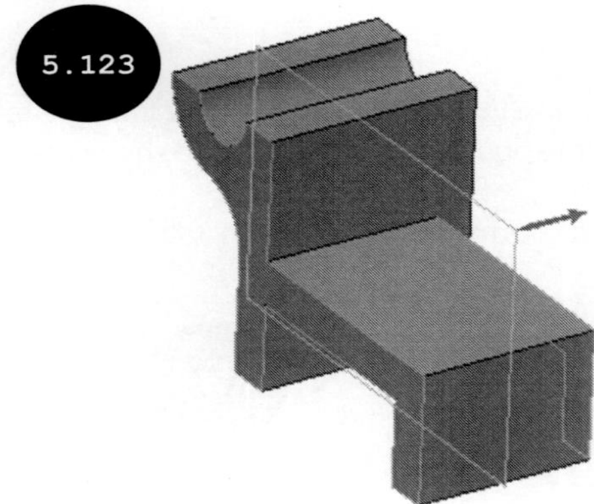

5. Click on the **OK** button in the dialog box and then change the current orientation of the model to the standard orientation. The datum plane passing through the middle of two selected faces is created.

   After creating the datum plane, create the third feature of the model.

6. Click on the **Sketch** tool in the **Datum** group. The **Sketch** dialog box appears.

7. Select the newly created datum plane as the sketching plane and then click on the **Sketch** button in the dialog box. The Sketching environment is invoked and the selected datum plane is oriented normal to the viewing direction.

8. Create the closed sketch of the third feature (three line entities), see Figure 5.124. The entities of the sketch shown in Figure 5.124 have been created by taking reference from the vertices of the existing geometry.

9. Click on the **OK** tool in the **Close** group to exit the Sketching environment.

10. Click on the **Extrude** tool in the **Shapes** group of the **Model** tab in the **Ribbon**. A preview of the extrude feature appears with default parameters.

11. Change the current orientation of the model to the standard orientation.

12. Select the **Symmetric** option of the **Side 1** drop-down list of the **Extrude** tab, see Figure 5.125.

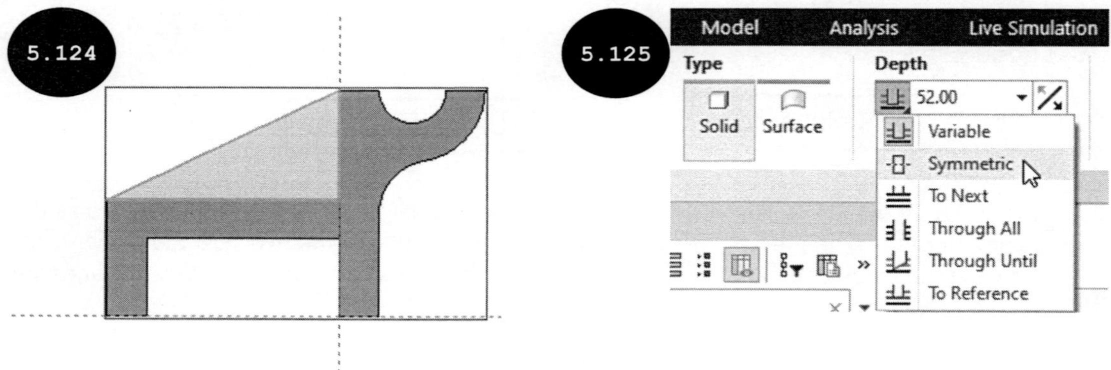

13. Enter **8** as the depth of extrusion in the **Value** field of the **Extrude** tab and then press ENTER. A preview of the extrude feature appears similar to the one shown in Figure 5.126.

14. Click on the green tick-mark button in the **Extrude** tab. The extrude feature is created, see Figure 5.127.

Section 7: Saving the Model

Now, you need to save the model.

1. Click on the **Save** tool in the **Quick Access Toolbar**. The **Save Object** dialog box appears.

2. Click on the **OK** button in the dialog box. The model is saved with the name **C05-Tutorial02** in the specified working directory (<<*Creo Parametric**Chapter 5*\).

Hands-on Test Drive 1

Create a model, as shown in Figure 5.128. All dimensions are in mm.

5.128

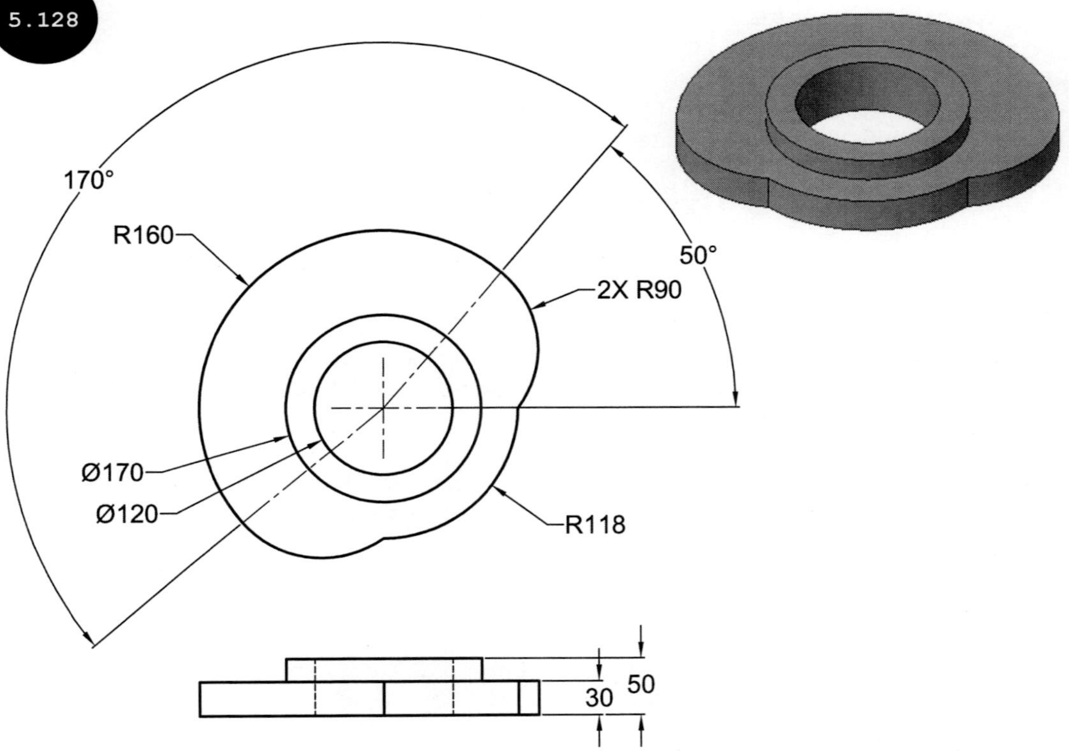

170°
R160
50°
2X R90
Ø170
Ø120
R118
30
50

Hands-on Test Drive 2

Create a model, as shown in Figure 5.129. All dimensions are in mm.

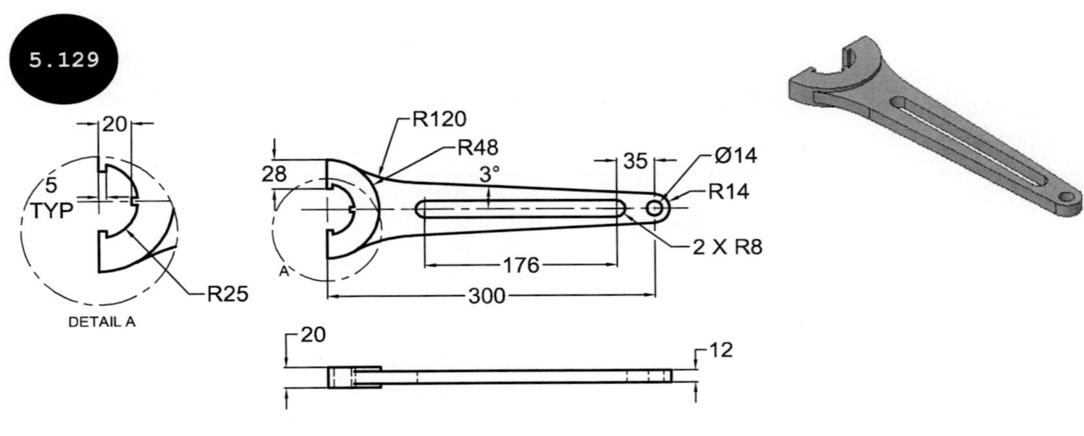

Summary

In this chapter, you have learned that the default planes; Front, Top, and Right may not be enough for creating models having multiple features, therefore, you need to create additional datum planes, methods for which are discussed. Methods for creating a datum axis, a datum coordinates system, and a datum point by using the respective tools are also discussed.

Questions

Complete and verify the following sentences:

- You can create datum planes by using the _________ tool.
- The _________ constraint is used for creating a datum plane at an offset distance from the selected reference.
- To create a datum plane parallel to a planar face of a model, you need to define two references. First reference can be a planar face and the second reference can be a _________, a _________, or a _________.
- To create a datum plane at an angle to a planar face/plane, you need to define two references. First reference can be a planar face/plane and the second reference can be a _________, an _________, or a _________.
- The _________ tool is used for creating a datum axis.
- The _________ tool is used for creating a datum coordinate system.
- You can create a datum point by using the _________, _________, and _________ tools.
- The _________ option allows you to define the location of the datum point on the selected edge by specifying the actual distance value, which measures from the start point of the edge.
- In Creo Parametric, you can create a datum point at the intersection of three faces or two edges. (True/False)
- You cannot select a planar face of existing features as the sketching plane for creating a feature. (True/False)

Advanced Modeling - I

In this chapter, the following topics will be discussed:

- Using Advanced Options of the Extrude Tool
- Using Advanced Options of the Revolve Tool
- Projecting Edges onto the Sketching Plane
- Editing a Feature
- Editing the Sketch of a Feature
- Measuring Geometries
- Assigning an Appearance
- Editing an Appearance
- Copying and Pasting an Appearance
- Removing Appearances
- Applying a Material
- Calculating Mass Properties

In the previous chapters, you learned how to create features using the **Extrude** and **Revolve** tools. In this chapter, you will explore the advanced options of these tools, including removing material. Additionally, you will learn how to measure distances between entities of a model, apply material properties, calculate the mass properties of a model, and more.

Using Advanced Options of the Extrude Tool

As discussed earlier, while extruding a sketch by using the **Extrude** tool, the **Extrude** tab appears in the **Ribbon**, see Figure 6.1. Some of the options of this **Extrude** tab have been discussed earlier while creating the base feature of a model. The remaining options are discussed next.

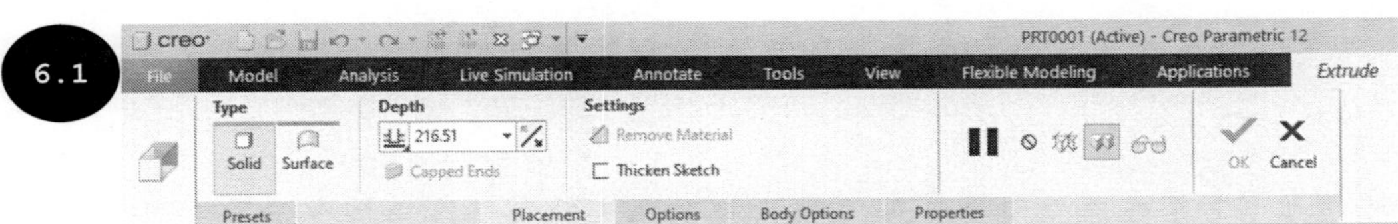

Side 1 Drop-down list

The **Side 1** drop-down list in the **Depth** area of the **Extrude** tab is used for selecting a depth option for extruding the feature on one side (side 1) of the sketching plane, see Figure 6.2. The **Variable** and **Symmetric** options of this drop-down list have been discussed earlier while creating the base feature of a model and the remaining options; **To Next**, **Through All**, **Through Until**, and **To Reference** are discussed next. Note that these options are not available while creating the base feature of a model.

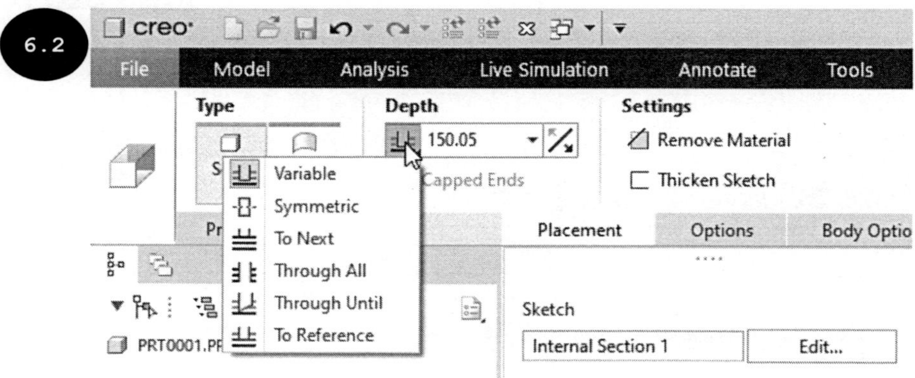

Note: You can also access the **Side 1** drop-down list in the **Options** panel of the **Extrude** tab, see Figure 6.3.

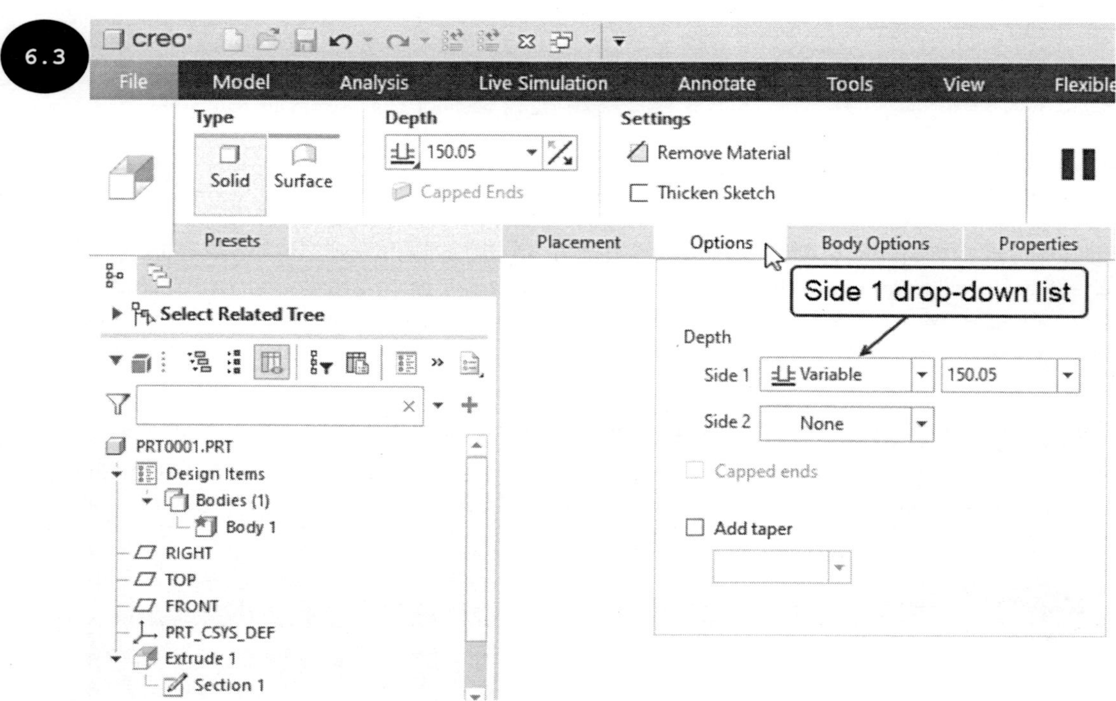

To Next

The **To Next** option of the **Side 1** drop-down list is used for defining the end condition or termination of the extrusion up to its next intersection. Figure 6.4 shows a sketch to be extruded and Figure 6.5 shows a preview of the extrude feature on selecting the **To Next** option in the **Side 1** drop-down list.

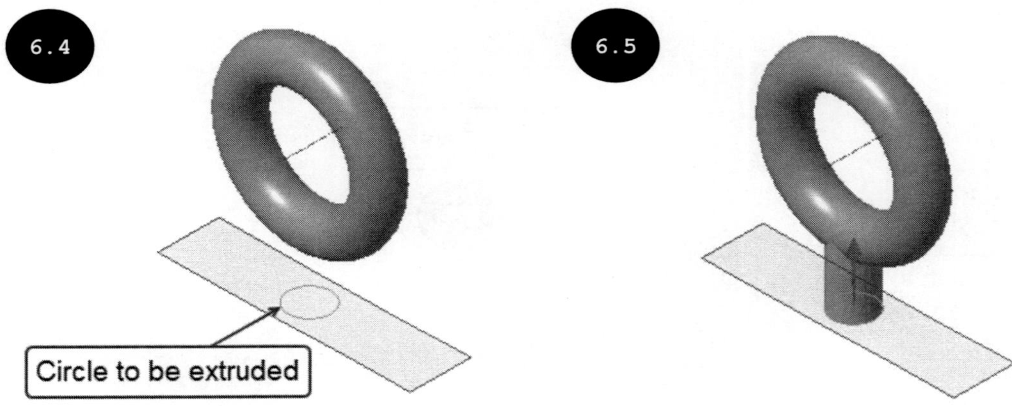

Note: The sketch terminates up to its next intersection encapsulating the entire sketch.

Through All

The **Through All** option of the **Side 1** drop-down list is used for defining the end condition or termination of the extrusion through all the faces of the model, see Figure 6.6.

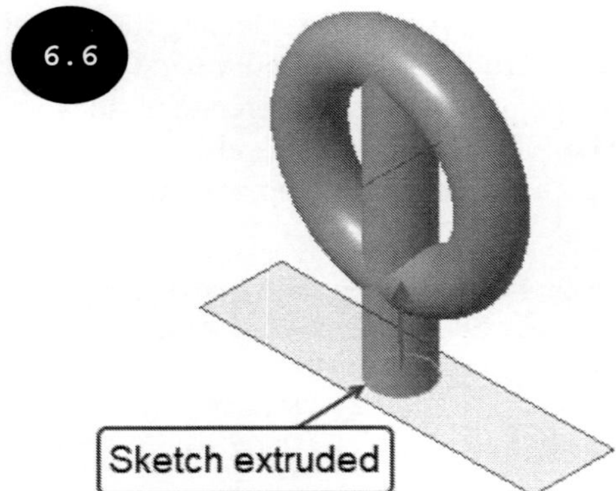

Through Until

The **Through Until** option is used for defining the end condition or termination of the extrusion up to a face (planar or curved). When you select the **Through Until** option, the **Depth Reference** collector appears in the **Extrude** tab (see Figure 6.7) and you are prompted to select a face as a reference up to which you want to extrude the feature. Figure 6.8 shows a sketch to be extruded and Figure 6.9 shows a preview of the feature whose end condition is defined by selecting a face of the model.

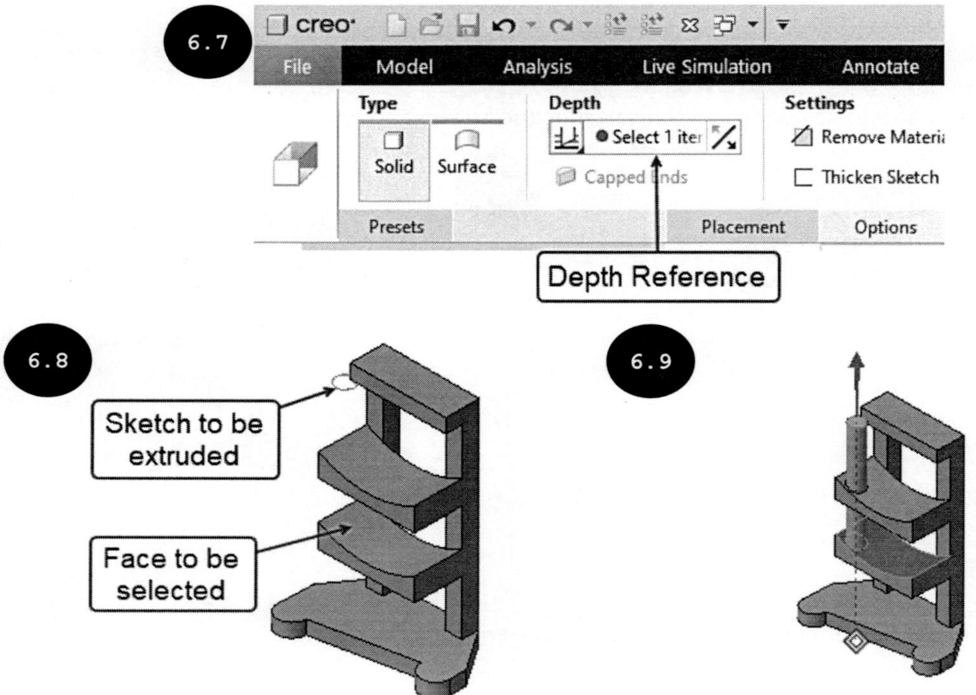

To Reference

The **To Reference** option is used for defining the end condition or termination of the extrusion up to a face, a plane, an edge, a curve, or a point/vertex. On selecting the **To Reference** option, the **Depth Reference** collector appears in the **Extrude** tab (see Figure 6.10) and you are prompted to select a face, a plane, an edge, a curve, or a point/vertex as a reference up to which you want to extrude the feature. Figure 6.11 shows the preview of a feature whose end condition is defined by selecting a vertex and Figure 6.12 shows the preview of a feature whose end condition is defined by selecting an edge.

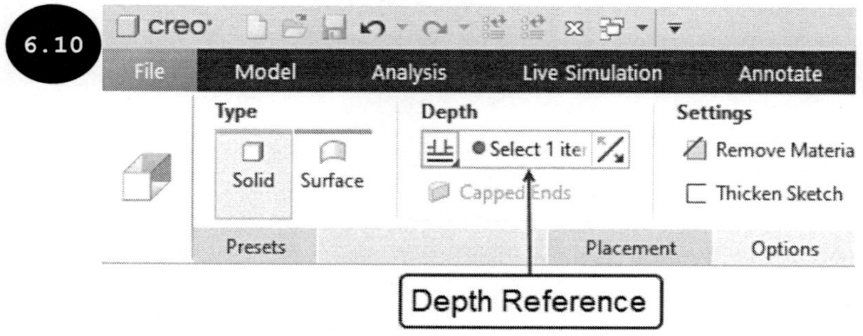

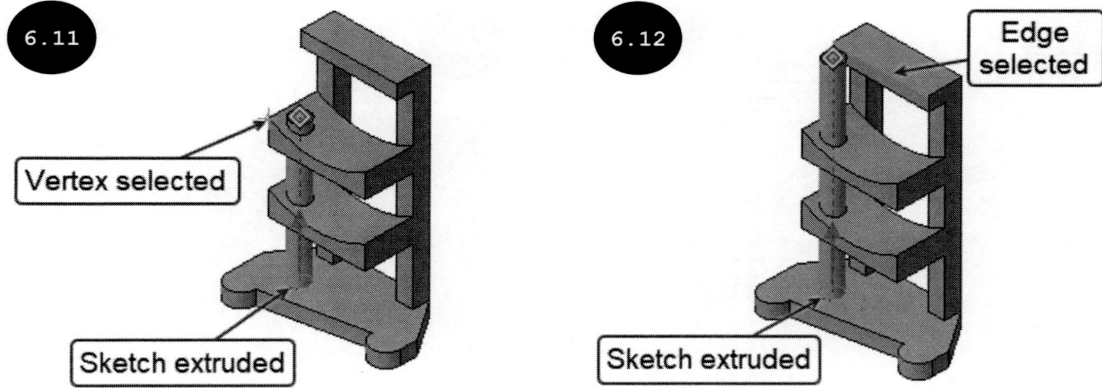

Side 2 Drop-down list

The **Side 2** drop-down list is used for selecting a depth option for extruding the feature on the other side (side 2) of the sketching plane. You can access the **Side 2** drop-down list in the **Options** panel of the **Extrude** tab, see Figure 6.13. The options available in the **Side 2** drop-down list are the same as those of the **Side 1** drop-down list with the only difference being that the options of the **Side 2** drop-down list are used for specifying the end condition of extrusion in the second direction of the sketching plane.

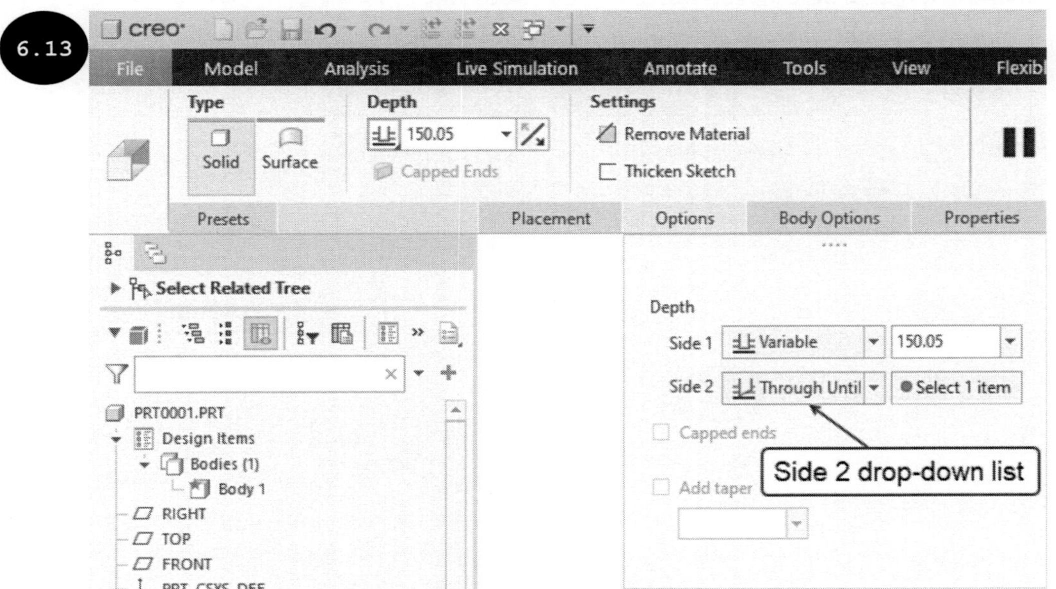

Remove Material

The **Remove Material** button is used for creating a cut feature by removing material from the existing solid feature. Note that the geometry of the material removed is defined by the sketch of the cut feature. Figure 6.14 shows a sketch and Figure 6.15 shows the resultant cut feature. Note that the **Remove Material** button is not enabled while creating the base/first feature of a model.

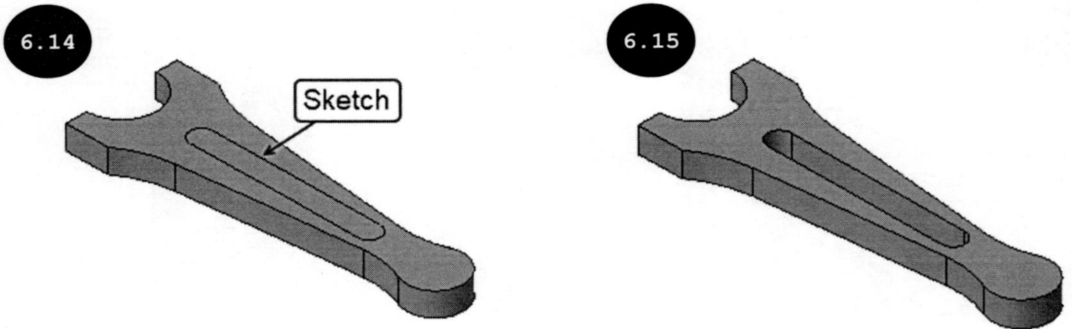

Change Material Direction

The **Change Material Direction** button in the **Settings** area of the **Extrude** tab is used for flipping the side of the material to be removed, see Figures 6.16 through 6.18. Figure 6.16 shows the **Change Material Direction** button in the **Settings** area in the **Extrude** tab. Figure 6.17 shows the sketch to be extruded and Figure 6.18 shows the resultant cut feature when the **Change Material Direction** button is activated. If the **Change Material Direction** button is not activated, the resultant cut feature appears similar to the one shown in Figure 6.19. Note that the **Change Material Direction** button is available only when the **Remove Material** button is activated in the **Extrude** tab.

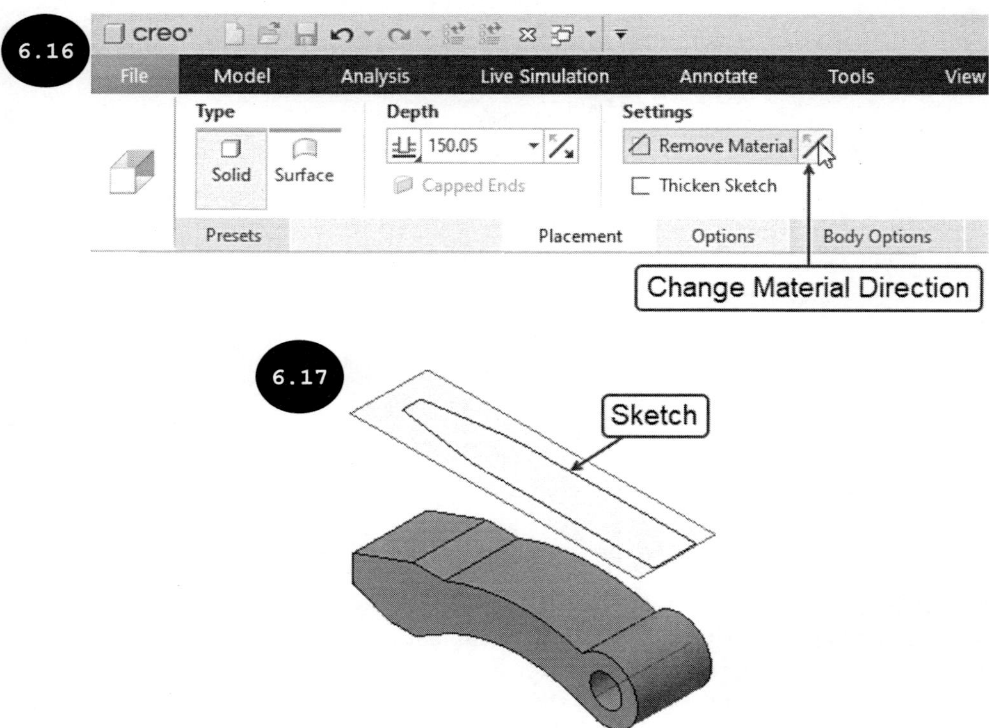

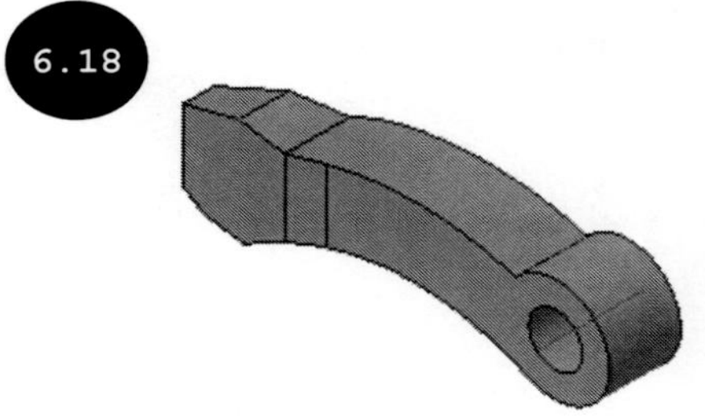

Change Material Direction button is activated

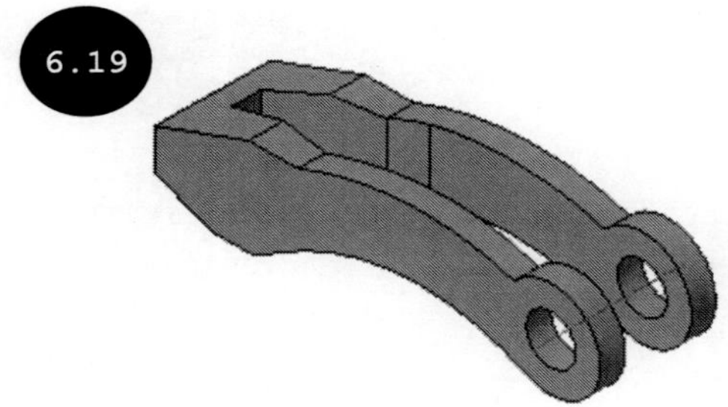

Change Material Direction button is not activated

Using Advanced Options of the Revolve Tool

As discussed earlier, while revolving a sketch by using the **Revolve** tool, the **Revolve** tab appears in the **Ribbon**, see Figure 6.20. Some of the options in the **Revolve** tab have been discussed earlier while creating the base revolved feature of a model. The remaining options such as **To Reference** and **Change Material Direction** are the same as discussed earlier while creating an extrude feature.

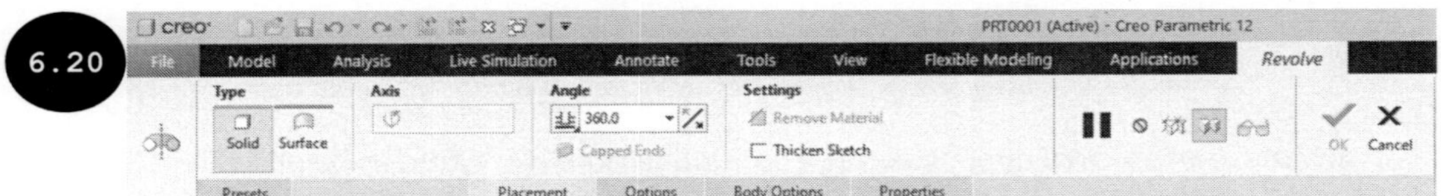

Projecting Edges onto the Sketching Plane

In Creo, while sketching, you can project edges of the existing features onto the current sketching plane as sketch entities by using the **Project** tool. Figure 6.21 shows a model in which the edges of the existing features have been projected as sketch entities onto the current sketching plane in the Sketching environment.

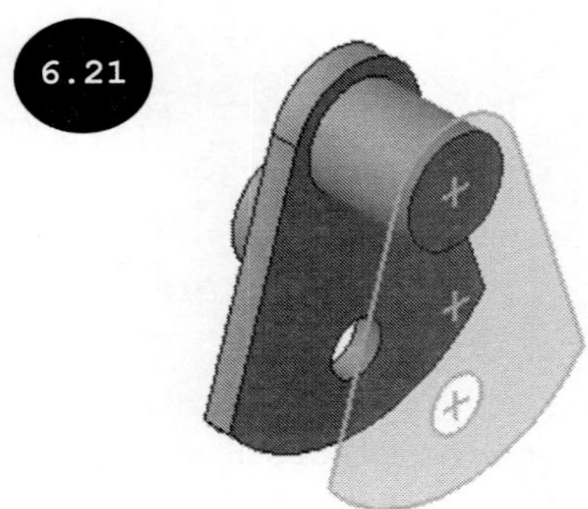

To project edges of existing features onto the current sketching plane, click on the **Project** tool in the **Sketching** group of the **Sketch** tab, see Figure 6.22. The **Type** dialog box appears, see Figure 6.23. The options in this dialog box are discussed next.

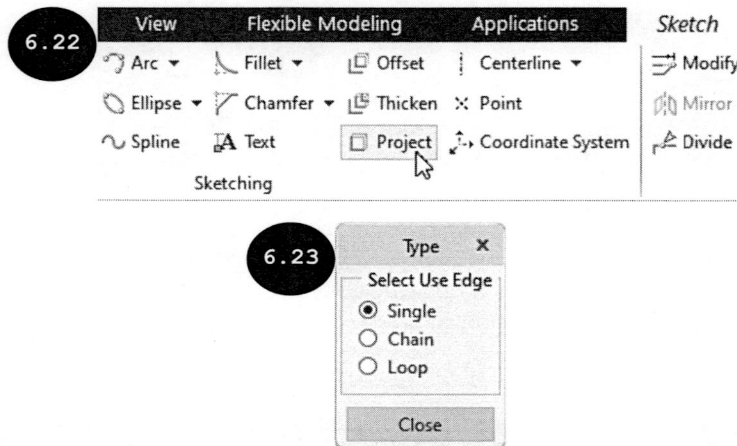

Single

The **Single** radio button of the **Type** dialog box is used for selecting a single edge of an existing feature to be projected onto the current sketching plane. To do so, select the **Single** radio button and then select an edge of the model. The selected edge gets projected onto the current sketching plane. Similarly, you can project other edges of the model, individually one after another.

Chain

The **Chain** radio button is used for selecting a continuous chain of edges to be projected. Note that a chain of edges is defined by a minimum of two edges or entities. To project a chain of edges, select the **Chain** radio button in the **Type** dialog box. Next, select two edges of the model one after the other to define a chain. A chain of edges defined by selected edges gets selected. Also, the **Menu Manager** dialog box appears, see Figure 6.24. In this dialog box, the **Accept** option accepts the currently selected chain of edges and projects them onto the current sketching plane. The **Next** and **Previous** options of this dialog box cycle through the other available chain of edges. You can select the desired chain of edges and then click on the **Accept** option. The selected edges get projected onto the current sketching plane.

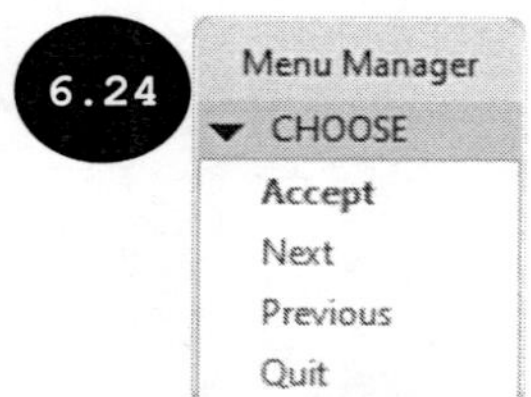

Loop

The **Loop** radio button is used for selecting a closed loop of edges to be projected. To do so, select the **Loop** radio button in the **Type** dialog box and then select the face of the model. The closed loop of edges of the selected face gets projected onto the current sketching plane. Note that if the selected face has more than one closed loop of edges (refer to Figure 6.25), then the **Menu Manager** dialog box appears. In this dialog box, you can cycle through different available loops by clicking the **Next** or **Previous** option. Click on the **Accept** option in the dialog box when the desired closed-loop gets selected in the graphics area. All the edges of the selected loop get projected onto the current sketching plane, see Figure 6.25. In this figure, the outer closed loop of edges is projected onto the current sketching plane.

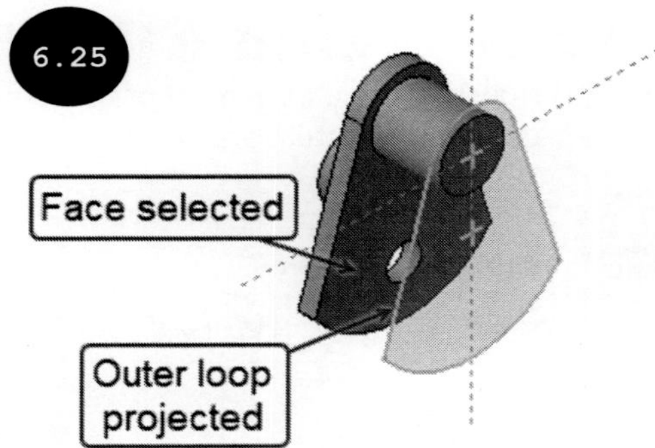

After projecting an edge, a chain of edges, or a loop onto the current sketching plane, click on the **Close** button in the **Type** dialog box to close it.

Editing a Feature

Creo allows you to edit the features of a model at any point of design. You can edit individual features and their sketches. You will learn about editing a sketch later in this chapter. The method for editing a feature is discussed below:

1. Click on a feature in the **Model Tree** or in the graphics area. A Mini toolbar appears, see Figure 6.26. In this figure, the extrude feature is selected in the Model Tree.

2. Click on the **Edit Definition** tool in the Mini toolbar, see Figure 6.26. A preview of the selected feature appears in the graphics area. Also, the respective tab appears in the **Ribbon**.

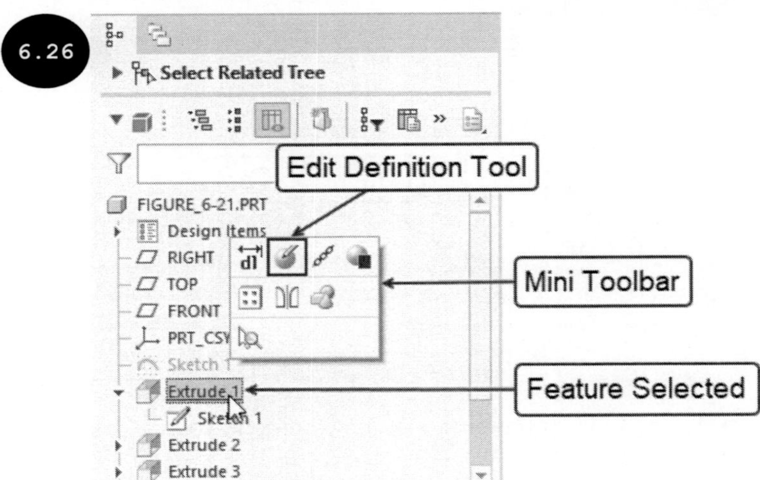

3. Change the feature parameters by using the options available in the tab that appears in the **Ribbon**.

4. Once you have edited the feature parameters, click on the green tick mark ✓. The selected feature gets edited.

Editing the Sketch of a Feature

1. In the **Model Tree**, click on the arrow that appears in front of the feature whose sketch needs to be edited, see Figure 6.27. The sketch of the feature appears in the **Model Tree**.

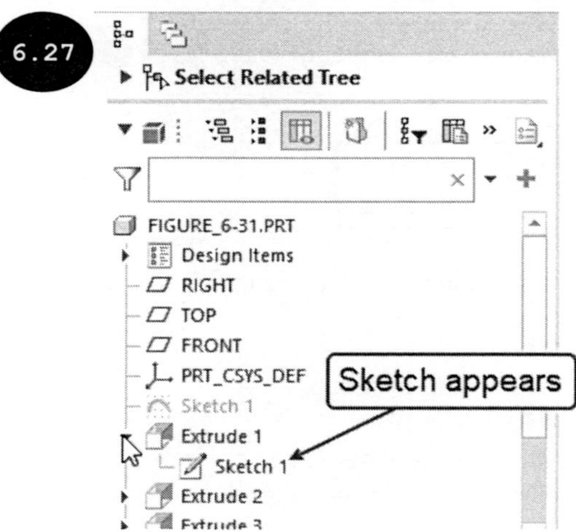

2. Click on the sketch in the **Model Tree**. A Mini toolbar appears, see Figure 6.28.

3. Click on the **Edit Definition** tool in the Mini toolbar, see Figure 6.28. The Sketching environment is invoked and the selected sketch is oriented normal to the viewing direction.

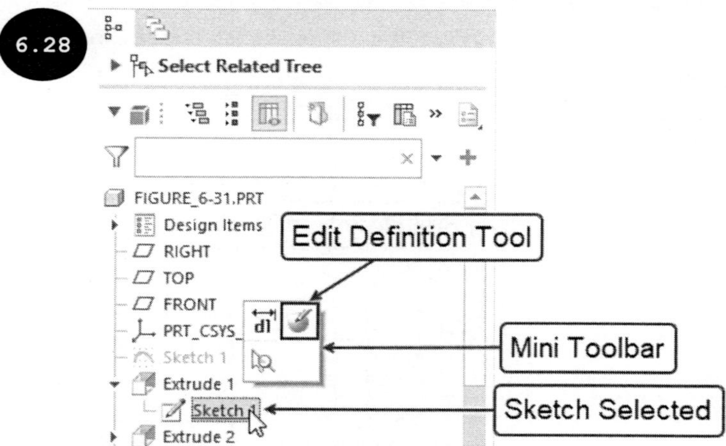

4. By using the sketching tools in the Sketching environment, you can modify the sketch of the feature as per your requirement.

5. Once you have edited the sketch of the feature, exit the Sketching environment.

Measuring Geometries

In Creo, you can measure different geometrical parameters such as length, angle, area, and volume by using the measuring tools, see Figure 6.29. The measuring tools are available in the **Measure** flyout of the **Analysis** tab in the **Ribbon**. All these tools are discussed next.

6.29

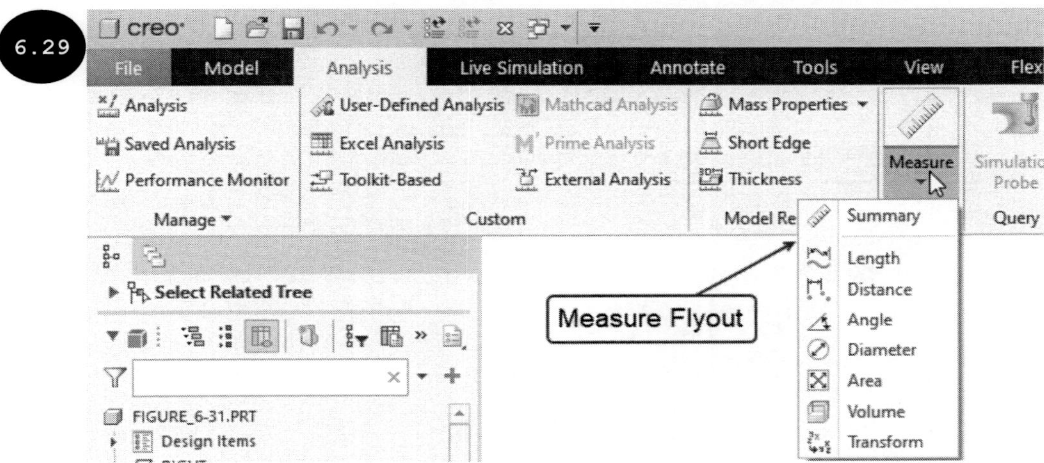

Measuring Multiple Parameters

You can measure multiple parameters such as the area, perimeter, diameter, and length of a selected geometry by using the **Summary** tool. Note that the display of results depends upon the selected geometry, see Figure 6.30. In this figure, a cylindrical face of a model is selected as the geometry and the respective results appear.

6.30

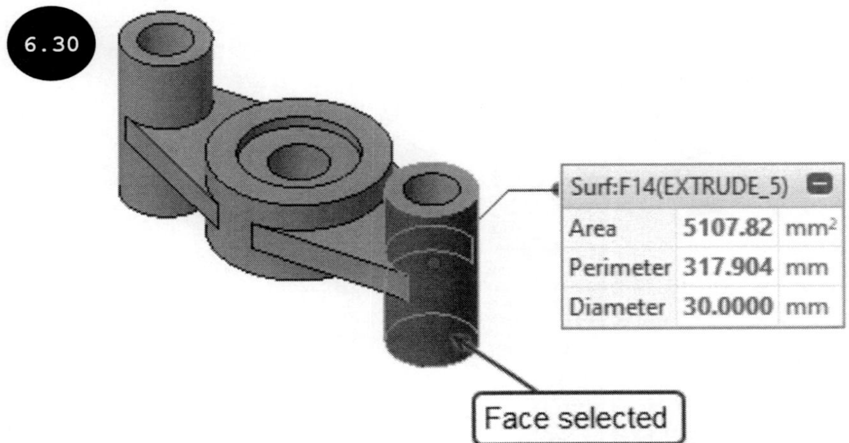

You can also calculate the measuring results between two selected geometries by using the **Summary** tool. To do so, click on the **Summary** tool in the **Measure** flyout of the **Analysis** tab, refer to Figure 6.29. The **Measure** dialog box appears in the graphics area. Next, select two geometries by pressing the CTRL key, see Figure 6.31. Results such as distance between the selected geometries, total area, and total perimeter appear in the graphics area. Also, the +sign appears on each of the selected geometry in the graphics area, see Figure 6.31. You can also click on the +sign of a geometry to display its individual results in the graphics area, see Figure 6.32.

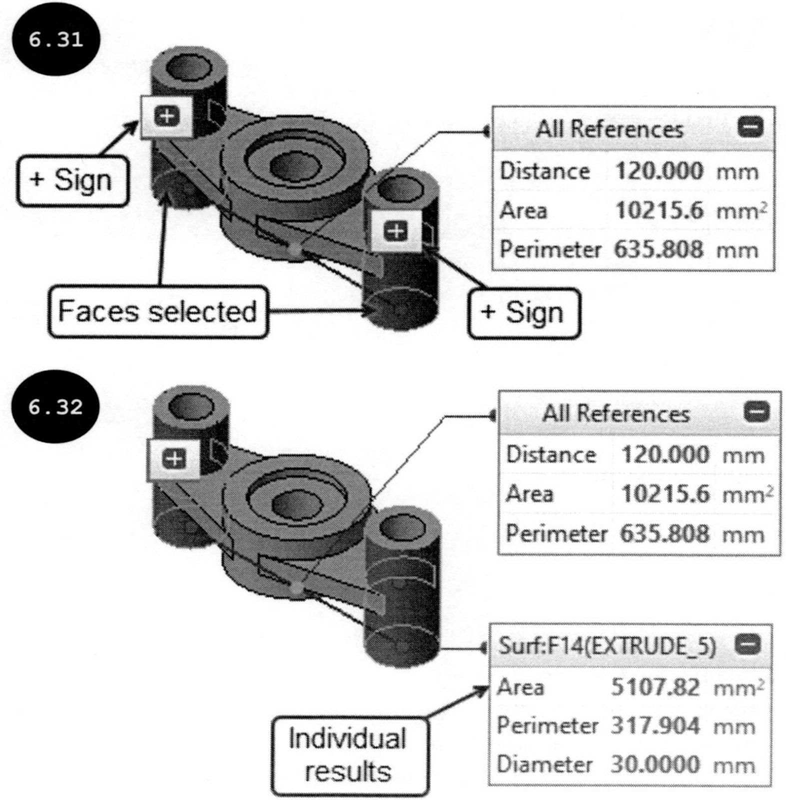

Tip: You can also expand the **Measure** dialog box by clicking on the +sign available at its end to display the measuring results, see Figure 6.33.

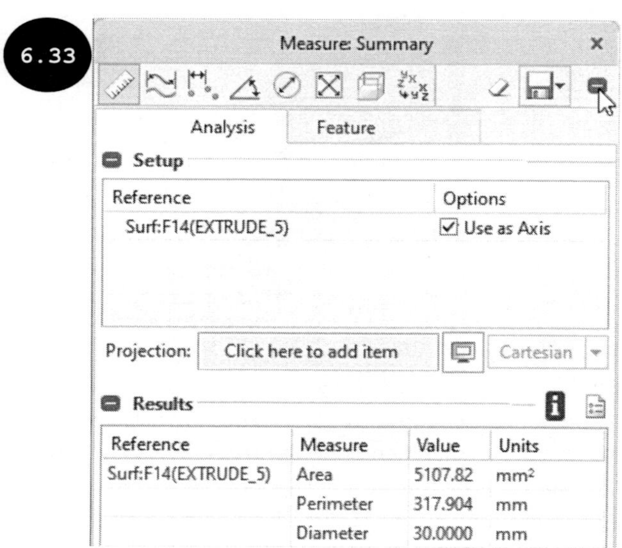

Measuring the Length

The **Length** tool is used for measuring the length of a geometry. To do so, invoke the **Measure** flyout in the **Analysis** tab of the **Ribbon**, see Figure 6.34. Next, click on the **Length** tool in the flyout. The **Measure Length** dialog box appears, see Figure 6.35. Next, select an edge (linear or curved). The length of the selected geometry appears in the graphics area, see Figure 6.36.

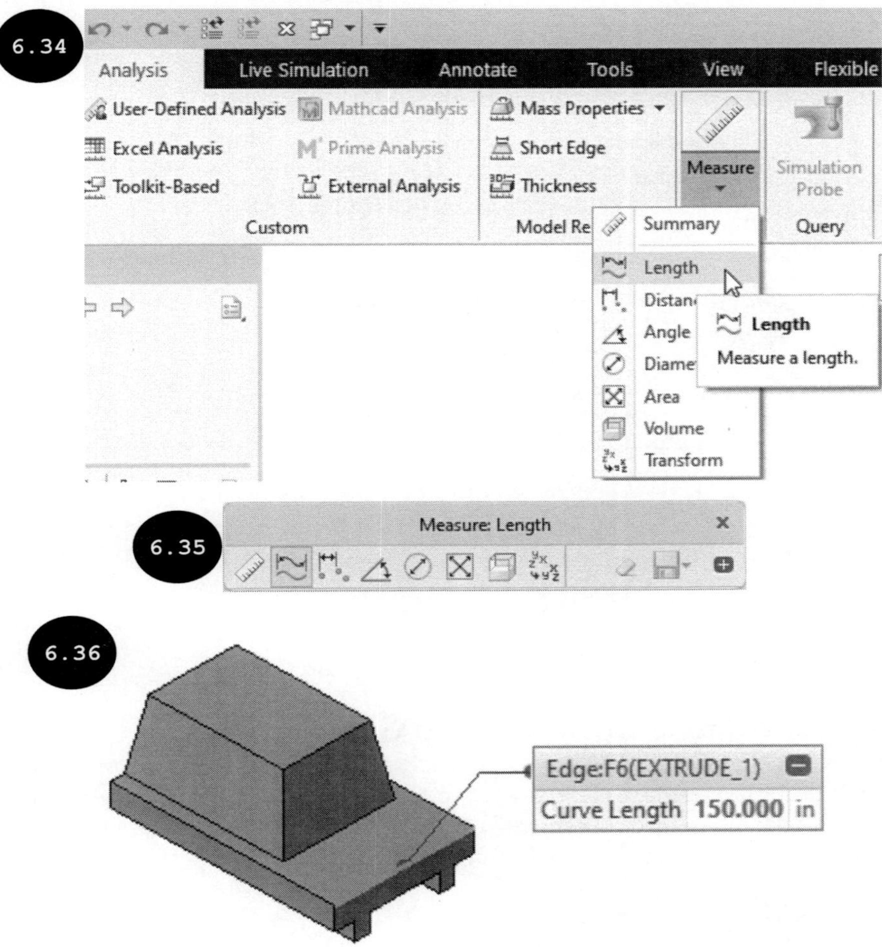

You can also select multiple edges by pressing the CTRL key. On doing so, the total length of the selected edges appears in the graphics area.

Measuring the Distance Between Two Geometries

To measure the distance between two geometries, click on the **Distance** tool in the **Measure** flyout of the **Analysis** tab in the **Ribbon**, see Figure 6.37. The **Measure Distance** dialog box appears, see Figure 6.38. Next, select two geometries (faces or edges) by pressing the CTRL key. The distance between the selected geometries appears in the graphics area, see Figure 6.39.

6.37

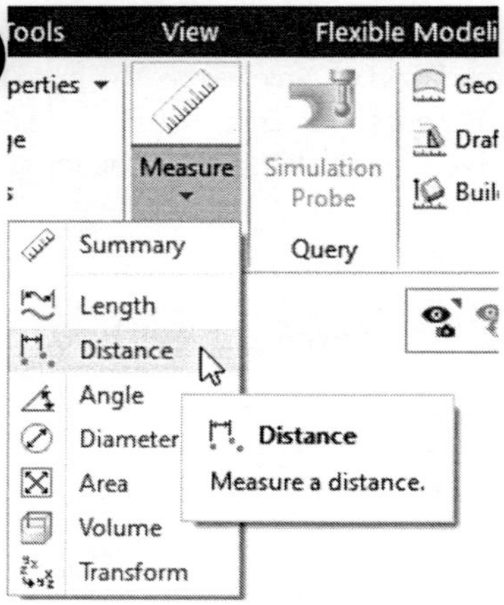

Tools
View
Flexible Modeli
perties
Measure
Simulation Probe
Query
Geo
Draf
Buil
Summary
Length
Distance
Angle
Diameter
Area
Volume
Transform
Distance
Measure a distance.

6.38

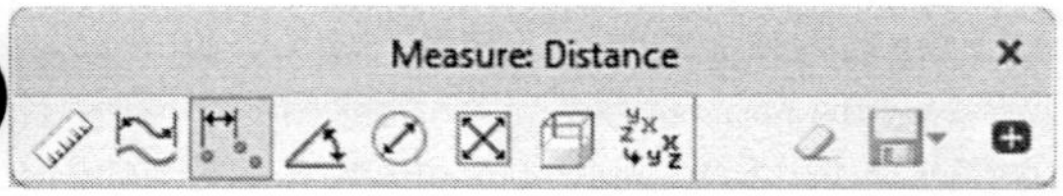

Measure: Distance

6.39

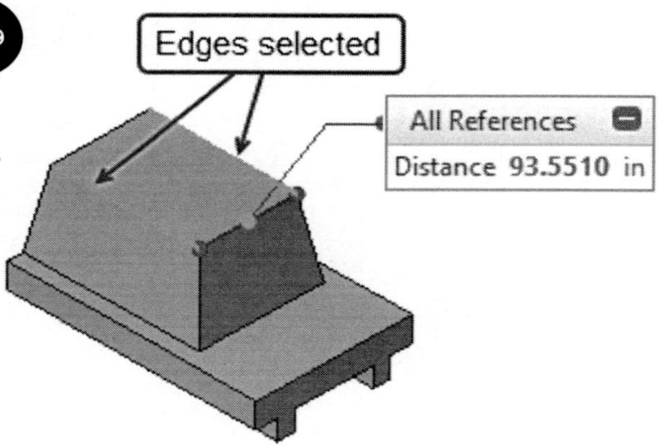

Edges selected
All References
Distance 93.5510 in

Measuring the Angle Between Two Geometries

To measure the angle between two geometries, click on the **Angle** tool in the **Measure** flyout. The **Measure Angle** dialog box appears. Next, select two geometries (faces or edges) by pressing the CTRL key. The angle between the selected geometries appears in the graphics area, see Figure 6.40. In this figure, two edges are selected to measure the angle between them.

6.40

All References
Angle 80.1489 deg
Edges selected

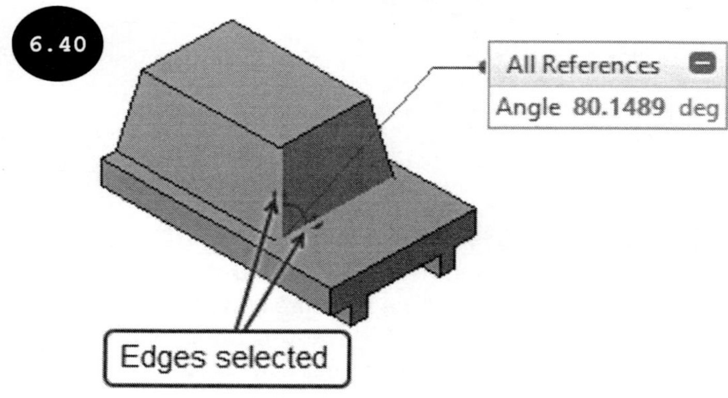

Measuring the Diameter and Radius

To measure the diameter and radius of a circular geometry, click on the **Diameter** tool in the **Measure** flyout and then select a cylindrical face or a round edge in the graphics area. The diameter and radius values of the selected geometry appear in the graphics area, see Figure 6.41.

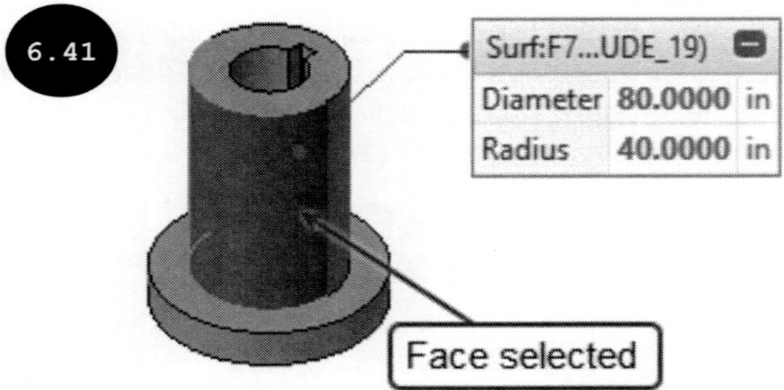

Measuring the Area

To measure the area of a geometry, click on the **Area** tool in the **Measure** flyout and then select a face in the graphics area. The area of the selected face appears in the graphics area, see Figure 6.42.

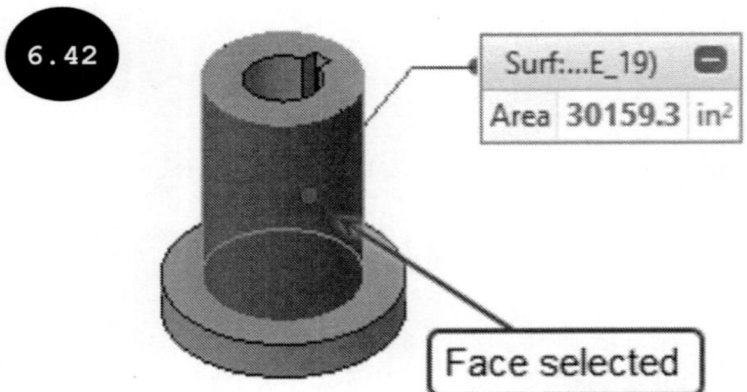

Measuring the Volume

To measure the volume of a model, click on the **Volume** tool in the **Measure** flyout. The volume of the model appears in the graphics area, see Figure 6.43.

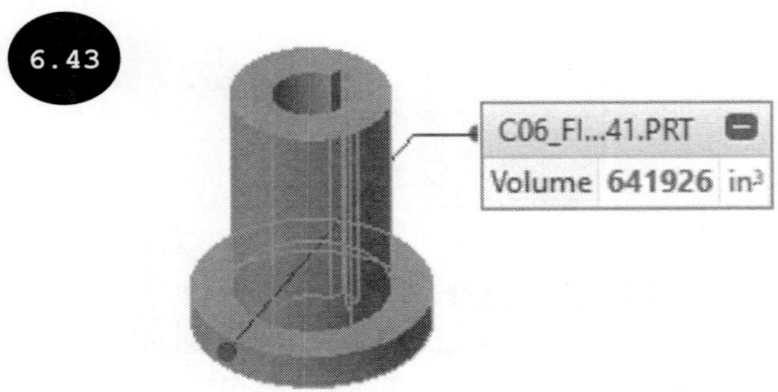

Measuring the Transformation Matrix

In Creo, you can also measure the transformation matrix between two coordinate systems by using the **Transform** tool. To do so, invoke the **Measure** flyout and then click on the **Transform** tool, see Figure 6.44. The **Measure Transform** dialog box appears. Next, select two coordinate systems by pressing the CTRL key. The transformation matrix callout appears in the graphics area, see Figure 6.45. Next, click on the **Matrix** option in the callout that appears in the graphics area. The **Measure Transform** dialog box gets expanded and the transformation matrix between the selected coordinate systems appears, see Figure 6.46. You can also expand the **Measure Transform** dialog box by clicking on the +sign available at its end to display the transformation matrix.

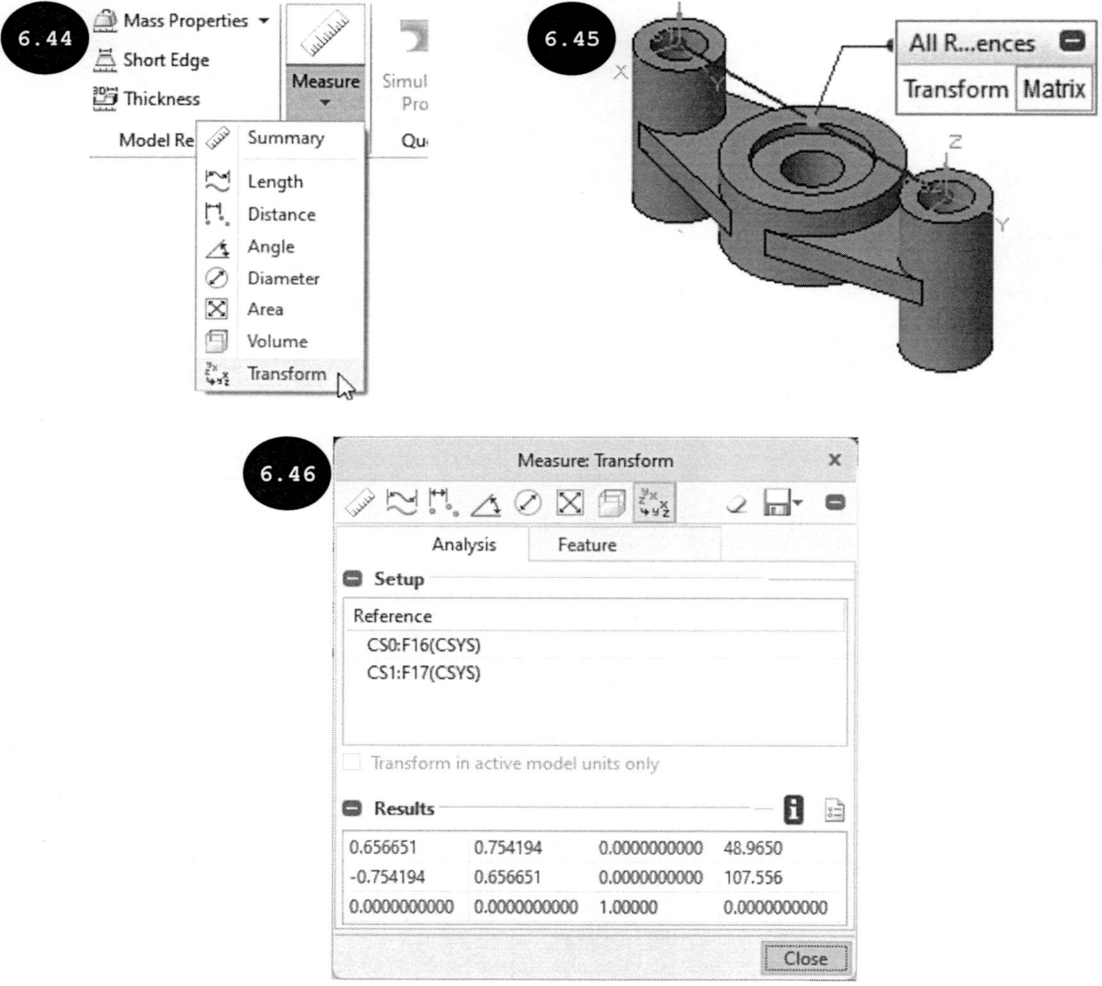

Assigning an Appearance

In Creo, you can change the default appearance of a model by assigning a predefined or customized appearance to the model or individual faces of the model. The methods for assigning a predefined and customized appearance are discussed next.

Assigning a Predefined Appearance

1. Click on the **View** tab in the **Ribbon** and then click on the arrow at the bottom of the **Appearances** tool, see Figure 6.47. The **Appearance** flyout appears.

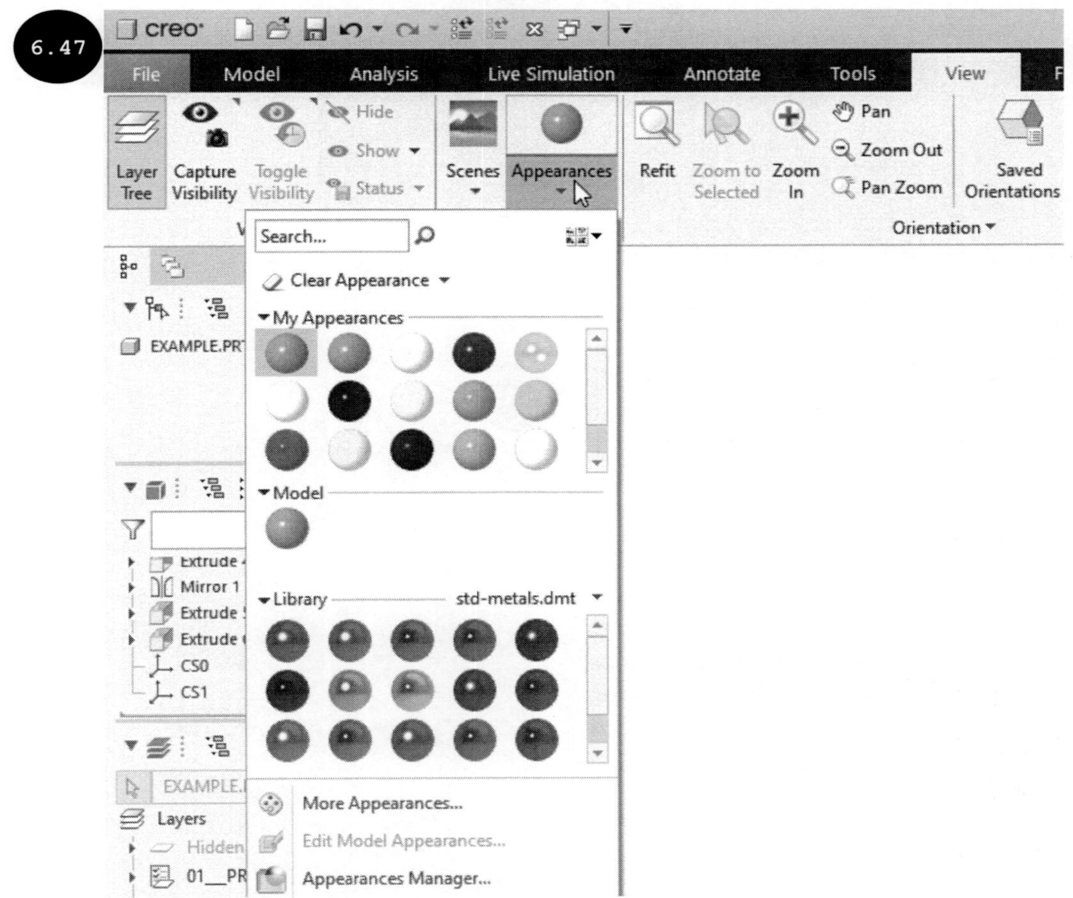

Note: In the **Appearance** flyout, the **My Appearances** area displays a list of predefined appearances that are stored in the startup directory. The **Model** area displays a list of appearances that are currently assigned to the model. The **Library** area displays a list of predefined appearances that are available in the system library.

2. Click on a predefined appearance available in the **My Appearances** area or **Library** area of the **Appearance** flyout. The cursor changes to paintbrush cursor. Also, the **Select** window appears in the graphics area and you are prompted to select one or more geometries.

3. Select one or more faces of the model to assign the appearance. Note that to select multiple faces, you need to press and hold the CTRL key. You can also select the entire model by clicking on its name at the top of the **Model Tree**. After selecting one or more faces, or a model, press the middle mouse button or click on the **OK** button in the **Select** window. The appearance is assigned to the selected faces or model, see Figure 6.48. In this figure, the appearance is assigned to the entire model.

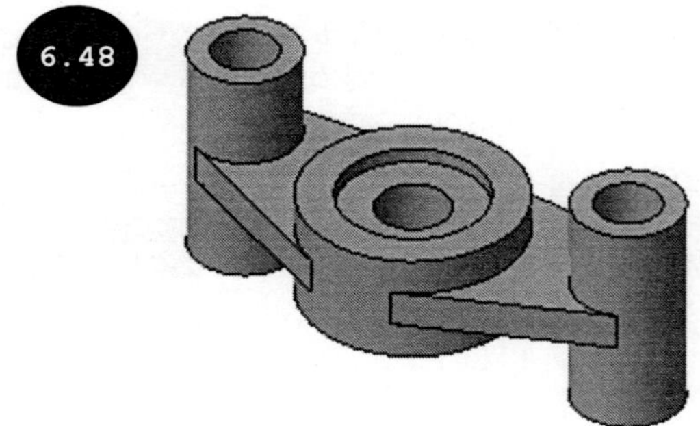

Assigning a Customized Appearance

In addition to assigning a predefined appearance, you can also customize the appearance properties as required before assigning it.

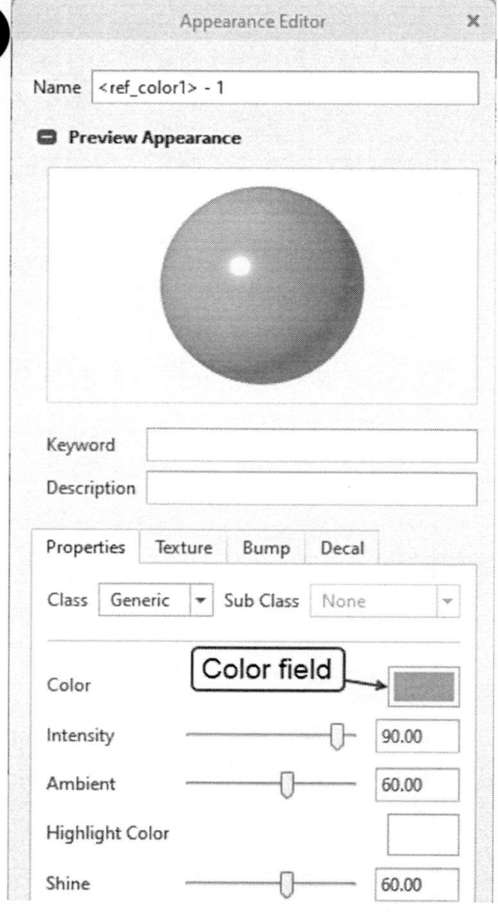

1. Invoke the **Appearance** flyout by clicking on the arrow at the bottom of the **Appearances** tool in the **View** tab of the **Ribbon**.

2. Click on the **More Appearances** option in the **Appearance** flyout. The **Appearance Editor** dialog box appears, see Figure 6.49.

3. Click on the **Color** field in the **Appearance Editor** dialog box. The **Color Editor** dialog box appears. Next, select the required color and then click on the **OK** button in the dialog box. A preview of the selected color appears in the **Preview** area of the **Appearance Editor** dialog box.

4. After selecting the required color, change the properties of the color as per requirement such as intensity, ambient, shine, and reflection by using the respective slider available in the **Properties** tab of the dialog box. You can also assign a texture, bump, and decal by using the respective tabs of the dialog box.

5. Click on the **Close** button in the **Appearance Editor** dialog box. The paintbrush cursor appears and you are prompted to select one or more geometries to assign the selected appearance.

6. Select one or more faces of the model to assign the selected appearance. To select multiple faces, you need to press and hold the CTRL key. You can also select the entire model by clicking on its name at the top of the **Model Tree**. After selecting a face, faces, or model, press the middle mouse button or click on the **OK** button in the **Select** window. The customized appearance is assigned to the selected face, faces, or model.

Editing an Appearance

After assigning a predefined or customized appearance to a model, you can further edit the appearance that is assigned to the model. The method for editing the model appearance is discussed below:

1. Invoke the **Appearance** flyout in the **View** tab of the **Ribbon** and then click on the **Edit Model Appearances** tool, see Figure 6.50. The **Model Appearance Editor** dialog box appears, see Figure 6.51. Alternatively, right-click on the appearance to be edited in the **Model** area of the **Appearance** flyout and then click on the **Edit** tool in the shortcut menu that appears to invoke the **Model Appearance Editor** dialog box.

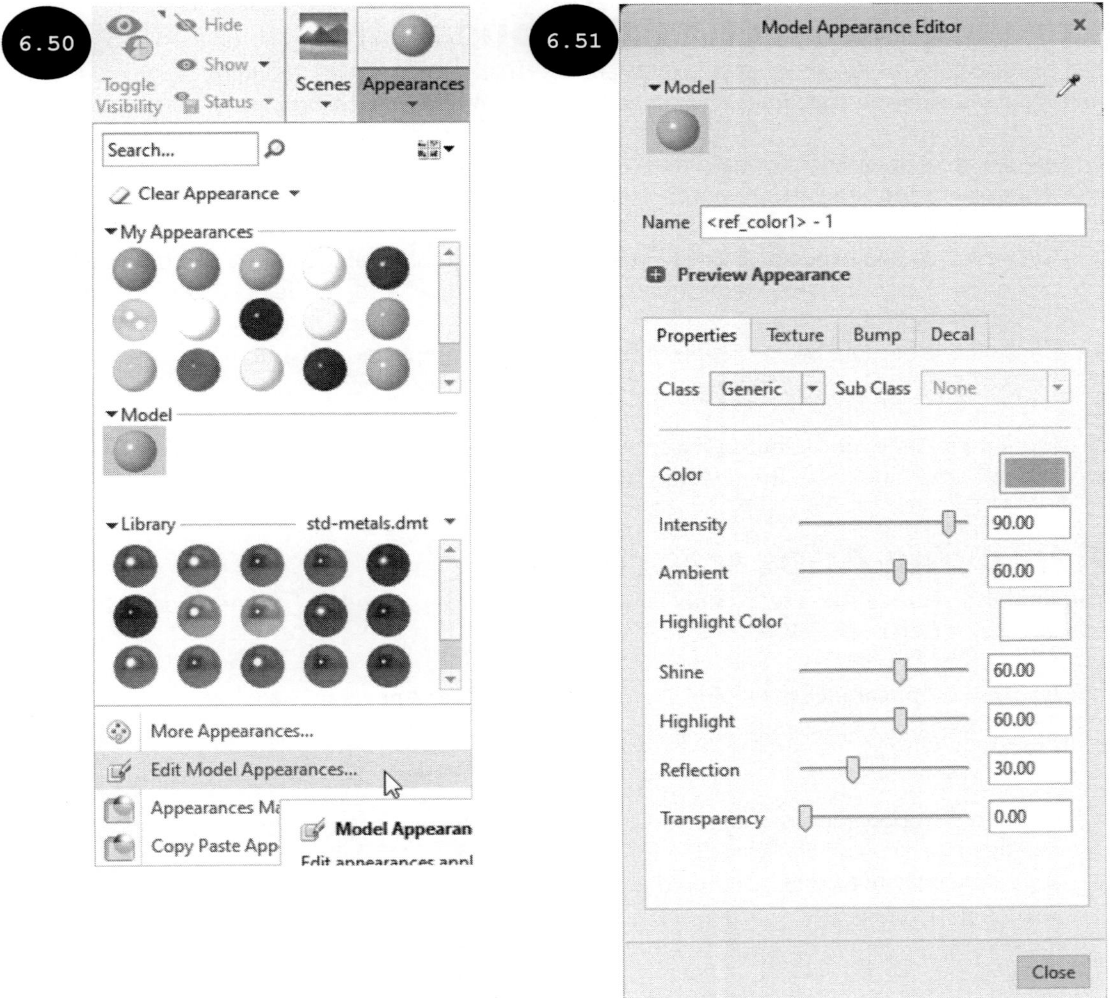

The **Model** area of the dialog box displays all the appearances that are currently assigned to the model.

2. Ensure that the appearance to be edited is selected in the **Model** area of the dialog box.

3. Click on the **Color** field of the **Properties** tab in the dialog box to edit the color of the selected appearance. The **Color Editor** dialog box appears. In this dialog box, select the required color and then click on the **OK** button.

4. After selecting a required color, change the properties of the color such as intensity, ambient, shine, and reflection by using the respective slider available in the **Properties** tab of the dialog box. You can also assign a texture, bump, and decal by using the respective tabs of the dialog box.

5. Click on the **Close** button in the **Model Appearance Editor** dialog box. The appearance of the model gets modified, as specified.

Copying and Pasting an Appearance

You can also copy an already assigned appearance and paste it on another geometry of the model. The method for copying an appearance from one geometry and pasting it on another is discussed below:

1. Invoke the **Appearance** flyout in the **View** tab of the **Ribbon** and then click on the **Copy Paste Appearance** tool. You are prompted to select an appearance of a face to be copied.

2. Click on the appearance of a face to be copied in the graphics area. You are prompted to select one or more faces to apply or paste the copied appearance. Also, the **Select** dialog box appears.

3. Click on one or more faces to apply or paste the copied appearance. Note that to select multiple faces of a model, you need to press and hold the CTRL key.

4. Press the middle mouse button or click on the **OK** button in the **Select** dialog box. The copied appearance is applied to the selected faces of the model.

Removing Appearances

You can also remove the already applied appearances from a model. The method for removing appearances is discussed below:

1. Invoke the **Appearance** flyout and then click on the **Clear Appearance** tool, see Figure 6.52. The **Select** dialog box appears and you are prompted to select the appearances of the faces to be removed.

2. Click on the appearances of the faces to be removed by pressing the CTRL key. Next, press the middle mouse button or click on the **OK** button in the **Select** dialog box. Note that to remove the appearances from a model, click on the name of the model at the top of the **Model Tree** and then press the middle mouse button. The appearance of the selected faces gets removed from the model.

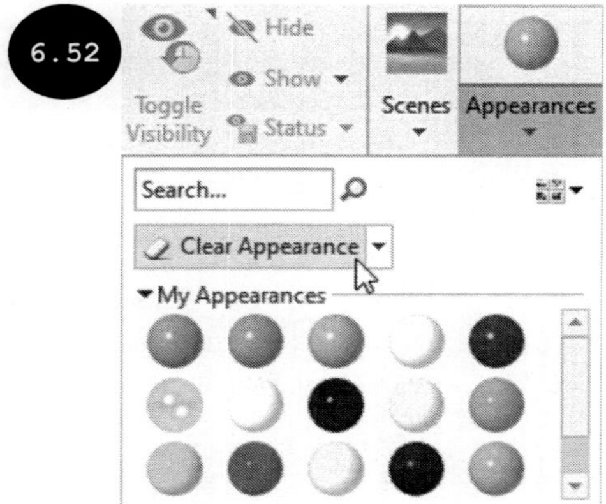

In addition to removing the individual appearances of the model, you can remove all the appearances that are assigned to the model by using the **Clear All Appearances** tool. To do so, invoke the **Appearance** flyout and then click on the arrow next to the **Clear Appearance** tool, see Figure 6.53. A drop-down list appears. In this drop-down list, click on the **Clear All Appearances** tool, see Figure 6.53. The **Confirm** dialog box appears, see Figure 6.54. In this dialog box, click on the **Yes** button to remove all the appearances of the model.

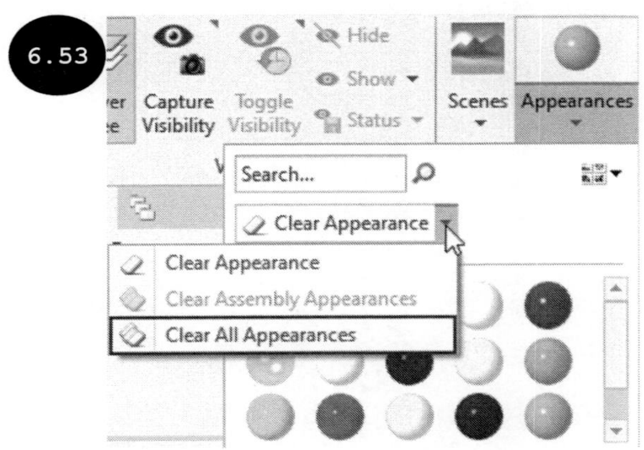

Applying a Material

In Creo, you can apply standard material properties such as density, elastic modulus, tensile strength to a model. Note that assigning standard material properties to a model is important in order to calculate its mass properties as well as to perform static and dynamic analysis. Creo contains standard materials in its material library. You can directly apply the required standard material to a model from the material library. You can also edit the material properties of the applied material as well as create a new material. The methods for applying a standard material, editing material properties, and creating a new material are discussed next.

Applying a Standard Material

1. Click on **File** > **Prepare** > **Model Properties** in the **File** menu, see Figure 6.55. The **Model Properties** dialog box appears, see Figure 6.56.

6.55

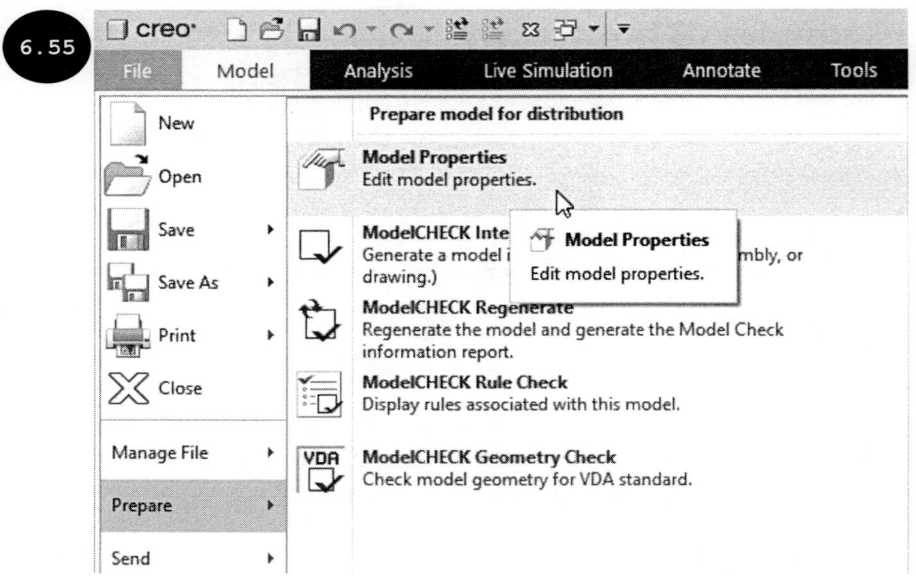

6.56

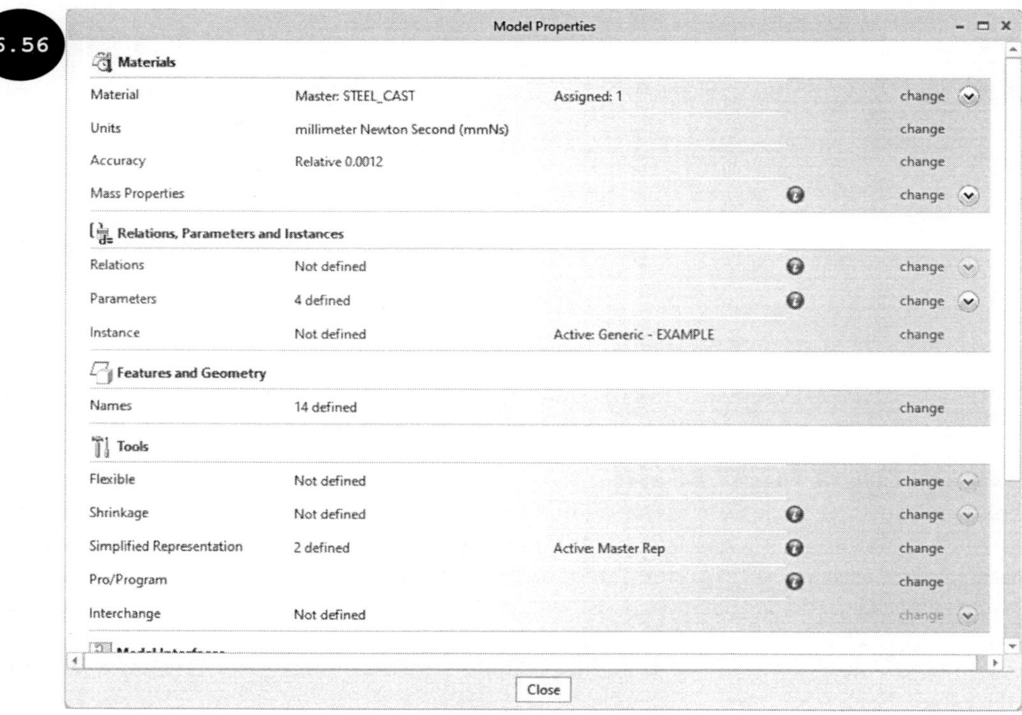

2. Click on the **change** option that appears on the right of the **Material** row in the dialog box, see Figure 6.57. The **Materials in Model** dialog box appears, see Figure 6.58.

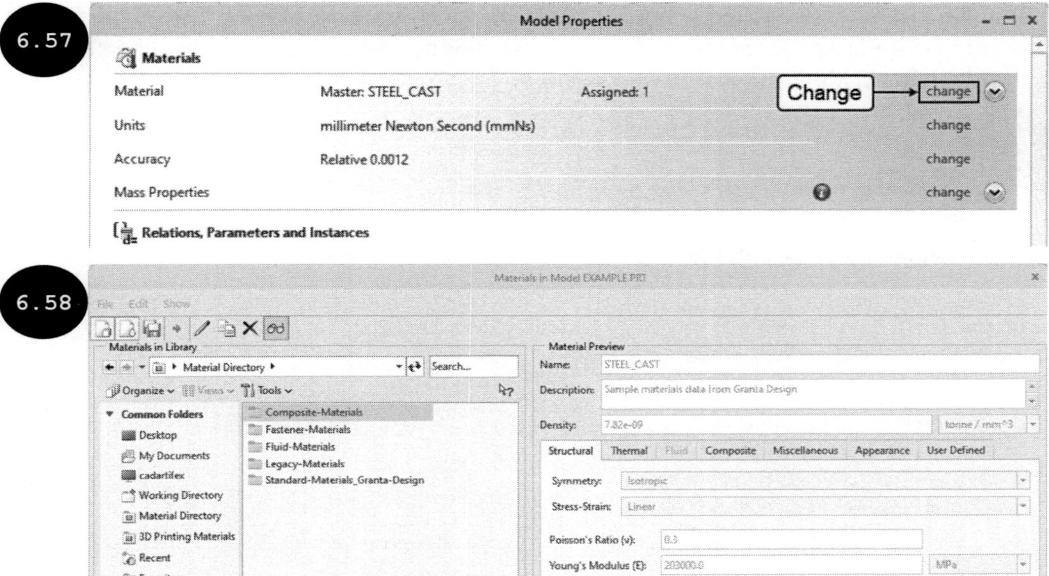

3. Expand the **Standard-Materials_Granta-Design** material folder of the **Material Directory** in the dialog box by double-clicking on it. The different material categories such as **Ferrous_metals, Non-ferrous_metals, Plastics,** and **Woods** appear in the dialog box.

4. Expand the required material category in the dialog box. The materials available in the expanded material category appear, see Figure 6.59. This figure shows the expanded **Ferrous_metals** material category.

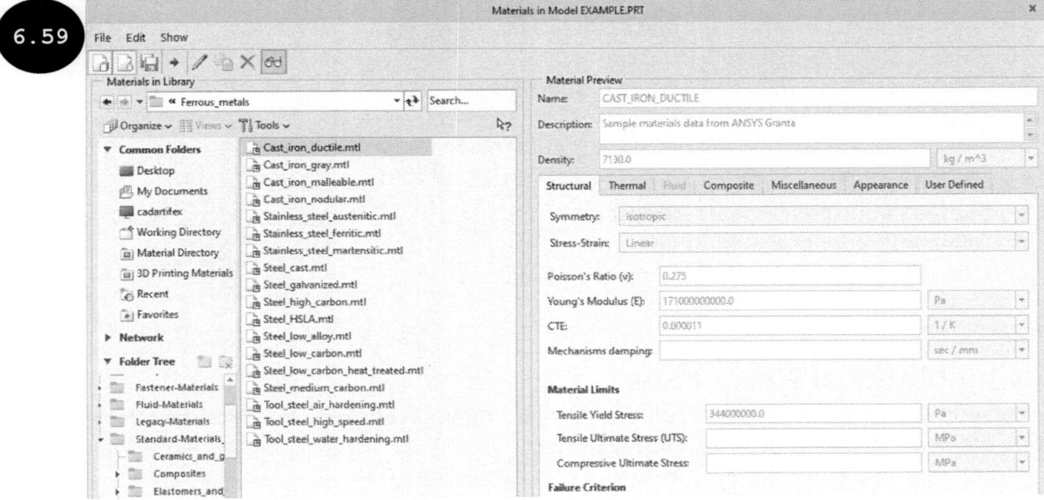

5. Double-click on the required material in the expanded material category. The properties of the selected material appear on the right half of the dialog box. Also, the selected material is added in the **Materials in Model** area of the dialog box. In Figure 6.60, the **Steel_cast** material is selected.

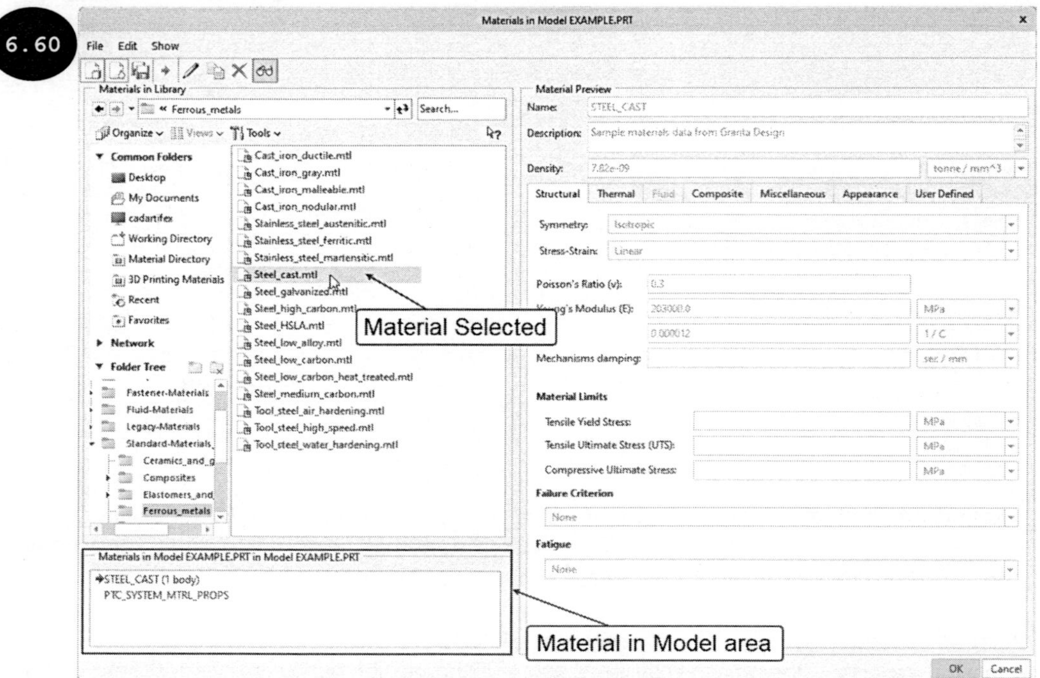

6. Click on the **OK** button in the dialog box. The selected material is assigned to the model and appears next to **Material** in the **Model Properties** dialog box.

7. Close the **Model Properties** dialog box by clicking on the **Close** button. The material properties of the selected material are assigned to the model and the **Materials** node is added to the **Model Tree**, see Figure 6.61.

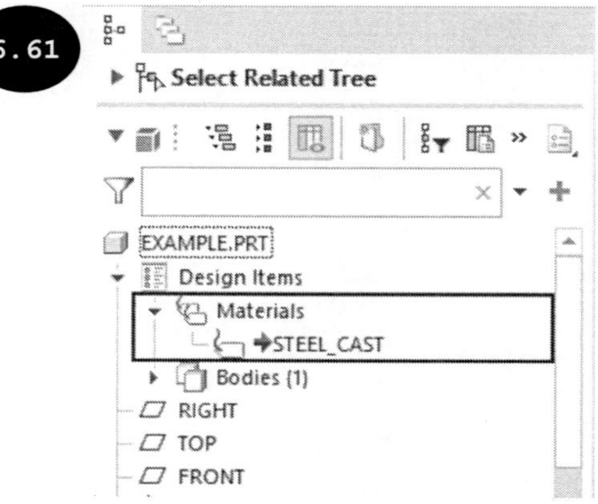

Editing Material Properties

You can edit the material properties of the standard material applied to the model. The method for editing the material properties is discussed below:

1. Expand the **Materials** node in the **Model Tree** and then right-click on the standard material to be edited. A shortcut menu appears, see Figure 6.62.

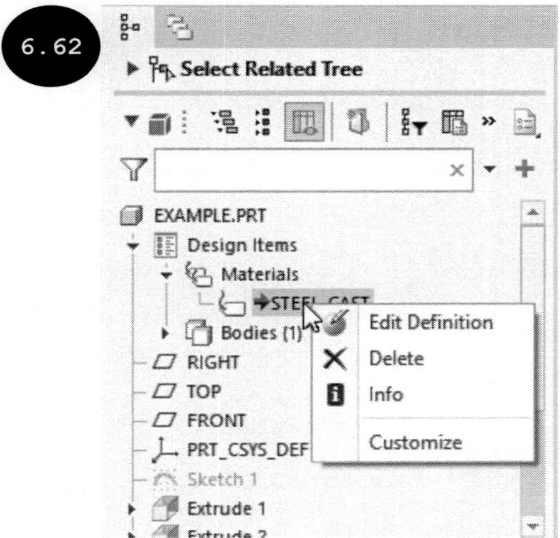

2. Click on the **Edit Definition** tool in the shortcut menu. The **Material Definition** dialog box appears, see Figure 6.63.

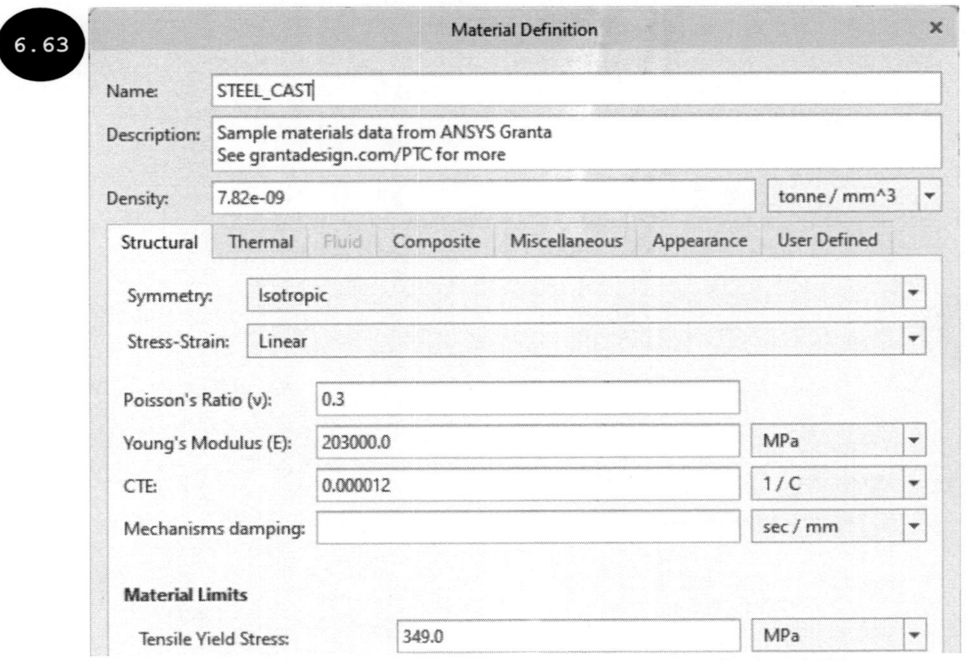

3. Specify new material properties such as Poisson's ratio, Density, and Young Modulus as required in the respective fields of the dialog box.

4. Click on the **OK** button in the dialog box. The material properties are changed, as specified.

Creating a New Material

You can also create a new material as per your requirement and save it in the **Material Directory**. The method for creating a new material is discussed below:

1. Click on **File > Prepare > Model Properties** in the **File** menu, see Figure 6.64. The **Model Properties** dialog box appears.

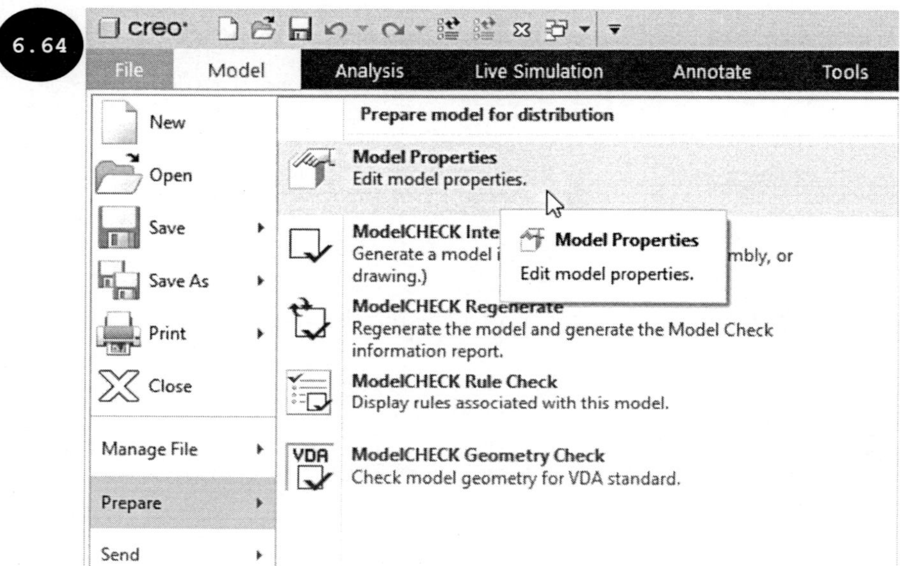

2. Click on the **change** option that appears on the right of the **Material** row in the dialog box, see Figure 6.65. The **Materials in Model** dialog box appears, see Figure 6.66.

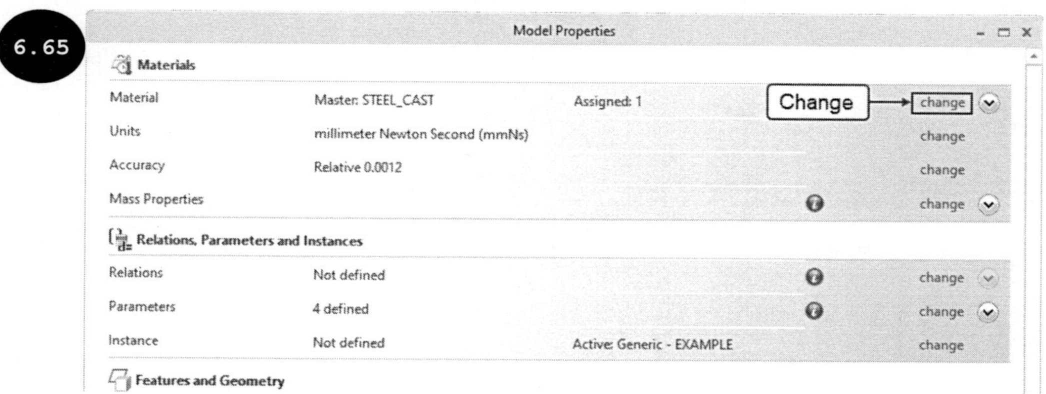

3. Click on the **Create new solid material** tool in the **Materials in Model** dialog box, see Figure 6.66. The **Material Definition** dialog box appears.

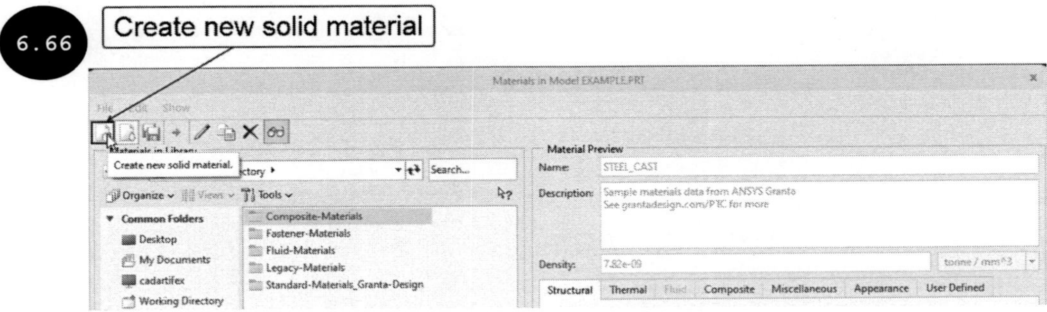

4. Specify material properties such as Poisson's ratio, Density, Young's Modulus, and Tensile Ultimate Stress, as required in the respective fields of the dialog box.

5. Click on the **Save to Library** button in the dialog box to save the material. The **Save a Copy** dialog box appears. In this dialog box, browse to the required location and then click on the **OK** button. The material is saved in the specified location as *.mtl* file. You can now apply this material to the model, as discussed earlier.

Calculating Mass Properties

After assigning material properties to a model, you can calculate its mass properties such as mass and volume by using the **Mass Properties** tool of the **Model Report** group in the **Analysis** tab, see Figure 6.67. The method for calculating the mass properties of a model is discussed below:

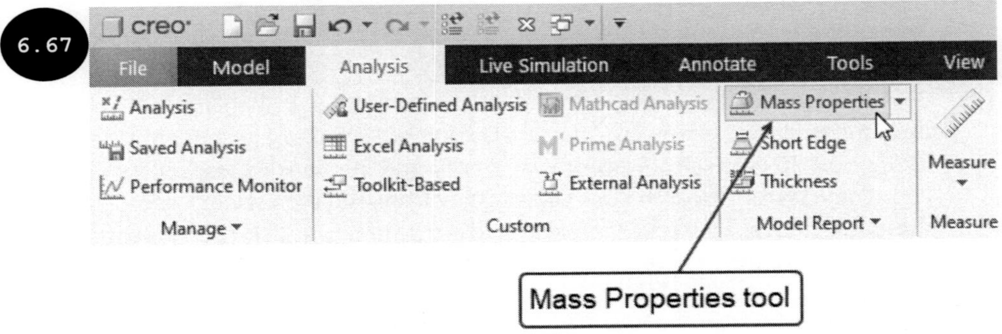

1. Click on the **Mass Properties** tool of the **Model Report** group in the **Analysis** tab, see Figure 6.67. The **Mass Properties** dialog box appears.

2. Click on the **Preview** button in the dialog box. Mass properties such as volume, surface area, mass, and center of gravity of the model appear in the **Mass Properties** dialog box, see Figure 6.68.

3. Review the results of the mass properties and then exit the dialog box.

6.68

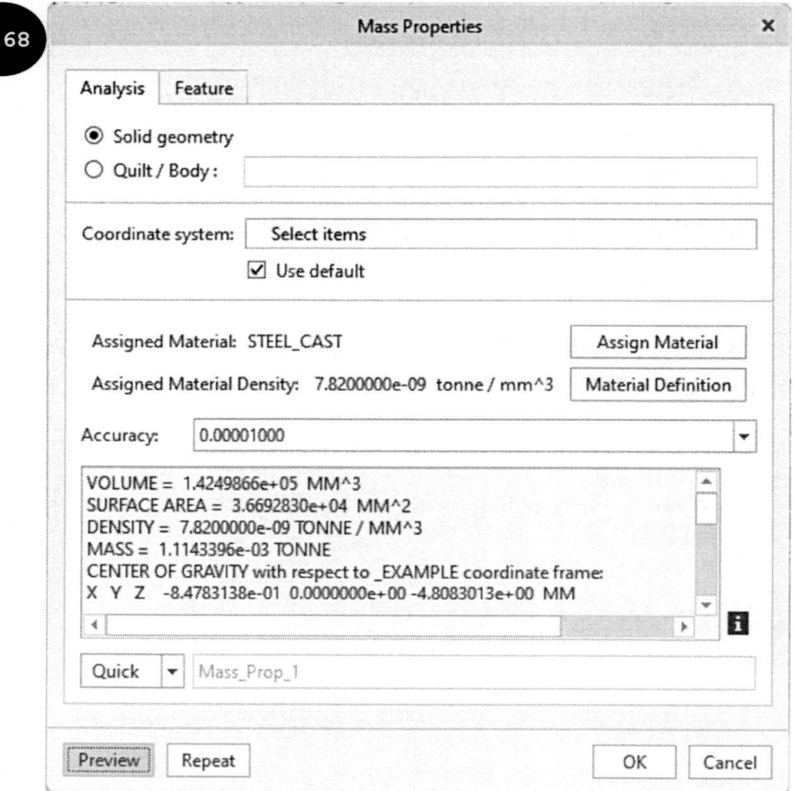

Note: By default, the center of gravity and inertia of the model is calculated with respect to the default coordinate system, since the **Use Default** check box is selected in the **Mass Properties** dialog box. To calculate the center of gravity and inertia with respect to a user-defined coordinate system, clear the **Use Default** check box and then select a coordinate system in the graphics area. The center of gravity and inertia of the model are changed and calculated with respect to the selected coordinate system.

Tip: You can also calculate the mass properties of the model by using the **Model Properties** dialog box. To do so, click on the **File > Prepare > Model Properties** in the **File** menu. Next, click on the **change** option that appears on the right of the **Mass Properties** row in the **Model Properties** dialog box that appears. The **Mass Properties** dialog box appears. In this dialog box, click on the **Calculate** button to calculate the mass properties of the model. You can also generate a report by clicking on the **Generate Report** button of the dialog box.

Tutorial 1

Create the model shown in Figure 6.69. You need to create the model by creating all its features one by one. After creating the model, assign the Steel High Carbon material and calculate the mass properties of the model. All dimensions are in mm.

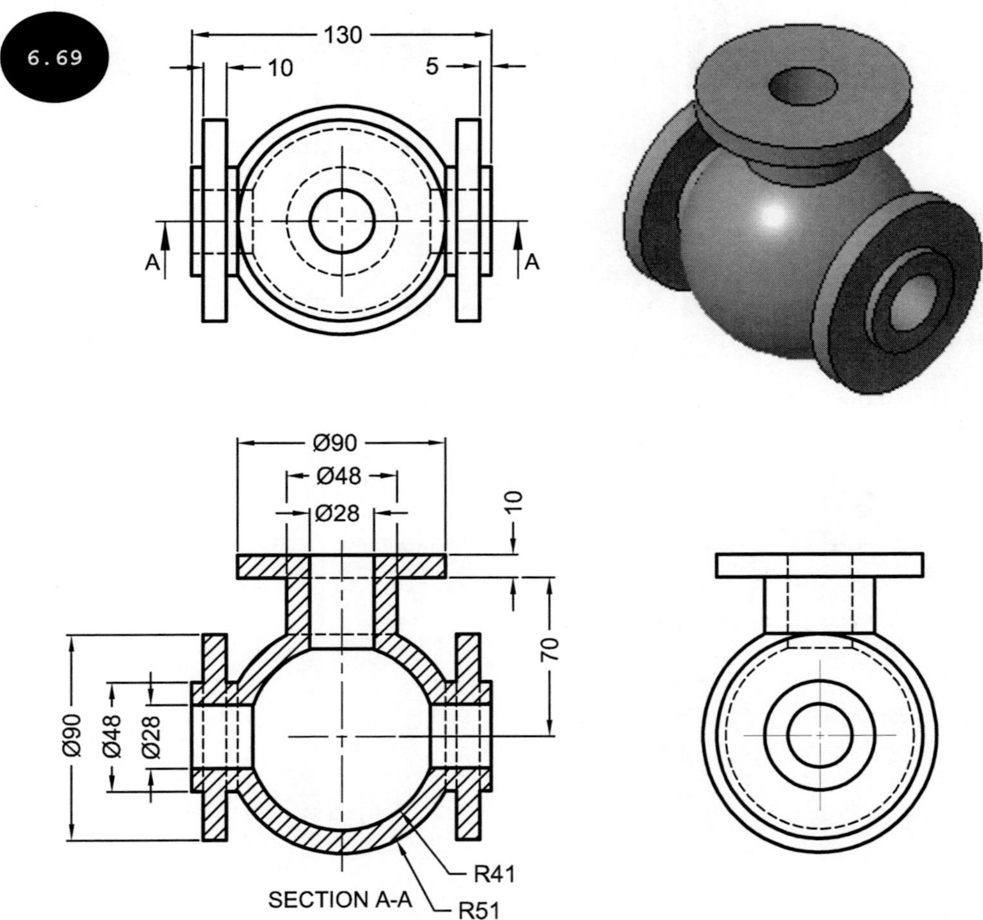

Section 1: Starting Creo Parametric

1. Start Creo Parametric by double-clicking on the Creo Parametric icon on your desktop.

Section 2: Setting the Working Directory

Now, you need to set the working directory to save the files of the current session of Creo Parametric. It is recommended to create a folder with the name "*Chapter 6*" inside the "*Creo Parametric*" folder in the local drive of your system. If the "*Creo Parametric*" folder has not already been created earlier then you need to create this folder.

1. Click on the **Select Working Directory** tool in the **Data** group of the **Home** tab, see Figure 6.70. The **Select Working Directory** window appears. In this window, browse to *Creo Parametric > Chapter 6*. You need to create these folders, if not created earlier. Next, click on the **OK** button in the dialog box. The working directory is set to <<*Creo Parametric**Chapter 6*\\.

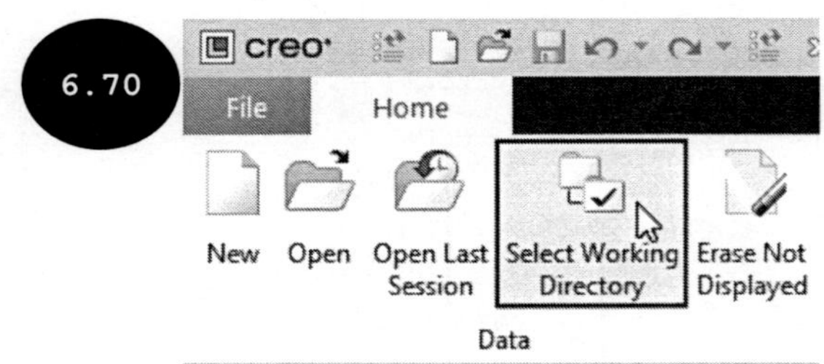

Section 3: Invoking the Part Mode

1. Click on the **New** tool in the **Data** group of the **Home** tab. The **New** dialog box appears, see Figure 6.71. Alternatively, press CTRL + N to invoke the **New** dialog box.

2. Ensure that the **Part** radio button is selected in the **Type** area and the **Solid** radio button is selected in the **Sub-type** area of the dialog box, see Figure 6.71.

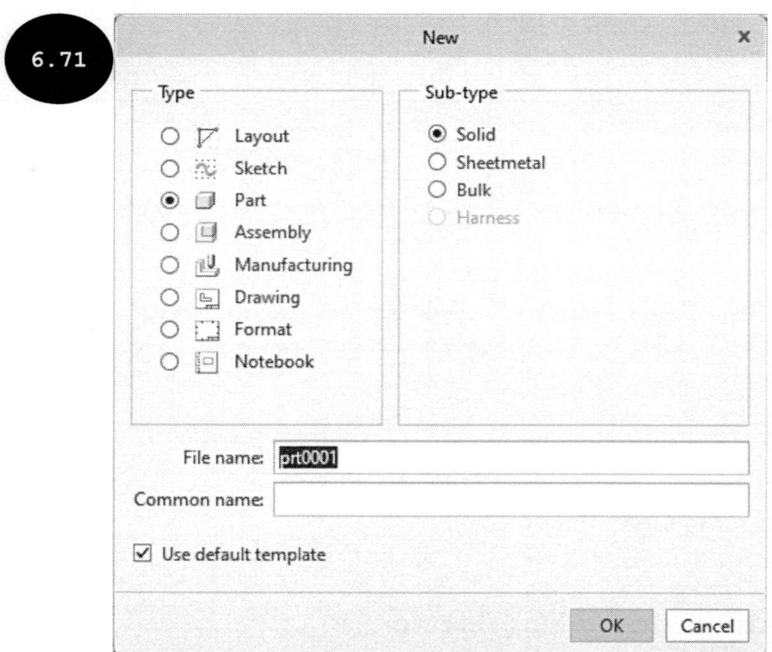

3. Enter **C06-Tutorial01** in the **File name** field of the dialog box as the name of the model.

4. Clear the **Use default template** check box and then click on the **OK** button in the dialog box. The **New File Options** dialog box appears, see Figure 6.72.

6.72

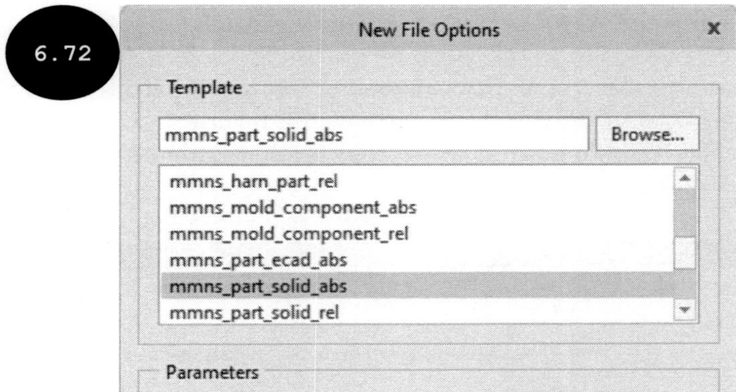

5. Select the **mmns_part_solid_abs** template in the **New File Options** dialog box and then click on the **OK** button. The Part mode is invoked with the **mmns_part_solid_abs** template. In this template, the length is measured in millimeters, mass is measured in Newton, and time is measured in seconds.

Section 4: Creating the Base Feature - Revolve Feature

1. Invoke the Sketching environment by selecting the Front plane as the sketching plane and then create the sketch of the base feature, see Figure 6.73.

6.73

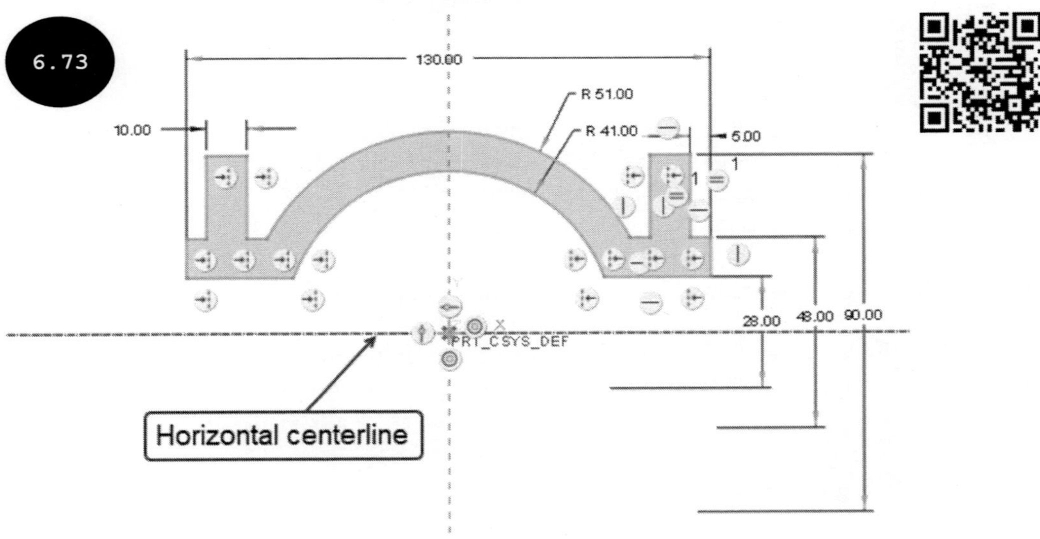

Note: In Figure 6.73, the horizontal centerline is created by using the **Centerline** tool for applying the linear diameter dimensions of the sketch. Also, equal constraints are applied between the entities that are of equal length. You can also create line entities on one side of the vertical centerline and then mirror them to create entities on the other side of the vertical centerline.

2. Click on the **OK** tool in the **Close** group of the **Ribbon** to exit the Sketching environment. The Part mode is invoked and the sketch is selected in the graphics area.

You can now revolve the sketch to create the revolve feature.

3. Click on the **Revolve** tool in the **Shapes** group of the **Model** tab. The **Revolve** tab appears in the **Ribbon**, see Figure 6.74. Also, a preview of the revolve feature appears in the graphics area such that the horizontal centerline of the sketch is automatically selected as the axis of revolution, see Figure 6.75.

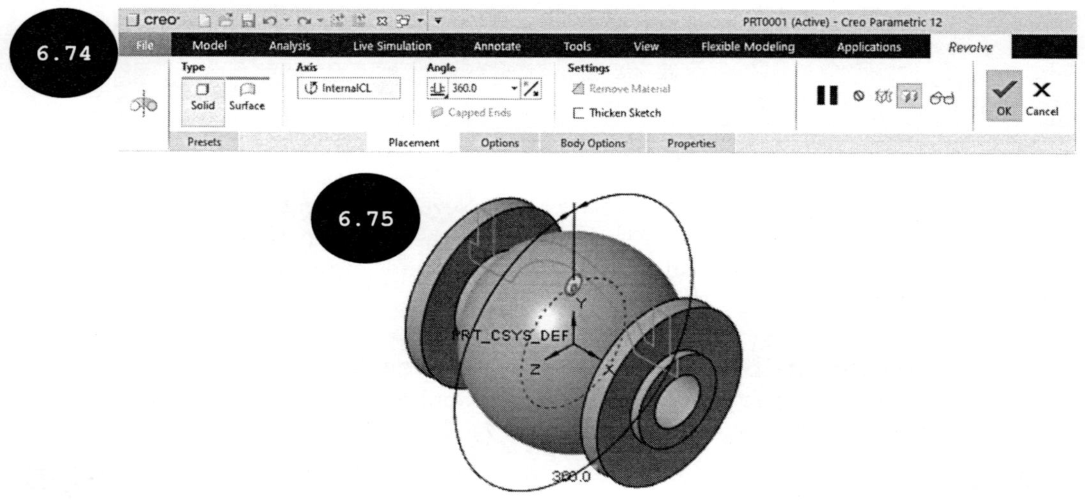

6.74

6.75

Note: If a sketch is not selected before invoking the **Revolve** tool then you will be prompted to select the sketch to be revolved. Select the sketch in the graphics window. A preview of the revolve feature appears in the graphics window.

4. Change the current orientation of the model to the standard orientation.

5. Ensure that the **Variable** option is selected in the **Side 1** drop-down list and the angle value is set to 360-degrees in the **Angle Value** field of the **Revolve** tab, see Figure 6.76.

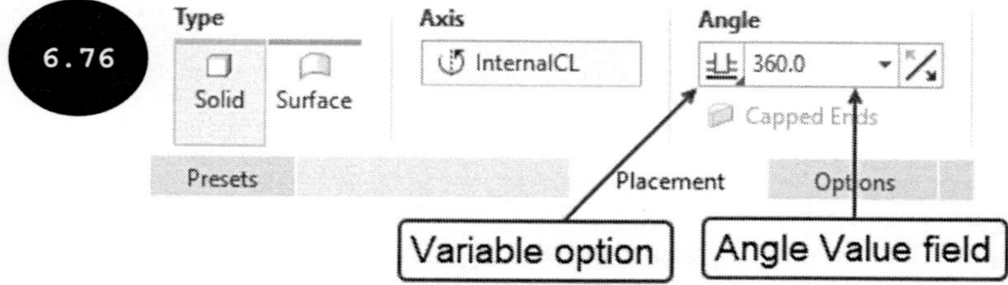

6.76

6. Click on the green tick-mark button in the **Revolve** tab. The revolve feature is created, see Figure 6.77.

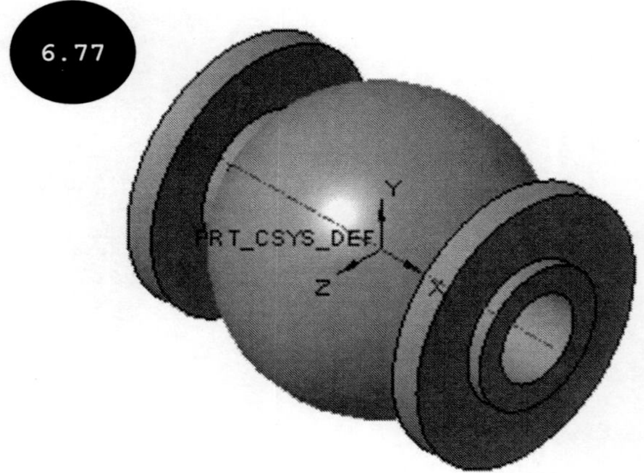

Section 5: Creating the Second Feature - Extrude Feature

To create the second feature of the model, you first need to create a datum plane at an offset distance of 70 mm from the Top plane.

1. Click on the **Plane** tool in the **Datum** group of the **Model** tab. The **Datum Plane** dialog box appears.

2. Select the Top plane as a reference in the **Model Tree** or in the graphics area. The preview of an offset datum plane appears, see Figure 6.78. Also, the **Offset** constraint is selected in the **Constraint** drop-down list in the **References** area of the **Datum Plane** dialog box, see Figure 6.79.

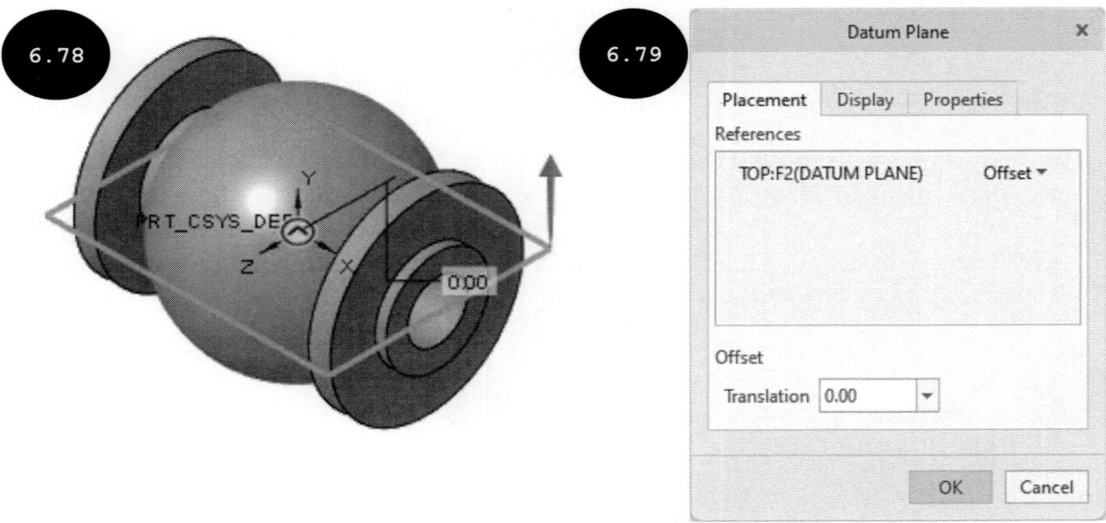

3. Enter **70** in the **Translation** field of the **Offset** area in the dialog box and then press ENTER. A preview of the offset datum plane appears as shown in Figure 6.80.

4. Click on the **OK** button in the dialog box. The offset datum plane is created, see Figure 6.81.

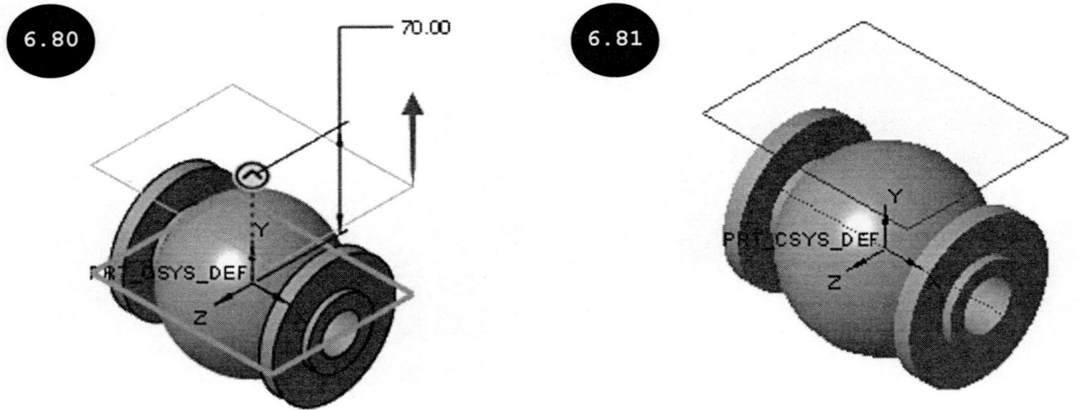

Note: In Figure 6.81, all other datum planes are turned off for clarity. To do so, click on the datum plane to be turned off and then click on the **Hide** tool in the Mini toolbar that appears in the graphics area.

You can now create the second feature of the model by using the newly created plane.

5. Invoke the Sketching environment by selecting the newly created datum plane as the sketching plane.

6. Create a sketch of the second feature (a circle of diameter 48 mm), see Figure 6.82.

7. Click on the **OK** tool in the **Close** group of the **Ribbon** to exit the Sketching environment. The Part mode is invoked and the sketch is selected in the graphics area. Next, change the current orientation of the model to the standard orientation.

   You can now extrude the sketch.

8. Click on the **Extrude** tool in the **Shapes** group of the **Model** tab. A preview of the extrude feature appears, see Figure 6.83. Also, the **Extrude** tab appears in the **Ribbon**. If the preview of the extrude feature does not appear, then select the sketch in the graphics area.

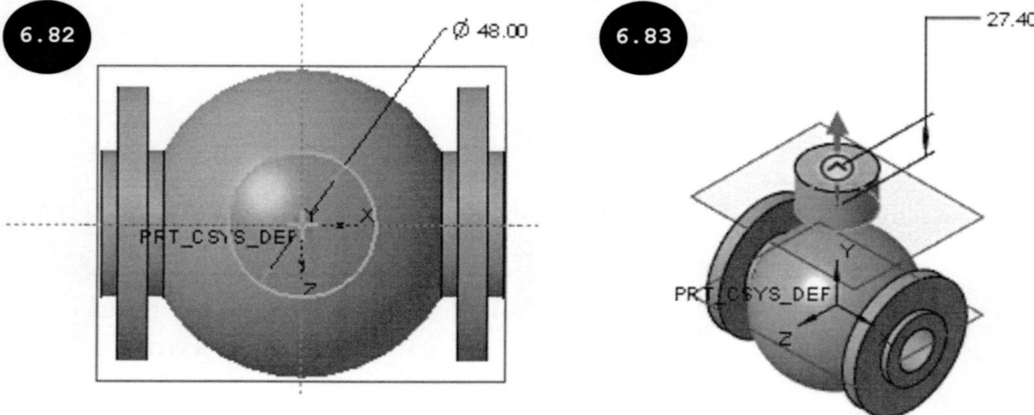

9. Click on the **Flip Direction** button in the **Extrude** tab, see Figure 6.84. The direction of extrusion changes downward.

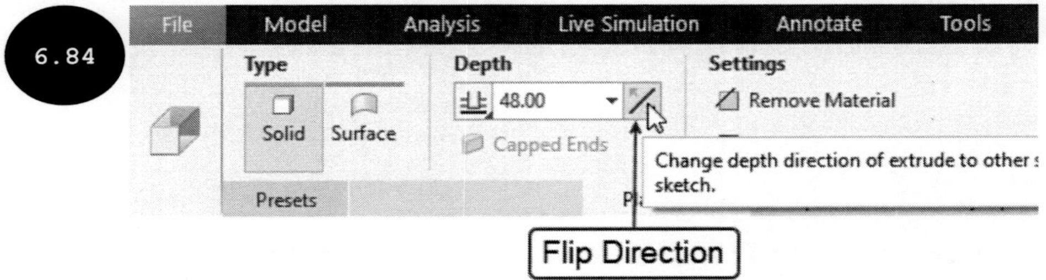

10. Select the **To Next** option in the **Side 1** drop-down list in the **Extrude** tab, see Figure 6.85. The preview of the feature gets modified in the graphics area such that it has been terminated at its next intersection.

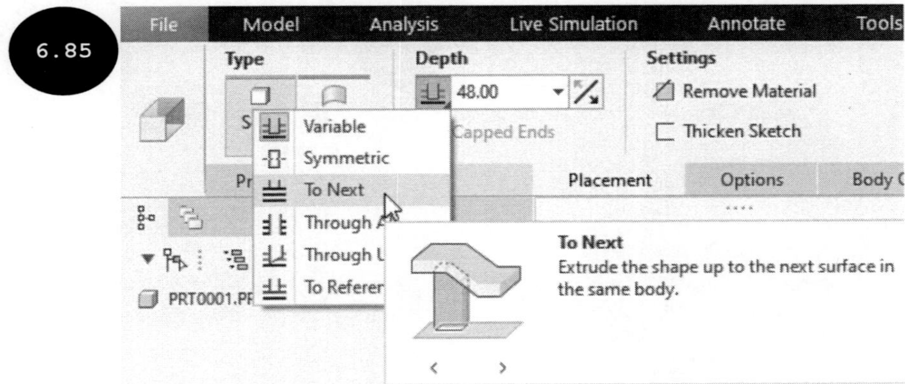

11. Click on the green tick-mark button in the **Extrude** tab. The extrude feature is created, see Figure 6.86.

Note: In Figure 6.86, the display of datum planes, datum axes, datum points, and coordinate systems is turned off. To do so, invoke the **Datum Display Filters** flyout in the **In-graphics** toolbar and then clear all the check boxes, see Figure 6.87.

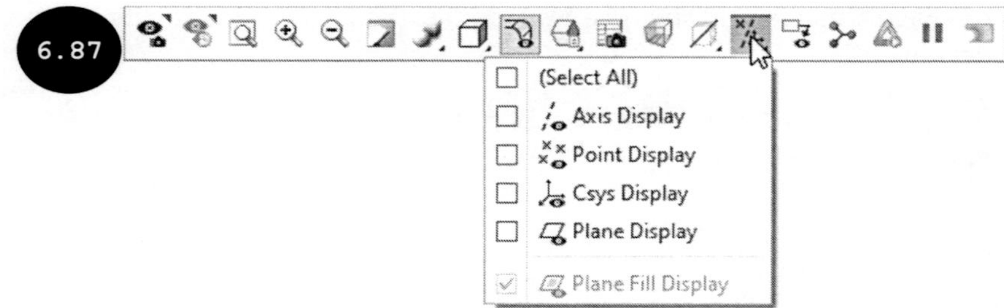

Section 6: Creating the Third Feature - Extrude Feature

1. Invoke the Sketching environment by selecting the top planar face of the second feature as the sketching plane, see Figure 6.88.

2. Create a sketch of the third feature (a circle of diameter 90 mm), see Figure 6.89.

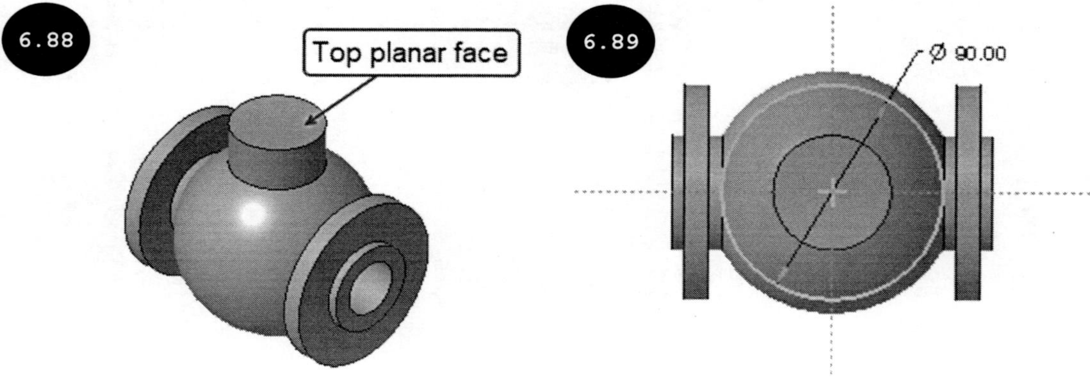

3. Click on the **OK** tool in the **Close** group of the **Ribbon** to exit the Sketching environment. The Part mode is invoked and the sketch is selected in the graphics area. Next, change the current orientation of the model to the standard orientation.

   You can now extrude the sketch.

4. Click on the **Extrude** tool in the **Shapes** group of the **Model** tab. A preview of the extrude feature appears. Also, the **Extrude** tab appears in the **Ribbon**. If the preview of the extrude feature does not appear in the graphics area, then select the sketch in the graphics area.

5. Enter **10** as the depth of extrusion in the **Value** field of the **Extrude** tab and then press ENTER. The preview of the extrude feature gets modified, see Figure 6.90.

6. Click on the green tick-mark button in the **Extrude** tab. The extrude feature is created, see Figure 6.91.

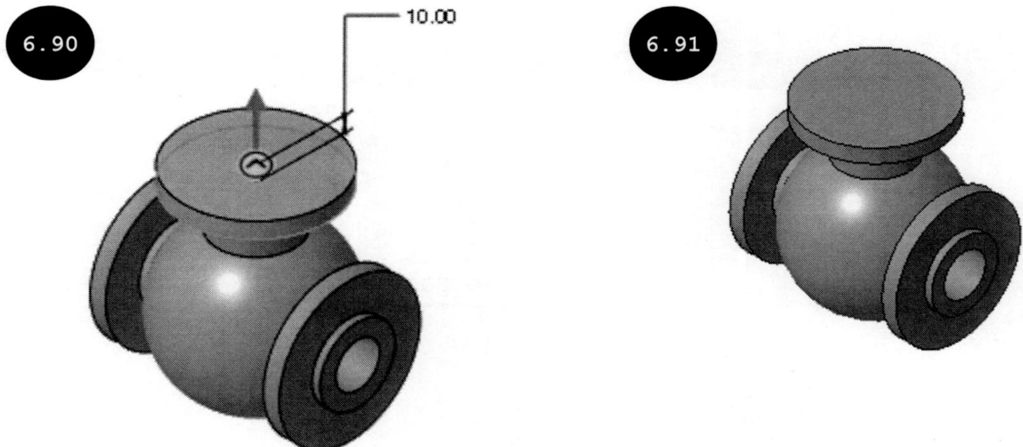

Section 7: Creating the Fourth Feature - Extrude Cut Feature

1. Invoke the Sketching environment by selecting the top planar face of the third feature as the sketching plane.

2. Create a sketch of the fourth feature (a circle of diameter 28 mm), see Figure 6.92.

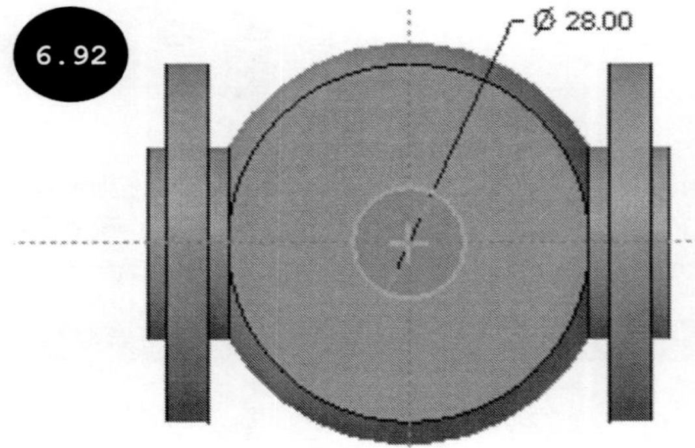

3. Click on the **OK** tool in the **Close** group of the **Ribbon** to exit the Sketching environment. The Part mode is invoked and the sketch is selected in the graphics area. Next, change the current orientation of the model to the standard orientation.

   You can now extrude the sketch.

4. Click on the **Extrude** tool in the **Shapes** group of the **Model** tab. A preview of the extrude feature appears. Also, the **Extrude** tab appears in the **Ribbon**.

5. Click on the **Flip Direction** button in the **Extrude** tab, see Figure 6.93. The direction of extrusion changes downward and the **Remove Material** button gets activated, automatically, see Figure 6.93. Also, a preview of the cut feature appears in the graphics area.

6. Ensure that the **Remove Material** button is activated to create the cut feature by removing the material, see Figure 6.94.

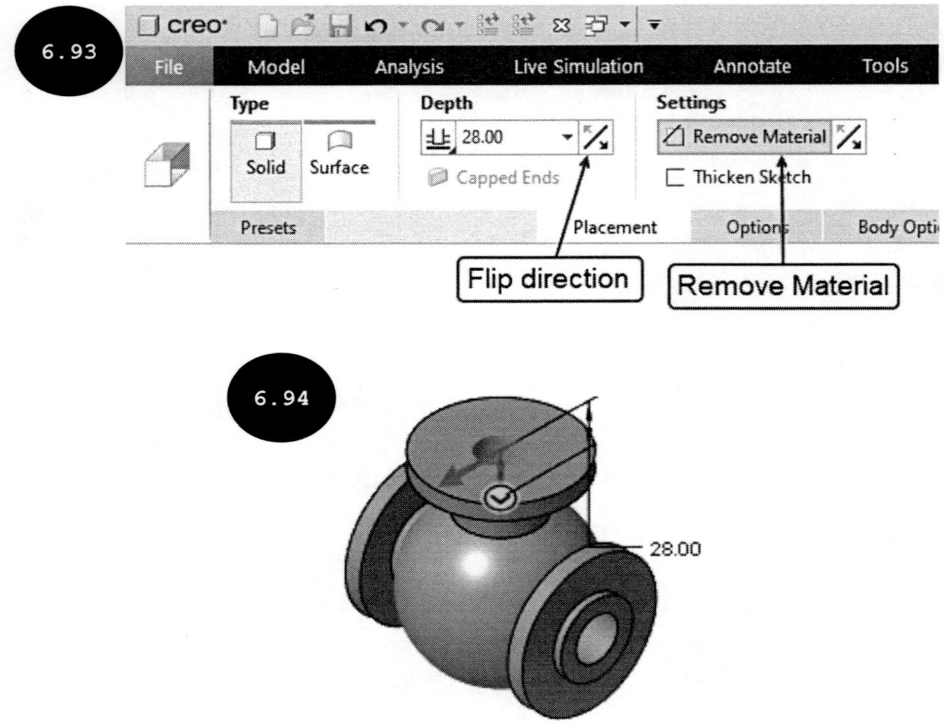

7. Invoke the **Options** panel of the **Extrude** tab and then select the **To Next** option in the **Side 1** drop-down list, see Figure 6.95. The preview of the feature gets modified in the graphics area such that it has been terminated at its next intersection (inner circular face of the base feature).

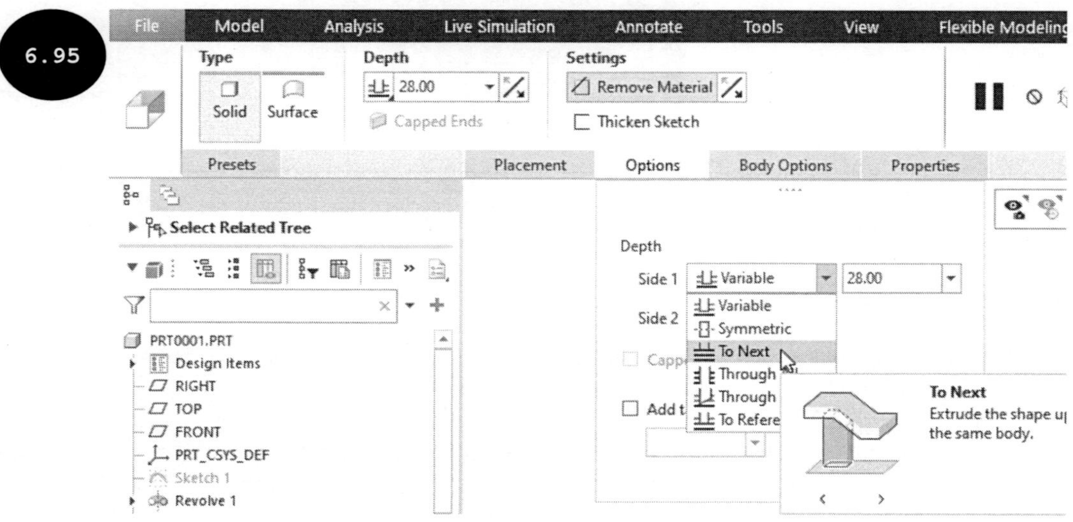

8. Click on the green tick-mark button in the **Extrude** tab. The extrude cut feature is created, see Figures 6.96 and 6.97.

Note: In Figure 6.96, the display style of the model has been changed to the 'Hidden Line' display style. Also, the orientation of the model has been changed to Front view for better understanding of the cut feature.

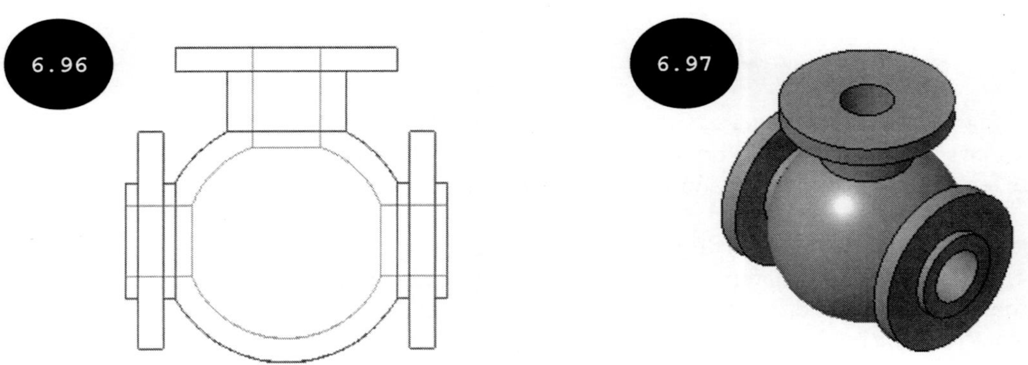

Section 8: Assigning the Material

1. Click on **File > Prepare > Model Properties** in the **File** menu, see Figure 6.98. The **Model Properties** dialog box appears, see Figure 6.99.

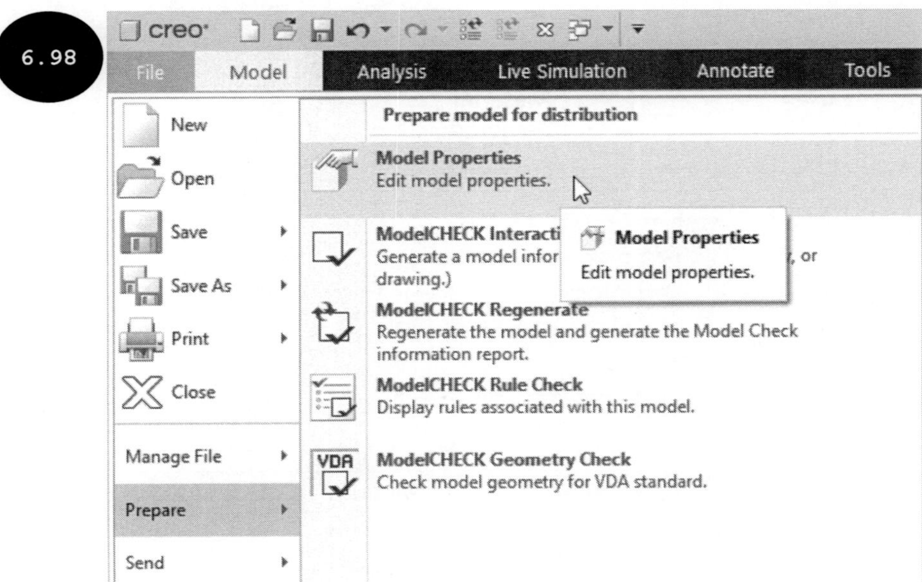

2. Click on the **change** option that appears on the right of the **Material** row in the dialog box, see Figure 6.99. The **Materials in Model** dialog box appears.

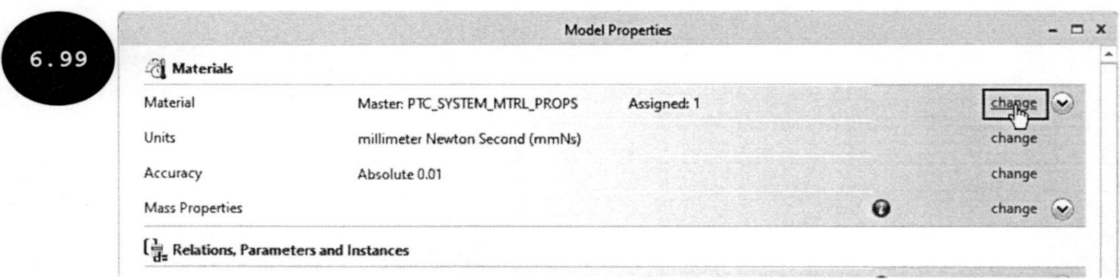

3. Expand the **Standard-Materials_Granta-Design** material folder of the **Material Directory** in the dialog box by double-clicking on it. The different material categories such as **Ferrous_metals**, **Non-ferrous_metals**, **Plastics**, and **Woods** appear in the dialog box.

4. Expand the **Ferrous_metals** material category in the dialog box and then double-click on the **Steel_high_carbon.mtl** material, see Figure 6.100. The properties of the selected material appear on the right half of the dialog box. Also, the selected material is added in the **Materials in Model** area of the dialog box, see Figure 6.100.

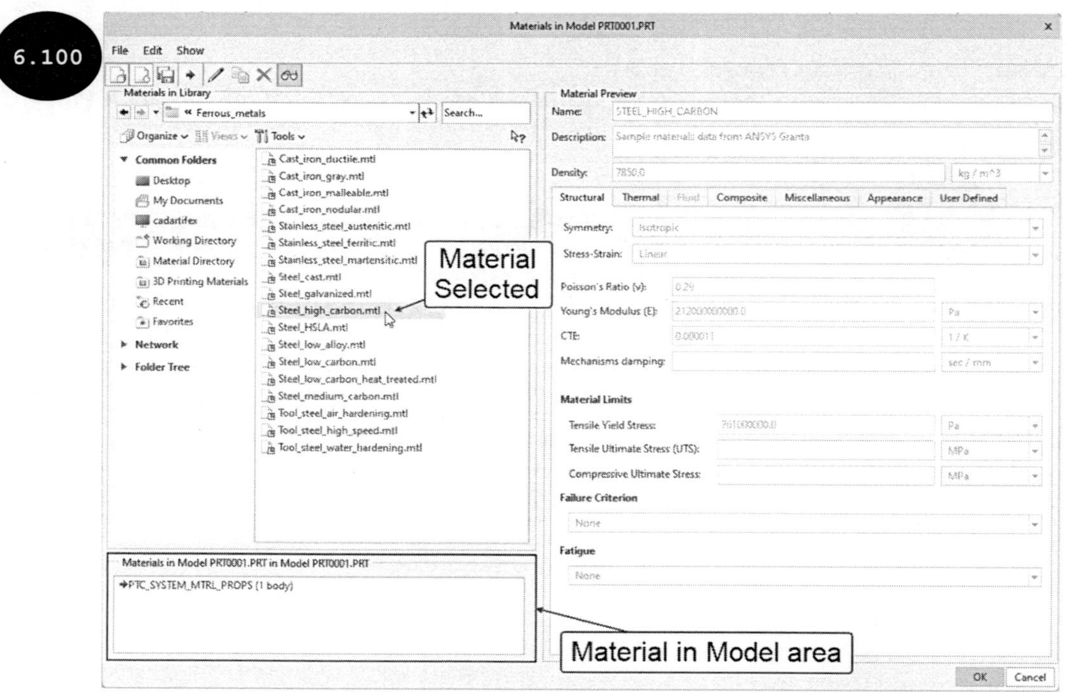

5. Click on the **OK** button in the dialog box. The Steel High Carbon material is assigned to the model and appears next to **Material** in the **Model Properties** dialog box.

6. Close the **Model Properties** dialog box by clicking on the **Close** button. The material properties of the selected material are assigned to the model.

Section 9: Calculating Mass Properties

1. Click on the **Analysis** tab in the **Ribbon** and then click on the **Mass Properties** tool in the **Model Report** group, see Figure 6.101. The **Mass Properties** dialog box appears.

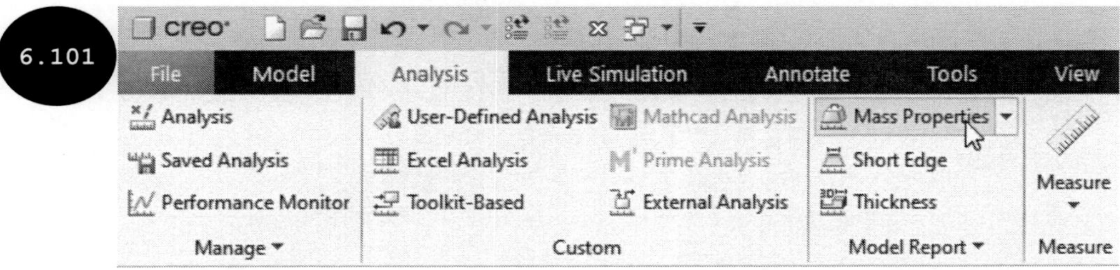

2. Click on the **Preview** button in the dialog box. The mass properties of the model appear in the dialog box, see Figure 6.102.

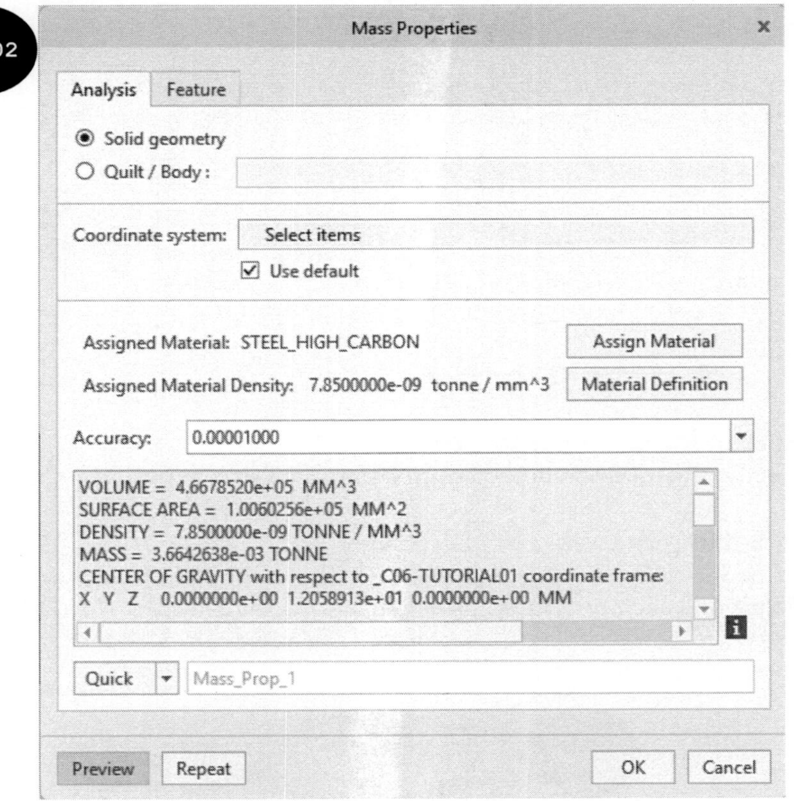

3. After reviewing the mass properties, exit the **Mass Properties** dialog box.

Section 10: Saving the Model

1. Click on the **Save** tool in the **Quick Access Toolbar**. The **Save Object** dialog box appears.

2. Click on the **OK** button in the dialog box. The model is saved with the name **C06-Tutorial01** in the specified working directory (<<*Creo Parametric**Chapter 6*\).

Tutorial 2

Create the model shown in Figure 6.103. After creating the model, assign the Steel Cast material and calculate the mass properties of the model. All dimensions are in mm.

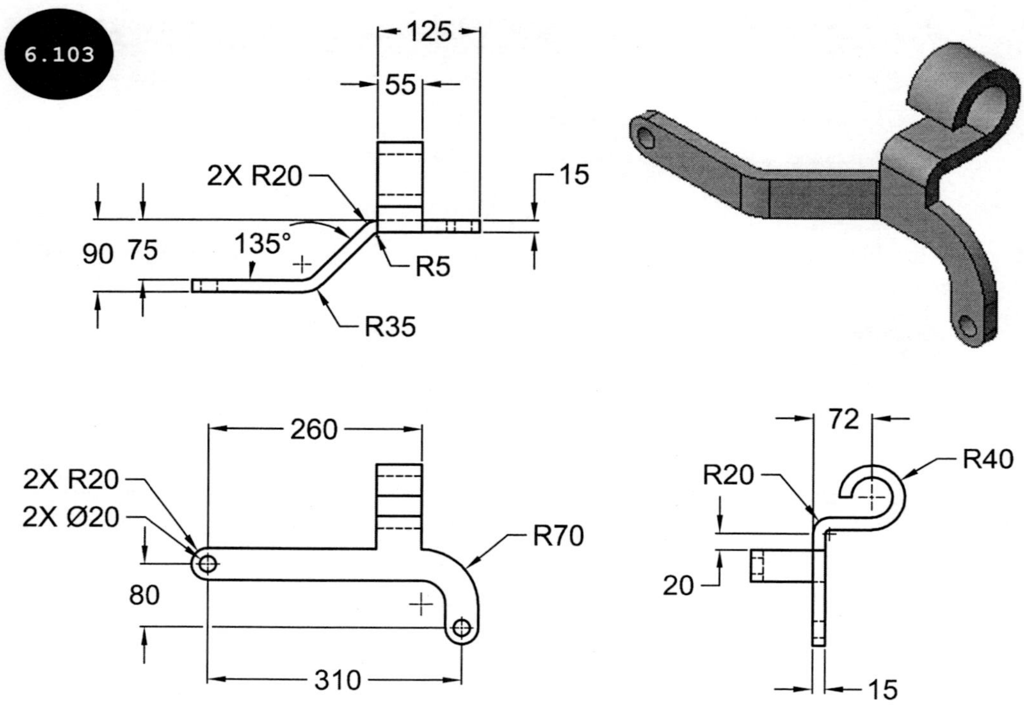

Section 1: Starting Creo Parametric

1. Start Creo Parametric by double-clicking on the Creo Parametric icon on your desktop.

Section 2: Setting the Working Directory

1. Click on the **Select Working Directory** tool in the **Data** group of the **Home** tab, see Figure 6.104. The **Select Working Directory** window appears. In this window, browse to *Creo Parametric > Chapter 6*. You need to create these folders, if not created earlier. Next, click on the **OK** button in the dialog box. The working directory is set to <<*Creo Parametric**Chapter 6*\.

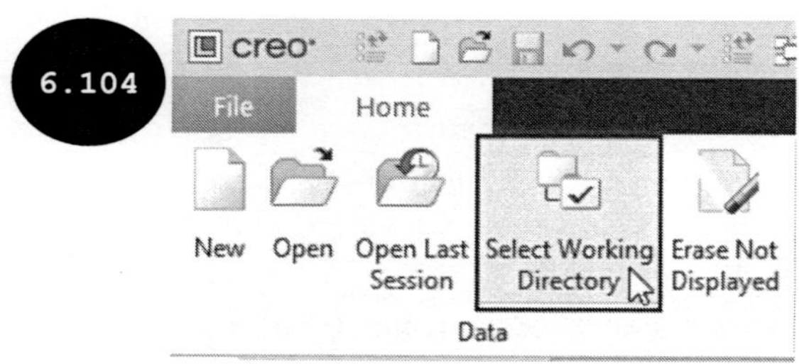

Section 3: Invoking the Part Mode

1. Click on the **New** tool in the **Data** group of the **Home** tab. The **New** dialog box appears, see Figure 6.105. Alternatively, press the CTRL + N to invoke the **New** dialog box.

2. Ensure that the **Part** radio button is selected in the **Type** area and the **Solid** radio button is selected in the **Sub-type** area of the dialog box, see Figure 6.105.

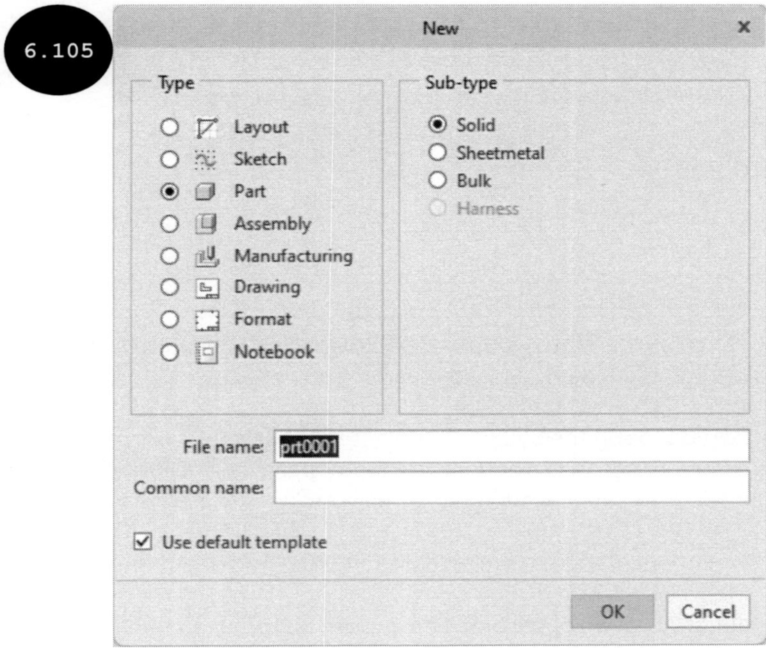

3. Enter **C06-Tutorial02** in the **File name** field of the dialog box as the name of the model.

4. Clear the **Use default template** check box and then click on the **OK** button in the dialog box. The **New File Options** dialog box appears, see Figure 6.106.

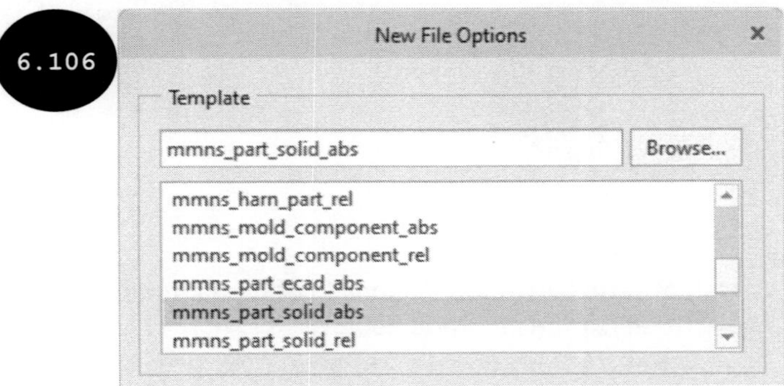

5. Select the **mmns_part_solid_abs** template in the **New File Options** dialog box and then click on the **OK** button. The Part mode is invoked with the **mmns_part_solid_abs** template. In this template, the length is measured in millimeters, mass is measured in Newton, and time is measured in seconds.

Section 4: Creating the Base Feature - Extrude Feature

1. Invoke the Sketching environment by selecting the Front plane as the sketching plane and then create the sketch of the base feature, see Figure 6.107.

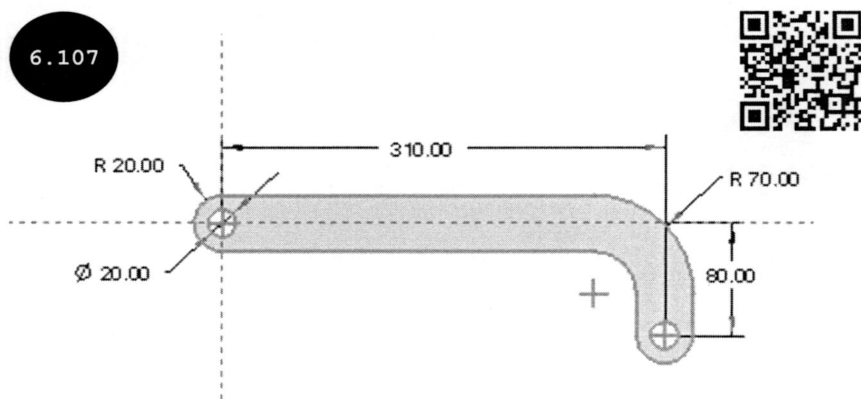

2. Click on the **OK** tool in the **Close** group of the **Ribbon** to exit the Sketching environment. The Part mode is invoked and the sketch is selected in the graphics area.

3. Click on the **Extrude** tool in the **Shapes** group of the **Model** tab. A preview of the extrude feature appears, see Figure 6.108. Also, the **Extrude** tab appears in the **Ribbon**. If the preview of the extrude feature does not appear, then select the sketch in the graphics area.

4. Change the current orientation of the model to the standard orientation, see Figure 6.108.

5. Select the **Symmetric** option of the **Side 1** drop-down list of the **Extrude** tab (see Figure 6.109), to add the material symmetrically on both sides of the sketching plane.

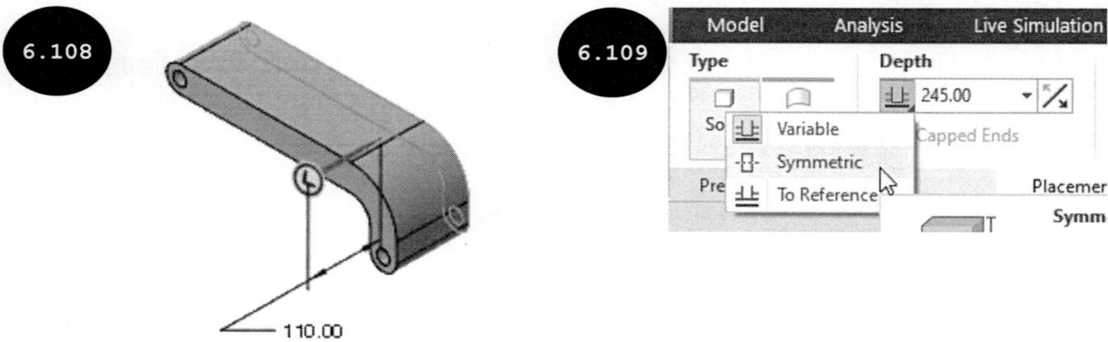

6. Enter **90** as the depth of extrusion in the **Value** field of the **Extrude** tab and then press ENTER. The preview of the extrude feature gets modified.

7. Click on the green tick-mark button in the **Extrude** tab. The extrude feature is created, see Figure 6.110.

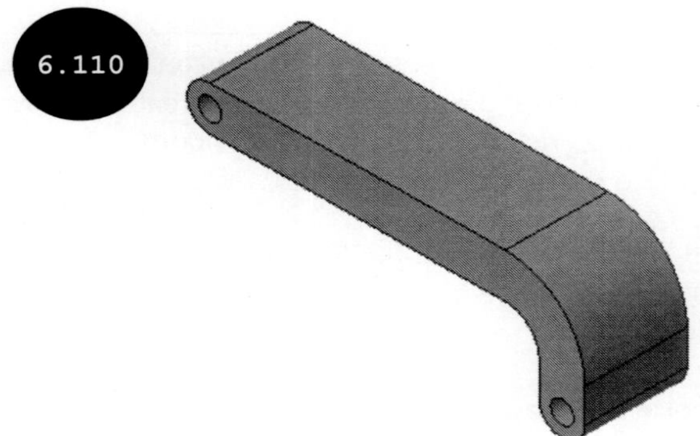

Section 5: Creating the Second Feature - Extrude Cut Feature

1. Invoke the Sketching environment by selecting the top planar face of the base feature as the sketching plane.

2. Click on the **References** tool in the **Setup** group of the **Sketch** tab to specify references for creating the sketch, see Figure 6.111. The **References** dialog box appears and you are prompted to select entities of the model to specify references.

3. Select the outer entities (1, 2, and 3) of the model, see Figure 6.112. The references are defined.

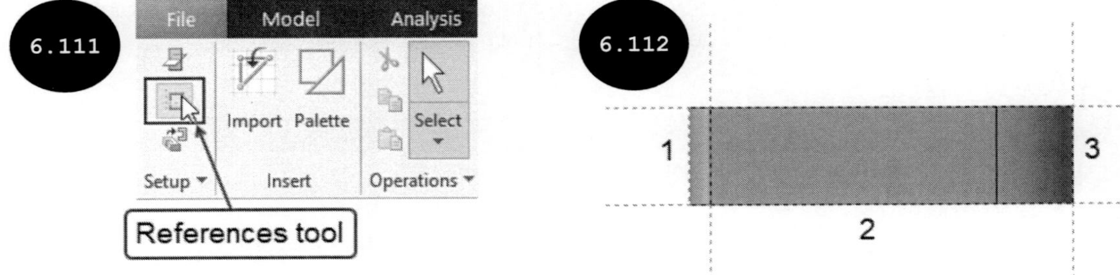

4. Close the **References** dialog box by clicking on the **Close** button.

   You can now create a sketch of the second feature.

5. Create a sketch of the second feature by using the defined references, see Figure 6.113.

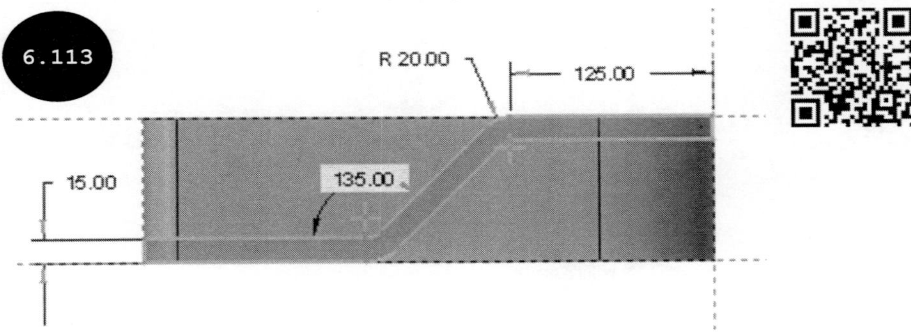

Tip: The sketch shown in Figure 6.113 is created by drawing an upper opened loop of the sketch and then offsetting it at an offset distance of 15 mm, to create the lower loop of the sketch by using the **Offset** tool. Also, line entities are created on both ends to create a closed sketch.

6. Click on the **OK** tool in the **Close** group of the **Ribbon** to exit the Sketching environment. The Part mode is invoked and the sketch is selected in the graphics area. Change the orientation of the model to standard orientation.

7. Click on the **Extrude** tool in the **Shapes** group of the **Model** tab. A preview of the extrude feature appears. Also, the **Extrude** tab appears in the **Ribbon**.

8. Click on the **Flip Direction** button in the **Extrude** tab, see Figure 6.114. The direction of extrusion changes to downward.

9. Click on the **Remove Material** button to create the cut feature by removing the material, see Figure 6.114.

10. Select the **Through All** option in the **Side 1** drop-down list to remove the material throughout the model, see Figure 6.114.

11. Click on the **Change Material Direction** button to flip the side of the material to be removed, see Figure 6.114. A preview of the model appears as shown in Figure 6.115.

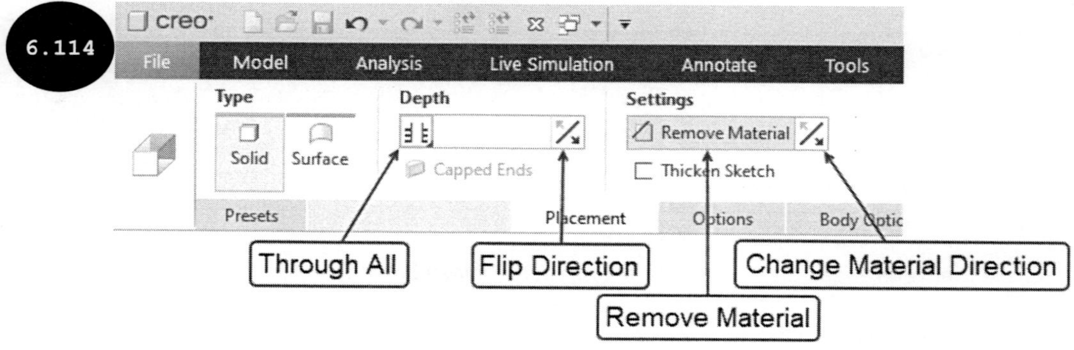

12. Click on the green tick-mark button in the **Extrude** tab. The extrude cut feature is created, see Figure 6.116.

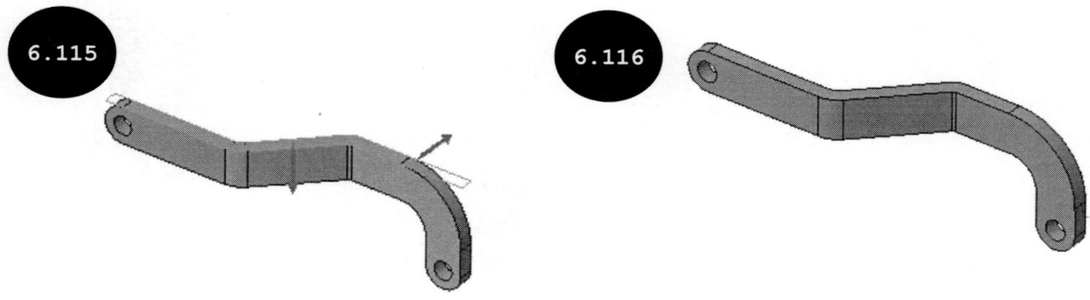

Section 6: Creating the Third Feature - Extrude Feature

To create the third feature of the model, you first need to create a datum plane at an offset distance of 205 mm from the Right plane.

1. Click on the **Plane** tool in the **Datum** group of the **Model** tab. The **Datum Plane** dialog box appears.

2. Select the Right plane as the reference in the **Model Tree** or in the graphics area. The preview of an offset datum plane appears.

3. Enter **205** in the **Translation** field of the **Offset** area in the dialog box and then press ENTER. The preview of the offset datum plane appears as shown in Figure 6.117. Note that in this figure, all other datum planes have been turned off for clarity of the image.

4. Click on the **OK** button in the dialog box. The offset datum plane is created.

   After creating the datum plane, you need to create the third feature of the model.

5. Invoke the Sketching environment by selecting the newly created datum plane as the sketching plane.

6. Create a sketch of the third feature, see Figure 6.118.

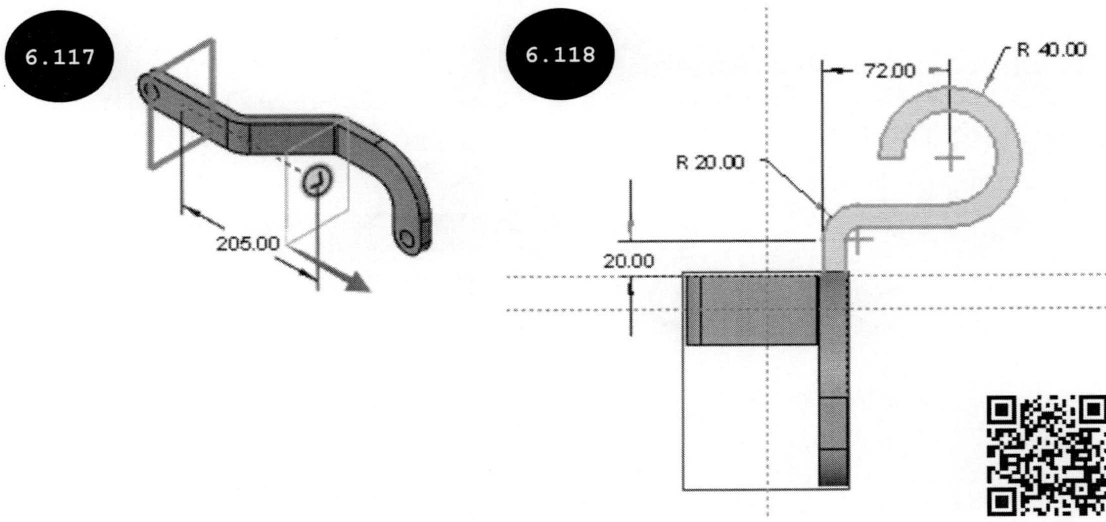

Tip: To make the sketch of the third feature fully defined as shown in Figure 6.118, you need to apply the required constraints such as tangent constraints between the sets of connecting lines and arcs. Also, the coincident constraints between the center points of the arcs that are sharing the same center point need to be applied.

7. Click on the **OK** tool in the **Close** group of the **Ribbon** to exit the Sketching environment. Next, change the orientation of the model to standard orientation.

8. Click on the **Extrude** tool in the **Shapes** group of the **Model** tab. A preview of the extrude feature appears, see Figure 6.119. Also, the **Extrude** tab appears in the **Ribbon**.

9. Enter **55** as the depth of extrusion in the **Value** field of the **Extrude** tab and then press ENTER. The preview of the extrude feature gets modified.

10. Click on the green tick-mark button in the **Extrude** tab. The extrude feature is created, see Figure 6.120.

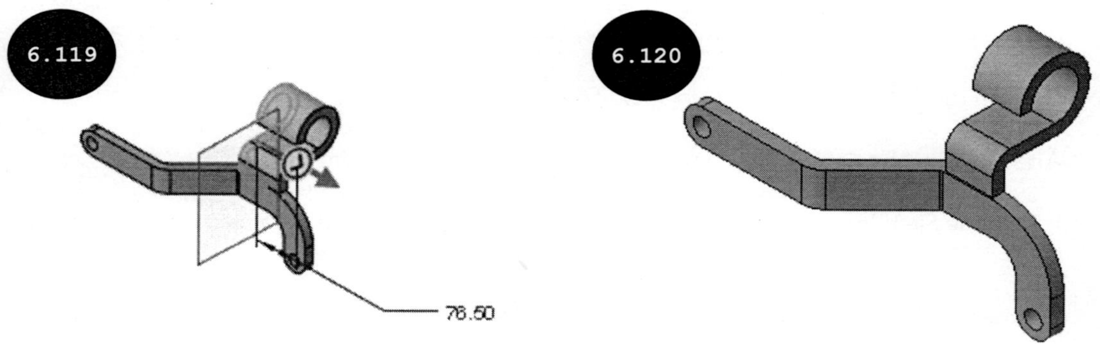

Section 7: Assigning the Material

1. Click on **File > Prepare > Model Properties** in the **File** menu, see Figure 6.121. The **Model Properties** dialog box appears, see Figure 6.121.

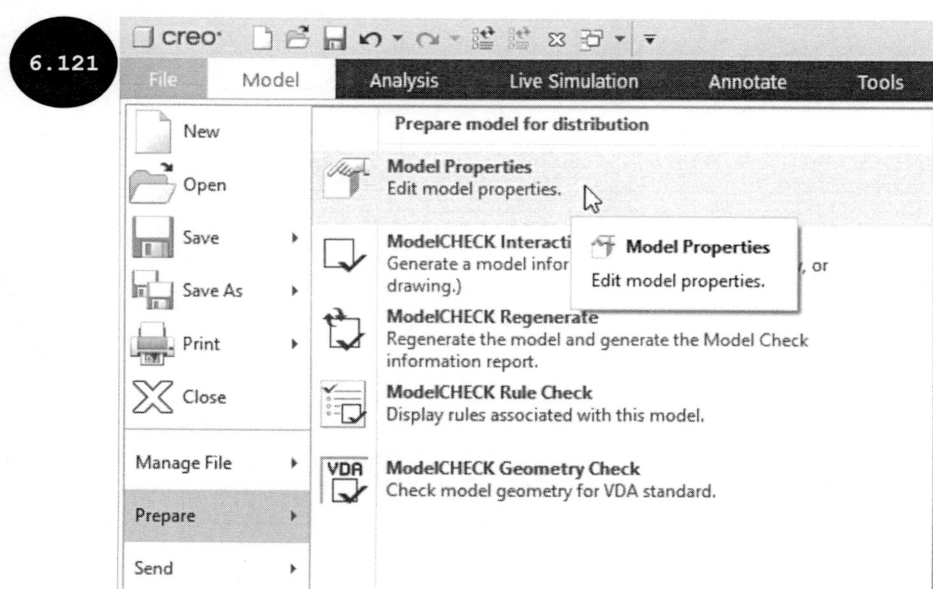

2. Click on the **change** option that appears on the right of the **Material** row in the dialog box, see Figure 6.122. The **Materials in Model** dialog box appears.

6.122

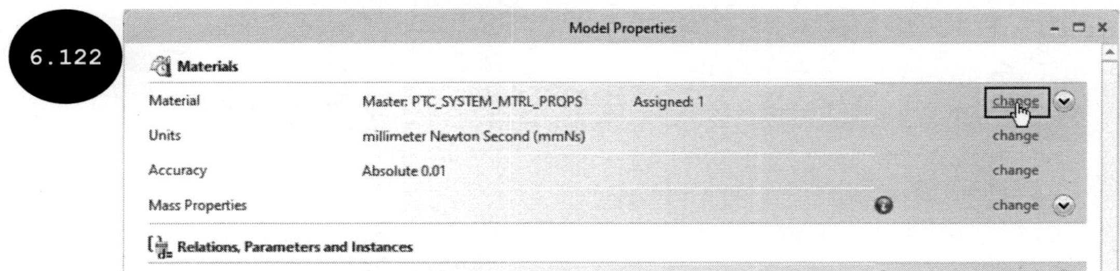

3. Expand the **Standard-Materials_Granta-Design** material folder of the **Material Directory** in the dialog box by double-clicking on it. The different material categories such as **Ferrous_metals**, **Non-ferrous_metals**, **Plastics**, and **Woods** appear.

4. Expand the **Ferrous_metals** material category in the dialog box and then double-click on the **Steel_cast.mtl** material, see Figure 6.123. The properties of the selected material appear on the right half of the dialog box. Also, the selected material is added in the **Materials in Model** area of the dialog box, see Figure 6.123.

6.123

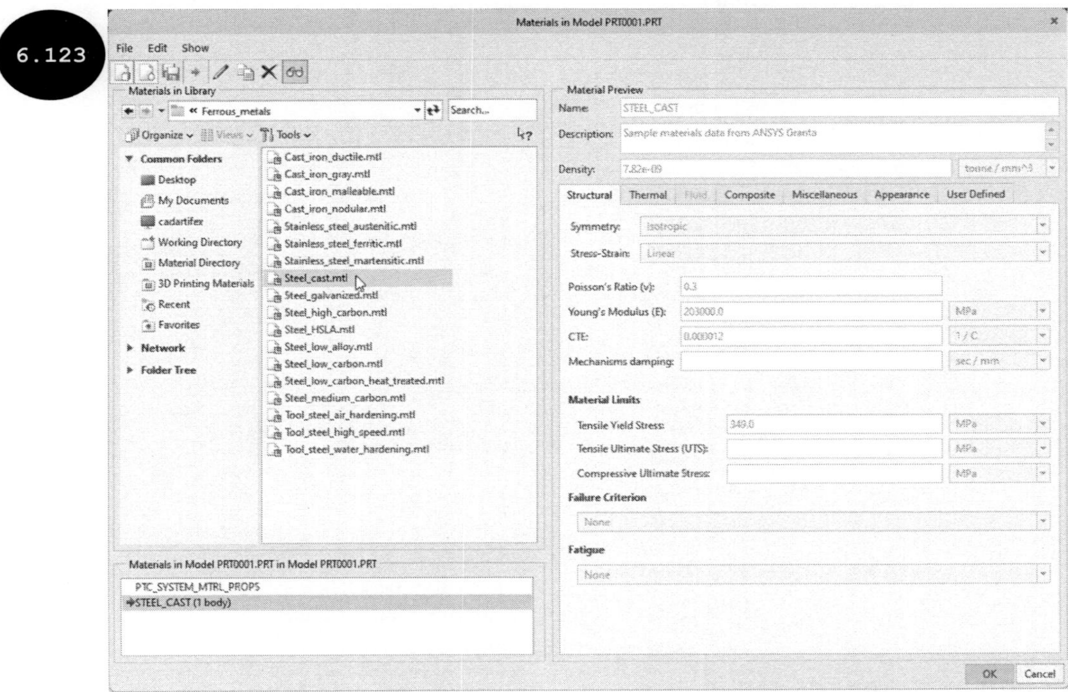

5. Click on the **OK** button in the dialog box. The Steel Cast material is assigned to the model and appears next to **Material** in the **Model Properties** dialog box.

6. Close the **Model Properties** dialog box by clicking on the **Close** button. The material properties of the selected material are assigned to the model.

Section 8: Calculating Mass Properties

1. Click on the **Analysis** tab in the **Ribbon** and then click on the **Mass Properties** tool in the **Model Report** group, see Figure 6.124. The **Mass Properties** dialog box appears.

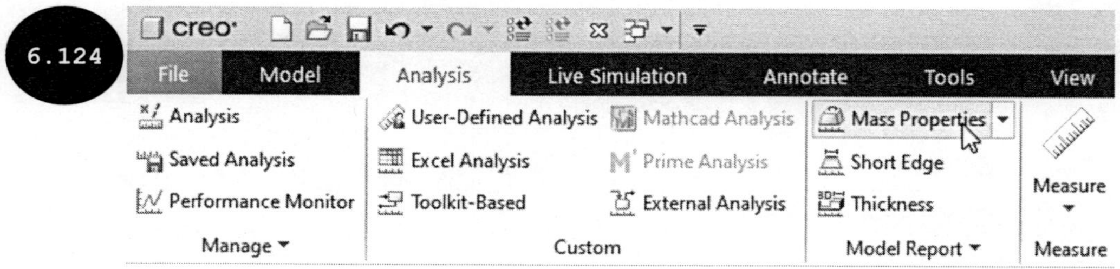

2. Click on the **Preview** button in the dialog box. The mass properties of the model appear in the dialog box, see Figure 6.125. After reviewing the mass properties, exit the **Mass Properties** dialog box.

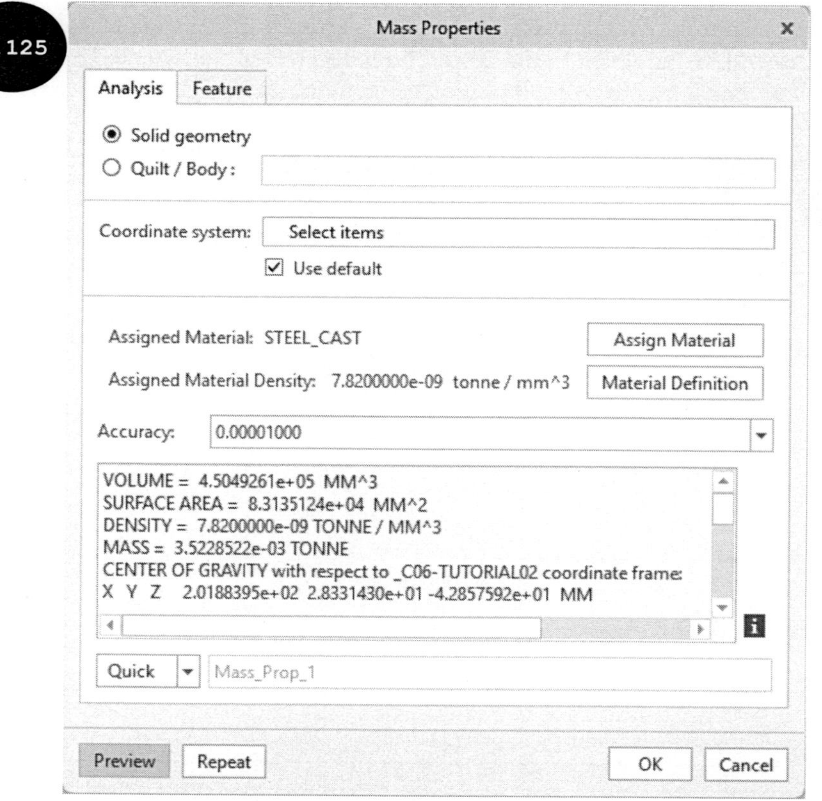

Section 9: Saving the Model

1. Click on the **Save** tool in the **Quick Access Toolbar**. The **Save Object** dialog box appears.

2. Click on the **OK** button in the dialog box. The model is saved with the name **C06-Tutorial02** in the specified working directory (<<*Creo Parametric**Chapter 6*\).

Hands-on Test Drive 1

Create the model shown in Figure 6.126. After creating the model, apply the Stainless Steel Austenitic material to the model and calculate its mass properties. All dimensions are in mm.

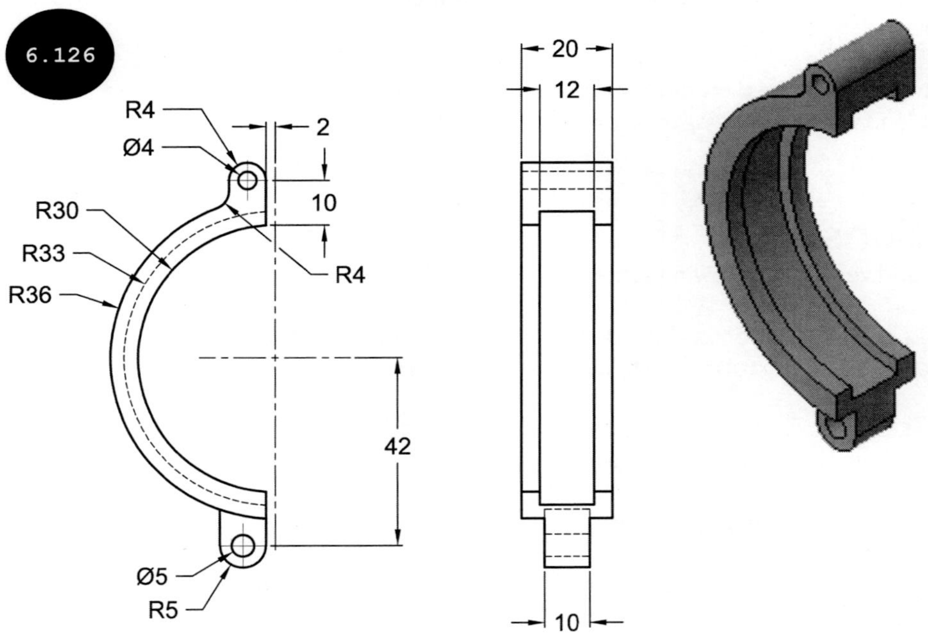

Hands-on Test Drive 2

Create the model shown in Figure 6.127. After creating the model, apply the Steel Low Alloy material to the model and calculate its mass properties. All dimensions are in mm.

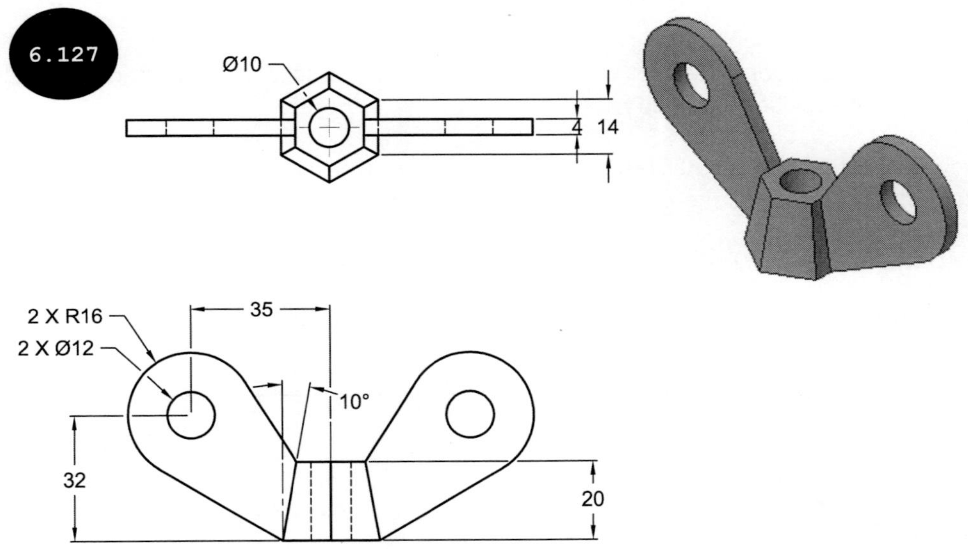

Summary

In this chapter, you have learned advanced options for creating extrude or revolve features. The chapter discussed methods for creating cut features by using the **Extrude** and **Revolve** tools, projecting the edges of existing features onto the current sketching plane by using the **Project** tool, and editing an existing feature and the sketch of a feature as per the design change.

The chapter also explained methods for measuring different geometrical parameters such as length, angle, area, and volume by using measuring tools, assigning appearance and material, and calculating the mass properties of a model.

Questions

Complete and verify the following sentences:

- The _________ option of the **Side 1** drop-down list of the **Extrude** tab is used for defining the termination of the extrusion up to its next intersection.
- The _________ button of the **Extrude** tab is used for creating a cut feature by removing the material from the existing solid feature.
- The _________ option is used for defining the termination of extrusion by selecting a vertex.
- The _________ button of the **Extrude** tab is used for flipping the side of the material to be removed.
- You can project the edges of existing features as sketch entities onto the current sketching plane by using the _________ tool.
- The _________ tool is used for calculating mass properties such as the mass and volume of a model.
- The _________ tool is used for measuring multiple results such as area, perimeter, diameter, and length of a selected geometry.
- A revolve cut feature is created by removing material from the model by revolving a sketch around a centerline or an axis. (True/False)
- You can edit individual features and their sketches as per your requirements. (True/False)
- In Creo Parametric, you cannot customize material properties. (True/False)

CHAPTER

7

Advanced Modeling - II

In this chapter, the following topics will be discussed:

- Creating a Sweep Feature
- Creating a Helical Sweep feature
- Creating a Volume Helical Sweep feature
- Creating a Blend feature
- Creating a Swept Blend feature
- Creating a Rotational Blend feature

In the previous chapters, you have learned about the primary modeling tools that are used for creating 3D parametric models. You have also learned about the basic workflow of creating models, which involves first creating the base feature of a model and then creating the remaining features of the model one by one.

In this chapter, you will explore some of the advanced modeling tools such as **Sweep**, **Helical Sweep**, **Volume Helical Sweep**, **Blend**, **Swept Blend**, and **Rotational Blend**.

Creating a Sweep Feature

A sweep feature is created by adding or removing material by sweeping a section along one or more trajectories. Figure 7.1 shows a section and a trajectory. Figure 7.2 shows the resultant sweep feature created by sweeping the section along the trajectory.

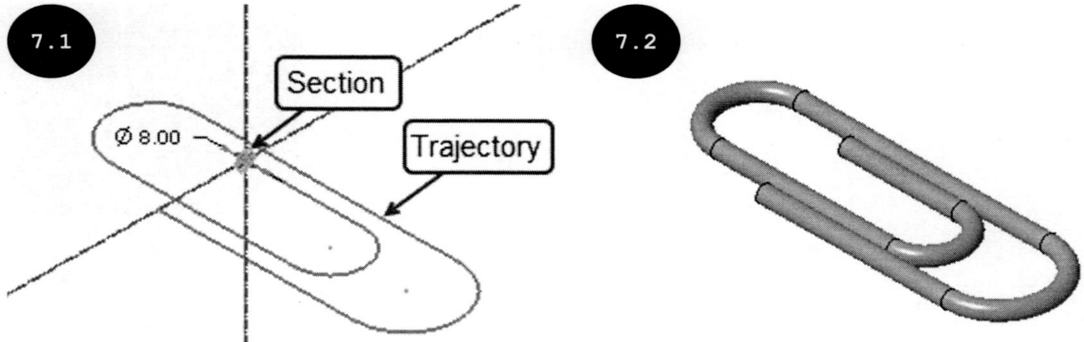

It is evident from the above figures that to create a sweep feature, you first need to create a trajectory and a section, where the section follows the trajectory and creates a sweep feature. To create a section, you need to identify the cross-section of the feature to be created. To create a trajectory, you need to identify the path taken by the section for creating the feature. In Creo, you can create a sweep feature by using the **Sweep** tool. Note that to create a solid sweep feature, you need to take care of the following points:

1. The section must be a closed sketch. In Creo, a section is created after invoking the **Sweep** tool.
2. The trajectory can be an open or a closed sketch, which is made up of a set of end to end connected sketch entities or a curve. You can also select an edge of the model as a trajectory.
3. The trajectory must be created before invoking the **Sweep** tool.
4. The section, trajectory, as well as the resultant sweep feature must not self-intersect. For example, if the arc or the spline radius of the trajectory is too small relative to the section, then the resultant feature self-intersects.

In Creo, you can create various types of sweep features such as constant section sweep and variable section sweep. The same are discussed next.

Creating a Constant Section Sweep Feature

A constant section sweep feature is a feature that has a constant section throughout the selected trajectory.

1. Create an open or a closed sketch/curve as a trajectory and then select it in the graphics area, see Figure 7.3.

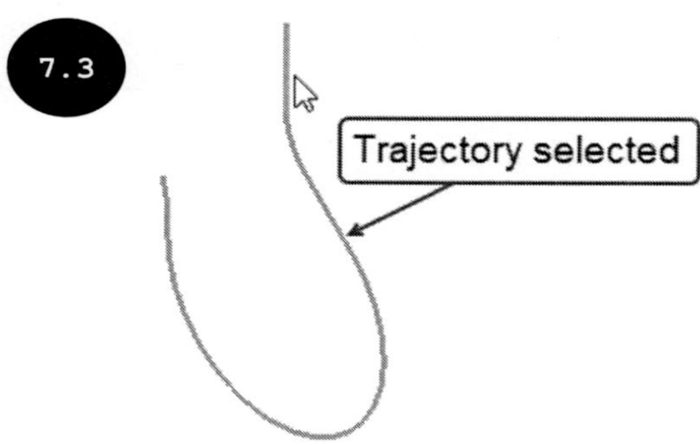

2. Click on the **Sweep** tool in the **Shapes** group of the **Model** tab, see Figure 7.4. The **Sweep** tab appears in the **Ribbon**, see Figure 7.5. Also, an arrow appears on one end of the selected trajectory, and dimension handles appear on both ends of the trajectory, see Figure 7.6.

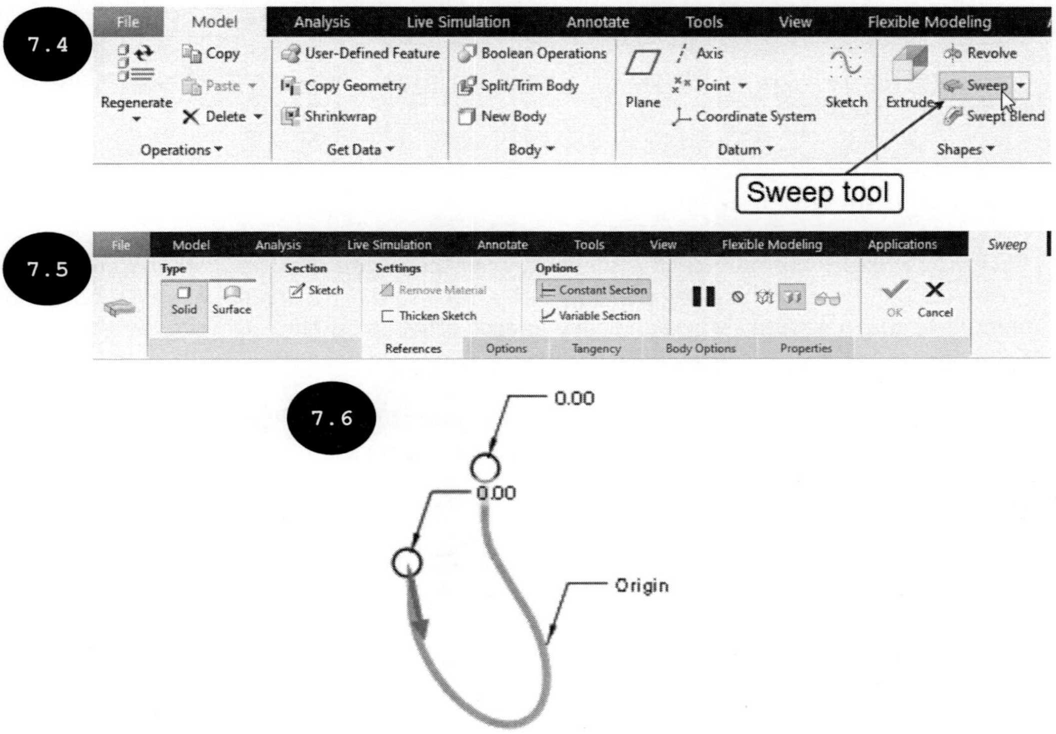

Note: The endpoint of the trajectory where the arrow appears is defined as the start point from where the section will start following the path to create the sweep feature. You can click on the arrow to flip the start point of the trajectory.

Sweep as solid : The **Sweep as solid** button of the **Sweep** tab is used for creating a solid sweep feature by sweeping a section along a trajectory. By default, this button is activated. As a result, you can create a solid sweep feature.

Sweep as surface : The **Sweep as surface** button is used for creating a surface sweep feature. Note that a surface feature has zero thickness and no mass properties. Also, the section of the surface feature can be an open or closed sketch.

Sketch : The **Sketch** button is used for creating or editing a section of the feature.

Constant Section : The **Constant Section** button is used for creating a constant section sweep such that the shape of the section remains constant as it is swept along the trajectory.

Variable Section : The **Variable Section** button is used for creating a variable section sweep feature such that the shape of the section varies as it is swept along the origin trajectory. To create a variable section sweep, you need to select two or more than two trajectories. You will learn about creating a variable section sweep later in this chapter.

3. Ensure that the **Sweep as solid** button is activated in the **Type** area of the **Sweep** tab to create a solid sweep feature.

4. Ensure that the **Constant Section** button is activated in the **Options** area of the **Sweep** tab to create a constant section sweep.

5. Click on the **Sketch** button in the **Section** area of the **Sweep** tab. The Sketching environment is invoked and the sketching plane is oriented normal to the viewing direction. Note that two centerlines that are mutually perpendicular to each other define the origin of the sketch at their point of intersection.

6. Create a closed sketch as the section of the sweep feature, see Figure 7.7. Next, change the orientation of the sketch to standard orientation, see Figure 7.8.

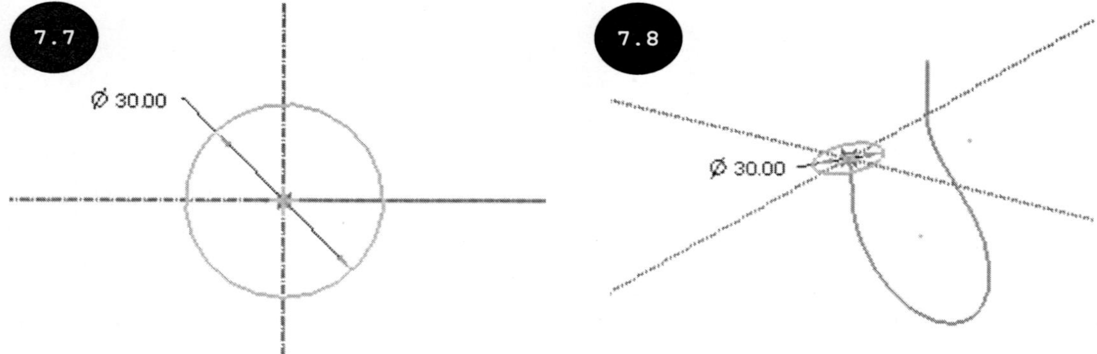

7. Exit the Sketching environment by clicking on the **OK** tool in the **Close** group of the **Sketch** tab. A preview of the constant sweep feature appears in the graphics area, see Figure 7.9.

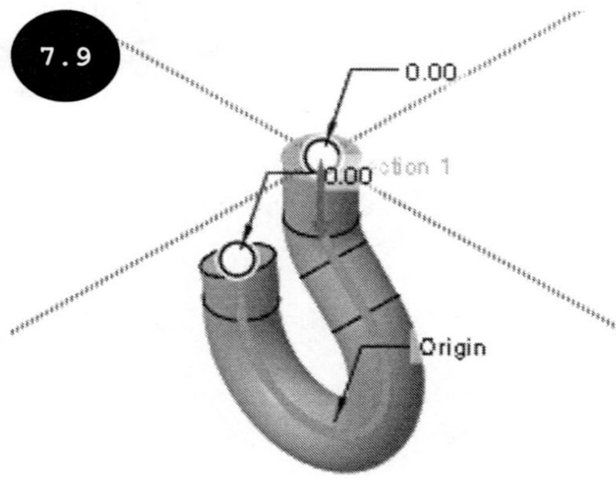

8. Expand the **References** panel of the **Sweep** tab if not expanded by default, see Figure 7.10. The options in this panel are discussed below:

 Trajectories: The **Trajectories** collector in the **References** panel displays a list of trajectories selected, see Figure 7.10. You can select one or more than one trajectory to create the sweep feature. You will learn about creating a sweep feature by selecting more than one trajectory later in this chapter.

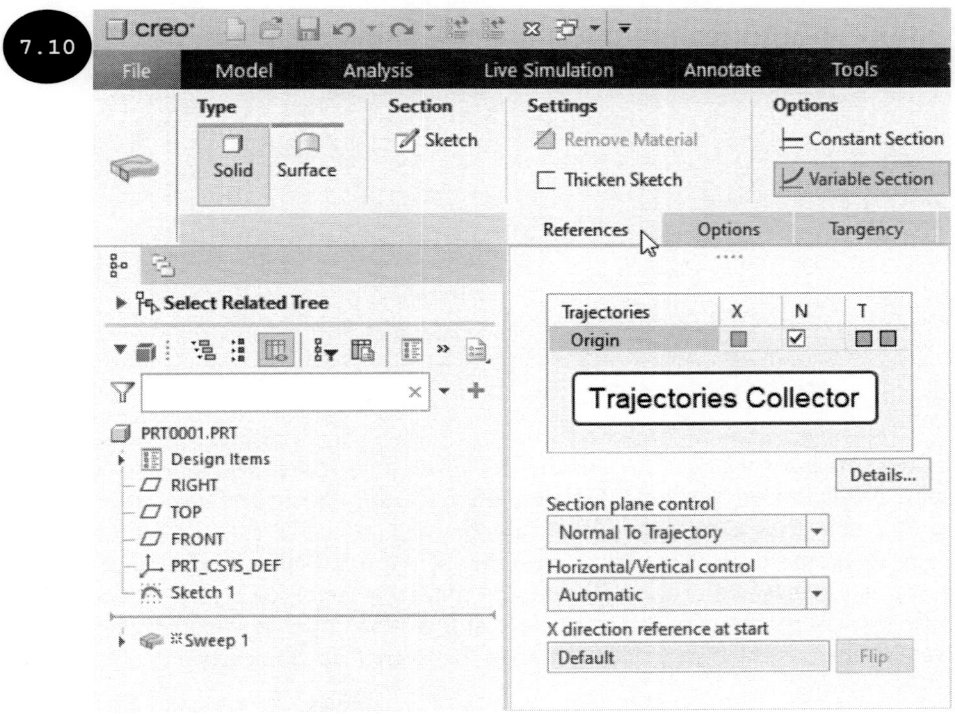

 Section plane control: By default, the **Normal To Trajectory** option is selected in the **Section plane control** drop-down list of the **References** panel. As a result, the section follows the trajectory by maintaining a normal constraint throughout the trajectory, see Figures 7.11 and 7.12.

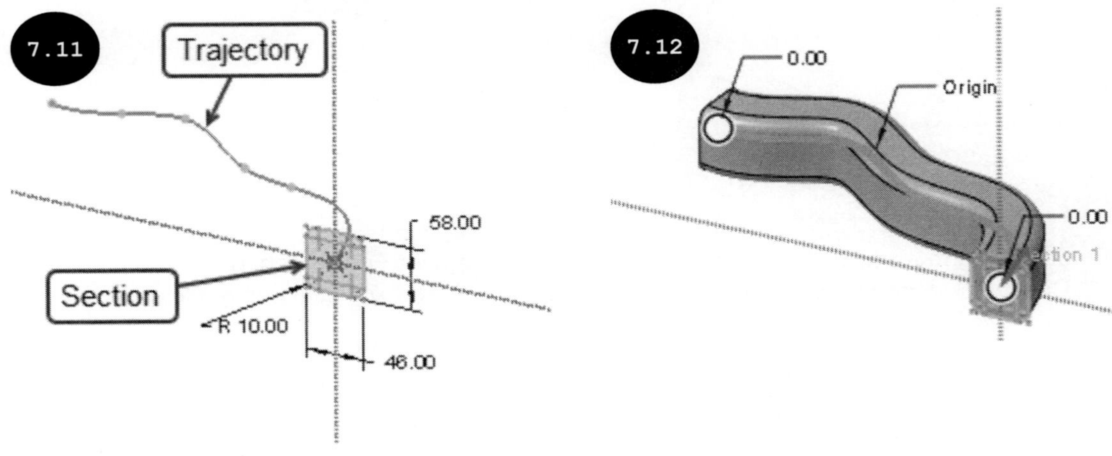

The **Normal to Projection** option is used for creating a sweep feature such that the section becomes normal to the projection of the trajectory along a specified direction reference, see Figures 7.13 and 7.14. When you select the **Normal To Projection** option in the **Section plane control** drop-down list, the **Direction reference** field appears and you are prompted to select a direction reference. You can select a plane, an axis, a coordinate system axis, or a straight entity as a direction reference. In Figure 7.14, a datum plane is selected as a direction reference.

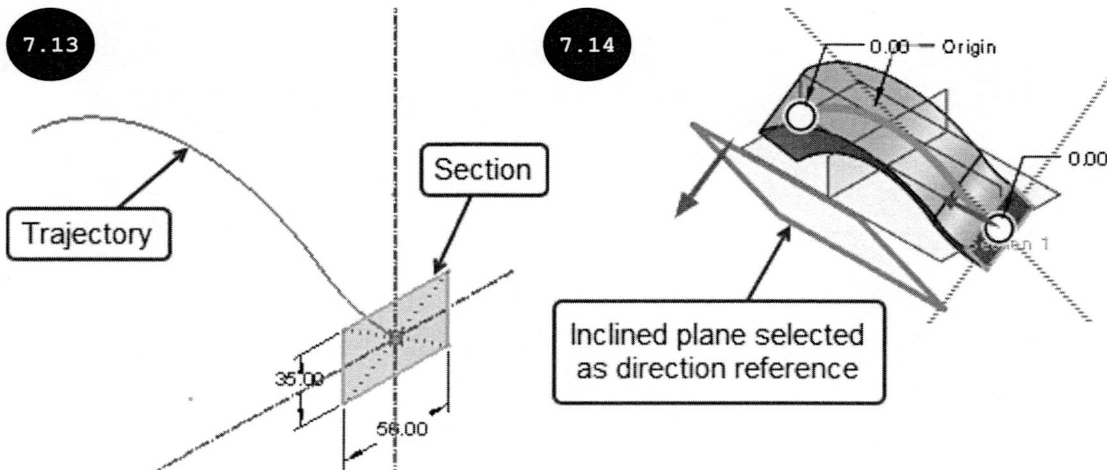

The **Constant Normal Direction** option is used for creating a sweep feature such that the section remains parallel to the specified direction reference throughout the trajectory, see Figure 7.15. When you select the **Constant Normal Direction** option, the **Direction reference** field appears and you are prompted to select a direction reference. You can select a plane, an axis, a coordinate system axis, a planar face, or a straight entity as a direction reference. Figure 7.15 shows the preview of a sweep feature when the **Constant Normal Direction** option is selected, whereas Figure 7.16 shows the preview of the sweep feature when the **Normal To Trajectory** option is selected.

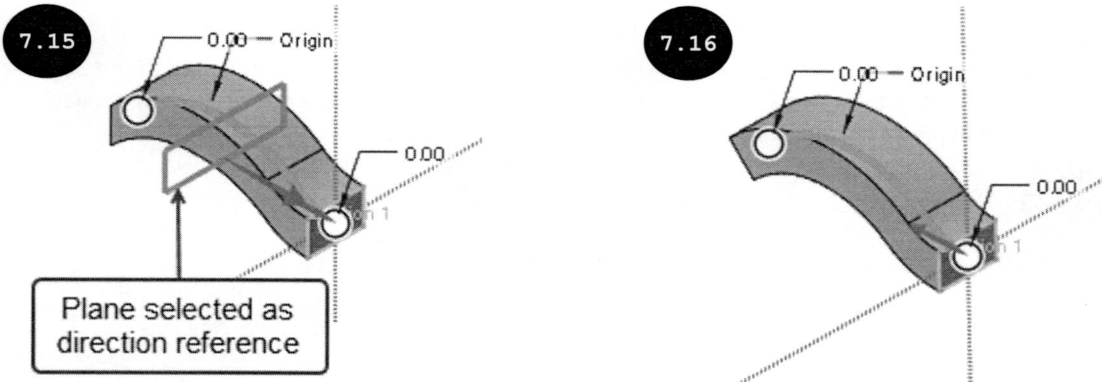

9. Select the required option (**Normal To Trajectory**, **Normal to Projection**, or **Constant Normal Direction**) in the **Section plane control** drop-down list of the expanded **References** panel.

Note: You can also define the start and end conditions of the sweep feature by using the dimension handles that appear on both ends of the trajectory in the preview of the sweep feature, see Figure 7.17. By default, a **0** dimension value is specified on both ends of the trajectory. As a result, the section starts exactly from the start point of the trajectory and ends at the endpoint of the trajectory. To define the end condition of the sweep feature, double-click on the end dimension handle and then enter the dimension value (positive or negative) in the edit field that appears, see Figure 7.18. Next, press ENTER. Similarly, you can change the start condition of the sweep feature. You can also drag the handles that appear on both ends of the trajectory to define the start and end conditions of the sweep feature.

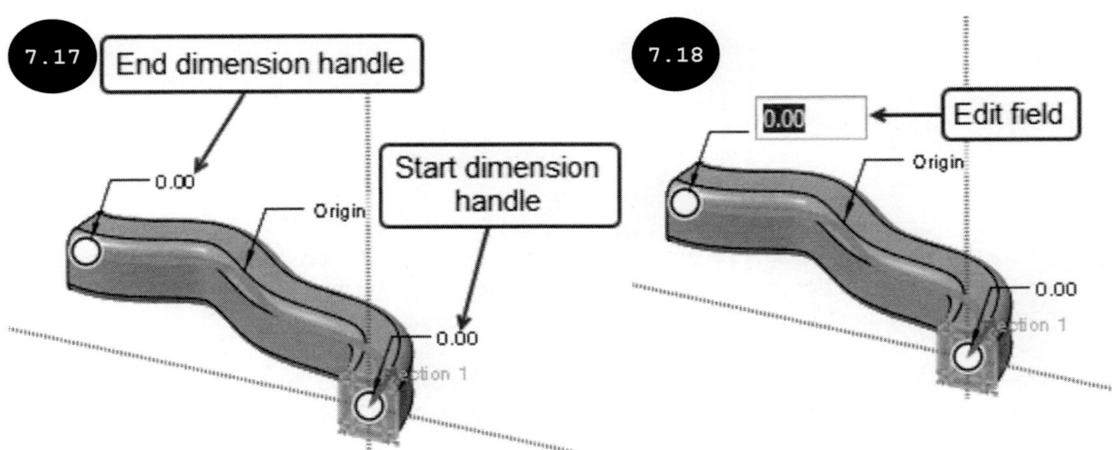

10. Click on the green tick-mark button in the **Sweep** tab of the **Ribbon**. A constant section sweep is created.

Creating a Variable Section Sweep Feature

A variable section sweep feature is a feature in which the section varies while being swept along the origin trajectory. To create a variable section sweep feature, you need to select two or more trajectories.

1. Create two or more open or closed curves as trajectories, see Figure 7.19.

2. Click on the **Sweep** tool in the **Shapes** group of the **Model** tab. The **Sweep** tab appears in the **Ribbon** and you are prompted to select trajectories. Most of the options of the **Sweep** tab have already been discussed earlier.

Tip: You can select trajectories before or after invoking the **Sweep** tool by pressing the CTRL key.

3. Select all the trajectories one by one by pressing the CTRL key. The first selected trajectory becomes the origin trajectory and the last selected trajectory becomes the X-trajectory, see Figure 7.20. The X-trajectory is used for controlling the start and end conditions of the sweep feature. Note that the section is swept along the origin trajectory and the variation of the section is controlled by the X-trajectory and other trajectories.

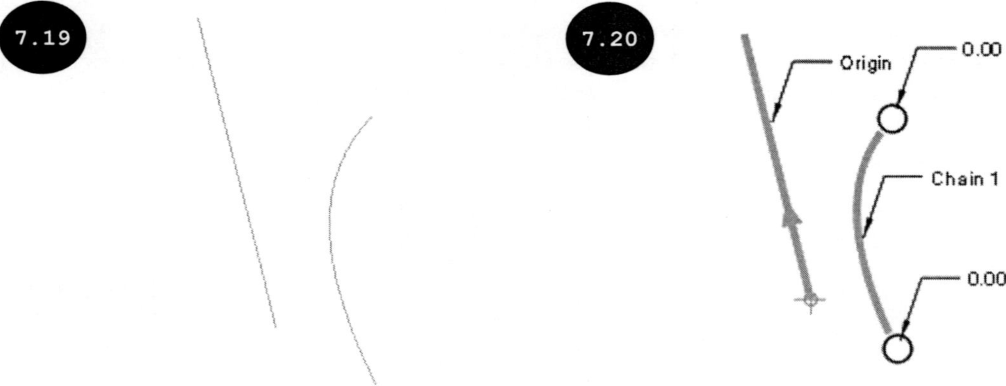

4. Ensure that the **Variable Section** button is activated in the **Options** area of the **Sweep** tab to create a variable section sweep. This button gets activated automatically on selecting two or more than two trajectories.

5. Click on the **Sketch** button in the **Section** area of the **Sweep** tab. The Sketching environment is invoked and the sketching plane is oriented normal to the viewing direction. Note that two centerlines which are mutually perpendicular to each other appear. Also, cross marks appear at the intersection of the section plane and trajectories, see Figure 7.21. In this figure, the orientation of the sketch has been changed to standard orientation to display the intersection points clearly.

6. Create a closed sketch as a section of the sweep feature such that it passes through the intersection points of all the trajectories, see Figure 7.22.

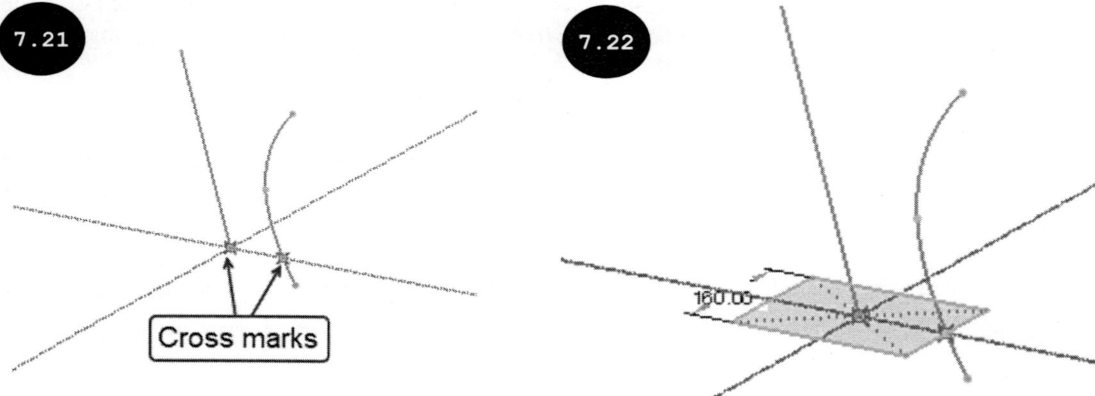

7. Exit the Sketching environment by clicking on the **OK** tool in the **Close** group of the **Sketch** tab. A preview of the variable sweep feature appears in the graphics area, see Figure 7.23.

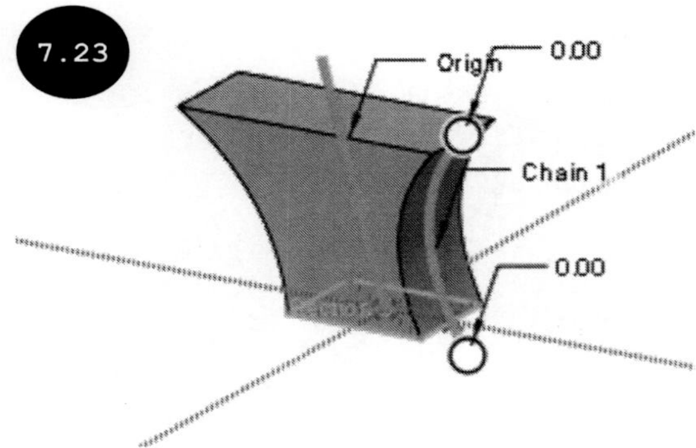

8. Expand the **References** panel of the **Sweep** tab if not expanded by default, see Figure 7.24. Most of the options of this panel have been discussed earlier.

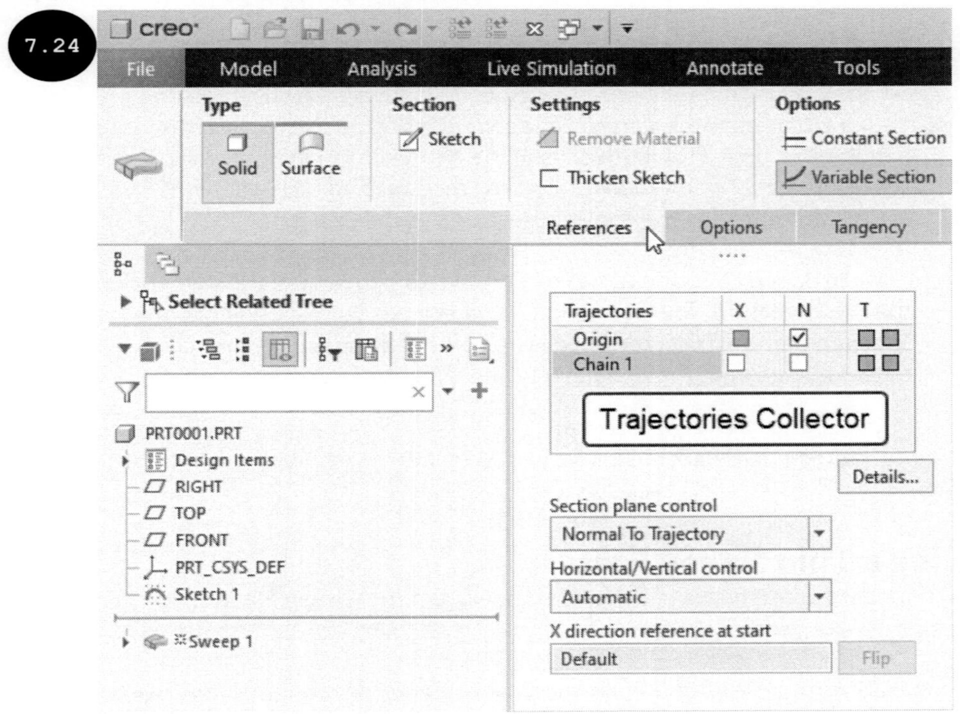

Note: By default, the **Normal To Trajectory** option is selected in the **Section plane control** drop-down list of the expanded **References** panel. As a result, the section follows the origin trajectory as well as maintains the normal constraint to it. You can define any other trajectory as a normal trajectory to which the section maintains normal constraint, see Figure 7.25. To do so, select the check box corresponding to the trajectory and the **N** column in the **Trajectories** collector, refer to Figure 7.24.

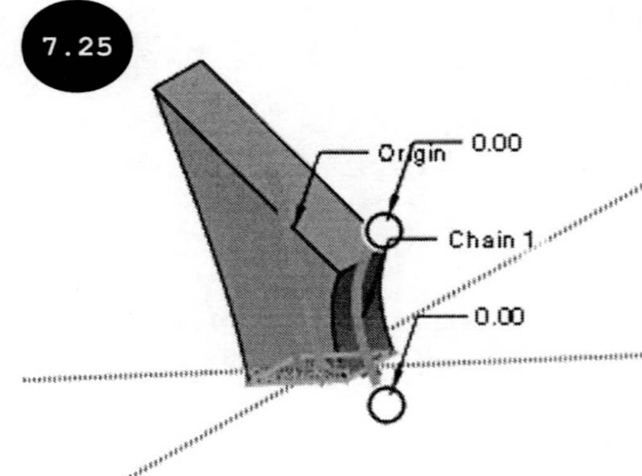

9. Select the required option (**Normal To Trajectory**, **Normal to Projection**, or **Constant Normal Direction**) in the **Section plane control** drop-down list of the expanded **References** panel. All these options are the same as discussed earlier while creating the constant section sweep.

Note: You can also define the start and end conditions of the sweep feature by using the dimension handles that appear on both ends of the X-trajectory in the preview of the sweep feature, see Figure 7.25. The method for defining the start and end conditions is same as discussed earlier while creating the constant section sweep feature.

You can define any trajectory as the X-trajectory to control the start and end conditions of the sweep feature. To do so, select the check box corresponding to the trajectory and the X column in the **Trajectories** collector of the expanded **References** panel. The selected trajectory becomes the X-trajectory and dimension handles appear on both its ends.

10. Click on the green tick-mark button in the **Sweep** tab of the **Ribbon**. A variable section sweep is created.

Creating a Thin Sweep Feature

A sweep feature of specified wall thickness is known as a thin sweep feature. The thin sweep feature can be a constant or variable section sweep.

1. Create one or more trajectories in the graphics area. To create a thin sweep feature of the constant section, you need to create a single trajectory, whereas to create a thin sweep feature of the variable section, you need to create multiple trajectories.

2. Click on the **Sweep** tool in the **Shapes** group of the **Model** tab. The **Sweep** tab appears in the **Ribbon** and you are prompted to select one or more trajectories. Most of the options of the **Sweep** tab have been discussed earlier.

3. Select one or more trajectories in the graphics area. To select multiple trajectories, you need to press the CTRL key. In Figure 7.26, three trajectories are selected to create a thin sweep feature of the variable section.

4. Click on the **Sketch** button in the **Section** area of the **Sweep** tab. The Sketching environment is invoked and the sketching plane is oriented normal to the viewing direction. In the Sketching environment, two centerlines appear that are mutually perpendicular to each other. Also, cross marks appear at the point of intersection of the section plane and the trajectories.

5. Change the current orientation of the sketch to standard orientation.

6. Create a closed sketch as the section of the sweep feature such that it passes through the intersection points of all the trajectories, see Figure 7.27. In this figure, the section is created by using the **Spline** tool.

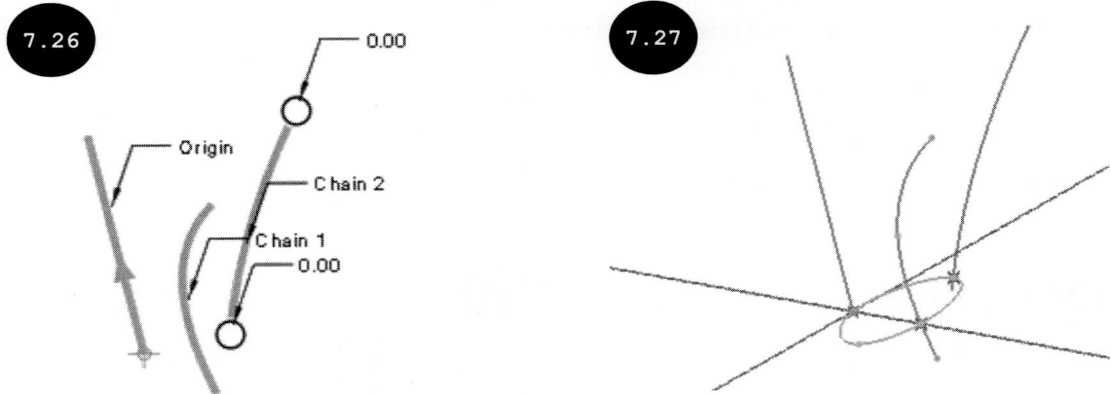

7. Exit the Sketching environment by clicking on the **OK** tool in the **Close** group of the **Sketch** tab. A preview of the sweep feature appears in the graphics area, see Figure 7.28.

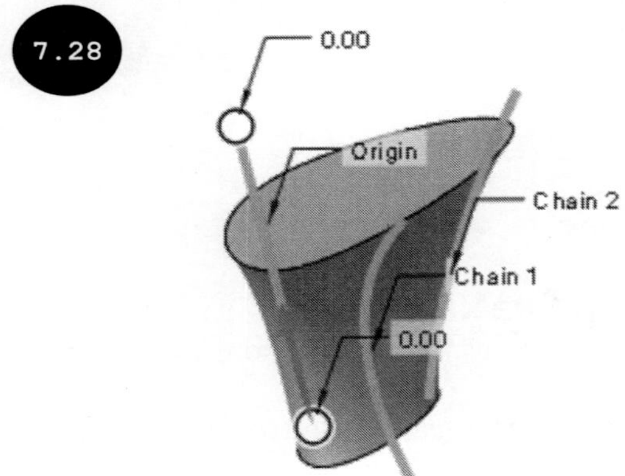

8. Click on the **Thicken Sketch** button in the **Settings** area of the **Sweep** tab to create a thin sweep feature. The **Thickness value** field appears next to the **Thicken Sketch** button in the **Settings** area of the **Sweep** tab, see Figure 7.29. Also, a preview of the thin sweep feature appears with the default thickness in the graphics area, see Figure 7.30.

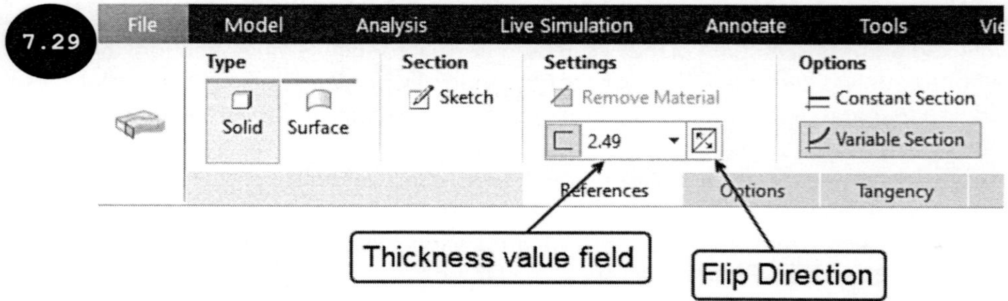

9. Enter the thickness value in the **Thickness value** field of the **Settings** area and then press ENTER. The preview of the sweep feature gets updated in the graphics area.

10. Click on the **Flip Direction** button in the **Settings** area of the **Sweep** tab to change the thickness direction to either one or both sides of the sketch.

11. Click on the green tick-mark button in the **Sweep** tab of the **Ribbon**. A thin section sweep of uniform wall thickness is created, see Figure 7.31.

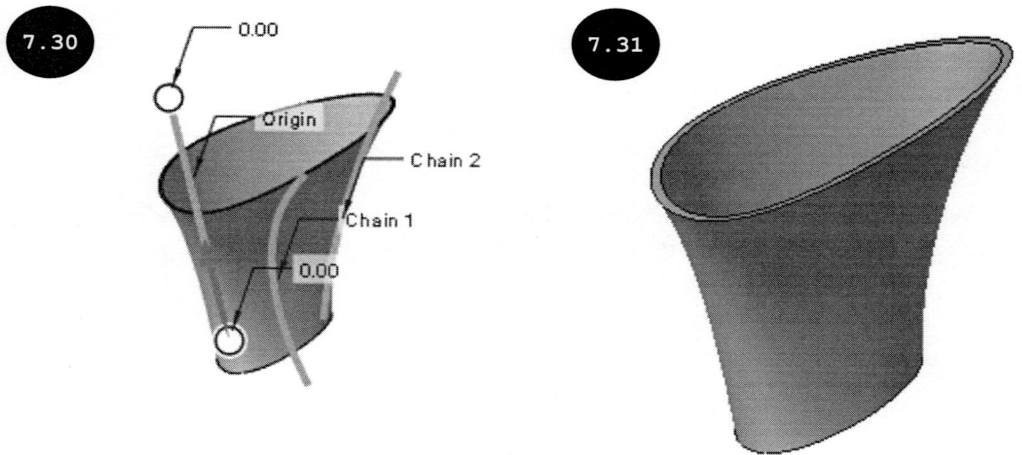

Creating a Cut Sweep Feature

A cut sweep feature is created by removing a material from an existing feature.

1. Create one or more trajectories in the graphics area, see Figure 7.32. In this figure, a single trajectory is created.

2. Invoke the **Sweep** tool and then select one or more trajectories in the graphics area.

3. Click on the **Sketch** button in the **Section** area of the **Sweep** tab. The Sketching environment is invoked and the sketching plane is oriented normal to the viewing direction.

4. Create a closed sketch as a section of the sweep feature such that it passes through the intersection points of all the trajectories, see Figure 7.33.

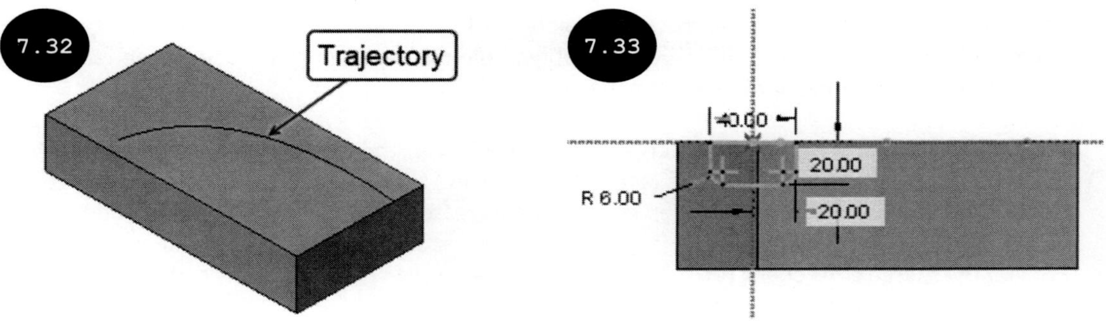

5. Change the current orientation of the model to standard orientation.

6. Exit the Sketching environment by clicking on the **OK** tool in the **Close** group of the **Sketch** tab. A preview of the sweep feature appears in the graphics area.

7. Click on the **Remove Material** button in the **Settings** area of the **Sweep** tab. A preview of the cut sweep feature appears such that the material is removed from the model, see Figure 7.34.

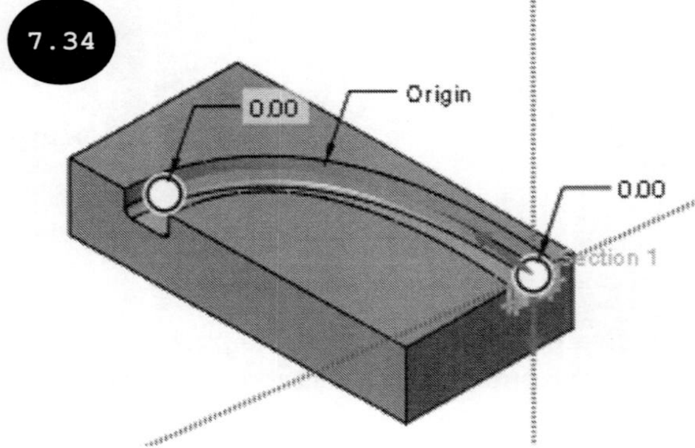

8. Expand the **Options** panel of the **Sweep** tab, see Figure 7.35. The options in this tab are discussed below:

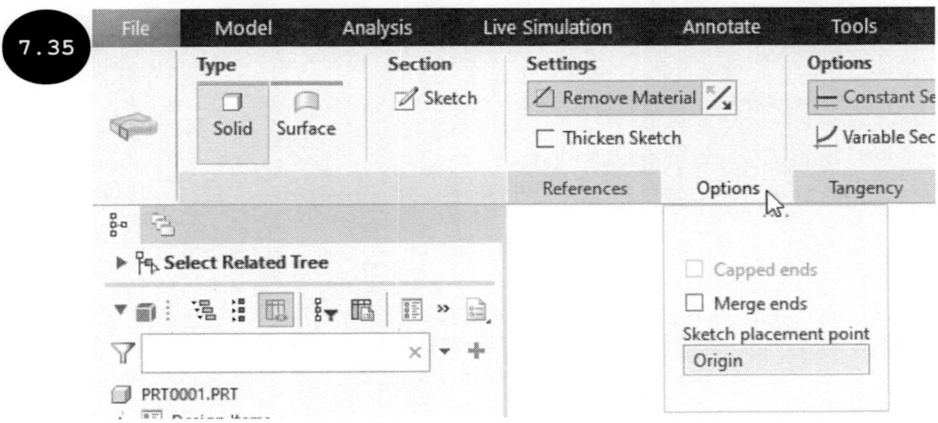

Capped ends: The **Capped ends** check box is used for creating a surface sweep feature with closed ends. Note that this check box is enabled only on creating the surface sweep feature by activating the **Sweep as surface** button in the **Sweep** tab.

Merge ends: On selecting the **Merge ends** check box in the **Options** panel, the ends of the sweep feature get aligned with the faces of the existing feature, see Figure 7.36. Note that this check box is not enabled if the sweep feature being created is the base feature of a model.

9. Select the **Merge ends** check box in the **Options** panel to align the ends of the sweep feature with the faces of the existing feature, see Figure 7.36.

10. Click on the green tick-mark button in the **Sweep** tab of the **Ribbon**. A cut-section sweep feature is created by removing the material from the model, see Figure 7.37.

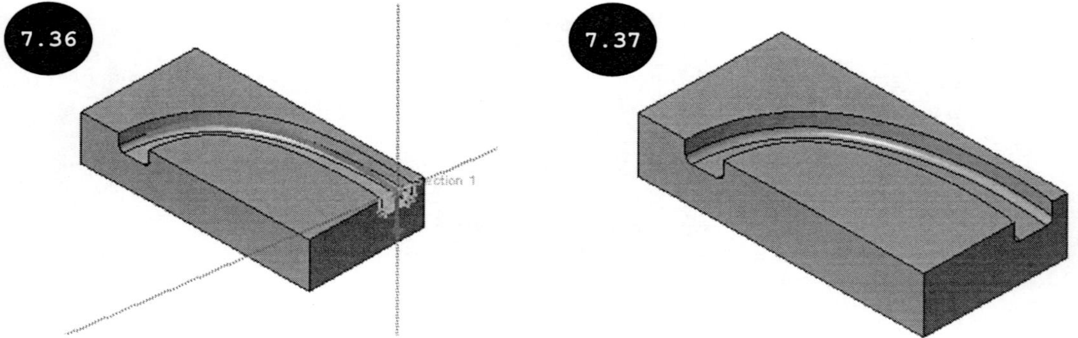

Creating a Helical Sweep feature

In Creo Parametric, you can create a constant or variable pitch helical sweep feature by using the **Helical Sweep** tool, see Figures 7.38 and 7.39. The methods for creating constant and variable pitch helical sweep features are discussed next.

Creating a Helical Sweep Feature with Constant Pitch

1. Create an open linear sketch entity with a centerline in the Sketching environment, see Figure 7.40. Next, exit the Sketching environment.

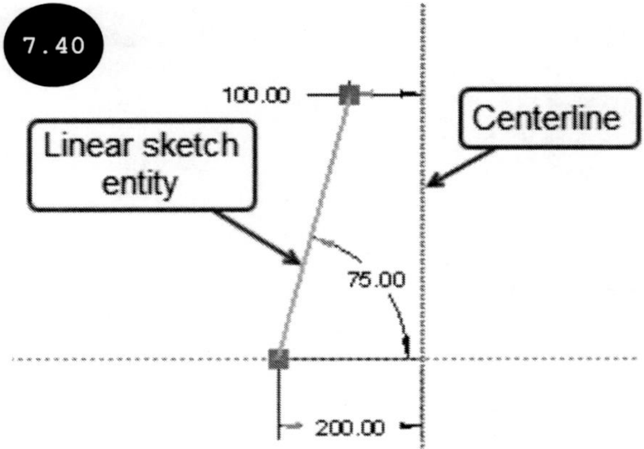

Note: The linear sketch entity is used as a trajectory which defines the shape and height of the helix. The centerline is used as the axis of revolution of the section. You can create a centerline by using the **Centerline** tool of the **Sketching** group in the Sketching environment. Also, the distance between the trajectory and the centerline defines the radius of the helix.

2. Click on the arrow next to the **Sweep** tool in the **Shapes** group of the **Model** tab. A flyout appears, see Figure 7.41.

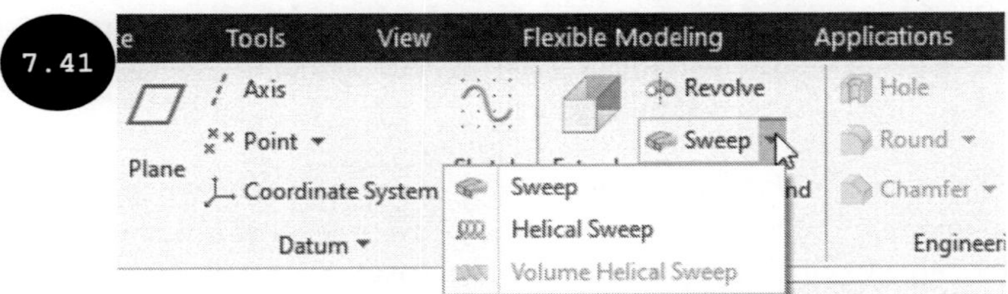

3. Click on the **Helical Sweep** tool in the flyout, see Figure 7.41. The **Helical Sweep** tab appears in the **Ribbon**, see Figure 7.42.

4. Select the linear sketch entity as a trajectory to define the shape and height of the helix, if not selected, by default. An arrow appears on one end of the trajectory which defines the start of the helix, see Figure 7.43. Also, the internal centerline of the sketch is automatically selected as the axis of revolution of the helix.

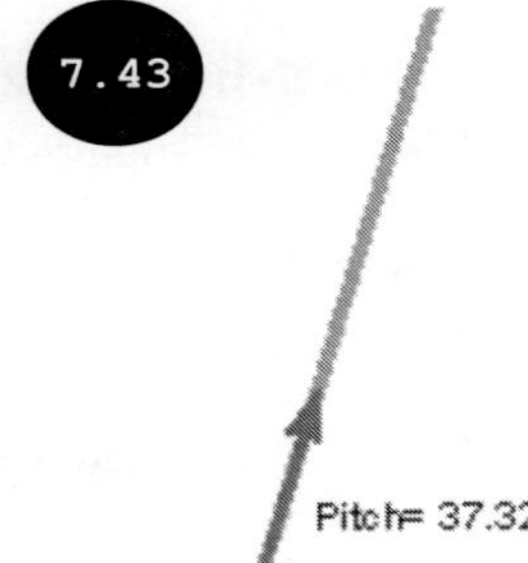

5. Expand the **References** panel of the **Helical Sweep** tab if not expanded by default, see Figure 7.44. The options of the **References** panel are discussed below:

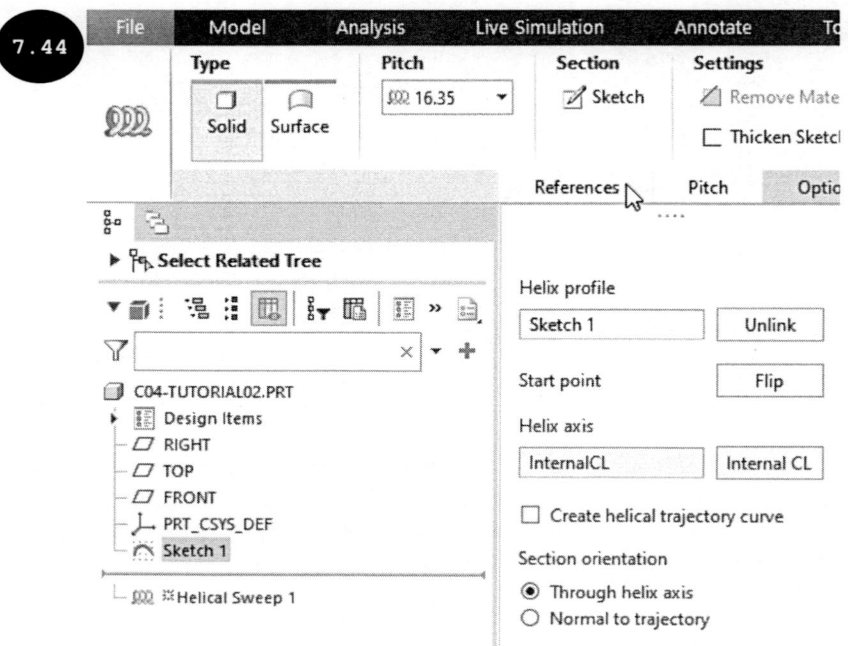

Helix profile: The **Helix profile** field of the **References** panel displays the name of the linear sketch entity that is selected as a trajectory. The **Unlink** button is used for breaking the association between the resultant feature and the sketch (trajectory) that is selected, and creates a copy of the sketch as an internal sketch of the feature.

Flip: The **Flip** button is used for flipping the starting point of the helix from one end of the trajectory to the other. You can also click on the arrow that appears on one end of the trajectory in the graphics area to flip the starting point of the helix.

Helix axis: The **Helix axis** field is used for selecting a centerline as the axis of revolution of the helix. By default, the internal centerline that is created with the sketch of the trajectory gets selected automatically as the axis of revolution.

Create helical trajectory curve: The **Create helical trajectory curve** check box is used for creating a curve from the helical trajectory after the feature has been created. This check box is cleared by default.

Through helix axis: By default, the **Through helix axis** radio button is selected. As a result, the helical sweep is created such that the section plane passes through the axis of revolution.

Normal to trajectory: The **Normal to trajectory** radio button is used for creating a helical sweep such that the section plane is oriented normal to the trajectory.

6. Ensure that a sketch is selected as a trajectory in the **Helix profile** field of the **References** panel.

7. Ensure that the axis of revolution of the helix is defined in the **Helix axis** field.

8. Select the **Through helix axis** radio button in the **References** panel to create a helical sweep feature such that the section plane passes through the axis of revolution.

9. Click on the **Sketch** button in the **Section** area of the **Helical Sweep** tab to create a section of the helical sweep feature. The Sketching environment is invoked and the sketching plane is oriented normal to the viewing direction. Also, two centerlines that are mutually perpendicular to each other appear at the starting point of the trajectory, see Figure 7.45.

10. Create a closed sketch as the section of the helical sweep feature, see Figure 7.46. In this figure, a circle is created as the sketch of the section.

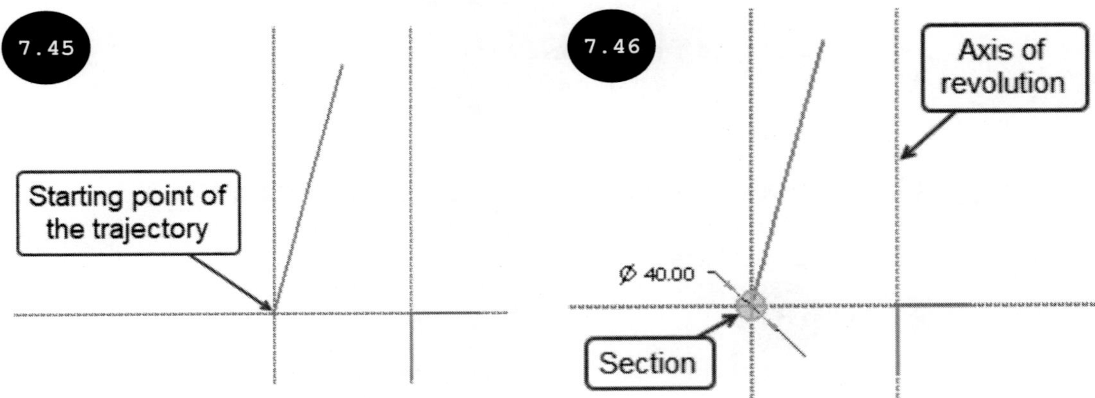

11. Exit the Sketching environment by clicking on the **OK** tool in the **Close** group of the **Sketch** tab. A preview of the helical sweep feature appears in the graphics area such that the shape and height of the feature are defined by the trajectory and the radius of the helix is defined by the distance between the trajectory and the axis of revolution, see Figure 7.47.

12. Enter the pitch value of the helical sweep feature in the **Pitch value** field in the **Pitch** area of the **Helical Sweep** tab, see Figure 7.48. The preview of the sweep feature having constant pitch gets modified in the graphics area.

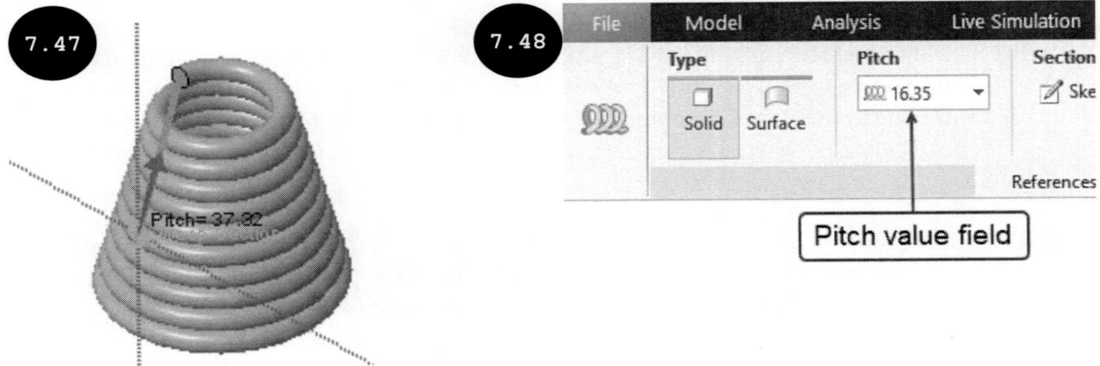

13. Specify the sweep direction from right to left or vice-versa by clicking on the **Left-handed Rule** or **Right-handed Rule** button in the **Options** area of the **Helical Sweep** tab.

14. Click on the green tick-mark button in the **Helical Sweep** tab of the **Ribbon**. A helical sweep feature with constant pitch is created, see Figure 7.49.

7.49

Creating a Helical Sweep Feature with Variable Pitch

1. Create an open linear sketch entity with a centerline in the Sketching environment, see Figure 7.50. Next, exit the Sketching environment.

7.50

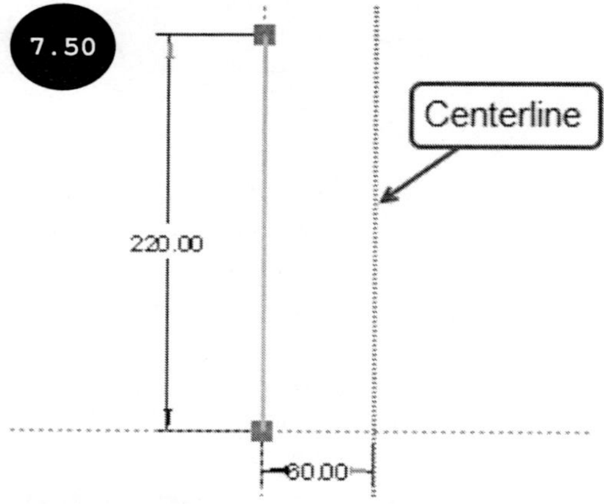

Note: The linear sketch entity is used as a trajectory which defines the shape and height of the helix. The centerline is used as the axis of revolution of the section. You can create a centerline by using the **Centerline** tool of the **Sketching** group in the Sketching environment. The distance between the trajectory and the centerline defines the radius of the helix.

2. Click on the arrow next to the **Sweep** tool in the **Shapes** group and then click on the **Helical Sweep** tool in the flyout that appears, see Figure 7.51. The **Helical Sweep** tab appears in the **Ribbon**, see Figure 7.52. Most of the options in this tab have been discussed earlier.

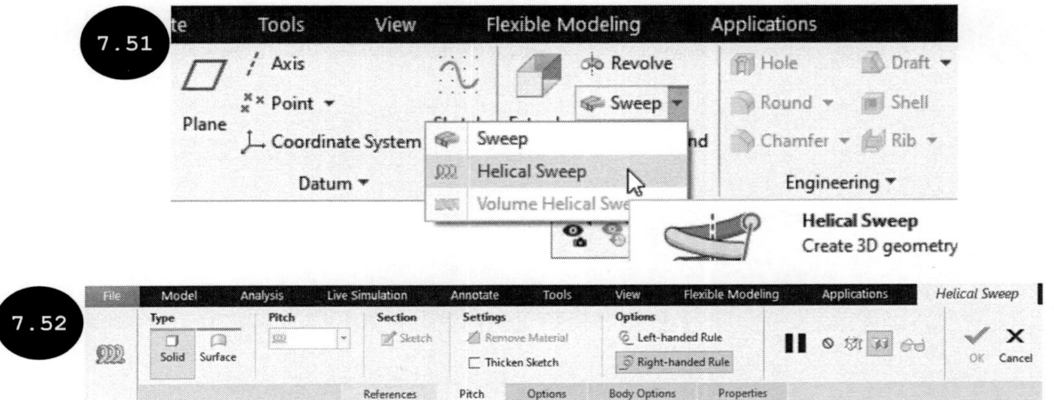

3. Select the linear sketch entity as a trajectory to define the shape and height of the helix, if not selected by default. An arrow appears on one end of the trajectory which defines the start of the helix and the internal centerline of the sketch is automatically selected as the axis of revolution of the helix.

4. Click on the **Sketch** button in the **Section** area of the **Helical Sweep** tab to create a section of the helical sweep feature. The Sketching environment is invoked and the sketching plane is oriented normal to the viewing direction.

5. Create a closed sketch as the section of the helical sweep feature, see Figure 7.53.

6. Exit the Sketching environment by clicking on the **OK** tool in the **Close** group of the **Sketch** tab. A preview of the helical sweep feature with default constant pitch appears, see Figure 7.54.

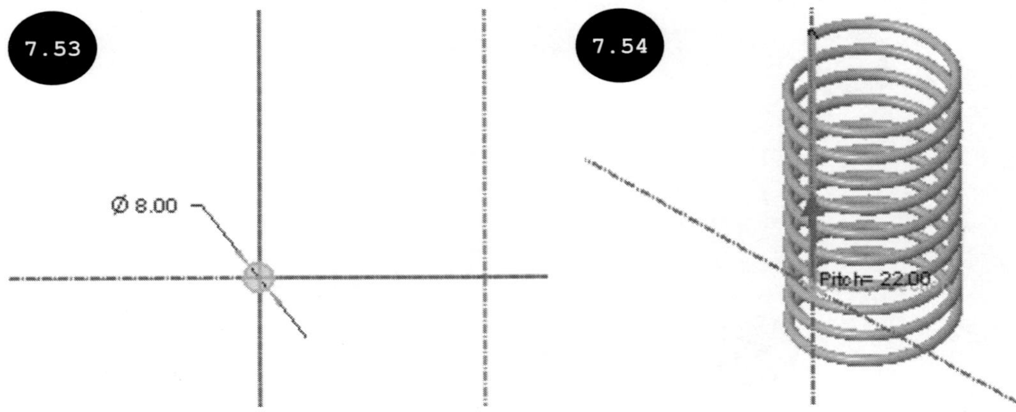

7. Expand the **Pitch** panel of the **Helical Sweep** tab, see Figure 7.55. By default, the pitch value at the start point of the trajectory is specified in the **Pitch** column of the first row (Row 1).

8. Click on the field corresponding to the first row (Row 1) and the **Pitch** column to specify the pitch value at the start point, as required. An edit field appears.

9. Enter the pitch value at the start point in the edit field that appears, see Figure 7.55.

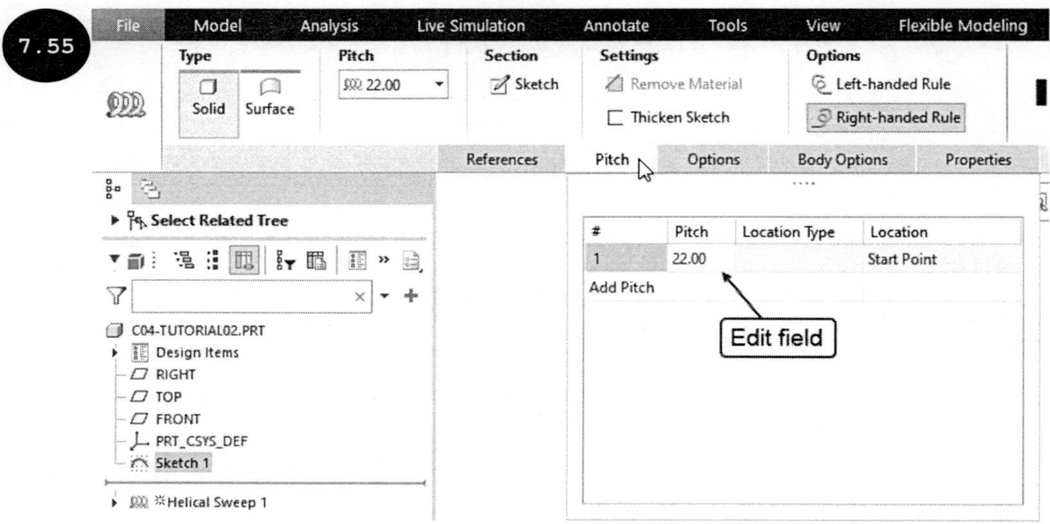

10. Click on the **Add Pitch** option that appears below the first row (Row 1) in the **Pitch** panel. The second row (Row 2) gets added which defines the pitch value at the endpoint of the trajectory, see Figure 7.56.

11. Click on the field corresponding to the second row (Row 2) and **Pitch** column, and then enter the pitch value at the endpoint of the trajectory in the edit field that appears, see Figure 7.56.

12. Click on the **Add Pitch** option to add another row for specifying a different pitch at a different location. The third row (Row 3) gets added in the **Pitch** panel, see Figure 7.56. Also, a location handle appears in the graphics area, see Figure 7.57.

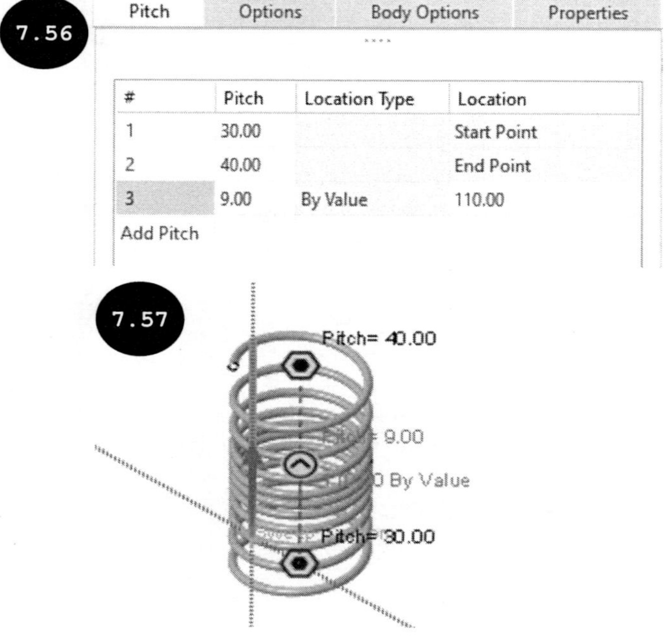

13. Specify the location value, where you want to define a different pitch along the trajectory, in the field corresponding to the third row (Row 3) and the **Location** column. Note that the location value is defined in terms of the total length of the trajectory. This is because the **By Value** option is selected in the **Location Type** drop-down list, by default. The **By Reference** option in this drop-down list is used for defining the pitch location by specifying a vertex or a point as a reference. The **By Ratio** option is used for defining the pitch location in terms of ratio (between 0 and 1) where 0 denotes the start point and 1 denotes the endpoint of trajectory. You can also drag the location handle that appears in the graphics area to define the location dynamically in the graphics area.

14. Specify the pitch value at the specified location in the third row (Row 3) and then press ENTER. A preview of the helical sweep with variable pitch at different locations appears, see Figure 7.58.

7.58

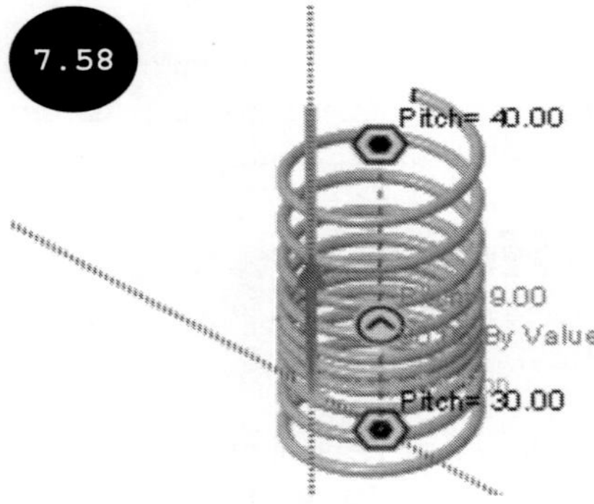

15. Similarly, you can add multiple rows in the **Pitch** panel and specify different pitch values at different locations of the trajectory.

16. Click on the green tick-mark button in the **Helical Sweep** tab of the **Ribbon**. A helical sweep feature with variable pitch is created, see Figure 7.59.

7.59

Creating a Cut Helical Sweep Feature

A cut helical sweep feature is created by removing material from an existing feature, see Figure 7.60. It is generally used for creating threads on a cylindrical feature. You can create a cut helical sweep feature by using the **Helical Sweep** tool. The method for creating the cut helical sweep feature is the same as discussed earlier with the only difference being that you need to activate the **Remove Material** button in the **Helical Sweep** tab to create the feature by removing the material.

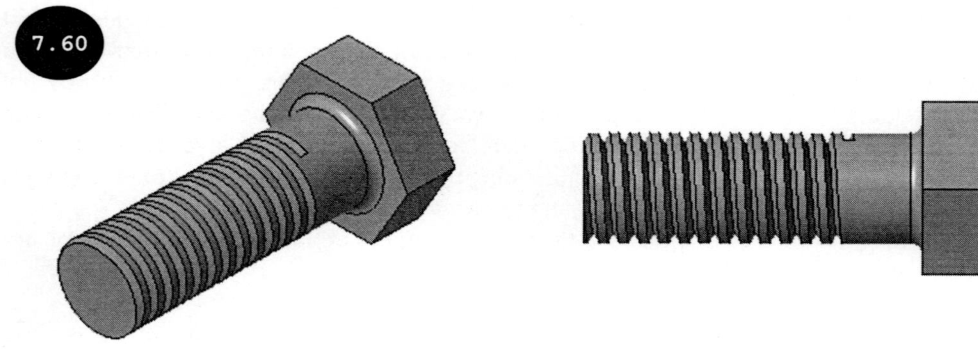
7.60

Tip: You can also create a thin helical sweep feature with uniform wall thickness by using the **Helical Sweep** tool. The method for creating a thin helical sweep feature is same as discussed earlier.

Creating a Volume Helical Sweep feature

A volume helical sweep feature is created by removing material from an existing feature by sweeping a 3D object along a helical trajectory as a cutting tool.

In Creo Parametric, you can create a constant or variable pitch volume helical sweep feature by using the **Volume Helical Sweep** tool. Note that this tool is enabled only after at least one 3D feature is available in the graphics area. The methods for creating constant and variable pitch volume helical sweep features are discussed next.

Creating a Volume Helical Sweep Feature with Constant Pitch

1. Click on the arrow next to the **Sweep** tool in the **Shapes** group of the **Model** tab. A flyout appears, see Figure 7.61.

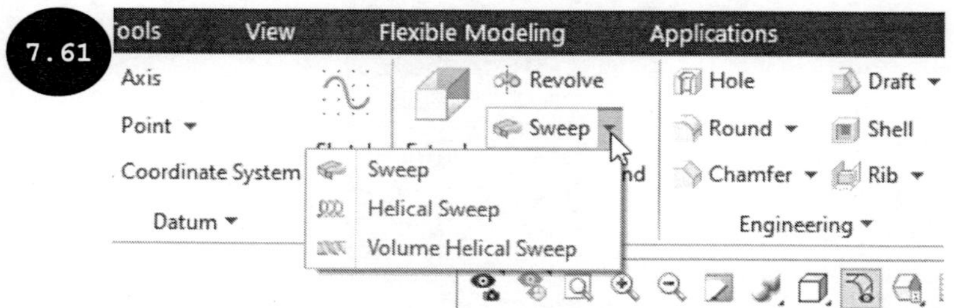

7.61

2. Click on the **Volume Helical Sweep** tool in the flyout, see Figure 7.61. The **Volume Helical Sweep** tab appears in the **Ribbon**, see Figure 7.62.

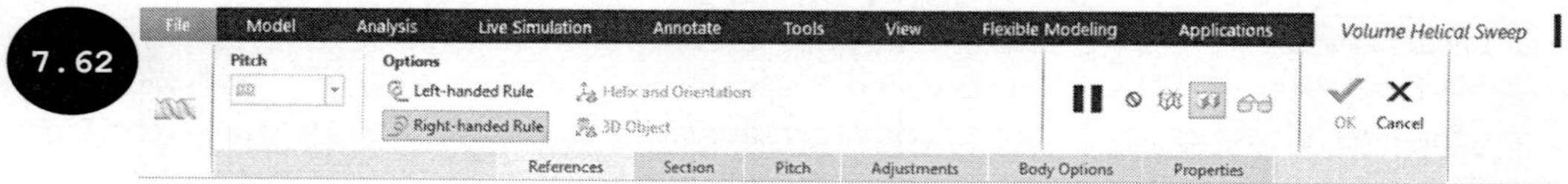

7.62

3. Expand the **References** panel of the **Volume Helical Sweep** tab if not expanded by default, see Figure 7.63. The options of the **References** panel are the same as discussed earlier.

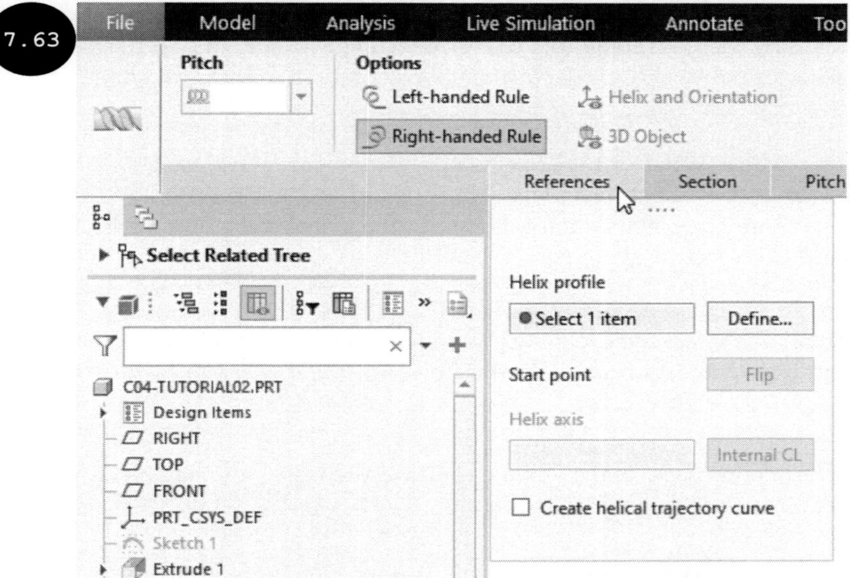

Now, you need to create an open sketch to define the helix trajectory. You can also select an already created sketch as a trajectory.

4. Click on the **Define** button in front of the **Helix profile** field to create an open sketch as a helix trajectory. The **Sketch** dialog box appears.

5. Invoke the Sketching environment by selecting a plane and then create a linear sketch entity with a centerline, see Figure 7.64.

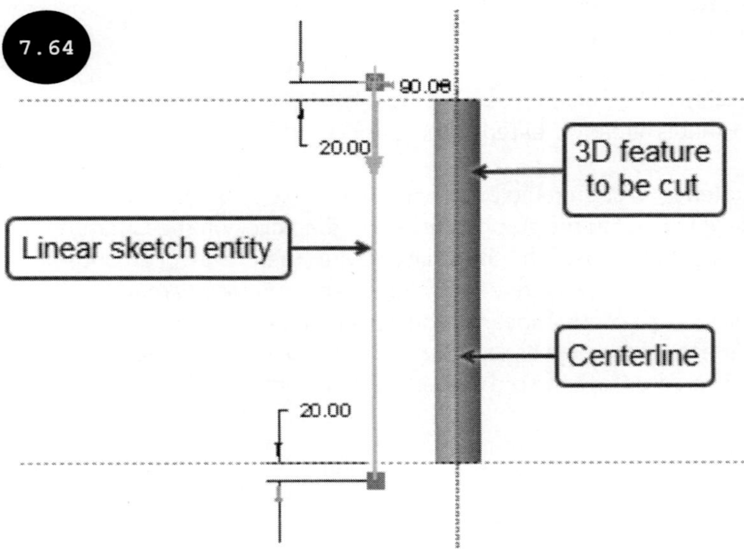

Note: The linear sketch entity is used as a trajectory which defines the shape and height of the helix. The centerline is used as the axis of revolution of the helix. You can create a centerline by using the **Centerline** tool of the **Sketching** group in the Sketching environment. The distance between the trajectory and the centerline defines the radius of the helix.

6. After creating the sketch, exit the Sketching environment. The linear sketch entity of the sketch gets defined as the trajectory and its name appears in the **Helix profile** field of the **References** panel. The centerline of the sketch is defined as the axis of revolution and its name appears in the **Helix axis** field of the panel.

Tip: You can also select the **Create helical trajectory curve** check box in the **References** panel to create a helical curve from the path followed by the tool, if required.

7. Expand the **Section** panel of the **Volume Helical Sweep** tab to define a revolved section of the 3D object for removing the material, see Figure 7.65. The options in this panel are discussed below:

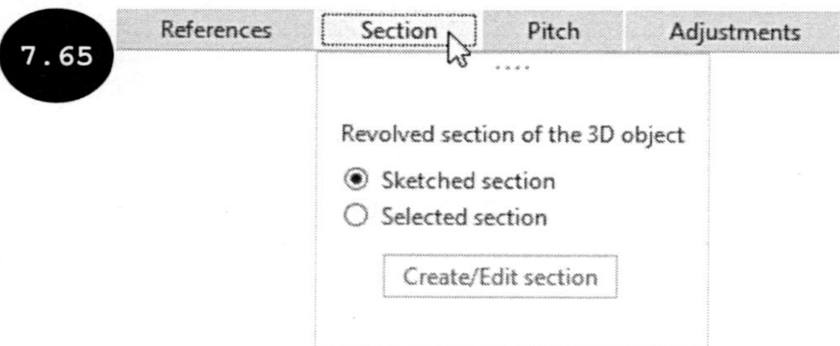

Sketched section: The **Sketched section** radio button is used for creating a revolved section of the 3D object for removing the material.

Selected section: The **Selected section** radio button is used for selecting a revolved section of the 3D object that is already created in the graphics area.

8. Select the **Sketched section** radio button in the expanded **Section** panel for creating a revolved section of the 3D object in the graphics area and then click on the **Create/Edit section** button in the expanded **Section** panel. The Sketching environment is invoked and the sketching plane is oriented normal to the viewing direction. Also, two centerlines green and red, that are mutually perpendicular to each other appear at the starting point of the trajectory, see Figure 7.66. The green centerline that is the Y-axis represents the axis of revolution for the revolved section of the 3D object to be created and the red centerline represents the X-axis.

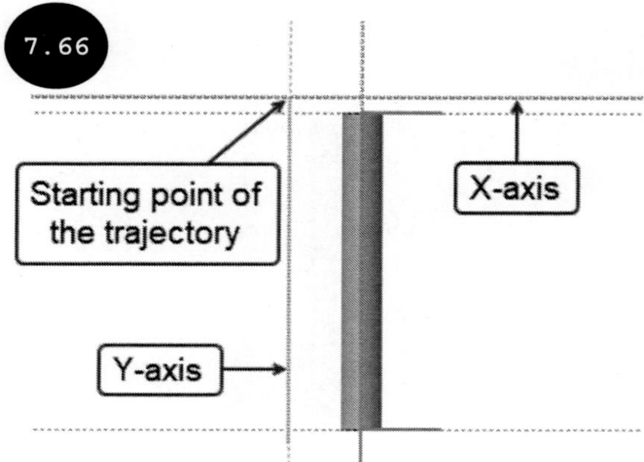

Now, you need to create a revolve section of a 3D object. However, before you create a revolve section, you need to take care of the following points:

- The section must be a closed sketch.
- The section must be on one side of the axis of revolution that is the Y-axis.
- The section must contain a line along the axis of revolution that is the Y-axis.
- The section can only contain line and circular arc entities.
- The section should not have a concave shape (arc entity) and should create a resultant feature with a convex shape.

9. Create a closed sketch as a revolved section of the 3D object, see Figure 7.67. In this figure, a rectangle is created as the sketch of the section.

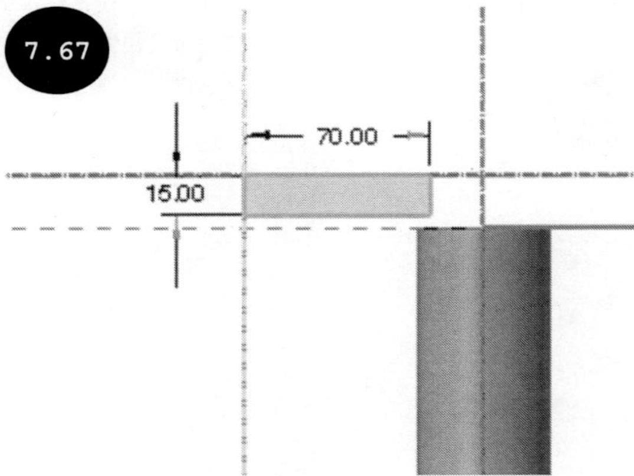

10. Exit the Sketching environment by clicking on the **OK** tool in the **Close** group of the **Sketch** tab. A preview of the volume helical sweep feature appears in the graphics area such that the shape and height of the feature are defined by the trajectory and the radius of the helix is defined by the distance between the trajectory and the axis of revolution, see Figure 7.68.

7.68

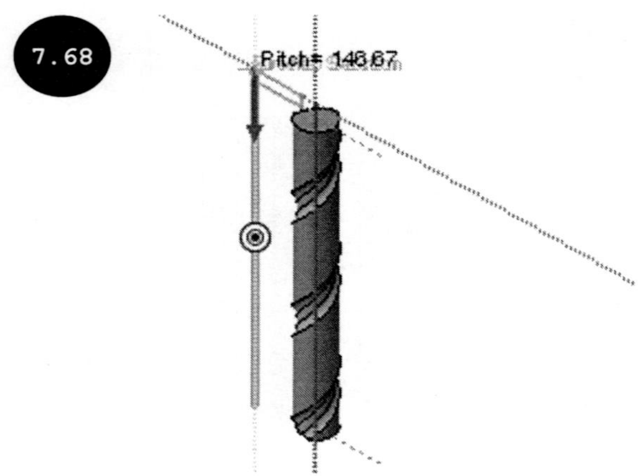

11. Enter the pitch value of the volume helical sweep feature in the **Pitch value** field in the **Pitch** area of the **Volume Helical Sweep** tab, see Figure 7.69. The preview of the sweep feature having constant pitch gets modified in the graphics area.

7.69

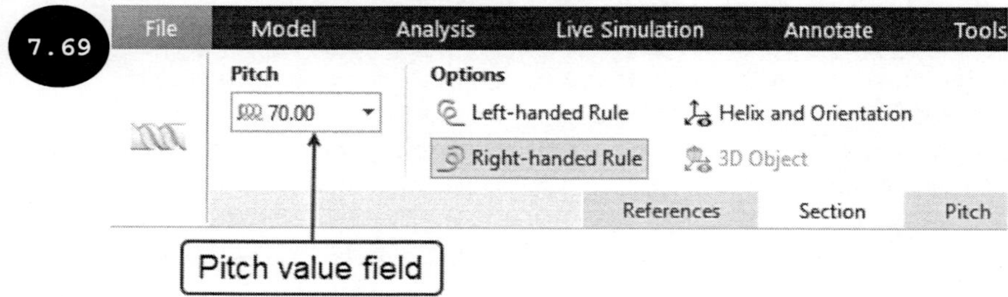

12. Click on the **Helix and Orientation** button in the **Options** area of the **Volume Helical Sweep** tab to show the helix and the orientation of the 3D object, see Figure 7.70.

7.70

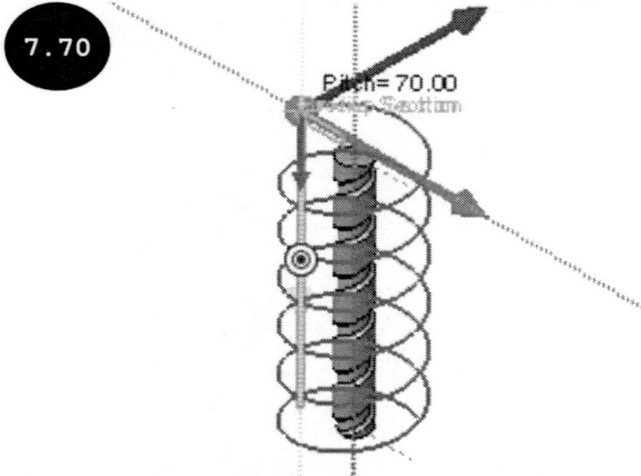

13. Click on the **3D Object** button in the **Options** area of the **Volume Helical Sweep** tab to show the 3D object formed by revolving the sketched section, see Figure 7.71. Note that this button is enabled after enabling the **Helix and Orientation** button.

14. Specify the sweep direction from right to left or vice-versa by clicking on the **Left-handed Rule** or **Right-handed Rule** button in the **Options** area of the **Volume Helical Sweep** tab. A preview of the sweep feature and the 3D tool appears in the graphics area, see Figure 7.71.

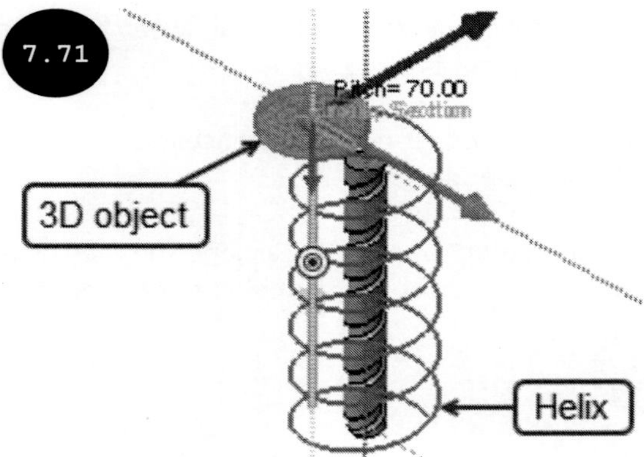

15. Click on the green tick-mark button in the **Volume Helical Sweep** tab of the **Ribbon**. A volume helical sweep feature with constant pitch is created, see Figure 7.72.

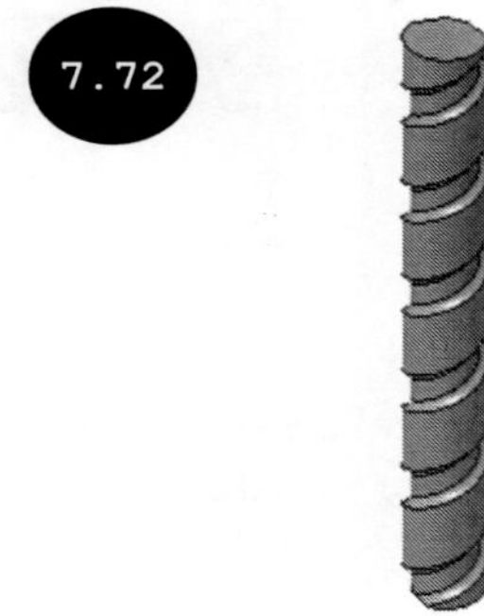

Creating a Volume Helical Sweep Feature with Variable Pitch

1. Click on the arrow next to the **Sweep** tool in the **Shapes** group of the **Model** tab. A flyout appears, see Figure 7.73.

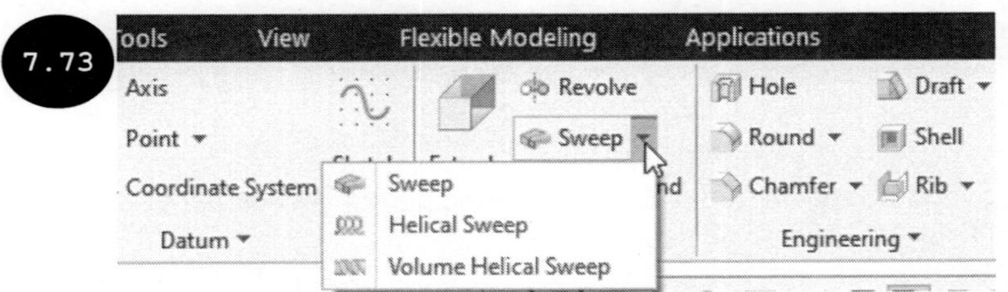

2. Click on the **Volume Helical Sweep** tool in the flyout, see Figure 7.73. The **Volume Helical Sweep** tab appears in the **Ribbon**, see Figure 7.74.

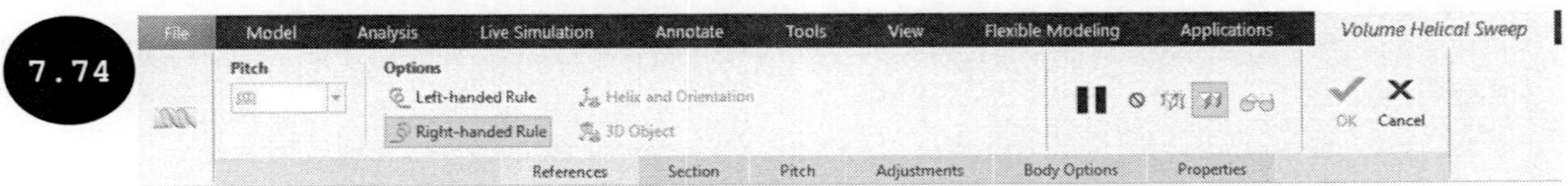

3. Expand the **References** panel of the **Volume Helical Sweep** tab, if not expanded by default. The options in this panel are the same as discussed earlier.

4. Click on the **Define** button in the expanded **References** panel to create an open sketch as a helix trajectory. The **Sketch** dialog box appears.

5. Invoke the Sketching environment by selecting a plane and then create a linear sketch entity with a centerline, see Figure 7.75. Next, exit the Sketching environment.

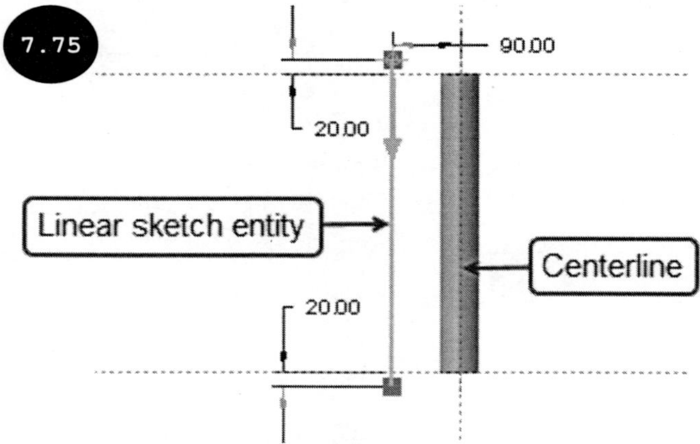

6. Expand the **Section** panel of the **Volume Helical Sweep** tab to define a revolved section of the 3D object for removing the material, see Figure 7.76. The options in this panel are the same as discussed earlier.

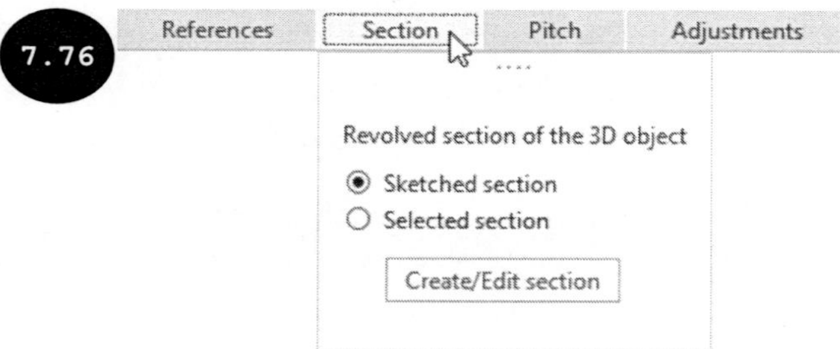

7. Select the **Sketched section** radio button in the expanded **Section** panel to create a section of the revolved 3D object in the graphics area.

8. Click on the **Create/Edit section** button in the expanded **Section** panel. The Sketching environment is invoked and the sketching plane is oriented normal to the viewing direction.

9. Create a closed sketch as a section of the volume helical sweep feature such that it fulfills all the section requirements, as discussed earlier, see Figure 7.77. In this figure, a sketch is created using lines.

10. Exit the Sketching environment by clicking on the **OK** tool in the **Close** group of the **Sketch** tab. A preview of the helical sweep feature with default constant pitch appears, see Figure 7.78.

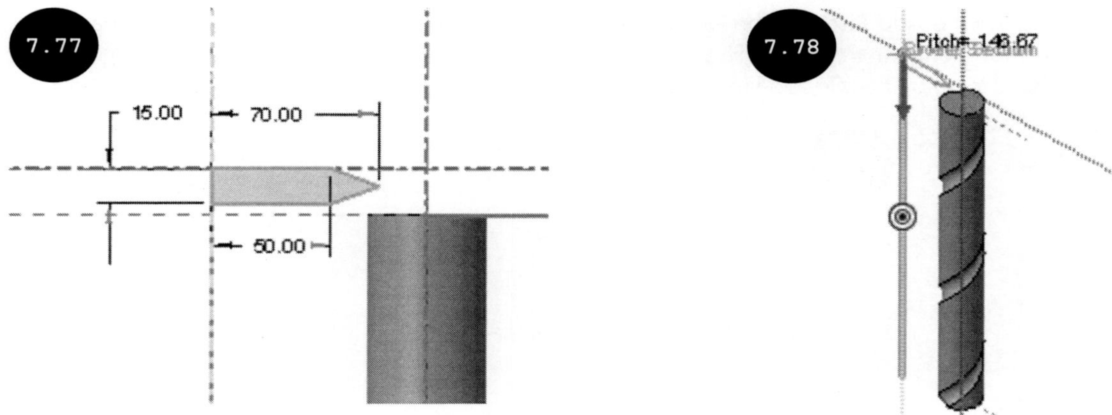

Now, you need to define a variable pitch for the feature.

11. Expand the **Pitch** panel of the **Volume Helical Sweep** tab, see Figure 7.79. By default, the pitch value at the start point of the trajectory is specified in the **Pitch** column of the first row (Row 1).

12. Click on the field corresponding to the first row (Row 1) and the **Pitch** column to specify the pitch value at the start point, as required. An edit field appears.

13. Enter the pitch value at the start point in the edit field that appears, see Figure 7.79.

7.79

14. Click on the **Add Pitch** option that appears below the first row (Row 1) in the **Pitch** panel. The second row (Row 2) gets added which defines the pitch value at the endpoint of the trajectory.

15. Click on the field corresponding to the second row (Row 2) and **Pitch** column and then enter the pitch value at the endpoint of the trajectory in the edit field that appears, see Figure 7.80.

16. Click on the **Add Pitch** option to add another row for specifying a different pitch at a particular location along the trajectory. The third row (Row 3) gets added to the **Pitch** panel, see Figure 7.80. Also, a location handle appears in the graphics area, see Figure 7.81.

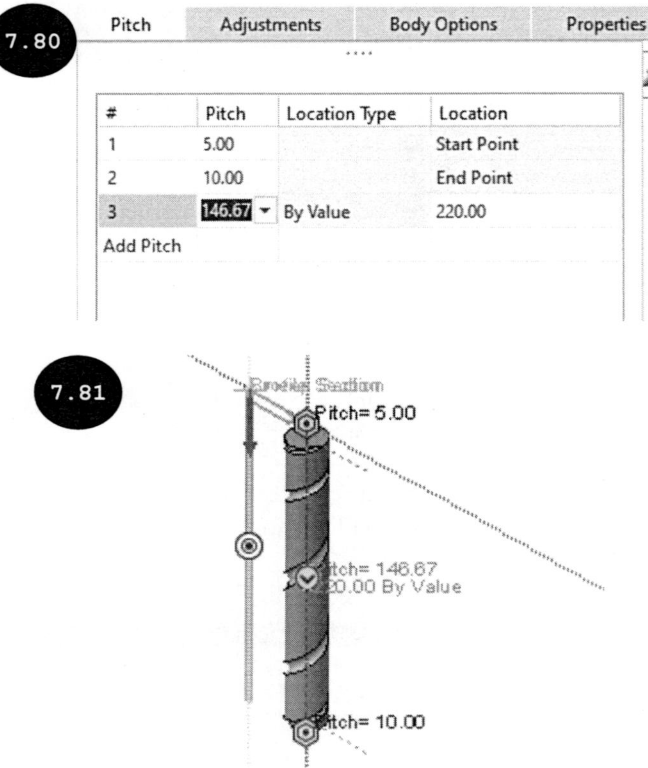

17. Specify the location value, where you want to define a different pitch along the trajectory, in the field corresponding to the third row (Row 3) and the **Location** column. Note that the location value is defined in terms of the total length of the trajectory. This is because the **By Value** option is selected in the **Location Type** drop-down list, by default. The **By Reference** option in this drop-down list is used for defining the pitch location by specifying a vertex or a point as a reference. The **By Ratio** option is used for defining the pitch location in terms of ratio (between 0 and 1) where 0 denotes the start point and 1 denotes the endpoint of the trajectory. You can also drag the location handle that appears in the graphics area to define the location dynamically in the graphics area.

18. Specify the pitch value at the specified location in the third row (Row 3) and then press ENTER. A preview of the helical sweep with variable pitch at different locations appears, see Figure 7.82.

19. Similarly, you can add multiple rows in the **Pitch** panel and specify different pitch values at different locations along the trajectory.

20. Click on the green tick-mark button in the **Volume Helical Sweep** tab of the **Ribbon**. A volume helical sweep feature with variable pitch is created, see Figure 7.83.

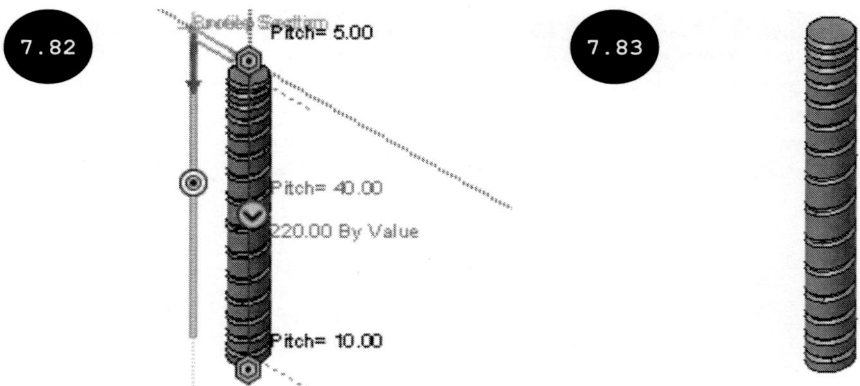

Creating a Blend feature

A blend feature is created by blending two or more than two sections such that the cross-sectional shape of the blend feature transits from one section to another. Figure 7.84 shows two dissimilar sections created on different planes having an offset distance between each other. Figure 7.85 shows the resultant blend feature created. The method for creating a blend feature is discussed below:

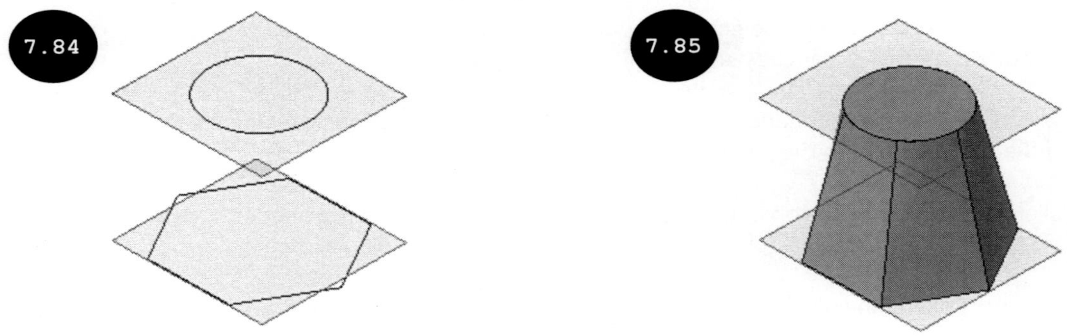

Note: To create a blend feature in Creo Parametric, the number of entities in each section should be the same. In Figure 7.84, the polygonal section is composed of 6 entities. As a result, to create a blend feature as shown in Figure 7.85, the circular section is divided into 6 entities by using the **Divide** tool of the **Editing** group in the Sketching environment.

1. Expand the **Shapes** group of the **Model** tab by clicking on the arrow (see Figure 7.86), and then click on the **Blend** tool. The **Blend** tab appears in the **Ribbon** with the **Sections** panel expanded, see Figure 7.87. The options in this panel are discussed below:

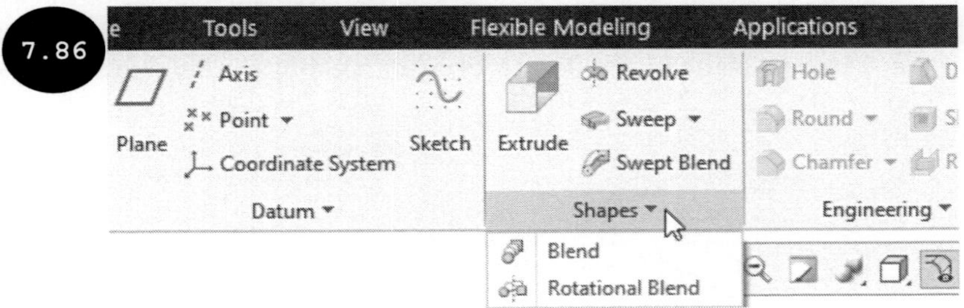

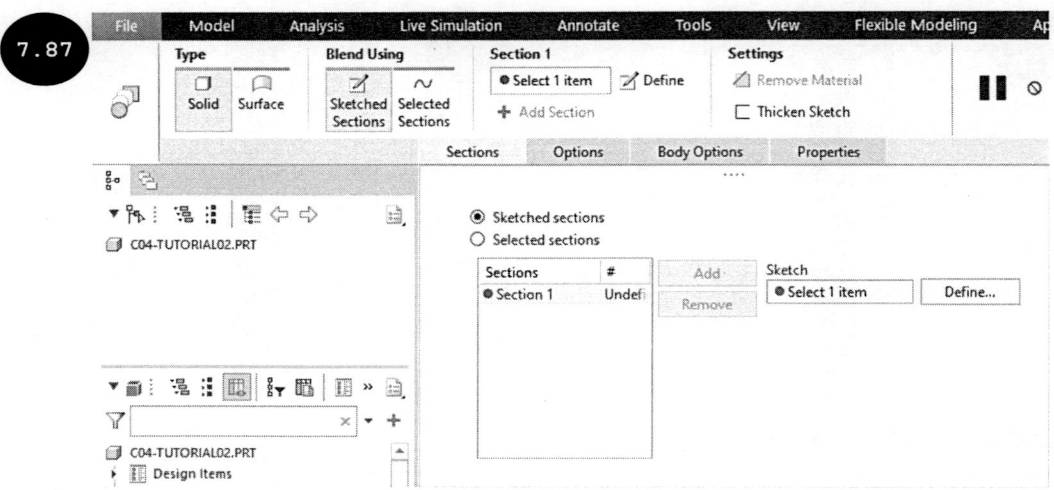

7.87

Sketched sections: The **Sketched sections** radio button is used for creating sections of the blend feature.

Selected sections: The **Selected sections** radio button is used for selecting sections of the blend feature that are already created in the graphics area.

2. Select the **Sketched sections** radio button in the expanded **Sections** panel to create the sections of the blend feature in the graphics area, see Figure 7.87.

3. Click on the **Define** button in the expanded **Sections** panel or in the **Section 1** area of the **Blend** tab to define the sketching plane for creating the first section. The **Sketch** dialog box appears.

4. Select the sketching plane and then click on the **Sketch** button in the dialog box. The Sketching environment is invoked and the sketching plane is oriented normal to the viewing direction.

5. Create the sketch of the first section, see Figure 7.88. Note that, an arrow appears on one of the vertices of the sketch which indicates the start point of the section. In Creo Parametric, you need to ensure that the start points of all sections are in the same direction to avoid twisting in the resultant blend feature.

6. After creating the first section, exit the Sketching environment.

7. Change the orientation of the sketch to the standard orientation. Notice that an offset handle appears in the graphics area (see Figure 7.89) and an **Offset** field appears in the **Blend** tab, see Figure 7.90. Also, you are prompted to specify the offset distance to create a new datum plane, parallel to the sketching plane of the first section, for creating the second section of the blend feature.

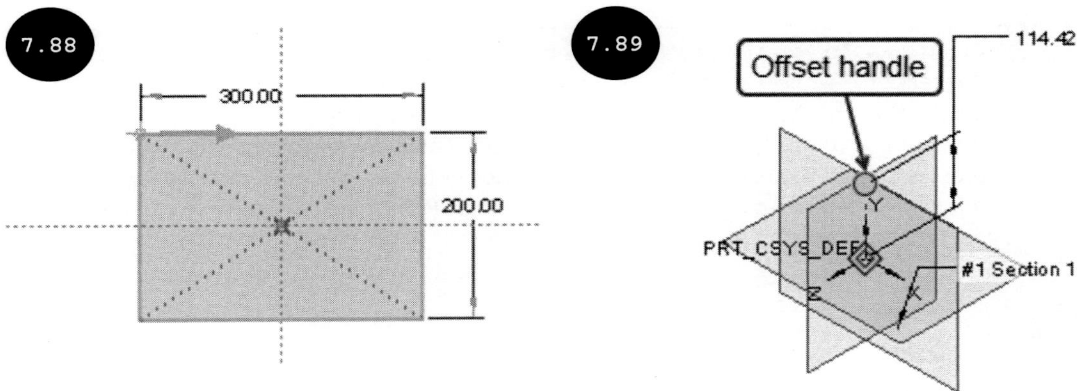

8. Expand the **Sections** panel of the **Blend** tab, see Figure 7.90. Notice that section 1 is created and the number of entities in section 1 are identified, see Figure 7.90.

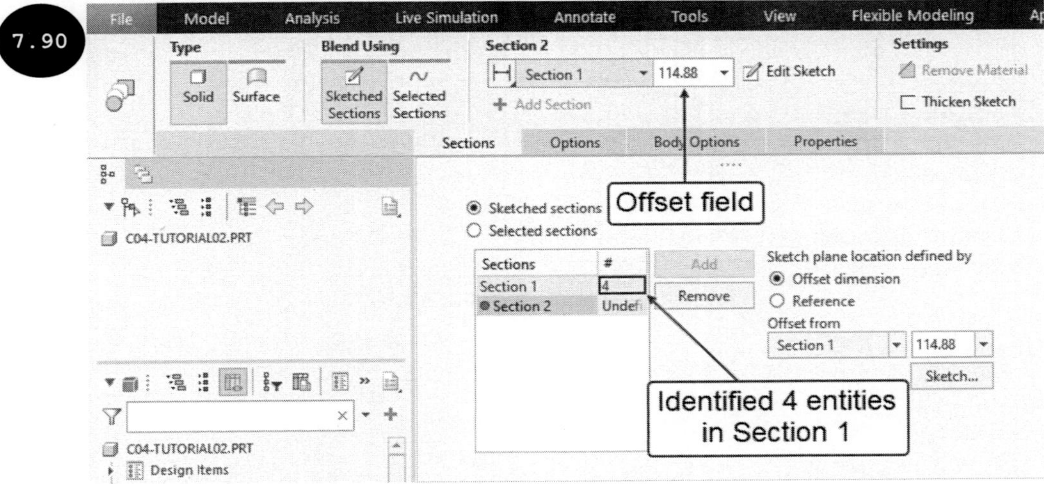

9. Enter offset distance in the **Offset** field to create a new datum plane for creating the second section of the blend feature.

10. Click on the **Sketch** button in the expanded **Sections** panel. A datum plane is created at the specified offset distance from the first section and becomes the sketching plane for creating the second section of the blend feature.

11. Create a sketch of the second section, see Figure 7.91. In this figure, a circle is created as the sketch of the second section. As mentioned earlier, to create a blend feature, the number of entities in each section should be the same. Therefore, the circle shown in Figure 7.91 has been divided into four entities by using the **Divide** tool of the **Editing** group in the **Sketch** tab.

Note: An arrow appears on one of the points of the section indicating that it is the start point of the section, see Figure 7.91. To avoid twisting in the resultant blend feature, you need to ensure that the start points of all sections are in the same direction. To change the start point of a section, click on a point of the section to be defined as the start point and then press and hold the right mouse button. A shortcut menu appears, refer to Figure 7.92. In this shortcut menu, click on **Feature Tools > Start Point**. The selected point of the section becomes the start point.

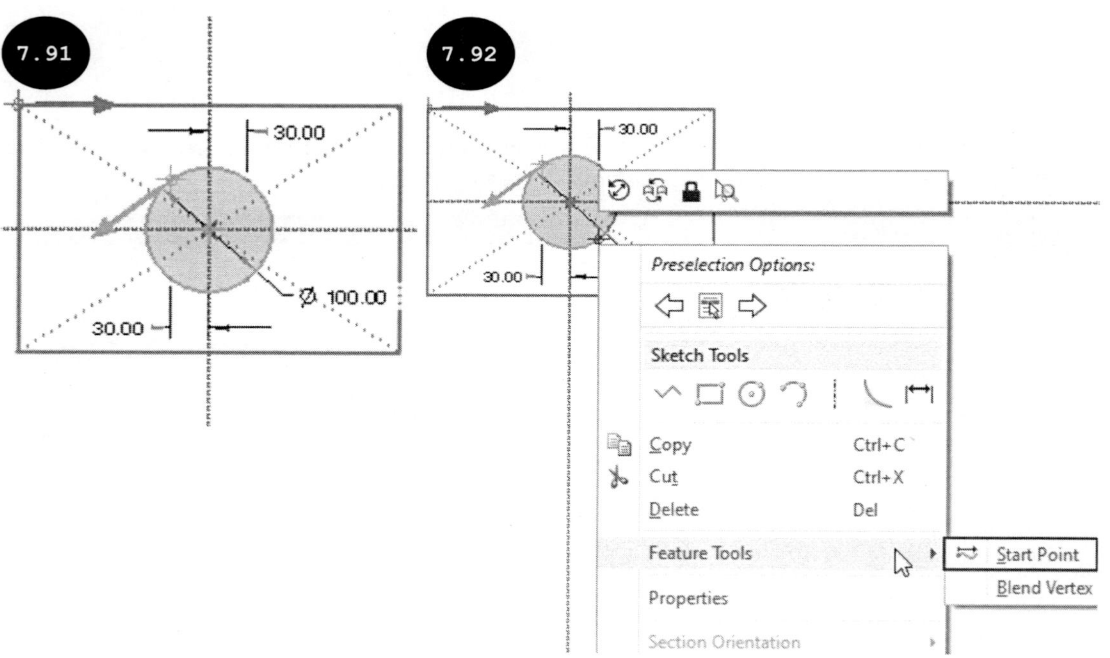

12. After creating the second section, exit the Sketching environment and then change the orientation of the model to standard orientation. The preview of the blend feature appears in the graphics area, see Figure 7.93.

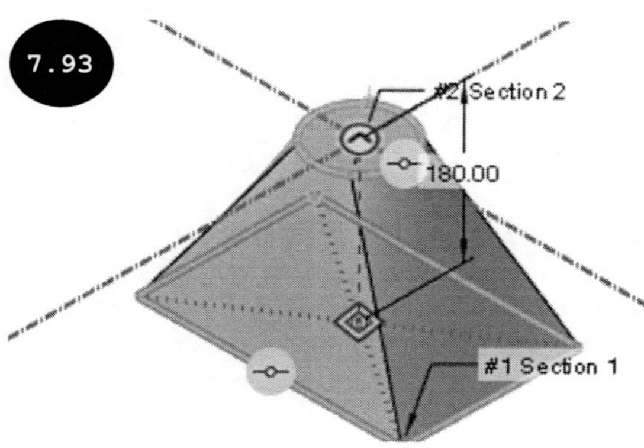

13. Expand the **Sections** panel of the **Blend** tab (see Figure 7.94), and then click on the **Add** button to create the third section of the blend feature. Alternatively, click on the **Add Section** button in the **Section 2** area of the **Blend** tab. **Section 3** is added to the section list of the **Sections** panel (see Figure 7.95), and an offset handle appears in the graphics area.

7.94

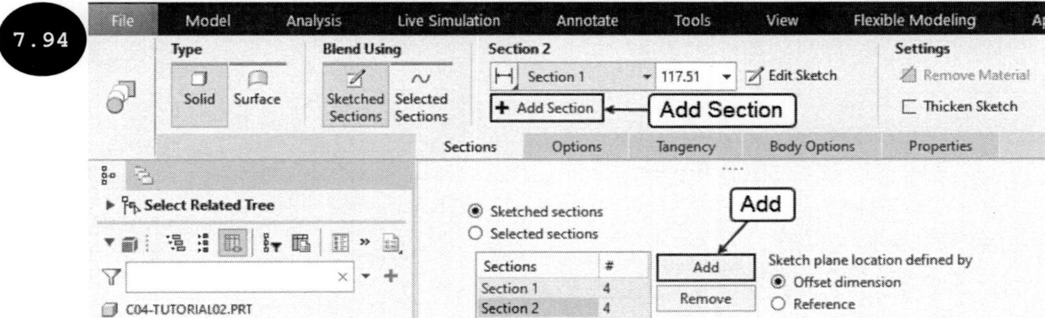

14. Select the **Section 1** or **Section 2** option in the **Offset from** drop-down list of the expanded **Sections** panel to measure the offset distance for creating a new datum plane, see Figure 7.95. In this figure, **Section 2** is selected in the **Offset from** drop-down list.

15. Enter the offset distance in the **Offset** field of the expanded **Sections** panel to create a new datum plane for creating the third section of the blend feature, see Figure 7.95.

7.95

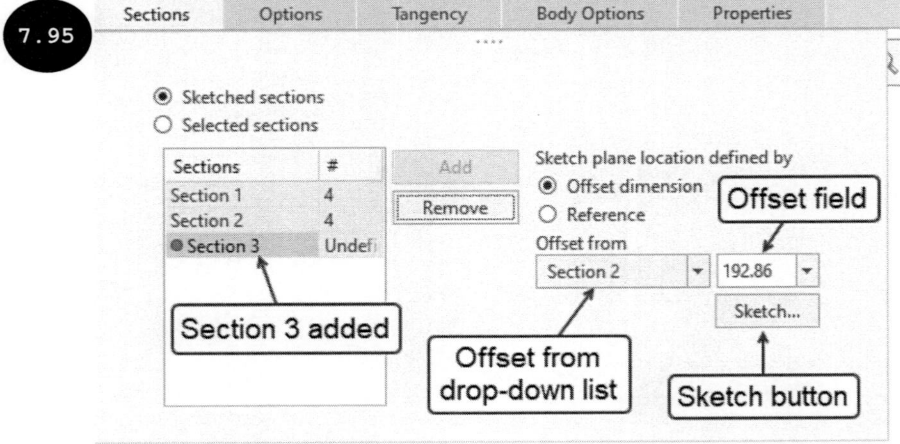

16. Click on the **Sketch** button in the expanded **Sections** panel. A datum plane at the specified offset distance from the selected section is created and becomes the sketching plane for creating the third section of the blend feature.

17. Create the sketch of the third section, see Figure 7.96. In this figure, a rectangle is created as the sketch of the third section. As discussed earlier, ensure that the start points of all sections are in the same direction to avoid twisting in the resultant blend feature.

18. Exit the Sketching environment and then change the orientation of the model to standard orientation. A preview of the blend feature appears in the graphics area, see Figure 7.97. You can create multiple sections one by one to create a blend feature in a similar manner.

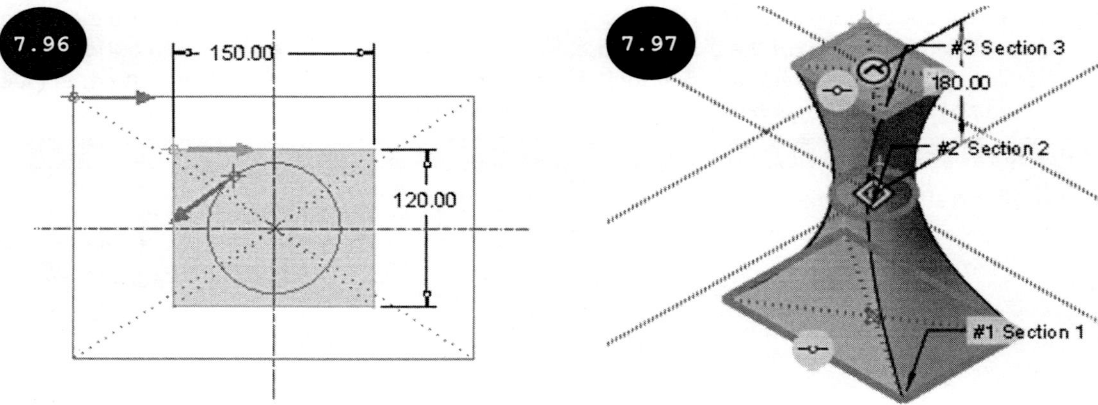

19. Expand the **Options** panel of the **Blend** tab (see Figure 7.98), and then either select the **Straight** or **Smooth** radio button. The **Straight** radio button is used for creating a blend feature with a straight transition from one section to another, see Figure 7.99. The **Smooth** radio button is used for creating a blend feature with smooth transition from one section to another, see Figure 7.100.

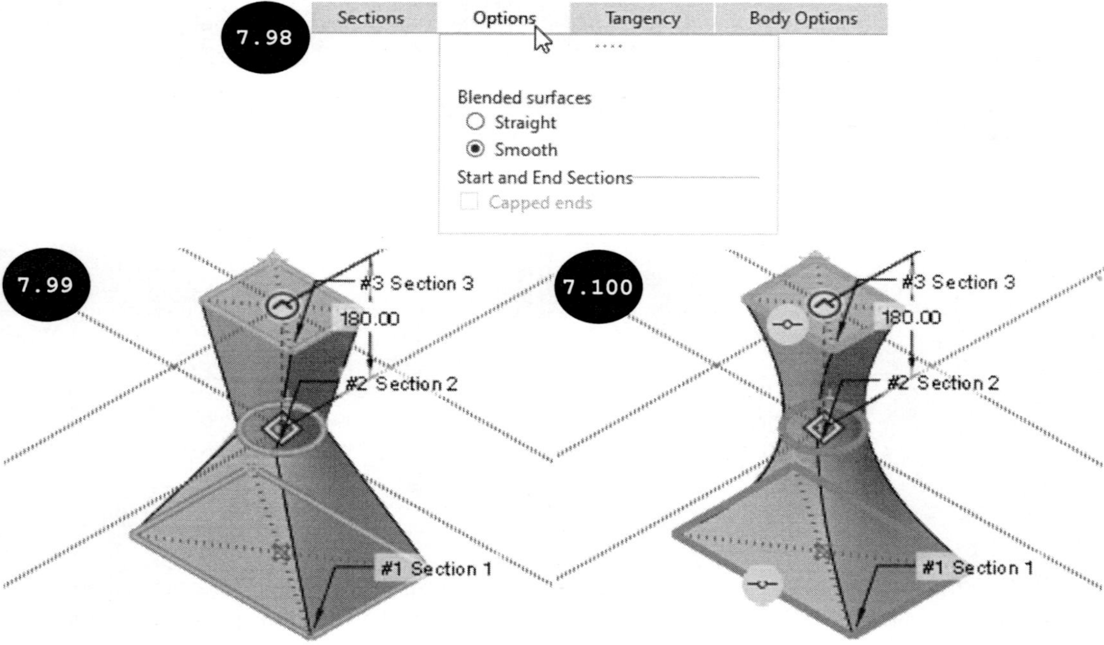

20. Click on the green tick-mark button in the **Blend** tab of the **Ribbon**. The blend feature is created, see Figure 7.101.

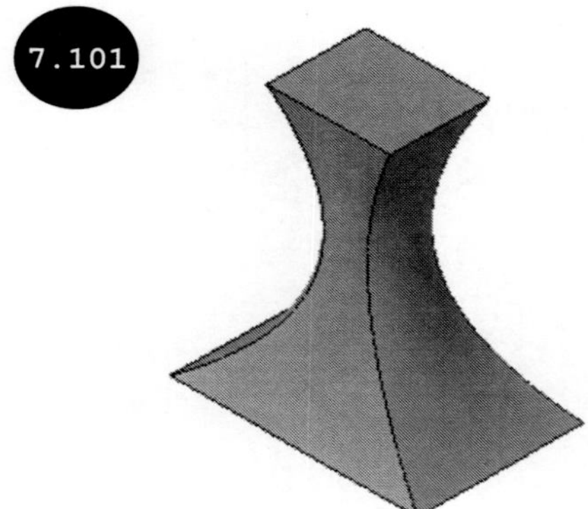

Note: You can create a thin blend feature with uniform wall thickness by using the **Thicken Sketch** button of the **Blend** tab. You can also create a cut blend feature by removing a material from an existing feature of the model using the **Remove Material** button of the **Blend** tab. The methods for creating a thin and a cut blend feature are same as discussed earlier.

Creating a Swept Blend feature

A swept blend feature is a combination of sweep and blend features in which a trajectory is created to guide the cross-sectional shape of the feature while transiting from one section to another, see Figures 7.102 and 7.103. Figure 7.102 shows a trajectory and two sections. Figure 7.103 shows the resultant swept blend feature. You can create a swept blend feature by using the **Swept Blend** tool. Note that to create a swept blend feature, you need to create a trajectory before invoking the **Swept Blend** tool. However, the sections can be created before or after invoking the tool. The method for creating a swept blend feature is discussed below:

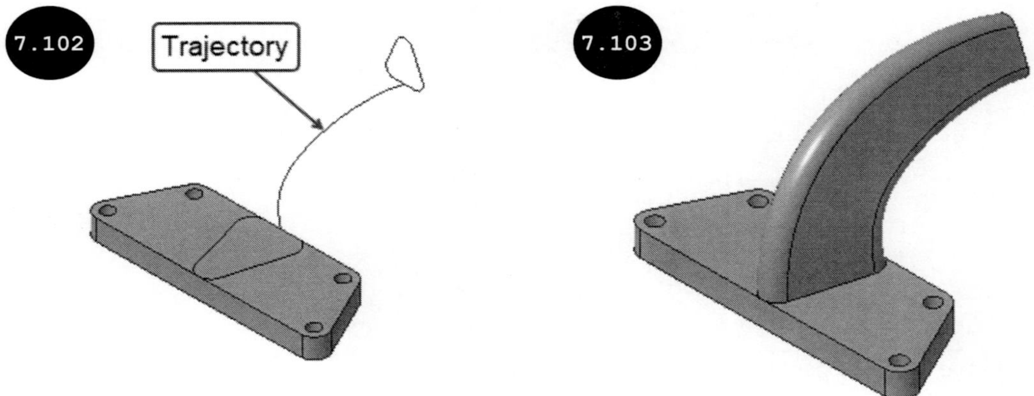

1. Create an open or closed sketch as a trajectory in the Sketching environment, see Figure 7.104. After creating the trajectory, exit the Sketching environment.

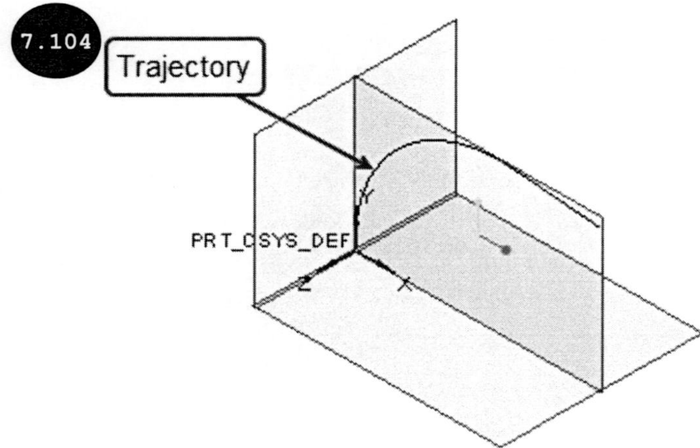

2. Select the trajectory in the graphics area and then click on the **Swept Blend** tool in the **Shapes** group of the **Model** tab, see Figure 7.105. The **Swept Blend** tab appears in the **Ribbon**. Also, an arrow appears in the graphics area representing the start point of the trajectory, see Figure 7.106. You can flip the start point to the other end of the trajectory by clicking on the arrow that appears in the graphics area.

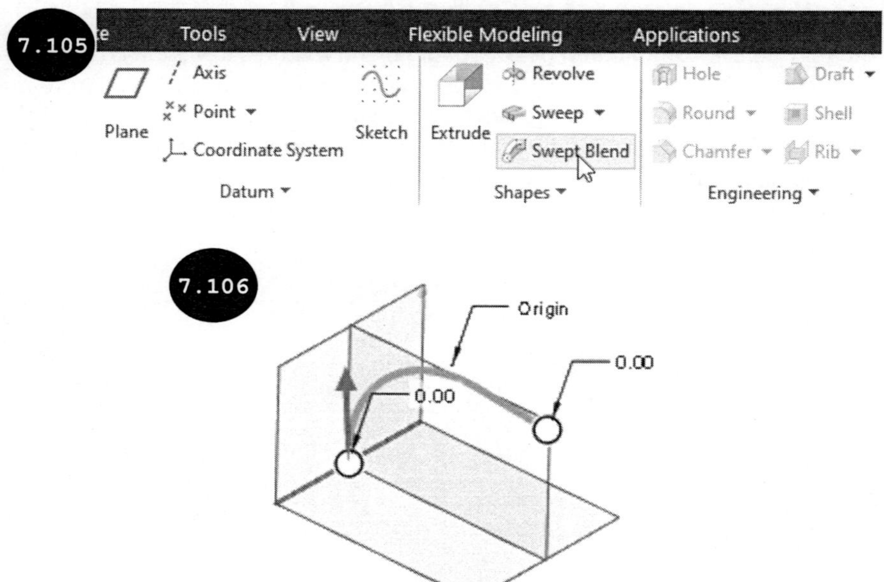

3. Expand the **Sections** panel of the **Swept Blend** tab, see Figure 7.107. Most of the options of the expanded **Sections** panel are the same as discussed earlier.

7.107

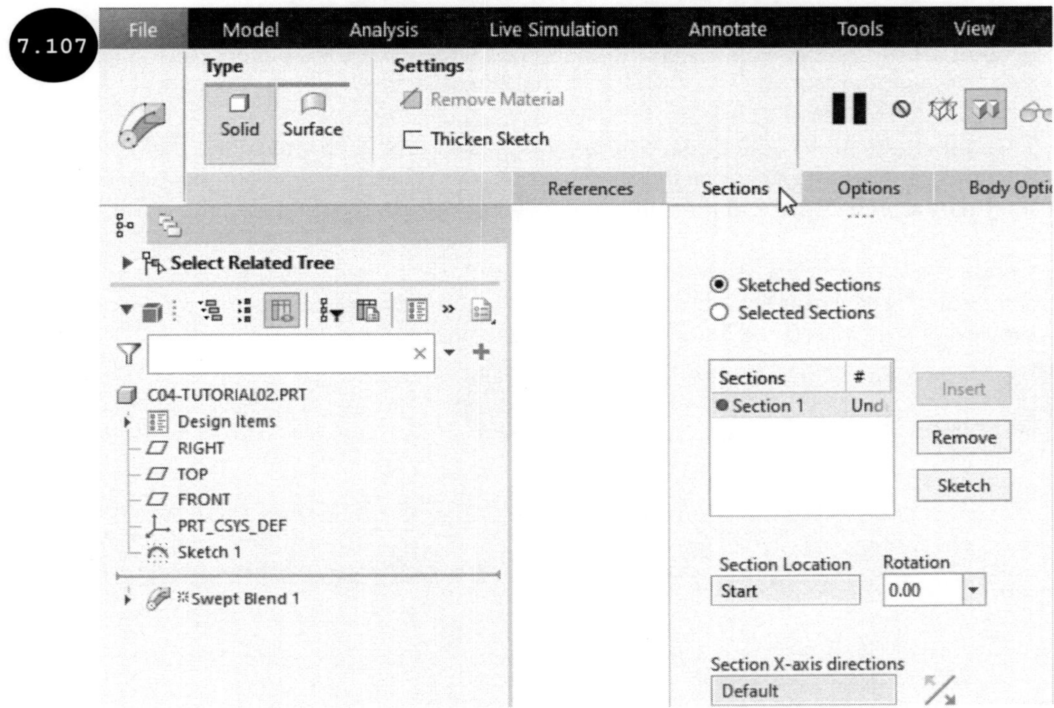

Tip: If the sections of the swept blend feature are already created in the graphics area then select the **Selected Sections** radio button in the expanded **Sections** panel. Next, select the first section of the blend feature in the graphics area. To select the second section of the feature, click on the **Insert** button in the expanded **Sections** panel and then select the second section of the feature. Similarly, you can select multiple sections to create a swept blend feature. As discussed, all sections should have the same number of entities.

4. Ensure that the **Sketched Sections** radio button is selected in the expanded **Sections** panel to create the sections of the swept blend feature.

   Section Location: The **Section Location** field of the expanded Sections panel displays the location for creating the section along the trajectory. The display of **Start** in this field indicates that the section will be created at the start point of the trajectory. Similarly, the display of **End** indicates that the section will be created at the endpoint of the trajectory.

5. Click on the **Sketch** button in the expanded **Sections** panel. The Sketching environment is invoked and an imaginary sketching plane normal to the start point of the trajectory is oriented normal to the viewing direction.

6. Create the sketch of the first section, see Figure 7.108. Next, exit the Sketching environment.

7. Click on the **Insert** button in the expanded **Sections** panel. The second section is added to the section list of the expanded **Sections** panel. **End** appears in the **Section Location** field which indicates that the second section will be created on the endpoint of the trajectory.

8. Ensure that the newly added section (**Section 2**) is selected in the section list of the expanded **Sections** panel and then click on the **Sketch** button. The Sketching environment is invoked and an imaginary sketching plane at the end of the trajectory is oriented normal to the viewing direction.

9. Create the sketch of the second section at the end of the trajectory, see Figure 7.109. Next, exit the Sketching environment and change the orientation of the model to standard orientation. The preview of the swept blend feature appears, see Figure 7.110.

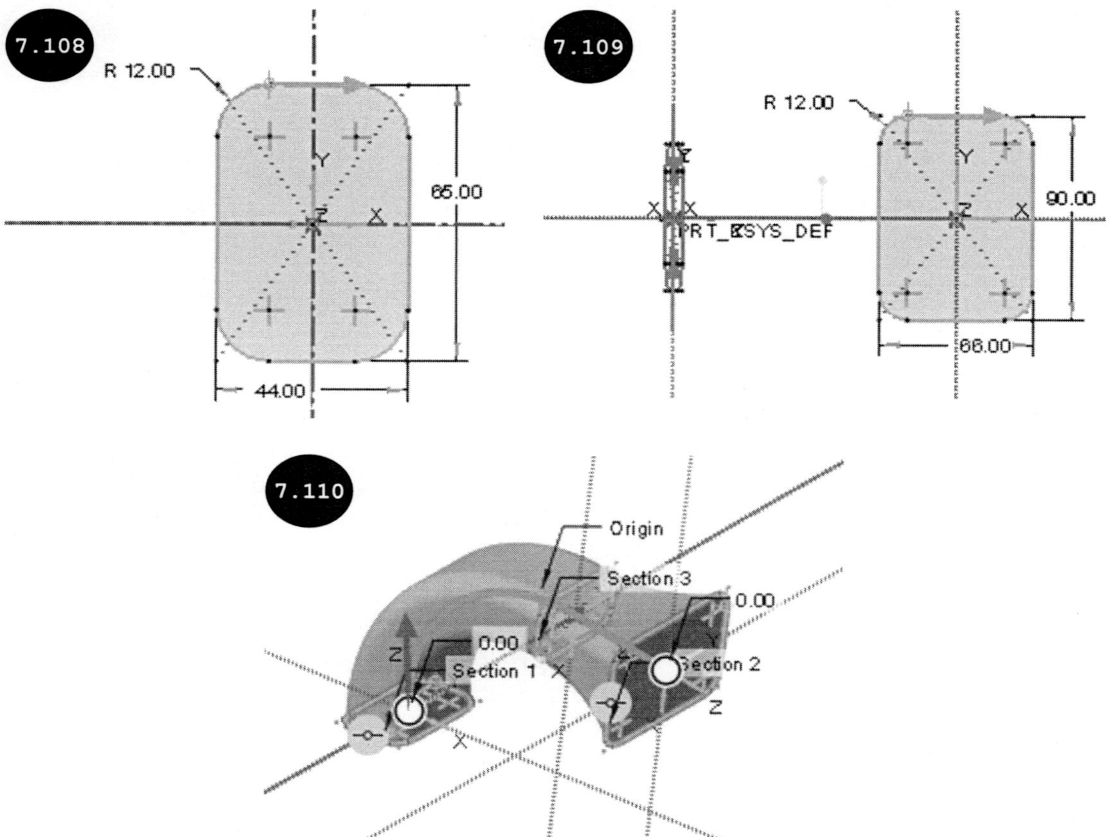

10. Click on the **Insert** button in the expanded **Sections** panel to create the third section of the feature. The third section is added to the section list of the expanded **Sections** panel. You are prompted to define the location of the section along the trajectory in the graphics area. You can define the location of the section by selecting a point in the graphics area.

Now, you need to create a datum point on the trajectory to define the location of the third section.

11. Ensure that the newly added section (**Section 3**) is selected in the expanded **Sections** panel. Next, click on the arrow below the **Datum** tool available on the right most end of the **Swept Blend** tab, see Figure 7.111. The **Datum flyout** appears.

12. Click on the **Point** tool in the **Datum** flyout, see Figure 7.111. The **Datum Point** dialog box appears.

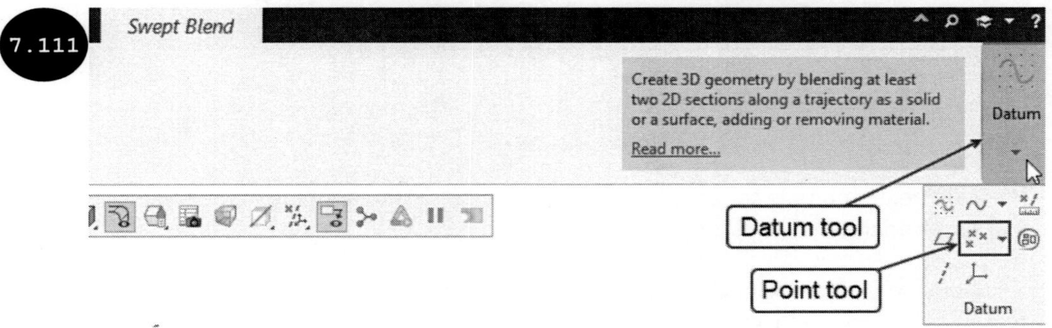

13. Move the cursor over the trajectory then click on the required location. The preview of a datum point appears on the trajectory in the specified location, see Figure 7.112.

14. Drag the datum point to the required location on the trajectory or enter the offset value/ratio in the **Datum Point** dialog box to specify the location of the datum point on the trajectory, see Figure 7.113. In this figure, the location of the datum point is specified at the end of the arc entity of the trajectory.

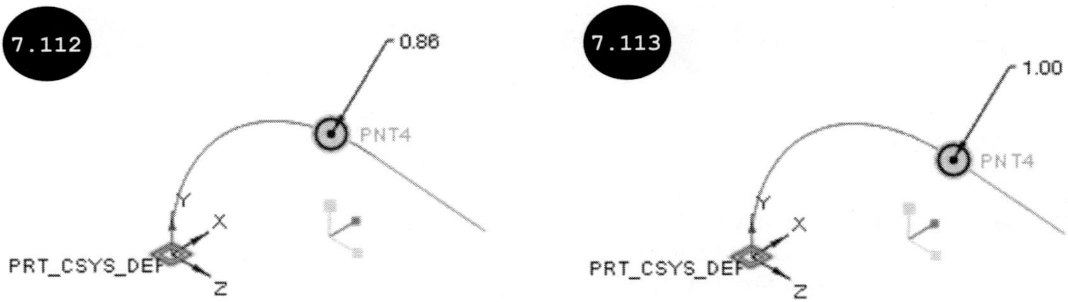

15. Click on the **OK** button in the **Datum Point** dialog box and then click on the **Play** ▶ button in the **Swept Blend** tab to resume the creation of the swept blend feature.

16. Expand the **Sections** panel of the **Swept Blend** tab and then click on the **Sketch** button. The Sketching environment is invoked and an imaginary sketching plane that is normal to the newly created datum point becomes parallel to the screen.

17. Create a sketch of the third section, see Figure 7.114. Next, exit the Sketching environment and change the orientation of the model to standard orientation. The preview of the swept blend feature appears, see Figure 7.115.

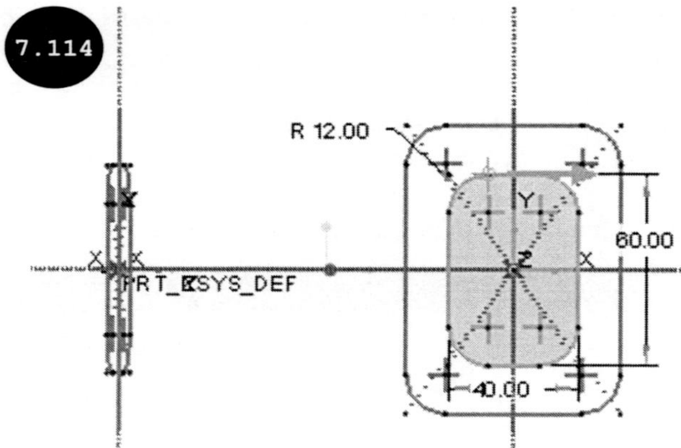

18. You can create multiple sections to control the cross-sectional shape of the swept blend feature in a similar manner.

19. Click on the green tick-mark button in the **Swept Blend** tab of the **Ribbon**. The swept blend feature is created, see Figure 7.116.

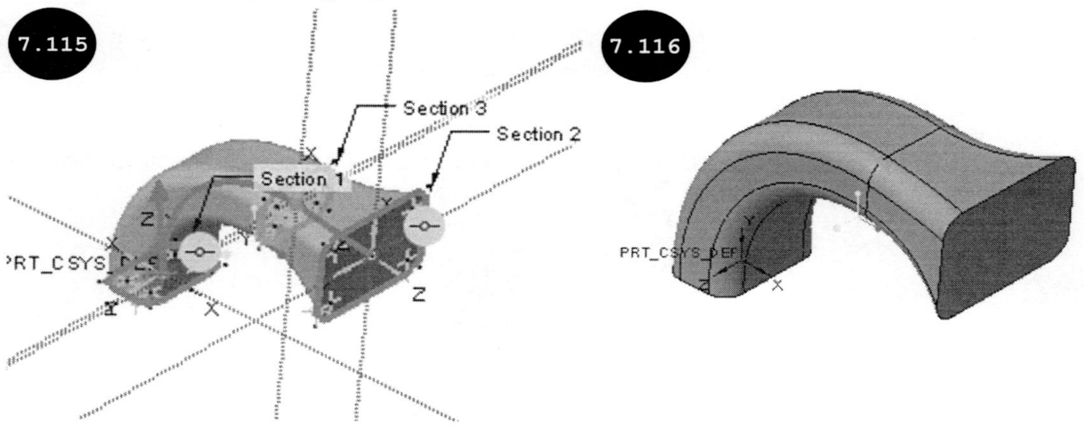

Note: You can create a thin swept blend feature with uniform wall thickness by using the **Thicken Sketch** button of the **Swept Blend** tab. You can also create a cut swept blend feature by removing material from an existing feature of the model using the **Remove Material** button of the **Swept Blend** tab. The methods for creating a thin and a cut swept blend feature are same as discussed earlier.

Creating a Rotational Blend feature

A rotational blend feature is created by rotating sections about an axis of revolution, see Figure 7.117. This figure shows the preview of a rotational blend feature in which three sections at different angles of rotation are blending about an axis of revolution. You can create a rotational blend feature by using the **Rotational Blend** tool. To create a rotational blend feature, you need to create two or more than two sections and a centerline as the axis of revolution. The method for creating a rotational blend feature is discussed below:

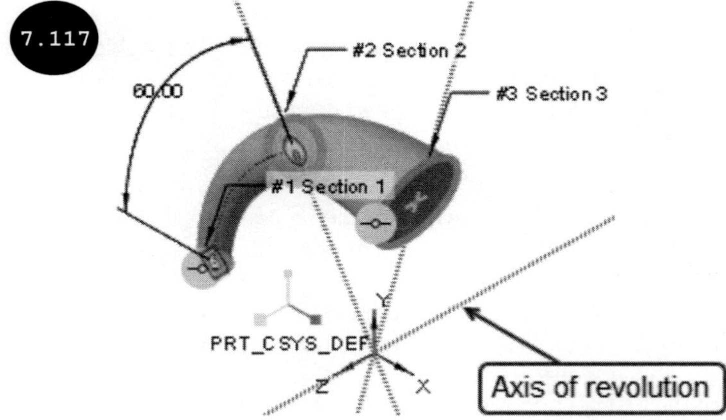

1. Expand the **Shapes** group of the **Model** tab by clicking on the arrow (see Figure 7.118) and then click on the **Rotational Blend** tool. The **Rotational Blend** tab appears in the **Ribbon**.

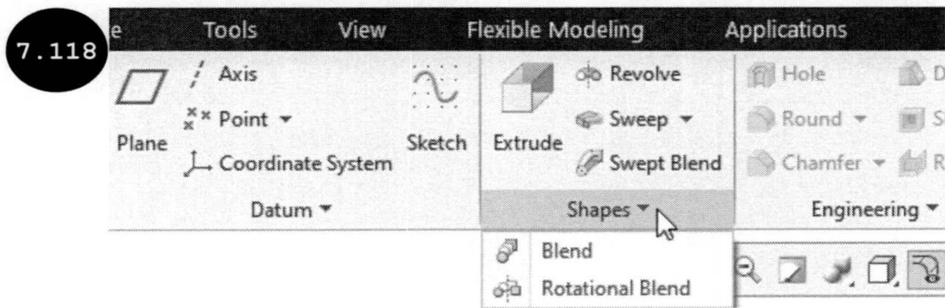

2. Expand the **Sections** panel of the **Rotational Blend** tab, if not expanded by default, see Figure 7.119. The options in this panel are the same as discussed earlier.

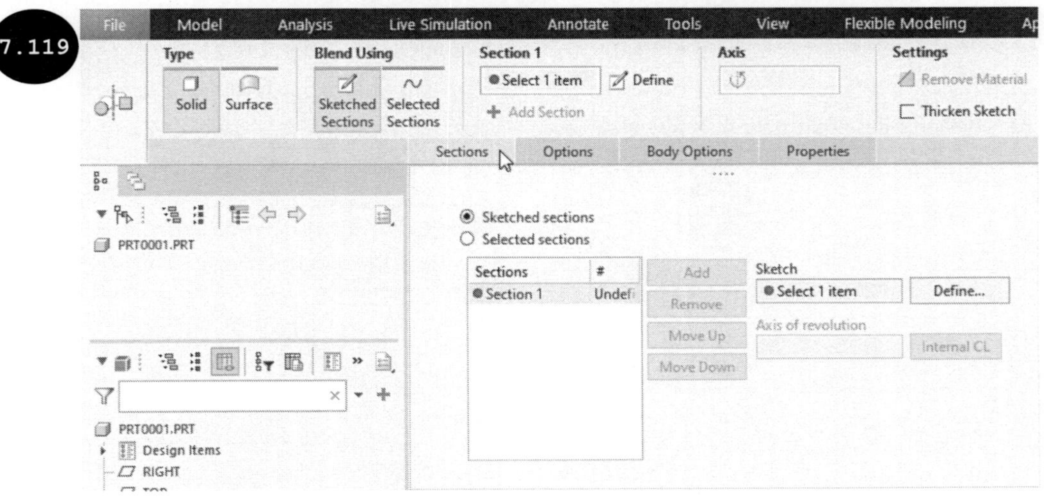

3. Select the **Sketched sections** radio button in the expanded **Sections** panel to create the sections of the blend feature in the graphics area.

You can also select sections that are already created in the graphics area by selecting the **Selected sections** radio button of the expanded **Sections** panel. To create all sections before invoking the **Rotational Blend** tool, you need to ensure that the sketching planes of all the sections intersect at the same axis of rotation.

4. Click on the **Define** button in the expanded **Sections** panel to define the sketching plane for creating the first section. The **Sketch** dialog box appears.

5. Select the sketching plane and then click on the **Sketch** button in the dialog box. The Sketching environment is invoked and the sketching plane is oriented normal to the viewing direction.

6. Create a sketch of the first section with a centerline, see Figure 7.120. Note that an arrow appears on one of the vertices of the sketch which indicates the start point of the section. You need to ensure that the start points of all sections are in the same direction to avoid twisting the resultant feature.

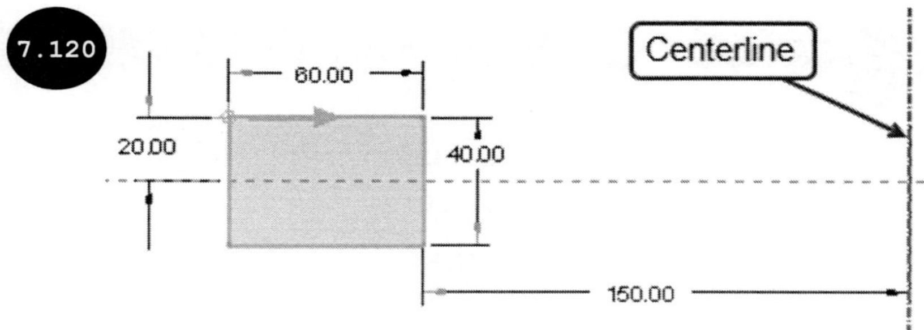

7. After creating the first section with a centerline, exit the Sketching environment. The first section is created and the internal centerline of the first section is selected as the axis of revolution, automatically. Also, you are prompted to specify the angle offset value about the axis of revolution for creating the second section of the feature.

8. Change the orientation of the sketch to the standard orientation and expand the **Sections** panel. Notice that an angle offset handle appears in the graphics area (see Figure 7.121), and an **Offset** field appears in the expanded **Sections** panel, see Figure 7.122.

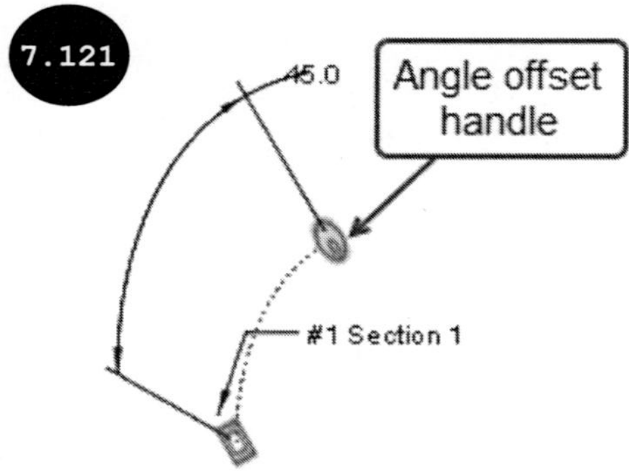

9. Enter the angle offset value in the **Offset** field and then click on the **Sketch** button in the expanded **Sections** panel, see Figure 7.122. The Sketching environment is invoked and an imaginary sketching plane at the specified angle about the axis of revolution becomes normal to the viewing direction for creating the second section. Also, the projected view of the first section appears on the imaginary sketching plane for your reference, see Figure 7.123.

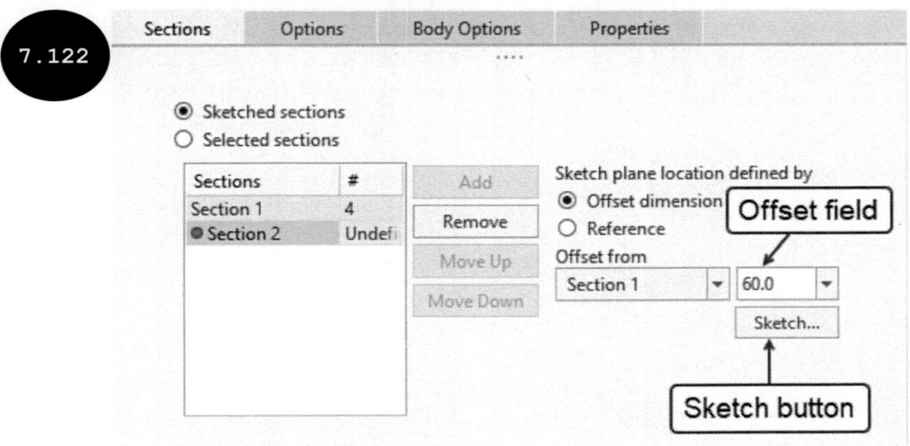

Note: You can enter an angle offset value in the range from **-120** to **120** degrees in the Offset field of the expanded **Sections** panel. You can also drag the angle offset handle that appears in the graphics area to define the angle offset value.

10. Create a sketch of the second section, see Figure 7.124. In this figure, a circle is created as the sketch of the second section. As mentioned earlier, the number of entities in each section should be the same. Therefore, the circle shown in Figure 7.124 has been divided into four entities by using the **Divide** tool of the **Editing** group in the **Sketch** tab.

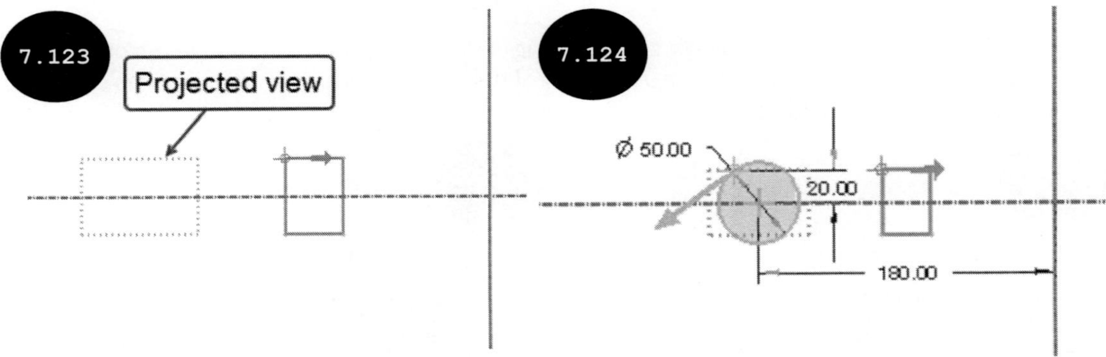

11. After creating the second section, exit the Sketching environment and then change the orientation of the model to standard orientation. A preview of the rotational blend feature appears in the graphics area such that both the sections are blending about the axis of revolution, see Figure 7.125.

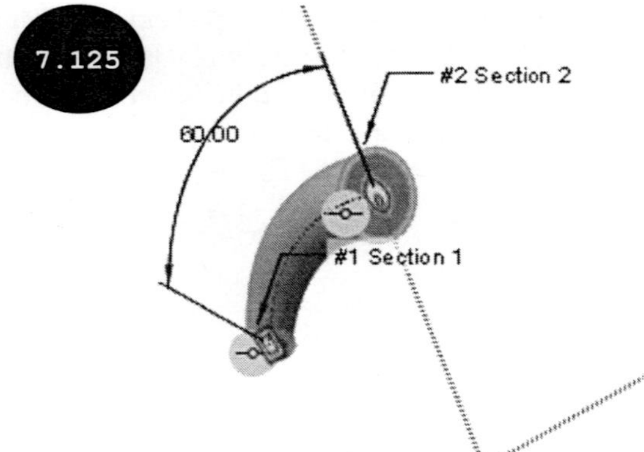

12. Expand the **Sections** panel and then click on the **Add** button to create the third section of the feature. The third section is added to the section list of the expanded **Sections** panel. You are then prompted to define the angle offset value about the axis of rotation for creating the third section of the feature.

13. Select the **Section 1** or **Section 2** option in the **Offset from** drop-down list of the expanded **Sections** panel.

14. Enter the angle offset value in the **Offset** field and then click on the **Sketch** button in the expanded **Sections** panel. The Sketching environment is invoked and an imaginary sketching plane at the specified angle about the axis of rotation becomes normal to the viewing direction for creating the third section. The projected view of the first and second sections appears on the imaginary sketching plane for your reference.

15. Create a sketch of the third section, see Figure 7.126. In this figure, a circle is created as the sketch of the third section which has been divided into four entities by using the **Divide** tool of the **Editing** group in the **Sketch** tab.

16. After creating the third section, exit the Sketching environment and then change the orientation of the model to standard orientation. A preview of the rotational blend feature appears such that all the sections are blending about the axis of revolution, see Figure 7.127.

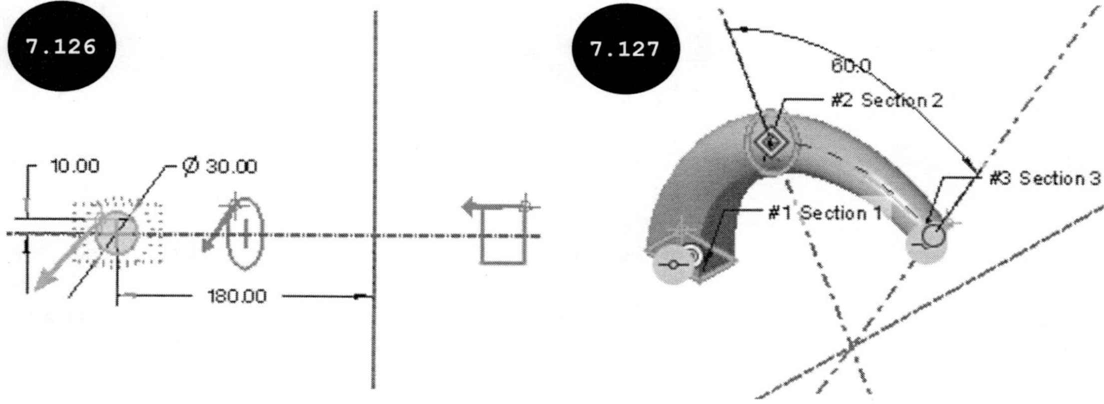

17. You can similarly create multiple sections to create a rotational blend feature.

Note: You can also create a closed rotational blend feature such that the start and end sections of the feature join automatically with each other and create a closed rotational blend feature. To do so, expand the **Options** panel of the **Rotational Blend** tab (see Figure 7.128), and then select the **Connect end and start sections** check box. A preview of the closed rotational blend feature appears, see Figure 7.129. Note that the **Connect end and start sections** check box is enabled only when minimum three sections are available.

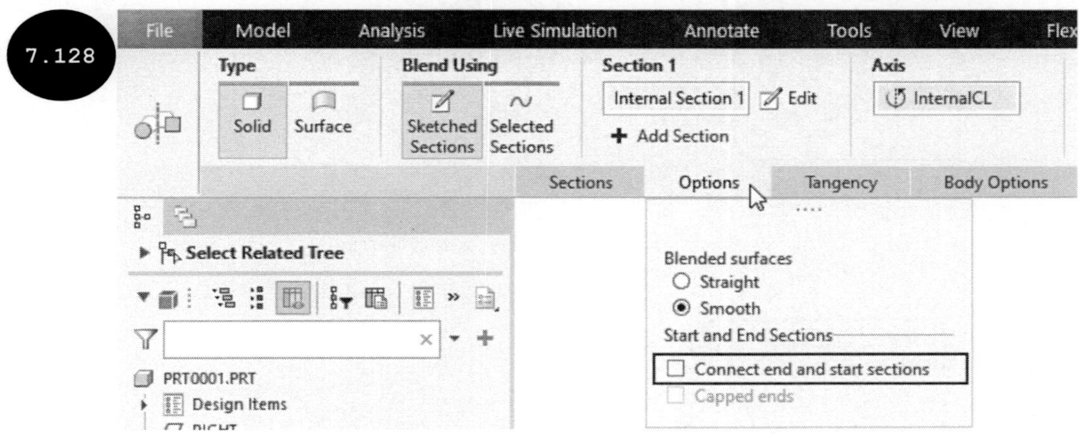

18. Click on the green tick-mark button in the **Rotational Blend** tab of the **Ribbon**. The rotational blend feature is created, see Figure 7.130.

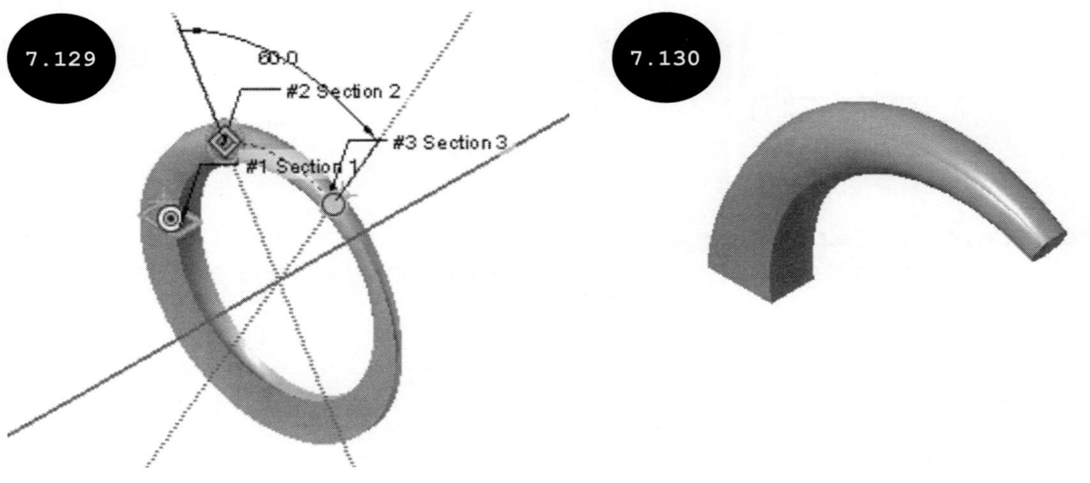

Tutorial 1

Create the model shown in Figure 7.131. The different views and dimensions are given in the same figure. All dimensions are in mm.

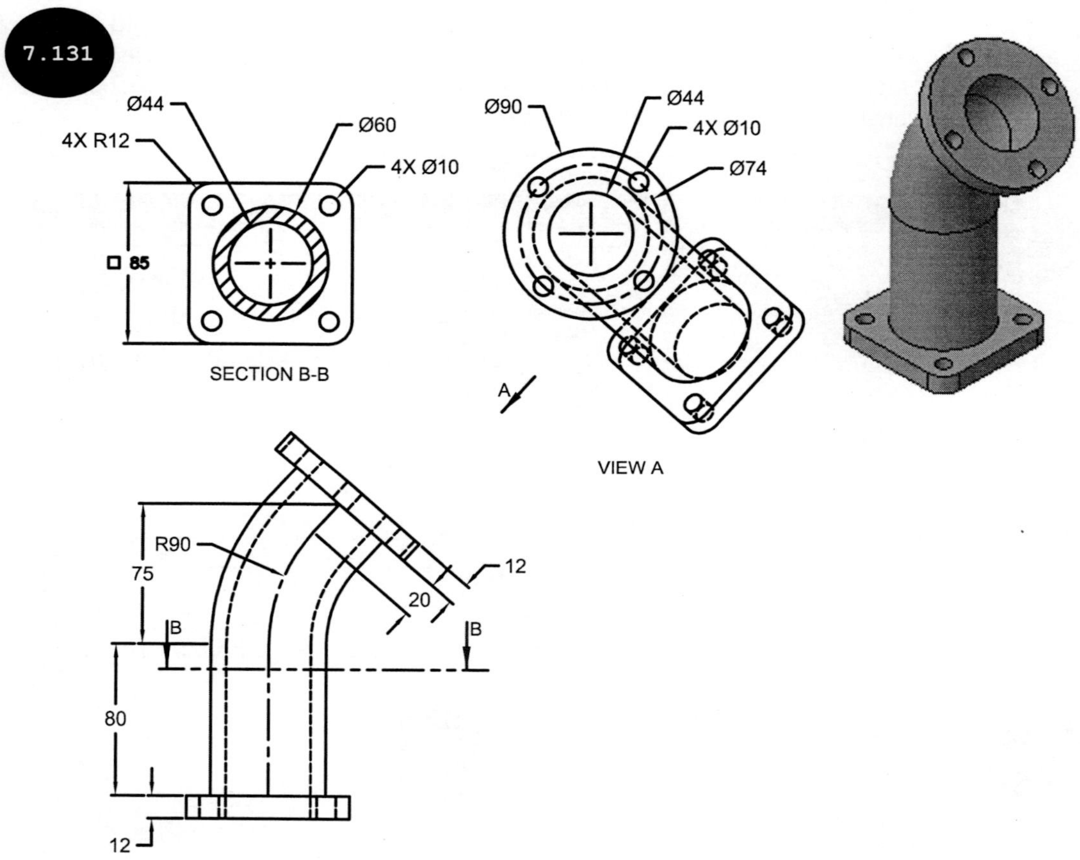

Section 1: Starting Creo Parametric

1. Start Creo Parametric by double-clicking on the Creo Parametric icon on your desktop.

Section 2: Setting the Working Directory

Now, you need to set the working directory to save the files of the current session of Creo Parametric. It is recommended to create a folder with the name "*Chapter 7*" inside the "*Creo Parametric*" folder in the local drive of your system. If the "*Creo Parametric*" folder has not been created earlier then you need to create this folder.

1. Click on the **Select Working Directory** tool in the **Data** group of the **Home** tab, see Figure 7.132. The **Select Working Directory** window appears. In this window, browse to *Creo Parametric > Chapter 7*. You need to create these folders, if not created earlier. Next, click on the **OK** button in the dialog box. The working directory is set to < <*Creo Parametric**Chapter 7*\\.

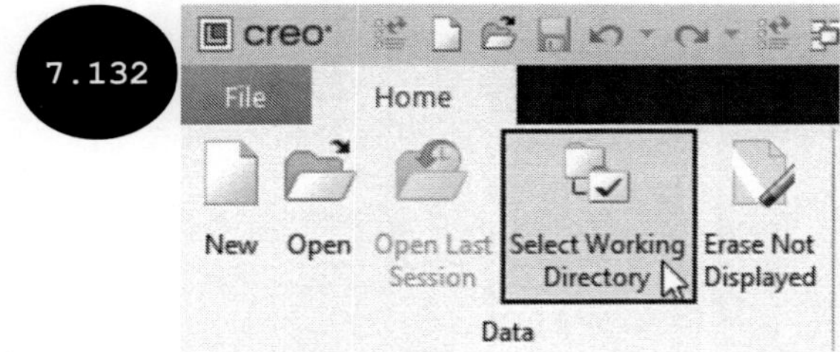

Section 3: Invoking the Part Mode

1. Click on the **New** tool in the **Data** group of the **Home** tab. The **New** dialog box appears, see Figure 7.133. Alternatively, press CTRL + N to invoke the **New** dialog box.

2. Ensure that the **Part** radio button is selected in the **Type** area and the **Solid** radio button is selected in the **Sub-type** area of the dialog box, see Figure 7.133.

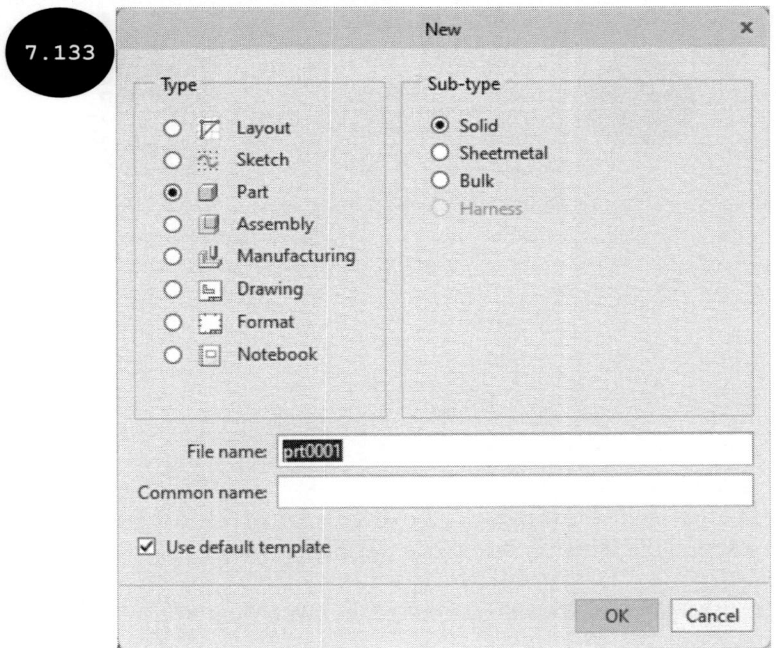

3. Enter **C07-Tutorial01** in the **File name** field of the dialog box as the name of the model.

4. Clear the **Use default template** check box and then click on the **OK** button in the dialog box. The **New File Options** dialog box appears, see Figure 7.134.

5. Select the **mmns_part_solid_abs** template in the **New File Options** dialog box and then click on the **OK** button. The Part mode is invoked with the **mmns_part_solid_abs** template. In this template, the length is measured in millimeters, mass is measured in Newton, and time is measured in seconds.

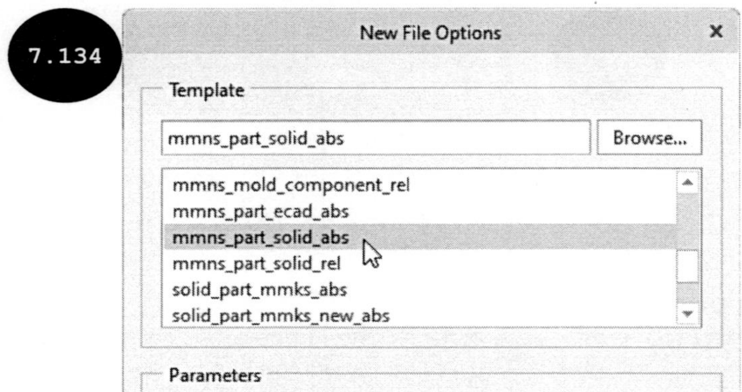

Section 4: Creating the Base Feature - Sweep Feature

1. Invoke the Sketching environment by selecting the Front plane as the sketching plane and then create a trajectory of the sweep feature, see Figure 7.135.

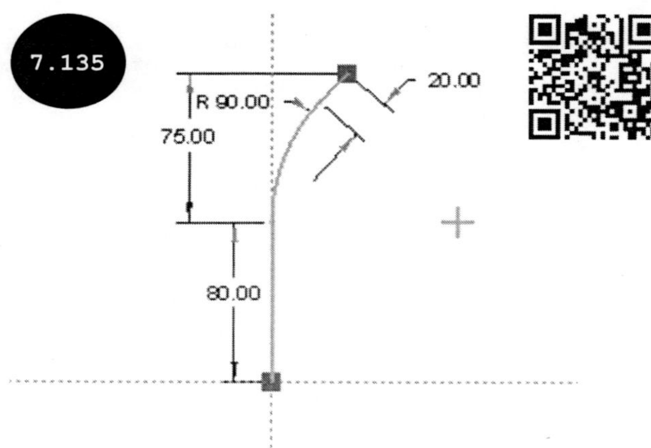

2. Click on the **OK** tool in the **Close** group of the **Ribbon** to exit the Sketching environment. The Part mode is invoked and the sketch is selected in the graphics area.

   After creating the trajectory, you need to create the sweep feature.

3. Click on the **Sweep** tool in the **Shapes** group of the **Model** tab, see Figure 7.136. The **Sweep** tab appears in the **Ribbon**, see Figure 7.137. Also, an arrow appears on one end of the selected trajectory, and dimension handles appear on both ends of the trajectory, see Figure 7.138.

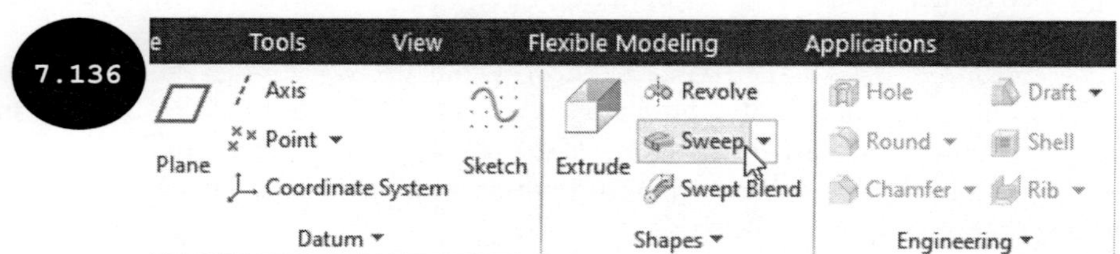

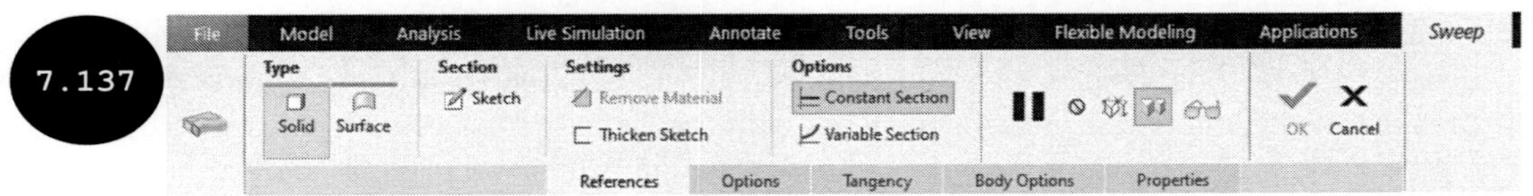

Note: The endpoint of the trajectory where the arrow appears is defined as the start point from where the section will start following the path to create the sweep feature.

4. Click on the arrow that appears on one end of the trajectory in the graphics area to flip the start point of the trajectory as shown in Figure 7.139.

Now, you need to create a section of the sweep feature.

5. Click on the **Sketch** button in the **Section** area of the **Sweep** tab. The Sketching environment is invoked and the sketching plane is oriented normal to the viewing direction.

6. Create a circle of diameter 60 mm as the section of the sweep feature, see Figure 7.140.

7. Exit the Sketching environment by clicking on the **OK** tool in the **Close** group of the **Sketch** tab and then change the orientation of the model to standard orientation. A preview of the sweep feature appears in the graphics area, see Figure 7.141.

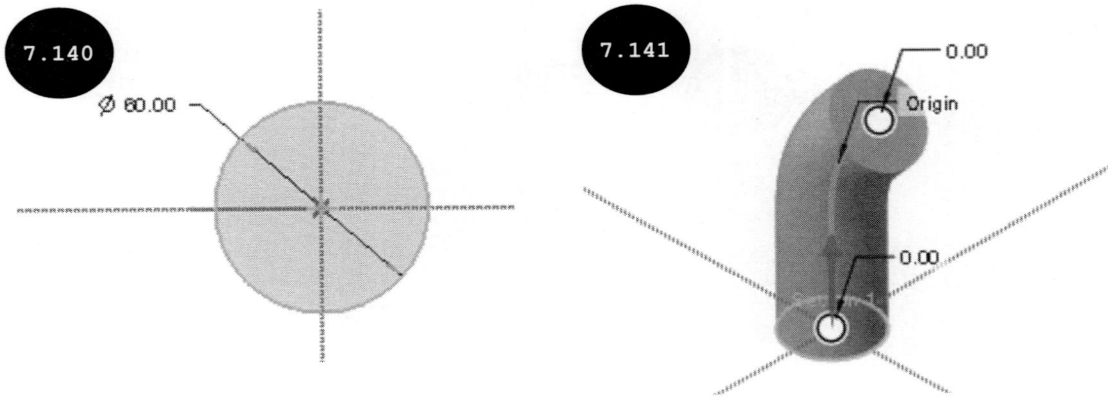

8. Click on the **Thicken Sketch** button in the **Settings** area of the **Sweep** tab to create a thin sweep feature. The **Thickness value** field appears in the **Sweep** tab, see Figure 7.142. Also, a preview of the thin sweep feature appears with the default thickness in the graphics area, see Figure 7.143.

7.142

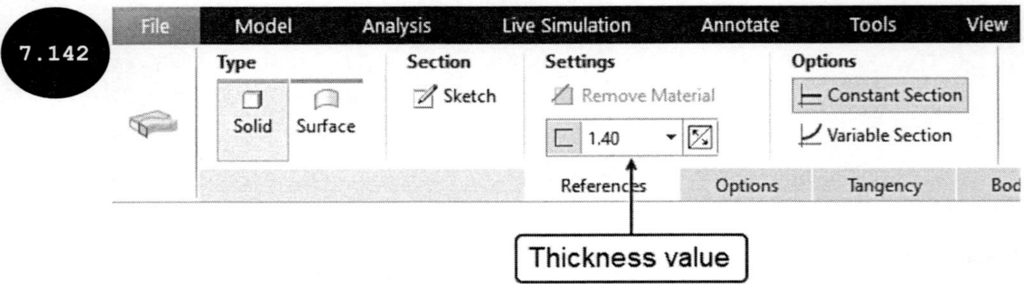

9. Enter **8** in the **Thickness value** field in the **Settings** area and then press ENTER. The preview of the sweep feature gets updated in the graphics area.

10. Ensure that the thickness is added inward to the section. As needed, you can change the thickness direction such that the material is added inward to the section by clicking on the **Flip Direction** button of the **Sweep** tab, see Figure 7.144.

7.143 7.144

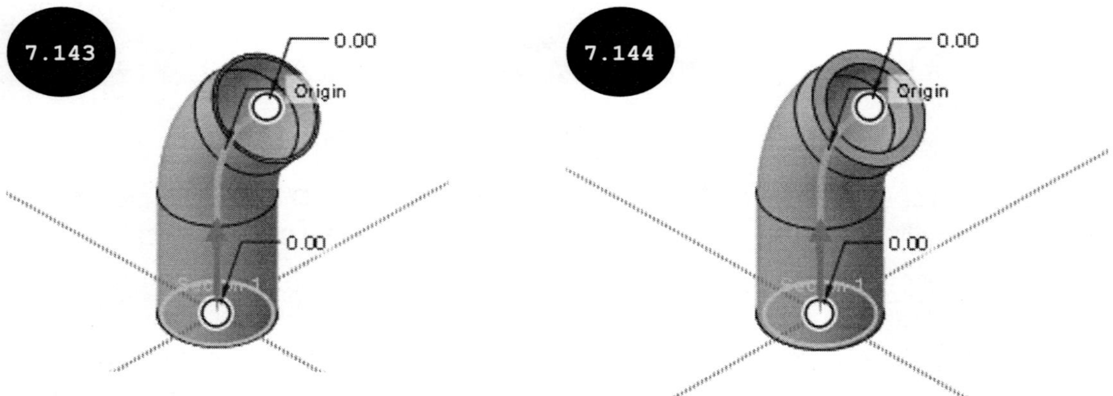

11. Click on the green tick-mark button in the **Sweep** tab of the **Ribbon**. A thin section sweep feature is created, see Figure 7.145.

7.145

Section 5: Creating the Second Feature - Extrude Feature

1. Rotate the model such that the bottom face of the base feature (sweep) can be viewed, see Figure 7.146. You can rotate the model by pressing and holding the middle mouse button and then dragging the cursor in the graphics area.

2. Invoke the Sketching environment by selecting the bottom face of the base feature (sweep) as the sketching plane.

3. Create a sketch of the second feature, see Figure 7.147. After creating the sketch of the second feature, exit the Sketching environment. Next, change the orientation of the model to standard orientation.

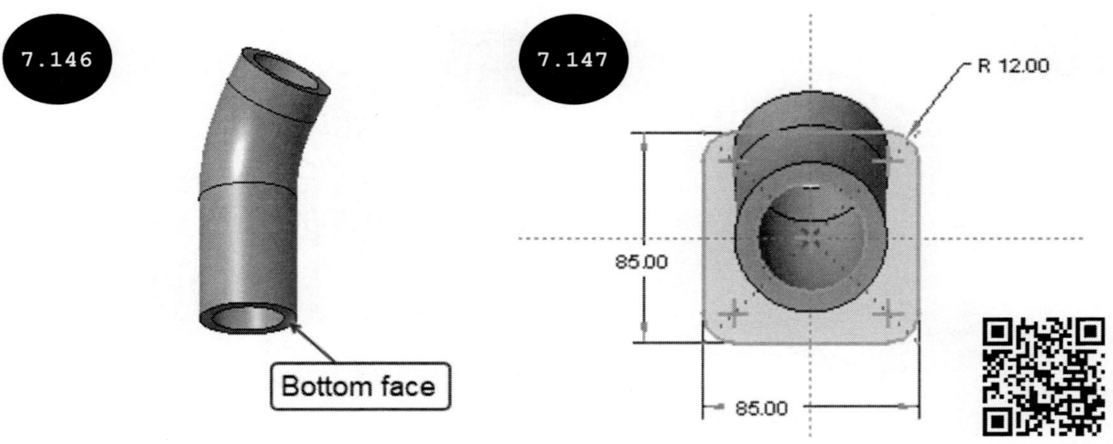

Tip: The arcs of the sketch shown in Figure 7.147 are of equal radius, therefore, an equal constraint is applied among all arcs. Also, the inner circle of the sketch has equal constraint with the inner circular edge of the base feature.

4. Click on the **Extrude** tool in the **Shapes** group of the **Model** tab. A preview of the extrude feature appears (see Figure 7.148) and the **Extrude** tab appears in the **Ribbon**. If the preview of the extrude feature does not appear, then select the sketch in the graphics area.

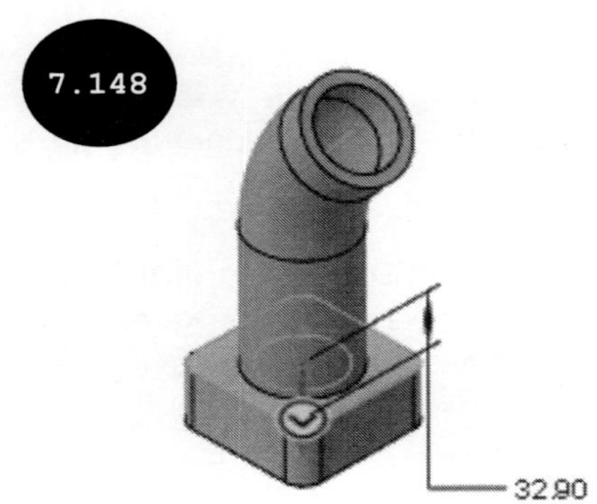

5. Enter **12** as the depth of extrusion in the **Value** field in the **Depth** area of the **Extrude** tab and then press ENTER. The preview of the extrude feature gets modified.

6. Click on the green tick-mark button in the **Extrude** tab. The extrude feature is created, see Figure 7.149.

Section 6: Creating the Third Feature - Extrude Cut Feature

1. Invoke the Sketching environment by selecting the top planar face of the second feature as the sketching plane.

2. Create the sketch (four circles of diameter 10 mm), see Figure 7.150.

Tip: The sketch of the third feature shown in Figure 7.150 has four circles of the same diameter; therefore, equal constraint is applied among all circles. Also, the center points of all circles are coincident with the center point of the respective semi-circular edge of the second feature. When you pause the cursor over a semi-circular edge of the feature, the center point of the semi-circular edge gets highlighted. You can click on the highlighted center point of the semi-circular edge to specify the center point of the circle.

3. Exit the Sketching environment and then change the orientation of the model to standard orientation.

4. Click on the **Extrude** tool in the **Shapes** group of the **Model** tab. A preview of the extrude feature appears. If the preview of the extrude feature does not appear, then select the sketch in the graphics area.

5. Click on the **Flip Direction** button in the **Depth** area of the **Extrude** tab, see Figure 7.151. The direction of extrusion changes to downward and the **Remove Material** button gets activated, automatically, see Figure 7.151. Also, a preview of the cut feature appears in the graphics area, see Figure 7.152.

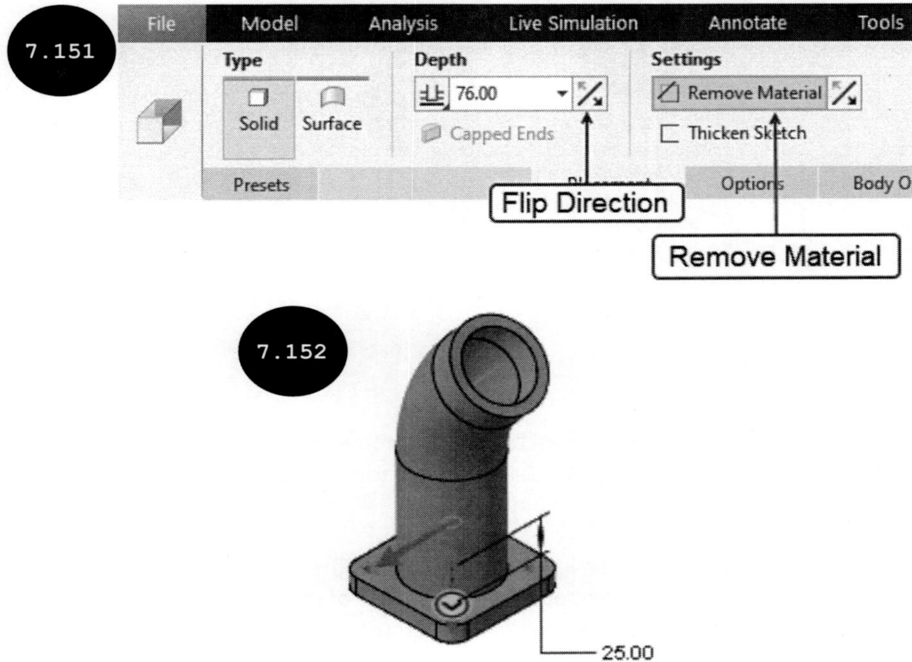

6. Invoke the **Options** panel of the **Extrude** tab and then select the **Through All** option in the **Side 1** drop-down list, see Figure 7.153.

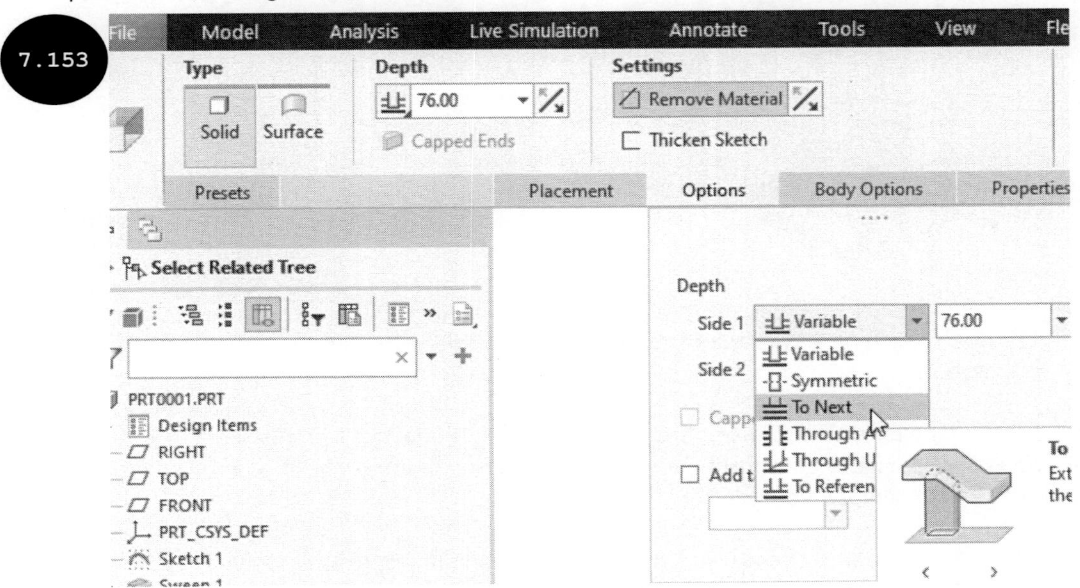

7. Click on the green tick-mark button in the **Extrude** tab. The extrude cut feature is created, see Figure 7.154.

Section 7: Creating the Fourth Feature - Extrude Feature

1. Invoke the Sketching environment by selecting the top planar face of the sweep feature (base feature) as the sketching plane, see Figure 7.155.

2. Create the sketch (two circles), see Figure 7.156. In this figure, the center points of both the circles are coincident with the center point of the circular edge of the base feature. Also, the inner circle of the sketch has equal constraint with the inner circular edge of the base feature.

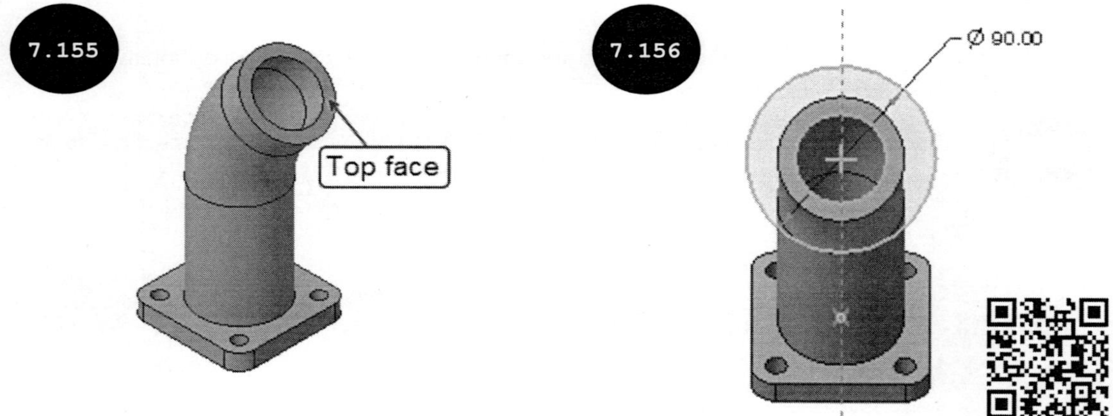

3. Exit the Sketching environment and then change the orientation of the model to standard orientation.

4. Click on the **Extrude** tool in the **Shapes** group of the **Model** tab. A preview of the extrude feature appears, see Figure 7.157. If the preview of the extrude feature does not appear, then select the sketch in the graphics area.

5. Enter **12** as the depth of extrusion in the **Value** field in the **Depth** area of the **Extrude** tab and then press ENTER. The preview of the extrude feature gets modified.

6. Click on the green tick-mark button in the **Extrude** tab. The extrude feature is created, see Figure 7.158.

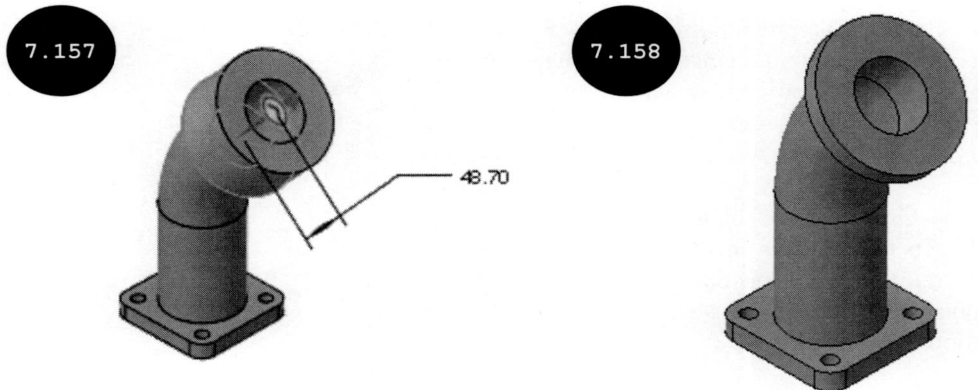

Section 8: Creating the Fifth Feature - Extruded Cut Feature

1. Invoke the Sketching environment by selecting the top planar face of the fourth feature as the sketching plane.

2. Create the sketch (four circles of equal diameter 10 mm), see Figure 7.159.

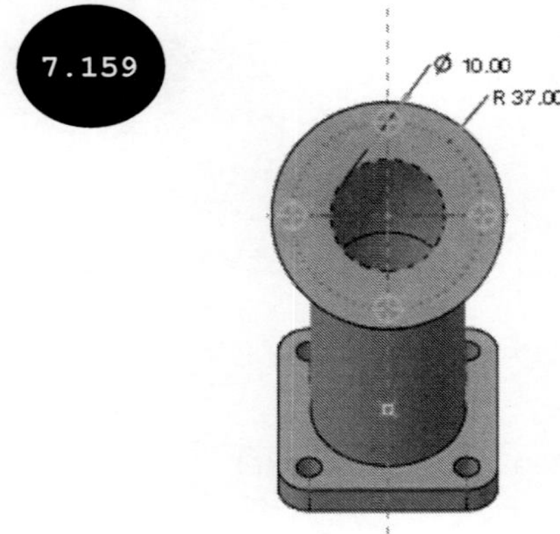

Tip: As the PCD (Pitch Circle Diameter) of all circles shown in Figure 7.159 is same, you can create a construction circle of radius 37 mm, whose center point is coincident with the center point of the circular edge of the fourth feature, by activating the **Construction Mode** tool. Next, you can deactivate the **Construction Mode** tool and then create circles of diameter 10 mm such that the center points of the circles are coincident with the construction circle.

3. Exit the Sketching environment and then change the orientation of the model to standard orientation.

4. Click on the **Extrude** tool in the **Shapes** group of the **Model** tab. A preview of the extrude feature appears.

5. Click on the **Flip Direction** button in the **Extrude** tab. The direction of extrusion changes to downward and the **Remove Material** button gets activated automatically. A preview of the cut feature also appears in the graphics area, see Figure 7.160.

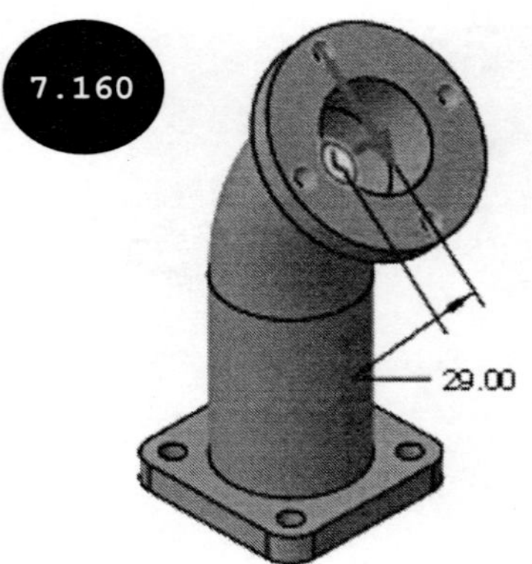

6. Expand the **Options** panel of the **Extrude** tab and then select the **To Next** option in the **Side 1** drop-down list, see Figure 7.161. The preview of the feature is modified in the graphics area such that it gets terminated at its next intersection.

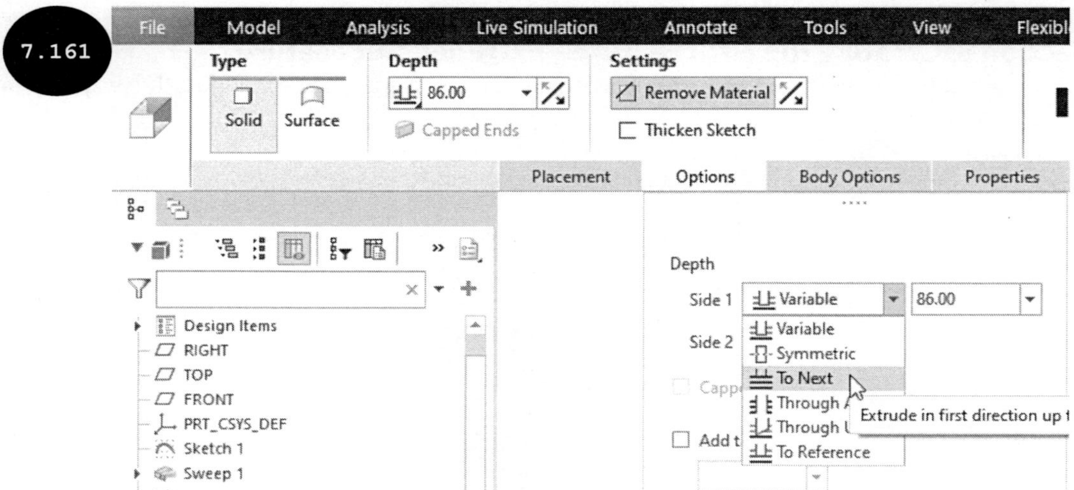

7. Click on the green tick-mark button in the **Extrude** tab. The extrude cut feature is created, see Figure 7.162.

Section 9: Saving the Model

1. Click on the **Save** tool in the **Quick Access Toolbar**. The **Save Object** dialog box appears.

2. Click on the **OK** button in the dialog box. The model is saved with the name **C07-Tutorial01** in the specified working directory (<<*Creo Parametric**Chapter 7*\).

Tutorial 2

Create the model shown in Figure 7.163. The different views and dimensions are given in the same figure. All dimensions are in mm.

7.163

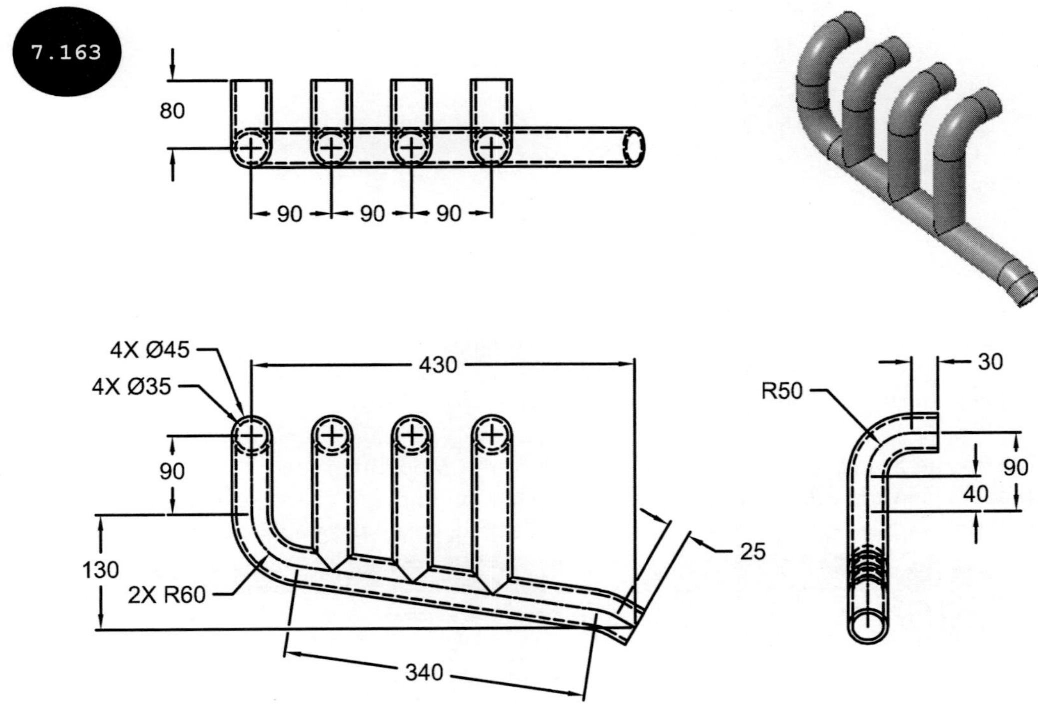

Section 1: Starting Creo Parametric

1. Start Creo Parametric by double-clicking on the Creo Parametric icon on your desktop.

Section 2: Setting the Working Directory

1. Set the working directory to <<*Creo Parametric**Chapter 7*. You need to create these folders, if not created earlier.

Section 3: Invoking the Part Mode

1. Click on the **New** tool in the **Data** group of the **Home** tab. The **New** dialog box appears.

2. Enter **C07-Tutorial02** in the **File name** field of the dialog box as the name of the model.

3. Clear the **Use default template** check box and then click on the **OK** button in the dialog box. The **New File Options** dialog box appears.

4. Select the **mmns_part_solid_abs** template in the **New File Options** dialog box and then click on the **OK** button. The Part mode is invoked with the **mmns_part_solid_abs** template.

Section 4: Creating the Base Feature - Sweep Feature

1. Invoke the Sketching environment by selecting the Right plane as the sketching plane and then create a trajectory of the sweep feature, see Figure 7.164.

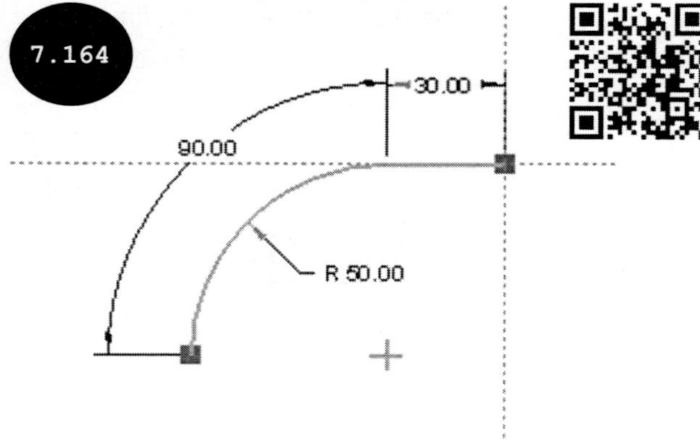

2. Click on the **OK** tool in the **Close** group of the **Ribbon** to exit the Sketching environment.

   After creating the trajectory, you need to create the sweep feature.

3. Click on the **Sweep** tool in the **Shapes** group of the **Model** tab, see Figure 7.165. The **Sweep** tab appears in the **Ribbon**. Also, an arrow appears on one end of the selected trajectory and dimension handles appear on both the ends of the trajectory in the graphics area, see Figure 7.166.

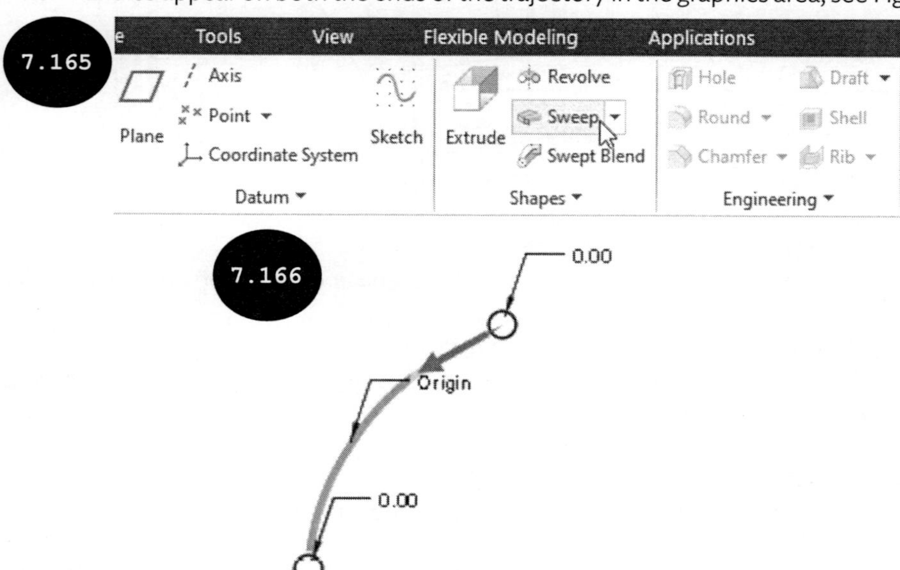

Now, you need to create the section of the sweep feature.

4. Click on the **Sketch** button in the **Section** area of the **Sweep** tab. The Sketching environment is invoked and the sketching plane is oriented normal to the viewing direction.

5. Create the sketch (two circles of diameter 45 mm and 35 mm) as the section of the sweep feature, see Figure 7.167.

6. Exit the Sketching environment by clicking on the **OK** tool in the **Close** group of the **Sketch** tab and then change the orientation of the model to standard orientation. A preview of the sweep feature appears in the graphics area, see Figure 7.168.

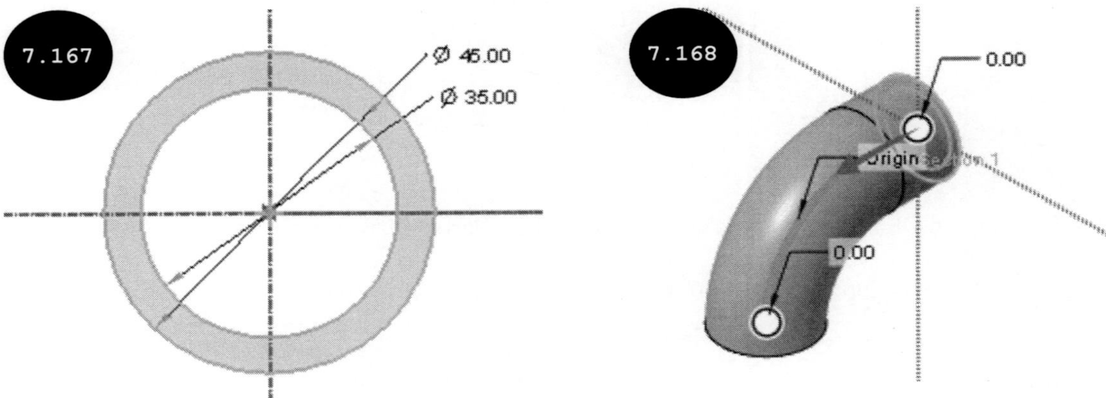

7. Click on the green tick-mark button in the **Sweep** tab of the **Ribbon**. The sweep feature is created, see Figure 7.169.

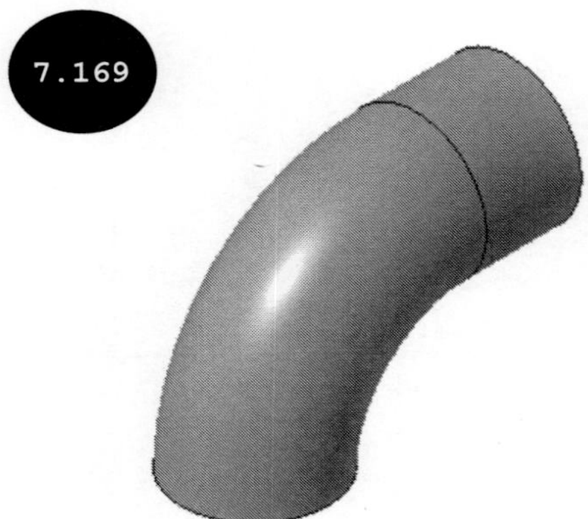

Section 5: Creating the Second Feature - Sweep Feature

To create the second feature of the model, you first need to create a datum plane at an offset distance of 80 mm from the Front plane.

1. Click on the **Plane** tool in the **Datum** group of the **Model** tab. The **Datum Plane** dialog box appears.

2. Click on the **Front Plane** as a reference. The preview of an offset datum plane appears.

3. Enter **80** in the **Translation** field of the **Offset** area in the dialog box and then press ENTER. Ensure that the direction of the plane creation is same as shown in the Figure 7.170. If needed, you can flip the direction of the plane by entering a negative offset value.

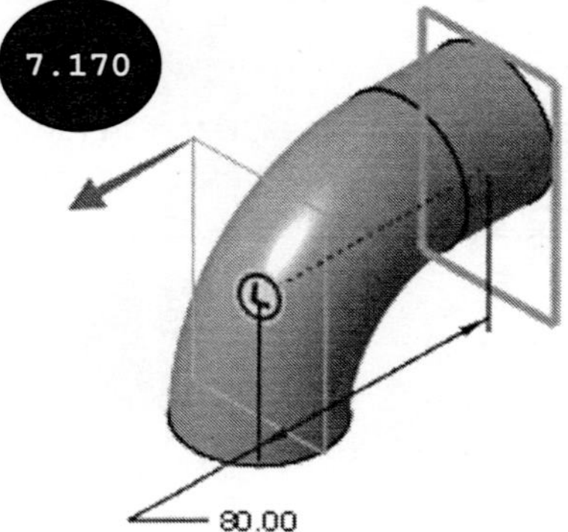

4. Click on the **OK** button in the dialog box. The offset datum plane is created.

5. Invoke the Sketching environment by selecting the newly created datum plane as the sketching plane.

6. Create the trajectory of the second sweep feature, see Figure 7.171.

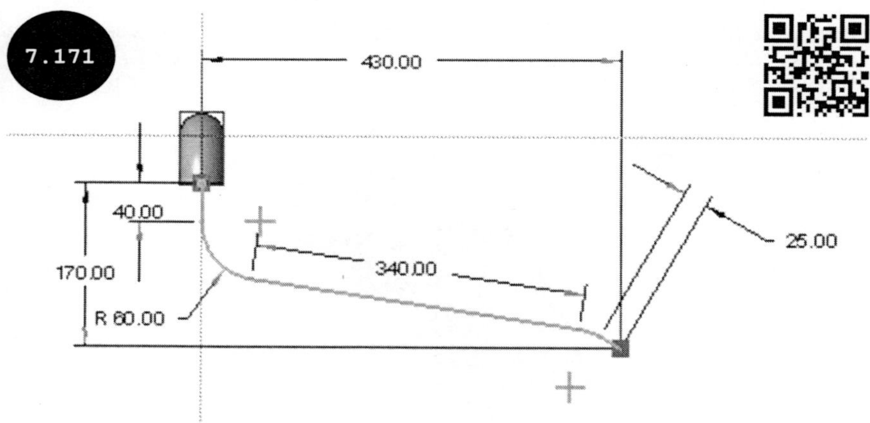

Note: Equal relation has been applied between both the arcs.

7. Click on the **OK** tool in the **Close** group of the **Ribbon** to exit the Sketching environment. Next, change the orientation of the model to standard orientation.

After creating the trajectory, you need to create the sweep feature.

8. Click on the **Sweep** tool in the **Shapes** group of the **Model** tab. The **Sweep** tab appears in the **Ribbon**. Also, an arrow appears on one end of the selected trajectory and dimension handles appear on both the ends of the trajectory in the graphics area, see Figure 7.172.

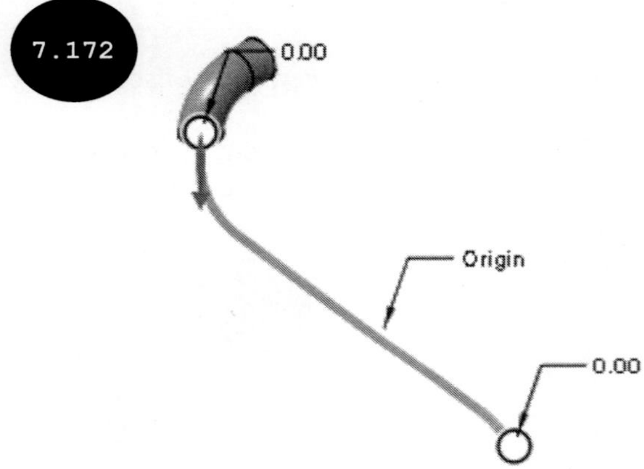

Now, you need to create a section of the sweep feature.

9. Click on the **Sketch** button in the **Section** area of the **Sweep** tab. The Sketching environment is invoked and the sketching plane is oriented normal to the viewing direction.

10. Create two circles as the section of the sweep feature by taking reference of the circular edges of the base feature, see Figure 7.173.

11. Exit the Sketching environment by clicking on the **OK** tool in the **Close** group of the **Sketch** tab and then change the orientation of the model to standard orientation. A preview of the sweep feature appears in the graphics area, see Figure 7.174.

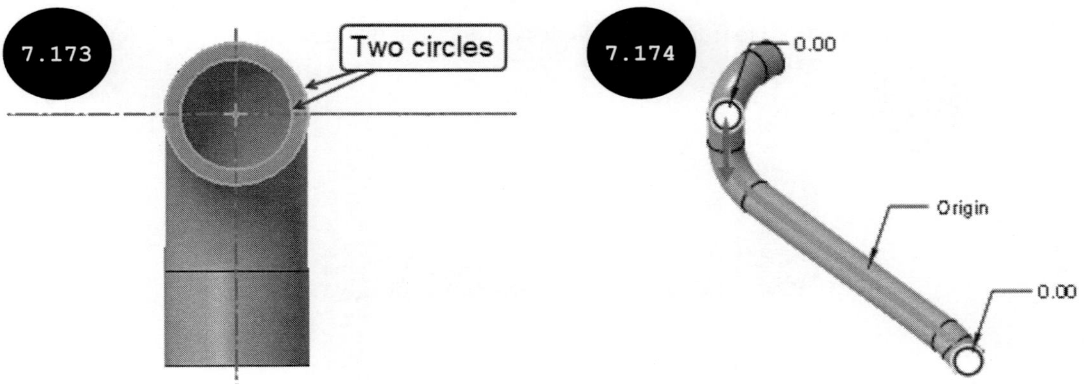

12. Click on the green tick-mark button in the **Sweep** tab of the **Ribbon**. The sweep feature is created, see Figure 7.175.

Section 6: Creating the Third Feature - Extrude Feature

To create the third feature of the model, you first need to create a datum plane at an offset distance of 50 mm from the Top plane.

1. Click on the **Plane** tool in the **Datum** group of the **Model** tab. The **Datum Plane** dialog box appears.

2. Click on the **Top Plane** as a reference. The preview of an offset datum plane appears.

3. Enter -50 in the **Translation** field of the **Offset** area in the dialog box and then press ENTER. A preview of the datum plane appears at an offset distance of 50 mm from the Top plane downward, see Figure 7.176.

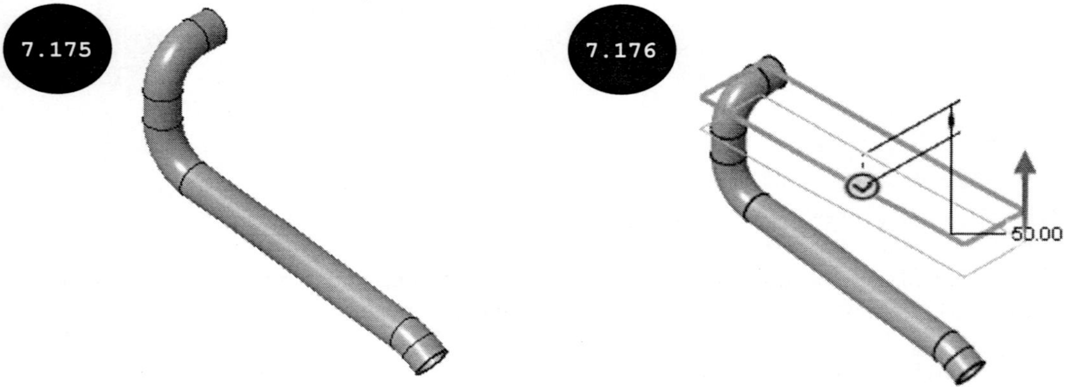

4. Click on the **OK** button in the dialog box. The offset datum plane is created.

5. Invoke the Sketching environment by selecting the newly created datum plane as the sketching plane.

6. Create a sketch of the third feature (three circles of the same diameter 45 mm), see Figure 7.177.

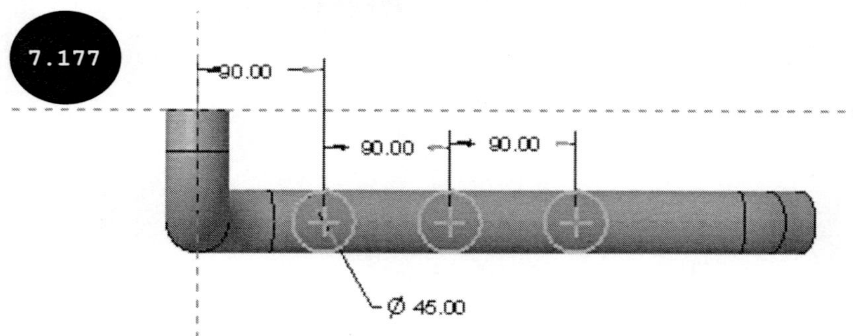

7. Exit the Sketching environment and then change the orientation of the model to standard orientation.

8. Click on the **Extrude** tool in the **Shapes** group of the **Model** tab. The preview of the extrude feature appears. If the preview does not appear, then select the sketch in the graphics area.

9. Click on the **Flip Direction** button in the **Depth** area of the **Extrude** tab to reverse the direction of extrusion downward.

10. Expand the **Options** panel of the **Extrude** tab and then select the **To Next** option in the **Side 1** drop-down list. The preview of the feature is modified in the graphics area such that it gets terminated at its next intersection, see Figure 7.178.

11. Click on the green tick-mark button in the **Extrude** tab. The extrude feature is created, see Figure 7.179.

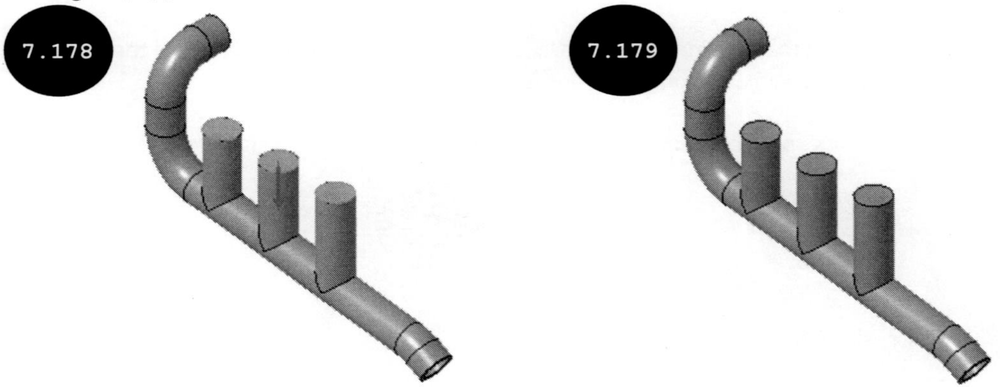

Section 7: Creating the Fourth Feature - Extruded Cut Feature

1. Invoke the Sketching environment by selecting the top planar face of the third feature as the sketching plane, see Figure 7.180.

2. Create a sketch of the fourth feature (a circle of diameter 35mm), see Figure 7.181.

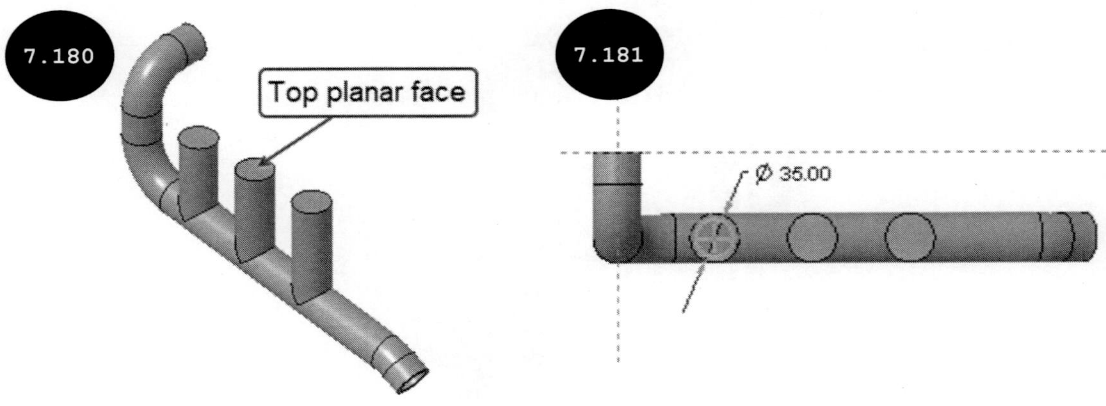

Tip: The sketch of the fourth feature shown in Figure 7.181 has a circle, which is concentric to the circular edges of the existing extrude feature.

3. Exit the Sketching environment and then change the orientation of the model to standard orientation.

4. Click on the **Extrude** tool in the **Shapes** group of the **Model** tab. A preview of the extrude feature appears.

5. Click on the **Flip Direction** button in the **Depth** area of the **Extrude** tab. The direction of extrusion changes to downward and the **Remove Material** button gets activated automatically. A preview of the cut feature also appears in the graphics area.

6. Expand the **Options** panel of the **Extrude** tab and then select the **To Reference** option in the **Side 1** drop-down list.

7. Rotate the model such that the inner circular face of the model can be viewed and then select it as the face to terminate the creation of the cut feature, see Figure 7.182.

8. Click on the green tick-mark button. The extrude feature is created, see Figure 7.183.

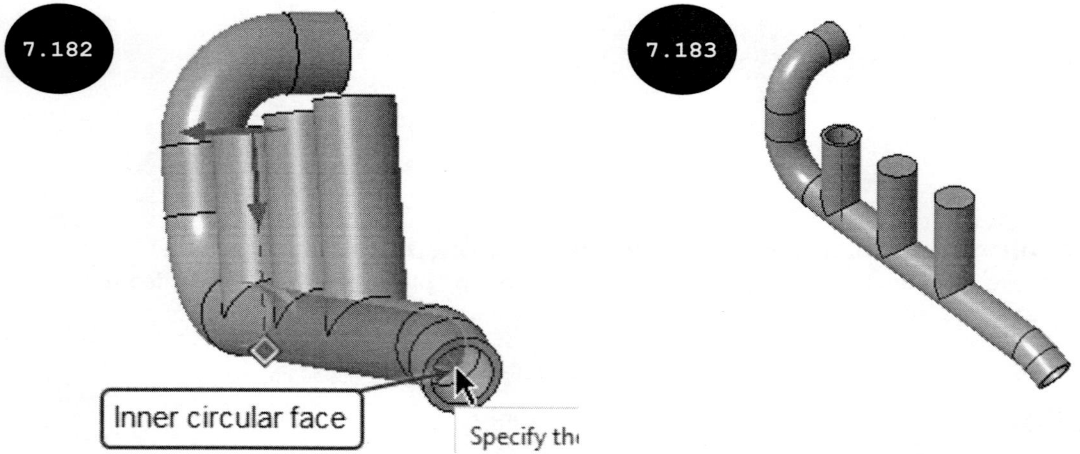

9. Similarly, create the other two extrude cut features, see Figure 7.184.

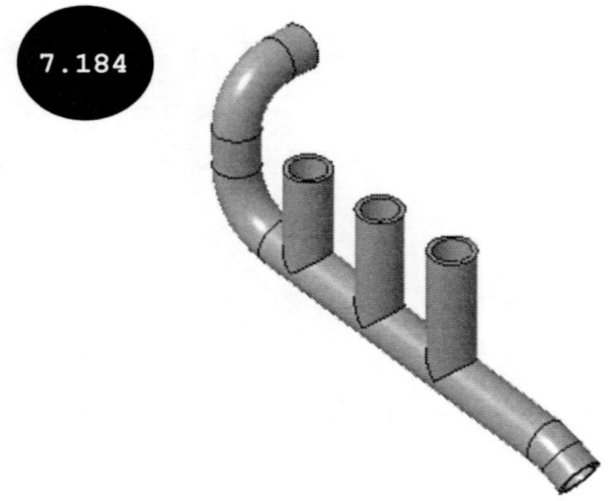

Section 8: Creating the Fifth Feature - Sweep Feature

To create the fifth feature of the model, you first need to create a reference plane at an offset distance of 90 mm from the Right plane.

1. Click on the **Plane** tool in the **Datum** group of the **Model** tab. The **Datum Plane** dialog box appears.

2. Click on the **Right Plane** as a reference. The preview of an offset datum plane appears.

3. Enter -**90** in the **Translation** field of the **Offset** area in the dialog box and then press ENTER. The preview of the datum plane appears at an offset distance of 90 mm from the Right plane, see Figure 7.185. In this figure, display of all other datum planes is turned off.

4. Click on the **OK** button in the dialog box. The offset datum plane is created.

5. Invoke the Sketching environment by selecting the newly created datum plane as the sketching plane.

6. Create a trajectory of the sweep feature, see Figure 7.186. In this figure, the sketch entities are created by taking reference from the existing entities (trajectory) of the base sweep feature.

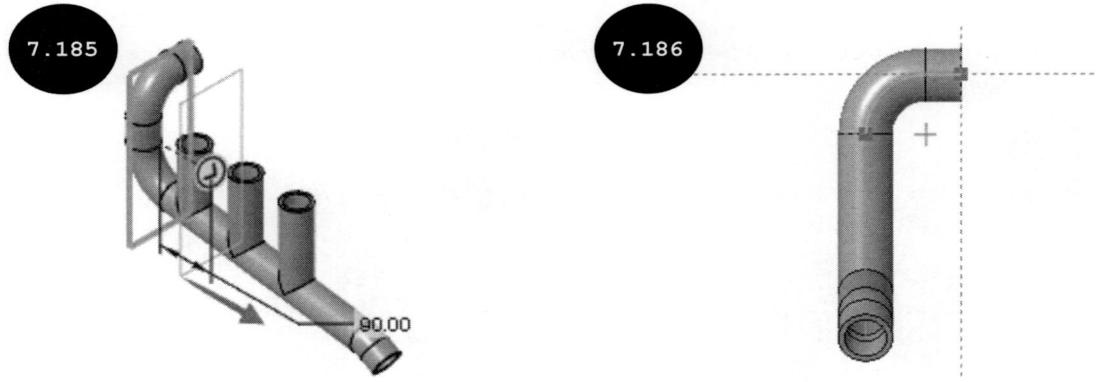

7. Click on the **OK** tool in the **Close** group of the **Ribbon** to exit the Sketching environment. Next, change the orientation of the model to standard orientation.

   After creating the trajectory, you need to create the sweep feature.

8. Click on the **Sweep** tool in the **Shapes** group of the **Model** tab. The **Sweep** tab appears in the **Ribbon**. Also, an arrow appears on one end of the selected trajectory, and dimension handles appear on both ends of the trajectory in the graphics area, see Figure 7.187.

   Now, you need to create a section of the sweep feature.

9. Click on the **Sketch** button in the **Section** area of the **Sweep** tab. The Sketching environment is invoked and the sketching plane is oriented normal to the viewing direction.

10. Create three sets of circles as the section of the sweep feature (two circles in each set), see Figure 7.188.

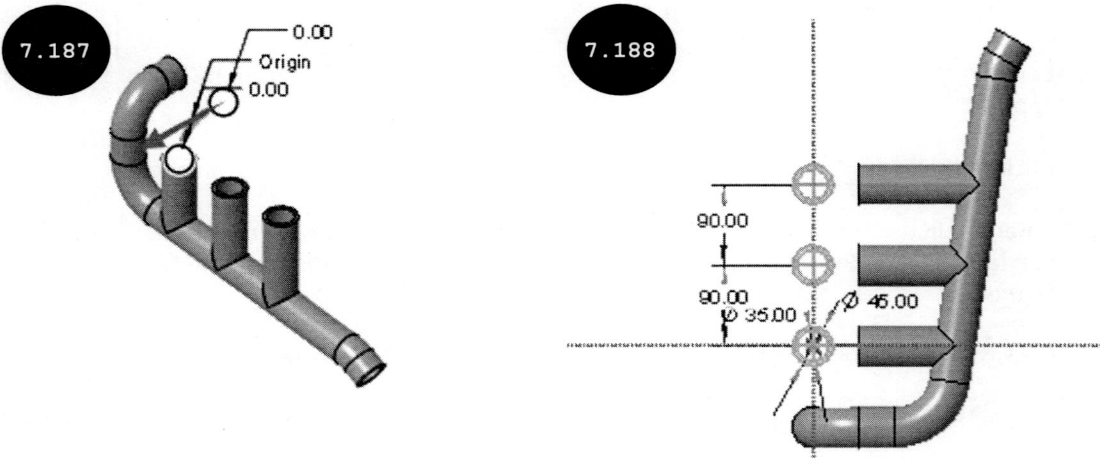

11. Exit the Sketching environment by clicking on the **OK** tool in the **Close** group and then change the orientation of the model to standard orientation. A preview of the sweep feature appears in the graphics area, see Figure 7.189.

12. Click on the green tick-mark button in the **Sweep** tab of the **Ribbon**. The sweep feature is created, see Figure 7.190.

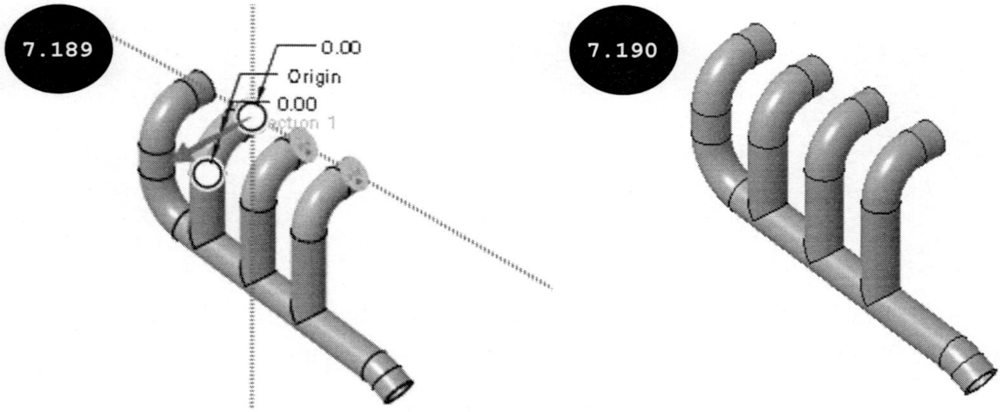

Section 9: Saving the Model

1. Click on the **Save** tool in the **Quick Access Toolbar**. The **Save Object** dialog box appears.

2. Click on the **OK** button in the dialog box. The model is saved with the name **C07-Tutorial02** in the specified working directory (<<*Creo Parametric**Chapter 7*\).

Tutorial 3

Create the model shown in Figure 7.191. All dimensions are in mm.

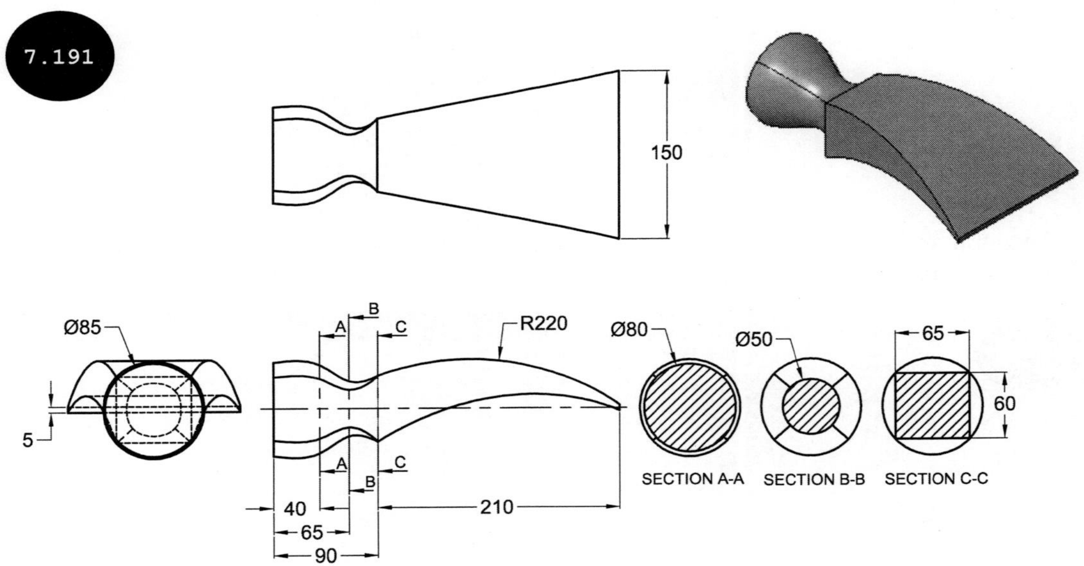

Section 1: Starting Creo Parametric

1. Start Creo Parametric by double-clicking on the Creo Parametric icon on your desktop.

Section 2: Setting the Working Directory

1. Set the working directory to <<*Creo Parametric\Chapter 7*.

Section 3: Invoking the Part Mode

1. Click on the **New** tool in the **Data** group of the **Home** tab. The **New** dialog box appears.

2. Enter **C07-Tutorial03** in the **File name** field of the dialog box as the name of the model.

3. Clear the **Use default template** check box and then click on the **OK** button in the dialog box. The **New File Options** dialog box appears.

4. Select the **mmns_part_solid_abs** template in the **New File Options** dialog box and then click on the **OK** button. The Part mode is invoked with the **mmns_part_solid_abs** template.

Section 4: Creating the Base Feature - Blend Feature

Now, you need to create the base feature of the model by using the **Blend** tool.

1. Expand the **Shapes** group of the **Model** tab and then click on the **Blend** tool, see Figure 7.192. The **Blend** tab appears in the **Ribbon** along with the expanded **Sections** panel, refer to Figure 7.193.

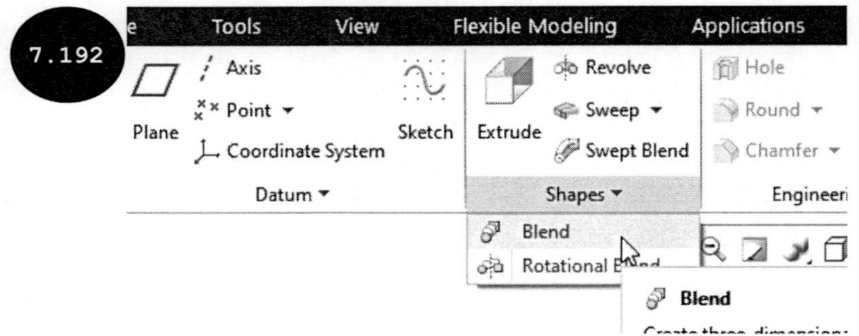

2. Ensure that the **Sketched sections** radio button is selected in the expanded **Sections** panel to create sections of the blend feature in the graphics area, see Figure 7.193.

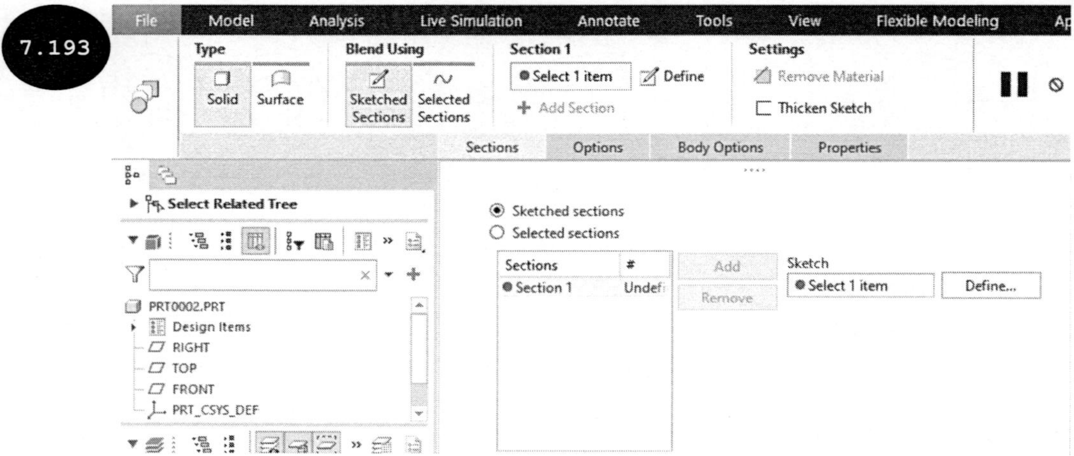

3. Click on the **Define** button in the expanded **Sections** panel to define the sketching plane for creating the first section. The **Sketch** dialog box appears.

4. Select the Right plane as the sketching plane and then click on the **Sketch** button in the dialog box. The Sketching environment is invoked and the Right plane is oriented normal to the viewing direction.

5. Create a sketch (a circle of diameter 85 mm) of the first section. Next, divide the circle into four entities by using the **Divide** tool of the **Editing** group in the **Sketch** tab. An arrow appears on one of the points of the sketch which indicates the start point of the section, see Figure 7.194.

6. After creating the first section, exit the Sketching environment.

7. Change the orientation of the sketch to standard orientation. Notice that an offset handle appears in the graphics area, see Figure 7.195. You are also prompted to specify the offset distance to create a new datum plane for creating the second section of the blend feature.

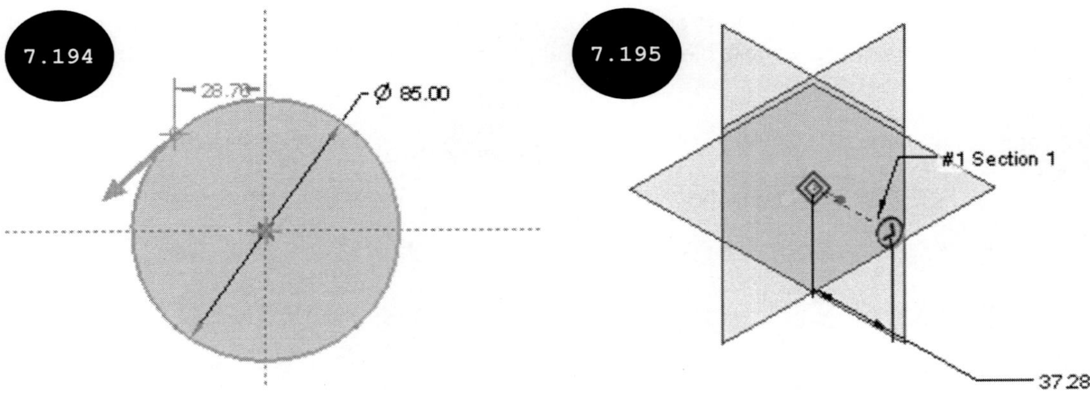

8. Expand the **Sections** panel of the **Blend** tab, see Figure 7.196. Notice that Section 1 is created and the number of entities of Section 1 are identified as 4.

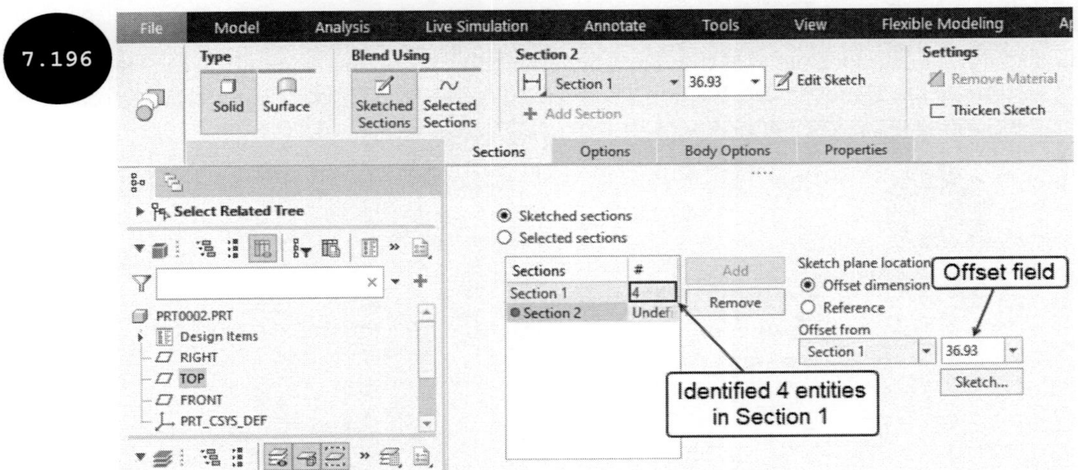

9. Ensure that the **Offset dimension** radio button is selected in the expanded **Sections** panel.

10. Enter **40** in the **Offset** field of the expanded **Sections** panel as the offset distance for creating a new datum plane for creating the second section of the blend feature.

11. Click on the **Sketch** button in the **Sections** panel. A datum plane at an offset distance of 40 mm is created and becomes the sketching plane for creating the second section.

12. Create the second section (a circle of diameter 80 mm) and then divide the circle into four entities by using the **Divide** tool of the **Editing** group, see Figure 7.197.

Note: Ensure that the start points of the first and second sections are in the same direction to avoid twisting in the resultant blend feature.

13. Exit the Sketching environment and then change the orientation of the model to standard orientation. The preview of the blend feature appears in the graphics area, see Figure 7.198.

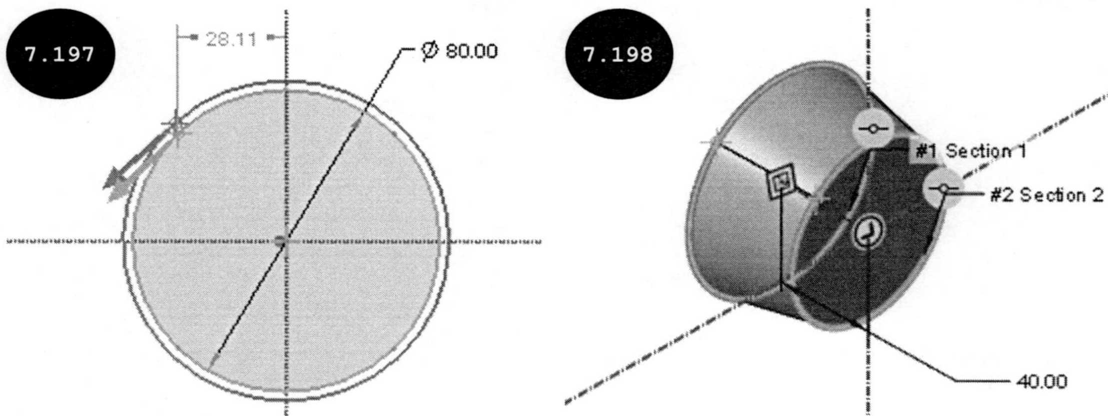

14. Expand the **Sections** panel of the **Blend** tab and then click on the **Add** button to create the third section of the blend feature. **Section 3** is added to the section list, see Figure 7.199. Also, an offset handle appears in the graphics area.

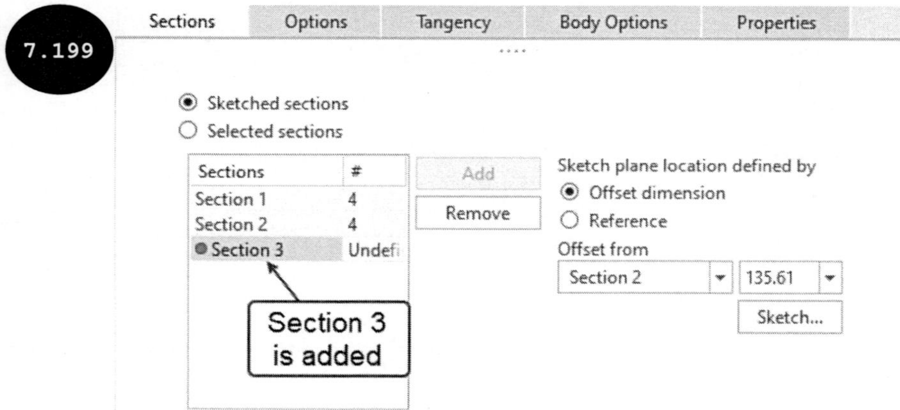

15. Select the **Section 1** option in the **Offset from** drop-down list of the expanded **Sections** panel.

16. Enter **65** in the **Offset** field of the expanded **Sections** panel and then click on the **Sketch** button. A datum plane is created at an offset distance of 65 mm and becomes the sketching plane for creating the third section of the blend feature.

17. Create the third section (a circle of diameter 50 mm) and then divide the circle into four entities by using the **Divide** tool of the **Editing** group, see Figure 7.200. Ensure that the start point of all the sections is in one direction as shown in Figure 7.200.

18. Exit the Sketching environment and then change the orientation of the model to standard orientation. The preview of the blend feature appears in the graphics area, see Figure 7.201.

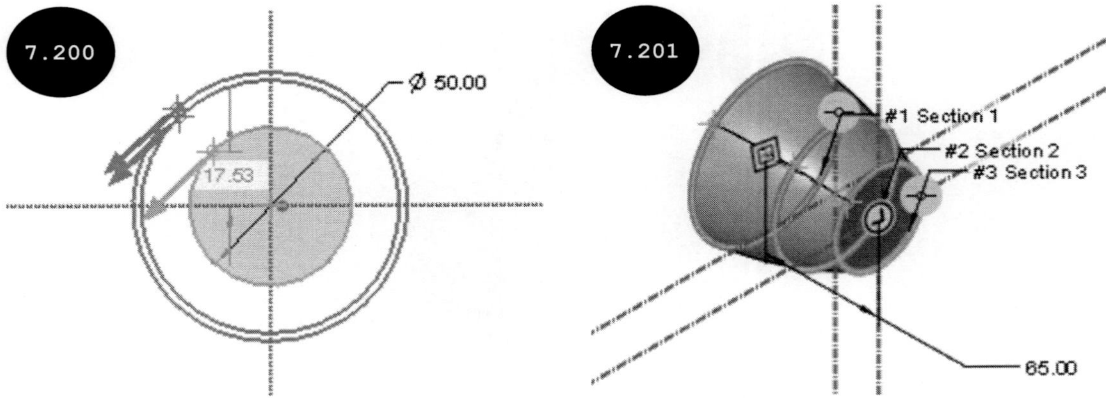

19. Expand the **Sections** panel of the **Blend** tab and then click on the **Add** button to create the fourth section of the blend feature. **Section 4** is added to the section list of the Sections panel.

20. Select the **Section 1** option in the **Offset from** drop-down list of the expanded **Sections** panel.

21. Enter **90** in the **Offset** field of the expanded **Sections** panel and then click on the **Sketch** button. A datum plane at an offset distance of 90 mm is created and becomes the sketching plane for creating the fourth section of the blend feature.

22. Create the fourth section (a rectangle of 65 mm X 60 mm), see Figure 7.202. Ensure that the start points of all the sections are in one direction as shown in Figure 7.202.

23. Exit the Sketching environment and then change the orientation of the model to standard orientation. A preview of the blend feature appears in the graphics area, see Figure 7.203.

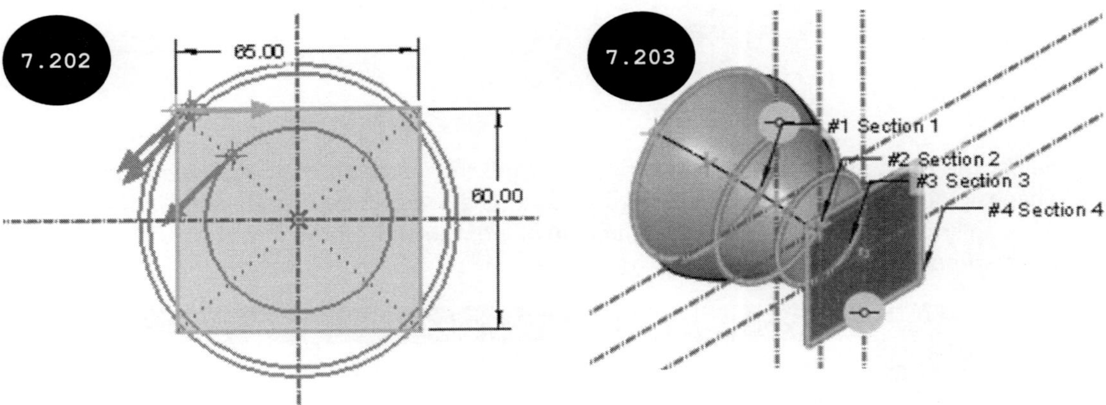

24. Click on the green tick-mark button in the **Blend** tab of the **Ribbon**. The blend feature is created, see Figure 7.204.

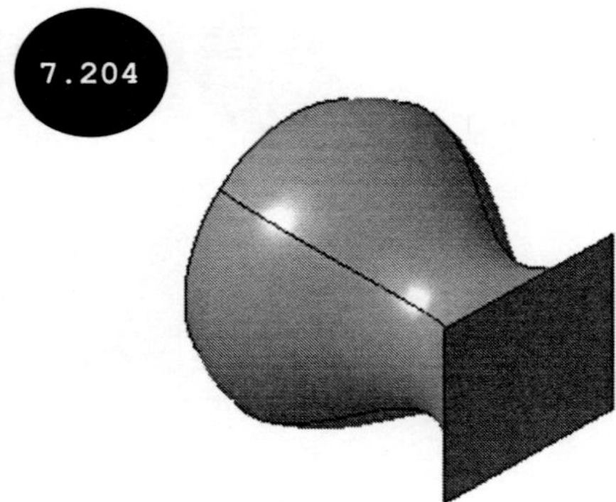

Section 5: Creating the Second Feature - Swept Blend Feature

Now, you need to create the second feature of the model, which is a swept blend feature.

1. Invoke the Sketching environment by selecting the Front plane as the sketching plane.

2. Create an arc of radius 220 mm as the trajectory of the sweep blend feature, see Figure 7.205. Next, exit the Sketching environment.

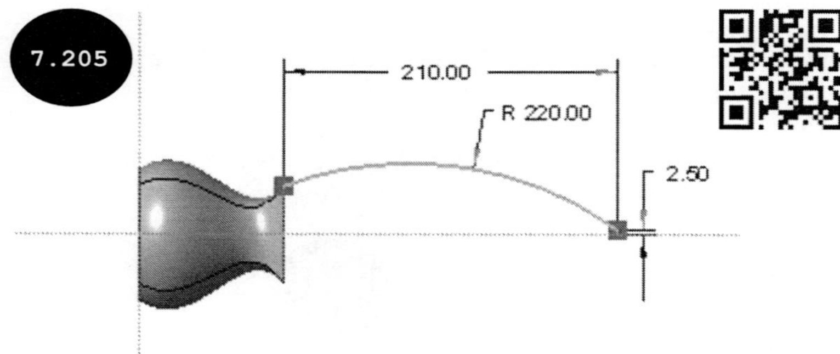

3. Select the trajectory (arc) in the graphics area and then click on the **Swept Blend** tool in the **Shapes** group of the **Model** tab, see Figure 7.206. The **Swept Blend** tab appears in the **Ribbon**. Also, an arrow appears in the graphics area on one of the ends of the trajectory that represents the start point of the trajectory, see Figure 7.207.

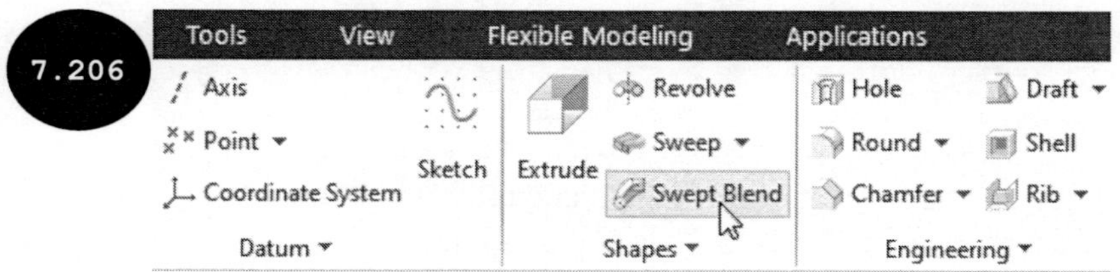

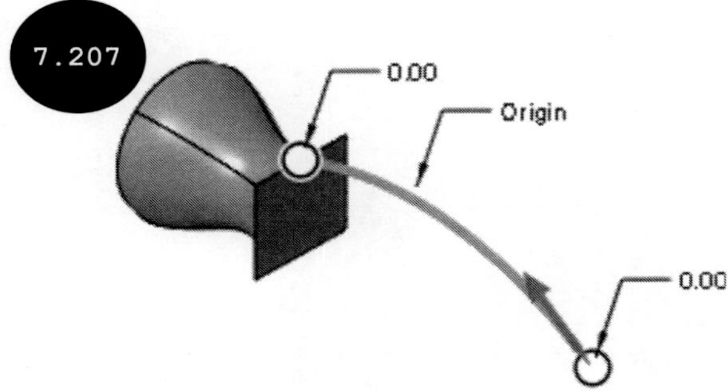

4. Expand the **Sections** panel of the **Swept Blend** tab and then click on the **Sketch** button in the expanded **Sections** panel. The Sketching environment is invoked and an imaginary sketching plane normal to the start point of the trajectory is oriented normal to the viewing direction.

5. Create the sketch of the first section, see Figure 7.208. Next, exit the Sketching environment.

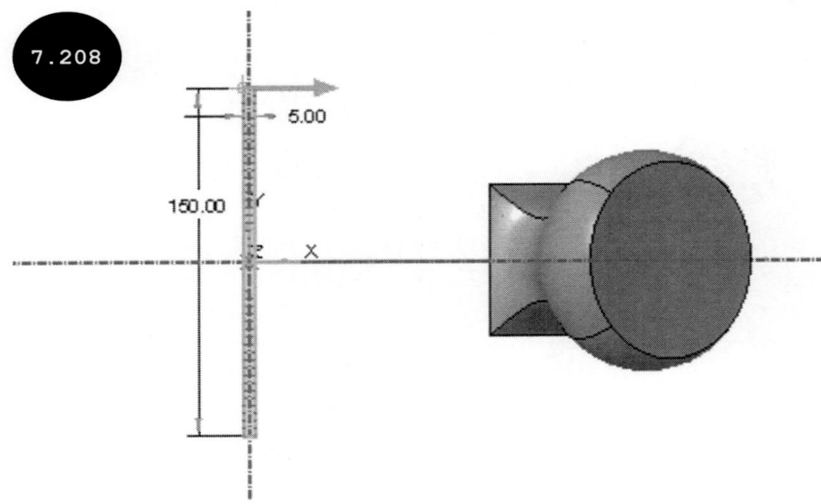

6. Click on the **Insert** button in the expanded **Sections** panel. The second section is added to the section list of the expanded **Sections** panel. Also, **End** appears in the **Section Location** field which indicates that the second section will be created at the end of the trajectory.

7. Ensure that the newly added section (**Section 2**) is selected in the section list of the expanded **Sections** panel and then click on the **Sketch** button. The Sketching environment is invoked and an imaginary sketching plane that is normal to the endpoint of the trajectory becomes parallel to the screen.

8. Create the sketch of the second section at the end of the trajectory, see Figure 7.209. In this figure, the rectangular sketch is created by taking reference from the existing geometries. Ensure that the start points of both the sections are in the same direction to avoid twisting in the resultant feature.

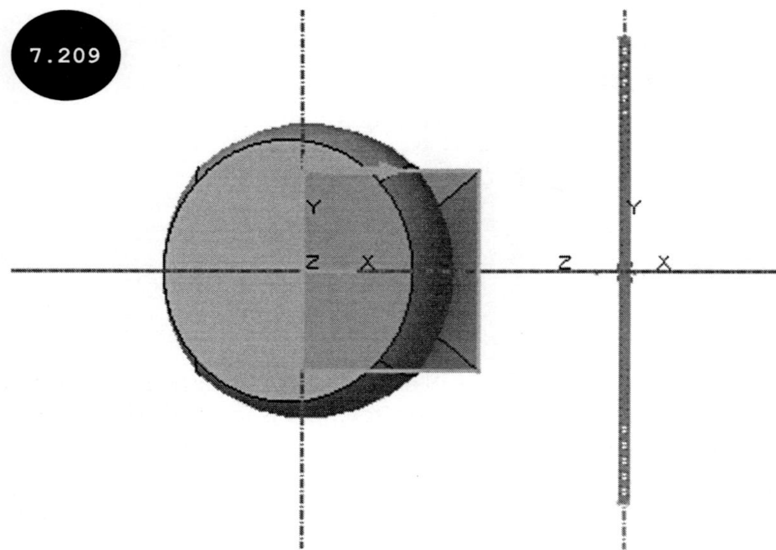

9. Exit the Sketching environment and change the orientation of the model to standard orientation. A preview of the swept blend feature appears, see Figure 7.210.

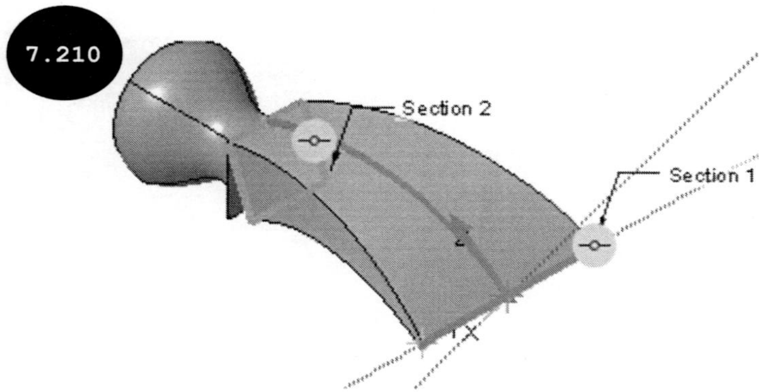

10. Expand the **References** panel of the **Swept Blend** tab, see Figure 7.211.

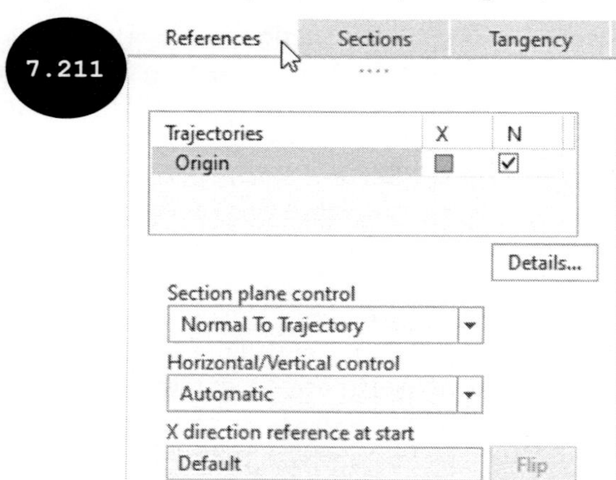

11. Select the **Constant Normal Direction** option in the **Section plane control** drop-down list of the expanded **References** panel. The **Direction reference** field appears (see Figure 7.212), and you are prompted to select a reference direction.

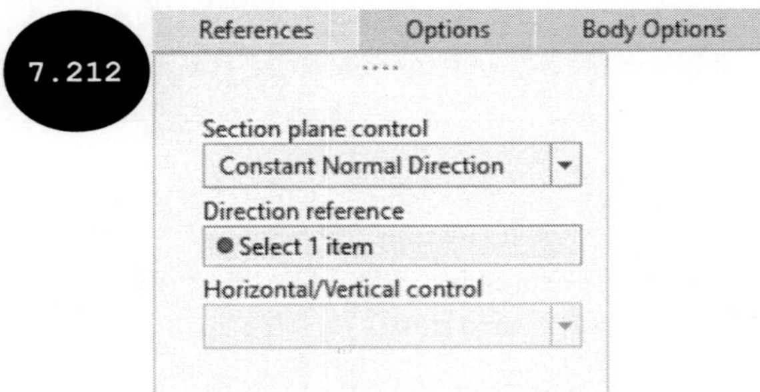

12. Select the Right plane as the reference direction. The preview of the swept blend feature appears such that the section remains parallel to the specified direction reference throughout the trajectory, see Figure 7.213.

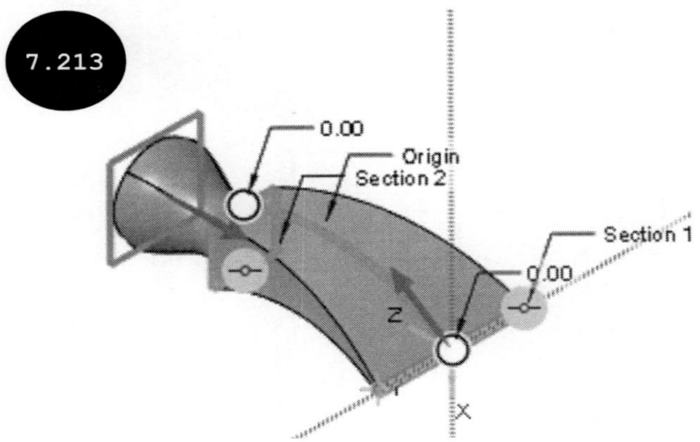

13. Click on the green tick-mark button in the **Swept Blend** tab of the **Ribbon**. The swept blend feature is created, see Figure 7.214.

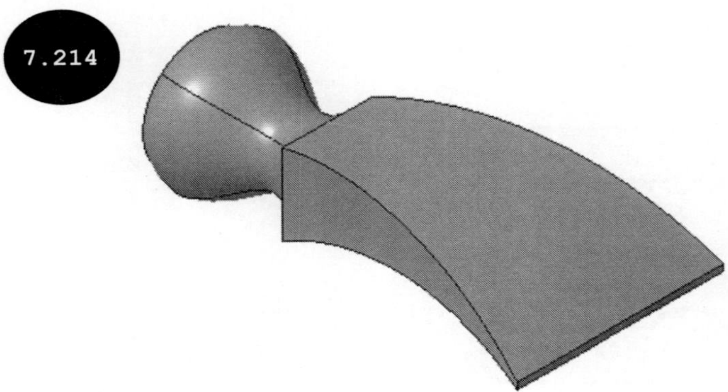

Section 6: Saving the Model

1. Click on the **Save** tool in the **Quick Access Toolbar**. The **Save Object** dialog box appears.

2. Click on the **OK** button in the dialog box. The model is saved with the name **C07-Tutorial03** in the specified working directory (<<*Creo Parametric**Chapter 7*\).

Hands-on Test Drive 1

Create the model shown in Figure 7.215, apply the Steel low carbon material, and calculate the mass properties of the model. All dimensions are in mm.

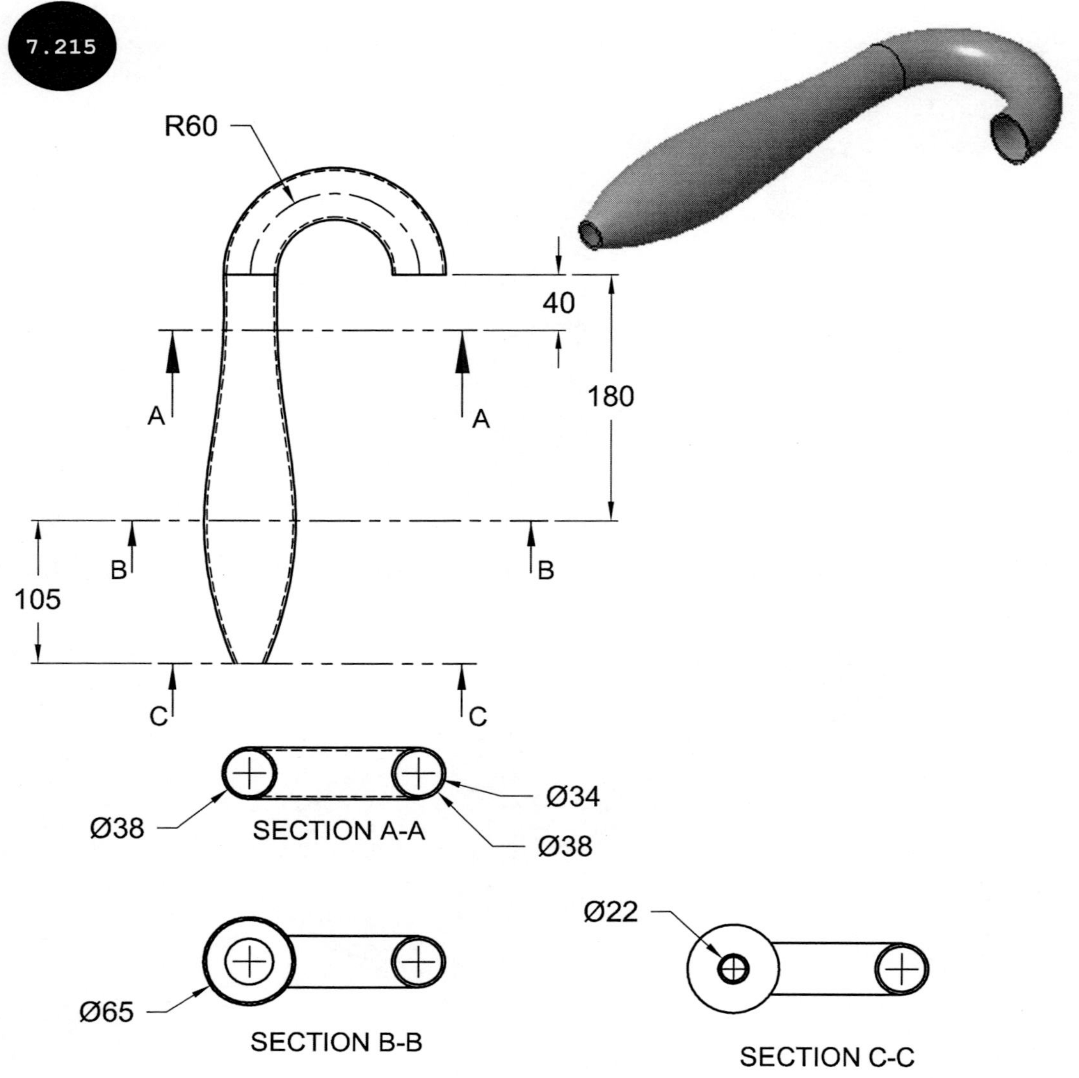

Hands-on Test Drive 2

Create the model shown in Figure 7.216 and then apply the Steel low alloy material. Also, calculate the mass properties of the model. All dimensions are in mm.

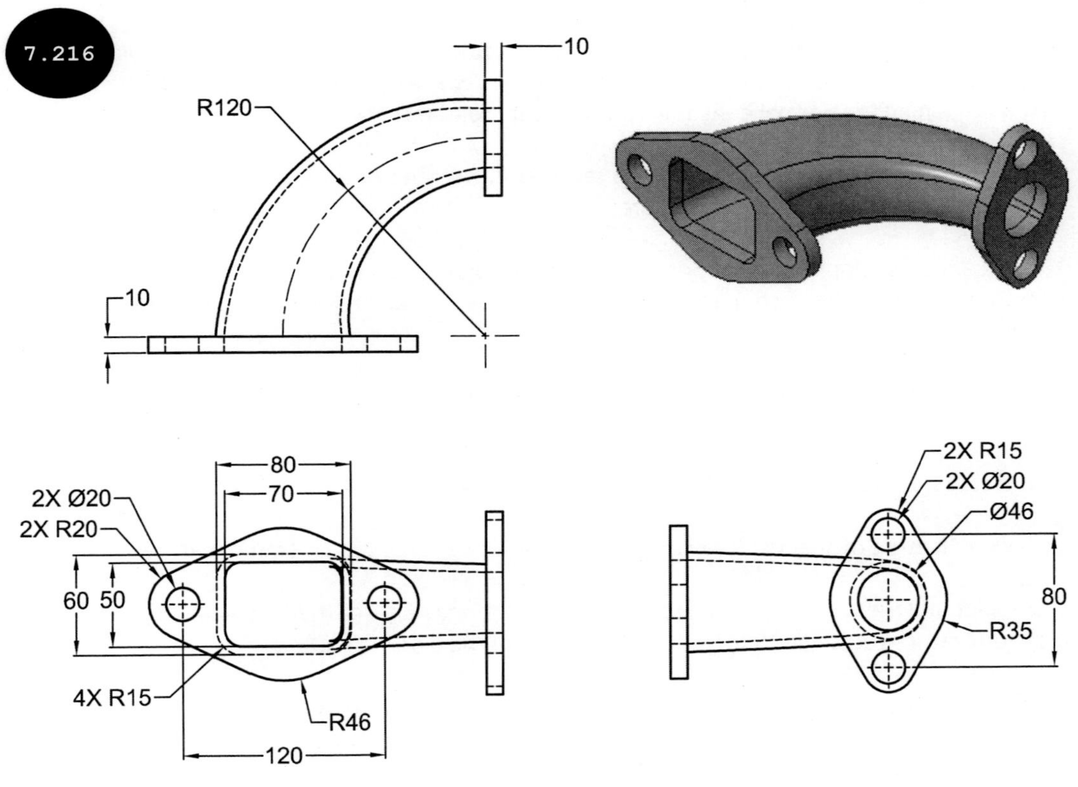

Summary

In this chapter, you have learned how to create sweep features, helical sweep features, volume helical sweep features, blend features, swept blend features, and rotational blend features.

Methods for creating various types of sweep features such as constant section sweep, variable section sweep, thin sweep feature, and cut sweep feature, by using the **Sweep** tool have been explained in the chapter. You have also learned how to create various types of helical sweep features by using the **Helical Sweep** tool, and various types of volume helical sweep features by using the **Volume Helical Sweep** tool. The chapter also describes the creation of Blend features.

Questions

Complete and verify the following sentences:

- The _________ tool is used for creating sweep features.
- While creating a sweep feature, the _________ option is selected in the **Section plane control** drop-down list of the **References** panel, by default. As a result, the section follows the trajectory by maintaining the normal constraint throughout the trajectory.
- The _________ button of the **Sweep** tab is used for invoking the Sketching environment to create the section of the sweep feature.
- The _________ option of the **Section plane control** drop-down list is used for creating a sweep feature such that the section remains parallel to a specified direction reference throughout the trajectory.
- You can control the start and end conditions of a sweep feature by using the _________ that appear on both ends of the trajectory.
- To create a _________ sweep feature, you need to select two or more than two trajectories.
- A sweep feature of specified wall thickness is known as _________ sweep feature.
- On selecting the _________ check box in the **Options** panel of the **Sweep** tab, the ends of the sweep feature get aligned/merged with the faces of the existing feature.
- You can create a constant or variable pitch helical sweep feature by using the _________ tool.
- The _________ radio button is used for creating a blend feature with a straight transition from one section to another.
- In Creo Parametric, to create a blend feature, the number of entities in each section should be the same. (True/False)
- To create a swept blend feature, you need to create a trajectory before invoking the **Swept Blend** tool. (True/False)
- In Creo Parametric, you cannot create a tapered helical sweep feature. (True/False)
- You cannot change the start point of a section from one point to another. (True/False)

CHAPTER

8

Patterning and Mirroring

In this chapter, the following topics will be discussed:

- Creating a Dimension Pattern
- Creating a Direction Pattern
- Creating an Axis Pattern
- Creating a Fill Pattern
- Creating a Table Pattern
- Creating a Reference Pattern
- Creating a Curve Pattern
- Creating a Point Pattern
- Creating a Variable Pattern
- Creating a Geometry Pattern
- Deleting a Pattern
- Mirroring a Feature
- Copying and Pasting a Feature

Patterning and mirroring tools are very powerful tools that help designers speed up the creation of a design, increase efficiency, and save time. For example, if a plate has 1000 holes of the same diameter, instead of creating each hole individually, you can create one hole and then pattern it to create all the remaining holes. Similarly, if the geometry is symmetric, you can create one of its sides and mirror it to create the other sides. The various methods used for patterning and mirroring features, faces, or bodies are discussed next.

In Creo Parametric, you can create different types of patterns such as Dimension Pattern, Direction Pattern, Axis Pattern, Fill Pattern, Table Pattern, Curve Pattern, and Point Pattern. The methods for creating various types of patterns are discussed next.

Creating a Dimension Pattern

Dimension pattern is used for creating multiple instances of a feature linearly, in one or two linear directions by selecting dimensions, see Figures 8.1 through 8.3. Note that in this pattern, the dimensions of the parent feature are used for defining the pattern directions. Figure 8.1 shows a feature to be patterned, including direction 1 and direction 2 dimensions. Figure 8.2 shows the resultant dimension pattern created in direction 1, whereas Figure 8.3 shows the resultant dimension pattern created in direction 1 and direction 2.

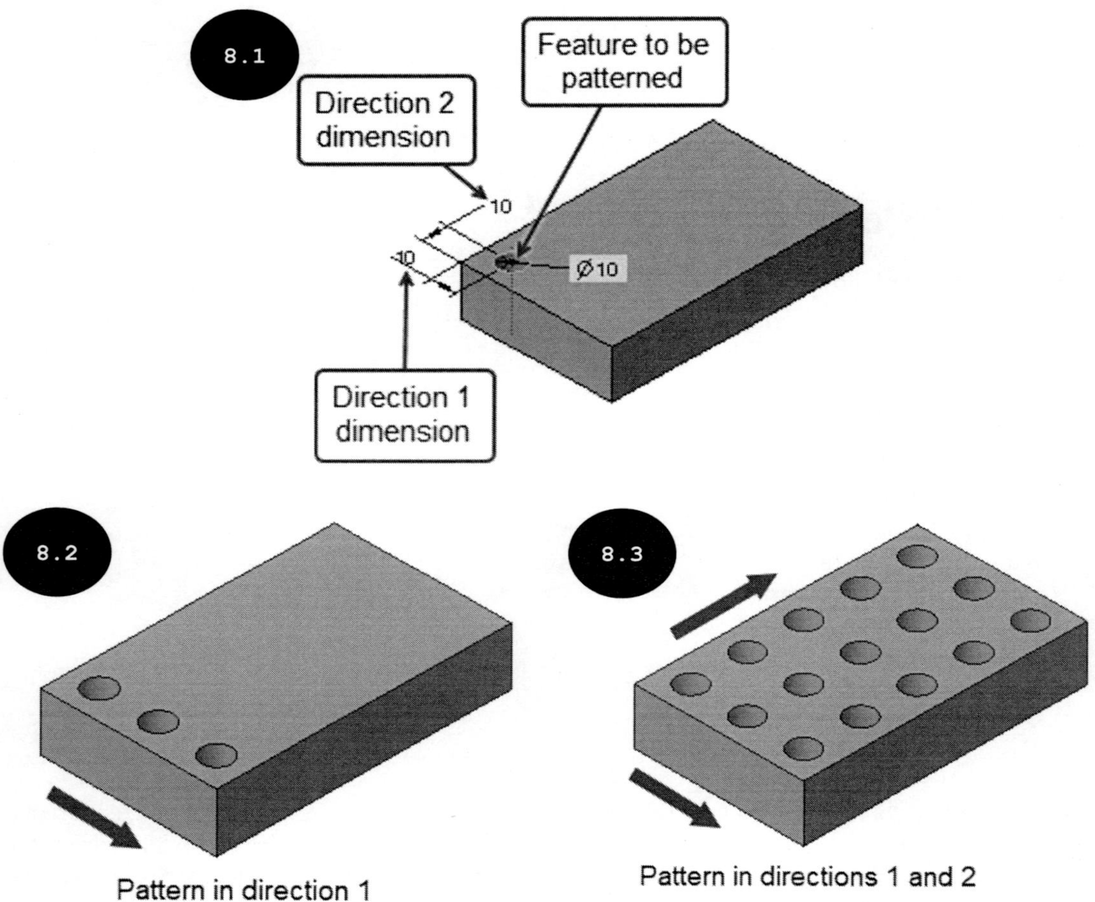

The method for creating a dimension pattern is discussed below:

1. Select a feature to be patterned in the graphics area or in the **Model Tree**.

2. Click on the **Pattern** tool in the **Editing** group of the **Model** tab, see Figure 8.4. The **Pattern** tab appears in the **Ribbon** which contains various options to create different types of patterns, see Figure 8.5.

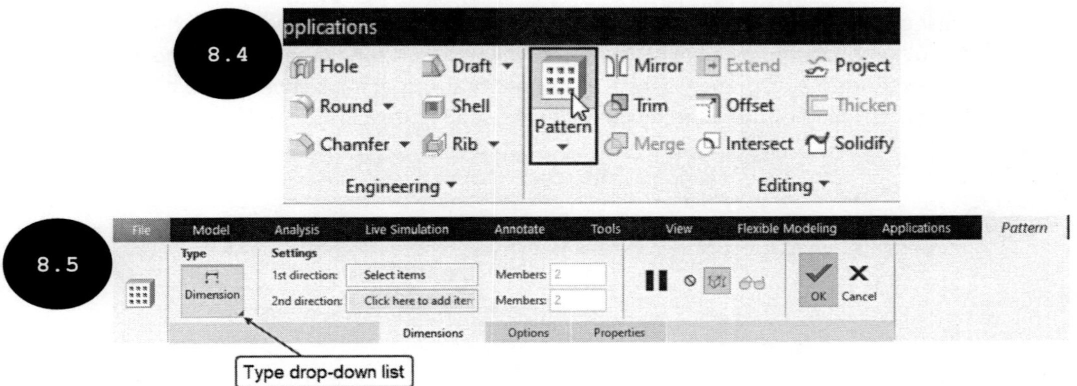

Type: By default, the **Dimension** option is selected in the **Type** drop-down list in the **Type** area of the **Pattern** tab, see Figure 8.5. As a result, the dimensions of the selected feature appear in the graphics area, since the **Dimension** option is used for creating a pattern by selecting the dimensions of the parent feature as the pattern directions. The other options of the **Type** drop-down list are discussed later in this chapter.

3. Ensure that the **Dimension** option is selected in the **Type** drop-down list of the **Type** area, see Figure 8.5.

4. Click on the dimension of the parent feature in the graphics area as the first pattern direction. An edit field appears in the graphics area, see Figure 8.6. Also, **1 item(s)** appears in the **First direction pattern dimensions** field in the **Settings** area of the **Pattern** tab (see Figure 8.7), which indicates that the dimension is selected as the first pattern direction.

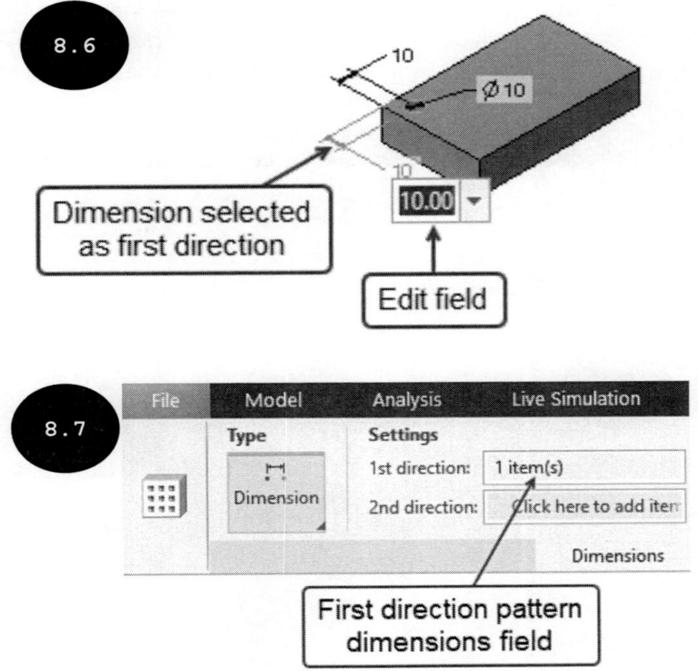

5. Enter the increment or spacing between two pattern instances in the edit field that appears in the graphics area and then press ENTER. Alternatively, expand the **Dimensions** panel of the **Pattern** tab, if not expanded automatically, and then specify the spacing between two pattern instances in the **Increment** field of the **Direction 1** collector, see Figure 8.8.

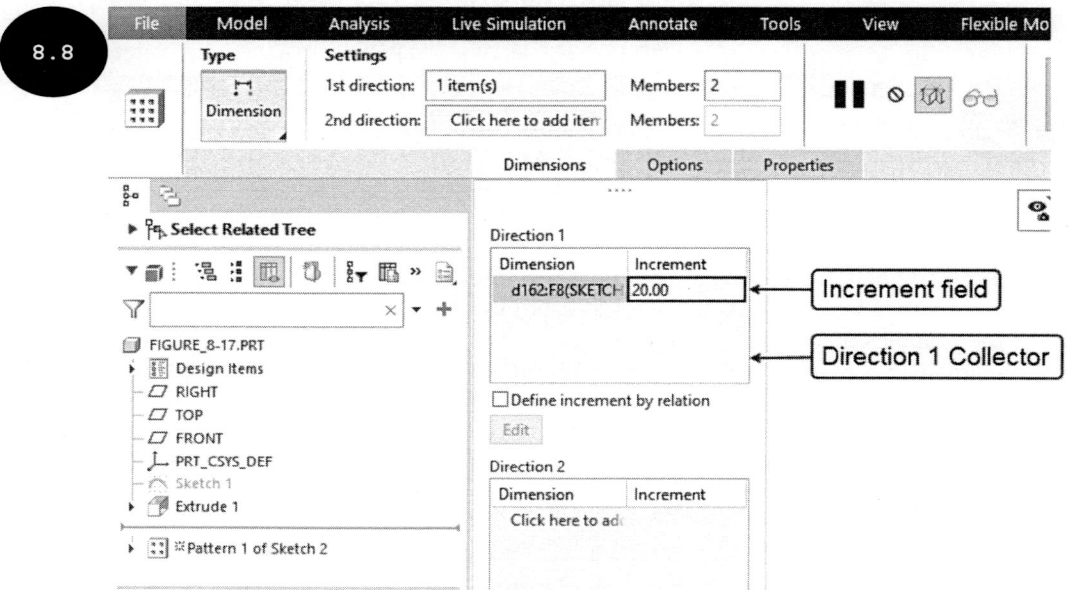

Now, you need to define the number of pattern instances to be created in the first direction.

6. Enter the number of pattern instances to be created in the **Members** field besides the **1st Direction** field in the **Settings** area of the **Pattern** tab and then press ENTER, see Figure 8.9. The dots appear in the graphics area representing the pattern instances in the first pattern direction, see Figure 8.10.

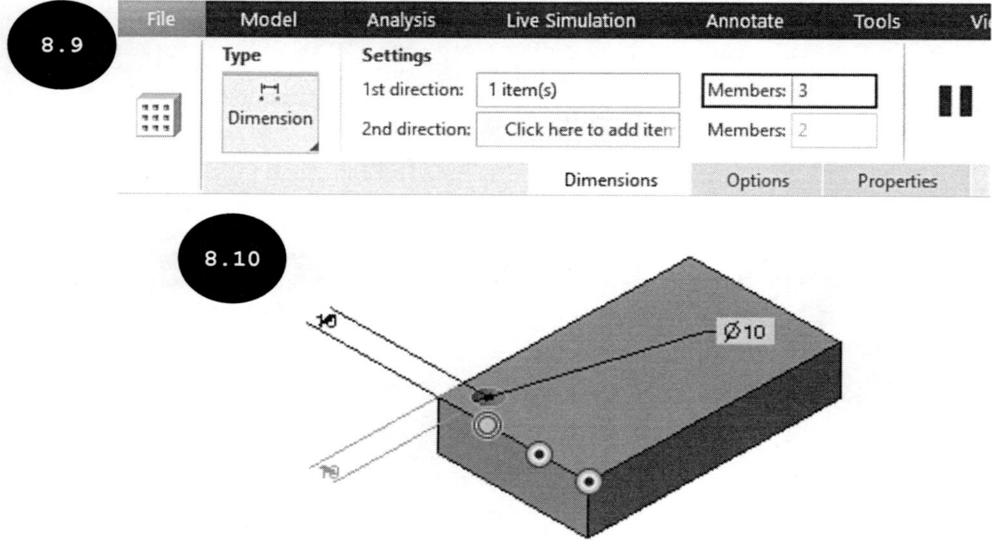

Note: The number of pattern instances specified in the **Members** field besides the **1st Direction** field in the **Pattern** tab also includes the parent feature.

After specifying the number of pattern instances in the first direction, you can define the second pattern direction and a number of instances in it.

7. Expand the **Dimensions** panel of the **Pattern** tab and then click on the **Direction 2** collector to activate it, see Figure 8.11.

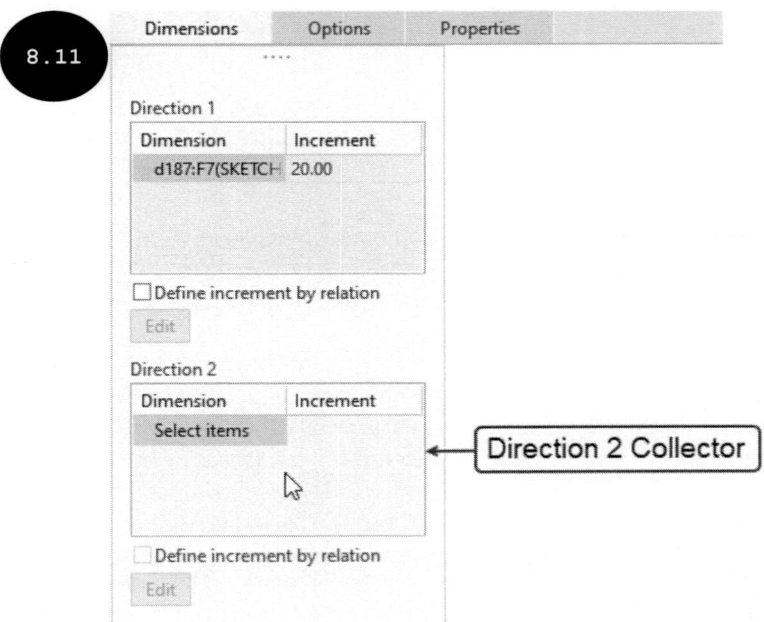

8. Click on the dimension of the parent feature in the graphics area as the second pattern direction. An edit field appears in the graphics area, see Figure 8.12. Also, the name of the selected dimension appears in the **Direction 2** collector of the expanded **Dimensions** panel, see Figure 8.13.

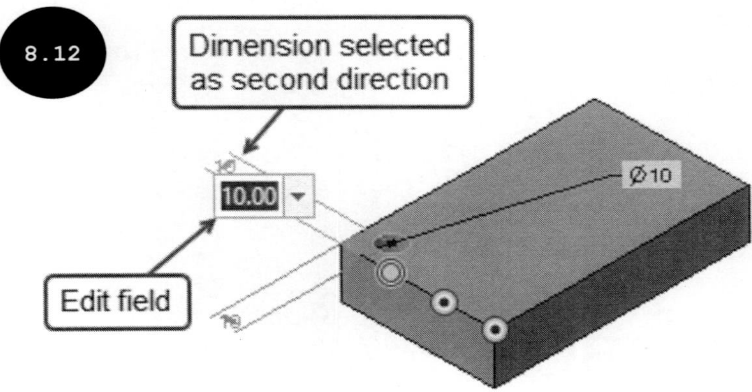

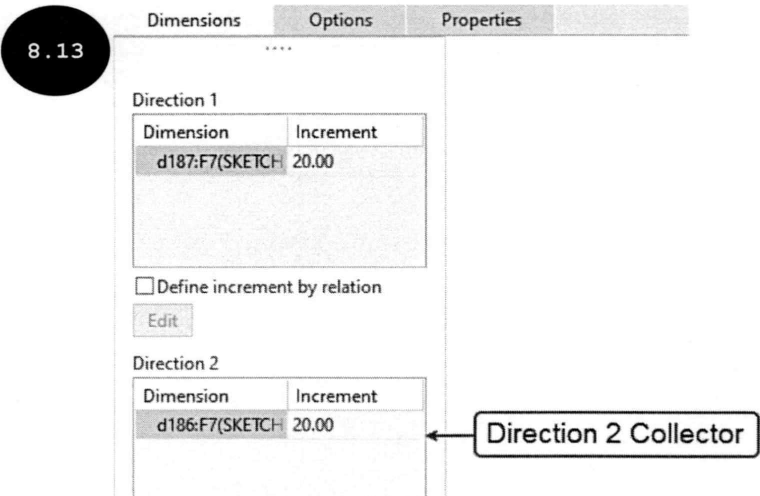

9. Enter the increment or spacing between two pattern instances in the second pattern direction in the edit field that appears in the graphics area and then press ENTER. Alternatively, you can also specify the spacing between two pattern instances in the **Increment** field of the **Direction 2** collector in the expanded **Dimensions** panel.

10. Enter the number of pattern instances to be created in the **Members** field besides the **2nd Direction** field in the **Settings** area of the **Pattern** tab and then press ENTER, see Figure 8.14. The dots appear in the graphics area representing the pattern instances in the second pattern direction, see Figure 8.15. Note that the number of pattern instances specified in the **Members** field besides the **2nd Direction** field also includes the parent feature.

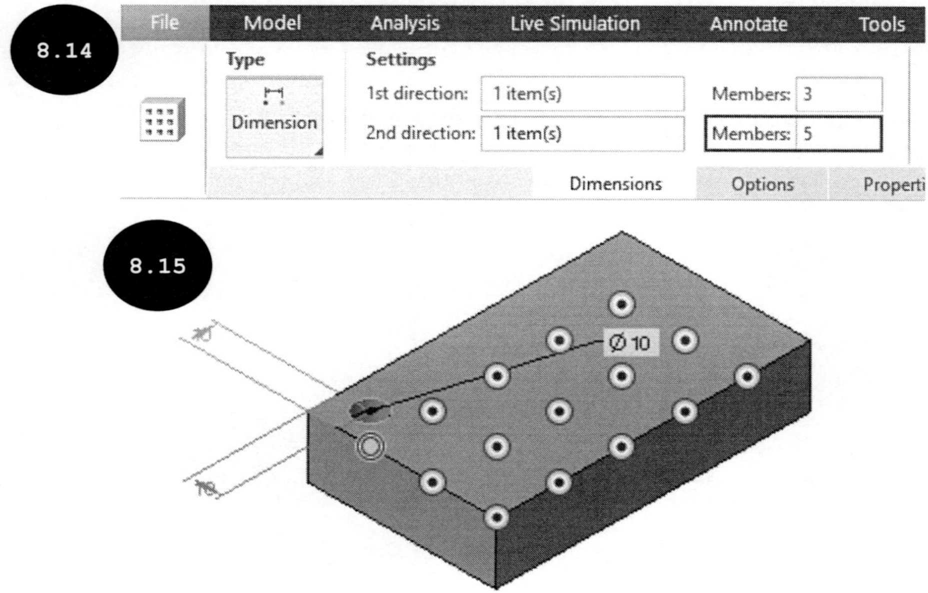

11. Expand the **Options** panel of the **Pattern** tab, see Figure 8.16. The options are discussed below:

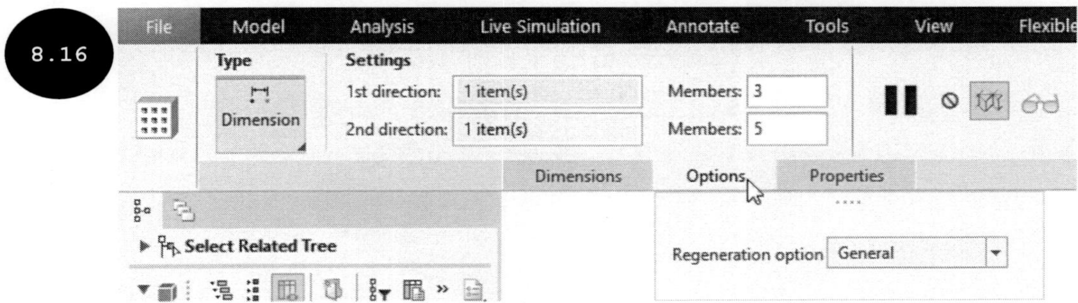

General: The **General** option of the **Regeneration option** drop-down list in the expanded **Options** panel allows to create a complex pattern in which pattern instances can touch or intersect each other as well as the edges of the placement face of the model.

Identical: The **Identical** option is used for creating an identical pattern in which all the instances are identical in size and shape. This option does not allow any intersection between the pattern instances or the edges of the placement face of the model.

Variable: The **Variable** option is used for creating a variable pattern in which you can vary the geometry or size of instances. You will learn more about variable pattern later in this chapter.

12. Select the **General** option in the **Regeneration option** drop-down list of the expanded **Options** panel.

13. Click on the green tick-mark button in the **Pattern** tab of the **Ribbon**. The dimension pattern in direction 1 and direction 2 is created, see Figure 8.17.

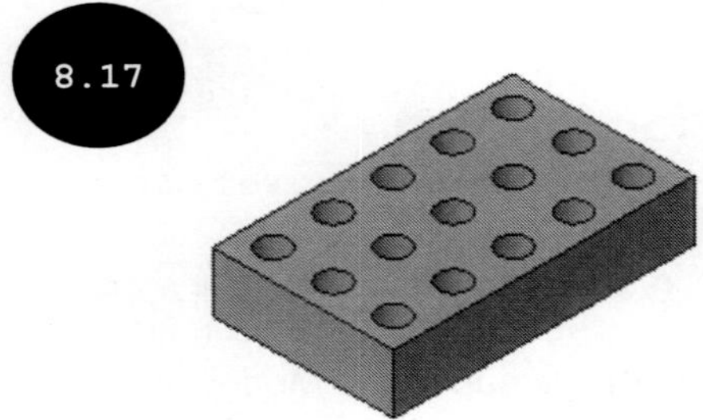

Creating a Direction Pattern

Direction pattern is used for creating multiple instances of a feature in one or two linear directions, see Figures 8.18 through 8.20. You can select a straight edge, a planar face, a linear curve, an axis of a coordinate system, or a datum axis to define a pattern direction. Figure 8.18 shows a feature to be patterned and two straight edges as direction 1 and direction 2. Figure 8.19 shows the resultant direction pattern created in direction 1, whereas Figure 8.20 shows the resultant direction pattern created in direction 1 as well as direction 2.

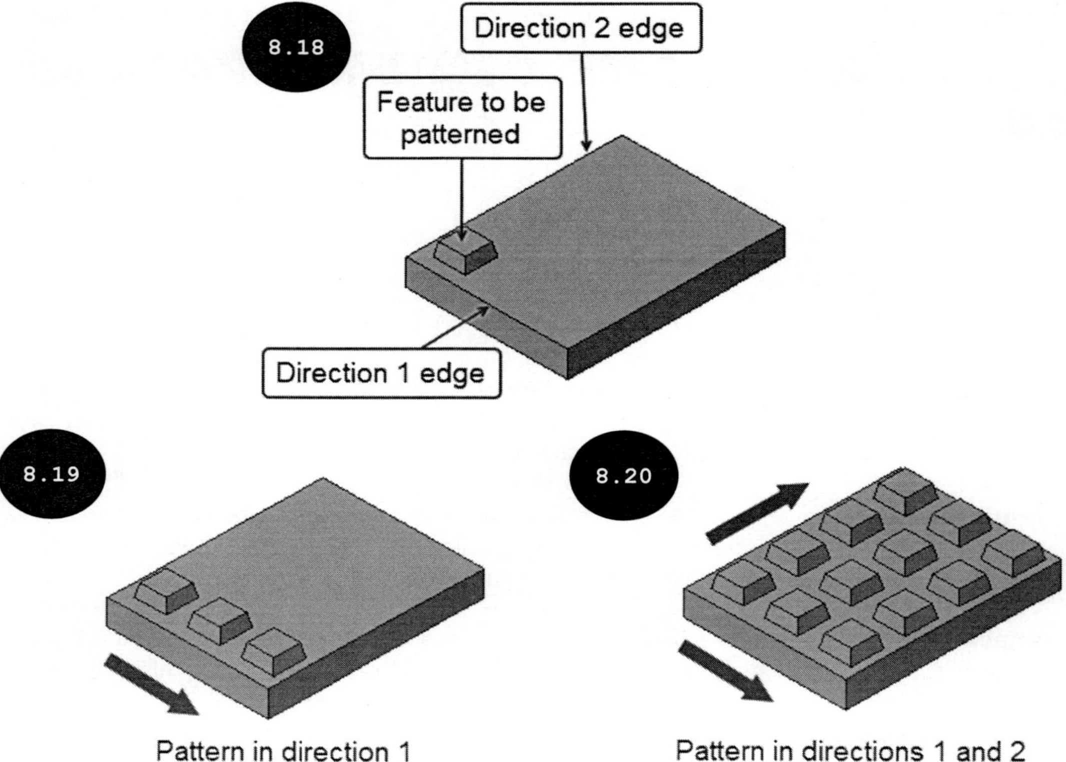

In addition to creating a direction pattern in one or two linear directions, you can also create a direction pattern circularly, as well as by selecting a coordinate system to define the direction vector of the pattern. The different types of direction patterns are discussed next.

Creating a Linear Direction Pattern

The method for creating a linear direction pattern is discussed below:

1. Select a feature to be patterned in the graphics area or in the **Model Tree**.

2. Click on the **Pattern** tool in the **Editing** group of the **Model** tab, see Figure 8.21. The **Pattern** tab appears in the **Ribbon**.

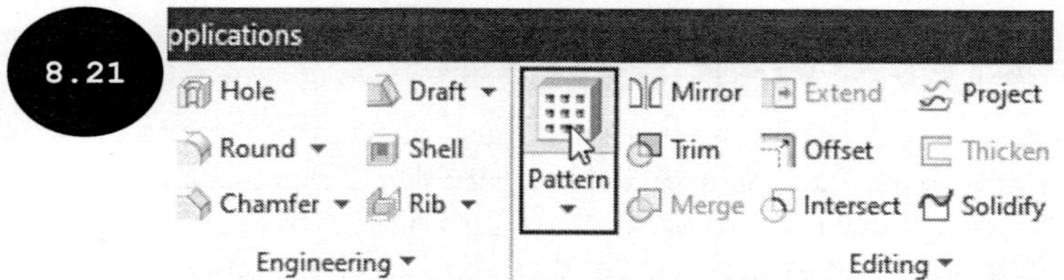

3. Select the **Direction** option in the **Type** drop-down list of the **Type** area, see Figure 8.22. The options for creating a direction pattern appear in the **Pattern** tab.

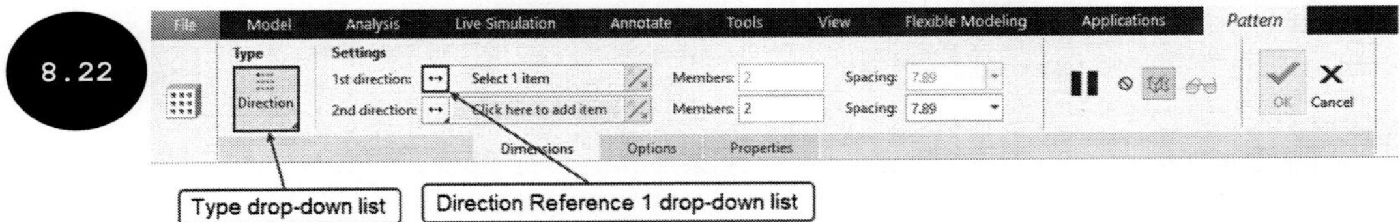

Direction Reference 1 drop-down list: By default, the **Translation** option is selected in the **Direction Reference 1** drop-down list in the **Settings** area of the **Pattern** tab, see Figure 8.22. As a result, you can create a linear direction pattern by selecting a straight edge, a linear curve, an axis, a planar face, or a plane to define a linear direction of the pattern. On selecting the **Rotation** option in the **Direction Reference 1** drop-down list, you can create a circular direction pattern by selecting a straight edge, a linear curve, or an axis as the axis of revolution of the pattern. On selecting the **Coordinate System** option , you need to select a coordinate system to define the direction vector in **X**, **Y**, and **Z** fields, see Figure 8.23. You will learn about creating a direction pattern by using the **Rotation** and **Coordinate System** options later in this chapter.

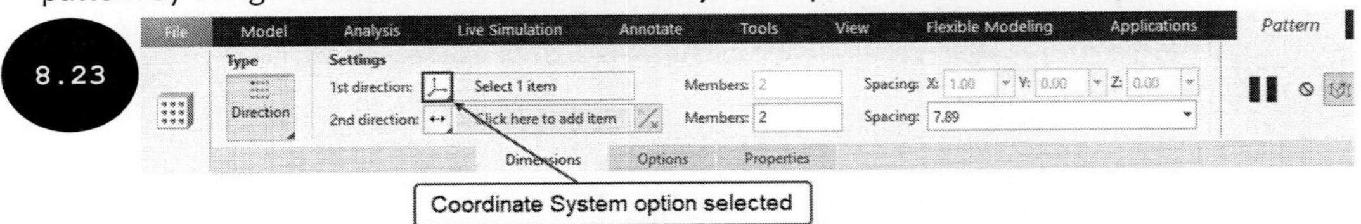

4. Ensure that the **Translation** option is selected in the **Direction Reference 1** drop-down list in the **Settings** area in the **Pattern** tab to create a linear direction pattern.

5. Select a straight edge, a linear curve, an axis, a planar face, or a plane as the first direction reference. The name of the selected entity appears in the **First Direction Reference** field in the **Settings** area of the **Pattern** tab, see Figure 8.24. Also, black dots appear in the graphics area representing the pattern instances along the selected direction reference, see Figure 8.25.

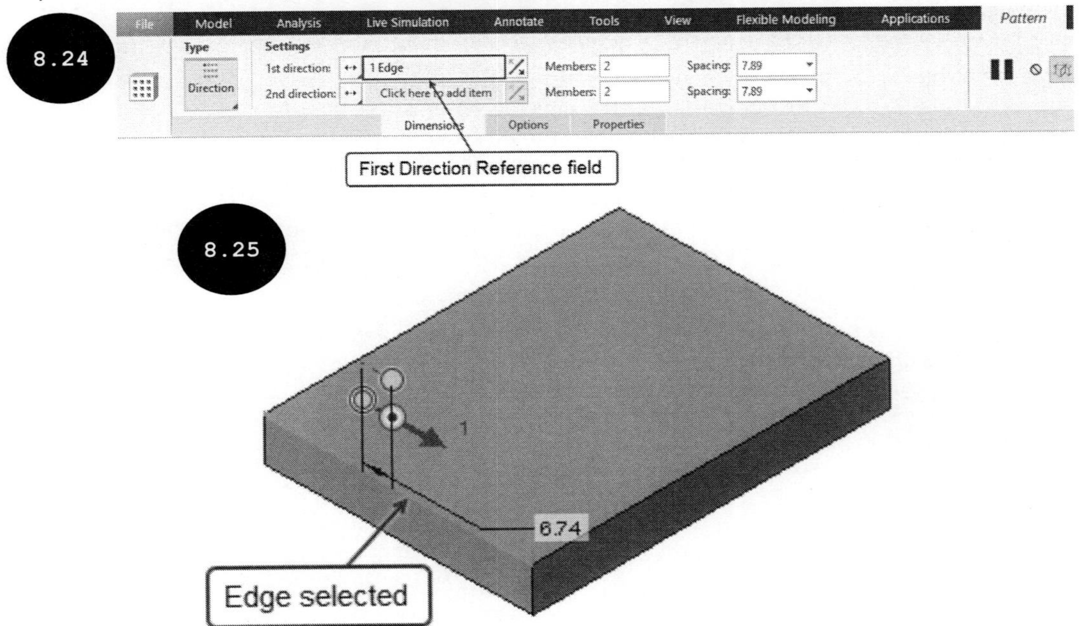

6. Enter a number of pattern instances to be created along the first direction reference in the **Members** field, see Figure 8.26. Next, press ENTER.

Note: The number of pattern instances specified in the **Members** field also includes the parent feature.

7. Enter the spacing between pattern instances in the **Spacing** field of the **Pattern** tab, see Figure 8.26. Next, press ENTER.

8. Click on the **Flip** button to reverse the direction of the pattern, if needed, see Figure 8.26.

9. Click on the **Second Direction Reference** field in the **Settings** area, see Figure 8.26. The **Second Direction Reference** field gets activated and you are prompted to select a second direction reference of the pattern.

8.26

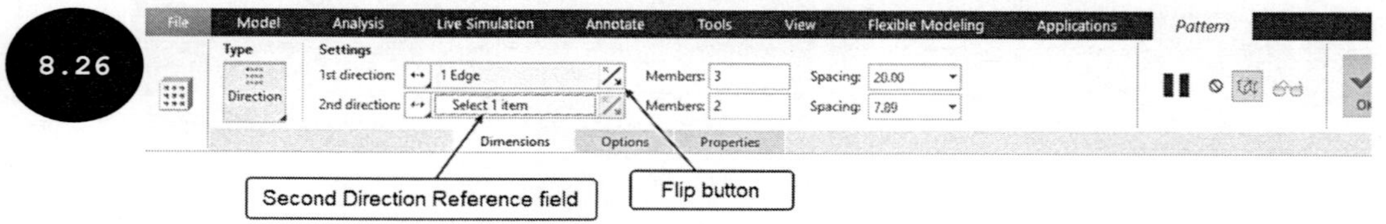

10. Select a straight edge, a linear curve, an axis, a planar face, or a plane as the second direction reference. The name of the selected entity appears in the **Second Direction Reference** field of the **Settings** area. Also, black dots appear in the graphics area along the selected second direction reference, representing the pattern instances, see Figure 8.27.

11. Specify the number of pattern instances and the spacing between pattern instances along the second pattern direction in the respective fields of the **Pattern** tab.

12. Click on the **Flip** button to reverse the direction of the pattern, if needed.

Note: In Creo Parametric, you can skip some of the instances of the pattern. To do so, click on the black dot to be skipped that appears in the graphics area. The selected black dot turns to white indicating that it is removed. You can similarly skip multiple pattern instances.

13. Click on the green tick-mark button in the **Pattern** tab. A linear direction pattern in two linear directions is created, see Figure 8.28.

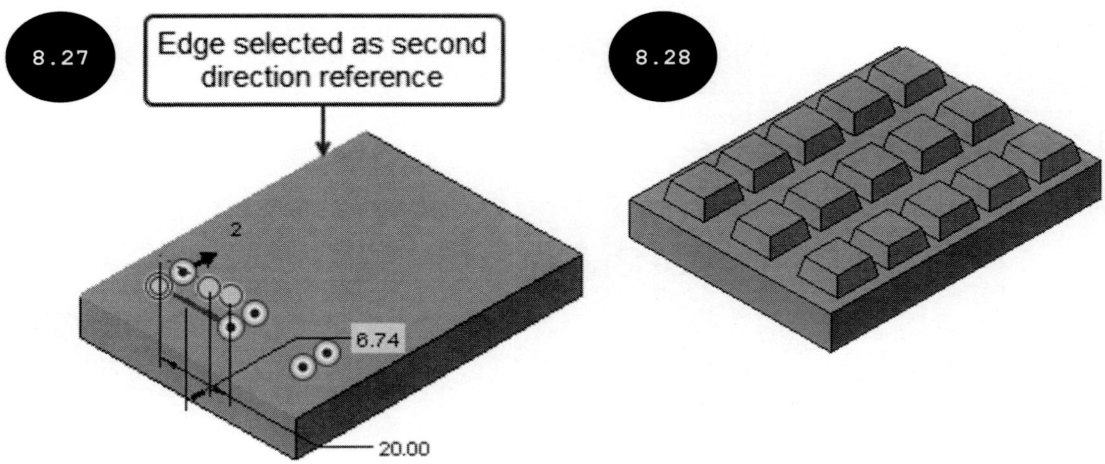

Creating a Circular Direction Pattern

The method for creating a circular direction pattern is discussed below:

1. Select a feature to be patterned in the graphics area or in the **Model Tree**.

2. Click on the **Pattern** tool in the **Editing** group of the **Model** tab. The **Pattern** tab appears in the **Ribbon**.

3. Select the **Direction** option in the **Type** drop-down list of the **Type** area, see Figure 8.29. The options for creating a direction pattern appear in the **Pattern** tab.

4. Select the **Rotation** option in the **Direction Reference 1** drop-down list of the **Settings** area to create a circular direction pattern, see Figure 8.29.

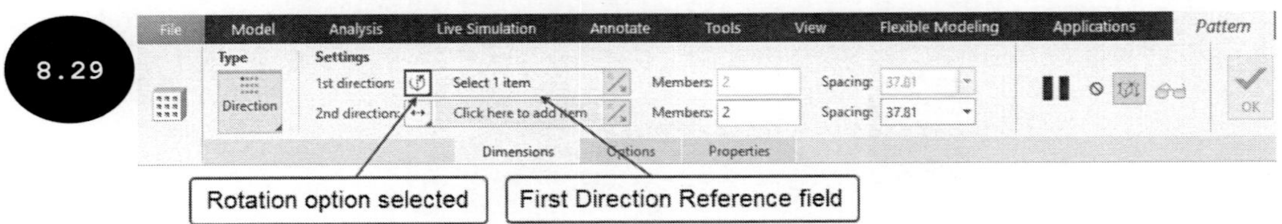

5. Select a straight edge, a linear curve, or an axis as the axis of revolution of the pattern, see Figure 8.30. In this figure, an axis of the coordinate system is selected as the axis of revolution. The name of the selected entity appears in the **First Direction Reference** field of the **Pattern** tab. Also, black dots appear in the graphics area representing the pattern instances around the axis of revolution selected, see Figure 8.30.

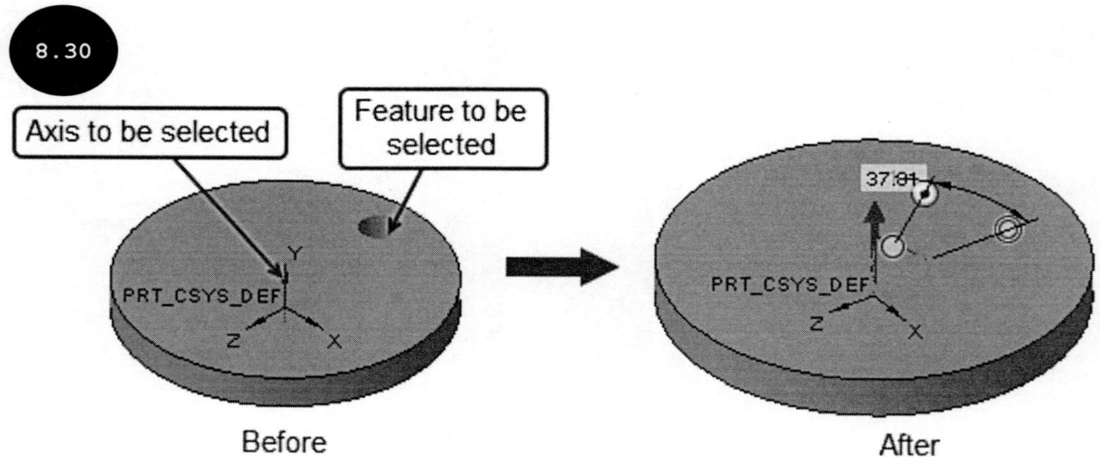

6. Enter the number of pattern instances to be created in the first direction and the angle between the instances in the respective fields of the **Pattern** tab. You can also reverse the first direction of the pattern by clicking on the **Flip** button.

Tip: You can similarly create a direction pattern in the second direction by selecting a second direction reference and the number of pattern instances to be created in the second direction as well as the angle between instances.

Note: To skip a pattern instance, click on the black dot to be skipped that appears in the graphics area. The selected black dot turns to white indicating that it is removed. You can similarly skip other pattern instances.

7. Click on the green tick-mark button in the **Pattern** tab. A circular direction pattern is created, see Figure 8.31.

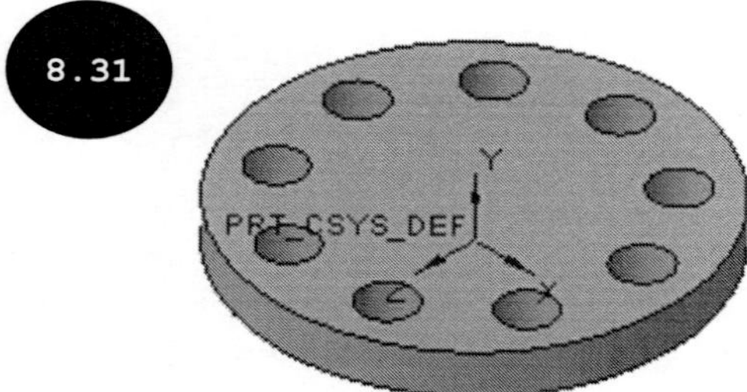

Creating a Direction Pattern by Selecting a Coordinate System

The method for creating a direction pattern by selecting a coordinate system is discussed below:

1. Select a feature to be patterned in the graphics area or in the **Model Tree**.

2. Click on the **Pattern** tool in the **Editing** group. The **Pattern** tab appears in the **Ribbon**.

3. Select the **Direction** option in the **Type** drop-down list of the **Type** area in the **Pattern** tab, see Figure 8.32. The options for creating a direction pattern appear in the **Pattern** tab.

4. Select the **Coordinate System** option in the **Direction Reference 1** drop-down list in the **Pattern** tab, see Figure 8.32.

8.32

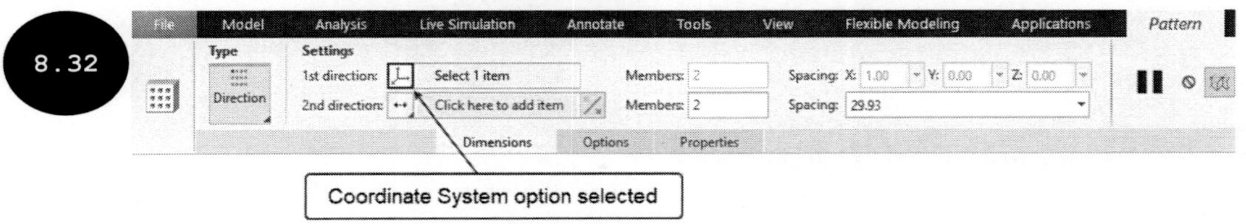

5. Select a coordinate system in the graphics area, see Figure 8.33. The selected coordinate system appears in the **First Direction Reference** field of the **Settings** area. Note that the coordinate system to be selected should be created before the feature is patterned.

6. Enter the number of pattern instances to be created in the **Members** field of the **Settings** area in the **Pattern** tab and then press ENTER. Black dots appear in the graphics area representing the number of pattern instances including the parent feature.

7. Specify the X, Y, and Z values in the respective **X**, **Y**, and **Z** fields of the **Pattern** tab to define the direction vector. In this figure, 46, 0, and 18 are defined as the X, Y, and Z values, respectively. As a result, the X axis distance between the pattern instances is 46 mm, Y axis distance between the pattern instances is 0 mm, and Z axis distance between the pattern instances is 18 mm.

8.33

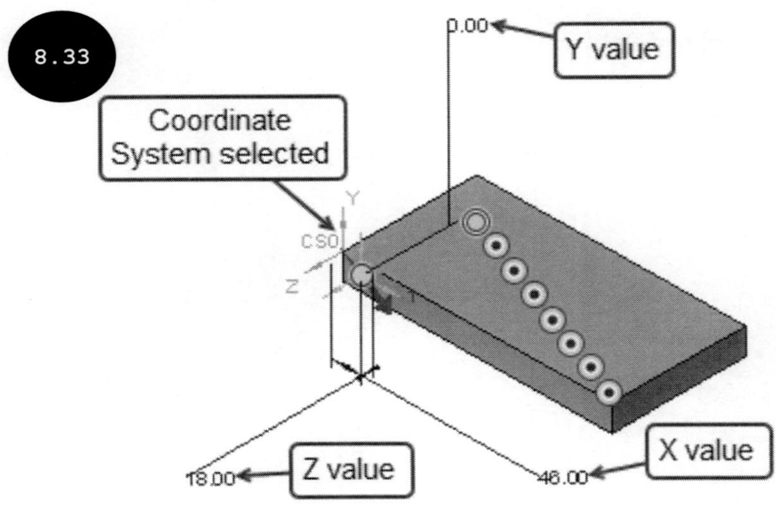

Tip: You can similarly specify the second direction reference and define the number of pattern instances to be created in the second direction.

8. Click on the green tick-mark button in the **Pattern** tab. The direction pattern is created by selecting a coordinate system, see Figure 8.34.

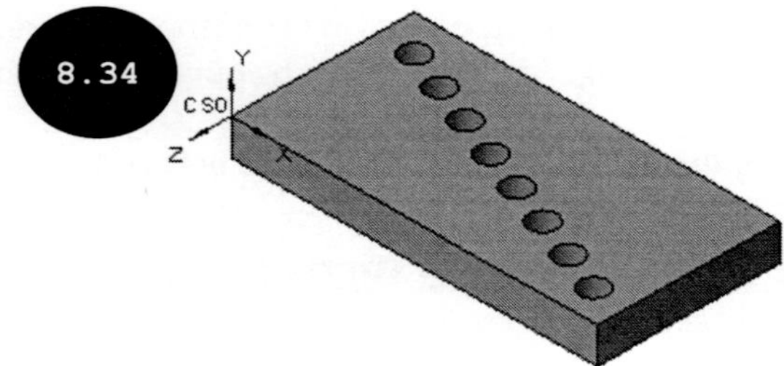

Creating an Axis Pattern

An axis pattern is used for creating multiple instances of a feature circularly, in an angular direction, see Figure 8.35. You can select an axis to define an angular direction for creating the pattern. You can also create an axis pattern in angular as well as in radial directions, see Figure 8.36. In this figure, the axis pattern is created in both directions. The method for creating an axis pattern is discussed below:

8.35

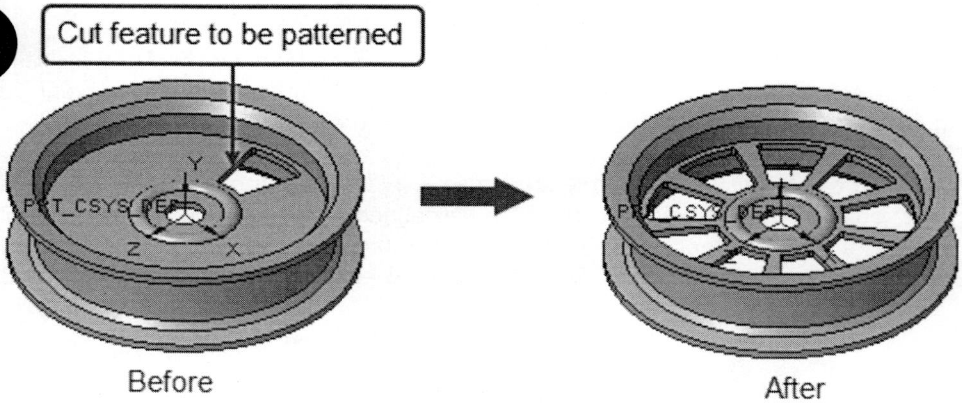

Cut feature to be patterned

Before After

8.36

Cut feature to be patterned

Before After

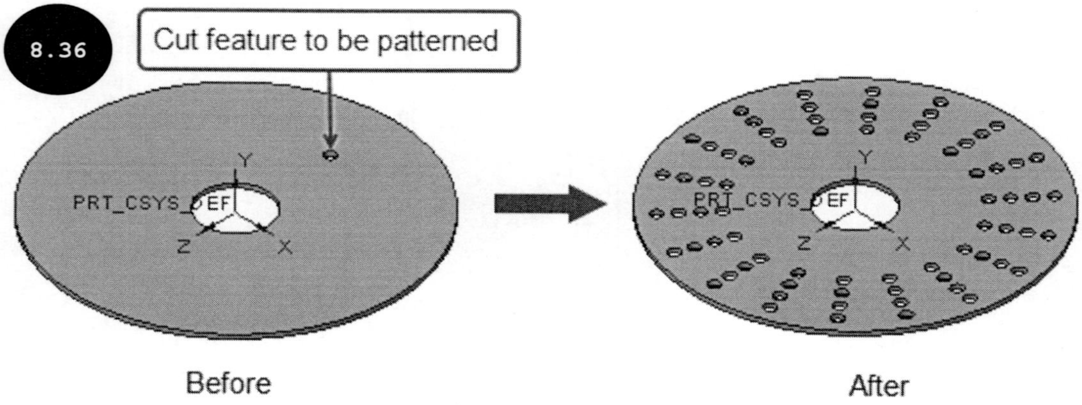

1. Select a feature to be patterned in the graphics area or in the **Model Tree**.

2. Click on the **Pattern** tool in the **Editing** group of the **Model** tab. The **Pattern** tab appears.

3. Select the **Axis** option in the **Type** drop-down list of the **Type** area in the **Pattern** tab, see Figure 8.37. The options for creating an axis pattern in angular and radial directions appear in the **Pattern** tab.

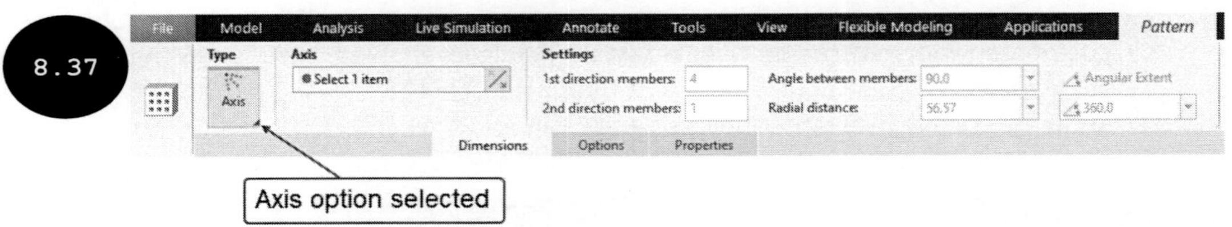

4. Select an axis to define the angular direction for creating the pattern instances around it, see Figure 8.38. Black dots appear in the graphics area representing the pattern instances.

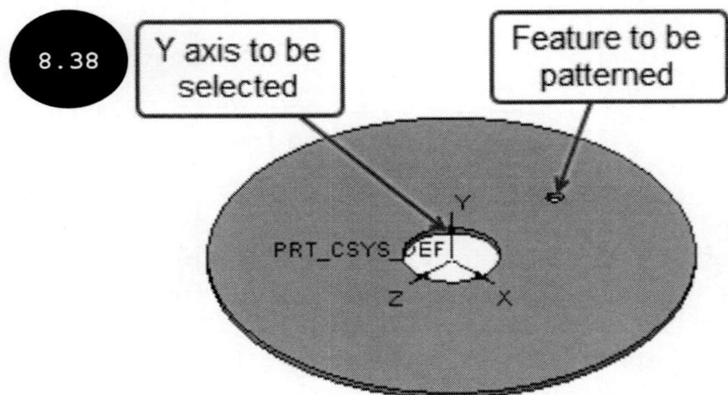

5. Enter the number of pattern instances to be created and the angle between the two pattern instances in the respective fields of the **Pattern** tab. Black dots representing the pattern instances appears, see Figure 8.39.

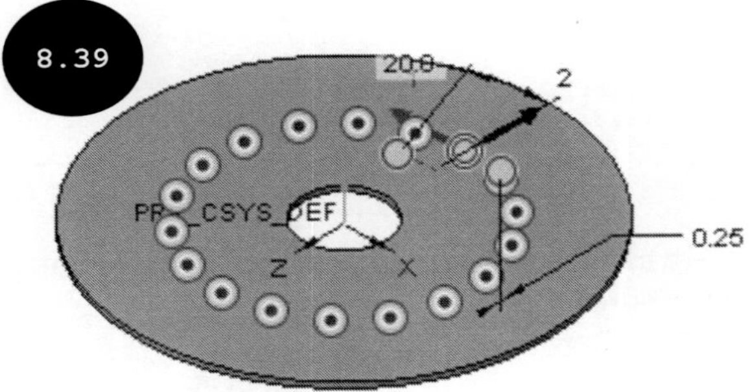

Note: To skip a pattern instance, click on the black dot to be skipped in the graphics area. The selected black dot turns to white indicating that it is removed. You can similarly skip the other pattern instances.

Note: Instead of specifying the angle between two pattern instances, you can specify the total angle value as angular extent to arrange all the pattern instances within the specified angle value with equal angular spacing among all instances. To do so, click on the **Angular extent** button, see Figure 8.40. The **Angular extent** field gets enabled. Next, enter the total angle value in the **Angular extent** field and then press ENTER. All the pattern instances get arranged equally within the specified angle value.

8.40

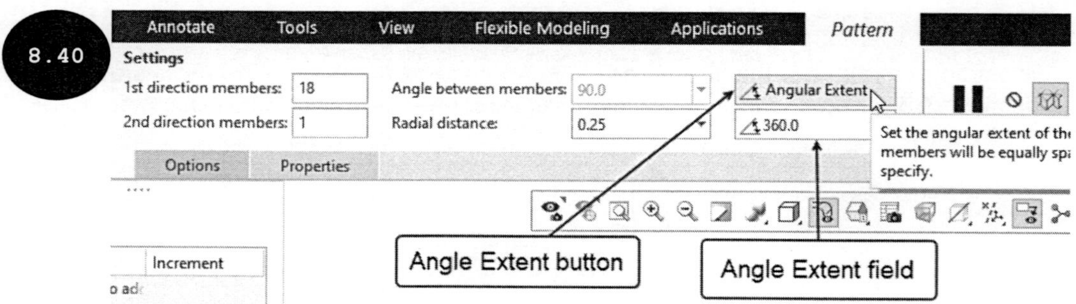

After specifying the number of pattern instances and the angle value, you can click on the green tick-mark button of the **Pattern** tab to create the axis pattern in angular direction only. For creating an axis pattern in angular as well as radial directions, you need to follow the steps given below:

6. Enter the number of instances to be created in the radial direction (second direction) and the radial distance between the pattern instances in the respective fields of the **Settings** area, see Figure 8.41. Black dots representing the pattern instances in the radial direction appear in the graphics area, see Figure 8.42.

8.41

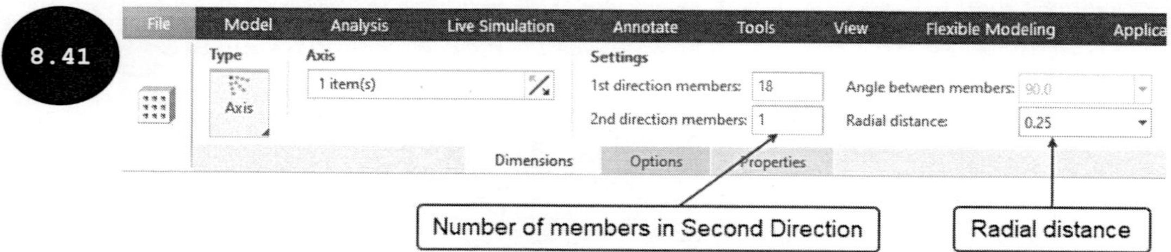

7. Click on the green tick-mark button in the Pattern tab. The axis pattern in angular and radial directions is created, see Figure 8.43.

8.42 8.43

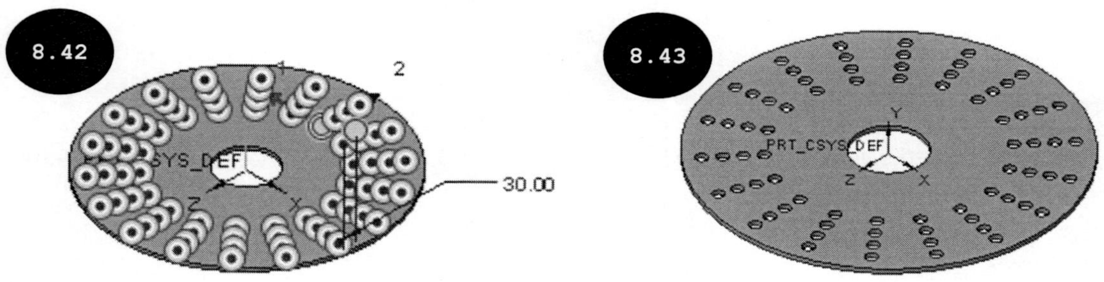

Creating a Fill Pattern

A fill pattern is created by populating an area with pattern instances. In the fill pattern, you can create multiple instances of a feature by filling in an area that is defined by a sketch, see Figure 8.44. The method for creating a fill pattern is discussed below:

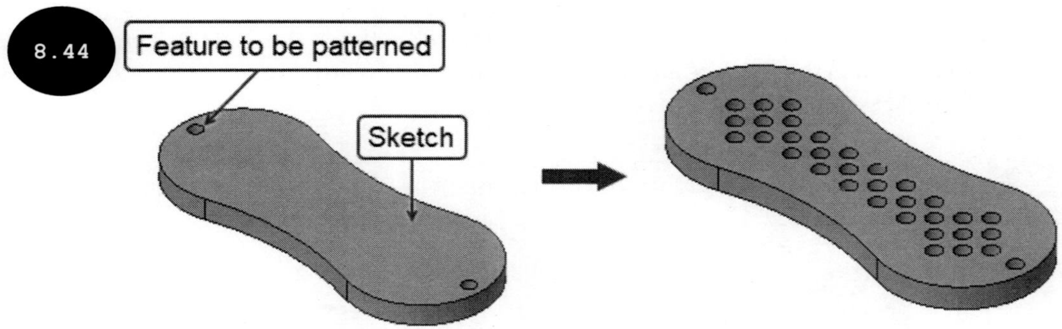

1. Select a feature to be patterned in the graphics area or in the **Model Tree**.

2. Click on the **Pattern** tool in the **Editing** group of the **Model** tab. The **Pattern** tab appears.

3. Select the **Fill** option in the **Type** drop-down list of the **Type** area, see Figure 8.45. The options for creating a fill pattern appear in the **Pattern** tab.

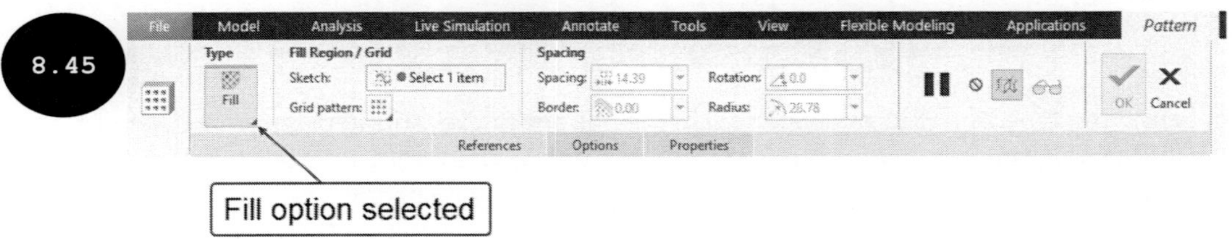

Now, you need to select a sketch to define an area to be filled. You can select an existing sketch or create a new sketch to define an area. Note that you can select or create an open or closed sketch to define an area to be filled.

4. Expand the **References** panel of the **Pattern** tab, see Figure 8.46.

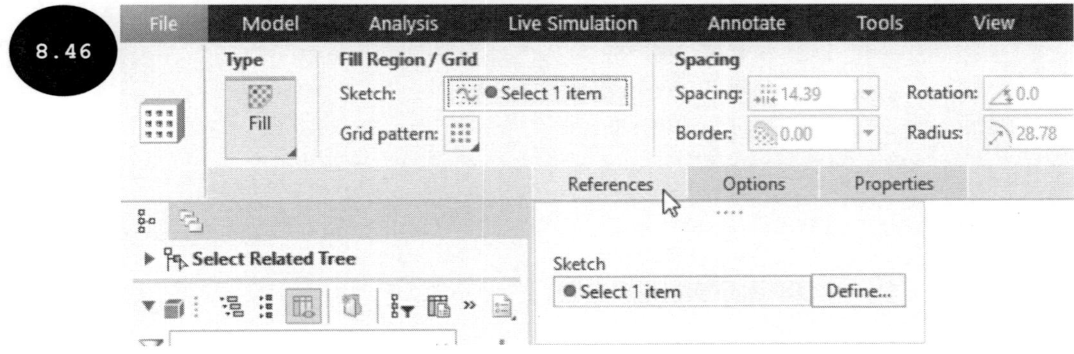

5. Select a sketch to be filled. The black dots representing pattern instances appear inside the area that is defined by the selected sketch. Note that the sketch to be selected should be created before the feature is patterned. If the sketch has not been created earlier then you need to create it. To do so, click on the **Define** button of the expanded **References** panel. The **Sketch** dialog box appears. Next, select a plane or a planar face as the sketching plane and then click on the **Sketch** button in the dialog box. The Sketching environment is invoked. Now, you can create a sketch to define the enclosed area to be filled. After creating the sketch, exit the Sketching environment. Black dots appear in the graphics area representing the pattern instances, see Figure 8.47. In this figure, a closed sketch is created.

Note: You can click on the black dots to skip the pattern instances, as discussed earlier.

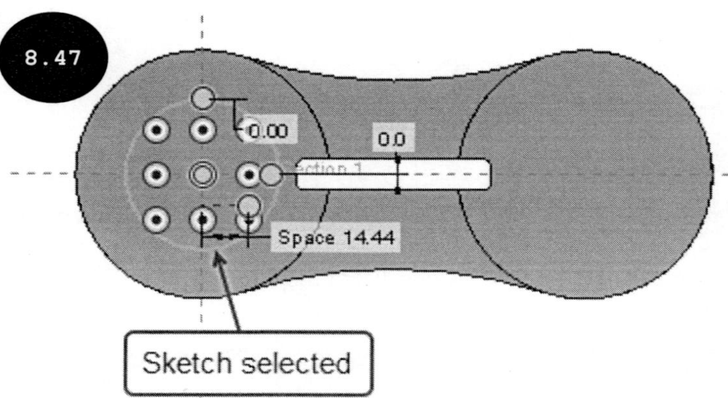

6. Select the type of layout or shape for the fill pattern in the **Grid Pattern** drop-down list of the **Fill Region/Grid** area, see Figure 8.48. You can define the layout for the fill pattern as square, diamond, hexagon, circle, spiral, or curve by selecting the respective option in the **Grid Pattern** drop-down list, see Figures 8.49 through 8.54.

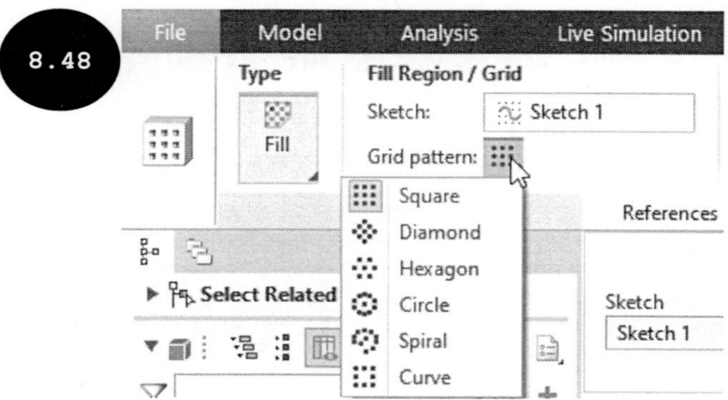

Figures 8.49 through 8.54 show the preview of the fill pattern with different pattern layouts.

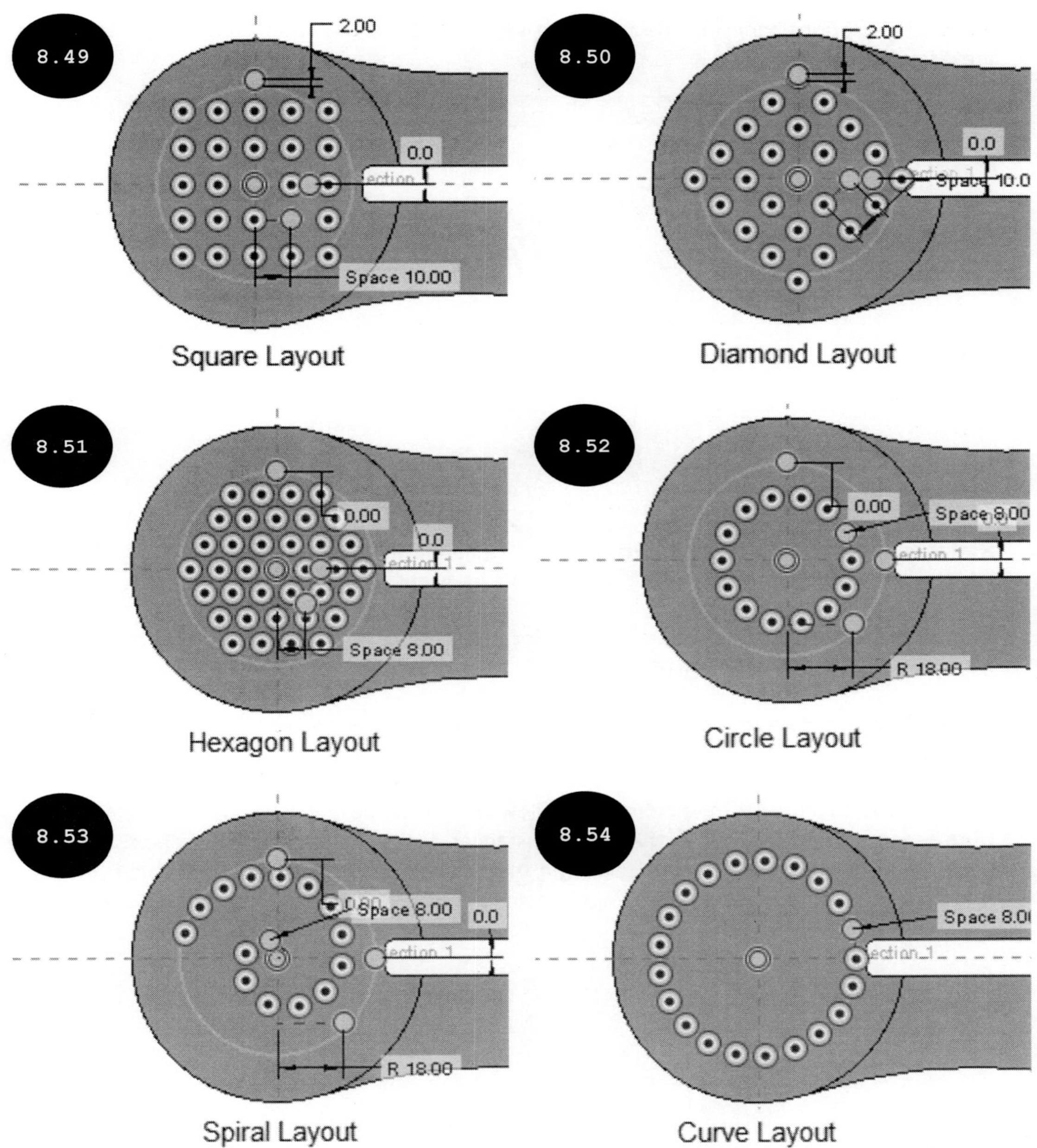

7. Specify the pattern parameters such as spacing between the pattern instances from center to center, distance between the center of an outermost pattern instance and the sketch boundary, and angle of orientation of the pattern instances from the origin in the respective fields of the **Pattern** tab.

8. Expand the **Options** panel of the **Pattern** tab, see Figure 8.55. The options available in this panel are discussed below:

8.55

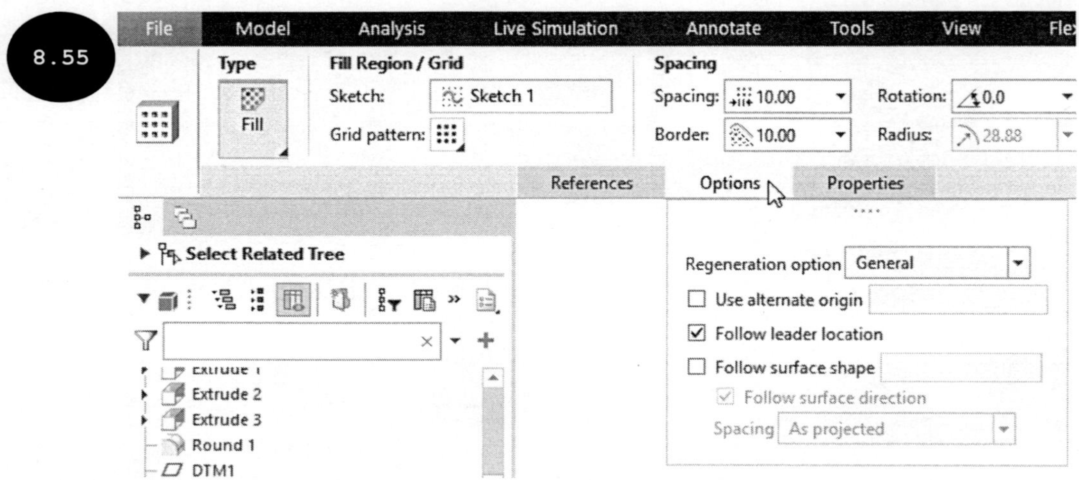

Regeneration option drop-down list: The **General**, **Identical**, and **Variable** options of the **Regeneration option** drop-down list are the same as discussed earlier.

Use alternate origin: On selecting the **Use alternate origin** check box, you can select an alternate origin point for the fill pattern.

Follow leader location: On selecting the **Follow leader location** check box, the pattern gets created on the placement face or plane of the sketch boundary.

Follow surface shape: On selecting the **Follow surface shape** check box, you can select a face whose shape is to be followed by the pattern instances. Note that when this check box is selected, the **Follow surface direction** check box and the **Spacing** drop-down list get enabled. You can select the required option for projecting/mapping the pattern instances onto the selected face in the **Spacing** drop-down list.

9. After specifying the required parameters, click on the green tick-mark button in the **Pattern** tab. The fill pattern is created, see Figure 8.56.

8.56

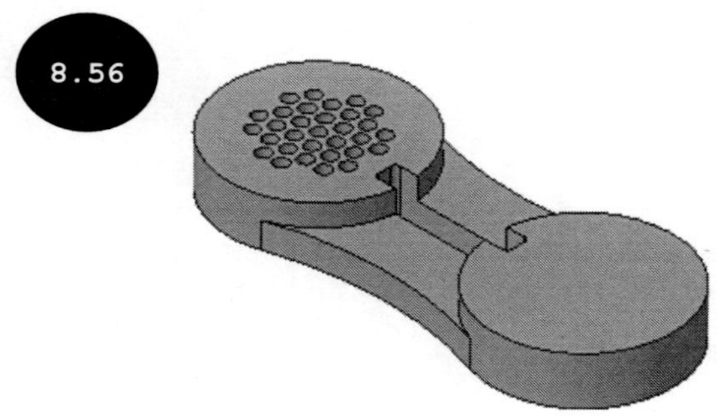

Creating a Table Pattern

A table driven pattern is created by defining the dimensions of the pattern instances with reference to the dimensions of the parent feature in a table. The method for creating a table driven pattern is discussed below:

1. Select a feature to be patterned in the graphics area or in the **Model Tree**.

2. Click on the **Pattern** tool in the **Editing** group of the **Model** tab. The **Pattern** tab appears.

3. Select the **Table** option in the **Type** drop-down list of the **Type** area in the **Pattern** tab, see Figure 8.57. The options for creating a table pattern appear in the **Pattern** tab. Also, the dimensions of the selected feature appear in the graphics area.

8.57

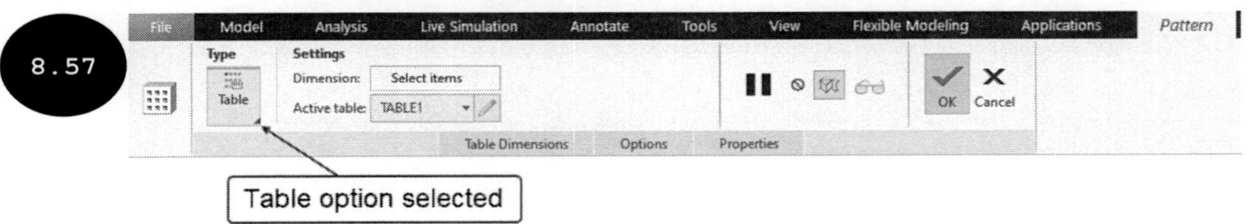

4. Select the dimensions that define the placement of the feature by pressing the CTRL key in the graphics area, see Figure 8.58. In this figure, dimensions 50 and 120 of the parent feature are selected to define the dimensions of the pattern instances.

8.58

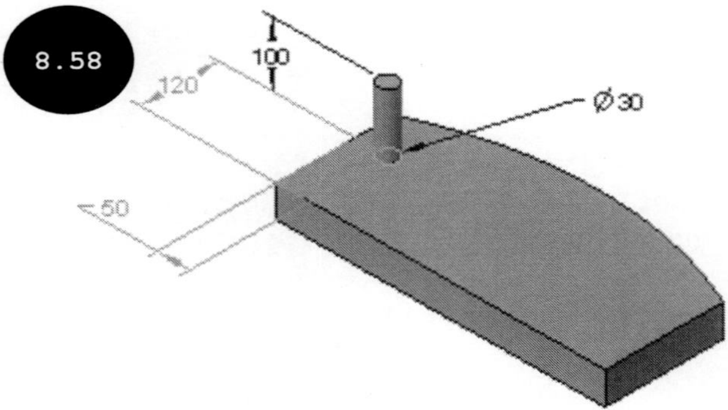

5. Click on the **Edit** button in the **Settings** area of the **Pattern** tab. The **Pro/TABLE** window appears in the graphics area, see Figure 8.59.

6. Click on the field corresponding to row R12 (below the **idx**) and column C1, and then enter **1**. The value **1** indicates the first pattern instance. Note that the rows below the **idx** represent the pattern instances in a sequential order.

7. Click on the field corresponding to the row R12 (representing the first pattern instance) and the column C2. Next, enter a distance value for the first pattern instance along the first selected dimension of the parent feature, see Figure 8.59.

8. Click on the field corresponding to row R12 (representing the first pattern instance) and the column C3. Next, enter a distance value for the first pattern instance along the second selected dimension of the parent feature, see Figure 8.59.

9. Similarly, enter the distance values for the remaining pattern instances in the table, see Figure 8.59. In this figure, total 8 pattern instances are defined.

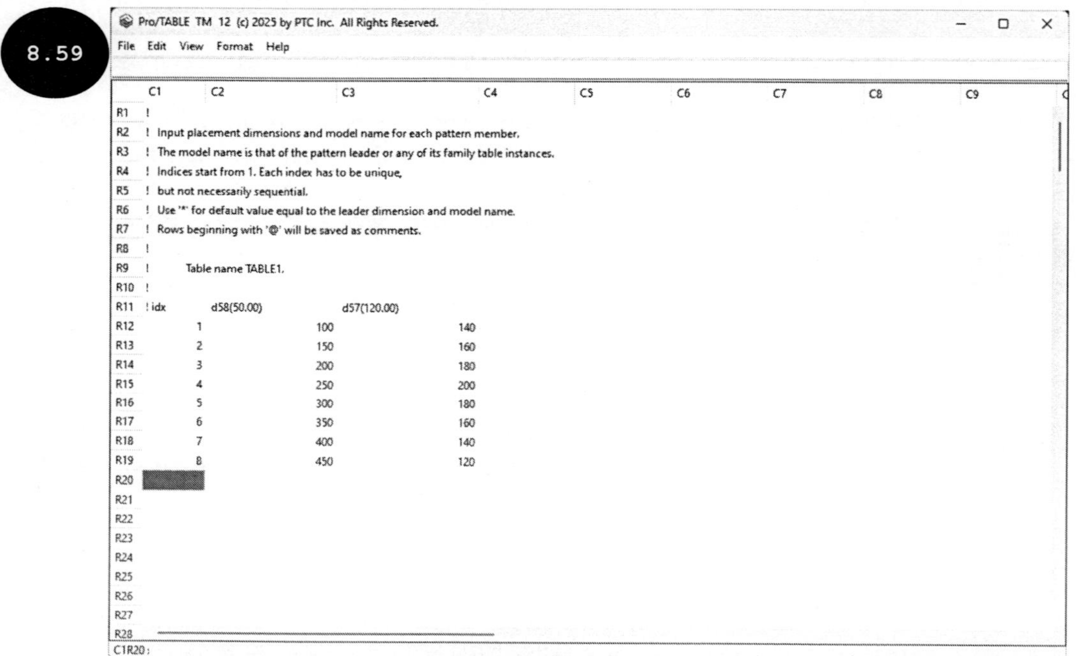

10. After defining the distance values for all the pattern instances, close the **Pro/TABLE** window. Black dots appear in the graphics area representing the pattern instances, see Figure 8.60.

11. Click on the green tick-mark button in the Pattern tab. The desired table driven pattern is created, see Figure 8.61.

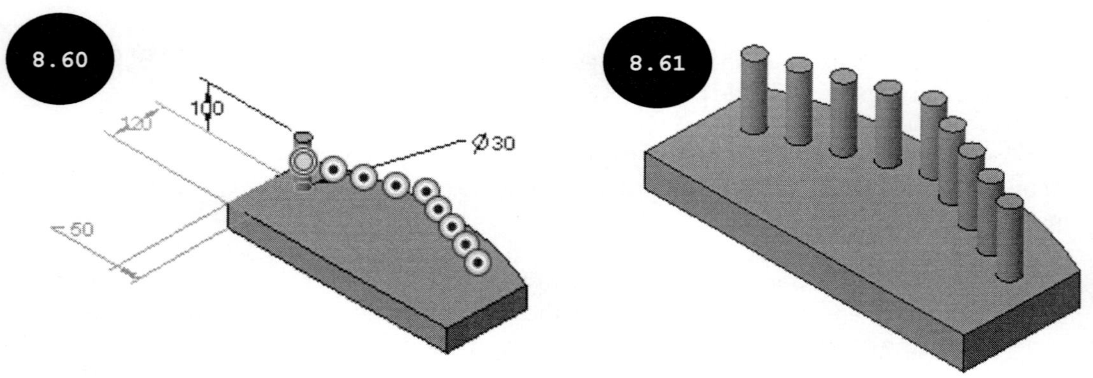

Creating a Reference Pattern

A reference pattern is used for creating multiple instances of a feature with reference to an existing pattern. Note that the feature to be patterned must have a relationship with any of the pattern instances of the existing pattern, see Figures 8.62 and 8.63. In Figure 8.62, the hole feature is created on the top planar face of an existing pattern instance. Figure 8.63 shows the resultant reference pattern of the hole feature created with reference to the existing pattern. The method for creating a reference pattern is discussed below:

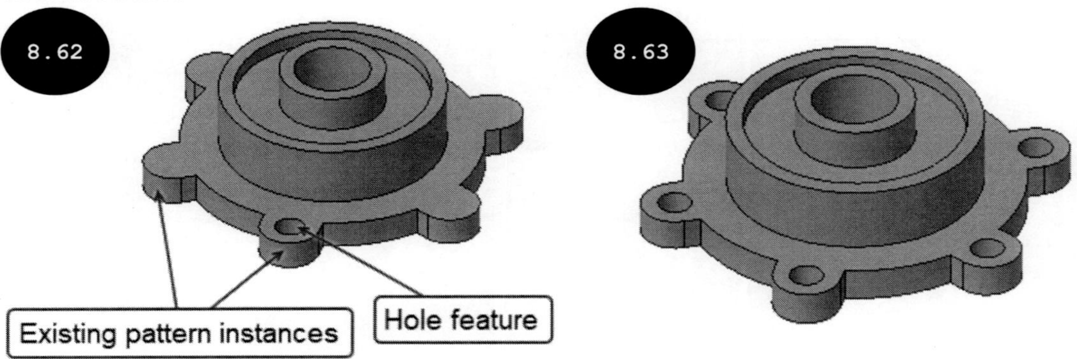

1. Select a feature to be patterned in the graphics area or in the **Model Tree**.

Note: To create a reference pattern, the feature to be patterned must have a relationship with a pattern instance of an existing pattern feature. Also, if the feature to be patterned is a sketch based feature then its sketch should be an internal sketch of the feature.

2. Click on the **Pattern** tool in the **Editing** group of the **Model** tab. The **Pattern** tab appears with the **Reference** option selected in the **Type** drop-down list, automatically, see Figure 8.64. Also, black dots appear in the graphics area representing the pattern instances with reference to the pattern instances of the existing pattern, see Figure 8.65.

3. Click on the green tick-mark button of the **Pattern** tab. The desired reference pattern is created, see Figure 8.66.

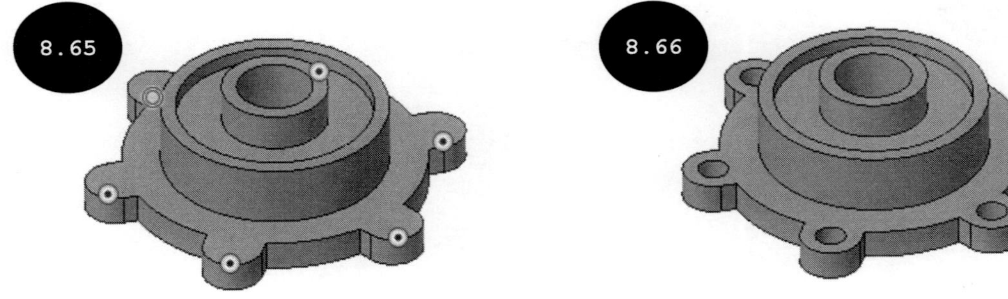

Creating a Curve Pattern

Curve driven pattern is used for creating multiple instances of a feature along a curve, see Figure 8.67. This figure shows a feature to be patterned, a closed sketch as a curve, and the resultant curve driven pattern. You can select an open or closed sketch as a curve to drive the pattern instances. The method for creating a curve driven pattern is discussed below:

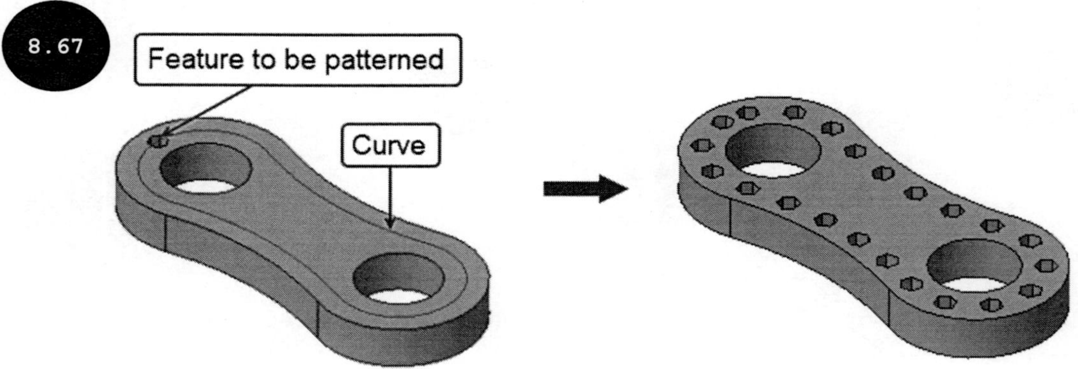

1. Select a feature to be patterned in the graphics area or in the **Model Tree**.

2. Click on the **Pattern** tool in the **Editing** group of the **Model** tab. The **Pattern** tab appears.

3. Select the **Curve** option in the **Type** drop-down list of the **Type** area in the **Pattern** tab, see Figure 8.68. The options for creating a curve driven pattern appear in the **Pattern** tab. Also, you are prompted to select a curve. You can select an existing open or closed sketch as a curve or create a new sketch.

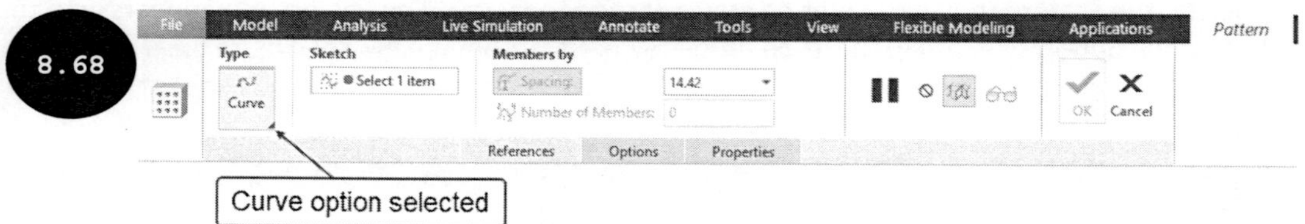

4. Expand the **References** panel of the **Pattern** tab (see Figure 8.69), and then click on the **Define** button to create a curve for driving the pattern instances. The **Sketch** dialog box appears.

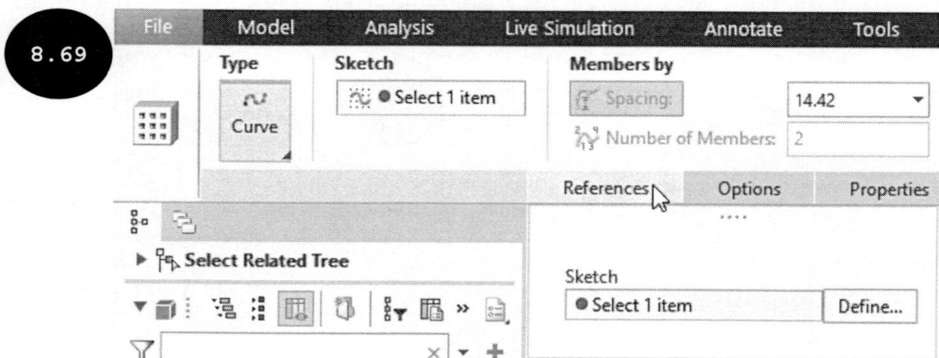

5. Select a planar face or a plane as the sketching plane and then click on the **OK** button in the **Sketch** dialog box. The Sketching environment gets invoked.

6. Create an open or closed sketch as a curve to drive the pattern instances, see Figure 8.70. In this figure, the curve is created by offsetting the outer edges of the model at an offset distance of 10 mm using the **Offset** tool. It is recommended to maintain the right orientation of the pattern instances, the curve should pass through the intersection point of the horizontal and vertical reference lines, see Figure 8.70.

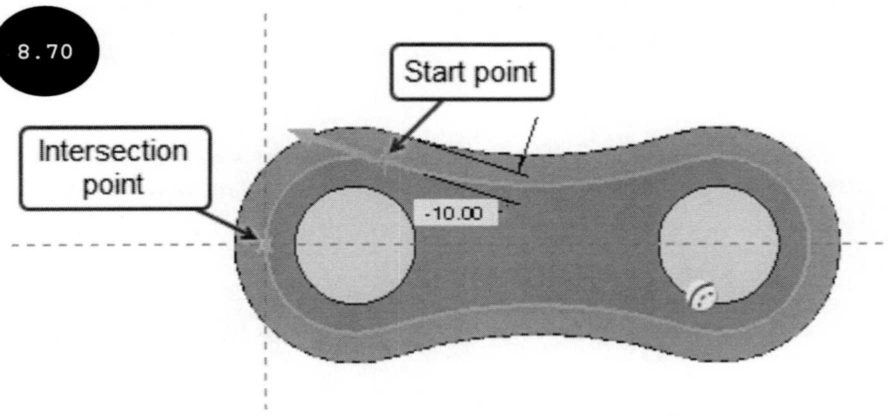

Note: An arrow appears on one of the points of the curve segment, which indicates the start point of the pattern. To change the start point of the pattern from one point to another, click on a point of the curve segment to be defined as the start point and then press and hold the right mouse button. A shortcut menu appears, see Figure 8.71. In the shortcut menu, click on **Features Tools > Start Point**, see Figure 8.71. The selected point of the curve section becomes the start point of the pattern, see Figure 8.72. Note that to create a point on the curve, you need to divide the curve segment at that location by using the **Divide** tool.

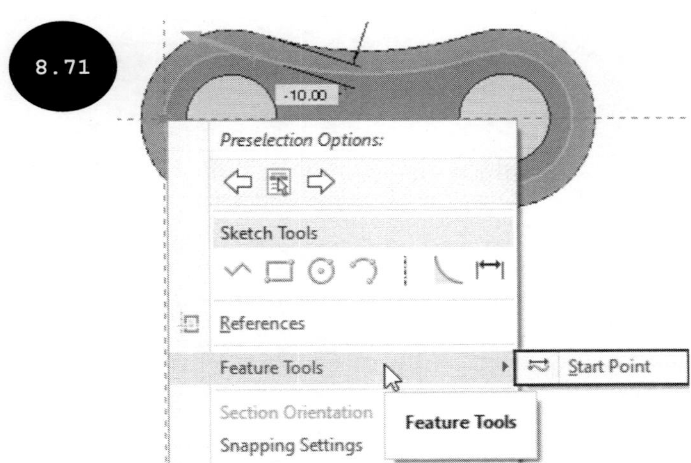

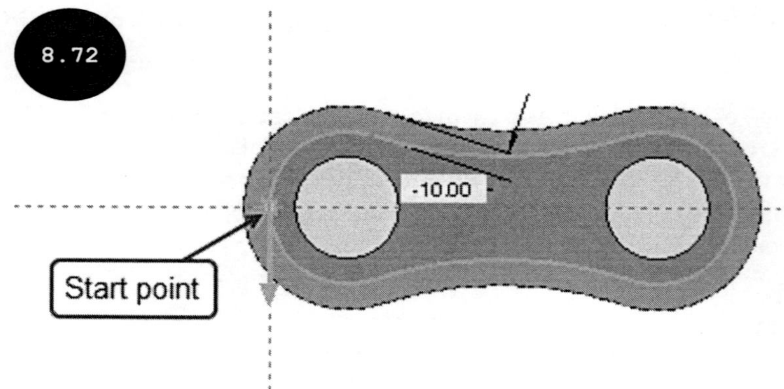

7. After creating the curve and defining the start point of the pattern, exit the Sketching environment. Black dots appear in the graphics area representing the preview of the pattern instances along the curve, see Figure 8.73.

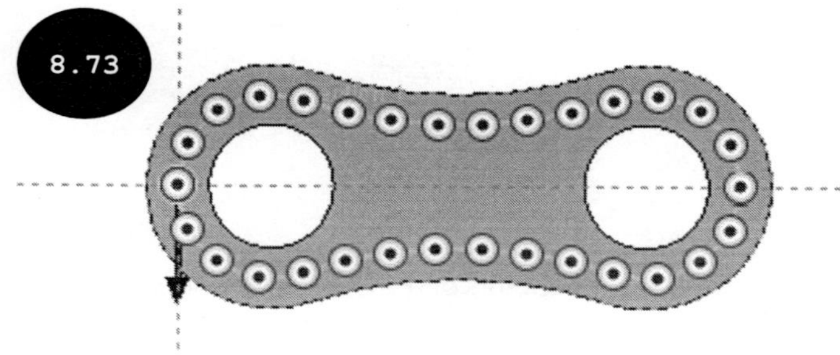

8. Specify the spacing between the pattern instances in the **Spacing** field of the **Members by** area in the **Pattern** tab, see Figure 8.74. On doing so, the number of pattern instances to be created along the curve gets automatically calculated.

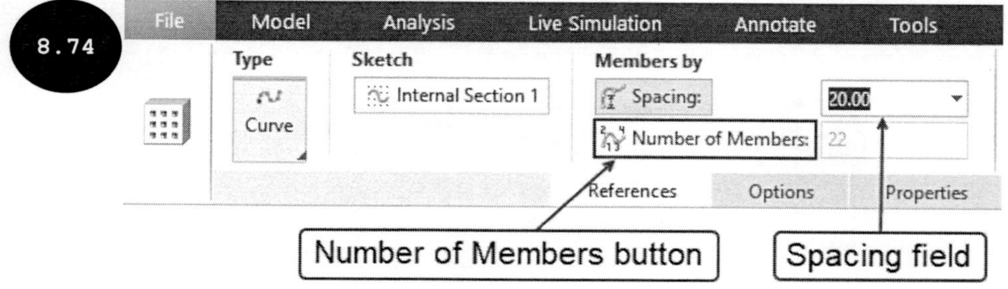

Note: Instead of specifying the spacing between the pattern instances, you can also define the number of pattern instances to be created along the curve. To do so, click on the **Number of Members** button in the **Pattern** tab, see Figure 8.74. A field next to this button gets enabled in the **Pattern** tab. In this field, you can specify the number of pattern instances to be created along the curve.

9. Click on the green tick-mark button in the **Pattern** tab. The curve driven pattern is created, see Figure 8.75.

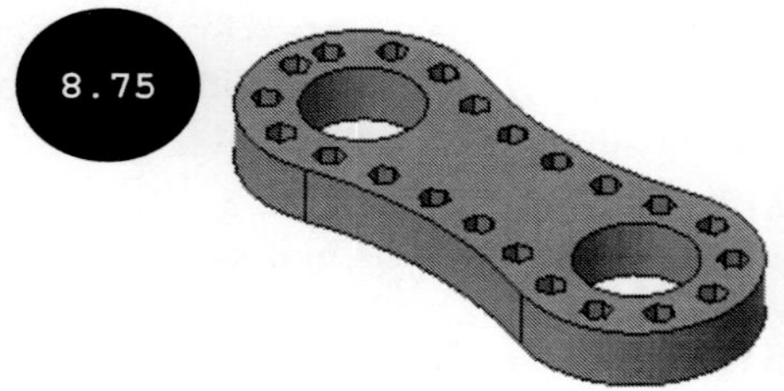

Creating a Point Pattern

Point driven pattern is used for creating multiple instances of a feature at sketch points, datum points, or coordinate systems, see Figures 8.76 and 8.77. Figure 8.76 shows sketch points and the feature to be patterned. Figure 8.77 shows the resultant pattern created by propagating the parent feature to each point. Note that you can create sketch points and coordinate systems in the Sketching environment by using the **Point** tool and **Coordinate System** tool of the **Datum** group.

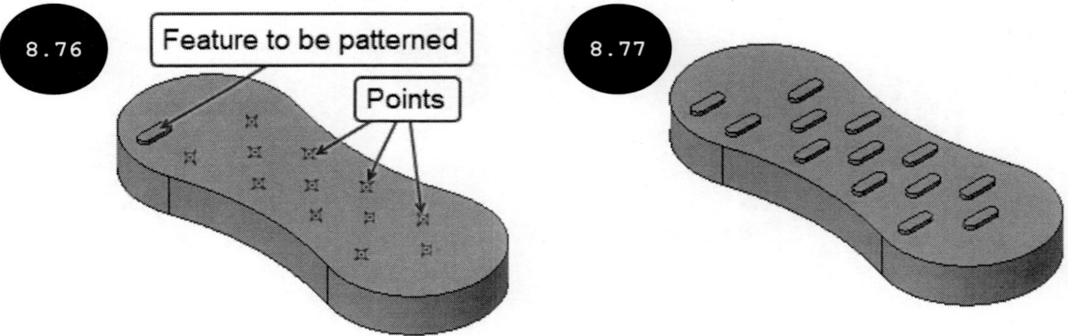

The method for creating a point driven pattern is discussed below:

1. Select a feature to be patterned in the graphics area or in the **Model Tree**.
2. Click on the **Pattern** tool in the **Editing** group of the **Model** tab. The **Pattern** tab appears.
3. Select the **Point** option in the **Type** drop-down list in the **Pattern** tab, see Figure 8.78. The options for creating a point driven pattern appear in the **Pattern** tab. Also, you are prompted to select points. You can select a sketch with sketch points or sketch coordinate systems. You can also select datum points or datum coordinate systems to create a point driven pattern.

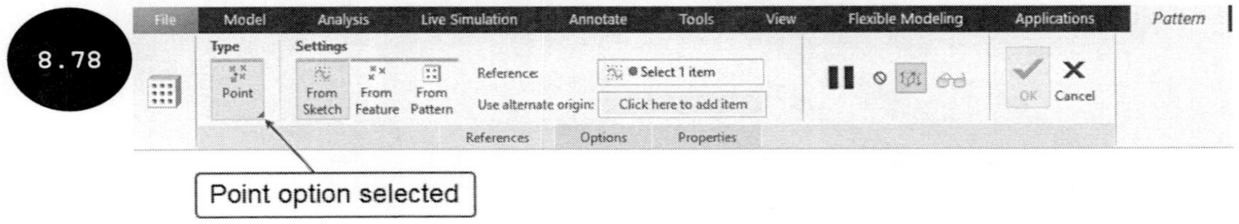

Note: As discussed earlier, you can create sketch points and sketch coordinate systems in the Sketching environment by using the **Point** tool and **Coordinate System** tool of the **Datum** group, respectively.

4. Select a sketch with sketch points or coordinate system in the **Model Tree**. Black dots appear in the graphics area representing the preview of the pattern instances, see Figure 8.79. Note that the sketch to be selected should be created before the parent feature.

Note: Instead of selecting an existing sketch containing sketch points or coordinate systems, you can also create a new sketch. To do so, expand the **References** panel of the **Pattern** tab and then click on the **Define** button. The **Sketch** dialog box appears. In this dialog box, select a planar face or a plane as the sketching plane and then click on the **Sketch** button. The Sketching environment gets invoked. Next, create sketch points or coordinate systems by using the **Sketch** or **Coordinate System** tools of the **Datum** group and then exit the Sketching environment.

5. Click on the green tick-mark button in the **Pattern** tab. The point driven pattern is created such that the parent feature gets propagated to each sketch point of the sketch, see Figure 8.80.

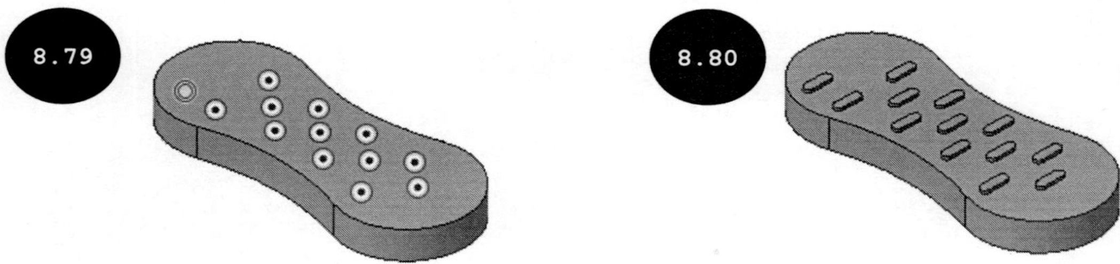

Creating a Variable Pattern

In Creo Parametric, you can create a variable pattern for Dimension, Direction, and Axis patterns. A variable pattern is created such that you can vary the size and spacing between the pattern instances, see Figure 8.81. This figure shows a variable pattern created for a Direction pattern in one direction by varying the size (length and diameter) as well as the spacing between the pattern instances. The method for creating a variable pattern is discussed below:

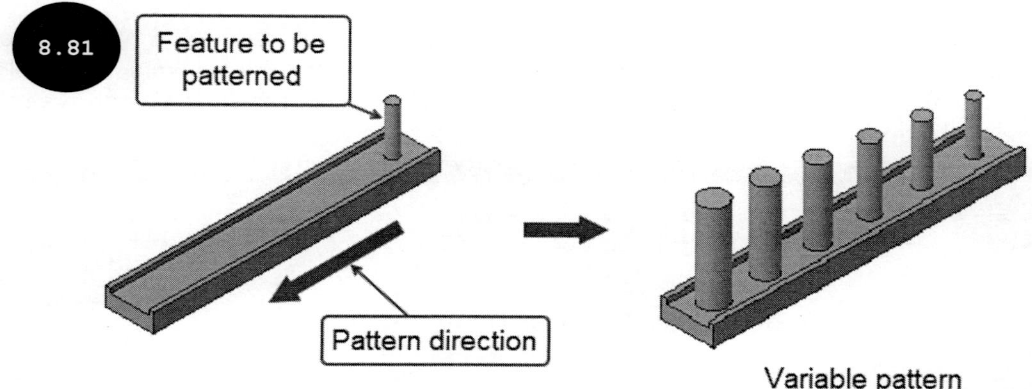

1. Select a feature to be patterned in the graphics area or in the **Model Tree**.

2. Click on the **Pattern** tool in the **Editing** group of the **Model** tab. The **Pattern** tab appears in the **Ribbon**, see Figure 8.82.

3. Select the type of pattern to be created (**Dimension**, **Direction**, or **Axis**) in the **Type** drop-down list of the **Type** area in the **Pattern** tab to create the respective variable pattern, see Figure 8.82. In this figure, the **Direction** option is selected as a pattern type to create a variable pattern. You can select **Dimension**, **Direction**, or **Axis** option to create a variable pattern, as required.

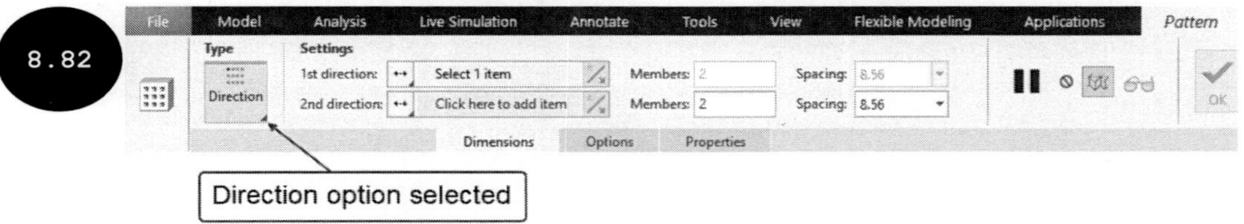

4. Specify the required parameters for creating the pattern such as pattern directions, number of pattern instances, spacing between pattern instances, and so on, in the **Pattern** tab, as discussed earlier. Black dots appear in the graphics area representing the preview of the pattern instances, see Figure 8.83. Note that the parameters required for creating a pattern depend upon the type of pattern selected in the **Type** drop-down list of the **Type** area. In Figure 8.83, the preview of a linear direction pattern appears on specifying a linear pattern direction, number of pattern instances, and spacing between pattern instances.

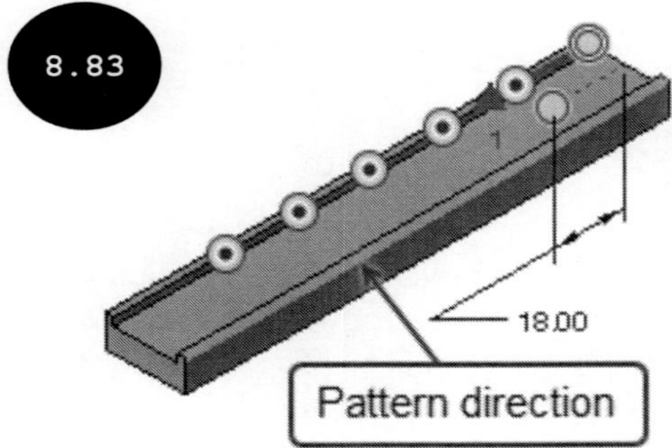

Now, you need to define the dimensions to be varied for creating the variable pattern.

5. Expand the **Dimensions** panel of the **Pattern** tab, if not expanded by default, and then click on the **Direction 1** collector, see Figure 8.84. All the dimensions of the parent feature appear in the graphics area, see Figure 8.85.

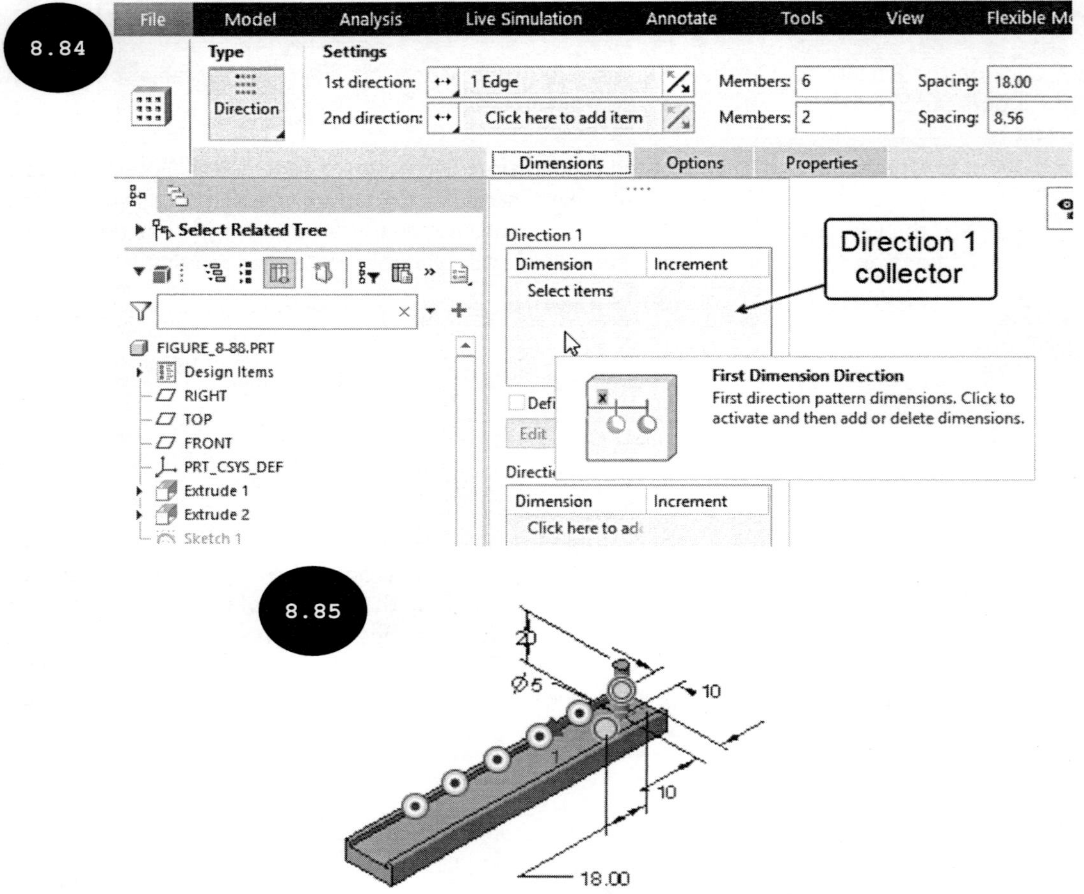

6. Select a dimension of the parent feature to be varied along direction 1 in the graphics area. An edit field appears. Next, enter the incremental value for the selected dimension in the edit field that appears in the graphics area and then press ENTER. The name of the selected dimensions and the incremental value appear in the **Direction 1** collector of the expanded **Dimensions** panel, see Figure 8.86.

7. Similarly, select the remaining dimensions to be varied along direction 1 by pressing the CTRL key and specify the incremental value for each dimension, individually. Figure 8.87 shows the **Direction 1** collector with three dimensions (length, diameter, and linear dimension) selected to be varied along direction 1.

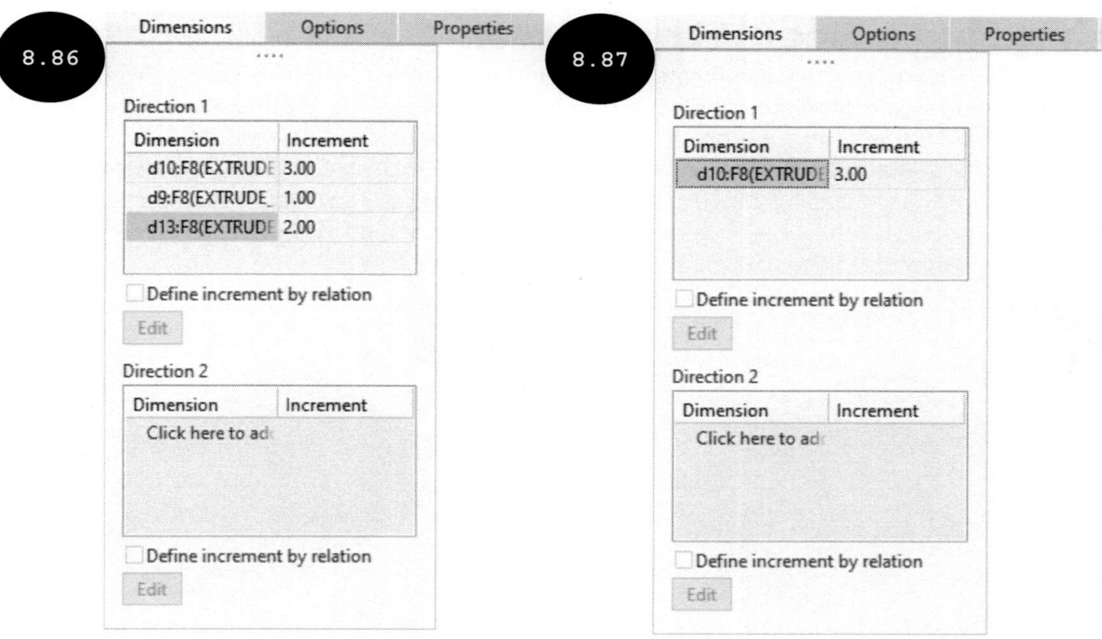

Tip: To edit the incremental value of a dimension, click on the **Increment** field of the dimension in the **Increment** column of the **Direction 1** collector and then enter the incremental value in the field that appears. Next, press ENTER.

Note: You can also vary the pattern instances along direction 2 by using the **Direction 2** collector of the expanded **Dimensions** panel.

8. Click on the green tick-mark button in the **Pattern** tab. The desired variable pattern is created, see Figure 8.88.

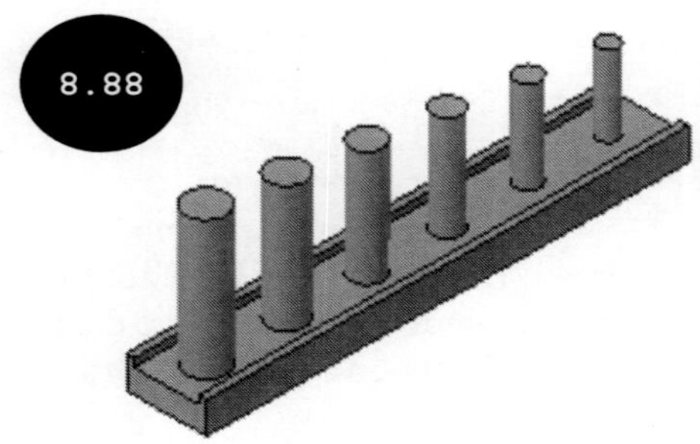

Creating a Geometry Pattern

In Creo Parametric, you can also create multiple instances of a geometry by using the **Geometry Pattern** tool. Using this tool, you can pattern a geometry instead of a feature, see Figures 8.89 and 8.90. Figure 8.89 shows two cut geometries that are created by using a single sketch. As a result, both the cut geometries act as a single feature. Figure 8.90 shows the resultant geometry pattern created in which only the smaller cut geometry is patterned. Note that you can create a geometry pattern for Direction, Axis, Fill, Table, Curve, and Point patterns only. The method for creating a geometry pattern is discussed below:

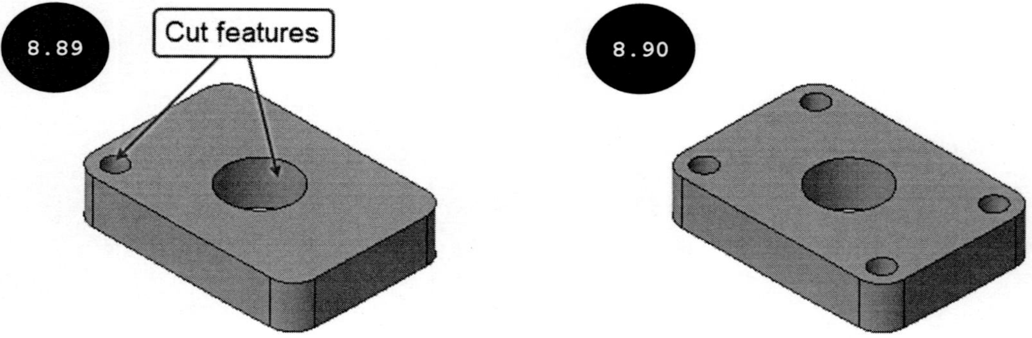

1. Select a geometry to be patterned in the graphics area. You can select multiple faces of a geometry to be patterned by pressing the CTRL key.

2. Click on the arrow at the bottom of the **Pattern** tool in the **Editing** group and then click on the **Geometry Pattern** tool in the flyout that appears, see Figure 8.91. The **Geometry Pattern** tab appears.

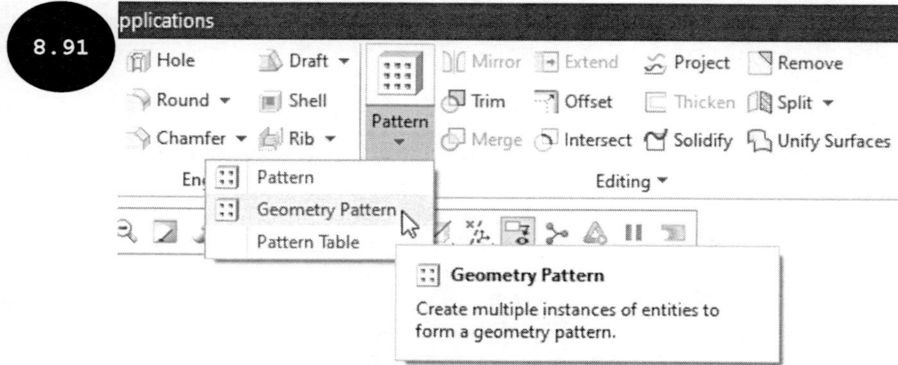

3. Select the type of pattern to be created (**Direction**, **Axis**, **Fill**, **Table**, **Curve**, or **Point**) in the **Type** drop-down list of the **Type** area in the **Geometry Pattern** tab to create the respective geometry pattern, see Figure 8.92. In this figure, the **Direction** option is selected as a pattern type to create a geometry pattern.

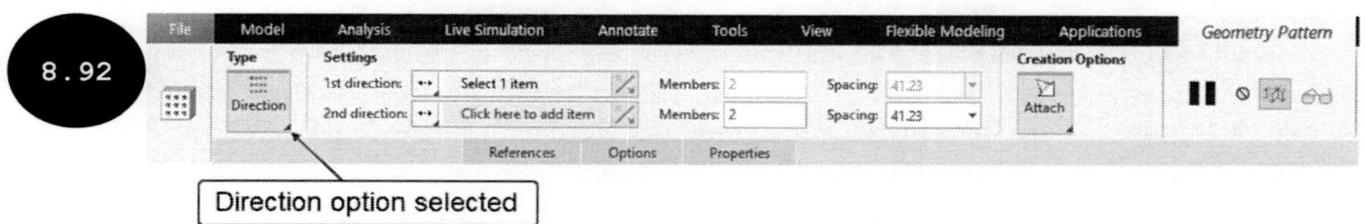

4. Specify the required parameters for creating the pattern such as pattern directions, number of pattern instances, spacing between pattern instances, and so on, in the **Settings** area of the **Geometry Pattern** tab, as discussed earlier. Black dots appear in the graphics area representing the preview of the pattern instances, see Figure 8.93. Note that the parameters required for creating a pattern depend upon the type of pattern selected in the **Type** drop-down list of the **Type** area and are same as discussed earlier. In Figure 8.93, the preview of a linear direction pattern appears on specifying two linear pattern directions, number of pattern instances, and spacing between pattern instances.

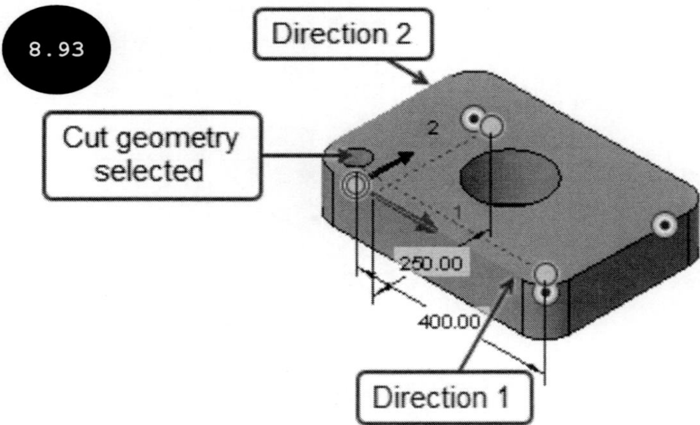

5. Click on the green tick-mark button in the **Geometry Pattern** tab. The selected geometry gets patterned, see Figure 8.94.

Deleting a Pattern

To delete an already created pattern, right-click on the name of the pattern feature in the **Model Tree** and then click on the **Delete Pattern** tool in the shortcut menu that appears, see Figure 8.95. The selected pattern gets deleted and the parent feature remains available in the model. To delete the parent feature along with the pattern instances, click on the **Delete** tool in the shortcut menu.

8.95

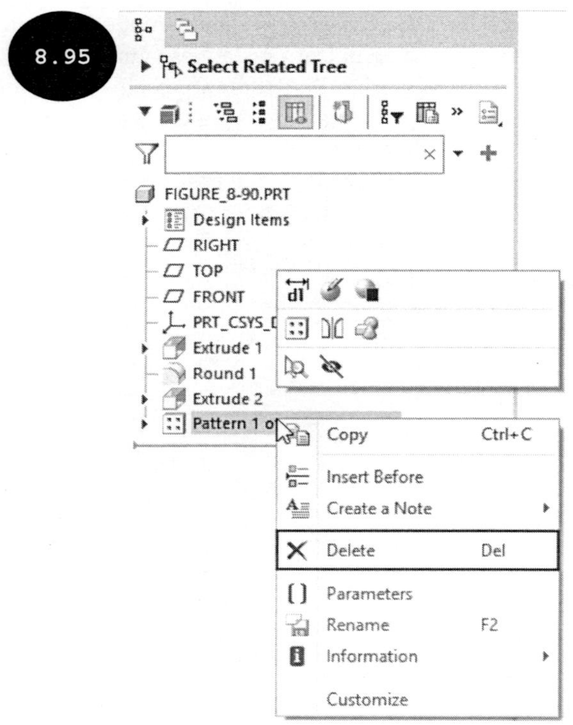

Mirroring a Feature

In Creo Parametric, you can mirror one or more features about a mirroring plane by using the **Mirror** tool. You can select a planar face or a plane as the mirroring plane. Figure 8.96 shows features to be mirrored and a mirroring plane. Figure 8.97 shows the resultant mirror feature created. The method for mirroring a feature is discussed below:

8.96 8.97

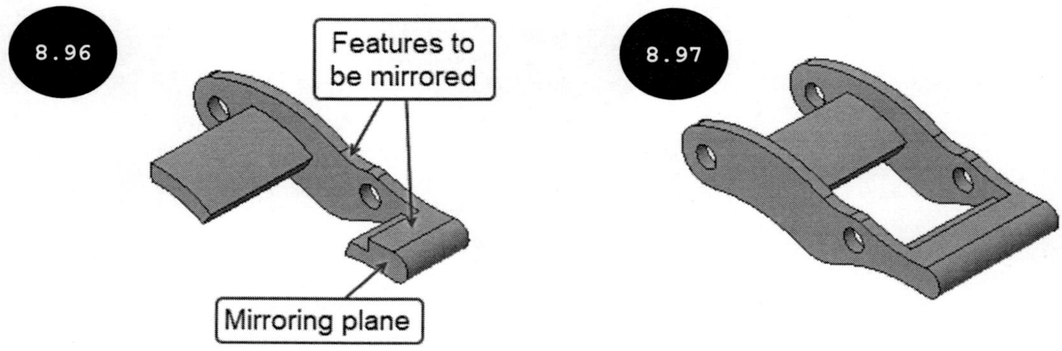

1. Select one or more features to be mirrored in the graphics area or in the **Model Tree**, see Figure 8.98. In this figure, three features are selected. You can select multiple features by pressing the CTRL key.

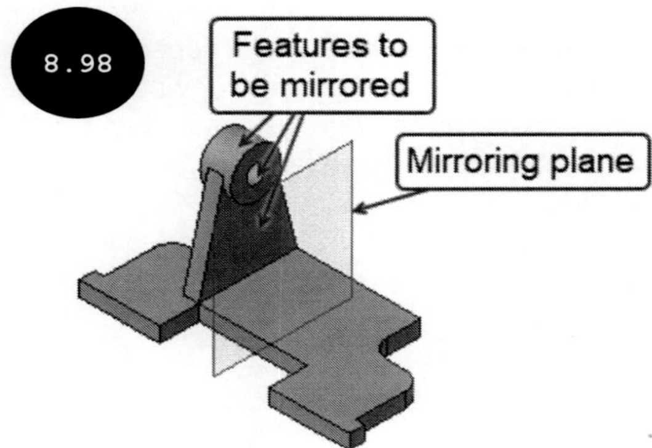

2. Click on the **Mirror** tool in the **Editing** group of the **Model** tab, see Figure 8.99. The **Mirror** tab appears in the **Ribbon** (see Figure 8.100), and you are prompted to select a mirroring plane.

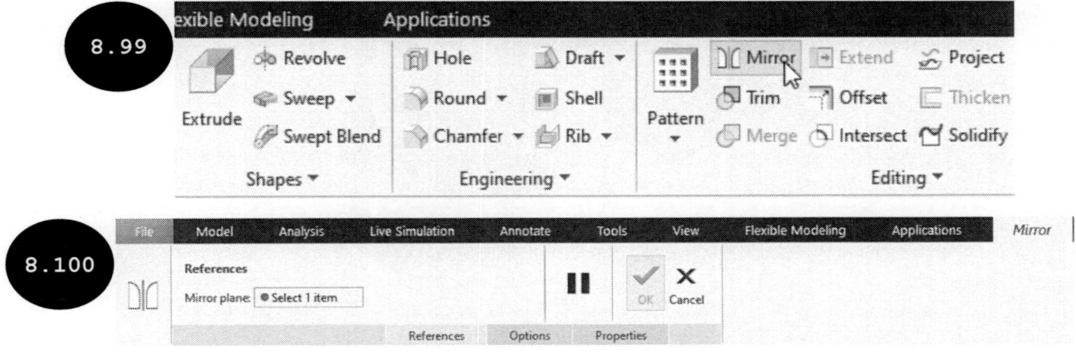

3. Select a planar face or a plane as the mirroring plane, refer to Figure 8.98.

4. Expand the **Options** panel of the **Mirror** tab, see Figure 8.101. The options are discussed below:

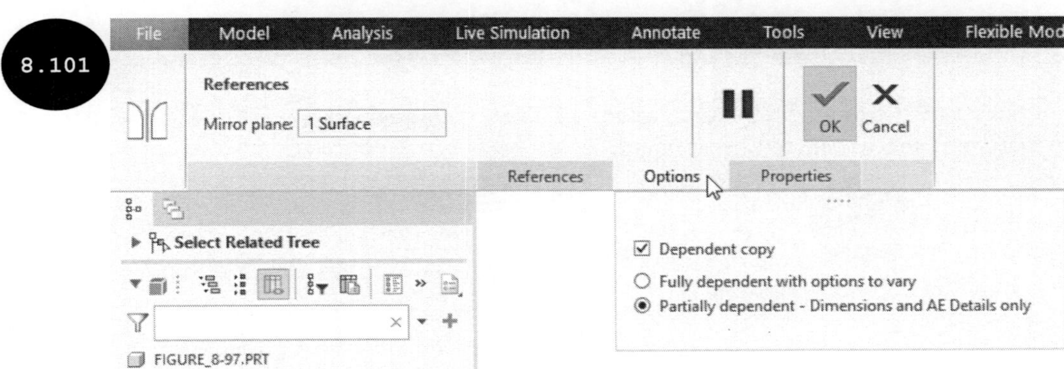

Dependent copy: By default, the **Dependent copy** check box is selected in the expanded **Options** panel of the **Mirror** tab. As a result, the resultant mirrored copy becomes dependent on the original features, partially or fully. When the **Fully dependent with options to vary** radio button is selected in the expanded **Options** panel, the resultant mirrored copy becomes fully dependent on the original features. When the **Partially dependent - Dimensions and AE Details only** radio button is selected, the resultant mirrored copy becomes partially dependent on the original features. This means that only the dimensions and annotation element details of the mirrored features are dependent on the original features.

5. Ensure that the **Dependent copy** check box and the **Fully dependent with options to vary** radio button are selected in the expanded **Options** panel.

6. Click on the green tick-mark button in the **Mirror** tab. The selected features get mirrored along the mirroring plane, see Figure 8.102.

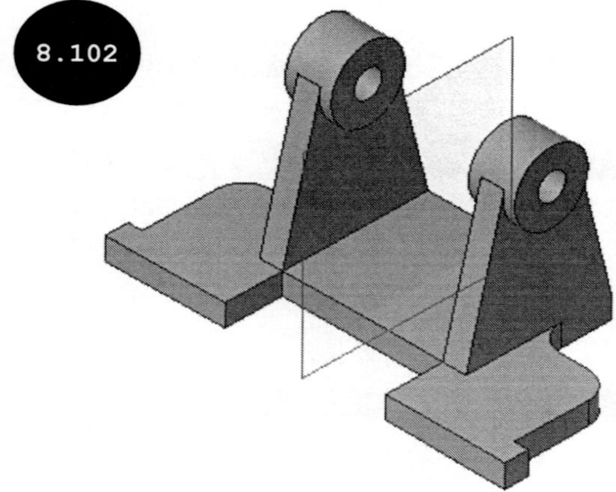

Copying and Pasting a Feature

In Creo Parametric, you can create an independent copy of one or more features by using the **Copy** tool and **Paste Special** tool. The method for creating an independent copy of a feature is discussed below:

1. Select one or more features to be copied in the **Model Tree**.

2. Click on the **Copy** tool in the **Operations** group of the **Model** tab, see Figure 8.103. The selected feature(s) gets copied to the clipboard.

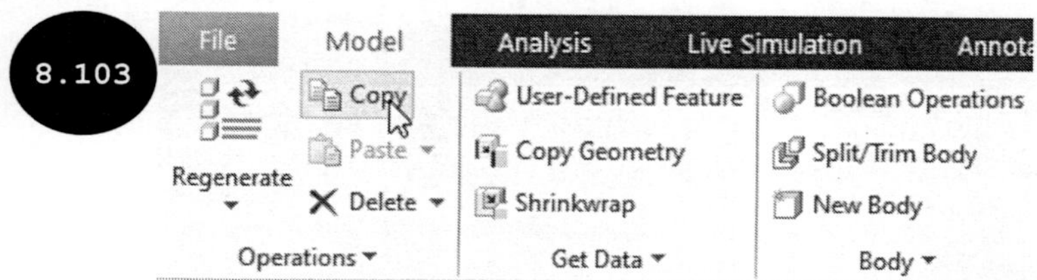

Now, you can paste the copied feature(s) by using the **Paste** or **Paste Special** tools. Both these tools are used for creating an independent copy of the selected feature(s) with the only difference being that the **Paste Special** tool provides more flexibility and additional options to paste the selected feature(s).

3. Click on the arrow next to the **Paste** tool in the **Operations** group and then click on the **Paste Special** tool in the flyout that appears, see Figure 8.104. The **Paste Special** dialog box appears, see Figure 8.105.

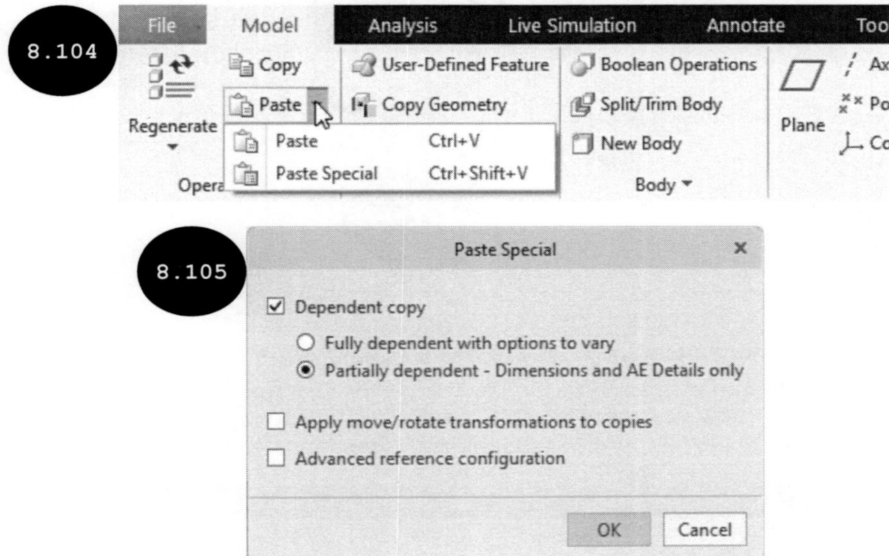

4. Clear the **Dependent copy** check box to create an independent copy of the selected feature(s). The **Fully dependent with options to vary** and the **Partially dependent - Dimensions and AE Details only** options get disabled. Both these options are same as discussed earlier.

   Apply move/rotate transformations to copies: On selecting the **Apply move/rotate transformations to copies** check box, you can move or rotate the copied feature by using the translation and rotation handles to define its placement location.

   Advanced reference configuration: On selecting the **Advanced reference configuration** check box, you can change or modify the references of the copied feature.

5. Select the **Apply move/rotate transformations to copies** check box to move or rotate the copied feature to the required location.

6. Click on the **OK** button in the **Paste Special** dialog box. The **Move (Copy)** tab appears in the **Ribbon** and you are prompted to select a direction reference for moving the copied feature.

7. Select a linear edge, a planar face, or a plane to define the direction reference, see Figure 8.106. The move handle appears in the graphics area, see Figure 8.106.

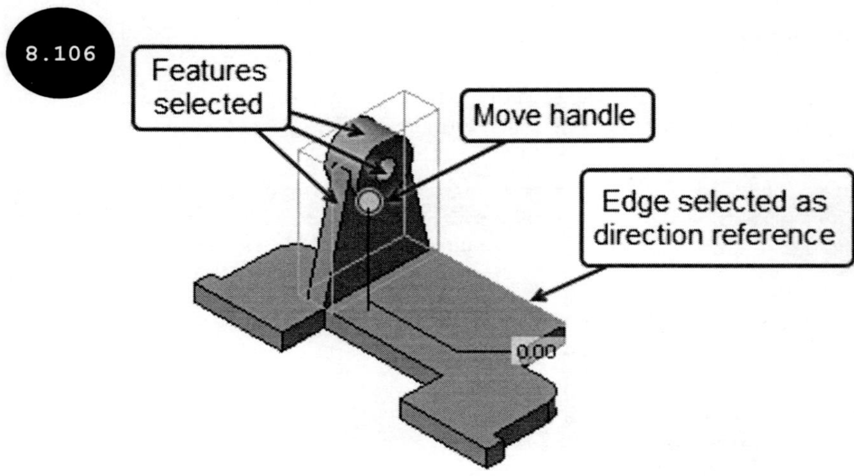

8. Expand the **Transformations** panel in the **Move (Copy)** tab, if not expanded by default, see Figure 8.107. Notice that the **Move** option is selected in the **Settings** drop-down list of the expanded **Transformations** panel, by default. As a result, the move handle appears in the graphics area to move the copied feature along the selected direction reference.

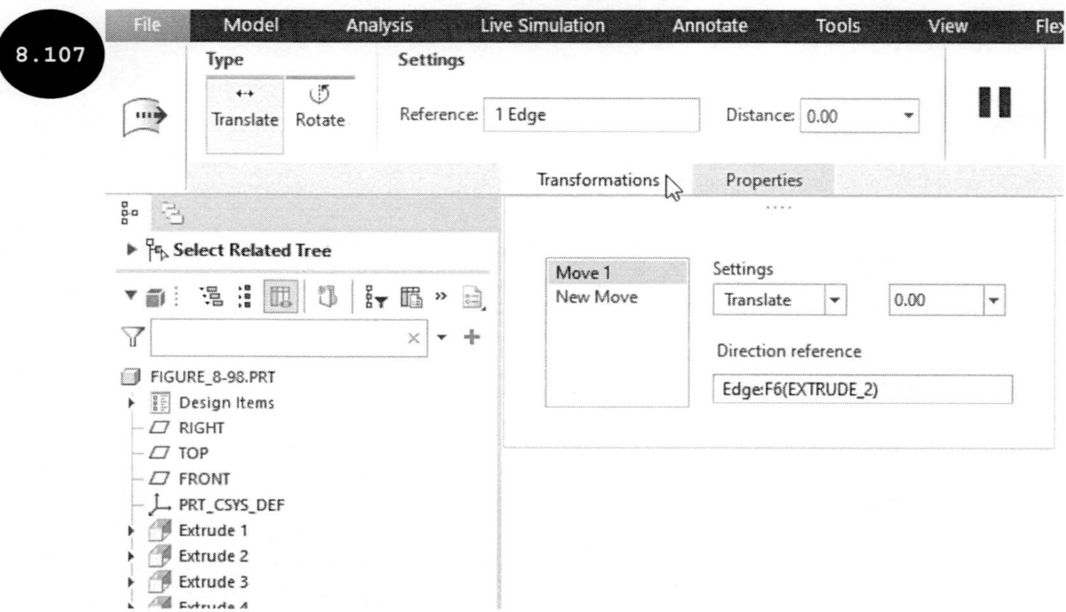

9. Drag the move handle or enter the translation value in the field that appears in front of the **Settings** drop-down list to move the copied feature along the selected direction reference at the required location.

Note: To rotate the copied feature about the selected direction reference, select the **Rotate** option in the **Settings** drop-down list of the expanded **Transformations** panel. Alternatively, select the **Rotate** button in the **Type** area of the **Move (Copy)** tab. On doing so, the rotate handle appears in the graphics area. Now, you can rotate the copied feature about the selected direction reference by dragging the rotate handle.

10. Click on the green tick-mark button in the **Move (Copy)** tab. The copied feature gets moved to the defined location, see Figure 8.108.

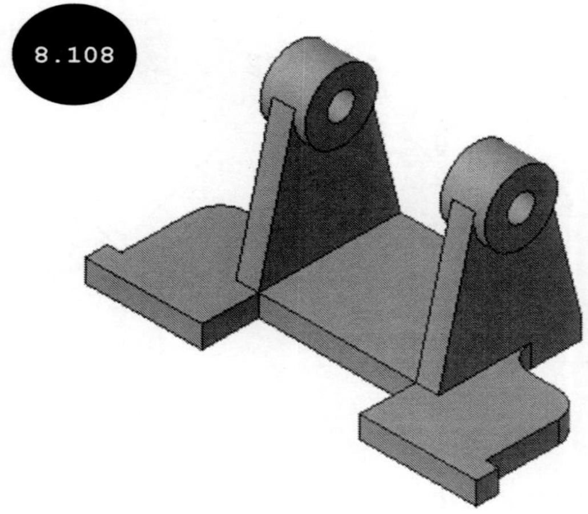

Note: You can also paste the copied feature by using the **Paste** tool. To do so, click on the **Paste** tool in the **Operations** group of the **Model** tab. The respective tab appears in the **Ribbon** depending upon the type of copied feature (extrude or revolve). Next, expand the **Placement** panel in the tab and then click on the **Edit** button to define the placement plane for pasting the copied feature. The **Sketch** dialog box appears. In this dialog box, select a plane or a planar face as the placement plane and then click on the **Sketch** button. The sketch of the copied feature gets attached to the cursor. Next, click to define the position of the sketch on the selected placement face. The Sketching environment gets invoked. Now, you can use the sketching tools to modify the sketch of the copied feature and define its position by applying dimensions, if needed. Next, exit the Sketching environment. The preview of the feature appears. Next, click on the green-tick mark button in the tab. The copied feature gets pasted onto the selected placement plane.

Tutorial 1

Create the model shown in Figure 8.109. All dimensions are in mm.

8.109

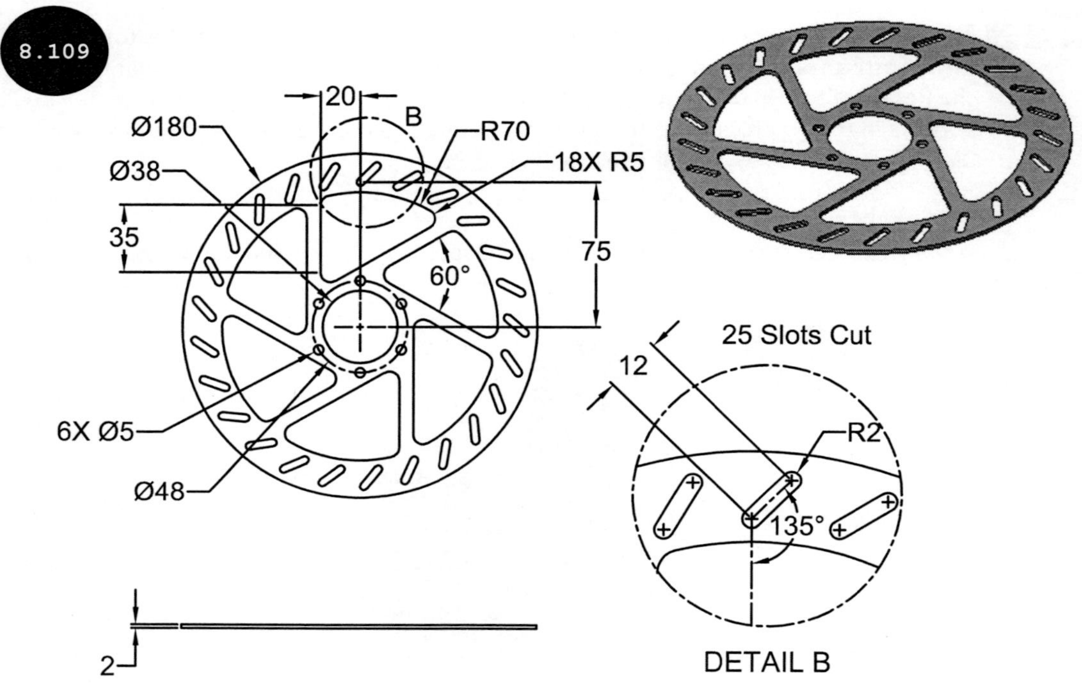

Section 1: Starting Creo Parametric

1. Start Creo Parametric by double-clicking on the Creo Parametric icon on your desktop.

Section 2: Setting the Working Directory

Now, you need to set the working directory to save the files of the current session of Creo Parametric.

1. Click on the **Select Working Directory** tool in the **Data** group of the **Home** tab, see Figure 8.110. The **Select Working Directory** window appears. In this window, browse to *Creo Parametric > Chapter 8*. You need to create these folders, if not created earlier. Next, click on the **OK** button. The working directory is set to <<*Creo Parametric**Chapter 8*\\.

8.110

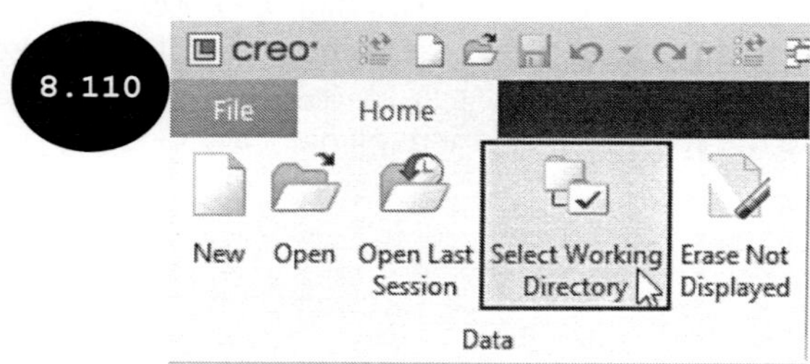

Section 3: Invoking the Part Mode

1. Click on the **New** tool in the **Data** group of the **Home** tab. The **New** dialog box appears, see Figure 8.111. Alternatively, press the CTRL + N to invoke the **New** dialog box.

2. Ensure that the **Part** radio button is selected in the **Type** area and the **Solid** radio button is selected in the **Sub-type** area of the dialog box, see Figure 8.111.

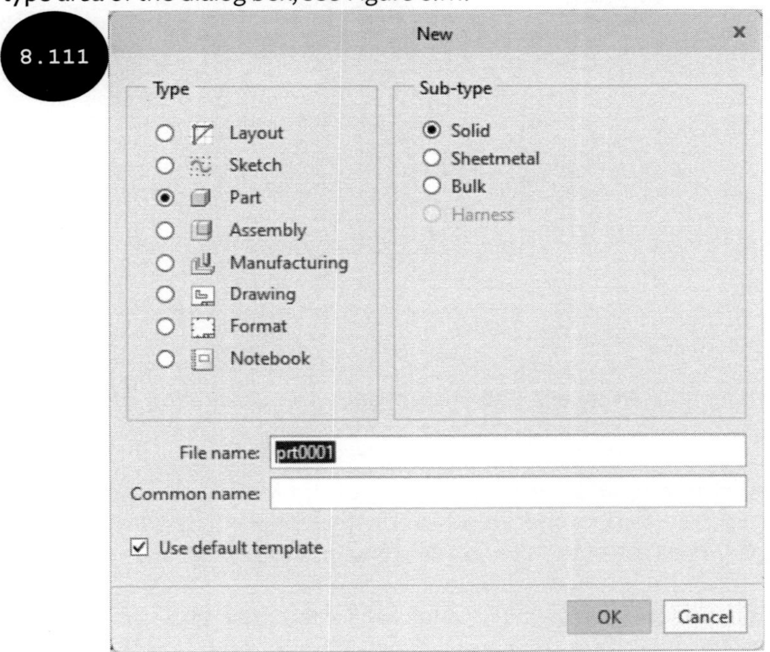

3. Enter **C08-Tutorial01** in the **File name** field of the dialog box as the name of the model.

4. Clear the **Use default template** check box and then click on the **OK** button in the dialog box. The **New File Options** dialog box appears, see Figure 8.112.

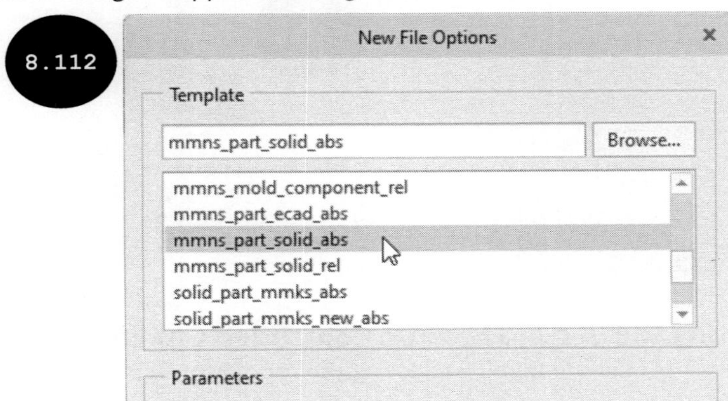

5. Select the **mmns_part_solid_abs** template in the **New File Options** dialog box and then click on the **OK** button. The Part mode is invoked with the **mmns_part_solid_abs** template.

Section 4: Creating the Base Feature - Extrude Feature

1. Invoke the Sketching environment by selecting the Top plane as the sketching plane and then create the sketch of the extrude feature, see Figure 8.113.

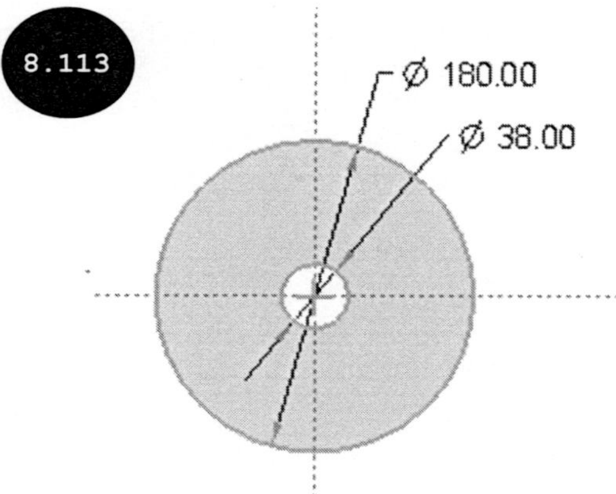

2. Exit the Sketching environment and then change the orientation of the sketch to standard orientation.

3. Click on the **Extrude** tool in the **Shapes** group of the **Model** tab. The preview of the extrude feature appears. Also, the **Extrude** tab appears in the **Ribbon**. If the preview of the extrude feature does not appear, then select the sketch in the graphics area.

4. Enter **2** as the depth of extrusion in the **Value** field of the **Extrude** tab and then press ENTER. The preview of the extrude feature appears as shown in Figure 8.114.

5. Click on the green tick-mark button in the **Extrude** tab. The extrude feature is created, see Figure 8.115.

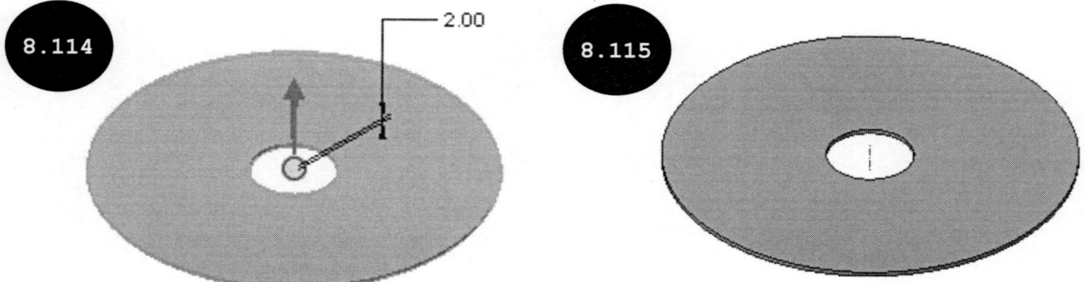

Section 5: Creating the Second Feature - Extruded Cut Feature

1. Invoke the Sketching environment by selecting the top planar face of the base feature as the sketching plane.

2. Create the sketch of the second feature, see Figure 8.116.

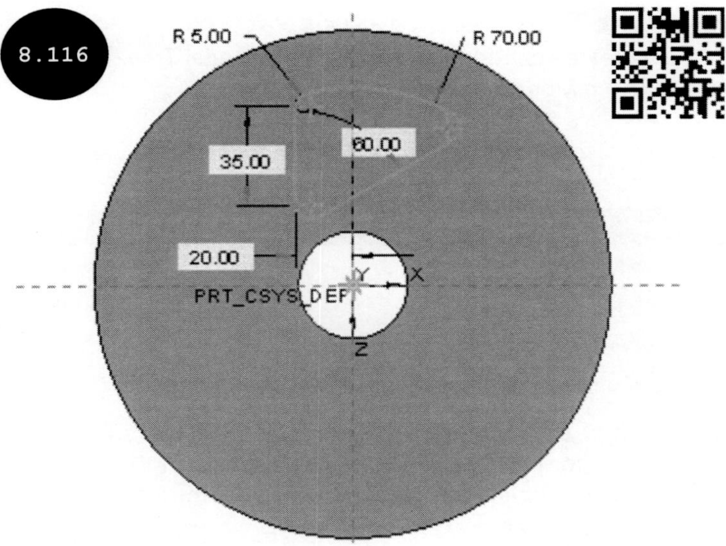

3. Exit the Sketching environment and then change the orientation of the sketch to standard orientation.

4. Ensure that the previously created sketch is selected in the graphics area.

5. Click on the **Extrude** tool in the **Shapes** group of the **Model** tab. The preview of the extrude feature appears. Also, the **Extrude** tab appears in the **Ribbon**.

6. Click on the **Flip Direction** button in the **Depth** area of the **Extrude** tab. The direction of extrusion changes to downward and the **Remove Material** button gets activated, automatically. Also, the preview of the cut feature appears in the graphics area.

7. Expand the **Options** panel of the **Extrude** tab and then select the **Through All** option in the **Side 1** drop-down list.

8. Click on the green tick-mark button. The extrude cut feature is created, see Figure 8.117.

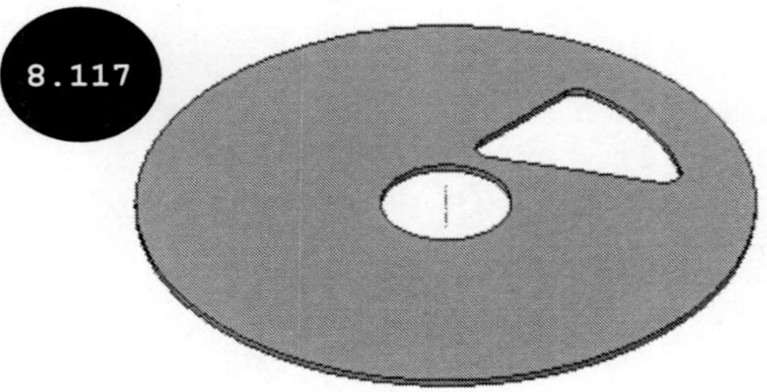

Section 6: Creating the Third Feature - Axis Pattern

1. Select the previously created extrude cut feature in the **Model Tree**. The **Pattern** tool is enabled in the **Editing** group of the **Model** tab.

2. Click on the **Pattern** tool in the **Editing** group of the **Model** tab, see Figure 8.118. The **Pattern** tab appears in the **Ribbon**.

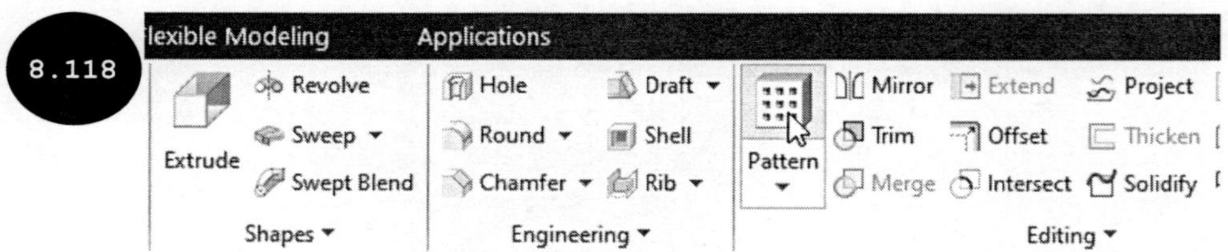

3. Select the **Axis** option in the **Type** drop-down list of the **Type** area in the **Pattern** tab, see Figure 8.119. The options for creating an axis pattern appear in the **Pattern** tab. Also, you are prompted to select an axis to define the angular direction of the axis pattern.

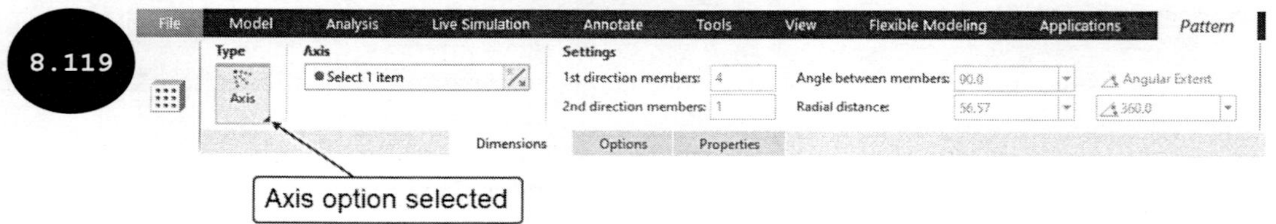

4. Select the **Y-axis** of the default coordinate system to define the angular direction of the pattern. Black dots appear in the graphics area representing the preview of the pattern instances, see Figure 8.120.

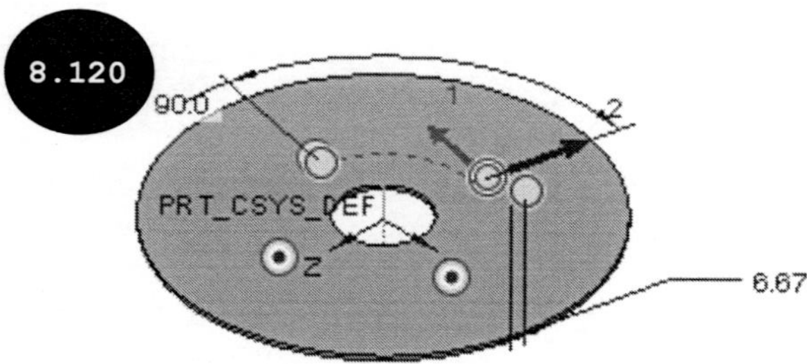

Note: If the default coordinate system is not visible in the graphics area, then you can turn on its visibility. To do so, ensure that the **Csys Display** check box is selected in the **Datum Display Filters** flyout of the **In-graphics** toolbar, see Figure 8.121.

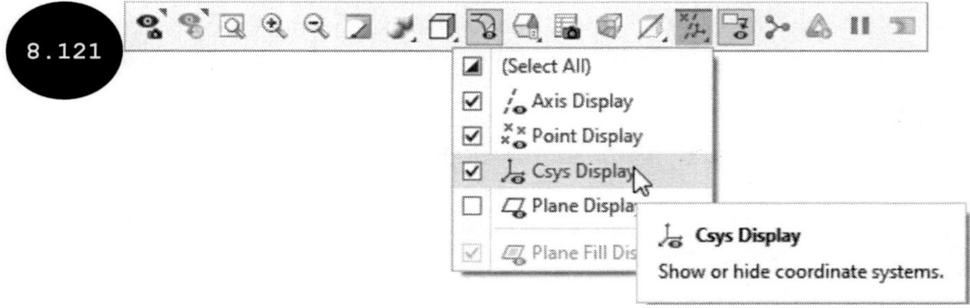

5. Click on the **Angular extent** button in the **Settings** area of the **Pattern** tab (see Figure 8.122,) to arrange all the pattern instances equally within a specified total angle value. The **Angular extent** field is enabled in the **Pattern** tab.

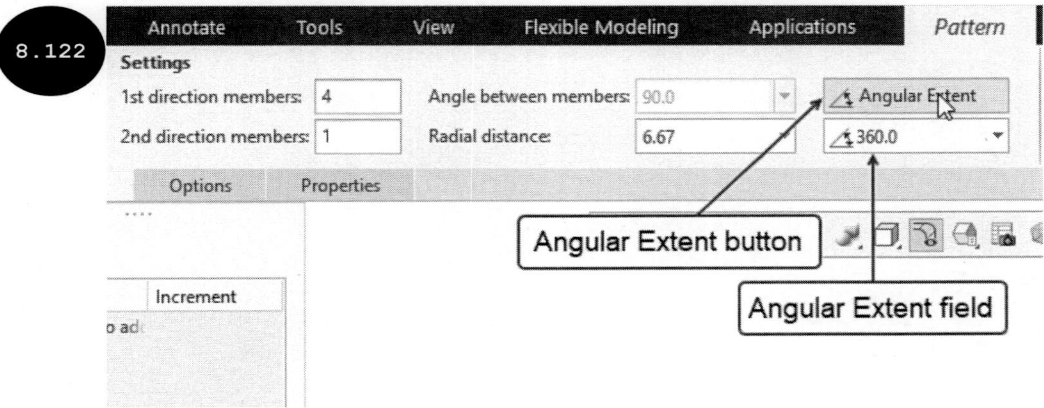

6. Ensure that a **360** degrees angle value is specified in the **Angular extent** field in the **Settings** area of the **Pattern** tab as the total angle value of the axis pattern.

7. Enter **6** as the number of pattern instances to be created, circularly in the **1st direction members** field in the **Settings** area of the **Pattern** tab, and then press ENTER. All the pattern instances get arranged equally within the specified total angle value.

8. Click on the green tick-mark button in the **Pattern** tab. The axis pattern is created, see Figure 8.123.

Section 7: Creating the Fourth Feature - Extrude Cut Feature

1. Invoke the Sketching environment by selecting the top planar face of the base feature as the sketching plane.

2. Create the sketch of the fourth feature of the model, see Figure 8.124.

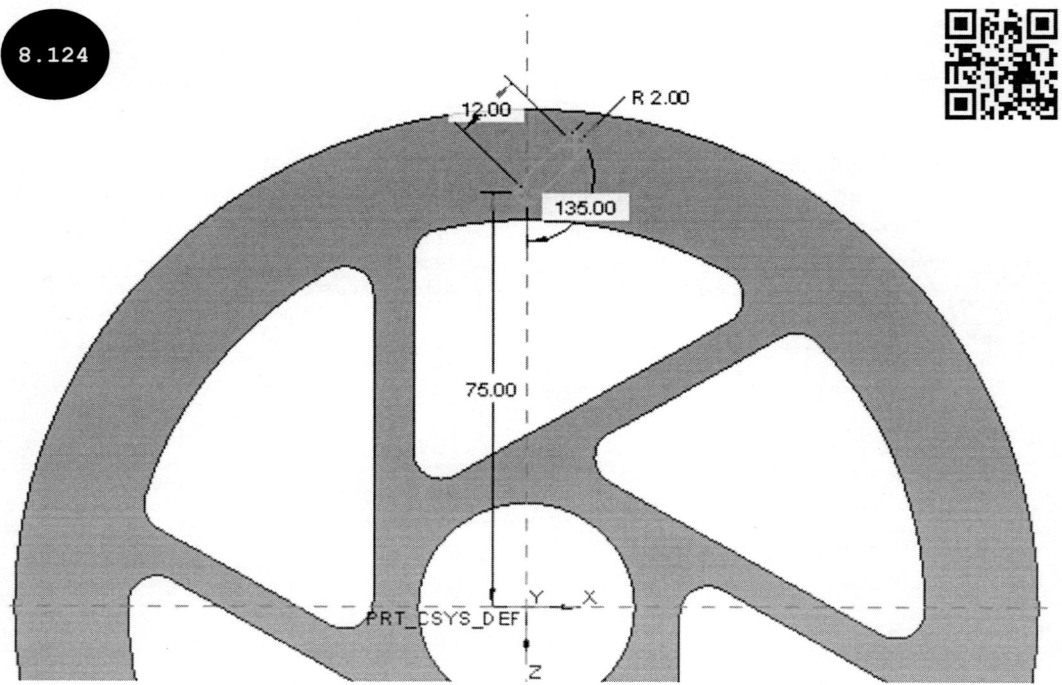

3. Exit the Sketching environment and then change the orientation of the sketch to standard orientation.

4. Ensure that the previously created sketch is selected in the graphics area.

5. Click on the **Extrude** tool in the **Shapes** group of the **Model** tab. The preview of the extrude feature appears. Also, the **Extrude** tab appears in the **Ribbon**.

6. Click on the **Flip Direction** button in the **Depth** area of the **Extrude** tab. The direction of extrusion changes to downward and the **Remove Material** button gets activated, automatically. Also, the preview of the cut feature appears in the graphics area.

7. Expand the **Options** panel of the **Extrude** tab and then select the **Through All** option in the **Side 1** drop-down list.

8. Click on the green tick-mark button. The extrude cut feature is created, see Figure 8.125.

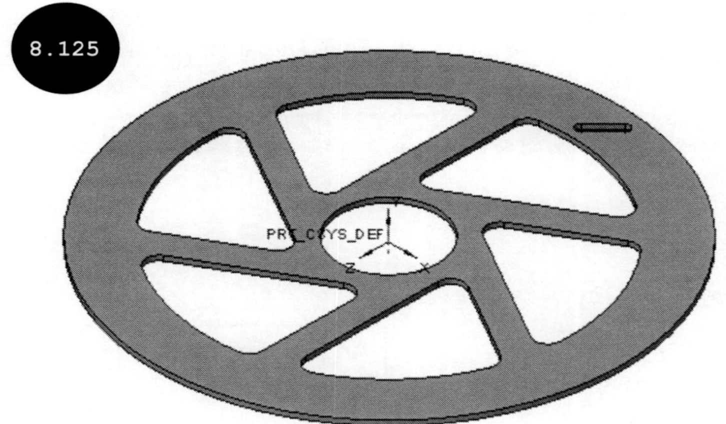

8.125

Section 8: Creating the Fifth Feature - Axis Pattern

1. Select the previously created extrude cut feature in the **Model Tree**. The **Pattern** tool is enabled in the **Editing** group of the **Model** tab.

2. Click on the **Pattern** tool in the **Editing** group of the **Model** tab. The **Pattern** tab appears in the **Ribbon**.

3. Select the **Axis** option in the **Type** drop-down list of the **Type** area, see Figure 8.126. The options for creating an axis pattern appear in the **Pattern** tab. Also, you are prompted to select an axis to define the angular direction of the axis pattern.

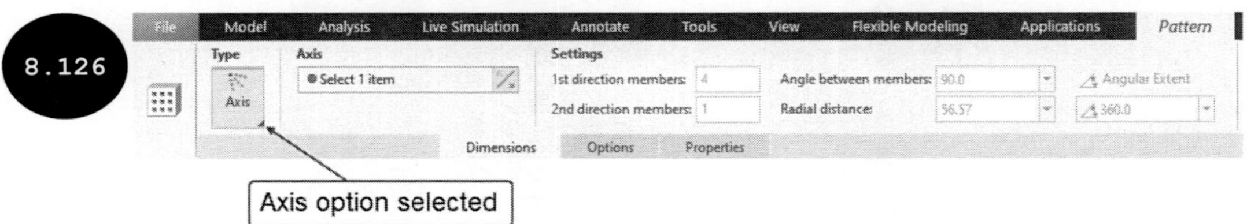

8.126

4. Select the **Y-axis** of the default coordinate system to define the angular direction of the pattern. Black dots appear in the graphics area representing the preview of the pattern instances, see Figure 8.127.

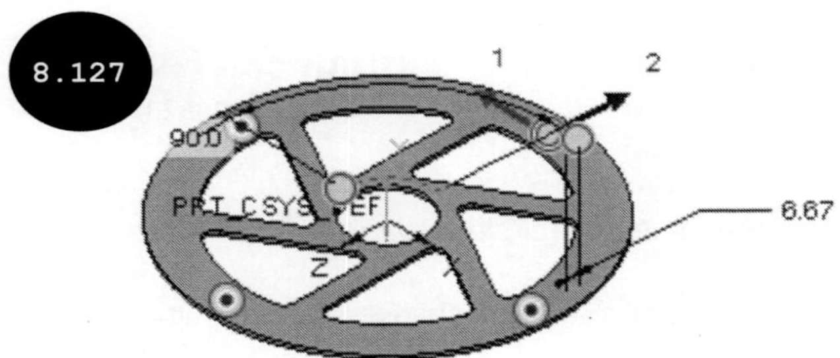

8.127

5. Click on the **Angular extent** button in the **Pattern** tab (see Figure 8.128) to arrange all the pattern instances equally within a specified total angle value. The **Angular extent** field gets enabled in the **Pattern** tab.

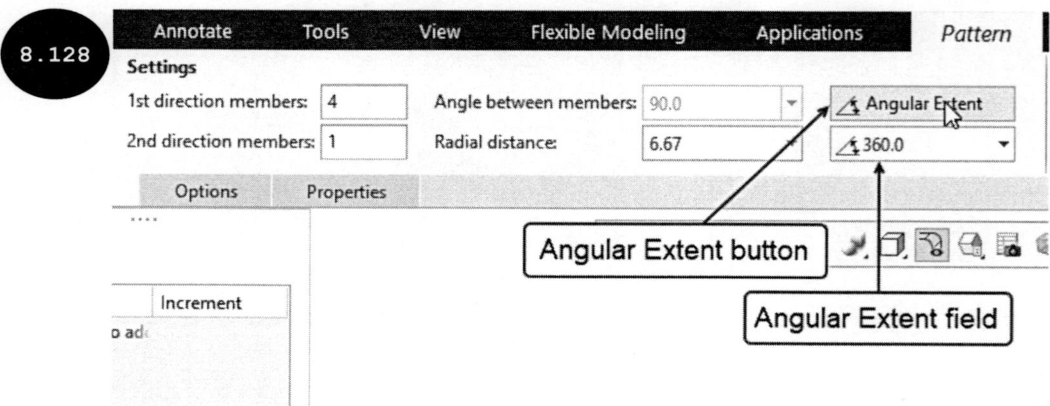

6. Ensure that a **360** degrees angle value is specified in the **Angular extent** field of the **Settings** area as the total angle value of the axis pattern.

7. Enter **25** as the number of pattern instances to be created, circularly in the **1st direction members** field of the **Settings** area, and then press ENTER. All the pattern instances get arranged equally within the specified total angle value.

8. Click on the green tick-mark button in the **Pattern** tab. The axis pattern is created, see Figure 8.129.

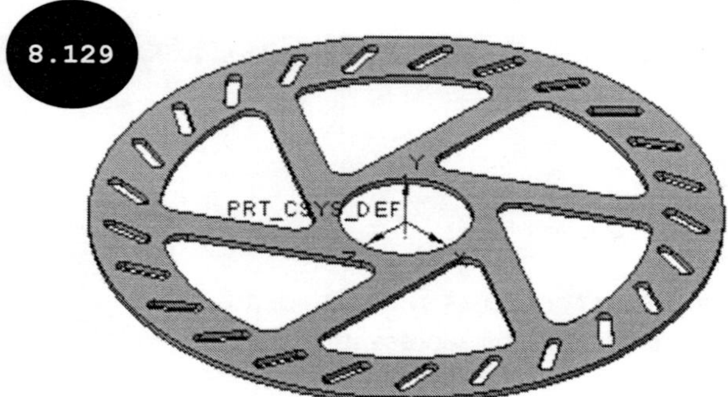

Section 9: Creating the Sixth Feature - Extrude Cut Feature

1. Invoke the Sketching environment by selecting the top planar face of the base feature as the sketching plane.

2. Create the sketch of the sixth feature (circle of diameter 5 mm), see Figure 8.130.

3. Exit the Sketching environment and then change the orientation of the sketch to standard orientation.

4. Ensure that the previously created sketch is selected in the graphics area.

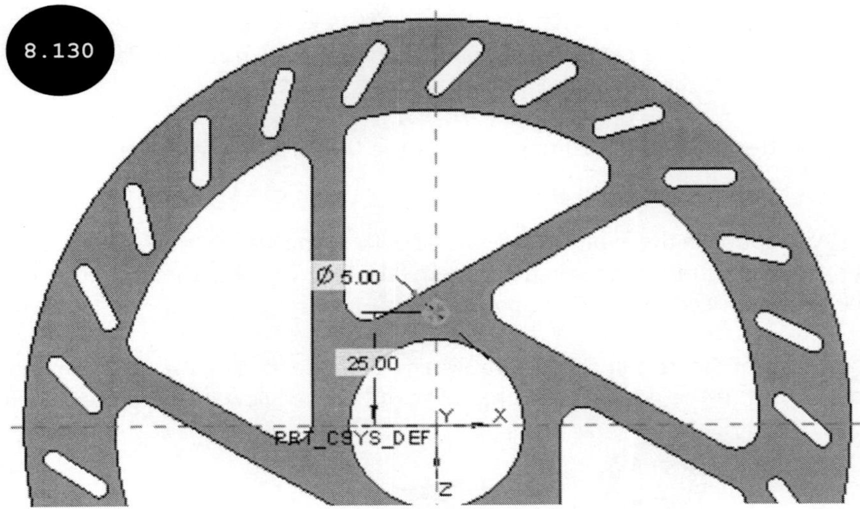

5. Click on the **Extrude** tool in the **Shapes** group of the **Model** tab. The preview of the extrude feature appears. Also, the **Extrude** tab appears in the **Ribbon**.

6. Click on the **Flip Direction** button in the **Depth** area of the **Extrude** tab. The direction of extrusion changes to downward and the **Remove Material** button gets activated in the **Settings** area, automatically. Also, the preview of the cut feature appears in the graphics area.

7. Expand the **Options** panel of the **Extrude** tab and then select the **Through All** option in the **Side 1** drop-down list.

8. Click on the green tick-mark button. The extrude cut feature is created, see Figure 8.131.

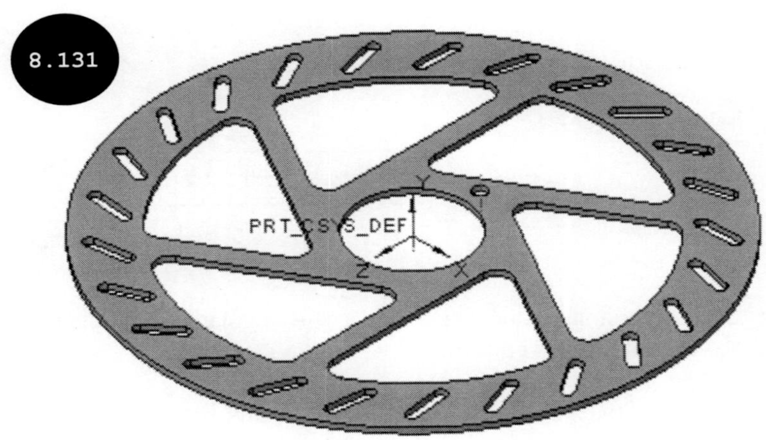

Section 10: Creating the Seventh Feature - Axis Pattern

1. Select the previously created extrude cut feature in the **Model Tree**. The **Pattern** tool is enabled in the **Editing** group of the **Model** tab.

2. Click on the **Pattern** tool in the **Editing** group of the **Model** tab. The **Pattern** tab appears in the **Ribbon**.

3. Select the **Axis** option in the **Type** drop-down list of the **Type** area in the **Pattern** tab. The options for creating an axis pattern appear in the **Pattern** tab. Also, you are prompted to select an axis to define the angular direction of the axis pattern.

4. Select the **Y-axis** of the default coordinate system to define the angular direction of the pattern. Black dots appear in the graphics area representing the preview of the pattern instances, see Figure 8.132.

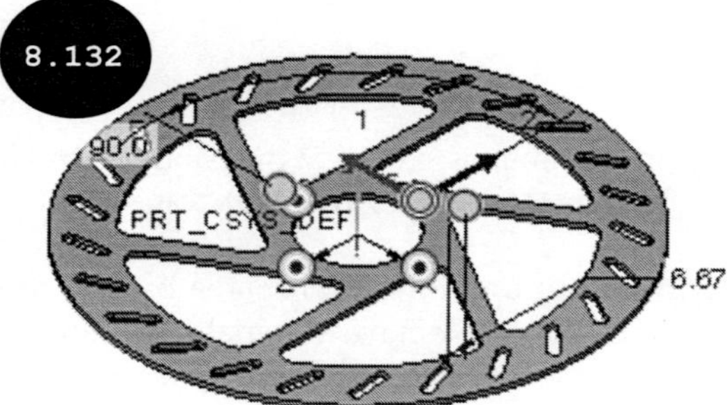

5. Click on the **Angular extent** button in the **Settings** area of the **Pattern** tab, see Figure 8.133. The **Angular extent** field gets enabled in the **Pattern** tab.

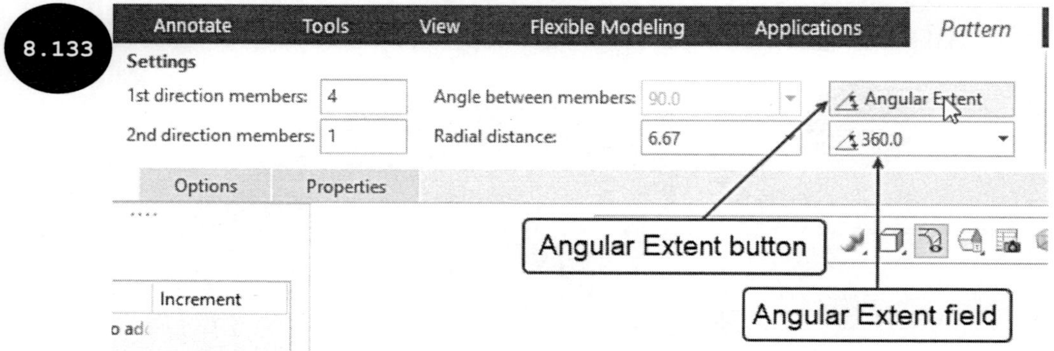

6. Ensure that a **360** degrees angle value is specified in the **Angular extent** field of the **Settings** area as the total angle value of the axis pattern.

7. Enter **6** as the number of pattern instances to be created circularly in the **1st direction members** field of the **Settings** area, and then press ENTER. All the pattern instances get arranged equally within the specified total angle value.

8. Click on the green tick-mark button in the **Pattern** tab. The axis pattern is created, see Figure 8.134.

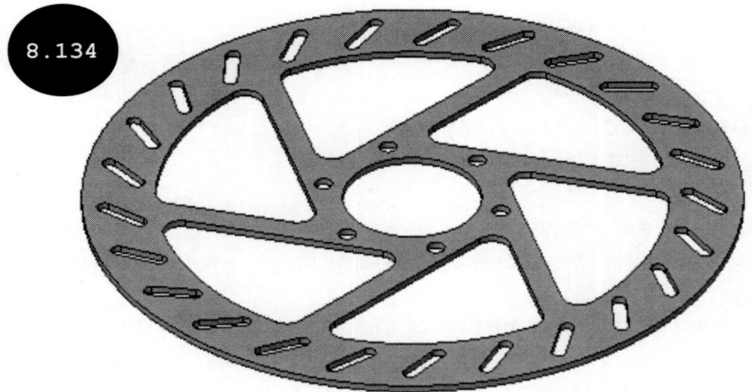

Section 11: Saving the Model

1. Click on the **Save** tool in the **Quick Access Toolbar**. The **Save Object** dialog box appears.

2. Click on the **OK** button in the dialog box. The model is saved with the name **C08-Tutorial01** in the specified working directory (<<*Creo Parametric**Chapter 8*\).

Tutorial 2

Create the model shown in Figure 8.135. The different views and dimensions are given in the same figure. All dimensions are in mm.

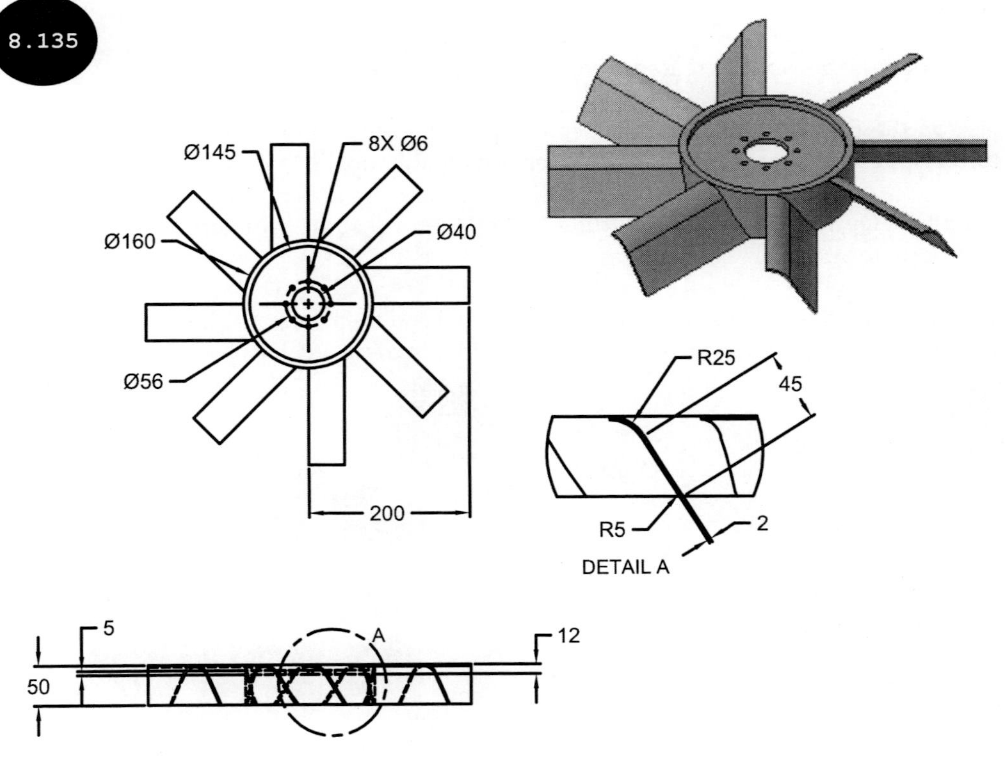

Section 1: Starting Creo Parametric

1. Start Creo Parametric by double-clicking on the Creo Parametric icon on your desktop.

Section 2: Setting the Working Directory

1. Set the working directory to <<\Creo Parametric\Chapter 8.

Section 3: Invoking the Part Mode

1. Click on the **New** tool in the **Data** group of the **Home** tab. The **New** dialog box appears.
2. Enter **C08-Tutorial02** in the **File name** field of the dialog box as the name of the model.
3. Clear the **Use default template** check box and then click on the **OK** button in the dialog box. The **New File Options** dialog box appears.
4. Select the **mmns_part_solid_abs** template in the **New File Options** dialog box and then click on the **OK** button. The Part mode is invoked with the **mmns_part_solid_abs** template.

Section 4: Creating the Base Feature - Extrude Feature

1. Invoke the Sketching environment by selecting the Top plane as the sketching plane.
2. Create the sketch of the base feature of the model, see Figure 8.136.
3. Exit the Sketching environment and then change the orientation of the sketch to standard orientation.
4. Ensure that the previously created sketch is selected in the graphics area.
5. Click on the **Extrude** tool in the **Shapes** group of the **Model** tab. The preview of the extrude feature appears. Also, the **Extrude** tab appears in the **Ribbon**.
6. Expand the **Options** panel of the **Extrude** tab and then select the **Symmetric** option in the **Side 1** drop-down list.
7. Enter **50** as the depth of extrusion in the **Value** field and then press ENTER. The preview of the extrude feature appears symmetrically on both sides of the sketching plane, see Figure 8.137.

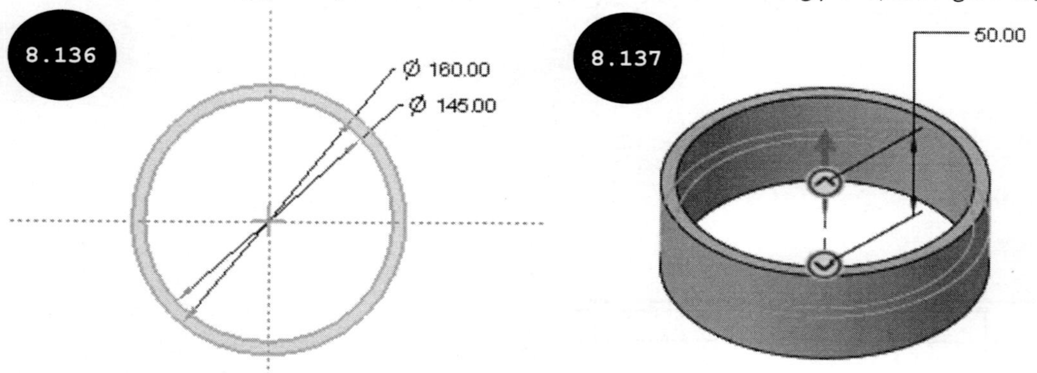

8. Click on the green tick-mark button in the **Extrude** tab. The extrude feature is created, see Figure 8.138.

Section 5: Creating the Second Feature - Extrude Feature

To create the second feature, you need to create a datum plane at an offset distance of 12 mm from the top planar face of the model downward.

1. Click on the **Plane** tool in the **Datum** group of the **Model** tab. The **Datum Plane** dialog box appears.

2. Select the top planar face of the base feature as a reference in the graphics area. The preview of an offset datum plane appears.

3. Enter **-12** in the **Translation** field of the **Offset** area in the dialog box and then press ENTER. The preview of the offset datum plane appears as shown in Figure 8.139. Note that the negative offset distance is used for reversing the direction of the offset plane downward.

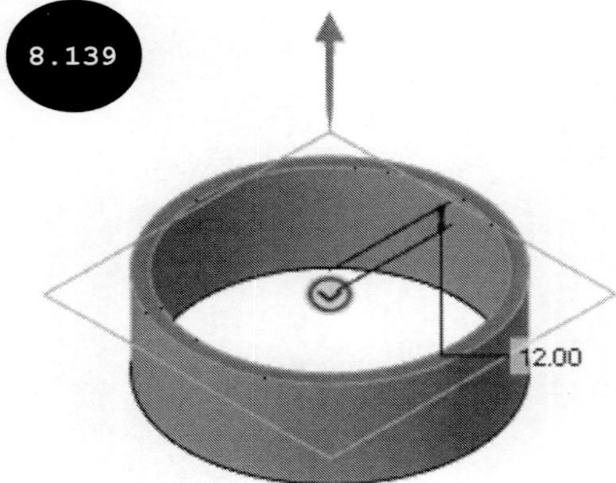

4. Click on the **OK** button in the dialog box. The offset datum plane is created.

   After creating the datum plane, you need to create the second feature of the model.

5. Invoke the Sketching environment by selecting the newly created datum plane as the sketching plane.

6. Create two circles, one of diameter 40 mm and the second, of the same diameter as that of the inner circular edge of the base feature, as the sketch of the second feature, see Figure 8.140.

7. Exit the Sketching environment and then change the orientation of the sketch to standard orientation.

8. Ensure that the previously created sketch is selected in the graphics area.

9. Click on the **Extrude** tool in the **Shapes** group of the **Model** tab. The preview of the extrude feature appears. Also, the **Extrude** tab appears in the **Ribbon**.

10. Enter **5** as the depth of extrusion in the **Value** field of the **Extrude** tab and then press ENTER. The preview of the extrude feature appears similar to the one shown in Figure 8.141.

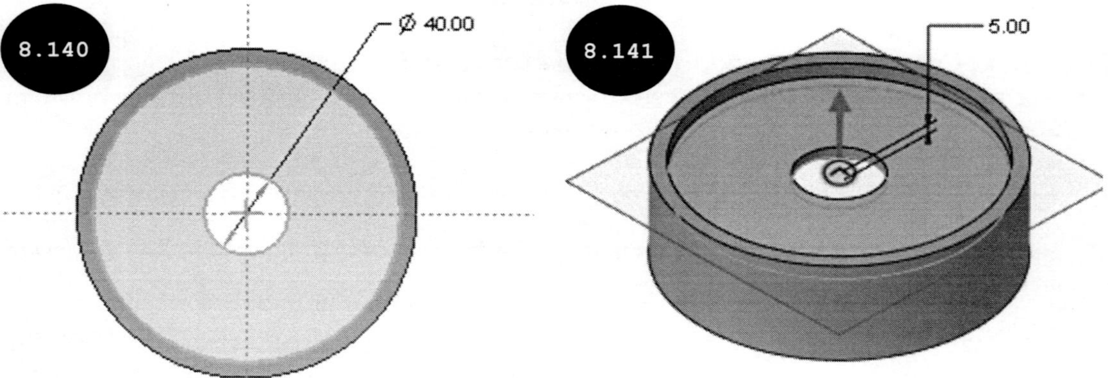

11. Click on the green tick-mark button in the **Extrude** tab. The extrude feature is created, see Figure 8.142.

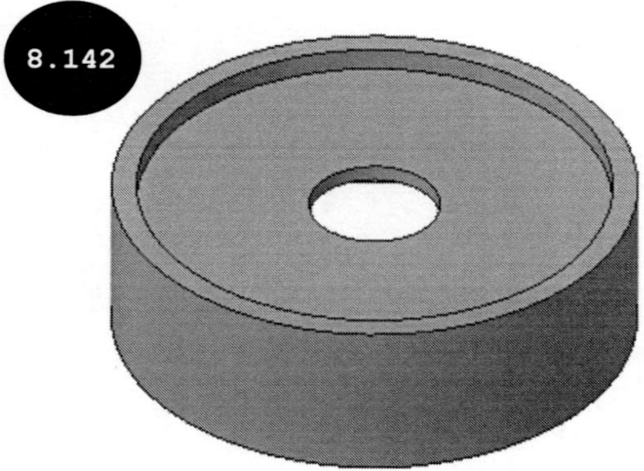

Section 6: Creating the Third Feature - Extrude Cut Feature

1. Invoke the Sketching environment by selecting the top planar face of the second feature (previously created extrude feature) as the sketching plane.

2. Create a circle of diameter 6 mm as the sketch of the third feature, see Figure 8.143.

3. Exit the Sketching environment and then change the orientation of the sketch to standard orientation.

4. Ensure that the previously created sketch is selected in the graphics area.

5. Click on the **Extrude** tool in the **Shapes** group of the **Model** tab. The preview of the extrude feature appears. Also, the **Extrude** tab appears in the **Ribbon**.

6. Click on the **Flip Direction** button in the **Depth** area of the **Extrude** tab. The direction of extrusion changes to downward and the **Remove Material** button gets activated in the **Settings** area, automatically. Also, the preview of the cut feature appears in the graphics area.

7. Expand the **Options** panel of the **Extrude** tab and then select the **Through All** option in the **Side 1** drop-down list.

8. Click on the green tick-mark button. The extrude cut feature is created, see Figure 8.144.

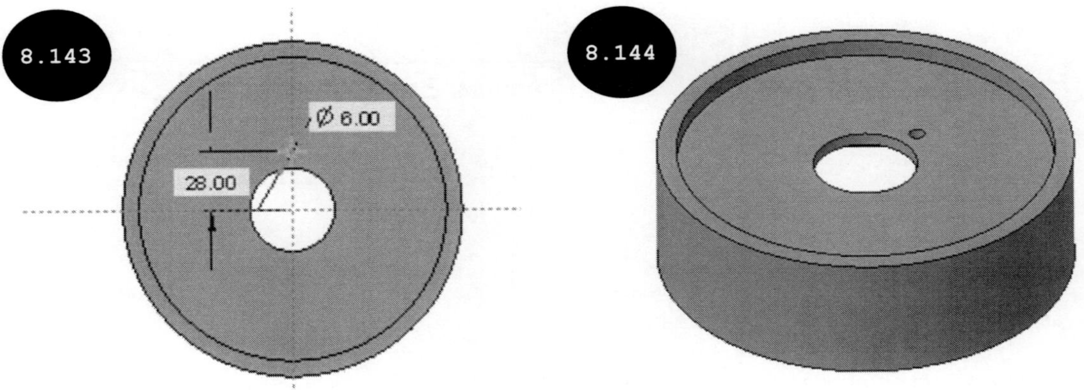

Section 7: Creating the Fourth Feature - Axis Pattern

1. Select the previously created extrude cut feature in the **Model Tree**. The **Pattern** tool is enabled in the **Editing** group of the **Model** tab.

2. Click on the **Pattern** tool in the **Editing** group of the **Model** tab. The **Pattern** tab appears in the **Ribbon**.

3. Select the **Axis** option in the **Type** drop-down list of the **Type** area in the **Pattern** tab. The options for creating an axis pattern appear in the **Pattern** tab. Also, you are prompted to select an axis to define the angular direction of the axis pattern.

4. Select the **Y-axis** of the default coordinate system to define the angular direction of the pattern. Black dots appear in the graphics area representing the preview of the pattern instances, see Figure 8.145.

8.145

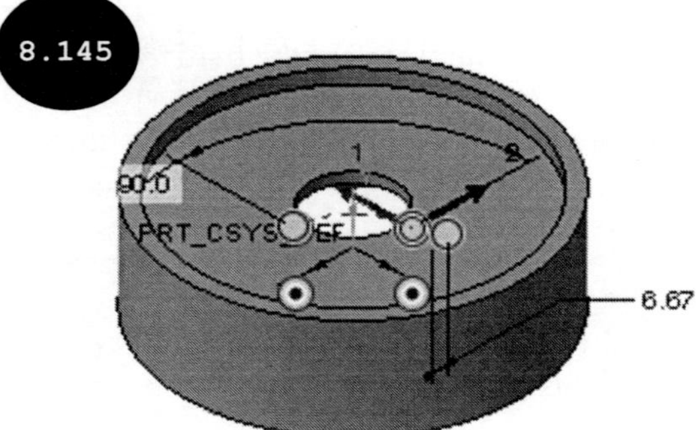

5. Click on the **Angular extent** button in the **Settings** area of the **Pattern** tab, see Figure 8.146. The **Angular extent** field gets enabled in the **Pattern** tab.

8.146

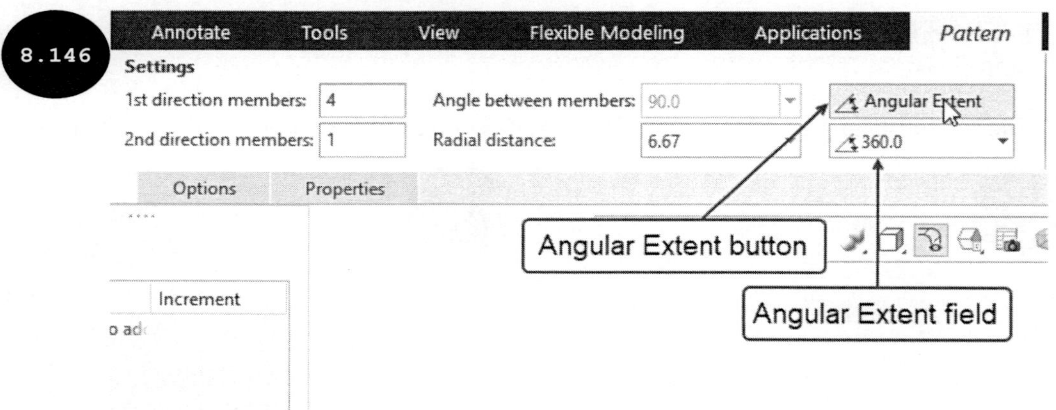

6. Ensure that a **360** degrees angle value is specified in the **Angular extent** field of the **Settings** area as the total angle value of the axis pattern.

7. Enter **8** as the number of pattern instances to be created, circularly in the **1st direction members** field of the **Settings** area, and then press ENTER. All the pattern instances get arranged equally within the specified total angle value.

8. Click on the green tick-mark button in the **Pattern** tab. The axis pattern is created, see Figure 8.147. Note that in Figure 8.147, the display of the coordinate system, datum planes, and axis, are turned off by using the **Datum Display Filters** flyout of the **In-graphics** toolbar.

8.147

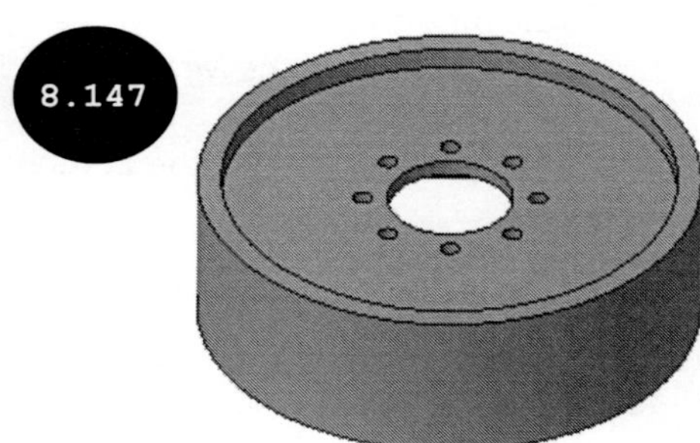

Section 8: Creating the Fifth Feature - Extrude Feature

The fifth feature of the model is an extrude feature and its sketch is to be created on a datum plane, which is at an offset distance of 200 mm from the Right plane.

1. Click on the **Plane** tool in the **Datum** group of the **Model** tab. The **Datum Plane** dialog box appears.

2. Select the Right Plane as a reference in the graphics area. The preview of an offset datum plane appears.

3. Enter -**200** in the **Translation** field of the **Offset** area in the dialog box and then press ENTER. The preview of the offset datum plane appears as shown in Figure 8.148.

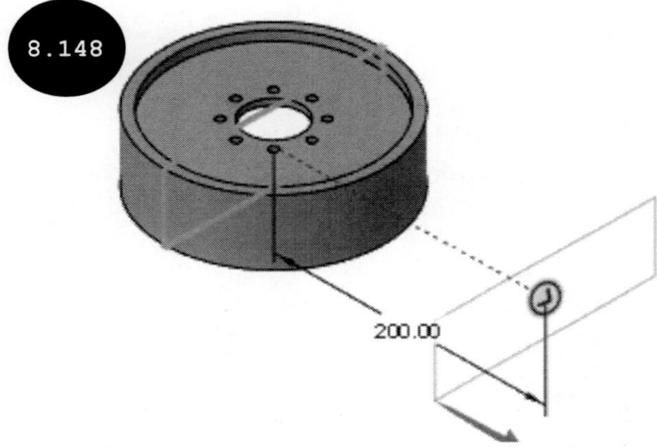

4. Click on the **OK** button in the dialog box. The offset datum plane is created.

   Now, you can create the sketch of the fifth feature on the newly created datum plane.

5. Invoke the Sketching environment by selecting the newly created datum plane as the sketching plane.

6. Create the sketch of the extrude feature, see Figure 8.149.

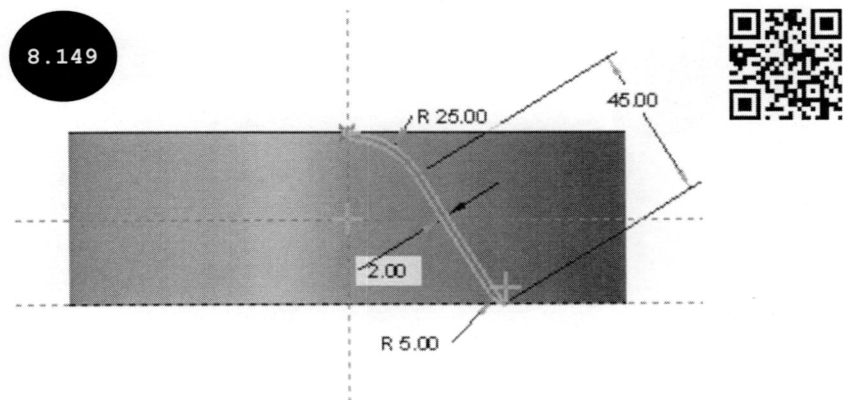

Note: In the sketch shown in Figure 8.149, the tangent constraint has been applied between the connecting arcs and lines of the sketch. Also, the center point of the arc having a radius of 25 mm is coincident with the origin.

7. Exit the Sketching environment and then change the orientation of the sketch to standard orientation.

8. Ensure that the previously created sketch is selected in the graphics area.

9. Click on the **Extrude** tool in the **Shapes** group of the **Model** tab. A preview of the extrude feature appears. Also, the **Extrude** tab appears in the **Ribbon**.

10. Click on the **Flip Direction** button in the **Depth** area of the **Extrude** tab to reverse the direction of extrusion toward the base feature, see Figure 8.150.

11. Expand the **Options** panel of the **Extrude** tab and then select the **To Next** option in the **Side 1** drop-down list. The preview of the extrude feature gets terminated at its nearest intersection, see Figure 8.151.

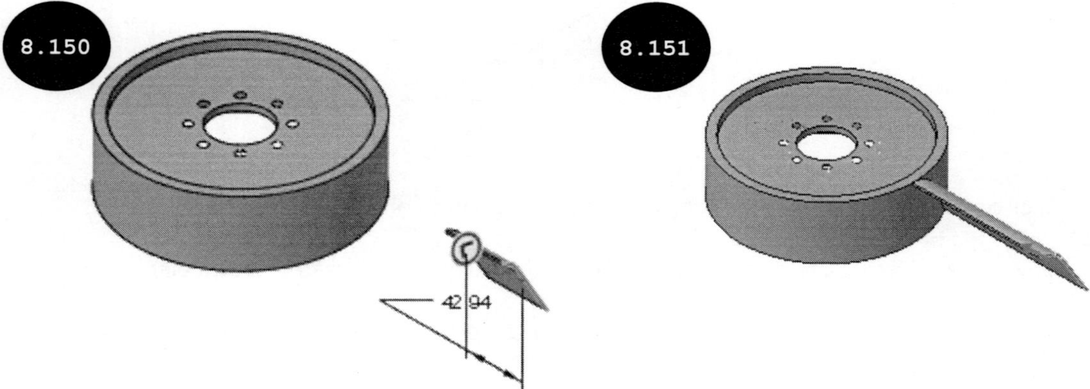

12. Click on the green tick-mark button in the **Extrude** tab. The extrude feature is created, see Figure 8.152.

Section 9: Creating the Sixth Feature - Axis Pattern

1. Select the previously created extrude feature in the **Model Tree**.

2. Click on the **Pattern** tool in the **Editing** group of the **Model** tab. The **Pattern** tab appears in the **Ribbon**.

3. Select the **Axis** option in the **Type** drop-down list of the **Type** area in the **Pattern** tab. The options for creating an axis pattern appear in the **Pattern** tab. Also, you are prompted to select an axis to define the angular direction of the axis pattern.

4. Select the **Y-axis** of the default coordinate system to define the angular direction of the pattern. Black dots appear in the graphics area representing the preview of the pattern instances.

5. Click on the **Angular extent** button in the **Pattern** tab, see Figure 8.153. The **Angular extent** field gets enabled in the **Pattern** tab.

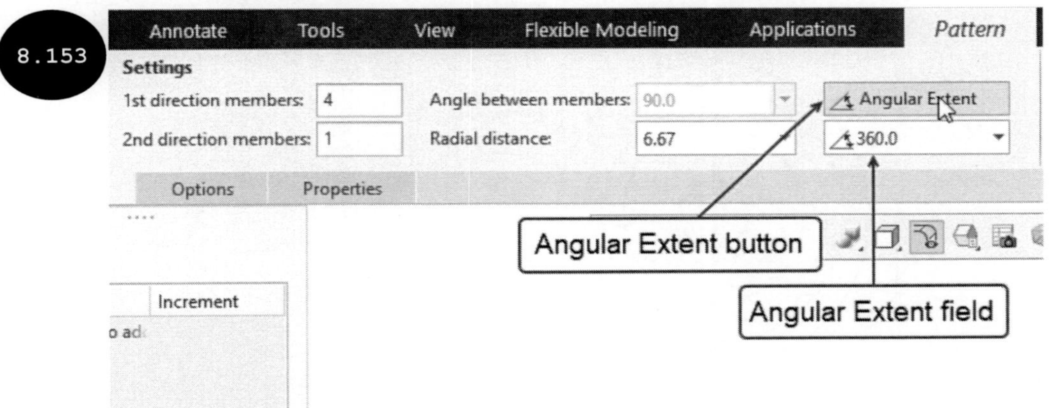

6. Ensure that a **360** degrees angle value is specified in the **Angular extent** field of the **Pattern** tab as the total angle value of the axis pattern.

7. Enter **8** as the number of pattern instances to be created circularly in the **1st direction members** field of the **Pattern** tab, and then press ENTER. All the pattern instances get arranged equally within the specified total angle value.

8. Click on the green tick-mark button in the **Pattern** tab. The axis pattern is created, see Figure 8.154.

Section 10: Saving the Model

1. Click on the **Save** tool in the **Quick Access Toolbar**. The **Save Object** dialog box appears.

2. Click on the **OK** button in the dialog box. The model is saved with the name **C08-Tutorial02** in the specified working directory (<<*Creo Parametric**Chapter 8*\\).

Hands-on Test Drive 1

Create the model shown in Figure 8.155. The different views and dimensions are given in the same figure for your reference.

8.155

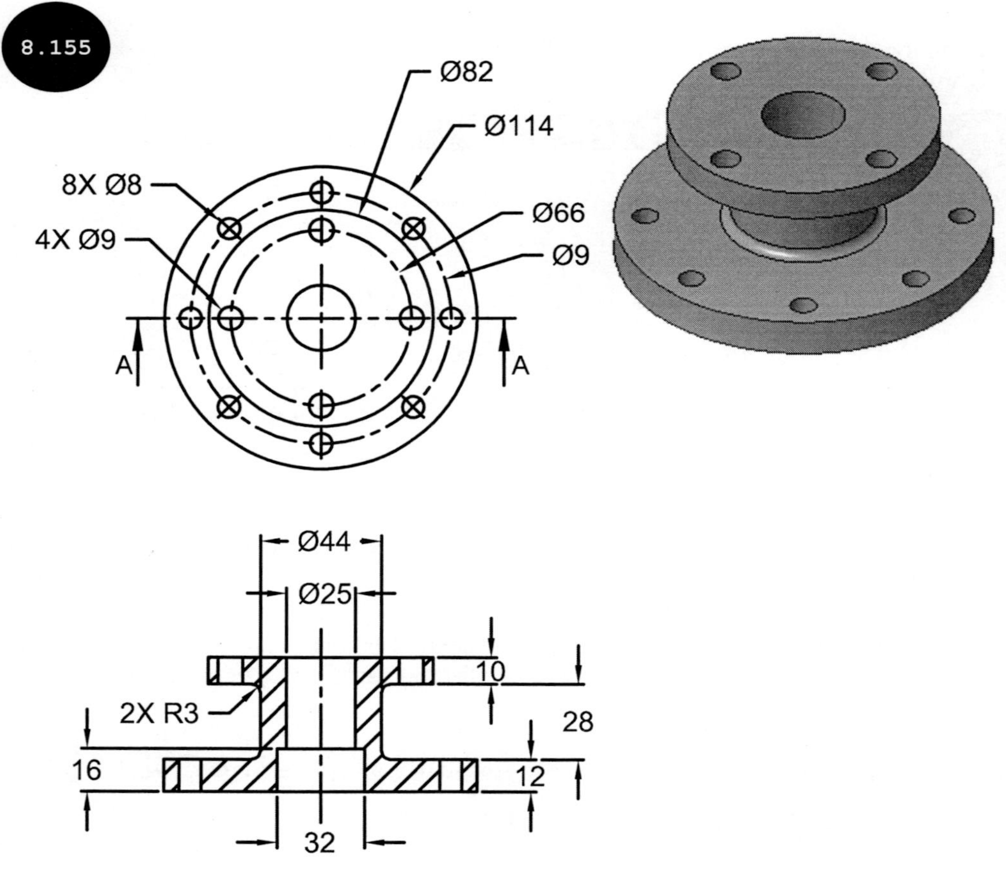

Hands-on Test Drive 2

Create the model shown in Figure 8.156. The different views and dimensions are given in the same figure for your reference.

8.156

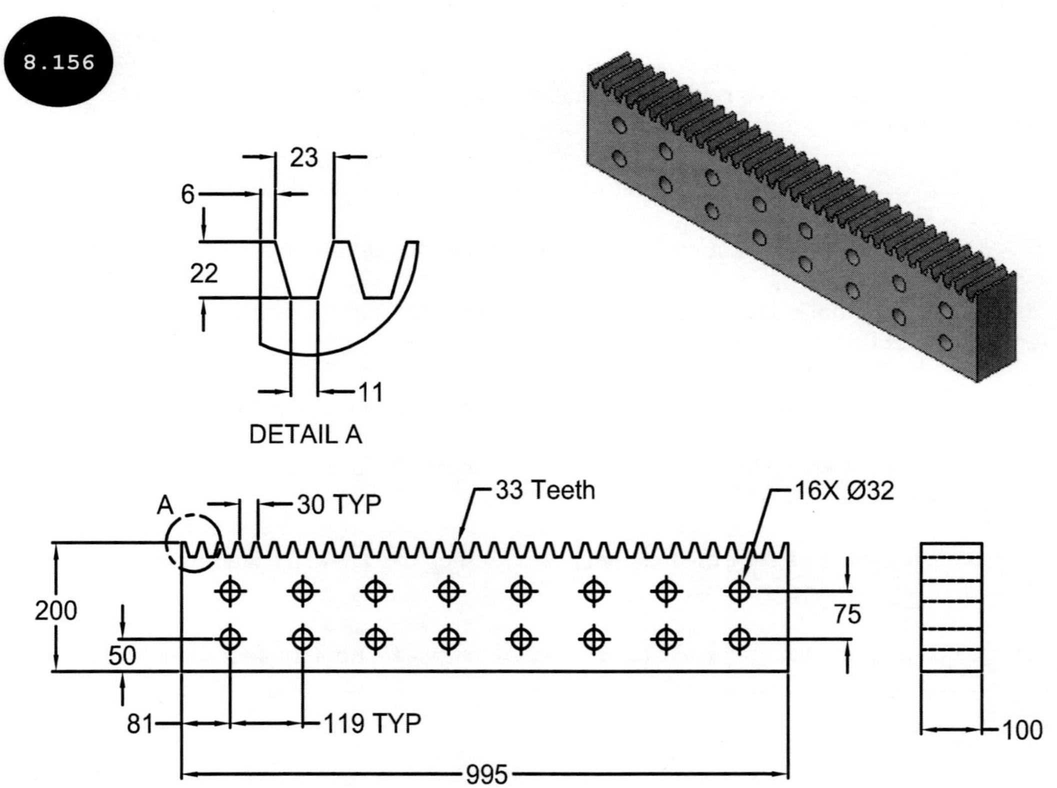

Summary

In this chapter, you have learned how to use various patterning and mirroring tools. Once you have read the chapter thoroughly, you can create different types of patterns such as dimension patterns, direction patterns, axis patterns, fill patterns, table patterns, reference patterns, curve patterns, variable patterns, and geometry patterns.

In addition to creating different patterns, you have also learned how to skip pattern instances, delete a pattern, mirror one or more features about a mirroring plane, and copy and paste a feature.

Questions

Complete and verify the following sentences:

- The ________ tool is used for creating multiple instances of a feature, linearly in one or two linear directions by selecting dimensions as the pattern directions.

- The _________ tool is used for creating multiple instances of a feature along a curve.
- You can create a variable pattern for _________ , _________, and _________ patterns.
- A variable pattern is created such that you can vary the _________ and _________ between the pattern instances.
- The _________ pattern is used for creating multiple instances of a feature in angular direction as well as in radial direction.
- The _________ pattern is used for patterning a geometry instead of a feature.
- The _________ tool is used for mirroring one or more features about a mirroring plane.
- The _________ tool is used for deleting an already created pattern such that the parent feature remains available in the model.
- The _________ tool is used for copying one or more selected features to the clipboard.
- The number of pattern instances specified in the **Members** field also includes the parent feature. (True/False).
- To create a reference pattern, the feature to be patterned must have a relationship with a pattern instance of an existing pattern feature. (True/False).
- In Creo Parametric, you cannot skip pattern instances that are not required. (True/False).

CHAPTER

9

Advanced Modeling - III

In this chapter, the following topics will be discussed:

- Creating Simple and Standard Holes
- Creating Cosmetic Threads
- Creating Rounds
- Creating Auto Rounds
- Creating Chamfers
- Creating Rib Features
- Creating Shell Features

In earlier chapters, you have learned about creating circular cut features representing holes by using the **Extrude** tool. In this chapter, you will learn about creating simple holes as well as standard holes such as tapped, tapered, drilled, and clearance as per the standard specifications by using the **Hole** tool. Additionally, you will learn about other engineering tools such as **Cosmetic Thread**, **Round**, **Chamfer**, **Rib**, and **Shell**.

Creating Simple and Standard Holes

In Creo Parametric, you can create simple, custom, and standard holes by using the **Hole** tool. The standard holes such as tapped, tapered, drilled, and clearance are created as per the standard specifications. The methods for creating simple and standard holes by using the **Hole** tool are discussed next.

Creating Simple Holes

In Creo Parametric, you can create a simple hole using a predefined rectangle profile, a standard hole profile (countersink, counterbore, or tip angle), or a sketched profile, see Figures 9.1 through 9.3. Figure 9.1 shows a predefined rectangle profile of a hole. Figure 9.2 shows different standard profiles such as counterbore, countersink, and tip angle. Figure 9.3 shows a sketched profile of a hole.

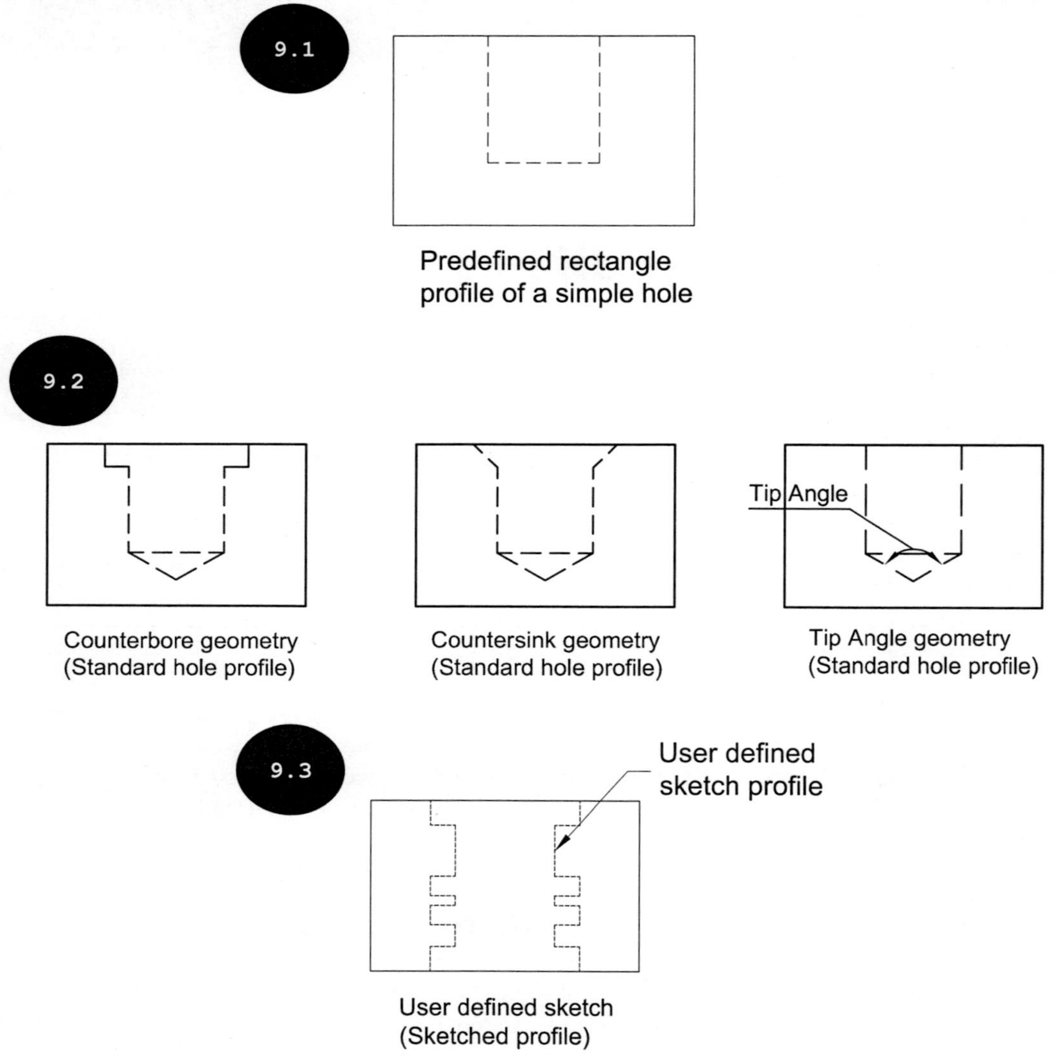

It is evident from the above figures that the predefined rectangle profile uses a rectangular geometry to define the hole profile. The standard hole profile uses countersink, counterbore, or tip angle geometry to define the hole profile, whereas, the sketched profile uses a user defined sketch as the hole profile. The methods for creating various types of simple holes by using the **Hole** tool are discussed next.

Creating Simple Holes Using the Predefined Rectangle Profile

The method for creating a simple hole using the predefined rectangle profile is discussed below:

1. Click on the **Hole** tool in the **Engineering** group of the **Model** tab, refer to Figure 9.4. The **Hole** tab appears in the **Ribbon**, see Figure 9.5.

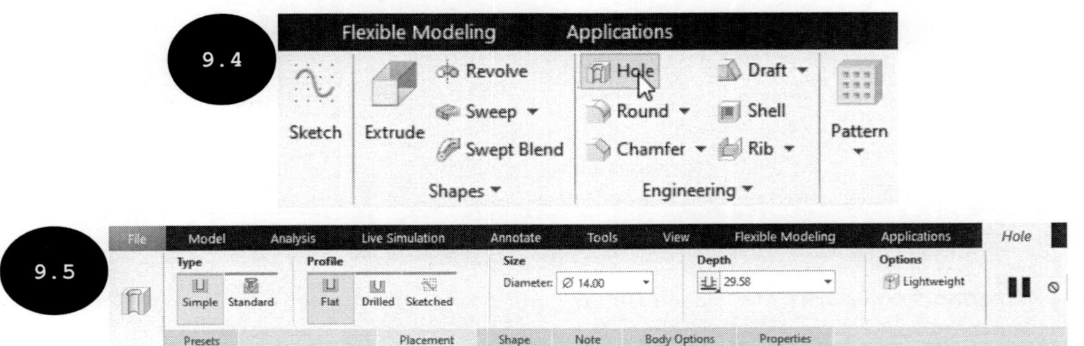

By default, the **Simple** button is activated in the **Type** area of the **Hole** tab. As a result, you can create simple holes by using a predefined rectangle profile, a standard hole profile, or a sketched profile.

2. Ensure that the **Simple** button is activated in the **Type** area of the **Hole** tab to create a simple hole, see Figure 9.5.

3. Ensure that the **Flat** button is activated in the **Profile** area of the **Hole** tab to create a simple hole using a predefined rectangle profile, see Figure 9.5.

4. Click on a face (planar or curved) of the model to define the placement of the hole. The preview of a simple hole appears in the graphics area with default parameters, see Figure 9.6.

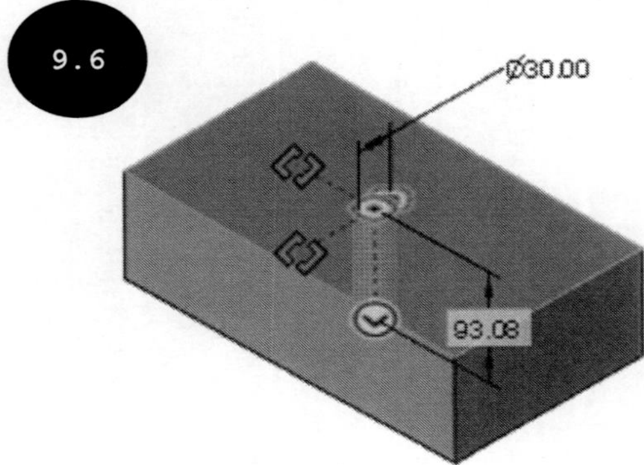

5. Expand the **Placement** panel of the **Hole** tab, if not expanded by default, see Figure 9.7. Notice that the name of the selected placement face appears in the **Placement** collector of the expanded **Placement** panel. The options in the expanded **Placement** panel are discussed below:

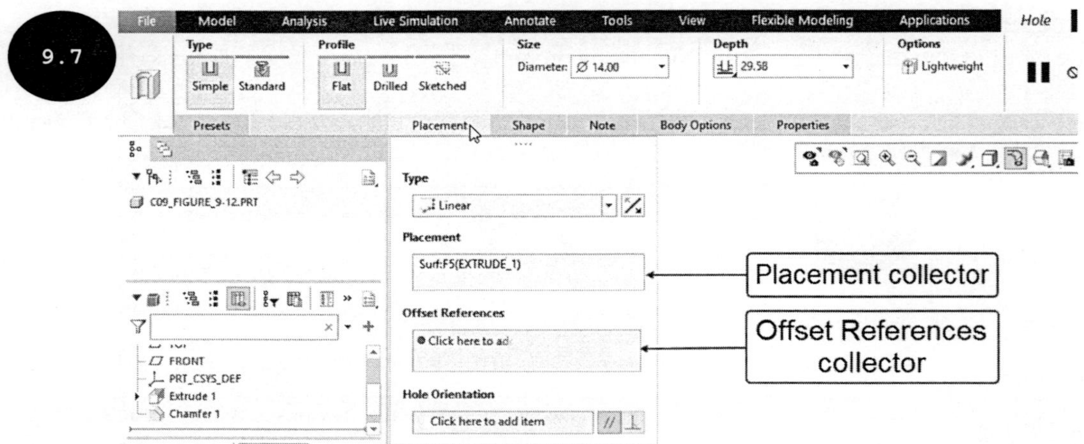

Placement collector: The **Placement** collector displays the name of the face selected as the placement face for creating the hole.

Type drop-down list: The **Type** drop-down list is used for selecting an option to define the placement of the hole on the selected face. The options are discussed below:

Linear: The **Linear** option is used for defining the placement of the hole by specifying two linear references, see Figure 9.8.

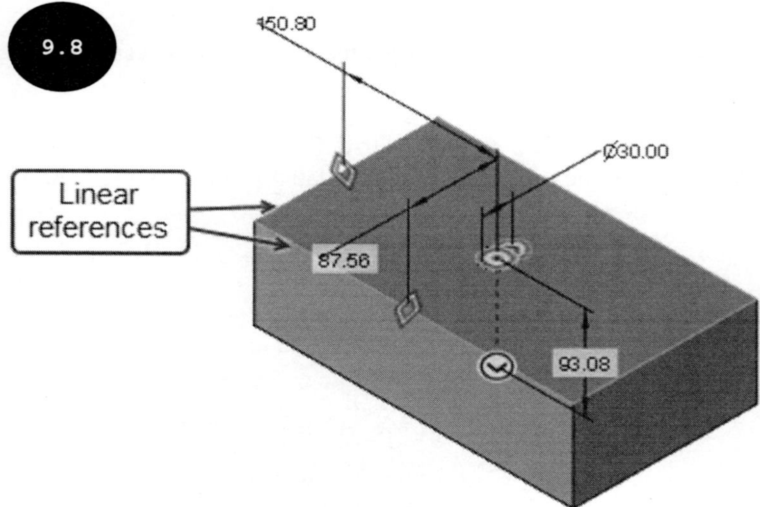

Radial: The **Radial** option is used for defining the placement of the hole by specifying a linear reference and an angular reference, see Figure 9.9. In this figure, the top face of the cylindrical feature is selected as the linear reference to define the distance between the center of the hole and the top face selected. Also, the side face is selected as the angular reference to define the angular dimension from the hole center to the face selected.

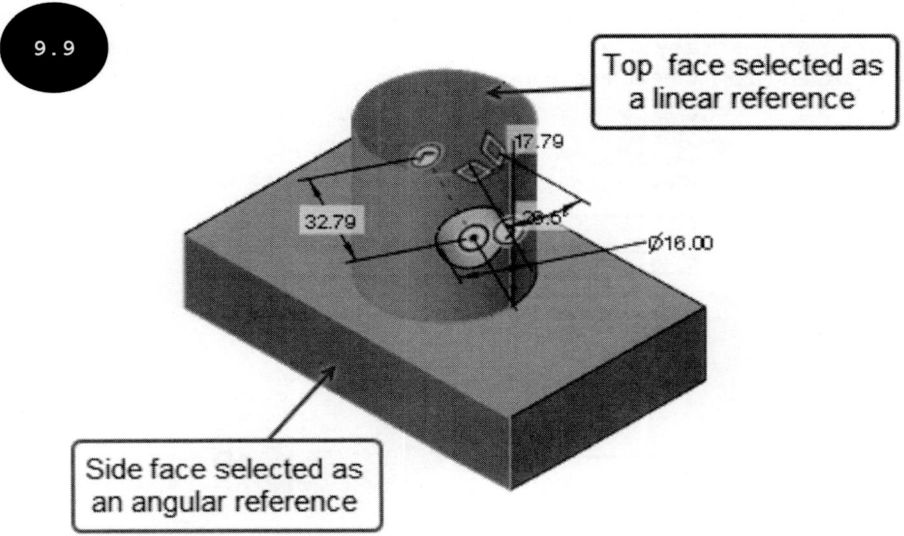

Diameter: The **Diameter** option is used for defining the placement of the hole, diametrically by specifying an angular reference and an axial reference, see Figure 9.10. In this figure, the side face is selected as the angular reference to define the angular dimension from the hole center to the face selected. Also, the axis of the cylindrical feature is selected as axial reference to define the diameter dimension with respect to the axis selected.

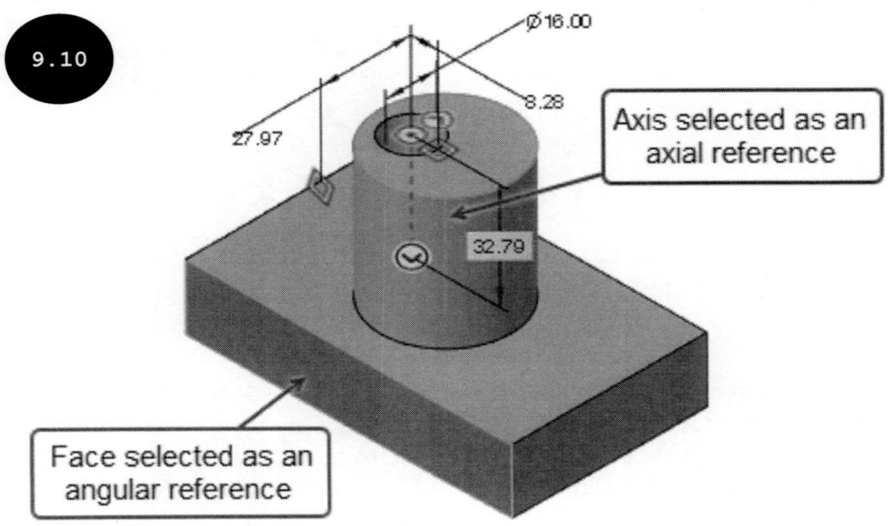

Coaxial: The **Coaxial** option is used for defining the placement of the hole along an existing datum axis or an axis of a cylindrical feature, see Figure 9.11. On selecting this option, you need to select an axis and a placement face (planar or curved) to create the hole.

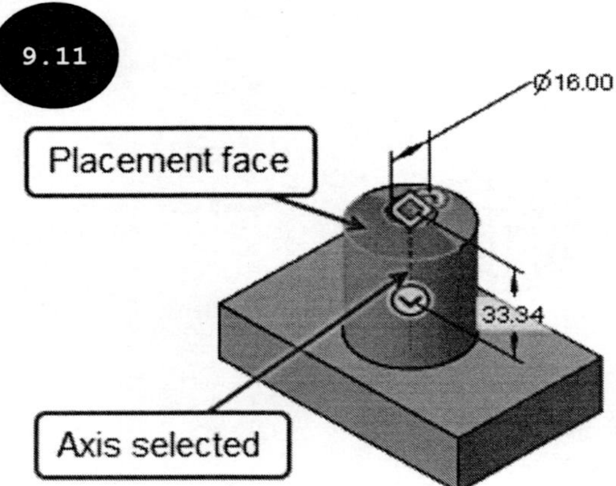

On Point: The **On Point** option is used for defining the placement of the hole on an existing datum point, see Figure 9.12. On selecting this option, you need to select a datum point and a placement face (planar or curved) to create the hole.

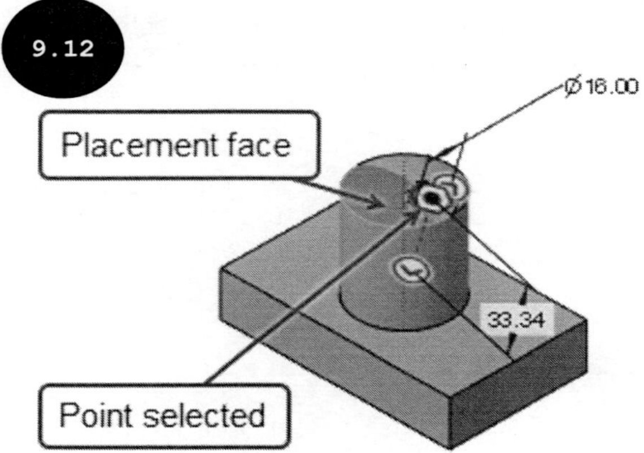

Sketched: The **Sketched** option is used for defining the placement of the hole on a plane or a planar face by using geometric entities. On selecting this option, you need to select a plane or a planar face for invoking the Sketching environment. Next, draw an entity such as a datum point or a sketch line in the Sketching environment. You can also draw multiple entities. After drawing entities, exit the Sketching environment. The preview of holes appears either on drawn points, endpoints of sketch lines, or midpoints of sketched lines in the graphics area depending upon the button selected (**Place holes on sketched points, Place holes on endpoints of sketched lines,** or **Place holes on midpoints of sketched lines**) in the **Place on** area of the expanded **Placement** panel.

Offset References collector: The **Offset References** collector of the expanded **Placement** panel is used for selecting references for defining the placement of the hole depending upon the option selected in the **Type** drop-down list. Note that to select the second reference, you need to press the CTRL key.

Flip: The **Flip** button is used for reversing the direction of hole creation to the other side of the placement face.

Hole orientation collector: The **Hole orientation** collector is used for changing the default orientation of the hole by selecting an orientation reference. By default, the orientation of the hole is defined based on the placement face selected, see Figure 9.13. You can select a linear edge, a planar face, a plane, or an axis as the orientation reference, see Figure 9.14. In this figure, an edge is selected as the orientation reference to define the orientation of the hole.

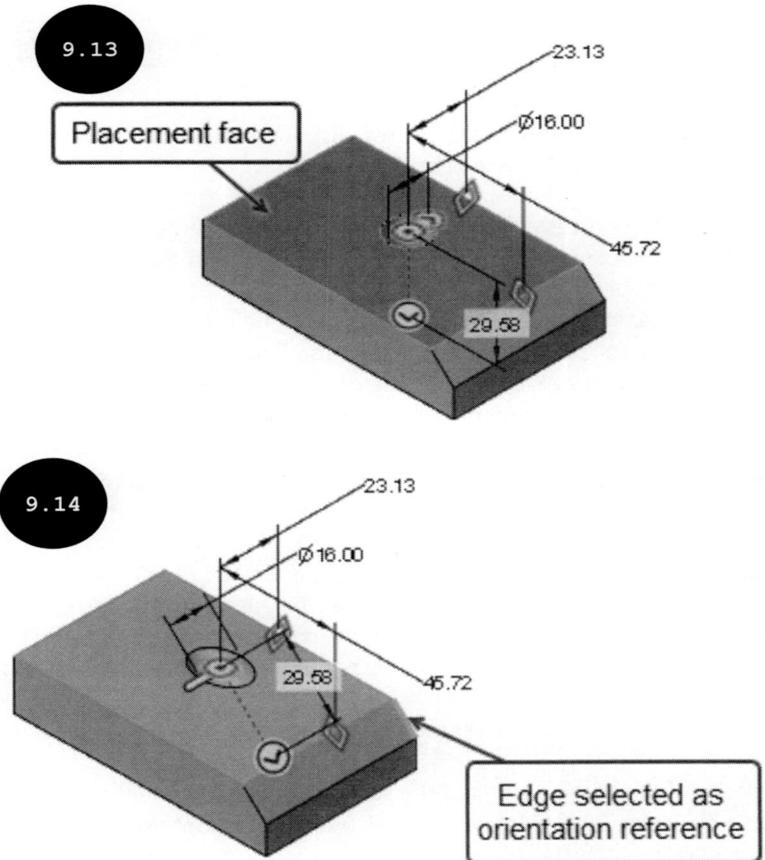

You can also specify whether the orientation of the hole is parallel or perpendicular to the orientation reference selected by selecting the required button available in front of the **Hole Orientation** collector, see Figure 9.15.

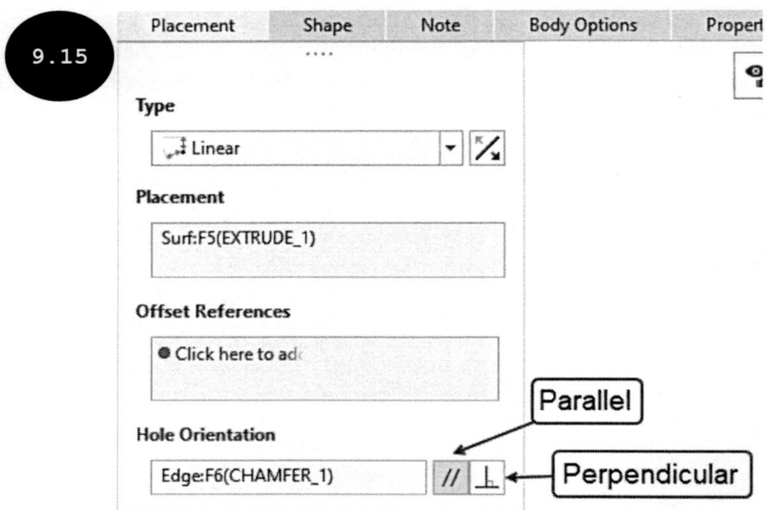

6. Select the required option in the **Type** drop-down list of the expanded **Placement** panel to define the placement of the hole, as discussed earlier.

7. Click on the **Offset References** collector of the expanded **Placement** panel and then select two references to define the placement of the hole depending upon the option selected in the **Type** drop-down list. You need to press the CTRL key to select the second reference. You can also drag the handles that appear in the preview of the hole to define the placement references. Note that the **Offset References** collector is not enabled, if the **Coaxial**, **On Point**, or **Sketched** option is selected in the **Type** drop-down list. In the case of the **Coaxial** option, you need to select an axis and a placement face in the **Placement** collector by pressing the CTRL key. Similarly, for the **On Point** option, you need to select a datum point and a placement face in the **Placement** collector. For the **Sketched** option, you need to select a placement face and draw entities such as datum points and sketch lines for defining the position of holes.

8. Edit the default dimension values to specify the placement of the hole with respect to the references selected in the **Offset References** collector. Alternatively, you can edit a dimension value in the graphics area by double-clicking on the respective dimension and then entering the required value in the edit field that appears. After entering the dimension value, press ENTER.

9. Enter the diameter of the hole in the **Diameter** field of the **Hole** tab, see Figure 9.16.

10. Specify the depth of the hole on side 1 of the sketching plane by selecting the required option in the **Side 1** drop-down list of the **Hole** tab, see Figure 9.16. The options in this drop-down list and the method for specifying the depth of a hole are the same as discussed earlier.

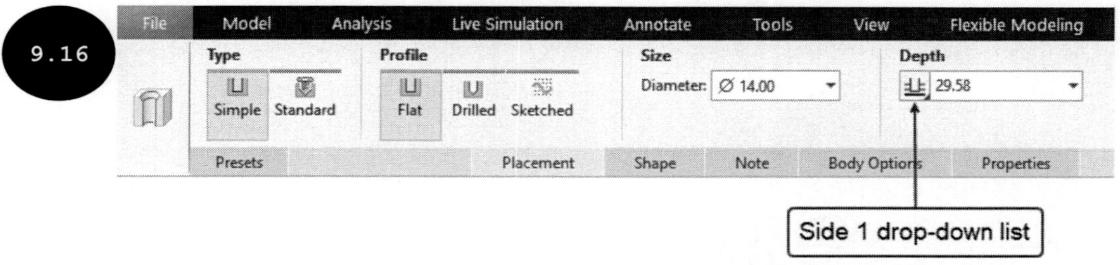

11. Expand the **Shape** panel of the **Hole** tab, see Figure 9.17. In the expanded **Shape** panel, you can specify the depth of the hole on side 1 as well as on side 2 of the sketching plane. Note that the depth of the hole on side 1 of the sketching plane can be defined without expanding the **Shape** panel, as discussed in earlier steps.

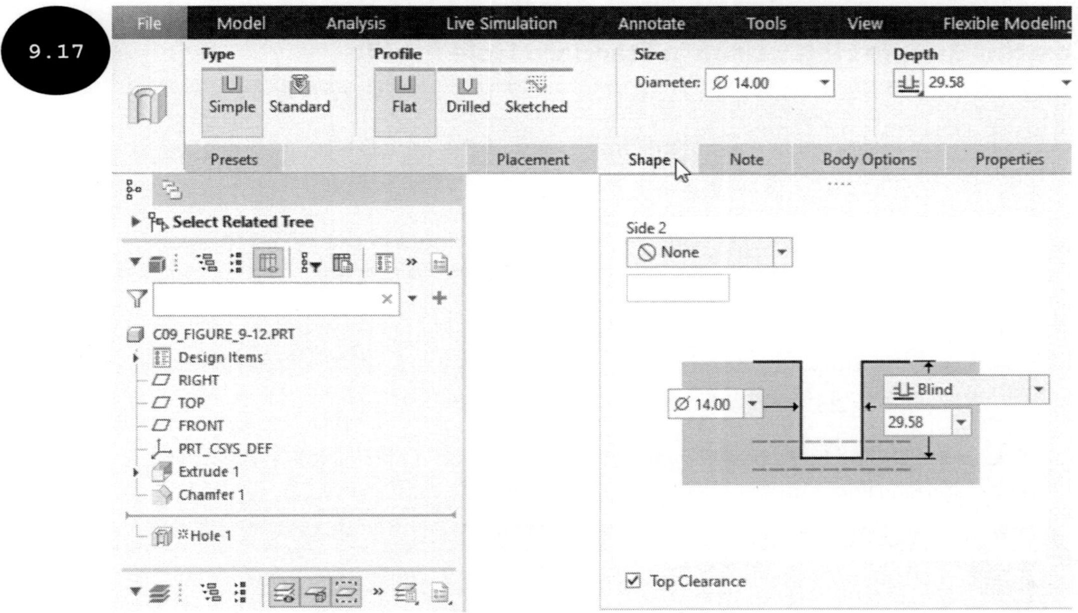

Top Clearance: The **Top Clearance** check box is used for making a clearance at the top of the hole such that the top of the hole is fully outside the model.

Lightweight: On activating the **Lightweight** button in the **Options** area of the **Hole** tab, the resultant holes will be represented as lightweight holes. A lightweight hole is a graphical representation of a hole without removing material from the model. It is represented by an orange circular curve and an axis, where the circular curve follows the hole circumference and lies on the hole placement plane. This helps in reducing the complexity of the model and improves the overall performance of the system. By default, this button is deactivated, hence the hole feature is created by removing material from the model.

12. After defining all the parameters, click on the green tick-mark button in the **Hole** tab. A hole with specified parameters is created using the predefined rectangle profile, see Figure 9.18.

9.18

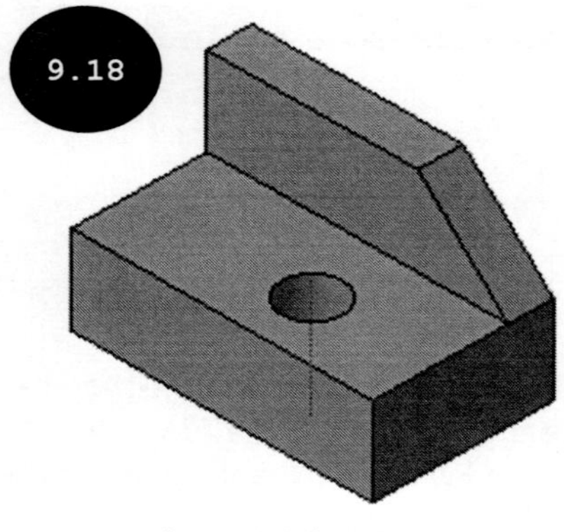

Isometric view

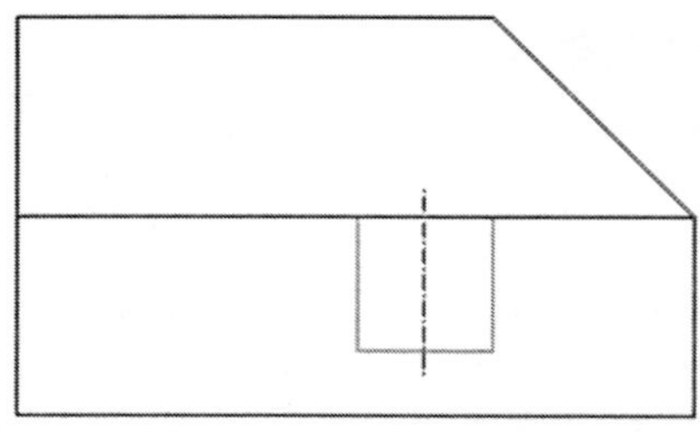

Front view in Hidden Line display

Creating Simple Holes Using a Standard Hole Profile

The method for creating a simple hole using a standard hole profile is discussed below:

1. Click on the **Hole** tool in the **Engineering** group of the **Model** tab. The **Hole** tab appears in the **Ribbon**.

   By default, the **Simple** button is activated in the **Type** area of the **Hole** tab. As a result, you can create simple holes by using a predefined rectangle profile, a standard hole profile, or a sketched profile.

2. Ensure that the **Simple** button is activated in the **Type** area of the **Hole** tab to create a simple hole, see Figure 9.19.

3. Click on the **Drilled** button to activate it in the **Profile** area of the **Hole** tab to create a simple hole using a standard hole profile such as counterbore and countersink, see Figure 9.19.

9.19

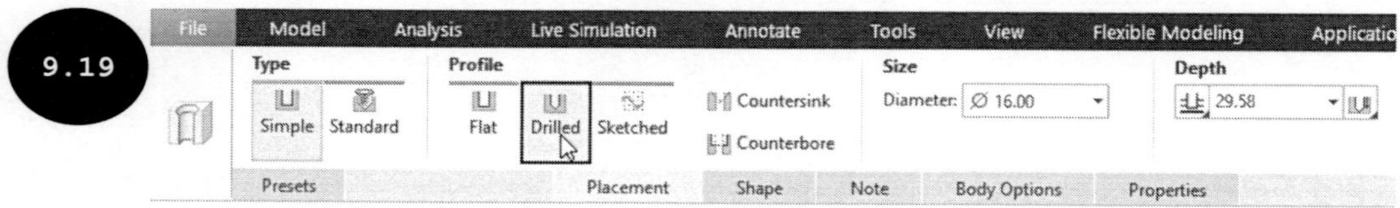

4. Click on a face (planar or curved) of the model as the placement face of the hole. The preview of a simple hole appears in the graphics area with default parameters.

5. Expand the **Placement** panel of the **Hole** tab, if not expanded by default, and then specify the placement references. Also, edit the dimension values to define the placement of the hole, as discussed earlier. You can also drag the handles that appear in the graphics area to define the placement references.

6. Click on the **Countersink** or **Counterbore** button in the **Hole** tab to create a hole using the countersink or counterbore standard profile, respectively, see Figure 9.20. The preview of the hole appears in the graphics area as per the selected standard profile, see Figures 9.21 and 9.22. Figure 9.21 shows the preview of the hole using the countersink standard profile, whereas Figure 9.22 shows the preview of the hole using the counterbore standard profile.

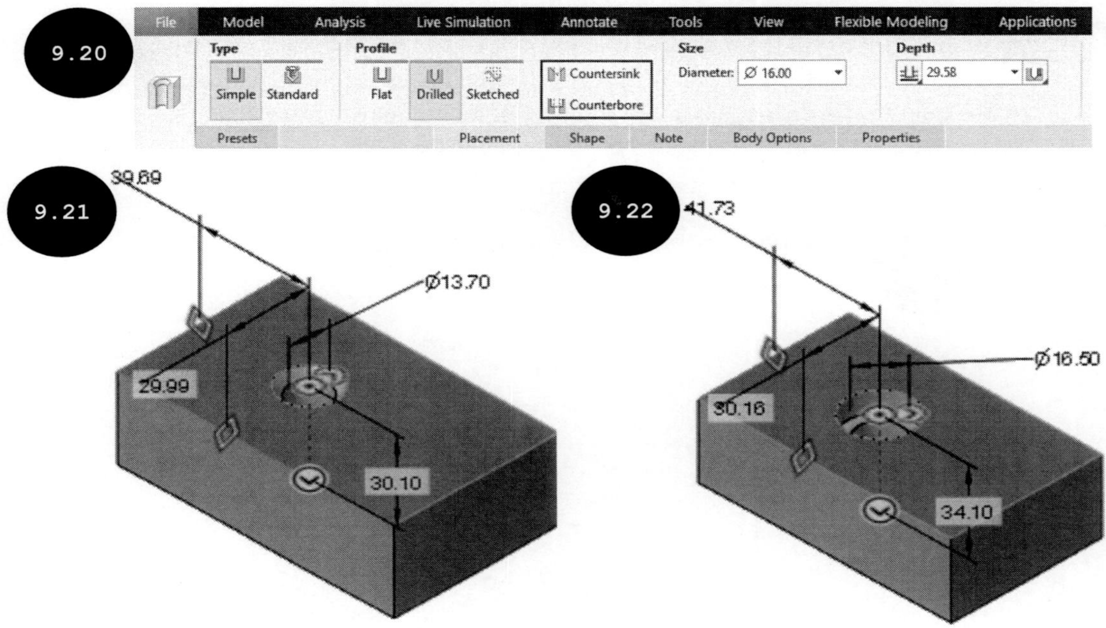

Note: You can also create a hole using a combination of the counterbore and countersink profiles by activating both the **Countersink** and **Counterbore** buttons in the **Profile** area of the **Hole** tab. On doing so, a counterbore hole will be created with the countersink shape under the hole head, see Figure 9.23.

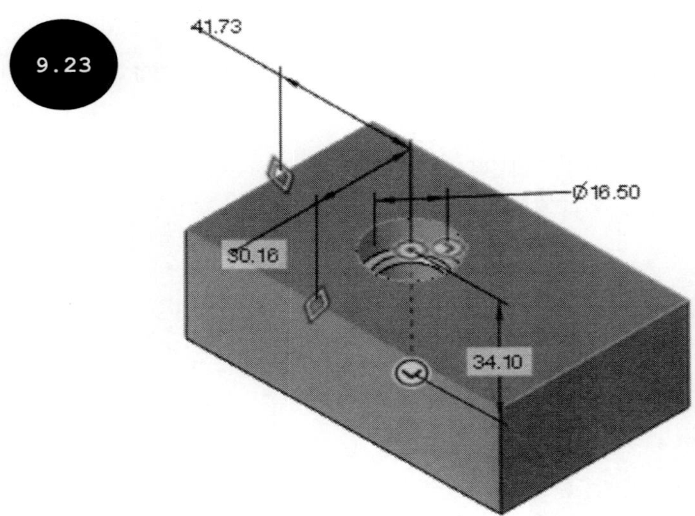

7. Expand the **Shape** panel of the **Hole** tab (see Figure 9.24), and then specify the hole parameters such as diameter, depth, tip angle, and so on in the respective dimension fields of the expanded **Shape** panel. Note that the shape of the hole and options for specifying the hole parameters depend upon the type of standard profile selected.

Note: When the **Blind** option is selected as the depth option in the expanded **Shape** panel, you can specify the depth as well as the tip angle of the hole, refer to Figure 9.24. The depth of the hole can be defined up to the shoulder or tip of the hole by selecting the **Shoulder** or **Tip** radio button in the expanded **Shape** panel, respectively.

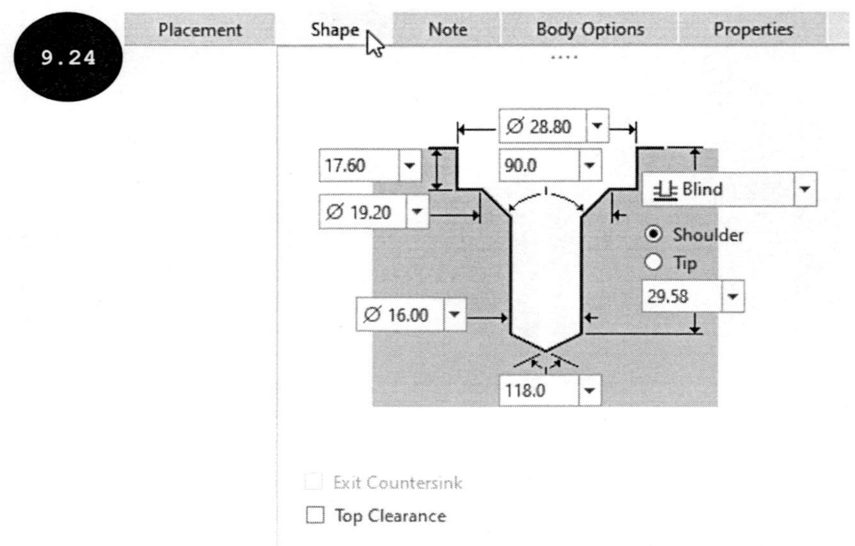

Top Clearance: The **Top Clearance** check box is used for making a clearance at the top of the hole such that the top of the hole is fully outside the model.

8. Select the **Top Clearance** check box in the expanded **Shape** panel to ensure that the top of the hole is fully outside the model.

9. Click on the green tick-mark button in the **Hole** tab. A hole is created using the standard profile, see Figure 9.25. In this figure, a counterbore hole is created with a tip angle.

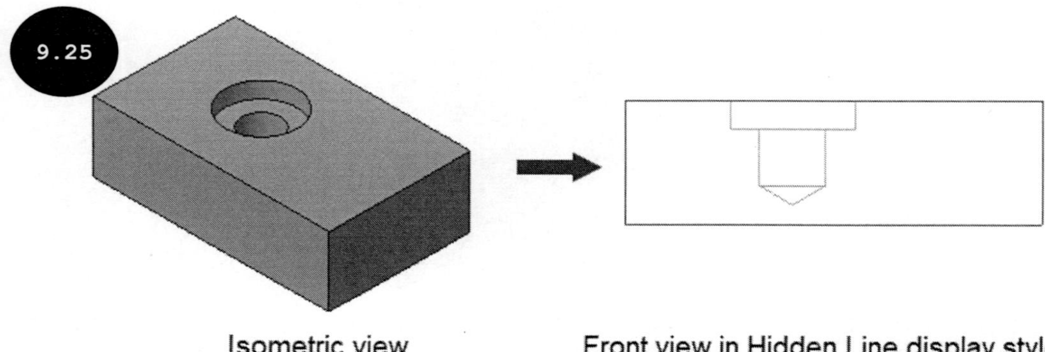

Creating Simple Holes Using a Sketched Profile

The method for creating a simple hole using a sketched hole profile is discussed below:

1. Click on the **Hole** tool in the **Engineering** group of the **Model** tab. The **Hole** tab appears in the **Ribbon**.

2. Ensure that the **Simple** button is activated in the **Type** area of the **Hole** tab to create a simple hole, see Figure 9.26.

3. Click on the **Sketched** button to activate it in the **Profile** area of the **Hole** tab to create a simple hole using a user defined sketched profile, see Figure 9.26

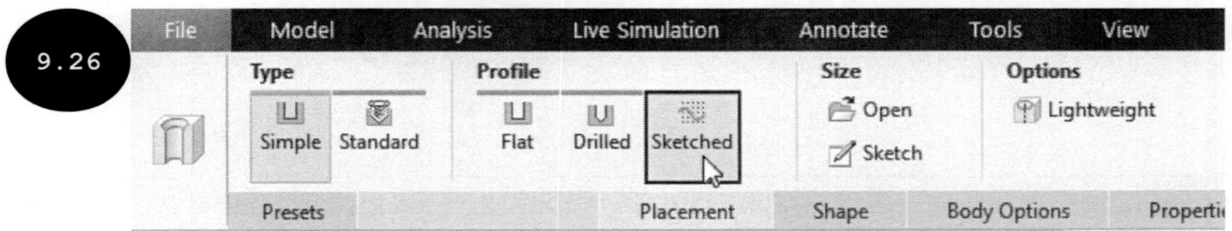

4. Click on a face (planar or curved) of the model as the placement face of the hole. The preview of a simple hole appears in the graphics area with default parameters.

5. Expand the **Placement** panel of the **Hole** tab, if not expanded by default, and then specify the placement references. Also, edit the dimension values to define the placement of the hole, as discussed earlier. You can also drag the handles that appear in the graphics area to define the placement references.

6. Click on the **Sketch** button in the **Hole** tab, see Figure 9.27. The Sketching environment gets invoked for creating the hole profile.

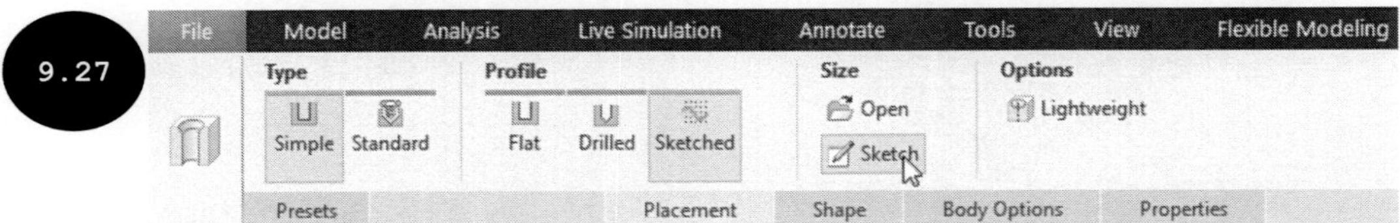

7. Create a closed sketch with a centerline on either side as the hole profile, see Figure 9.28. The sketch of the hole profile must contain a centerline as the axis of revolution of the hole. Note that the depth of the hole depends upon the overall height of the sketch created.

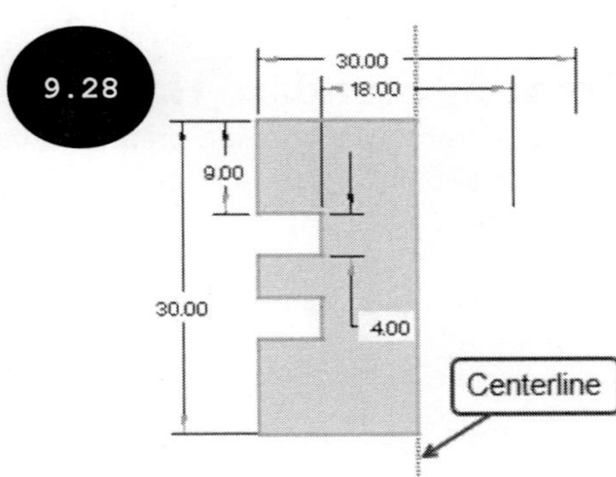

8. After creating the sketch, exit the Sketching environment. A preview of the hole using the sketched profile appears in the graphics area, see Figure 9.29.

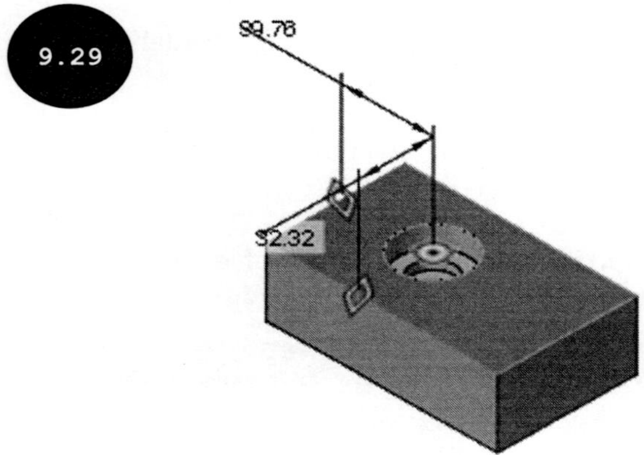

Tip: In Creo Parametric, you can also create a hole using an existing saved sketch as the hole profile by using the **Open** button in the **Hole** tab.

9. Click on the green tick-mark button in the **Hole** tab. A simple hole using a sketched profile is created, see Figure 9.30.

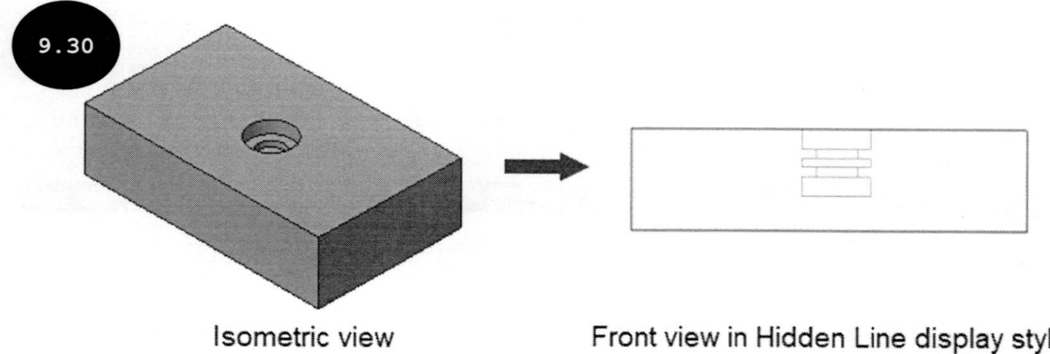

Creating Standard Holes

In Creo Parametric, you can create industry-standard holes such as tapped, tapered, drilled, and clearance as per the standard specifications by using the **Hole** tool. The method for creating a standard hole is discussed below:

1. Click on the **Hole** tool in the **Engineering** group of the **Model** tab. The **Hole** tab appears in the **Ribbon**.

2. Click on the **Standard** button in the **Type** area of the **Hole** tab to create a standard hole, see Figure 9.31. The options for creating different types of standard holes are discussed below:

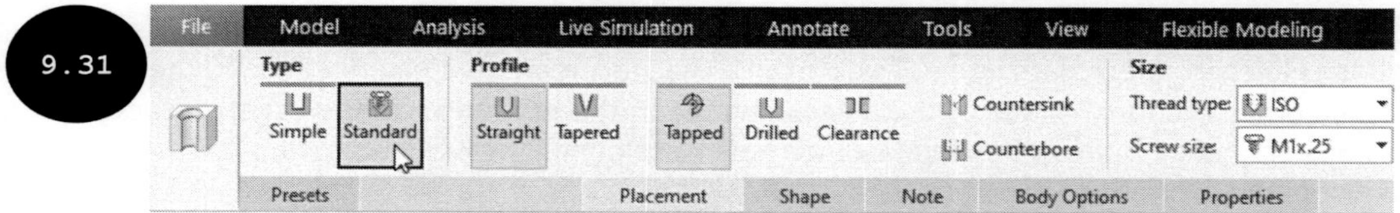

Tapped: The **Tapped** button is available when the **Straight** profile of the hole is selected in the **Hole** tab. By default, the **Tapped** button is activated in the **Hole** tab. As a result, you can create an industry-standard tapped hole. A tapped hole is created by cutting threads in the hole. Figure 9.32 shows the cross-section of the tapped hole in the expanded **Shape** panel. Note that the dotted lines in the cross-section of the hole represent threads. In Creo Parametric, the threads of the tapped holes are represented as cosmetic threads. A Cosmetic thread represents the real thread of a feature without removing the material. You will learn more about cosmetic threads later in this chapter.

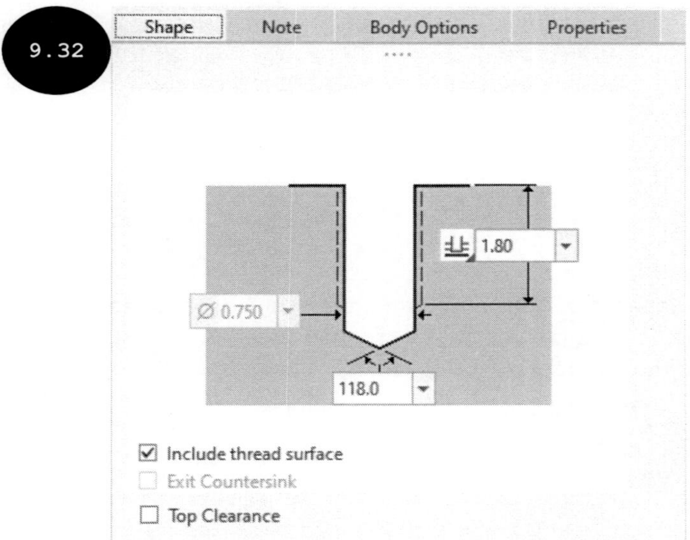

Drilled: The **Drilled** button is available when the **Straight** profile of the hole is selected in the **Hole** tab, refer to Figure 9.31. This button is used for creating a drilled hole. Figure 9.33 shows the cross-section shape of the drilled hole in the expanded **Shape** panel.

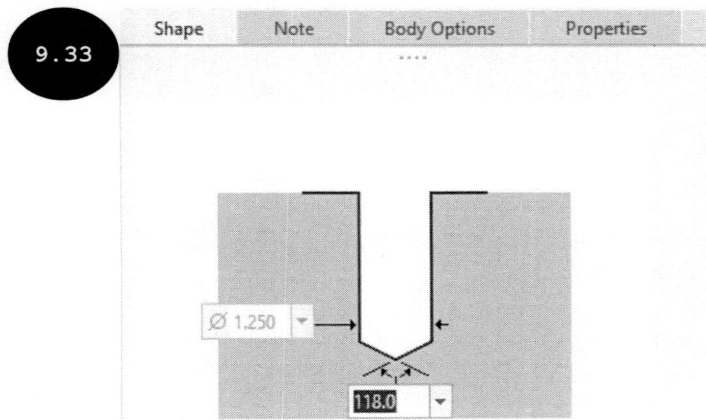

Clearance: The **Clearance** button is available when the **Straight** profile of the hole is selected in the **Hole** tab, refer to Figure 9.31. This button is used for creating a clearance hole. Figure 9.34 shows the cross-sectional shape of the clearance hole in the expanded **Shape** panel. You can create close fit, medium fit, or free fit clearance hole by selecting the required option in the drop-down list of the expanded **Shape** panel.

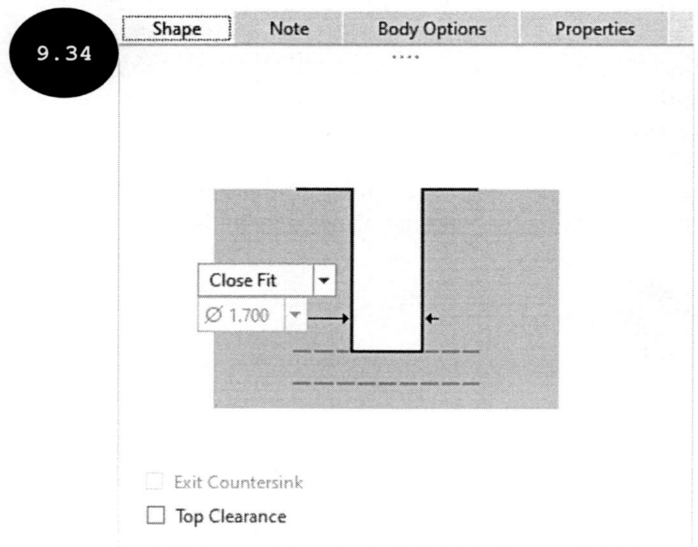

Tapered: The **Tapered** button is used for creating a tapered threaded hole. Figure 9.35 shows the cross-section of the tapered hole in the expanded **Shape** panel. The dotted lines in the cross-section of the hole represent threads.

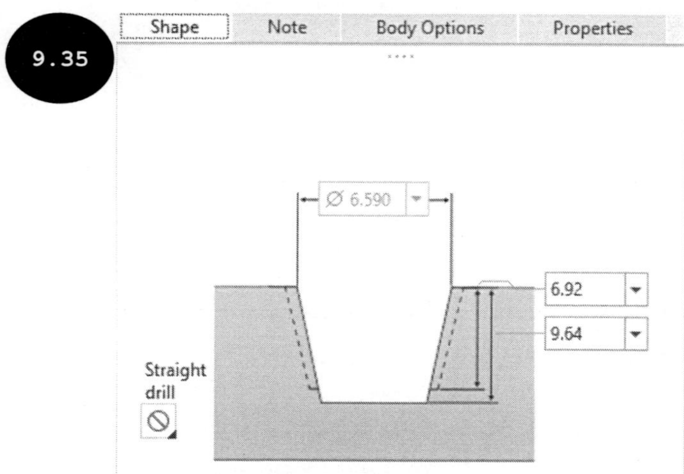

3. Click on the required standard hole button (**Tapped**, **Drilled**, **Clearance**, or **Tapered**) to be created in the **Hole** tab, as discussed above.

4. Expand the **Placement** panel of the **Hole** tab, if not expanded by default, and then specify the placement references. Also, edit the dimension values to define the placement of the hole, as discussed earlier. The options available in the **Placement** panel are the same as discussed earlier. You can also drag the handles that appear in the graphics area to define the placement references.

5. Select the required industry-standard hole chart such as **ISO**, **UNC**, or **UNF** in the **Thread type** drop-down list in the **Size** area of the **Hole** tab, see Figure 9.36.

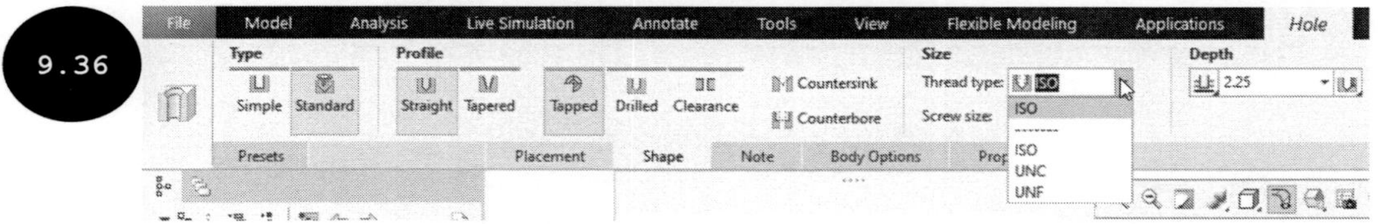

6. Select the size of the screw to be inserted into the hole in the **Screw size** drop-down list in the **Size** area of the **Hole** tab, see Figure 9.37. The availability of options in this drop-down list depends upon the type of standard hole chart selected. Figure 9.37 shows the **Screw size** drop-down list when the **ISO** hole chart is selected. Note that you can also enter the size of the screw that is not available in the drop-down list. On doing so, the system selects the closest screw size as per the standard specifications.

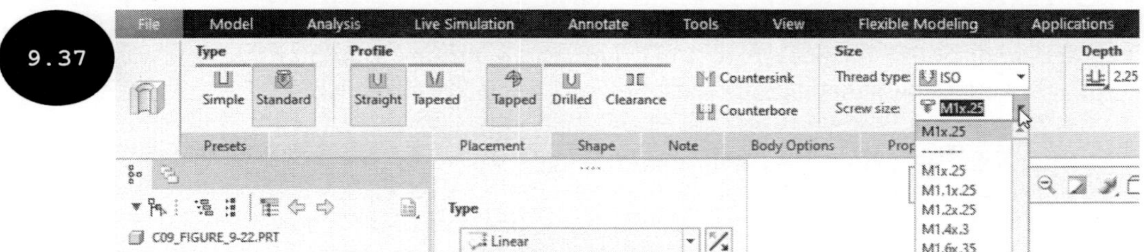

7. Specify the depth of the hole by selecting the required option in the **Side 1** drop-down list in the **Depth** area of the **Hole** tab, see Figure 9.38. The options in this drop-down list and the method for specifying the depth of a hole are the same as discussed earlier.

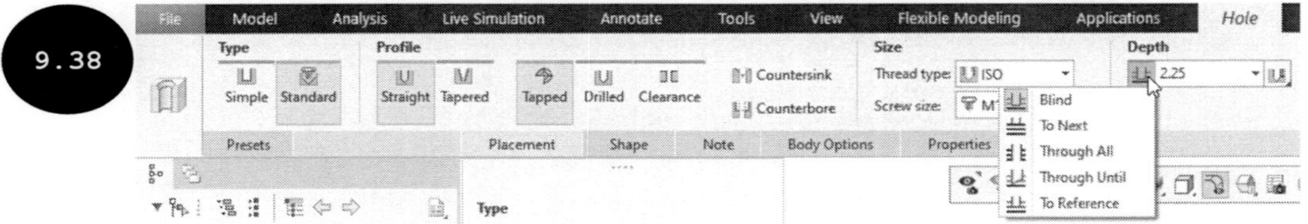

8. Expand the **Shape** panel of the **Hole** tab to review the hole parameters and the cross-sectional shape of the hole, see Figure 9.39. Note that the hole parameters and the cross-sectional shape of the hole that appears in the expanded **Shape** panel depend upon the type of standard hole and screw size specified. Some of the hole parameters such as hole depth and tip angle, can also be edited or specified in the expanded **Shape** panel.

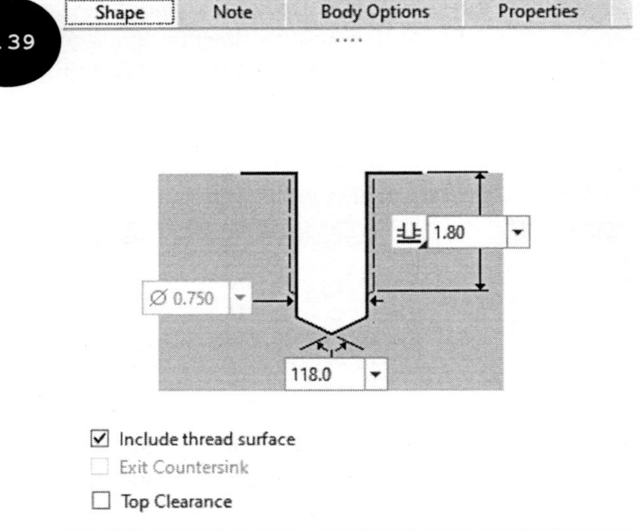

9. Click on the **Countersink** or **Counterbore** button in the **Hole** tab to create a countersink or counterbore hole as per the industry-standard specifications, respectively, if required. Note that on activating both the **Countersink** and **Counterbore** buttons, a counterbore hole will be created with the countersink shape under the hole head, as discussed earlier.

10. Expand the **Note** tab in the **Hole** tab, see Figure 9.40. The expanded **Note** tab displays the standard specifications of the hole. Also, the **Add a note** check box is selected, by default. As a result, after the hole is created, the standard specifications of the hole will appear in text format attached to the hole in the graphics area, refer to Figure 9.41.

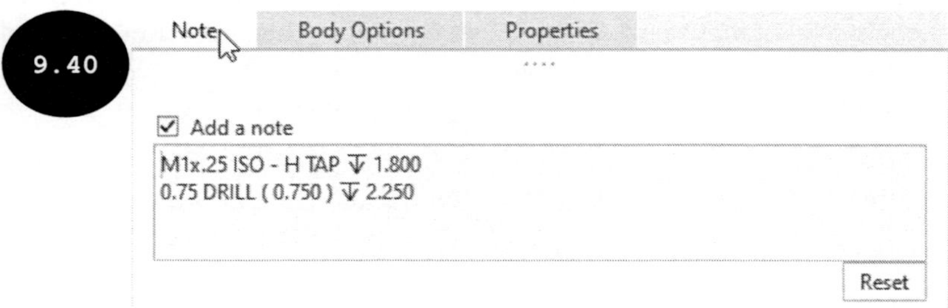

11. Click on the green tick-mark button in the **Hole** tab. The standard hole of the specified specification is created, see Figure 9.41. Note that in Figure 9.41, the cosmetic thread of the hole is represented as line entities in the front view of the model.

Note: In Creo, while editing a hole feature, you can change its hole type from simple to standard or vice-versa. To do so, click on the hole to be edited in the **Model Tree** and then click on the **Edit Definition** tool in the **Mini** toolbar that appears. The **Hole** tab appears in the **Ribbon**. Now, you can change the hole type as required by using the **Hole** tab.

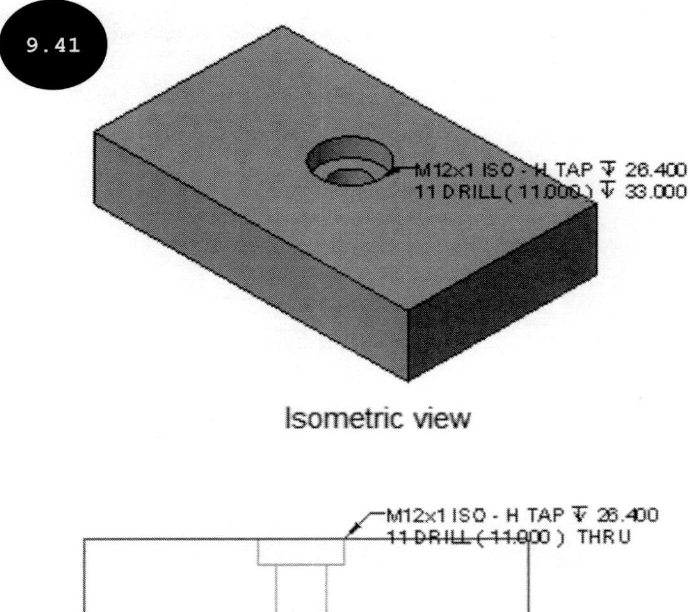

Creating Cosmetic Threads

A Cosmetic thread represents the real thread of a feature without removing the material. It helps in reducing the complexity of the model and improves the overall performance of the system. Note that the cosmetic threads are not visible in the model, however in the 'Hidden Line' display style, the cosmetic threads are visible as light colored lines. Figure 9.42 shows a cosmetic thread created on a cylindrical feature. The method for creating a cosmetic thread is discussed below:

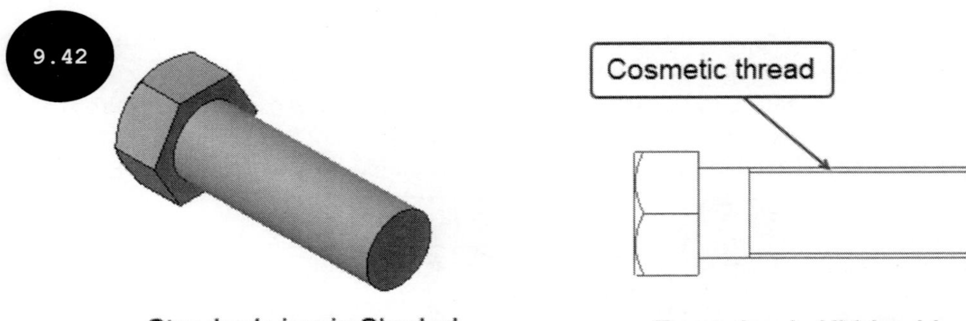

1. Expand the **Engineering** group of the **Model** tab by clicking on the arrow next to it (see Figure 9.43), and then click on the **Cosmetic Thread** tool. The **Thread** tab appears in the **Ribbon**, see Figure 9.44.

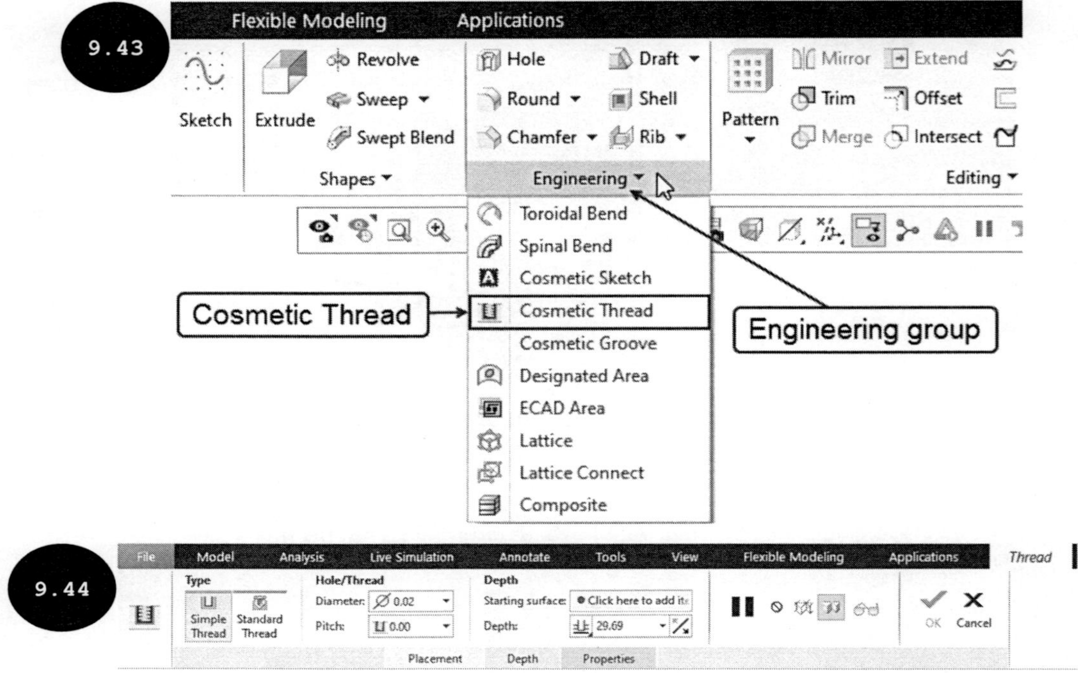

By default, the **Simple Thread** button is activated in the **Type** area of the **Thread** tab. As a result, you can create a simple cosmetic thread on a cylindrical feature or a hole feature. On activating the **Standard Thread** button, you can create a standard thread on a cylindrical or circular cut feature as per the standard specifications.

2. Select the required button (**Simple Thread** or **Standard Thread**) in the **Type** area of the **Thread** tab to create a cosmetic thread. The options for creating a cosmetic thread appear in the **Thread** tab depending upon the type selected.

3. Expand the **Placement** panel of the **Thread** tab, if not expanded by default, and then select the placement face for creating the cosmetic thread. You can select a cylindrical or a circular face of an extrude or a cut feature to create a cosmetic thread, see Figure 9.45. In this figure, a circular face of a cut feature is selected. As soon as you select a placement face, the name of the selected face appears in the **Threaded surface** collector of the expanded **Placement** panel, see Figure 9.46.

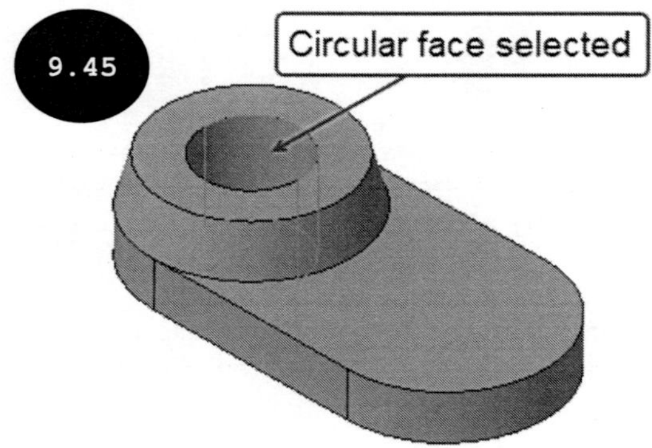

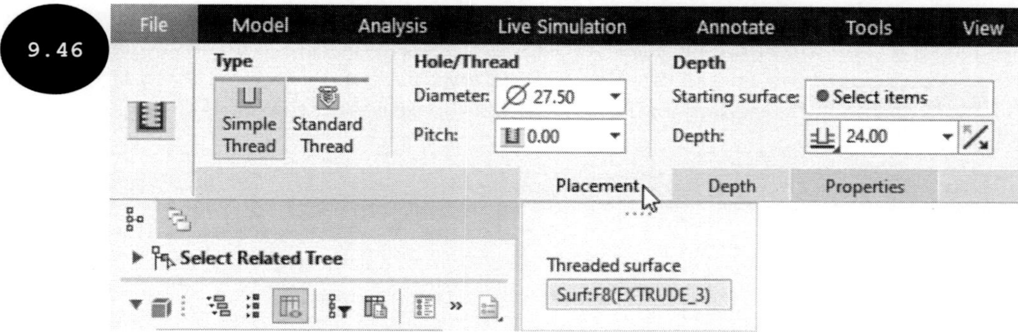

4. Expand the **Depth** panel (see Figure 9.47), and then select a planar face to define the start face of the thread. A preview of the cosmetic thread starting from the selected start face appears in the graphics area, see Figure 9.48.

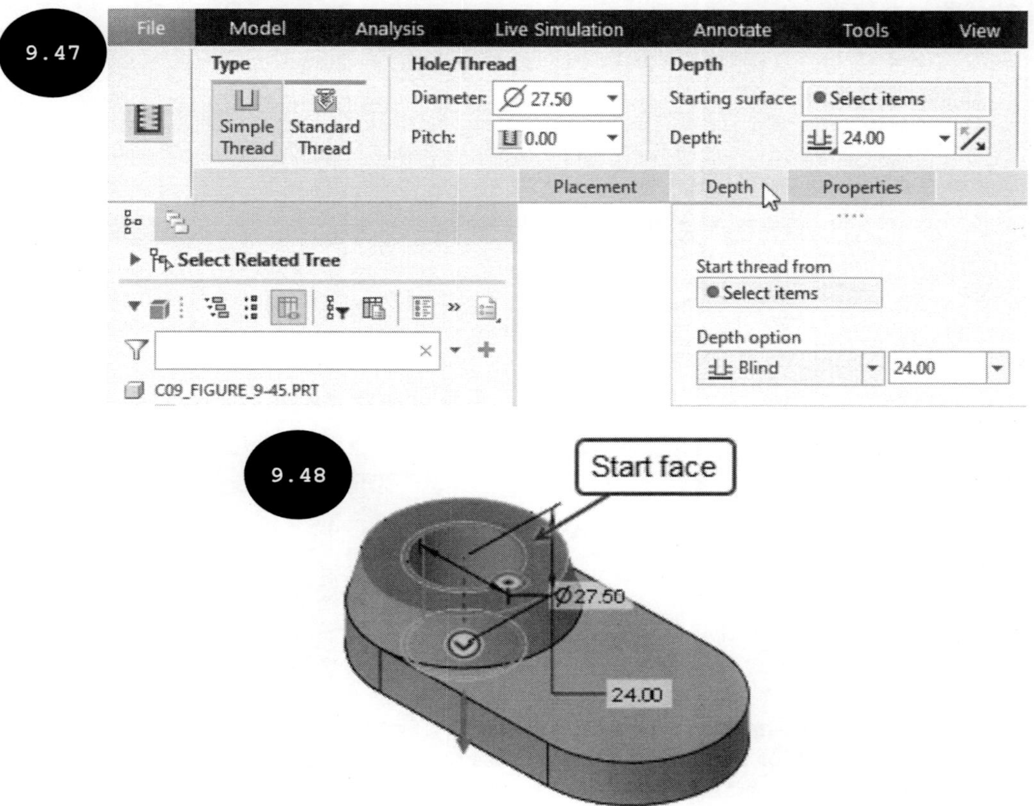

5. Specify the depth of the thread by selecting the required option from the **Depth option** drop-down list of the expanded **Depth** panel. By default, the **Blind** option is selected. As a result, you can specify a depth value of the thread in the field that appears in front of the **Depth option** drop-down list. The options for specifying the depth of the thread are the same as discussed earlier.

6. Specify other parameters such as diameter and pitch for creating a simple cosmetic thread, thread type (ISO, UNF, or UNC) and, thread size for creating a standard cosmetic thread in the respective fields of the **Thread** tab. Figure 9.49 shows the options in the **Thread** tab for creating a simple cosmetic thread and Figure 9.50 shows the options for creating a standard cosmetic thread.

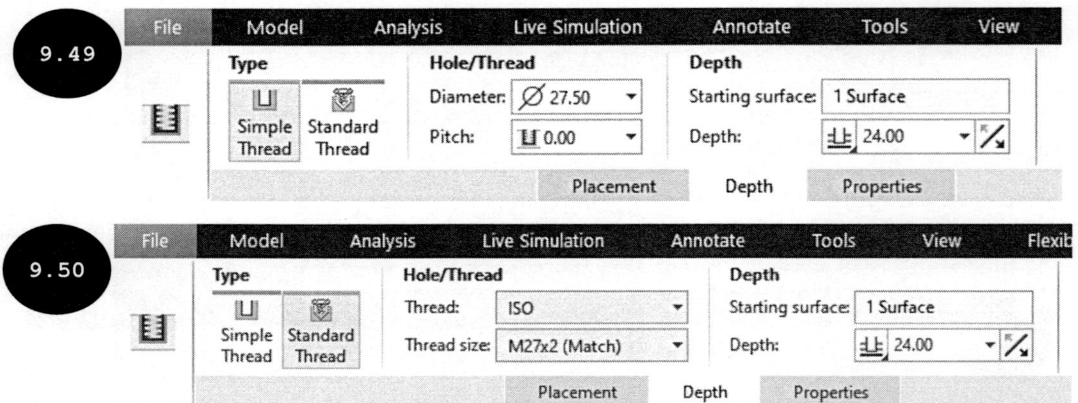

7. Expand the **Properties** panel of the **Thread** tab to review or edit the properties of the cosmetic thread, see Figure 9.51.

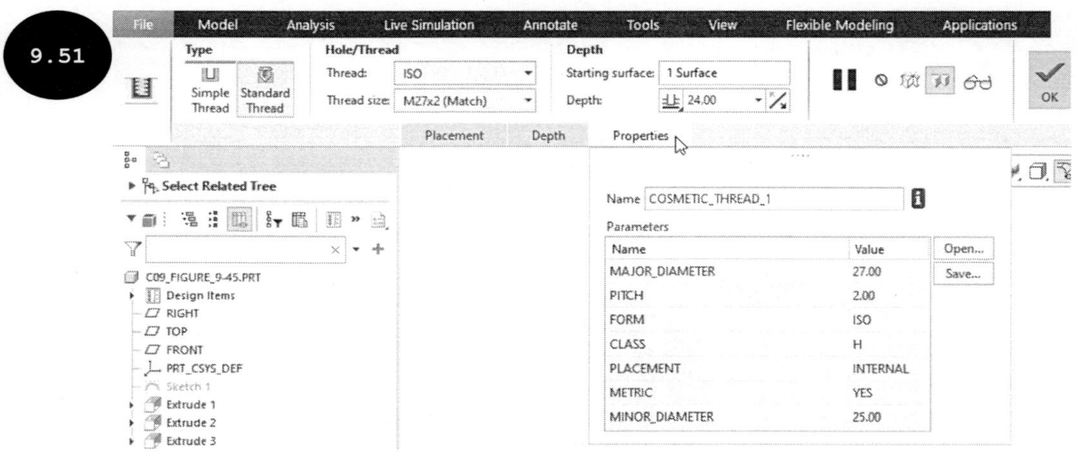

Tip: You can save the specified properties of the cosmetic thread in *.thr* file for future use by using the **Save** button of the expanded **Properties** panel. You can also open an existing *.thr* file containing thread parameters for creating the cosmetic thread by using the **Open** button.

8. Click on the green tick-mark button in the **Thread** tab. A cosmetic thread with specified parameters is created on the selected face of the feature, see Figure 9.52. As discussed earlier, cosmetic threads are not visible in the model, however in the 'Hidden Line' display style, the cosmetic threads are visible as light-colored lines.

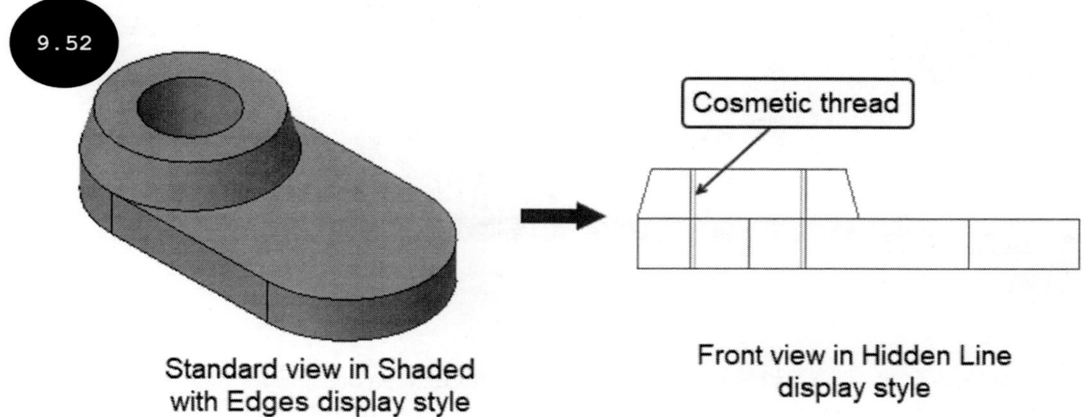

Creating Rounds

A round is defined as a fillet of a circular or a conical profile and is used for removing sharp edges of a model that may cause injury while handling the model. Figure 9.53 shows a model before and after creating a round of circular profile.

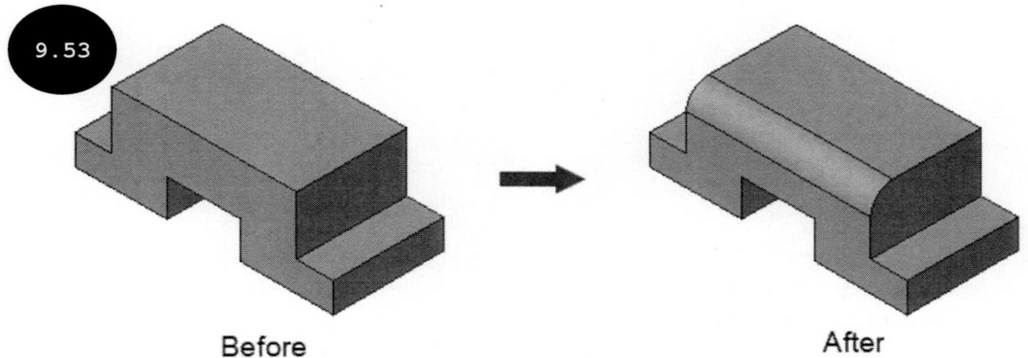

In Creo Parametric, you can create four types of rounds: constant radius round, variable radius round, curve driven round, and full round by using the **Round** tool. The methods for creating various types of rounds are discussed next.

Creating a Constant Radius Round

A constant radius round is a fillet that has a constant radius throughout the selected edge, refer to Figure 9.53. You can create a constant radius fillet by using the **Round** tool. The method for creating a constant radius round is discussed below:

1. Click on the **Round** tool in the **Engineering** group of the **Model** tab, see Figure 9.54. The **Round** tab appears in the **Ribbon**, see Figure 9.55. Some of the options of the **Round** tab are discussed below:

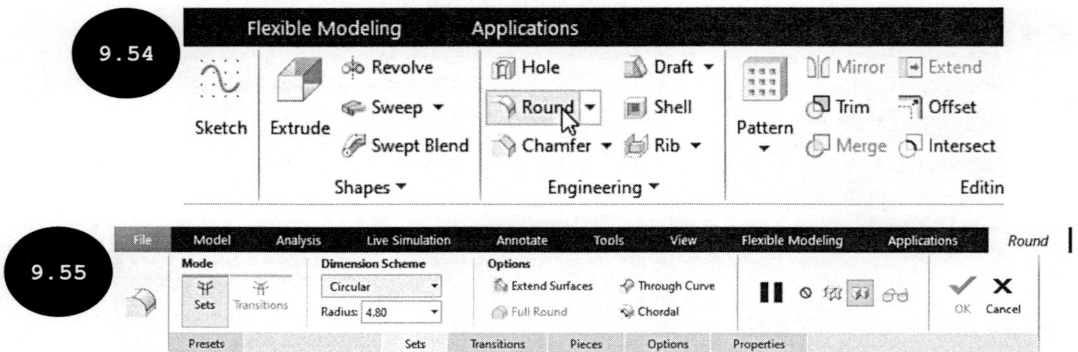

Sets: By default, the **Sets** button is activated in the **Mode** area of the **Round** tab. As a result, you can create rounds by defining multiple sets. For each set of round, you can specify a different radius value, see Figure 9.56.

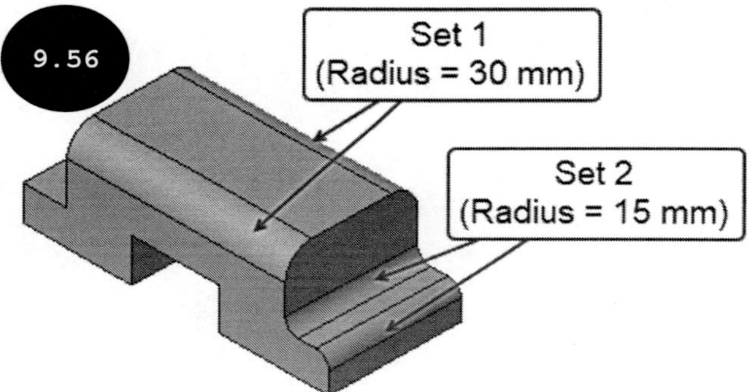

Transitions: On activating the **Transitions** button, you can define the shape of a setback, round at the vertex, that is formed at the intersection of three or more than three edges. To do so, select three edges that are intersecting at a common vertex by pressing the CTRL key (see Figure 9.57), and then click on the **Transitions** button in the **Mode** area of the **Round** tab to activate it. Different transitions appear on the selected edges of the model, see Figure 9.58. Next, click on the transition that appears at the vertex. A drop-down list appears in the **Round** tab with the **Default (Round Only 2)**, **Intersect**, **Corner Sphere**, **Round Only 1**, and **Patch** options, see Figure 9.59.

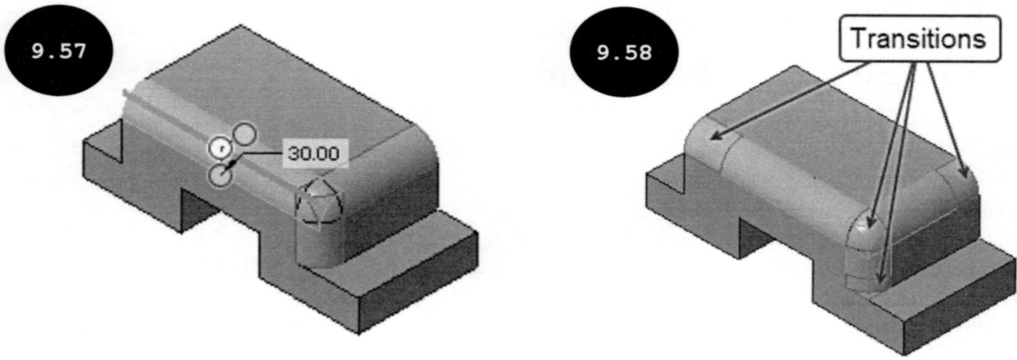

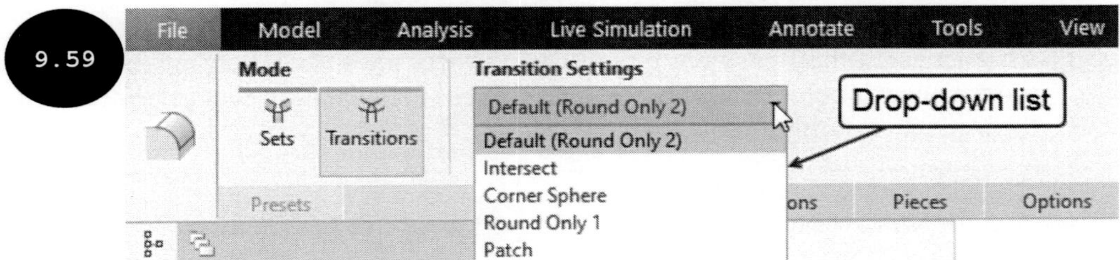

Select the option in this drop-down list for applying the required transition type to the selected vertex. The **Default (Round Only 2)** option is used for applying the default transition type to the vertex. The **Intersect** option is used for applying the intersect transition such that the sharp edges are created at the vertex, see Figure 9.60. The **Corner Sphere** option is used for creating a smooth spherical corner at the vertex. You can also increase the default radius value of the spherical corner by dragging the spherical handle that appears in the graphics area, see Figure 9.61. On doing so, a length handle appears on each edge of the round, see Figure 9.61. You can control the length of the round along each edge by dragging these handles, dynamically or by entering the required values in the fields that appear in the **Round** tab.

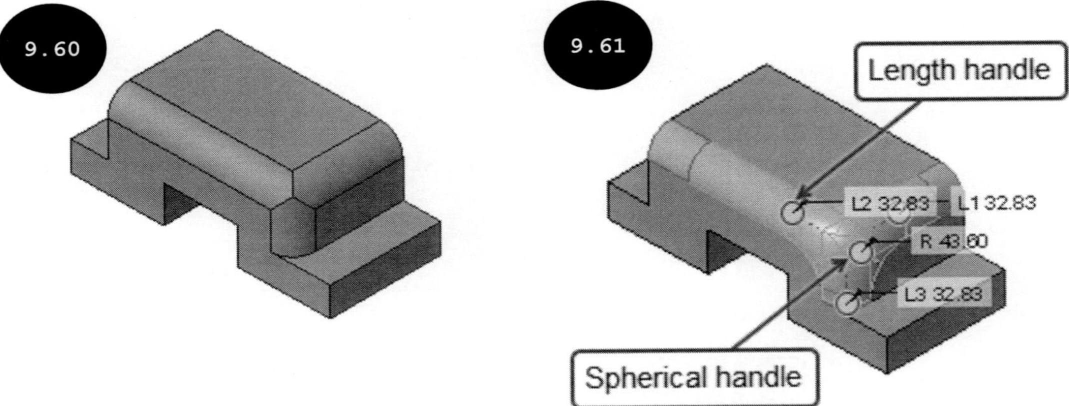

The **Patch** option is used for creating a patch transition at the vertex with respect to an adjacent face of the model. On selecting this option, the **Optional surface** field appears in the **Transition Settings** area of the **Round** tab. Click on this field and then select an adjacent face of the model to define the patch transition, see Figure 9.62. You can also drag the handle that appears in the graphics area to control the patch radius.

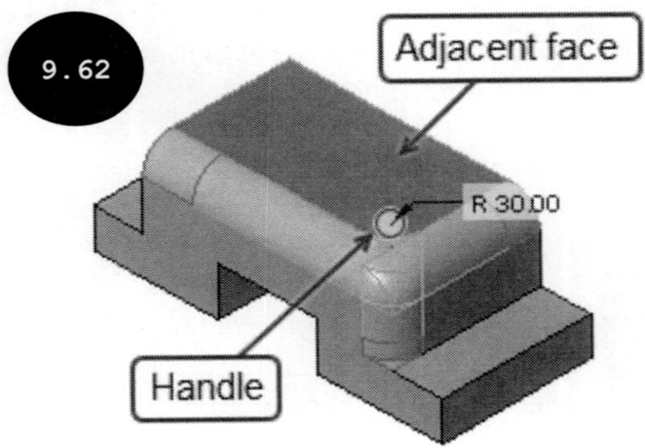

Note: After activating the **Transitions** button, if you select a transition other than the vertex, then the options available in the drop-down list are used for defining the limit of the round along the respective transition edge.

2. Ensure that the **Sets** button is activated in the **Round** tab for creating rounds by defining multiple sets.

3. Expand the **Sets** panel of the **Round** tab, if not expanded by default, see Figure 9.63. The options available in the expanded **Sets** panel are used for creating rounds by defining multiple sets with different profiles and radius values. Some of the options are discussed below:

9.63

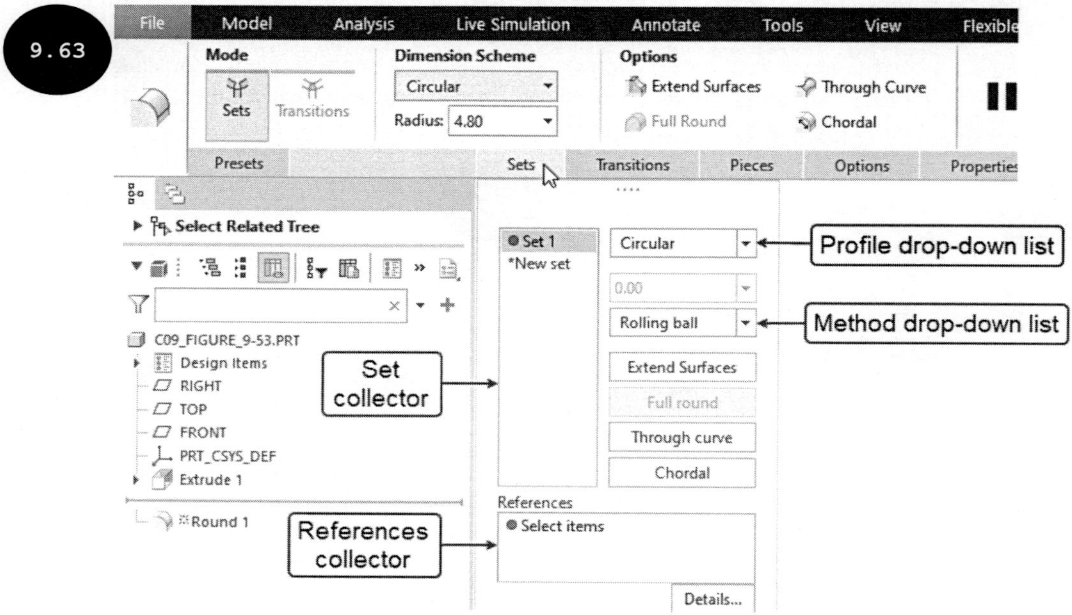

Set collector: By default, **Set 1** is added to the **Set** collector of the expanded **Sets** panel. As a result, you can select one or more edges as set 1 in the **References** collector to create rounds of the same radius. Note that you need to press the CTRL key to select multiple edges as set 1. You can also select two adjacent faces of a model by pressing the CTRL key as set 1. The **New set** option in the **Set** collector is used for creating a new set of rounds. For each set of round, you can specify a different radius value in the **Radius** field.

References collector: The **References** collector is used for selecting one or more edges, or two adjacent faces of a model to create rounds. Note that to select multiple edges or two adjacent faces in a single set, you need to press the CTRL key.

Radius field: The **Radius** field is used for defining the radius value of an active set.

4. Ensure that the **Set 1** option is selected in the **Set** collector.

5. Select one or more edges by pressing the CTRL key as set 1. The names of the selected edges appear in the **References** collector of the expanded **Sets** panel. Also, the preview of the rounds appears in the graphics area with a radius handle on the first selected edge, see Figure 9.64. In this figure, four edges are selected as set 1.

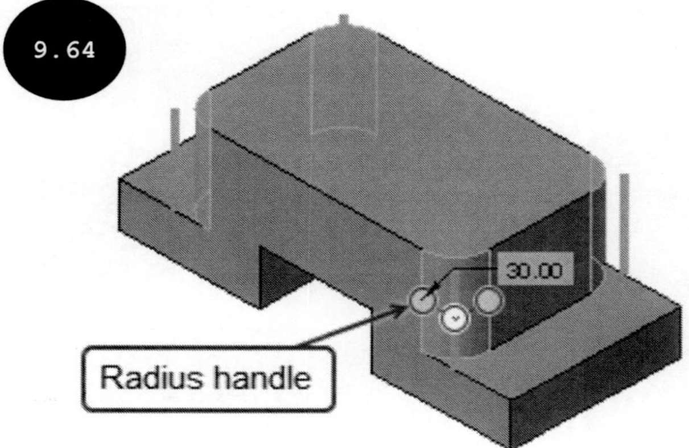

Note: By dragging the radius handle that appears in the graphics area, you can control the radius value of all the edges since all edges are selected as a single set.

6. Enter the radius value of the rounds in the **Radius** field of the **Round** tab or drag the radius handle that appears in the graphics area to define the radius value of all the rounds, dynamically.

7. Select the required option in the **Profile** drop-down list of the expanded **Sets** panel to define the cross-sectional shape of the set 1 rounds. You can select the **Circular**, **Conic**, **C2 Continuous**, **D1 x D2 Conic**, or **D1 x D2 C2** option in this drop-down list to define the profile of the set 1 rounds. All these options are discussed below:

   Circular: By default, the **Circular** option is selected in the **Profile** drop-down list. As a result, a round of circular profile is created, see Figure 9.65.

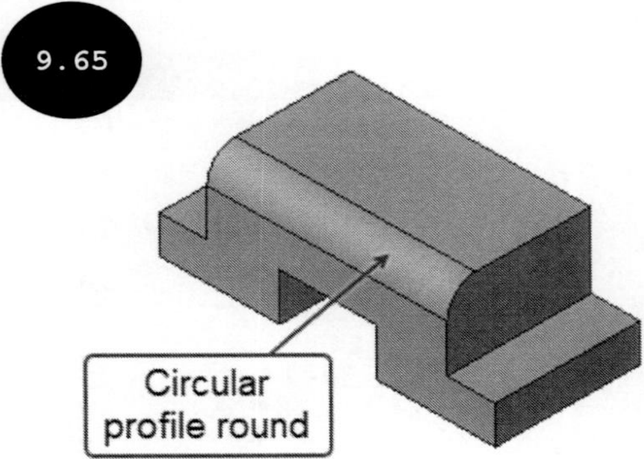

Conic: The **Conic** option is used for creating a round of conic profile. When you select this option, the **Rho** field becomes available below the **Profile** drop-down list in the **Dimension Scheme** area of the **Round** tab. In this field, you can specify the Rho value for the round in the range from 0.05 to 0.95. Note that the Rho value defines the sharpness of the round, see Figures 9.66 and 9.67. You can also define the Rho value by dragging the handle that appears in the graphics area.

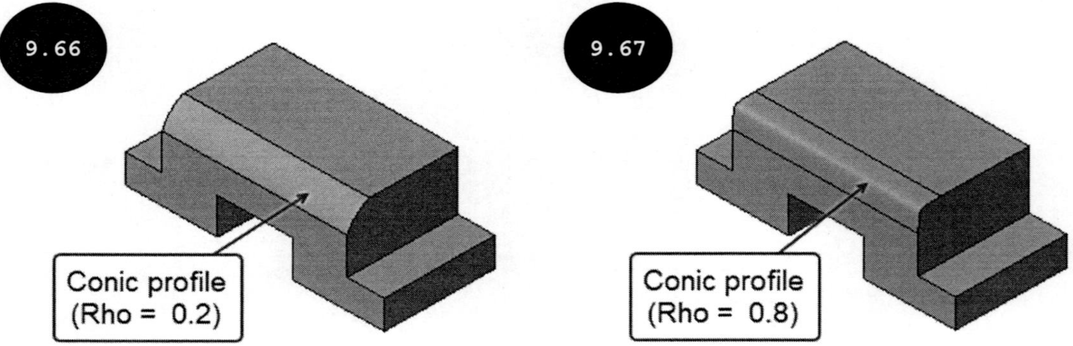

C2 Continuous: The **C2 Continuous** option is used for creating a round of curvature continuous profile that is similar to a conic profile with the only difference that it maintains curvature continuity with the adjacent faces of the selected edge to improve the aesthetic quality of the geometry. On selecting this option, the **C2** field appears below the **Profile** drop-down list in the **Dimension Scheme** area of the **Round** tab, which is used for specifying the C2 shape factor in the range from 0.05 to 0.95. Note that the C2 shape factor defines the curvature continuity with the adjacent faces of the model. You can also define the C2 shape factor by dragging the handle that appears in the graphics area.

D1 x D2 Conic: The **D1 x D2 Conic** option is used for creating a round of conic profile by specifying different conic distance values on both sides of the edge selected and a rho value that defines the sharpness of the round. On selecting this option, the **Rho**, **D1**, and **D2** fields become available in the **Dimension Scheme** area of the **Round** tab, see Figure 9.68. In these fields, you can specify different conic distance values and a rho value, respectively for creating a round, see Figure 9.69. Alternatively, you can also drag the handles that appear in the graphics area to define different conic distance values and a conic parameter value.

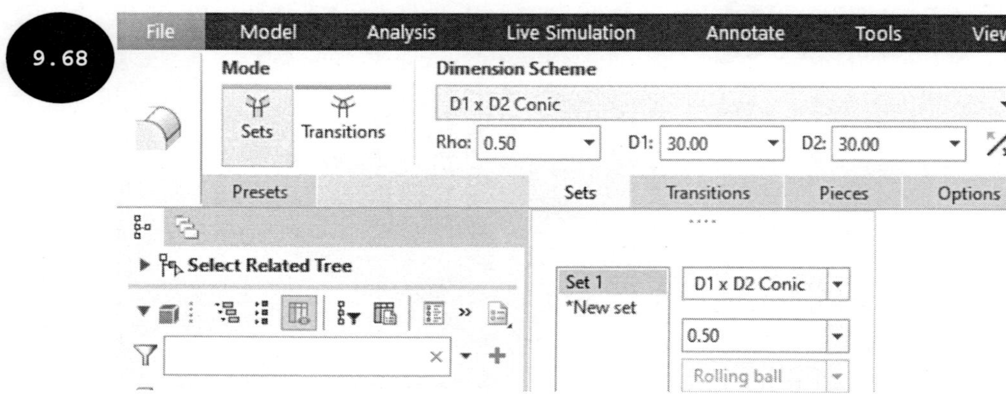

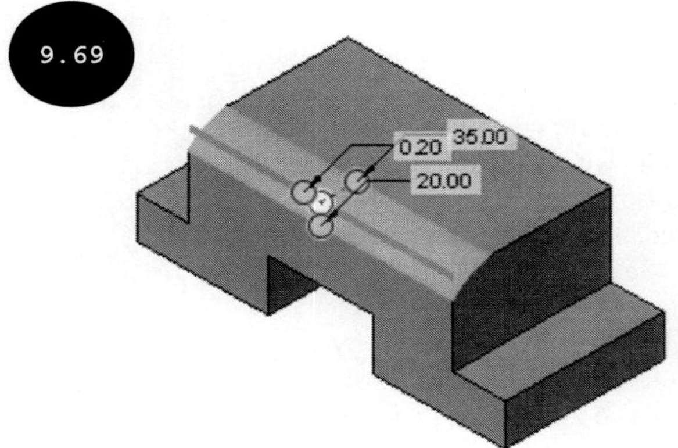

D1 x D2 C2: On selecting the **D1 x D2 C2** option, the **C2**, **D1**, and **D2** fields become available in the **Dimension Scheme** area of the **Round** tab. The **C2** field is used for defining the C2 shape factor in the range from 0.05 to 0.95 to control the curvature continuity of the round with its adjacent faces. The **D1** and **D2** fields are used for specifying different conic distance values on both sides of the edge selected, see Figure 9.70. You can also drag the handles that appear in the graphics area to define different conic distance values and a C2 shape factor for creating a round.

8. Select the required option (**Rolling ball** or **Normal to spine**) in the **Method** drop-down list of the expanded **Sets** panel as the method to be used for creating the round, see Figure 9.71. Note that this drop-down list is enabled only when the **Circular** or **Conic** option is selected in the **Profile** drop-down list. The options of this drop-down list are discussed below:

   Rolling ball: By default, the **Rolling ball** option is selected. As a result, the round is created such that an imaginary spherical ball is rolled along the faces to which it stays tangent.

   Normal to spine: On selecting the **Normal to spine** option, the round is created such that an arc or a conic profile is swept along the edges that are normal to the selected spine.

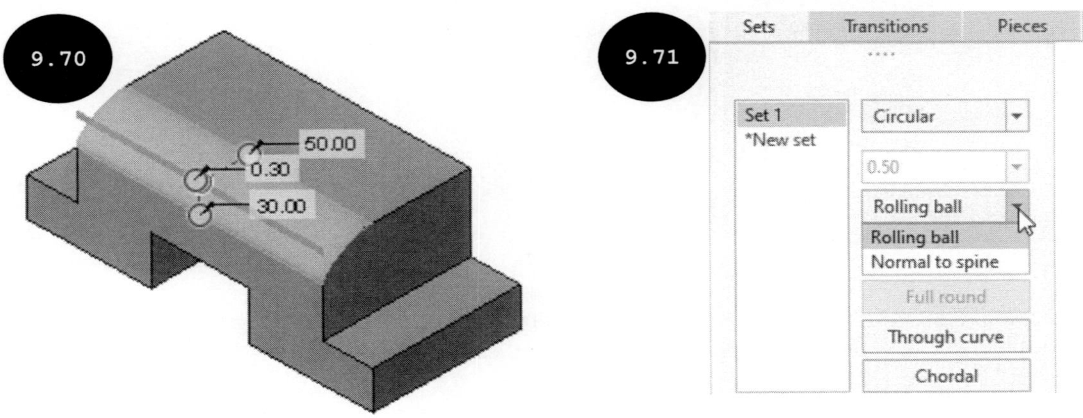

After defining all the parameters for creating rounds as set 1 in the expanded **Sets** panel of the **Round** tab, you can create multiple sets of rounds.

9. Similar to creating rounds as set 1, you can create multiple sets of rounds with different radius values and profiles. To do so, click on the **New set** option in the **Set** collector of the expanded **Sets** panel. A new set "**Set 2**" is added to it and becomes an active set, see Figure 9.72. Next, select edges or two adjacent faces of the model by pressing the CTRL key to create rounds as set 2. The preview of the rounds appears in the graphics area. Next, specify other parameters for creating the rounds, as discussed earlier. You can similarly create multiple sets of rounds by using the **New set** option.

10. Click on the green tick-mark button in the **Round** tab. Rounds of constant radius with specified parameters is created.

Creating a Variable Radius Round

A variable radius round is a fillet that has variable radii along an edge of a model, see Figure 9.73. You can create a variable radius round by using the **Round** tool. The method for creating a variable radius round is discussed below:

1. Click on the **Round** tool in the **Engineering** group of the **Model** tab, see Figure 9.74. The **Round** tab appears in the **Ribbon**.

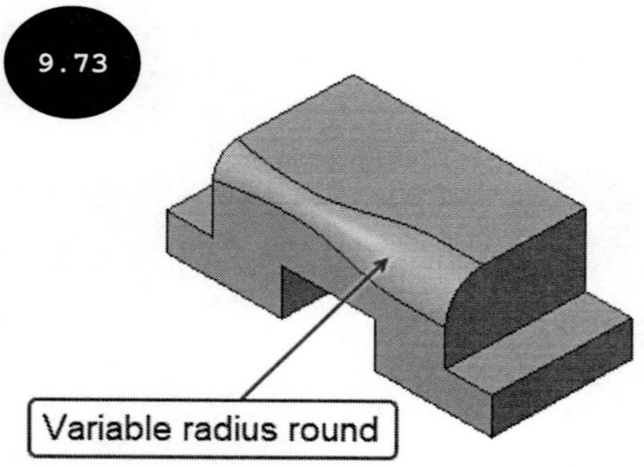

2. Expand the **Sets** panel of the **Round** tab, if not expanded by default, see Figure 9.75. Some of the options of the expanded **Sets** panel are discussed earlier and the options for creating a variable radius round are discussed below:

9.75

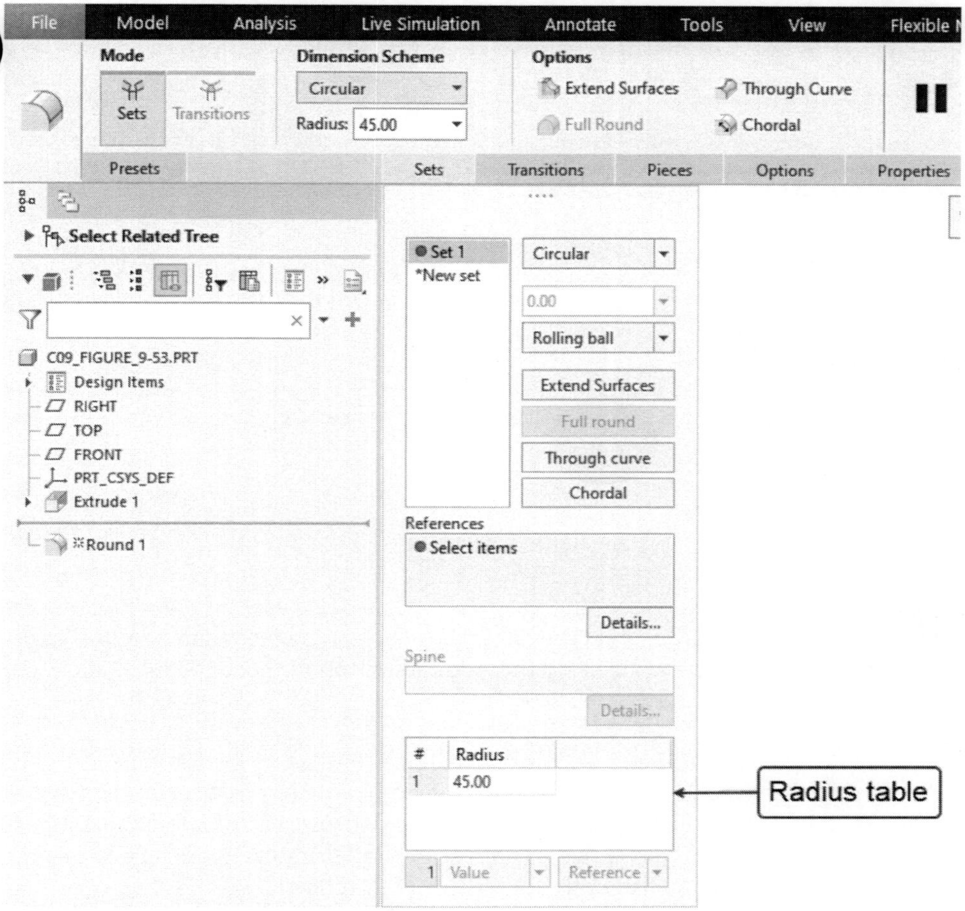

Radius table

3. Select an edge of the model to create a variable radius round as set 1. The name of the selected edge appears in the **References** collector of the expanded **Sets** panel. Also, a preview of the constant radius round with the default radius value appears in the graphics area, see Figure 9.76.

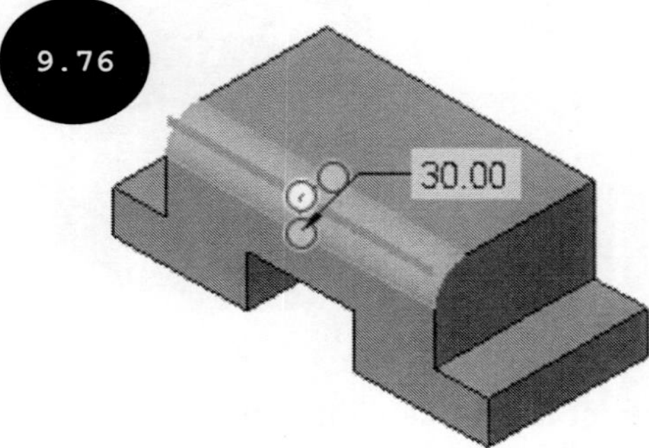

4. Right-click on the **Radius** table of the expanded **Sets** panel and then click on the **Add radius** option that appears, see Figure 9.77. The radius handles appear on each end/vertex of the edge selected in the graphics area, see Figure 9.78. Also, the radius values appear in the **Radius** table for each vertex of the edge selected, see Figure 9.79.

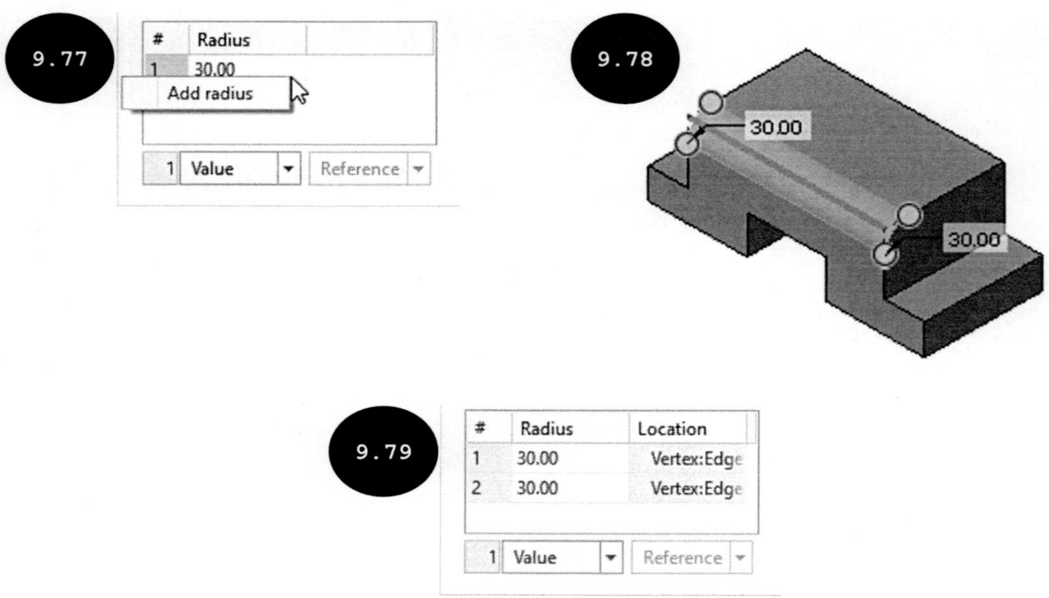

Tip: You can also press and hold the right mouse button on the radius handle that appears in the graphics area and then click on the **Add radius** option that appears to add radius values on both vertices of the edge selected.

5. Specify different radius values as required, at both vertices of the edge by dragging the radius handles that appear in the graphics area. Alternatively, enter different radius values in the corresponding fields in the **Radius** column of the **Radius** table. Figure 9.80 shows the preview of a round with different radii at both the vertices of the edge.

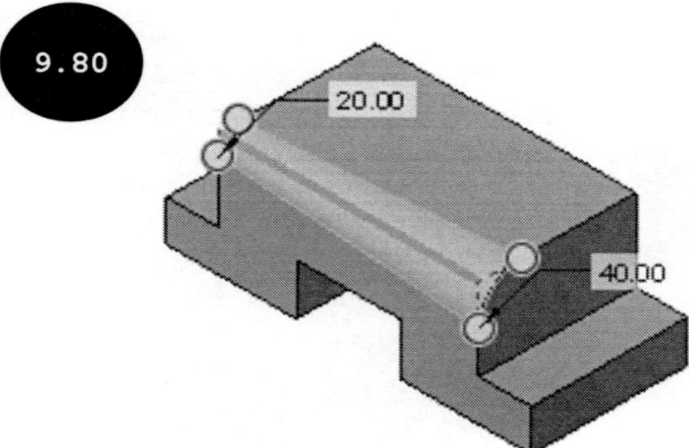

In addition to specifying different radius values at each end of the edge selected, you can add multiple control points along it and specify different radius values at each control point. The steps for adding multiple control points along an edge are discussed below:

6. Right-click on the **Radius** table of the expanded **Sets** panel and then click on the **Add radius** option that appears, see Figure 9.81. A radius handle appears at a default location along the edge of the graphics area, see Figure 9.82. Also, the default radius and its location values appear in the **Radius** table, see Figure 9.83.

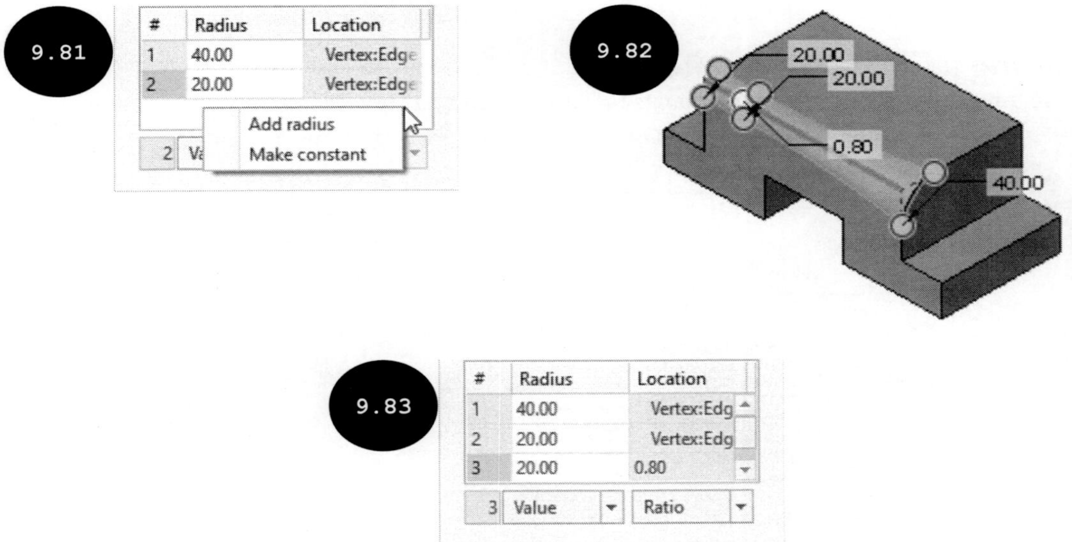

7. Specify a new radius value and its location in terms of percentage value in the respective fields of the **Radius** table. Alternatively, you can drag the radius handle that appears in the graphics area to specify the radius value and its location along the edge selected. Figure 9.84 shows the preview of a round with different radius values at both vertices and the middle of the edge selected.

8. You can similarly add multiple control points along the edge and specify different radius values, as required.

9. Click on the green tick-mark button in the **Round** tab. The variable radius round on the edge selected is created, see Figure 9.85.

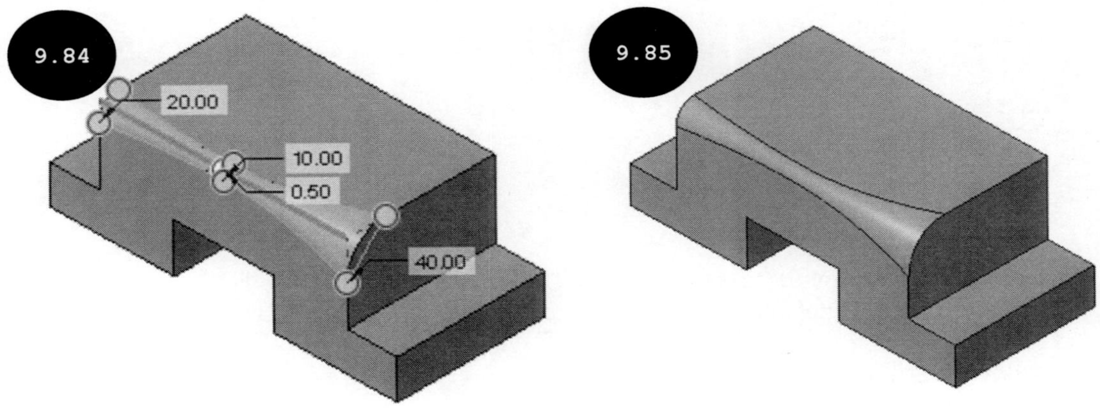

Tip: You can also delete an already added control point in the variable radius round. To do so, press and hold the right-mouse button on the respective radius handle that appears in the preview of the round and then click on the **Delete** option in the shortcut menu that appears.

Creating a Curve Driven Round

A curve driven round is created such that its radius is driven by a curve along the edge of a model, see Figure 9.86. The method for creating a curve driven round is discussed below:

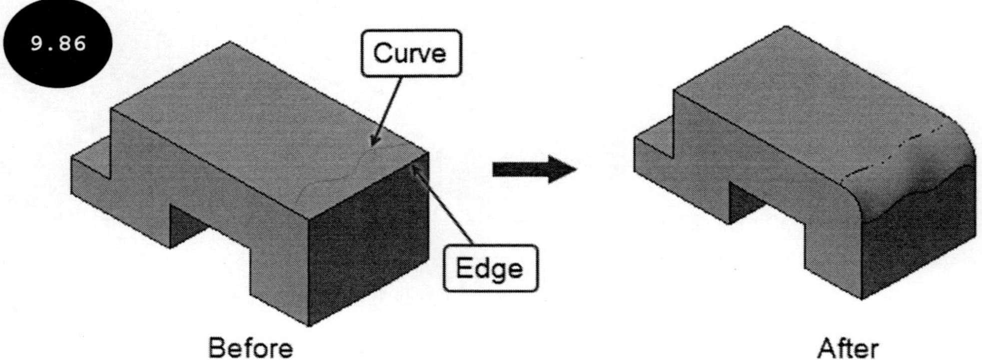

1. Create a sketch as a curve on an adjacent face of the edge to be selected for creating the round. Note that all segments of the curve must be tangent to each other, see Figure 9.87. You can create a curve in the Sketching environment by using sketching tools such as **Spline**, **Line**, and **Arc**.

2. Click on the **Round** tool in the **Engineering** group of the **Model** tab, see Figure 9.88. The **Round** tab with the expanded **Sets** panel appears in the **Ribbon**.

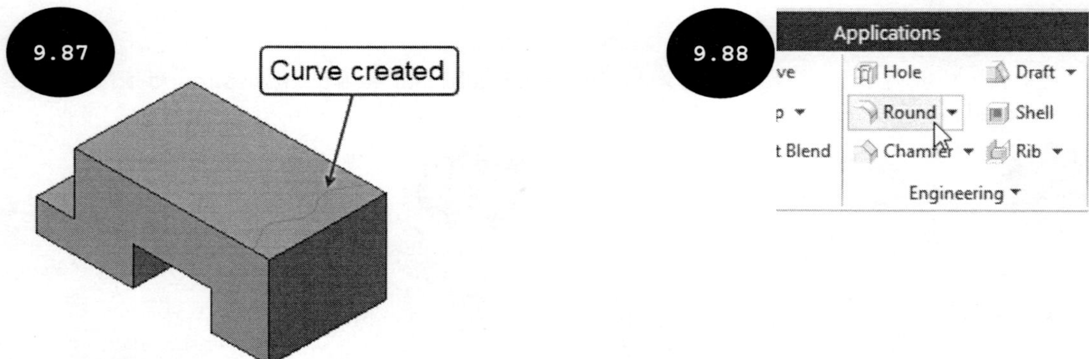

3. Select an edge of the model to create a round. The preview of a constant radius round appears on the selected edge, by default, see Figure 9.89.

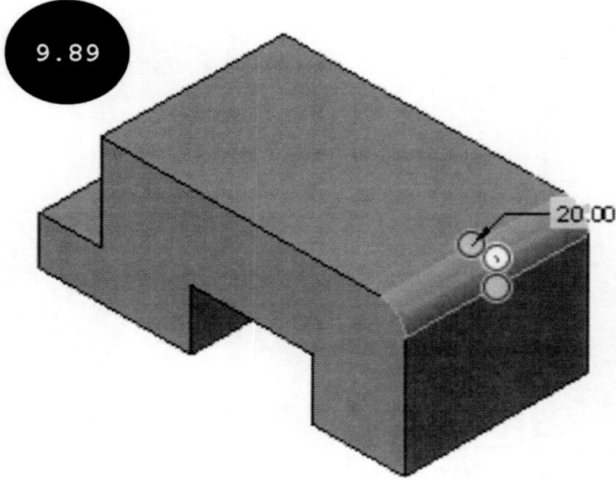

4. Click on the **Through Curve** button in the **Options** area of the **Round** tab, see Figure 9.90. The **Driving curve** field gets enabled and you are prompted to select a chain of tangent entities.

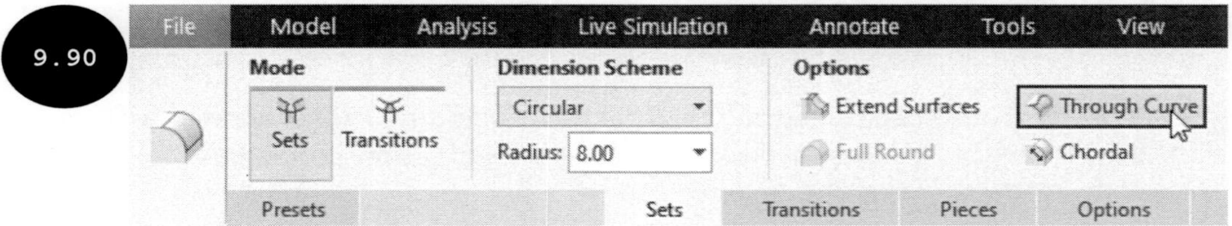

5. Select a sketch as a curve in the graphics area. The preview of the round appears such that its radius is driven by the curve selected, see Figure 9.91.

6. Click on the green tick-mark button in the **Round** tab. The curve driven round is created, see Figure 9.92.

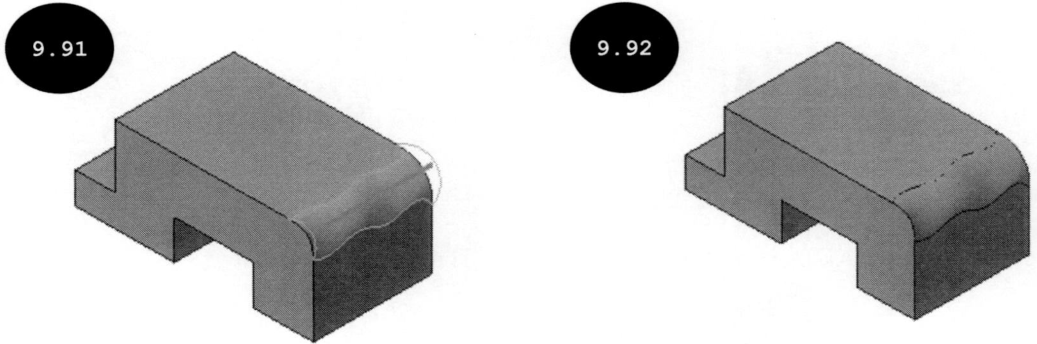

Creating a Full Round

A full round is created tangent to three adjacent faces of a model, see Figure 9.93. The method for creating a full round is discussed below:

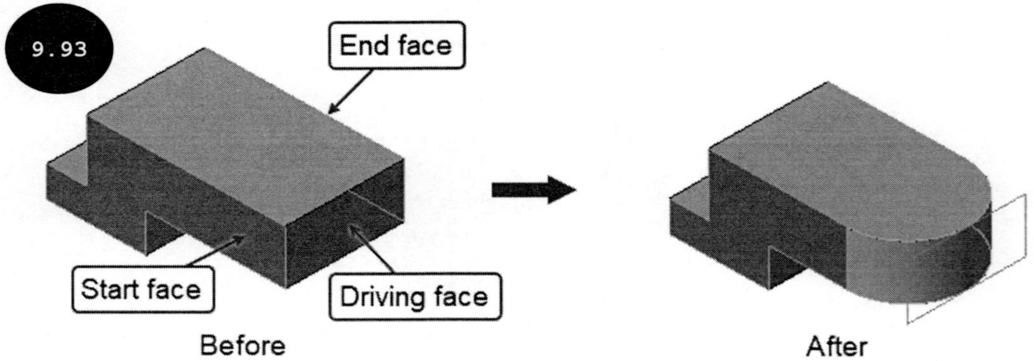

1. Click on the **Round** tool in the **Engineering** group of the **Model** tab. The **Round** tab appears in the **Ribbon**.

2. Select two faces of a model as start and end faces by pressing the CTRL key as set 1, see Figure 9.94. The **Driving surface** field gets enabled in the **Model** tab and you are prompted to select a driving face of the model to create a full round.

3. Select a face that is in the middle of the selected faces as a driving face, see Figure 9.94. The preview of the full round appears in the graphics area, see Figure 9.95.

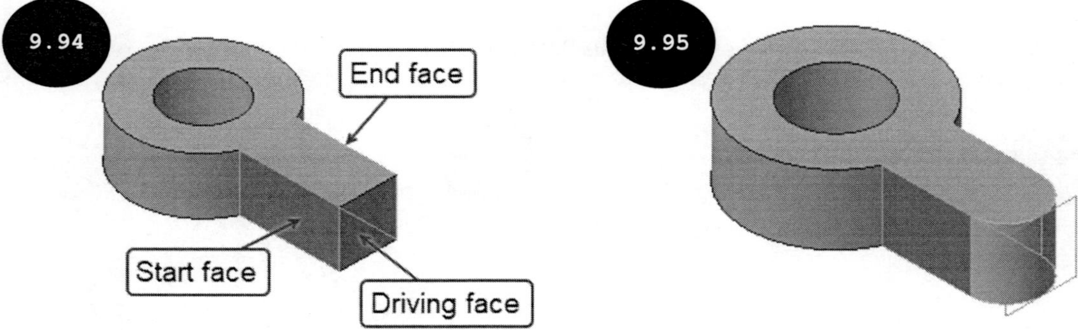

4. Click on the green tick-mark button in the **Round** tab. The full round is created, see Figure 9.96.

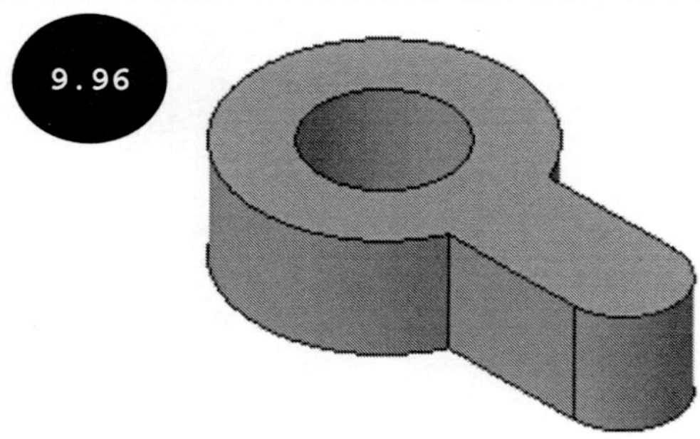

Creating Auto Rounds

In Creo Parametric, you can also create rounds of constant radii on all the edges (convex and concave) or selected edges of the model, automatically by using the **Auto Round** tool. Figure 9.97 shows a model with convex and concave edges and Figure 9.98 shows the resultant model after creating rounds on all the convex and concave edges of the model. The method for creating rounds by using the **Auto Round** tool is discussed below:

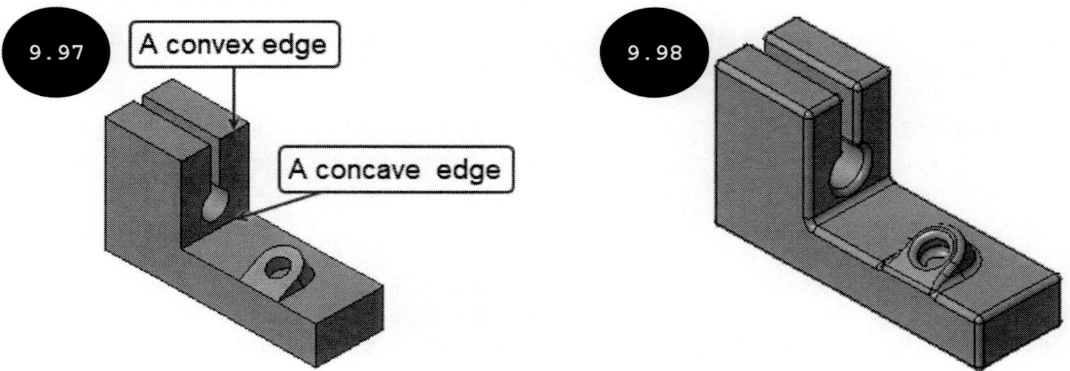

1. Click on the arrow next to the **Round** tool in the **Engineering** group of the **Model** tab. A flyout appears, see Figure 9.99.

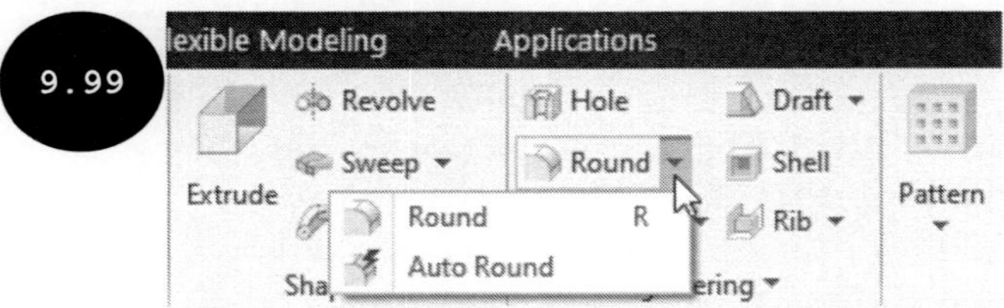

2. Click on the **Auto Round** tool in the flyout that appears. The **Auto Round** tab appears in the **Ribbon**, see Figure 9.100.

   By default, both the **Convex** and **Concave** buttons are activated in the **Auto Round** tab. As a result, Creo Parametric identifies all the convex and concave edges of the model for creating rounds.

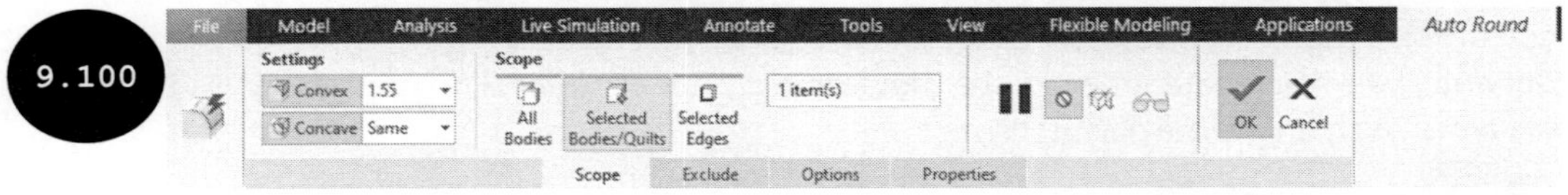

3. Ensure that the **Convex** and **Concave** buttons are selected in the **Auto Round** tab for creating rounds of constant radii on both these types of edges of the model. Note that if you do not want to create rounds on any of the edge types (convex or concave), then you need to deactivate the respective button in the **Auto Round** tab.

4. Specify the radius value for both the edge types in the fields that appear in front of the **Convex** and **Concave** buttons, respectively. You can specify the same or different radius values for creating rounds on the convex and concave edges of the model.

   Scope Area: The options in the **Scope** area of the **Auto Round** tab are used for defining a scope for creating auto rounds (refer to Figure 9.100) and the same are discussed below:

   All Bodies: On selecting the **All Bodies** button, the convex and concave edges of all the bodies get identified for creating rounds, automatically with specified radius values.

   Selected Bodies/Quilts: By default, the **Selected Bodies/Quilts** button is selected in the **Scope** area. As a result, you can create auto rounds on the convex and concave edges of the selected solid and quilt/surface models. Note that you can select multiple bodies by pressing the CTRL key.

   Selected Edges: The **Selected Edges** button is used for selecting edges of the model to create rounds. When you select this button, the **Selected Edges** collector gets enabled in the **Scope** area for selecting the edges. Note that you can select multiple edges by pressing the CTRL key.

5. Select the required button (**All Bodies**, **Selected Bodies/Quilts**, or **Selected Edges**) in the **Scope** area for creating rounds of specified radius values, automatically, as discussed above.

Note: You can also exclude some of the edges of the model from creating rounds, automatically. To do so, expand the **Exclude** panel of the **Auto Round** tab and then select the edges to be excluded in the **Excluded Edges** collector that appears. You need to press the CTRL key to select multiple edges.

6. Click on the green tick mark in the **Auto Round** tab. The **Auto-Round Player** window appears and the process of creating rounds on the edges of the model gets started. After it is down, the rounds of a specified radius are created on the edges of the model and the **Auto-Round Player** window disappears.

Creating Chamfers

A chamfer is a bevel face that is non-perpendicular to its adjacent faces, see Figure 9.101. In Creo Parametric, you can create an edge chamfer and a corner chamfer. The methods for creating both these types of chamfers are discussed next.

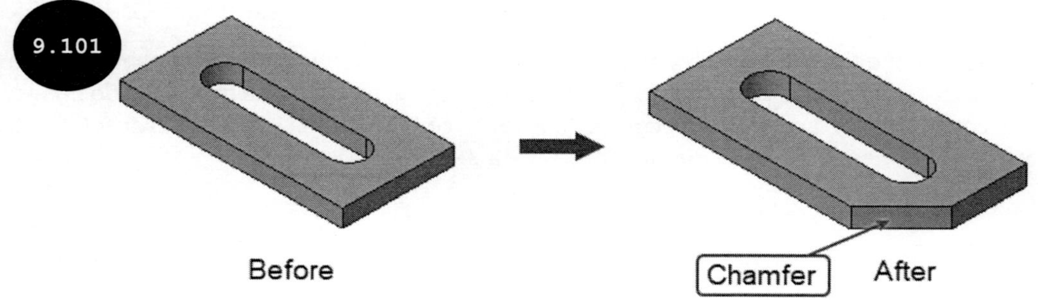

Creating an Edge Chamfer

The chamfers that are created on the edges of a model are known as edge chamfers. In Creo Parametric, you can create an edge chamfer by using various dimension schemes. The method for creating an edge chamfer by using various dimension schemes is discussed below:

1. Click on the **Chamfer** tool in the **Engineering** group of the **Model** tab, see Figure 9.102. The **Edge Chamfer** tab appears in the **Ribbon**, see Figure 9.103.

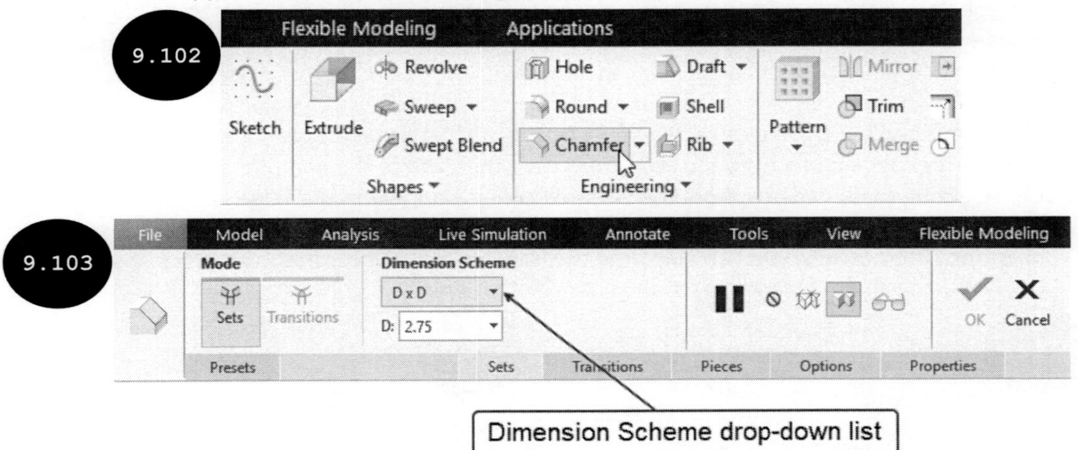

By default, the **Sets** button is activated in the **Edge Chamfer** tab. As a result, you can create chamfers by defining multiple sets and for each set of chamfer, you can use a different dimension scheme.

2. Expand the **Sets** panel of the **Edge Chamfer** tab, if not expanded by default, and then select an edge to create a chamfer. A preview of the chamfer appears on the selected edge as per the default parameters, see Figure 9.104. Also, the name of the selected edge appears in the **References** collector of the expanded **Sets** panel, see Figure 9.105. You can select multiple edges by pressing the CTRL key to create chamfers of the same parameters as set 1.

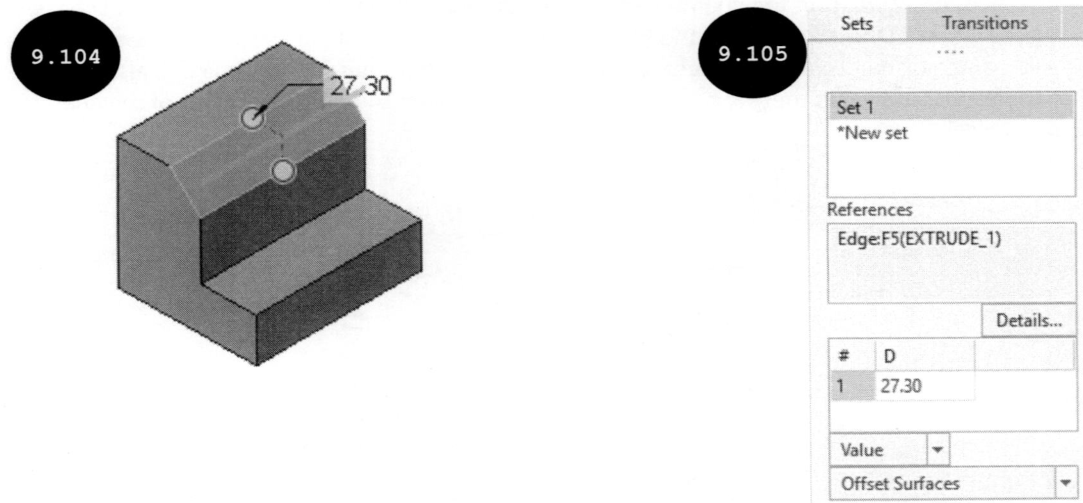

3. Select the required dimension scheme (D x D, D1 x D2, Angle x D, 45 x D, O x O, or O1 x O2) for creating the chamfer in the **Dimension Scheme** drop-down list. The various dimension schemes are discussed below:

D x D: The D x D option is used for creating a chamfer at an equal distance "D" from both sides of the chamfer edge, see Figure 9.106. By default, the **D x D** option is selected in the **Dimension Scheme** drop-down list. As a result, the **D** field appears in the **Edge Chamfer** tab. In this field, you can specify a distance value that measures equally from both sides of the selected edge to create a chamfer. Alternatively, you can also drag the handle that appears in the graphics area to specify the distance value (D) of the chamfer, dynamically.

D1 x D2: The D1 x D2 option is used for creating a chamfer at a distance "D1" from one side of the chamfer edge and a distance "D2" from the other side of the chamfer edge, see Figure 9.107. On selecting the **D1 x D2** option, the **D1** and **D2** fields appear in the **Edge Chamfer** tab. In these fields, you can specify different distance values from both sides of the selected edge to create a chamfer. Alternatively, you can also drag the handles that appear in the graphics area to specify the distance values (D1 and D2) of the chamfer, dynamically.

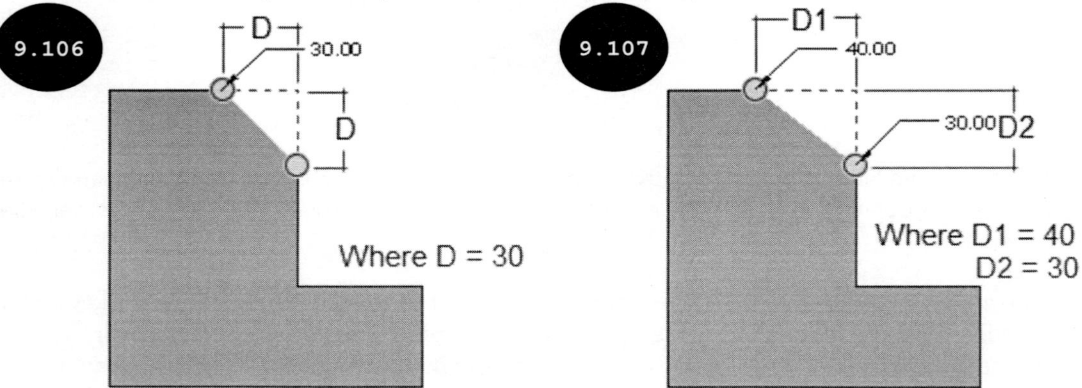

Angle x D: The Angle x D option is used for creating a chamfer by specifying an angle and a distance "D" value from the chamfer edge, see Figure 9.108. On selecting the **Angle x D** option, the **Angle** and **D** fields appear in the **Edge Chamfer** tab. In these fields, you can specify an angle value and a distance value respectively to create a chamfer. Alternatively, you can also drag the handles that appear in the graphics area to specify the angle and distance values of the chamfer, dynamically.

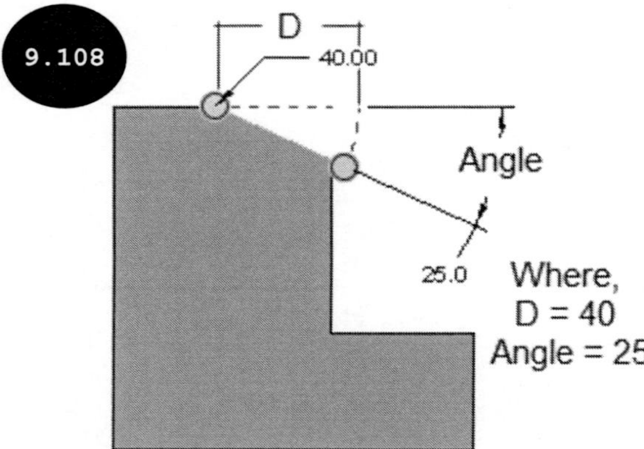

45 x D: The 45 x D option is used for creating a chamfer at an angle of 45-degrees to both the adjacent faces of the chamfer edge and a distance "D" that measures from both sides of the chamfer edge, see Figure 9.109. On selecting the **45 x D** option, the **D** field appears in the **Edge Chamfer** tab. In this field, you can specify a distance value that measures equally from both sides of the selected edge to create a chamfer. Alternatively, you can also drag the handle that appears in the graphics area to specify the distance values of the chamfer, dynamically. Note that the angle to both the adjacent faces of the chamfered edge remains 45 degrees.

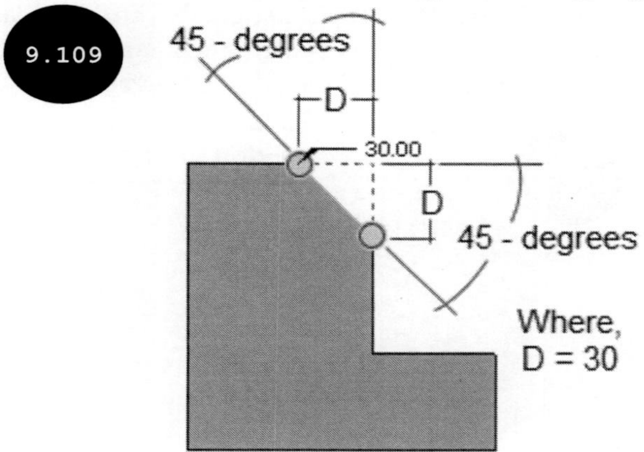

O x O: The O x O option is used for creating a chamfer at an equal offset distance "O" from the adjacent faces of the chamfer edge, see Figure 9.110. Note that this option is available only when the **Offset Surfaces** creation method is selected in the drop-down list of the expanded **Sets** panel. On selecting the **O x O** option, the **O** field appears in the **Edge Chamfer** tab. In this field, you can specify an offset distance. You can also drag the handle that appears in the graphics area to specify the offset distance value of the chamfer, dynamically.

O1 x O2: The O1 x O2 option is used for creating a chamfer at an offset distance "O1" from one side of the chamfer edge and an offset distance "O2" from the other side of the chamfer edge, see Figure 9.111. On selecting the **O1 x O2** option, the **O1** and **O2** fields appear in the **Edge Chamfer** tab. In these fields, you can specify different offset values from both sides of the selected edge to create a chamfer. You can also drag the handles that appear in the graphics area to specify the offset distance values (O1 and O2) of the chamfer, dynamically. Note that this option is available only when the **Offset Surfaces** creation method is selected in the drop-down list of the expanded **Sets** panel.

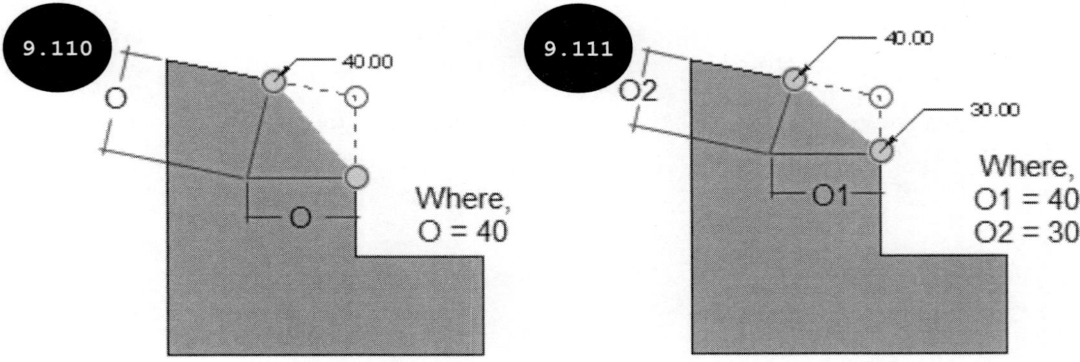

4. After selecting the required option in the **Dimension Scheme** drop-down list, the respective fields for specifying chamfer parameters such as distance and angle appear in the **Edge Chamfer** tab, as discussed above.

5. Specify the chamfer parameters depending on the option selected in the **Dimension Scheme** drop-down list.

6. Click on the green tick-mark button in the **Edge Chamfer** tab. The edge chamfer is created on the selected edge of the model as per the selected dimension scheme, see Figure 9.112. In this figure, the edge chamfer is created by using the D x D dimension scheme.

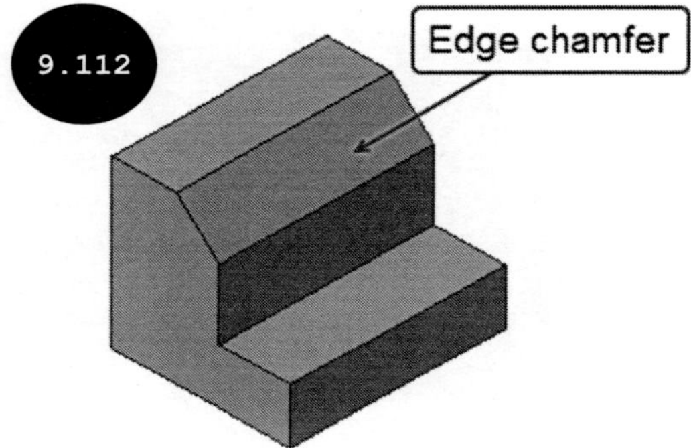

Creating a Corner Chamfer

A chamfer that is created on the vertex formed at the intersection of three edges of a model is known as a corner chamfer, see Figure 9.113. In Creo Parametric, you can create a corner chamfer by using the **Corner Chamfer** tool. The method for creating a corner chamfer is discussed below:

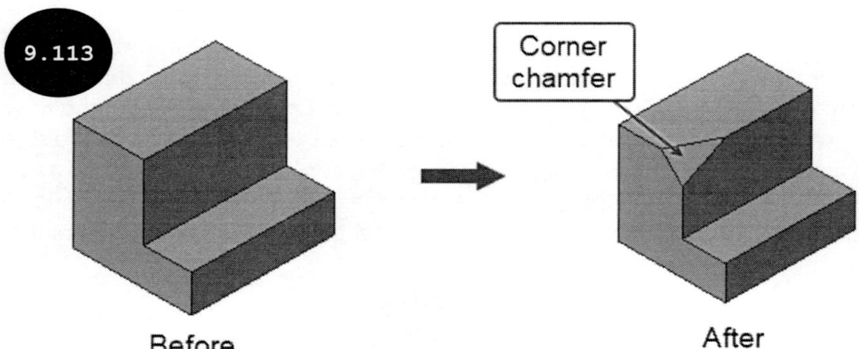

1. Click on the arrow next to the **Chamfer** tool in the **Engineering** group of the **Model** tab. A flyout appears, see Figure 9.114.

9.114

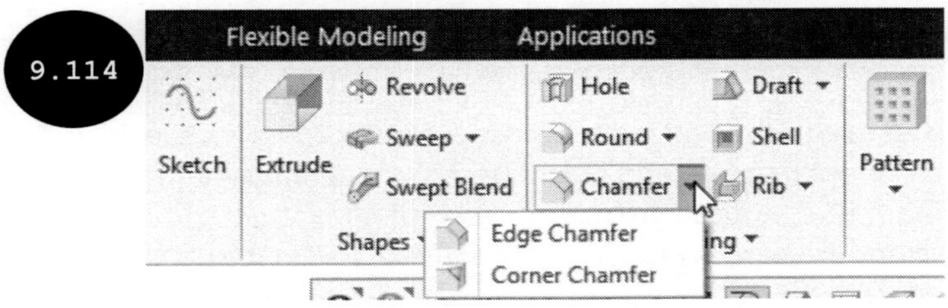

2. Click on the **Corner Chamfer** tool in the flyout that appears. The **Corner Chamfer** tab appears in the **Ribbon** (see Figure 9.115), and you are prompted to select a vertex of the model. Note that the **D1**, **D2**, and **D3** fields of the **Corner Chamfer** tab are enabled only after selecting a vertex.

9.115

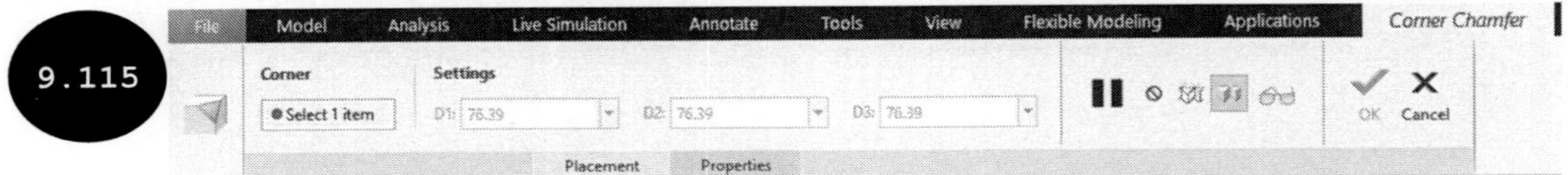

3. Click on a vertex of the model that is formed at the intersection of three edges. A preview of the corner chamfer with distance handles appears in the graphics area, see Figure 9.116. Also, the **D1**, **D2**, and **D3** fields of the **Corner Chamfer** tab are enabled for specifying distance values along each edge of the vertex selected.

9.116

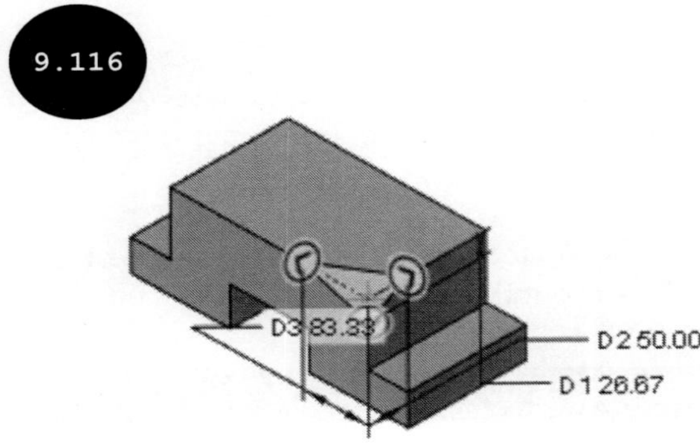

4. Specify distance values along each edge of the vertex selected in the **D1**, **D2**, and **D3** fields of the **Corner Chamfer** tab, respectively. Alternatively, drag the distance handles that appear in the graphics area to define distance values along each edge of the vertex, dynamically.

5. Click on the green tick-mark button in the **Corner Chamfer** tab. The corner chamfer is created at the selected vertex of the model.

Creating Rib Features

Rib features act as supporting features and are generally used for increasing the strength of a model. You can create a rib feature from an open sketch by adding thickness in a specified direction. Figure 9.117 shows a model with an open sketch and Figure 9.118 shows the resultant model with the rib feature created. In Creo Parametric, you can create two types of rib features: profile rib and trajectory rib by using the **Profile Rib** and **Trajectory Rib** tools, respectively. The methods for creating both types of rib features are discussed next.

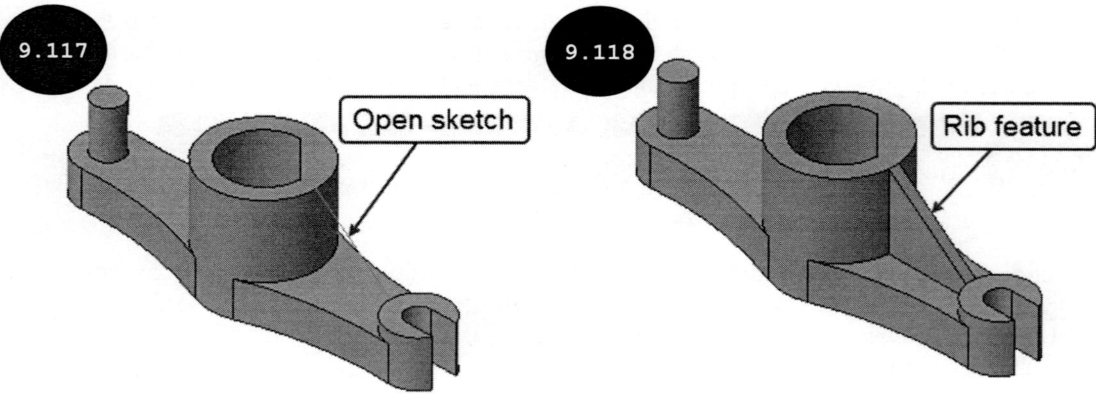

Creating a Profile Rib Feature

A profile rib feature is a thin protrusion that is attached to a solid model to increasing its strength. Figure 9.118 shows an example of a profile rib feature. The method for creating a rib feature is discussed below:

1. Click on the arrow next to the **Rib** tool in the **Engineering** group of the **Model** tab and then click on the **Profile Rib** tool in the flyout that appears, see Figure 9.119. The **Profile Rib** tab appears in the **Ribbon**, see Figure 9.120.

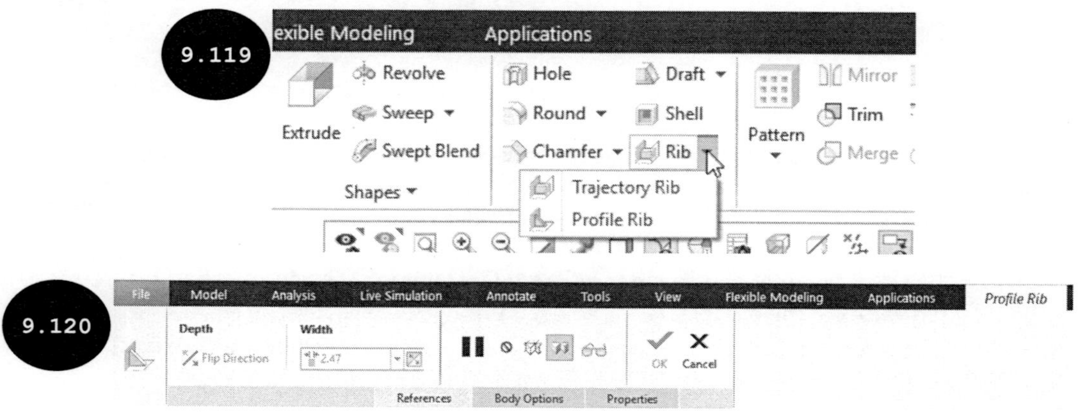

2. Click on the **Define** button in the expanded **References** panel of the **Profile Rib** tab to create an open sketch for creating the rib feature, see Figure 9.121. The **Sketch** dialog box appears. Note that if you have already created an open sketch, then you can select it in the **Model Tree** or in the graphics area for creating the rib feature.

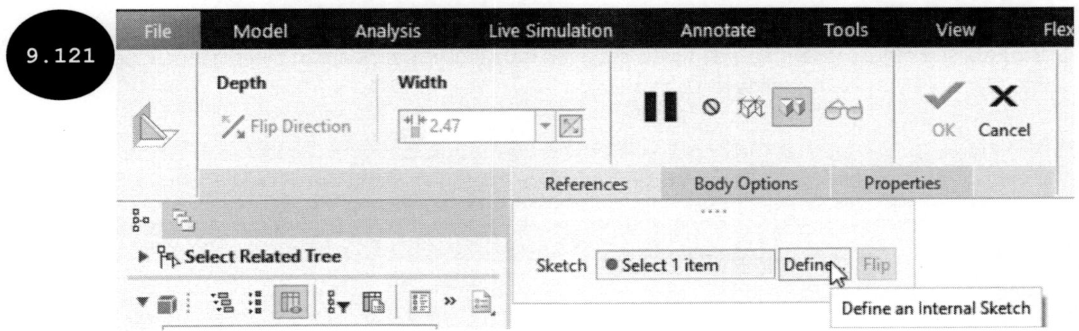

Note: The sketch of the rib feature must be on a plane that intersects with the model, see Figure 9.122. Also, the projection of both the ends of the sketch should lie on the geometry of the model.

3. Select a plane as the sketching plane for creating the sketch of the rib in the graphics area and then click on the **Sketch** button in the **Sketch** dialog box. The Sketching environment is invoked and the sketching plane becomes normal to the viewing direction.

4. Create an open sketch such that the projection of both ends of the sketch lies on the geometry of the model, see Figure 9.122.

5. Exit the Sketching environment by clicking on the **OK** button in the **Close** group. The preview of the rib feature appears in the graphics area with the default thickness value, see Figure 9.123.

Note: The arrow that appears in the preview of the rib feature should be pointing toward the geometry of the model, see Figure 9.123.

6. Click on the arrow that appears in the graphics area to reverse the direction of extrusion of the rib feature toward the geometry of the model, if needed. Alternatively, you can also reverse the direction of extrusion of the rib feature by clicking on the **Flip** button in the expanded **References** panel.

7. Enter the thickness value of the rib feature in the **Thickness** field in the **Width** area of the **Profile Rib** tab, see Figure 9.124. You can also drag the handle that appears in the graphics area to define the thickness of the rib feature, dynamically.

8. You can also change the thickness side of the rib feature between both sides, side 1, or side 2 of the rib profile by using the **Thickness Side** button of the **Profile Rib** tab, see Figure 9.124.

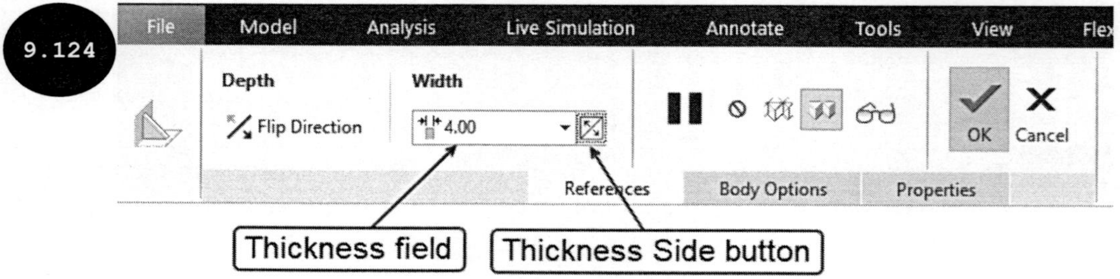

9. Click on the green tick-mark button in the **Profile Rib** tab. The profile rib feature of specified thickness is created, see Figure 9.125.

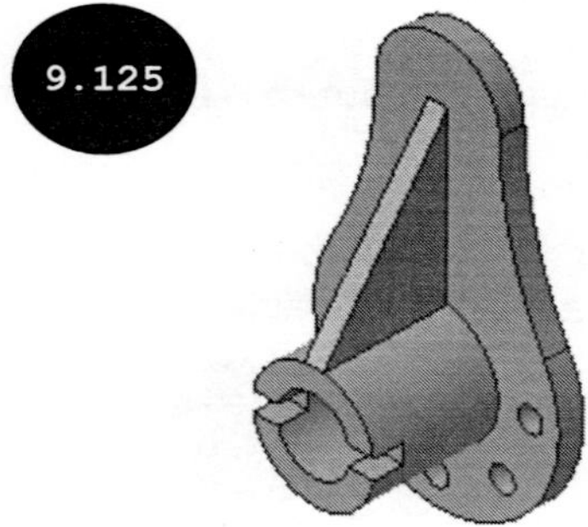

Creating a Trajectory Rib Feature

A trajectory rib feature is a thin protrusion that is mostly used for increasing the strength of the plastic parts. Figure 9.126 shows an example of a trajectory rib feature created on the model that represents a plastic part. The method for creating a trajectory rib feature is discussed below:

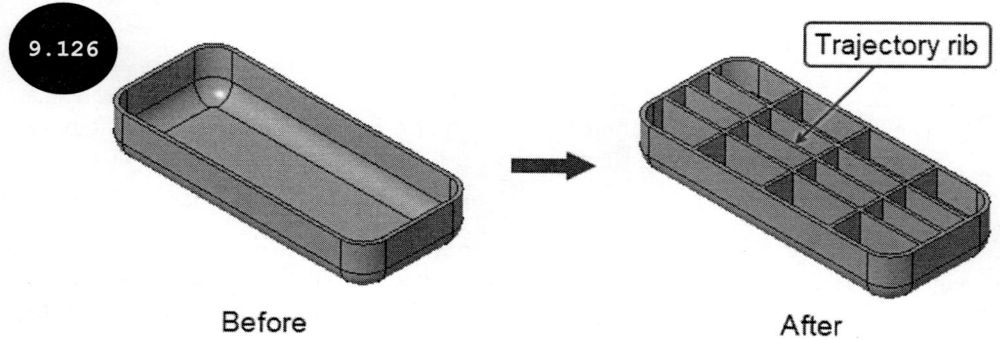

1. Click on the arrow next to the **Rib** tool in the **Engineering** group and then click on the **Trajectory Rib** tool in the flyout that appears, see Figure 9.127. The **Trajectory Rib** tab appears in the **Ribbon**.

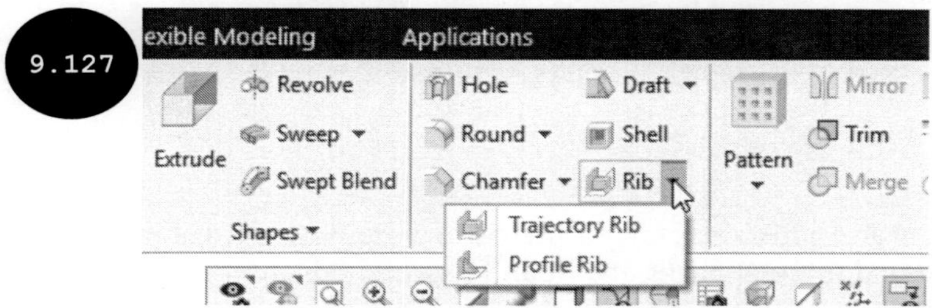

2. Click on the **Define** button in the expanded **Placement** panel of the **Trajectory Rib** tab to create an open or closed sketch for creating the rib feature. The **Sketch** dialog box appears.

3. Invoke the Sketching environment by selecting a plane or a planar face as the sketching plane for creating the sketch of the rib feature. Note that you can also select an existing open or closed sketch to create the trajectory rib feature.

4. Create an open or closed sketch in the Sketching environment by using the sketching tools, see Figure 9.128. In this figure, an open sketch is created on the top planar face of the model.

5. Exit the Sketching environment. A preview of the trajectory rib appears in the graphics area with default thickness value, see Figure 9.129.

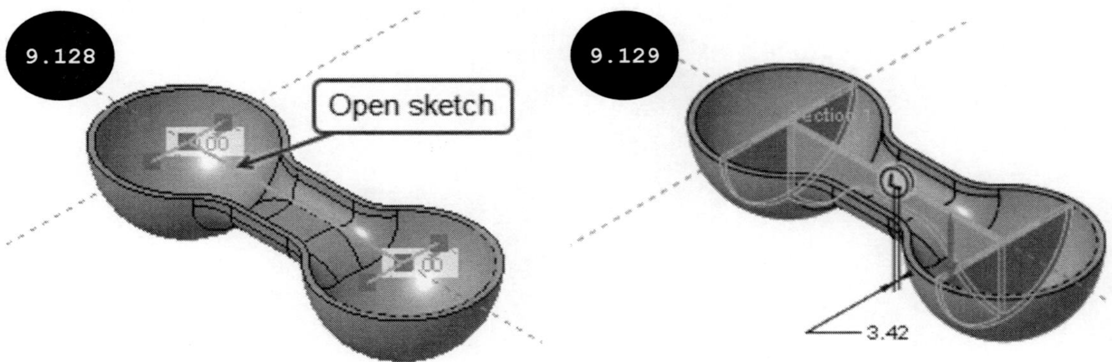

6. Enter the width value of the rib feature in the **Width** field of the **Trajectory Rib** tab, see Figure 9.130. Alternatively, you can drag the handle that appears in the graphics area to define the width, dynamically.

7. Ensure that the direction of the rib feature is toward the geometry of the model. If needed, you can change the depth direction of the rib to the other side of the sketch by clicking on the **Flip Direction** button, see Figure 9.130.

9.130

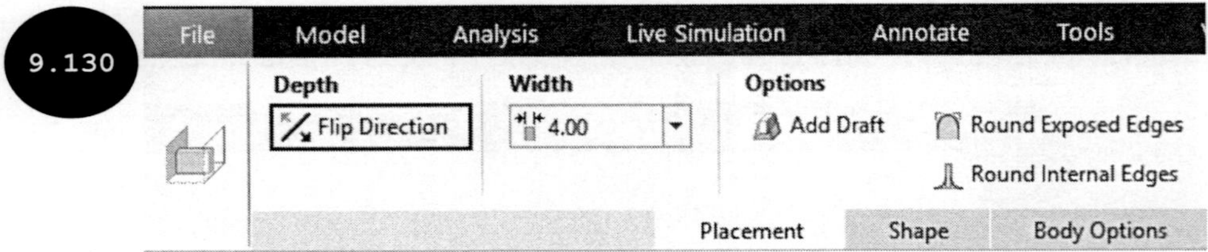

Note: You can also add rounds on the internal and exposed edges of the rib feature by activating the **Round Internal Edges** and **Round Exposed Edges** buttons of the **Trajectory Rib** tab, respectively. Moreover, you can add tapering to the rib feature by activating the **Add Draft** button. You can edit the radius value of the rounds and angle value of the draft in the respective fields that appear in the expanded **Shape** panel of the **Trajectory Rib** tab. Alternatively, you can also drag the respective handles that appear in the graphics area to edit the radius value of rounds and angle value of the draft.

8. Expand the **Shape** panel of the **Trajectory Rib** tab and then specify the required values in the respective fields that appear to control the shape of the rib feature. Note that the fields available in the expanded **Shape** panel for controlling the shape of the rib feature depend upon the buttons activated in the **Trajectory Rib** tab.

9. Click on the green tick-mark button in the **Trajectory Rib** tab. The trajectory rib feature is created, see Figure 9.131. In this figure, the rib feature is created by adding rounds on the internal edges of the rib feature.

9.131

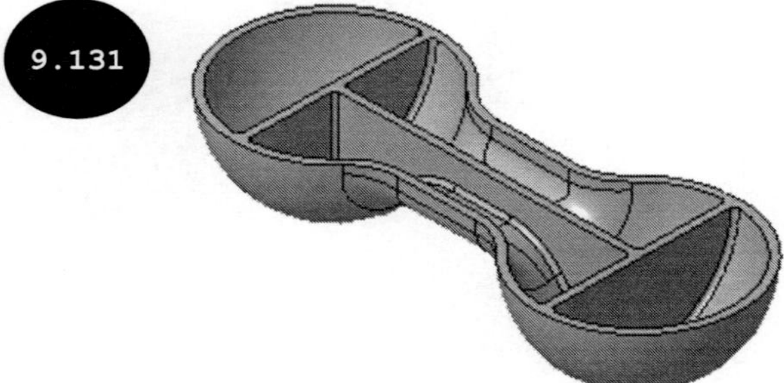

Creating Shell Features

A shell feature is a thin walled feature, that is created by making a model hollow from inside, see Figure 9.132. In this figure, the models are shown in 'Hidden Line' display style for clarity. In Creo Parametric, you can create a uniform thickness or multi thickness shell feature by using the **Shell** tool. You can also remove one or more faces of the model in the shell feature. The method for creating a shell feature is discussed below:

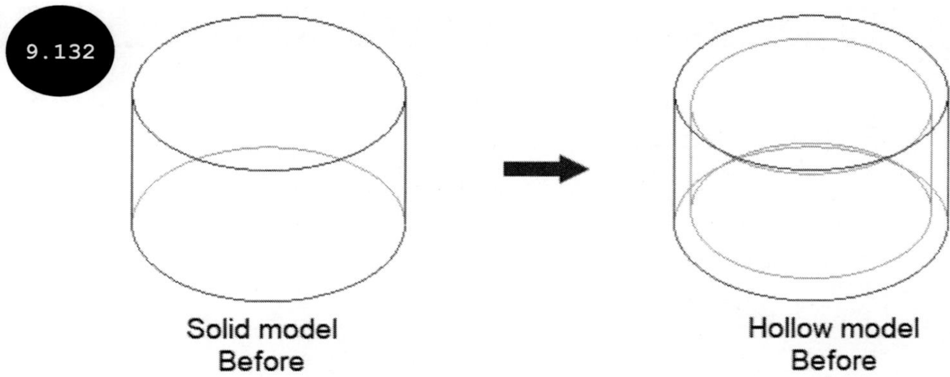

1. Click on the **Shell** tool in the **Engineering** group of the **Model** tab, see Figure 9.133. The **Shell** tab appears in the **Ribbon**.

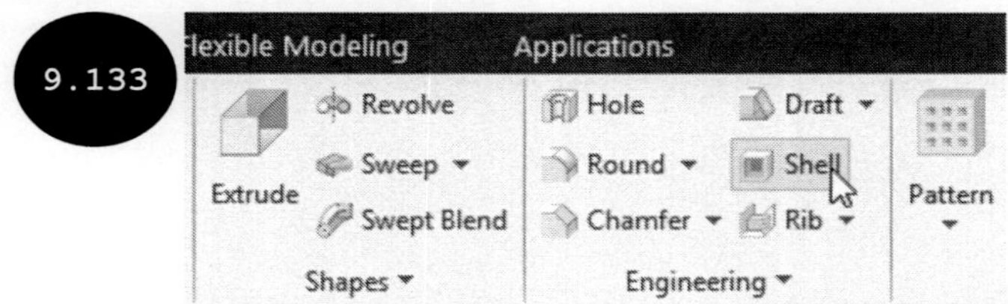

2. Specify a thickness value for the shell feature in the **Thickness** field in the **Settings** area of the **Shell** tab. Note that the thickness value specified in this field is applied to all walls of the feature, such that a shell feature with uniform thickness will be created.

3. Expand the **References** panel of the **Shell** tab, if not expanded by default, see Figure 9.134. The options in this panel are discussed below:

   Bodies to shell: The **All** radio button in the **Bodies to shell** area is used for creating shell features on all the bodies that are present in the graphics area. The **Selected** radio button in this area is used for creating shell features on the selected bodies only.

   Removed surfaces: The **Removed surfaces** collector is used for selecting faces of the model to be removed. Note that if you do not select any face of the model to be removed then a hollow solid model will be created.

   Non-default thickness: The **Non-default thickness** collector is used for selecting faces of the model on which different thickness is to be applied. Note that if you do not select any face of the model in this collector then a shell feature with uniform wall thickness will be created.

4. Ensure that the **Removed surfaces** collector is activated in the expanded **References** panel of the **Shell** tab to select the faces of the model to be removed.

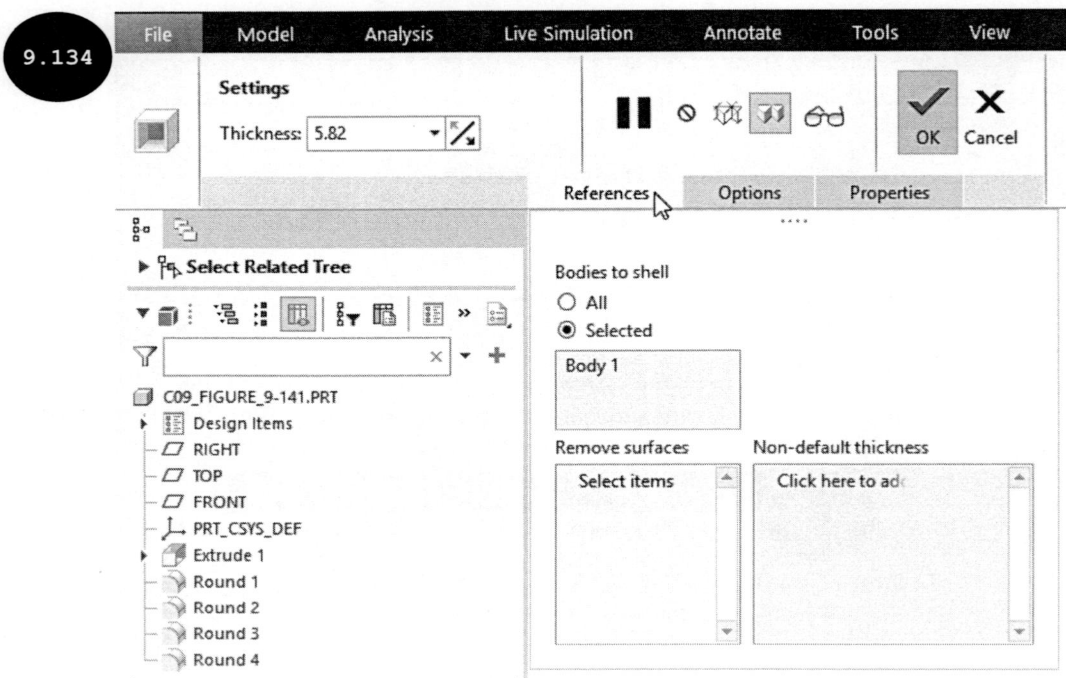

5. Click on the face of the model to be removed in the graphics area, see Figure 9.135. The selected face of the model gets removed from the model, see Figure 9.136. You can select a single face or multiple faces of the model to be removed. You can select multiple faces to be removed by pressing the CTRL key. Note that the names of the faces selected to remove appear in the **Removed surfaces** collector. If you do not select any face of the model to be removed, then a hollow shell feature will be created.

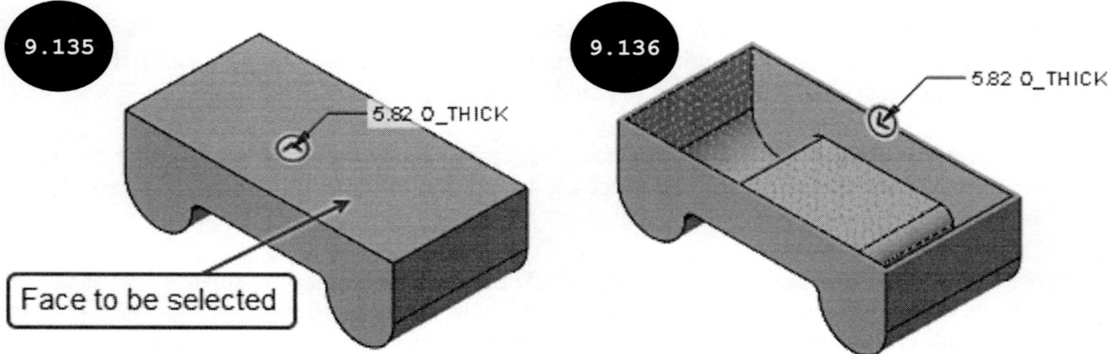

6. To specify different wall thickness for a face of the model, click on the **Non-default thickness** collector of the expanded **References** panel and then select a face of the model. The name of the selected face appears in the **Non-default thickness** collector with the default specified thickness value, see Figure 9.137. Next, enter a new thickness value for the selected face in the field that appears in front of its name in the **Non-default thickness** collector. Similarly, you can select multiple faces of the model by pressing the CTRL key and specifying different thickness value for each selected face of the model. Figure 9.138 shows the preview of a shell feature with different thickness values specified for the front and back faces of the model.

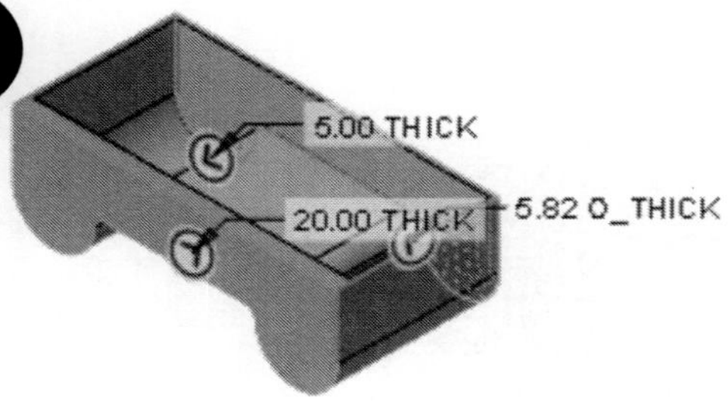

In Creo Parametric, you can also select the faces of the model to be excluded from a shell feature by using the **Options** panel of the **Shell** tab. The method for excluding faces from a shell feature is discussed below:

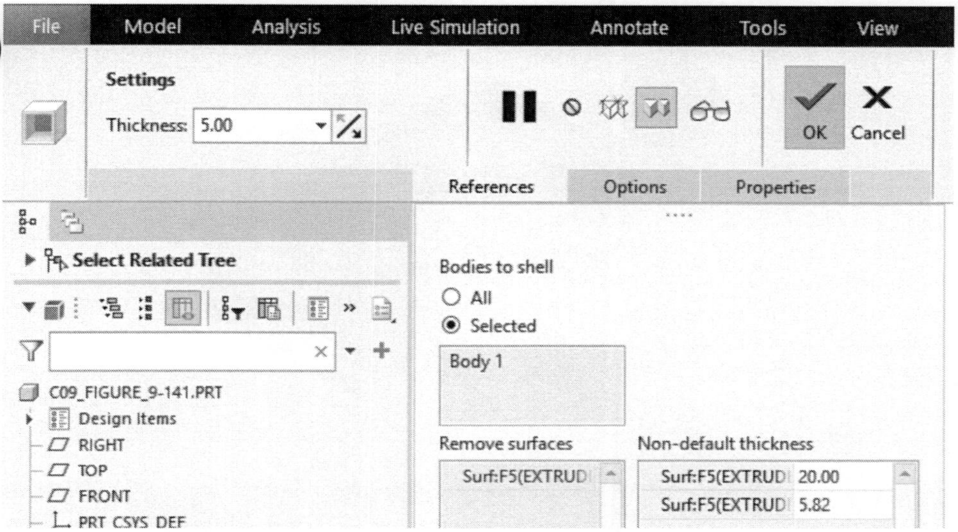

7. Expand the **Options** panel of the **Shell** tab and then activate the **Excluded surfaces** collector by clicking on it to select faces to be excluded from the shell feature. Next, select one or more faces of the model by pressing the CTRL key. The preview of the shell feature appears after excluding the selected faces, see Figure 9.139. In this figure, two faces are selected as the faces to be excluded. Note that the faces to be excluded should define a closed volume.

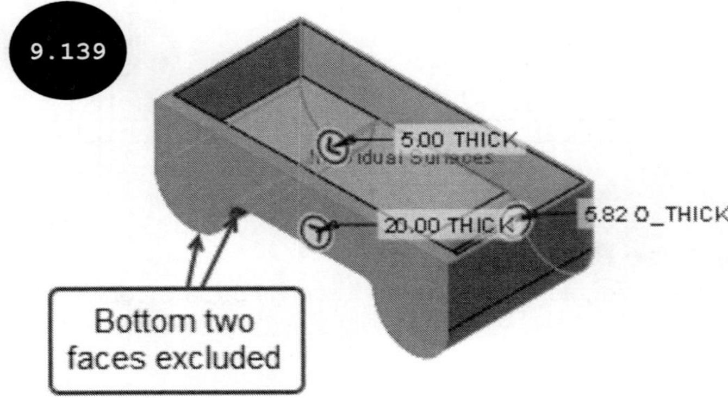

9.139

8. Click on the green tick-mark button. The shell feature is created, see Figure 9.140.

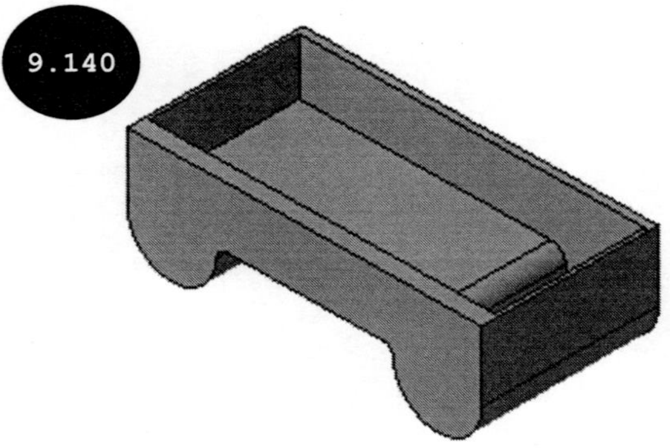

Tutorial 1

Create the model shown in Figure 9.141. All dimensions are in mm.

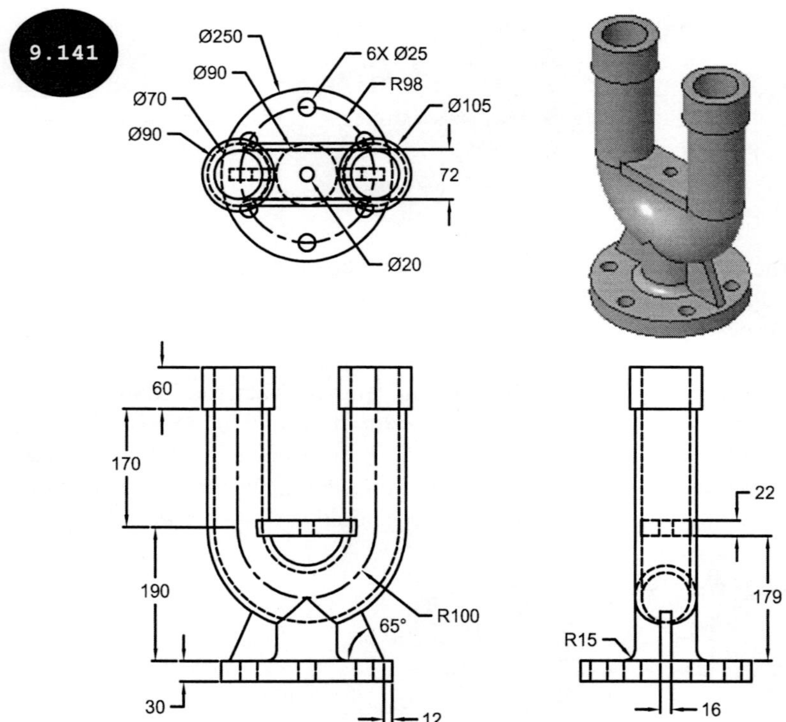

Section 1: Starting Creo Parametric

1. Start Creo Parametric by double-clicking on the Creo Parametric icon on your desktop.

Section 2: Setting the Working Directory

Now, you need to set the working directory to save the files of the current session of Creo Parametric.

1. Click on the **Select Working Directory** tool in the **Data** group of the **Home** tab, see Figure 9.142. The **Select Working Directory** window appears. In this window, browse to the *Creo Parametric > Chapter 9*. You need to create the *Chapter 9* folder inside the *Creo Parametric* folder. Next, click on the **OK** button. The working directory is set to <<*Creo Parametric\Chapter 9*\.

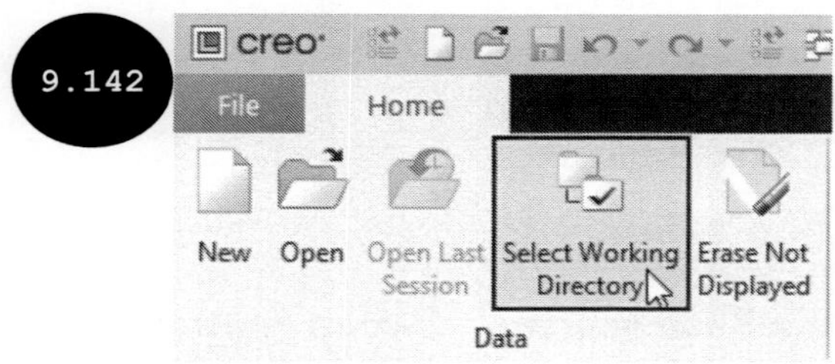

Section 3: Invoking the Part Mode

1. Click on the **New** tool in the **Data** group of the **Home** tab. The **New** dialog box appears, see Figure 9.143. Alternatively, press the CTRL + N to invoke the **New** dialog box.

2. Ensure that the **Part** radio button is selected in the **Type** area and the **Solid** radio button is selected in the **Sub-type** area of the dialog box, see Figure 9.143.

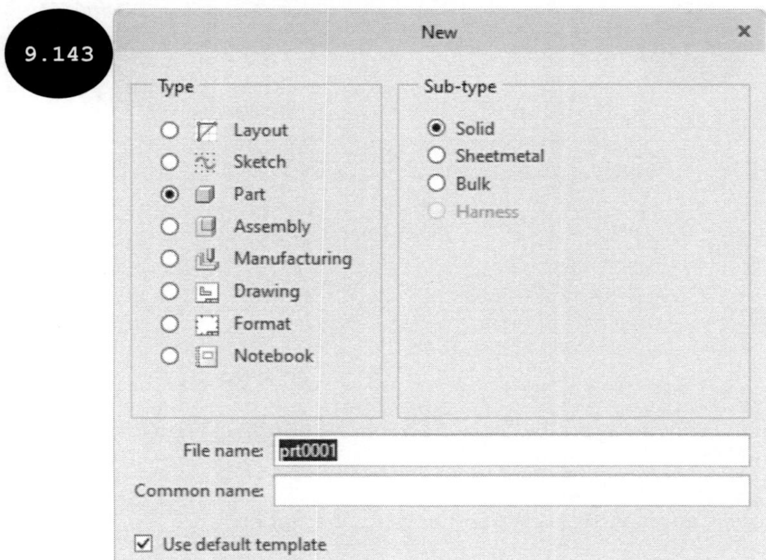

3. Enter **C09-Tutorial01** in the **File name** field of the dialog box as the name of the model.

4. Clear the **Use default template** check box and then click on the **OK** button in the dialog box. The **New File Options** dialog box appears, see Figure 9.144.

5. Select the **mmns_part_solid_abs** template in the **New File Options** dialog box and then click on the **OK** button. The Part mode is invoked with the **mmns_part_solid_abs** template.

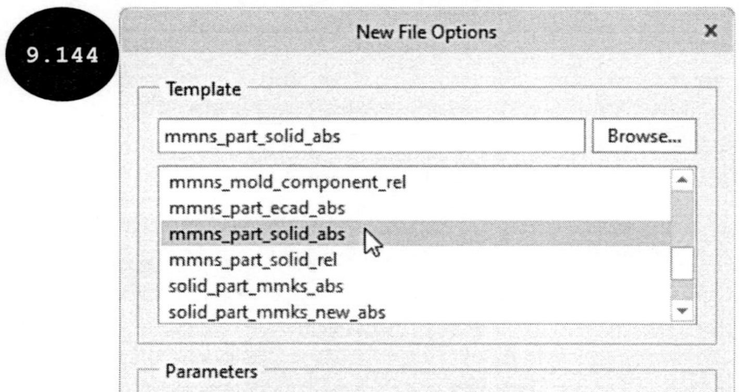

Section 4: Creating the Base Feature - Sweep Feature

The base feature of the model is a sweep feature.

1. Invoke the Sketching environment by selecting the Front plane as the sketching plane.

2. Create a sketch of the sweep feature as a trajectory, see Figure 9.145. In this figure, an equal constraint has been applied between the vertical lines of the sketch. Also, the connecting line and arc entities of the sketch have tangent constraints with each other.

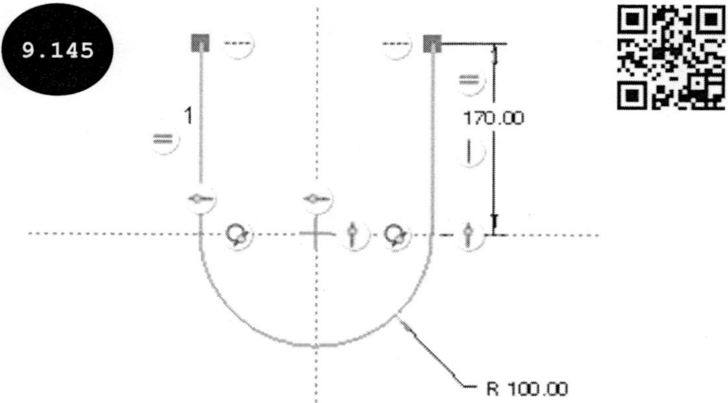

3. Exit the Sketching environment by clicking on the **OK** button in the **Close** group of the **Sketch** tab in the **Ribbon**.

4. Change the orientation of the sketch to standard orientation.

   After creating the trajectory of the sweep feature, you need to create the sweep feature.

5. Select the sketch that is created in the graphics area as the trajectory of the sweep feature, if not selected, by default.

6. Click on the **Sweep** tool in the **Shapes** group of the **Model** tab. The **Sweep** tab appears in the **Ribbon**. Also, an arrow appears on one end of the selected trajectory, and dimension handles appear on both ends of the trajectory, see Figure 9.146.

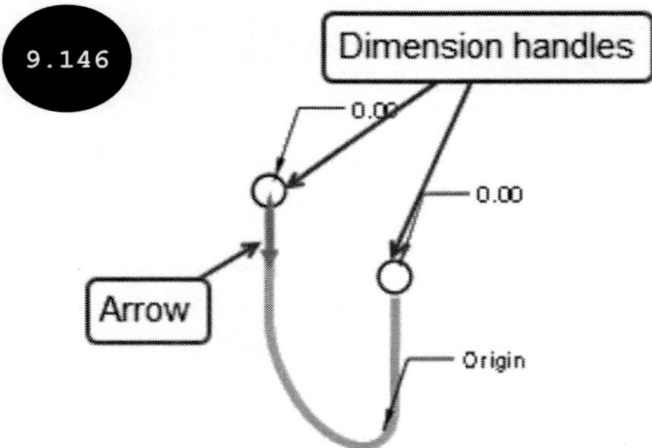

7. Ensure that the **Constant Section** button is activated in the **Options** area of the **Sweep** tab to create a constant section sweep.

8. Click on the **Sketch** button in the **Section** area of the **Sweep** tab. The Sketching environment is invoked and the sketching plane is oriented normal to the viewing direction. Note that two centerlines that are mutually perpendicular to each other define the origin of the sketch at their intersection.

9. Create a circle of diameter 90 mm as the section of the sweep feature, see Figure 9.147. Next, change the orientation of the sketch to standard orientation.

10. Exit the Sketching environment by clicking on the **OK** tool in the **Close** group of the **Sketch** tab. A preview of the constant sweep feature appears in the graphics area, see Figure 9.148.

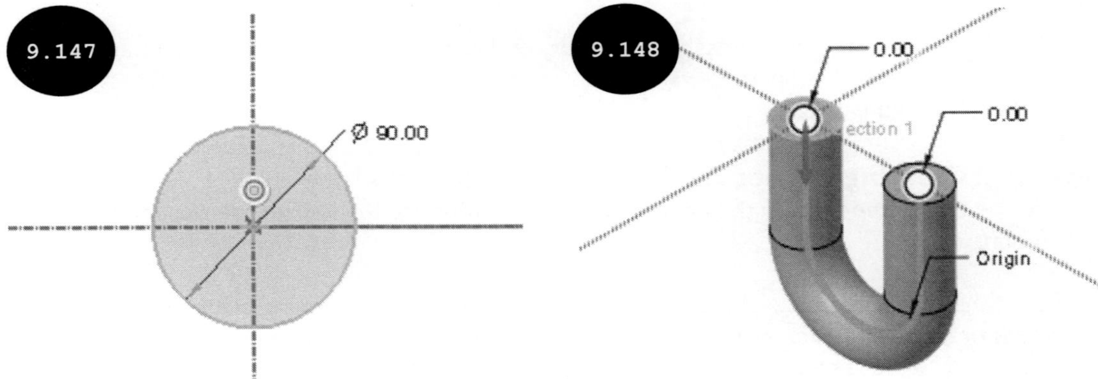

11. Click on the **Thicken Sketch** button in the **Settings** area of the **Sweep** tab to create a thin sweep feature, see Figure 9.149. The **Thickness value** field appears next to the **Thicken Sketch** button. Also, a preview of the thin sweep feature appears with the default thickness value in the graphics area.

12. Enter **10** in the **Thickness value** field of the **Sweep** tab and then press ENTER. A preview of the sweep feature appears as shown in Figure 9.150.

13. Change the thickness direction of the sweep feature inward by clicking on the **Flip Direction** button in the **Settings** area of the **Sweep** tab. Note that the **Flip Direction** button is used for changing the thickness direction along one side (inward), other side (outward), or both sides of the section.

14. Click on the green tick-mark button in the **Sweep** tab. A sweep feature of thickness 10 mm is created, see Figure 9.151.

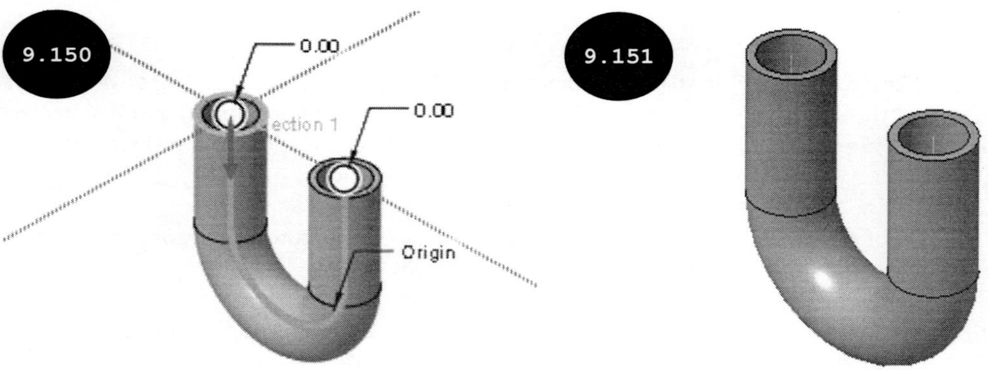

15. Hide the sketch that is created as the trajectory of the sweep feature in the graphics area. To do so, click on **Sketch 1** in the **Model Tree** and then click on the **Hide** tool in the Mini toolbar that appears, see Figure 9.152.

Section 5: Creating the Second Feature - Extrude Feature

1. Click on the **Extrude** tool in the **Shapes** group of the **Model** tab. The **Extrude** tab appears in the **Ribbon**.

2. Select the top planar face of the base feature (sweep) as the sketching plane for creating the sketch of the extrude feature, see Figure 9.153. The Sketching environment is invoked and the selected planar face becomes normal to the viewing direction.

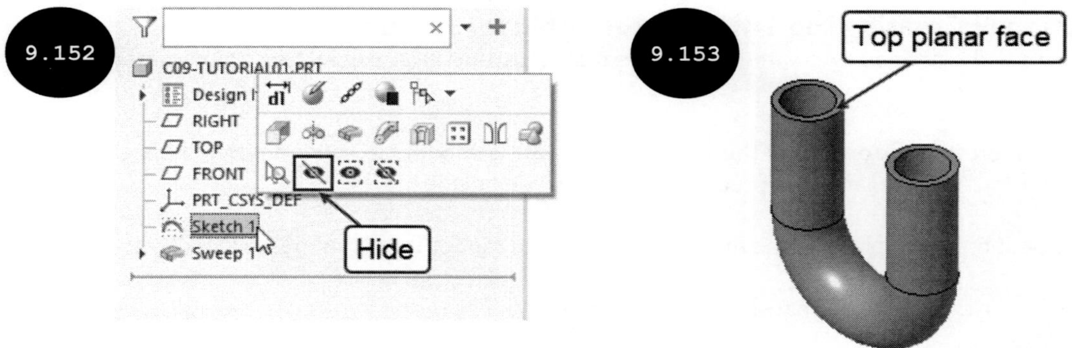

3. Create two circles as the sketch of the second feature, see Figure 9.154.

Note: The sketch of the second feature shown in Figure 9.154 has two circles: outer circle is of diameter 105 mm and the inner circle has equal constraint with the inner circular edge of the sweep feature. This is because the inner circle of the sketch has the same diameter as the inner circular edge of the feature also sharing the same center point.

4. Exit the Sketching environment. A preview of the extrude feature appears in the graphics area with default parameters, see Figure 9.155. Change the orientation of the model to standard orientation.

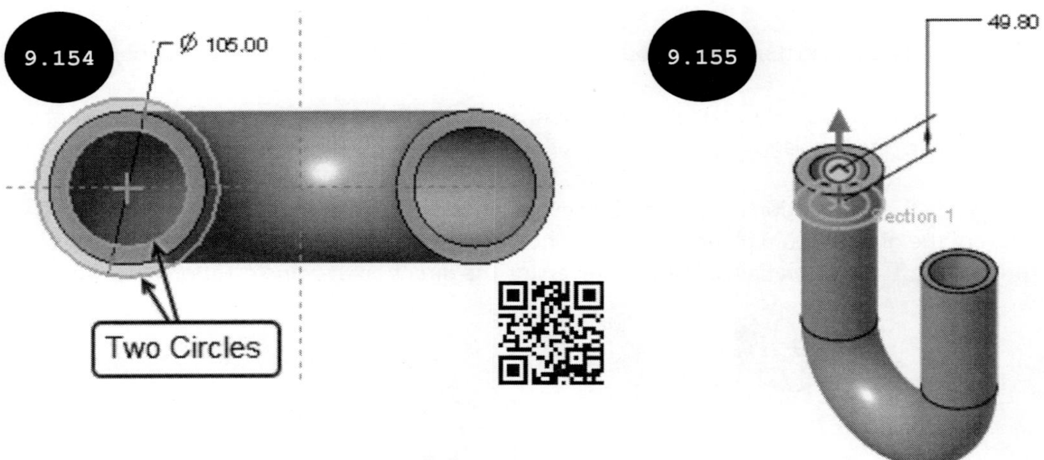

5. Enter **60** as the depth of extrusion in the **Value** field of the **Extrude** tab and then press ENTER. The preview of the extrude feature gets modified.

6. Click on the green tick-mark button in the **Extrude** tab. The extrude feature is created, see Figure 9.156.

Section 6: Creating the Third Feature - Mirror Feature

1. Select the previously created extrude feature (**Extrude 1**) as the feature to be mirrored in the **Model Tree**.

2. Click on the **Mirror** tool in the **Editing** group of the **Model** tab. The **Mirror** tab appears in the **Ribbon**. Also, you are prompted to select a mirroring plane.

3. Select the Right plane as the mirroring plane in the **Model Tree** or in the graphics area.

4. Click on the green tick-mark button in the **Mirror** tab. The mirror feature is created, see Figure 9.157.

Section 7: Creating the Fourth Feature - Extrude Feature

To create the sketch of the fourth feature (extrude), you need to create a datum plane at an offset distance of 190 mm from the Top plane.

1. Click on the **Plane** tool in the **Datum** group of the **Model** tab. The **Datum Plane** dialog box appears.

2. Select the Top Plane as a reference in the **Model Tree** or in the graphics area. The preview of an offset datum plane appears.

3. Enter **-190** in the **Translation** field of the **Offset** area in the dialog box and then press ENTER. The preview of the offset datum plane appears as shown in Figure 9.158. Note that the negative value entered in the **Translation** field is used for reversing the direction of plane creation to downward.

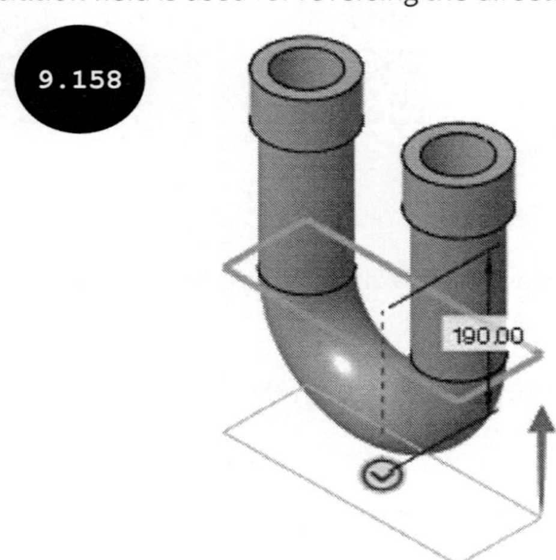

4. Click on the **OK** button in the dialog box. The offset datum plane is created, see Figure 9.159.

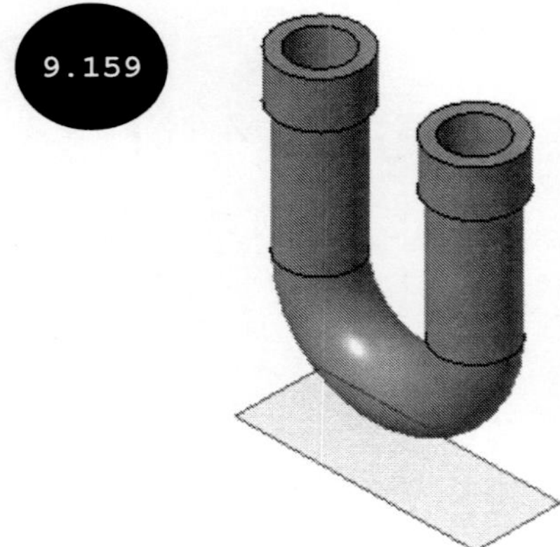

Note: In Figure 9.159, all datum planes are turned off except the newly created datum plane for clarity of the image.

After creating the datum plane, create the fourth feature of the model.

5. Click on the **Extrude** tool in the **Shapes** group of the **Model** tab. The **Extrude** tab appears in the **Ribbon**.

6. Select the newly created datum plane as the sketching plane for creating the sketch of the fourth feature (extrude). The Sketching environment is invoked and the selected datum plane becomes normal to the viewing direction.

7. Create a circle of diameter 90 mm as the sketch of the fourth feature, see Figure 9.160. Note that the center point of the circle is at the origin.

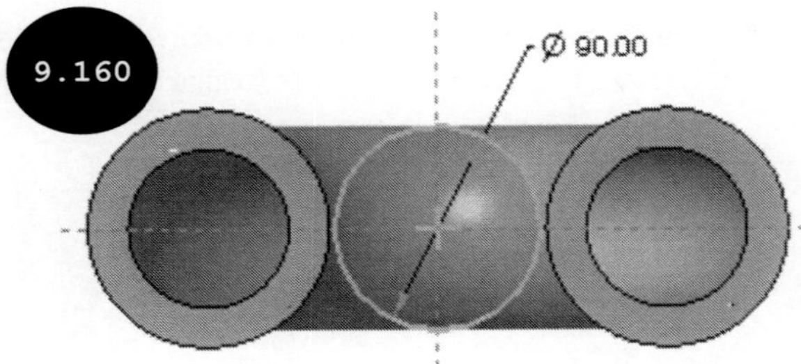

8. Exit the Sketching environment. The preview of the extrude feature appears in the graphics area with default parameters. Next, change the orientation of the model to standard orientation.

9. Expand the **Options** panel of the **Extrude** tab and then select the **To Next** option in the **Side 1** drop-down list. The preview of the extrude feature gets terminated at its nearest intersection, see Figure 9.161.

10. Click on the green tick-mark button in the **Extrude** tab. The extrude feature is created, see Figure 9.162.

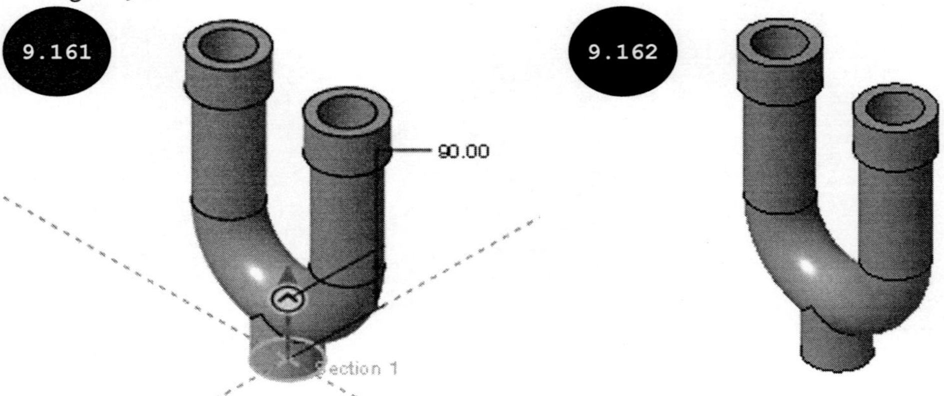

Section 8: Creating the Fifth Feature - Extrude Feature

1. Click on the **Extrude** tool in the **Shapes** group of the **Model** tab. The **Extrude** tab appears in the **Ribbon**.

2. Select the datum plane (**DTM1**) as the sketching plane, which is created at an offset distance of 190 mm from the Top plane. The Sketching environment is invoked and the selected datum plane becomes normal to the viewing direction.

3. Create a circle of diameter 250 mm as the sketch of the fifth feature, see Figure 9.163.

4. Exit the Sketching environment. The preview of the extrude feature appears in the graphics area with default parameters. Next, change the orientation of the model to standard orientation.

5. Enter **30** as the depth of extrusion in the **Value** field of the **Extrude** tab and then press ENTER. The preview of the extrude feature gets modified.

6. Click on the **Flip Direction** button in the **Extrude** tab to reverse the direction of extrusion downward. The preview of the extrude feature appears similar to the one shown in Figure 9.164.

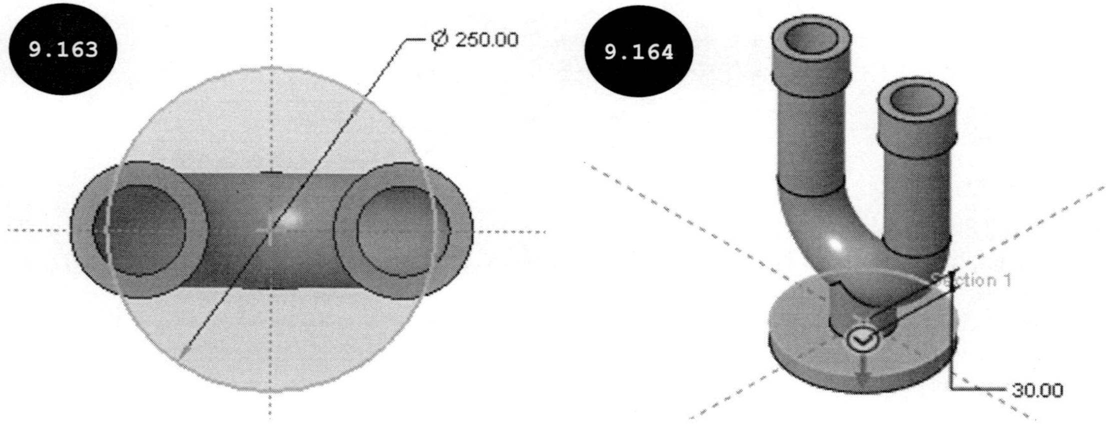

7. Click on the green tick-mark button in the **Extrude** tab. The extrude feature is created, see Figure 9.165.

Section 9: Creating the Sixth Feature - Extrude Cut Feature

1. Click on the **Extrude** tool in the **Shapes** group of the **Model** tab. The **Extrude** tab appears in the **Ribbon**.

2. Select the top planar face of the fifth feature (previously created extruded feature) as the sketching plane.

3. Create a circle of diameter 25 mm as the sketch of the sixth feature, see Figure 9.166.

4. Exit the Sketching environment. The preview of the extrude feature appears in the graphics area with default parameters. Next, change the orientation of the model to standard orientation.

5. Click on the **Flip Direction** button in the **Extrude** tab. The direction of extrusion changes to downward and the **Remove Material** button gets activated, automatically. Also, the preview of the cut feature appears in the graphics area.

6. Select the **Through All** option in the **Side 1** drop-down list.

7. Click on the green tick-mark button in the **Extrude** tab. The extrude cut feature is created, see Figure 9.167.

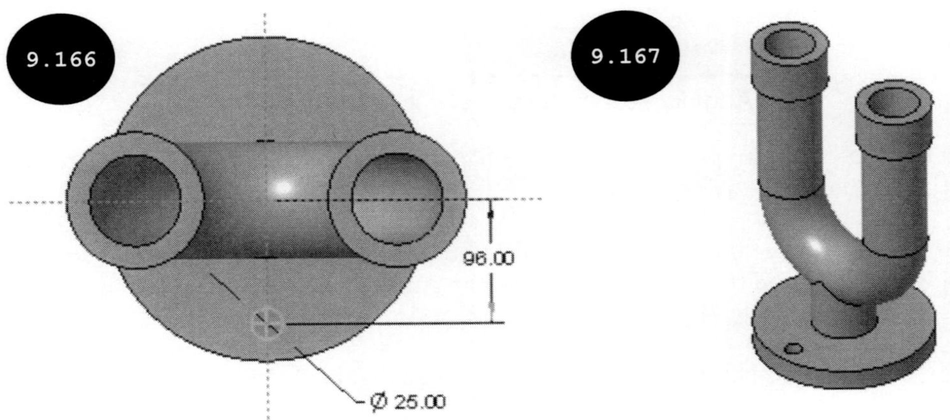

Section 10: Creating the Seventh Feature - Axis Pattern

1. Select the previously created extrude cut feature (sixth feature) in the **Model Tree**.

2. Click on the **Pattern** tool in the **Editing** group of the **Model** tab. The **Pattern** tab appears in the **Ribbon**.

3. Select the **Axis** option in the **Type** drop-down list of the **Pattern** tab. The options for creating an axis pattern appear in the **Pattern** tab. Also, you are prompted to select an axis to define the angular direction of the axis pattern.

4. Select the Y-axis of the default coordinate system to define the angular direction of the pattern. Black dots appear in the graphics area representing the preview of the pattern instances, see Figure 9.168.

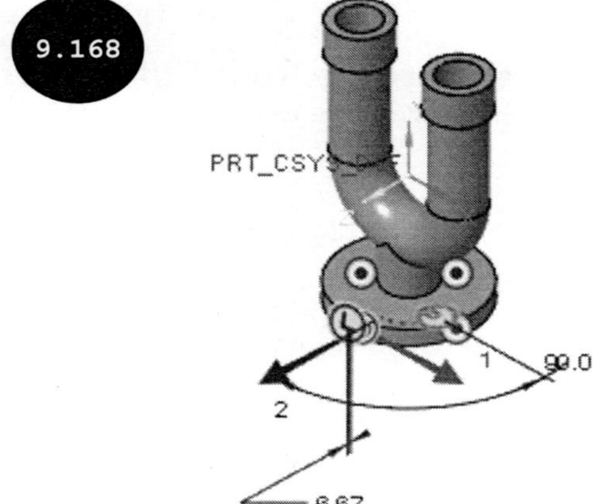

5. Click on the **Angular extent** button in the **Pattern** tab (see Figure 9.169), to arrange all the pattern instances equally within a specified total angle value. The **Angular extent** field gets enabled in the **Pattern** tab.

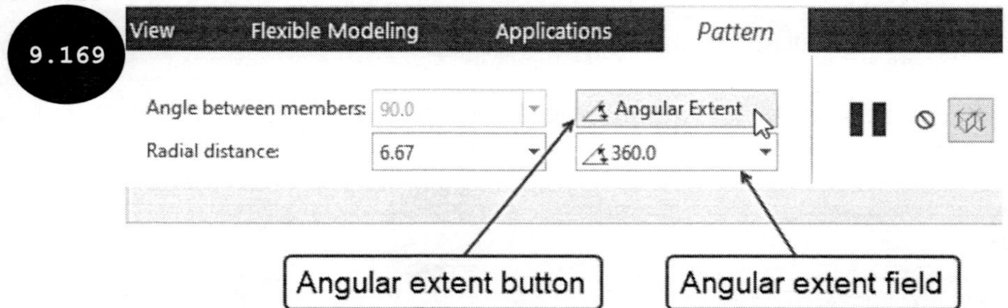

6. Ensure that the **360**-degree angle value is specified in the **Angular extent** field of the **Pattern** tab as the total angle value of the axis pattern.

7. Enter **6** as the number of pattern instances to be created, circularly in the **1st direction members** field of the **Pattern** tab, and then press ENTER. All the pattern instances get arranged equally within the specified total angle value.

8. Click on the green tick-mark button in the **Pattern** tab. The axis pattern is created, see Figure 9.170.

9.170

Section 11: Creating the Eighth Feature - Round

1. Click on the **Round** tool in the **Engineering** group. The **Round** tab appears.

2. Select the circular edge of the model to create a round, see Figure 9.171. The preview of the fillet appears in the graphics area with the default radius.

3. Enter **15** in the **Radius** field in the **Dimension Scheme** area of the **Round** tab.

4. Expand the **Sets** panel of the **Round** tab and then ensure that the **Circular** option is selected in the **Profile** drop-down list.

5. Click on the green tick-mark button in the **Round** tab. A fillet of radius 15 mm is created, see Figure 9.172.

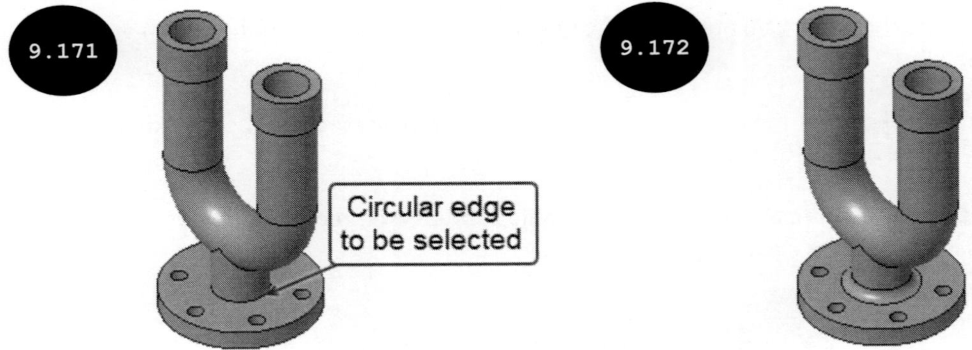

9.171 9.172

Section 12: Creating the Ninth Feature - Rib Feature

1. Click on the arrow next to the **Rib** tool in the **Engineering** group and then click on the **Profile Rib** tool in the flyout that appears, see Figure 9.173. The **Profile Rib** tab appears in the **Ribbon**.

9.173

2. Select the Front plane in the **Model Tree** or in the graphics area as the sketching plane to create the sketch of the rib feature. The Front plane becomes normal to the sketching plane.

3. Create an inclined line as the sketch of the rib feature, see Figure 9.174. Note that both the open ends of the sketch lie on the edges of the model, see Figure 9.174.

4. Exit the Sketching environment and click on the **Flip Direction** button in the **Depth** area of the **Profile Rib** tab, if needed. A preview of the rib feature appears with the default thickness value, see Figure 9.175.

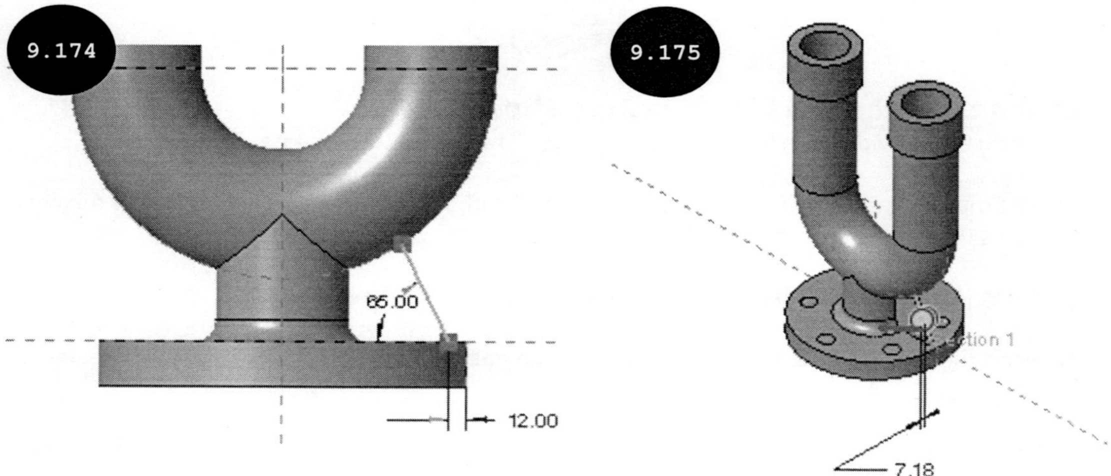

5. Enter **16** as the thickness value of the rib feature in the **Thickness** field in the **Width** area of the **Profile Rib** tab.

6. Change the thickness of the rib to both sides of the rib profile by using the **Thickness Option** button of the **Profile Rib** tab.

7. Click on the green tick-mark button in the **Profile Rib** tab. The profile rib feature of specified thickness is created, see Figure 9.176.

Section 13: Creating the Tenth Feature - Mirror Feature

1. Select the previously created rib feature (**Profile Rib 1**) as the feature to be mirrored in the **Model Tree**.

2. Click on the **Mirror** tool in the **Editing** group of the **Model** tab. The **Mirror** tab appears in the **Ribbon**. Also, you are prompted to select a mirroring plane.

3. Select the Right plane as the mirroring plane in the **Model Tree** or in the graphics area.

4. Click on the green tick-mark button in the **Mirror** tab. The mirror feature is created, see Figure 9.177.

Section 14: Creating the Eleventh Feature - Extrude Feature

1. Click on the **Extrude** tool in the **Shapes** group of the **Model** tab. The **Extrude** tab appears.

2. Select the Right plane as the sketching plane in the **Model Tree** or in the graphics area. The Sketching environment is invoked.

3. Create a rectangle (72 x 22) as the sketch of the eleventh feature, see Figure 9.178. Note that the center of the rectangle is at the origin.

4. Exit the Sketching environment. A preview of the extrude feature appears in the graphics area with default parameters. Next, change the orientation of the model to standard orientation.

5. Expand the **Options** panel of the **Extrude** tab. Next, select the **To Next** options in the **Side 1** and **Side 2** drop-down lists of the expanded **Options** panel.

6. Click on the green tick-mark button in the **Extrude** tab. The extrude feature is created, see Figure 9.179.

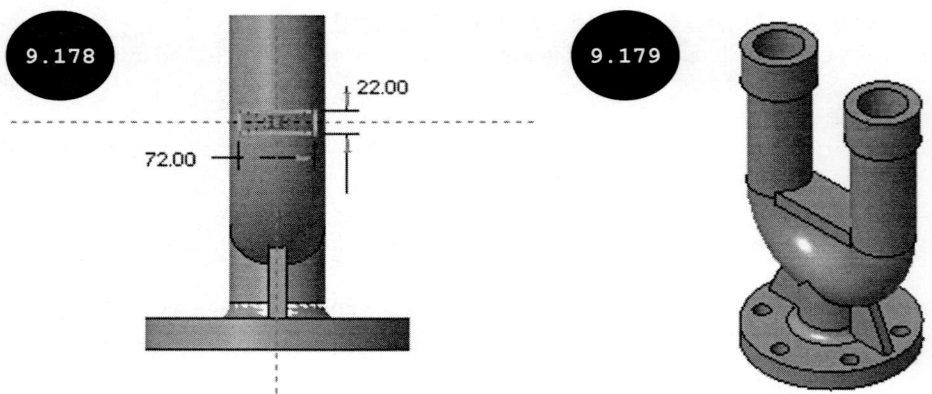

Section 15: Creating the Twelfth Feature - Extrude Cut Feature

1. Click on the **Extrude** tool in the **Shapes** group of the **Model** tab. The **Extrude** tab appears.

2. Click on the top planar face of the eleventh feature (previously created extrude feature) as the sketching plane.

3. Create a circle of diameter 20 mm, whose center point is at the origin, as the sketch of the twelfth feature, see Figure 9.180.

4. Exit the Sketching environment. A preview of the extrude feature appears in the graphics area with default parameters. Next, change the orientation of the model to standard orientation.

5. Click on the **Flip Direction** button in the **Depth** area of the **Extrude** tab. The direction of extrusion changes to downward and the **Remove Material** button gets activated in the **Settings** area of the **Extrude** tab, automatically. Also, the preview of the cut feature appears in the graphics area.

6. Expand the **Options** panel of the **Extrude** tab and then select the **To Next** option in the **Side 1** drop-down list.

7. Click on the green tick-mark button in the **Extrude** tab. The extrude cut feature is created, see Figure 9.181.

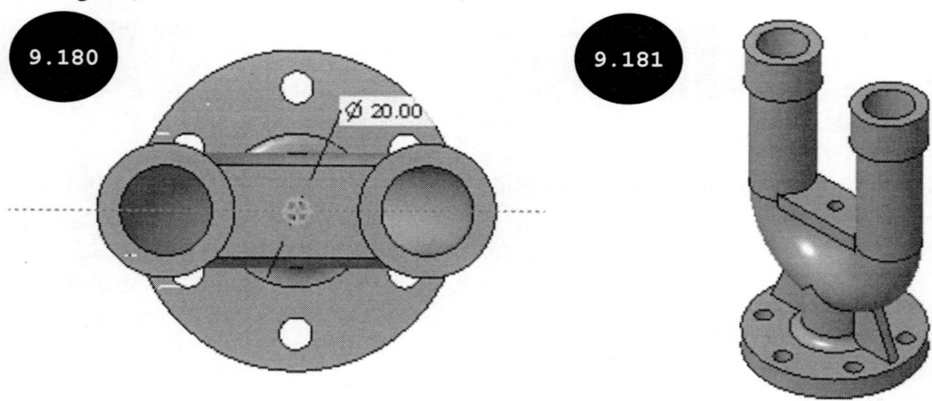

Section 16: Saving the Model

1. Click on the **Save** tool in the **Quick Access Toolbar**. The **Save Object** dialog box appears.

2. Click on the **OK** button in the dialog box. The model is saved with the name **C09-Tutorial01** in the specified working directory (*<<\Creo Parametric\Chapter 9*).

Tutorial 2

Create the model shown in Figure 9.182. All dimensions are in mm.

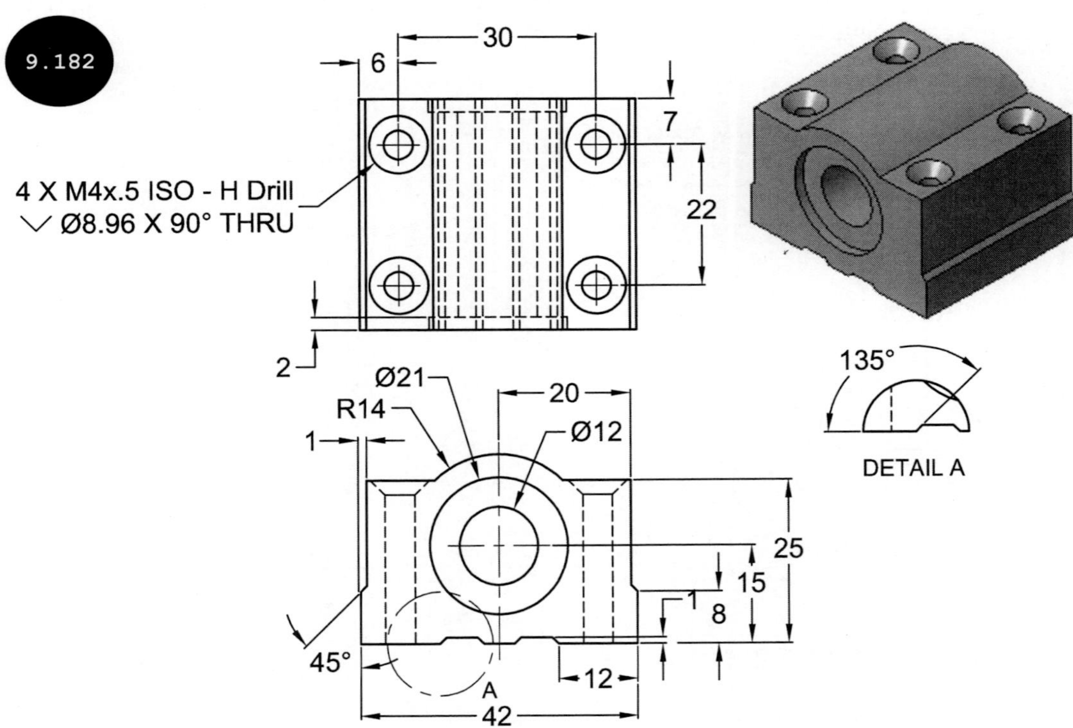

Section 1: Starting Creo Parametric and Setting the Working Directory

1. Start Creo Parametric by double-clicking on the Creo Parametric icon on your desktop.

2. Set the working directory to <<\Creo Parametric\Chapter 9\.

Section 2: Invoking the Part Mode

1. Invoke the Part mode with the **mmns_part_solid_abs** template by using the **New** tool. Note that you need to specify the **C09-Tutorial02** as the name of the model while invoking the Part mode.

Section 3: Creating the Base Feature - Extrude Feature

The base feature of the model is an extruded feature.

1. Click on the **Extrude** tool in the **Shapes** group of the **Model** tab. The **Extrude** tab appears.

2. Select the Front plane as the sketching plane to create the sketch of the extruded feature. The Sketching environment is invoked and the selected plane becomes normal to the viewing direction.

3. Create the sketch of the extrude feature, see Figure 9.183. Note that you need to apply the required constraints to make the sketch fully defined.

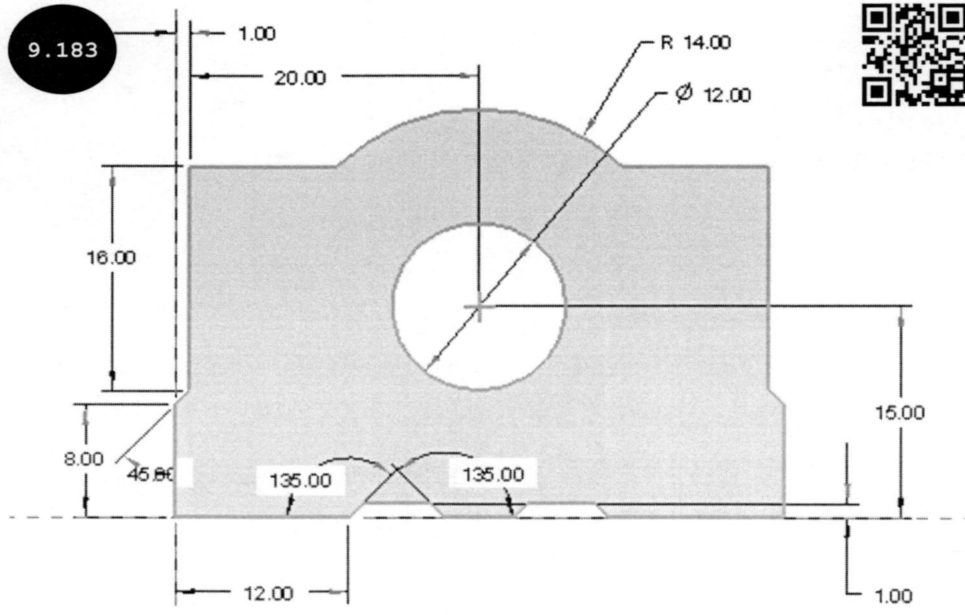

4. Exit the Sketching environment. A preview of the extrude feature appears in the graphics area with default parameters. Next, change the orientation of the model to standard orientation.

5. Enter **36** as the depth of extrusion in the **Value** field in the **Depth** area of the **Extrude** tab and then press ENTER. The preview of the extrude feature gets modified.

6. Expand the **Options** panel of the **Extrude** tab and then select the **Symmetric** option in the **Side 1** drop-down list to add the material symmetrically on both sides of the sketching plane, see Figure 9.184.

7. Click on the green tick-mark button in the **Extrude** tab. The extrude feature is created, see Figure 9.185.

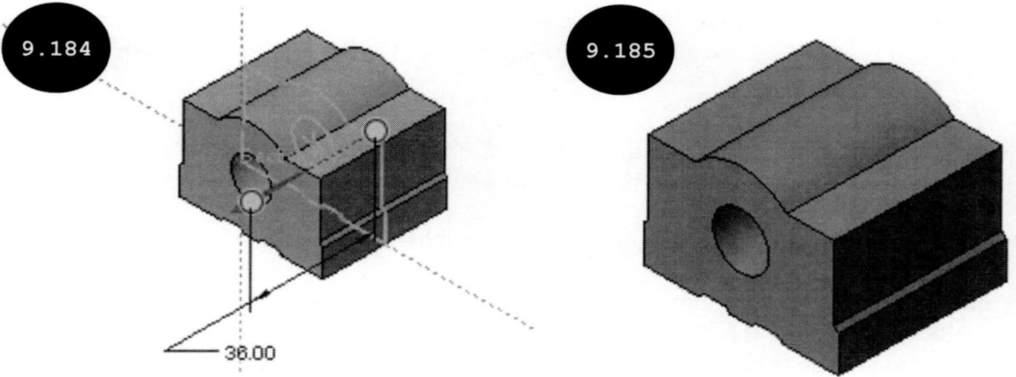

Section 4: Creating the Second Feature - Extrude Cut Feature

1. Click on the **Extrude** tool in the **Shapes** group of the **Model** tab. The **Extrude** tab appears.

2. Select the front planar face of the previously created extrude feature as the sketching plane.

3. Create a circle of diameter 21 mm as the sketch of the second feature, see Figure 9.186.

4. Exit the Sketching environment. A preview of the extrude feature appears in the graphics area with default parameters. Next, change the orientation of the model to standard orientation.

5. Click on the **Flip Direction** button in the **Depth** area of the **Extrude** tab to reverse the direction of extrusion.

6. Ensure that the **Remove Material** button is activated in the **Settings** area of the **Extrude** tab to create a feature by removing the material from the model. Also, the preview of the cut feature appears in the graphics area.

7. Enter **2** as the depth of extrusion in the **Value** field in the **Depth** area of the **Extrude** tab and then press ENTER. The preview of the extrude feature gets modified.

8. Click on the green tick-mark button in the **Extrude** tab. The extrude cut feature is created, see Figure 9.187.

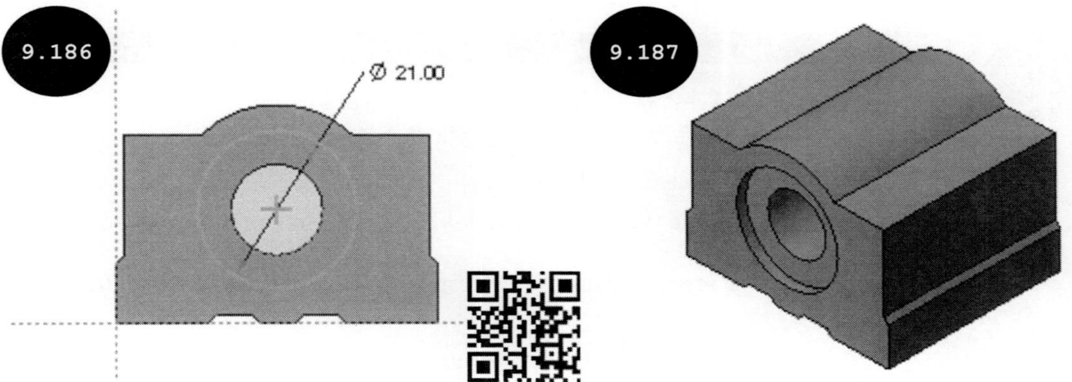

Section 5: Creating the Third Feature - Mirror Feature

1. Select the previously created extrude cut feature (**Extrude 2**) as the feature to be mirrored in the **Model Tree**.

2. Click on the **Mirror** tool in the **Editing** group of the **Model** tab. The **Mirror** tab appears in the **Ribbon**. Also, you are prompted to select a mirroring plane.

3. Select the Front plane as the mirroring plane in the **Model Tree** or in the graphics area.

4. Click on the green tick-mark button in the **Mirror** tab. The mirror feature is created, see Figure 9.188. In this figure, the display style of the model has been changed to the 'Wireframe' display style to view the mirror feature that is created at the back face of the model.

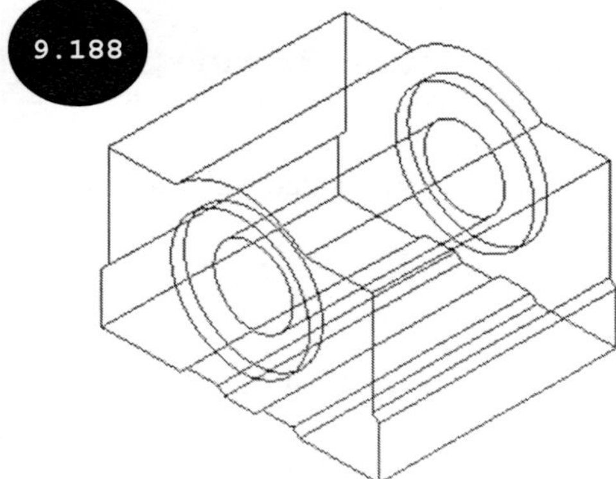
9.188

Section 6: Creating the Fourth Feature - Hole Feature

The fourth feature of the model is a standard hole feature.

1. Click on the **Hole** tool in the **Engineering** group of the **Model** tab. The **Hole** tab appears in the **Ribbon**.

2. Click on the **Standard** button in the **Type** area of the **Hole** tab to activate it for creating a standard hole, see Figure 9.189.

3. Click on the **Drilled** button in the **Profile** area of the **Hole** tab to activate it for creating a drilled hole, see Figure 9.189.

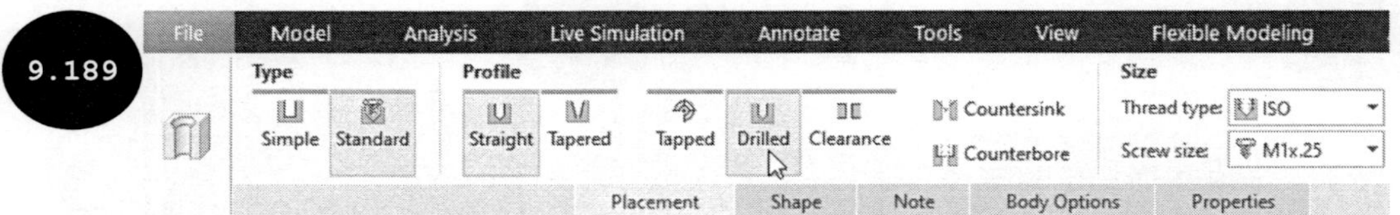

9.189

4. Select the **ISO** option in the **Thread type** drop-down list in the **Size** area of the **Hole** tab.

5. Select the **M4x.5** option in the **Screw size** drop-down list of the **Hole** tab as the size of the screw to be inserted into the hole.

6. Select the **Through All** option in the **Side 1** drop-down list of the **Hole** tab to create a through hole, see Figure 9.190.

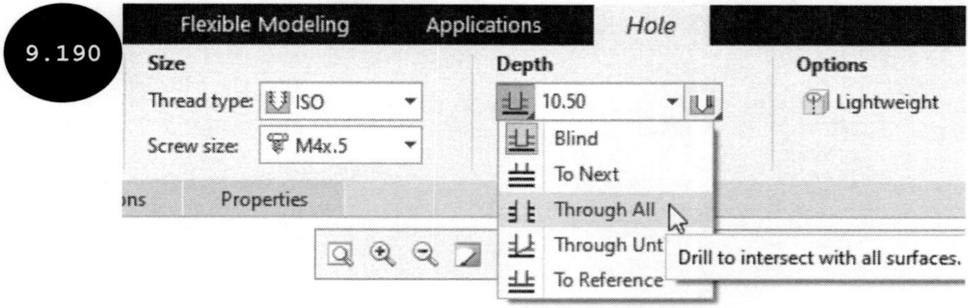

7. Click on the **Countersink** button in the **Profile** area of the **Hole** tab to create a countersink hole.

   After specifying all the required specifications for the standard hole to be created, you need to define its placement face on the model.

8. Click on the top planar face of the model as the placement face of the hole, see Figure 9.191. A preview of the hole appears with default specifications and two placement handles, see Figure 9.192.

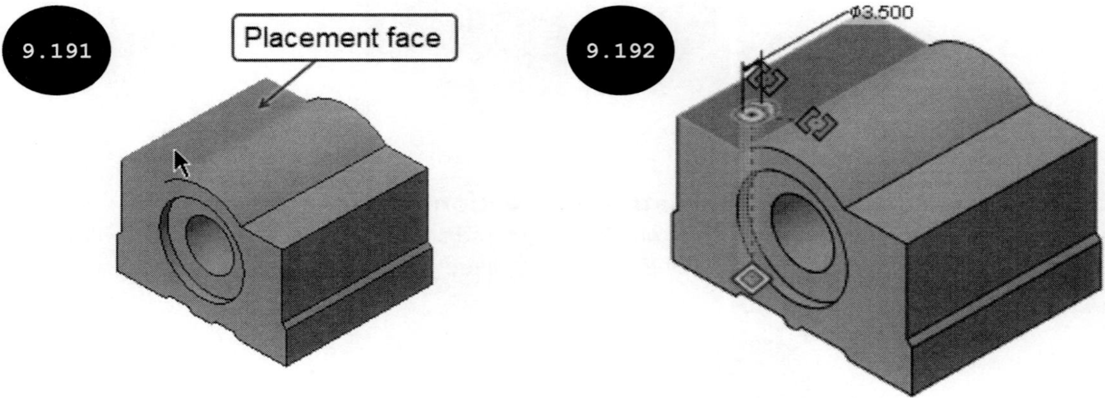

9. Drag and drop the placement handle that appears in the preview of the hole on the front face of the model as the first reference to define the placement of the hole.

10. Similarly, drag and drop the second placement handle to the left face of the model as the second reference to define the placement of the hole. A preview of the hole appears as per the required specifications, see Figure 9.193.

11. Edit the dimension values that define the placement of the hole in the graphics area such that the center of the hole measures 7 mm from the front reference face and 5 mm from the left reference face of the model, see Figure 9.194. Note that you can edit a dimension value by double-clicking on it in the graphics area.

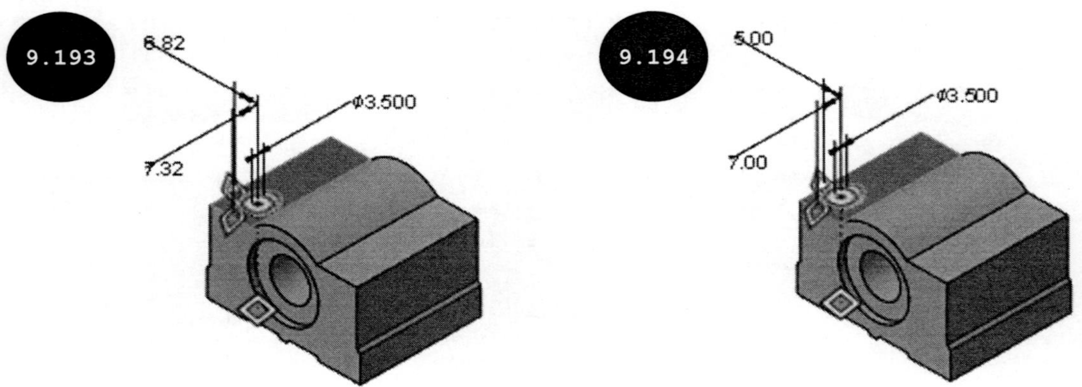

12. Click on the green tick-mark button in the **Hole** tab. A standard hole of the required specification is created, see Figure 9.195.

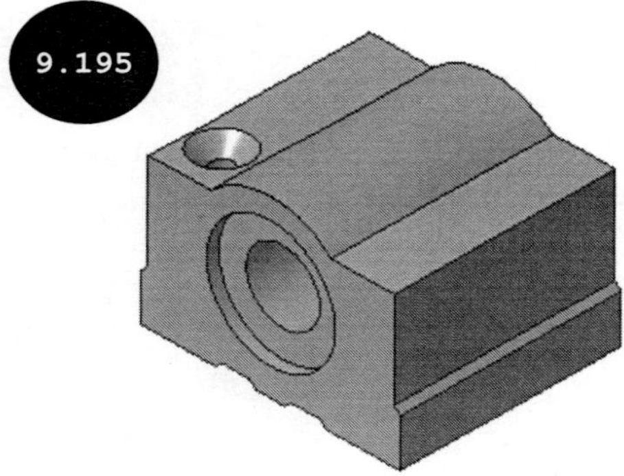

Section 7: Creating the Fifth Feature - Direction Pattern

1. Create the direction pattern of the previously created standard hole by using the **Pattern** tool to create the remaining instances of the hole, see Figure 9.196. This figure shows the final model after creating all its features.

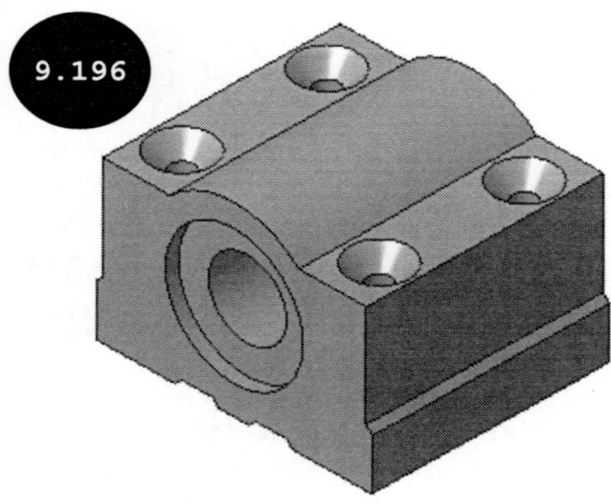

Section 8: Saving the Model

1. Click on the **Save** tool in the **Quick Access Toolbar**. The **Save Object** dialog box appears.
2. Click on the **OK** button in the dialog box. The model is saved with the name **C09-Tutorial02** in the specified working directory (<<*Creo Parametric**Chapter 9*\).

Hands-on Test Drive 1

Create the model shown in Figure 9.197. All dimensions are in mm.

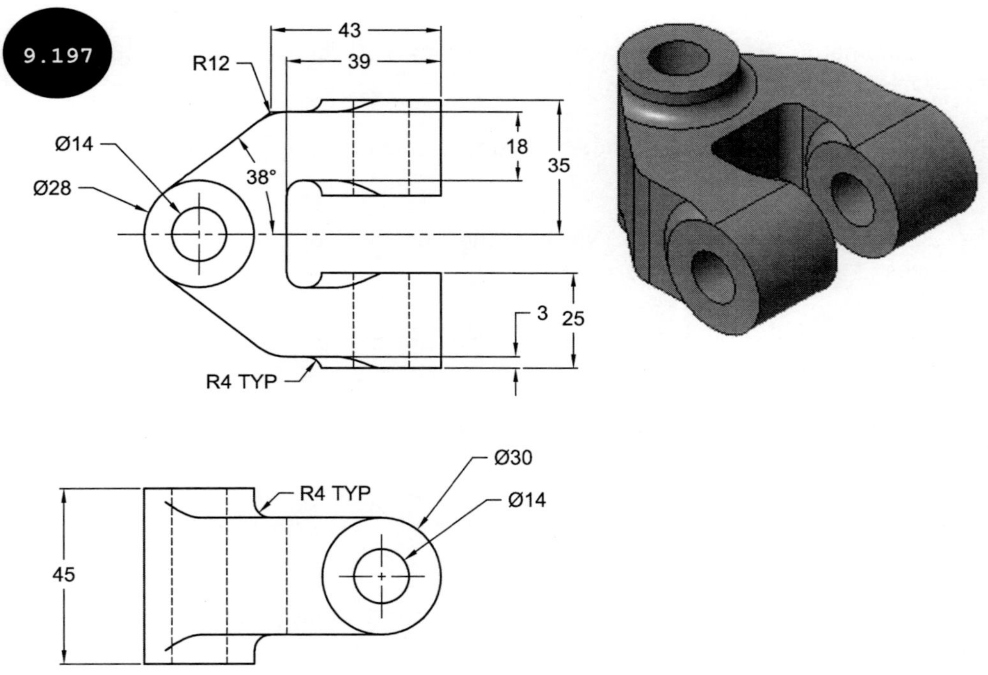

Summary

The chapter discussed how to create simple holes using a predefined rectangle profile, a standard hole profile (countersink, counterbore, or tip angle), and a sketched profile. It also explained how to create industry-standard holes such as tapped, tapered, drilled, and clearance as per the standard specifications by using the **Hole** tool, how to create cosmetic threads that are used to represent real threads on the holes, fasteners, and cylindrical features, reducing the complexity of a model and improving the overall performance of the system.

The chapter also discussed various types of rounds: constant radius round, variable radius round, curve driven round, and full round, along with the methods for creating rounds of constant radii on all the edges (convex and concave) of the model, automatically by using the **Auto Round** tool, creating an edge chamfer and a corner chamfer by using the **Edge Chamfer** and **Corner Chamfer** tools, respectively. Also, methods for creating a profile rib and a trajectory rib by using the **Profile Rib** and **Trajectory Rib** tools, respectively, and creating shell features were discussed.

Questions

Complete and verify the following sentences:

- In Creo Parametric, you can create a simple hole using a predefined rectangle profile, a standard hole profile, or a _________ profile.
- The _________ tool is used for adding cosmetic threads to holes, fasteners, and cylindrical features of a model.
- The _________ option is used for defining the placement of a hole by specifying two linear references.
- The _________ button of the **Hole** tab is used for creating a simple hole with a user-defined sketched profile.
- In Creo Parametric, you can create industry-standard holes such as tapped, tapered, _________, and _________ by using the **Hole** tool.
- A _________ round is created such that its radius is driven by a curve along the edge of a model.
- The _________ tool is used for creating rounds of constant radii on all the edges (convex and concave) of the model, automatically.
- A _________ feature acts as a supporting feature and is generally used for increasing the strength of a model.
- The _________ tool is used for creating a thin-walled feature.
- You can create a profile rib feature by using an open or closed sketch. (True/False).
- You cannot create a trajectory rib feature by using a closed sketch. (True/False).
- In Creo Parametric, you can create a shell feature by removing one or more faces of a model. (True/False).

10

Working with Assemblies - I

In this chapter, the following topics will be discussed:

- Bottom-up Assembly Approach
- Top-down Assembly Approach
- Invoking the Assembly Mode
- Creating an Assembly by using Bottom-up Approach
- Fixing the First Assembly Component
- Applying Constraints
- Moving/Rotating Individual Components
- Editing Constraints

In the earlier chapters, you have learned about the basic and advanced techniques of creating real world mechanical components. In this chapter, you will learn about different techniques for creating mechanical assemblies. An assembly is made up of two or more than two components joined together by applying constraints. You will learn about applying constraints later in this chapter. Figure 10.1 shows an assembly, in which multiple components are assembled with respect to each other by applying the required constraints.

10.1

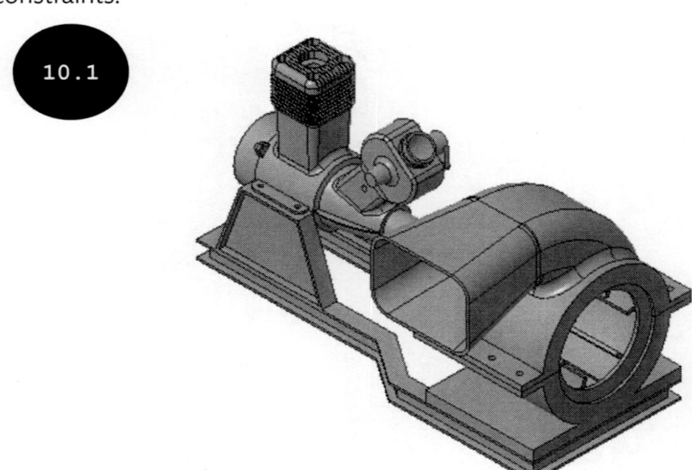

In Creo Parametric, you can create assemblies in the Assembly mode by using two approaches: Bottom-up Assembly Approach and Top-down Assembly Approach. You can also use a combination of these approaches for creating an assembly. Both approaches are discussed next.

Bottom-up Assembly Approach

The Bottom-up Assembly Approach is the most widely used approach for assembling components. In this approach, first, all the components of the assembly are created one by one in the Part mode and saved in a common location. Later, all the components are inserted one by one in the Assembly mode and then assembled with respect to each other by applying the required constraints.

Tip: Creo Parametric has bidirectional association between all its modes. As a result, if any change or modification is made to a component in the Part mode, the same change automatically replicates or reflects in the Assembly and Drawing modes as well, and vice-versa.

Top-down Assembly Approach

In the Top-down Assembly Approach, all the components of the assembly are created within the Assembly mode. It helps in creating a concept-based design, in which new components of an assembly are created by taking reference from the existing components.

Invoking the Assembly Mode

In Creo Parametric, to invoke the Assembly mode for creating assemblies, click on the **New** tool in the **Data** group of the **Home** tab or in the **Quick Access Toolbar**. The **New** dialog box appears, see Figure 10.2. Alternatively, press CTRL + N to invoke the **New** dialog box.

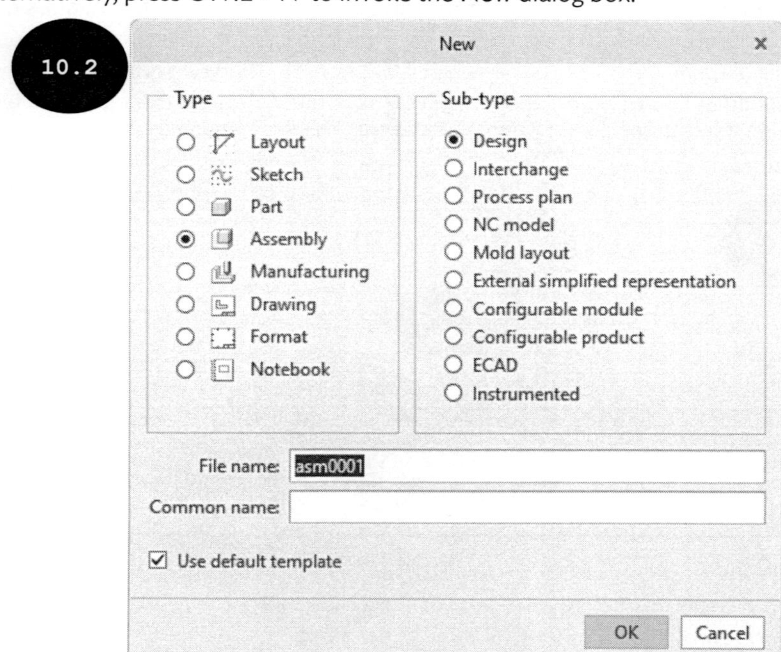

In the **New** dialog box, select the **Assembly** radio button in the **Type** area and the **Design** radio button in the **Sub-type** area, see Figure 10.2. Next, enter the name of the assembly file in the **File name** field of the dialog box. By default, the **Use default template** check box is selected in the dialog box. As a result, the default Creo template with a predefined unit system is used for the assembly file. To select a template other than the default one, clear the **Use default template** check box and then click on the **OK** button in the dialog box. The **New File Options** dialog box appears, see Figure 10.3. In this dialog box, you can select the required template for the assembly file. For example, to open the assembly file with the Metric unit system, you can select the **mmns_asm_design_abs** template in the dialog box. In this template, length is measured in millimeters, mass is measured in Newton, and time is measured in seconds. After selecting the required template, click on the **OK** button in the dialog box. The Assembly mode is invoked and three default assembly datum planes: Front, Top, and Right, which are mutually perpendicular to each other appear in the graphics area, see Figure 10.4.

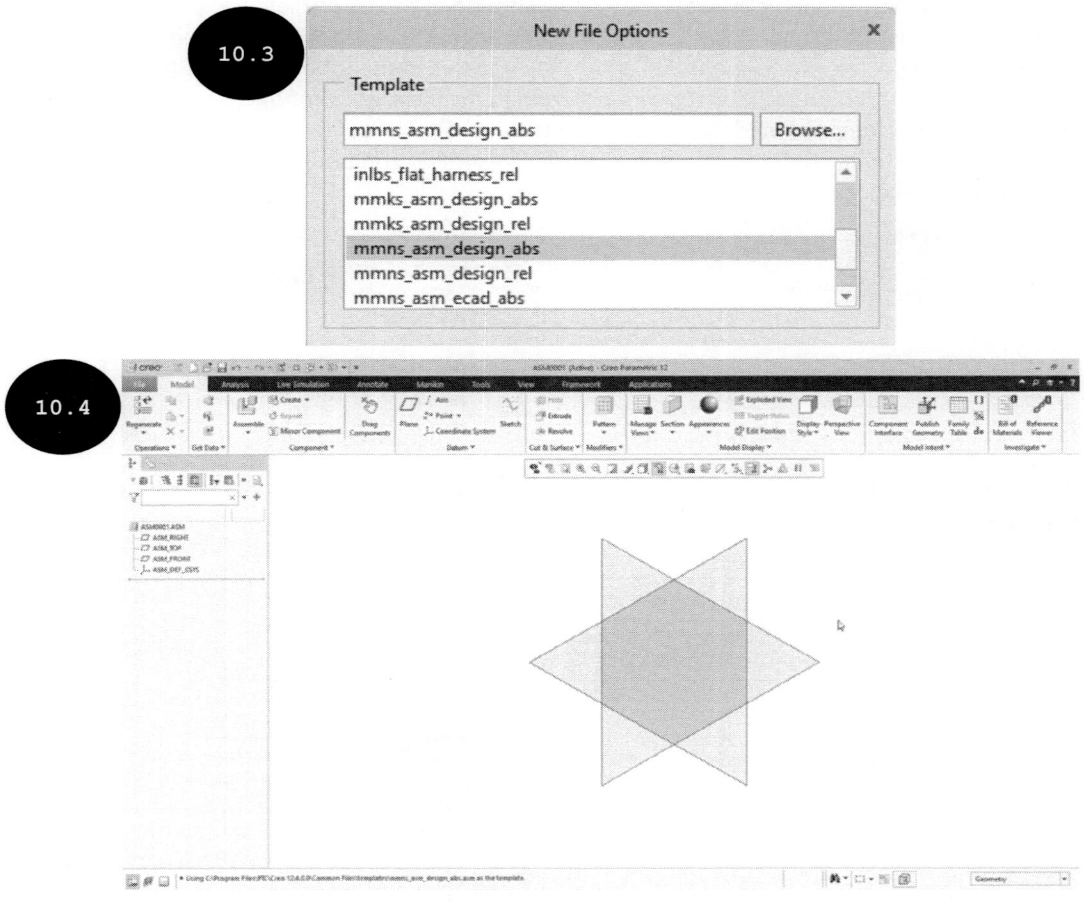

Tip: If you invoke the Assembly mode by selecting the **Empty** template in the **New File Options** dialog box, the default assembly datum planes will not be available in the graphics area.

After invoking the Assembly mode, you can create assemblies by using the Bottom-up Assembly Approach or Top-down Assembly Approach. The method for creating an assembly by using the Bottom-up Assembly Approach is discussed next.

Creating an Assembly by using Bottom-up Approach

To create an assembly by using the Bottom-up Assembly Approach, you need to insert the components one by one in the Assembly environment by using the **Assemble** tool and apply the required constraints to assemble them with each other. The method for inserting the components in the Assembly environment is discussed next.

Inserting Components in the Assembly Environment

To insert a component in the Assembly environment, click on the **Assemble** tool in the **Component** group of the **Model** tab, see Figure 10.5. The **Open** dialog box appears. In this dialog box, browse to the location where all components of the assembly are saved and then select the first component to be inserted in the Assembly environment. You can also preview the selected component before inserting it in the Assembly environment by using the **Preview** option of the **Open** dialog box. Next, click on the **Open** button in the dialog box. The selected component gets inserted in the Assembly environment, see Figure 10.6. Also, the **Component Placement** tab appears in the **Ribbon** and the 3D Dragger with translational and rotational handles appears attached to the inserted component in the graphics area. The options in the **Component Placement** tab are used for applying constraints to define the position of the component or its relationship relative to other assembly components. Some of the options of the **Component Placement** tab are discussed below:

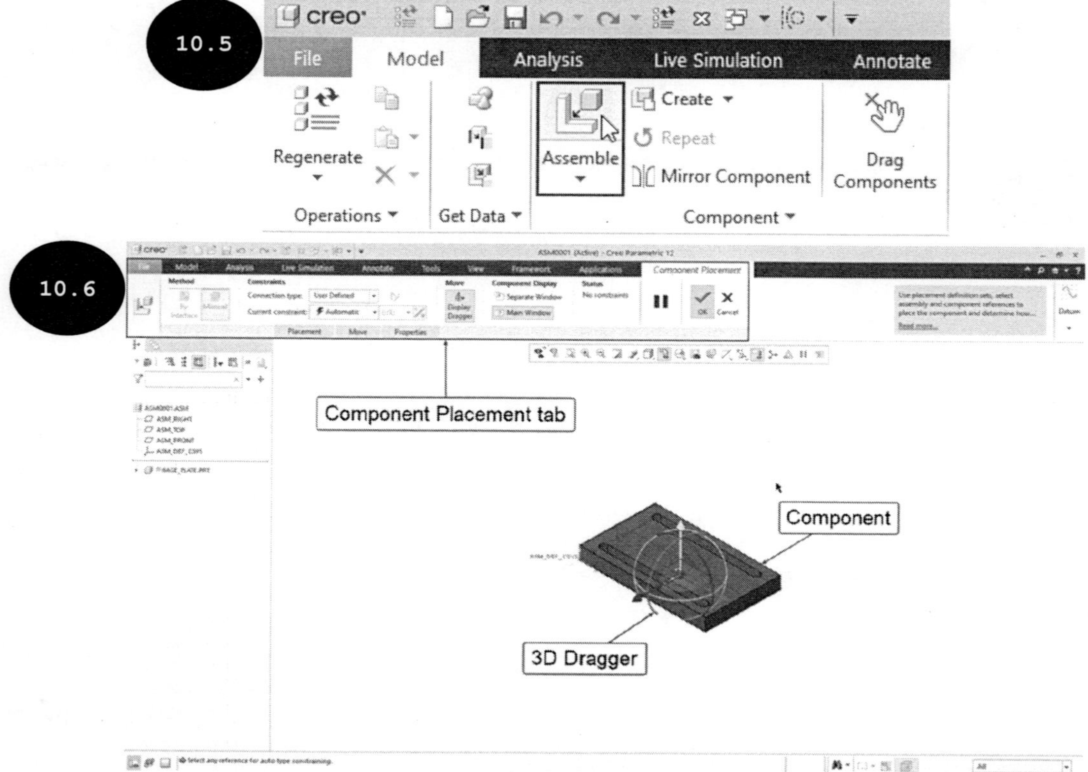

Display Dragger

By default, the **Display Dragger** button is activated in the **Move** area of the **Component Placement** tab. As a result, the **3D Dragger** with translational and rotational handles appears attached to the inserted component in the graphics area. You can drag the translational and rotational handles of the 3D Dragger to change the position and orientation of the component before applying a constraint in the Assembly environment. Note that if the movement of a component is restricted to a direction by applying a constraint, then the component cannot move in that direction. You will learn about restricting the component movements by applying constraints later in this chapter.

Main Window

By default, the **Main Window** button is activated in the **Component Display** area of the **Component Placement** tab. As a result, the component appears in the Assembly window itself for applying constraints with other components of the assembly. It helps to preview the change in the component position when you apply a constraint. Note that the first component needs to be assembled with the assembly datum planes by applying the required constraints. You will learn about applying constraints later in this chapter.

Separate Window

On activating the **Separate Window** button in the **Component Display** area of the **Component Placement** tab, the inserted component appears in a separate window for applying constraints. It helps to easily select a component reference and an assembly reference to apply a constraint. Note that to apply a constraint, you need to select two references such as faces, planes, datum planes, and axes. You will learn about applying constraints by selecting two references later in this chapter.

Note: In Creo Parametric, you can display the component in the Assembly window as well as in a separate window for applying constraints by activating both the buttons: **Main Window** and **Separate Window** at the same time in the **Component Placement** tab.

Connection type drop-down list

The **Connection type** drop-down list in the **Constraints** area of the **Component Placement** tab displays a list of predefined constraint sets such as Rigid, Pin, Slider, Cylinder, Planar, and Bearing, see Figure 10.7. A predefined constraint set contains constraints that are used for maintaining a particular relationship between the components of the assembly and forms a mechanism. You will learn about applying various predefined constraints later in this chapter.

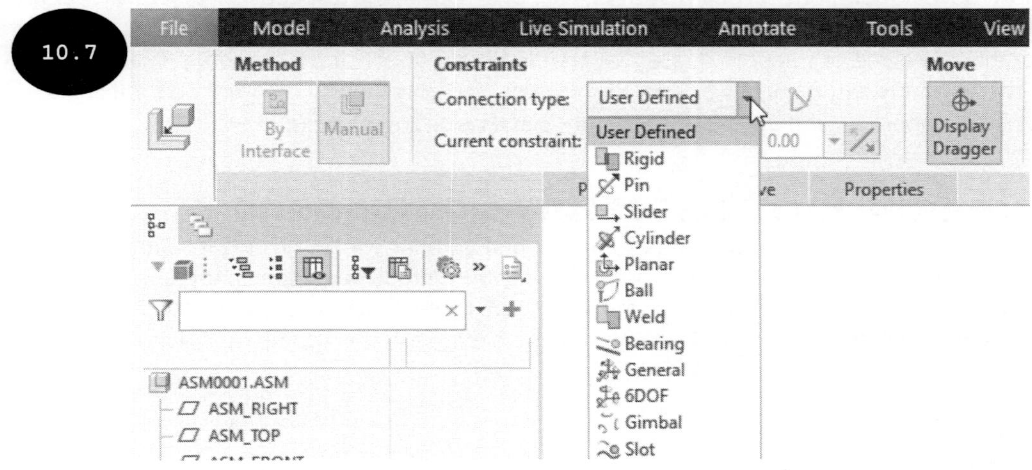

Current constraint drop-down list

The **Current constraint** drop-down list in the **Constraints** area of the **Component Placement** tab displays a list of constraints such as Distance, Angle Offset, Parallel, Coincident, Normal, and Tangent, see Figure 10.8. These constraints are used for defining the position of the components relative to each other by restricting or reducing their degrees of freedom. These constraints are also known as user defined constraints or placement constraints. Note that the **Current constraint** drop-down list displays a complete list of available constraints when the **User Defined** or **Rigid** option are selected in the **Connection type** drop-down list in the **Constraints** area of the **Component Placement** tab. You will learn about applying different user-defined constraints later in this chapter.

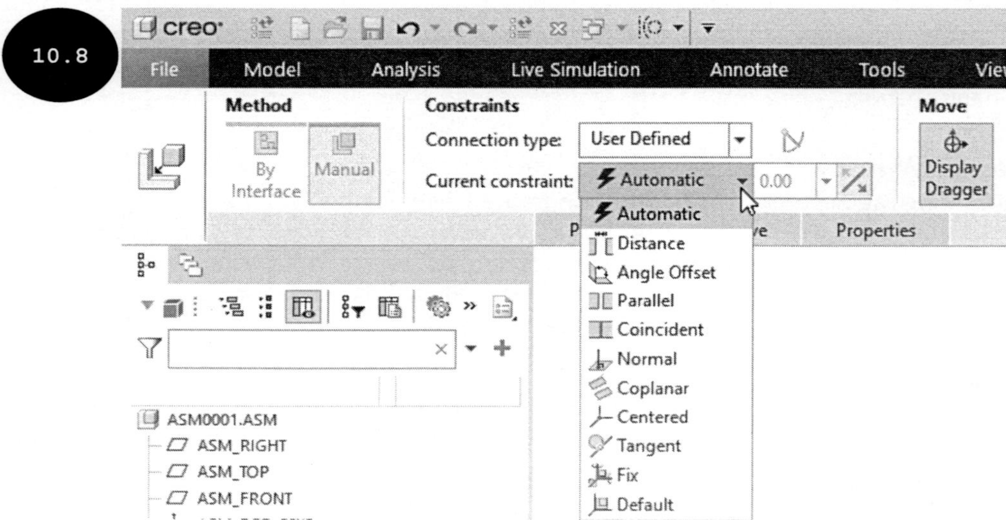

In Creo Parametric, every component you insert in the Assembly environment has six free degrees of freedom: three translational and three rotational. This means that the components in the Assembly environment can move along the X, Y, and Z axes and rotate about the X, Y, and Z axes. You need to fix these free degrees of freedom of a component by applying the required constraints with other components of the assembly. It is not just about fixing the degrees of freedom of components, you need to maintain actual relationships between them exactly as it is in real-world assembly. You need to allow movable components of an assembly to move freely in the respective movable directions. For example, the function of a shaft in an assembly is to rotate about its axis therefore, you need to retain its rotational degree of freedom. Note that the first component of the assembly needs to be fixed with the assembly datum planes by applying the required constraints. The method for fixing the first assembly component with the assembly datum planes is discussed next.

Fixing the First Assembly Component

In Creo Parametric, it is recommended to fix the first component by aligning its coordinate system with the assembly coordinate system. To do so, select the **Default** constraint in the **Current constraint** drop-down list in the **Constraints** area of the **Component Placement** tab, see Figure 10.9. The component moves toward the assembly coordinate system and becomes a fixed component with respect to the assembly coordinate system, see Figure 10.10. Also, the status of the components appears as **Fully constrained** in the **Component Placement** tab. The fully constrained status of a component indicates that it is a fixed component and cannot move in any direction. Next, click on the green tick-mark button in the **Component Placement** tab.

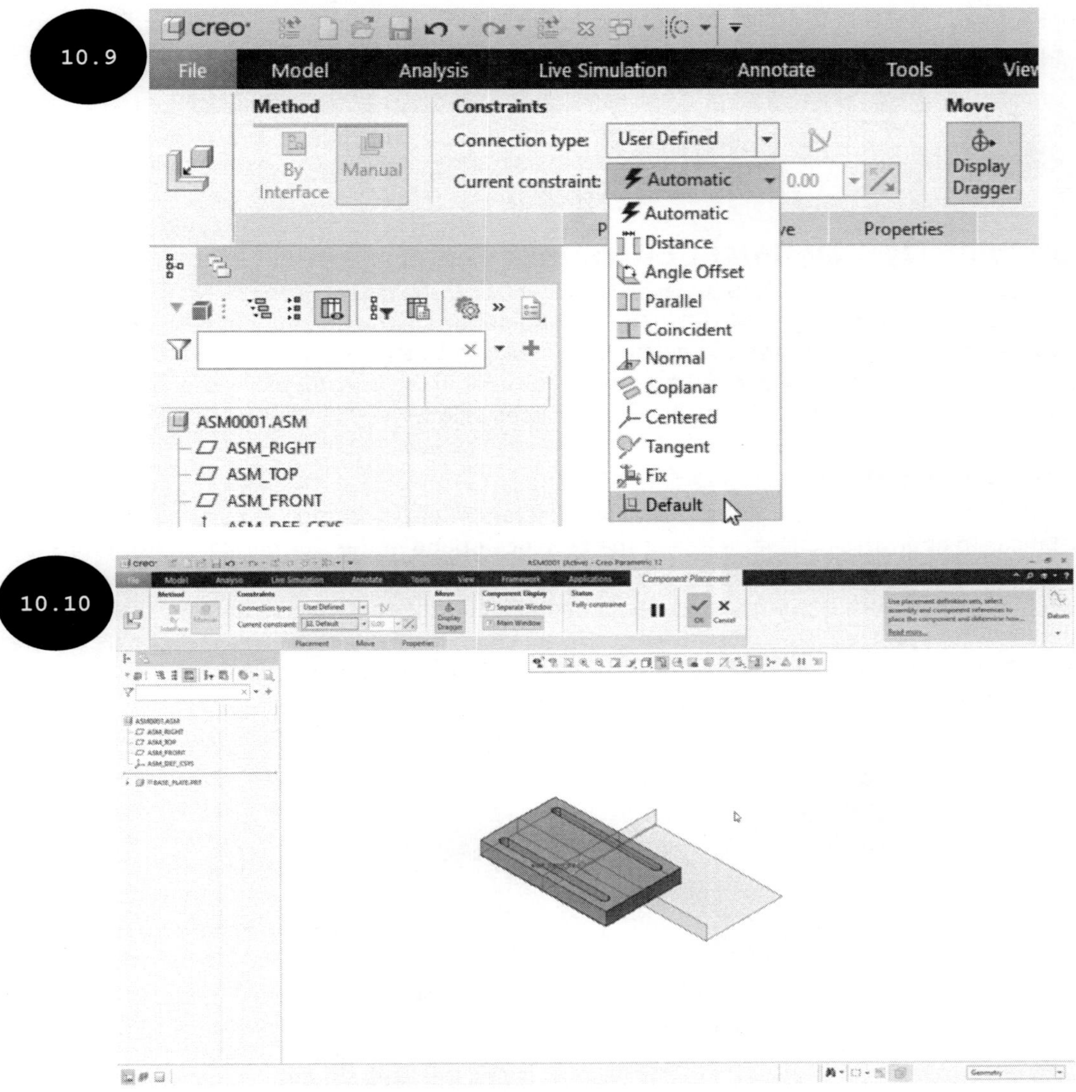

After inserting the first component in the Assembly environment and fixing its coordinate system with the default assembly coordinate system, you can insert the second component by using the **Assemble** tool and then apply the required constraints. The methods for applying constraints are discussed next.

Applying Constraints

In Creo Parametric, you can apply two types of constraints: predefined constraint sets and user defined constraints by using the **Connection type** and **Current constraint** drop-down lists in the **Constraints** area of the **Component Placement** tab, respectively, see Figure 10.11. The **Component Placement** tab appears in the **Ribbon**, every time you insert a component in the Assembly environment. The methods for applying user-defined constraints and predefined constraint sets are discussed next.

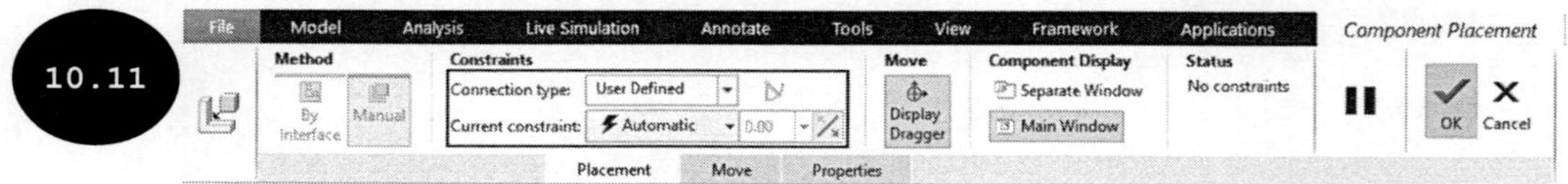

Applying User Defined Constraints

As discussed, you can apply various types of user-defined constraints between two components by using the **Current constraint** drop-down list in the **Constraints** area of the **Component Placement** tab. Note that this drop-down list displays a complete list of available constraints when the **User Defined** or **Rigid** option is selected in the **Connection type** drop-down list in the **Constraints** area of the **Component Placement** tab. The different constraints are discussed below.

Distance Constraint

The Distance constraint is used for restricting references of two components at a specified offset distance. To apply this constraint, select the **Distance** option in the **Current constraint** drop-down list and then select two references of different components one by one in the graphics area. You can select two planar faces, datum planes, axes, or a combination of a datum plane and a planar face as the references to apply the Distance constraint, see Figure 10.12. In this figure, two planar faces are selected. Next, enter a required offset distance value between the selected references of the components in the **Set constraint offset** field of the **Component Placement** tab, see Figure 10.13. Alternatively, you can also specify the offset distance value by dragging the distance handle that appears in the graphics area.

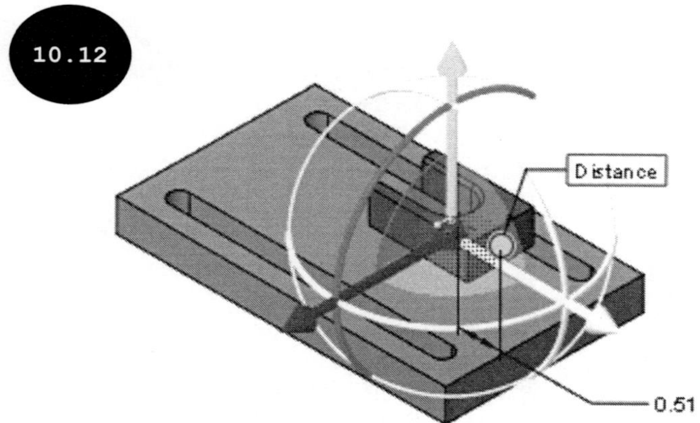

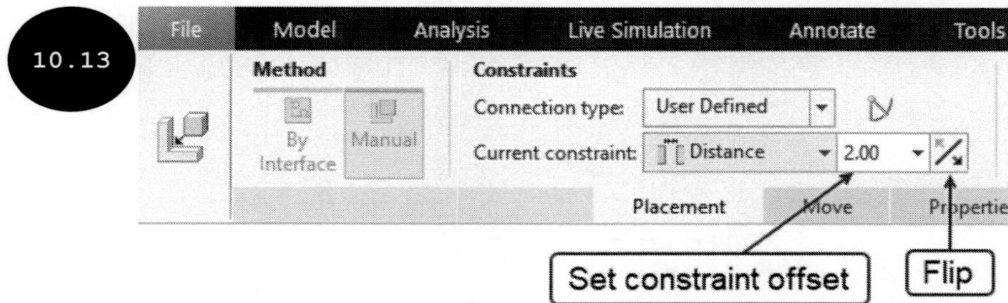

You can also reverse the offset direction by clicking on the **Flip** button in the **Component Placement** tab, see Figure 10.14.

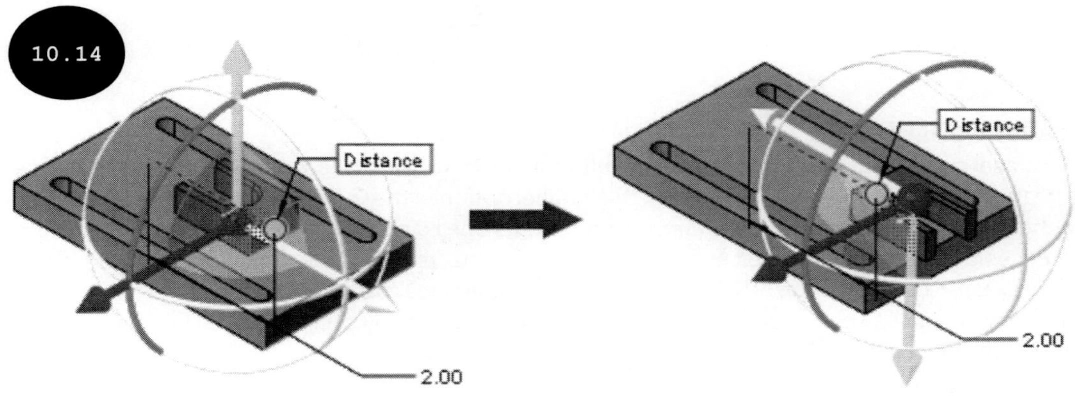

Tip: The expanded **Placement** panel of the **Component Placement** tab displays a list of constraints applied to the component. You can also edit the references and parameters of a constraint, delete a constraint, or apply a new constraint by using the expanded **Placement** panel. You will learn about editing and deleting a constraint later in this chapter.

Note: You need to apply multiple constraints to a component with respect to other assembly components to make it fully defined.

Angle Offset Constraint

The Angle Offset constraint is used for restricting references of two components at a specified angular distance, see Figure 10.15. To apply this constraint, select the **Angle Offset** option in the **Current constraint** drop-down list and then select two references of different components one by one in the graphics area. You can select two planar faces, datum planes, axes, or a combination of a datum plane and a planar face as the references to apply the Angle Offset constraint, see Figure 10.15. In this figure, two planar faces are selected. Next, enter a required angular value between the selected references of the components in the **Set constraint offset** field of the **Component Placement** tab. You can also specify the angular value by dragging the handle that appears in the graphics area. To reverse the orientation of the constraint, click on the **Flip** button in the **Component Placement** tab.

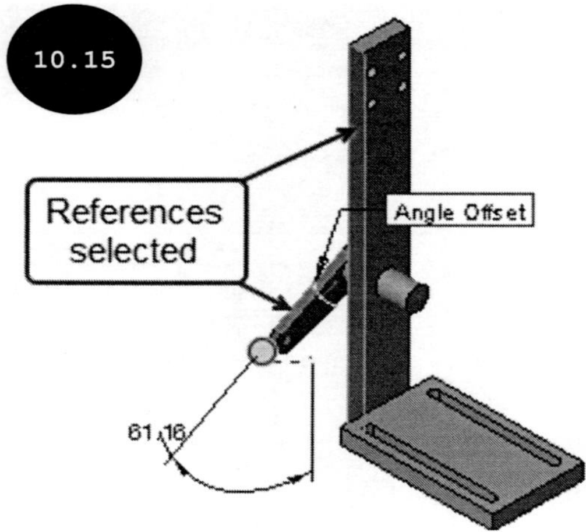

Parallel Constraint

The Parallel constraint is used for restricting references of two components parallel to each other, see Figure 10.16. To apply this constraint, select the **Parallel** option in the **Current constraint** drop-down list and then select two references of different components one by one in the graphics area. The selected references become parallel to each other, see Figure 10.16. You can select two planar faces, datum planes, axes, or a combination of a datum plane and a planar face as references for applying the Parallel constraint. You can also reverse the orientation of the constraint by clicking on the **Flip** button in the **Component Placement** tab.

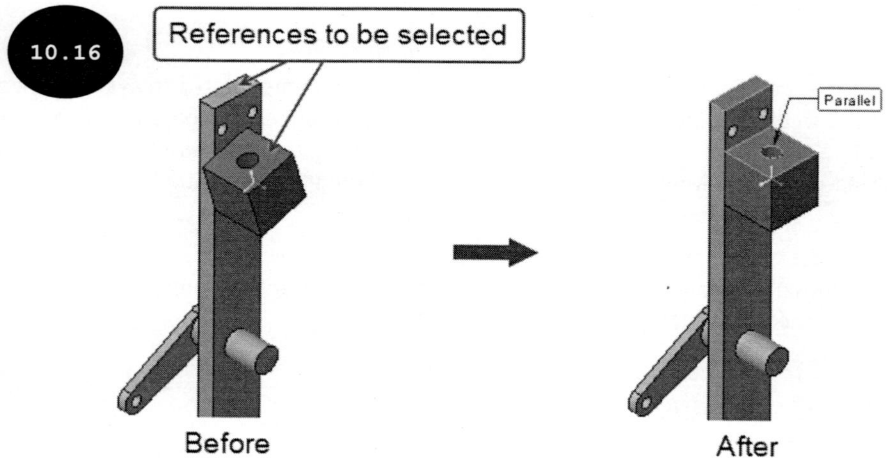

Coincident Constraint

The Coincident constraint is used for making references of the two components coincident with each other, see Figures 10.17 and 10.18. You can select two faces, datum planes, axes, or a combination of these entities as references to apply the Coincident constraint. Note that if you select circular faces as references to apply this constraint, then the axes of both the selected faces become coincident with each other, see Figure 10.17. To apply this constraint, select the **Coincident** option in the **Current constraint** drop-down list and then select two references of different components one by one in the graphics area. The selected references become coincident with each other. You can also reverse the orientation of the constraint by clicking on the **Flip** button in the **Component Placement** tab.

10.17

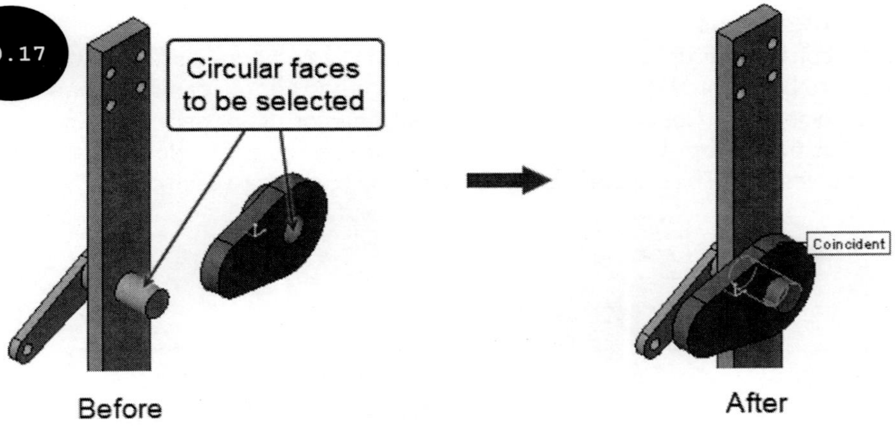

Circular faces
to be selected
Coincident
Before
After

10.18

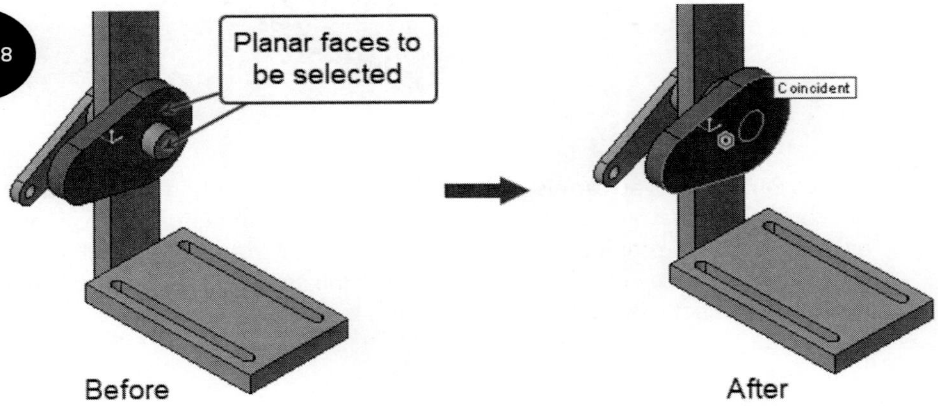

Planar faces to
be selected
Coincident
Before
After

Normal Constraint

The Normal constraint is used for making references of two components perpendicular to each other, see Figure 10.19. You can select two faces, datum planes, axes, or a combination of these entities as references for applying the Normal constraint. To apply this constraint, select the **Normal** option in the **Current constraint** drop-down list and then select two references of different components one by one in the graphics area. The selected references become perpendicular to each other. You can also reverse the orientation of the constraint by clicking on the **Flip** button in the **Component Placement** tab.

10.19

References to
be selected
Normal
Before
After

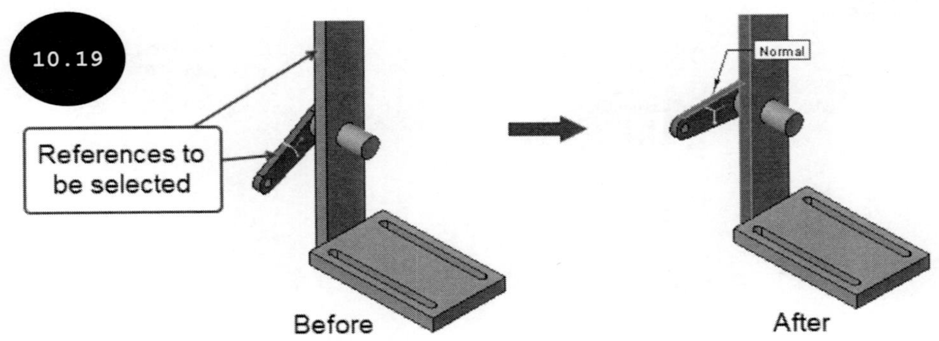

Coplanar Constraint

The Coplanar constraint is used for making references of two components aligned to each other and allowing them to be oriented on the same plane, see Figure 10.20. You can select two edges, or axes as references to apply the Coplanar constraint. To apply this constraint, select the **Coplanar** option in the **Current constraint** drop-down list and then select two references of different components one by one in the graphics area. The selected references become coplanar to each other.

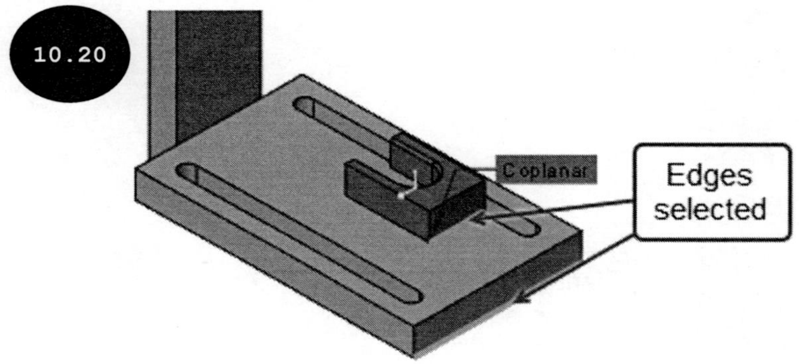

Note: In Creo Parametric, you can also use the Query selection method to select faces and edges of a component that are hidden by other faces of the component. To do so, move the cursor over an entity of the component and then right-click. With each right-click, Creo Parametric cycles through each entity that is located near the cursor tip. Once the required entity is highlighted, select it by clicking the left mouse button.

Centered Constraint

The Centered constraint is used for making two references (conical, spherical, or toroidal faces) centered to each other, see Figure 10.21. In this figure, two conical faces are selected. You can also select two coordinate systems as references to apply this constraint. On doing so, the origins of both the coordinate systems get aligned to each other and the translational degrees of freedom of the component get restricted. However, the component can rotate around the origin.

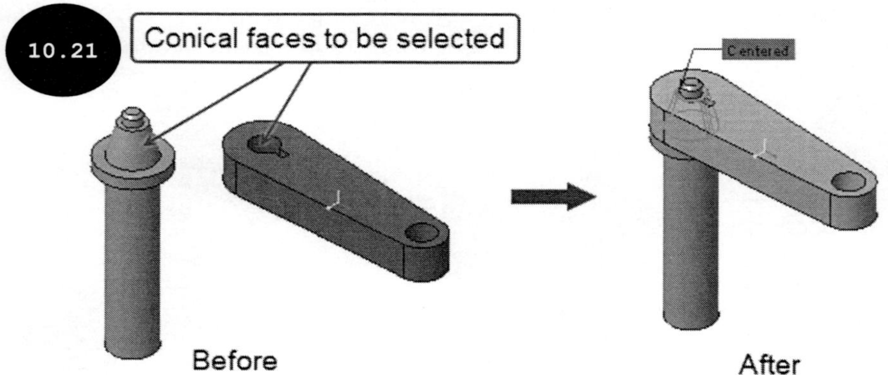

Tangent Constraint

The Tangent constraint is used for making a circular face tangent to another circular face, planar face, or datum plane, see Figure 10.22. In this figure, two circular faces are selected.

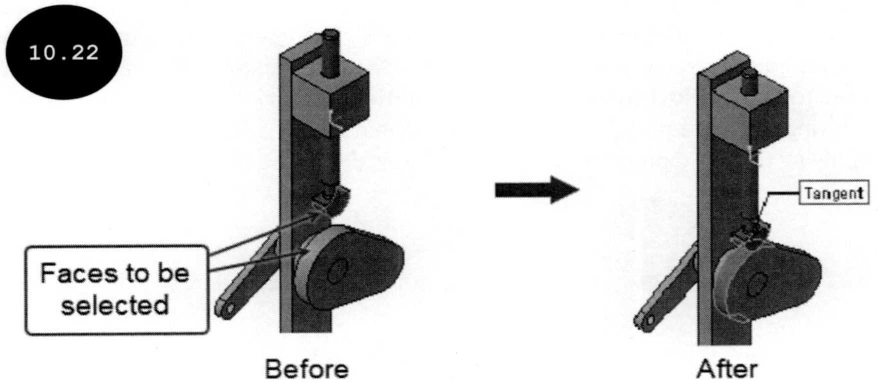

Fix Constraint

The Fix constraint is used for fixing the component in its current position.

Default Constraint

The Default constraint is used for aligning the coordinate system of the component with the default assembly coordinate system.

Automatic Constraint

The Automatic constraint is used for applying the best suitable constraints, automatically depending upon the references selected. By default, the **Automatic** option is selected in the **Current constraint** drop-down list. As a result, depending upon the type of references selected, Creo Parametric identifies the most suitable constraint for the selected references and applies it.

Note: You need to apply multiple constraints to a component with respect to other assembly components to make it fully defined.

Applying Predefined Constraint Set

In Creo Parametric, you can apply various predefined constraint sets such as Rigid, Pin, Slider, Cylinder, Planar, and Bearing between components by using the **Connection type** drop-down list in the **Constraints** area of the **Component Placement** tab. The various predefined constraint sets are discussed below.

Rigid

The Rigid predefined constraint set is used for connecting two components together by removing all degrees of freedom and not allowing any relative motion between the components, see Figure 10.23. The rigid predefined constraint set is mainly applied between the components that are welded or bolted together with no allowable motion between them. In the Rigid predefined constraint set, you need to apply all the required constraints such as Coincident, Distance, Angle Offset, and Parallel between the components to make a rigid connection. Note that this is the same as making a component fully defined by applying all the required user defined constraints with other assembly components. The method for applying the Rigid predefined constraint set is discussed below:

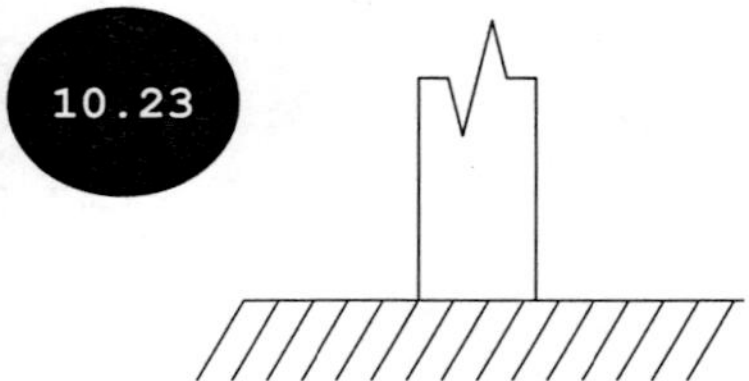

Rigid predefined constraint set
(No translation and rotational movements)

1. Select the **Rigid** option in the **Connection type** drop-down list in the **Constraints** area of the **Component Placement** tab that appears, every time when you insert a component in the Assembly environment, see Figure 10.24.

2. Ensure that the **Automatic** option is selected in the **Current constraint** drop-down list in the **Constraints** area of the **Component Placement** tab to apply the constraint automatically depending upon the references selected, see Figure 10.24.

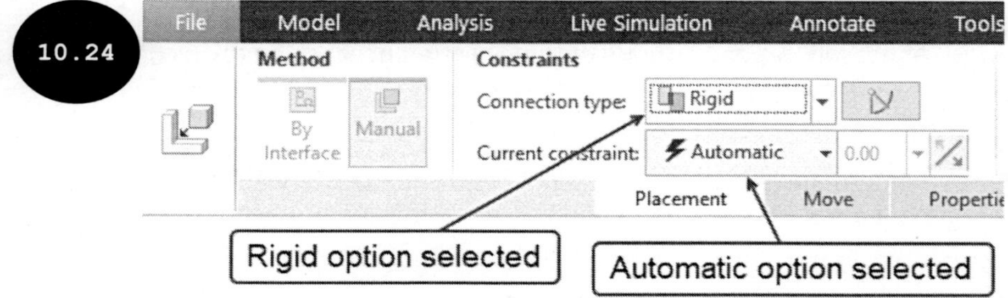

3. Select references of two different components one by one in the graphics area, see Figure 10.25 (a). The most suitable constraint gets applied, automatically, depending upon the references selected, see Figure 10.25 (b). In this figure, two planar faces are selected and the Coincident constraint is applied between them automatically.

Note: You can also select a constraint other than the one applied automatically between the selected references. To do so, select the required constraint in the **Current constraint** drop-down list of the **Component Placement** tab. Alternatively, double-click on the constraint callout that appears in the graphics area and then select the required constraint in the drop-down list of the Mini toolbar that appears, see Figure 10.26.

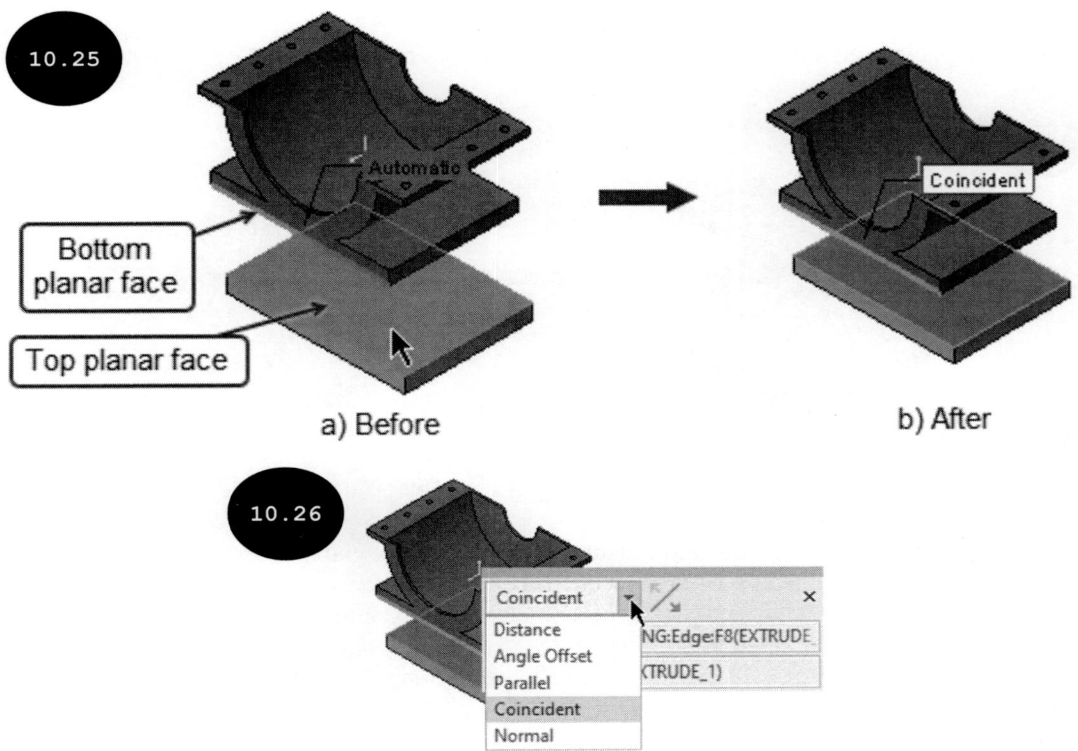

After applying the first constraint, some degrees of freedom of the component get restricted. However, you need to restrict all degrees of freedom of the component to make it fully defined by applying other constraints.

Tip: In the 3D Dragger, the white colored translational and rotational handles indicate that the degrees of freedom are fixed and the component cannot move or rotate in that direction, see Figure 10.27. You can turn on or off the display of the 3D Dragger in the graphics area by clicking on the **Display Dragger** button in the **Move** area of the **Component Placement** tab.

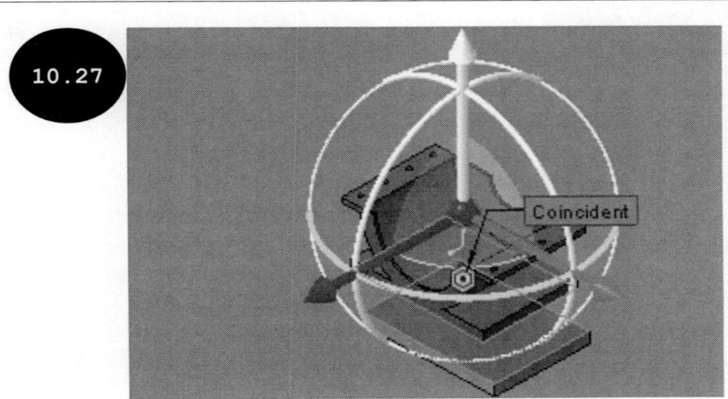

4. Select other references of the components one by one in the graphics area, see Figure 10.28. In this figure, two planar faces are selected and the Coincident constraint is applied between them.

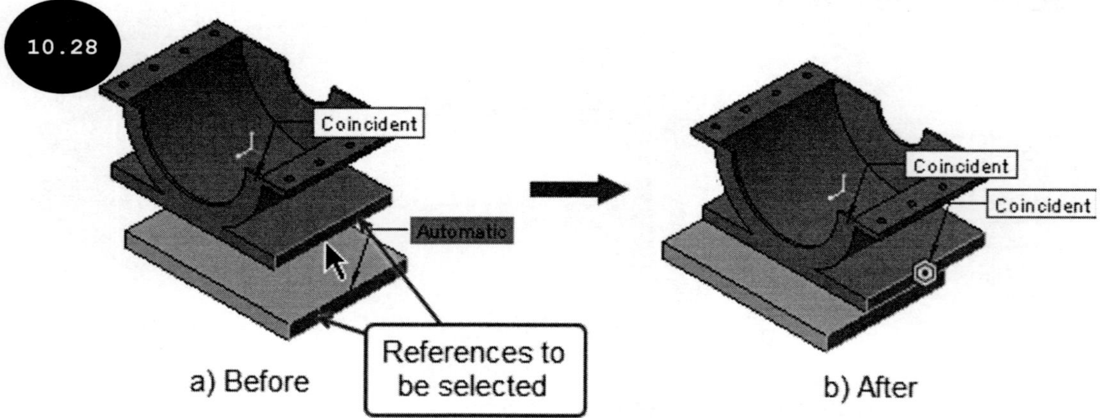

5. Select other references of the components one by one in the graphics area, see Figure 10.29. In this figure, two planar faces are selected and the Coincident constraint is applied between them. Also, in this example, after applying three Coincident constraints, the status of the component appears as **Fully constrained** in the **Status** area of the **Component Placement** tab. This means that all degrees of freedom of the component are restricted and the component cannot move or rotate in any direction.

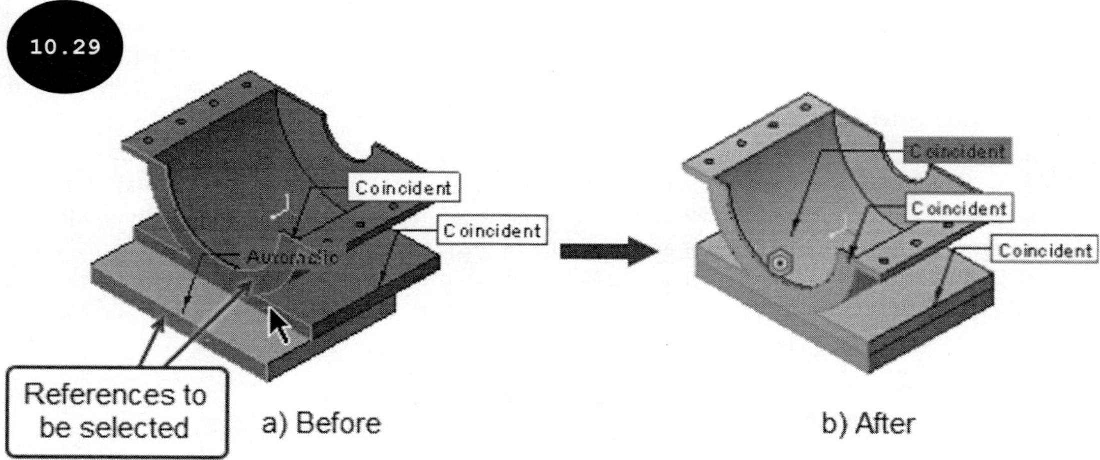

6. Click on the green tick-mark button in the **Component Placement** tab, when all degrees of freedom of the component get restricted and a rigid connection is formed with the assembly component.

Pin

The Pin predefined constraint set allows the component to rotate about an axis by removing all degrees of freedom except one rotational degree of freedom, see Figure 10.30. The method for applying the Pin predefined constraint set is discussed below:

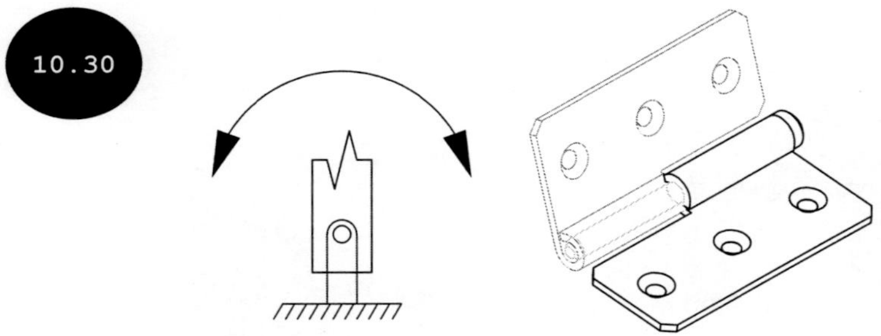

Pin predefined constraint set
(Only one rotational movement is allowed)

1. Select the **Pin** option in the **Connection type** drop-down list in the **Constraints** area of the **Component Placement** tab that appears, every time when you insert a component in the Assembly environment, see Figure 10.31.

2. Expand the **Placement** panel of the **Component Placement** tab, if not expanded by default, see Figure 10.31. You are prompted to apply an axis alignment connection between the references of the components.

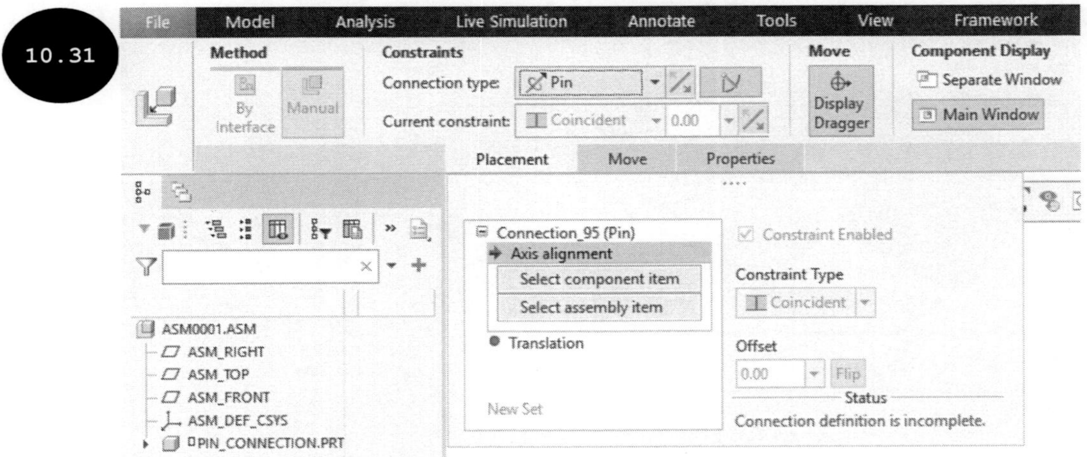

3. Select references of two different components one by one in the graphics area to apply the axis alignment connection between them, see Figure 10.32 (a). You can select axes, edges, or circular faces as references to apply this connection. The selected references get aligned with each

other, see Figure 10.32 (b). Also, you are prompted to apply a translation connection between the references of the components. In Figure 10.32 (a), two circular faces are selected as references to apply the axis alignment connection, and in Figure 10.32 (b), the axes of both the selected references become aligned with each other.

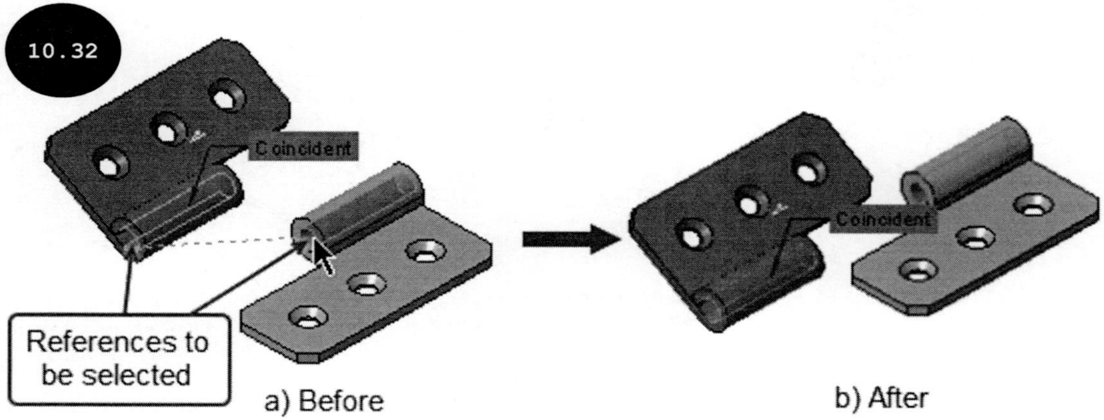

4. Select references of the components one by one in the graphics area to apply the translation connection between them, see Figure 10.33. The selected references become coincident with each other and the status appears as **Connection Definition Complete** in the **Status** area of the **Component Placement** tab. This means that the Pin predefined constraint set is defined and the component can only rotate about its axis.

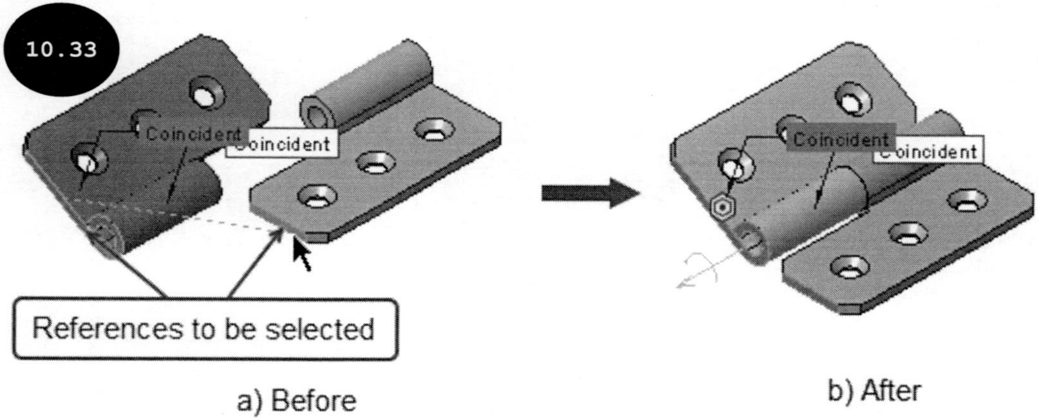

Note: By default, after applying the Pin predefined constraint set, the component can rotate 360 degrees around its axis. To limit the angle of rotation of the component, expand the **Placement** panel and then click on the **Rotation Axis/Rotation 1** connection for defining the references to limit the angle of rotation of the component, see Figure 10.34. Next, select two planar references one by one in the graphics area, see Figure 10.35 (a). The current angle value between the selected references appears, see Figure 10.35 (b). Next, enter the required angle value in the **Current Position** field of the expanded **Placement** panel to define the position of the component and then press ENTER. The angle between the selected references gets changed, as specified. You can also drag the handle that appears in the graphics area to define the position of the component, dynamically. You can set the current defined position (angle) of the component as the zero position by clicking on the **Set Zero Position** button. Next, select the **Minimum Limit** and **Maximum Limit** check boxes and then specify the minimum and maximum angle of rotation in the respective fields of the expanded **Placement** panel. On doing so, the component will rotate within the specified minimum and maximum angle of rotation values.

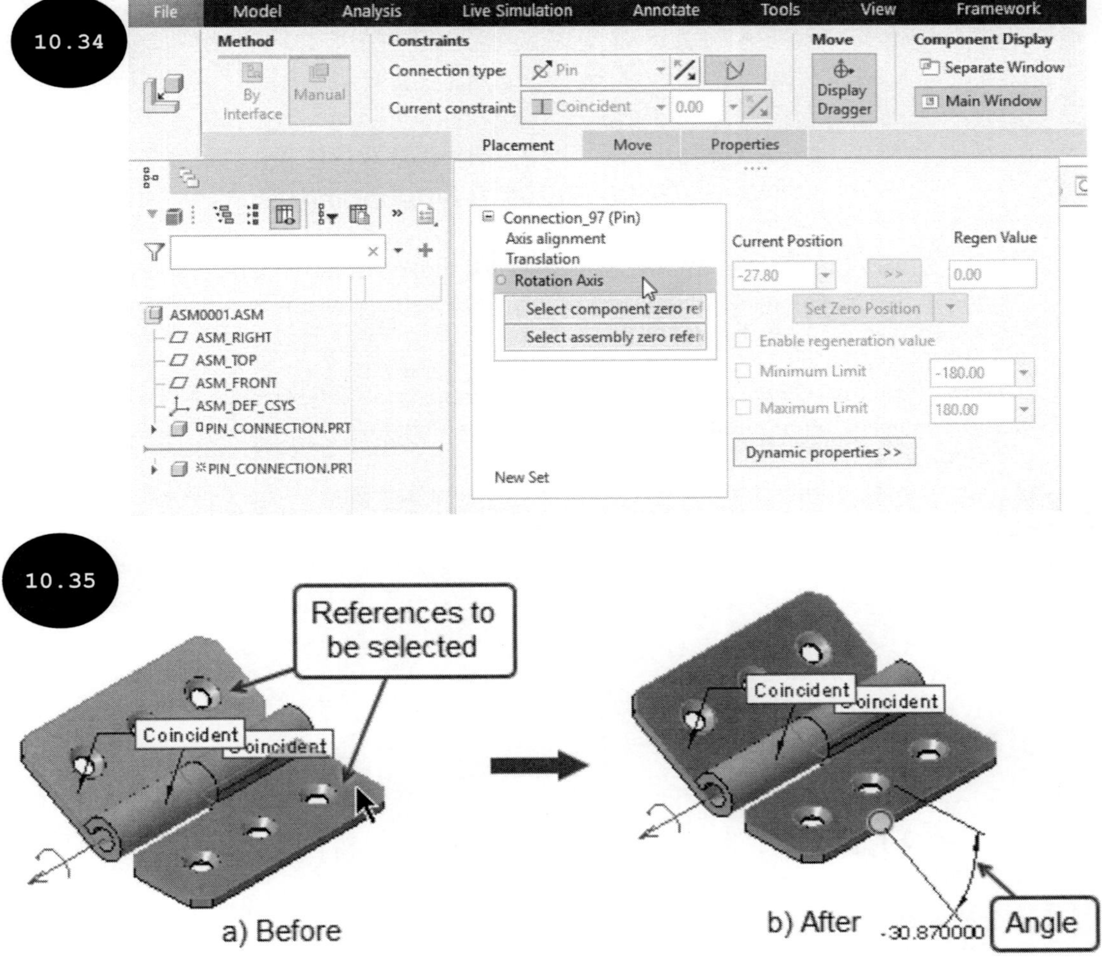

5. Click on the green tick-mark button in the **Component Placement** tab, when the status appears as **Connection Definition Complete** in the **Status** area of the **Component Placement** tab. The Pin predefined constraint set is defined and the component can only rotate about its axis.

You can rotate the component about its free degrees of freedom by using the **Drag Components** tool of the **Model** tab in the **Ribbon**. You can also press and hold the CTRL + ALT + left mouse button and then drag the cursor to rotate the component.

Slider

The Slider predefined constraint set allows the component to translate/slide along an axis by removing all degrees of freedom except one translational degree of freedom, see Figure 10.36. The method for applying the Slider predefined constraint set is discussed below:

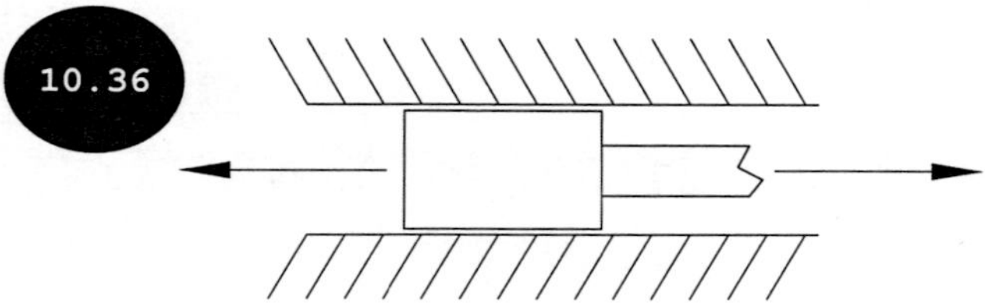

Slider predefined constraint set
(Moves freely along a single axis)

1. Select the **Slider** option in the **Connection type** drop-down list in the **Constraints** area of the **Component Placement** tab that appears, every time when you insert a component in the Assembly environment, see Figure 10.37.

2. Expand the **Placement** panel of the **Component Placement** tab, if not expanded by default, see Figure 10.37. You are prompted to apply an axis alignment connection between the references of the components.

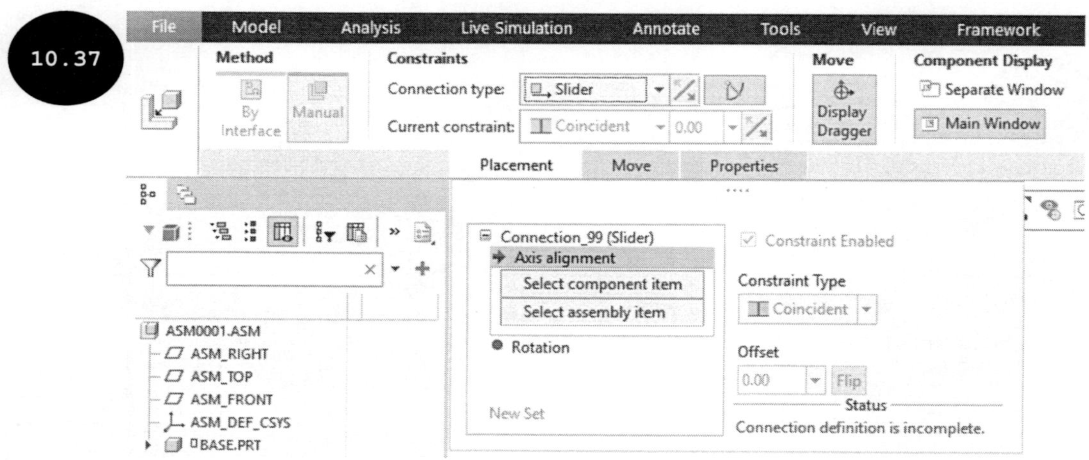

3. Select references of two different components one by one in the graphics area to apply the axis alignment connection between them, see Figure 10.38. You can select axes, edges, or circular faces as the references to apply this connection. The selected references get aligned with each other, see Figure 10.38. Also, you are prompted to apply a rotation connection between the references of the components.

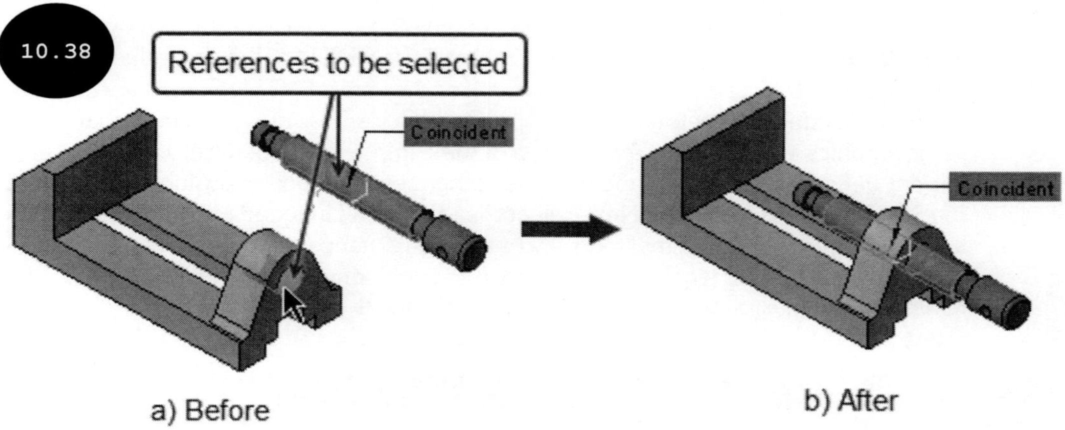

4. Select references of the components one by one in the graphics area to apply the rotation connection between them, see Figure 10.39. You can select faces, planes, and datum planes as the references. In Figure 10.39, two datum planes are selected. The selected references become coincident with each other and the status appears as **Connection Definition Complete** in the **Status** area of the **Component Placement** tab. It means that the Slider predefined constraint set is defined and the component can only translate about its axis.

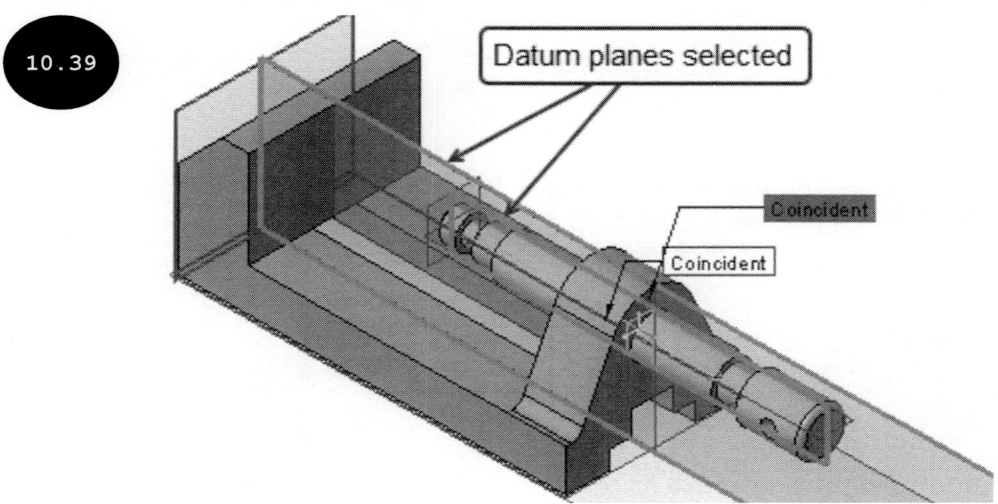

Note: By default, after applying the Slider predefined constraint set, the component can translate freely along its axis. To limit the translational movement, expand the **Placement** panel and then click on the **Translation Axis/Translation 1** connection for defining the references to limit the translational movement of the component, see Figure 10.40. Next, select two references one by one in the graphics area, see Figure 10.41 (a). The current distance value between the selected references appears in the graphics area, see Figure 10.41 (b). Next, enter the required distance value in the **Current Position** field of the expanded **Placement** panel to define the position of the component and then press ENTER. The distance between the selected references gets changed, as specified. You can also drag the handle that appears in the graphics area to define the position of the component, dynamically. You can set the current defined position (distance) of the component as the zero position by clicking on the **Set Zero Position** button. Next, select the **Minimum Limit** and **Maximum Limit** check boxes and then specify the minimum and maximum distance values in the respective fields of the expanded **Placement** panel. On doing so, the component will move within the specified minimum and maximum distance values.

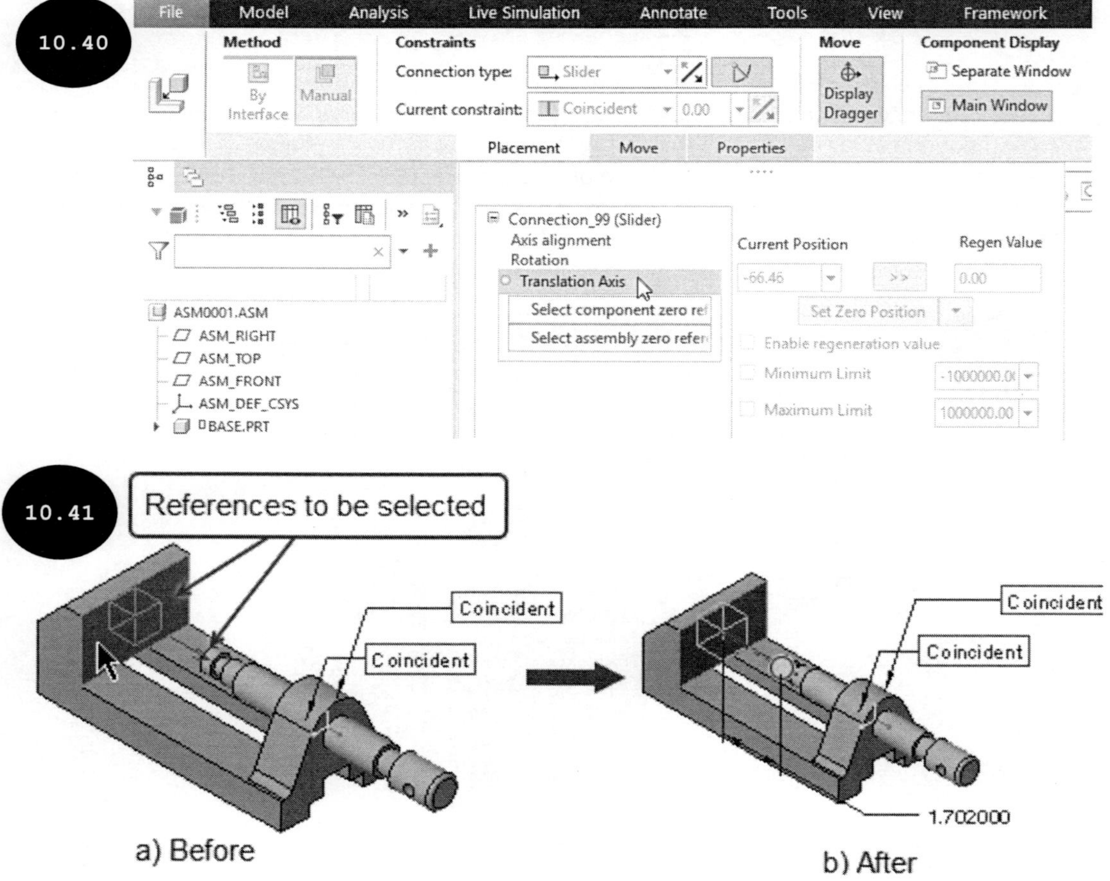

5. Click on the green tick-mark button in the **Component Placement** tab, when the status appears as **Connection Definition Complete** in its **Status** area. The Slider predefined constraint set is defined and the component can only translate along its axis.

Tip: You can move the component along its free degrees of freedom by using the **Drag Components** tool of the **Model** tab in the **Ribbon**.

Cylinder

The Cylinder predefined constraint set allows the component to translate as well as rotate about the same axis by removing all degrees of freedom except one translational and one rotational degree of freedom, see Figure 10.42. The method for applying the Cylinder predefined constraint set is discussed below:

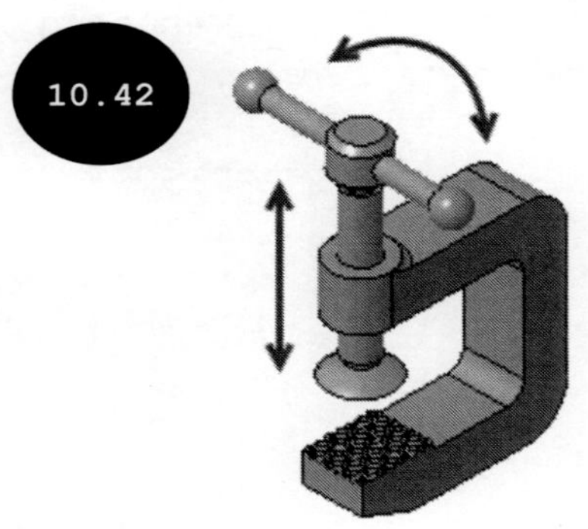

1. Select the **Cylinder** option in the **Connection type** drop-down list in the **Constraints** area of the **Component Placement** tab that appears every time you insert a component in the Assembly environment, see Figure 10.43.

2. Expand the **Placement** panel of the **Component Placement** tab, if not expanded by default, see Figure 10.43. You are prompted to apply an axis alignment connection between the references of the components.

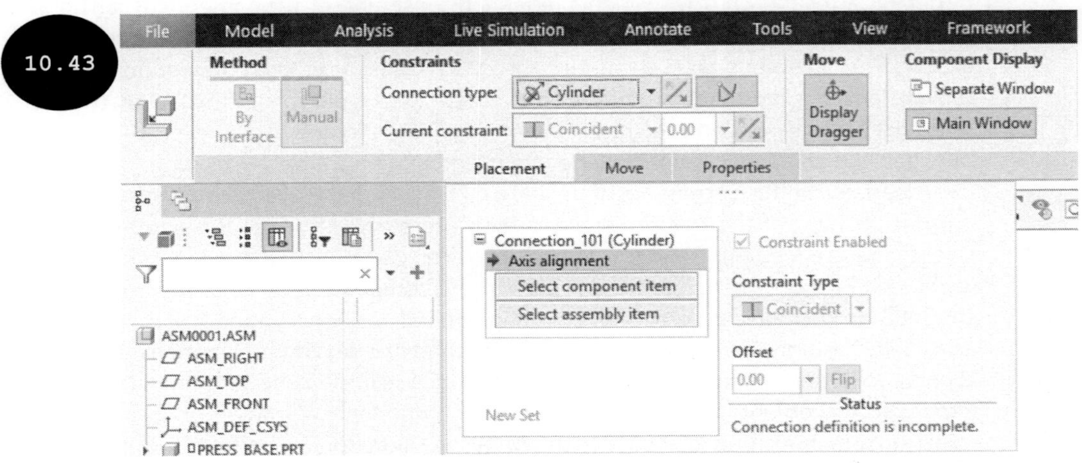

3. Select references of two different components one by one in the graphics area to apply the axis alignment connection between them, see Figure 10.44. You can select axes, edges, or circular faces as the references to apply this connection. The selected references get aligned with each other and the status appears as **Connection Definition Complete** in the **Status** area of the **Component Placement** tab. This means that the Cylinder predefined constraint set is defined and the component can translate as well as rotate about its axis.

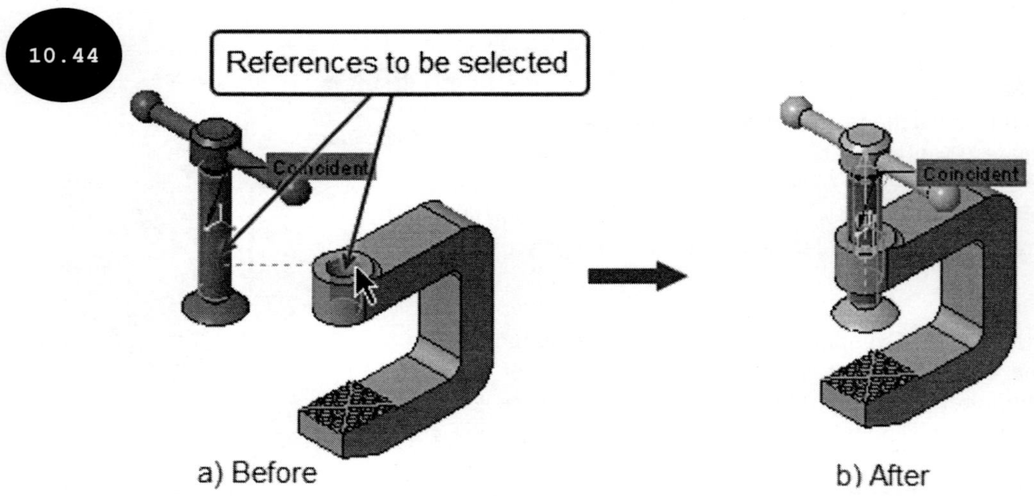

Note: By default, after applying the Cylinder predefined constraint set, the component can translate as well as rotate freely along an axis. To limit the translational movement of the component, expand the **Placement** panel and then click on the **Translation Axis** connection for defining the references to limit the translational movement, see Figure 10.45. Next, select two planar references one by one in the graphics area, see Figure 10.46. The current distance value between the selected references appears in the graphics area. Next, enter the required distance value in the **Current Position** field of the expanded **Placement** panel to define the current position of the component and then press ENTER. The distance between the selected references gets changed, as specified. You can also drag the handle that appears in the graphics area to define the position of the component, dynamically. Next, click on the **Set Zero Position** button to set the current defined position (distance) of the component as its zero position. Next, select the **Minimum Limit** and **Maximum Limit** check boxes and then specify the minimum and maximum distance values in the respective fields of the expanded **Placement** panel. On doing so, the component will move within the specified minimum and maximum distance values only, see Figure 10.46. Similarly, you can also limit the rotational movement of the component by using the **Rotation Axis** connection of the expanded **Placement** panel.

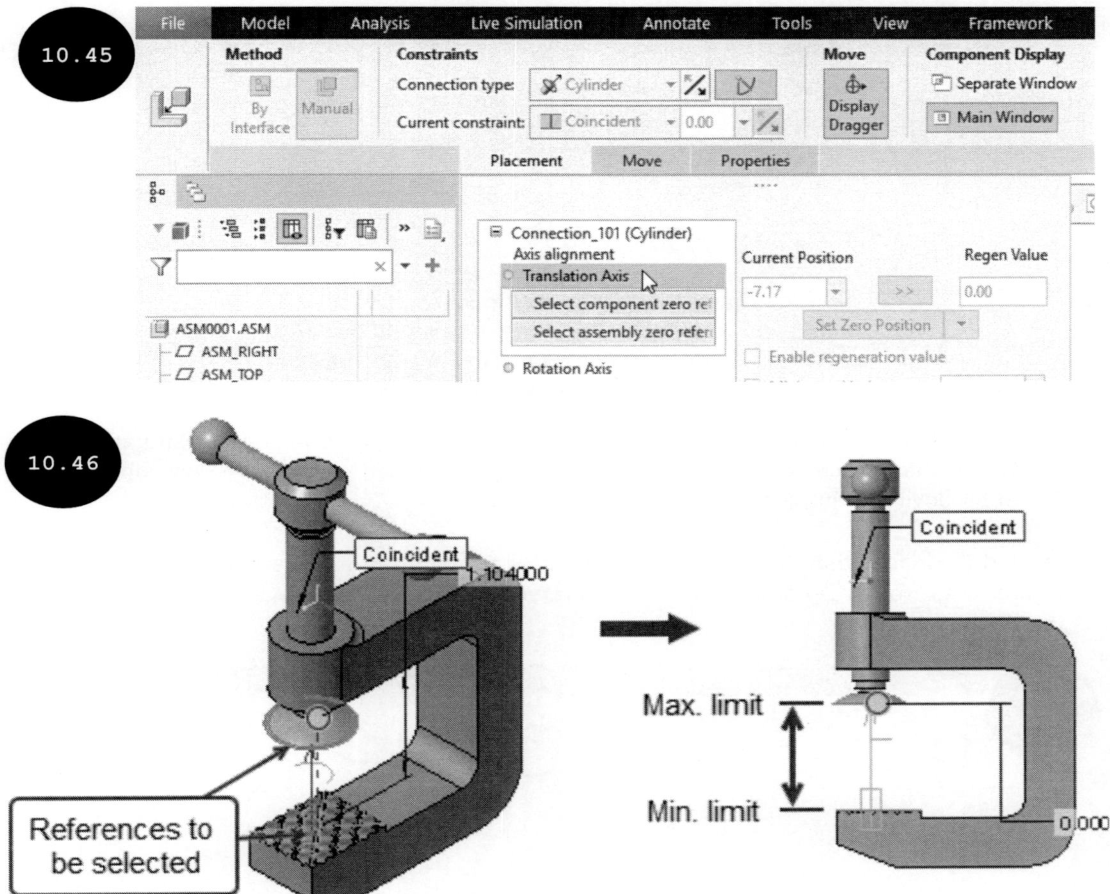

4. Click on the green tick-mark button in the **Component Placement** tab. The Cylinder predefined constraint set is defined and the component can translate and rotate about its axis.

Planar

The Planar predefined constraint set allows the component to translate along two axes as well as rotate about a single axis on a plane, see Figure 10.47. In this joint, you can restrain the component to a planar face of another component such that its movement in the direction normal to the planar face gets restricted and allows movement within the plane of the face. Also, it allows a rotational movement along an axis normal to the planar face. For example, an object moves on the planar face of a table top as well as rotates about an axis normal to the planar face. The method for applying the Planar predefined constraint set is discussed below:

10.47

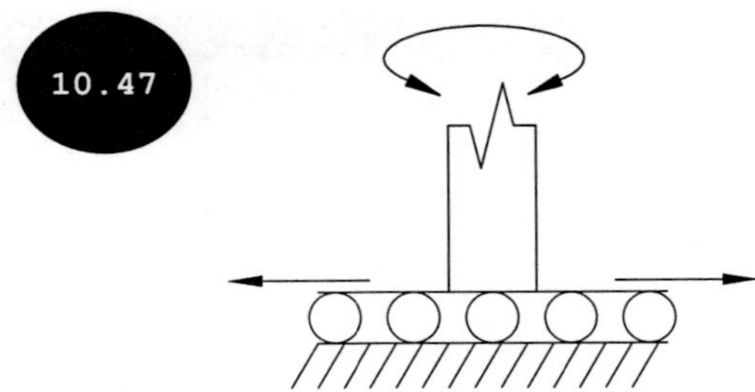

Planar predefined constraint set
(Moves freely within the plane of face and no movements in the direction normal to the planar face. Also, allows a rotational movement about an axis)

1. Select the **Planar** option in the **Connection type** drop-down list in the **Constraints** area of the **Component Placement** tab that appears, every time when you insert a component in the Assembly environment, see Figure 10.48.

2. Expand the **Placement** panel of the **Component Placement** tab, if not expanded by default, see Figure 10.48. You are prompted to select references to apply the planar connection between them.

10.48

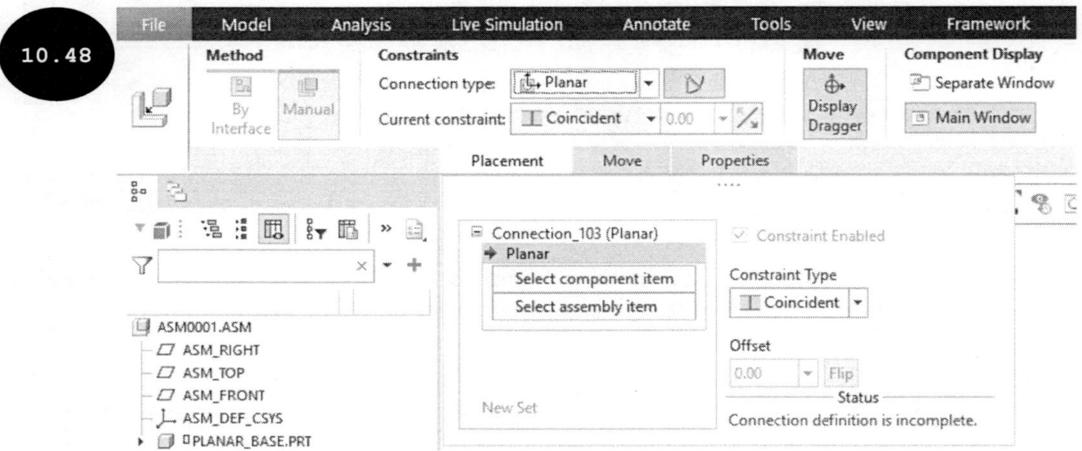

3. Select references of two different components one by one in the graphics area, see Figure 10.49. You can select faces, planes, and datum planes as the references to apply the planar connection. The selected references get aligned with each other and the status appears as **Connection Definition Complete** in the **Status** area of the **Component Placement** tab. This means that the Planar predefined constraint set is defined and the component can translate along two axes and rotate about an axis normal to the plane of the face.

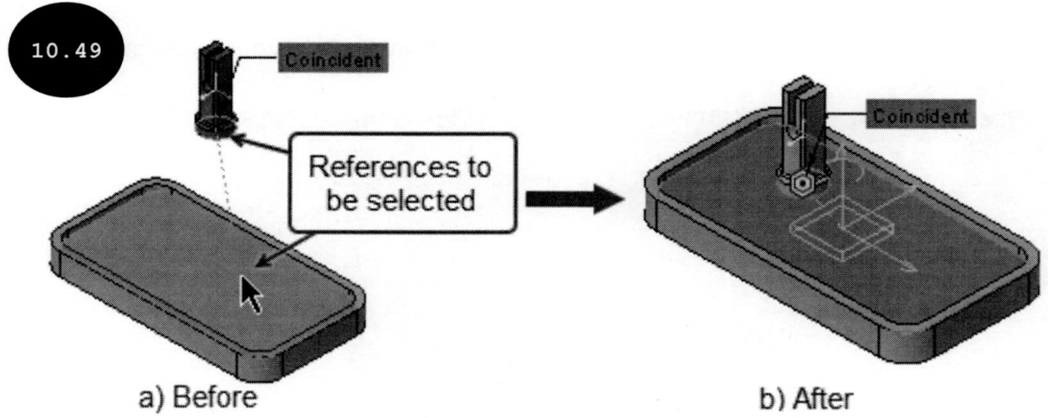

Note: By default, after applying the Planar predefined constraint set, the component can translate along two axes and rotate about an axis normal to the plane of face. However, as discussed earlier, you can limit these translation and rotational movements by applying the additional **Translation Axis 1**, **Translation Axis 2**, and **Rotation Axis** connections that appear in the expanded **Placement** panel.

4. Click on the green tick-mark button in the **Component Placement** tab. The Planar predefined constraint set is defined and the component can translate along two axes and rotate about an axis normal to the plane of the face.

Ball

The Ball predefined constraint set allows the component to rotate about all three rotational axes, see Figure 10.50. In this predefined constraint set, all translational degrees of freedom of the component get restricted and the component can rotate about the three axes with respect to a point. The method for applying the Ball predefined constraint set is discussed below:

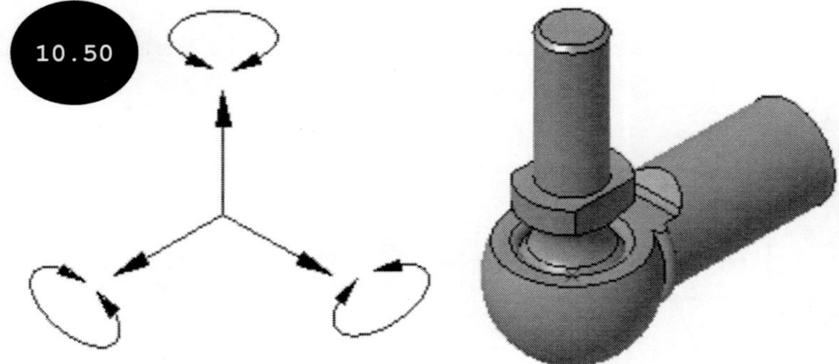

1. Select the **Ball** option in the **Connection type** drop-down list in the **Constraints** area of the **Component Placement** tab that appears, every time you insert a component in the Assembly environment.

2. Expand the **Placement** panel of the **Component Placement** tab, if not expanded by default, see Figure 10.51. You are prompted to select references to apply the point alignment connection between them.

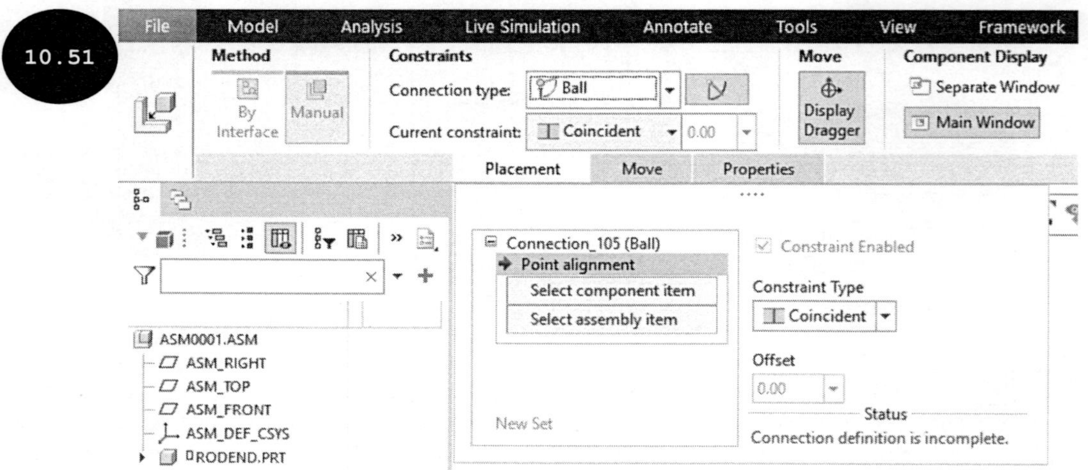

3. Select references of two different components one by one in the graphics area, see Figure 10.52. You can select points, datum points, or vertex as the references to apply the point alignment connection. The selected references get aligned with each other and the status appears as **Connection Definition Complete** in the **Status** area of the **Component Placement** tab. This means that the Ball predefined constraint set is defined and the component can rotate about the three axes with respect to the point selected.

Note: To easily select a reference of the component being inserted for applying a constraint, turn off the display of dragger handles by clicking on the **Display Dragger** button in the **Move** area of the **Component Placement** tab. Note that it is a toggle tool. Alternatively, you can display the component being inserted in a separate window by clicking on the **Separate Window** button in the **Component Placement** tab for easily selecting its reference for applying the constraint.

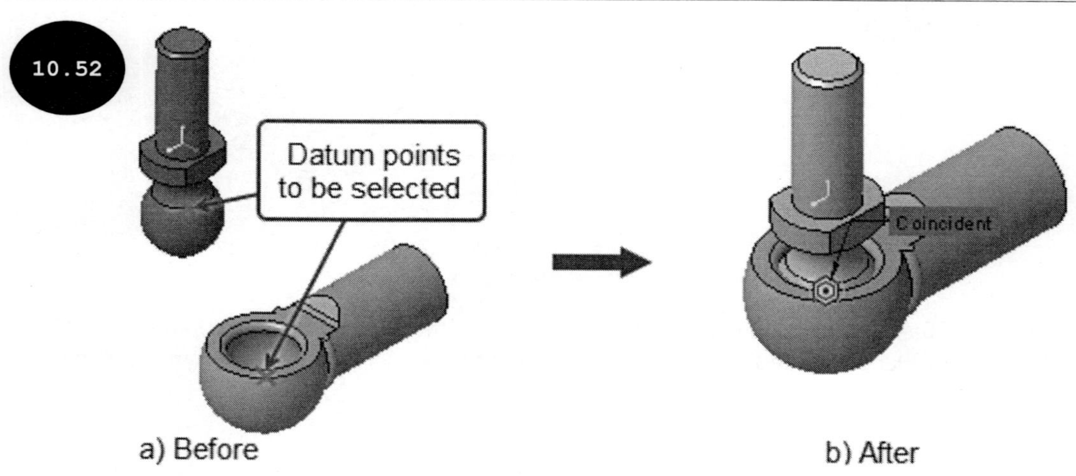

4. Click on the green tick-mark button in the **Component Placement** tab. The Ball predefined constraint set is defined and the component can rotate about three axes and all its translational movements are restricted.

Weld

The Weld predefined constraint set is used for connecting the components together so that they do not have any relative motion to each other and form a weld connection. In this predefined constraint set, all degrees of freedom of the component get restricted by aligning the coordinate systems of two components together. The method for applying the Weld predefined constraint set is discussed below:

1. Select the **Weld** option in the **Connection type** drop-down list in the **Constraints** area of the **Component Placement** tab.

2. Expand the **Placement** panel of the **Component Placement** tab, if not expanded by default. You are prompted to select coordinate systems, see Figure 10.53.

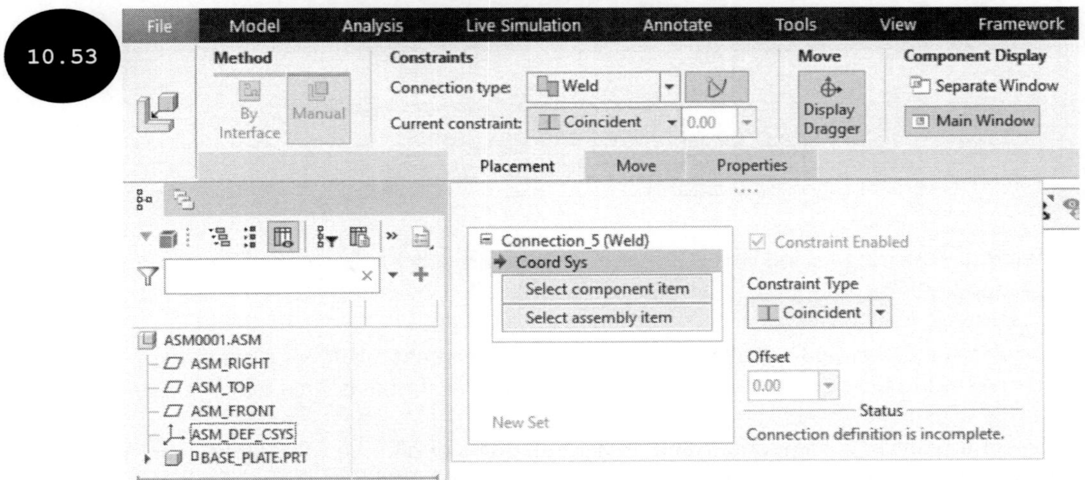

3. Select coordinate systems of two components one by one in the graphics area, see Figure 10.54. Both the coordinate systems get aligned with each other (see Figure 10.54), and the status appears as **Connection Definition Complete** in the **Status** area of the **Component Placement** tab.

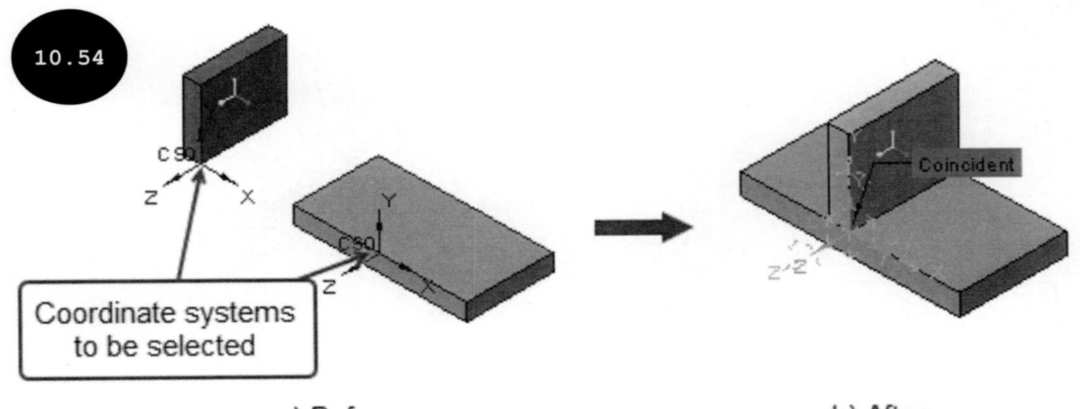

a) Before b) After

4. Click on the green tick-mark button in the **Component Placement** tab. The Weld predefined constraint set is defined and all degrees of freedom of the component get restricted, which means the component cannot move in any direction.

Bearing

The Bearing predefined constraint set is used for defining the bearing connection between the components such that the moveable component can rotate about all its three rotational axes and translate along a specified axis, see Figure 10.55. The method for applying the Bearing predefined constraint set is discussed below:

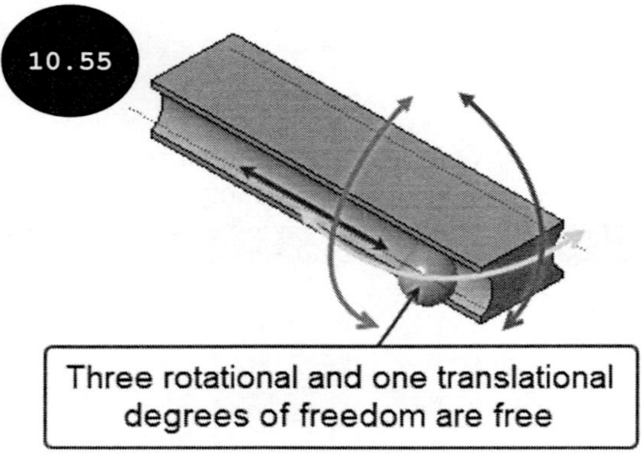

1. Select the **Bearing** option in the **Connection type** drop-down list in the **Constraints** area of the **Component Placement** tab.

2. Expand the **Placement** panel of the **Component Placement** tab, if not expanded by default. You are prompted to select references to apply the point alignment connection between them.

3. Select a point of a component and an axis, an edge, or a curve of another component as the references. The selected references get aligned with each other (see Figure 10.56), and the status appears as **Connection Definition Complete** in the **Component Placement** tab.

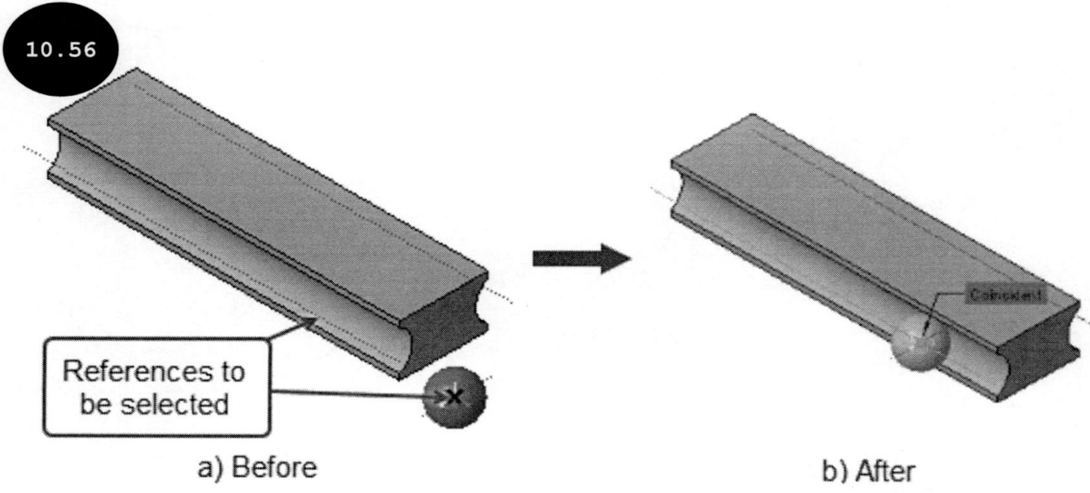

4. Click on the green tick-mark button in the **Component Placement** tab. The Bearing predefined constraint set is defined and the moveable component can rotate about all its three rotational axes and translate along the specified axis.

General

The General predefined constraint set is used for applying one or two user defined constraints. Note that you can only apply a Distance, Parallel, or Coincident constraint as a user defined constraint. The method for applying the General predefined constraint set is the same as applying user defined constraints.

6DOF

The 6DOF predefined constraint set is used for defining a connection between the coordinate systems of two components such that the motion between the components does not get affected. Also, the components remain free to rotate and translate in six degrees of freedom, see Figure 10.57.

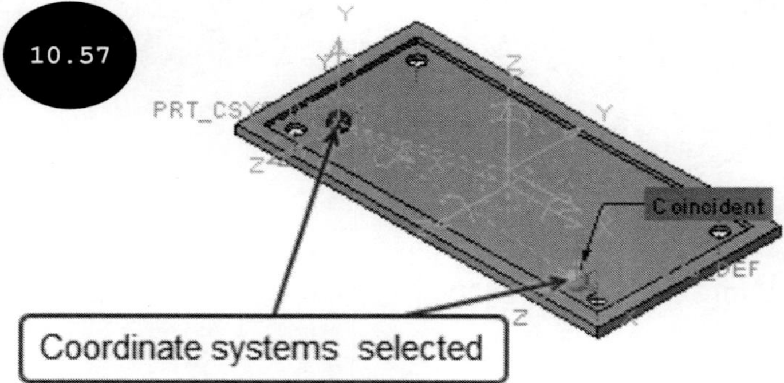

Gimbal

The Gimbal predefined constraint set is used for aligning the origins of the coordinate systems of two components such that the moveable component can rotate around the origin freely. Also, all the translational degrees of freedom of the component get restricted and the component cannot translate in any direction.

Slot

The Slot predefined constraint set is used for translating a point of the component along a trajectory/path of another component, see Figure 10.58. The method for applying the Slot predefined constraint set is discussed below:

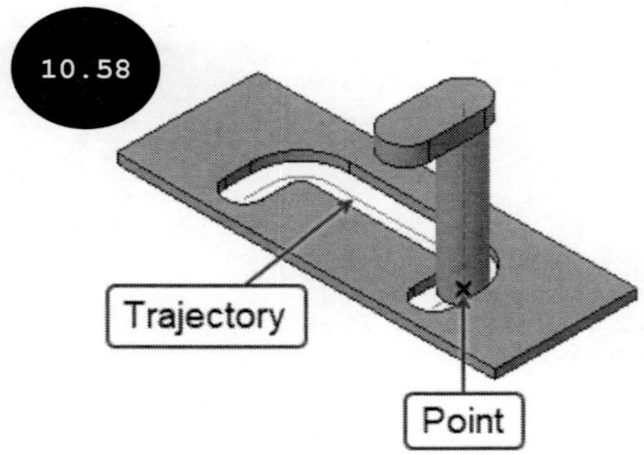

1. Select the **Slot** option in the **Connection type** drop-down list.

2. Expand the **Placement** panel of the **Component Placement** tab, if not expanded by default. You are prompted to select references to apply the point on line connection between them.

3. Select a point or a vertex of a component as the first reference, see Figure 10.59. Next, select end to end connected edges or curves by pressing the CTRL key as the second reference to define the trajectory, see Figure 10.59. The selected point/vertex gets aligned to trajectory and the status appears as **Connection Definition Complete** in the **Component Placement** tab.

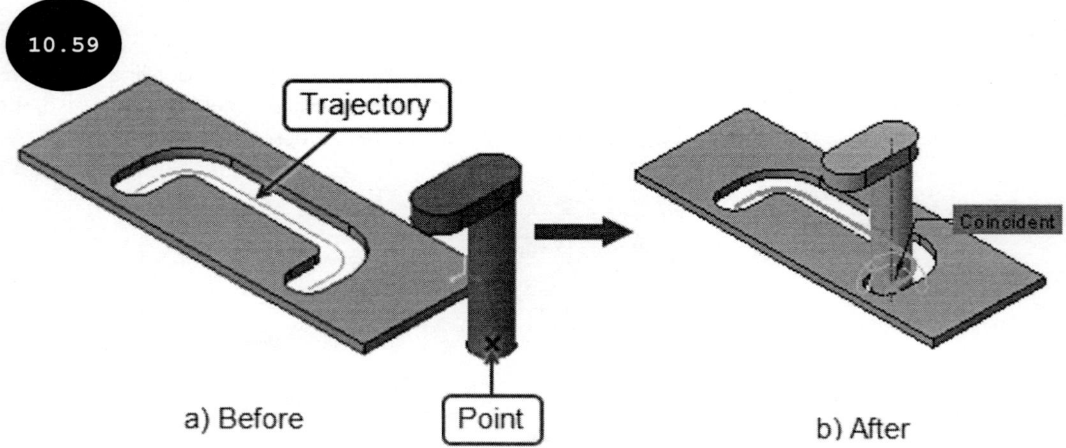

4. Click on the green tick-mark button in the **Component Placement** tab. The Slot predefined constraint set is defined and the selected point/vertex can follow the trajectory in three directions.

Moving/Rotating Individual Components

In Creo Parametric, you can move and rotate individual components of an assembly about their free degrees of freedom by using the **Drag Components** tool. The method for moving and rotating a component is discussed below:

1. Click on the **Drag Components** tool in the **Component** group of the **Model** tab, see Figure 10.60. The **Drag** dialog box appears along with the **Select** window in the graphics area, see Figure 10.61. Also, you are prompted to select a component.

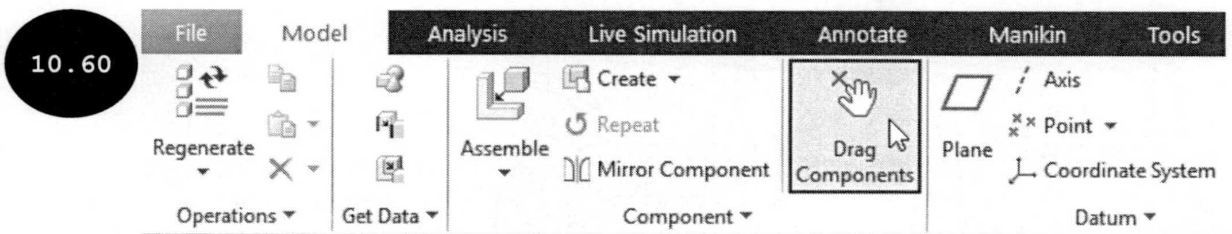

2. Click on the component to be moved or rotated in the graphics area. An indicator point appears on the component, see Figure 10.62.

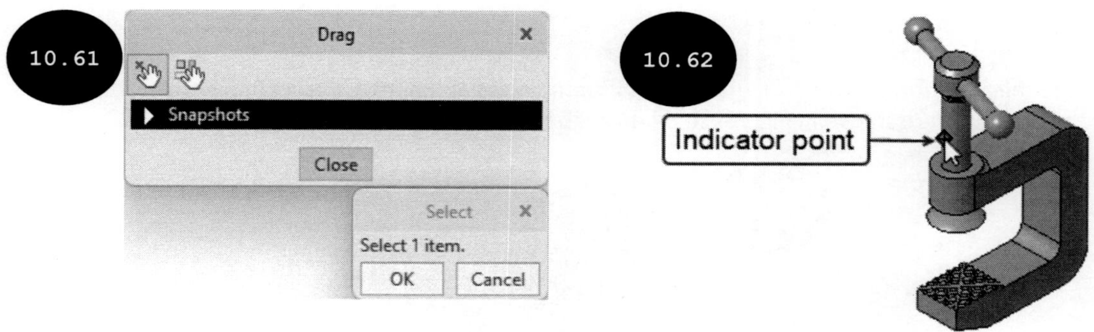

3. Move the cursor pointer in the graphics area. The indicator point follows the cursor movement and the selected component moves/rotates, accordingly along its free degrees of freedom.

4. Click the left mouse button to end the movement of the component.

5. Similarly, you can move other components of the assembly.

6. Press the middle mouse button twice to exit the tool.

Editing Constraints

In Creo Parametric, after assembling the components of an assembly by applying the required constraints, you may need to edit them. To do so, select the component in the **Model Tree** or in the graphics area. The Mini toolbar appears, see Figure 10.63. In the Mini toolbar, click on the **Edit Definition** tool . The **Component Placement** tab appears in the **Ribbon** and the components that are assembled after the selected component become invisible in the graphics area. Now, by using the options of the **Component Placement** tab, you can edit the existing constraints or apply new constraints, as required.

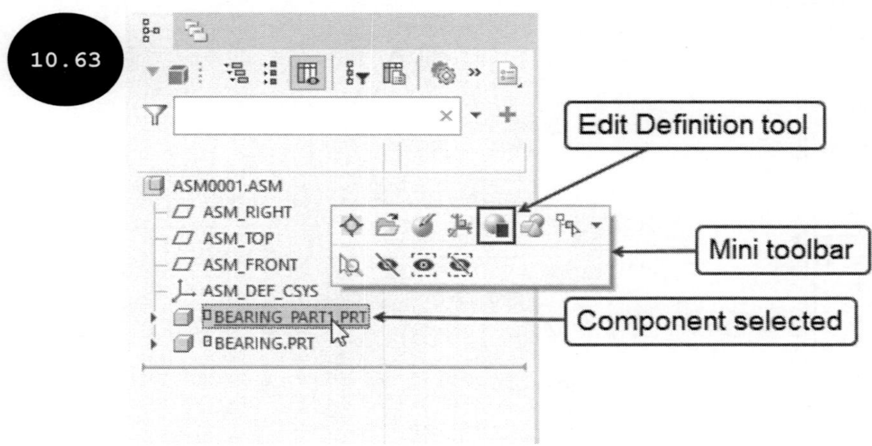

Tutorial 1

Create the assembly shown in Figure 10.64. Different views and dimensions of individual components of the assembly are shown in Figures 10.65 through 10.69. All dimensions are in mm.

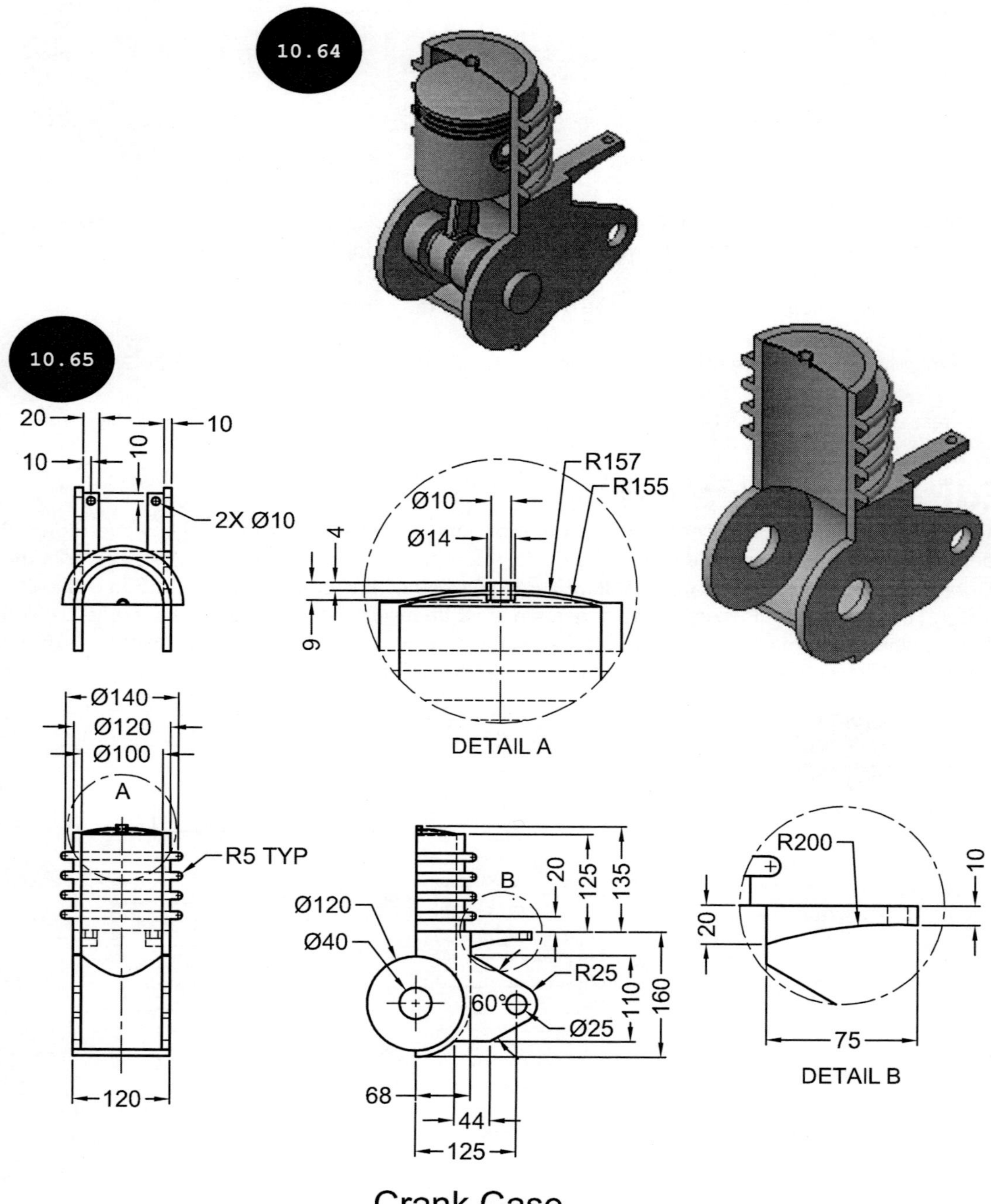

Crank Case

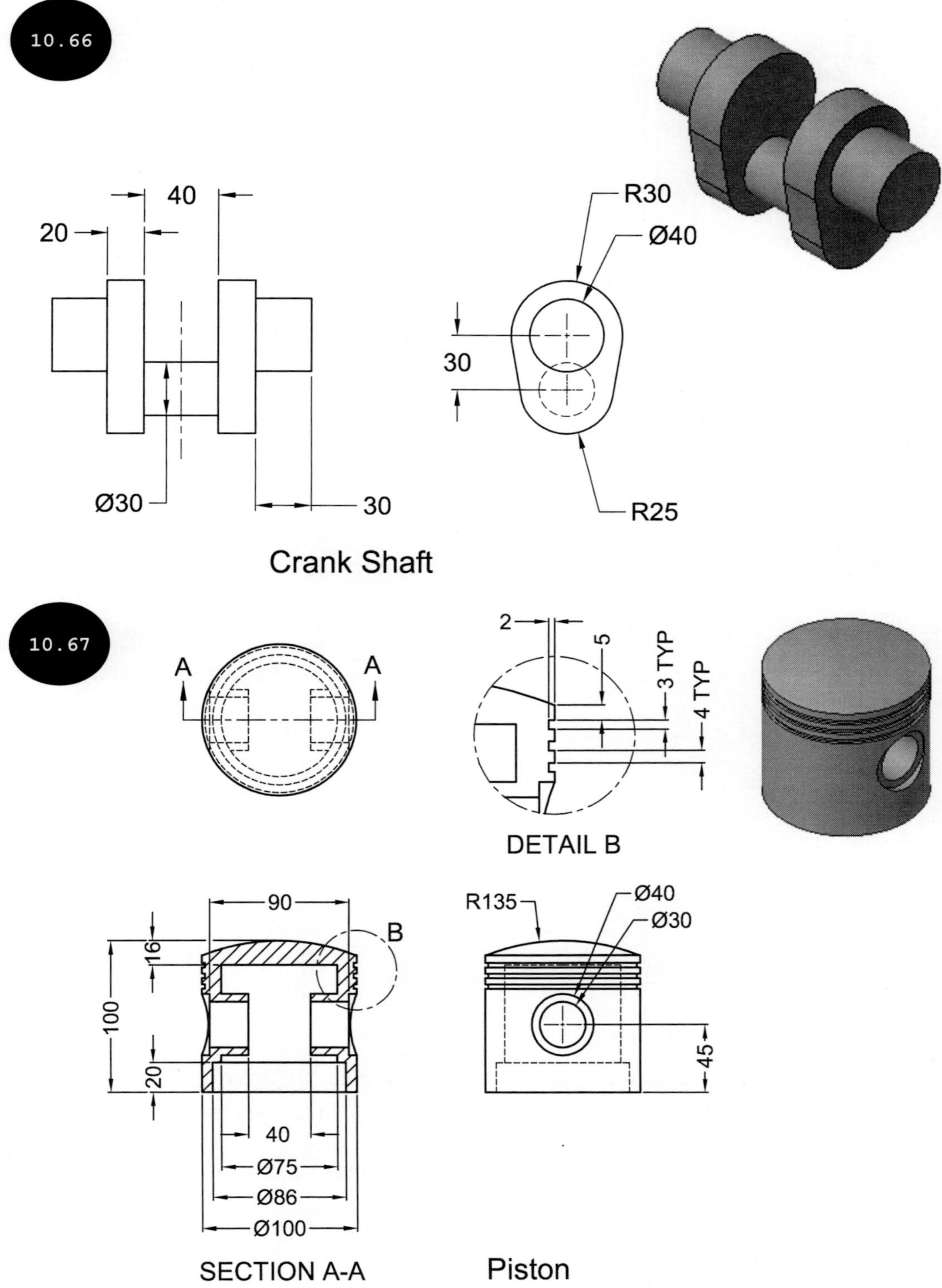

Crank Shaft

SECTION A-A

Piston

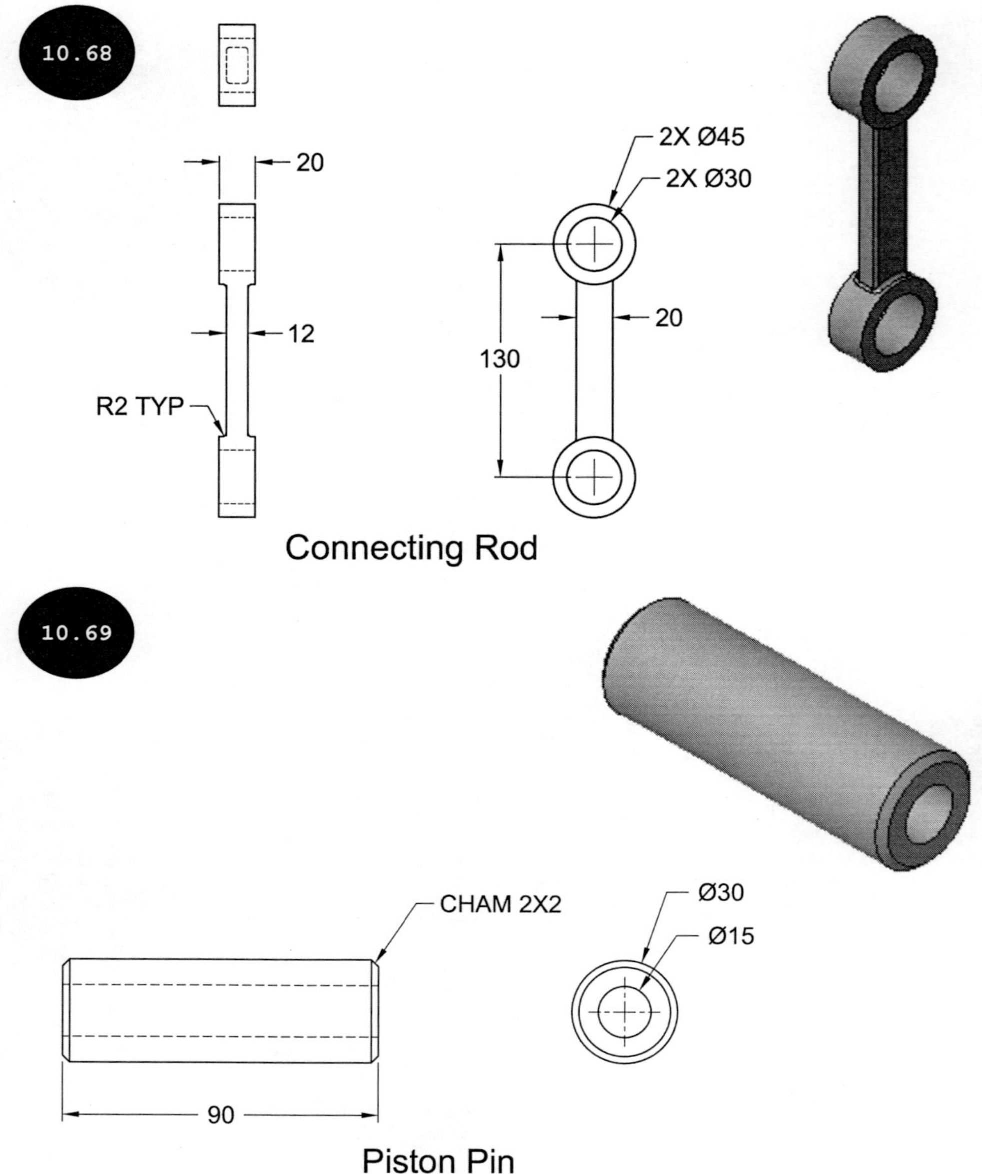

Section 1: Starting Creo and Creating Assembly Components

In this section, you will create all the components of the assembly in the Part mode one by one.

1. Start Creo Parametric by double-clicking on the Creo Parametric icon on your desktop.

2. Set the working directory to <<*Creo Parametric**Chapter 10**Tutorial 1*\\. You need to create these folders in the *Creo Parametric* folder.

3. Create all components of the assembly one by one in the Part mode. Refer to Figures 10.65 through 10.69 for the dimensions of each component. After creating the components, save them in the *Tutorial 1* folder of the *Chapter 10* folder.

Note: You can also download all the assembly components by logging in to your account on the CADArtifex website (***cadartifex.com/login***). If you are a new user, you must first register on the CADArtifex website (***cadartifex.com/register***) to access the online resources.

Section 2: Invoking the Assembly Mode

After creating all the components, you need to assemble them in the Assembly mode.

1. Click on the **New** tool in the **Data** group of the **Home** tab. The **New** dialog box appears. Alternatively, press CTRL + N to invoke the **New** dialog box.

2. Select the **Assembly** radio button in the **Type** area and **Design** radio button in the **Sub-type** area of the **New** dialog box, see Figure 10.70.

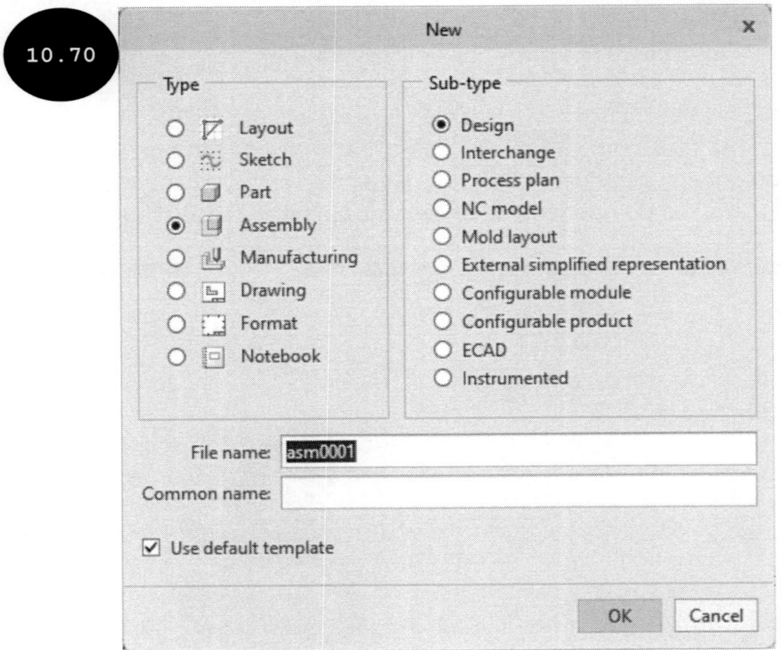

3. Enter **C10-Tutorial01** in the **File name** field of the dialog box as the name of the assembly.

4. Clear the **Use default template** check box and then click on the **OK** button in the dialog box. The **New File Options** dialog box appears, see Figure 10.71.

5. Select the **mmns_asm_design_abs** template in the **New File Options** dialog box and then click on the **OK** button. The Assembly mode is invoked with the **mmns_asm_design_abs** template.

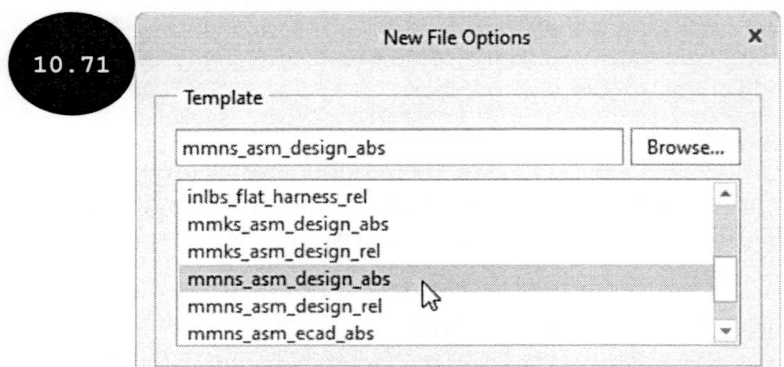

Section 3: Inserting the First Component - Crank Case

1. Click on the **Assemble** tool in the **Component** group of the **Model** tab, see Figure 10.72. The **Open** dialog box appears.

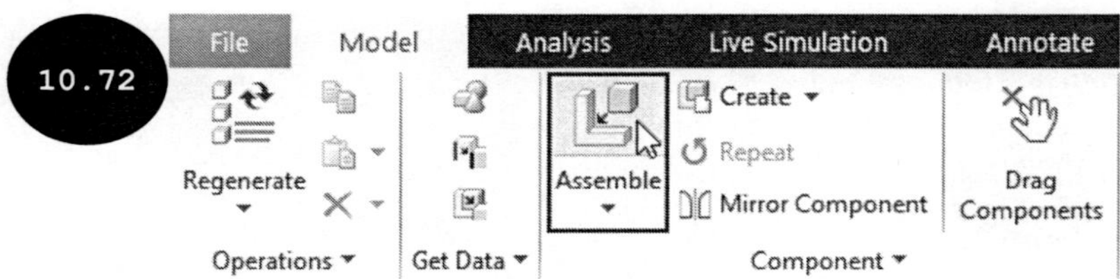

2. Select the *Crank Case* component and then click on the **Open** button in the dialog box. The selected component gets inserted in the Assembly environment with the 3D Dragger, see Figure 10.73. Also, the **Component Placement** tab appears in the **Ribbon**.

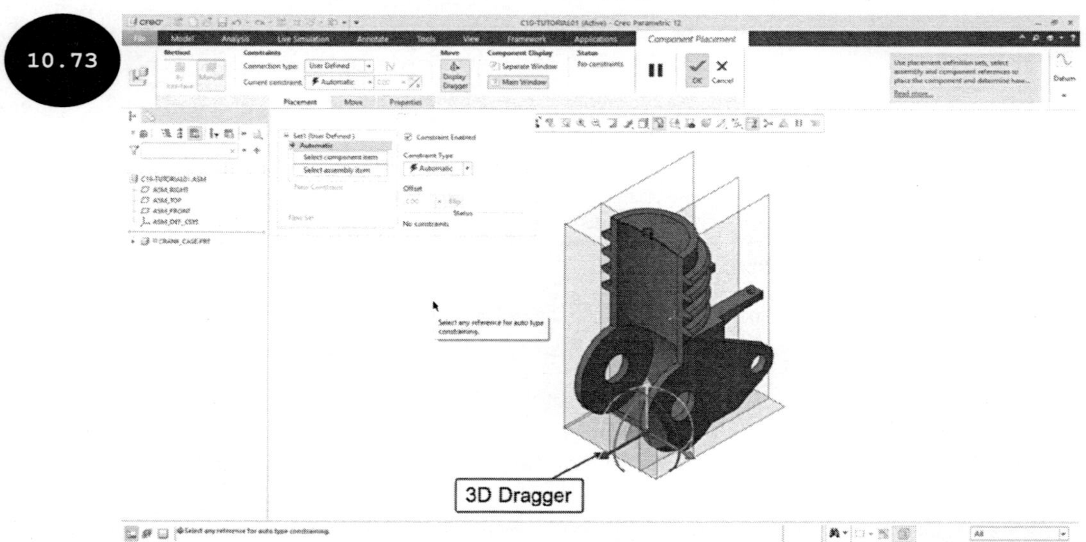

3. Select the **Default** constraint in the **Current constraint** drop-down list of the **Component Placement** tab, see Figure 10.74. The component moves toward the assembly coordinate system and becomes a fixed component with respect to the assembly coordinate system. Also, the status of the components appears as **Fully constrained** in the **Component Placement** tab.

10.74

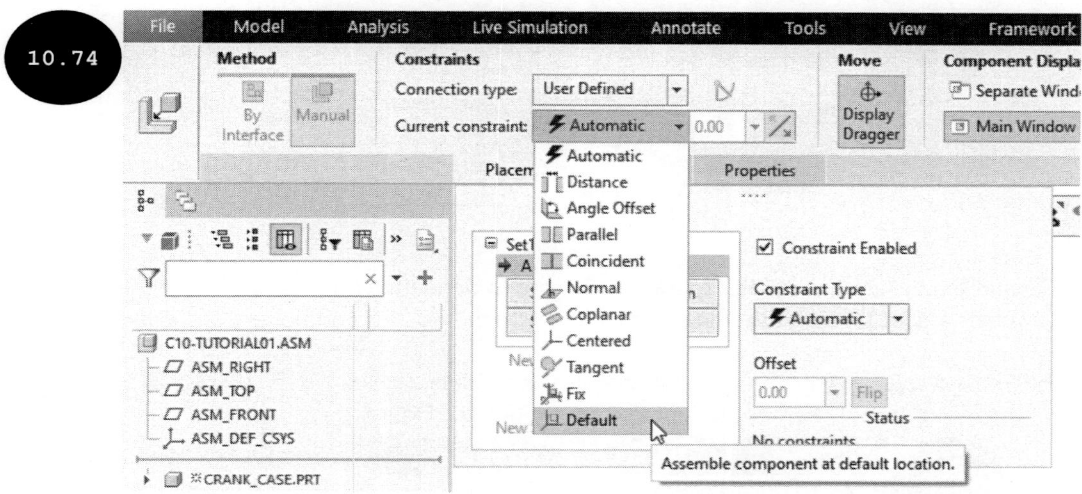

4. Click on the green tick-mark button in the **Component Placement** tab. The ***Crank Case*** component gets inserted in the Assembly environment and becomes a fixed component with respect to the assembly coordinate system.

Section 4: Inserting the Second Component - Crank Shaft

1. Click on the **Assemble** tool in the **Component** group of the **Model** tab. The **Open** dialog box appears.

2. Select the ***Crank Shaft*** component and then click on the **Open** button in the dialog box. The selected component gets inserted in the Assembly environment with the 3D Dragger, see Figure 10.75. Also, the **Component Placement** tab appears in the **Ribbon**.

10.75

Note: In Figure 10.75, the display of datum axes, points, coordinate systems, and planes is turned off. To do so, invoke the **Datum Display Filters** flyout of the **In-graphics** toolbar and then clear the **Select All** check box, see Figure 10.76.

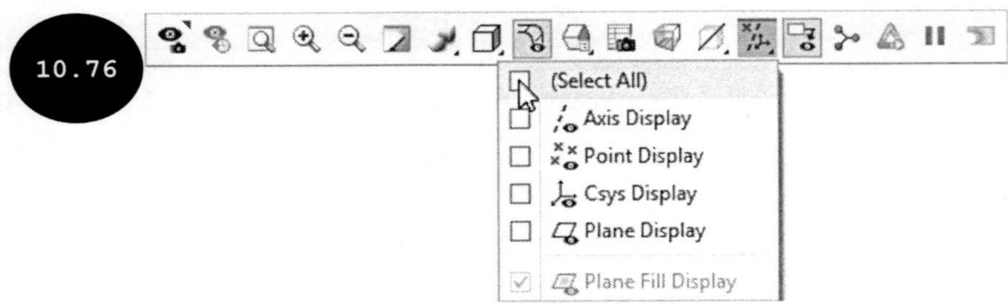

3. Drag the translational handles of the 3D Dragger to define the position of the component in the graphics area such that it should not intersect with the existing component of the assembly.

4. Hide the display of the 3D Dragger in the graphics area by clicking on the **Display Dragger** button in the **Move** area of the **Component Placement** tab, see Figure 10.77.

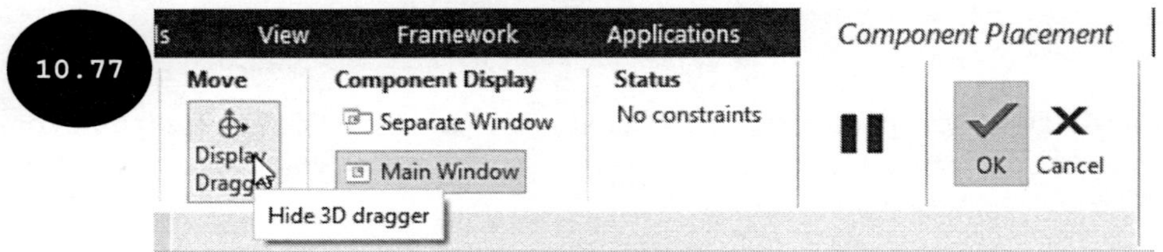

5. Select the **Pin** option in the **Connection type** drop-down list of the **Constraints** area to apply the Pin predefined constraint between the components, see Figure 10.78.

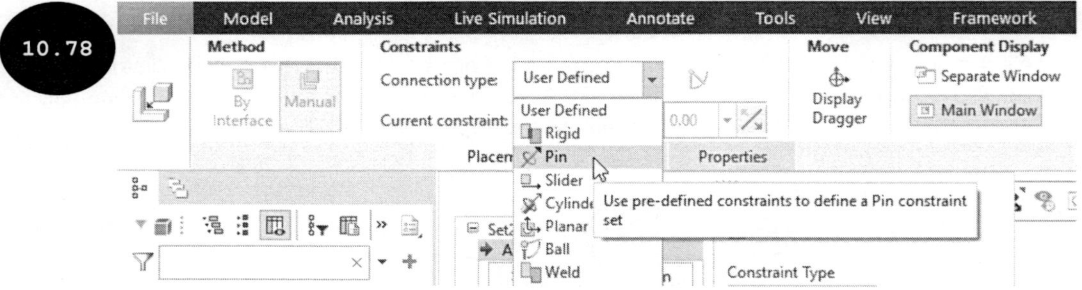

6. Expand the **Placement** panel of the **Component Placement** tab, see Figure 10.79. You are prompted to select references for applying the axis alignment connection.

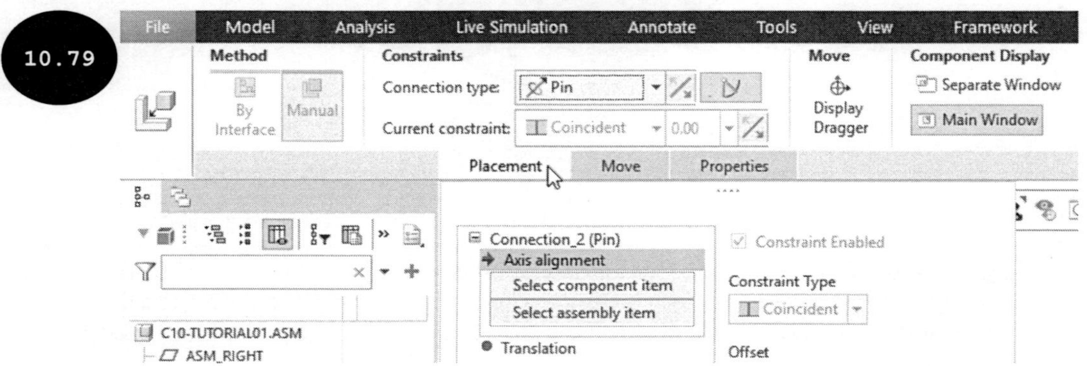

7. Select the circular face of the second component (*Crank Shaft*) as the component reference and then select the circular face of the first component (*Crank Case*) as the assembly reference, see Figure 10.80. The axes of both the selected references get aligned to each other by applying the Coincident constraint between them. Also, you are prompted to select references for applying the translation connection.

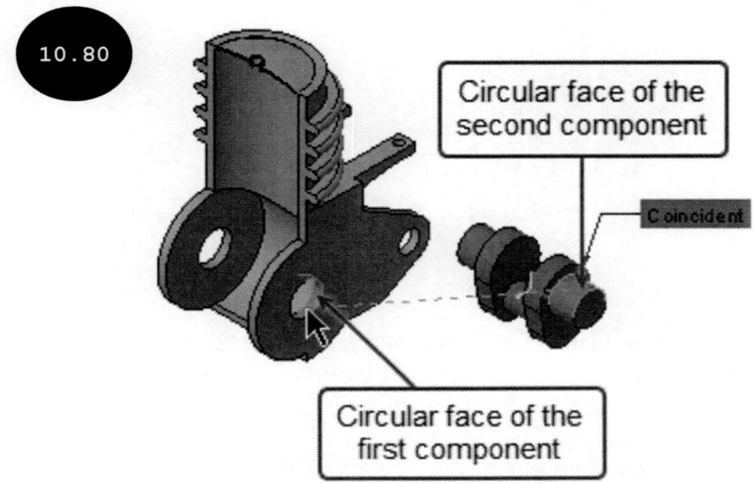

8. Ensure that the display of datum planes is turned on in the graphics area. To turn on the display of datum planes, invoke the **Datum Display Filters** flyout of the **In-graphics** toolbar and then select the **Plane Display** check box, see Figure 10.81.

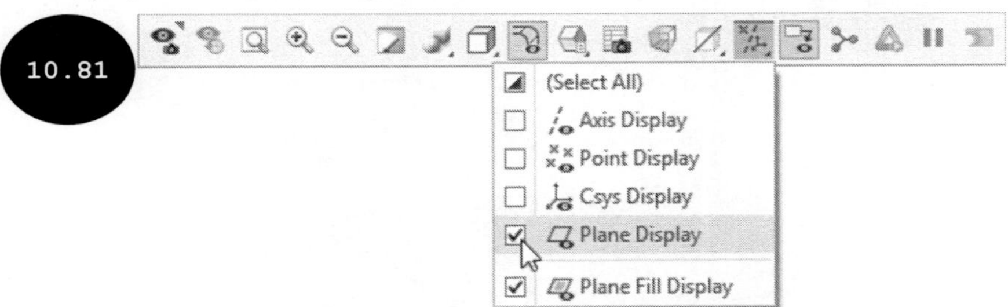

9. Select the Right datum plane of the second component (*Crank Shaft*) as the component reference and then select the Right datum plane of the first component (*Crank Case*) as the assembly reference to apply the translation connection between them, see Figure 10.82. The selected references become coincident with each other and the status appears as **Connection Definition Complete** in the **Status** area of the **Component Placement** tab. This means that the Pin predefined constraint set is defined and the second component (*Crank Shaft*) can only rotate about its axis, see Figure 10.83.

Note: In Figure 10.83, the display of datum planes is turned off for clarity of the image.

10. Click on the green tick-mark button in the **Component Placement** tab. The Pin predefined constraint set is defined and the *Crank Shaft* component can only rotate about its axis.

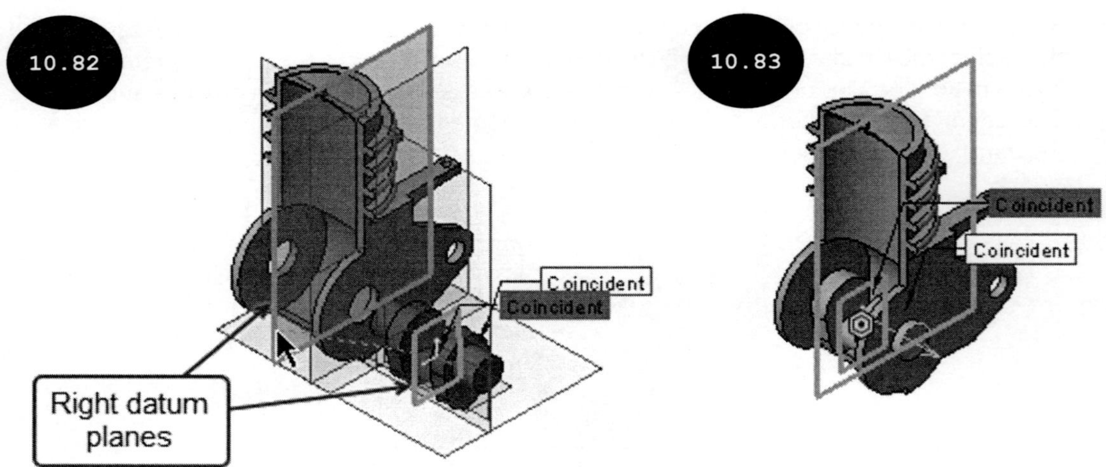

Section 5: Inserting the Third Component - Connecting Rod

1. Click on the **Assemble** tool in the **Component** group of the **Model** tab. The **Open** dialog box appears.

2. Select the *Connecting Rod* component and then click on the **Open** button in the dialog box. The selected component gets inserted in the Assembly environment, see Figure 10.84. Also, the **Component Placement** tab appears in the **Ribbon**.

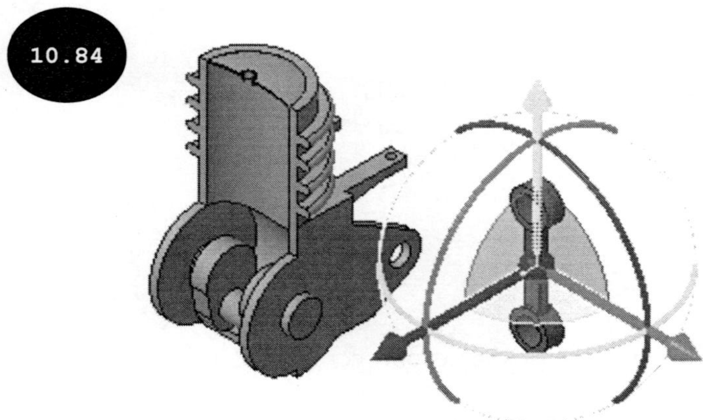

3. Drag the translational handles of the 3D Dragger to define the position of the component in the graphics area such that it should not intersect with the existing components of the assembly.

4. Hide the display of the 3D Dragger in the graphics area. You can turn on or off the display of the 3D Dragger by clicking on the **Display Dragger** button in the **Move** area of the **Component Placement** tab.

5. Select the **Pin** option in the **Connection type** drop-down list of the **Component Placement** tab and then expand the **Placement** panel, if not expanded by default, see Figure 10.85. You are prompted to select references for applying the axis alignment connection.

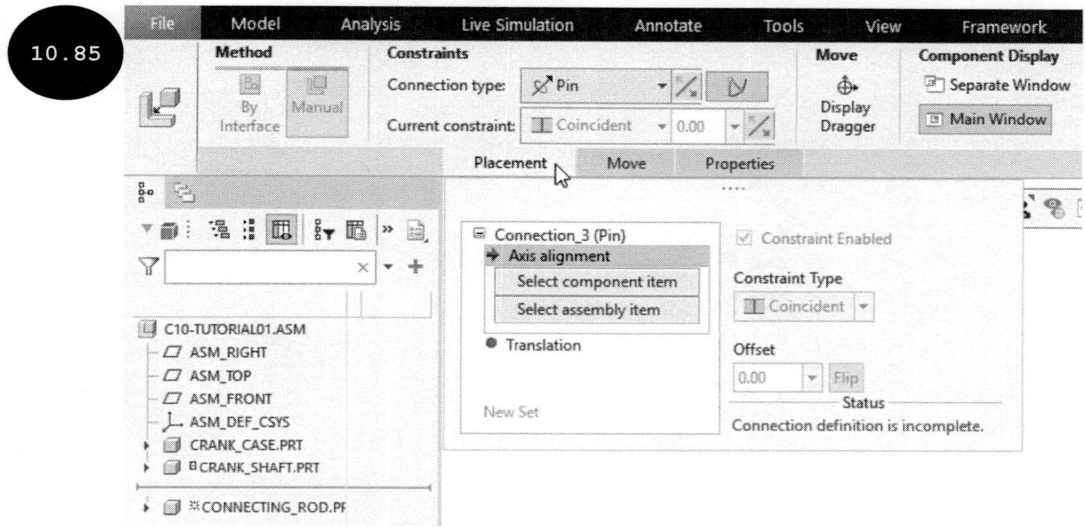

6. Select the circular face of the bottom hole of the third component (*Connecting Rod*) as the component reference and then select the circular face of the second component (*Crank Shaft*) as the assembly reference, see Figure 10.86. The axes of both the selected references get aligned to each other by applying the Coincident constraint between them. Also, you are prompted to select references for applying the translation connection.

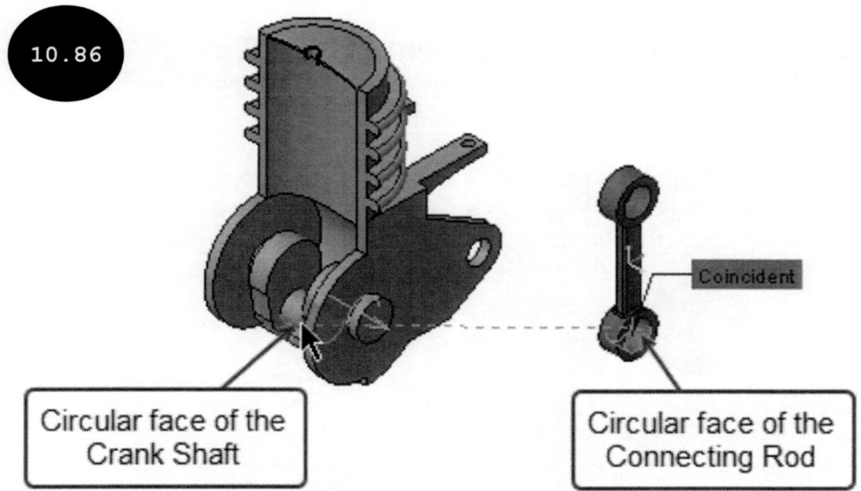

7. Ensure that the display of datum planes is turned on in the graphics area.

8. Select the Right datum plane of the third component (*Connecting Rod*) as the component reference and then select the Right datum plane of the second component (*Crank Shaft*) as the assembly reference to apply the translation connection between them, see Figure 10.87. The selected references become coincident with each other and the status appears as **Connection Definition Complete** in the **Status** area of the **Component Placement** tab. This means that the Pin predefined constraint set is defined and the *Connecting Rod* component can only rotate about its axis, see Figure 10.88.

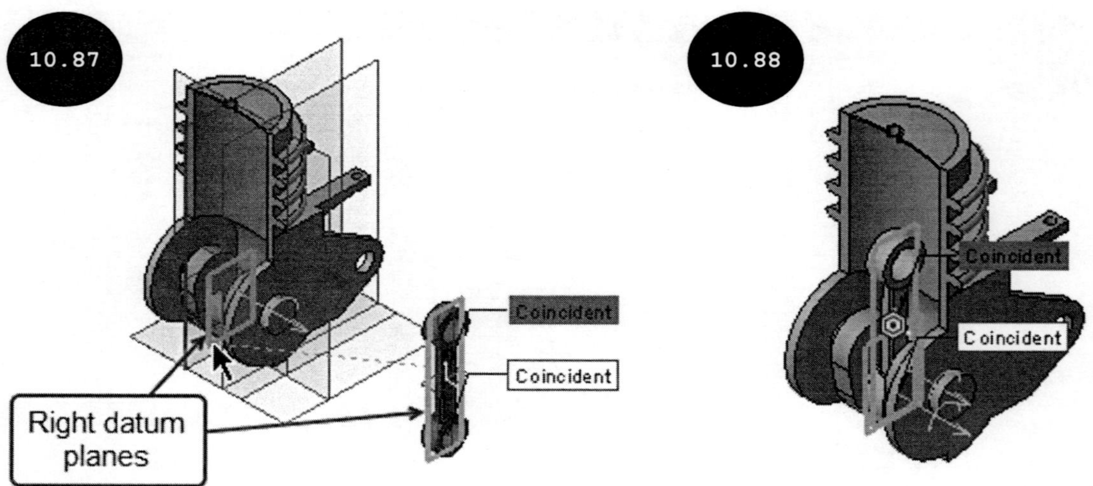

Note: In Figure 10.88, the display of datum planes is turned off for clarity of the image.

9. Click on the green tick-mark button in the **Component Placement** tab. The Pin predefined constraint set is defined and the *Connecting Rod* component can only rotate about its axis.

Section 6: Inserting the Fourth Component - Piston Pin

1. Click on the **Assemble** tool in the **Component** group of the **Model** tab. The **Open** dialog box appears.

2. Select the *Piston Pin* component and then click on the **Open** button in the dialog box. The selected component gets inserted in the Assembly environment, see Figure 10.89. Also, the **Component Placement** tab appears in the **Ribbon**.

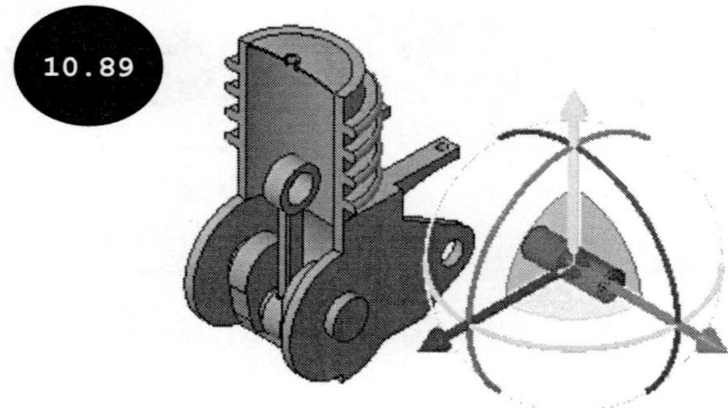

3. Drag the translational handles of the 3D Dragger to define the position of the component in the graphics area such that it should not intersect with the existing components of the assembly.

4. Hide the display of the 3D Dragger in the graphics area. You can turn on or off the display of the 3D Dragger by clicking on the **Display Dragger** button in the **Component Placement** tab.

5. Ensure that the **User Defined** option is selected in the **Connection type** drop-down list and the **Automatic** option is selected in the **Current constraint** drop-down list to apply placement constraints, automatically, see Figure 10.90.

10.90

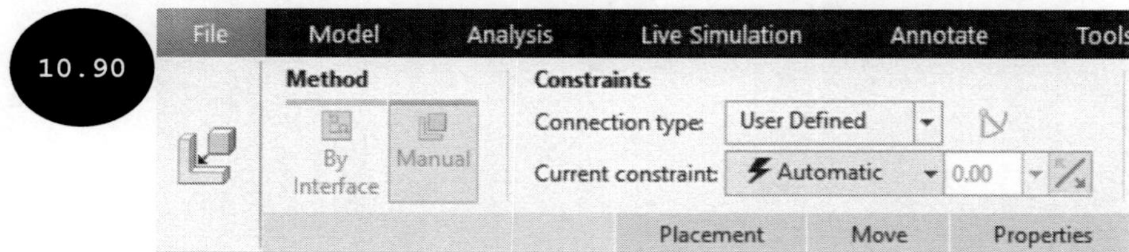

6. Select the circular face of the fourth component (*Piston Pin*) as the component reference and then select the upper circular face of the third component (*Connecting Rod*) as the assembly reference, see Figure 10.91. The axes of both the selected references get aligned to each other by applying the Coincident constraint between them. Also, you are prompted to select references for applying the translation connection.

10.91

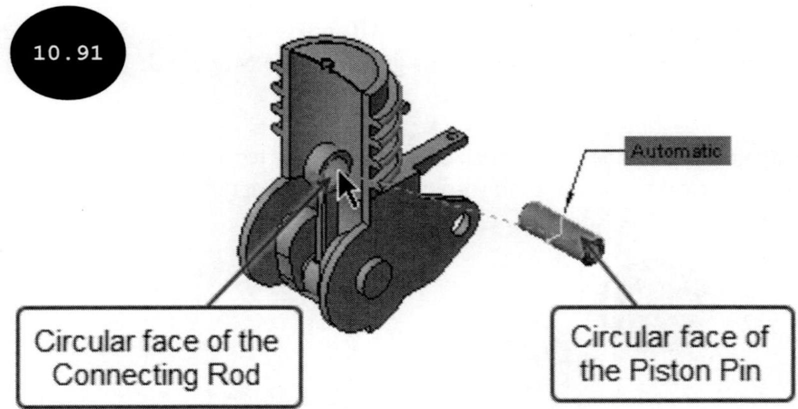

7. Ensure that the display of datum planes is turned on in the graphics area.

8. Select the Right datum plane of the fourth component (*Piston Pin*) as the component reference and then select the Right datum plane of the third component (*Connecting Rod*) as the assembly reference to apply the translation connection between them, see Figure 10.92. Select the **Coincident** option in the **Current constraint** drop-down list. The selected references become coincident with each other (see Figure 10.93), and the status appears as **Fully constrained using assumptions** in the **Status** area of the **Component Placement** tab.

Note: In Figure 10.93, the display of datum planes is turned off for clarity of the image.

9. Click on the green tick-mark button in the **Component Placement** tab. The *Piston Pin* component is assembled in the assembly.

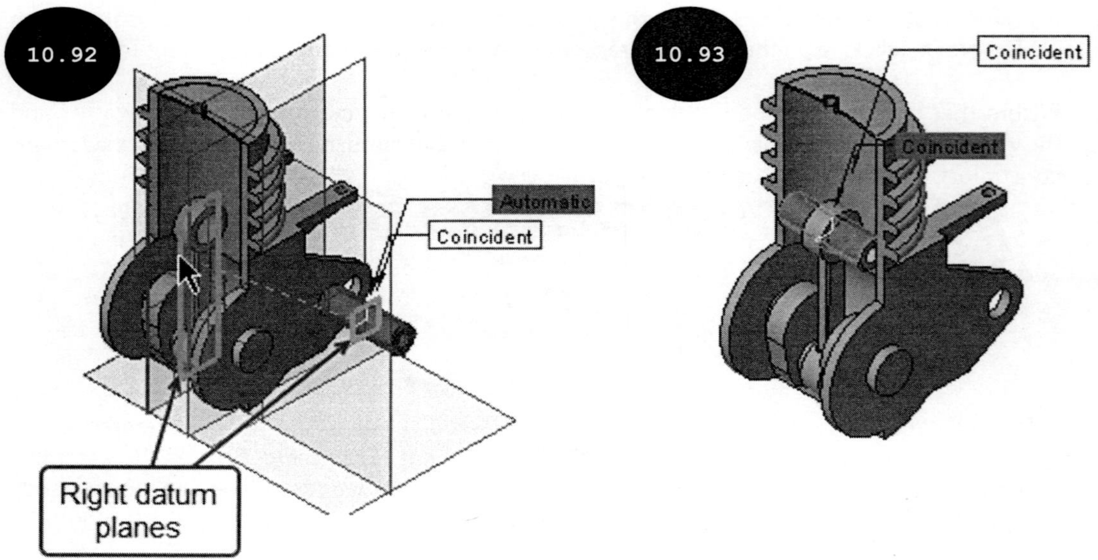

Section 7: Inserting the Fifth Component - Piston

1. Click on the **Assemble** tool in the **Component** group of the **Model** tab. The **Open** dialog box appears.

2. Select the *Piston* component and then click on the **Open** button in the dialog box. The selected component gets inserted in the Assembly environment, see Figure 10.94. Also, the **Component Placement** tab appears in the **Ribbon**.

3. Select the **Cylinder** option in the **Connection type** drop-down list in the **Constraints** area of the **Component Placement** tab and then expand the **Placement** panel, if not expanded by default, see Figure 10.95. You are prompted to select references for applying the axis alignment connection.

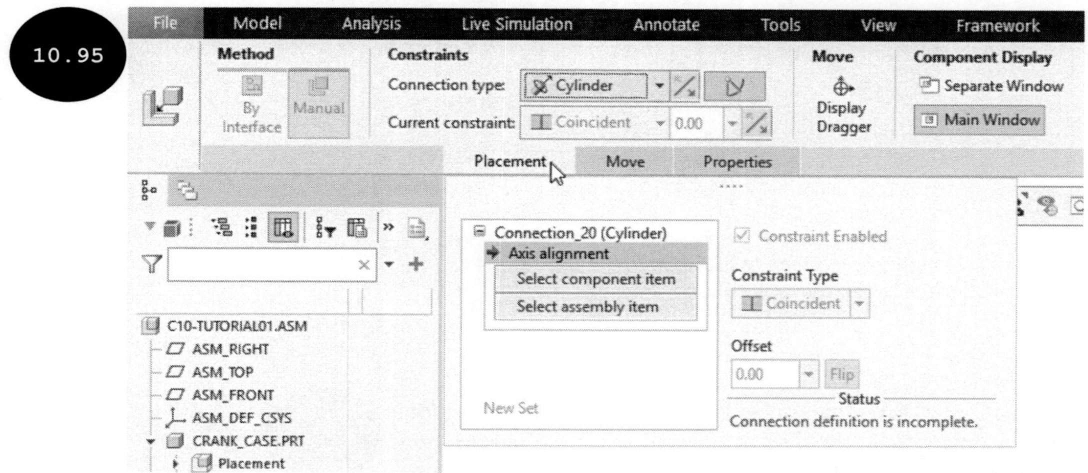

4. Select the outer circular face of the fifth component (Piston) as the component reference and then select the inner circular face of the first component (Crank Case) as the assembly reference, see Figure 10.96. The axes of both the selected references get aligned with each other, see Figure 10.97. Also, the status appears as **Connection Definition Complete** in the **Status** area of the **Component Placement** tab. This means that the Cylinder predefined constraint set is defined and the Piston can translate as well as rotate about its axis.

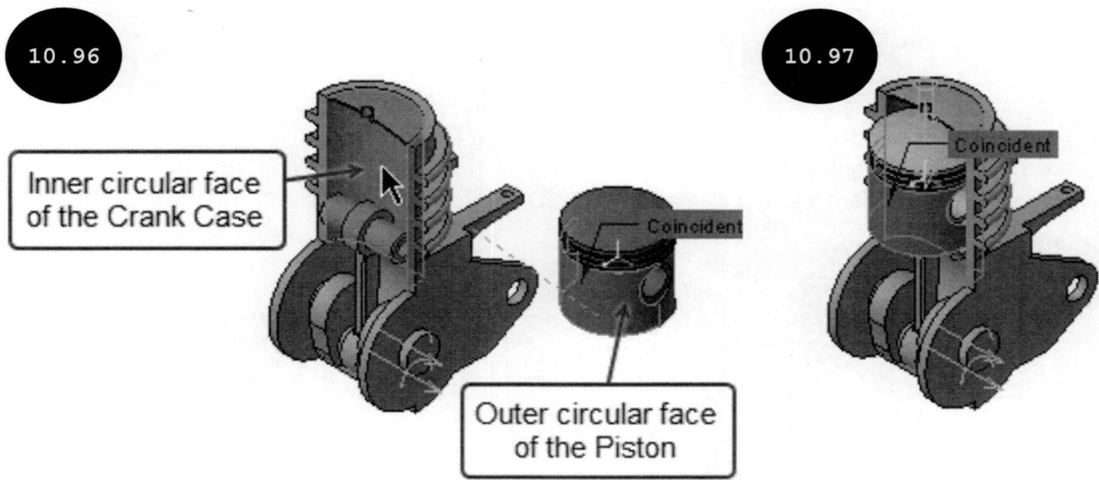

Now, you need to apply an additional constraint set to connect the Piston and the Connecting Rod.

5. Click on the **New Set** option in the expanded **Placement** panel of the **Component Placement** tab, see Figure 10.98. A new connection set is added in the expanded **Placement** panel.

10.98

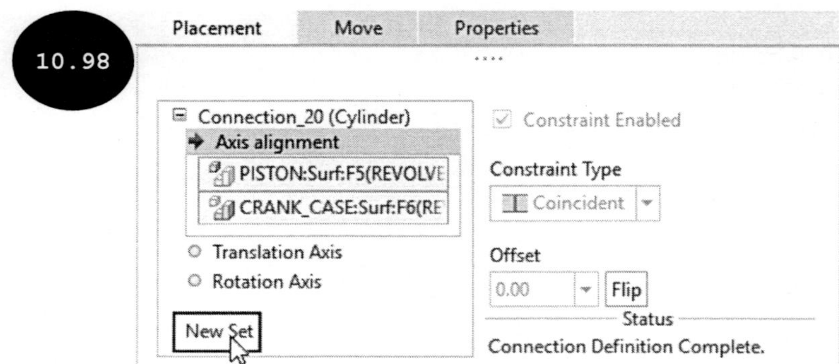

6. Select the **General** option in the **Connection type** drop-down list in the **Constraints** area of the **Component Placement** tab as the newly added constraint set to be applied.

10.99

7. Move the Piston component outside the assembly by dragging the translational handle of the 3D Dragger, see Figure 10.99. Note that you can turn on or off the display of 3D Dragger in the graphics area by clicking on the **Display Dragger** button in the **Move** area of the **Component Placement** tab.

8. Select the circular face of the hole of the Piston component and then the outer circular face of the **Piston Pin** component, see Figure 10.100. The Coincident constraint is applied such that the axes of both the selected circular faces get aligned with each other, see Figure 10.101.

10.100 10.101

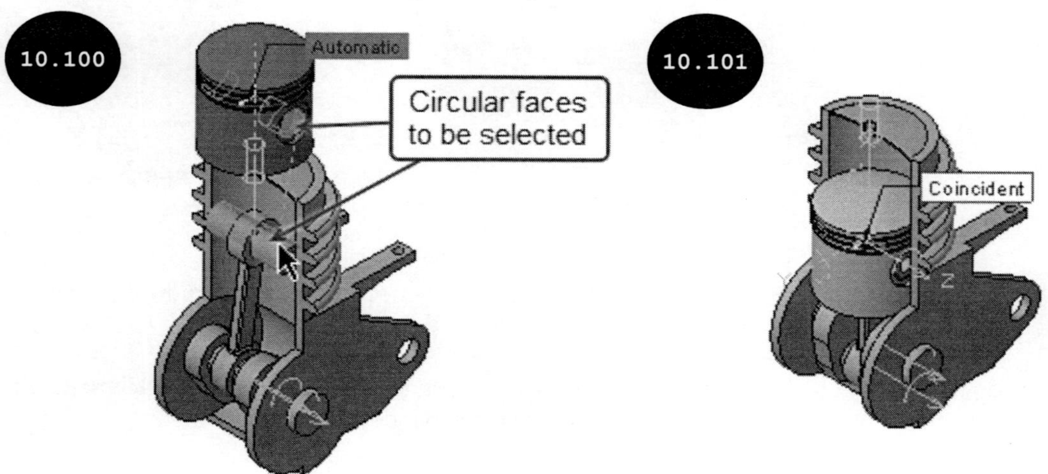

9. Click on the green tick-mark button in the **Component Placement** tab. The Cylinder and General predefined constraint sets are defined. Figure 10.102 shows the final assembly.

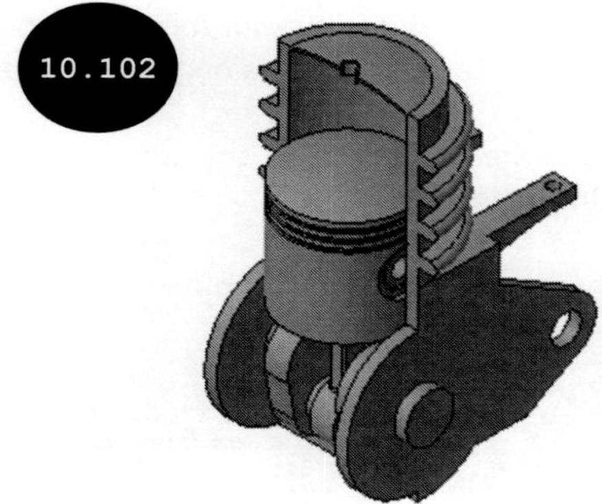

Section 8: Reviewing the motion of the assembly

After assembling all the components of the assembly, you can move its components along their free degrees of freedom to review the motion.

1. Click on the **Drag Components** tool in the **Component** group, see Figure 10.103. The **Drag** dialog box appears along with the **Select** window in the graphics area.

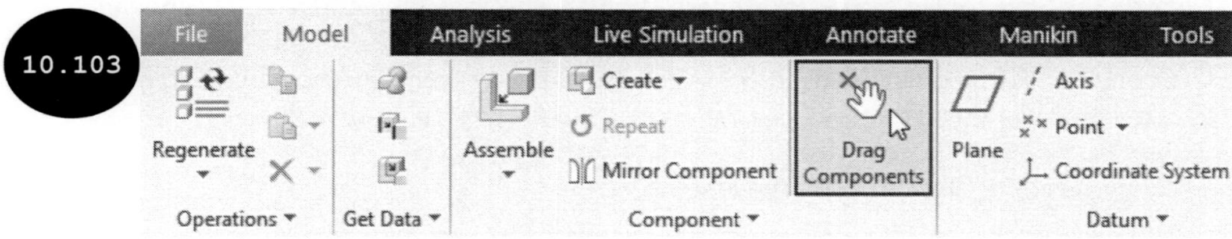

2. Click on the second component (*Crank Shaft*) of the assembly as the component to be moved. An indicator point appears on the selected component (*Crank Shaft*), see Figure 10.104.

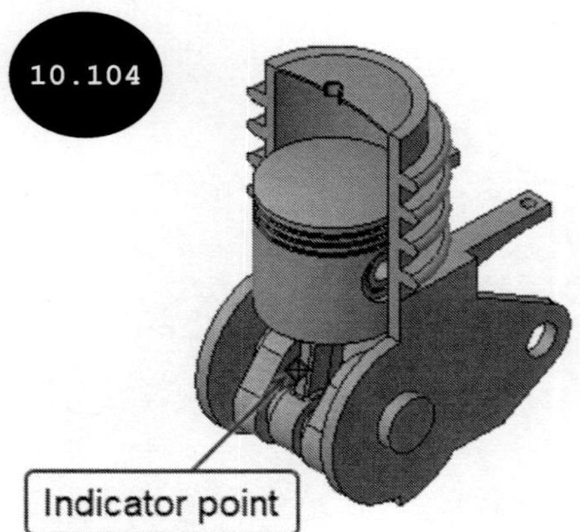

3. Move the cursor in the graphics area. The indicator point follows the cursor movement and the components of the assembly move/rotate, accordingly along their free degrees of freedom.

4. Click the left mouse button to end the movement of the component. Next, press the middle mouse button twice to exit the **Drag Components** tool.

5. Click on the **Regenerate** tool in the **Quick Access Toolbar** to regenerate the assembly, see Figure 10.105.

10.105

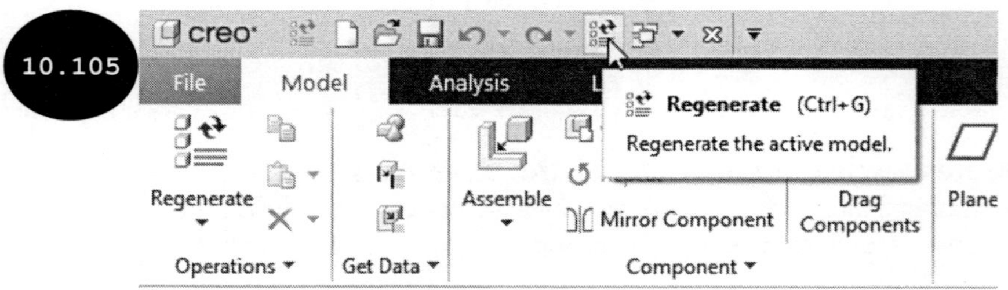

Section 9: Saving the Assembly

1. Click on the **Save** tool in the **Quick Access Toolbar**. The **Save Object** dialog box appears.

2. Click on the **OK** button in the dialog box. The assembly is saved with the name **C10-Tutorial01** in the specified working directory (<<*\Creo Parametric\Chapter 10\Tutorial 1*).

3. Click on the **File > Close** to close the assembly.

Tutorial 2

Create the assembly shown in Figure 10.106. Different views and dimensions of individual components of the assembly are shown in Figures 10.107 through 10.114. All dimensions are in mm.

10.106

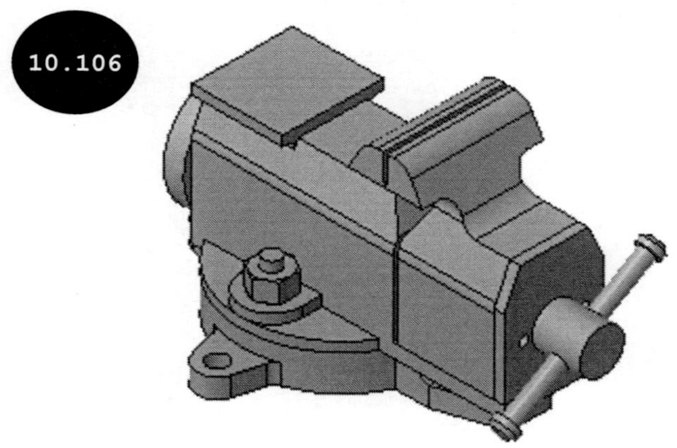

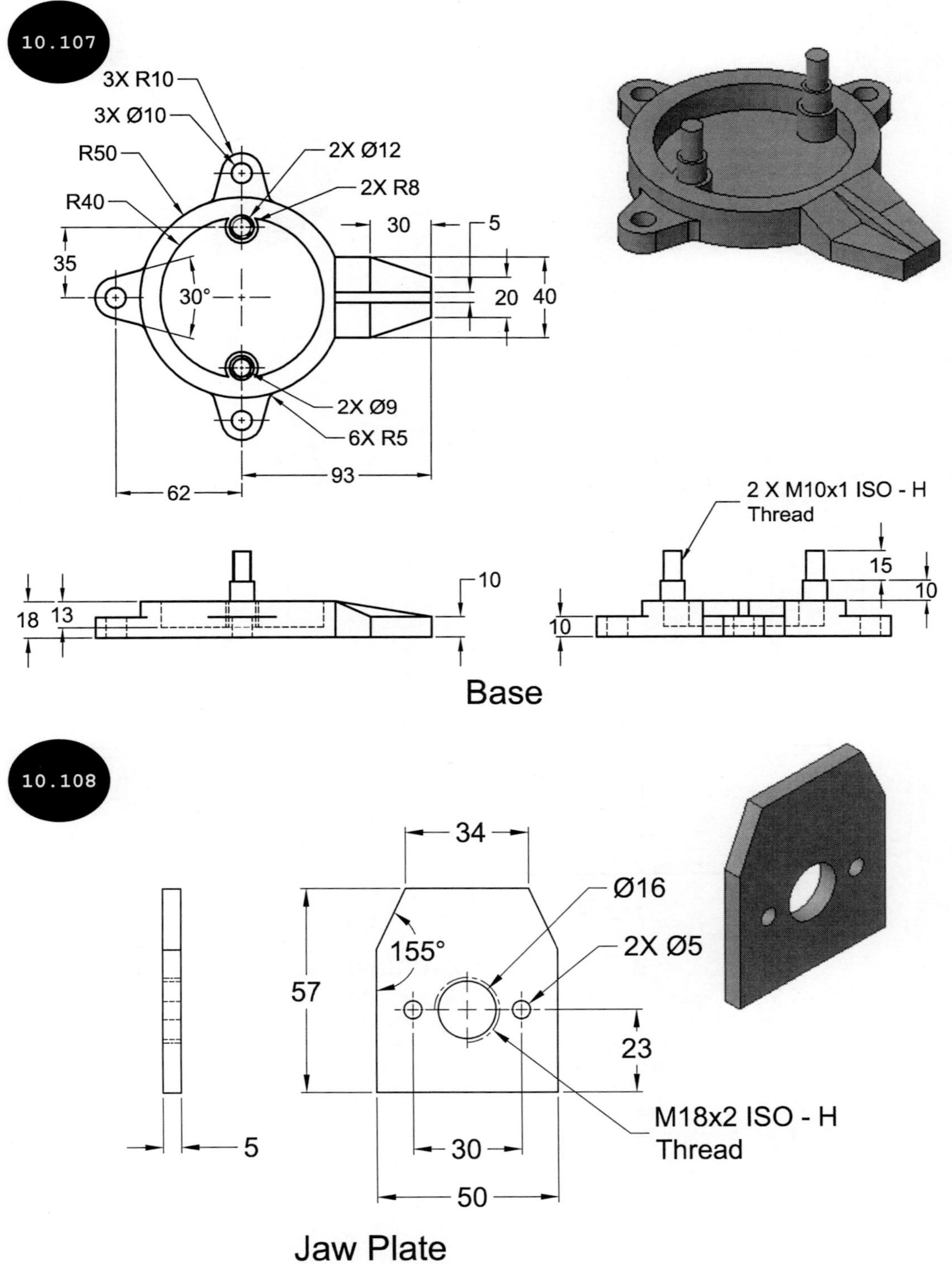
10.107
3X R10
3X Ø10
R50
R40
2X Ø12
2X R8
30
5
35
30°
20
40
2X Ø9
6X R5
93
62
2 X M10x1 ISO - H
Thread
15
10
18
13
10
10
Base
10.108
34
Ø16
2X Ø5
155°
57
23
M18x2 ISO - H
Thread
5
30
50
Jaw Plate

10.109

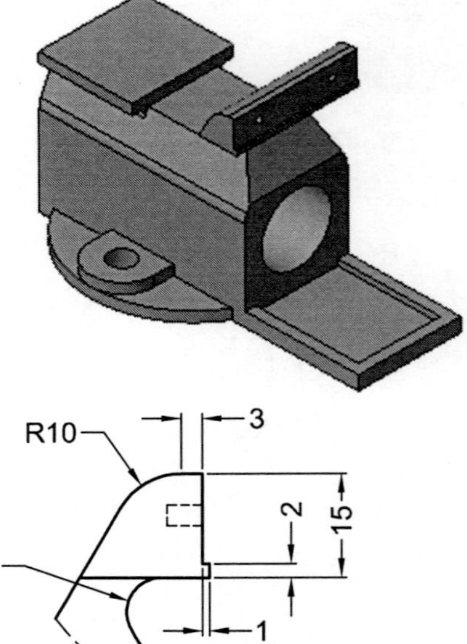

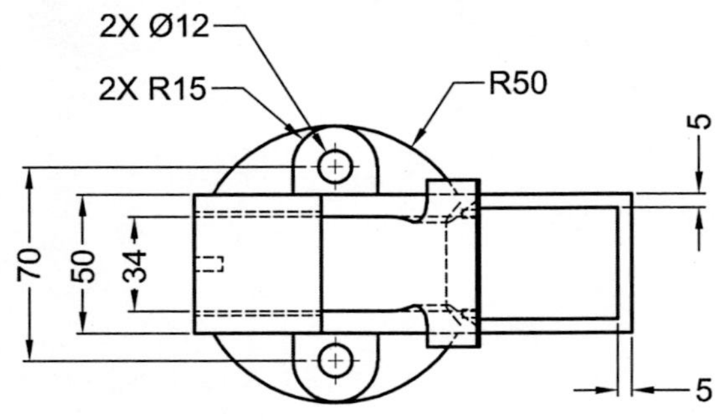
2X Ø12
2X R15
R50
70
50
34
5
5

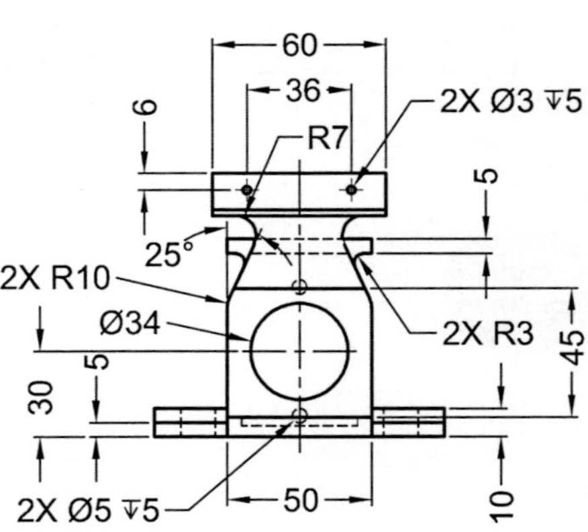
R10
3
R5
2
15
1
Detail A

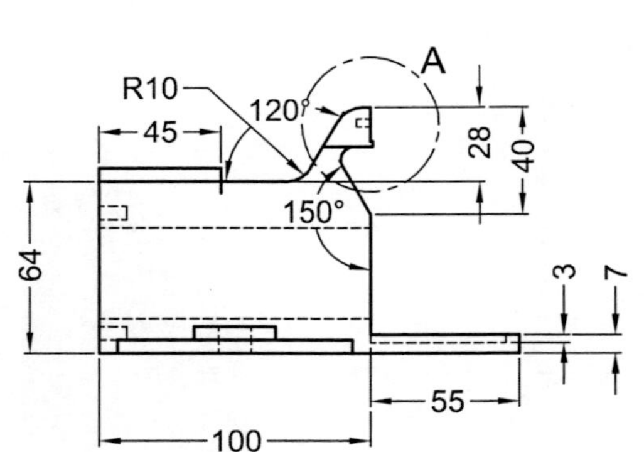
R10
120°
A
45
28
40
150°
64
3
7
55
100

60
36
2X Ø3 ⊽5
6
R7
5
25°
2X R10
Ø34
2X R3
45
5
30
2X Ø5 ⊽5
50
10

Fixed Jaw

10.110

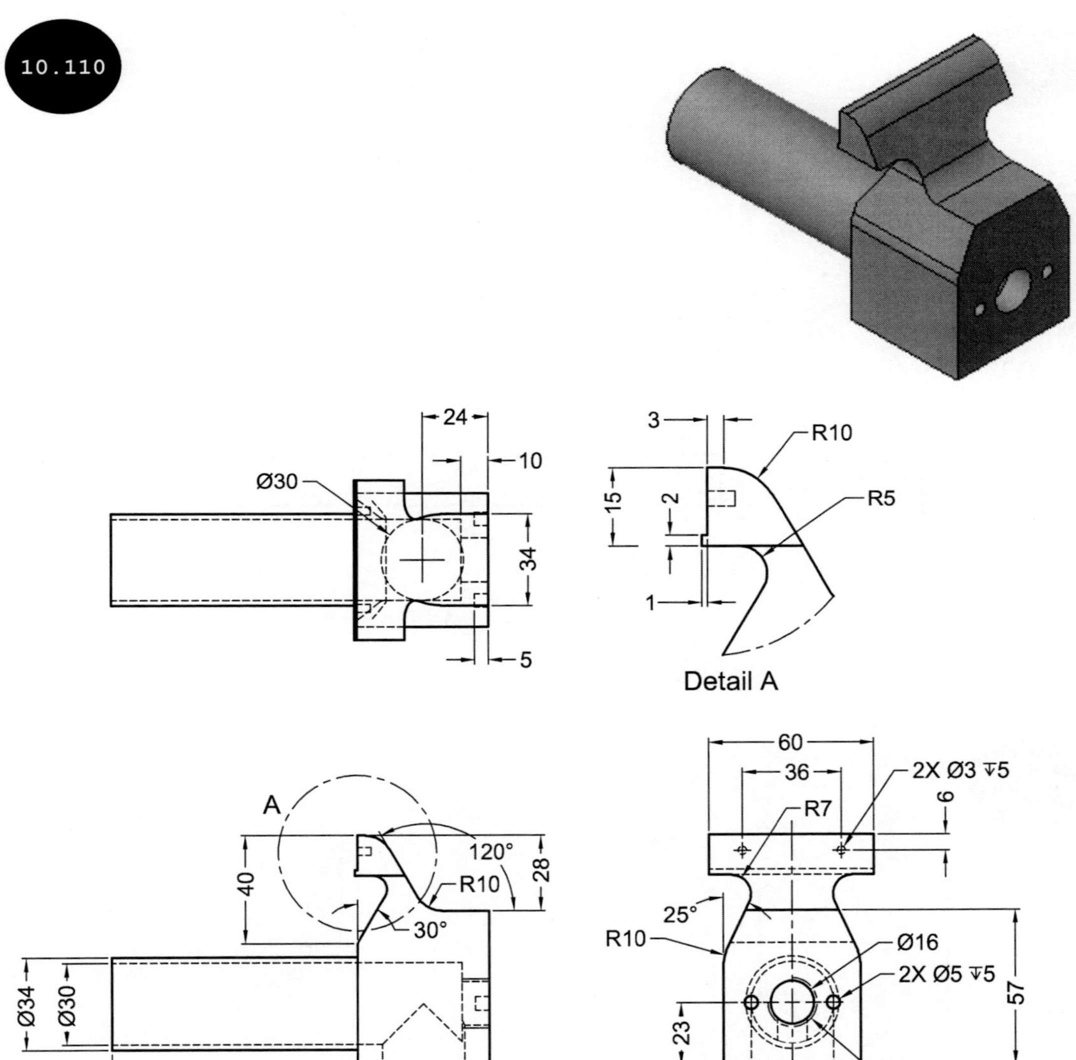

Sliding Jaw

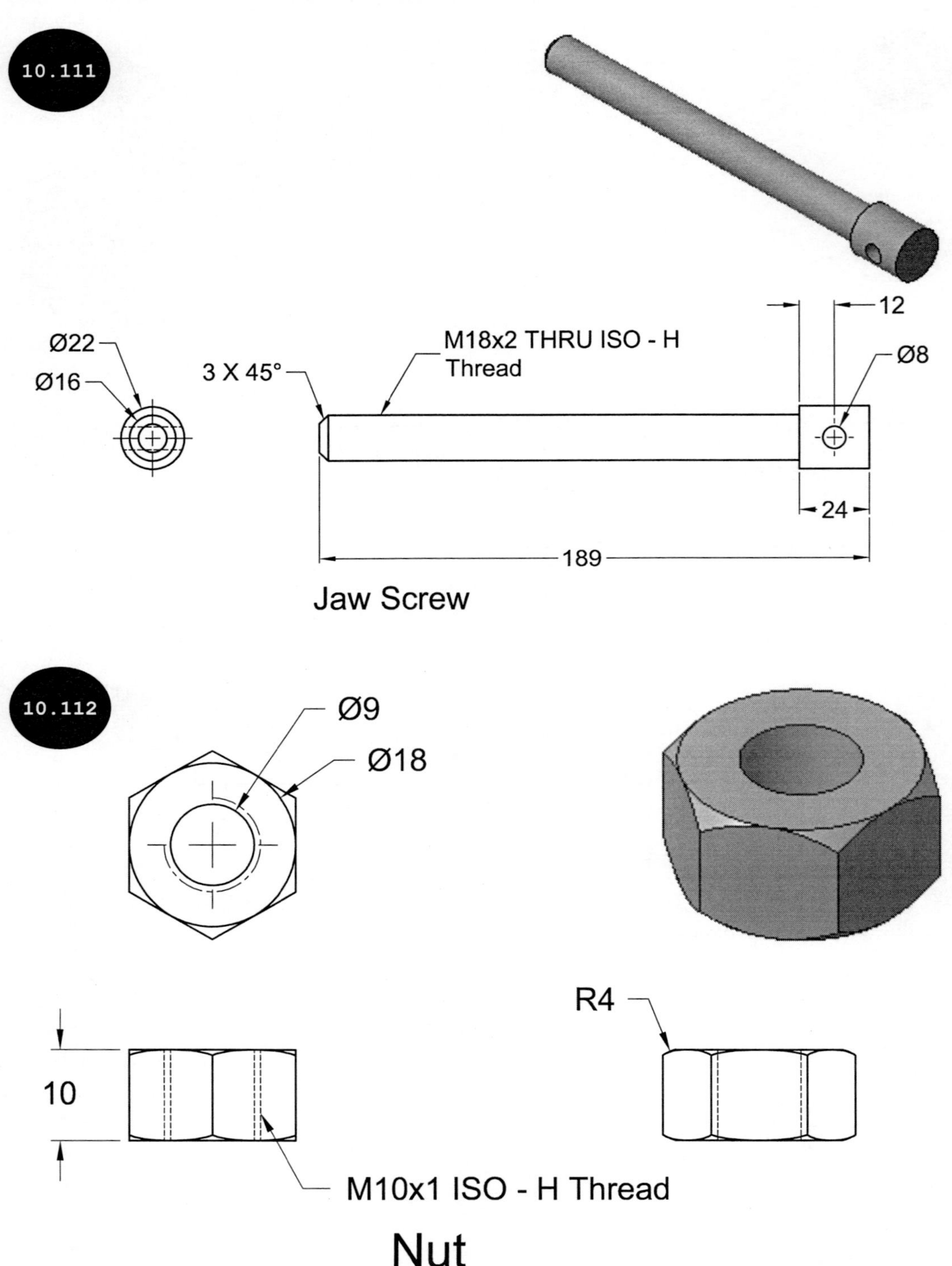
10.111
Ø22
Ø16
3 X 45°
M18x2 THRU ISO - H
Thread
12
Ø8
24
189
Jaw Screw
10.112
Ø9
Ø18
R4
10
M10x1 ISO - H Thread
Nut

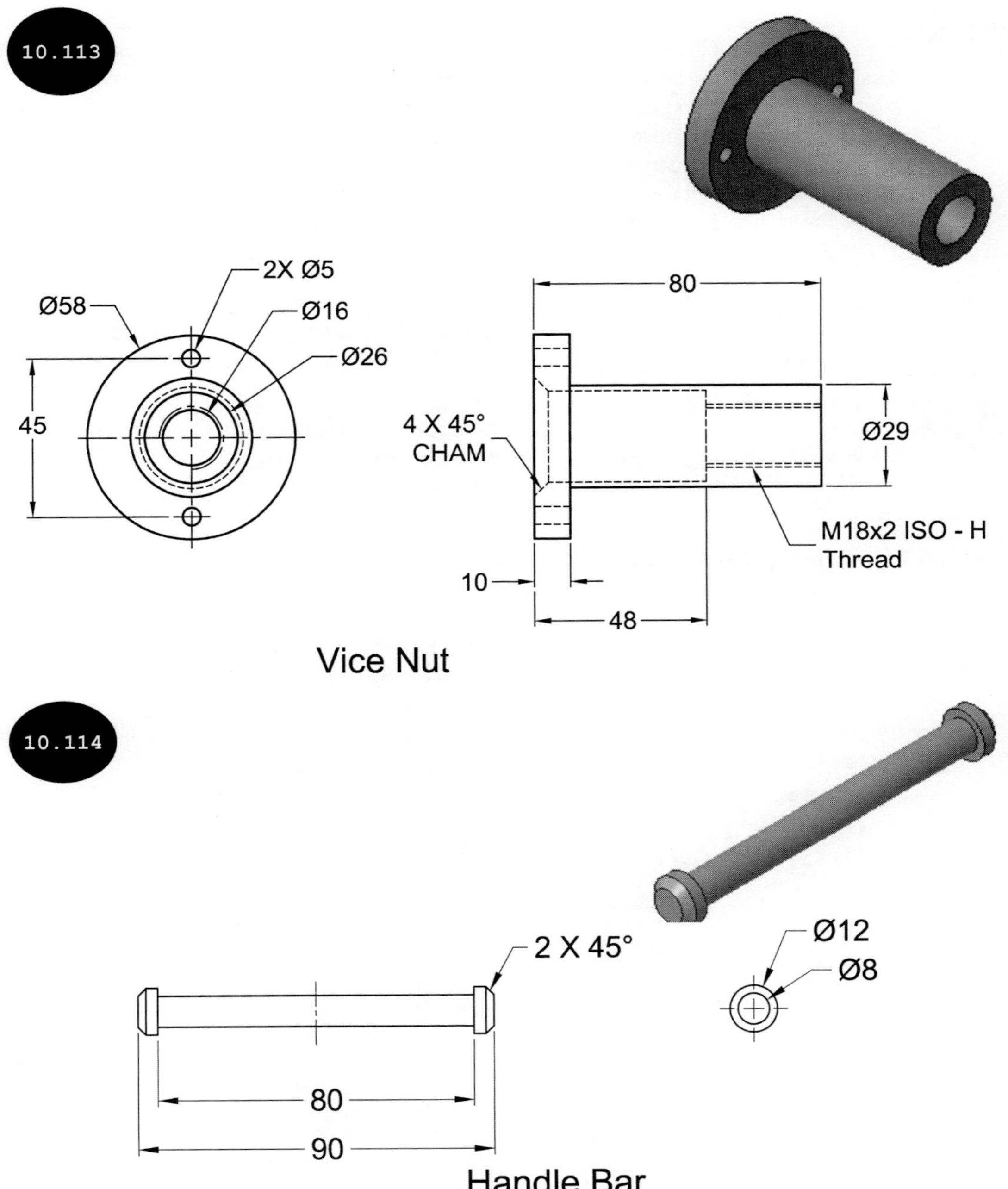

Section 1: Starting Creo and Creating Assembly Components

1. Start Creo Parametric by double-clicking on the Creo Parametric icon on your desktop.

2. Set the working directory to <<*Creo Parametric**Chapter 10**Tutorial 2*\\. You need to create these folders in the *Creo Parametric* folder.

Note: In Creo Parametric, before you create a component or open an existing component or assembly, it is recommended to remove all the files that are not currently displayed in the current session of Creo Parametric by clicking on the **File > Manage Session > Erase Not Displayed**. This is because, Creo Parametric does not allow you to specify a name for a component that has been previously used in the session. Also, when you open an assembly, the previously created or opened components in the session will be opened, if the names of the components being opened match with them.

3. Create all components of the assembly one by one in the Part mode. Refer to Figures 10.107 through 10.114 for the dimensions of each component. After creating the components, save them in the *Tutorial 2* folder of the *Chapter 10* folder.

Note: You can also download all the assembly components by logging in to your account on the CADArtifex website (***cadartifex.com/login***). If you are a new user, you must first register on the CADArtifex website (***cadartifex.com/register***) to access the online resources.

Section 2: Invoking the Assembly Mode

After creating all the components, you need to assemble them in the Assembly mode.

1. Click on the **New** tool in the **Data** group of the **Home** tab. The **New** dialog box appears. Alternatively, press the CTRL + N to invoke the **New** dialog box.

2. Select the **Assembly** radio button in the **Type** area and **Design** radio button in the **Sub-type** area of the **New** dialog box, see Figure 10.115.

10.115

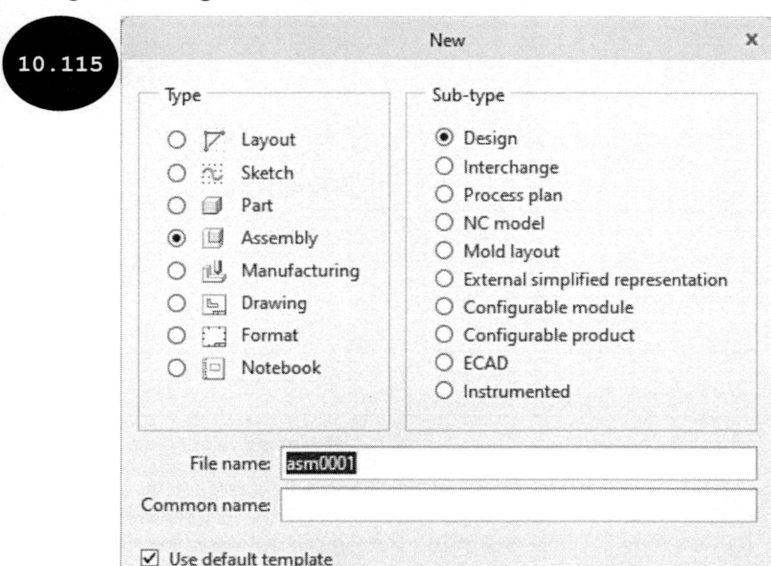

3. Enter **C10-Tutorial02** in the **File name** field of the dialog box as the name of the assembly.

4. Clear the **Use default template** check box and then click on the **OK** button in the dialog box. The **New File Options** dialog box appears, see Figure 10.116.

5. Select the **mmns_asm_design_abs** template in the **New File Options** dialog box and then click on the **OK** button. The Assembly mode is invoked with the **mmns_asm_design_abs** template.

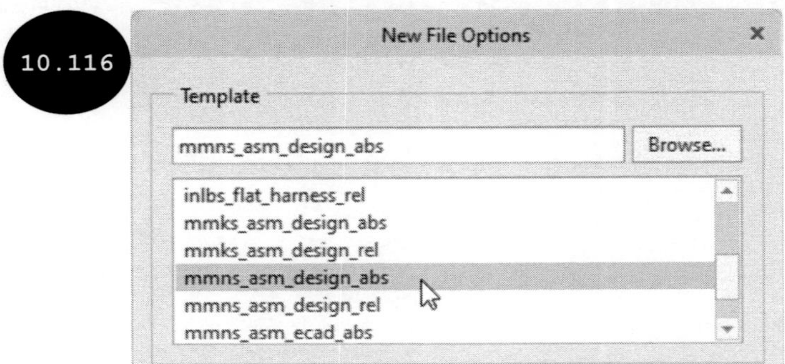

Section 3: Inserting the First Component - Base

1. Click on the **Assemble** tool in the **Component** group, see Figure 10.117. The **Open** dialog box appears.

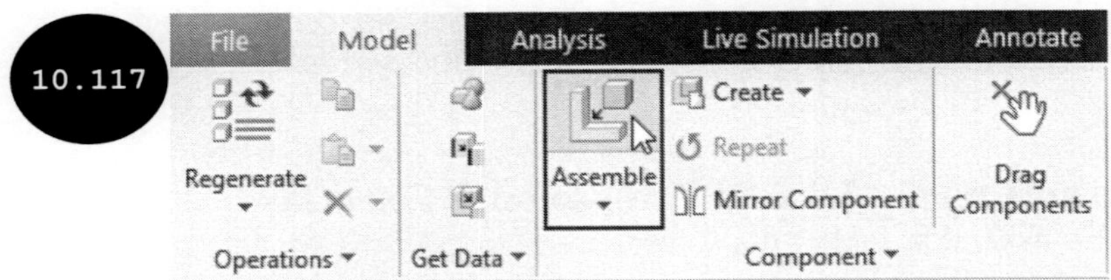

2. Select the ***Base*** component and then click on the **Open** button in the dialog box. The selected component gets inserted in the Assembly environment with the 3D Dragger, see Figure 10.118. Also, the **Component Placement** tab appears in the **Ribbon**.

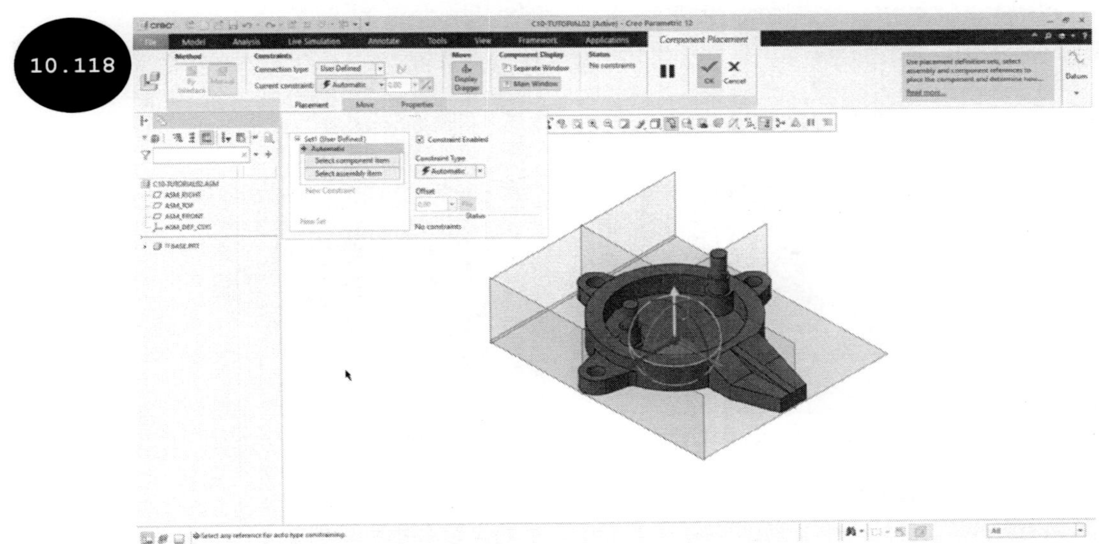

3. Select the **Default** constraint in the **Current constraint** drop-down list of the **Component Placement** tab, see Figure 10.119. The component moves toward the assembly coordinate system and becomes a fixed component with respect to the assembly coordinate system. Also, the status of the components appears as **Fully constrained** in the **Component Placement** tab.

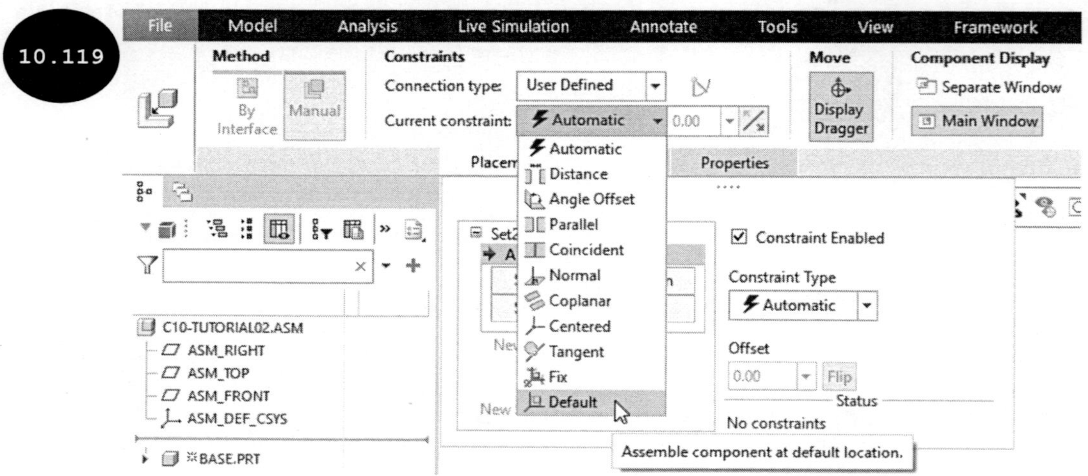

10.119

4. Click on the green tick-mark button in the **Component Placement** tab. The *Base* component gets inserted in the Assembly environment and becomes a fixed component with respect to the assembly coordinate system.

Section 4: Inserting the Second Component - Fixed Jaw

1. Click on the **Assemble** tool in the **Component** group of the **Model** tab. The **Open** dialog box appears.

2. Select the *Fixed Jaw* component and then click on the **Open** button in the dialog box. The selected component gets inserted in the Assembly environment with the 3D Dragger, see Figure 10.120. Also, the **Component Placement** tab appears in the **Ribbon**.

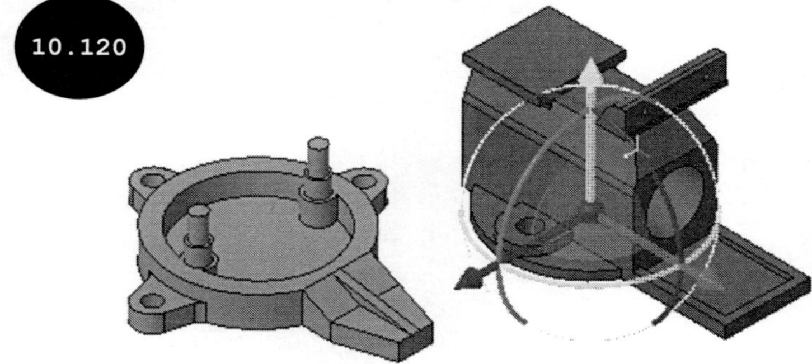
10.120

Note: In Figure 10.120, the display of datum axes, points, coordinate systems, and planes is turned off. To do so, invoke the **Datum Display Filters** flyout of the **In-graphics** toolbar and then clear the **Select All** check box, see Figure 10.121.

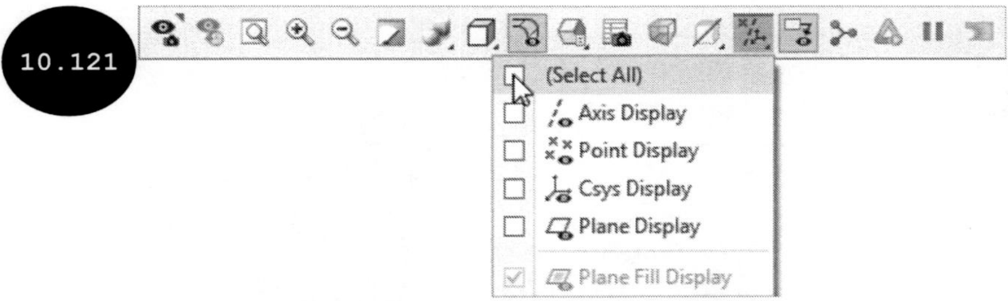

3. Drag the translational handles of the 3D Dragger to define the position of the component in the graphics area such that it should not intersect with the existing component of the assembly.

4. Hide the display of the 3D Dragger in the graphics area by clicking on the **Display Dragger** button in the **Component Placement** tab, see Figure 10.122.

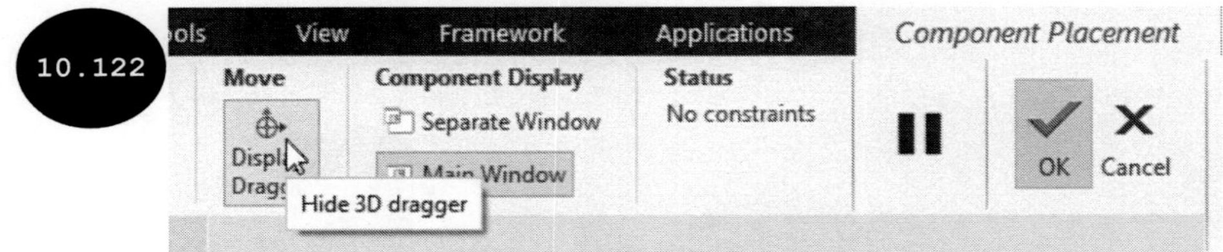

5. Ensure that the **User Defined** option is selected in the **Connection type** drop-down list and the **Automatic** option is selected in the **Current constraint** drop-down list to apply placement constraints, automatically, see Figure 10.123.

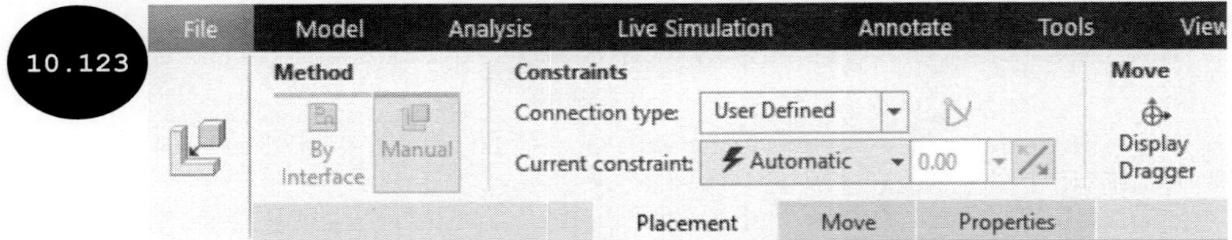

6. Select the bottom planar face of the second component (*Fixed Jaw*) and the top planar face of the first component (*Base*) as references to apply the constraint, see Figure 10.124. Both the selected faces get coincident with each other and the Coincident constraint is applied, automatically. Note that you need to rotate the assembly to select the bottom planar face of the Fixed Jaw component.

7. Select the inner circular face of the hole of the second component (*Fixed Jaw*) and the outer circular face of the first component (*Base*) as references to apply the second constraint, see Figure 10.125. The axes of both the selected faces get coincident to each other and the Coincident constraint is applied, automatically, see Figure 10.126. Also, the **Fully constrained using assumptions** status appears in the **Status** area of the **Component Placement** tab. This indicates that the component is fully defined and it cannot move in any direction.

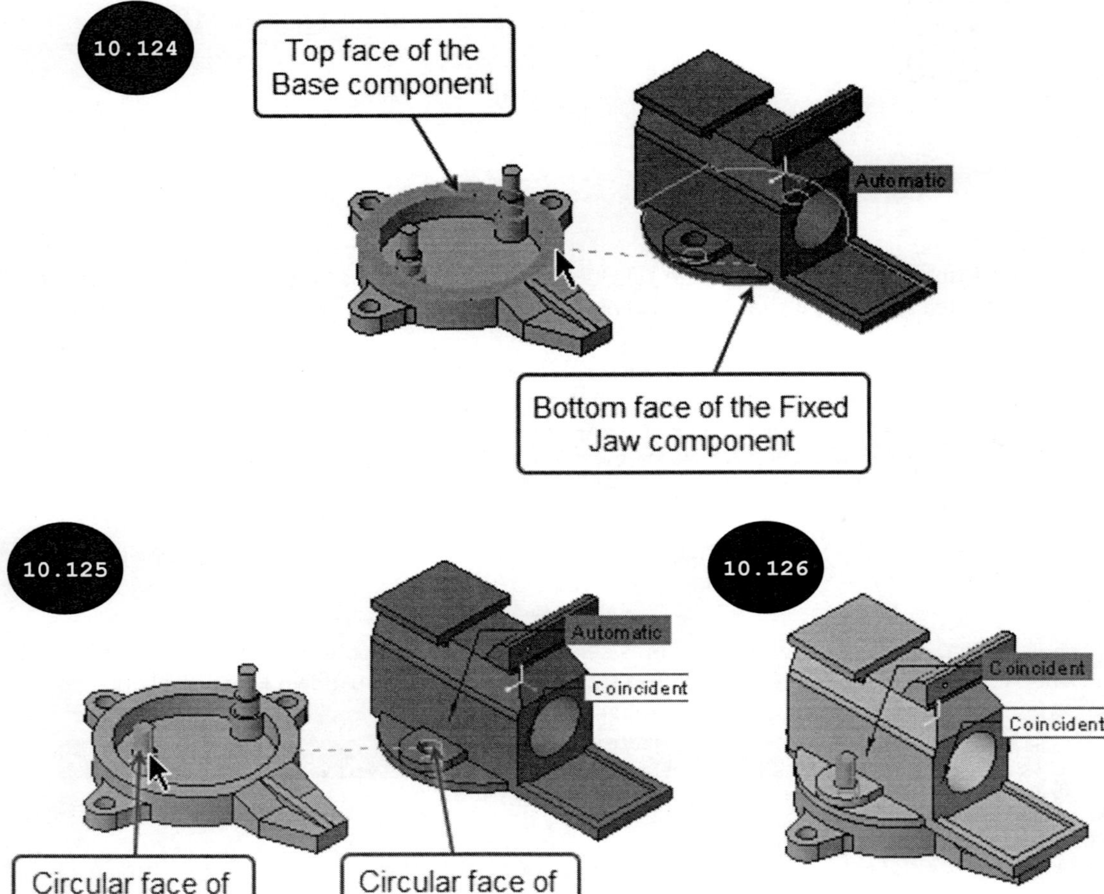

Note: The component becomes fully defined by applying two Coincident constraints. This is because, the **Allow Assumptions** check box is selected in the expanded **Placement** panel of the **Component Placement** tab, by default. If you clear this check box, then you need to apply an additional constraint to restrict the rotational degree of freedom of the component.

8. Click on the green tick-mark button in the **Component Placement** tab. The second component is assembled in the assembly and all its degrees of freedom are restricted.

Section 5: Inserting the Third Component - Sliding Jaw

1. Click on the **Assemble** tool in the **Component** group of the **Model** tab. The **Open** dialog box appears.

2. Select the *Sliding Jaw* component and then click on the **Open** button in the dialog box. The selected component gets inserted in the Assembly environment, see Figure 10.127. Also, the **Component Placement** tab appears in the **Ribbon**.

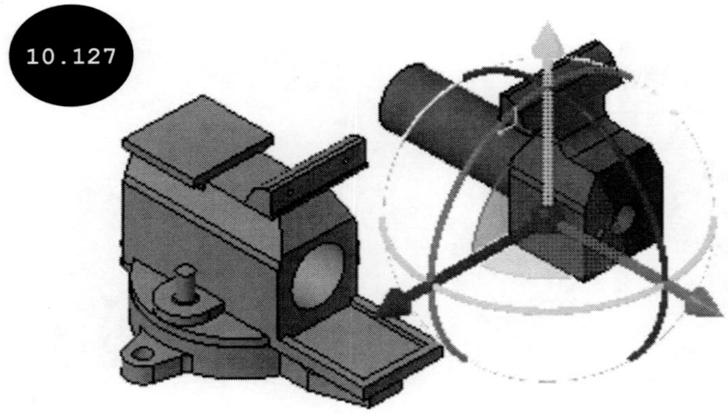

3. Drag the translational handles of the 3D Dragger to define the position of the component in the graphics area such that it should not intersect with the existing components of the assembly.

4. Hide the display of the 3D Dragger in the graphics area. You can turn on or off the display of the 3D Dragger by clicking on the **Display Dragger** button in the **Move** area of the **Component Placement** tab.

5. Select the **Slider** option in the **Connection type** drop-down list of the **Component Placement** tab and then expand the **Placement** panel, if not expanded by default, see Figure 10.128. You are prompted to select references for applying the axis alignment connection.

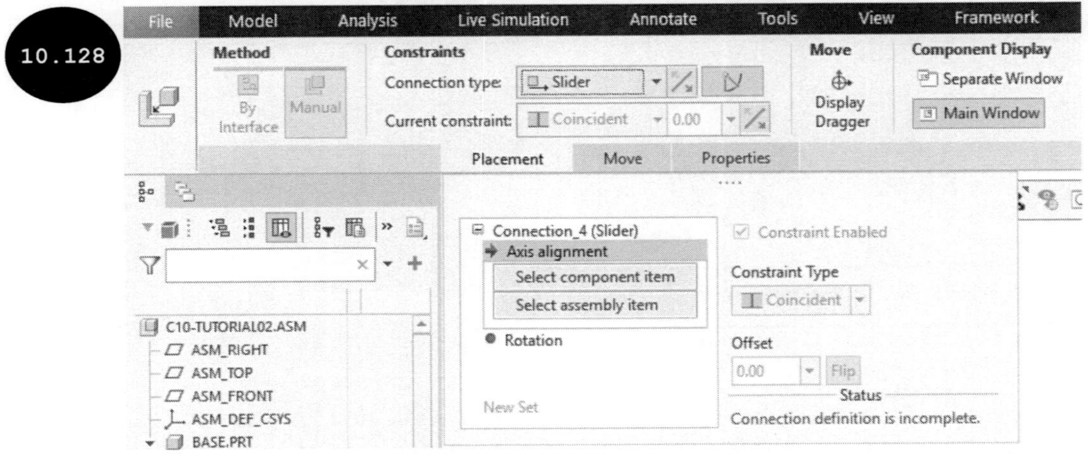

6. Select the outer circular face of the third component (*Sliding Jaw*) and the inner circular face of the second component (*Fixed Jaw*) as the references, see Figure 10.129. The axes of both the selected references get aligned with each other, see Figure 10.130. Also, you are prompted to select references for applying the rotation connection.

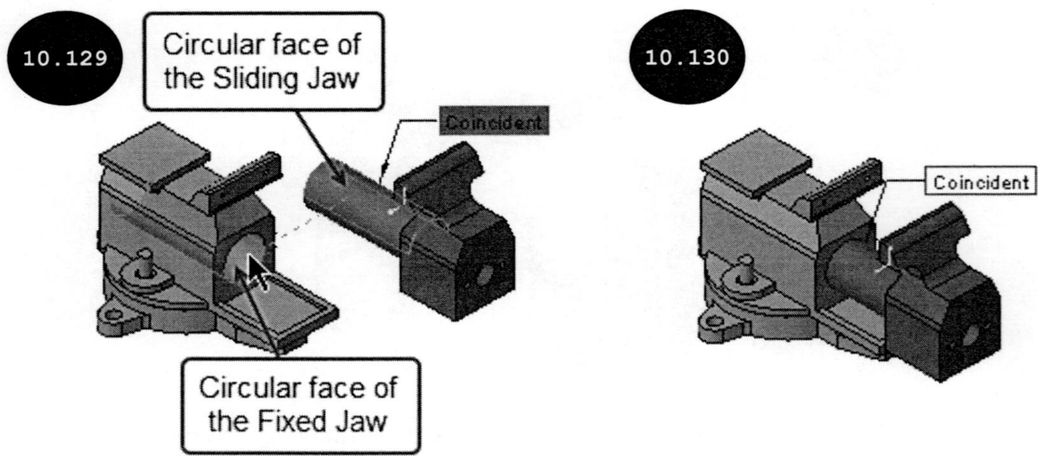

7. Select the planar face of the third component (*Sliding Jaw*) and the planar face of the second component (*Fixed Jaw*) as the references, see Figure 10.131. The selected references become coincident with each other and the status appears as **Connection Definition Complete** in the **Status** area of the **Component Placement** tab. This means that the Slider predefined constraint set is defined and the *Sliding Jaw* component can only translate along its axis, see Figure 10.132.

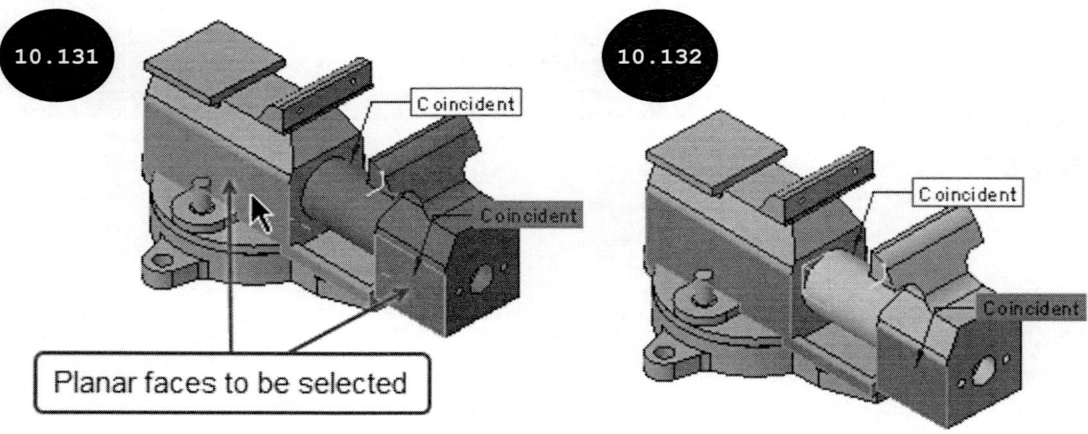

By default, after applying the Slider predefined constraint set, the component can translate freely along its axis. Now, you need to define the limit for the translation movement of the *Sliding Jaw* component.

8. Click on the **Translation Axis** connection in the expanded **Placement** panel to define the references to limit the translational movement of the component.

9. Select the planar face of the third component (*Sliding Jaw*) and the planar face of the second component (*Fixed Jaw*) as references, see Figure 10.133. The current distance value between the selected references appears in the graphics area, see Figure 10.134. Also, the options to define the translation limits between the selected references are enabled in the expanded Placement panel of the **Component Placement** tab.

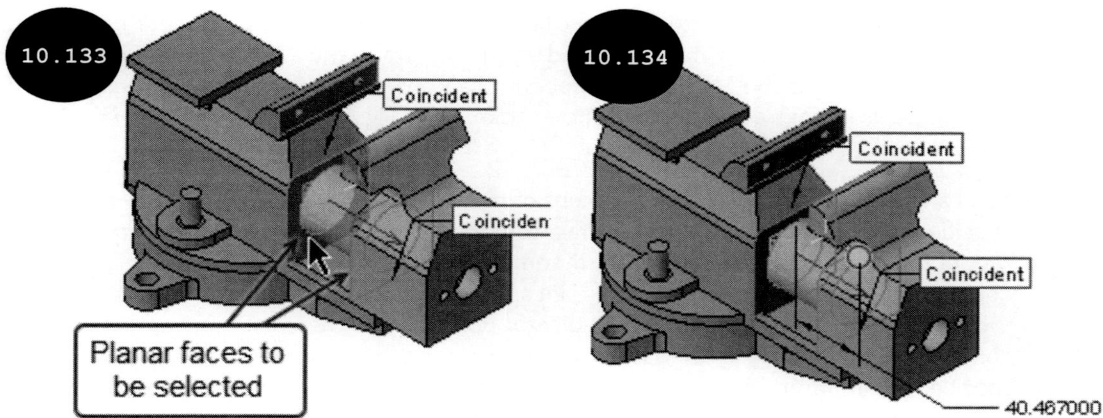

10. Enter **2** in the **Current Position** field of the expanded **Placement** panel and then click on the **Set Zero Position** button. The distance between the selected references gets changed, as specified, see Figure 10.135. Also, the distance of 2 mm becomes the zero position of the component.

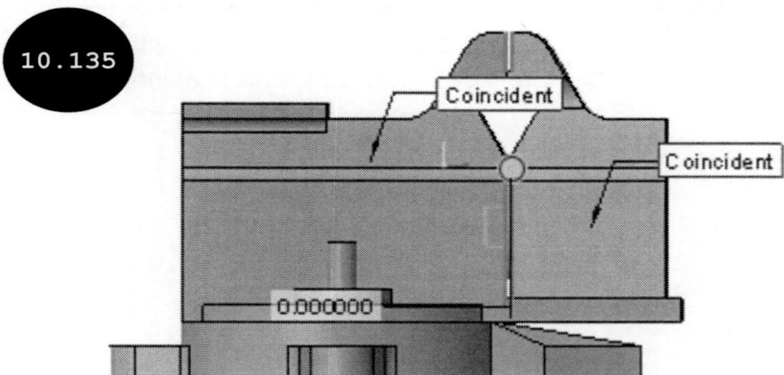

11. Select the **Minimum Limit** check box in the expanded **Placement** panel and then enter **0** as the minimum limit for the translation movement, see Figure 10.136.

12. Select the **Maximum Limit** check box in the expanded **Placement** panel and then enter **30** as the maximum limit for the translation movement, see Figure 10.136.

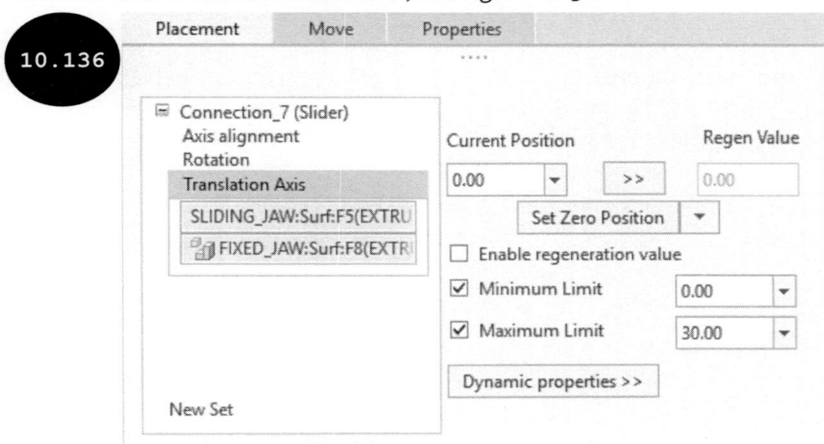

13. Click on the green tick-mark button in the **Component Placement** tab. The Slider predefined constraint set is defined with minimum and maximum translation limits as 0 and 30 mm, respectively. This means the *Slider Jaw* component can only be translated within the specified minimum and maximum translation limit of 0 to 30 mm, see Figure 10.137.

Tip: You can review the translation movement of the third component (*Sliding Jaw*) within the specified limit. To do so, click on the **Drag Components** tool in the **Component** group of the **Model** tab and then click on the third component (*Sliding Jaw*) of the assembly as the component to be moved. An indicator point appears on the selected component. Next, move the cursor in the graphics area. The indicator point follows the cursor movement and the component (*Sliding Jaw*) of the assembly moves along its free degrees of freedom within the specified minimum and maximum translation limits, see Figure 10.137. Next, click the left mouse button to end the movement of the component and then press the middle mouse button twice to exit the **Drag Components** tool.

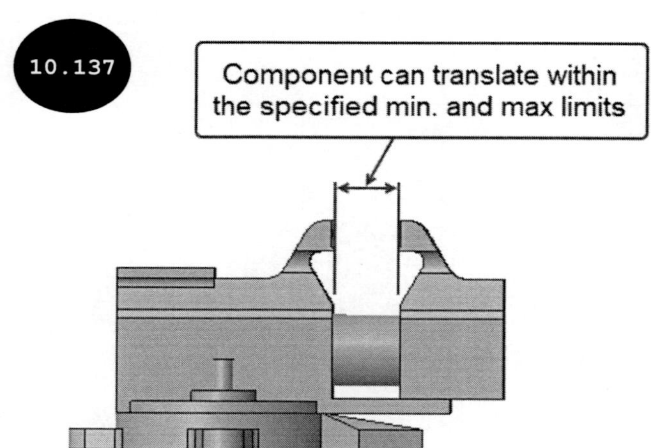

Section 6: Inserting the Fourth Component - Jaw Plate

1. Click on the **Assemble** tool in the **Component** group of the **Model** tab. The **Open** dialog box appears.

2. Select the *Jaw Plate* component and then click on the **Open** button in the dialog box. The selected component gets inserted in the Assembly environment, see Figure 10.138. Also, the **Component Placement** tab appears in the **Ribbon**.

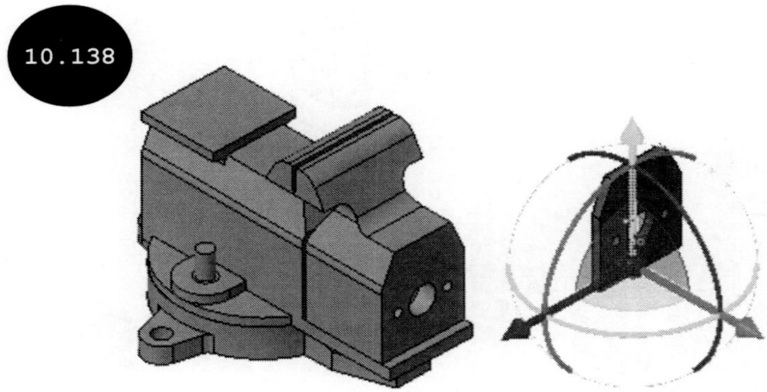

3. Hide the display of the 3D Dragger in the graphics area. You can turn on or off the display of the 3D Dragger by clicking on the **Display Dragger** button in the **Component Placement** tab.

4. Ensure that the **User Defined** option is selected in the **Connection type** drop-down list and the **Automatic** option is selected in the **Current constraint** drop-down list to apply placement constraints, automatically.

5. Select the circular face of the fourth component (*Jaw Plate*) and the circular face of the third component (*Sliding Jaw*) as references to apply the constraint, see Figure 10.139. The axes of both the selected references get aligned to each other and the Coincident constraint is applied, automatically.

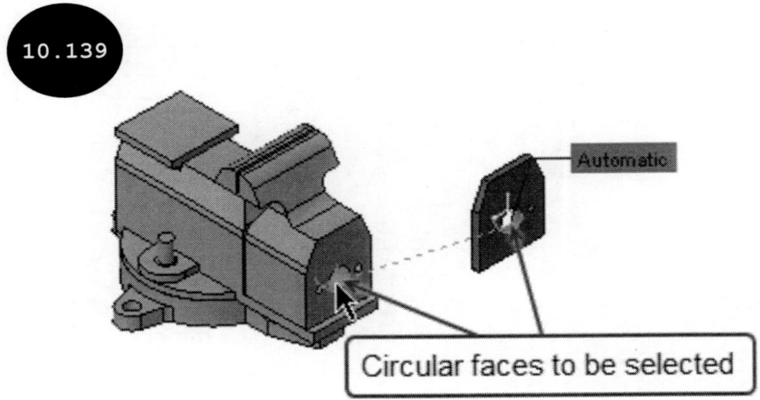

6. Select the back planar face of the fourth component (*Jaw Plate*) and the right planar face of the third component (*Sliding Jaw*) as the references to apply the constraint, see Figure 10.140. The Distance constraint is applied between the selected references, automatically, see Figure 10.141.

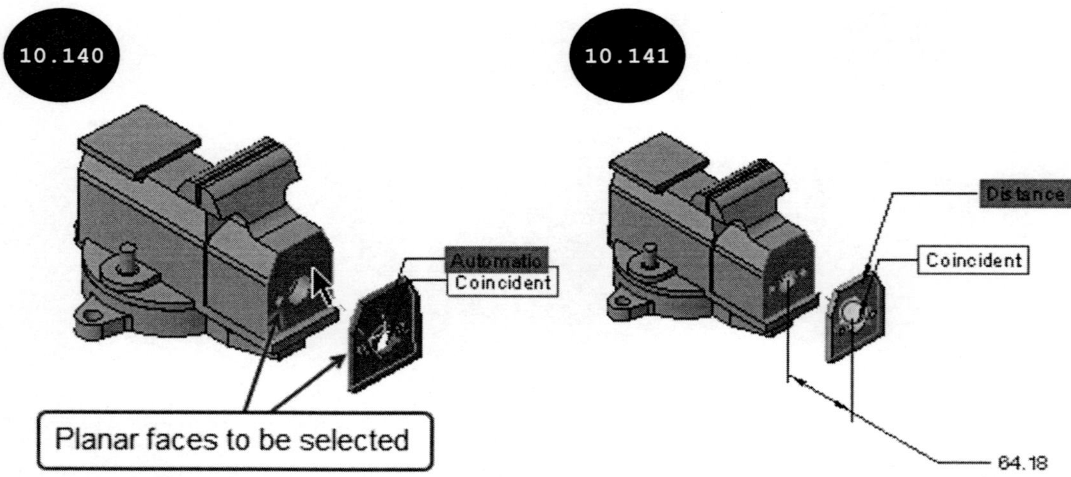

7. Select the **Coincident** option in the **Current constraint** drop-down list in the **Constraints** area of the **Component Placement** tab to apply the Coincident constraint between the selected references. The selected references become coincident with each other, see Figure 10.142. Also, the status appears as **Fully constrained using assumptions** in the **Status** area of the **Component Placement** tab.

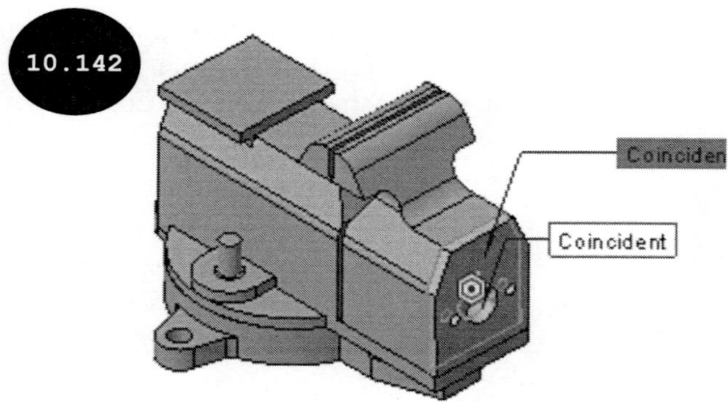

Tip: The *Jaw Plate* component becomes fully defined by applying two Coincident constraints. This is because, the **Allow Assumptions** check box is selected in the expanded **Placement** panel of the **Component Placement** tab, by default. If you clear this check box, then you need to apply an additional constraint to restrict the rotational degree of freedom of the component.

8. Click on the green tick-mark button in the **Component Placement** tab. The fourth component (*Jaw Plate*) is assembled in the assembly and all its degrees of freedom are restricted.

Section 7: Inserting the Fifth Component - Vice Nut

1. Click on the **Assemble** tool in the **Component** group of the **Model** tab. The **Open** dialog box appears.

2. Select the ***Vice Nut*** component and then click on the **Open** button in the dialog box. The selected component gets inserted in the Assembly environment, see Figure 10.143. Also, the **Component Placement** tab appears in the **Ribbon**.

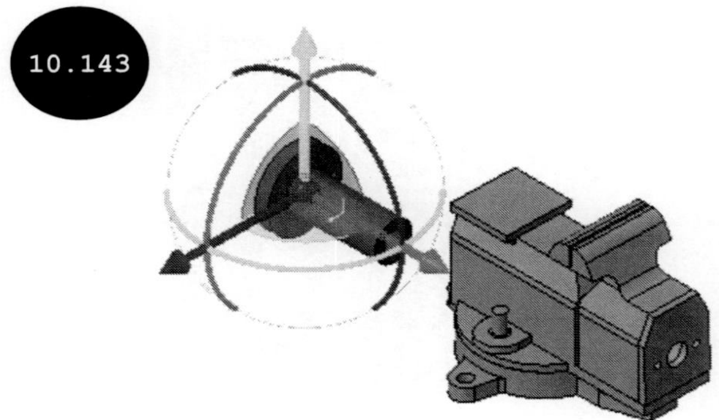

3. Ensure that the **User Defined** option is selected in the **Connection type** drop-down list and the **Automatic** option is selected in the **Current constraint** drop-down list to apply placement constraints, automatically.

4. Rotate the assembly such that you can view its back face, see Figure 10.144. Next, select the circular face of the fifth component (*Vice Nut*) and the circular face of the second component (*Fixed Jaw*) as references to apply the constraint, see Figure 10.144. The axes of both the selected references get aligned to each other and the Coincident constraint is applied, automatically.

5. Select the planar face of the fifth component (*Vice Nut*) and the planar face of the second component (*Fixed Jaw*) as references to apply the second constraint, see Figure 10.145. The Distance constraint is applied between the selected references, automatically.

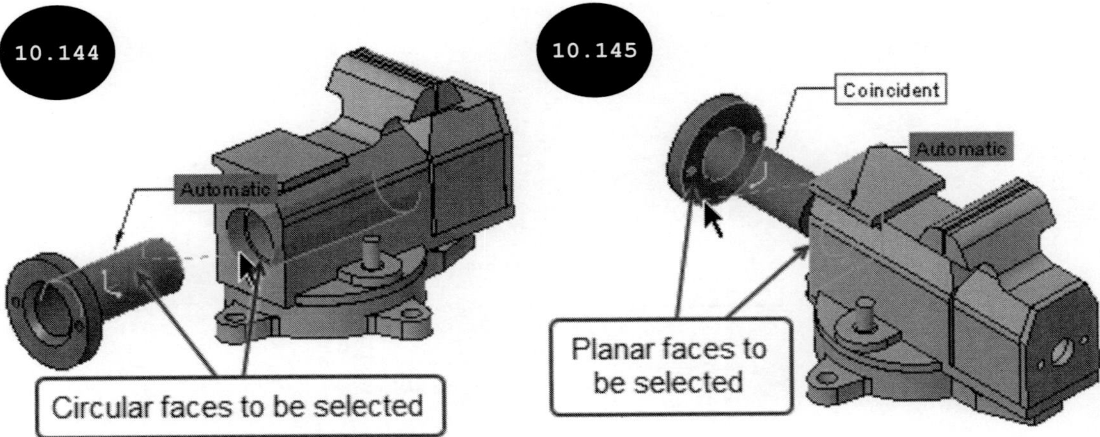

6. Select the **Coincident** option in the **Current constraint** drop-down list in the **Constraints** area of the **Component Placement** tab to apply the Coincident constraint between the selected references. The selected references become coincident with each other, see Figure 10.146.

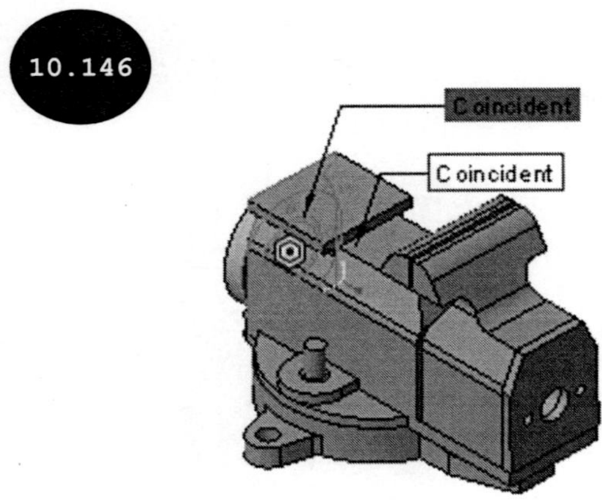

7. Click on the **Separate Window** button in the **Component Placement** tab to open the *Vice Nut* in a separate window, see Figure 10.147. Also, click on the **Main Window** button to deactivate it and turn off the display of the *Vice Nut* in the assembly window, see Figure 10.147.

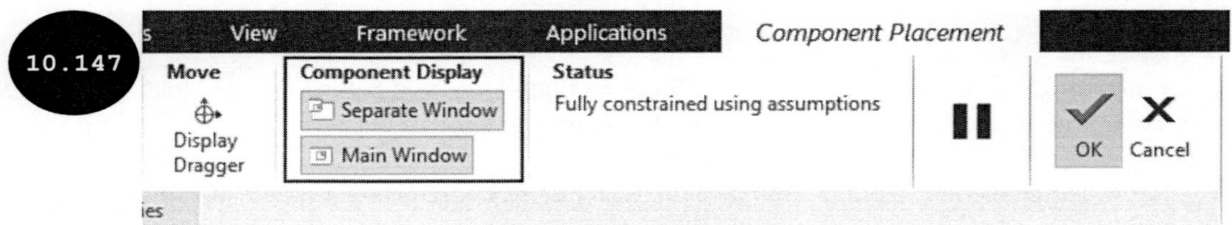

Now, you need to apply a constraint to restrict the rotational degree of freedom of the *Vice Nut* component.

8. Click on the **New Constraint** option in the expanded **Placement** panel, see Figure 10.148.

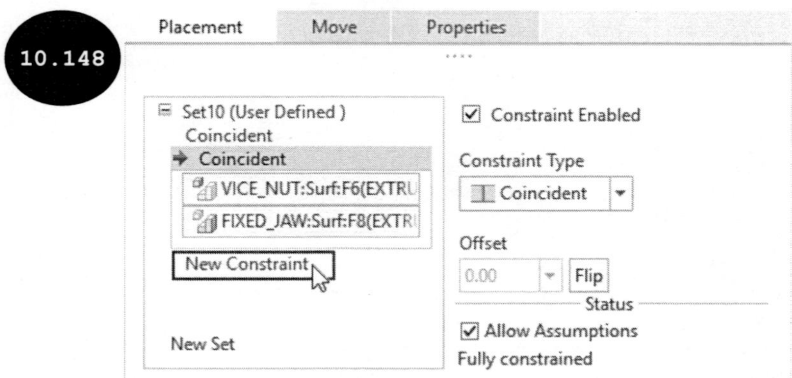

9. Select the circular face of the fifth component (*Vice Nut*) as a first reference, which is opened in a separate window, see Figure 10.149.

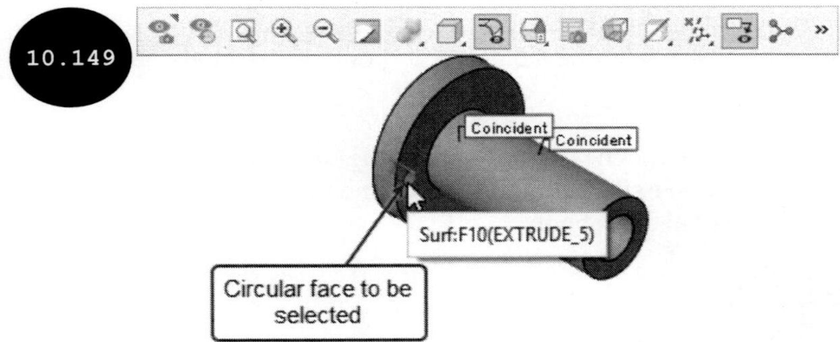

10. Select the circular face of the hole available at the back planar face of the second component (*Fixed Jaw*) as the second reference in the assembly window, see Figure 10.150. The axes of both the selected references become oriented to each other and the status appears as **Fully constrained** in the **Status** area of the **Component Placement** tab.

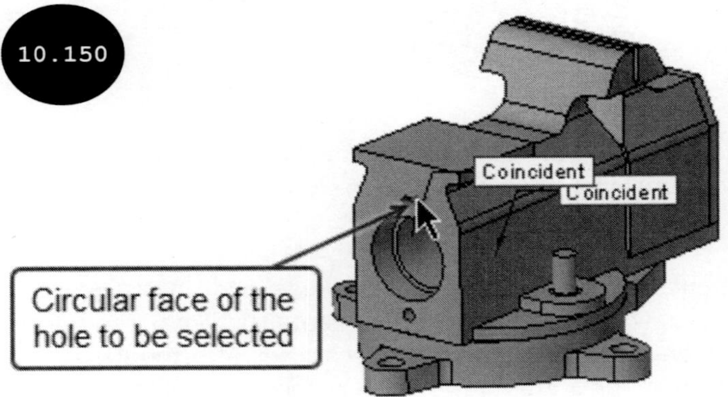

11. Click on the **Main Window** button in the **Component Placement** tab to turn on the display of the *Vice Nut* in the assembly window, see Figure 10.151. Also, click on the **Separate Window** button to deactivate it and turn off the display of the *Vice Nut* in a separate window.

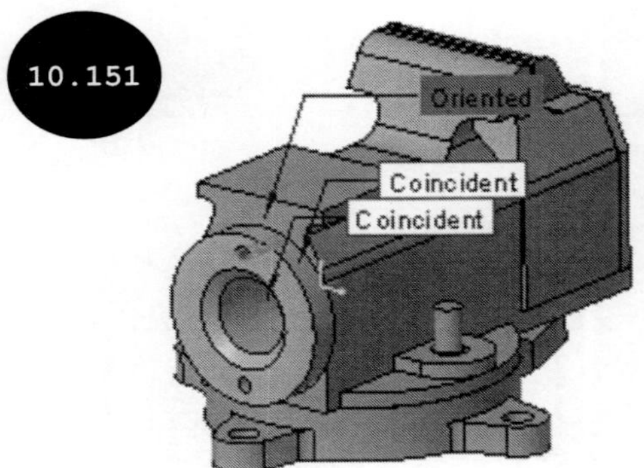

12. Click on the green tick-mark button in the **Component Placement** tab. The fifth component (*Vice Nut*) is assembled in the assembly and all its degrees of freedom are restricted.

13. Change the current orientation of the assembly to standard orientation.

Section 8: Inserting the Sixth Component - Jaw Screw

1. Click on the **Assemble** tool in the **Component** group of the **Model** tab. The **Open** dialog box appears.

2. Select the *Jaw Screw* component and then click on the **Open** button in the dialog box. The selected component gets inserted in the Assembly environment, see Figure 10.152. Also, the **Component Placement** tab appears in the **Ribbon**.

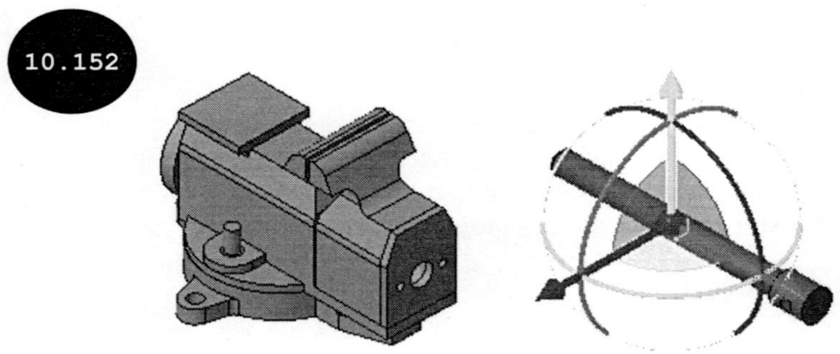

3. Select the **Cylinder** option in the **Connection type** drop-down list in the **Constraints** area of the **Component Placement** tab. You are prompted to select references for applying the axis alignment connection.

4. Select two references to apply the Cylinder predefined constraint set between the sixth component (Jaw Screw) and the fourth component (*Jaw Plate*), see Figure 10.153. The axes of both the selected references get aligned with each other. Also, the status appears as **Connection Definition Complete** in the **Status** area of the **Component Placement** tab. This means that the *Jaw Screw* can translate as well as rotate about its axis.

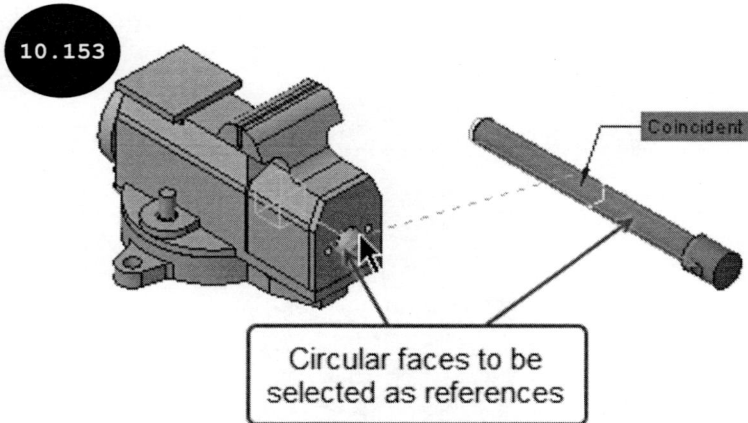

Now, you need to apply an additional constraint set to connect the *Jaw Screw* and the *Jaw Plate* component.

5. Click on the **New Set** option in the expanded **Placement** panel of the **Component Placement** tab, see Figure 10.154. A new connection set is added in the expanded **Placement** panel.

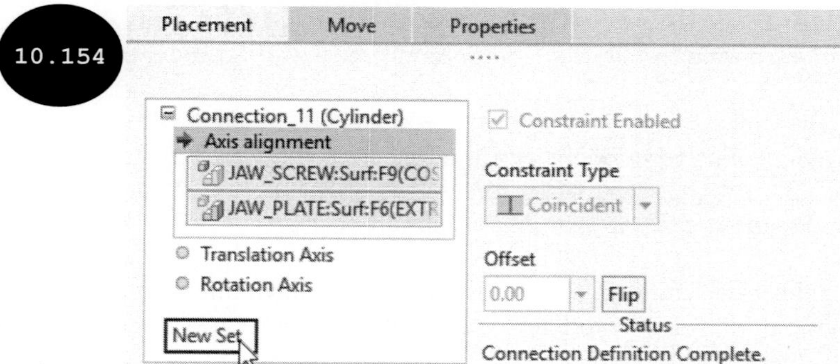

6. Select the **General** option in the **Connection type** drop-down list in the **Constraints** area of the **Component Placement** tab as the new constraint set to be applied.

7. Select two references to apply the General predefined constraint set between the planar faces of the sixth component (Jaw Screw) and the fourth component (*Jaw Plate*), see Figure 10.155. The Distance constraint is applied between the selected references, automatically.

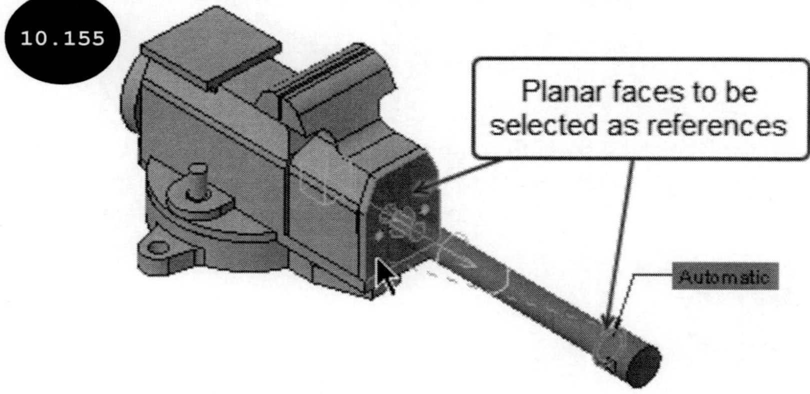

8. Select the **Coincident** option in the **Current constraint** drop-down list in the **Constraints** area of the **Component Placement** tab to apply the Coincident constraint between the selected references. The selected references become coincident with each other, see Figure 10.156.

9. Click on the green tick-mark button in the **Component Placement** tab. The Cylinder and General predefined constraint sets are defined and the assembly appears similar to the one shown in Figure 10.157.

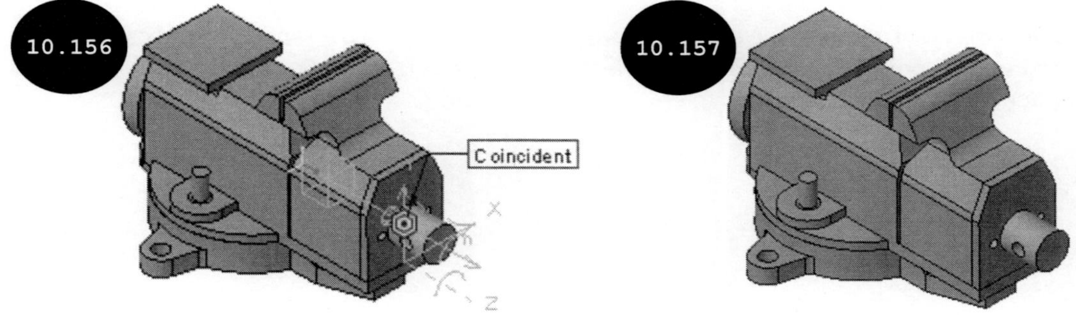

Section 9: Inserting the seventh Component - Handle Bar

1. Click on the **Assemble** tool in the **Component** group of the **Model** tab. The **Open** dialog box appears.

2. Select the ***Handle Bar*** component and then click on the **Open** button in the dialog box. The selected component gets inserted in the Assembly environment, see Figure 10.158. Also, the **Component Placement** tab appears in the **Ribbon**.

3. Ensure that the **User Defined** option is selected in the **Connection type** drop-down list and the **Automatic** option is selected in the **Current constraint** drop-down list to apply placement constraints, automatically.

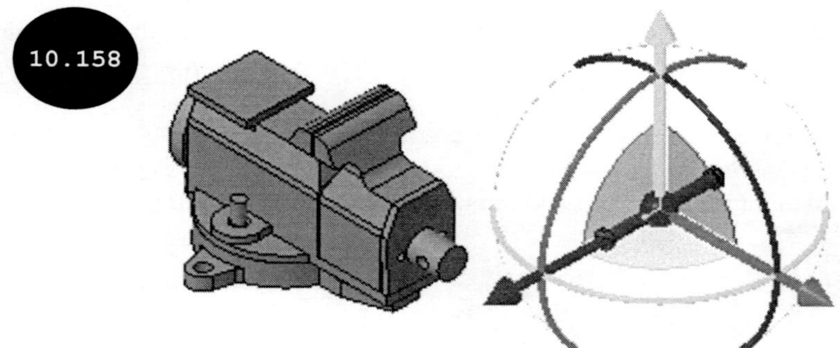

4. Select the circular face of the seventh component (*Handle Bar*) and the circular face of the sixth component (*Jaw Screw*) as references to apply the constraint, see Figure 10.159. The axes of both the selected references get aligned to each other and the Coincident constraint is applied, automatically.

5. Ensure that the display of datum planes is turned on in the graphics area.

6. Select the Front datum plane of the seventh component (*Handle Bar*) and the Front datum plane of the sixth component (*Jaw Screw*) as the references, see Figure 10.160. The Distance constraint is applied between the selected references, automatically.

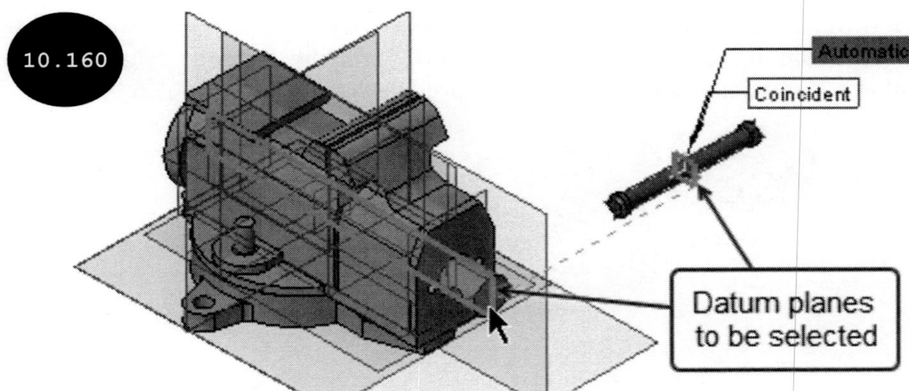

7. Select the **Coincident** option in the **Current constraint** drop-down list in the **Constraints** area of the **Component Placement** tab. The selected references become coincident with each other, see Figure 10.161. Also, the status appears as **Fully constrained using assumptions** in the **Status** area of the **Component Placement** tab.

Tip: Ensure that the **Allow Assumptions** check box is selected in the expanded **Placement** panel if the status does not appear as **Fully constrained using assumptions**.

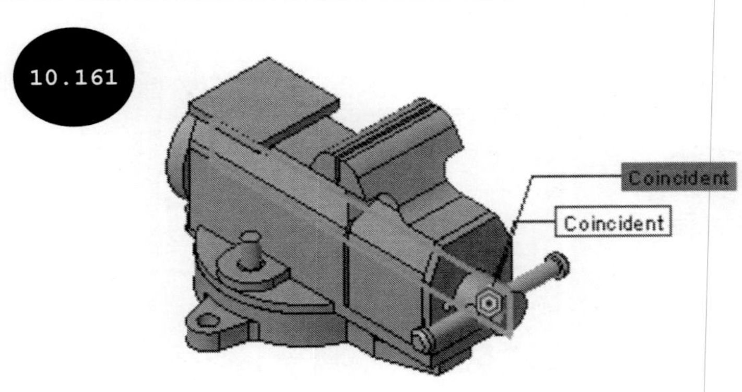

Note: In Figure 10.161, the display of datum planes is turned off for clarity of the image.

8. Click on the green tick-mark button in the **Component Placement** tab. The seventh component (*Handle Bar*) is assembled in the assembly.

Section 10: Inserting the Remaining Components

1. Insert the eighth component (*Nut*) in the assembly by using the **Assemble** tool.

2. Select the **Pin** option in the **Connection type** drop-down list in the **Constraints** area of the **Component Placement** tab.

3. Select the circular face of the eighth component (*Nut*) and the circular face of the first component (*Base*) as the references, see Figure 10.162. The axes of both the selected references get aligned to each other and the Coincident constraint is applied between them.

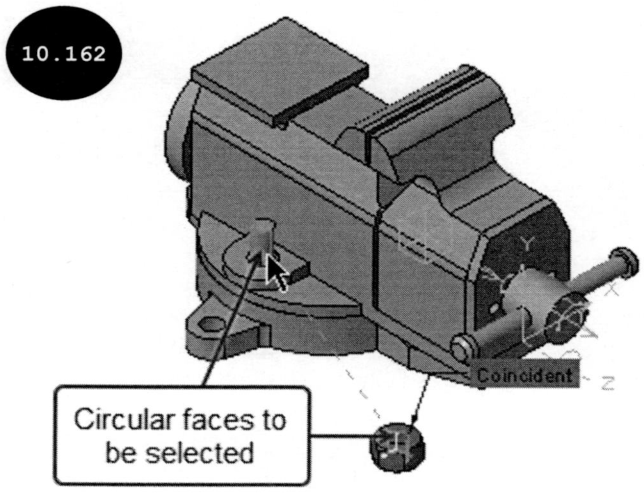

4. Move the *Nut* outside the assembly such that it does not intersect with assembly components by dragging the translational handle of the 3D Dragger.

5. Select the bottom planar face of the eighth component (*Nut*) and the top planar face of the second component (*Fixed Jaw*) as references, see Figure 10.163.

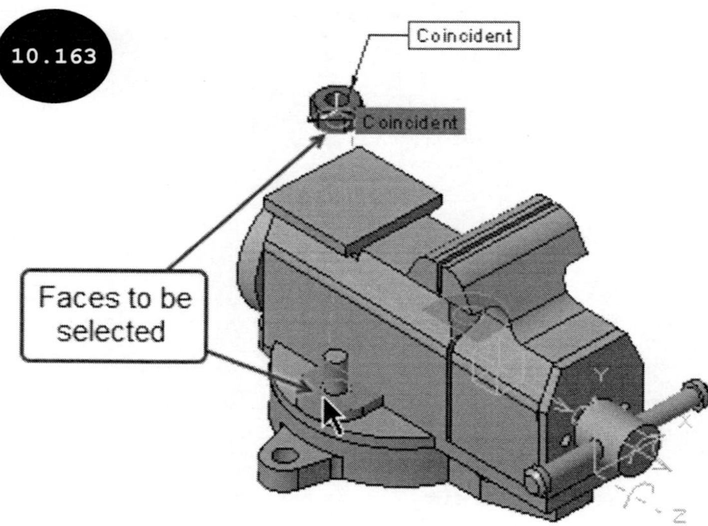

6. Ensure that the **Coincident** option is selected in the **Current constraint** drop-down list of the **Constraints** area as the constraint to be applied between the selected references. The selected references become coincident with each other, see Figure 10.164. Also, the status appears as **Connection Definition Complete** in the **Status** area of the **Component Placement** tab.

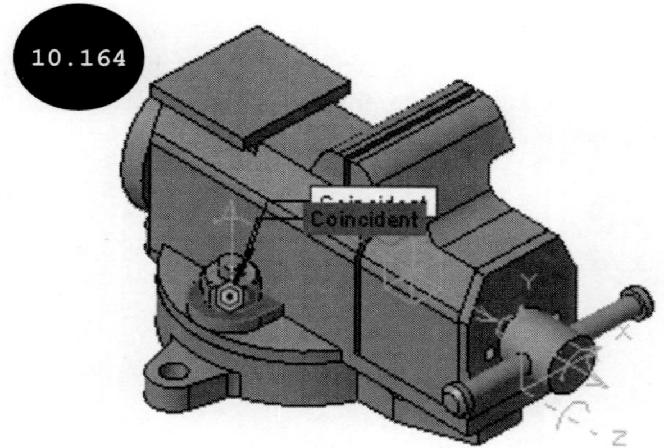

7. Click on the green tick-mark button in the **Component Placement** tab. The eighth component (*Nut*) is assembled in the assembly.

8. Similarly, insert another instance of the *Nut* as the ninth component and assemble in the assembly. Figure 10.165 shows the final assembly after assembling all its components.

9. Click on the **Regenerate** tool in the **Quick Access Toolbar** to regenerate the assembly.

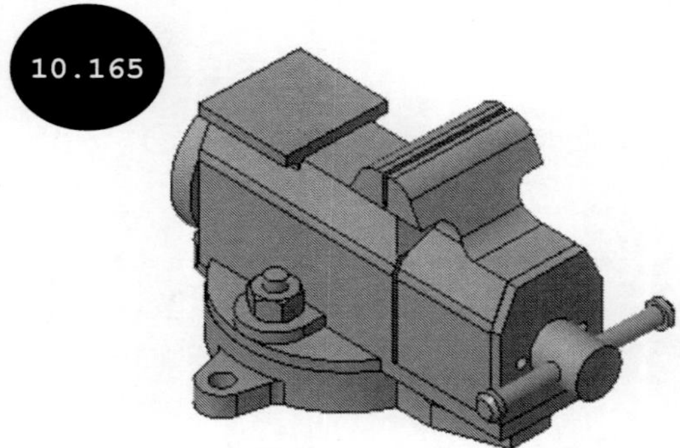

Section 11: Saving the Assembly

1. Click on the **Save** tool in the **Quick Access Toolbar**. The **Save Object** dialog box appears.

2. Click on the **OK** button in the dialog box. The assembly is saved with the name **C10-Tutorial02** in the specified working directory (<<*Creo Parametric**Chapter 10**Tutorial 2*\).

3. Click on the **File** > **Close** to close the assembly.

Hands-on Test Drive 1

Create the assembly shown in Figure 10.166. The exploded view of the assembly is shown in Figure 10.167 for your reference only. Different views and dimensions of individual components of the assembly are shown in Figures 10.168 through 10.175. All dimensions are in mm.

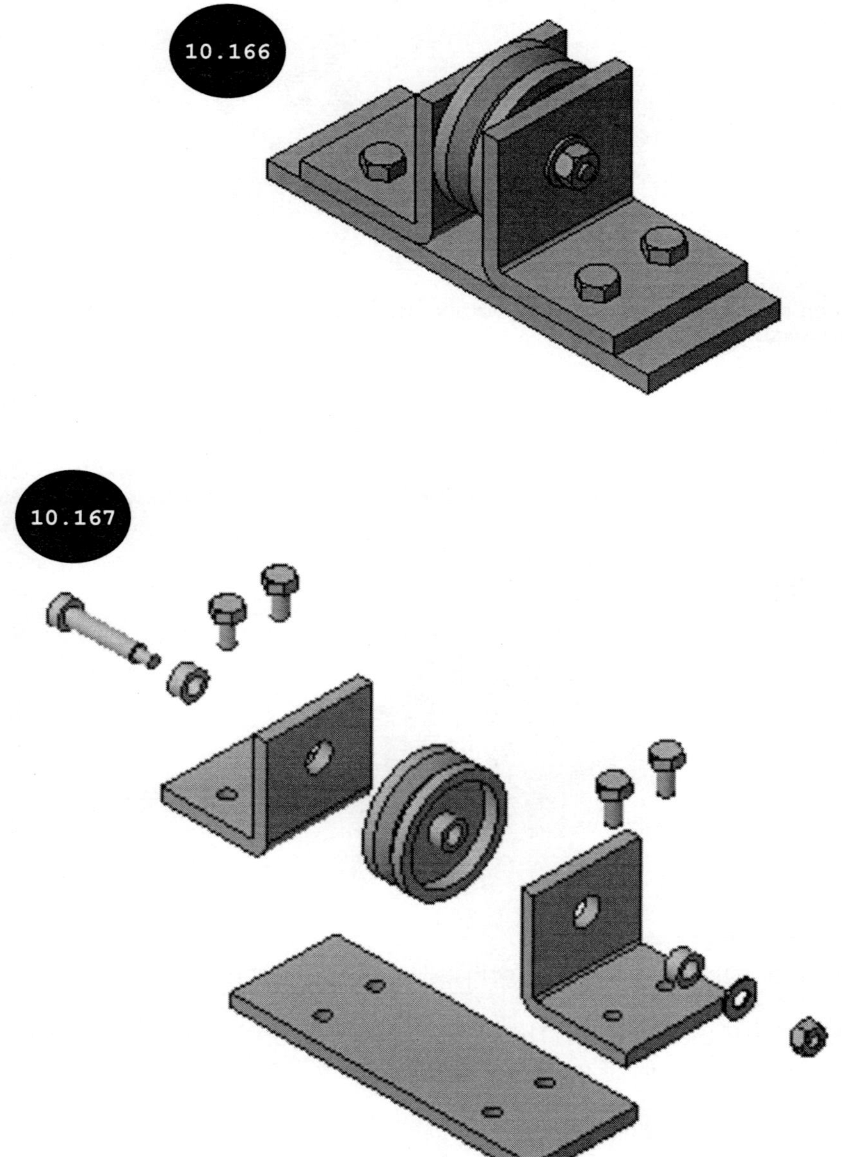

10.168

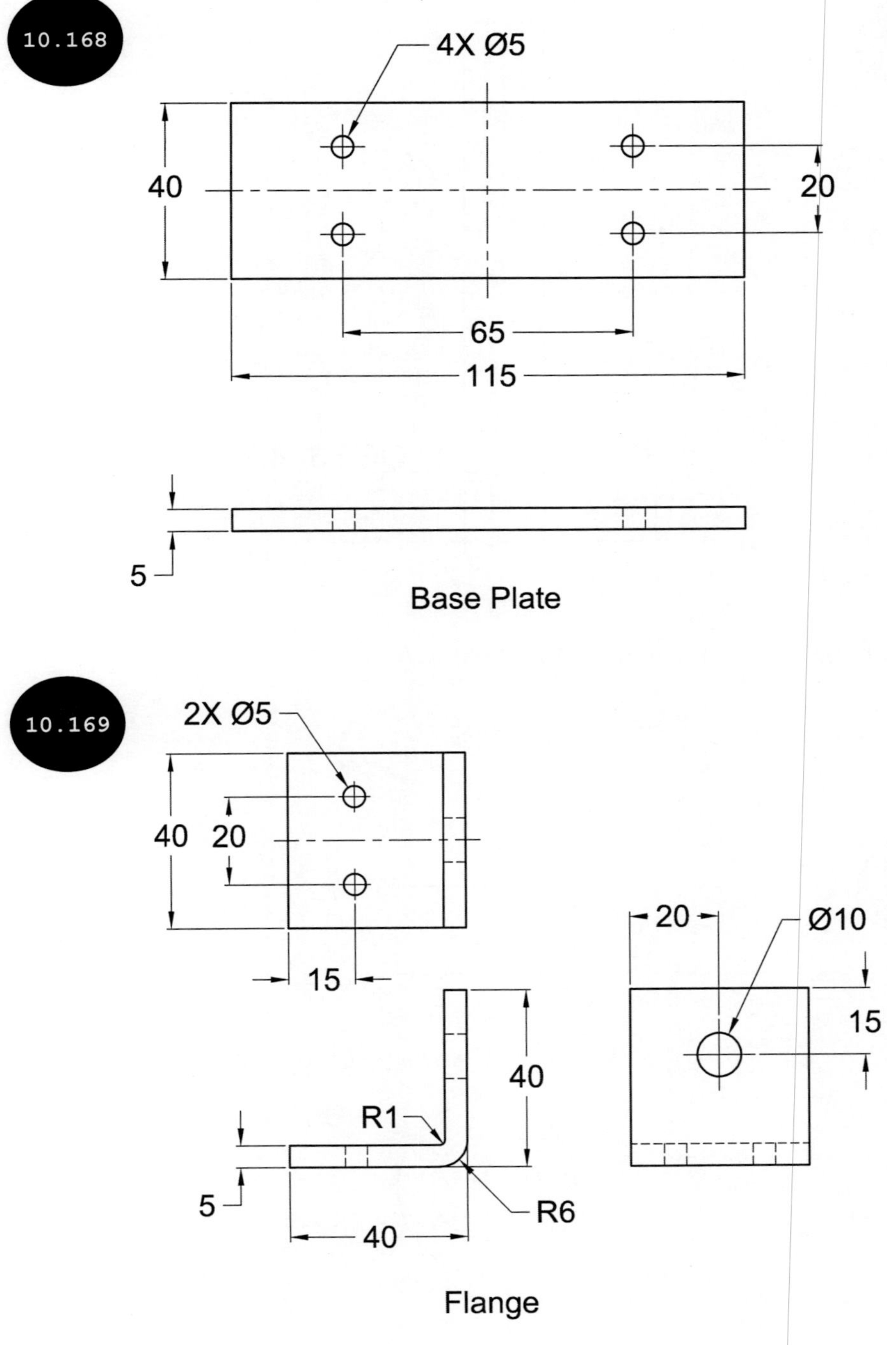

Base Plate

Flange

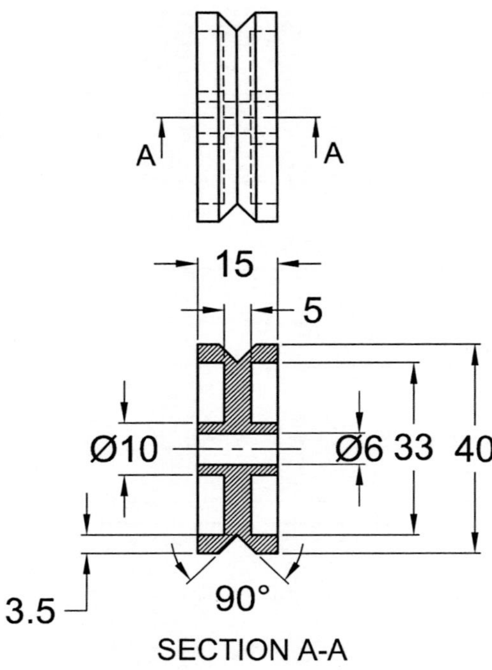

Wheel

10.171

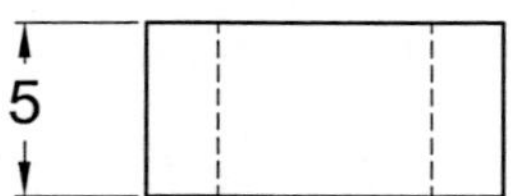

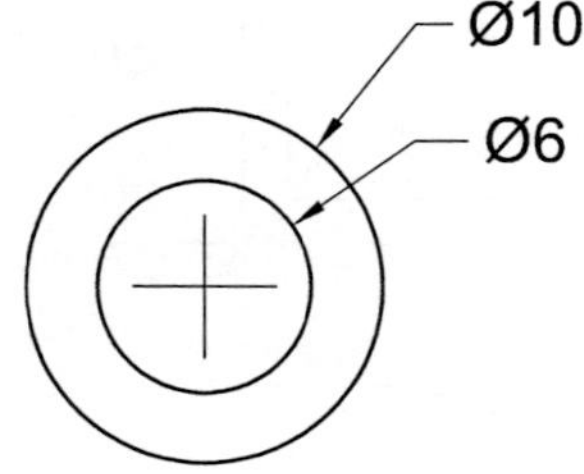

Bushing

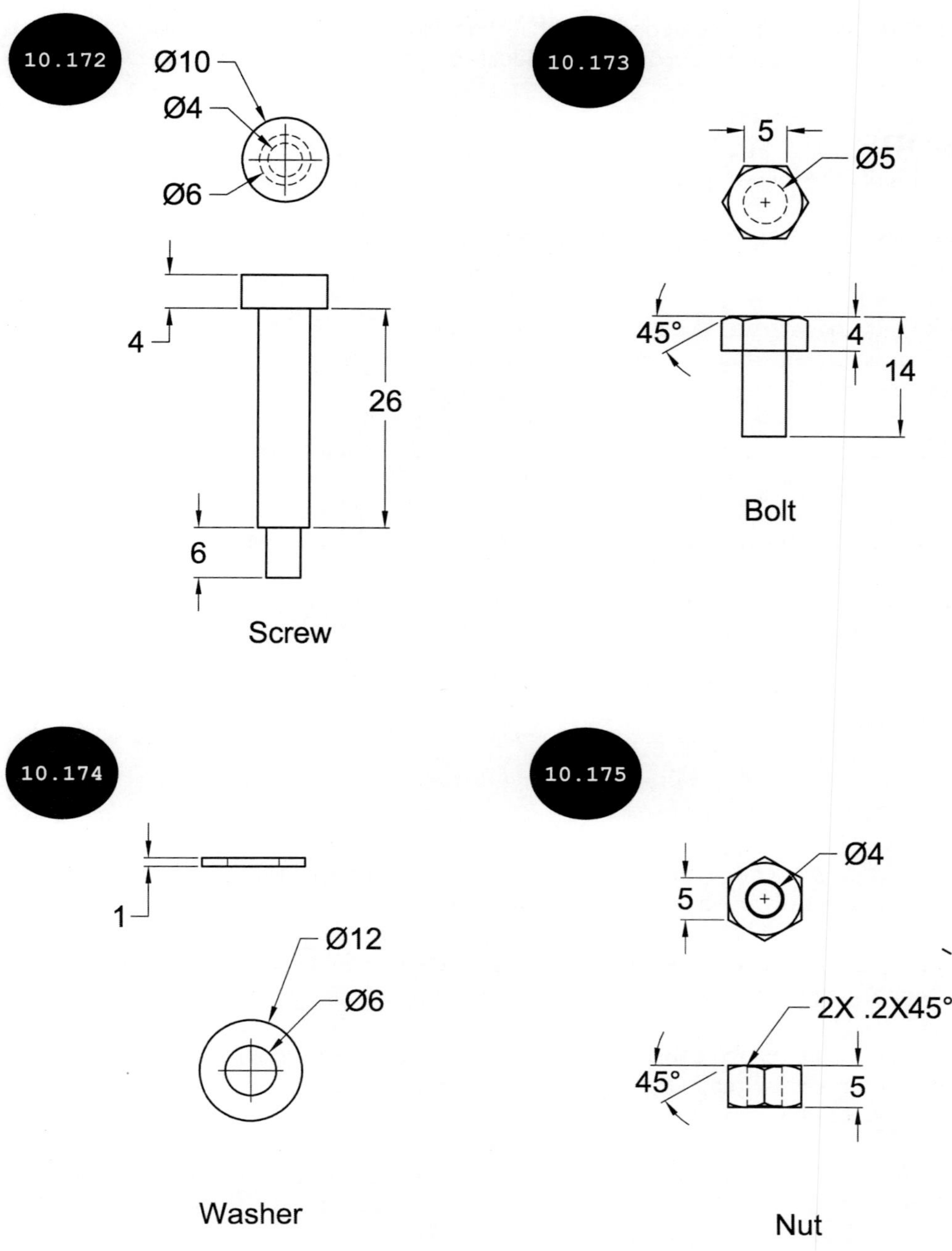

Summary

In this chapter, you have learned about creating assemblies by using the bottom-up assembly approach. The chapter explained methods for applying different types of predefined constraint sets such as Pin, Slider, Cylinder, and Planar as well as the user defined constraints such as Distance, Angle Offset, Parallel, and Coincident to assemble the components with respect to each other. You have also learned how to edit constraints as well as move and rotate individual components in the Assembly environment.

Questions

Complete and verify the following sentences:

- In Creo Parametric, you can create assemblies by using the ________ and ________ approaches.
- Creo Parametric has a ________ association between all its modes. As a result, if any change or modification is made to a component in the Part mode, the same change automatically reflects in the Assembly and Drawing modes as well, and vice-versa.
- The ________ allows you to change the position and orientation of the component before applying a constraint in the Assembly environment.
- A free component within the Assembly environment has ________ degrees of freedom.
- The ________ constraint is used for aligning the coordinate system of the component with the default assembly coordinate system.
- The ________ constraint is used for restricting references of two components at a specified angular distance.
- The ________ constraint is used for making two references (conical, spherical, or toroidal faces) of components centered to each other.
- The ________ predefined constraint set allows the component to rotate about an axis by removing all degrees of freedom except one rotational degree of freedom.
- The ________ predefined constraint set allows the component to translate/slide along an axis by removing all degrees of freedom except one translational degree of freedom.
- The ________ predefined constraint set allows the component to translate as well as rotate about the same axis by removing all degrees of freedom except one translational and one rotational degrees of freedom.
- You can move an individual component of an assembly along its free degrees of freedom. (True/False).
- In the Pin predefined constraint set, you cannot define the minimum and maximum limits for the angle of rotation. (True/False).

CHAPTER

11

Working with Assemblies - II

In this chapter, the following topics will be discussed:

- Creating an Assembly using the Top-down Approach
- Editing Assembly Components
- Displaying Constraints in Model Tree
- Patterning Assembly Components
- Mirroring a Component of an Assembly
- Creating Assembly Features
- Suppressing or Resuming Components
- Assembling Multiple Copies of a Component
- Checking Interference between Components
- Creating an Exploded View
- Switching Between Exploded and Unexploded Views
- Specifying Settings for Animating Exploded View
- Creating Bill of Material (BOM)

In the previous chapter, you have learned about creating assemblies by using the Bottom-up Assembly Approach. You have also learned about different types of constraints and how to move or rotate individual components of an assembly. In this chapter, you will learn about creating assemblies by using the Top-down Assembly Approach, editing assembly components, patterning and mirroring components, creating assembly features, suppressing/resuming components, assembling multiple copies of a component, checking interference between components, creating an exploded view of an assembly, and so on.

Creating an Assembly using the Top-down Approach

In the Top-down Assembly Approach, all components of an assembly are created within the Assembly environment itself. Creating components in the Assembly environment helps in taking reference from the existing components of the assembly. Using this approach, you can create a concept-based design, where new components of an assembly can be created by taking reference from the existing components and maintaining the relationships between them. The method for creating an assembly by using the Top-down Assembly Approach is discussed below:

Creating an Assembly using the Top-down Approach

1. Invoke the Assembly environment by using the **New** tool of the **Quick Access Toolbar**, as discussed earlier, see Figure 11.1. Note that while invoking the assembly file, you can specify its name and select a required template file.

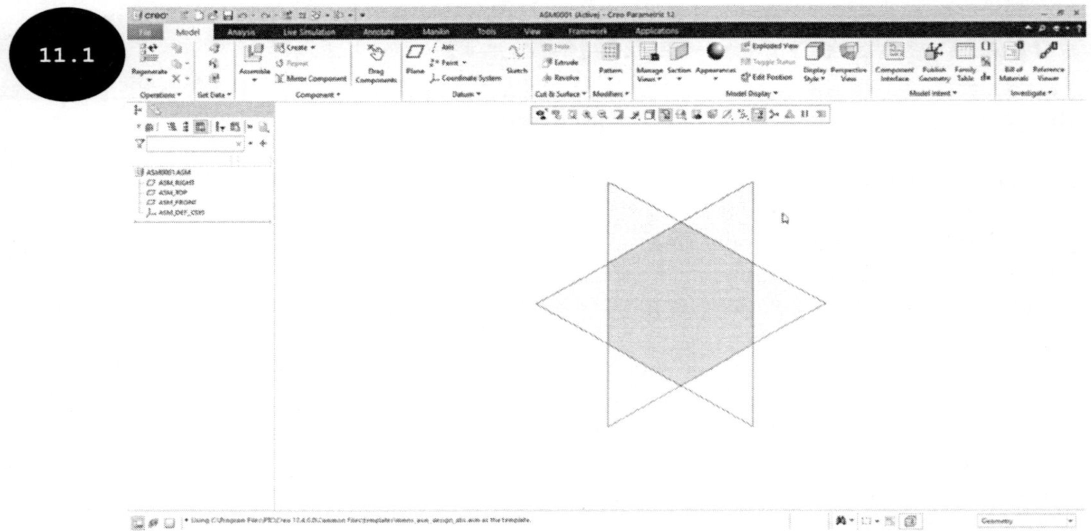

Now, you need to create components within the Assembly environment.

2. Click on the **Create** tool in the **Component** group of the **Model** tab, see Figure 11.2. The **Create Component** dialog box appears in the graphics area, see Figure 11.3.

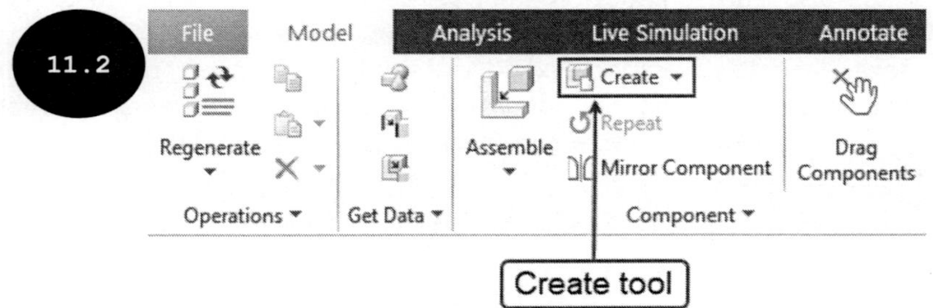

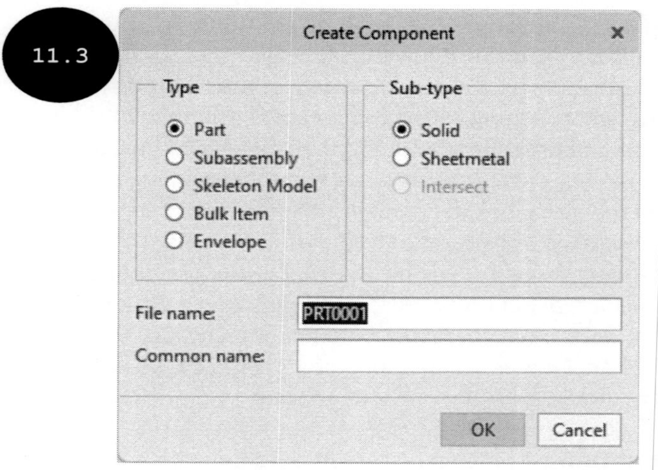

Note: By default, the **Part** radio button is selected in the **Type** area and the **Solid** radio button is selected in the **Sub-type** area of the **Create Component** dialog box. As a result, you can create a solid part/component. On selecting the **Sheetmetal** radio button in the **Sub-type** area, you can create a sheetmetal component and on selecting the **Intersect** radio button, you can create a component by intersecting two or more than two components. Note that the **Intersect** radio button is enabled only when the components are already available in the Assembly environment. Besides creating a solid, a sheetmetal, or an intersect component, you can also create a sub-assembly in the Assembly environment by selecting the **Subassembly** radio button in the **Type** area of the **Create Component** dialog box.

3. Ensure that the **Part** radio button is selected in the **Type** area and the **Solid** radio button is selected in the **Sub-type** area of the dialog box to create a solid component, see Figure 11.3.

4. Enter the name of the component in the **File name** field and then click on the **OK** button in the dialog box. The **Creation Options** dialog box appears, see Figure 11.4. The options in this dialog box are used for specifying a method for creating the component. The options are discussed below:

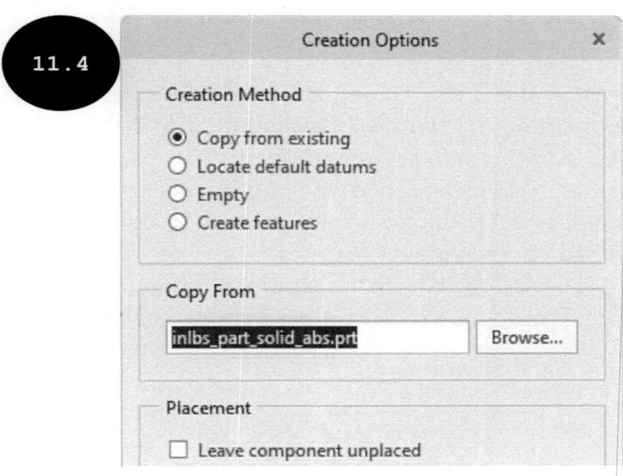

Copy from existing: The Copy from existing radio button is used for creating a copy of an existing component and inserting it in the assembly. To do so, select this radio button and then click on the Browse button in the Copy From area of the dialog box. The Choose template dialog box appears. Next, select a component to be copied and then click on the Open button in the dialog box. The name of the selected component appears in the Copy From field of the Creation Options dialog box. Next, ensure that the Leave component unplaced check box is cleared in the Placement area of the dialog box to define the placement of the new component in the assembly by specifying the required constraints. Note that if you select the Leave component unplaced check box, then the component will be inserted in the assembly without defining placement constraints and will act as an unplaced component. Next, click on the OK button. A preview of the component appears in the assembly environment and the Component Placement tab appears in the Ribbon. Now, you can apply the required constraints to define the placement of the component, as discussed in the previous chapter.

Locate default datums: The Locate default datums radio button is used for creating a new component by assembling it automatically to the selected assembly references. When this radio button is selected in the Creation Options dialog box, the Locate Datums Method area appears with three radio buttons: Three planes, Axis normal to plane, and Align csys to csys in the dialog box, see Figure 11.5. These radio buttons are discussed below:

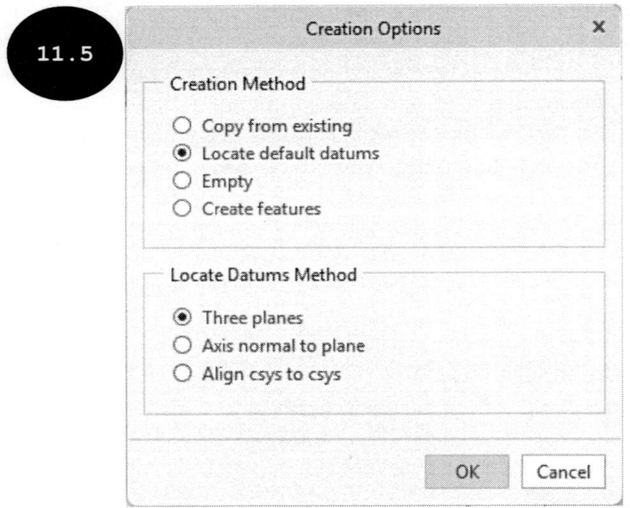

Three planes: When you select the Three planes radio button and click on the OK button in the Creation Options dialog box, you will be prompted to select three datum planes of the assembly individually. On doing so, a new empty component is created in the assembly with three datum planes that are assembled or aligned with the selected datum planes of the assembly. Also, the newly created component becomes an active assembly component, and the Part modeling environment is invoked for creating its features. After creating all the features of the newly created component, you need to activate the Assembly mode. To do so, click on the name of the assembly in the Model Tree and then click on the Activate tool in the Mini toolbar that appears, see Figure 11.6.

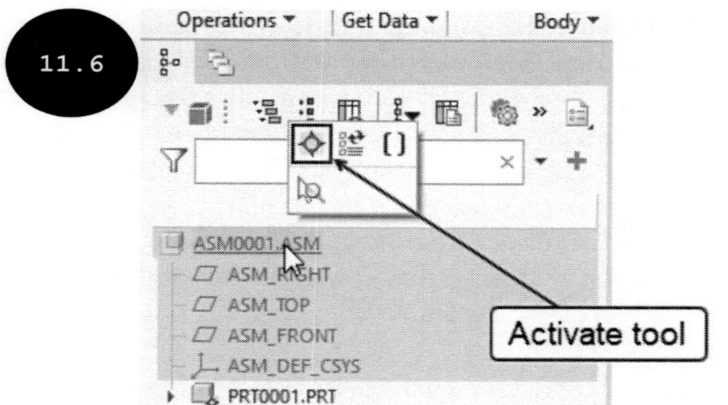

Axis normal to plane: When you select the **Axis normal to plane** radio button and click on the **OK** button in the **Creation Options** dialog box, you will be prompted to select a datum plane of the assembly and an axis normal to it one by one. On doing so, a new empty component is created in the assembly with datum planes and an axis concerning the selected datum plane and axis of the assembly. Also, the name of the newly created component appears in the **Model Tree**. Besides, it becomes an active component, and the Part modeling environment is invoked for creating its features. After creating all the features of the newly added component, you need to activate the Assembly mode. To do so, click on the name of the assembly in the **Model Tree** and then click on the **Activate** tool in the Mini toolbar that appears.

Align csys to csys: When you select the **Align csys to csys** radio button and click on the **OK** button in the **Creation Options** dialog box, you will be prompted to select a coordinate system of the assembly. On doing so, a new empty component is created in the assembly with datum planes and a coordinate system that is assembled or aligned to the assembly coordinate system. Also, the name of the newly created component appears in the **Model Tree**. Besides, it becomes an active component, and the Part modeling environment is invoked for creating its features. After creating all the features of the newly added component, you need to activate the Assembly mode. To do so, click on the name of the assembly in the **Model Tree** and then click on the **Activate** tool in the Mini toolbar that appears.

Empty: The **Empty** radio button is used for creating an empty component in the assembly. When you select this radio button in the **Creation Options** dialog box and click **OK**, a new empty component is added to the assembly and its name appears in the **Model Tree**. Note that to add features to an empty component, you need to activate it by clicking on the **Activate** tool in the Mini toolbar that appears on clicking its name in the **Model Tree**.

Tip: To create default datum planes of an empty component, you need to open it in the Part modeling environment. To do so, click on the name of the empty component in the **Model Tree** and then click on the **Open** tool in the Mini toolbar that appears. The empty component is opened in the Part modeling environment. Now, you can create its default datum planes by using the **Plane** tool.

Create features: The **Create features** radio button is used for creating a new component by creating its features using the existing assembly references. When you select this radio button in the **Creation Options** dialog box and click **OK**, a new component is created in the assembly and its name appears in the **Model Tree**. Also, it becomes an active component and the Part modeling environment is invoked for creating its features by using the assembly references.

5. Select the **Locate default datums** radio button and then the **Align csys to csys** radio button in the **Creation Options** dialog box to create a new component by aligning its coordinate system to the assembly coordinate system, see Figure 11.7.

Note: You can select any of the required radio buttons (**Copy from existing, Locate default datums, Empty**, or **Create features**) in the **Creation Options** dialog box, as discussed earlier, for creating a new component in the assembly.

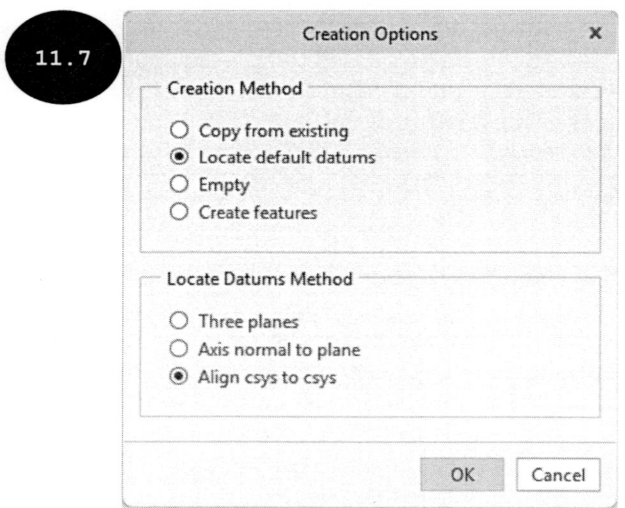

6. Click on the **OK** button in the **Creation Options** dialog box. You are prompted to select an assembly coordinate system.

7. Select the coordinate system of the assembly. The new component is created in the assembly with datum planes and a coordinate system that is aligned to the assembly coordinate system. The name of the newly created component appears in the **Model Tree**. Also, it becomes an active component and the Part modeling environment is invoked for creating its features, see Figure 11.8. Note that the datum planes of an active component appear dark in the graphics area.

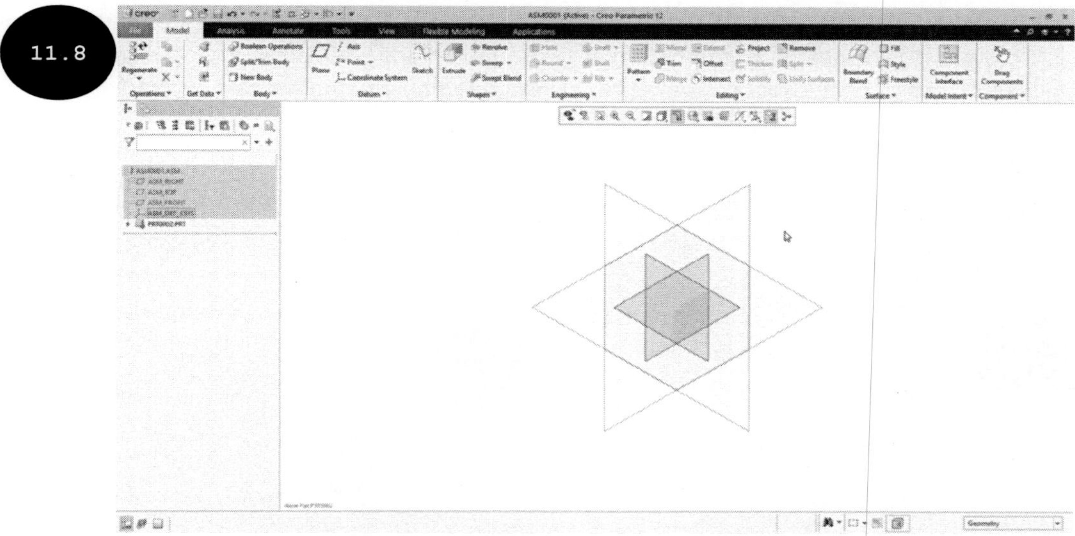

Now, you can add features to the newly created component in the assembly.

8. Click on the **Sketch** tool in the **Datum** group of the **Model** tab to create the sketch of the base feature of the newly added component. The **Sketch** dialog box appears.

9. Select a datum plane of the component as the sketching plane in the graphics area and then click on the **Sketch** button in the dialog box. The Sketching environment is invoked and the selected datum plane is oriented normal to the viewing direction, see Figure 11.9. In this figure, the top datum plane of the active component is selected as the sketching plane.

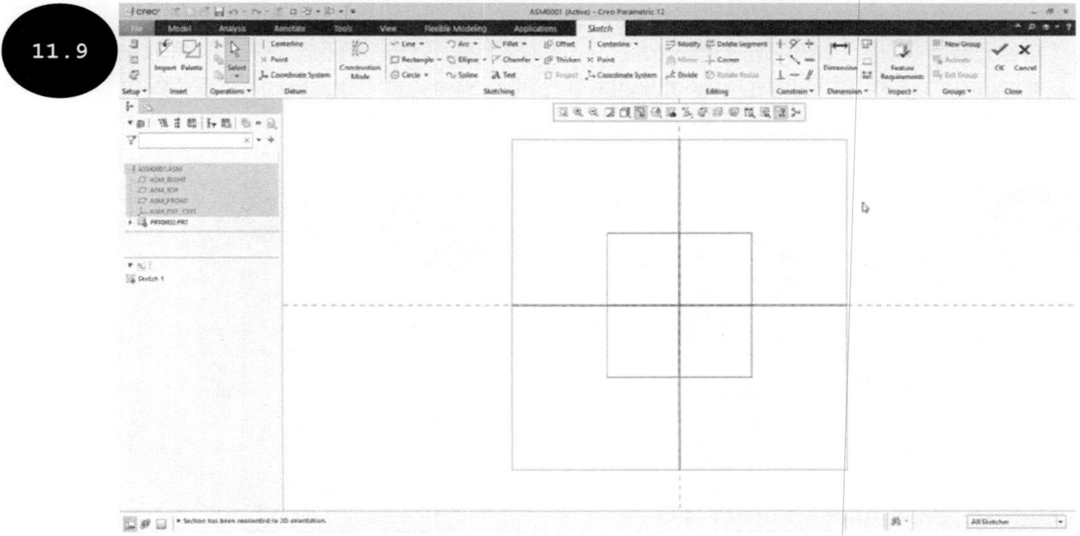

10. Create the sketch of the base feature of the component by using the sketching tools, refer to Figure 11.10.

11. After creating the sketch, exit the Sketching environment by clicking on the **OK** button in the **Close** group. The sketch of the base feature is created and the Part modeling environment is invoked. Next, change the orientation of the sketch to standard orientation.

    After creating the sketch, you need to convert it into a solid feature by using solid modeling tools.

12. Convert the sketch into a solid feature by using a solid modeling tool such as **Extrude** or **Revolve**, refer to Figure 11.11. In this figure, the sketch is extruded to a depth of 15 mm by using the **Extrude** tool.

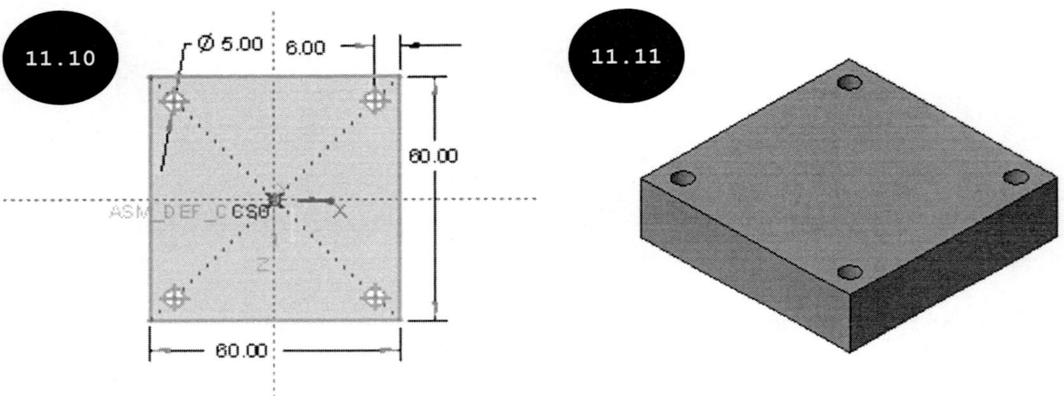

Now, you need to create the second feature of the component.

13. Invoke the Sketching environment again by selecting a planar face or a datum plane as the sketching plane for creating a sketch of the second feature.

14. Create the sketch of the second feature (refer to Figure 11.12) and then convert it into a feature by using a solid modeling tool, refer to Figure 11.13. In Figure 11.12, the sketch of the feature is created on the top planar face of the base feature. In Figure 11.13, the sketch is extruded to a depth of 75 mm by using the **Extrude** tool.

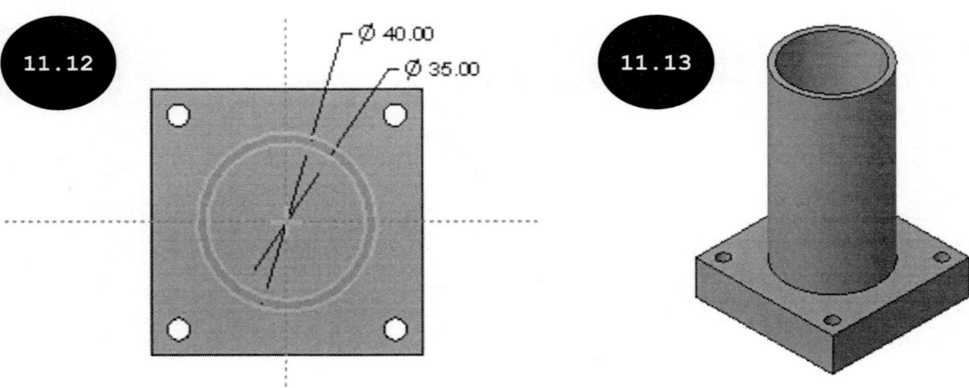

15. Similarly, you can create the remaining features of the component one after the other.

16. After creating all features of the first component, click on the name of the assembly in the **Model Tree**. A Mini toolbar appears, see Figure 11.14.

17. Click on the **Activate** tool in the Mini toolbar that appears, see Figure 11.14. The assembly mode gets activated.

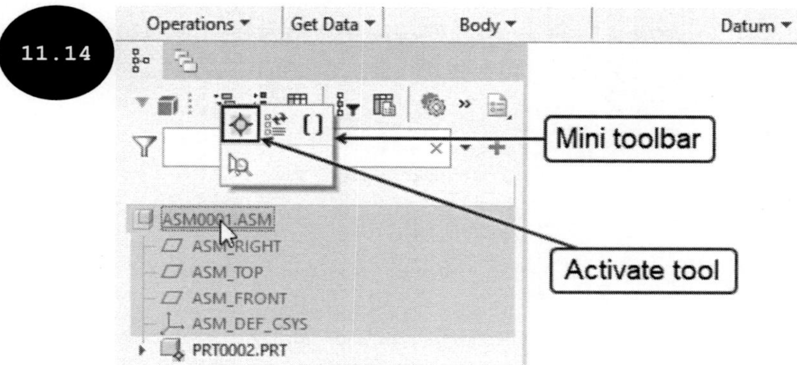

Note: In Creo Parametric, the components created in the Assembly environment are fixed components and all their degrees of freedom are restricted.

After creating the first component, you can create the second component of the assembly.

18. Click on the **Create** tool in the **Component** group of the **Model** tab, see Figure 11.15. The **Create Component** dialog box appears in the graphics area.

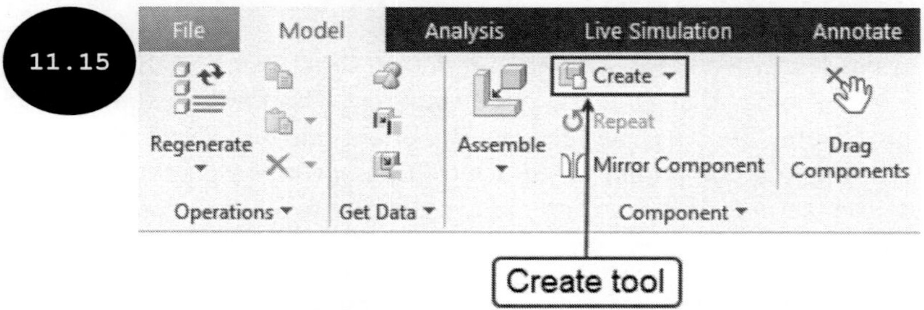

19. Ensure that the **Part** radio button is selected in the **Type** area and the **Solid** radio button is selected in the **Sub-type** area of the dialog box to create a solid component.

20. Enter a name for the component in the **Name** field and then click on the **OK** button in the dialog box. The **Creation Options** dialog box appears, see Figure 11.16. The options of this dialog box have been discussed earlier.

21. Select the **Empty** radio button in the **Creation Options** dialog box to create the second component as an empty component, see Figure 11.16.

Note: You can select any of the available radio buttons (**Copy from existing, Locate default datums, Empty**, or **Create features**) in the **Creation Options** dialog box, as discussed earlier, for creating a new component in the assembly.

11.16

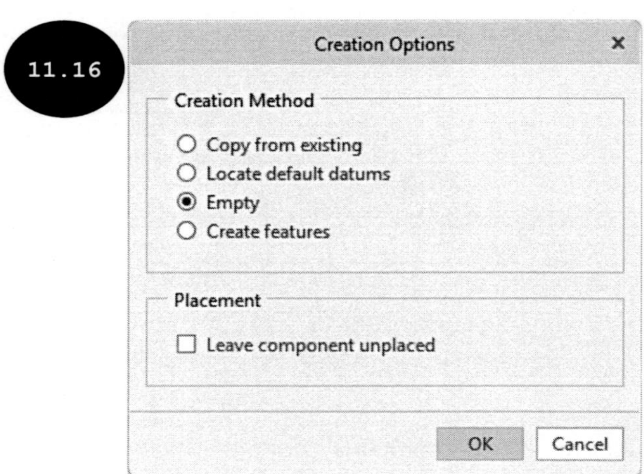

22. Ensure that the **Leave component unplaced** check box is cleared in the **Placement** area of the dialog box. Next, click on the **OK** button. A new empty component is created in the assembly and its name appears in the **Model Tree**.

    Now, you need to add features to the newly created empty component. To do so, you need to first activate the component in the assembly.

23. Click on the newly created empty component in the **Model Tree** and then click on the **Activate** tool in the Mini toolbar that appears, see Figure 11.17. The newly created empty component (second component) becomes the active component and the Part modeling environment is invoked. Also, the first component becomes transparent in the graphics area so that you can easily create the features of the second component and take reference of the first component, refer to Figure 11.18.

11.17

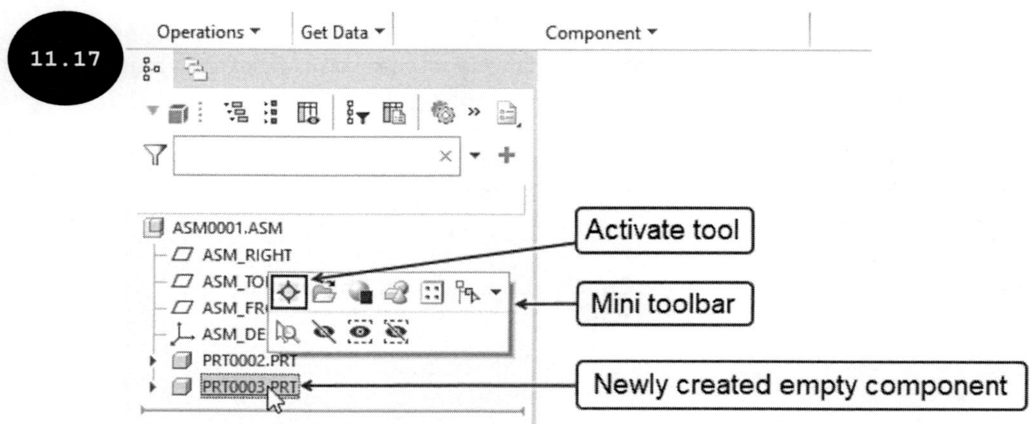

11.18

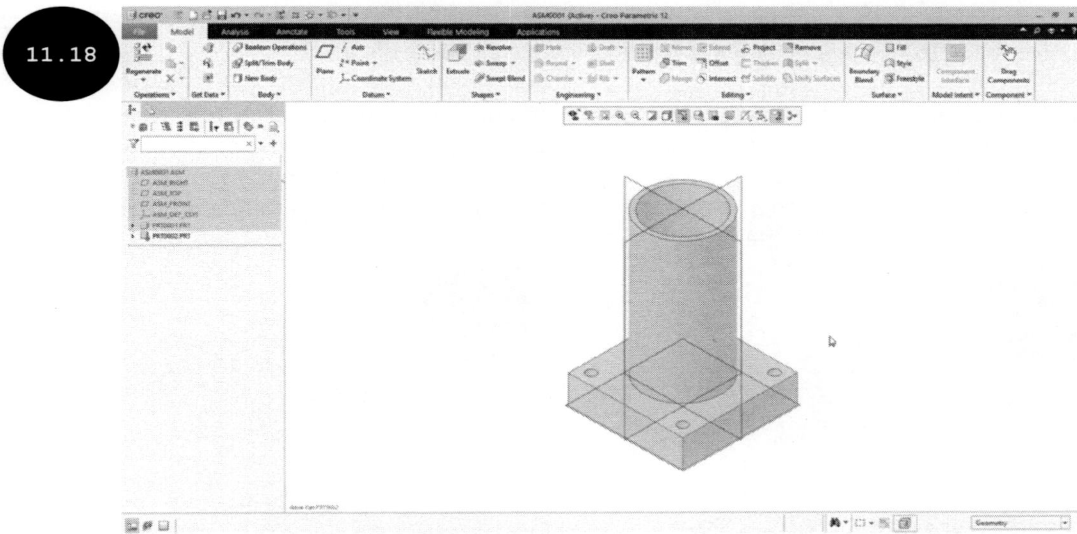

Now, you can add features to the second component.

24. Click on the **Sketch** tool in the **Datum** group of the **Model** tab to create the sketch of the base feature of the second component. The **Sketch** dialog box appears.

25. Select a plane or a planar face of the first component as the sketching plane in the graphics area and then click on the **Sketch** button in the dialog box. The Sketching environment is invoked and the selected plane/planar face is oriented normal to the viewing direction, refer to Figure 11.19. In this figure, the top planar face of the first component is selected as the sketching plane.

11.19

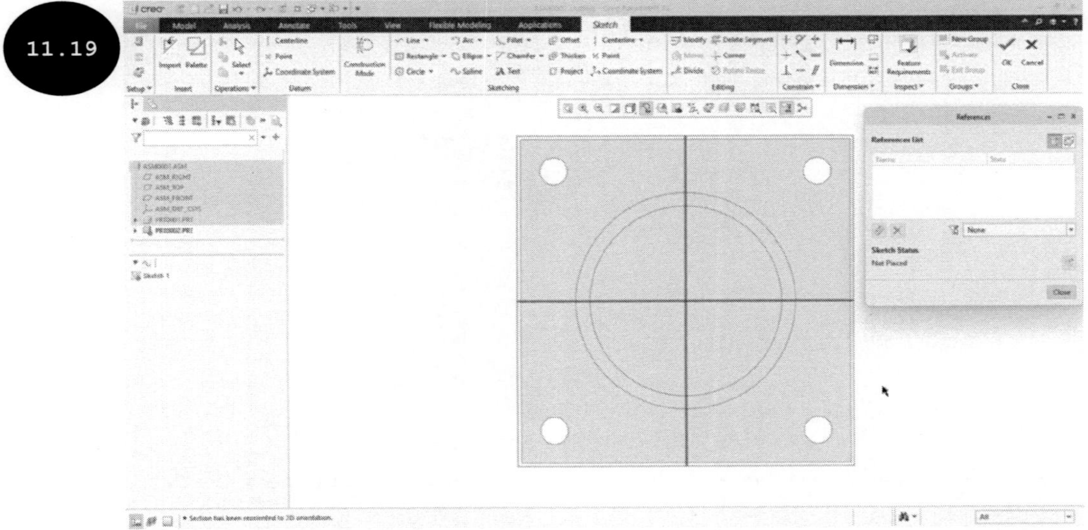

26. Invoke the **References** dialog box to specify references for creating the sketch, if not invoked by default. You can invoke the **References** dialog box by clicking on the **References** tool in the **Setup** group of the **Sketch** tab.

27. Select the required entities of the first component to specify references for creating the sketch (refer to Figure 11.20) and then close the **References** dialog box.

28. Create the sketch of the base feature of the second component by taking reference of the first component, refer to Figure 11.21. In this figure, the rectangle and the outer four circles of the sketch have been created by projecting the edges of the first component onto the sketching plane. Also, the orientation of the model has been changed to the standard orientation for a better understanding of the sketch.

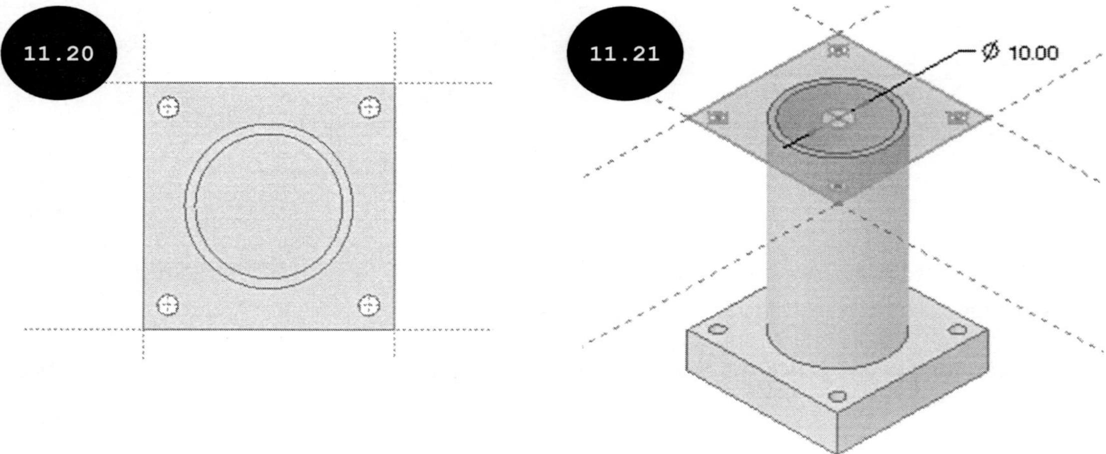

29. Exit the Sketching environment and then convert the sketch into a solid feature by using a solid modeling tool such as **Extrude** or **Revolve**, refer to Figure 11.22. In this figure, the sketch is extruded to a depth of 15 mm by using the **Extrude** tool.

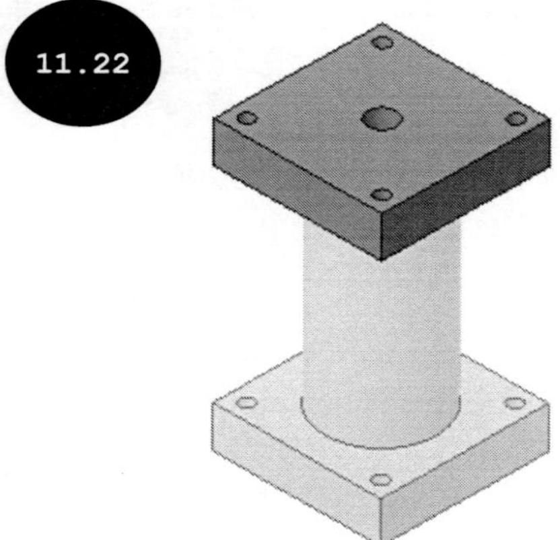

30. Similarly, you can create the remaining features of the second component one by one.

31. After creating all features of the second component, you need to activate the Assembly model. To do so, click on the name of the assembly in the **Model Tree** and then click on the **Activate** tool in the Mini toolbar that appears. Figure 11.23 shows the assembly components after activating the Assembly mode.

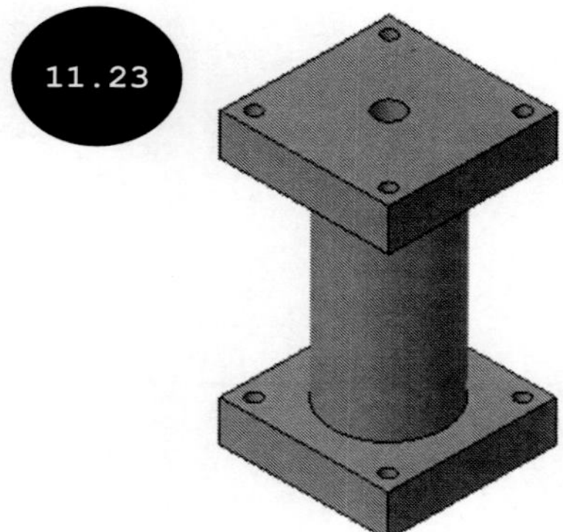

After creating the second component, you can create the third component of the assembly.

32. Click on the **Create** tool in the **Component** group of the **Model** tab, see Figure 11.24. The **Create Component** dialog box appears in the graphics area.

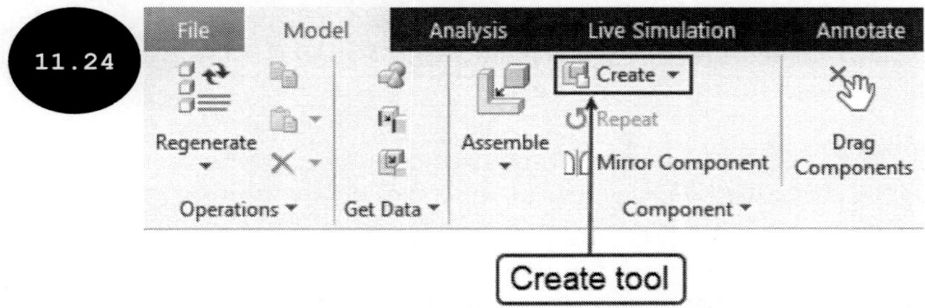

33. Ensure that the **Part** radio button is selected in the **Type** area and the **Solid** radio button is selected in the **Sub-type** area of the dialog box to create a solid component.

34. Enter a name for the component in the **Name** field and then click on the **OK** button in the dialog box. The **Creation Options** dialog box appears.

35. Select the **Empty** radio button in the **Creation Options** dialog box to create the third component as an empty component.

36. Ensure that the **Leave component unplaced** check box is cleared in the **Placement** area of the **Creation Options** dialog box. Next, click on the **OK** button. A new empty component is created in the assembly and its name appears in the **Model Tree**.

    Now, you need to add features to the newly created empty component (third component). To do so, you need to first activate it in the assembly.

37. Click on the newly created empty component (third component) in the **Model Tree** and then click on the **Activate** tool in the Mini toolbar that appears, see Figure 11.25. The newly created empty component (third component) becomes the active component and the Part modeling environment is invoked. Also, the existing components become transparent in the graphics area so that you can easily create the third component by taking reference from the existing components, refer to Figure 11.26.

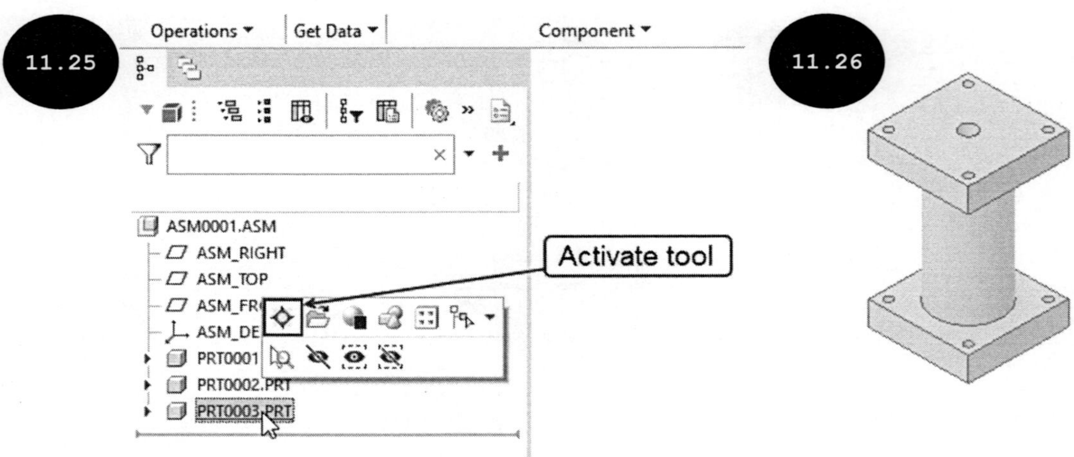

Now, you can add features to the newly added empty component (third component).

38. Invoke the Sketching environment by selecting a plane or a planar face of the existing component as the sketching plane, refer to Figure 11.27. In this figure, the top planar face of the second component is selected as the sketching plane.

39. Create the sketch of the first feature of the third component, refer to Figure 11.27. In this figure, a circle has been created by projecting the circular edges of the second component onto the sketching plane.

40. Exit the Sketching environment and then convert the sketch into a solid feature by using a solid modeling tool such as **Extrude** or **Revolve**, refer to Figure 11.28. In this figure, the circle is extruded to a distance of 120 mm, symmetrically on both sides of the sketching plane.

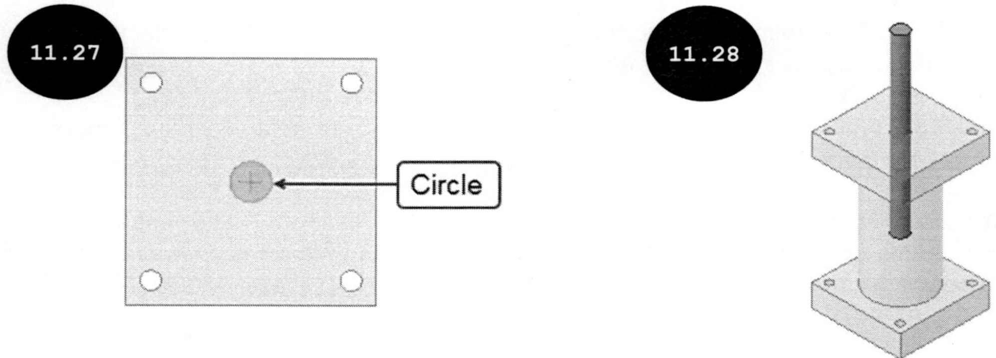

Now, you can create the second feature of the third component.

41. Create the second feature of the third component, refer to Figure 11.29. In this figure, the sketch (circle) of the second feature is created on the bottom planar face of the first feature of the component and extruded to a distance of 6 mm.

42. Similarly, create the remaining features of the third component one by one, refer to Figure 11.30.

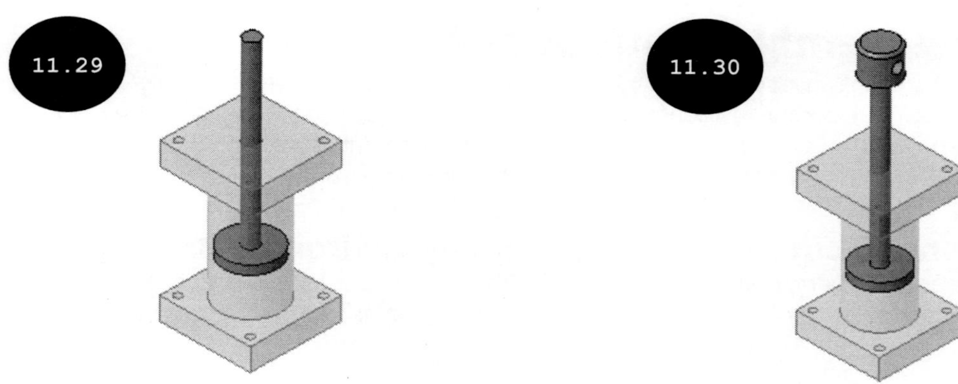

43. After creating all features of the third component, activate the Assembly model by clicking on the **Activate** tool in the Mini toolbar that appears on clicking the name of the assembly in the **Model Tree**.

    After creating the third component, you can create the remaining components.

44. Similarly, you can create the remaining components of the assembly one by one, refer to Figure 11.31.

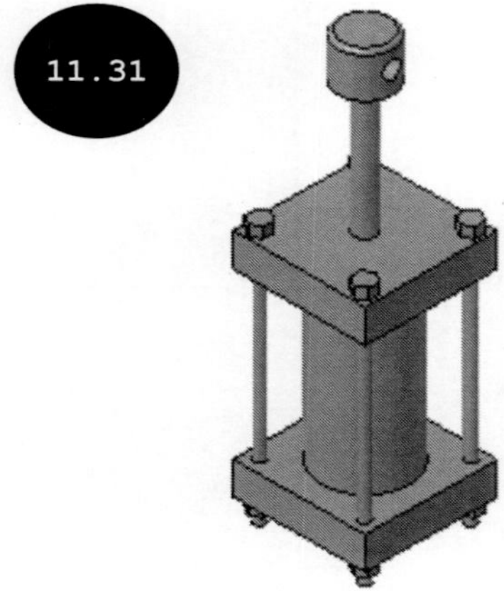

Note: In Creo Parametric, the components created in the Assembly environment are fixed components and all their degrees of freedom are restricted.

After creating all the components of the assembly, you can save the assembly file and its components.

45. Click on the **Save** tool in the **Quick Access Toolbar** toolbar. The **Save Object** dialog box appears.

46. Click on the **OK** button in the dialog box. The assembly and its individual components are saved in the specified working directory.

Editing Assembly Components

In the process of creating an assembly, you may need to edit its components several times depending upon the changes in the design, revisions, or validation of the design. Creo Parametric allows you to edit each component of an assembly within the Assembly environment as well as in the Part modeling environment. Different methods for editing assembly components are discussed next.

Editing Components within the Assembly Environment

To edit the features of a component within the Assembly environment, you first need to ensure that the features of each assembly component are displayed in the **Model Tree**, see Figure 11.32.

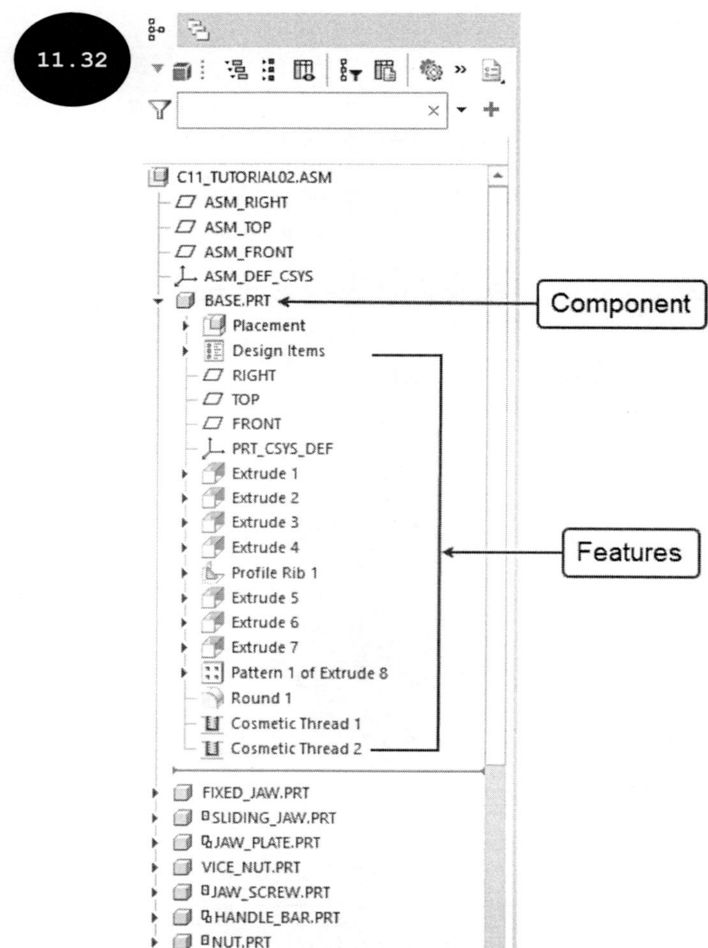

The method for displaying the features of each component of the assembly in the **Model Tree** is discussed below:

1. Click on the **Tree Filters** in the **Navigator**, see Figure 11.33. The **Tree Filters** dialog box appears, refer to Figure 11.34.

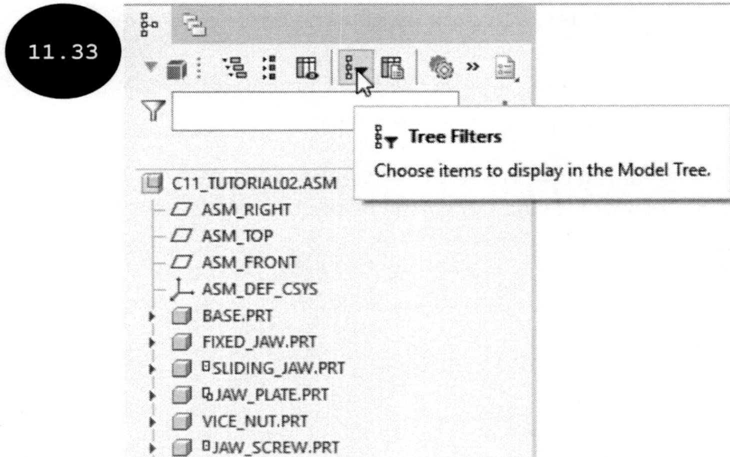

2. Ensure that the **General** option is selected in the left panel of the dialog box. Next, select the **Features** check box in the **General Items** area that appears on the right panel of the dialog box, see Figure 11.34.

3. After selecting the **Features** check box, click on the **Apply** button in the dialog box. All features of the individual components of the assembly including datum planes and coordinate systems appear in the **Model Tree**. Next, exit the dialog box by clicking on the **OK** button.

Now, you can edit the features of a component in the Assembly environment.

4. Click on a feature of a component to be edited in the **Model Tree**. A Mini toolbar appears, see Figure 11.35.

5. Click on the **Edit Definition** tool in the Mini toolbar, see Figure 11.35. The preview of the selected feature appears in the graphics area. Also, the respective tab appears in the **Ribbon**.

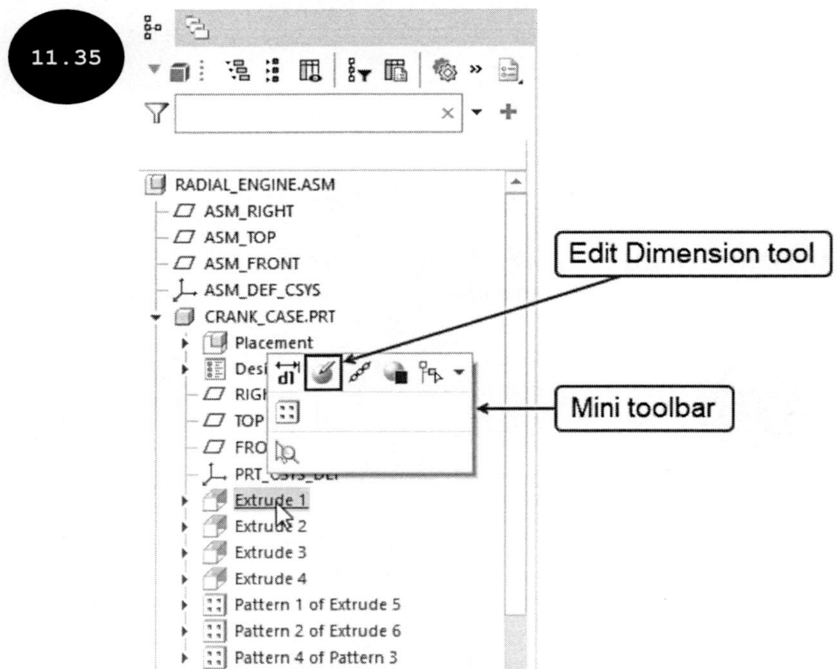

6. Change the feature parameters by using the options available in the tab that appears in the **Ribbon**.

7. Once you have edited the feature parameters, click on the green tick-mark ✓. The selected feature gets edited, as specified.

8. Similarly, you can edit the sketch of a feature.

Editing Components in the Part Modeling Environment

In addition to editing components of an assembly in the Assembly environment, you can also open a component of an assembly in the Part modeling environment and then perform the editing operations. The method for editing a component in the Part Modeling environment is discussed below:

1. Click on the component to be edited in the **Model Tree** or in the graphics area. A Mini toolbar appears, see Figure 11.36.

2. Click on the **Open** tool in the Mini toolbar, see Figure 11.36. The selected component is opened in the Part modeling environment.

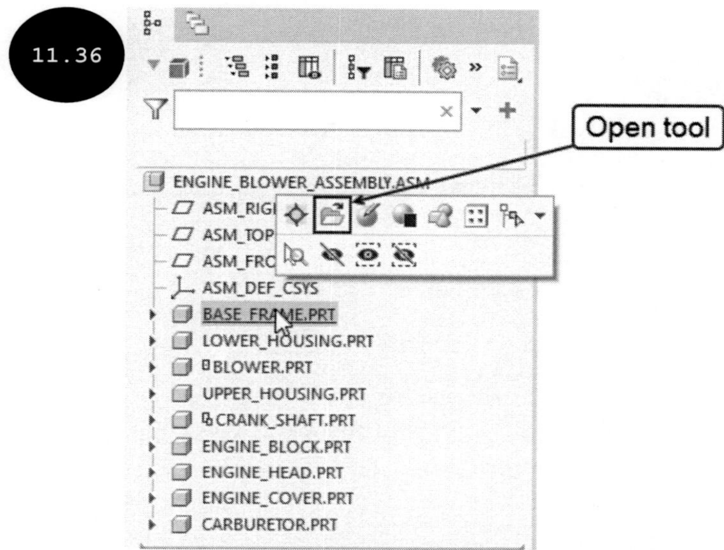

Now, you can edit the component in the Part modeling environment by editing its features and sketches.

3. Edit the features of the component, as required in the Part modeling environment. The methods for editing a feature and its sketch are the same as discussed earlier.

4. Once you have edited the component in the Part modeling environment, click on the **Save** tool in the **Quick Access Toolbar** to save the modified component. Next, click on **Windows** > *name of the assembly* in the **Quick Access Toolbar** to switch to the Assembly environment, see Figure 11.37.

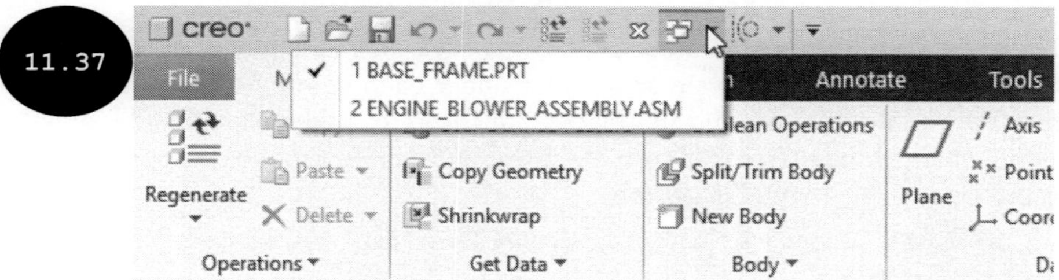

Displaying Constraints in Model Tree

In the **Model Tree**, the constraints applied to a component of an assembly appear in the **Placement** folder. The method for displaying the **Placement** folder in the **Model Tree** is discussed below:

1. Click on the **Tree Filters** in the **Navigator**, see Figure 11.38. The **Tree Filters** dialog box appears, refer to Figure 11.39.

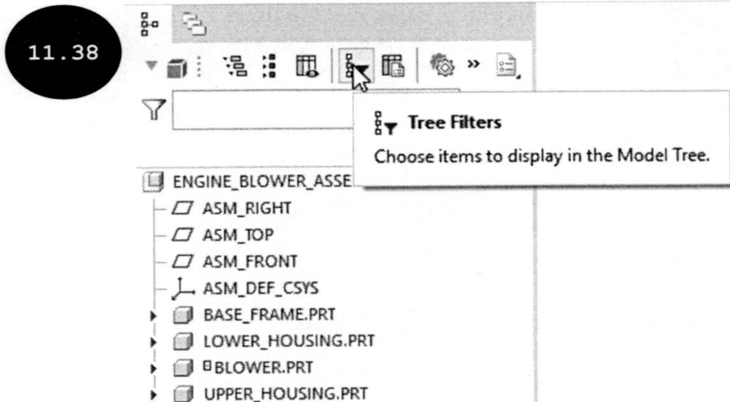

2. Ensure that the **General** option is selected in the left panel of the dialog box. Next, select the **Placement folder** check box in the **General Items** area that appears on the right panel of the dialog box, see Figure 11.39.

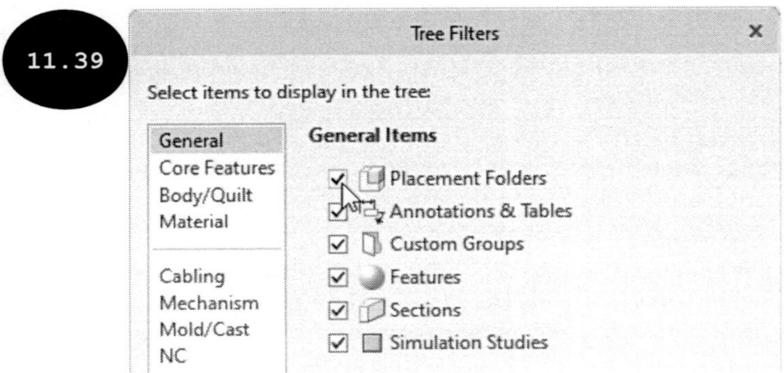

3. After selecting the **Placement folder** check box, click on the **Apply** button in the dialog box. The **Placement** folder is displayed as a folder under each component in the **Model Tree**, see Figure 11.40. You need to expand the **Placement** folder and then the **Set** sub-folder under the component in the **Model Tree** to display the constraints applied to the component. Next, exit the dialog box by clicking on the **OK** button.

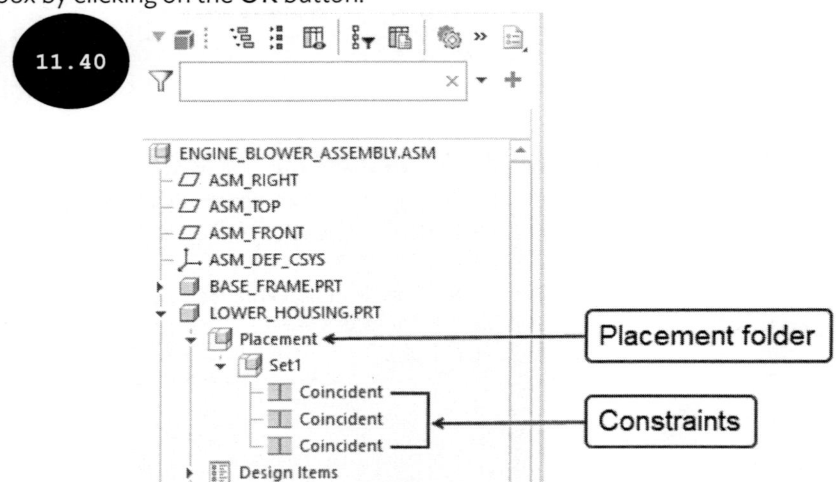

Patterning Assembly Components

Similar to patterning a feature of a component in the Part modeling environment, you can also pattern a component of an assembly in the Assembly environment, see Figure 11.41. In this figure, a component of the assembly is patterned to create its other instances. The methods for patterning a component in the Assembly environment are discussed below:

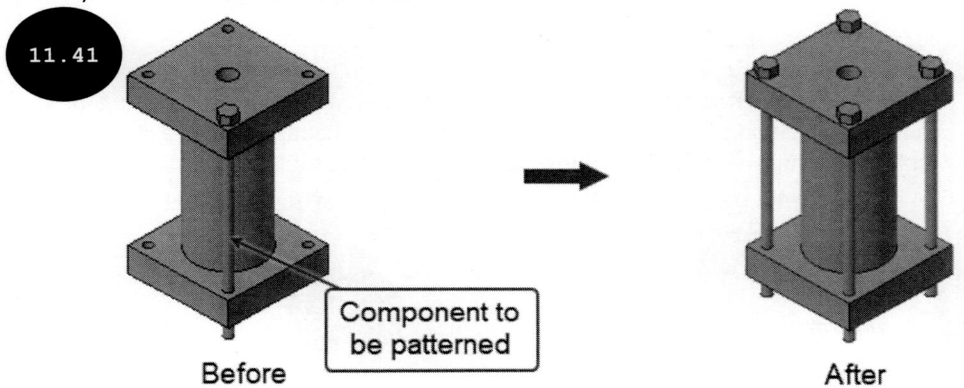

1. Click on a component to be patterned in the **Model Tree** or in the graphics area. A Mini toolbar appears, see Figure 11.42.

2. Click on the **Pattern** tool in the Mini toolbar, see Figure 11.42. The **Pattern** tab appears in the **Ribbon**, see Figure 11.43. Alternatively, you can also click on the **Pattern** tool in the **Modifiers** group of the **Model** tab.

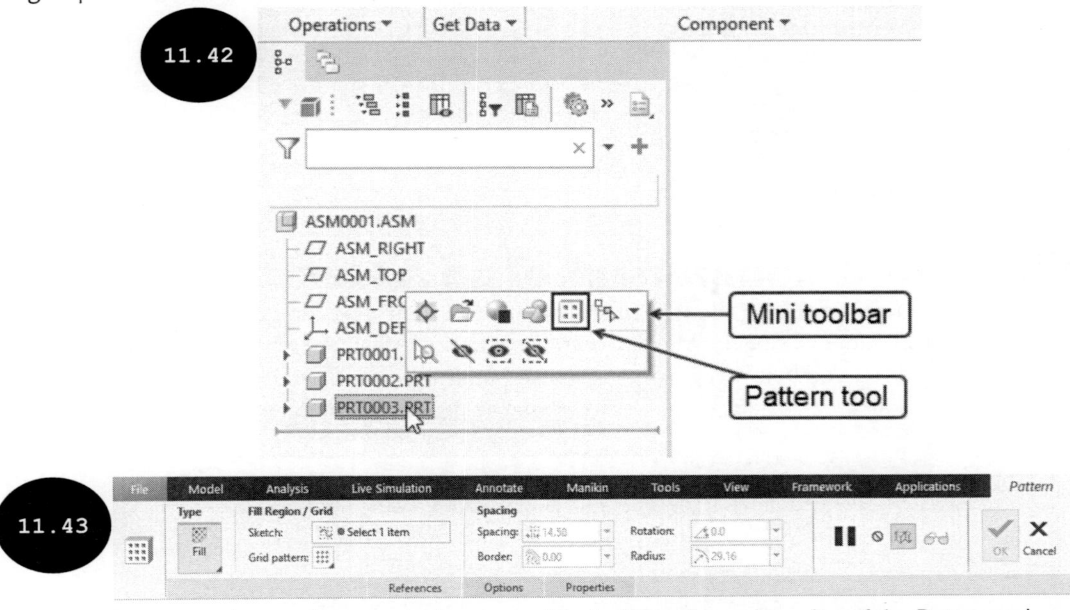

3. Select the required type of pattern to be created in the **Type** drop-down list of the **Pattern** tab and then specify the required parameters. In Creo Parametric, you can create various types of patterns such as Dimension Pattern, Direction Pattern, Axis Pattern, Fill Pattern, Table Pattern, Reference Pattern, Curve Pattern, and Point Pattern. The methods for creating different types of patterns

are the same as discussed earlier while creating patterns in the Part modeling environment with the only difference that in the Part modeling environment, you pattern a feature, while in the Assembly environment, you pattern a component to create multiple instances.

4. After specifying all the parameters to pattern a component, click on the green tick-mark button in the **Pattern** tab of the **Ribbon**. The respective pattern type is created.

Note: In Creo Parametric, you can also create a group of multiple components and pattern them together. To do so, select multiple components in the **Model Tree** by pressing the CTRL key and then click on the **Group** tool in the Mini toolbar that appears, see Figure 11.44. All the selected components are grouped together and a group folder is created in the **Model Tree**, see Figure 11.45. Now, you can pattern the group to pattern all its components together.

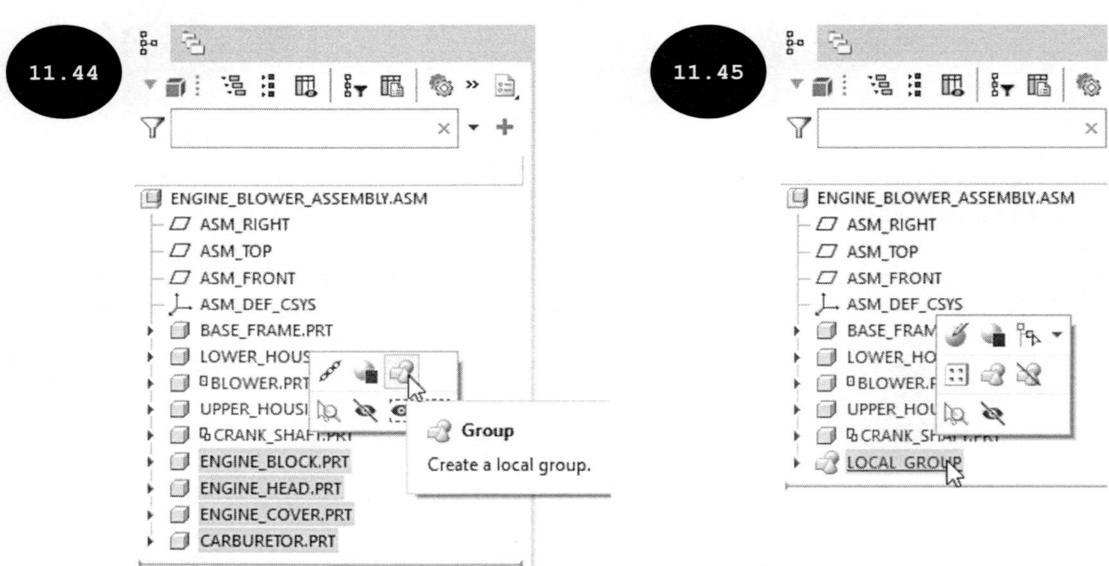

Mirroring a Component of an Assembly

Similar to mirroring a feature in the Part modeling environment, you can mirror a component in the Assembly environment by using the **Mirror Component** tool, see Figure 11.46. The method for mirroring a component is discussed below:

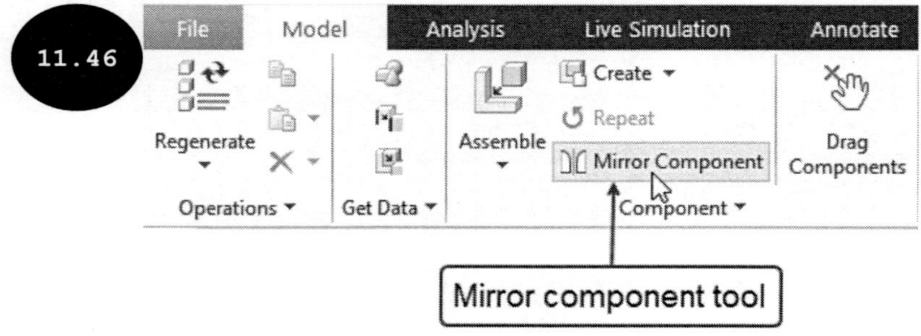

1. Click on the **Mirror Component** tool in the **Component** group, see Figure 11.46. The **Mirror Component** dialog box appears, see Figure 11.47.

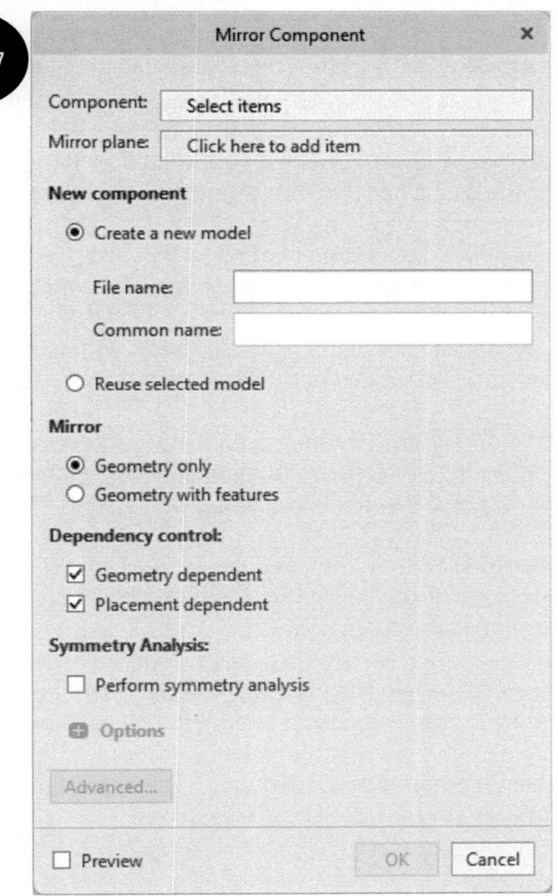

2. Select a component to be mirrored in the **Model Tree** or the graphics area, see Figure 11.48. The name of the selected component appears in the **Component** field of the dialog box. Also, you are prompted to select a mirroring plane.

3. Select a plane or a planar face as the mirroring plane in the graphics area, see Figure 11.48.

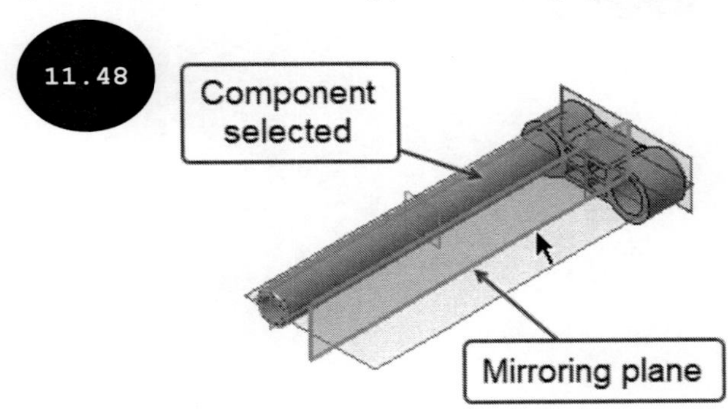

Create a new model: By default, the Create a new model radio button is selected in the New component area of the dialog box. As a result, a new mirrored component will be created. You can specify a name for the new mirrored component in the Name field.

Reuse selected model: On selecting the Reuse selected model radio button in the New component area, the selected component will be reused as the mirrored component.

4. Select the required radio button (Create a new model or Reuse selected model) in the New component area of the dialog box to mirror the selected component.

   Geometry only: By default, the Geometry only radio button is selected in the Mirror area of the dialog box. As a result, the mirrored copy of the selected component geometry is created.

   Geometry with features: On selecting the Geometry with features radio button, the mirrored copy of the selected component geometry and features is created.

5. Select the required radio button (Geometry only or Geometry with features) in the Mirror area of the dialog box. Note that both these radio buttons are enabled only when the Create a new model radio button is selected in the New component area of the dialog box.

   Geometry dependent: When the Geometry dependent check box is selected in the Dependency control area of the dialog box, the mirrored component geometry gets updated, if the original component geometry is modified.

   Placement dependent: When the Placement dependent check box is selected, the mirrored component placement or position gets updated, if the original component placement is modified.

6. Select or clear the Geometry dependent and Placement dependent check boxes in the Dependency control area of the dialog box, as required.

7. Select the Preview check box available at the lower left corner of the dialog box to display the preview of the mirror component.

8. Click on the OK button in the dialog box. The mirrored component is created, see Figure 11.49.

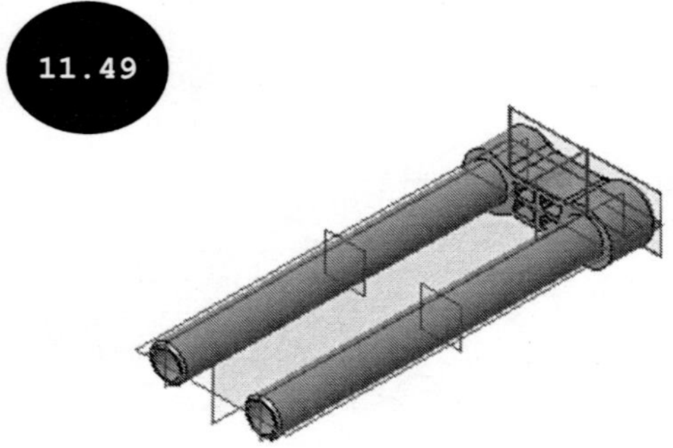

Creating Assembly Features

In a manufacturing unit or a shop floor, after assembling all components of an assembly, several cut operations may take place in components in order to give a final touch-up and align components perfectly with respect to each other. For this, Creo Parametric has tools to create cut features in the Assembly environment. Cut features created in the Assembly environment are known as assembly features and do not affect the original geometry of the components. For example, if you create an assembly feature (cut feature) on a component of an assembly in the Assembly environment; the assembly feature created will exist only in the assembly level and if you open the same component in the Part modeling environment, you will not find the existence of the assembly feature. This means that the assembly features exist in the assembly level only and will not affect the original geometry of the component, by default. However, you can also create an assembly feature such that it gets displayed in both, the assembly level as well as in the part level.

In Creo Parametric, you can create assembly features such as a hole, extrude cut, revolve cut, sweep cut, and blend cut. The tools for creating assembly features are available in the **Cut & Surface** group of the **Model** tab in the Assembly environment, see Figure 11.50. Note that to access all the tools of the **Cut & Surface** group, you need to expand it by clicking on the arrow available in its title bar.

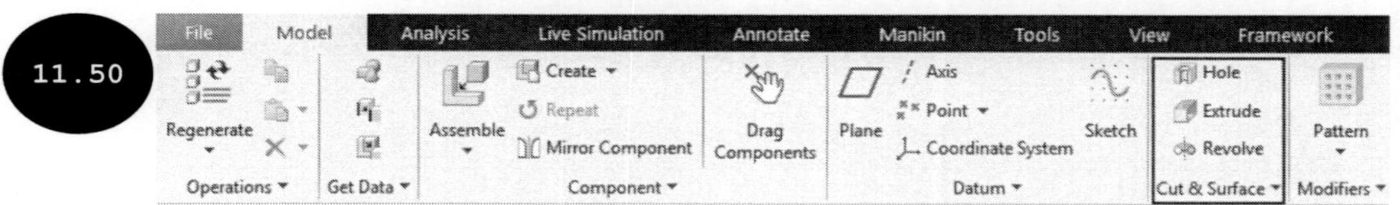

The method for creating an assembly feature is the same as that for creating a feature in the Part modeling environment. For example, the method for creating an extrude cut as an assembly feature is discussed below:

1. Click on the **Extrude** tool in the **Cut & Surface** group. The **Extrude** tab appears in the **Ribbon**, see Figure 11.51.

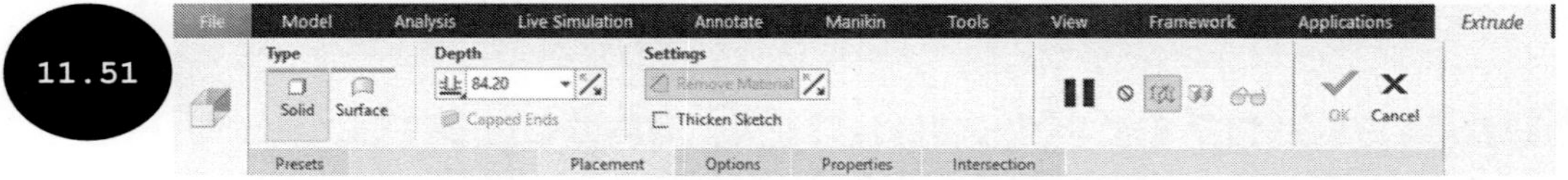

2. Select a plane or a planar face of an assembly component as the sketching plane. The Sketching environment is invoked.

3. Create a sketch of the extrude cut feature and then exit the Sketching environment. The preview of the cut feature appears in the graphics area.

4. Specify the required parameters for extrusion in the **Extrude** tab and then click on the green tick mark. The extrude cut feature is created on the selected component in the Assembly environment. However, if you open the same component in the Part modeling environment, you will not find the existence of the assembly feature (extrude cut feature).

Note: As discussed, the assembly features exist in the assembly level only and will not affect the original geometry of the component, by default. To display the assembly feature in both, the assembly level as well as in the part level, expand the **Intersection** panel of the **Extrude** tab and then clear the **Automatic Update** check box, see Figure 11.52. Next, select the **Part Level** option in the **Set Display Level** drop-down list of the expanded **Intersection** panel.

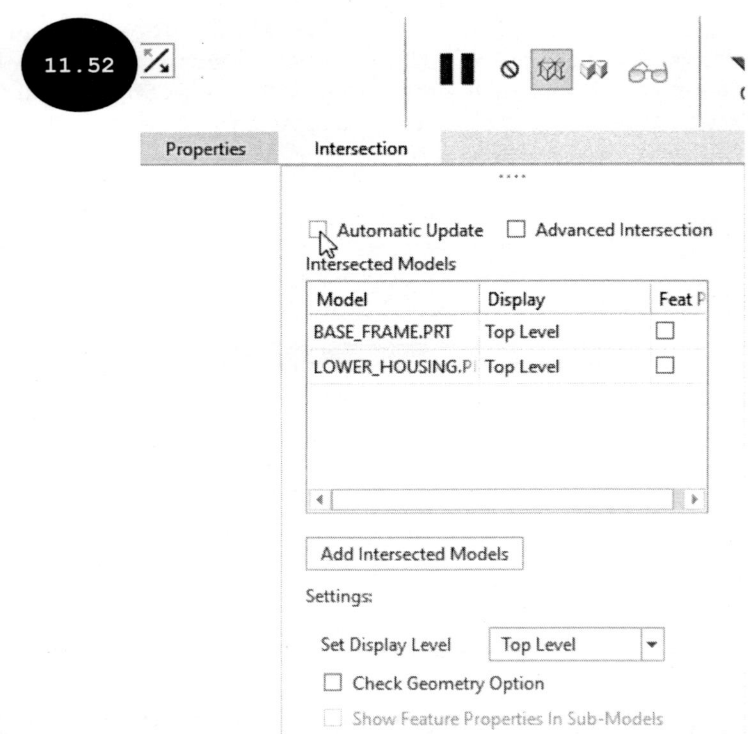

Suppressing or Resuming Components

In Creo Parametric, you can suppress or resume components of an assembly. A suppressed component is removed from the assembly and does not appear in the graphics area. Note that a suppressed component is not deleted from the assembly, it is only removed or hidden such that it is not loaded into the RAM (random access memory) while regenerating the assembly. This helps to speed up the overall performance of the system when you are working with large assemblies.

To suppress a component of an assembly, select the component to be suppressed either in the graphics area or in the **Model Tree**. A Mini toolbar appears, see Figure 11.53. In this Mini toolbar, click on the **Suppress** tool. The **Suppress** window appears to confirm the suppression of the highlighted component in the graphics area. Click on the **OK** button to confirm the suppression of the highlighted component. The selected component is suppressed and removed from the graphics area. Also, in the **Model Tree**, a black square appears in front of the name of the suppressed component, see Figure 11.54.

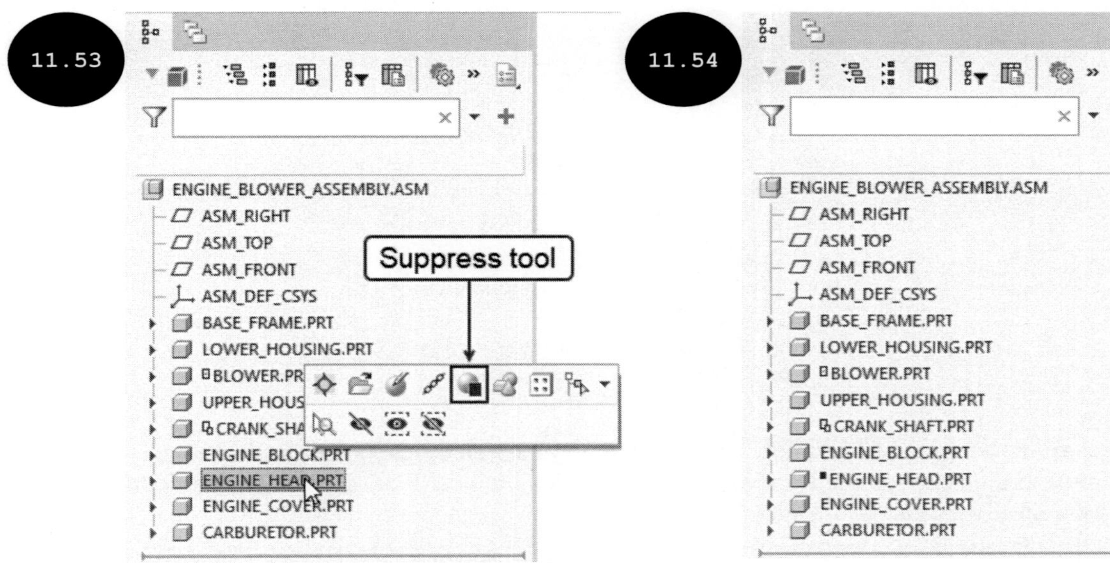

If the component to be suppressed has dependent or child components, then the **Suppress** window will appear with the **Suppress all** and **Suspend all** radio buttons, see Figure 11.55. The **Suppress all** radio button is used to suppress all the child components along with the selected parent component, whereas the **Suspend all** radio button is used to suppress only the parent component. You can also click on the **Edit Details** button to define a separate method (suppress or suspend) for each child component.

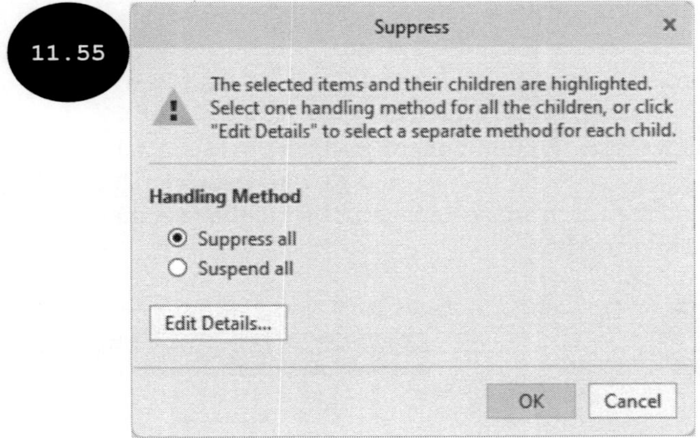

Note: If the suppressed component is not displayed in the **Model Tree**, then you need to turn on its display in the **Model Tree**. To do so, click on **Tree Filters** in the **Navigator**, see Figure 11.56. The **Tree Filters** dialog box appears. In this dialog box, ensure that the **General** option is selected in its left panel and then select the **Suppressed** check box in the **Items by State** area that appears on the right panel of the dialog box. Next, click on the **Apply** button and then **OK** button in the dialog box. The suppressed component appears in the **Model Tree** with a black square in front of its name.

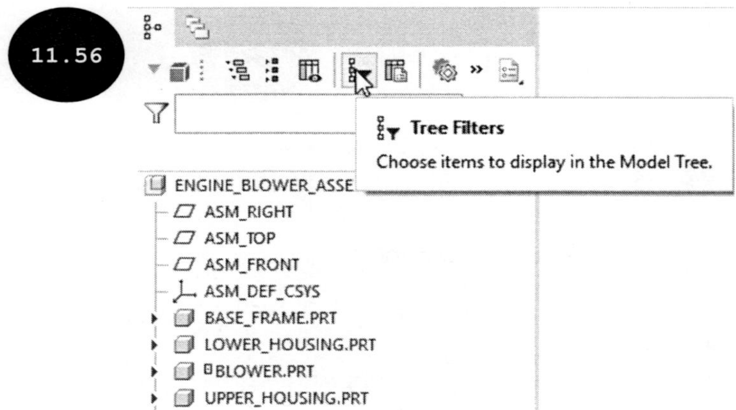

To resume a suppressed component in the assembly, click on the suppressed component in the **Model Tree** and then click on the **Resume** tool in the Mini toolbar that appears. The component is now resumed and appears in the assembly.

Assembling Multiple Copies of a Component

Sometimes, in an assembly, a particular component needs to be assembled repeatedly with other assembly components. One way of doing this is that you assemble the same component by applying the required constraints again and again. However, this is a time consuming process and to avoid it, in Creo Parametric, you can use the **Repeat** tool to assemble multiple copies of a component in the assembly. The method for assembling multiple copies of a component in an assembly is discussed below:

1. Select the assembly component to be repeated in the **Model Tree**.

2. Click on the **Repeat** tool in the **Component** group of the **Model** tab, see Figure 11.57. The **Repeat Component** dialog box appears, see Figure 11.58. Alternatively, right-click on the component in the **Model Tree** and then click on the **Repeat** tool in the shortcut menu that appears to invoke the **Repeat Component** dialog box.

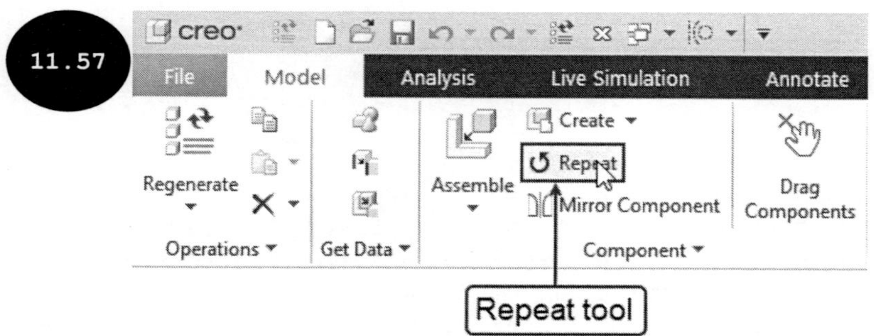

11.58

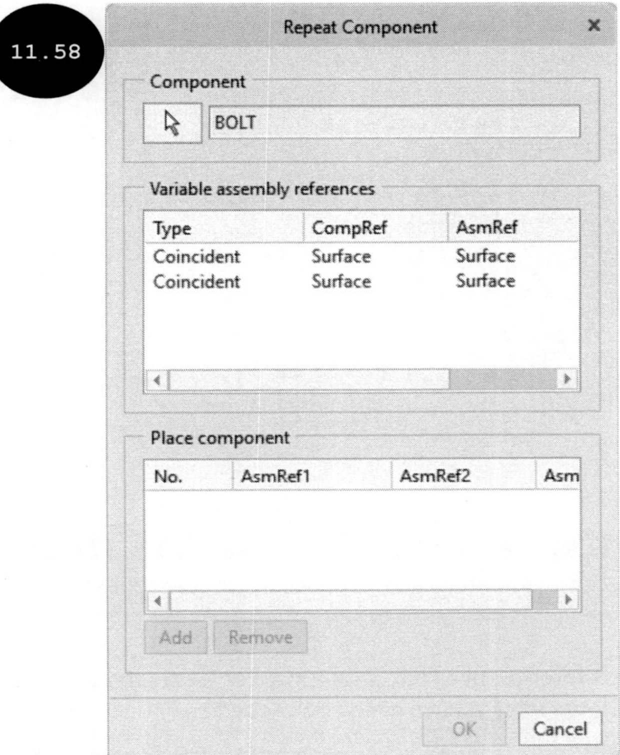

Variable assembly references: The **Variable assembly references** area of the **Repeat Component** dialog box displays a list of constraints that are applied to the selected component. Also, the **CompRef** and **AsmRef** columns of the **Variable assembly references** area display component and assembly references that are used for assembling the component.

3. Select the required constraints in the **Variable assembly references** area to define their new assembly references for creating a new copy of the selected component. The references of the selected constraints are highlighted in the graphics area. In Figure 11.59, only one coincident constraint is selected that aligns the axis of the bolt with the hole.

4. Click on the **Add** button in the dialog box and then select new assembly references for the selected constraints one by one in the graphics area. After selecting the assembly references for all the constraints, a new copy of the selected component is assembled in the assembly. Also, the newly selected references appear in the **Place component** area of the dialog box.

5. Similarly, you can continue specifying new references for the selected constraints to create multiple copies of the selected component in the assembly, see Figure 11.59. In this figure, the bolt component is assembled multiple times in the assembly by specifying new references for the coincident constraint that aligns the axis of the bolt with the hole.

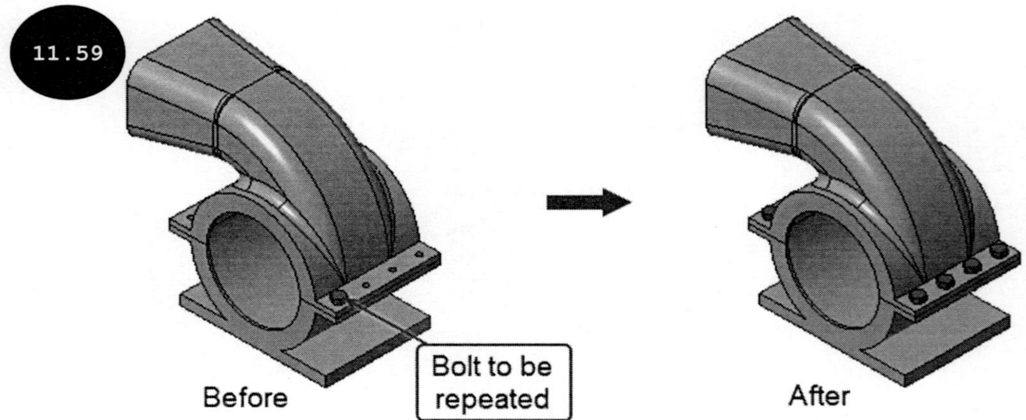

6. Click on the **OK** button to exit the dialog box.

Checking Interference between Components

In Creo Parametric, you can check interferences between the components of the assembly. The method for checking the interferences is discussed below:

1. Click on the **Global Interference** tool of the **Inspect Geometry** group in the **Analysis** tab, see Figure 11.60. The **Global Interference** dialog box appears.

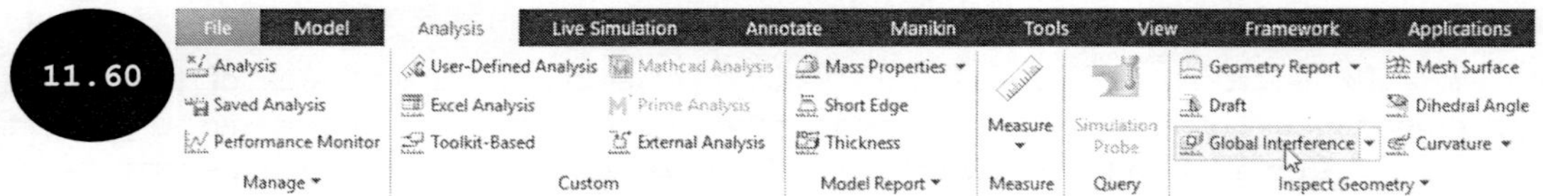

2. Select the required radio button: **Parts only** or **Sub-assembly only** to analyse the parts or the sub-assemblies, respectively in the **Setup** area of the dialog box.

3. Select the **Include quilts** and **Include facets** check boxes in the **Setup** area of the dialog box.

4. Ensure that the **Exact** radio button is selected in the **Compute** area of the dialog box to calculate accurate results.

5. Click on the **Preview** button in the dialog box. The interference detected between different component sets, appears in the dialog box, see Figure 11.61. Also, the detected interference gets highlighted in the graphics area, see Figure 11.62.

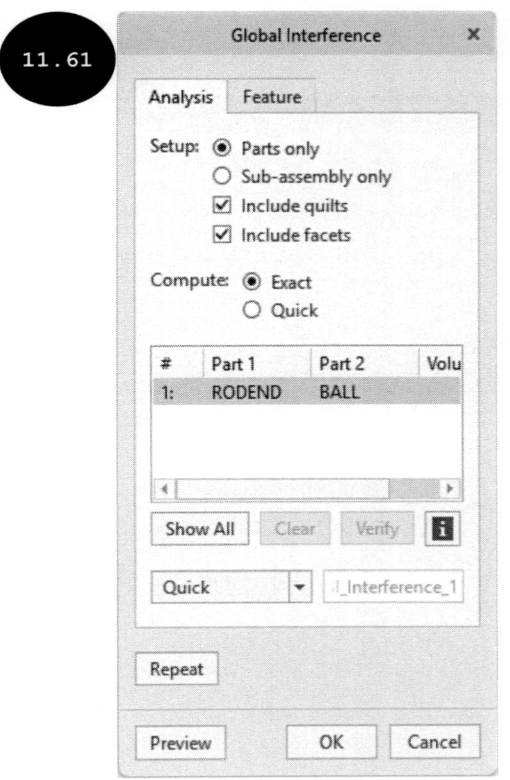

6. Review the interference result and then exit the dialog box.

Creating an Exploded View

Creating an exploded view of an assembly is important from the presentation point of view. Also, an exploded view of an assembly helps you easily identify the position of each component of an assembly. Moreover, an exploded view helps in making technical documentation and helps technical and non-technical clients easily understand the various components of the assembly. Figure 11.63 shows an assembly and Figure 11.64 shows an exploded view of the assembly. The method for creating an exploded view of an assembly is discussed below:

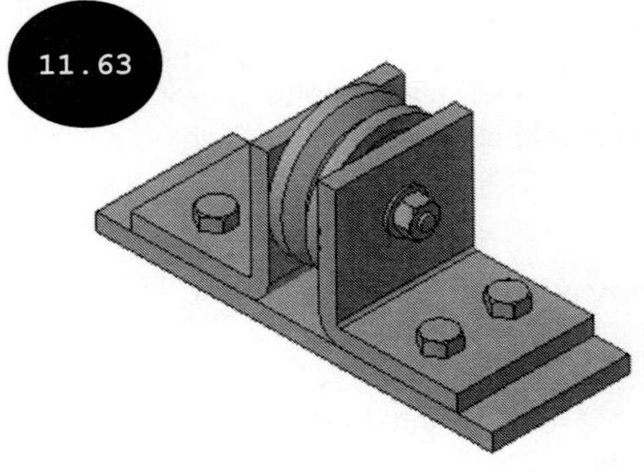

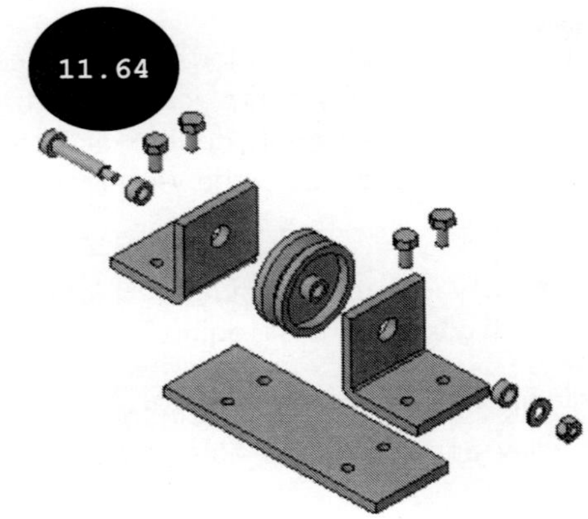

1. Click on the **Manage Views** tool in the **Model Display** group of the **Model** tab, see Figure 11.65. The **View Manager** dialog box appears, see Figure 11.66.

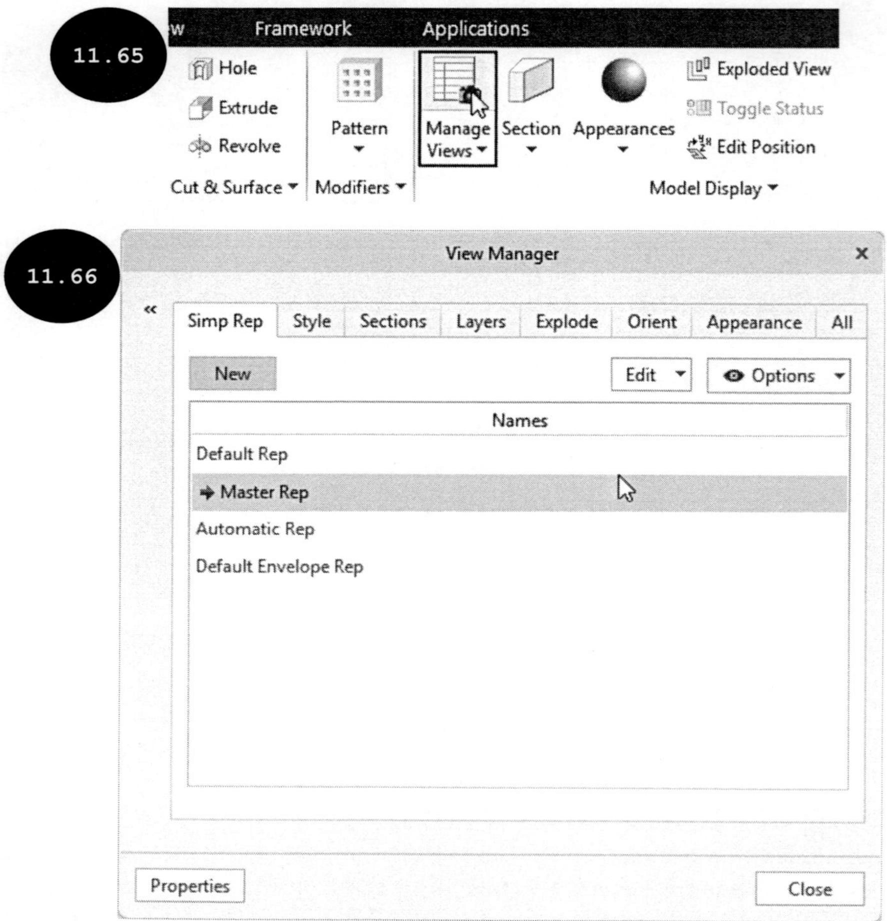

2. Click on the **Explode** tab in the **View Manager** dialog box. The name of the default exploded view appears as **Default Explode** in the **Names** column of the dialog box.

Note: The default exploded view is created such that it explodes each component of the assembly according to its placement constraints in the assembly. To display the default exploded view of an assembly, double-click on **Default Explode** that appears in the **Names** column of the **Explode** tab in the **View Manager** dialog box.

Now, you can create a new exploded view for an assembly by defining the exploded position of each component, as required.

3. Click on the **New** button in the **Explode** tab of the dialog box. A default name for the exploded view appears in the **Names** column of the dialog box, see Figure 11.67.

4. Press ENTER to accept the default name or type a new name for the exploded view. The new exploded view is created and becomes an active exploded view. Note that a green arrow in front of the name of an exploded view in the dialog box indicates that it is an active exploded view.

   Now, you can define the position of each component for the active exploded view.

5. Click on **Edit > Edit Position** in the dialog box, see Figure 11.68. The **Explode Tool** tab appears in the **Ribbon**, see Figure 11.69.

Translate: By default, the **Translate** button is activated in the **Explode Tool** tab. As a result, you can translate one or more components to explode along an axis.

Rotate: On activating the **Rotate** button in the **Explode Tool** tab, you can rotate one or more components around an axis.

View Plane: On activating the **View Plane** button in the **Explode Tool** tab, you can move one or more components along the viewing plane.

6. Select the required button (**Translate**, **Rotate**, or **View Plane**) in the **Explode Tool** tab as the motion type to explode the component.

7. Select a component of the assembly to explode. The translational handles appear in the graphics area, see Figure 11.70. Note that the translational handles appear only when the **Translate** button is activated in the **Explode Tool** tab of the **Ribbon**.

Tip: You can also select multiple components by pressing the CTRL key to explode them as a group.

Note: If the **Rotate** button is activated in the **Explode Tool** tab, then on choosing a component, you need to select an edge or an axis to define the axis of rotation to rotate the selected component. After defining the axis of rotation, the rotational handle appears in the graphics area, see Figure 11.71. You can drag this rotational handle to rotate the selected component around the axis of rotation.

If the **View Plane** button is activated, then on selecting a component, the manipulate handle appears in the graphics area, see Figure 11.72. You can drag this handle to move the selected component along the viewing plane.

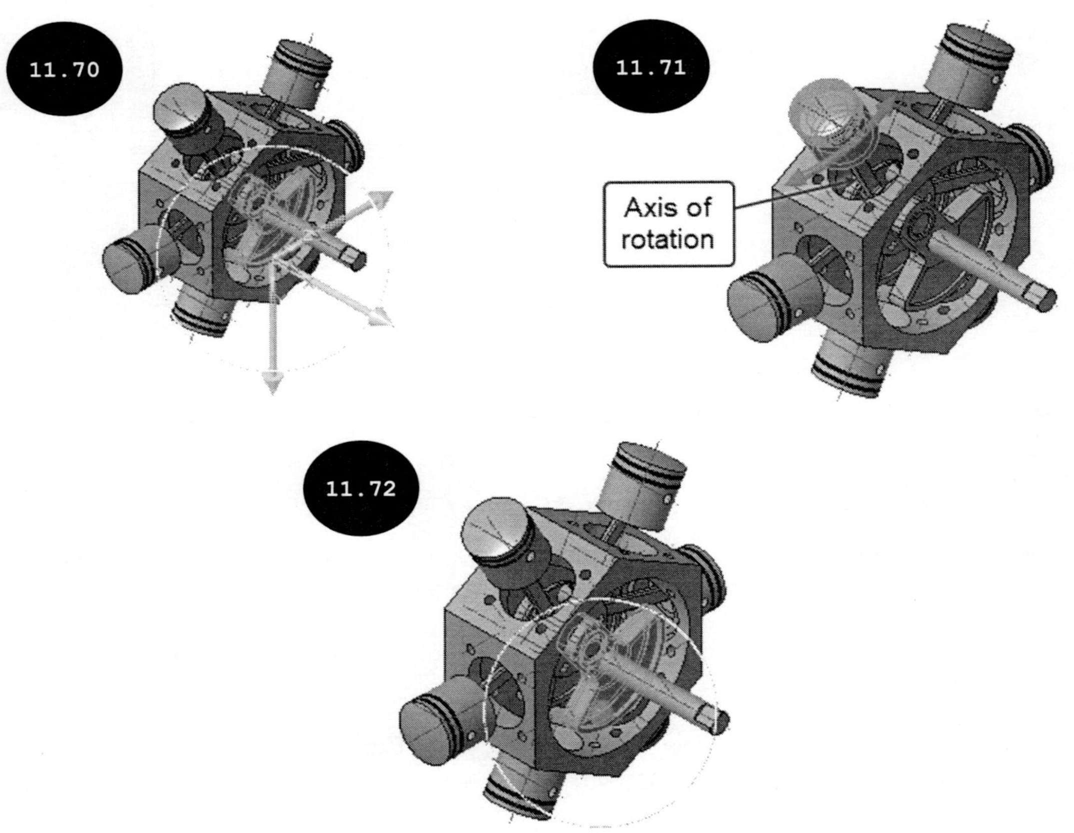

8. Drag the required handle in the graphics area to define the new position of the component in the graphics area, see Figure 11.73. In this figure, the component is being translated by dragging a translational handle. Note that the display of handles in the graphics area depends on the button (**Translate**, **Rotate**, or **View Plane**) that is activated in the **Explode Tool** tab.

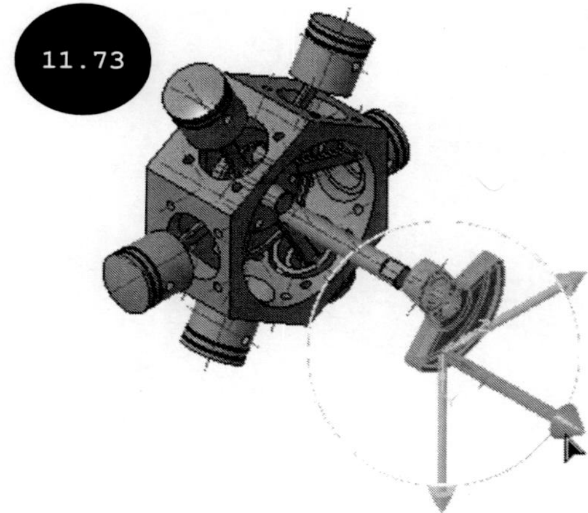

9. Expand the **Options** panel of the **Explode Tool** tab, see Figure 11.74. The options in this panel are discussed below:

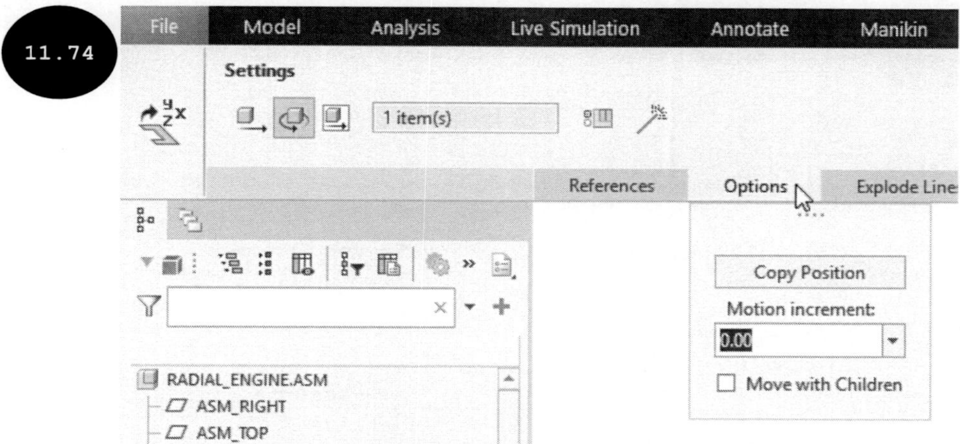

Motion increment: The **Motion increment** field of the expanded **Options** panel is used for specifying an increment value for the movement of the selected component. For example, if the incremental value is specified as 30 mm in this field, then on dragging the handle, the component translates/rotates at an incremental distance of 30 mm only.

Move with Children: On selecting the **Move with Children** check box, the selected component translates/rotates along with all its child components, see Figure 11.75. In this figure, on moving the flange component, all its child components are also being moved along with it.

11.75

10. Expand the **References** panel, see Figure 11.76. The options in the expanded **References** panel are discussed below:

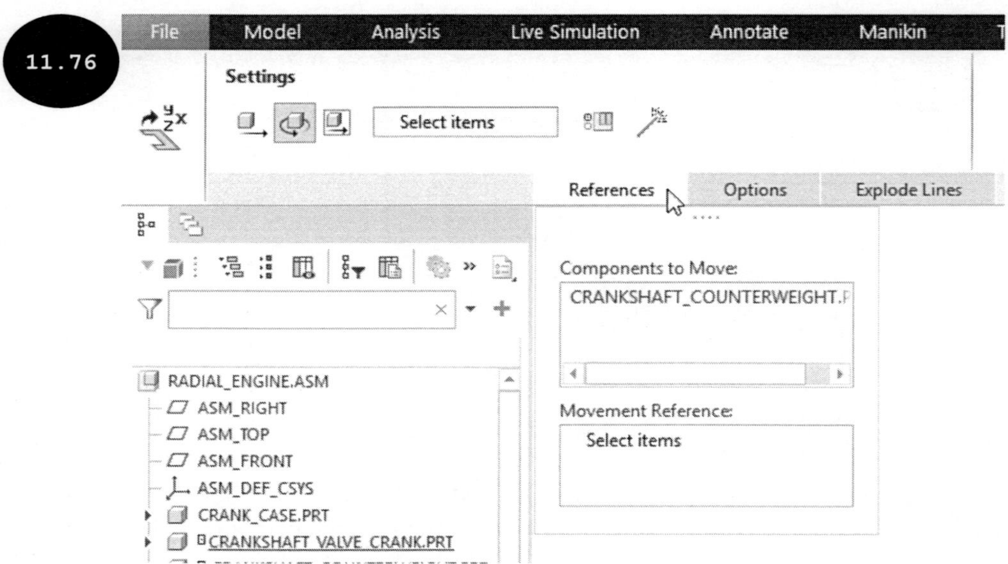

Components to Move: The **Components to Move** field of the expanded **References** panel displays the name of the selected component to be exploded. Note that you can also select multiple components by pressing the CTRL key to explode them as a group.

Movement Reference: The **Movement Reference** field is used for defining a reference for moving the selected component in other than the default directions. To do so, click on the **Movement Reference** field and then select an edge, an axis, a plane normal, a planar face normal, or 2 points to define the direction reference for moving the selected component. On doing so, a translational handle gets aligned to the selected direction reference. Figure 11.77 shows the default translational handles that appear on selecting the Connecting Rod component of the assembly and Figure 11.78 shows the translational handles that appear on selecting the planar face as the reference. Now, you can drag the translational handle to move the component along or normal to the selected reference, respectively, see Figure 11.79.

11. Define a direction reference for moving the selected component by using the **Movement Reference** field of the expanded **References** panel, if required.

12. Explode the components of the assembly, as required by dragging their respective handles, see Figure 11.79.

13. Expand the **Explode Lines** panel to create exploded lines, see Figure 11.80. The options in this panel are discussed below:

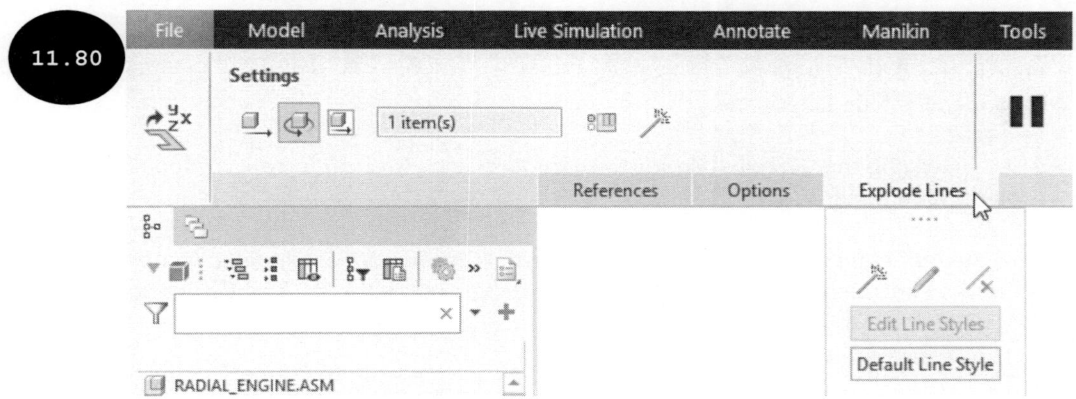

Create cosmetic offset lines to illustrate movement of exploded component : This button is used for creating cosmetic exploded lines in the exploded view of the assembly, see Figure 11.81. In an exploded view, the exploded lines are used for showing relationships between components and illustrating their assembly lines.

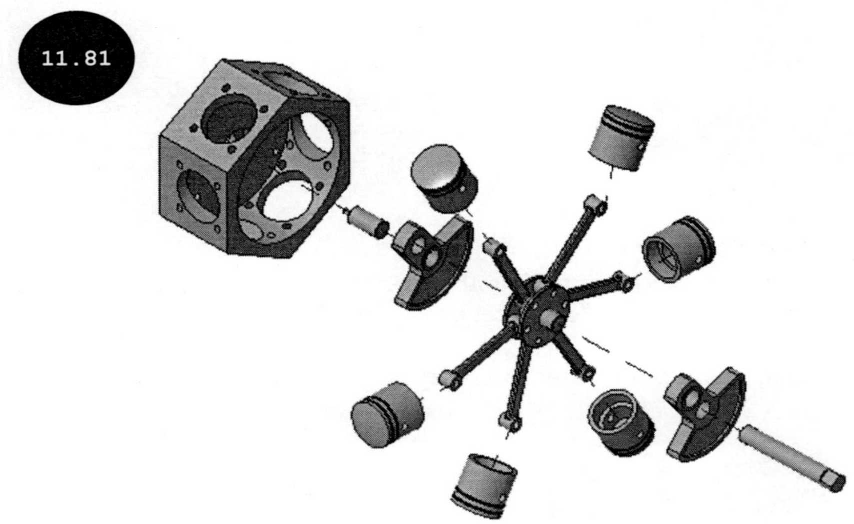

11.81

Default Line Style: The **Default Line Style** button is used for specifying the default line style for the exploded lines. To do so, click on the **Default Line Style** button in the expanded **Explode Lines** panel. The **Line Style** dialog box appears, see Figure 11.82. By using this dialog box, you can specify style, line font, and color as the default style of the exploded lines.

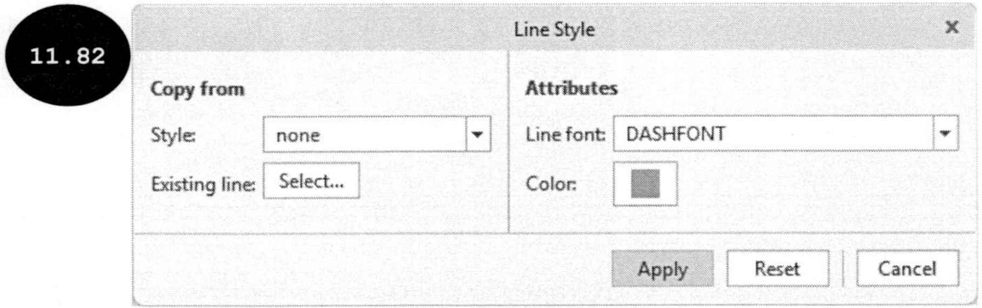

11.82

14. Specify the default style for the exploded lines by using the **Default Line Style** button of the expanded **Explode Lines** panel.

    After specifying the default style for the exploded lines, you can create exploded lines in the exploded components of the assembly.

15. Click on the **Create cosmetic offset lines to illustrate movement of exploded component** button in the expanded **Explode Tool** tab to create the exploded lines. The **Cosmetic Offset Line** dialog box appears, see Figure 11.83.

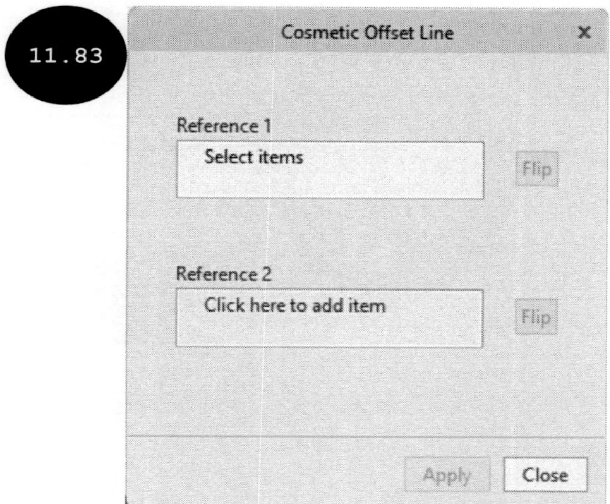

16. Select faces, circular edges, straight edges, or planar faces of the two different components having the same assembly line one after the other as Reference 1 and Reference 2 to connect them with a cosmetic exploded line, see Figure 11.84.

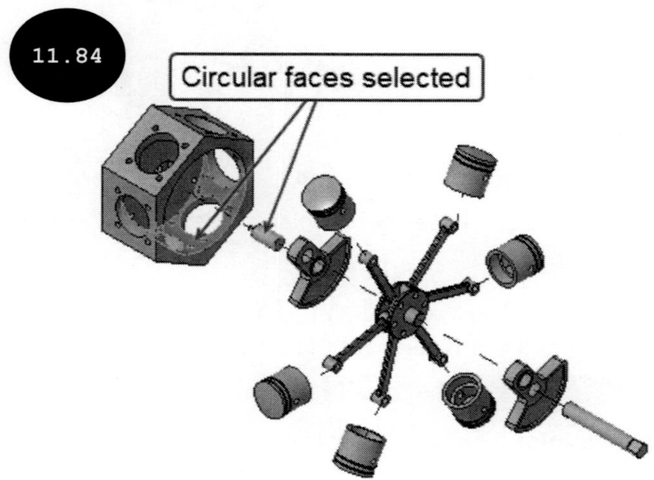

17. Click on the **Apply** button in the **Cosmetic Offset Line** dialog box. A cosmetic exploded line is created, which represents the assembly line of the selected components, see Figure 11.85. Also, the **Cosmetic Offset Line** dialog box is still displayed in the graphics area.

Note: On selecting a circular reference to create an exploded line, you can define whether to route the exploded line along its axis or normal to the face selected by selecting the **Use cylinder axis** or **Normal to surface** radio button in the **Cosmetic Offset Line** dialog box, respectively.

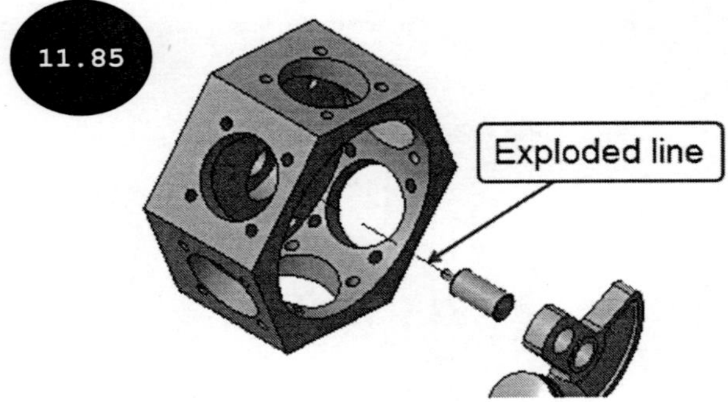

18. Similarly, create exploded lines between the other components of the assembly, see Figure 11.86.

19. After creating cosmetic exploded lines between the components, close the **Cosmetic Offset Line** dialog box.

    Edit the selected explode line : The **Edit the selected explode line** button is used for editing the selected exploded line. Note that this button is enabled only when an exploded line is selected in the graphics area.

    Delete the selected explode lines : The **Delete the selected explode lines** button is used for deleting the selected exploded line. Note that this button is enabled only when an exploded line is selected in the graphics area.

    Edit Line Styles: The **Edit Line Styles** button of the expanded **Explode Lines** panel is used for editing the line style of the selected exploded lines. This button is enabled only when an exploded line is selected in the graphics area.

20. Edit the required exploded lines if needed, by using the respective buttons of the expanded **Explode Lines** panel of the **Explode Tool** tab.

    Toggle the exploded state of selected component(s) : The **Toggle the exploded state of selected component(s)** button of the **Explode Tool** tab is used for switching between the exploded or unexploded state of a selected component or components in the graphics area.

21. Click on the **Toggle the exploded state of selected component(s)** button in the **Explode Tool** tab to view the exploded or unexploded state of the selected component, if required. Note that this button is activated only when a component is selected in the graphics area.

22. After creating the exploded view of the assembly, click on the green tick-mark button in the **Explode Tool** tab of the **Ribbon**. The **View Manager** dialog box appears with the name of the exploded view created.

    Now, you need to save the exploded view.

23. Click on **Edit > Save** in the **View Manager** dialog box, see Figure 11.87. The **Save Display Elements** dialog box appears. In this dialog box, click on the **OK** button to save the exploded view of the assembly.

Note: In Creo Parametric, you can also display a list of all exploded steps that are created in the currently active exploded view. To do so, click on the **Properties** button of the **View Manager** dialog box. A list of all the exploded steps appears in the dialog box, see Figure 11.88. Now, you can edit or delete an individual exploded step. To edit an exploded step, select it in the list and then click on the **Edit Position** button in the dialog box. The translational handles appear in the graphics area and the **Explode Tool** tab appears in the **Ribbon**. Now, you can drag the translational handle to change the position of the component. Next, click on the green tick-mark button. To delete an exploded step, select it in the list of the exploded steps and then click on the **Remove** button in the dialog box.

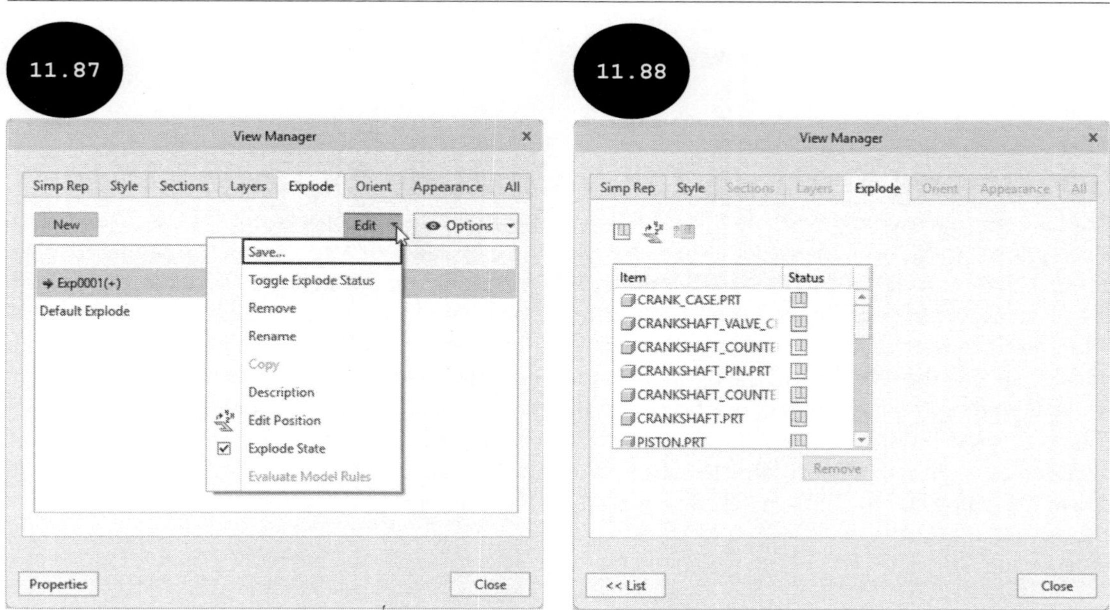

24. After saving the exploded view, close the **View Manager** dialog box.

Switching Between Exploded and Unexploded Views

In Creo Parametric, you can switch between the exploded and unexploded views of the assembly by using the **Exploded View** tool of the **Model Display** group in the **Model** tab, see Figure 11.89. Figure 11.90 shows the exploded view, whereas Figure 11.91 shows the unexploded view of the assembly.

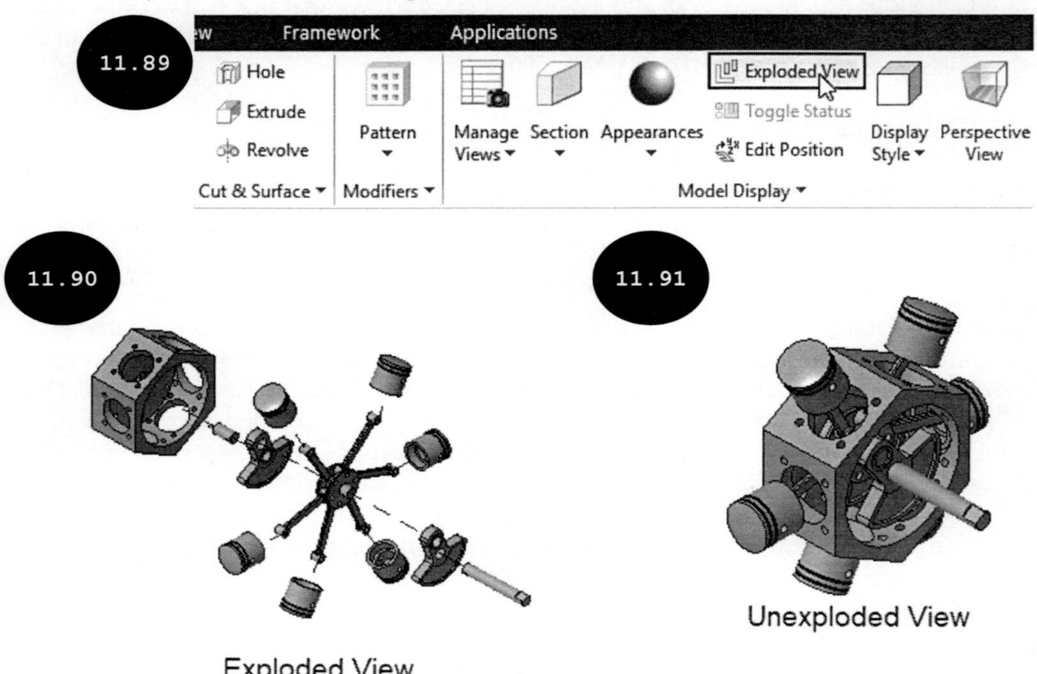

Specifying Settings for Animating Exploded View

After creating an exploded view of an assembly, you can animate the components of the assembly to display its exploded and unexploded views by using the **Exploded View** tool of the **Model Display** group. However, you need to ensure that the option for animating the exploded/unexploded view of the assembly is turned on in the **Creo Parametric Options** dialog box. To do so, click on **File > Options**. The **Creo Parametric Options** dialog box appears. In this dialog box, click on the **Entity Display** option that appears on the left panel of the dialog box, see Figure 11.92. Next, ensure that the **Show animation while exploding the assembly** check box is selected in the dialog box, see Figure 11.92. You can also specify the maximum duration of the animated transition in the **Maximum seconds an animation takes between explode states** field of the dialog box. You can also select the **Follow explode sequence** check box in the dialog box to animate the exploded steps of the assembly in the order they are created.

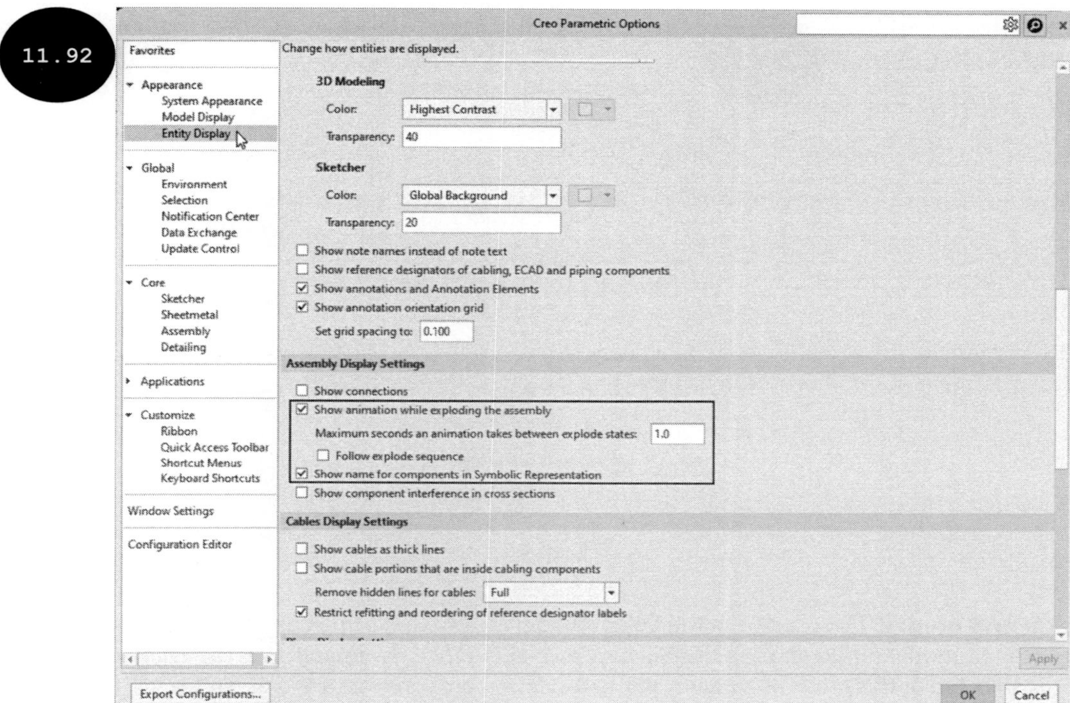

Creating Bill of Material (BOM)

A Bill of Material (BOM) is one of the most important features of any drawing. It contains information related to the number of components, material, quantity, and so on. In addition to creating Bill of Material (BOM) in a drawing, Creo Parametric also allows you to create BOM in the Assembly environment. You will learn about creating Bill of Material (BOM) in a drawing in Chapter 12. The method for creating BOM in the Assembly environment is discussed below:

1. Click on the **Bill of Materials** tool in the **Investigate** group of the **Model** tab, see Figure 11.93. The **Bill of Materials (BOM)** dialog box appears, see Figure 11.94. The options in this dialog box are discussed below:

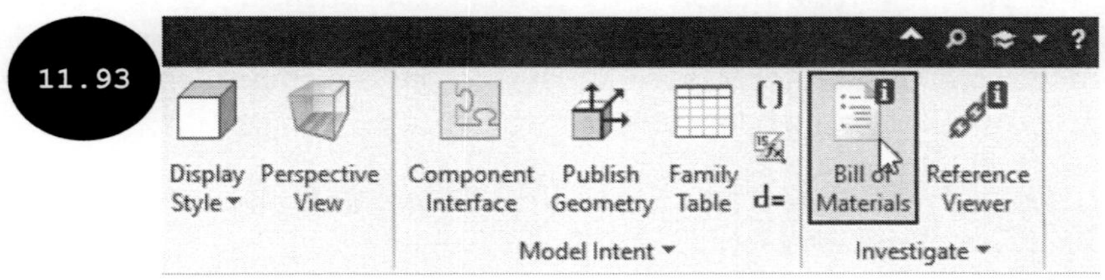

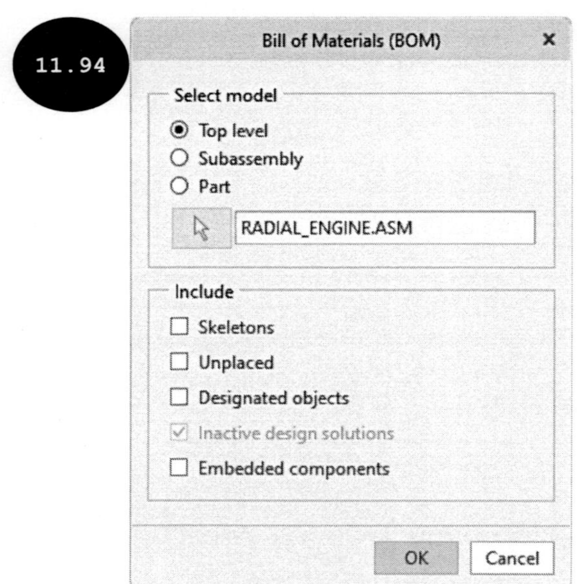

Select model: The options in the **Select model** area of the dialog box are used for selecting the type of model for generating the **Bill of Material (BOM)**. By default, the **Top level** radio button is selected in this area. As a result, all the top level components of the assembly will be included in the BOM. Also, the sub-assemblies of the current assembly will be included in the BOM as components. On selecting the **Subassembly** radio button, you can select a subassembly of the main assembly in the graphics area or in the **Model Tree** to generate the BOM of its components. On selecting the **Part** radio button, you can select a part in the graphics area or in the **Model Tree** to generate its BOM.

Include: On selecting the **Skeletons** check box in the **Include** area of the dialog box, the assembly features that are available in the current assembly will also be included in the BOM. On selecting the **Unplaced** check box, the unplaced components of the assembly will also be included in the BOM. On selecting the **Designated objects** check box, the bulk items such as glue and paint if available in the assembly, will also be included in the BOM. Bulk items are non-solid representations of components in the assembly. You can create bulk items in an assembly by selecting the **Bulk Item** radio button in the **Create Component** dialog box. On selecting the **Embedded components** check box, the embedded components will be included in the BOM. An embedded component is a component that is copied and embedded into an assembly. It is independent of the original component.

2. Select the required options in the **Bill of Materials (BOM)** dialog box and then click on the **OK** button. The BOM of the assembly appears in the browser, see Figure 11.95. Also, the file of the BOM is automatically saved in the working directory with the name of the assembly as *.bom* file extension.

11.95

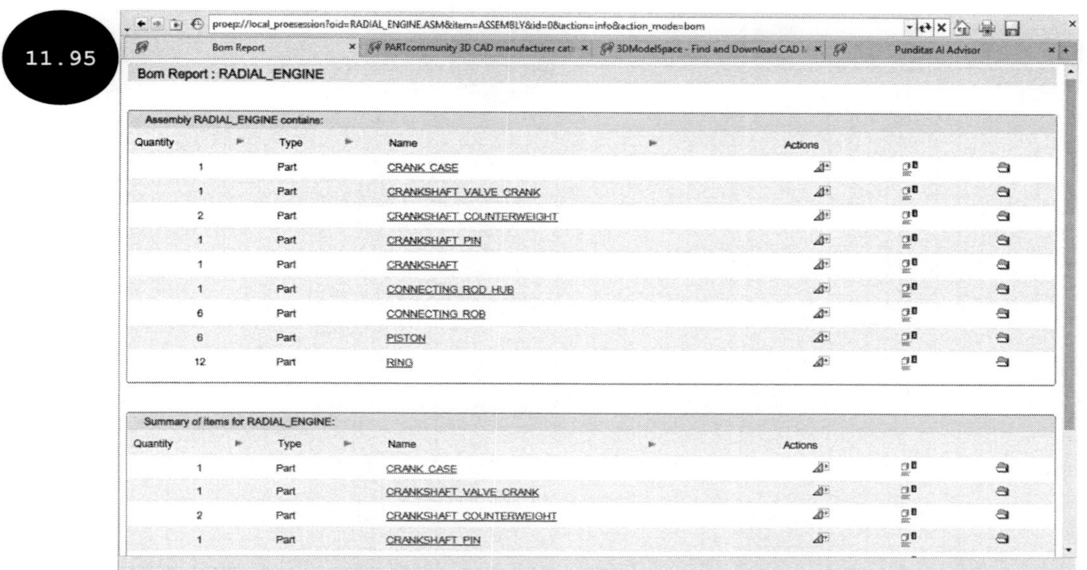
proep://local_proesession?oid=RADIAL_ENGINE.ASM&item=ASSEMBLY&id=0&action=info&action_mode=bom

Bom Report : RADIAL_ENGINE

Assembly RADIAL_ENGINE contains:

Quantity	Type	Name	Actions
1	Part	CRANK_CASE	
1	Part	CRANKSHAFT_VALVE_CRANK	
2	Part	CRANKSHAFT_COUNTERWEIGHT	
1	Part	CRANKSHAFT_PIN	
1	Part	CRANKSHAFT	
1	Part	CONNECTING_ROD_HUB	
6	Part	CONNECTING_ROD	
6	Part	PISTON	
12	Part	RING	

Summary of items for RADIAL_ENGINE:

Quantity	Type	Name	Actions
1	Part	CRANK_CASE	
1	Part	CRANKSHAFT_VALVE_CRANK	
2	Part	CRANKSHAFT_COUNTERWEIGHT	
1	Part	CRANKSHAFT_PIN	

Tutorial 1

Create the assembly shown in Figure 11.96 by using the Top-down Assembly approach. Different views and dimensions of each assembly component are shown in Figures 11.97 through 11.99. All dimensions are in mm.

11.96

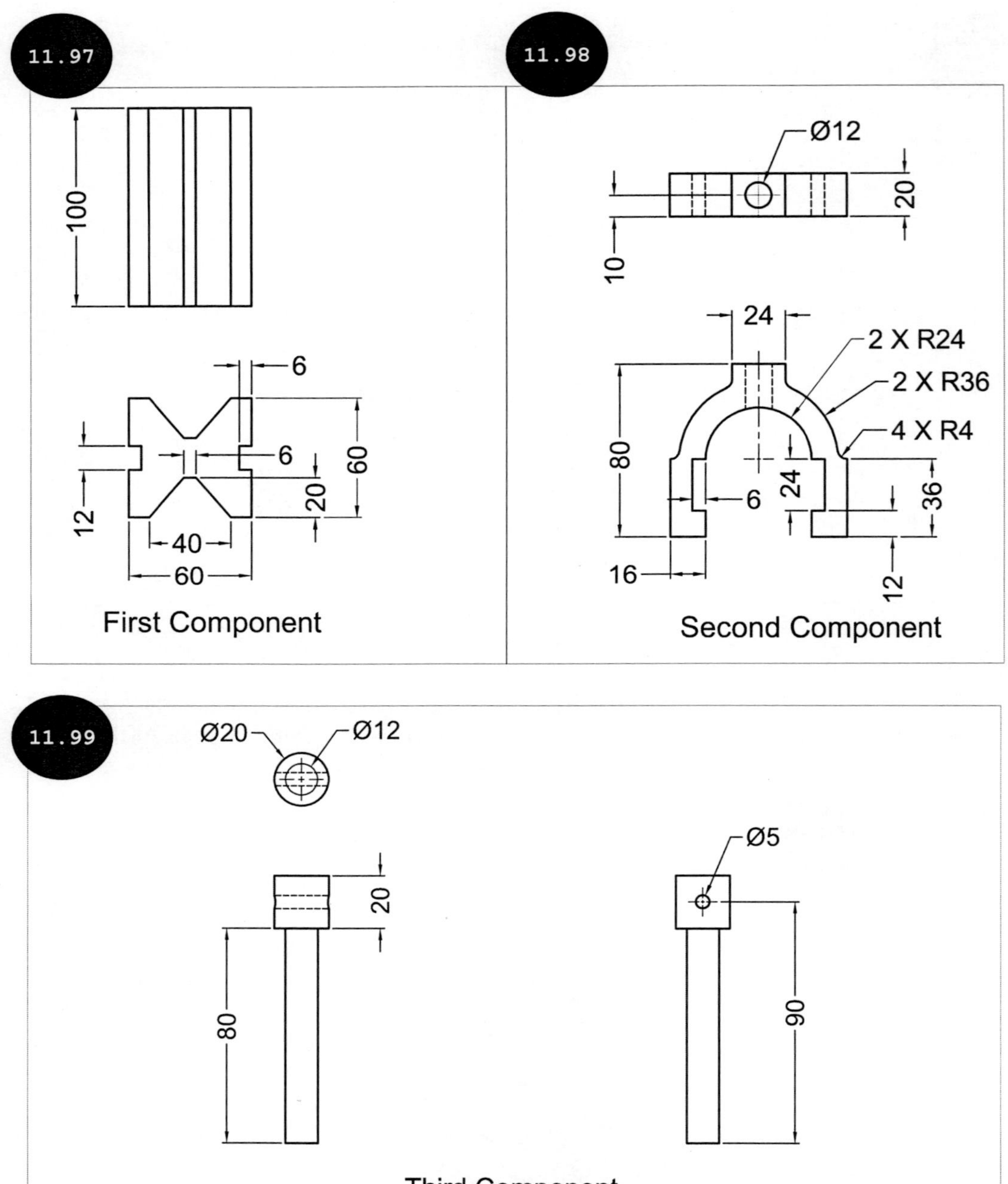

Section 1: Starting Creo and Invoking Assembly Mode

1. Start Creo Parametric by double-clicking on the Creo Parametric icon on your desktop.

2. Set the working directory to <<*Creo Parametric\Chapter 11\Tutorial 1*\. You need to create these folders in the *Creo Parametric* folder.

Now, you need to invoke the Assembly mode to create the assembly by using the Top-down Assembly approach.

3. Click on the **New** tool in the **Data** group of the **Home** tab. The **New** dialog box appears. Alternatively, press CTRL + N to invoke the **New** dialog box.

4. Select the **Assembly** radio button in the **Type** area and **Design** radio button in the **Sub-type** area of the **New** dialog box, see Figure 11.100.

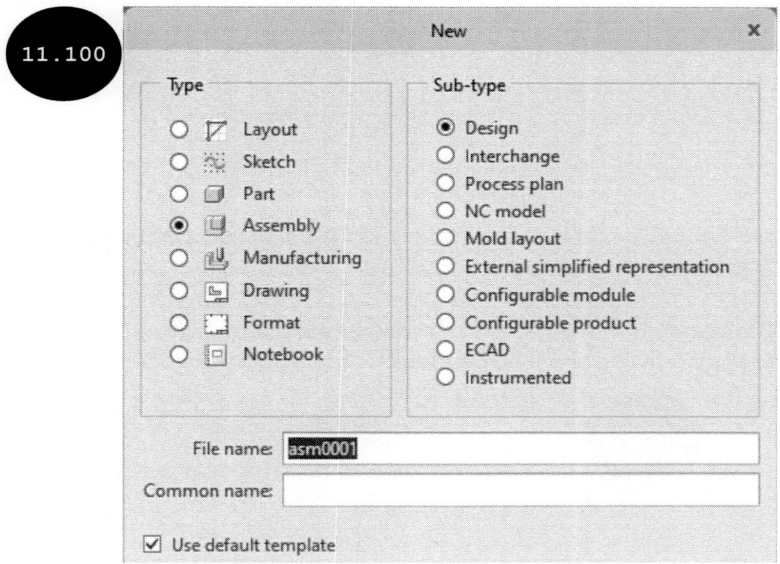

5. Enter **C11-Tutorial01** in the **File name** field of the dialog box as the name of the assembly.

6. Clear the **Use default template** check box and then click on the **OK** button in the dialog box. The **New File Options** dialog box appears.

7. Select the **mmns_asm_design_abs** template in the **New File Options** dialog box and then click on the **OK** button. The Assembly mode is invoked with the **mmns_asm_design_abs** template.

Section 2: Creating the First Component

1. Click on the **Create** tool in the **Component** group of the **Model** tab, see Figure 11.101. The **Create Component** dialog box appears in the graphics area, see Figure 11.102.

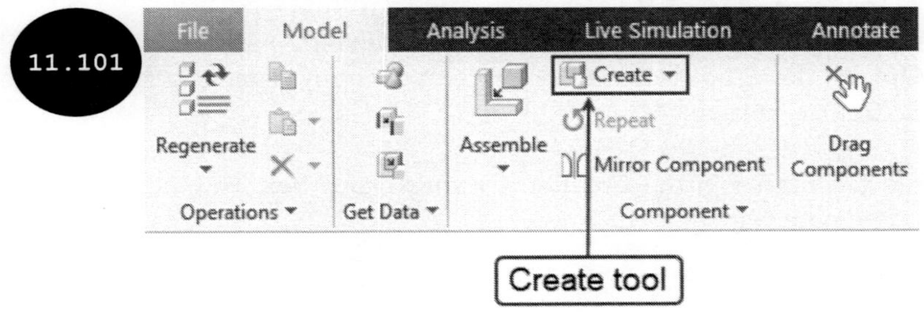

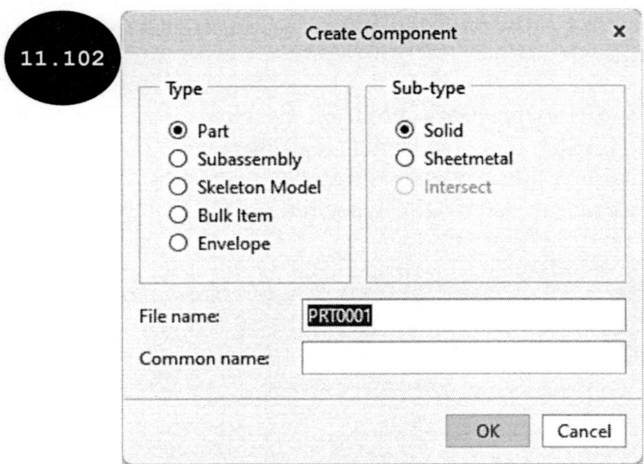

2. Ensure that the **Part** radio button is selected in the **Type** area and the **Solid** radio button is selected in the **Sub-type** area of the dialog box to create a solid component, see Figure 11.102.

3. Enter **First_Component** as the name of the component in the **File name** field and then click on the **OK** button in the dialog box. The **Creation Options** dialog box appears, see Figure 11.103.

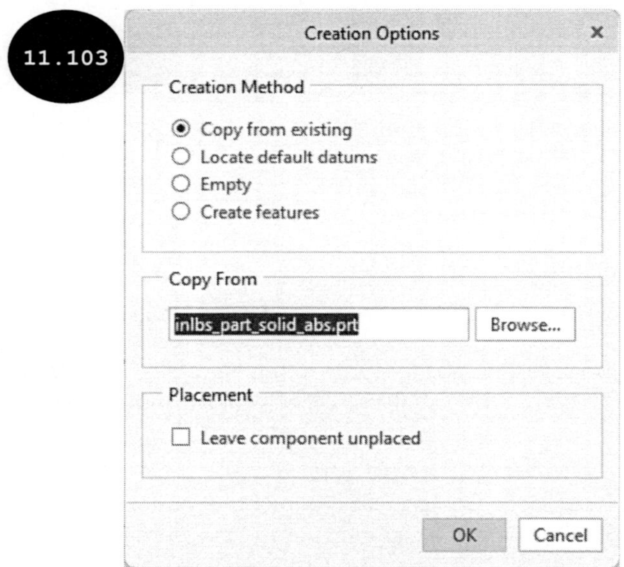

4. Select the **Locate default datums** radio button and then the **Align csys to csys** radio button in the **Creation Options** dialog box to create a new component by aligning its coordinate system to the assembly coordinate system.

5. Click on the **OK** button in the **Creation Options** dialog box. You are prompted to select an assembly coordinate system.

6. Select the coordinate system of the assembly. The new component is created in the assembly with datum planes and a coordinate system that is aligned to the assembly coordinate system. The name of the newly created component appears in the **Model Tree**. Also, it becomes an active component and the Part modeling environment is invoked for creating its features, see Figure 11.104. Note that the datum planes of an active component appear dark in the graphics area.

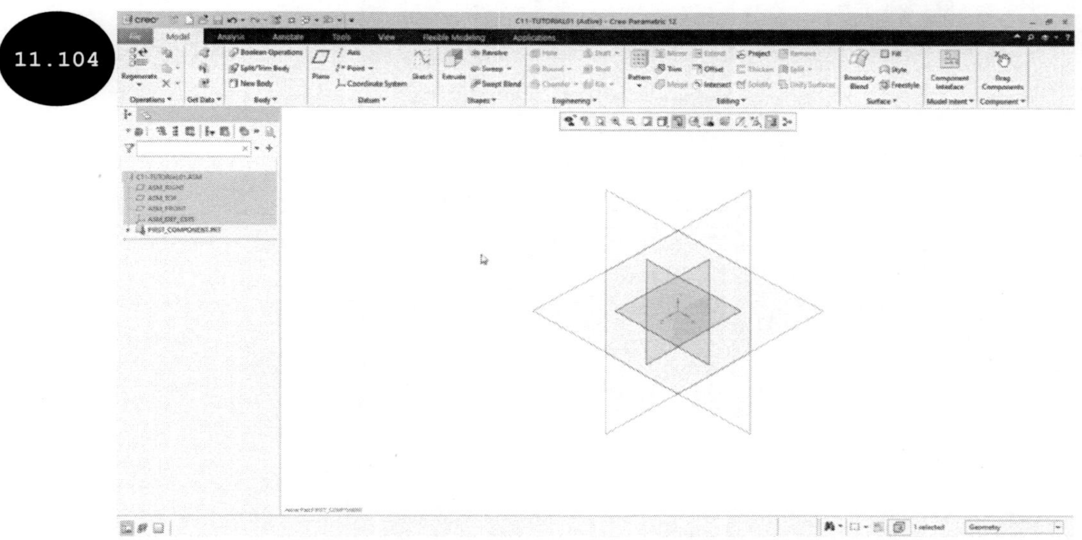

Now, you can create features of the newly created component in the assembly.

7. Click on the **Extrude** tool in the **Shapes** group of the **Model** tab. The **Extrude** tab appears in the **Ribbon**. Also, you are prompted to select a sketching plane.

8. Select the Front Plane of the component as the sketching plane in the graphics area, see Figure 11.105. The Sketching environment is invoked and the selected datum plane is oriented normal to the viewing direction.

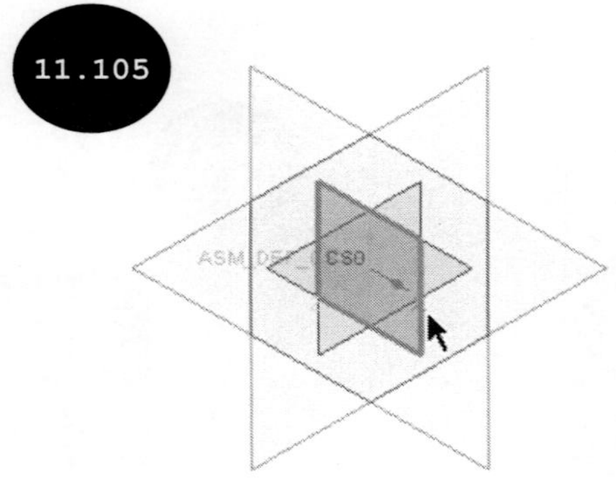

Now, you can create a sketch of the first feature of the component.

9. Create the sketch of the first feature of the component by using the sketching tools, see Figure 11.106.

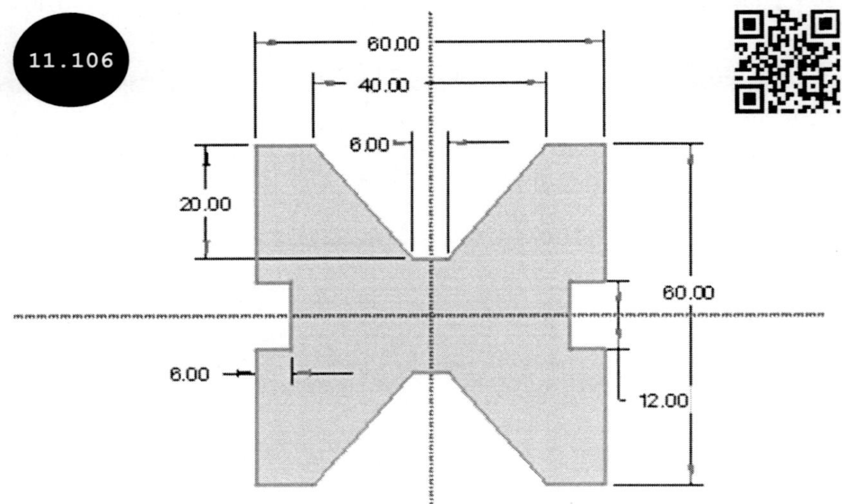

10. Exit the Sketching environment by clicking on the **OK** tool in the **Close** group of the **Sketch** tab. A preview of the extrude feature appears in the graphics area, see Figure 11.107. Change the current orientation of the model to the standard orientation.

11. Expand the **Options** panel of the **Extrude** tab and then select the **Symmetric** option in the **Side 1** drop-down list.

12. Enter **100** as the depth of extrusion in the **Value** field and then press ENTER. A preview of the extrude feature appears symmetrically on both sides of the sketching plane.

13. Click on the green tick-mark button in the **Extrude** tab. The first component is created, see Figure 11.108.

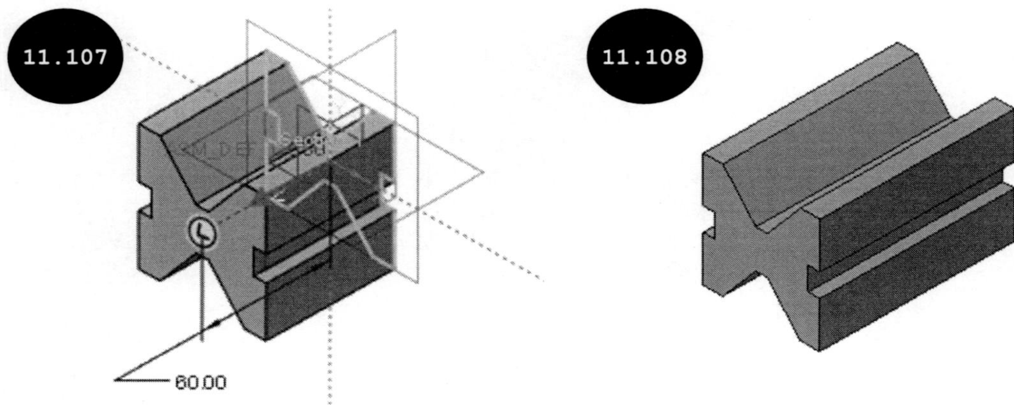

Note: In some of the figures of this tutorial, the display of datum planes is turned off for the clarity of images.

Section 3: Creating the Second Component

To create the second component of the assembly, you first need to activate the assembly file.

1. Click on the name of the assembly (**C11-TUTORIAL01**) in the **Model Tree**. The Mini toolbar appears, see Figure 11.109.

2. Click on the **Activate** tool in the Mini toolbar, see Figure 11.109. The assembly gets activated.

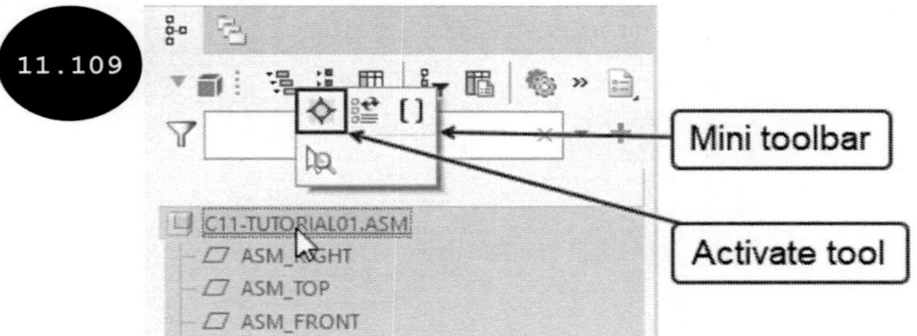

Now, you can create the second component of the assembly.

3. Click on the **Create** tool in the **Component** group of the **Model** tab, see Figure 11.110. The **Create Component** dialog box appears in the graphics area.

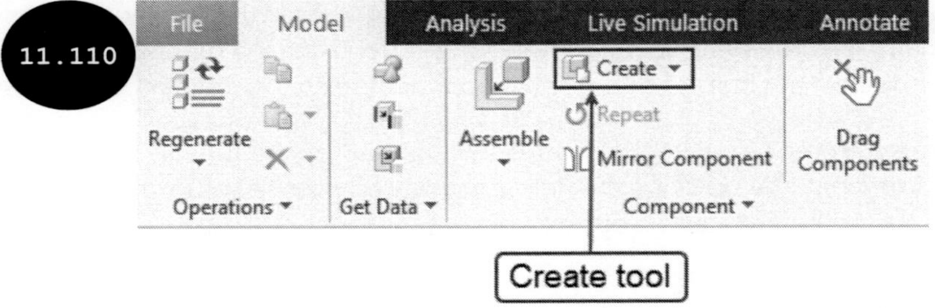

4. Ensure that the **Part** radio button is selected in the **Type** area and the **Solid** radio button is selected in the **Sub-type** area of the dialog box to create a solid component.

5. Enter **Second_Component** as the name of the component in the **File name** field and then click on the **OK** button in the dialog box. The **Creation Options** dialog box appears.

6. Select the **Empty** radio button in the dialog box to create the second component as an empty component.

7. Ensure that the **Leave component unplaced** check box is cleared in the dialog box.

8. Click on the **OK** button in the **Creation Options** dialog box. The second component is created and its name appears in the **Model Tree**, see Figure 11.111.

Now, you need to create the features of the second component. To do so, you need to first activate it in the assembly.

9. Click on the newly created empty component (second component) in the **Model Tree** and then click on the **Activate** tool in the Mini toolbar that appears, see Figure 11.111. The newly created empty component (second component) becomes the active component and the Part modeling environment is invoked. Also, the first component becomes transparent in the graphics area so that you can easily create the features of the second component by taking its reference.

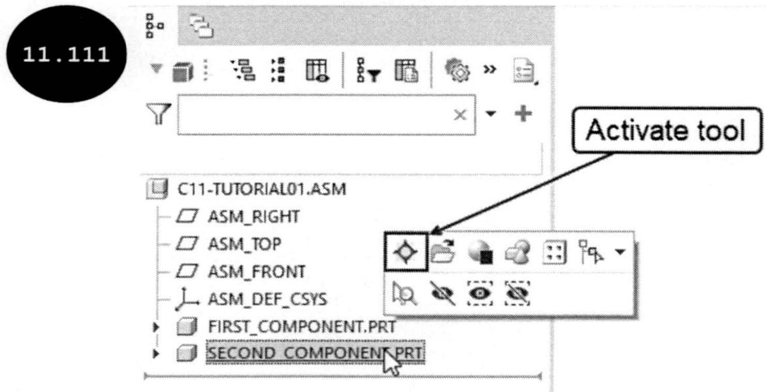

Now, you can add features to the second component.

10. Click on the **Extrude** tool in the **Shapes** group of the **Model** tab. The **Extrude** tab appears in the **Ribbon**. Also, you are prompted to select a sketching plane.

11. Select the Front Plane of the assembly as the sketching plane in the graphics area, see Figure 11.112. The Sketching environment is invoked and the **References** dialog box appears. Also, you are prompted to select geometries of the first component to specify references.

Note: If the **References** dialog box does not appear, by default on invoking the Sketching environment, then click on the **References** tool in the **Setup** group of the **Sketch** tab to display the **References** dialog box.

12. Select the outer geometries of the first component to define the references for creating the first feature of the second component, see Figure 11.113. Next, close the **References** dialog box.

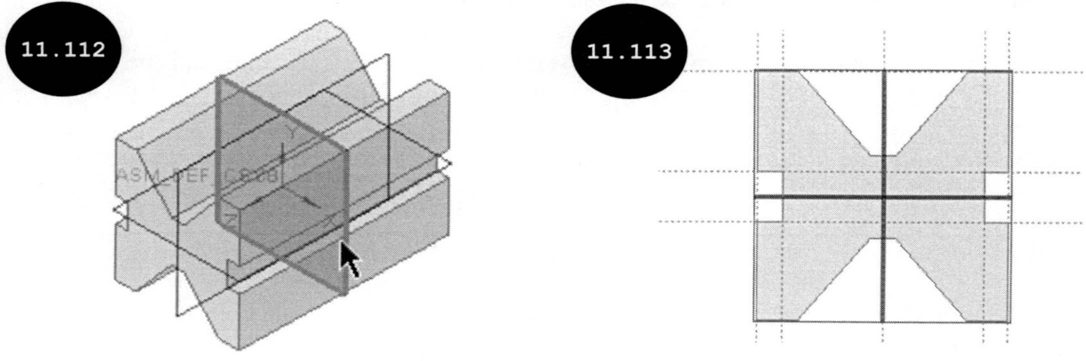

13. Create a sketch of the first feature of the second component, see Figure 11.114.

14. Exit the Sketching environment. A preview of the extrude feature appears in the graphics area. Next, change the current orientation of the model to the standard orientation.

15. Expand the **Options** panel of the **Extrude** tab and then select the **Symmetric** option in the **Side 1** drop-down list.

16. Enter **20** as the depth of extrusion in the **Value** field and then press ENTER. A preview of the extrude feature appears symmetrically on both sides of the sketching plane.

17. Click on the green tick-mark button in the **Extrude** tab. The first feature of the second component is created, see Figure 11.115.

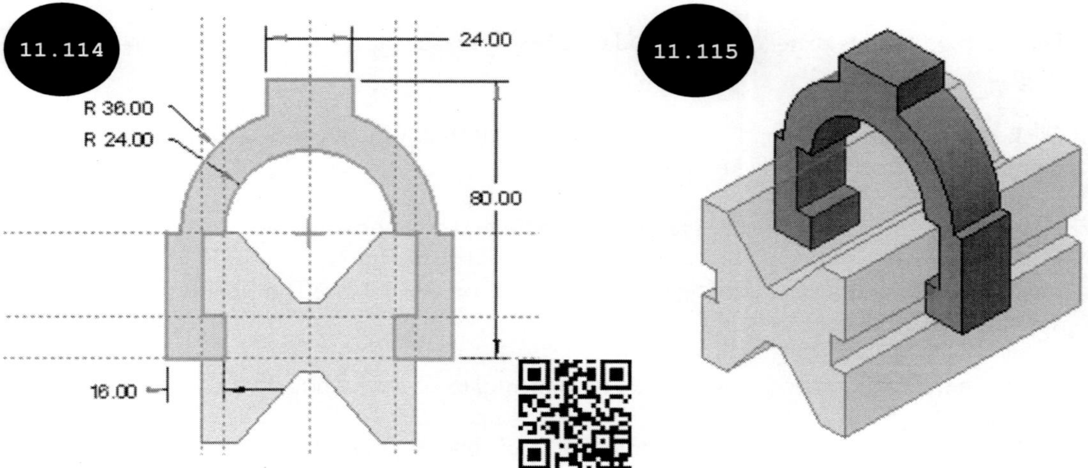

Now, you need to create the second feature of the second component.

18. Click on the **Extrude** tool in the **Shapes** group of the **Model** tab. The **Extrude** tab appears in the **Ribbon**. Also, you are prompted to select a sketching plane.

19. Select the top planar face of the first feature of the second component as the sketching plane and then create a circle of diameter 12 mm as the sketch of the second feature, see Figure 11.116.

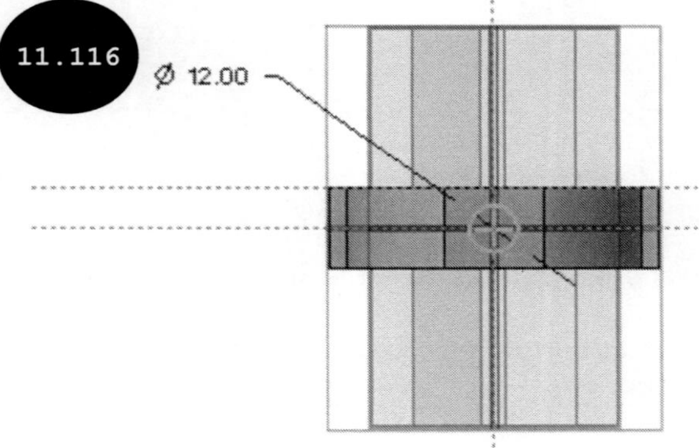

Note: The **References** dialog box appears on invoking the Sketching environment to define references. Select the datum planes that pass through the origin as the geometries and then close this dialog box.

20. Exit the Sketching environment. A preview of the extrude feature appears in the graphics area. Next, change the current orientation of the model to the standard orientation.

21. Click on the **Flip Direction** button in the **Depth** area of the **Extrude** tab. The direction of extrusion changes to downward and the **Remove Material** button gets activated in the **Settings** area of the **Extrude** tab, automatically. Also, a preview of the cut feature appears in the graphics area.

22. Expand the **Options** panel of the **Extrude** tab and then select the **To Next** option in the **Side 1** drop-down list.

23. Click on the green tick-mark button in the **Extrude** tab. The second feature of the second component is created, see Figure 11.117.

    Now, you need to create the third feature of the second component.

24. Click on the **Round** tool in the **Engineering** group of the **Model** tab. The **Round** tab appears in the **Ribbon**.

25. Enter **4** in the **Radius** field of the **Round** tab as the radius of the round and then press ENTER.

26. Click on the required edges (4 edges) of the second component by pressing the CTRL key as the edges to create rounds of the same radius. The preview appears, see Figure 11.118.

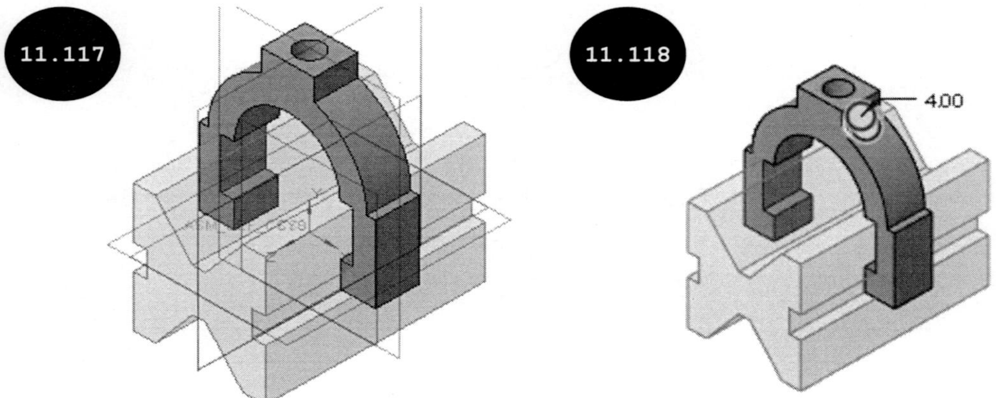

11.117
11.118

27. Ensure that the **Circular** option is selected in the **Profile** drop-down list of the **Round** tab.

28. Click on the green tick-mark button in the **Round** tab. The third feature of the second component is created, see Figure 11.119.

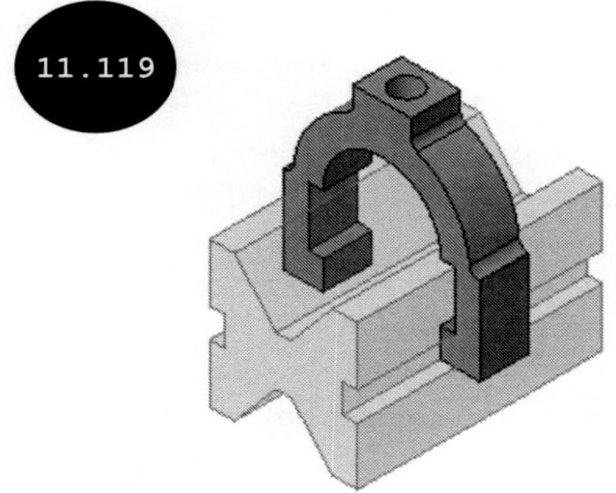

After creating all features of the second component, you need to create the third component of the assembly.

Section 4: Creating the Third Component

To create the third component of the assembly, you first need to activate the assembly file.

1. Click on the name of the assembly (**C11-TUTORIAL01**) in the **Model Tree** and then click on the **Activate** tool in the Mini toolbar that appears, see Figure 11.120.

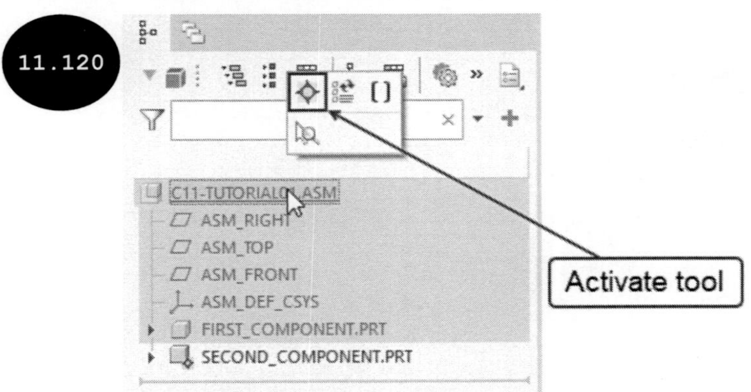

Now, you can create the third component of the assembly.

2. Click on the **Create** tool in the **Component** group of the **Model** tab, see Figure 11.121. The **Create Component** dialog box appears in the graphics area.

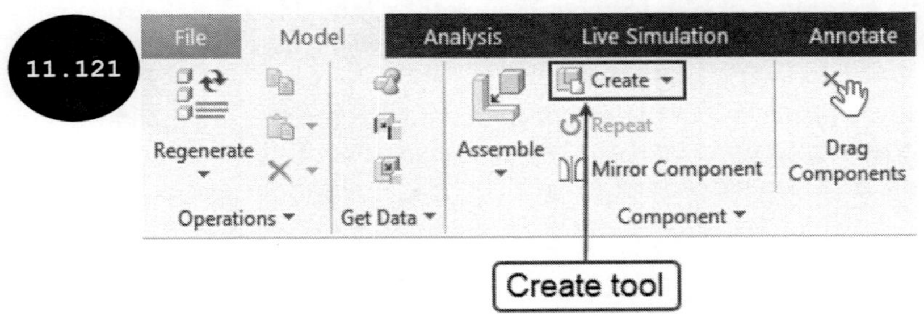

3. Ensure that the **Part** radio button is selected in the **Type** area and the **Solid** radio button is selected in the **Sub-type** area of the dialog box to create a solid component.

4. Enter **Third_Component** as the name of the component in the **File name** field and then click on the **OK** button in the dialog box. The **Creation Options** dialog box appears.

5. Select the **Empty** radio button in the dialog box to create the third component as an empty component.

6. Ensure that the **Leave component unplaced** check box is cleared in the dialog box.

7. Click on the **OK** button in the **Creation Options** dialog box. The third component is created and its name appears in the **Model Tree**.

   Now, you need to create the features of the third component. To do so, you need to first activate it in the assembly.

8. Click on the newly created empty component (third component) in the **Model Tree** and then click on the **Activate** tool in the Mini toolbar that appears, see Figure 11.122. The newly created empty component (third component) becomes the active component and the Part modeling environment is invoked. Also, the remaining components become transparent in the graphics area.

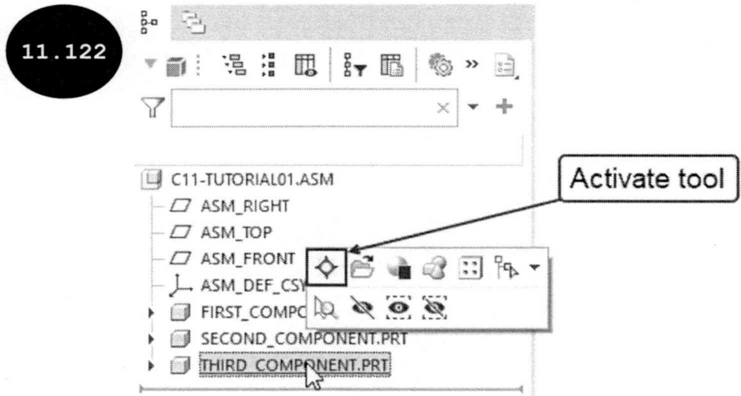

   Now, you can add features to the third component.

9. Click on the **Extrude** tool in the **Shapes** group of the **Model** tab. The **Extrude** tab appears in the **Ribbon**. Also, you are prompted to select a sketching plane.

10. Click on the top planar face of the second component as the sketching plane for creating the base feature of the third component. The Sketching environment is invoked and the **References** dialog box appears. Also, you are prompted to select geometries of the existing components to specify references.

Note: If the **References** dialog box does not appear by default on invoking the Sketching environment, then click on the **References** tool in the **Setup** group of the **Sketch** tab to display the **References** dialog box.

11. Select the circular edge of the hole of the second component to define the references for creating the first feature of the third component. Next, close the **References** dialog box.
12. Create a circle by taking reference of the circular edge of the second component as the sketch of the base feature, see Figure 11.123.
13. Exit the Sketching environment. A preview of the extrude feature appears in the graphics area. Next, change the current orientation of the model to the standard orientation.
14. Expand the **Options** panel of the **Extrude** tab and then select the **Symmetric** option in the **Side 1** drop-down list.
15. Enter **80** as the depth of extrusion in the **Value** field and then press ENTER. A preview of the extrude feature appears symmetrically on both sides of the sketching plane.
16. Click on the green tick-mark button in the **Extrude** tab. The first feature of the third component is created, see Figure 11.124.

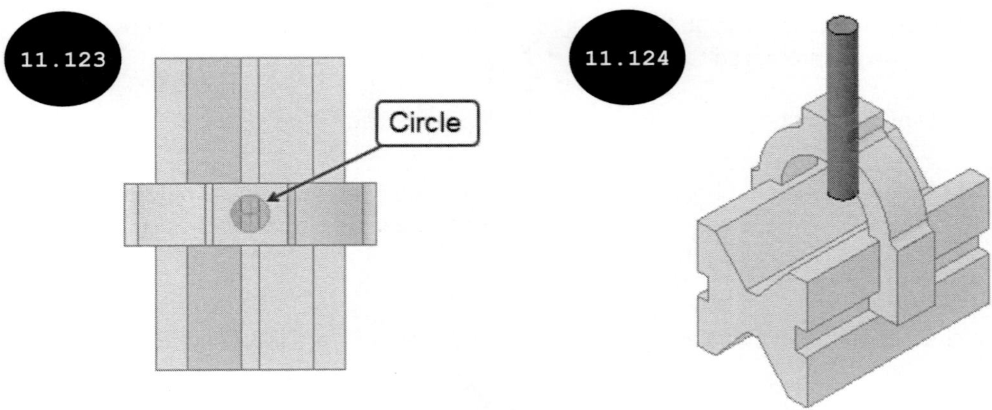

Now, you need to create the second feature of the third component.

17. Click on the **Extrude** tool in the **Shapes** group of the **Model** tab and then select the top planar face of the first feature of the third component as the sketching plane.

Note: The **References** dialog box appears on invoking the Sketching environment to define references. Select the circular edge of the previously created first feature as the geometry and then close the dialog box.

18. Create a circle of diameter 20 mm as the sketch of the second feature, see Figure 11.125.

19. Exit the Sketching environment. The preview of the extrude feature appears in the graphics area. Next, change the current orientation of the model to the standard orientation.

20. Enter **20** as the depth of extrusion in the **Value** field of the **Extrude** tab and then press ENTER.

21. Click on the green tick-mark button in the **Extrude** tab. The second feature of the third component is created, see Figure 11.126.

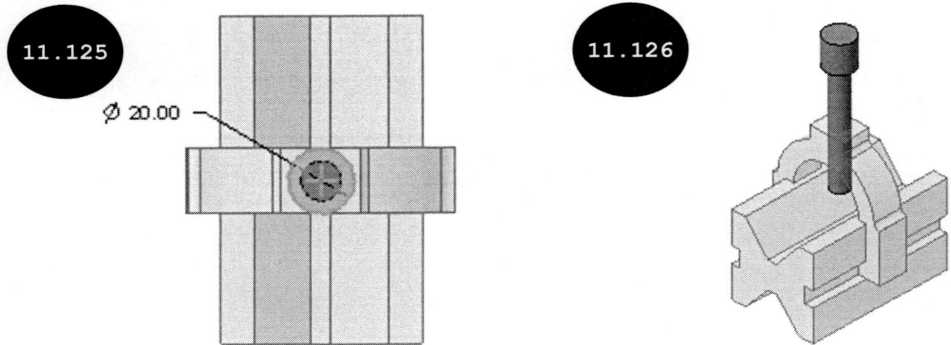

Now, you need to create the third feature of the third component.

22. Click on the **Extrude** tool in the **Shapes** group of the **Model** tab. The **Extrude** tab appears in the **Ribbon**. Also, you are prompted to select a sketching plane.

23. Select the Right Plane of the assembly as the sketching plane, see Figure 11.127.

Note: The **References** dialog box appears on invoking the Sketching environment to define references. Select the required geometries of the existing components to define the references and then close the dialog box.

24. Create a circle of diameter 5 mm as the sketch of the third feature, see Figure 11.128.

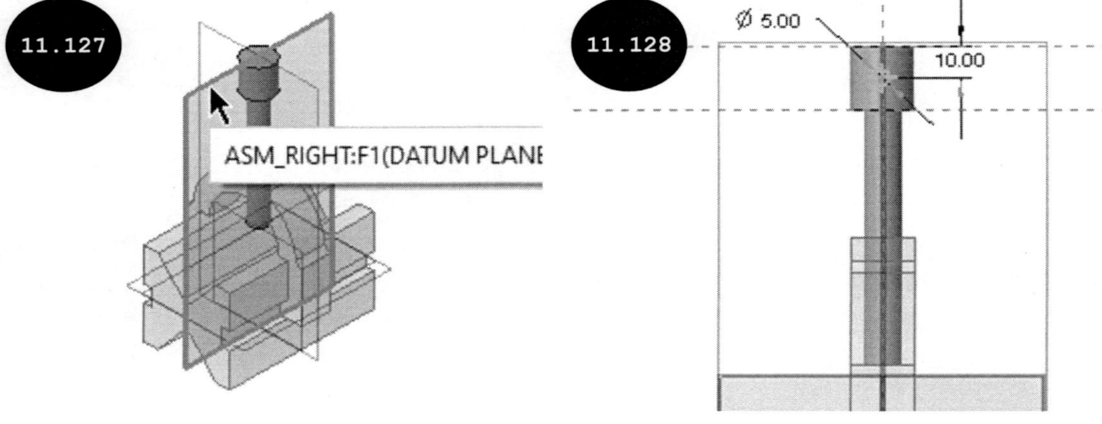

25. Exit the Sketching environment. A preview of the extrude feature appears in the graphics area. Next, change the current orientation of the model to the standard orientation.

26. Expand the **Options** panel of the **Extrude** tab and then select the **Through All** option in the **Side 1** and **Side 2** drop-down lists.

27. Ensure that the **Remove Material** button is activated in the **Extrude** tab.

28. Click on the green tick-mark button in the **Extrude** tab. The third feature of the third component is created, see Figure 11.129.

    After creating all the features of the third component, you need to activate the assembly file to switch back to the Assembly mode.

29. Click on the name of the assembly (**C11-TUTORIAL01**) in the **Model Tree** and then click on the **Activate** tool in the Mini toolbar that appears. The Assembly mode is invoked and the final assembly appears after creating all its components, as shown in Figure 11.130.

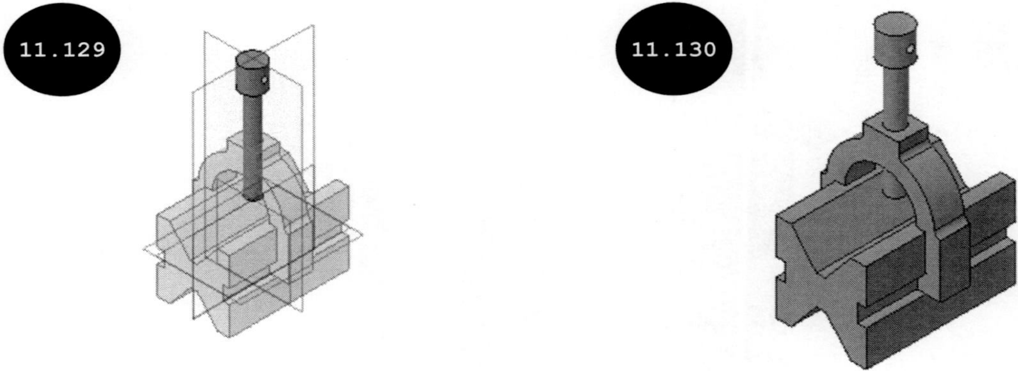

Note: By default, the components created by using the Top-down approach become fixed components in the Assembly environment.

Section 5: Saving Assembly and its Component

1. Click on the **Save** tool in the **Quick Access Toolbar**. The **Save Object** dialog box appears.

2. Click on the **OK** button in the dialog box. The assembly file and all its components are saved individually in the specified working directory (<<*Creo Parametric\\Chapter 11\\Tutorial 1*\\).

Tutorial 2

Open the assembly, created in Tutorial 2 of Chapter 10 (see Figure 11.131), and then create its exploded view similar to the one shown in Figure 11.132. You need to create exploded lines in the exploded view of the assembly and also animate the exploded view.

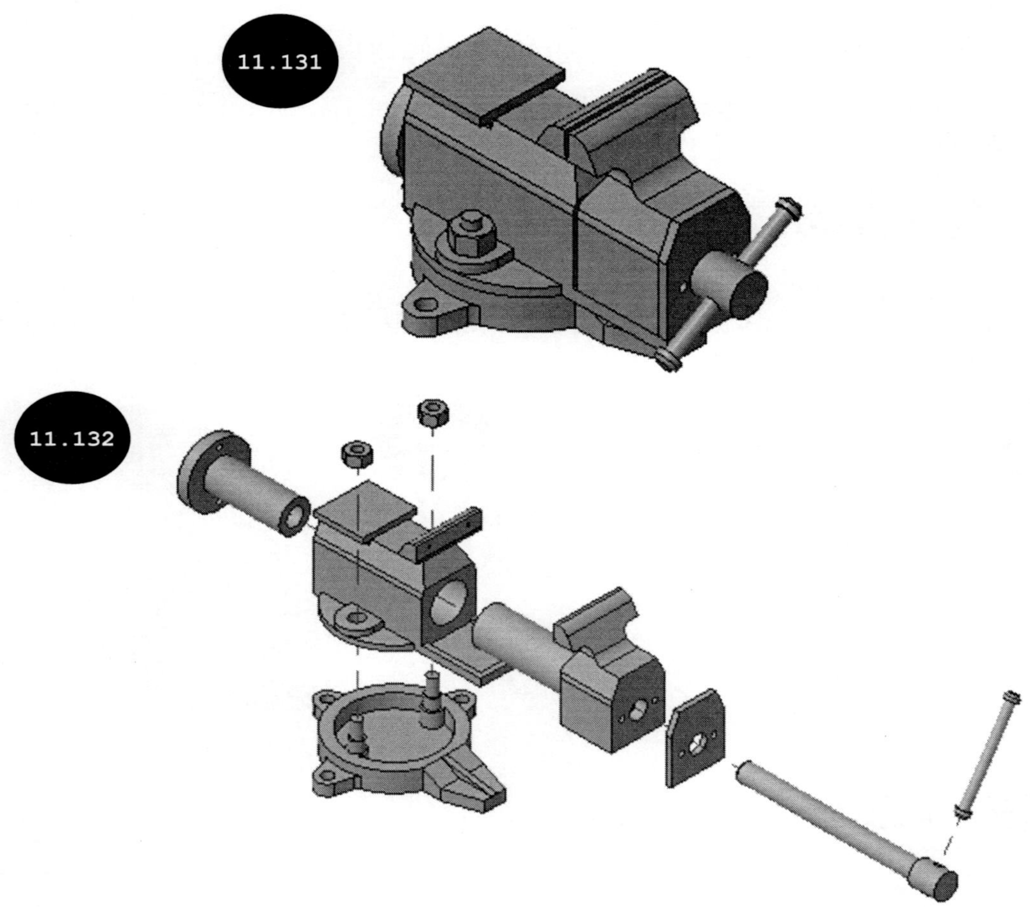

Section 1: Opening Tutorial 2 of Chapter 10

1. Start Creo Parametric by double-clicking on the Creo Parametric icon on your desktop.
2. Open the assembly, created in Tutorial 2 of Chapter 10 by using the **Open** tool of the **Quick Access Toolbar**.

Note: In Creo Parametric, before you open an existing component or assembly, it is recommended to remove all the files that were previously created or opened in the current session of Creo Parametric by clicking on the **File > Manage Session > Erase Not Displayed**. This needs to be done because, when you open an assembly, the previously created or opened components in the session will be opened if the names of the components being opened match them.

Section 2: Creating Exploded View

Now, you can create the exploded view of the assembly.

1. Click on the **Manage Views** tool in the **Model Display** group of the **Model** tab, see Figure 11.133. The **View Manager** dialog box appears, see Figure 11.134.

2. Click on the **Explode** tab in the **View Manager** dialog box, refer to Figure 11.135.

3. Click on the **New** button in the **Explode** tab of the dialog box. A default name for the exploded view appears in the **Names** column of the dialog box.

4. Accept the default name of the exploded view and then press ENTER. The new exploded view is created and becomes an active exploded view. Note that a green arrow in front of the name of the exploded view in the dialog box indicates that it is an active exploded view.

   Now, you can define the position of each component of the assembly in the active exploded view.

5. Click on **Edit > Edit Position** in the dialog box, see Figure 11.135. The **Explode Tool** tab appears in the **Ribbon**, see Figure 11.136.

11.135

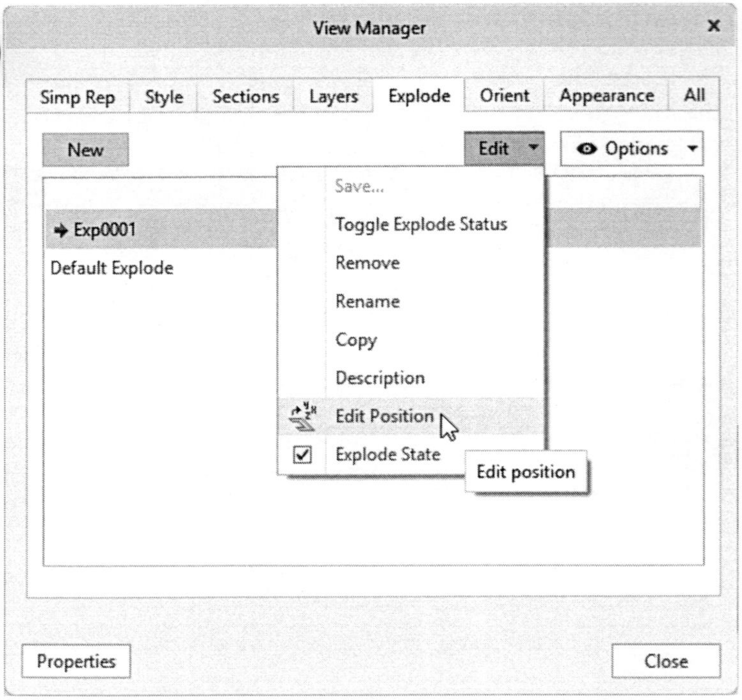

11.136

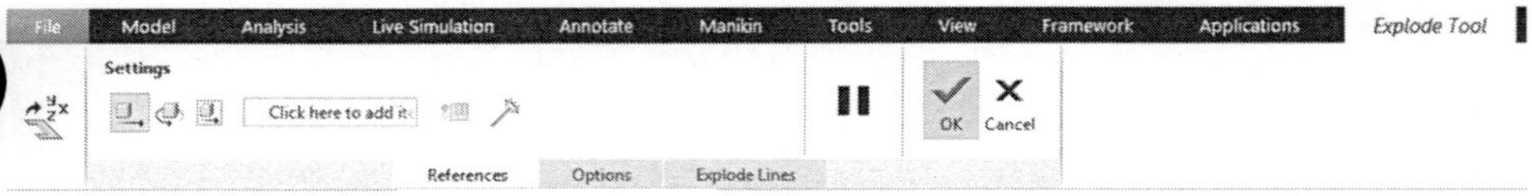

6. Ensure that the **Translate** button is activated in the **Settings** area of the **Explode Tool** tab as the motion type to explode the component.

7. Select the Base component of the assembly to explode. The translational handles appear in the graphics area, see Figure 11.137.

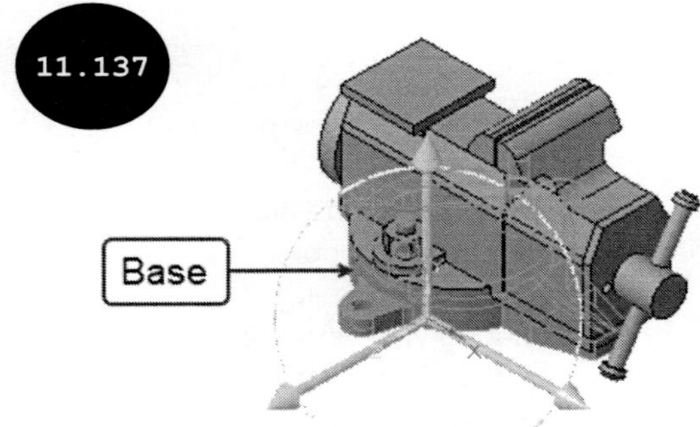

8. Drag the vertical translational handle downward to create the first exploded step, similar to the one shown in Figure 11.138.

9. Expand the **Options** panel of the **Explode Tool** tab and then select the **Move with Children** check box.

10. Select the Sliding Jaw component of the assembly. The translational handles appear in the graphics area, see Figure 11.139.

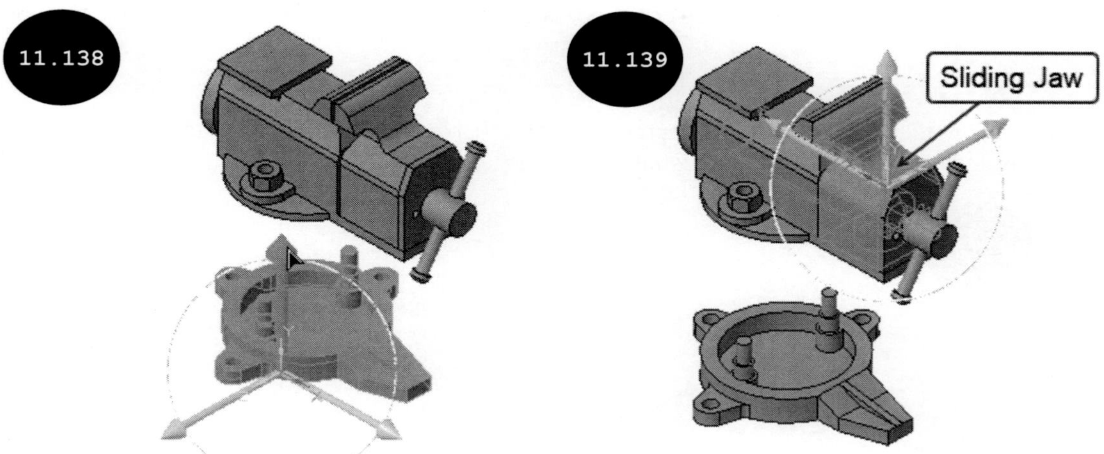

11. Move the Sliding Jaw similar to the one shown in Figure 11.140 by dragging the translational handle. Note that on moving the Sliding Jaw, all its child components also move along with it. This happens because, the **Move with Children** check box is selected in the **Options** panel.

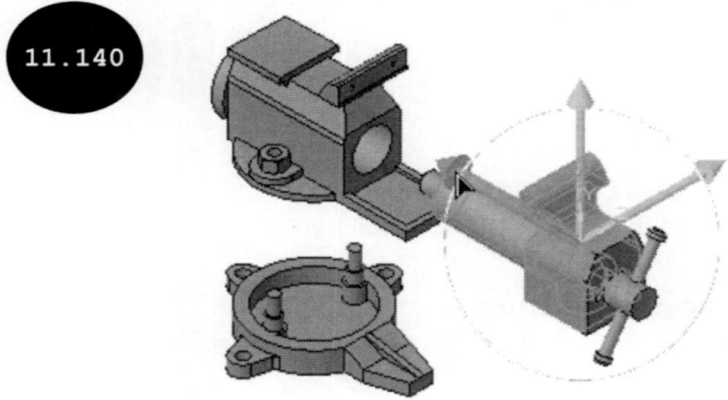

12. Similarly, explode the Jaw Plate, Jaw Screw, Handle, and Vice Nut components by dragging the respective translational handles, see Figure 11.141.

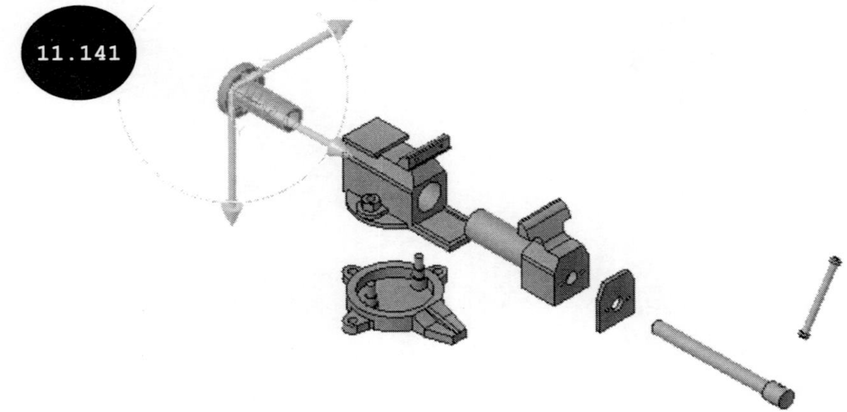

Note: To move the components individually without their child components, you need to ensure that the **Move with Children** check box is cleared in the **Options** panel of the **Explode Tool** tab.

13. Select both the Nut components by pressing the CTRL key and then drag the translational handle for exploding them together, see Figure 11.142.

11.142

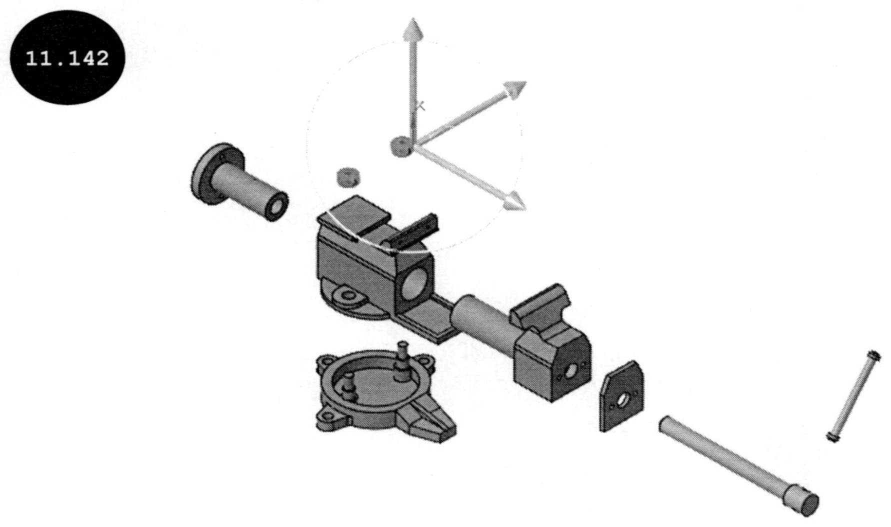

After exploding all the components of the assembly, you need to create the exploded lines.

Section 3: Creating Exploded Lines

Now, you can create cosmetic exploded lines in the exploded view of the assembly.

1. Click on the **Create cosmetic offset lines to illustrate movement of exploded component** button in the **Settings** area of the **Explode Tool** tab to create the exploded lines. The **Cosmetic Offset Line** dialog box appears, see Figure 11.143.

11.143

2. Select the outer circular face of the Handle and the inner circular face of the hole of the Jaw Screw as references to connect them with a cosmetic exploded line, see Figure 11.144.

3. Ensure that the **Use cylinder axis** radio buttons are selected in the **Cosmetic Offset Line** dialog box to define the route for the exploded line along the axes of the selected components.

4. Click on the **Apply** button in the dialog box. A cosmetic exploded line is created, see Figure 11.145. Also, the **Cosmetic Offset Line** dialog box is still displayed in the graphics area.

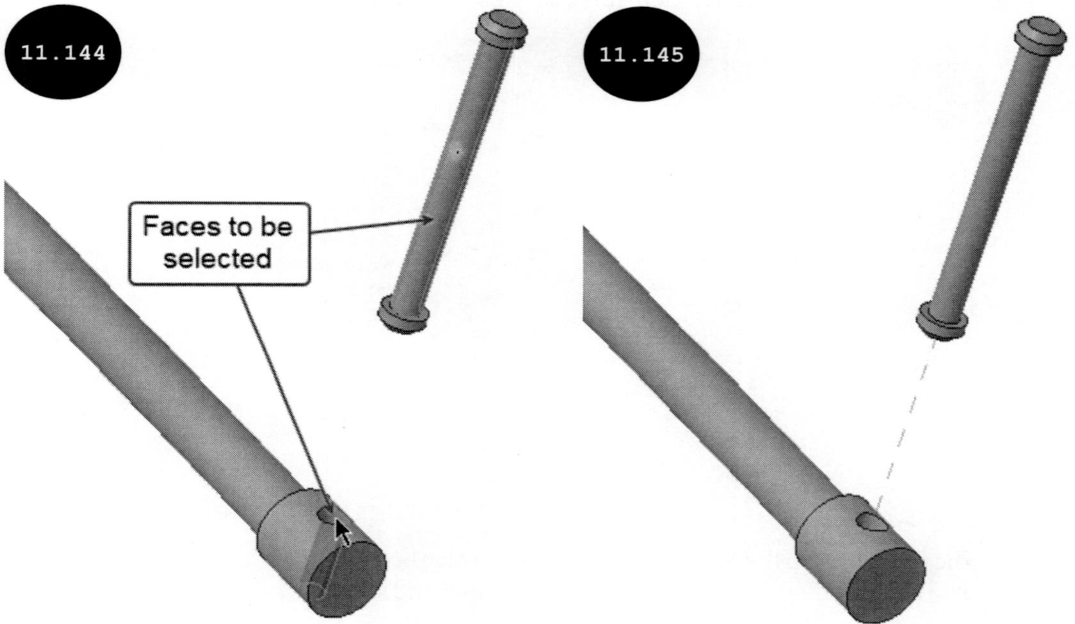

5. Similarly, create the exploded lines between the remaining components of the assembly, see Figure 11.146.

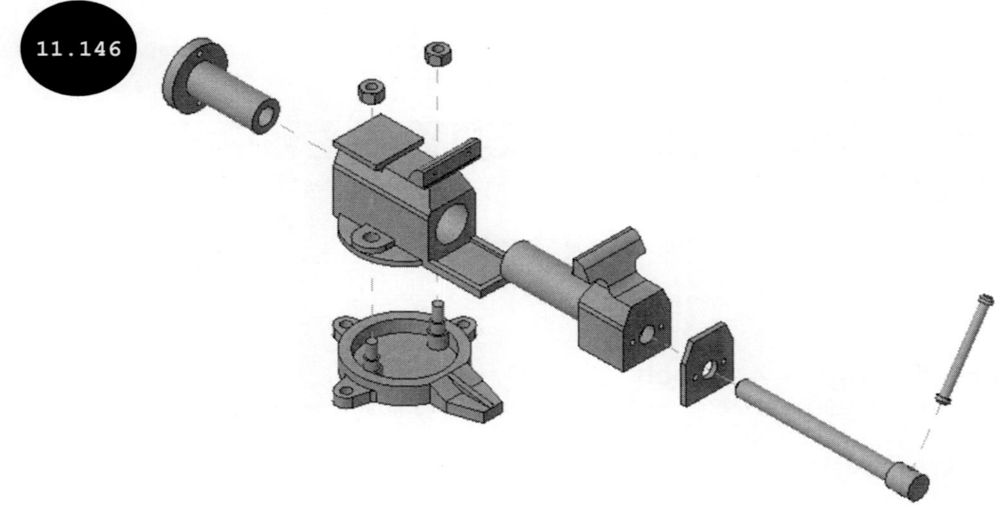

6. After creating the exploded lines, close the **Cosmetic Offset Line** dialog box.

7. Click on the green tick-mark button in the **Explode Tool** tab. The exploded view of the assembly is created and the **View Manager** dialog box appears.

   Now, you need to save the exploded view of the assembly.

8. Click on **Edit > Save** in the **View Manager** dialog box to save the exploded view of the assembly, see Figure 11.147. The **Save Display Elements** dialog box appears.

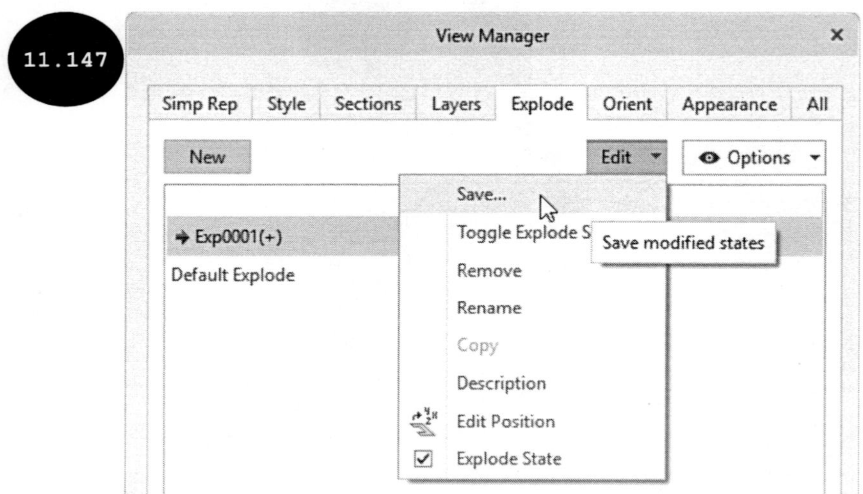

9. Click on the **OK** button in the **Save Display Elements** dialog box and then close the **View Manager** dialog box. The exploded view of the assembly is created and saved.

Section 4: Animating the Exploded View

Now, you can animate the exploded view of the assembly.

1. Click on the **Exploded View** tool of the **Model Display** group in the **Model** tab to animate the exploded/unexploded view of the assembly, see Figure 11.148

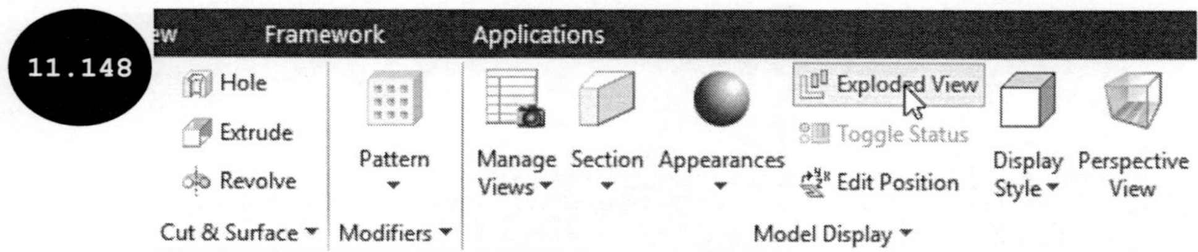

Section 5: Saving the Assembly

1. Click on the **Regenerate** tool in the **Quick Access Toolbar** to regenerate the assembly.

2. Click on the **Save** tool in the **Quick Access Toolbar** toolbar. The assembly is saved.

Hands-on Test Drive 1

Create the assembly shown in Figure 11.149 by using the Top-down approach. Different views and dimensions of the individual components of the assembly are shown in Figures 11.150 through 11.153. All dimensions are in mm.

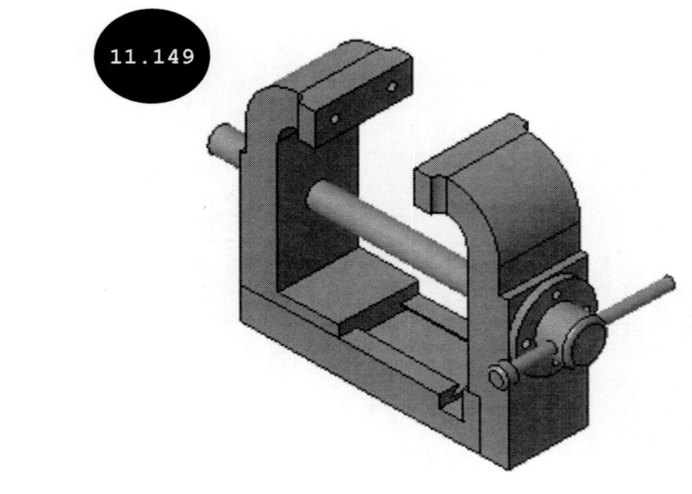

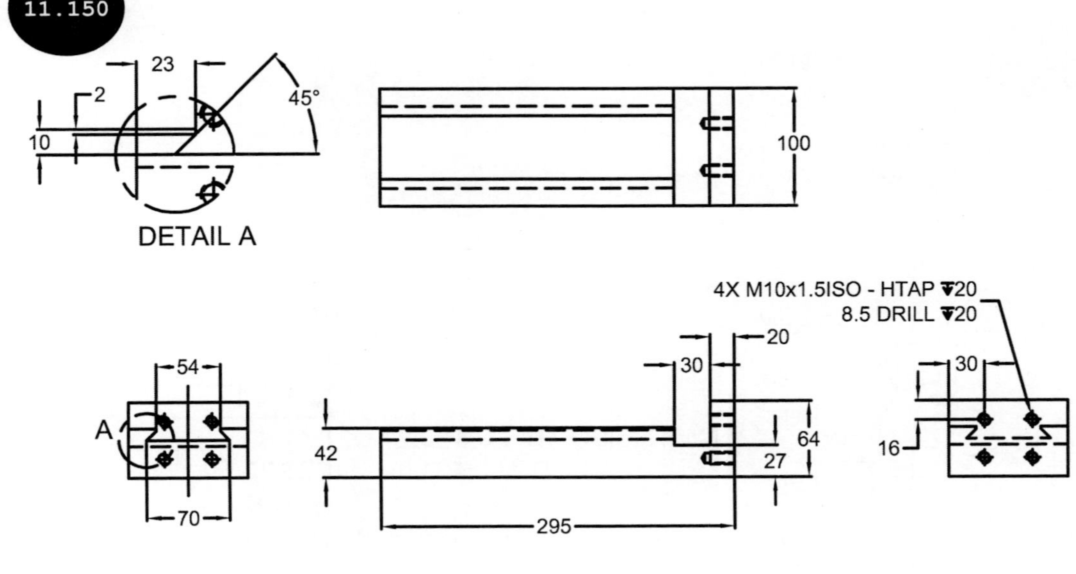

Base

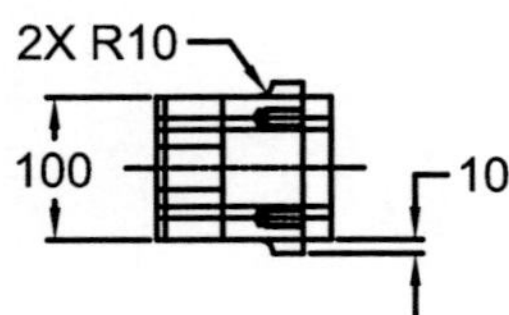

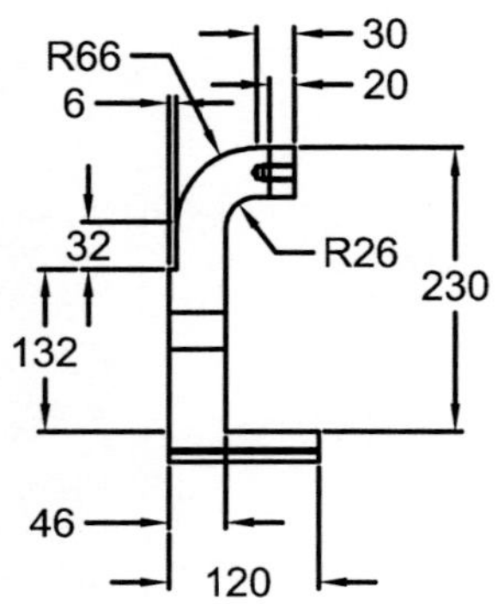

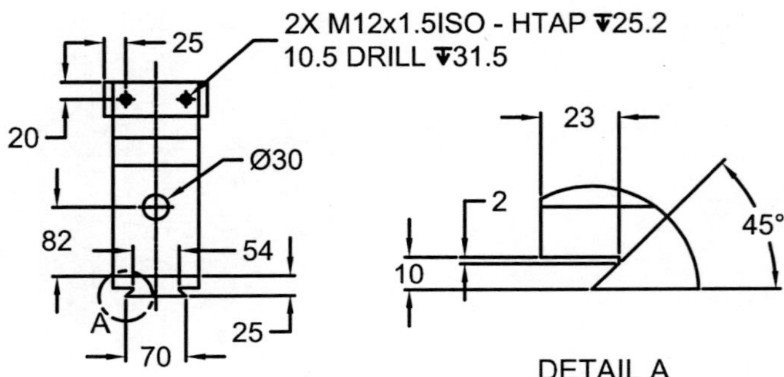

Moving Jaw

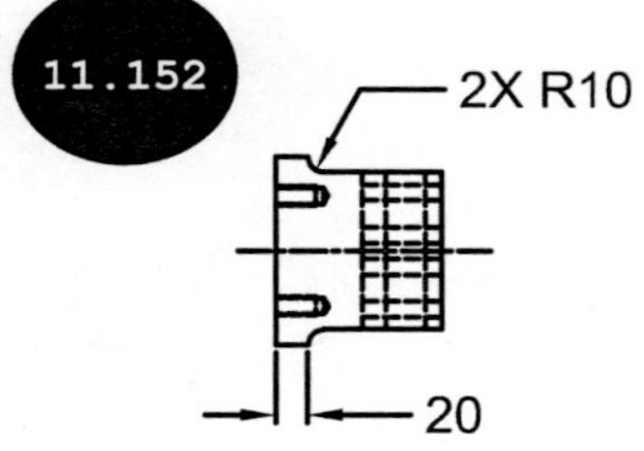

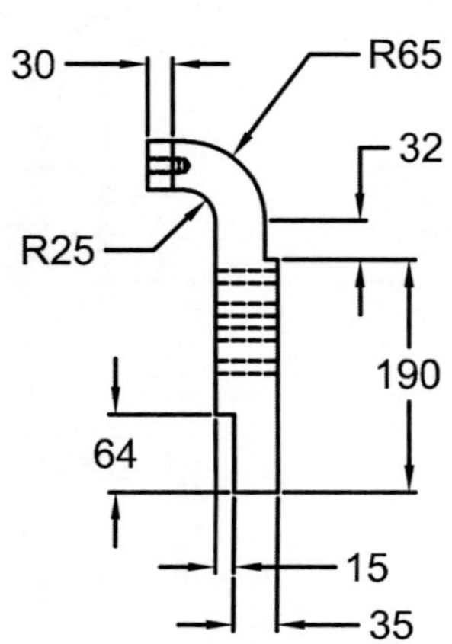

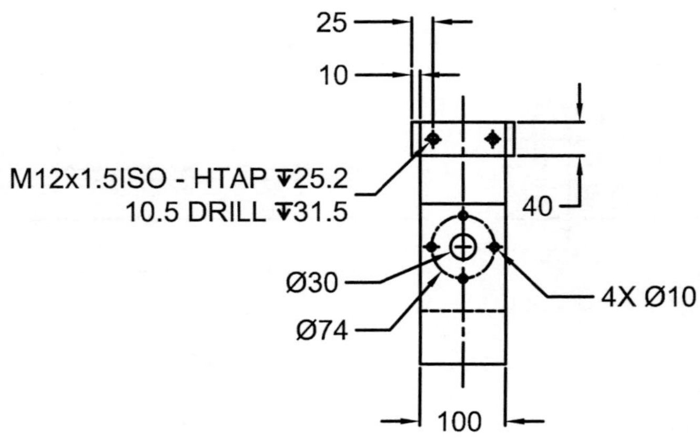

Fixed Jaw

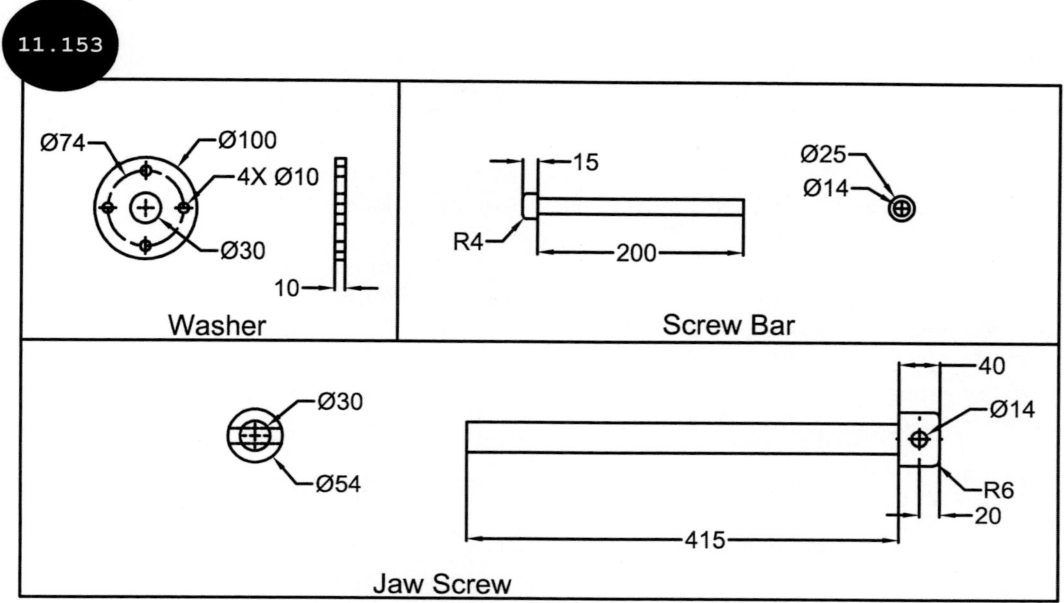

Summary

In this chapter, you have learned about creating assemblies by using the Top-down assembly approach, editing components of an assembly, editing constraints, displaying constraints and features of components in the **Model Tree**, patterning and mirroring assembly components, creating assembly features, suppressing or resuming the components of an assembly, inserting multiple copies of a component into an assembly, and checking interference between components of an assembly. Moreover, you have learned how to create exploded views of an assembly, switch between exploded and unexploded views of an assembly, and create the Bill of Materials (BOM).

Questions

Complete and verify the following sentences:

- In the _________ approach, you create all the components of an assembly in the Assembly environment.
- The _________ tool is used for creating an exploded view of an assembly.
- The _________ tool is used for creating a component within the Assembly environment.
- In the **Model Tree**, the constraints applied between the components of an assembly appear in the _________ folder.
- The _________ tool is used for assembling multiple copies of a component in the assembly.

- The ________ tool is used for checking interferences between the components of the assembly.
- The ________ button of the **Explode Tool** tab is used for creating cosmetic exploded lines in the exploded view of the assembly.
- The ________ tool is used for switching between exploded and unexploded views of an assembly.
- The ________ tool is used for displaying Bill of Materials (BOM) of an assembly in the Assembly environment.
- While creating an exploded view, you can move a component along with its child components by selecting ________ check box.
- The ________ tool is used to suppress a component from the assembly in the graphics area.
- You can edit the components of an assembly within the Assembly environment. (True/False)
- In Creo Parametric, you can create cut features in the Assembly environment. (True/False)
- In Creo Parametric, you cannot create sub-assemblies within a main assembly. (True/False)
- In Creo Parametric, the components created in the Assembly environment are fixed components and all their degrees of freedom are restricted. (True/False)

CHAPTER

12

Working with Drawings

In this chapter, the following topics will be discussed:

- Invoking Drawing Mode
- Adding a Model for Generating its Views
- Creating a General View
- Creating Projection Views
- Working with Angle of Projection
- Defining the Angle of Projection
- Creating a Detailed View
- Creating an Auxiliary View
- Creating a Revolved View
- Creating a Section View
- Controlling the Visibility of a View
- Creating a 3D Cross-Section View
- Creating a Copy and Align View
- Modifying Properties of a View
- Modifying Hatching of a View
- Moving, Erasing, and Deleting a View
- Creating a New Drawing Template/Format
- Applying Dimensions
- Editing the Text Style
- Adding Tolerances in the Drawing Views
- Adding Notes
- Creating the Bill of Material (BOM)
- Adding Balloons

In earlier chapters, you have learned about creating parts and assemblies. In this chapter, you will learn about creating 2D drawings. 2D drawings are technical drawings, which fully and clearly communicate the information about the end product to be manufactured. It is not only a drawing but also a language used by engineers to communicate ideas and information about engineered products. By using 2D drawings, a designer can communicate the information about the components to be manufactured to the engineers on the shop floor. Underscoring the importance of 2D drawings, the role of designers becomes very important in generating accurate and error-free drawings for production. Inaccurate or missing information about a component in drawings can lead to defective production. In Creo Parametric, you can generate error-free 2D drawings in the Drawing mode. The method for invoking the Drawing mode is discussed next.

Invoking Drawing Mode

To invoke the Drawing mode, click on the **New** tool in the **Quick Access Toolbar**, see Figure 12.1. The **New** dialog box appears, see Figure 12.2. Alternatively, press the CTRL + N to invoke the **New** dialog box.

In the **New** dialog box, select the **Drawing** radio button and then enter the name of the drawing file in the **File name** field of the dialog box. Next, click on the **OK** button in the dialog box. The **New Drawing**

dialog box appears, see Figure 12.3. The options in the **New Drawing** dialog box are used for selecting a drawing template; default, format, or empty for creating drawing views. The options are discussed below:

Default Model

The **Default Model** area of the **New Drawing** dialog box is used for selecting a model or an assembly whose drawing views are to be created. To select a model or an assembly, click on the **Browse** button in the **Default Model** area of the dialog box. The **Open** dialog box appears. In this dialog box, browse to the location where the model, whose drawing views are to be created, has been saved, and then select it. Next, click on the **Open** button in the dialog box. The name of the selected model appears in the **Default Model** area of the dialog box. Note that if a part or an assembly is already opened in the current session of Creo Parametric, then its name automatically appears in the **Default Model** area of the dialog box, which indicates that the model is selected for creating its drawing views.

Specify Template

The **Specify Template** area of the dialog box is used for selecting a drawing template for creating drawing views. The options in this area are discussed below:

Use template

When the **Use template** radio button is selected in this area, a list of standard templates/sheet sizes appears in the **Template** area of the dialog box, see Figure 12.3. You can select the required standard template in the **Template** area of the dialog box.

Empty with format

The **Empty with format** radio button is used for selecting a predefined format for creating drawing views. When this radio button is selected, the **Format** area appears in the dialog box, see Figure 12.4. In the **Format** area, click on the **Browse** button to select a predefined format of *.frm* or *.sec* file extension.

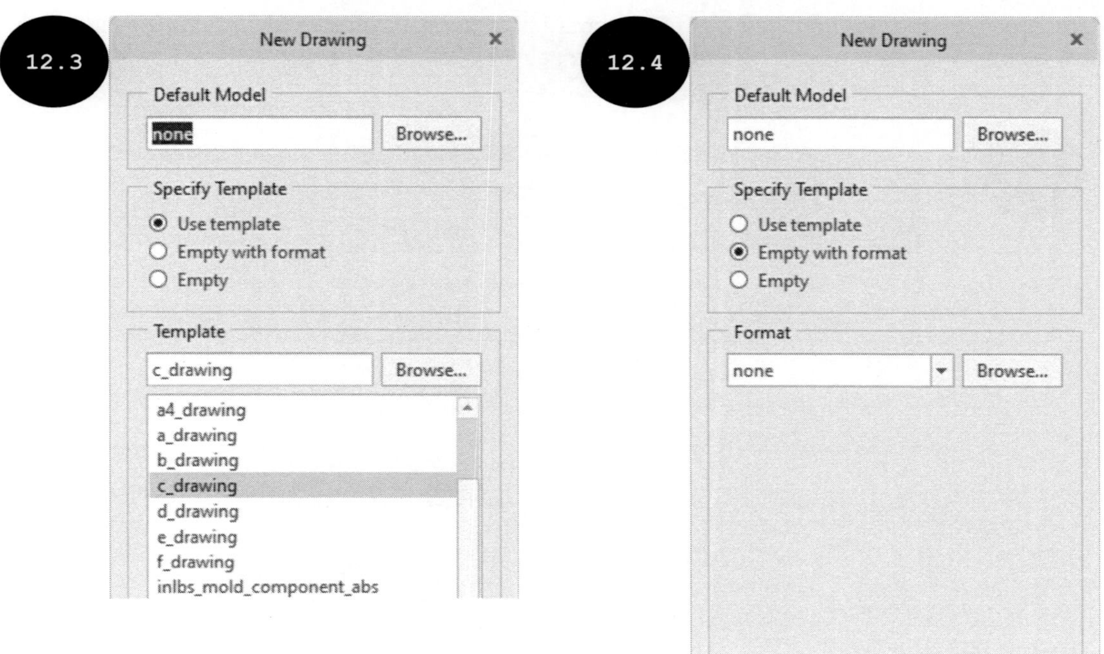

Empty

The **Empty** radio button of the **Specify Template** area is used for defining an empty sheet with custom size and orientation for creating drawing views. When the **Empty** radio button is selected, the **Orientation** and **Size** areas appear in the dialog box, see Figure 12.5. The options in the **Orientation** area are used for specifying the orientation of the drawing sheet. The **Portrait** and **Landscape** buttons of the **Orientation** area are used for defining standard sheet sizes with portrait and landscape orientations, respectively. You can select the required standard sheet size by using the **Standard Size** drop-down list of the **Size** area. The **Variable** button is used for defining a sheet with custom sizes and units. You can define the custom sheet size in the **Width** and **Height** fields of the **Size** area. Also, you can define the units by selecting the **Inches** or **Millimeters** radio button, respectively.

12.5

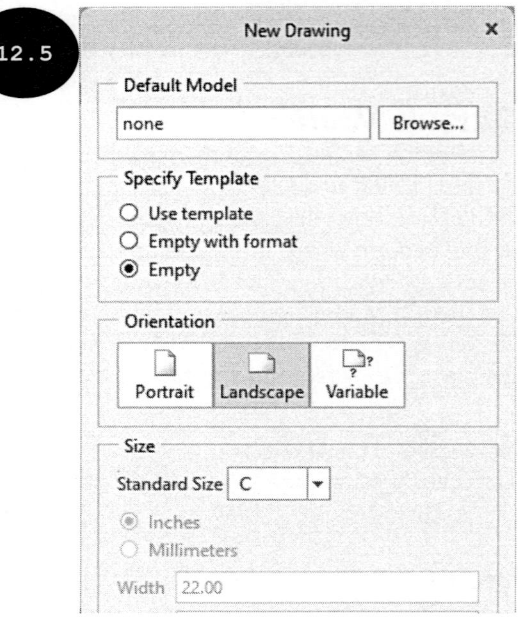

Note: The **Standard Size** drop-down list of the **Size** area is enabled only when the **Portrait** or **Landscape** button is selected in the **Orientation** area of the dialog box. The **Inches** and **Millimeters** radio buttons as well as the **Width** and **Height** fields of the **Size** area are enabled when the **Variable** button is selected in the **Orientation** area of the dialog box.

After specifying the required sheet size and orientation by using the options of the **New Drawing** dialog box, click on the **OK** button. The Drawing mode gets invoked with the display of a drawing sheet of specified size and orientation, see Figure 12.6.

12.6

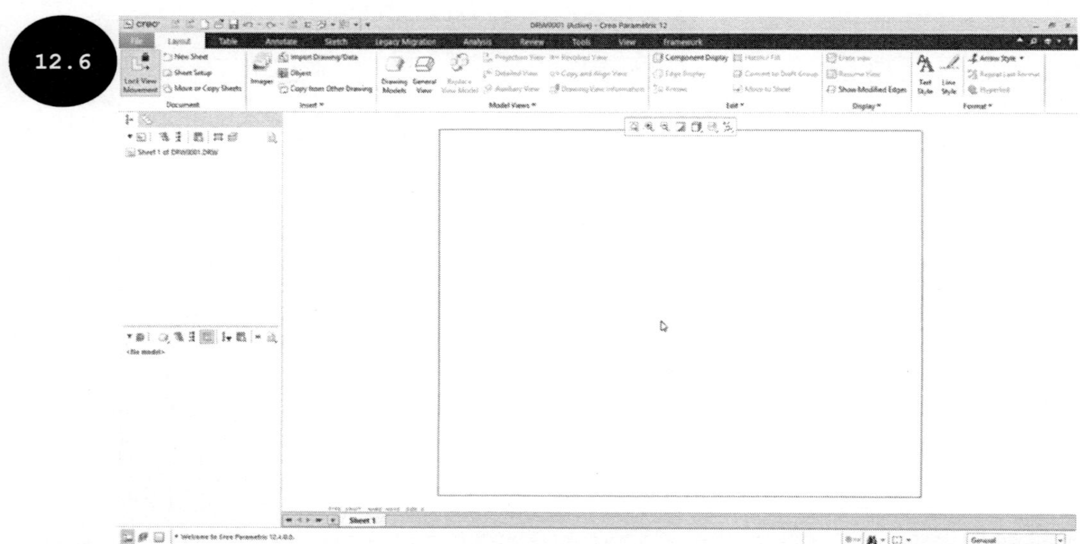

Note: If you invoke the Drawing mode with a default template by using the **Use template** radio button in the **New Drawing** dialog box, then the three standard orthogonal views: front, top, and side of the selected model get generated automatically on the drawing sheet, see Figure 12.7.

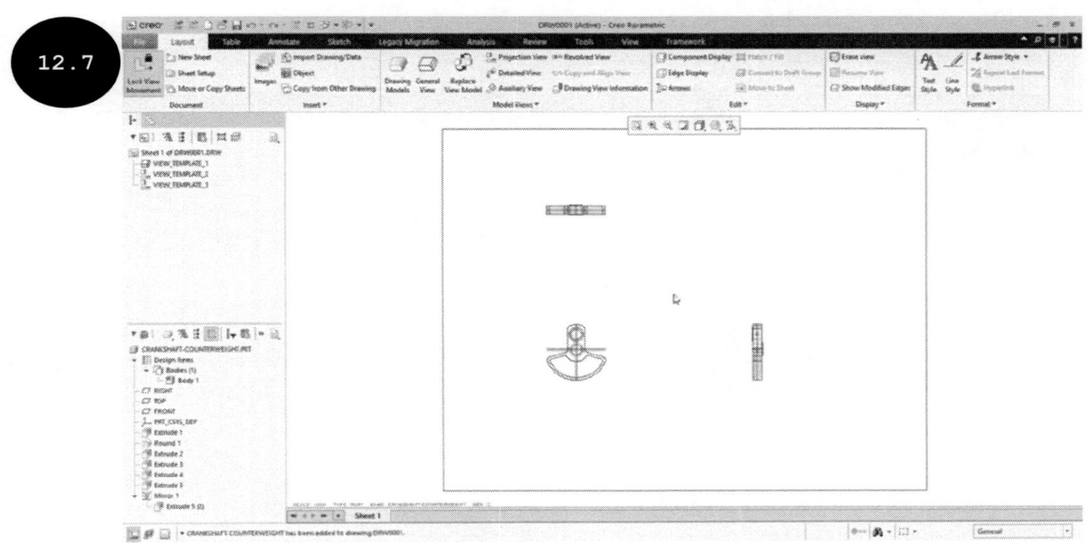

Adding a Model for Generating its Views

As discussed earlier, you can add a model whose drawing views are to be generated by using the **Default Model** area in the **New Drawing** dialog box. However, if you have not added a model, you can add it after invoking the Drawing mode by using the **Drawing Models** tool of the **Layout** tab, see Figure 12.8. The **DWG MODELS** menu appears, see Figure 12.9.

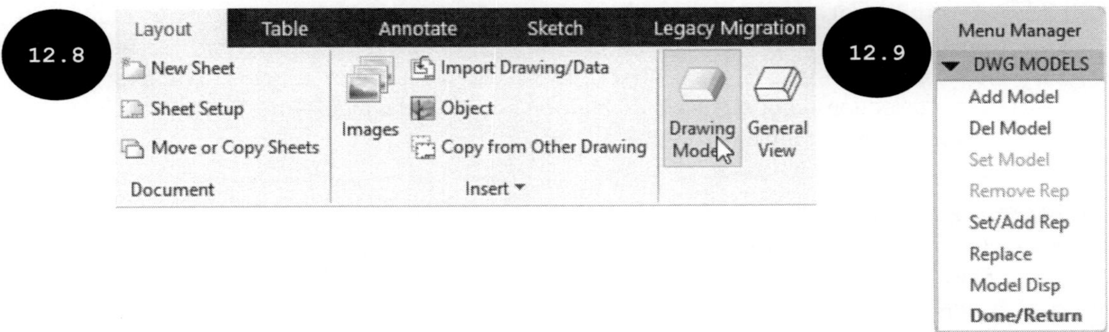

In the **DWG MODELS** menu, click on the **Add Model** option. The **Open** dialog box appears. In this dialog box, select a model (part or assembly) and then click on the **Open** button. The selected model gets added and appears in the **Model Tree** just below the **Drawing Tree** on the lower left side of the drawing sheet. Next, click on the **Done/Return** option in the **DWG MODELS** menu.

Creating a General View

A general view is an independent view of a model. It is also known as the base, first or parent view. In Creo Parametric, you can create a general view by using the **General View** tool of the **Layout** tab in the **Ribbon**. The method for creating a general view is discussed below:

1. Click on the **General View** tool in the **Layout** tab of the **Ribbon**, see Figure 12.10. The **Select Combined State** dialog box appears, see Figure 12.11. The options in this dialog box are discussed below.

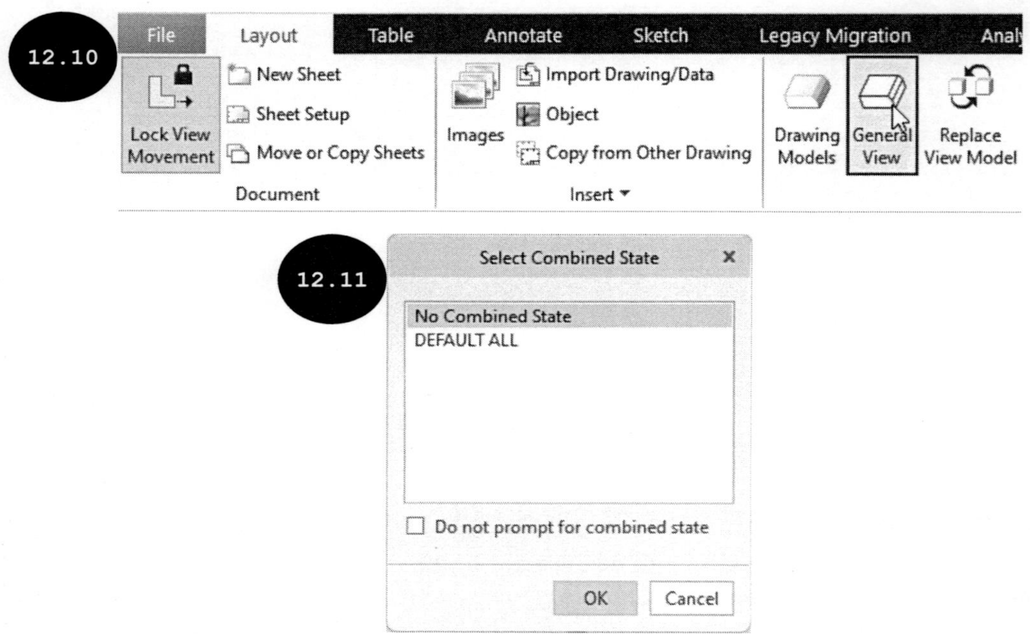

Note: If you have not added any model for generating its drawing views by using the **Default Model** area in the **New Drawing** dialog box or by using the **Drawing Models** tool as discussed earlier, then on clicking the **General View** tool, the **Open** dialog box appears for adding a model. After selecting a model, click on the **Open** button in the dialog box. The **Select Combined State** dialog box appears.

No Combined State: The No Combined State option of the **Select Combined State** dialog box is used for generating a drawing view of a component or an assembly without any combined state. Note that if the selected model is an assembly, then its unexploded view will be generated in default orientation on selecting this option.

DEFAULT ALL: The DEFAULT ALL option of the **Select Combined State** dialog box is used for generating a drawing view of a model with all its combined states. Note that if the selected model is an assembly, then its exploded view will be generated upon selecting this option.

Do not prompt for combined state: On selecting the **Do not prompt for combined state** check box, the **Select Combined State** dialog box will not appear the next time on generating a drawing view.

2. Select the **No Combined State** option in the **Select Combined State** dialog box for generating a drawing view without any combined state.

3. Click on the **OK** button in the **Select Combined State** dialog box. You are prompted to specify a center point for placing the drawing view on the drawing sheet.

4. Click on the drawing sheet to specify a center point of the drawing view. A preview of the drawing view appears on the drawing sheet. Also, the **Drawing View** dialog box appears, see Figure 12.12. Some of the options in this dialog box are discussed below:

12.12

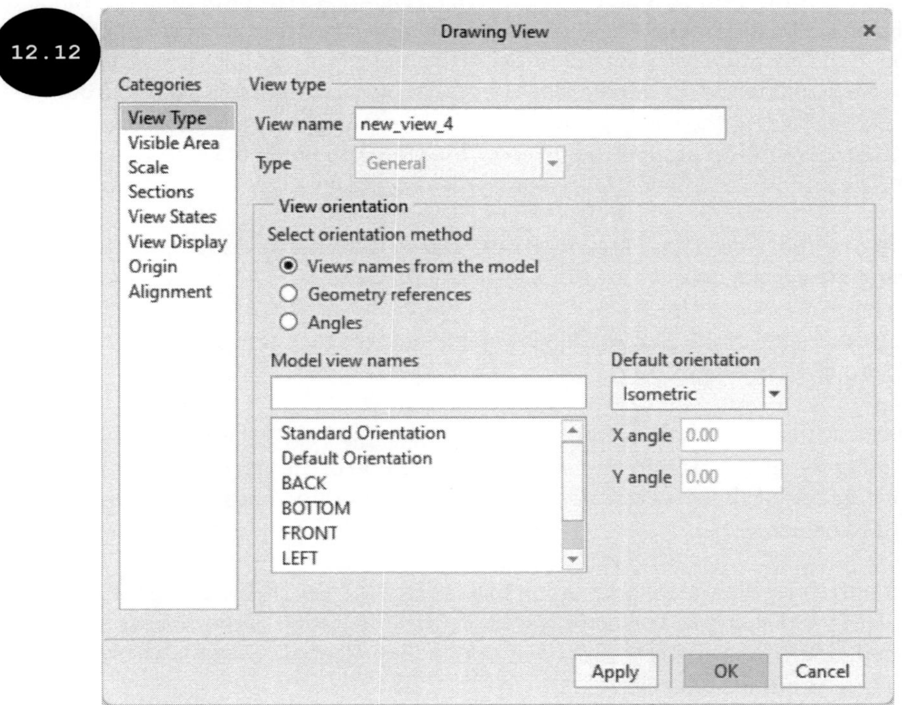

View Type: By default, the **View Type** category is selected in the **Categories** area on the left panel of the dialog box. As a result, the options for specifying the view type and orientation appear on the right panel of the dialog box, see Figure 12.12. The options are discussed below.

View name: By default, the name of the view appears in the **View name** field in the dialog box. You can also specify a new name for the view in this field, as required.

Views names from the model: By default, the **Views names from the model** radio button is selected in the **View orientation** area of the dialog box. As a result, a list of standard view orientations such as FRONT, BACK, and BOTTOM appear in the **Model view names** section of the dialog box. You can select the required orientation in this section. You can also specify the orientation of the view as isometric, trimetric, or user defined by selecting the required option in the **Default orientation** drop-down list, respectively. Note that on selecting the **User Defined** option in the **Default orientation** drop-down list, the **X angle** and **Y angle** fields get enabled in the dialog box. In these fields, you can specify X and Y angle values to define the orientation.

Geometry references: On selecting the **Geometry references** radio button in the **View orientation** area of the dialog box, you can define the orientation of the view by specifying references. To do so, select the required view such as **Front**, **Top**, or **Back** in the **Reference 1** drop-down list that appears in the dialog box and then select a geometry of the model in the drawing sheet to be oriented to the selected view. Similarly, select the required view in the **Reference 2** drop-down list and then select a geometry of the model to be oriented to the selected view.

Angles: On selecting the **Angles** radio button in the **View orientation** area, you can define the orientation of the view by specifying a rotation reference in the **Rotation reference** drop-down list and an angle value in the **Angle value** field that appears in the dialog box. Note that the **Normal** option in the **Rotation reference** drop-down list is used for rotating the model around the origin of the view and normal to the drawing sheet. The **Vertical** option is used for rotating the model around the origin of the view and vertically to the drawing sheet. The **Horizontal** option is used for rotating the model around the origin of the view and horizontally to the drawing sheet. The **Edge/Axis** option is used for rotating the model around an edge/axis selected.

5. Ensure that the **View Type** category is selected in the **Categories** area on the left panel of the **Drawing View** dialog box.

6. Enter a new name of the view in the **View name** field that appears on the right panel of the dialog box, if required.

7. Ensure that the **Views names from the model** radio button is selected in the **View orientation** area of the dialog box to define the standard orientation of the view. Note that you can also define the orientation of the view by selecting the **Geometry references** and **Angles** radio buttons, as discussed earlier.

8. Select the required standard orientation such as FRONT, BACK, or TOP in the **Model view names** section of the dialog box. You can also specify the orientation of the view as isometric, trimetric, or user defined by selecting the required option in the **Default orientation** drop-down list of the dialog box, as discussed earlier.

9. After specifying the required orientation of the view, click on the **Apply** button in the **Drawing View** dialog box. The view gets oriented in the drawing sheet as specified in the dialog box.

Note: By default, the view is generated as per the default scale of the sheet. However, you can change the default scale of the view by using the options available in the **Scale** category of the dialog box.

Now, you need to define the scale factor of the drawing view.

10. Click on the **Scale** category in the **Categories** area of the dialog box. The options for defining the scale of the drawing view appear on the right panel of the dialog box, see Figure 12.13.

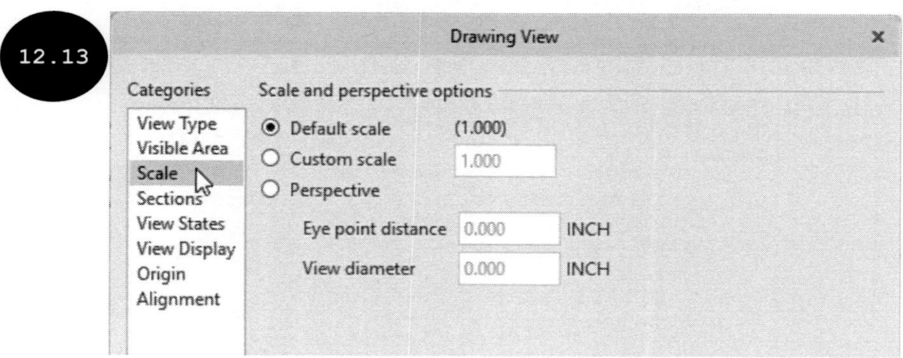

Scale: The options in the **Scale** category are used for defining the scale of the view and are discussed below.

Default scale: By default, the **Default scale** radio button is selected in the dialog box. As a result, the default scale of the view is defined as per the size of the sheet.

Custom scale: On selecting the **Custom scale** radio button, you can specify a custom scale for the drawing view in the field that appears on its right in the dialog box.

Perspective: On selecting the **Perspective** radio button, you can define the size of the drawing view by entering the eye-point distance (focal length) and view diameter values in the respective fields that appear in the dialog box.

11. Ensure that the **Default scale** radio button is selected in the dialog box to define the default scale of the view as per the sheet size. If needed, you can also define the custom scale for the view, as discussed above.

12. After specifying the scale of the view, click on the **Apply** button in the dialog box.

    Now, you need to define the display style of the view such as Wireframe, Hidden Line, No Hidden, Shaded, or Shaded With Edges. You can define the display style of the view by using the options of the **View Display** category in the **Drawing View** dialog box.

13. Click on the **View Display** category in the **Categories** area on the left panel of the dialog box. The options for defining the display style of the view appear on the right panel of the dialog box, see Figure 12.14.

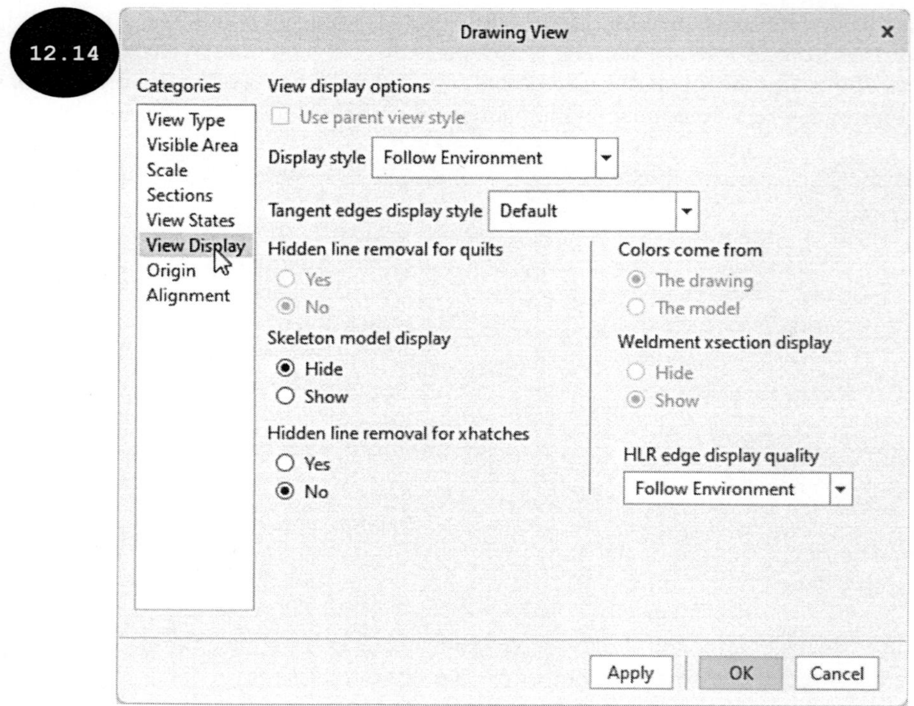

View Display: The options in the **View Display** category are used for defining the display style of the view and are discussed below.

Display style: By default, the **Follow Environment** option is selected in the **Display style** drop-down list. As a result, the view follows the display style that is selected in the **Display Style** flyout of the **In-graphics** toolbar in the Drawing mode, see Figure 12.15.

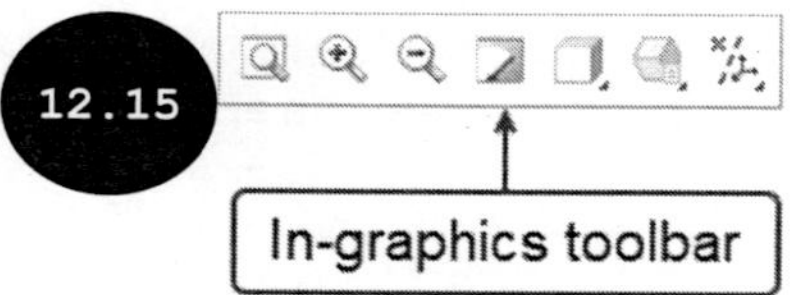

On selecting the **Wireframe** option in the **Display style** drop-down list, all visibility and hidden edges of the model appear in the 'Wireframe' display style, see Figure 12.16 (a). On selecting the **Hidden** option, the model appears in the 'Hidden Line' display style, where the hidden edges of the model become visible and appear faded in the view, see Figure 12.16 (b). On selecting the **No Hidden** option, the model appears in the 'No Hidden' display style, where the hidden edges of the model are not visible in the view, see Figure 12.16 (c). On selecting the **Shading** option, the drawing view appears in the 'Shaded' display style without the display of model edges, see Figure 12.16 (d). On selecting the **Shading With Edges** option, the view appears in the 'Shaded With Edges' display style with the display of model edges, see Figure 12.16 (e).

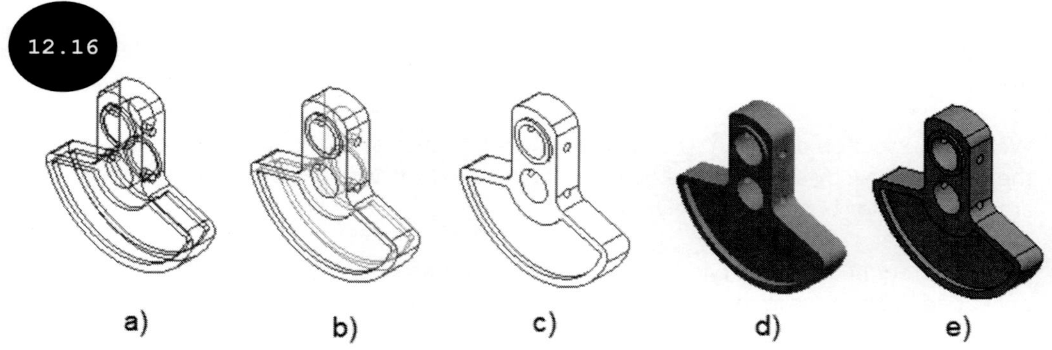

Tangent edges display style: The options in the **Tangent edges display style** drop-down list of the dialog box are used for defining the display style for the tangent edges of the model in the drawing view. By default, the **Default** option is selected. As a result, the tangent edges of the model appear in default display style in the view. On selecting the **None** option, the display of the tangent edges of the model gets turned off in the view, see Figure 12.17 (a). On selecting the **Solid** option, the tangent edges of the model appear as solid lines, see Figure 12.17 (b). On selecting the **Dimmed** option, the tangent edges of the model appear in a dimmed color, see Figure 12.17 (c). On selecting the **Centerline** option, the tangent edges of the model appear as centerlines, see Figure 12.17 (d). On selecting the **Phantom** option, the tangent edges of the model appear as phantom lines, see Figure 12.17 (e). Note that in Figure 12.17, the orientation of the view is defined as isometric and the display style is defined as 'No Hidden' display style.

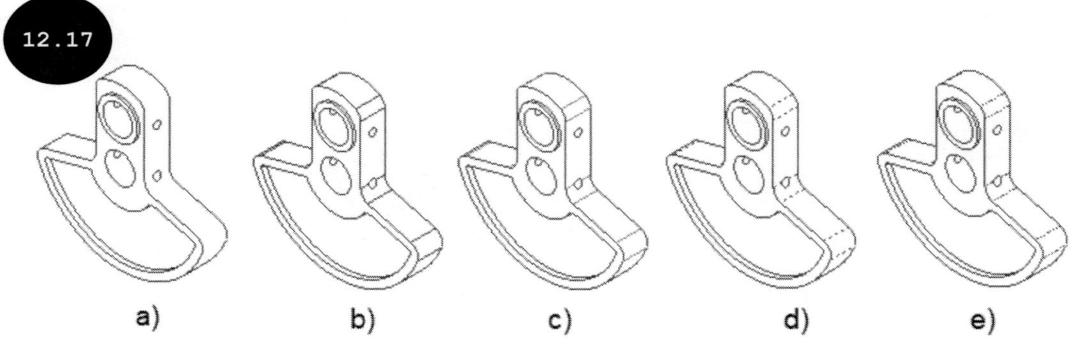

Hidden line removal for quilts: In Creo Parametric, you can remove or keep the hidden lines from the surface model by selecting the **Yes** or **No** radio button in the **Hidden line removal for quilts** area of the dialog box, respectively.

Skeleton model display: You can hide or show the skeleton model in the drawing view by selecting the **Hide** or **Show** radio button in the **Skeleton model display** area of the dialog box, respectively.

Hidden line removal for xhatches: You can remove or keep the display of hidden lines from the cross-hatches view by selecting the **Yes** or **No** radio button in the **Hidden line removal for xhatches** area of the dialog box, respectively.

Colors come from: You can define the drawing colors by using the drawing settings or model settings by selecting the **The drawing** or **The model** radio button in the **Colors come from** area of the dialog box, respectively.

Weldment xsection display: You can hide or show the display of the weldment cross-sections in the drawing view by selecting the **Hide** or **Show** radio button in the **Weldment xsection display** area of the dialog box, respectively.

14. Select the required display style of the view such as Wireframe, Hidden Line, No Hidden, Shaded, or Shaded With Edges in the **Display style** drop-down list of the dialog box.

15. Select the required display style for the tangent edges of the model in the **Tangent edges display style** drop-down list of the dialog box.

Note: The remaining options of the **Drawing View** dialog box are discussed later in this chapter.

16. You can similarly specify the other attributes for the drawing view and then click on the **Apply** button. Next, click on the **OK** button. The general view of specified orientation and attributes is created in the specified location of the drawing sheet and the dialog box is closed.

Creating Projection Views

Projection views are orthogonal views of an object, which are created by viewing an object from different projection sides such as top, front, and side. Figures 12.18 and 12.19 show different projection views of an object.

12.18

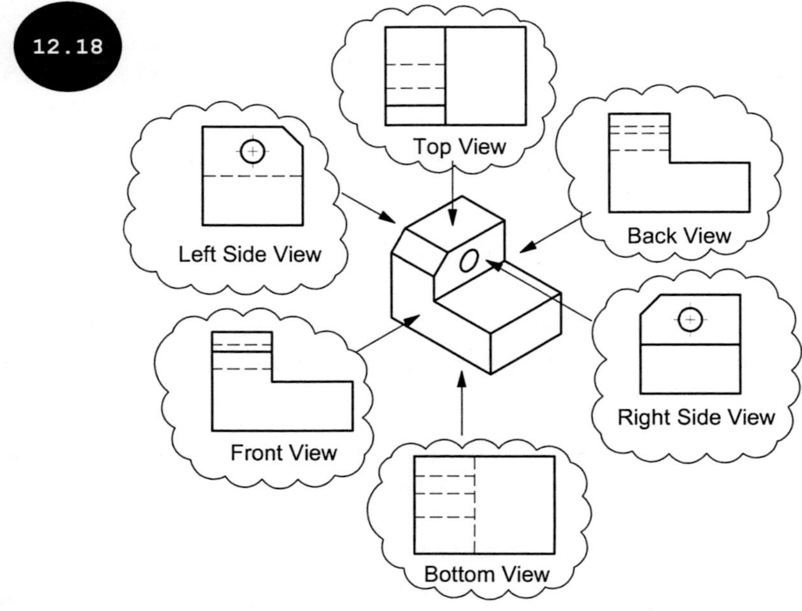

Projected Views

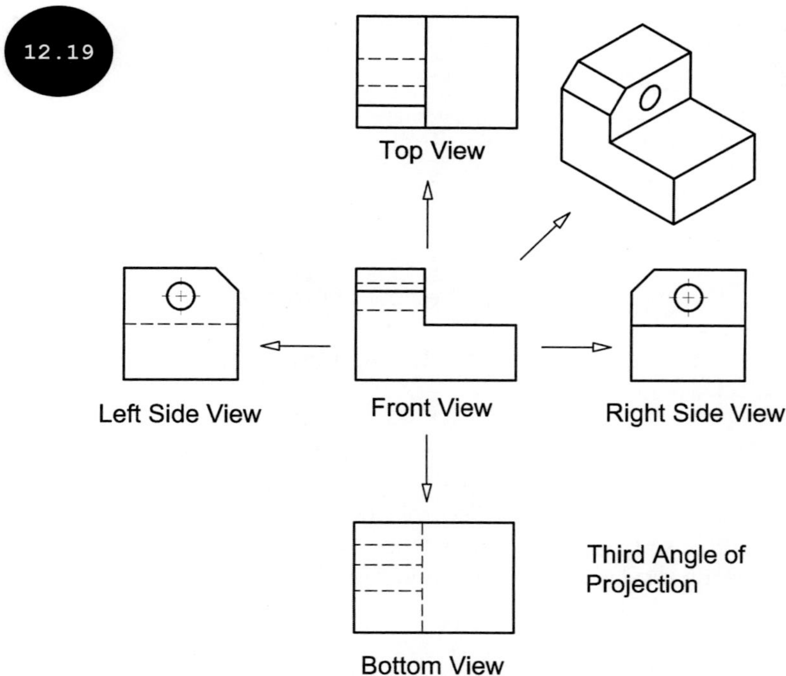

In Creo Parametric, you can create projection views by using the **Projection View** tool of the **Model Views** group, see Figure 12.20. The method for creating projection views is discussed below:

1. Click on the **Projection View** tool in the **Model Views** group in the **Layout** tab, see Figure 12.20. You are prompted to select a drawing view as the parent view whose projection view is to be created.

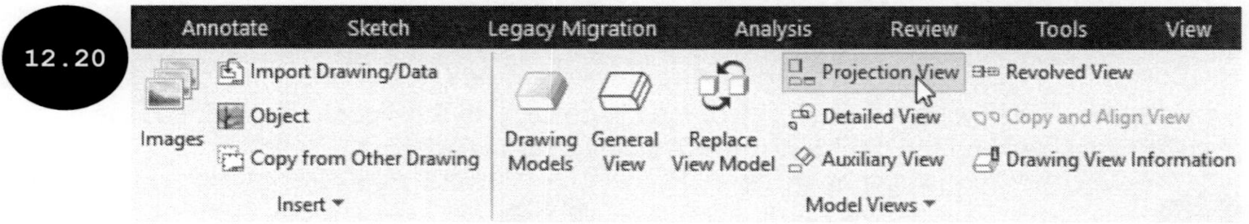

Note: If only one drawing view is available in the drawing sheet then it is automatically selected for creating its projection view. Also, the preview of the projection view is attached to the cursor. However, if two or more than two views are available in the drawing sheet, then you need to select a view whose projection view is to be created.

2. Select a drawing view in the sheet whose projection view is to be created. A rectangular box representing the preview of the projection view gets attached to the cursor, see Figure 12.21.

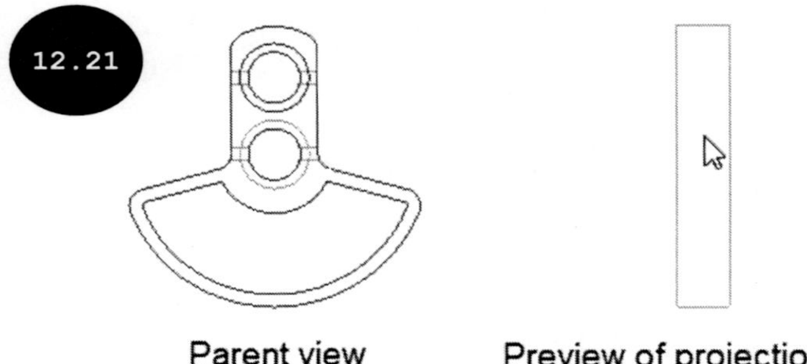

3. Move the cursor to the required side of the parent view in the drawing sheet for creating top, front, right, or left projection views, respectively.

4. Click to specify the placement point for the projection view at the required location in the drawing sheet. Depending on the placement point specified, the respective projection view gets created, see Figure 12.22. Note that the scale factor of the projection view is the same as the scale of the parent view. However, the display style of the projection view is as per the default display style. You can change the default display style of the Projection view by invoking the **Drawing View** dialog box.

   Now, you need to change the display style of the projection view, as required.

5. Double-click on the projection view in the drawing sheet. The **Drawing View** dialog box appears.

6. Click on the **View Display** category in the **Categories** area of the dialog box to display the options for defining the display style of the selected view.

7. Select the required display style in the **Display style** drop-down list of the dialog box. You can also define other attributes for the selected view, as discussed earlier.

8. Click on the **Apply** button in the dialog box and then the **OK** button. The display style of the projection view is changed as specified, see Figure 12.23. In this figure, the 'Hidden Line' display style is specified and the display of tangent edges is turned off.

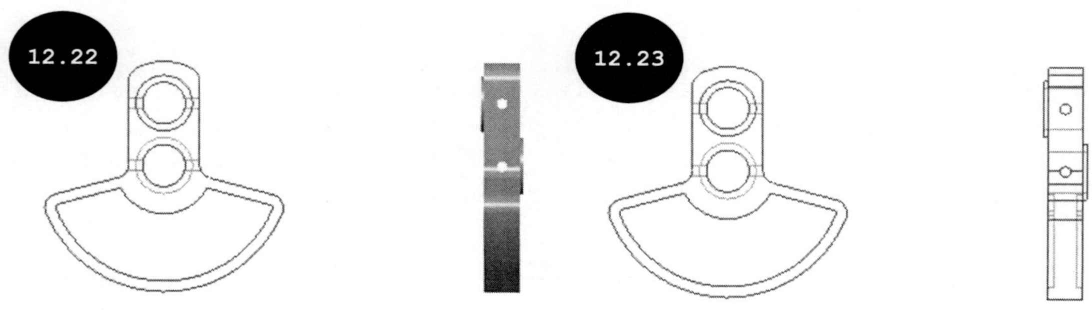

9. Similarly, you can create other projection views by using the **Projection View** tool and change their display style.

Note: The creation of projection views depends upon the angle of projection defined for the drawing sheet. You can define the first angle of projection or the third angle of projection for creating the projection views. The concept of angle of projection and the method to define the angle of projection for the drawing are discussed next.

Working with Angle of Projection

Engineering drawings follow two types of angles of projection: the first angle of projection and the third angle of projection. In the first angle of projection, the object is assumed to be kept in the first quadrant and the viewer views the object from the direction as shown in Figure 12.24. As the object has been kept in the first quadrant, its projections of views are on the respective planes as shown in Figure 12.24. Now on unfolding the planes of projections, the front view appears on the upper side and the top view appears on the bottom side. Also, the right side view appears on the left and the left side view appears on the right side of the front view, see Figure 12.25. Similarly, in the third angle of projection, the object is assumed to be kept in the third quadrant, see Figure 12.24. In this angle of projection, the projection of the front view appears on the bottom and the projection of the top view appears on the top side in the drawing. Also, the right side view appears on the right and the left side view appears on the left of the front view, see Figure 12.26.

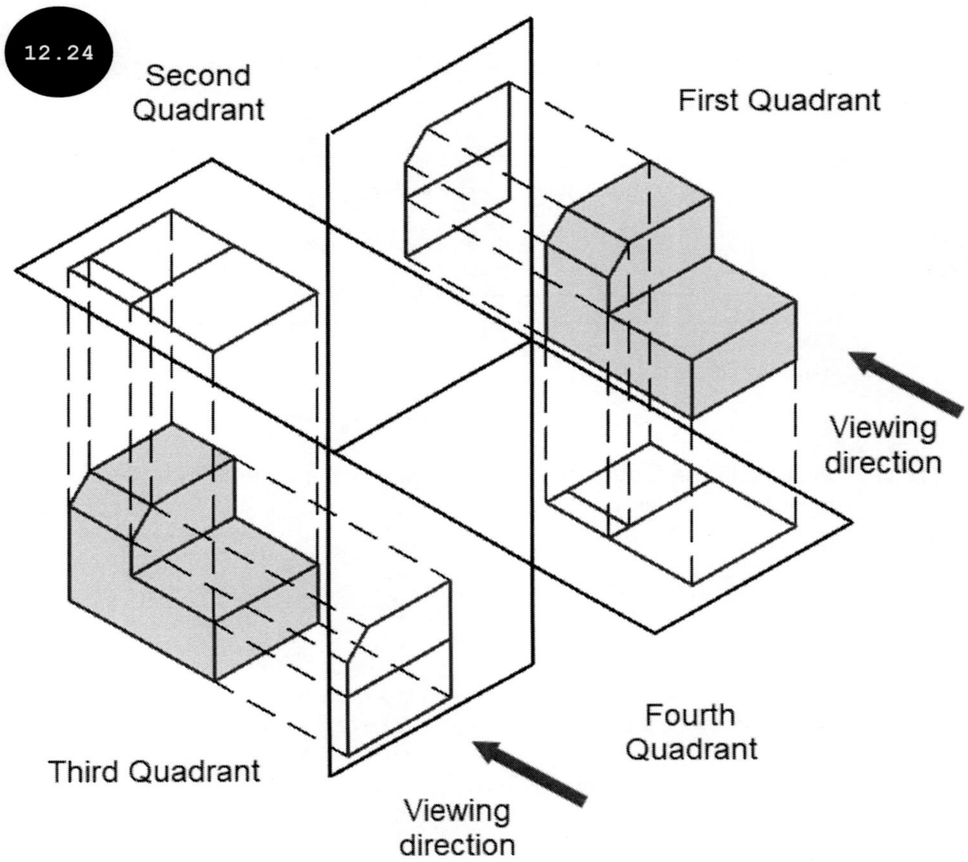

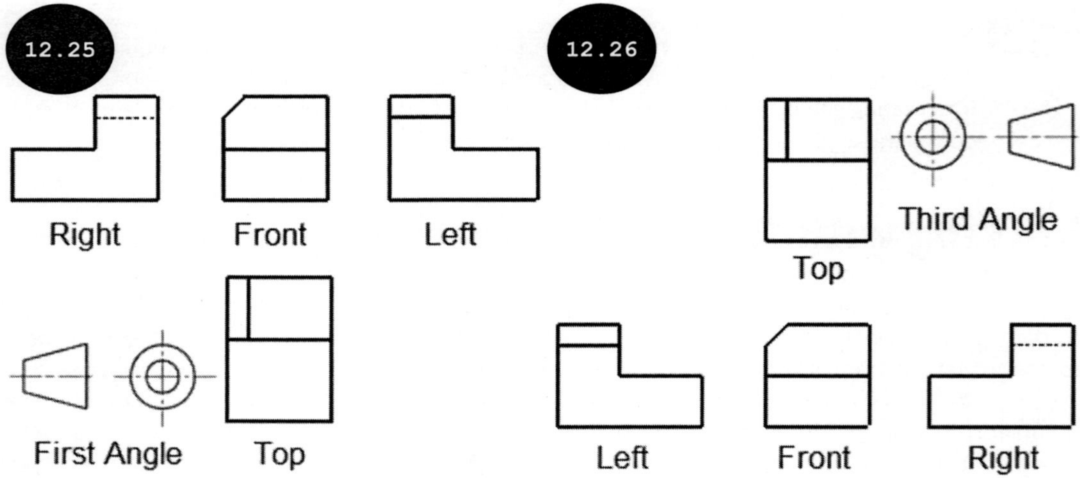

Defining the Angle of Projection

In Creo Parametric, you can define the required angle of projection for creating drawing views by using the **Drawing Properties** dialog box. The method for defining the angle of projection is discussed below:

1. Click on **File > Prepare > Drawing Properties**. The **Drawing Properties** dialog box appears, see Figure 12.27.
2. Click on the **change** option that appears on the right of **Detail Options** in the dialog box, see Figure 12.27. The **Options** dialog box appears, see Figure 12.28.

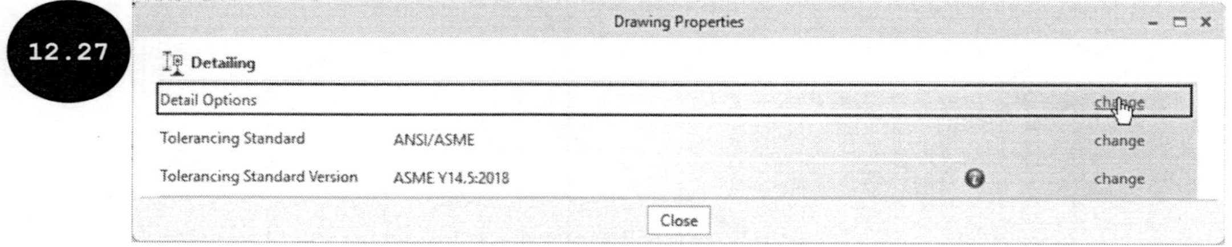

3. Enter **projection_type** in the **Option** field that appears at the lower left corner of the **Options** dialog box (see Figure 12.28), and then click on the **Find** button. The **Find Option** dialog box appears, see Figure 12.29.
4. Select the required angle of projection (**third_angle** or **first_angle**) in the **Set value** drop-down list of the **Find Option** dialog box, see Figure 12.29.
5. After selecting the required angle of projection, click on the **Add / Change** button in the **Find Option** dialog box and then click on the **Close** button to exit the dialog box.
6. Close the **Options** dialog box by clicking on the **Close** button.

12.28

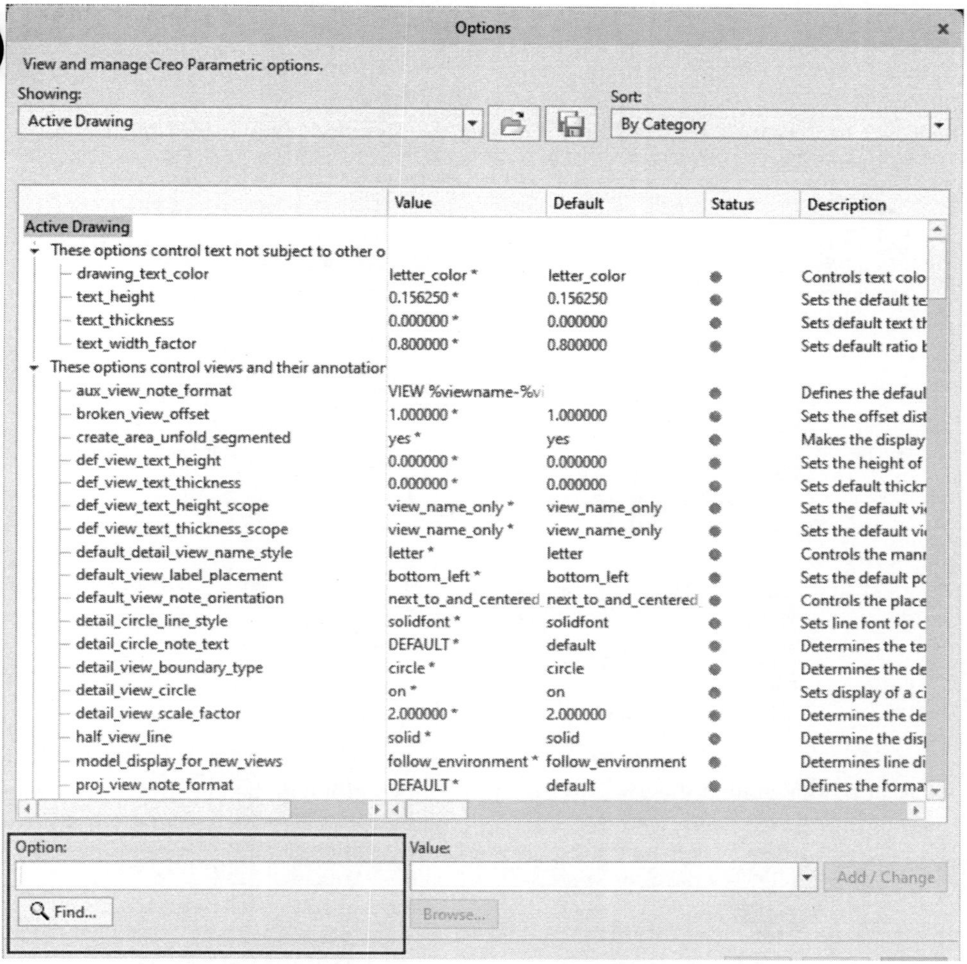

Options

View and manage Creo Parametric options.

Showing: Active Drawing

Sort: By Category

	Value	Default	Status	Description
Active Drawing				
These options control text not subject to other o				
drawing_text_color	letter_color *	letter_color	●	Controls text colo
text_height	0.156250 *	0.156250	●	Sets the default te
text_thickness	0.000000 *	0.000000	●	Sets default text th
text_width_factor	0.800000 *	0.800000	●	Sets default ratio b
These options control views and their annotatior				
aux_view_note_format	VIEW %viewname-%v		●	Defines the defaul
broken_view_offset	1.000000 *	1.000000	●	Sets the offset dist
create_area_unfold_segmented	yes *	yes	●	Makes the display
def_view_text_height	0.000000 *	0.000000	●	Sets the height of
def_view_text_thickness	0.000000 *	0.000000	●	Sets default thickr
def_view_text_height_scope	view_name_only *	view_name_only	●	Sets the default vi
def_view_text_thickness_scope	view_name_only *	view_name_only	●	Sets the default vi
default_detail_view_name_style	letter *	letter	●	Controls the mann
default_view_label_placement	bottom_left *	bottom_left	●	Sets the default pc
default_view_note_orientation	next_to_and_centered	next_to_and_centered	●	Controls the place
detail_circle_line_style	solidfont *	solidfont	●	Sets line font for c
detail_circle_note_text	DEFAULT *	default	●	Determines the te
detail_view_boundary_type	circle *	circle	●	Determines the de
detail_view_circle	on *	on	●	Sets display of a ci
detail_view_scale_factor	2.000000 *	2.000000	●	Determines the de
half_view_line	solid *	solid	●	Determine the disp
model_display_for_new_views	follow_environment *	follow_environment	●	Determines line di
proj_view_note_format	DEFAULT *	default	●	Defines the forma

Option: [ ] Find...

Value: [ ] Add / Change Browse...

12.29

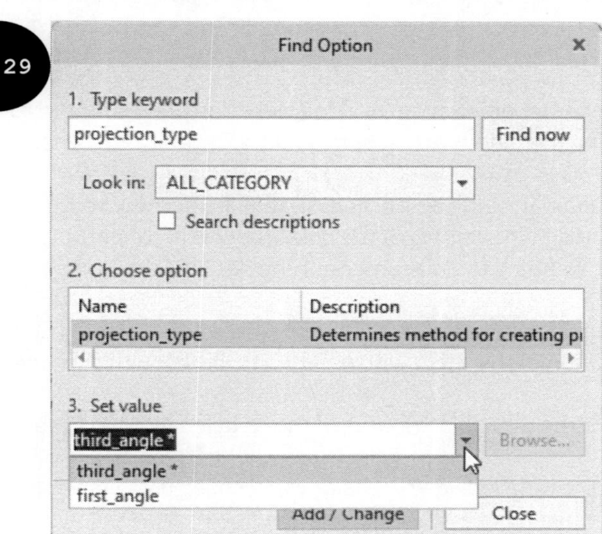

Creating a Detailed View

A detailed view is used for showing a portion of an existing drawing view in an enlarged scale, see Figure 12.30. You can define a portion of an existing drawing view to be enlarged by creating a closed spline. You can create a detailed view by using the **Detailed View** tool. The method for creating a detailed view is discussed below:

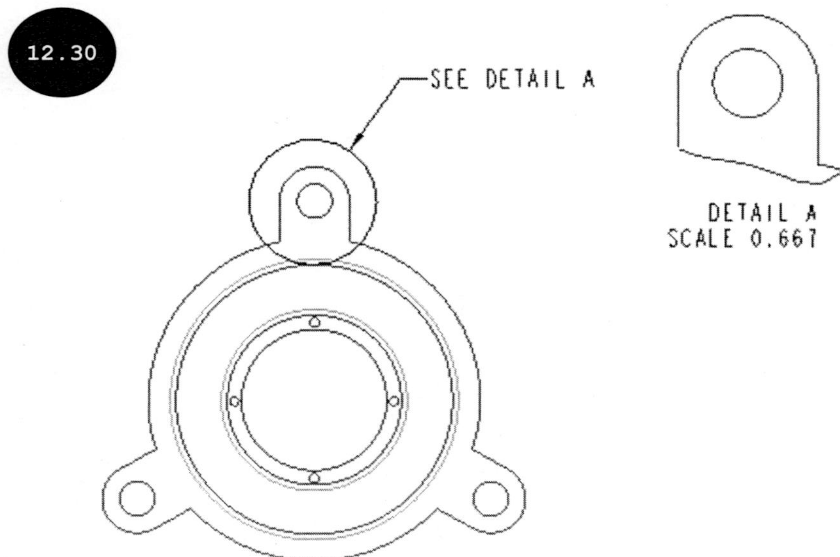

1. Click on the **Detailed View** tool in the **Model Views** group in the **Layout** tab, see Figure 12.31. You are prompted to specify a center point for creating a detailed view of an existing view.

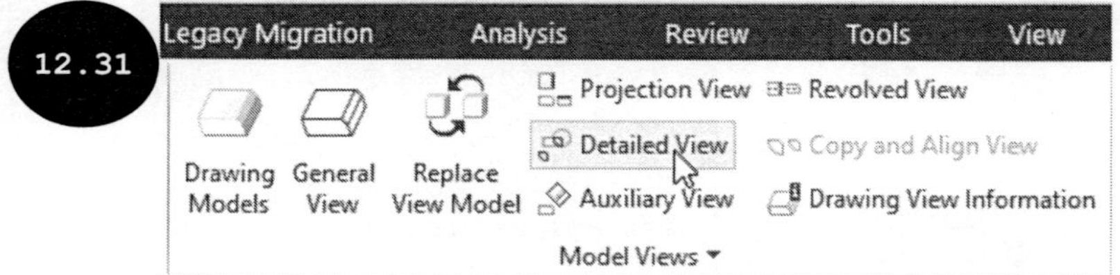

2. Click to specify a center point on an existing view. You are prompted to draw a spline to define an outline for creating the detailed view without intersecting with other splines.

3. Draw a closed spline around the portion of an existing view to be enlarged and then press the middle mouse button. The outline of the detailed view is defined and you are prompted to specify a center point for defining the placement of the detailed view on the sheet.

4. Click to define the placement of the detailed view on the sheet. The detailed view is created on the specified location of the sheet with default attributes such as name, scale, and boundary type.

   Now, you can edit the default attributes of the detailed view, as required.

5. Double-click on the detailed view in the drawing sheet. The **Drawing View** dialog box appears.

6. Ensure that the **View Type** category is selected in the **Categories** area of the dialog box.
7. Enter a new name for the detailed view in the **View name** field of the dialog box, if needed.
8. Select the required option in the **Boundary type on parent view** drop-down list to define the type of boundary on the parent view.
9. Select or clear the **Show boundary on detailed view** check box in the dialog box to show or hide the boundary on the detailed view, respectively.
10. Click on the **Apply** button in the dialog box and then the **OK** button to apply the changes and close the dialog box.

Tip: To edit the text font or size, double-click on the text to be edited. The **Format** tab appears in the **Ribbon**. By using the options of this tab, you can change the font, height, alignment, color, etc. of the selected text. After editing the text, click anywhere on the sheet.

Creating an Auxiliary View

An auxiliary view is a projected view, which is created by projecting the edges of an object normal to the edge of an existing drawing view, see Figure 12.32. The method for creating an auxiliary view is discussed below:

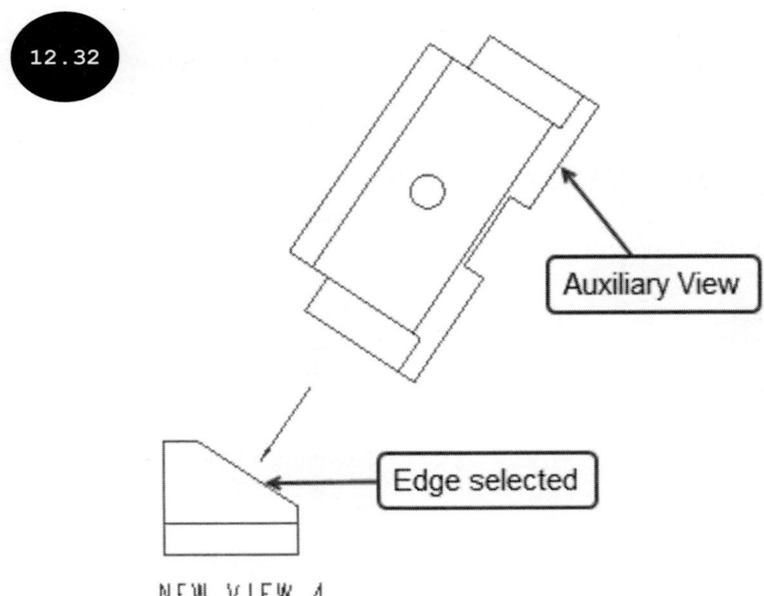

1. Click on the **Auxiliary View** tool in the **Model Views** group in the **Layout** tab. You are prompted to select an edge, an axis, or a datum plane of the parent view.

2. Select an edge of an existing drawing view to create an auxiliary view by projecting the edges of the model normal to the edge selected. You are prompted to specify a center point for defining the placement of the auxiliary view on the sheet.

3. Click to define the placement of the auxiliary view on the sheet. The auxiliary view is created on the specified location. Note that the scale factor of the auxiliary view is the same as the scale of the parent view. However, its display style is as per the default display style. You can change the default display style and display of the projection arrow by using the **Drawing View** dialog box.

   Now, you need to change the display style of the auxiliary view and the projection arrow.

4. Double-click on the auxiliary view in the drawing sheet. The **Drawing View** dialog box appears.

5. Ensure that the **View Type** category is selected in the **Categories** area of the dialog box.

6. Select the required radio button in the **Projection Arrows** area of the dialog box. On selecting the **None** radio button, the projection arrow is not displayed on the sheet. On selecting the **Single** radio button, a single projection arrow appears on the sheet. On selecting the **Double** radio button, double projection arrows appear on the sheet.

7. Click on the **Apply** button in the dialog box and then click on the **View Display** category in the **Categories** area of the dialog box to display the options for defining the display style.

8. Select the required display style for the auxiliary view by using the options in the dialog box.

9. Click on the **Apply** button in the dialog box and then the **OK** button. The display style of the auxiliary view is changed, as specified.

Creating a Revolved View

A revolved view is used for showing the cross-sectional slice of an existing view by revolving the section 90 degrees about the cutting plane, see Figure 12.33. The method for creating a revolved view is discussed below:

12.33

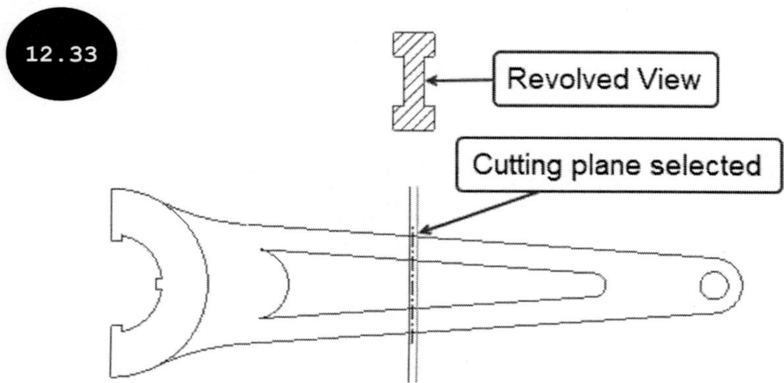

1. Click on the **Revolved View** tool in the **Model Views** group in the **Layout** tab, see Figure 12.34. You are prompted to select an existing view as the parent view for creating its revolved section.

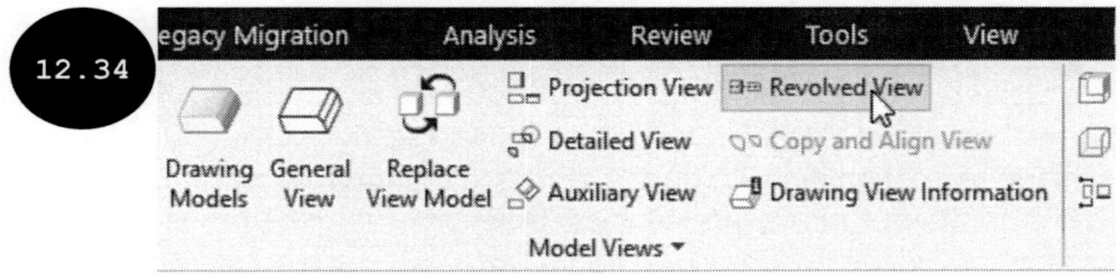

2. Click on an existing view in the drawing sheet. You are prompted to specify a center point on the drawing sheet to define the placement of the revolved view.

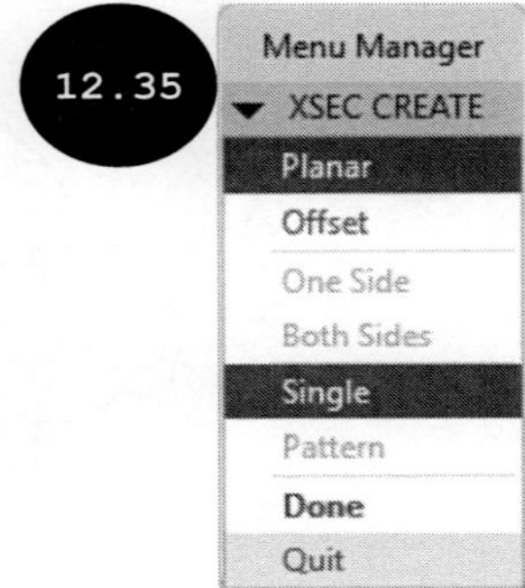

3. Click anywhere on the drawing sheet. The **Drawing View** dialog box appears. Also, the **XSEC CREATE** menu appears on the lower right corner of the sheet, see Figure 12.35. Note that the **XSEC CREATE** menu appears if the **Create New** option is selected in the **Cross-section** drop-down list of the **View Type** category in the dialog box, by default.

4. Ensure that the **View Type** category is selected in the **Drawing View** dialog box.

5. Ensure that the **Create New** option is selected in the **Cross-section** drop-down list of the **Revolved view properties** area in the dialog box.

6. Click on the **Planar** > **Single** > **Done** in the **XSEC CREATE** menu, see Figure 12.35. The **Message Input** window appears at the top middle area of the sheet and you are prompted to specify the name of the cross-section to be created.

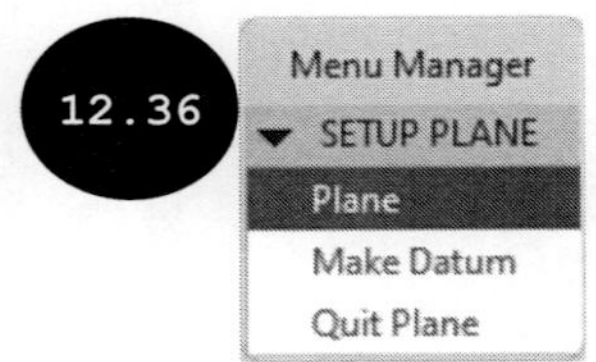

7. Enter the name of the cross-section in the **Message Input** window and then click on the green tick-mark button that appears on its right. The **SETUP PLANE** menu appears (see Figure 12.36), and you are prompted to select a planar face or a datum plane as the cutting plane for creating the revolved view.

8. Select a datum plane of the parent view as the cutting plane, refer to Figure 12.33. The resultant revolved view gets placed in line with the selected cutting plane.

9. Click on the **Apply** button and then close the dialog box.

Note: If the revolved view is placed on an existing view, then you can move it to define its placement on the sheet. To do so, click on the revolved view on the sheet and then press and hold the right-click to display a shortcut menu. Next, click on the **Lock View Movement** option in the shortcut menu to lock or unlock the movement of the view on the sheet. After unlocking the movement of the view, you can change its position on the sheet by dragging it to a new location on the sheet.

Creating a Section View

A section view is created cutting an object by using a cutting plane and then viewing the object from the direction normal to the cutting plane. Figure 12.37 shows a section view created by cutting an object using a cutting plane. A section view is used to illustrate the internal features of the object clearly. It also reduces the number of hidden-detail lines, facilitates the dimensioning of internal features, shows cross-section, and so on. In Creo Parametric, you can create a full section view, half section view, offset section view, local section view, full (aligned) section view, and full (unfold) section view on a projection view by using the options in the **Drawing View** dialog box. The various types of section views are discussed below:

12.37

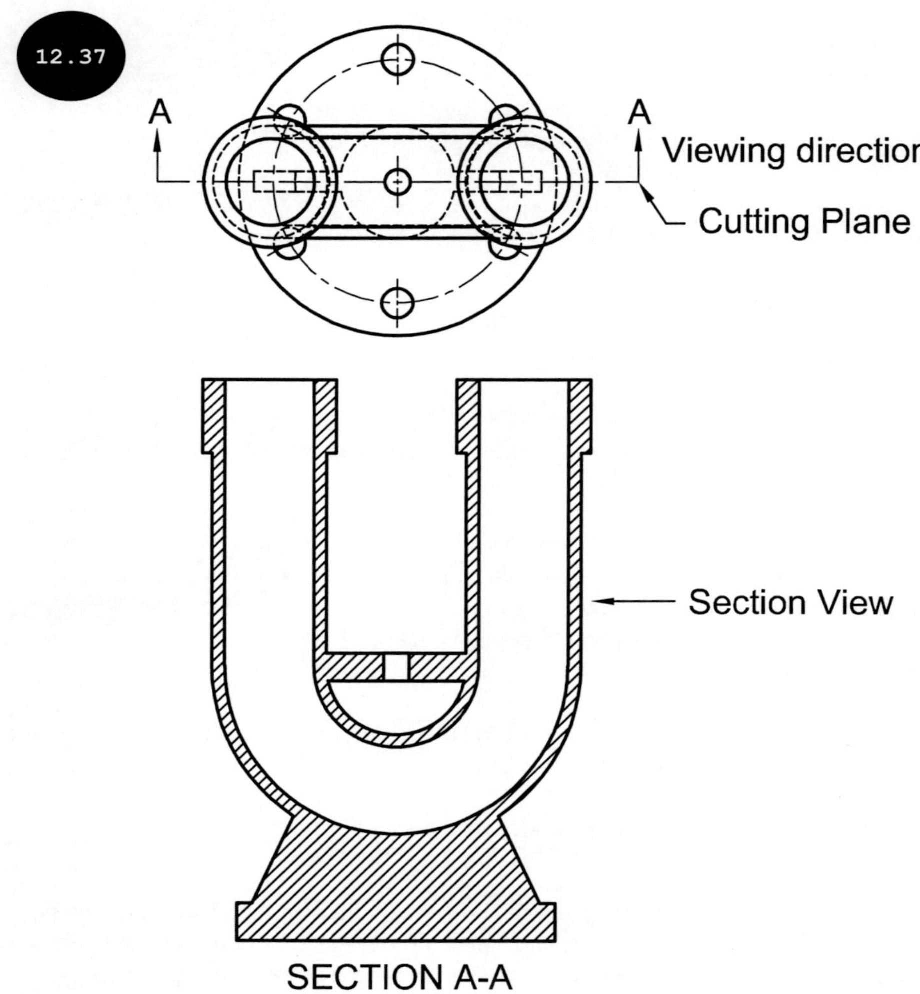

Creating a Full Section View

Full section views are the most widely used section views in engineering drawings. In a full section view, an object is assumed to be cut through all its length by a cutting plane, refer to Figure 12.37. The method for creating a full section view is discussed below:

1. Create a projection view from an existing view in the drawing sheet for creating the section view, see Figure 12.38.

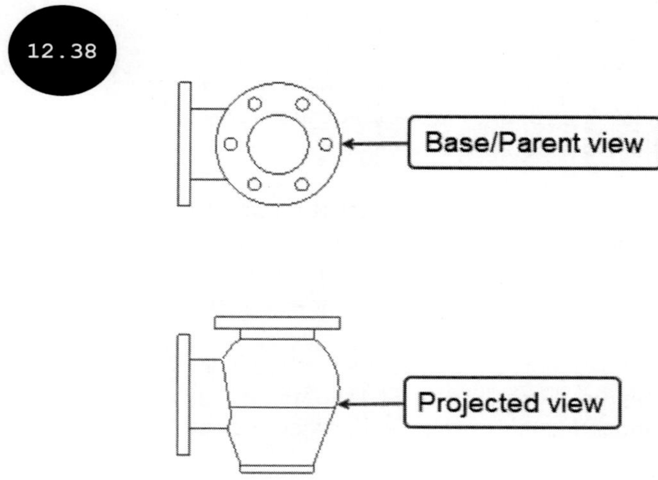

2. Double-click on the projection view to creating the section view. The **Drawing View** dialog box appears.

3. Click on the **Sections** category in the **Categories** area of the dialog box. The options for creating a section view appear on the right panel of the dialog box, see Figure 12.39.

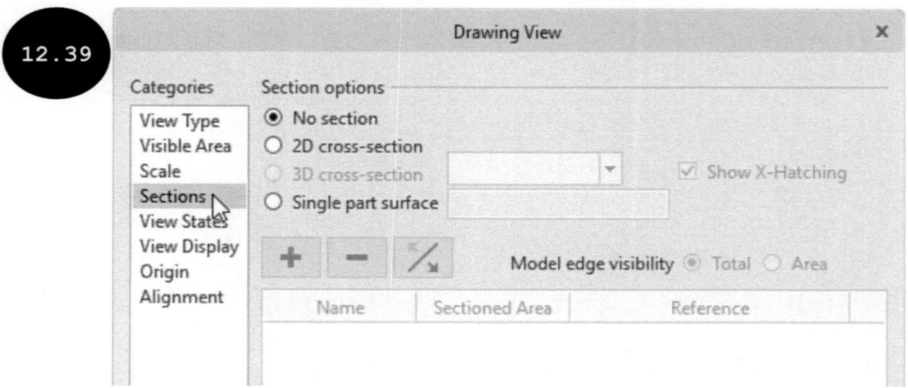

4. Select the **2D cross-section** radio button in the dialog box. The **Add cross-section to view** button gets enabled in the dialog box. This button is used for defining a section plane for creating a section view.

5. Click on the **Add cross-section to view** button in the dialog box. The **Name** and **Sectioned Area** drop-down lists are added in the **Drawing View** dialog box. Also, the **XSEC CREATE** menu appears on the lower right corner of the sheet, see Figure 12.40. Note that the **XSEC CREATE** menu appears if the **Create New** option is selected in the **Name** drop-down list of the **Drawing View** dialog box, by default.

6. Ensure that the **Create New** option is selected in the **Name** drop-down list of the dialog box for creating a new section view.

12.40

Menu Manager
XSEC CREATE
Planar
Offset
One Side
Both Sides
Single
Pattern
Done
Quit

7. Click on the **Planar** > **Single** > **Done** in the **XSEC CREATE** menu to define a cutting plane, see Figure 12.40. The **Message Input** window appears at the top middle area of the sheet and you are prompted to specify the name of the cross-section to be created.

8. Enter the name of the cross-section in the **Message Input** window and then click on the green tick-mark button that appears on its right. The **SETUP PLANE** menu appears, see Figure 12.41. Also, you are prompted to select a planar face or a datum plane as the cutting plane.

9. Select a datum plane from the parent view as the cutting plane, see Figure 12.42. The name of the section view appears in the **Name** drop-down list of the dialog box. Note that the display of the green tick-mark in front of the name of the section view indicates that the section view has been generated.

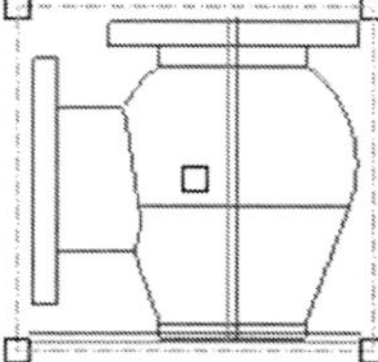

Now, you need to define the type of section view to be created such as full, half, or local.

10. Ensure that the **Full** option is selected in the **Sectioned Area** drop-down list of the dialog box to create a full section view.

Now, you need to define a view for displaying the section arrows.

11. Scroll to the right to display the **Arrow Display** collector in the dialog box. Next, click on the **Arrow Display** collector to activate it. You are prompted to select the parent view for displaying the section arrows.

12. Click on the parent view to display the section arrows on it. The name of the view selected appears in the **Arrow Display** collector of the dialog box.

13. Click on the **Apply** button in the dialog box. The section view is created and the section arrows appear on the selected parent view, see Figure 12.43.

Note: In Figure 12.43, the display of datum planes is turned off for clarity of image. To turn off the display of datum planes, invoke the **Datum Display Filters** flyout in the **In-graphics** toolbar and then clear the **Plane Display** check box.

14. Click on the **Flip** button in the dialog box to reverse the viewing direction, if needed. Next, click on the **Apply** button.

    You can also control the display of the model edges in the section view by selecting the **Total** or **Area** radio button in the dialog box. By default, the **Total** radio button is selected. As a result, the section view is created such that it displays cross-sectional edges as well as the edges of the model that are visible after the model is sectioned, see Figure 12.43. On selecting the **Area** radio button, only the cross-sectional edges appear in the section view, see Figure 12.44.

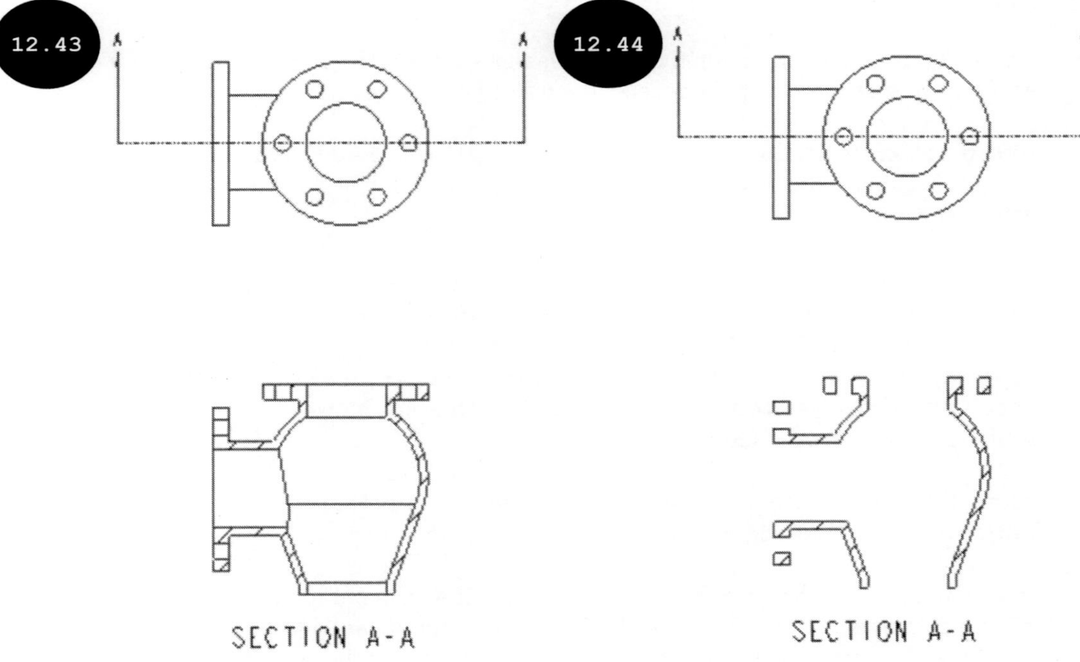

15. Select the **Total** or **Area** radio button in the dialog box, as required.

16. Click on the **OK** button to close the dialog box.

Creating a Half Section View

A half section view is created by cutting an object halfway through its length, see Figure 12.45. The method for creating a half section view is discussed below:

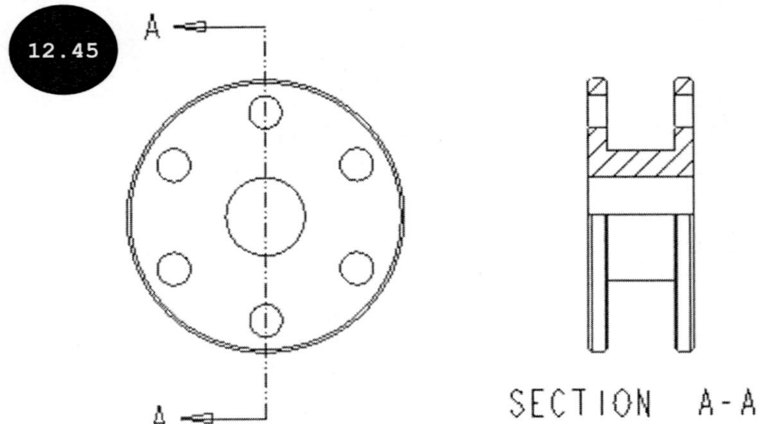

1. Double-click on a projection view for creating a half section view. The **Drawing View** dialog box appears.

2. Click on the **Sections** category in the **Categories** area of the dialog box. The options for creating a section view appear on the right panel of the dialog box.

3. Select the **2D cross-section** radio button in the dialog box. The **Add cross-section to view** button + gets enabled in the dialog box. This button is used for defining a section plane for creating a section view.

4. Click on the **Add cross-section to view** button + in the dialog box. The **Name** drop-down list is added in the **Drawing View** dialog box. Also, the **XSEC CREATE** menu appears on the lower right corner of the sheet, see Figure 12.46. Note that the **XSEC CREATE** menu appears if the **Create New** option is selected in the **Name** drop-down list of the dialog box, by default.

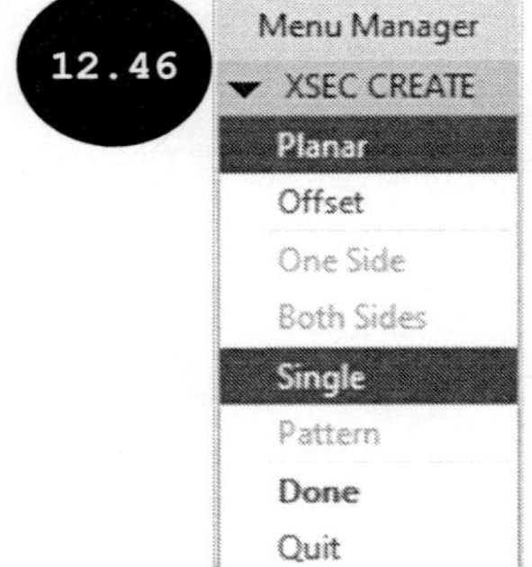

5. Ensure that the **Create New** option is selected in the **Name** drop-down list of the dialog box for creating a new section view.

6. Click on the **Planar > Single > Done** in the **XSEC CREATE** menu to define a cutting plane, see Figure 12.46. The **Message Input** window appears at the top middle area of the sheet and you are prompted to specify the name of the cross-section to be created.

7. Enter the name of the cross-section in the **Message Input** window and then click on the green tick-mark button that appears on its right. The **SETUP PLANE** menu appears, see Figure 12.47. Also, you are prompted to select a planar face or a datum plane as the cutting plane.

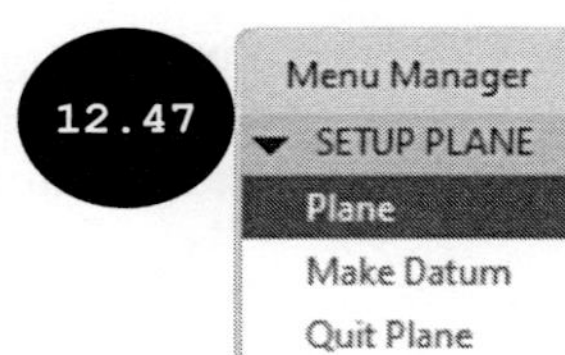

8. Select a datum plane from the parent view as the cutting plane, see Figure 12.48. The name of the section view appears in the **Name** drop-down list of the dialog box. Note that the display of the green tick-mark in front of the name of the section view indicates that the section view is generated correctly.

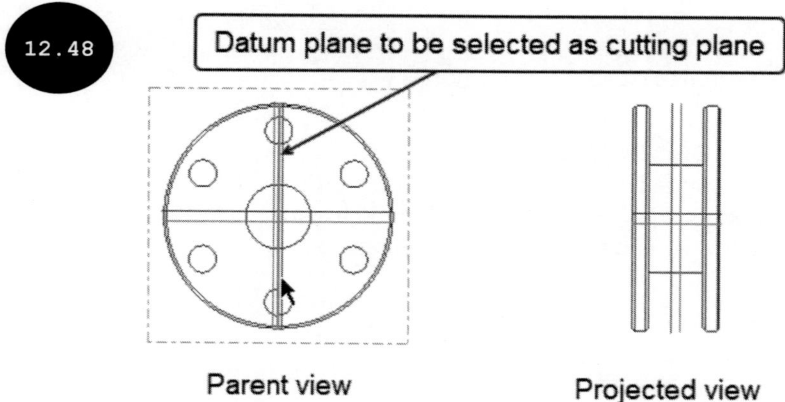

Now, you need to define the type of section view as half section view.

9. Select the **Half** option in the **Sectioned Area** drop-down list of the dialog box to create a half section view. The **Reference** collector gets enabled in the dialog box and you are prompted to select a reference plane for creating the half section view.

10. Select a reference plane that is non parallel to the cutting plane selected, see Figure 12.49. The **Boundary** collector gets enabled in the dialog box and you are prompted to specify the side of the reference plane to be sectioned in the view. Also, an arrow appears in the view that is pointing toward the side to be sectioned. Note that you can select a reference plane in the parent view or in the view to be sectioned.

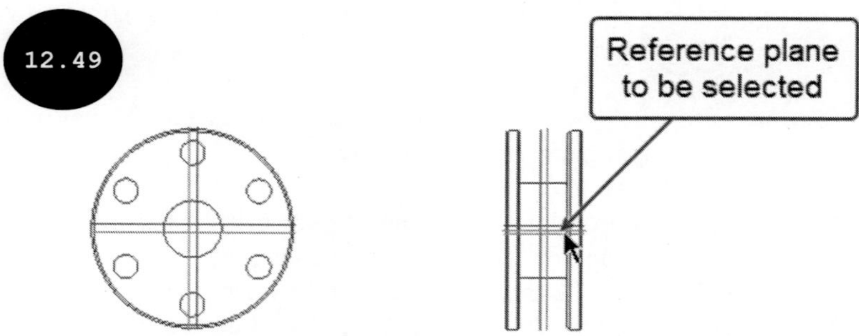

11. Click on the side of the reference plane to be sectioned in the view.

    Now, you need to select a view for displaying the section arrows.

12. Scroll to the right of the dialog box to display the **Arrow Display** collector. Next, click on the **Arrow Display** collector to activate it. You are prompted to select the parent view for displaying the section arrows.

13. Click on the parent view to display the section arrows on it. The name of the selected view appears in the **Arrow Display** collector of the dialog box.

14. Click on the **Apply** button in the dialog box. The half section view is created. You can also reverse the direction of arrows by using the **Flip** button of the dialog box.

15. Click on the **OK** button to close the dialog box.

Creating an Offset Section View

An offset section view is created by bending the imaginary cutting plane or section line such that it cuts the portion of the object that cannot be sectioned through a straight cutting plane, see Figure 12.50. The method for creating an offset section view is discussed below:

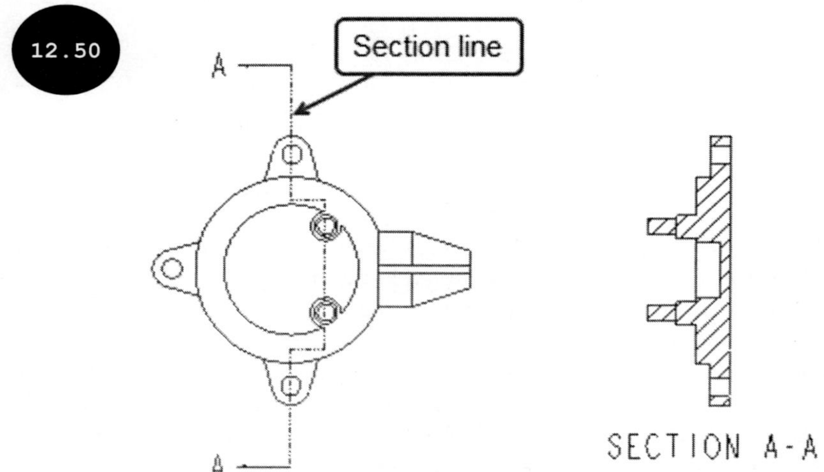

1. Double-click on a projection view to create an offset section view. The **Drawing View** dialog box appears.

2. Click on the **Sections** category in the **Categories** area of the dialog box. The options for creating a section view appear on the right panel of the dialog box.

3. Select the **2D cross-section** radio button in the dialog box and then click on the **Add cross-section to view** button **+** in the dialog box. The **Name** drop-down list is added in the **Drawing View** dialog box. Also, the **XSEC CREATE** menu appears on the lower right corner of the sheet, if the **Create New** option is selected in the **Name** drop-down list of the dialog box, by default.

4. Ensure that the **Create New** option is selected in the **Name** drop-down list of the dialog box for creating a new section view.

5. Click on the **Offset > Both Sides > Single > Done** in the **XSEC CREATE** menu to define a cutting plane, see Figure 12.51. The **Message Input** window appears at the top middle area of the sheet and you are prompted to specify the name of the cross-section to be created.

6. Enter the name of the cross-section in the **Message Input** window and then click on the green tick-mark button that appears on its right. The **SETUP SK PLN** menu appears, see Figure 12.52. Also, the 3D model of the view selected appears on the screen and you are prompted to select a sketching plane for creating the sketch of the section line.

7. Select the sketching plane for creating the sketch of the section line. The options in the **SETUP SK PLN** menu get changed (see Figure 12.53), and you are prompted to define the viewing direction to orient the sketching plane normal to the screen.

8. Click on the **Okay** option in the **SETUP SK PLN** menu or press the middle mouse button. Next, click on the **Default** option in the menu.

Note: If the **References** dialog box appears, select the required edges of the model to define references for creating the section line and then close the dialog box.

9. Click on **View > Orientation > Sketch Orientation** in the **Menu Bar**. The sketching plane gets oriented normal to the viewing direction, and you are prompted to create the sketch of the section line.

10. Create a sketch of the section line by using the sketching tools available in the **Sketch** tab or **Sketch** menu, see Figure 12.54.

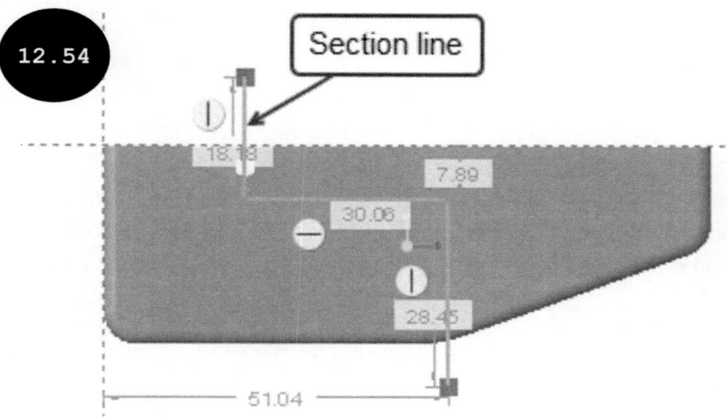

Note: The **Sketch** tab or **Sketch** menu appears for creating the sketch of the section line depending upon whether the 3D model was already opened in the current session of Creo Parametric. If the 3D model was already opened in the current session, then the **Sketch** tab appears in the **Ribbon** for creating the sketch.

11. After creating the section line, exit the Sketching environment by clicking on the **OK** tool in the **Close** group of the **Sketch** tab or the **Done** tool in the **Sketch** menu. The name of the section view appears in the **Name** drop-down list of the **Drawing View** dialog box.

12. Ensure that the **Full** option is selected in the **Sectioned Area** drop-down list of the dialog box.

    Now, you need to display the offset section arrows.

13. Scroll to the right of the dialog box to display the **Arrow Display** collector. Next, click on the **Arrow Display** collector to activate it. You are prompted to select the parent view for displaying the section arrows.

14. Click on the parent view to display the section arrows on it. The name of the selected view appears in the **Arrow Display** collector of the dialog box.

15. Click on the **Apply** button in the dialog box. The offset section view is created, see Figure 12.55. You can also reverse the direction of arrows by using the **Flip** button of the dialog box.

16. Click on the **OK** button to close the dialog box.

12.55

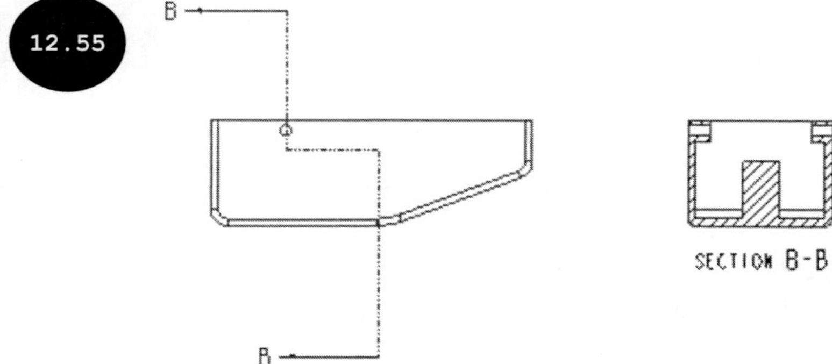

Creating a Local Section View

A local section view is created by removing or breaking out a portion of an existing view up to the cutting plane in order to view inner details of the object, see Figure 12.56. You can define the portion of an existing view to be removed by drawing a closed spline. The method for creating a local section view is discussed below:

1. Double-click on a projection view to create a local section view. The **Drawing View** dialog box appears.

2. Click on the **Sections** category in the **Categories** area of the dialog box. The options for creating a section view appear on the right panel of the dialog box.

3. Create a full section view on the selected view by using the **Drawing View** dialog box, as discussed earlier, see Figure 12.57. Note that to create a local section view, you first need to create a full section view. After creating the full section view, do not exit the **Drawing View** dialog box. In Figures 12.56 and 12.57, the display of datum planes is turned off for clarity of images.

4. After creating the full section view, select the **Local** option in the **Sectioned Area** drop-down list of the dialog box. The **Reference** collector gets enabled in the dialog box and you are prompted to specify a center point for the local section.

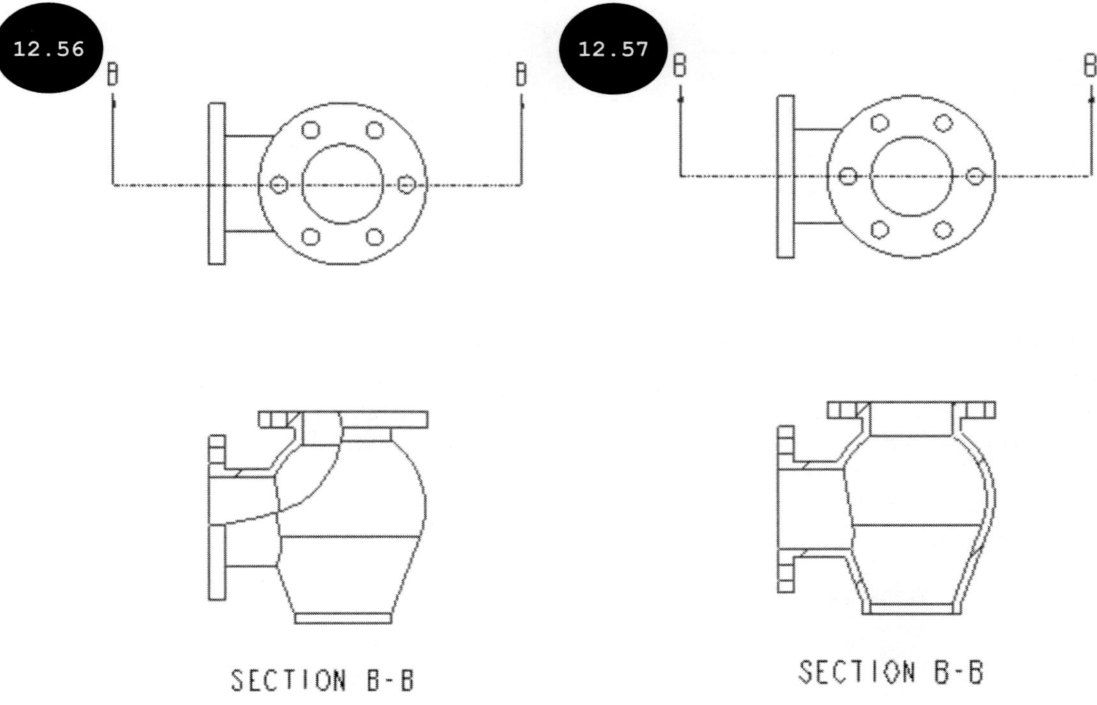

5. Click to define a center point for the local section on the view and then draw a closed spline around the portion to be broken out, see Figure 12.58.

6. After drawing a spline, press the middle mouse button. Next, click on the **Apply** button in the dialog box. The local section view is created such that only the portion lying inside the spline gets sectioned, see Figure 12.59.

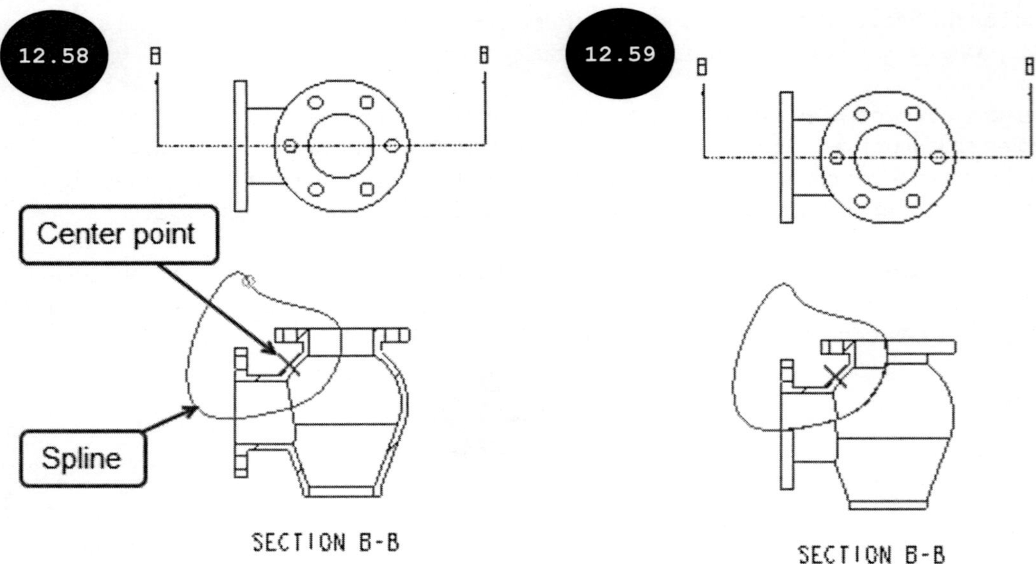

7. Click on the **OK** button to exit the dialog box.

Creating a Full (Aligned) Section View

A full (aligned) section view is created by cutting an object using the section line, which comprises two non-parallel lines, and then straightening the cross-section by revolving it around the center point of the section line, see Figure 12.60. The method for creating a full (aligned) section view is the same as that of creating an offset section view with the only difference being that in the full (aligned) section view the section gets straightened by revolving it around an axis. The method for creating a full (aligned) section view is discussed below:

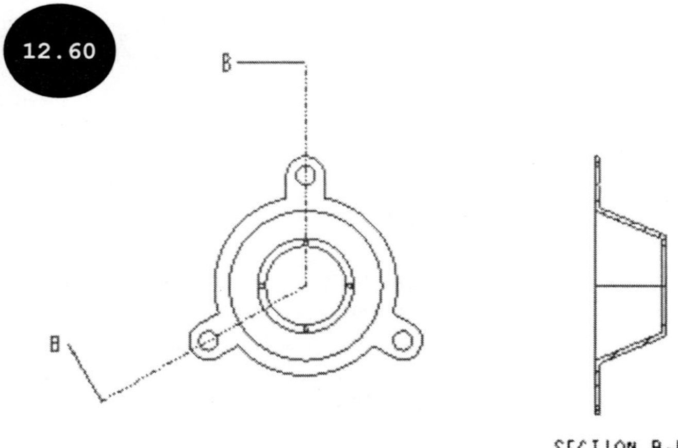

1. Double-click on a projection view to create a full (aligned) section view. The **Drawing View** dialog box appears.

2. Click on the **Sections** category in the **Categories** area of the dialog box. The options for creating a section view appear on the right panel of the dialog box.

3. Select the **2D cross-section** radio button in the dialog box and then click on the **Add cross-section to view** button **+** in the dialog box. The **Name** drop-down list is added in the **Drawing View** dialog box. Also, the **XSEC CREATE** menu appears on the lower right corner of the sheet, if the **Create New** option is selected in the **Name** drop-down list of the dialog box, by default.

4. Ensure that the **Create New** option is selected in the **Name** drop-down list of the dialog box.

5. Click on the **Offset > Both Sides > Single > Done** in the **XSEC CREATE** menu. The **Message Input** window appears at the top middle end of the sheet.

6. Enter the name of the cross-section in the **Message Input** window and then click on the green tick-mark button that appears on its right. The **SETUP SK PLN** menu appears. Also, the 3D model of the view selected appears on the screen and you are prompted to select a sketching plane for creating the sketch of the section line.

7. Select the sketching plane for creating the sketch of the section line. After selecting the sketching plane, click on the **Okay** option in the **SETUP SK PLN** menu. Next, click on the **Default** option in the menu.

8. Click on **View > Orientation > Sketch** Orientation in the Menu Bar. The sketching plane gets oriented normal to the viewing direction, and you are prompted to create the sketch of the section line.

Note: If the **References** dialog box appears, select the required edges of the model to define references for creating the section line and then close the dialog box.

9. Create a sketch, that comprises two non-parallel lines by using the sketching tools available in the **Sketch** tab or **Sketch** menu, see Figure 12.61.

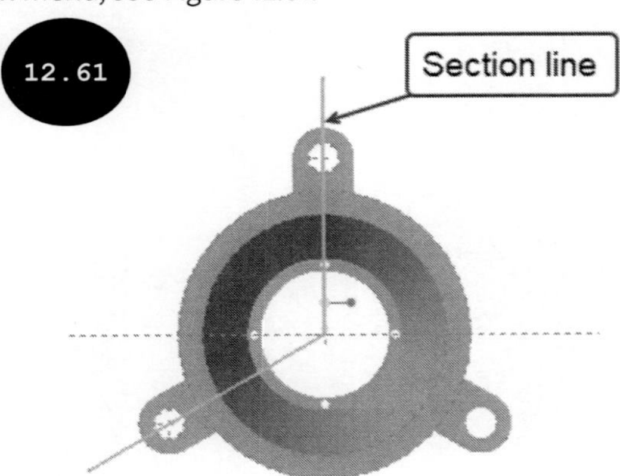

Note: The **Sketch** tab or **Sketch** menu appears for creating the sketch of the section line depending upon whether the 3D model was already opened in the current session of Creo Parametric. If the 3D model was already opened in the current session, then the **Sketch** tab appears in the **Ribbon** for creating the sketch.

10. After creating the section line, exit the Sketching environment by clicking on the **OK** tool in the **Close** group of the **Sketch** tab or the **Done** tool in the **Sketch** menu. The name of the section view appears in the **Name** drop-down list of the **Drawing View** dialog box.

11. Select the **Full(Aligned)** option in the **Sectioned Area** drop-down list of the dialog box. The **Reference** collector gets enabled in the dialog box and you are prompted to select an axis for revolving the section. Note that the axis should lie at the intersection of two line segments of the section line and normal to the parent view.

12. Ensure that the display of axes is turned on in the drawing views and then select an axis that lies at the intersection of two line segments of the section line, see Figure 12.62.

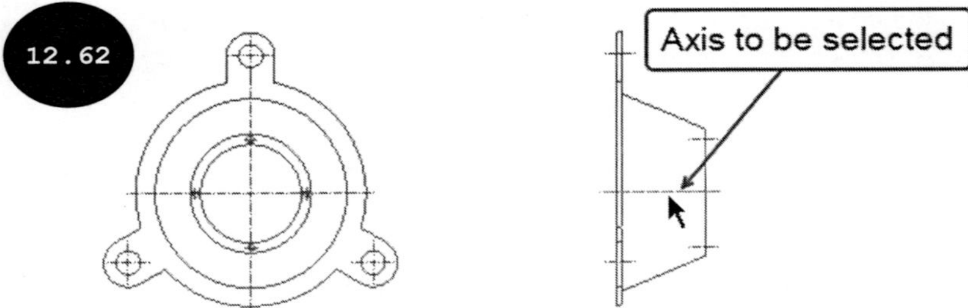

Now, you need to display the full (aligned) section arrows on the parent view.

13. Scroll to the right of the dialog box to display the **Arrow Display** collector. Next, click on the **Arrow Display** collector to activate it. You are prompted to select the parent view for displaying the section arrows.

14. Click on the parent view to display the section arrows and then click on the **Apply** button. The full (aligned) section view is created, see Figure 12.63. Next, close the dialog box.

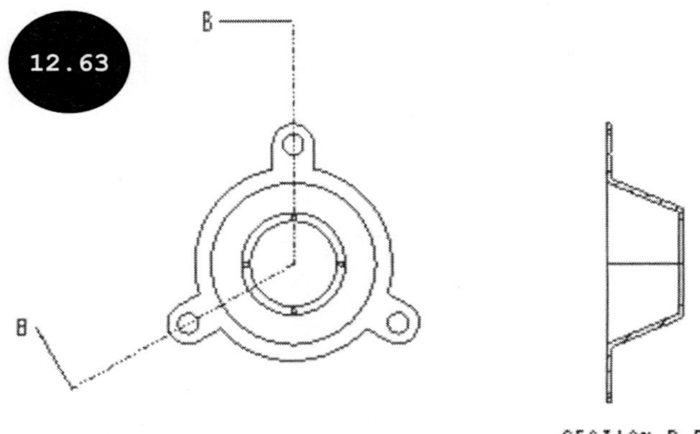

Creating a Full (Unfold) Section View

A full (unfold) section view is created by unfolding the cross-sectional area of an offset section view. Figure 12.64 shows an offset section view and Figure 12.65 shows a full (unfold) section view. Note that in Creo Parametric, you can only create a full (unfold) section view by using a general view. The method for creating a full (unfold) section view is discussed below:

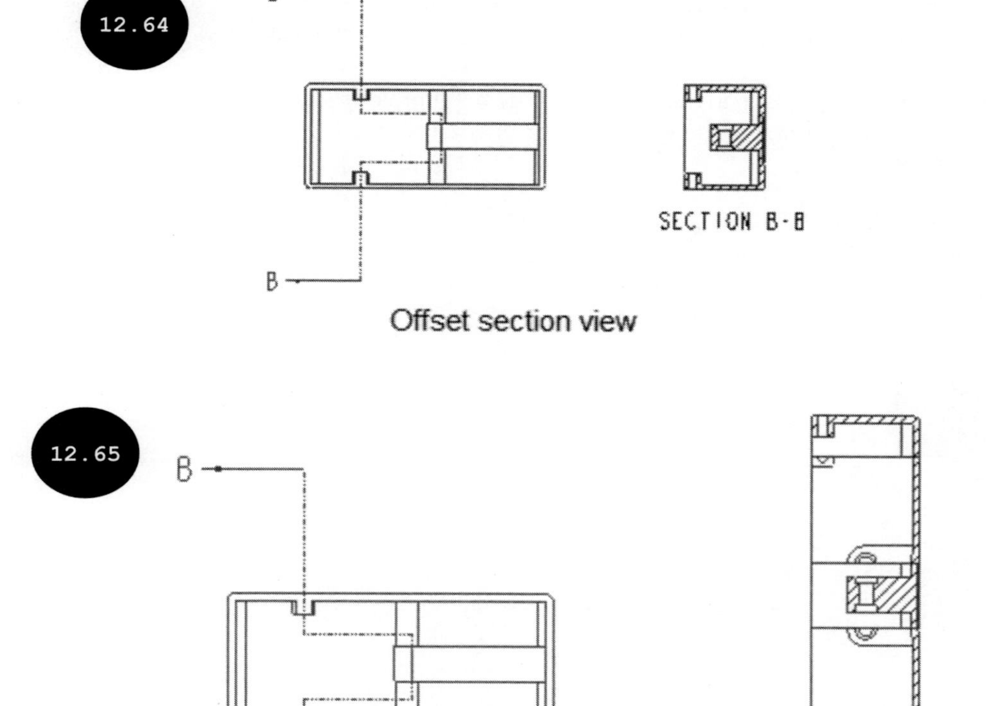

Offset section view

Full (Unfold) section view

1. Create an offset section view by using the **Drawing View** tool, refer to Figure 12.64. The method for creating an offset section view is discussed earlier.

   After creating an offset section view, you can convert it into a full (unfold) section view.

2. Double-click on the offset section view to invoke the **Drawing View** dialog box, if not already invoked.

3. Ensure that the **View Type** category is selected in the **Categories** area of the dialog box.

4. Select the **General** option in the **Type** drop-down list of the dialog box to convert the selected view type to the general view. This is done because the full (unfold) section view can only be created on the general view.

5. Click on the **Apply** button in the dialog box. The selected view type changes to general view.

6. Click on the **Sections** category in the **Categories** area of the dialog box and then select the **Full(Unfold)** option in the **Sectioned Area** drop-down list of the dialog box.

7. Click on the **Apply** button in the dialog box. The full (unfold) section view is created by unfolding the cross-sectional area of the view. Also, the orientation of the view is changed to normal to the section line.

8. Click on the **View Type** category in the dialog box and then enter **90** degrees in the **Angle value** field of the dialog box. Next, click on the **Apply** button. The orientation of the view is changed similar to the one shown in Figure 12.66.

9. Click on the **OK** button to close the dialog box.

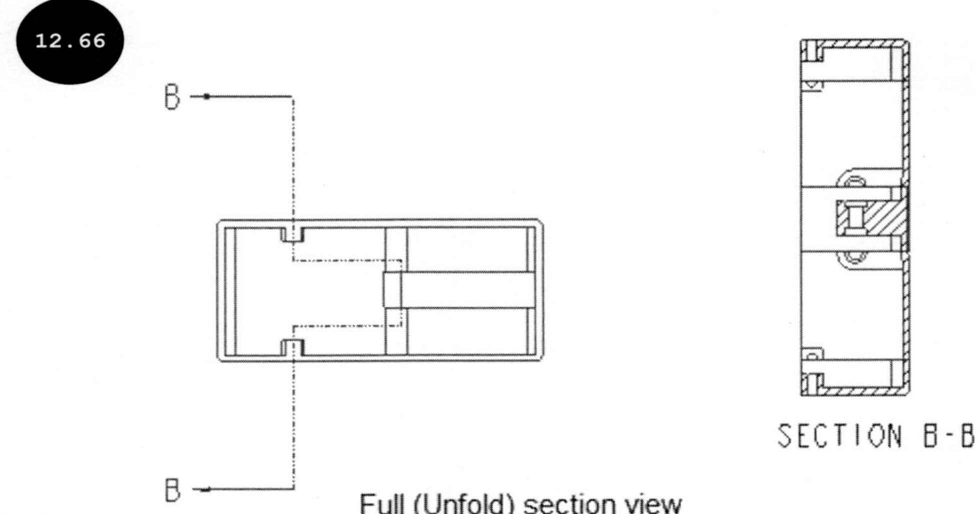

Note: Similar to creating various types of section views for components, you can also create section views for assemblies, see Figure 12.67.

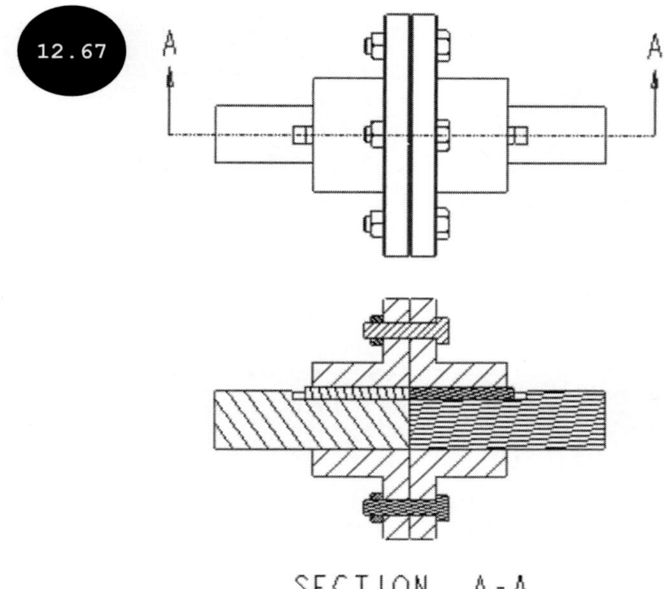

Tip: In Creo Parametric, you can also create an isometric section view, see Figure 12.68. To do so, create a general view of a model in the drawing sheet and then change its orientation to isometric. Next, click on the **Sections** category in the dialog box and then select the **2D cross-section** radio button. Ensure that the **Create New** option is selected in the **Name** drop-down list and then click on **Offset > Both Sides > Single > Done** in the **XSEC CREATE** menu that appears. Next, specify a name for the section view and press the middle mouse button. The 3D model appears in a separate window. Select the sketching plane for creating the section line and then press the middle mouse button twice. Create a sketch of the section line and then exit the 3D environment. Next, activate the **Arrow Display** collector in the **Drawing View** dialog box and then select a view to display section arrows. Next, click on the **Apply** and then **OK** button in the dialog box. The isometric section view is created.

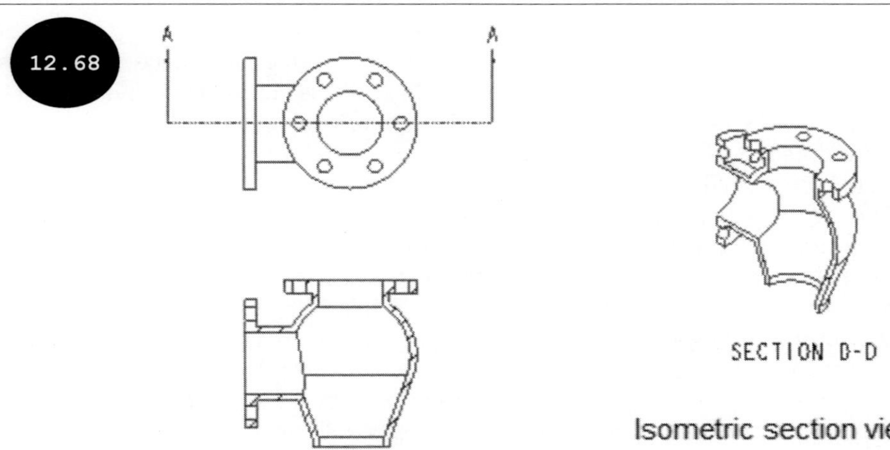

Controlling the Visibility of a View

In Creo Parametric, you can also control the display of a drawing view as a full view, a partial view, a half view, or a broken view by using the **Drawing View** dialog box. To do so, double-click on a view in the drawing sheet to invoke the **Drawing View** dialog box. Next, click on the **Visible Area** category in the **Categories** area of the dialog box. The **View visibility** drop-down list appears on the right panel of the dialog box, see Figure 12.69. The options in this drop-down list are used for controlling the visibility of the selected view. These options are discussed below.

12.69

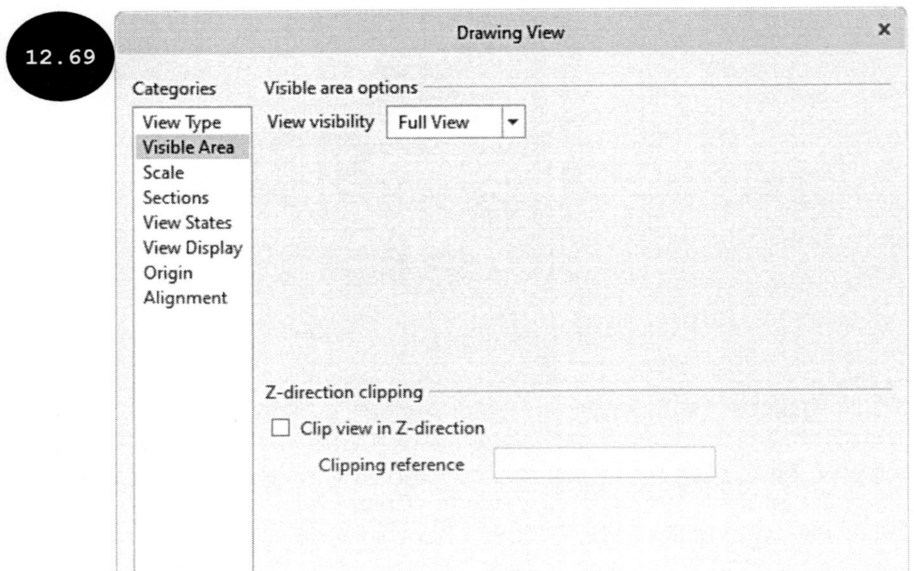

Full View

By default, the **Full View** option is selected in the **View Visibility** drop-down list in the dialog box. As a result, on creating a view such as a general view or a projection view, it display as a full or complete view in the drawing sheet, by default.

Half View

The **Half View** option is used for displaying only half the portion of an existing general, projection, or auxiliary view by cutting the object at a reference plane. To do so, select the **Half View** option in the **View Visibility** drop-down list of the dialog box. The **Half view reference plane** field appears in the dialog box and you are prompted to select a reference plane for creating the half view. Select a reference plane that is normal to the screen in the selected view, see Figure 12.70. Ensure that the display of reference planes is turned on for selection. After selecting a reference plane, an arrow appears in the drawing view such that it is pointing toward the portion to be kept in the drawing view. You can reverse the direction of arrow by clicking on the **Side to keep** button in the dialog box. Next, select the **Symmetry line** option in the **Symmetry line standard** drop-down list of the dialog box to display the symmetry line representation at the cutting area of the view, see Figure 12.71. Note that you can display no lines, solid lines, symmetry line, symmetry line as per ISO standard, symmetry line as per ASME standard at the cutting area of the view by selecting the required option in the **Symmetry line standard** drop-down list, respectively. Next, click on the **Apply** button in the dialog box. The half view is created in the sheet by removing the other half of the view, see Figure 12.71.

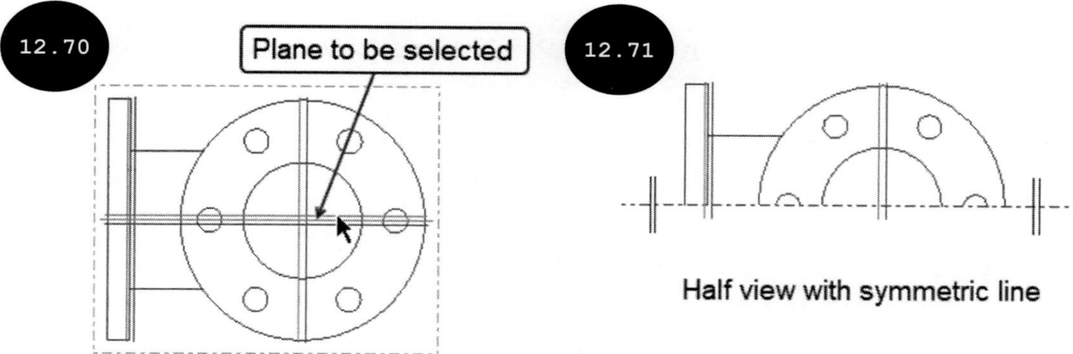

Partial View

The **Partial View** option is used for displaying a particular portion of an existing general, projection, auxiliary, or revolved view. To do so, select the **Partial View** option in the **View Visibility** drop-down list of the dialog box. The **Reference point on geometry** field appears in the dialog box and you are prompted to specify a reference point. Click to specify a point on the selected view, see Figure 12.72. The **Spline boundary** field gets activated in the dialog box and you are prompted to draw a closed spline around the specified point as the boundary to define the portion to be kept in the view. Draw a closed spline and then press the middle mouse button. Ensure that the **Show spline boundary on view** check box is selected in the dialog box to display the spline boundary on the partial view. If you do not want to display the spline boundary on the view, you can clear this check box. Next, click on the **Apply** button in the dialog box. The partial view is created such that only the portion that lies inside the spline appears in the view, see Figure 12.73.

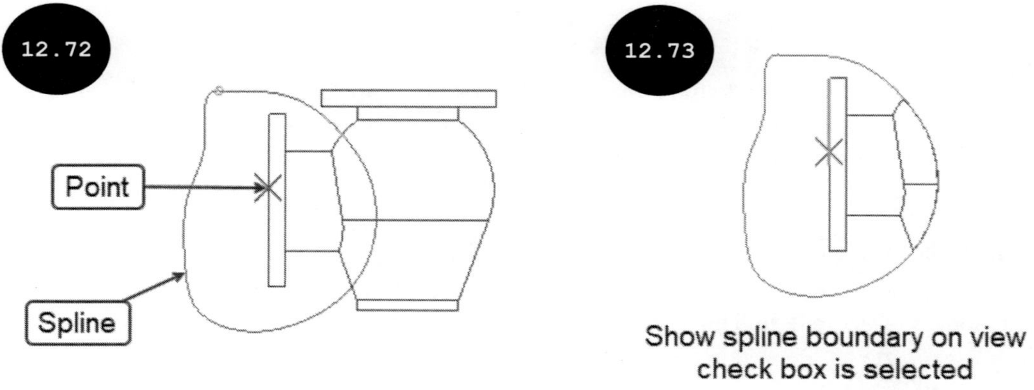

Broken View

The **Broken View** option is used for creating a broken view by breaking an existing general or projection view using a pair of horizontal or vertical lines such that the portion existing between the break lines is removed from the view. It is generally used for displaying a large scaled view on a small scale sheet by removing a portion of the view that has the same cross-section, see Figures 12.74 and 12.75. To create a broken view, select the **Broken View** option in the **View Visibility** drop-down list of the dialog box. Next, click on the **Add break** button + in the dialog box to add break lines. The **1st Break Line** collector gets activated in the dialog box and you are prompted to sketch a horizontal or vertical break line. Click on an edge of the selected view to create the start point of the first break line. Next, move the cursor vertically or horizontally to define the second point of the break line depending upon the edge selected. Note that if you have specified the start point of the break line on a horizontal edge then you can move the cursor vertically up or down to define the second point of the break line, whereas if you have specified the start point of the break line on a vertical edge then you can move the cursor horizontally toward left or right. Next, click to specify the second point of the break line on the sheet. The first break line is defined, see Figure 12.74. Also, the **2nd Break Line** collector gets activated in the dialog box and you are prompted to specify a point to define the second break line. Click to specify a point on the edge of the view up to which you want to break the view. The second break line is defined, see Figure 12.74. You can also select the required style for the break lines in the view. To do so, scroll to the right of the dialog box and then select the required option in the **Break Line Style** drop-down list that appears next to the **2nd Break Line** collector in the dialog box. Next, click on the **Apply** button in the dialog box. The broken view is created such that the portion existing between the break lines is removed from the view, see Figure 12.75.

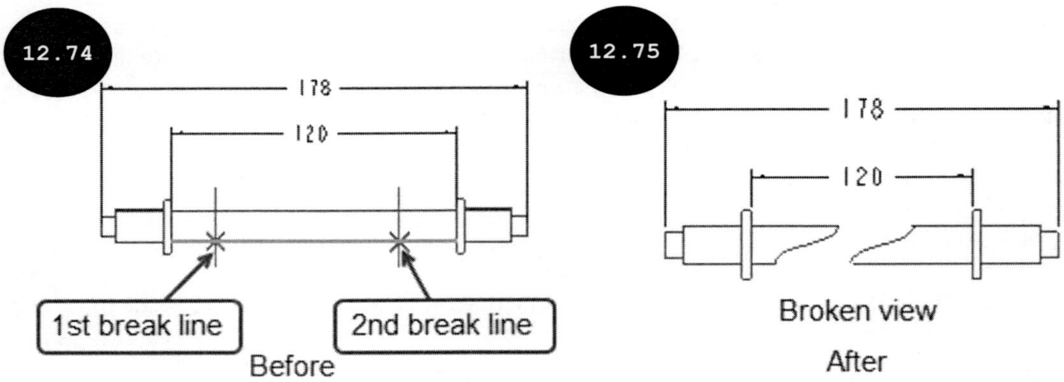

Note: The dimension applied to the broken view represents its actual dimension, see Figure 12.75. It is evident from this figure that even on breaking the view, the dimension value associated with it remains the same. You will learn more about applying dimensions later in this chapter.

Creating a 3D Cross-Section View

In Creo Parametric, you can also create a 3D cross-section view in the Drawing mode by defining zones in the Part mode, see Figure 12.76. The method for creating a 3D cross-section view is discussed below:

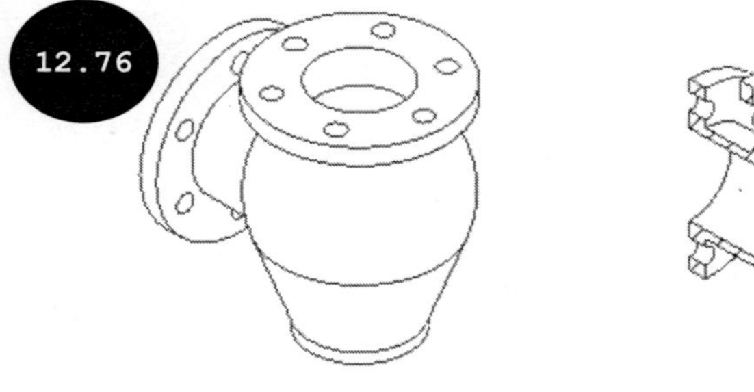

1. Open the component in the Part mode whose 3D cross-section view is to be created in the Drawing mode.

2. Click on the **View** tab in the **Ribbon** and then click on the **Manage Views** tool in the **Model Display** group of the **View** tab. The **View Manager** dialog box appears.

3. Click on the **Sections** tab in the **View Manager** dialog box and then invoke the **New** drop-down list in the dialog box, see Figure 12.77.

4. Select the **Zone** option in the **New** drop-down list to define a new zone for creating the 3D cross-section view. A default name for the zone such as Xsec0001, Xsec0002, ... or Xsec000n appears in the dialog box.

5. Enter a new name for the zone to be created and then press ENTER. A dialog box with the name you have specified for the zone appears, refer to Figure 12.78.

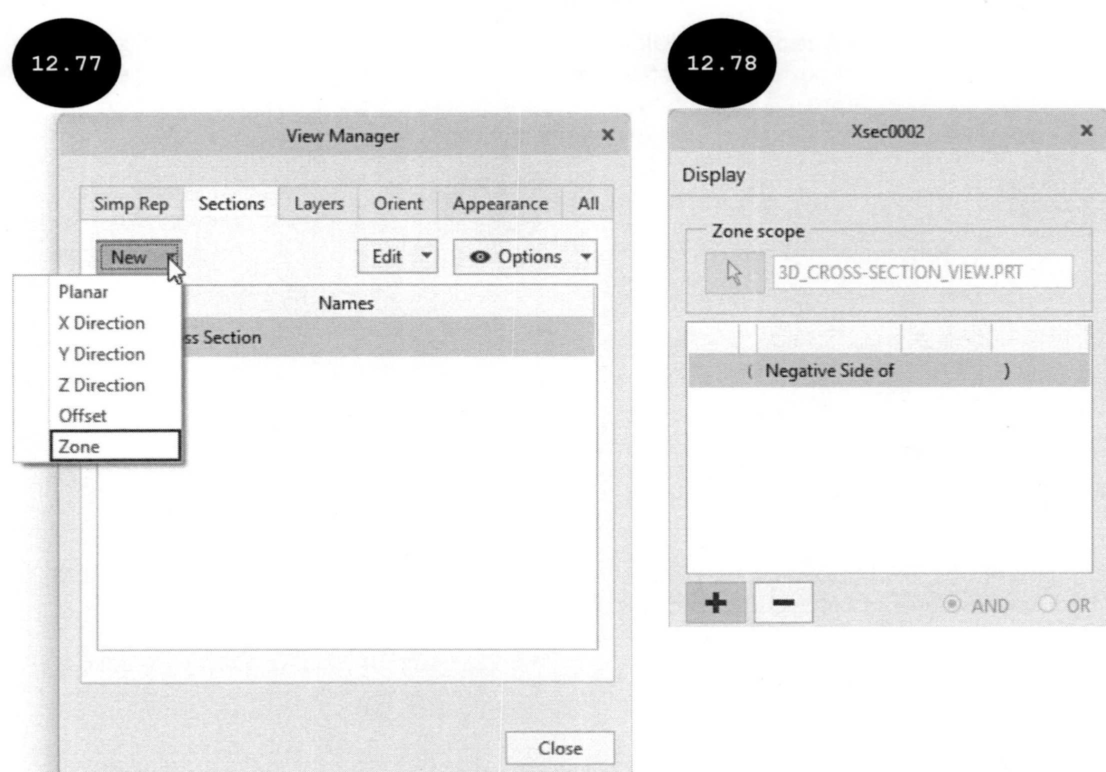

6. Select a datum plane or reference entity of the model for defining a zone. The datum plane is selected and arrows appear in the graphics area such that they are pointing toward the direction of creation of the zone, see Figure 12.79. By default, the negative side of the selected datum plane is used for defining the direction of creation of the zone. You can also reverse the direction of the creation of the zone to the positive side of the datum plane by clicking on the **Change orientation** button in the dialog box.

After selecting the first datum plane, you need to select the second datum plane for defining a zone. Note that you need to select two or more than two datum planes or reference entities for defining a zone.

7. Click on the **Add a reference to the zone** button in the dialog box to select a second datum plane or reference entity for defining a zone.

8. Select the second datum plane or reference entity of the model for defining a zone. The datum plane is selected and arrows appear in the graphics area such that they are pointing toward the direction of creation of the zone.

9. Reverse the direction of creation of the zone by clicking on the **Change orientation** button in the dialog box.

10. You can similarly select multiple datum planes or reference entities for defining a zone.

11. Click on the **Preview** button in the dialog box to preview the creation of a zone, see Figure 12.80. Note that the direction of arrows of the datum planes defines the creation of the zone. In Figure 12.80, two datum planes are selected and the direction arrows have been reversed toward the positive side of the datum planes for defining the zone.

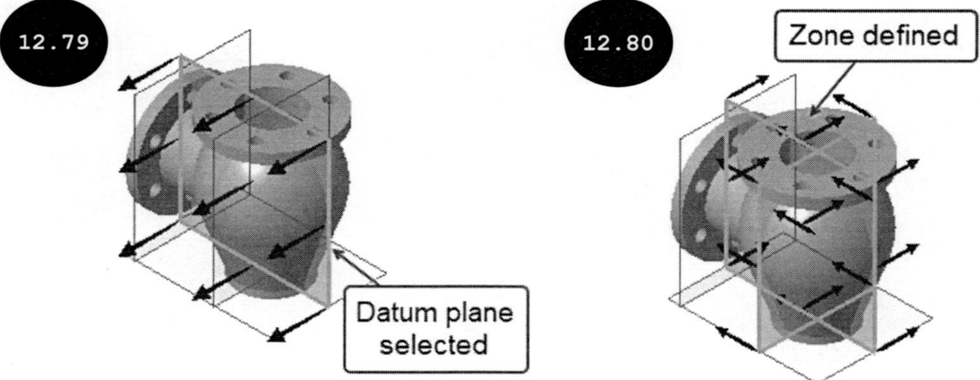

12. Click on the **OK** button in the dialog box to accept the specified settings. The **View Manager** dialog box appears. Next, close the dialog box.

    After creating a zone in the Part mode, you can create a 3D cross-section view in the Drawing mode by using it.

13. Invoke the Drawing mode and then create a general view of the model in the drawing sheet, see Figure 12.81. In this figure, the general view is created in isometric orientation.

14. Click on the **Sections** category in the **Categories** area of the **Drawing View** dialog box.

15. Select the **3D cross-section** radio button in the **Section options** area of the **Drawing View** dialog box. A drop-down list appears next to the **3D cross-section** radio button with a list of zones created for the component in the Part mode.

16. Select a required zone in the drop-down list that appears next to the **3D cross-section** radio button in the dialog box.

17. Ensure that the **Show X-Hatching** check box is selected in the dialog box to display hatching on the section area of the model in the view.

18. Click on the **Apply** button in the dialog box. The 3D cross-section view is created on the selected view by using the zone, see Figure 12.82.

19. Close the **Drawing View** dialog box.

Creating a Copy and Align View

A copy and align view is created by copying an existing partial or a detailed view of the drawing. This means that if a partial or detailed view is created in the drawing sheet, then you can copy it to create another aligned partial view with a different breakout boundary. The method for creating a copy and align view is discussed below:

1. Ensure that a partial or detailed view is already created in the drawing sheet for creating a copy and align view.

2. Click on the **Copy and Align View** tool in the **Model Views** group of the **Layout** tab, see Figure 12.83. You are prompted to select an existing partial view.

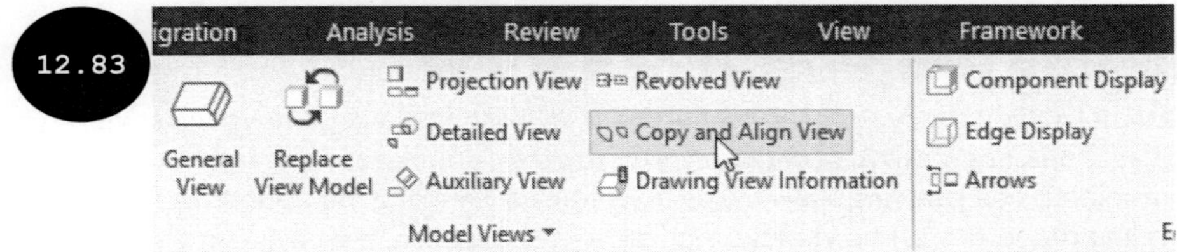

3. Select an existing partial view in the drawing sheet. You are prompted to specify a center point for the drawing view in the drawing sheet.

4. Click to specify a point anywhere in the drawing sheet to create the placement of the view. The full view of the model is placed at the specified location and you are prompted to specify a center point for defining the breakout boundary on the current view.

5. Click to specify a point on the current view, see Figure 12.84. You are prompted to draw a closed spline around the specified point as the boundary to define the portion to be kept in the view.

6. Draw a closed spline, see Figure 12.84. Next, press the middle mouse button. The view is created such that only the portion that lies inside the spline appears in the view, see Figure 12.85. Also, you are prompted to select a straight line (axis, segment, datum curve) of the current view to align it to the original/parent view.

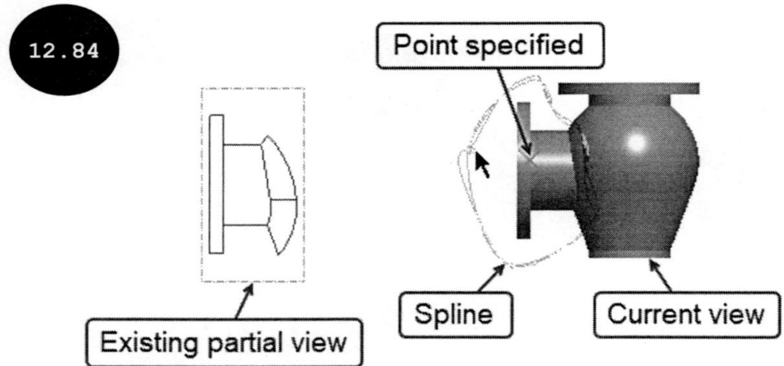

7. Select an edge or an axis of the current view to align it with the original/parent view, see Figure 12.85. The copy and align view is created such that it aligns with its parent partial view, see Figure 12.86.

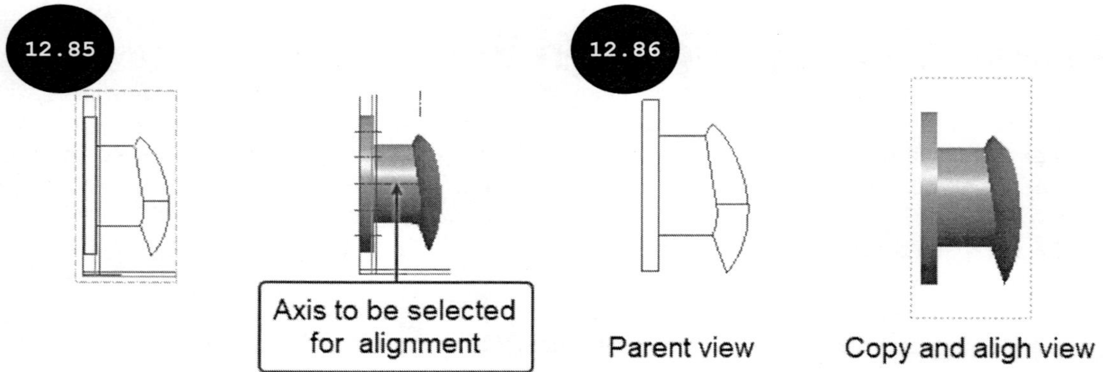

Modifying Properties of a View

In Creo Parametric, you can modify the properties of an existing drawing view such as view type, visible area, scale, sections, orientation, view display, etc. To do so, double-click on the view whose properties are to be modified. The **Drawing View** dialog box appears. By using the options of this dialog box, you can modify the properties of the view, as required. The options of the **Drawing View** dialog box have already been discussed earlier.

Modifying Hatching of a View

In Creo Parametric, you can also modify the cross-section hatching parameters such as hatch pattern, rotation angle, scale, horizontal translation, vertical translation, and color of hatching lines of a section view. To do so, double-click on the hatching of an existing view in the drawing sheet. The **Edit Hatching** tab appears in the **Ribbon**, see Figure 12.87. By using the options of this tab, you can modify the parameters of the selected cross-section hatching of the view. For example, to modify the angle of rotation of the hatching lines, enter the required angle value in the **Rotate Angle** field of the **Editing** group in the **Edit Hatching** tab, see Figure 12.87. Similarly, to modify the scale of the hatching lines, enter the required scale value in the **Scale** field of the **Edit Hatching** tab, see Figure 12.87.

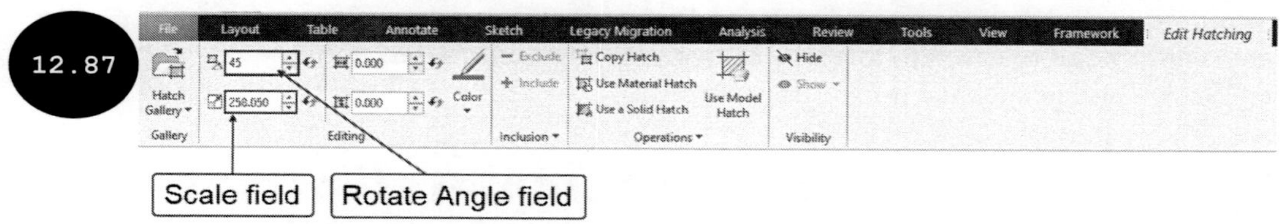

To modify the hatch pattern of the hatching, invoke the **All Pattern** flyout by clicking on the **Hatch Gallery** tool in the **Gallery** group, see Figure 12.88. Next, select the required hatch pattern in the **All Pattern** flyout. After selecting the required hatch pattern, click anywhere in the graphics area to exit the **Edit Hatching** tab.

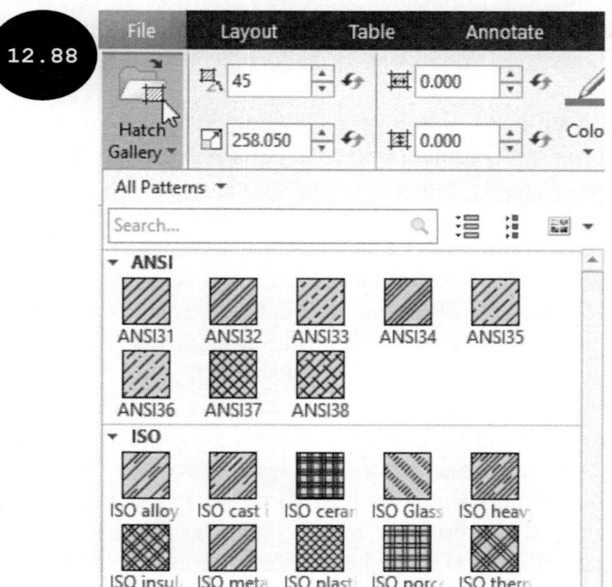

Moving, Erasing, and Deleting a View

To move a view on the sheet, click on the view to be moved and then press and hold the right mouse button to invoke a shortcut menu. Next, click on the **Lock View Movement** option in the shortcut menu to lock or unlock the movement of the view on the sheet. After unlocking the movement of the view, you can change its position on the sheet by dragging it to a new location.

To erase a view from the drawing sheet, click on the **Erase View** tool in the **Display** group of the **Layout** tab. You are prompted to select a view to be erased. Click on the view in the drawing sheet. The selected view gets erased and a rectangular box with the name of the erased view appears in its place. Note that the erased view is temporarily removed from the drawing sheet and all its information remains available in the memory of the drawing. You can regain the erased view at any point by clicking on the **Resume View** tool in the **Display** group of the **Layout** tab. As the view is temporarily erased from the drawing sheet, it does not affect its child views.

To delete a view from the drawing sheet, select the view to be deleted and then click on the **Delete** tool in the Mini toolbar that appears, see Figure 12.89. The selected view gets deleted from the drawing and none of its information remains in the memory of the drawing. Note that if any child view is associated with it, then that will also get deleted from the drawing.

Creating a New Drawing Template/Format

Creo Parametric is provided with several standard drawing templates for various sheet sizes. When you start a new drawing, you can select the required standard drawing template for creating the drawing. In Creo Parametric, you can also create a new drawing template/format as per your company standard which includes items such as tables for the company name, project name, revision number, revision date, created by, approved by, etc. You can create a new drawing template in the Format mode of Creo Parametric. In addition to creating a new drawing template, you can also import an existing template that is saved in .DWG, .DXF, .SET, .IGES, or etc. file format.

To create a new drawing template, click on the **New** tool in the **Quick Access Toolbar** to invoke the **New** dialog box. Next, select the **Format** radio button in the **New** dialog box and then enter a name of the format in the **Name** field of the dialog box. Next, click on the **OK** button. The **New Format** dialog box appears. In this dialog box, select the required orientation and size for the format and then click on the **OK** button. The Format mode is invoked. Now, you can create a new format by using the sketching tools available in the **Sketch** tab of the **Ribbon**. You can also create tables in the format by using the tools available in the **Table** tab of the **Ribbon**. After creating the format, you can save it in the required location as *.frm* file for using it as a format while creating a drawing in the Drawing mode.

In addition to creating a new format, you can also import a *.DWG, .DXF, .STP, .IGES*, etc. file in the Format mode and save it as *.frm* file. To do so, click on the **Import Drawing/Data** tool in the **Insert** group of the **Layout** tab in the **Format** mode, see Figure 12.90. The **Open** dialog box appears. In this dialog box, browse to the location where the file to be imported is saved and then select it. Next, click on the **Import** button in the dialog box. The **Import** dialog box appears, see Figure 12.91. In this dialog box, select the required attributes of the selected file to be imported. Next, click on the **OK** button. The **Confirmation** window appears, see Figure 12.92. In this window, click on the **Yes** button to scale the imported file such that it fits in the size of the format. The selected file gets imported, see Figure 12.93.

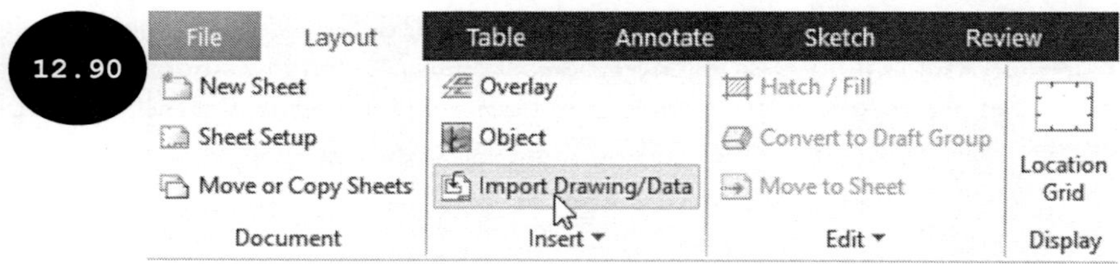

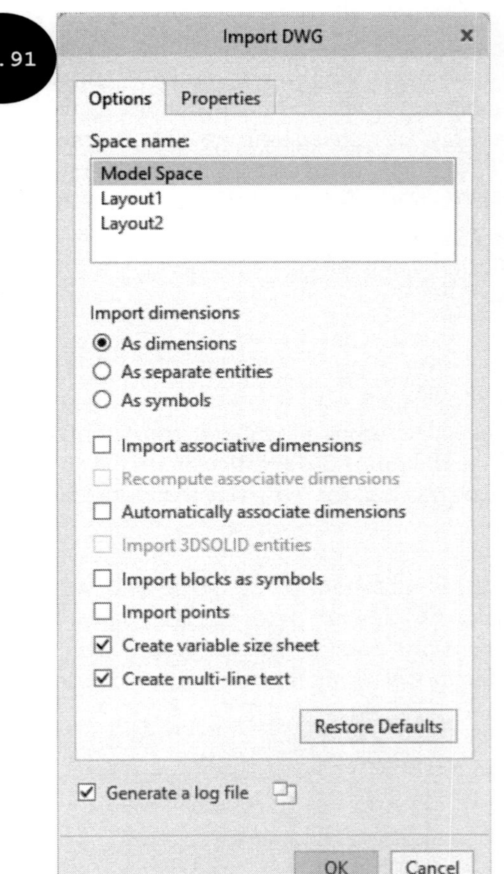
12.91
Import DWG
Options
Properties
Space name:
Model Space
Layout1
Layout2
Import dimensions
As dimensions
As separate entities
As symbols
Import associative dimensions
Recompute associative dimensions
Automatically associate dimensions
Import 3DSOLID entities
Import blocks as symbols
Import points
Create variable size sheet
Create multi-line text
Restore Defaults
Generate a log file
OK
Cancel

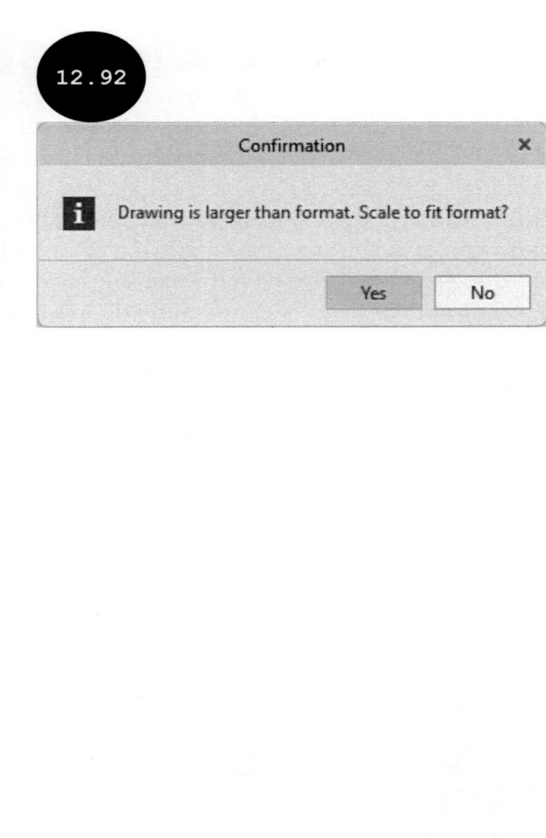
12.92
Confirmation
Drawing is larger than format. Scale to fit format?
Yes
No

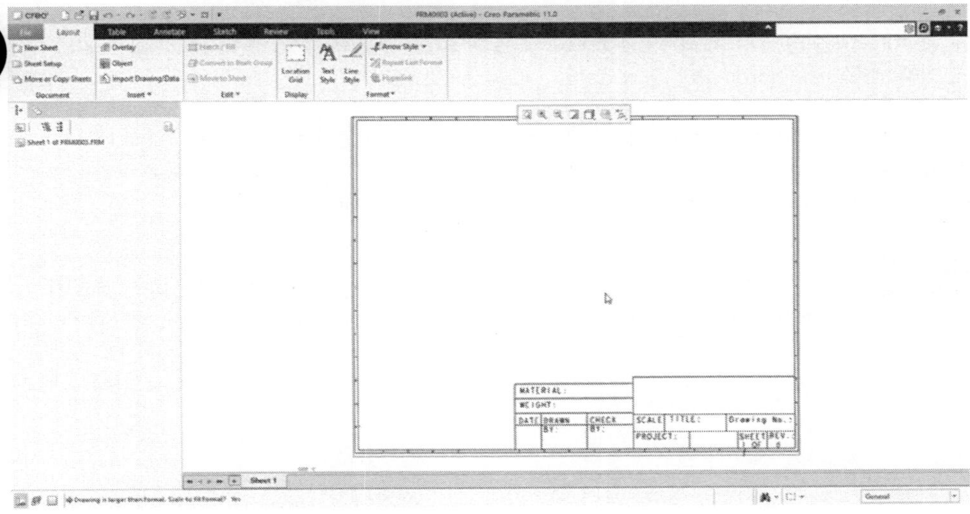
12.93

Applying Dimensions

After creating various drawing views of a part or an assembly in the Drawing mode, you need to apply dimensions to them. In Creo Parametric, you can apply two types of dimensions: driving dimensions and driven/reference dimensions. The driving dimensions are applied automatically in drawing views by retrieving the model dimensions, which are applied in the sketches and features of the model. Note that on modifying a driving dimension, the respective sketch or feature of the model is also modified and vice-versa. On the other hand, the driven/reference dimensions are applied manually by using the **Dimension** tool. The driven dimension cannot drive the dimension of the model. The methods for applying both types of dimensions are discussed next.

Applying Driving Dimensions

As discussed earlier, the driving dimensions are applied automatically in drawing views by retrieving the model dimensions. In Creo Parametric, you can retrieve dimensions and other properties of the model such as tolerances, notes, surface finishes, symbols, and datums on a particular view in the drawing sheet by using the **Show Model Annotations** tool. The method for retrieving the model dimensions and other properties is discussed below:

1. Click on the **Show Model Annotations** tool in the **Annotations** group of the **Annotate** tab, see Figure 12.94. The **Show Model Annotations** dialog box appears, refer to Figure 12.95. Note that this dialog box has six tabs; **Show the model dimensions, Show the model gtols, Show the model notes, Show the model surface finishes, Show the model symbols,** and **Show the model datums.**

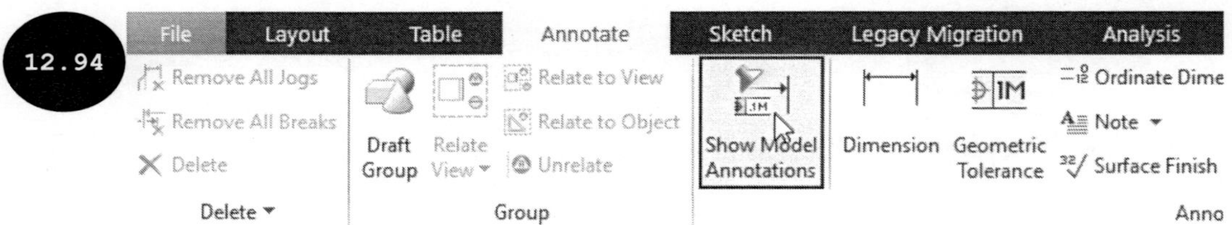

2. Ensure that the **Show the model dimensions** tab is activated in the dialog box to retrieve model dimensions in a drawing view.

3. Select a drawing view in the sheet for retrieving the model dimensions. A list of model dimensions appears in the dialog box with a check box on the left of each dimension name, see Figure 12.95. Also, the dimensions appear on the selected view in the sheet.

Note: You can also select multiple views for retrieving dimensions by pressing the CTRL key. In addition to selecting views, you can also select a particular feature of a view for retrieving its relative dimensions.

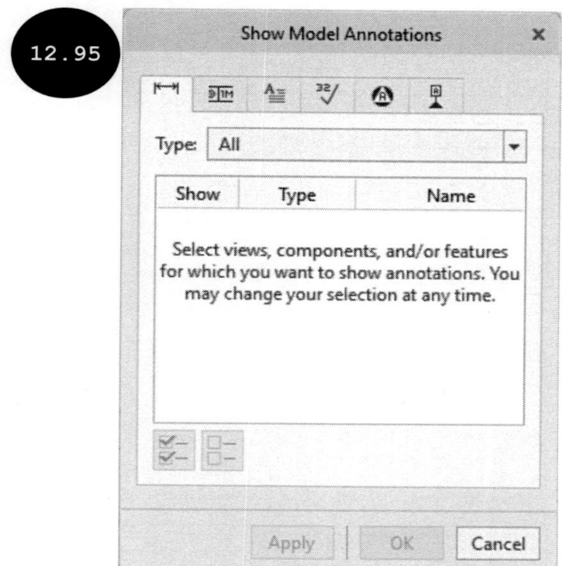

12.95

4. Select the required option in the **Type** drop-down list of the dialog box to filter the display of dimensions on the selected view.

Tip: By default, the **All** option is selected in the **Type** drop-down list in the dialog box. As a result, all the dimensions of the model get listed in the dialog box as well as appear on the selected view in the sheet. You can select the **All**, **Driving dimension annotation elements**, **All driving dimensions**, **Strong driving dimensions**, **Driven dimensions**, **Reference dimensions**, or **Ordinate dimensions** option to display the respective dimensions.

5. Select the check boxes of the dimensions in the dialog box to retain the corresponding dimensions in the selected view. You can also select the dimensions in the drawing view that you want to retain in the view. Note that to retain all the dimensions in the view, click on the **Select All** button in the dialog box.

6. Click on the **Apply** button in the dialog box. All the selected dimensions are retrieved and appear faded in the view.

7. Similarly, you can retrieve other properties of the model such as tolerances, notes, surface finishes, symbols, or datums on the selected view or views in the drawing sheet by using the options available in the respective tab (**Show the model gtols**, **Show the model notes**, **Show the model surface finishes**, **Show the model symbols**, or **Show the model datums**) of the **Show Model Annotations** dialog box.

8. Click on the **Close** button in the dialog box. The selected dimensions and the properties of the model get retrieved and applied to the selected views in the drawing sheet, see Figure 12.96.

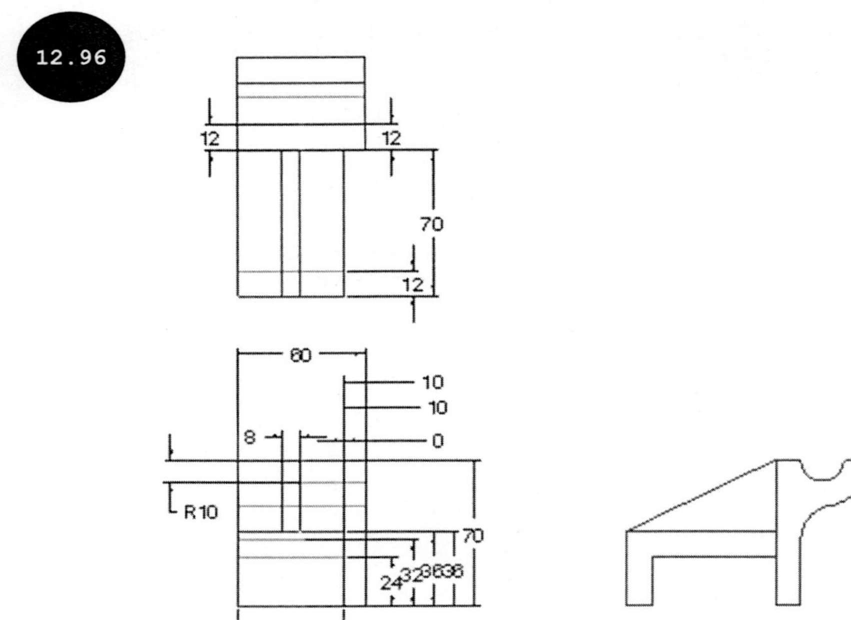

Note: Sometimes the driving dimensions applied in the drawing views neither appear in the required positions, nor do they maintain uniform spacing in the drawing views. You can select the dimension and then drag it to the required position for maintaining proper spacing between them.

Applying Driven/Reference Dimensions

Applying driven dimension is the manual method of applying dimensions to drawing views by using the **Dimension** tool. Note that a driven dimension cannot drive the dimension of the model and acts as a reference dimension only. The method for applying driven dimensions is discussed below:

1. Click on the **Annotate** tab in the **Ribbon**. All the tools of the **Annotate** tab appear, see Figure 12.97.

2. Click on the **Dimension** tool in the **Annotations** group of the **Annotate** tab, see Figure 12.97. The **Select Reference** window appears and you are prompted to select an entity for applying the dimension.

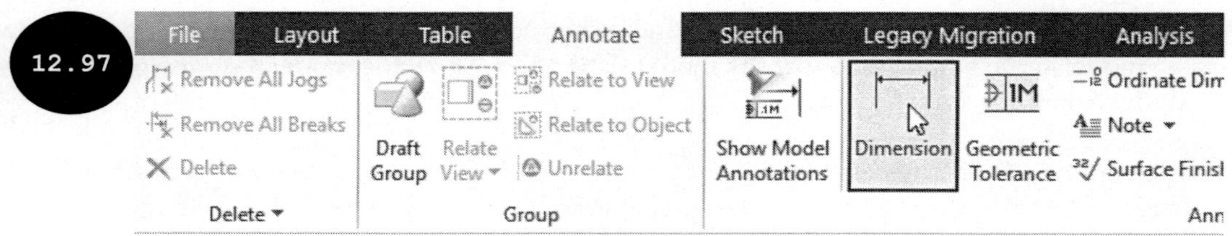

3. Select an entity of a drawing view to apply a dimension. The dimension value of the selected entity gets attached to the cursor.

Note: To apply a dimension between two entities, you need to select both the entities one by one by pressing the CTRL key.

4. After selecting one or more entities to apply a dimension, press the middle mouse button at the required location in the drawing sheet to define its placement. The dimension is applied and the **Dimension** tab appears in the **Ribbon**, see Figure 12.98. Next, click anywhere in the drawing sheet to exit the **Dimension** tab.

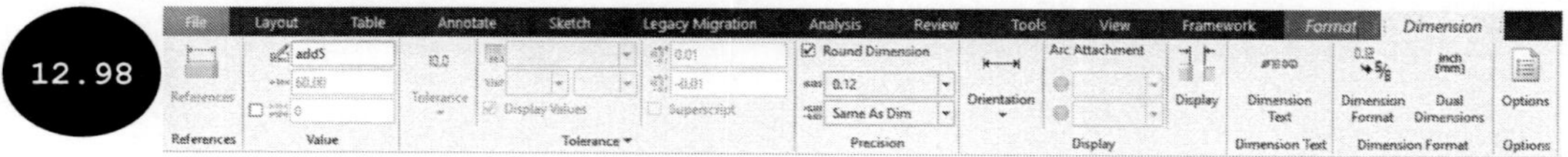

12.98

Tip: By using the tools of the **Dimension** tab, you can define the dimension properties such as tolerance, precision, display style, dimension text, dimension format, override dimension value, and so on.

5. You can similarly apply dimensions to other entities one by one. After applying all the required dimensions, press the middle mouse button to exit the **Dimension** tool.

Editing the Text Style

In Creo Parametric, you can edit the text style properties of dimensions and annotations such as font, height, thickness, width factor, and color by using the **Text Style** tool. The method for editing the text style properties is discussed below:

1. Select the dimensions or annotations in the drawing sheet whose text style needs to be edited. You can select multiple dimensions or annotations by drawing a window around them.

2. Click on the **Text Style** tool in the **Format** group of the **Annotate** tab, see Figure 12.99. The **Text Style** dialog box appears, see Figure 12.100.

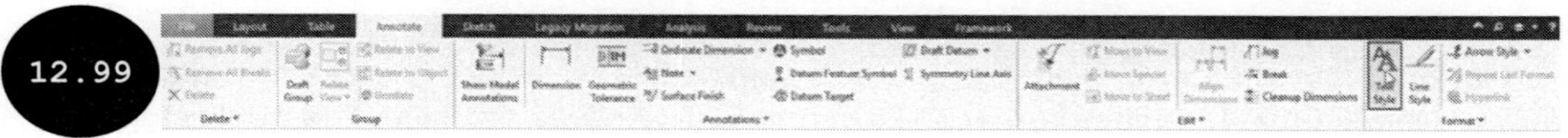

12.99

12.100

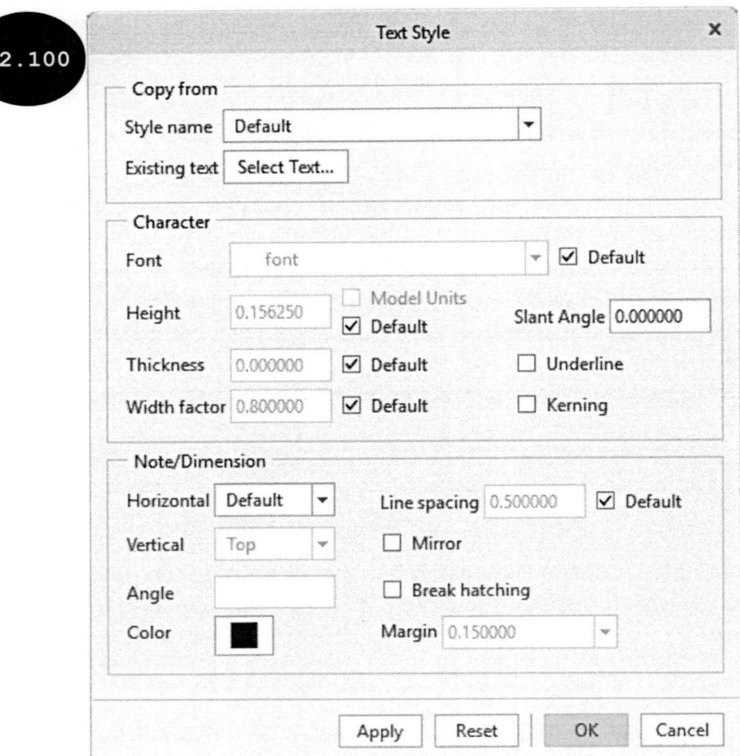

3. Clear the **Default** check boxes of the properties to be edited in the dialog box. The respective fields/drop-down lists get enabled for editing. For example, to change the text font, clear the **Default** check box that appears in front of the **Font** drop-down list in the dialog box. On doing so, the **Font** drop-down list gets enabled and allows you to select a required font for the selected dimensions or annotations.

4. After editing the required text style properties of the selected dimensions, click on the **Apply** button to accept the change and then click on the **OK** button in the dialog box.

Adding Tolerances in the Drawing Views

In Creo Parametric, you can add dimension tolerances and geometric tolerances in the drawing views. The dimension tolerances are used for defining the maximum and minimum accepted variations in the dimension values for manufacturing a component. The geometric tolerances provide additional information about the component for manufacturing such as critical surfaces of the component, surface profile, material condition, orientation, geometric condition, and so on. The methods for adding dimension tolerances and geometric tolerances in the drawing views are discussed next.

Adding Dimension Tolerances

In Creo Parametric, to add dimensions tolerances, you first need to ensure that the **tol_display** value is set to **yes**. To do so, click on the **File** > **Prepare** > **Drawing Properties** in the **File** menu. The **Drawing Properties** dialog box appears. In this dialog box, click on the **change** option that appears on the right of the **Detail Options** row in the dialog box, see Figure 12.101. The **Options** dialog box appears. Next, enter **tol_display** in the **Option** field in the lower left corner of the dialog box and then press ENTER. The default value of the **tol_display** option is selected in the **Value** drop-down list of the dialog box. Select the **yes** option in the **Value** drop-down list of the dialog box and then click on the **Add / Change** button. Next, click on the **Apply** button in the dialog box. The **tol_display** value changes to **yes**. Next, close the dialog box. Next, close the **Drawing Properties** dialog box.

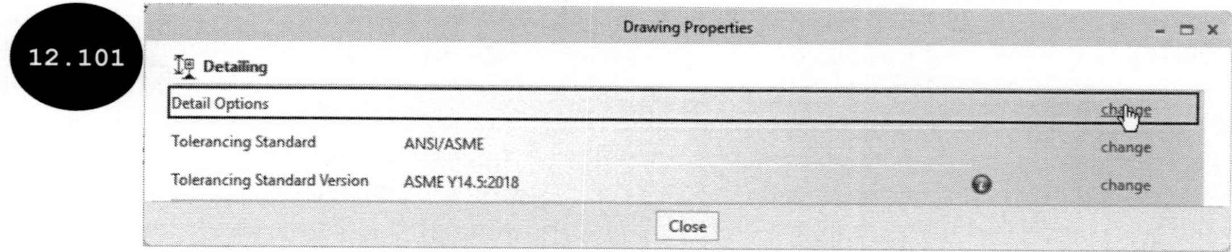

After defining the **tol_display** value as yes, you can add tolerances in the dimensions of the drawing views. To do so, select the dimension of a drawing view to add tolerance. The **Dimension** tab appears in the **Ribbon**. Next, in the **Tolerance** flyout of the **Dimension** tab, select the required type of tolerance for the selected dimension, see Figure 12.102. By default, the **Nominal** option is selected in the **Tolerance** flyout. As a result, the nominal dimension value is displayed with no tolerance. Depending upon the type of tolerance selected in this flyout, the corresponding fields are enabled in the **Tolerance** group of the **Dimension** tab for specifying tolerance values. Figure 12.103 shows a dimension with symmetric tolerance value of 0.05 mm added. Similarly, you can add tolerances to the remaining dimensions of a drawing.

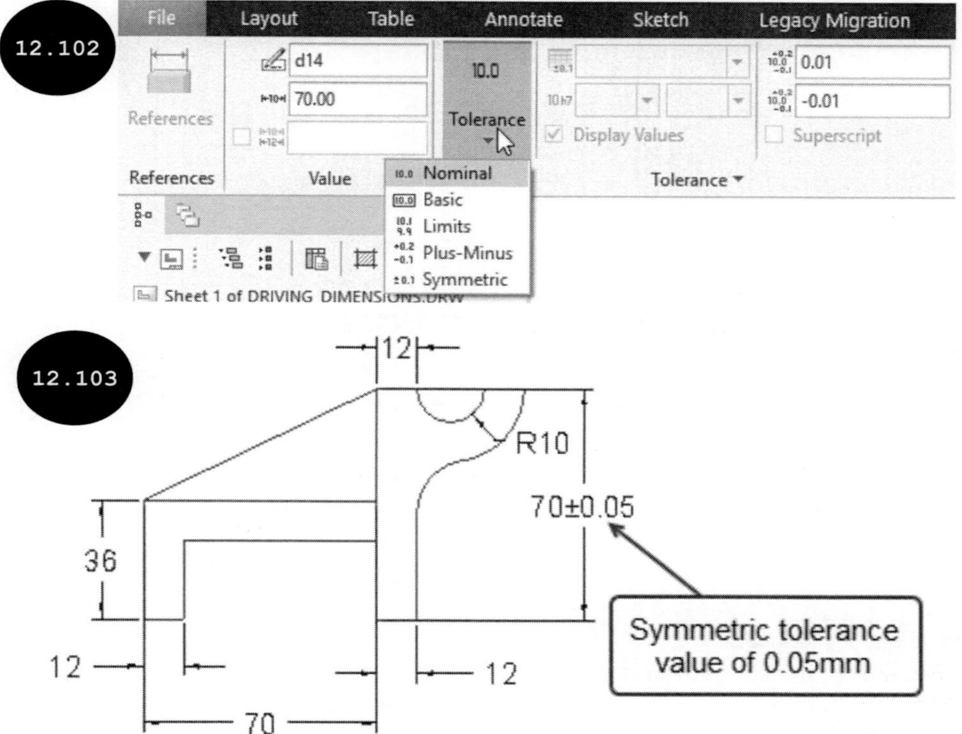

Adding Geometric Tolerances

As discussed earlier, the geometric tolerances (GTOLs) are used to provide additional information about the component for manufacturing such as critical surfaces of the component, surface profile, material condition, orientation, geometric condition, and so on. In Creo Parametric, you can add geometric tolerances (GTOLs) in drawing views by using the **Geometric Tolerance** tool. To do so, click on the **Geometric Tolerance** tool in the **Annotations** group of the **Annotate** tab. A GTOLs symbol appears attached to the cursor with default properties. Next, select an edge of a drawing view for adding GTOL. The GTOL is attached to the selected edge with a leader and you are prompted to define its placement point. Next, press the middle mouse button anywhere in the drawing sheet to define the placement for the GTOL. The GTOL is placed at the specified location with a leader attached to the selected edge, see Figure 12.104. Also, the **Geometric Tolerance** tab appears in the **Ribbon**, see Figure 12.105. Next, you can define the parameters for GTOL such as geometric characteristic symbol, geometric tolerance values, GTOL name, datum references, and so on by using the tools available in the **Geometric Tolerance** tab of the **Ribbon**. After defining the GTOL parameters, click anywhere in the drawing sheet to exit the **Geometric Tolerance** tab.

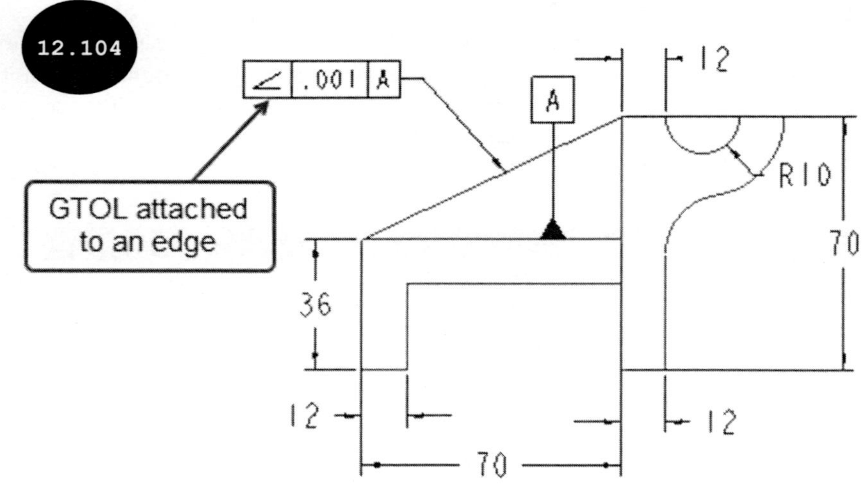

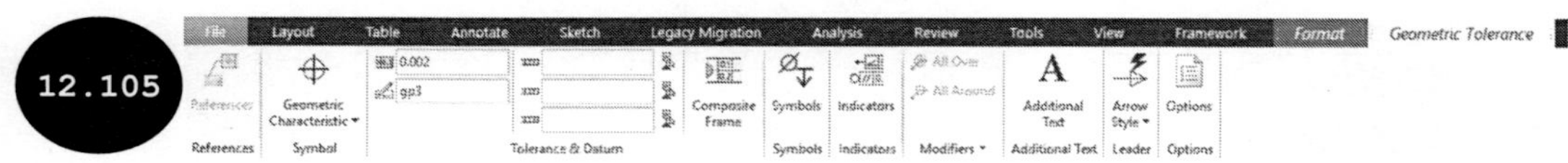

Note: You can attach the GTOL symbol to an edge, existing dimension, existing GTOL, as well as display it as a note in the drawing.

Adding Notes

In Creo Parametric, you can add notes on a drawing sheet by using the tools available in the **Note** flyout of the **Annotations** group, see Figure 12.106. Generally, adding notes in drawings is used for conveying or providing additional information that is not available in the drawing views.

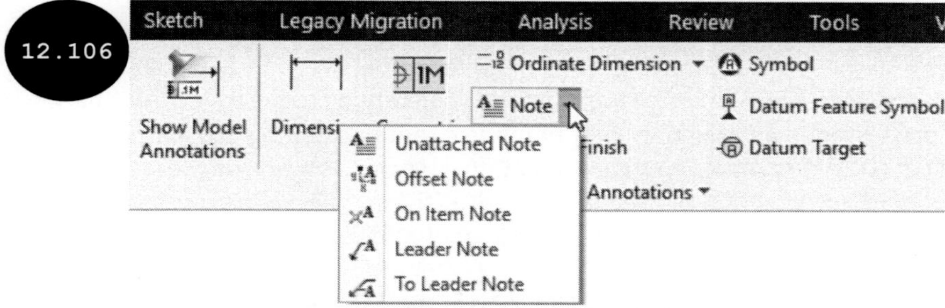

The **Unattached Note** tool of the **Note** flyout is used for adding notes anywhere on the drawing sheet such that it does not get attached to any entity in the drawing. To do so, click on the **Unattached Note** tool in the **Note** flyout. The **Select Point** dialog box appears, see Figure 12.107. Also, the preview of a note gets attached to the cursor. Note that the **Select a free point on the drawing** button is activated in the **Select Point** dialog box, by default. As a result, you can specify a placement for the note anywhere in the drawing sheet by clicking the left mouse button. On specifying the placement for the note, an edit box appears. Also, the **Format** tab is displayed in the **Ribbon**. Now, you can type the text in the edit box, as required. After entering the text, you can modify the text settings or format by using the tools in the **Format** tab of the **Ribbon**. Note that you can also specify the placement for the note by entering the absolute coordinates values, selecting an object or entity of the drawing view, or selecting a vertex of a view by activating the respective button in the **Select Point** dialog box. After adding a note, you can exit the **Format** tab by clicking the left mouse button twice anywhere in the drawing sheet.

The **Offset Note** tool of the **Note** flyout is used for adding a note at an offset distance from an existing dimension, GTOL, note, datum point, axis endpoint, or symbol. The **On Item Note** tool is used for adding a note on an object or entity of a drawing view. The **Leader Note** tool is used for adding a note to an object or entity of a drawing view with a leader. This tool also allows you to add tangent and normal leader notes to the selected entity. Figure 12.108 shows a note with a leader attached to an edge of a view. The **To Leader Note** tool is used for adding a note to an existing leader in the drawing sheet.

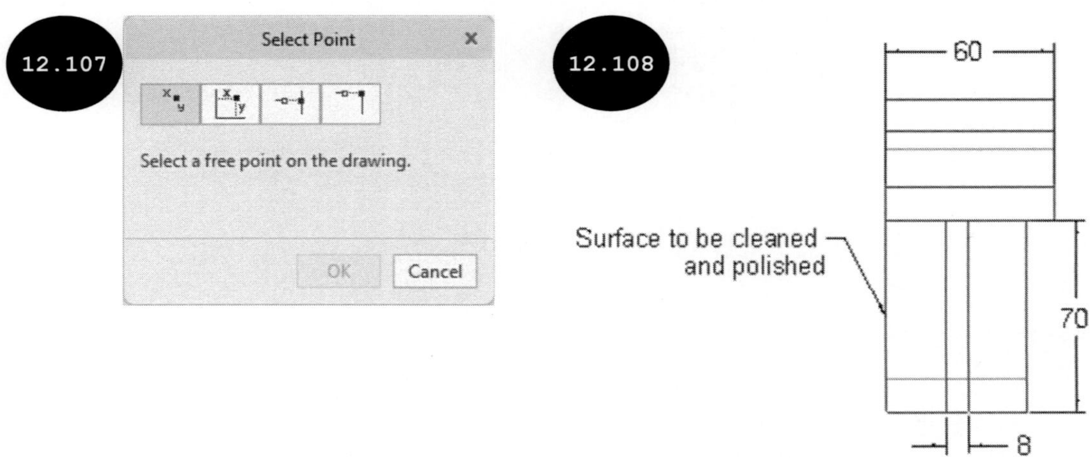

Creating the Bill of Material (BOM)

After creating all the required drawing views of an assembly in the Drawing environment, you need to create a Bill of Material. A Bill of Material (BOM) contains all the required information such as the number of parts used in an assembly, part number, quantity of each part, material, and so on. Since Bill of Material (BOM) contains all the information, it serves as a primary source of communication between the manufacturer and the vendors as well as the suppliers. The method for creating a Bill of Material (BOM) in the Drawing mode of Creo Parametric is discussed below:

1. Click on the **Table** tab in the **Ribbon**. The tools in the **Table** tab appear.

   Now, you need to create a table for the BOM in the drawing sheet. This needs to be done because, to create a Bill of Material (BOM) in Creo Parametric, you first need to create a table.

2. Invoke the **Table** flyout in the **Table** group of the **Table** tab, see Figure 12.109.

3. Hover the cursor over the number of columns to be added in the table and 2 rows in the **Table** flyout, see Figure 12.109. In this figure, the cursor is hovered on 5 columns and 2 rows (5X2) for creating a table. Next, click the left mouse button. A table is attached to the cursor. Next, click on the drawing sheet to specify its placement point. A table of specified columns and rows is added to the drawing sheet, see Figure 12.110.

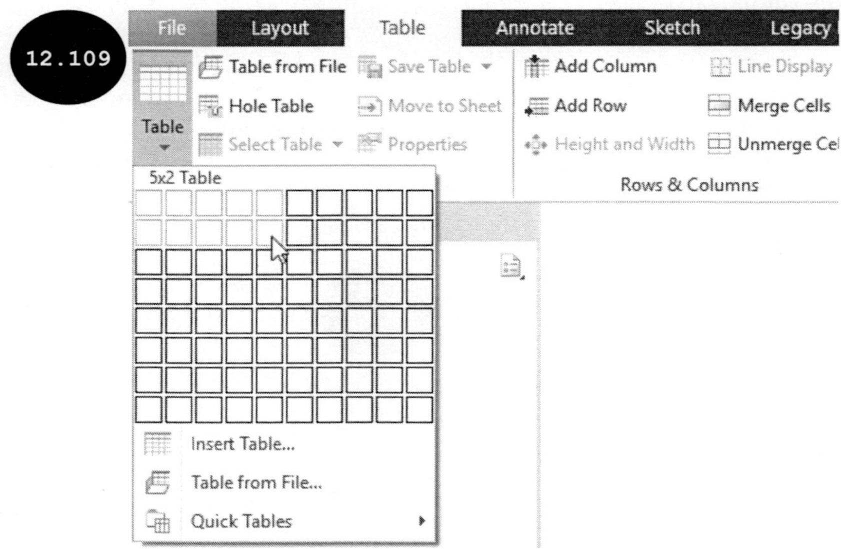

Tip: You can also add a table of specified columns and rows in the sheet by using the **Insert Table** dialog box. To do so, click on the **Insert Table** tool in the **Table** flyout, see Figure 12.109. The **Insert Table** dialog box appears. In this dialog box, enter the number of columns to be added in the table in the **Number of Columns** field and **2** in the **Number of Rows** field. Next, click on the **OK** button in the dialog box. A table gets attached to the cursor. Next, click to specify its placement point in the drawing sheet. A table of specified columns and rows is added in the sheet.

12.110

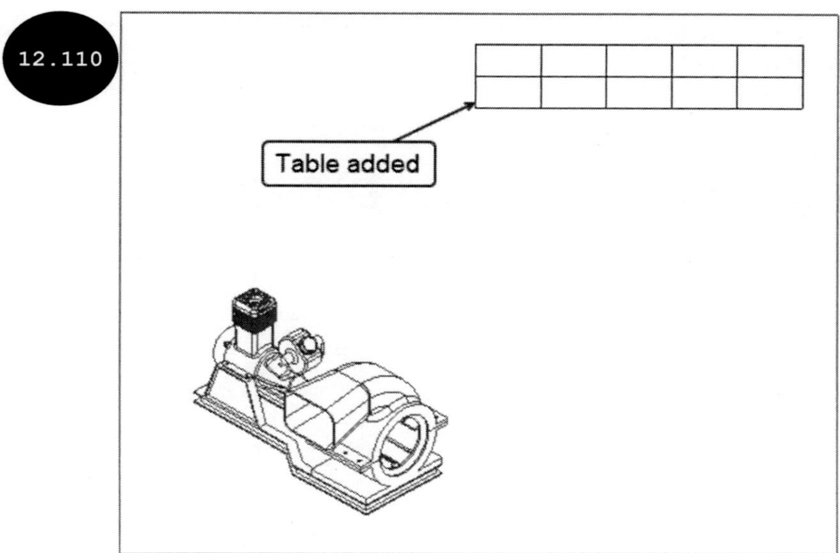

After adding the table, you need to define the item names of the table in the first row.

4. Double-click on the first cell of the first row in the table to define the item name. The **Format** tab appears in the **Ribbon** and you are prompted to enter an item name in the cell.

5. Enter **Part No.** as the item name in the first cell. Similarly, double-click on the remaining cells of the first row one by one and specify the item names, as required, see Figure 12.111. In this figure, the **Part No.**, **Part Name**, **Description**, **Material**, and **Quantity** are defined as item names.

12.111

Part No	Part Name	Description	Material	Quantity

Note: To change the height and width of a cell in the table, click on the cell whose height and width needs to be changed and then click on the **Height and Width** tool in the **Row & Columns** group of the **Table** tab. The **Height and Width** dialog box appears. In this dialog box, clear the **Automatic height adjustment** check box and then enter the height of the row in the **Height (characters)** field of the dialog box. Next, enter the width of the column in the **Width (characters)** field. After changing the height and width values, click on the **OK** button. You can also select multiple cells to change their height and width at the same time.

Tip: You can also change the default font of the table text as shown in Figure 12.111. To do so, select the entire text of the table by drawing a window around it and then click on the **Text Style** tool in the **Format** group of the **Table** tab. The **Text Style** dialog box appears. In this dialog box, clear the **Default** check box available in front of the **Font** drop-down list and then select the required font for the selected texts in the **Font** drop-down list. You can also specify other parameters of the text by using this dialog box and then click on the **OK** button.

Now, you need to define the cells of the second row of the table as repeat regions to specify data to be filled in the BOM.

6. Click on the **Repeat Region** tool in the **Data** group of the **Table** tab, see Figure 12.112. The **TBL REGIONS** menu appears, see Figure 12.113.

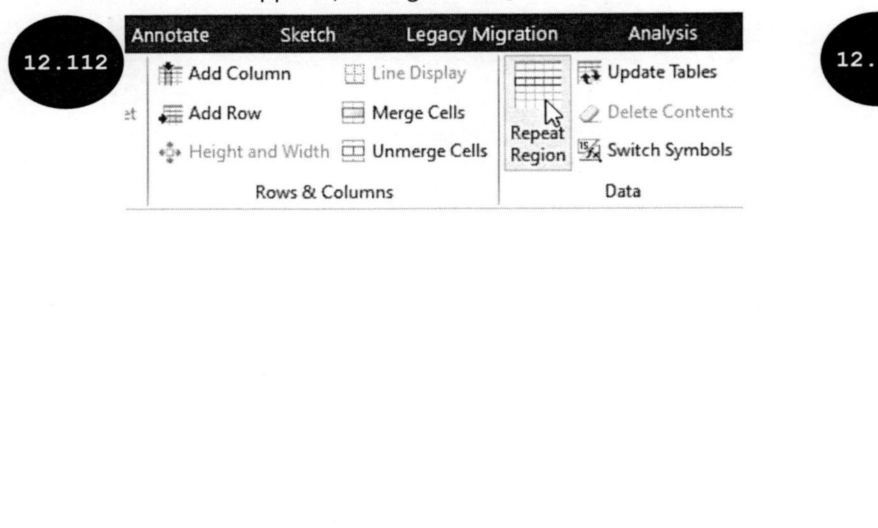

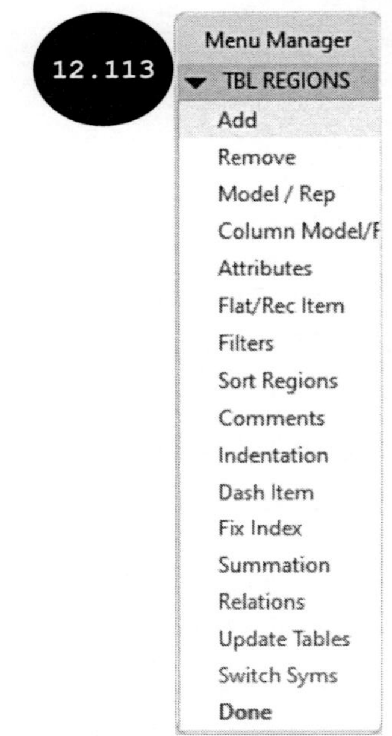

7. Click on the **Add** option in the **TBL REGIONS** menu. The **REGION TYPE** sub-menu appears at its bottom with the **Simple** option selected and you are prompted to locate the corners of the region.

8. Click on the first and last cells of the second row in the table by pressing the CTRL key to define the corners of the region. Next, click on the **Done** option in the **TBL REGIONS** menu. The second row of the table is defined as the region.

   Now, you need to define the data or information to be filled in the BOM table by assigning the report symbols to each cell of the second row that is defined as the repeat region.

9. Double-click on the first cell of the second row in the table to define the part index as the data to be filled in the first column of the table. The **Report Symbol** dialog box appears, see Figure 12.114.

10. Click on **rpt > index** in the **Report Symbol** dialog box. The **rpt.index** is displayed in the selected cell of the table, see Figure 12.115. This indicates that the part index (Part No.) information will be filled in the first column of the BOM table.

12.115

Part No	Part Name	Description	Material	Quantity
rpt.index				

Note: If the rpt.index text does not fit completely inside the selected cell of the table as shown in Figure 12.115, then you can ignore it.

11. Similarly, you can define the data or information to be filled in the remaining columns of the BOM table by assigning the respective report symbol. In the below steps, you will define part name, description, material, and quantity as the data to be filled in the second, third, fourth, and fifth column of the table, respectively.

    Now, you need to define the part name as the data to be filed in the second column.

12. Double-click on the second cell of the second row in the table to define the part name as the data to be filled in the second column of the table. The **Report Symbol** dialog box appears, refer to Figure 12.114.

13. Click on **asm > mbr > name** in the **Report Symbol** dialog box. The **asm.mbr.name** is displayed in the selected cell of the table. This indicates that the part name will be filled in the second column of the BOM table.

    Now, you need to define the part description as the data to be filled in the third column.

14. Double-click on the third cell of the second row of the table. The **Report Symbol** dialog box appears.

15. Click on **asm > mbr > User Defined** in the **Report Symbol** dialog box. The **Message Input** window appears at the top middle area of the sheet.

16. Enter a **description** in the **Message Input** window and then click on its green tick-mark button. The **asm.mbr.description** is displayed in the selected cell of the table.

    Now, you need to define the part material as the data to be filled in the fourth column.

17. Double-click on the fourth cell of the second row in the table. The **Report Symbol** dialog box appears.

18. Click on **asm > mbr > ptc_material > PTC_MATERIAL_NAME** in the **Report Symbol** dialog box. The **asm.mbr.ptc_material.PTC_MATERIAL_NAME** is displayed in the selected cell of the table.

    Now, you need to define the part quantity as the data to be filled in the fifth column.

19. Double-click on the fifth cell of the second row in the table. The **Report Symbol** dialog box appears.

20. Click on **rpt > qty** in the **Report Symbol** dialog box. The **rpt.qty** is displayed in the selected cell of the table.

    After defining data information to be filled in all the columns of the table, you need to update the table to create the BOM.

21. Click on the **Update Tables** tool in the **Data** group of the **Table** tab, see Figure 12.116. The BOM of the assembly gets created such that all the information of the assembly gets filled in the table, see Figure 12.117. Note that in the BOM, the components that are more than one in quantity get repeated. You need to avoid the repeated instances of the components and update the quantity information in the BOM.

12.116

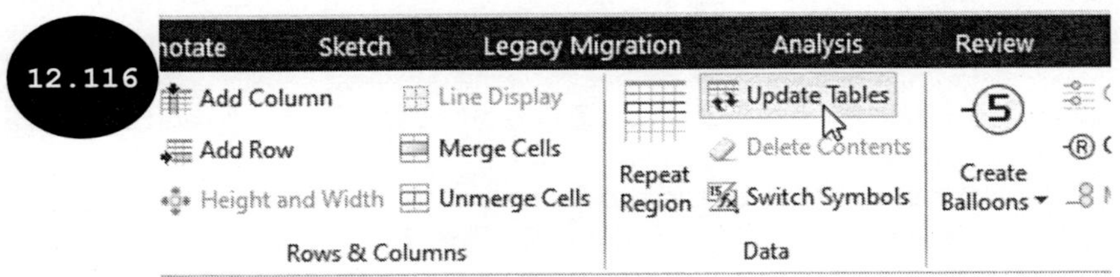

12.117

Part No.	Part Name	Description	Material	Quantity
1	BASE_FRAME		STEEL_CAST	
2	LOWER_HOUSING		SS	
3	UPPER_HOUSING		SS	
4	BOLT		STEEL_CAST	
5	BOLT		STEEL_CAST	
6	BOLT		STEEL_CAST	
7	BOLT		STEEL_CAST	
8	BOLT		STEEL_CAST	
9	BOLT		STEEL_CAST	
10	BOLT		STEEL_CAST	
11	BOLT		STEEL_CAST	
12	NUT		STEEL_CAST	
13	NUT		STEEL_CAST	
14	NUT		STEEL_CAST	
15	NUT		STEEL_CAST	
16	NUT		STEEL_CAST	
17	NUT		STEEL_CAST	
18	NUT		STEEL_CAST	
19	NUT		STEEL_CAST	
20	BLOWER		AL2014	
21	CRANK_SHAFT		STEEL	
22	ENGINE_BLOCK		STEEL_CAST	
23	ENGINE_COVER		STEEL_CAST	
24	ENGINE_HEAD		STEEL_CAST	

22. To avoid the repeated instances of the components in the BOM, click on the **Repeat Region** tool in the **Data** group of the **Table** tab, see Figure 12.118. The **TBL REGIONS** menu appears, see Figure 12.119.

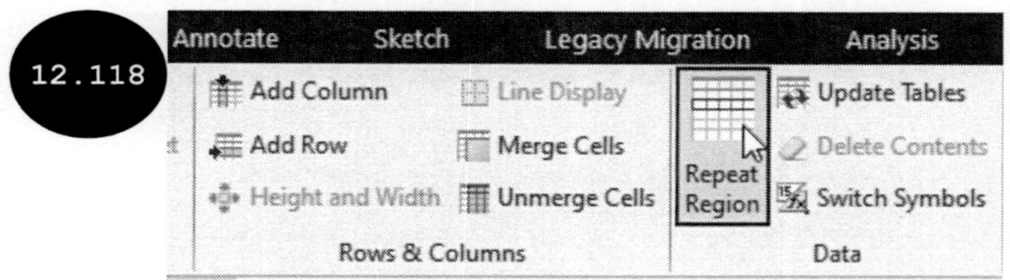

23. Click on the **Attributes** option in the **TBL REGIONS** menu. You are prompted to select a region.

24. Click on the repeat region of the BOM table. The **REGION ATTR** sub-menu appears, see Figure 12.120.

25. Click on the **No Duplicates** option in the **REGION ATTR** sub-menu and then click on the **Done/Return** option. The BOM gets updated such that the repeated instances of the components get removed and the quantity information appears in the **Quantity** column of the table, see Figure 12.121. Next, click on the **Done** option in the **TBL REGIONS** menu to close the menu.

12.121

Part No.	Part Name	Description	Material	Quantity
1	BASE_FRAME		STEEL_CAST	1
2	BLOWER		AL2014	1
3	BOLT		STEEL_CAST	8
4	CRANK_SHAFT		STEEL	1
5	ENGINE_BLOCK		STEEL_CAST	1
6	ENGINE_COVER		STEEL_CAST	1
7	ENGINE_HEAD		STEEL_CAST	1
8	LOWER_HOUSING		SS	1
9	NUT		STEEL_CAST	8
10	UPPER_HOUSING		SS	1

Adding Balloons

A Balloon is attached to a component with a leader line and displays the respective part number assigned in the Bill of Material (BOM), see Figure 12.122. In the drawings, balloons are generally added to the individual components of an assembly in order to identify them easily with respect to the part number assigned in the Bill of Materials (BOM).

12.122

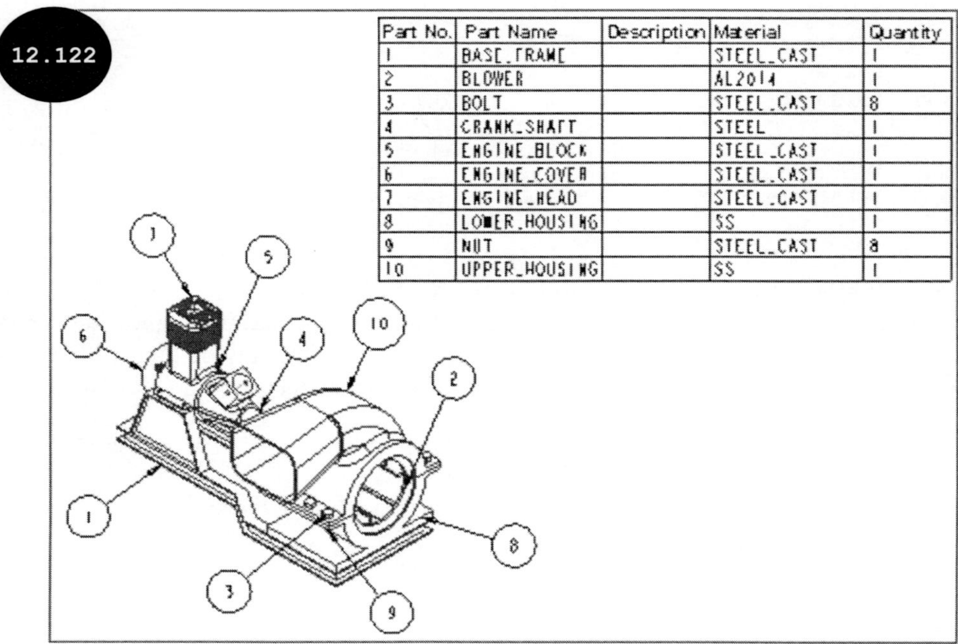

Part No.	Part Name	Description	Material	Quantity
1	BASE_FRAME		STEEL_CAST	1
2	BLOWER		AL2014	1
3	BOLT		STEEL_CAST	8
4	CRANK_SHAFT		STEEL	1
5	ENGINE_BLOCK		STEEL_CAST	1
6	ENGINE_COVER		STEEL_CAST	1
7	ENGINE_HEAD		STEEL_CAST	1
8	LOWER_HOUSING		SS	1
9	NUT		STEEL_CAST	8
10	UPPER_HOUSING		SS	1

In Creo Parametric, you can add balloons to all components of an assembly, all components of a selected view, selected components, selected components of a selected view, or components by selecting a record in the BOM table by using the respective tools available in the **Create Balloons** flyout, see Figure 12.123. The method for adding balloons to all components of an assembly is discussed below:

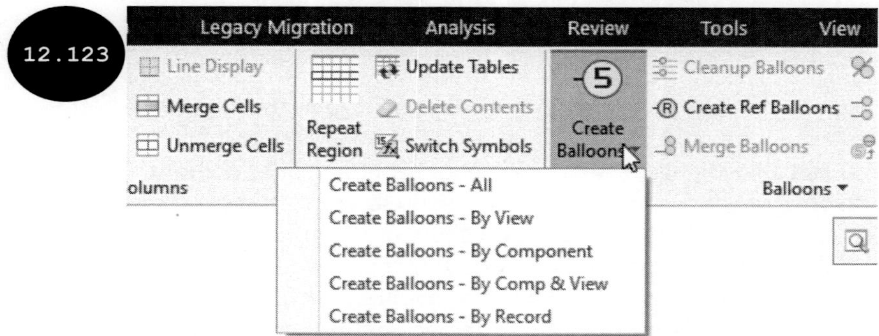

1. Invoke the **Create Balloons** flyout in the **Balloons** group of the **Table** tab, refer to Figure 12.123.

2. Click on the **Create Balloons - All** tool in the **Create Balloons** flyout.

3. The balloons get attached to all the components of the assembly in the drawing view, see Figure 12.124.

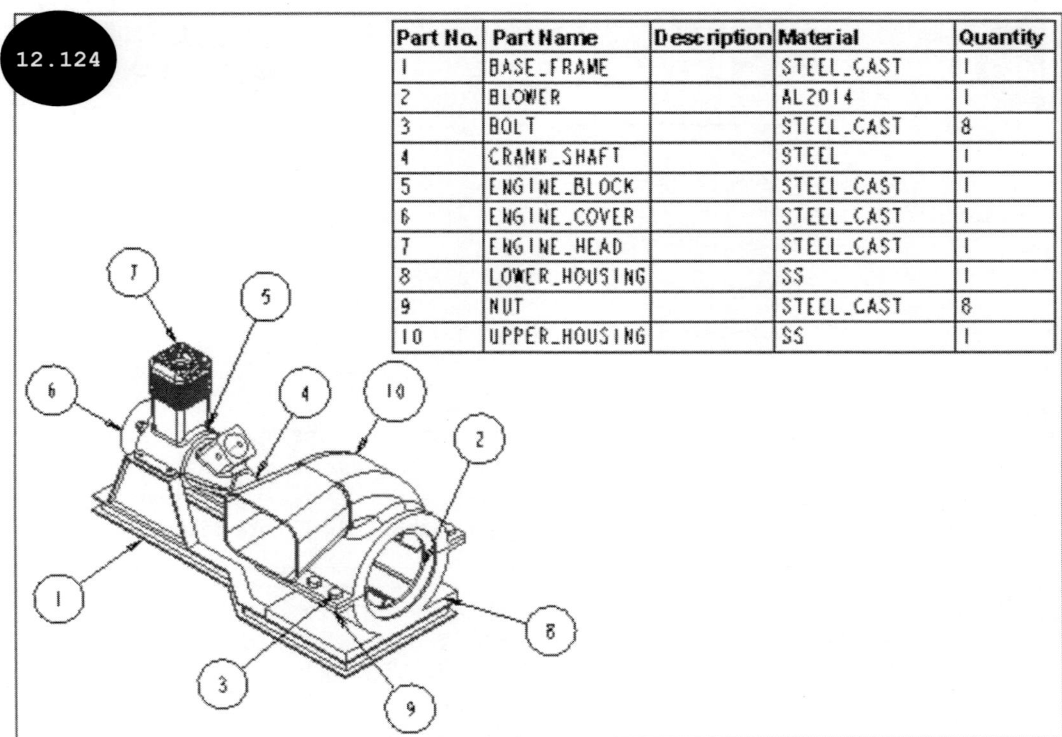

Part No.	Part Name	Description	Material	Quantity
1	BASE_FRAME		STEEL_CAST	1
2	BLOWER		AL2014	1
3	BOLT		STEEL_CAST	8
4	CRANK_SHAFT		STEEL	1
5	ENGINE_BLOCK		STEEL_CAST	1
6	ENGINE_COVER		STEEL_CAST	1
7	ENGINE_HEAD		STEEL_CAST	1
8	LOWER_HOUSING		SS	1
9	NUT		STEEL_CAST	8
10	UPPER_HOUSING		SS	1

Tip: If the balloons are not attached automatically on invoking the **Create Balloons - All** tool then you need to select a repeat region of the BOM table for adding balloons.

Note: After adding balloons to all components of an assembly in a drawing, you may need to change the position of balloons in the drawing sheet. To do so, select the balloon and then drag it to the desired location by pressing and holding the left mouse button.

You can also change or relocate the leader attachment point of a balloon to a desired reference or entity of the component. To do so, select the balloon and then press and hold the right mouse button to display a shortcut menu, see Figure 12.125. Next, click on the **Edit Attachment** option in the shortcut menu. The **MOD OPTIONS** menu appears see Figure 12.126. The **Same Ref** option of the menu is used for changing the position of the leader attachment point along the same reference of the component that is selected by default, whereas, the **Change Ref** option is used for changing the position of the leader attachment point to a different reference or entity of the component. Click on the **Change Ref** option in the menu and then select an entity of the component as a reference to define the position of the leader attachment point of the balloon. The position of the leader attachment point of the balloon gets changed to the selected entity of the component. Next, click on the **Done/Return** option in the **MOD OPTIONS** menu.

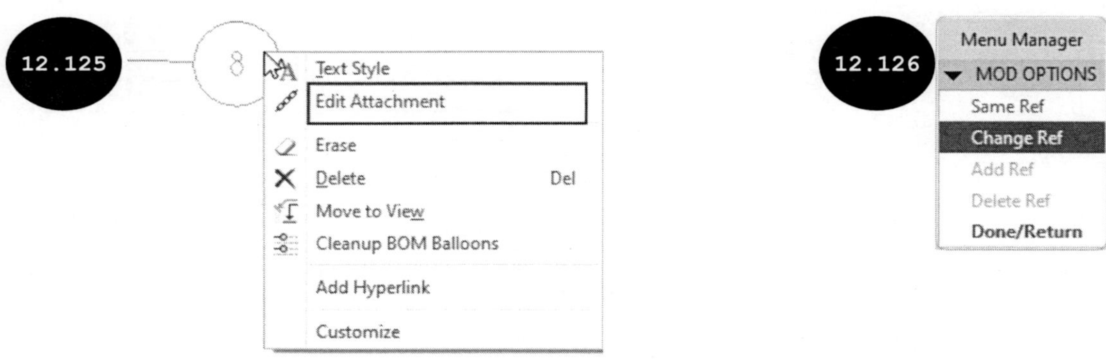

Tip: Similar to adding balloons to all components of an assembly in the drawing by using the **Create Balloons - All** tool, you can add balloons to all components of a selected view, selected components, selected components of a selected view, or components by selecting a record in the BOM table by using the respective tools available in the **Create Balloons** flyout.

Note: In case a drawing contains multiple general views, then on invoking the **Create Balloons - All** tool, the balloons get added to the first created general view. To add balloons to any other general view, you can use the **Create Balloons - By View** tool.

Tutorial 1

Open the model created in Tutorial 1 of Chapter 6 and then create different drawing views: front, top, side, isometric, section, and detailed as shown in Figure 12.127 in the A3 landscape standard sheet size. You also need to apply driving dimensions to the drawing views.

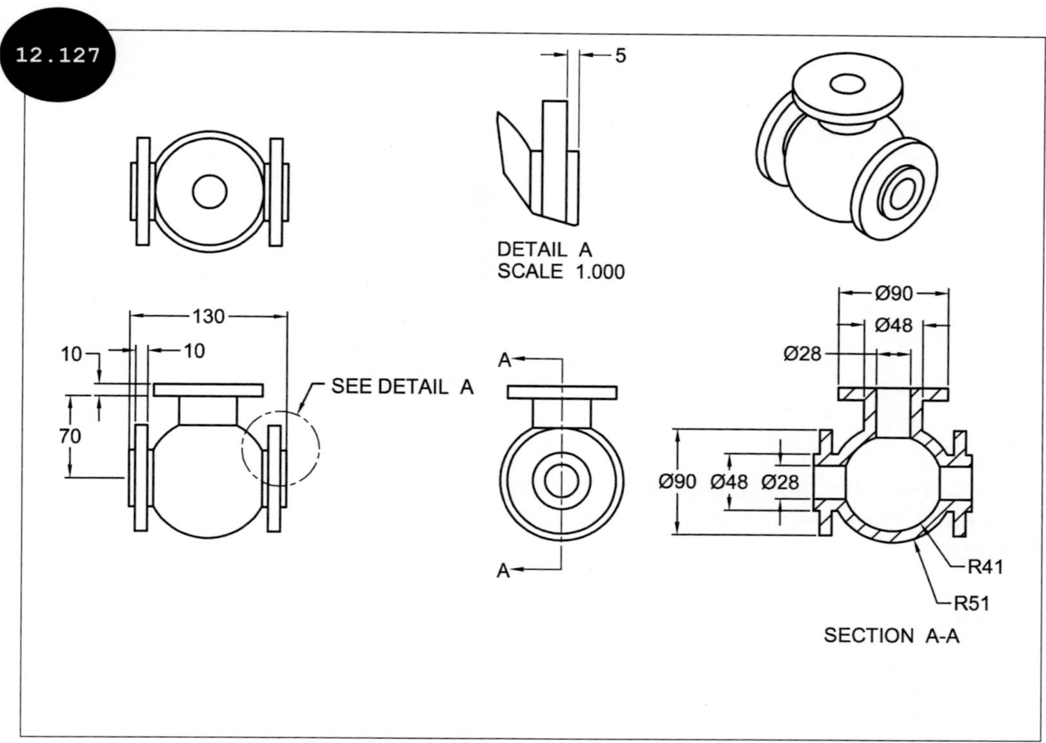

Section 1: Starting Creo Parametric and Setting the Working Directory

1. Start Creo Parametric by double-clicking on the Creo Parametric icon on your desktop.

2. Set the working directory to <<*Creo Parametric\Chapter 12\Tutorial 1*\. You need to create these folders in the *Creo Parametric* folder.

Section 2: Opening and Saving Model Created in Tutorial 1 of Chapter 6

1. Open the model created in Tutorial 1 of Chapter 6 by using the **Open** tool of the **Quick Access Toolbar**, see Figure 12.128.

   Now, you need to save the model with the name "Tutorial 1" in the *Chapter 12* folder in order to avoid any modification in the original file.

2. Click on **File > Save As** in the **File** menu. The **Save a Copy** dialog box appears.

3. Click on the **Working Directory** folder that appears on the left panel of the dialog box for accessing the current working directory (<<*Creo Parametric\Chapter 12\Tutorial 1*\).

4. Enter **C12-Tutorial01** in the **New file name** field of the **Save a Copy** dialog box and then click on the **OK** button. A copy of the model is saved with the name **C12-Tutorial01** in the specified working directory (<<*Creo Parametric**Chapter 12**Tutorial 1*\\).

12.128

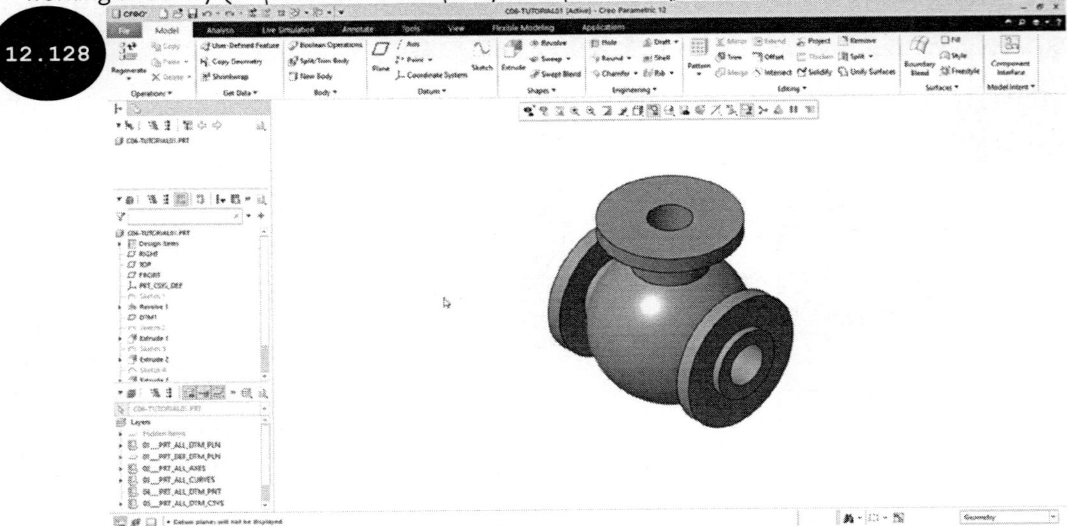

Section 3: Invoking Drawing Environment

1. Click on the **New** tool in the **Quick Access Toolbar** or press CTRL + N. The **New** dialog box appears.

2. Select the **Drawing** radio button in the **New** dialog box and then enter **C12-Tutorial01** in the **File name** field, see Figure 12.129.

12.129

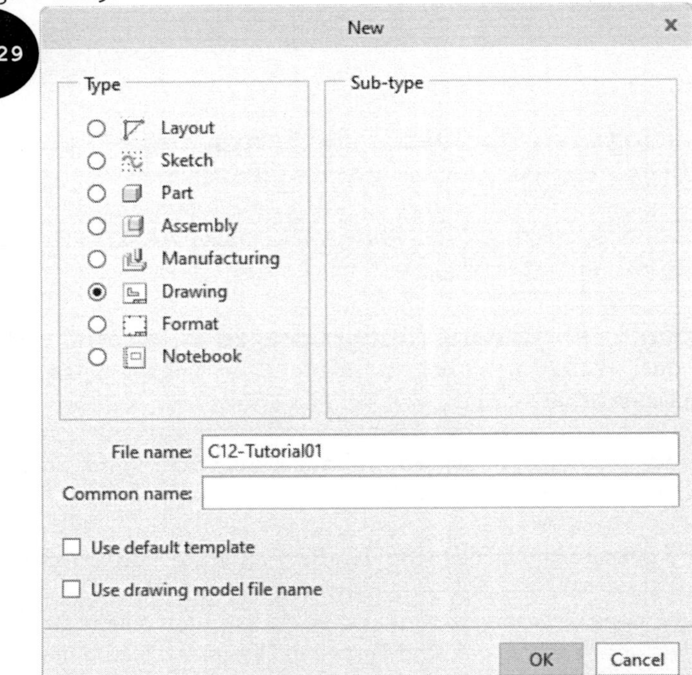

3. Clear the **Use default template** check box in the **New** dialog box and then click on the **OK** button. The **New Drawing** dialog box appears, see Figure 12.130.

   By default, Tutorial 1 of Chapter 6 (**c06-tutorial01.prt**) is selected as the default model in the **Default Model** area of the dialog box for creating a drawing, since it is opened in the current session of Creo Parametric. Now, you can select Tutorial 1 of Chapter 12 as the default model for creating a drawing.

4. Click on the **Browse** button in the **Default Model** area. The **Open** dialog box appears. Next, select the **C12-tutorial01** file which is saved at the location <<*Creo Parametric\Chapter 12\Tutorial 1*. The name of the selected file appears in the **Default Model** area of the **New Drawing** dialog box.

5. Ensure that the **Empty** radio button is selected in the **Specify Template** area of the dialog box to create a drawing on an empty sheet.

12.130

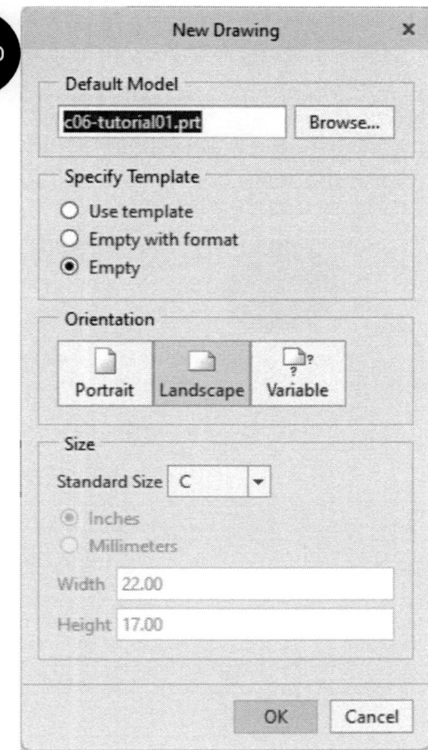

6. Ensure that the **Landscape** button is activated in the **Orientation** area of the dialog box.

7. Select the **A3** option to define the sheet size in the **Standard Size** drop-down list of the dialog box.

8. Click on the **OK** button in the dialog box. The Drawing mode gets invoked with an empty sheet of standard A3 sheet size (420 mm X 297 mm).

Section 4: Creating Front, Top, and Right Views

1. Click on the **General View** tool in the **Model Views** group of the **Layout** tab, see Figure 12.131. The **Select Combined State** dialog box appears.

12.131

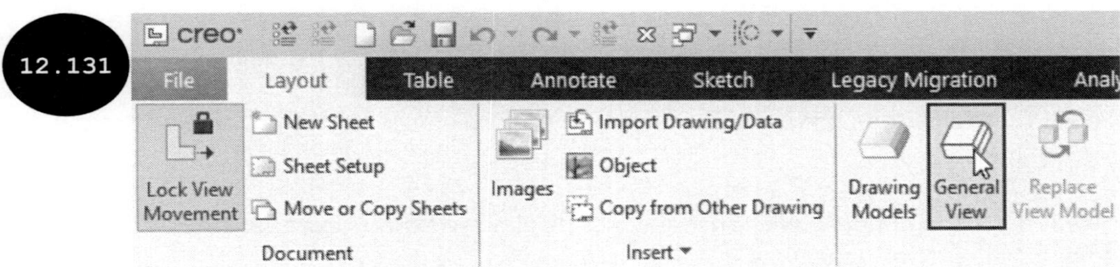

2. Select the **No Combined State** option in the **Select Combined State** dialog box and then click on the **OK** button. You are prompted to specify a center point for placing the drawing view on the drawing sheet.

3. Click on the lower left side of the drawing sheet to place the drawing view. The preview of the drawing view appears on the drawing sheet. Also, the **Drawing View** dialog box appears, see Figure 12.132.

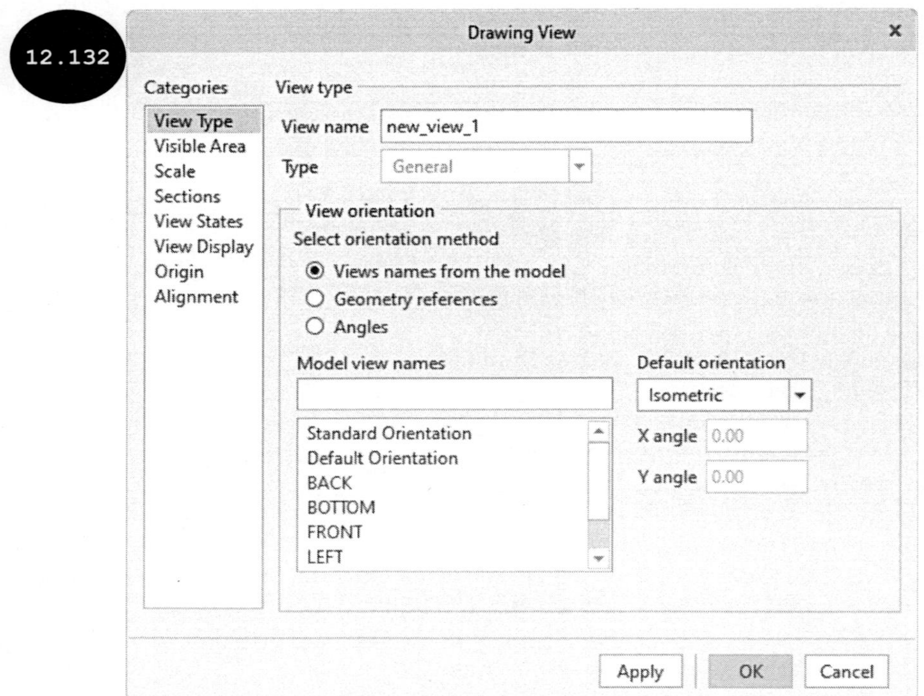

4. Select the **FRONT** option in the **Model view names** section of the dialog box for creating the front view of the model. Next, click on the **Apply** button in the dialog box. The preview of the view changes to the front view on the drawing sheet.

   Now, you need to define the display style for the drawing view.

5. Click on the **View Display** category in the **Categories** area of the dialog box. The options for defining the display style of the view appears on the right panel of the dialog box.

6. Select the **No Hidden** option in the **Display style** drop-down list of the dialog box as the display style of the view.

7. Select the **None** option in the **Tangent edges display style** drop-down list to remove the tangent edges of the model in the view.

8. Click on the **Apply** button in the dialog box. The display style of the front view gets changed as specified, see Figure 12.133.

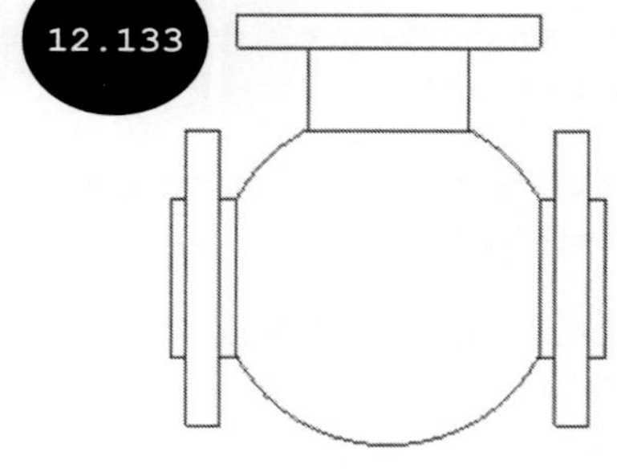

9. Click on the **OK** button to close the dialog box. The front view is created.

   Now, you need to create the top and right side views as projection views on the sheet.

10. Click on the **Projection View** tool in the **Model Views** group of the **Layout** tab. The front view of the sheet gets selected automatically as the parent view for creating a projection view and a rectangular box representing the preview of a projection view gets attached to the cursor.

11. Move the cursor to a location vertically above the front view where the top view is to be placed.

12. Click on the drawing sheet to specify the position for the top view. The top view is created and placed in the specified position on the sheet.

    Now, you need to change the display style of the top view.

13. Double-click on the top view to invoke the **Drawing View** dialog box.

14. Click on the **View Display** category in the **Categories** area of the dialog box. The options for defining the display style of the view appear on the right panel of the dialog box.

15. Select the **No Hidden** option in the **Display style** drop-down list of the dialog box and the **None** option in the **Tangent edges display style** drop-down list.

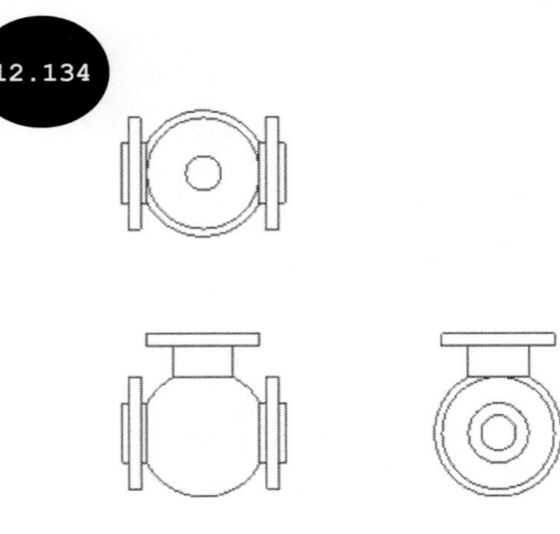

16. Click on the **Apply** button and then the **OK** button in the dialog box. The display style of the top view gets changed, refer to Figure 12.134. Also, the dialog box gets closed.

17. Similarly, create the right side view by selecting the front view as the parent view using the **Projection View** tool and then change its display style. Figure 12.134 shows the front, top, and right side views created on the sheet.

Section 5: Creating the Section View

To create a section view, you need to first create a projection view by selecting the existing right side view as the parent view.

1. Click on the **Projection View** tool in the **Model Views** group of the **Layout** tab. You are prompted to select a parent view.

2. Click to select the right side view as the parent view and then move the cursor horizontally toward the right. A rectangular box representing the preview of a projection view appears attached to the cursor.

3. Click on the drawing sheet to specify the position for the projection view. The projection view is created and placed in the specified position on the sheet, refer to Figure 12.135. In this figure, the drawing views are labeled for your reference only.

4. Change the display style of the newly created projection view to 'No Hidden' display style with no tangent edges by using the **Drawing View** dialog box, see Figure 12.135.

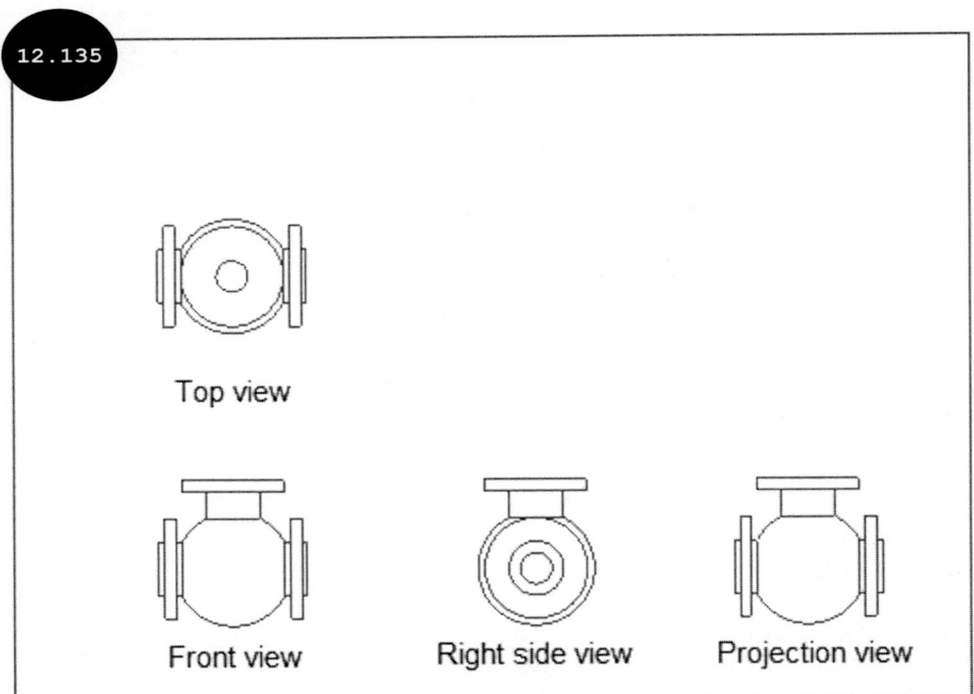

Now, you can create the section view of the newly created projection view.

5. Double-click on the newly created projection view to invoke the **Drawing View** dialog box.

6. Click on the **Sections** category in the **Drawing View** dialog box. The options for creating section view appear on the right panel of the dialog box.

7. Select the **2D cross-section** radio button in the dialog box. The **Add cross-section to view** button gets enabled in the dialog box. This button is used for creating a new cross-section of the selected view.

8. Click on the **Add cross-section to view** button in the dialog box. The **Name** and **Sectioned Area** drop-down lists are displayed in the **Drawing View** dialog box, see Figure 12.136. Also, the **XSEC CREATE** menu appears on the lower right corner of the sheet, see Figure 12.137. Note that the **XSEC CREATE** menu appears if the **Create New** option is selected in the **Name** drop-down list of the dialog box by default, refer to Figure 12.136.

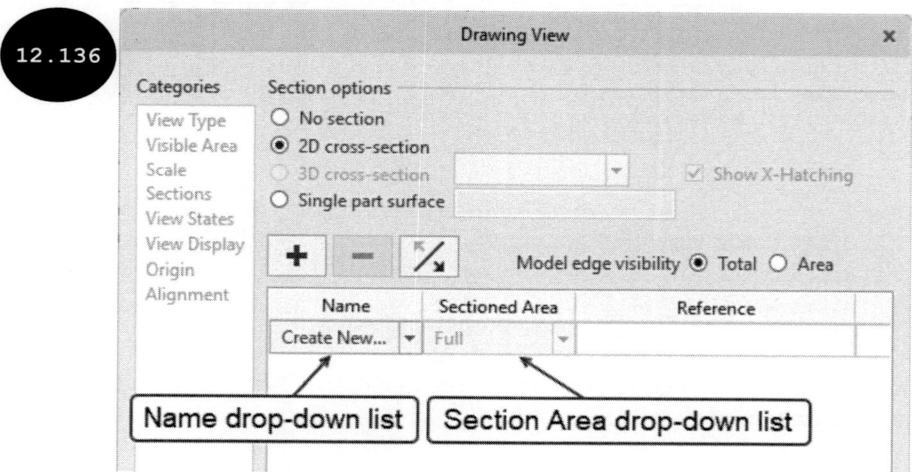

9. Ensure that the **Create New** option is selected in the **Name** drop-down list of the dialog box for creating a new section view, refer to Figure 12.136.

10. Click on the **Planar** > **Single** > **Done** in the **XSEC CREATE** menu to define a section or cutting plane for creating a section view, see Figure 12.137. The **Message Input** window appears at the top middle area of the sheet and you are prompted to specify the name of the cross-section to be created.

11. Enter A as the name of the cross-section view in the **Message Input** window and then click on the green tick-mark button that appears on its right. The **SETUP PLANE** menu appears (see Figure 12.138), and you are prompted to select a planar face or a datum plane as the section or cutting plane.

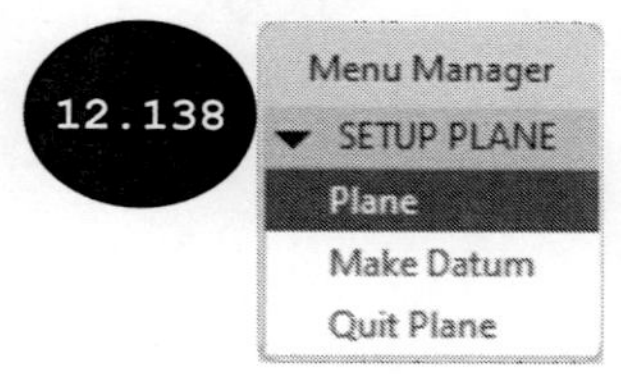

12. Select a datum plane from the parent view (right side view) of the selected projection view as the cutting plane, see Figure 12.139. The name of the section view appears in the **Name** drop-down list of the dialog box. Note that if the datum planes are not visible in the drawing area, then you need to turn on the display of datum planes. To do so, invoke the **Datum Display Filters** flyout of the **In-graphics** toolbar and then select the **Plane Display** check box.

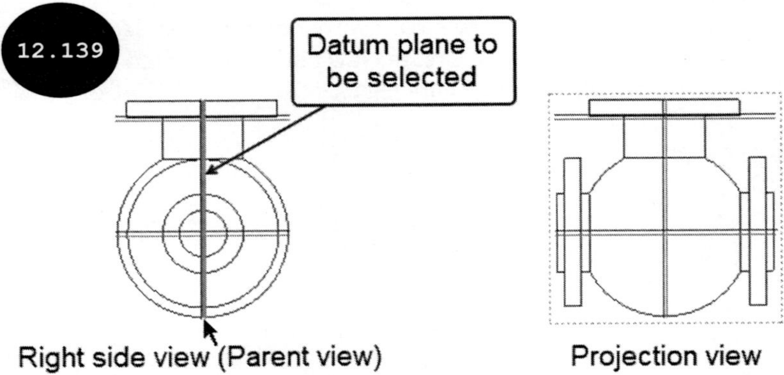

Now, you need to define the type of section view as full.

13. Ensure that the **Full** option is selected in the **Sectioned Area** drop-down list of the dialog box to create a full section view.

Now, you need to define a view for displaying the section arrows.

14. Scroll to the right of the **Drawing View** dialog box to display the **Arrow Display** collector. Next, click on the **Arrow Display** collector to activate it. You are prompted to select the parent view for displaying the section arrows.

15. Select the right side view as the parent view for displaying the section arrows.

16. Click on the **Apply** button in the dialog box and then the **OK** button. The section view is created and the section arrows appear on the selected parent view, see Figure 12.140.

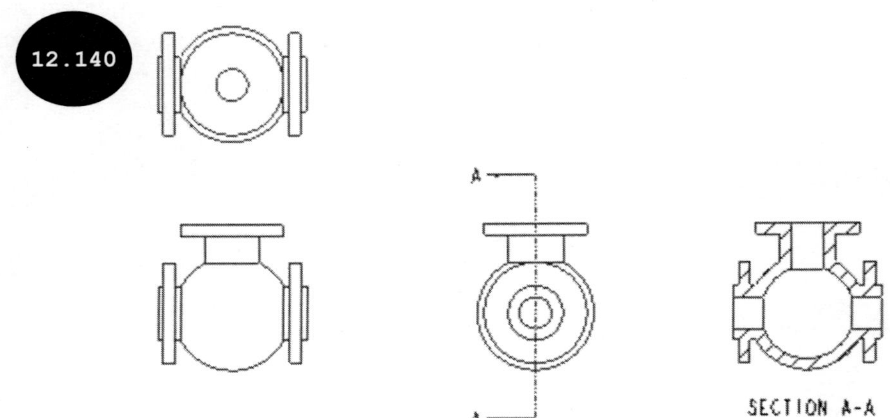

Section 6: Creating the Detailed View

Now, you need to create a detailed view of the right side portion of the front view to display it in an enlarged scale.

1. Click on the **Detailed View** tool in the **Model Views** group of the **Layout** tab. You are prompted to define a center point for creating the detailed view.

2. Click to specify a center point on the front view of the drawing for creating the detailed view, refer to Figure 12.141. You are prompted to draw a closed spline.

3. Draw a closed spline around the portion of the front view to be enlarged and then press the middle mouse button, see Figure 12.141. The outline of the detailed view is defined and you are prompted to specify a center point for defining the placement of the detailed view.

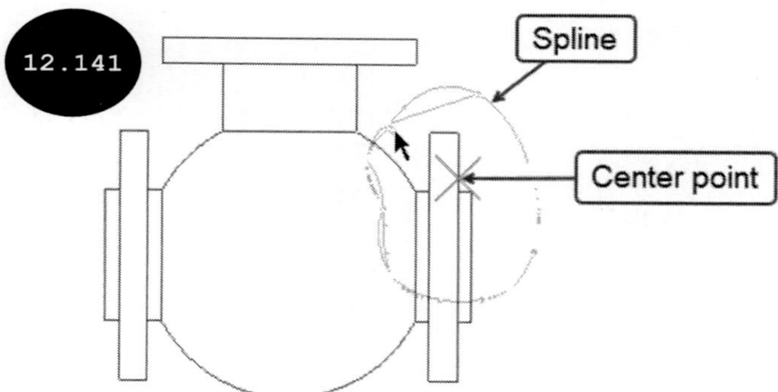

4. Click to define the placement of the detailed view on the sheet. The detailed view is created on the specified location of the sheet with default attributes, refer to Figure 12.142.

Section 7: Creating the Isometric View

Now, you need to create an isometric view of the model on the drawing sheet.

1. Click on the **General View** tool in the **Model Views** group of the **Layout** tab. The **Select Combined State** dialog box appears.

2. Click on the **OK** button in the **Select Combined State** dialog box. You are prompted to specify a center point for placing the drawing view on the drawing sheet.

3. Click on the upper right side in the drawing sheet to place the drawing view. The preview of the isometric view appears on the drawing sheet. Also, the **Drawing View** dialog box appears.

4. Ensure that the orientation of view appears as isometric on the drawing sheet and then click on the **Apply** button in the dialog box.

5. Click on the **View Display** category in the dialog box and then select the **No Hidden** option in the **Display style** drop-down list. Next, select the **None** option in the **Tangent edges display style** drop-down list of the dialog box.

6. Click on the **Apply** button and then the **OK** button in the dialog box. The isometric view of the model is created at the specified location on the sheet, see Figure 12.142.

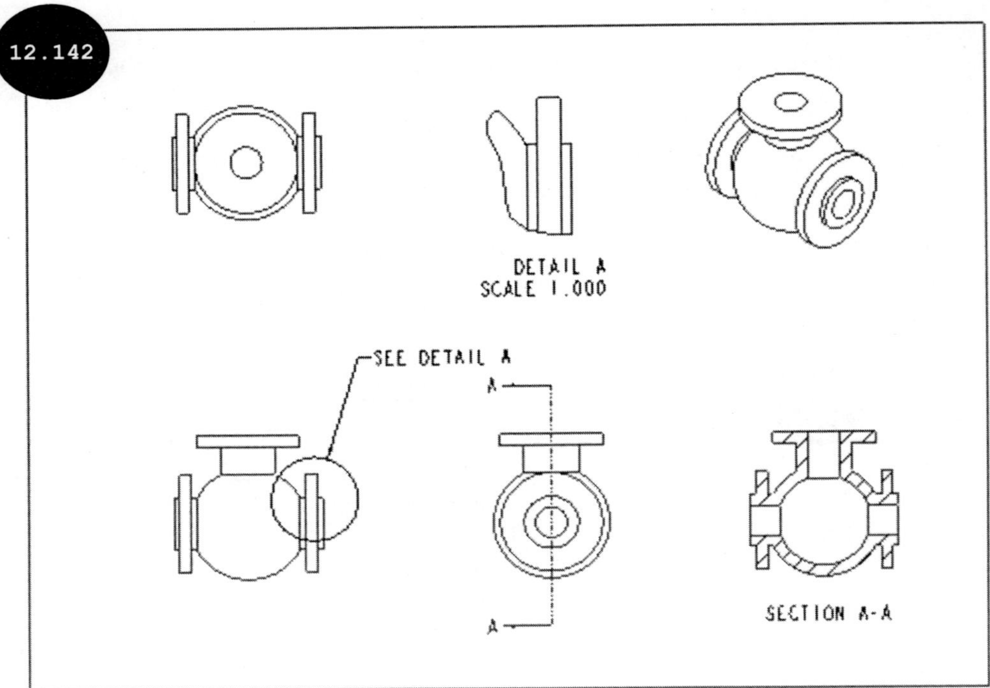

Section 8: Applying Driving Dimensions

1. Click on the **Annotate** tab in the **Ribbon**. The tools of the **Annotate** tab appear in the **Ribbon**.

2. Click on the **Show Model Annotations** tool in the **Annotations** group of the **Annotate** tab, see Figure 12.143. The **Show Model Annotations** dialog box appears.

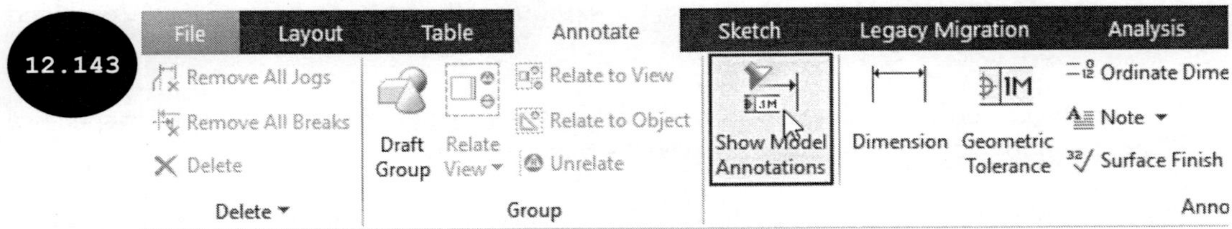

3. Select the section view of the drawing to apply the dimensions. The dimensions of the model get retrieved and applied on the selected section view, see Figure 12.144. Also, a list of the dimensions appears in the dialog box with a check box to the left of each dimension.

4. Select the diameter and radius dimensions that appear on the section view as the dimensions to be kept in the view.

5. Click on the **Apply** button and then the **Cancel** button in the dialog box. The selected diameter and radius dimensions are applied on the section view, see Figure 12.145.

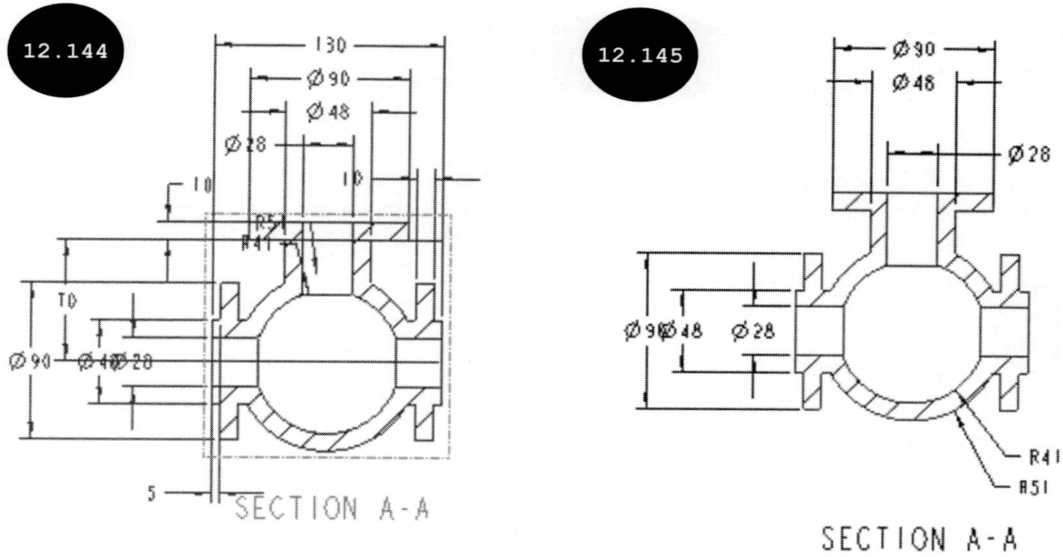

Note: In Figure 12.145, the position of the dimensions has been changed to avoid overlapping and to maintain spacing between the dimensions. To change the position of a dimension, click on a dimension and drag it to the required location on the sheet.

Now, you need to apply the remaining dimensions to the front view of the drawing.

6. Click on the **Show Model Annotations** tool in the **Annotations** group of the **Annotate** tab. The **Show Model Annotations** dialog box appears.

7. Select the front view of the drawing. The dimensions of the model get retrieved and applied on the selected front view. Also, a list of the dimensions appears in the dialog box.

8. Select all the dimensions that appear on the front view, except the dimension of 5 mm. Next, click on the **Apply** button in the dialog box and then the **Cancel** button. All the selected dimensions get applied on the front view of the drawing, see Figure 12.146.

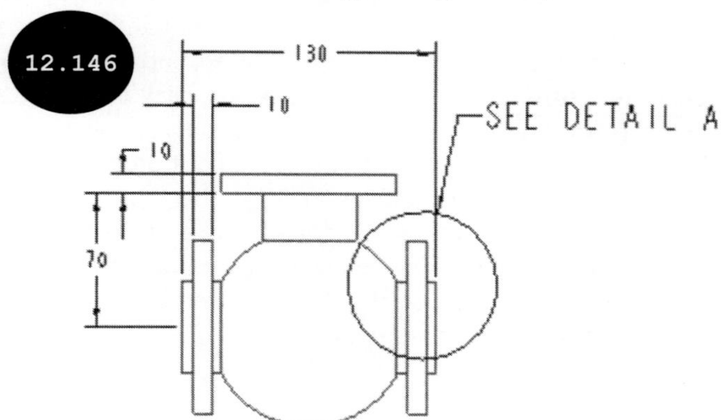

Now, you need to apply the dimensions on the detailed view of the drawing.

9. Click on the **Show Model Annotations** tool in the **Annotations** group and then select the detailed view of the drawing for applying dimensions. The dimension 5 mm appears on the detailed view.

10. Select the dimension (5 mm) that appears on the detailed view and then click on the **Apply** button in the dialog box. Next, click on the **Cancel** button. The selected dimension of 5 mm is applied to the detailed view. Figure 12.147 shows the final drawing after applying all the dimensions.

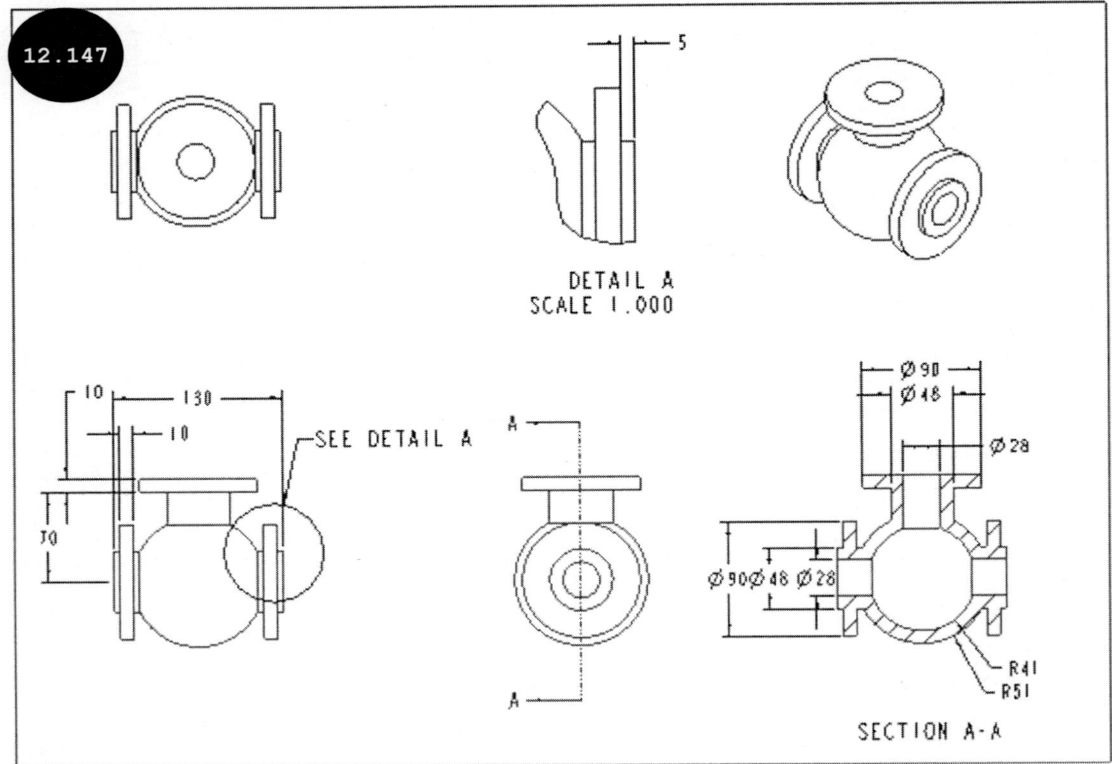

Note: In Figure 12.147, the text style of the dimensions such as font and height have been changed. To do so, select the dimensions by drawing a window around them. Ensure that you do not select the section line. After selecting the dimensions, click on the **Text Style** tool in the **Format** group of the **Annotate** tab. The **Text Style** dialog box appears. In this dialog box, clear the **Default** check box available in front of the **Font** drop-down list and then select the **Arial WGL** option in the **Font** drop-down list as the font of the text. Next, clear the **Default** check box available in front of the **Height** field and then specify a height value in the **Height** field of the dialog box. Similarly, you can change the other parameters of the selected dimensions and then click on the **Apply** button in the dialog box. Next, click on the **OK** button to close the **Text Style** dialog box.

Section 9: Saving the Model

1. Click on the **Save** tool in the **Quick Access Toolbar**. The **Save Object** dialog box appears.

2. Click on the **OK** button in the dialog box. The model is saved with the name **C12-Tutorial01** in the specified working directory (<<*Creo Parametric**Chapter 12**Tutorial 1*\).

Hands-on Test Drive 1

Open the assembly created in Tutorial 2 of Chapter 10 and then create different drawing views on a sheet of A1 size as shown in Figure 12.148. Also, create a Bill of Material (BOM) and add balloons in the isometric view of the assembly.

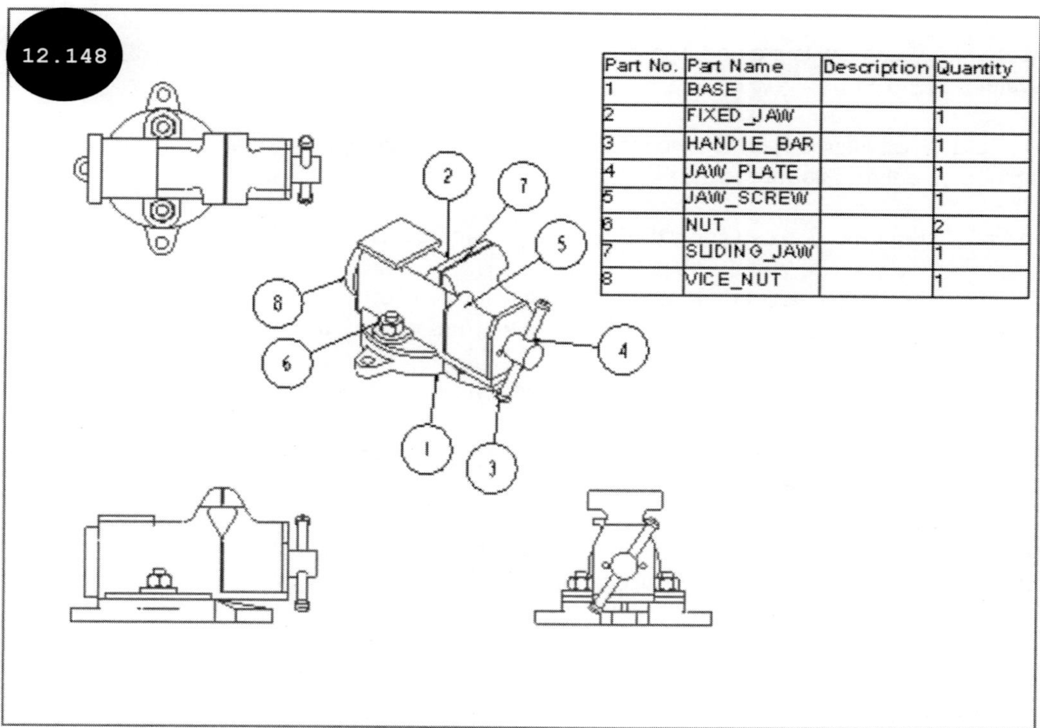

Part No.	Part Name	Description	Quantity
1	BASE		1
2	FIXED_JAW		1
3	HANDLE_BAR		1
4	JAW_PLATE		1
5	JAW_SCREW		1
6	NUT		2
7	SLIDING_JAW		1
8	VICE_NUT		1

Summary

In this chapter, you have learned about creating 2D drawings from parts and assemblies. The methods for creating various drawing views such as general views, projection views, section views, auxiliary views, and detailed views of a component or an assembly by using the respective tools have been discussed. You have also learned about the concept of angle of projection, defining the angle of projection for a drawing, and creating a new drawing template or format. After creating the required drawing views of a component or an assembly, you can apply reference and driving dimensions.

In addition, you have learned about modifying properties, hatching, and text style of a view. You have also learned about adding notes, bill of material (BOM), and balloons.

Questions

Complete and verify the following sentences:

- In the _________ mode of Creo Parametric, you can generate 2D drawings of a component or an assembly.
- A _________ view is an independent drawing view.
- The _________ views are orthogonal views of an object, which are created by viewing an object from different projection sides such as top, front, and side.
- Engineering drawings follow the _________ and the _________ angle of projection.
- A _________ view is created in order to show the portion of an existing view at an enlarged scale.
- A _________ view is used for showing a cross-section slice of an existing view by revolving the section 90 degrees about the cutting plane.
- In Creo Parametric, you can apply the _________ and _________ dimensions in a view.
- The _________ tool is used for retrieving dimensions and other properties of the model such as tolerances, notes, surface finishes, symbols, and datums on a particular view in the sheet.
- The _________ tool is used for editing the text style properties of dimensions and annotations.
- In Creo Parametric, after invoking the Drawing mode, you cannot add a model for generating its drawing views. (True/False).
- You can modify the cross-section hatching parameters such as spacing, angle, offset value, and line style of a section view. (True/False).
- In Creo Parametric, on modifying a driving dimension, the respective sketch or feature of the model is also modified. (True/False).

INDEX

Symbols

A

B

C

D

E

F

G

H

I

Q

R

S

T

U

V

W

Z

Other Publications by CADArtifex

Some of the other Publications by CADArtifex are given below:

AutoCAD Textbooks

AutoCAD 2026: A Power Guide for Beginners and Intermediate Users
AutoCAD 2025: A Power Guide for Beginners and Intermediate Users
AutoCAD 2024: A Power Guide for Beginners and Intermediate Users
and more

AutoCAD For Architectural Design Textbooks

AutoCAD 2023 for Architectural Design: A Power Guide for Beginners and Intermediate Users
AutoCAD 2022 for Architectural Design: A Power Guide for Beginners and Intermediate Users
AutoCAD 2021 for Architectural Design: A Power Guide for Beginners and Intermediate Users
and more

Autodesk Fusion 360 Textbooks

Autodesk Fusion 360: A Power Guide for Beginners and Intermediate Users (7th Edition)
Autodesk Fusion 360: A Power Guide for Beginners and Intermediate Users (6th Edition)
Autodesk Fusion 360: A Power Guide for Beginners and Intermediate Users (5th Edition)
and more

Autodesk Fusion 360 Surface and T-Spline Textbooks

Autodesk Fusion 360 Surface Design and Sculpting with T-Spline Surfaces (7th Edition)
Autodesk Fusion 360 Surface Design and Sculpting with T-Spline Surfaces (6th Edition)
and more

Autodesk Inventor Textbooks

Autodesk Inventor 2026: A Power Guide for Beginners and Intermediate Users
Autodesk Inventor 2025: A Power Guide for Beginners and Intermediate Users
Autodesk Inventor 2024: A Power Guide for Beginners and Intermediate Users
and more

FreeCAD Textbooks

FreeCAD 1.0: A Power Guide for Beginners and Intermediate Users
FreeCAD 0.21: A Power Guide for Beginners and Intermediate Users

Onshape Textbooks

Onshape 2025: A Power Guide for Beginners and Intermediate Users

PTC Creo Parametric Textbooks

Creo Parametric 12.0: A Power Guide for Beginners and Intermediate Users
Creo Parametric 11.0: A Power Guide for Beginners and Intermediate Users
Creo Parametric 10.0: A Power Guide for Beginners and Intermediate Users
and more

SOLIDWORKS Textbooks

SOLIDWORKS 2025: A Power Guide for Beginners and Intermediate User
SOLIDWORKS 2024: A Power Guide for Beginners and Intermediate User
SOLIDWORKS 2023: A Power Guide for Beginners and Intermediate User
and more

SOLIDWORKS Sheet Metal and Surface Design Textbooks

SOLIDWORKS Sheet Metal and Surface Design 2025 for Beginners and Intermediate Users
SOLIDWORKS Sheet Metal and Surface Design 2024 for Beginners and Intermediate Users
and more

SOLIDWORKS Simulation Textbooks

SOLIDWORKS Simulation 2025: A Power Guide for Beginners and Intermediate User
SOLIDWORKS Simulation 2024: A Power Guide for Beginners and Intermediate User
SOLIDWORKS Simulation 2023: A Power Guide for Beginners and Intermediate User
and more

Exercises Books

Some of the exercises books are given below:

100 AutoCAD Exercises - Learn by Practicing (2 Edition)
Autodesk Inventor Exercises - Learn by Practicing
Autodesk Fusion 360 Exercises Learn by Practicing (2023-24)
SOLIDWORKS Exercises - Learn by Practicing (3 Edition)

Project-Based Video Courses by CADArtifex

- SOLIDWORKS for Beginners and Intermediate Users
- Learn SOLIDWORKS Sheet Metal: From Concept to Creation
- Complete Fusion 360 All-in-One Course for Beginners (2025)
- Learn Fusion 360 with Real-World Mechanical Projects
- Fusion 360 Surface Design & T-Spline Sculpting
- Mastering AutoCAD 2D & 3D for Beginners
- Complete Onshape for Beginners: Project-Based Approach
- Complete FreeCAD for Beginners – No Experience Needed

For full course details, visit: cadartifex.com
